Psychology
BRIEF EDITION

John W. Santrock

UNIVERSITY OF TEXAS AT DALLAS

Boston   Burr Ridge, IL   Dubuque, IA   Madison, WI   New York   San Francisco   St. Louis
Bangkok   Bogotá   Caracas   Lisbon   London   Madrid
Mexico City   Milan   New Delhi   Seoul   Singapore   Sydney   Taipei   Toronto

McGraw-Hill Higher Education

A Division of The McGraw-Hill Companies

PSYCHOLOGY, BRIEF EDITION

Published by McGraw-Hill, an imprint of The McGraw-Hill Companies, Inc., 1221 Avenue of the Americas, New York, NY 10020. Copyright © 2000 by The McGraw-Hill Companies, Inc. All rights reserved. No part of this publication may be reproduced or distributed in any form or by any means, or stored in a database or retrieval system, without the prior written consent of The McGraw-Hill Companies, Inc., including, but not limited to, in any network or other electronic storage or transmission, or broadcast for distance learning.

♲ This book is printed on recycled, acid-free paper containing 10% postconsumer waste.

3 4 5 6 7 8 9 0 QPD/QPD 0 9 8 7 6 5 4 3 2 1

ISBN 0–07–240372–1

Vice president and editor-in-chief: *Thalia Dorwick*
Executive editor: *Joseph Terry*
Editorial director: *Jane Vaicunas*
Editorial coordinator: *Barbara Santoro*
Developmental editor: *Mindy De Palma*
Senior marketing manager: *Chris Hall*
Media technology project manager: *Sean Crowley*
Senior project manager: *Marilyn Rothenberger*
Senior production supervisor: *Sandra Hahn*
Coordinator of freelance design: *Michelle D. Whitaker*
Freelance cover designer: *Maureen McCutcheon*
Freelance interior designer: *Diane Beasley*
Senior photo research coordinator: *Carrie K. Burger*
Photo research: *LouAnn K. Wilson*
Senior supplement coordinator: *David A. Welsh*
Compositor: *GTS Graphics, Inc.*
Typeface: *10.5/12 Minion*
Printer: *Quebecor Printing Book Group/Dubuque, IA*

Cover images: (left) *"Sweet Pink" by Wassily Kandinsky (1866–1944), Sotheby's London/SuperStock*; (center) *"Female of the Species" by John W. Santrock*; (right) *Erich Lessing/Art Resource, NY, Klimt Gustav (1862–1918). The Kiss. 1907–1908. Oesterreichische Galerie, Vienna, Austria*

The credits section for this book begins on page C-1 and is considered an extension of the copyright page.

Library of Congress Cataloging-in-Publication Data

Santrock, John W.
    Psychology : brief edition / John W. Santrock. — 1 st ed.
      p.   c m.
    Includes bibliographical references and index.
    ISBN 0–07–240372–1
    1. Psychology.   I. Title.

BF121.S264   2000
150—dc21
                                            99–089679
                                            CIP

Brief Contents

Contents

CHAPTER

6

Memory   174

CHAPTER

7

Thinking, Language, and Intelligence   208

CHAPTER

8

Human Development   246

CHAPTER

12 Therapies 398

CHAPTER

13 Social Psychology 432

Preface

I have taught introductory psychology since 1967. Over the past four decades, my motivation and love for imparting psychology as a relevant science—one that is empirically sound yet meaningful for people's lives—has not wavered. Even when I first began teaching introductory psychology, I supplemented the text I used by having students read about such relevant topics as Erikson's theory of human development, case studies in abnormal psychology, and topics in applied psychology. In no other discipline (I am admittedly biased) will you find so many opportunities to better understand yourself and the people around you than in the discipline of psychology. This belief not only has been a foundation of my teaching introductory psychology for four decades, but also is the heart of this book.

What Do Instructors Really Want in a Brief Introductory Psychology Text?

In our extensive inquiries with instructors who use a brief book when teaching introductory psychology, they consistently told us that most of the so-called "brief" books are not brief enough. The instructors underscored that most of the brief books have too many pages and too many chapters.

In response to instructors' requests for a solid yet briefer book than others, *Psychology: Brief Edition* has 13 chapters and 476 main text pages, considerably briefer than virtually all other brief introductory psychology texts. The 13 chapters fit perfectly into most instructors' quarter or semester calendars and with less than 500 pages *Psychology: Brief Edition* is a book that students will welcome.

To keep the book as brief as possible, we have placed the material on health psychology and a statistical appendix on the McGraw-Hill Santrock *Psychology: Brief Edition* web site. The coverage of these topics on the web site follows exactly the same format as in the main text and can be accessed free by students and instructors.

In addition, four chapters, most of which have a strong applications emphasis, can be bundled with the main text of *Psychology: Brief Edition*. The additional chapters that can be bundled with the text are:

> Evolution and Heredity
> Gender and Sex
> Applied Psychology
> Psychology of Religion

These chapters are in full color and have the same design/layout as the chapters in the main text.

Psychology: The Relevant Science

As many instructors (and authors) know, it is quite a challenge to perceive what is needed to fulfill students' expectations, and then to fulfill them. How can we ensure that every page of a textbook has relevance? As we revise each sentence and each feature in the book, we must constantly ask ourselves: Why is this important? Is this a meaningful issue for today's students?

Psychology: Brief Edition has been infused with content, exercises, and resources that focus on psychology as a relevant science. The discipline of psychology is ideally suited to address some of the most important aspects of our lives. We don't have the answers to all of life's questions, but psychology can tell us much about matters like these:

- How our biological heritage affects our behavior
- How, and to what extent, our environmental experiences can change our lives
- How we perceive, remember, solve problems, and can become more creative
- How the social worlds of people and relationships affect the way we behave
- How the culture we live in influences us
- How we are similar to and different from others
- How science can provide us with more objective information about many aspects of life
- How to draw on conceptually diverse ideas in thinking about problems and issues
- How to understand controversies about mind and behavior
- How to think critically about many aspects of mind and behavior

The above ten areas are featured in a section in chapter 1 called "Psychology and Life: What Matters." They also are woven through the remainder of the text where appropriate. In addition, as you will see shortly, some of the book's main features emphasize psychology's relevance.

Every chapter of the book includes these "Psychology of Life" features:

Images of Psychology and Life
This section appears at the beginning of each chapter and introduces students to some aspect of the chapter in an interesting way. Examples of topics include: "Why Youth Kill" (chapter 1), "The Human Versus Big Blue, Cog, and CYC" (chapter 7), and "Showering Seven Times a Day, Looking at a Bleak Future, and Avoiding Breathing on People" (chapter 11).

Explorations in Psychology

These boxes, seamlessly interwoven with the text, provide an expanded look at many fascinating ideas and issues related to the content at that particular point in the chapter. Examples of topics include: "From Horoscopes to the Sex Lives of Tigers" (chapter 1), "Can we learn while we are asleep?" (chapter 4), and "The power of touch and massage in development" (chapter 8).

Thinking About Psychology and Life

These boxes appear several times in each chapter and encourage students to think critically or evaluate themselves in regard to content in that part of the chapter. Examples of topics include: "Nature, Nurture, and Politics" (chapter 2), "Are you a sensation seeker?" (chapter 9), and "Are You Introverted or Extroverted?" (chapter 10).

Development

The content of *Psychology: Brief Edition* was extensively overhauled and fine-tuned. Two types of consultants went over every sentence and section with a fine-tooth comb, making countless recommendations for what to add, subtract, revise, update, and rephrase.

Expert Research Consultants. A number of leading research experts in psychology evaluated individual chapters in their areas of expertise. Their detailed recommendations significantly improved the currency and accuracy of the text's research content.

Expert Teaching Consultants. They gave us an overall "big picture" view and detailed, line-by-line comments about what should go into an introductory psychology text and how it should be said. Their feedback has substantially reshaped this book in very positive ways.

Student Reviews and Focus Groups

We involved students in almost every facet of this revision. After all, they are the ultimate consumers of its content.

In addition to their part in determining the "relevance" theme for this edition, they told us (in focus groups) what elements worked and did not work for them in the various texts they used. They reacted to and advised us regarding several ideas we had developed for new substantive as well as pedagogical features. They critiqued the illustration program and gave numerous suggestions that helped guide the new format and design you see featured in this edition. All in all, their preferences are evident throughout the book.

∾ *"I really enjoy the layout of the book. I think the design, graphics are the most appealing part of this book. They make it interesting and they make it easier to turn the page."*
Heather Shafer, Student

∾ *"I like how the author is writing on a personal level. It's easy to read . . . [the text is] . . . well laid out, easy for eyes to move through the book, adds to the overall effect quite positively. . . ."*
Kelly Murphy, Student

∾ *"[The text is] very easy to comprehend. It is coherent . . . box titles are very attention-grabbing . . . good explanations. [The design] is the best part. The art is really cool, attention getting and visually appealing."*
Erica Mezi, Student

Acknowledgments

I owe debts to many people who substantially improved this book but two individuals deserve special thanks. Joseph Terry, Psychology Editor, was especially influential in supporting and shaping the book. I also benefited enormously from Glenn Turner's extensive, detailed analysis and recommendations. I value not only the extraordinary, competent professional input of these individuals, but also their friendship.

A number of leading experts in different subfields of psychology have provided me with invaluable advice about their areas of expertise.

Chapter 1: What Is Psychology: *Ludy Benjamin, Texas A&M, Charles Brewer, Clemson University; Keith E. Stanovich, University of Toronto;* Chapter 2: Biological Foundations and Neuroscience: *Jackson Beatty, UCLA;* Chapter 3: Sensation and Perception: *Alice O'Toole, University of Texas at Dallas;* Chapter 4: States of Consciousness: *G. William Domhoff;* Chapter 5: Learning: *Michelle Perry, U. of Illinois at Urbana, Champaign;* Chapter 6: Memory: *James Bartlett, University of Texas at Dallas; Daniel Schacter, Harvard University; Steven Smith, Texas A&M;* Chapter 7: Thinking, Language, and Intelligence: *Karen A. Luh; Jean Berko Gleason, Boston University; Mihalyi Csiksentmihalyi, University of Chicago;* Chapter 8: Human Development: *Illene Noppe, University of Wisconsin—Green Bay;* Chapter 9: Motivation and Emotion: *Laura King, SMU;* Chapter 10: Personality: *N.C. Higgins, University of North British Columbia;* Chapter 11: Abnormal Psychology: *Lillian Comas-Diaz, Transcultural Institute;* Chapter 12: Therapies: *Richard P. Halgin, University of Massachusetts, Amherst;* Chapter 13: Social Psychology: *Stanley Gaines, Pomona College; James Jones, U. of Delaware; John Harvey, U. of Iowa; Richard Brislin, East-West Center.*

In addition, many instructors who teach introductory psychology made special efforts to provide detailed feedback, in many cases on a line-by-line basis, about *Psychology: Brief Edition.* They were:

Valerie Ahl, *University of Wisconsin-Madison*
Susan Amato, *Boise State University*
Jim Backlund, *Kirtland Community College*
John Best, *Eastern Illinois University*
Michelle Boyer-Pennington, *Middle Tennessee State University*
James Calhoun, *University of Georgia*
Ellen Dennehy, *University of Texas-Dallas*
Kim Dielmann *University of Central Arkansas*
James Francis, *San Jacinto College*
James Greer, *Louisiana State University*
Jean Berko Gleason, *Boston University*
James J. Johnson, *Illinois State University*
Paul R. Kleinginna, *Georgia Southern University*
Linda Kline, *California State University-Chico*
Karen Kopera-Frye, *The University of Akron*
Phil Kraemer, *University of Kentucky*
Eric Landrum, *Boise State University*
Gary D. Laver, *California Polytechnic, San Luis Obispo*
Marta Losonczy, *Salisbury State University*
Karen E. Luh, *University of Wisconsin-Madison*
Jerry Marshall, *University of Central Florida*
Vicki Mays, *University of California-Los Angeles*
Carol Nemeroff, *Arizona State University*
Cindy Nordstrom, *Illinois State University*
David Penn *Louisiana State University*
Jeffrey Pedroza, *Lansing Community College*
Lawrence A. Pervin, *Rutgers University*
Vincent Punzo, *Earlham College*
Ed Raymaker, *Eastern Main Technical College*
Judith A. Sheiman, *Kutztown University*

Paula Shear, *University of Cincinnati*
Cynthia Sifonis, *University of Illinois*
Charles M. Slem, *California Polytech University*
Jutta M. Street, *Wake Technical Community College*
Roger M. Tarpy, Jr., *Bucknell University*
Christopher Taylor, *University of Arizona*
Leonard Williams, *Rowan University*
Michael Zickar, *Bowling Green State*

Another group of psychologists also deserve thanks. They wrote material for individual chapters in previous editions and some of this material served as a base for the development of chapters in the *Brief* edition. In this regard, thanks go to:

Alice O'Toole, *U. of Texas at Dallas* (What Is Psychology?; Sensation and Perception)
James Bartlett, *U. of Texas at Dallas* (Memory; Thinking, Language, and Intelligence)
Laura King, *Southern Methodist University* (Motivation and Emotion)
Barry Stein, *Tennessee Technological U.* (Thinking, Language, and Intelligence)

Student-Driven Pedagogy

Students not only should be challenged to study hard and think more deeply and productively about psychology, they should also be provided with an extensive pedagogical framework to help them learn. Each of the learning and study aids that follow, some of which are unique to this text, have been tested and endorsed by the majority of students attending our focus groups. As a consequence, we are more confident than ever before that your students will find this edition of *Psychology: Brief Edition* to be very student friendly.

Images of Psychology and Life

Opens each chapter with an imaginative, high-interest discussion that focuses on a topic related to the chapter content.

Chapter Outline

Shows the organization of topics by heading levels.

NEW!
Mini Cognitive Maps

These mini-maps appear three to five times per chapter and provide students with a more detailed, visual look at the organization of the chapter.

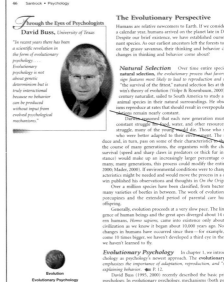

Preview

A brief look at what the chapter is about, including a series of questions that will be explored.

NEW!
Through the Eyes of Psychologists

This feature, appearing several times throughout each chapter, includes a photograph and quotation from leading psychologists to stimulate further thinking about the content.

Cartoons

Students like cartoons—perhaps because learning works best when the learner is in a good mood. To that end, cartoons appear several times in each chapter.

Summary Tables

These within-the-chapter reviews are coordinated with, and have the same headings as, the within-the-chapter cognitive maps. They give students a handle on information before they reach the end of the chapter.

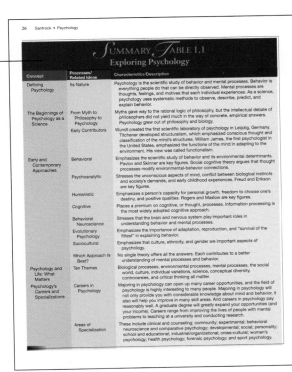

Explorations in Psychology

This feature addresses many controversial issues in psychology and science, asking the student to think critically and evaluate their own stance on these issues.

NEW! Key Terms

These are boldfaced in the text and their definition is italicized.

NEW! Cross-Linkage

This system, unique to this text and new in this edition, refers students to the primary discussion of all key concepts. A specific page reference appears in the text with a backward pointing arrow each time a key concept occurs in a chapter subsequent to its initial coverage.

NEW! McGraw-Hill web site

A web site icon appearing in the margin next to content guides student to the *Psychology: Brief Edition* Web site where they will find connecting Internet links that provide them with additional information. The label for each Web icon corresponds to the same label on the Santrock web site.

Thinking About Psychology and Life

This feature emphasizes the relevance of psychology to a student's everyday life through use of surveys and illustrative problems.

Overview

This consists of 2 parts: (1) an overall cognitive map of the entire chapter, and (2) a brief summary of the chapter.

NEW! Key People

The most important theorists and researchers in the chapter are listed and page-referenced.

End of Chapter Key Terms

The key terms are listed and page-referenced to the chapter in addition to a comprehensive glossary at the end of the book.

NEW! Taking It to the Net

Students are presented with questions to explore on the Internet, related to the chapter. From the *Psychology: Brief Edition* Web site under Taking It to the Net, students will find links to other Web sites providing information that will help them to think more deeply about the questions posed.

Illustration Program

The illustrations in introductory psychology texts have, in theory, always been important—but as almost any student will tell you, it is rare that the majority of photographs and figures are consistently relevant in a pedagogical context. This is usually because the authors and publishers place a far greater emphasis on the narrative content. However as more and more students become visual learners, the illustrative half of this equation must be accorded more attention. Failure to do so will result in texts that are unnecessarily more difficult for some students.

In this edition, we worked hard to give the illustration manuscript more relevance than the usual facelift would produce. Each photograph and figure was carefully selected and/or developed for its pedagogical significance, including those that open each chapter. Virtually every two-page spread contains one or more illustrations, providing visual interest and reinforcement for all key concepts. Many of the photo captions now contain critical thinking questions designed to encourage students to think more thoroughly about and apply the topic of the illustration to their own lives or related events.

Ancillaries

Print Media

Student Study Guide   The Study Guide to accompany *Psychology: Brief Edition* includes fill-in-the-blank activities, critical thinking, true/false, and multiple-choice exercises for students to get the most from their Introductory Psychology course. Take your mastery of psychology to the next level with the following resources and activities: The Big Picture: Chapter Overview, Learning Objectives, Guided Review, Explorations in Psychology, In Your Own Words, Correct the Incorrect, and Practice Test with Feedback.

Test Item File   Finally a Test Item File that works. It contains thoughtful, well-structured questions designed to foster true understanding, not rote memorization. While revised to accompany Santrock's *Psychology: Brief Edition*, this Test Item File is ideal for all instructors of introductory psychology. The test items found here cover a wide range of test-item types, including 125 multiple choice, 20 true/false, 20 fill-in-the-blanks, 20 matching, and 8 essay for each and every chapter!

Instructor's Course Planner   Creative, comprehensive, and fully integrated with the Student Study Guide and Test Item File, this teaching tool is ideal for both seasoned and first-year instructors of introductory psychology. Found within each chapter of this new and improved edition of the *Instructor's Course Planner* are the following features: Chapter Overview, Teaching Objectives, Teaching the Chapter, Explorations in Psychology, Thinking About Psychology in Everyday Life, Learning Style Activities, Activities Handouts, and Connections.

Multimedia

Computerized Test Bank (Macintosh and Windows)   This computerized test bank contains all of the questions in the print version and is available in both Macintosh and Windows platforms.

Interactive e-Source   The Santrock Interactive e-Source is a cutting edge CD-ROM consisting of the *Psychology: Brief Edition* textbook with interactive links to the supplement package within the text. The Interactive e-Source includes an abundance of interactive activities and special features such as, Psychology in the Reel World, primers, web resources, an audio glossary, interactive end-of-chapter quizzes, audio introductions to each chapter, Learning Style Assessment, and much more.

PRISM   The state-of-the-art PRISM CD-ROM combines 60 interactive simulations and exercises with text-specific study materials including learning objectives, review exercises, key terms, and practice quizzes to create a truly interactive learning experience. In addition to all of this, standard features include Psychology Around the Globe interactive articles, Web Links, Frequently Asked Questions, Internet Primer, Statistics Primer, Study Skills and Time Management Primer, and a Psychology Careers Appendix. Experience the next generation of Psychology study tools. Experience PRISM.

Web Site and Online Learning Center   The *Psychology: Brief Edition* Web site features a variety of instructor and student resources including an Online Learning Center with key terms, quizzes, chapter overviews, learning objectives, PowerPoint® Slides, web resources, primers and more.

Presentation Manager CD-ROM   Includes the contents of the Instructor's Manual, Test Bank, and PowerPoint® slides. The Presentation Manager provides an easy-to-use interface for the design and delivery of multimedia classroom presentations.

PageOut Image Bank   The McGraw-Hill Introductory Psychology Image Bank provides instructors with over 150 images from which to choose, including several from *Psychology: Brief Edition*.

Psychology

Chapter 1

CHAPTER OUTLINE

Images of Psychology and Life
Why Youth Kill

> *My* friend . . . care for your psyche, and . . . make it as good as possible. . . . Know thyself, for once we know ourselves, we may learn how to care for ourselves, but otherwise we never shall.*

Socrates
Greek Philosopher, 5th Century B.C.

Preview

PSYCHOLOGY IS A FASCINATING FIELD that contains some of the most interesting inquiries you will encounter in any area you study in college. In the following Images of Psychology section we will introduce you to one of those interesting areas of inquiry: Why do youth kill? Some of the other intriguing questions we will explore in this chapter are these:
- How did psychology come into being?
- What are psychology's main approaches?
- Why is critical thinking important in psychology?
- What is psychology's scientific approach like?

IN THE LATE 1990s, a series of school shootings gained national attention. In April 1999, at Columbine High School, in Littleton, Colorado, two students, Eric Harris (18) and Dylan Klebold (17), shot and killed 12 students and a teacher, wounded 23 others, and then killed themselves. In May 1998, slightly built Kip Kinkel strode into a cafeteria at Thurston High School in Springfield, Oregon, and opened fire on his fellow students, murdering two and injuring many others. Later that day, police went to Kip's home and found his parents lying dead on the floor, also victims of Kip's violence. In 1997, three students were killed and five others wounded in a hallway at Heath High School in West Paducah, Kentucky, by a 14-year-old student. These are but three of many school shooting incidents that have occurred in recent years.

Is there any way that psychologists can predict whether a youth will turn violent? It's a complex task but they have pieced together some clues (Cowley, 1998). The violent youth are overwhelmingly male and many are driven by feelings of powerlessness. Violence seems to infuse these youths with a sense of power. Sixteen-year-old Luke Woodham was known as a chubby nerd at his school in Pearl, Mississippi. But in the fall of 1997, he shed that image by stabbing his mother to death and shooting nine of his classmates, killing two of them. Woodham wrote in

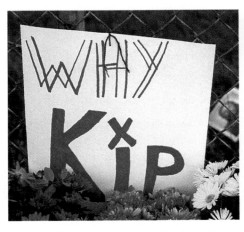

A sign at the entrance of the high school where the shooting spree took place asks Kip "why?" What are some possible reasons Kip Kinkel committed these brutal acts of violence?

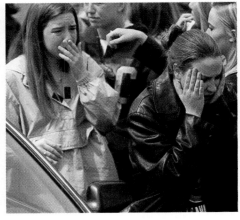

Students from Columbine High School in Littleton, Colorado, leave the school after two classmates went on a shooting rampage in April, 1999.

3

a letter: "I killed because people like me are mistreated every day. Murder is not weak and slow-witted. Murder is gutsy and daring."

Small-town shooting sprees attract attention but youth violence is far greater in poverty-infested areas of inner cities. Urban poverty fosters powerlessness and the rage that goes with it. Living in poverty is frustrating and many inner-city neighborhoods provide almost daily opportunities to observe violence. Many urban youth who live in poverty also lack adequate parent involvement and supervision.

University of Virginia psychologist Dewey Cornell (1998) says that many youth give clear indications of their future violence but aren't taken seriously. Cornell University psychologist James Garbarino (1999) says there is a lot of ignoring that goes on in these kinds of situations. Parents often don't want to acknowledge what might be a very upsetting reality. Harris and Klebold were members of the Trenchcoat Mafia clique of Columbine outcasts. The two even had made a video for a school video class the previous fall that depicted them walking down the halls at the school and shooting other students. Allegations were made that a year earlier the sheriff's department had been given information that Harris had bragged openly on the Internet that he and Klebold had built four bombs. Kip Kinkel had an obsession with guns and explosives, a history of abusing animals, and a nasty temper when crossed. When police examined his room, they found two pipe bombs, three larger bombs, and bomb-making recipes that Kip had downloaded from the Internet. Clearly, some signs were presented in these students' lives to suggest some serious problems, but it is still very difficult to predict whether youth like these will actually act on their anger and sense of powerlessness to commit murder.

Garbarino (1999) has interviewed a number of youth killers. He concludes that nobody really knows precisely why a tiny minority of youth kill but that it might be a lack of a spiritual center. In the youth killers he interviewed, Garbarino often found a spiritual or emotional emptiness in which the youth sought meaning in the dark side of life.

Exploring Psychology

Trying to figure out what motivates people like Kip Kinkel to commit murder is one of the many things psychologists do. What else do psychologists do?

Imagine that you are seated at dinner next to someone you have never met and learn that she is a psychologist. What comes to mind when you find out she is a psychologist? To many people, it means that she analyzes people's problems. When my wife is asked what her husband does for a living and she says "psychologist," they commonly respond, "Does he psychoanalyze you all the time?" When I meet people and they find out I'm a psychologist, you can see a reaction, like, "Uh oh, I'd better be on my guard or he will find out what I'm really like."

Many psychologists do analyze people's problems and try to help them cope with them. However, many psychologists are researchers, not therapists. No single image encompasses psychologists' varied activities. Consider the following descriptions of some contemporary psychologists at work:

- A research psychologist trained in cognitive psychology painstakingly constructs the thousands of steps of a computer program that, presented with hundreds of sentences, will learn language as an infant does.
- Another research psychologist trained in physiological psychology and neuroscience injects epinephrine into a rat that has learned a maze, to determine how the hormone affects its memory.
- A clinical psychologist probes a depressed client's thoughts for clues about the cause of the depression and thinks about ways to help the client cope more effectively.
- A school psychologist gives children a number of psychological tests and recommends the most effective learning environment for each child.

PEANUTS reprinted by permission of United Feature Syndicate, Inc.

- A psychologist interested in gender and women's issues teaches at a small college and works with her college and the community to eliminate sexual harassment.
- An organizational psychologist has a consulting firm that advises corporations on ways to improve communication and work productivity.

These are but a few of the many different portraits of psychologists. As you read this book, you will discover that psychology is a diverse field and psychologists have heterogeneous interests. Let's now see how psychologists define their field.

Defining Psychology

To some extent, psychology's findings may strike you as being simple common sense, but studies often turn up the unexpected in human behavior. For example, it may seem obvious that couples who live together before marriage have a better chance of making the marriage last. After all, practice makes perfect, doesn't it? But researchers have found a higher success rate for couples who marry before living together (Teachman & Polonko, 1990). It might also seem obvious that we would experience more stress and be less happy if we had to function in many different roles than if we only functioned in a single role. However, women who engage in multiple roles (such as wife, mother, and career woman) report more satisfaction with their lives than do women who engage in a single or fewer roles (such as wife or wife and mother) (Cozby, 1991). As you can see, psychology doesn't accept assumptions about human nature at face value, however reasonable they may sound. It is a rigorous discipline that tests assumptions.

Psychology *is the scientific study of behavior and mental processes.* There are three aspects to this definition: science, behavior, and mental processes.

As a **science,** *psychology uses systematic methods to observe, describe, predict, and explain behavior.* Psychology's methods are not casual. They are carefully and precisely planned and conducted. They are often verified by checking to see if they *describe* the behavior of many different people. For example, researchers might construct a questionnaire on sexual attitudes and give it to 500 individuals. They might spend considerable time devising the questions and determining the background of the people who are chosen to participate in the survey. The researchers may try to *predict* the sexual activity of college students based on their liberal or conservative religious attitudes, or on their sexual knowledge, for example. After the psychologists analyze their data, they will also want to *explain* what they *observe.* If the researchers discover from their survey that college students are less sexually active than they were a decade ago, they seek to explain why this change has occurred. They might ask, "Is it because of increased fear of sexually transmitted diseases?" As can be seen, psychology is recognized as a scientific discipline.

Let's now examine what behavior and mental processes are. **Behavior** *is everything we do that can be directly observed*—two people kissing, a baby crying, a college student riding a motorcycle.

Mental processes *are trickier to define than behavior; they are the thoughts, feelings, and motives that each of us experiences privately but that cannot be observed directly.* Though we cannot directly see thoughts and feelings, they are nonetheless real.

APA PsycNET
The American Psychological Society

*F*igure 1.1
Psychology's Beginnings
Psychology's seeds were sown in the nineteenth century by merging ideas from philosophy and natural sciences such as biology and physiology. *Why did psychology emerge as a hybrid offspring from these areas?*

History and Philosophy of Psychology
History of Psychology
Exploring the History of Psychology

Wilhelm Wundt (1832–1920), a philosopher-physician, who founded the first psychology laboratory at the University of Leipzig in Germany in 1879. Psychology Archives–University of Akron

They include *thinking* about kissing someone, a baby's *feelings* when its mother leaves the room, and a college student's *memory* of the motorcycle episode.

Psychology is not a cure-all for every knotty problem, and it doesn't tell us the meaning of life. It does, however, contribute enormously to our knowledge about why people are the way they are, why they think and act the way they do, and how they can cope more effectively with their lives. Many of life's problems today are psychological problems: death caused by unhealthy lifestyles (such as lack of exercise, poor eating habits, and inability to cope with stress), pollution, violence, racism, and employment in a changing information age. Psychologists are enthusiastic about psychology's potential to improve our lives in these and many other areas as we move into the twenty-first century. *It is an exciting time of discovery in the field of psychology.*

The Beginnings of Psychology as a Science

Now that we have defined psychology, let's explore the development and evolution of the field of psychology. How did a field so varied as psychology emerge? Who were its earliest contributors?

From Myth to Philosophy to Psychology
Ever since our ancestors first gathered around a fire to create and embellish myths, we've been trying to explain why things are the way they are. Myths attributed most events to the pleasure or displeasure of the gods: When a volcano erupted, the gods were angry; if two people fell in love, they were the target of Cupid's arrows. As we became more sophisticated, myths gave way to *philosophy*, the rational investigation of the underlying principles of being and knowledge.

For centuries, philosophers enjoyed arguing and debating (and still do today) questions like these: Do we acquire knowledge? Does information come to us through our senses and our experiences with the environment, or is it inborn? Although such speculation fuels a great deal of intellectual passion, psychologists always have searched for more concrete evidence than philosophers. Philosophers think about thinking and discuss thinking. So do psychologists, but psychologists also do something else. They systematically obtain and interpret evidence about thinking.

Philosophy was not the only discipline out of which psychology emerged. Psychology's roots also are in the natural sciences of biology and physiology (Benjamin, 1999). The intellectual atmosphere when psychology emerged as a science was heavily flavored by the work of British naturalist Charles Darwin. He developed the concept of **natural selection,** *that the organisms that are best adapted to their world are the most likely to survive, reproduce, and pass on their characteristics to their offspring.* Later in this chapter and in subsequent chapters, you will see that psychology has recently rediscovered Darwin's evolutionary approach. In addition to Darwin's influence on psychology's emergence, physiologists such as the German Johannes Müller already were proposing in the middle of the nineteenth century that the brain's role is to associate incoming sensory information with appropriate motor response.

Thus, by the late nineteenth century, conditions were ripe for psychology to emerge as a scientific discipline, a hybrid offspring of philosophy and natural science (Leahey, 1997) (see figure 1.1). Indeed, as we will see shortly, it was a philosopher-physician who put the pieces of the philosophy–natural science puzzle together to create the academic discipline of psychology.

Early Contributors
What was the first psychology lab like? What conceptual orientation did psychology's earliest contributors have?

Wundt's Laboratory Imagine a room in Leipzig, Germany, in the year 1879, where a bearded man with a wrinkled forehead and pensive expression is sitting on a chair. He turns his head toward a soft sound coming from the far side of the room.

After several seconds, he turns his head again, this time toward a loud sound. The activity is repeated with sounds of varying intensity. The man is Wilhelm Wundt, a philosopher-physician, who is credited with developing the first scientific laboratory in psychology. By systematically varying his experiences and then recording his reactions, Wundt was studying awareness of immediate experience, or what psychologists call *consciousness.*

Titchener and Structuralism The year is 1892. You are a student sitting in a class at Cornell University in Ithaca, New York. You and the other students wait with anticipation as a man wearing a flowing black gown strides into the lecture hall. Three assistants follow him. Instruments that demonstrate psychological experimentation are laid out on the stage. This was the protocol of E. B. Titchener, an Englishman and a student of Wundt's, who put his own spin on Wundt's psychology of consciousness after he immigrated to the United States. Titchener attempted to classify the structures of the mind, not unlike the way a chemist breaks down chemicals into their component parts—water into hydrogen and oxygen, for example. Thus, for Titchener, just as hydrogen and oxygen were structures, so were sensations and thoughts. He conceived of hydrogen and oxygen as structures of a chemical compound, and of sensations and thoughts as structures of the mind. This approach became known as **structuralism,** *an early theory of psychology developed by Wundt and Titchener that emphasized the importance of conscious thought and classification of the mind's structures.*

James and Functionalism The first psychologist in the United States was not Titchener, but William James. James (1890/1950) did not believe in the existence of the elementary, rigid structures of the mind for which Titchener searched. James argued that our minds are characterized by a continuous flow of information about our experiences rather than by discrete components. Following in the steps of Darwin, James emphasized the mind's ability to continuously evolve as it adapts to information about the environment. James's view shifted attention away from the mind's content to the mind's functions. James especially believed that the function of choosing was important in adapting to a changing world (Leahey, 1997). This approach became known as **functionalism,** *William James' theory that psychology's role is to study the functions of the mind and behavior in adapting to the environment.*

Edward Titchener (1876–1927), in the long, flowing black gown that he liked to wear when he lectured at Cornell University. When Titchener immigrated to the United States, he developed his own brand of psychology. What was Titchener's psychology like?
Psychology Archives–University of Akron

William James

Early and Contemporary Approaches to Psychology

The two approaches we just discussed—structuralism and functionalism—no longer are listed among psychology's main approaches, although most psychologists today continue to stress functionalism's emphasis on the importance of mind and behavior in adapting to the environment. Currently, seven main approaches compete in trying to explain psychology's subject matter: behavioral, psychoanalytic, humanistic, cognitive, behavioral neuroscience, evolutionary psychology, and sociocultural. Some of these approaches (behavioral, psychoanalytic) emerged very early in the twentieth century, others (evolutionary and sociocultural) are of very recent vintage. We will briefly study each of the seven approaches here, then return to them in greater depth later in this book.

Through the Eyes of Psychologists

William James, *author of*

Principles of
Psychology *(1890)*

*"Psychology is the
science of mental
life . . . of such
things as feelings,
desires, cognition,
reasoning,
decisions, and the
like."*

The Behavioral Approach

The year is 1898. You are ushered into a room, where you see a dog salivating profusely, and you wonder what is going on. A gentleman in a white laboratory coat walks over and quietly informs you that an experiment on learning is taking place. He explains that it is a very simple form of learning, in this case documented by the dog's salivation in anticipation of being fed. The man is Ivan Pavlov, who shows you that if he puts the dog's tray down or allows the dog to catch a glimpse of the attendant who fed him the previous day, the dog will begin to salivate.

Pavlov's experiments emphasized careful observation of overt behavior following precise manipulation of the environment. The observations were very different from the information collected through Wundt's introspection, which emphasized inferences about the conscious mind. Pavlov's interest in the overt behavior of organisms and the precise manner in which he observed behavior impressed a young American psychologist by the name of John B. Watson. Watson believed that conscious thought and mental processes had no place in psychology—they lacked objectivity and could not be measured, he said. The view of Pavlov and Watson is called the **behavioral approach,** *which emphasizes the scientific study of behavior and its environmental determinants.* According to behaviorists, we do well in school because of the rewards we experience; we behave in a well-mannered fashion for our parents because of the controls they place on us; and we work hard at our jobs because of the money we receive for our effort. We don't do these things, according to behaviorists, because of an inborn motivation to be a competent person or because a reward makes us feel better about ourselves. We do them because of the environmental conditions we have experienced and are continuing to experience.

Although an emphasis on observable behavior and environmental determinants is characteristic of all behavioral views today, different forms of behaviorism have developed. One form is close to the beliefs of Watson and is best represented by the well-known behaviorist B. F. Skinner (1938). Like Watson, Skinner argued that looking into the mind for the determinants of behavior detracts the investigator from the true cause of behavior—the external environment. Behaviorists who follow Skinner's approach modify and rearrange environmental experiences to determine their effects on an organism, whether rat, pigeon, or human. A father complains that his son misbehaves at home. Careful observation reveals that the father rarely rewards his son, even though his son gets good grades in school, is well liked by his peers, and does a number of chores around the house. The behaviorist calls the father's attention to this pattern of behavior and instructs him to tell the child how pleased he is whenever the child behaves positively, such as when the child does a chore. In this example, the behaviorist is not interested in what the father or the son is thinking or feeling. The behaviorist is only interested in their behavior, which can be directly observed.

Contemporary behaviorism also emphasizes the importance of observing behavior to understand an individual, and the rigorous methods for obtaining information about behavior advocated by Pavlov and Watson remain a cornerstone of the behavioral approach (Martin & Pear, 1999). Contemporary behaviorists continue to stress the importance of environmental determinants of behavior as well (Cantania, 2000; Pierce & Epling, 1999).

Not every behaviorist accepts Skinner's rejection of thought processes. **Social cognitive theory,** *as proposed by Albert Bandura (1986, 1998, 2000), stresses that behavior is determined not only by its controlling environmental conditions but also by how thoughts modify the impact of environment on behavior.* Perhaps the son in our example has observed and remembers other children misbehaving. The son might imitate their behavior, especially if the children are popular with peers. Bandura believes that imitation is one of the main ways we learn about our world. To reproduce a model's behavior, we must code and store the information in memory, which is a

Bandura's Theory

B. F. Skinner was a tinkerer who liked to make new gadgets. The younger of his two daughters, Deborah, was raised in Skinner's enclosed Air-Crib. Some critics accused Skinner of monstrous experimentation with his children; however, the early controlled environment has not had any noticeable harmful effects. Debbie, shown here as a child with her parents, is currently a successful artist, is married, and lives in London. Where do you stand on the ethics involved in Skinner's use of the enclosed Air-Crib to rear his infant daughter?

mental, or cognitive, process. Thus, social cognitive theorists broadened the scope of behaviorism to include not only observed behavior but also the ways in which information about the environment is cognitively processed.

The Psychoanalytic Approach

The year is 1904. You are lying on an incredibly comfortable couch in an office in Vienna, Austria. A gentleman with a stern look on his face walks in and sits down near you. He asks you to close your eyes. After several minutes of silence, he inquires about your childhood experiences. The man asking the questions is Sigmund Freud.

Unlike many pioneer psychologists, Freud was intrigued by the abnormal aspects of people's lives. Others were interested in either the conscious aspects of mind or in directly observable (overt) behavior. For Freud, the key to understanding mind and behavior rested in the unconscious aspects of mind—the aspects of which we are unaware. Freud compared the human mind to an iceberg. The conscious mind is only the tip of the iceberg, the portion above water; the unconscious mind is the huge bulk of the iceberg, the portion under water.

Freud (1917) believed that unlearned biological instincts influence the way individuals think, feel, and behave. These instincts, especially sexual and aggressive impulses, often conflict with the demands of society. For example, in Freud's view, a child inherits the tendency to act aggressively. The aggressive instinct is located in the child's unconscious mind; it is responsible, for example, for the aggressive energy a boy shows in destroying a friend's sand castle, in punching his brother in the nose, or in running wildly through a neighbor's flower garden. The aggressive instinct conflicts with acceptable social behavior, so the child must learn to adapt.

Although Freud saw much of psychological development as instinctually based, he argued that our early relationships with parents were the chief environmental contribution to our personality. That is why he asked you about your childhood as you relaxed on the couch. By getting you to talk about your early family life, Freud

The Psychoanalytic Approach

hoped you would unconsciously reveal clues about the conflicts causing your problems. The **psychoanalytic approach,** *then, emphasizes the unconscious aspects of the mind, conflict between biological instincts and society's demands, and early family experiences.*

The psychoanalytic approach has survived, although its form has changed somewhat from Freud's original theory. Many contemporary psychoanalytic theorists place less emphasis on sexual instincts and more emphasis on cultural experiences as determinants of personality. Unconscious thought remains a central theme, but contemporary psychoanalytic theorists believe conscious thought makes up more of the iceberg than Freud did.

Erik Erikson (1968) is an important revisionist of Freud's views. Erikson believes we progress through a series of personality stages over the human life span, unlike Freud, who thought personality virtually was etched in stone by 5 years of age. Erikson believes Freud shortchanged the role of culture in personality. Consider, for example, the adolescent years. In Erikson's approach, the key developmental task to be achieved during adolescence is identity, a search for who one is, what one is all about, and where one is going in life. For Freud, adolescents were primarily sexual beings, not wrapped, as Erikson believes, in an exploration of many different roles, some sexual but also some vocational, ideological, religious, lifestyle, and gender. Erikson believes that, by exploring alternatives in many different roles, an adolescent moves toward an identity. Erikson's view fits with our achievement-oriented culture, where exploration of alternative career options is a salient part of finding out who one is and where one is headed in life.

The Humanistic Approach

The Humanistic Approach

Some psychologists are not satisfied with either the behavioral approach, with its emphasis on environmental determinants of behavior, or the psychoanalytic approach, with its focus on instincts, abnormality, and unconscious thoughts. The **humanistic approach** *stresses a person's capacity for personal growth, freedom to choose his or her destiny, and positive qualities.* Humanistic psychologists take particular opposition to behaviorists, saying that individuals have the ability to control their lives rather than be manipulated by the environment. Humanists stress that our subjective, personal perception of ourselves and the world is more important than behavior itself. Humanists believe we have a tremendous potential for self-understanding. They also think we can help others achieve this self-understanding by providing a nurturant, warm social climate—in other words, by being supportive.

Carl Rogers (1961) and Abraham Maslow (1971) were the main architects of the humanistic approach. Rogers placed special emphasis on improving an individual's self-conception by providing a warm, supportive therapeutic environment. Maslow stressed the importance of achieving our potential, which he thinks is virtually limitless. Maslow called humanistic psychology the "third force" in psychology, believing it deserved the attention accorded the first two forces, behaviorism and psychoanalytic theory. The humanistic approach is a more recent view than behaviorism and psychoanalytic theory, so its staying power in psychology is yet to be determined. Critics call the humanistic approach unscientific, but it has been applauded for helping us reach our human potential and cope more effectively with our problems.

The humanists believe that we have a natural tendency to be loving toward each other and that each of us has the capacity to be a loving person if we would recognize it.

The Cognitive Approach   For many contemporary psychologists, the cognitive approach is an extremely important force in psychology. The **cognitive approach** *emphasizes the mental processes involved in knowing*: How we direct our attention, how we perceive, how we remember, and how we think and solve problems. For example, cognitive psychologists want to know how we solve algebraic equations, why we remember some things only for a short time but remember others for a lifetime, and how we can use imagery to plan for the future.

A cognitive psychologist views the mind as an active and aware problem-solving system (Baddeley, 1998; Haberlandt, 1999; Simon, 1996; Solso, 2000). This positive view contrasts with the pessimism of the psychoanalytic approach, which sees the individual as controlled by instincts, and the behavioral view, which portrays behavior as controlled by external environmental forces. In the cognitive view, an individual's mental processes are in control of behavior. The use of memories, perceptions, images, and thinking allows greater cognitive control over behavior than is possible in either the psychoanalytic or the behavioral approach. In the humanistic approach, emotions play a much stronger role than in the cognitive approach, and the humanistic approach does not emphasize the scientific study of mental processes, as does the cognitive approach.

Information processing *is the most widely adopted cognitive approach. Information-processing psychologists study how individuals process information—how they attend to information, how they perceive it, how they store it, how they think about it, and how they retrieve it for further use.* Computers played an important role in the development of the information-processing perspective. Essentially, computers are high-speed information-processing systems. In the 1950s, it was discovered that if computers were programmed appropriately, they could perform tasks that previously only humans could perform, such as playing chess or computing the answers to complex math problems. Computers provide a logical and concrete, though perhaps oversimplified, model of how information is processed in the mind.

Herbert Simon (1969) was among the pioneers of the information-processing approach. He reasoned that the human mind is best understood by comparing it to a computer processing information. In this model, the sensory and perceptual systems provide an "input channel," similar to data being entered into a computer. As information (input) comes into the mind, mental processes, or operations, act on it, just as the computer's software program acts on data. The transformed input generates information that remains in memory much in the way a computer stores what it has worked on. Finally, the information is retrieved from memory and put to use in the form of an overt response that can be observed, not unlike a computer searching for, finding, and printing out information.

The Behavioral Neuroscience Approach   According to the **behavioral neuroscience approach,** *the brain and nervous system are central to understanding behavior, thought, and emotion.* Our remarkable capabilities as human beings would not be possible without our brains. The human brain and nervous system constitute the most complex, intricate, and elegant system imaginable. Rather than study only thoughts, as cognitive psychologists do, neurobiologists believe that thoughts have a physical basis in the brain (Jausovec, 1999; Kolb & Whishaw, 1999). The human brain is only a 3-pound lump of matter, but in this lump are more than 100 billion interconnected nerve cells. Electrical impulses zoom throughout our brain cells, and chemical substances are released as we think, feel, and act.

Behavioral neuroscientists do study human brains, but much of their work is with simpler brains having far fewer nerve cells (Changeux & Chavillion, 1995). Consider the memory of the sea slug, a tiny snail with only about 10,000 nerve cells. The sea slug is a slow creature, but if given an electric shock to its tail, the sea slug

Neuroscientists have studied the memory of the sea slug, a tiny snail with only about 10,000 nerve cells. How did they investigate the sea slug's memory?

The Cognitive Approach
The Behavioral Science Approach

Calvin and Hobbes   **by Bill Watterson**

withdraws its tail quickly. It withdraws the tail even faster if it was previously shocked. In a primitive way, the sea slug remembers. The memory is written in chemicals. Shocking the sea slug's tail releases a chemical that basically provides a reminder that the tail was shocked. This memory informs the nerve cells to send out chemical commands to retract the tail the next time it is touched (Kandel & Schwartz, 1982). If nature builds complexity out of simplicity, the mechanism used by the sea slug might work in the human brain as well. In humans, the memory might come from the sight of a close friend, a dog's bark, or the sound of a car horn. Chemicals, then, might be the ink with which memories are written.

The human brain is divided into left and right sides. Roger Sperry (1964) made one of the most exciting discoveries in neuroscience when he revealed that some aspects of our behavior are controlled more by one side of the brain than by the other. Our own human gift of speech, for example, primarily involves the left side of our brain.

The Evolutionary Psychology Approach

The Evolutionary Psychology Approach

Although Darwin introduced the theory of evolution by natural selection in 1859, his ideas about evolution only recently have emerged as a popular framework for explaining behavior. Psychology's newest approach, the **evolutionary psychology approach,** *emphasizes the importance of adaptation, reproduction, and "survival of the fittest" in explaining behavior.* Evolutionary psychology's emphasis on adaptation reflects the earlier views of functionalism. Evolution favors organisms that are best adapted to survive and reproduce in a particular environment (Buss & Greiling, 1999). The evolutionary psychology approach focuses on conditions that allow individuals to survive or to fail. In this view, the evolutionary process of natural selection favors behaviors that increase organisms' reproductive success and their ability to pass their genes to the next generation.

David Buss' (1995, 1999, 2000) ideas on evolutionary psychology have ushered in a whole new wave of interest in how evolution is involved in explaining human behavior. He believes that just as evolution shapes our physical features, such as body shape and height, it also pervasively influences how we make decisions, how aggressive we are, our fears, and our mating patterns.

Steven Pinker (1997, 1999) recently argued that "how the mind works" can be summarized by three main points: (1) The mind computes, (2) the mind was designed to compute by evolution, and (3) these computations are performed by specialized brain systems that natural selection has designed to achieve specific kinds of goals, such as survival. Thus, in Pinker's view, the mind analyzes sensory input in ways that would have benefited the hunters and gatherers of human prehistory. Minds that understood causes and effects, built tools, set traps, and avoided poisonous mushrooms had the best chance of surviving and having offspring that would someday be able to invent mathematics and make movies about robots.

Through the Eyes of Psychologists

Steven Pinker, *MIT*

"The mind is a system of organs of computation that allowed our ancestors to outsmart plants and animals."

The Sociocultural Approach

The **sociocultural approach** *emphasizes that culture, ethnicity, and gender are essential to understanding behavior, thought, and emotion.* **Culture** *is the behavior patterns, beliefs, and other products of a particular group of people, such as values, work patterns,*

In Xinjiang, China, a woman prepares for horseback courtship. Her suitor must chase her, kiss her, and evade her riding crop—all on the gallop. A new marriage law took effect in China in 1981. The law sets a minimum age for marriage—22 years for males, 20 years for females. Late marriage and late childbirth are critical efforts in China's attempt to control population growth. What do you think about such laws?

The tapestry of American culture has changed dramatically in recent years. Nowhere is the change more noticeable than in the increasing ethnic diversity of America's citizens. Ethnic minority groups—African American, Latino, Native American, and Asian, for example—made up approximately one-third of all individuals under the age of 17 in the United States in the year 2000. Two of psychology's challenges are to become more sensitive to race and ethnic origin and to provide improved services to ethnic minority individuals. What might these communication strategies be like?

music, dress, diet, and ceremonies, that are passed on from generation to generation. A cultural group can be as large and complex as the United States, or it can be as small as an African hunter-gatherer tribe, but whatever its size, the group's culture influences the identity, learning, and social behavior of its members (Matsumoto, 1996; Triandis, 1994, 2000).

Ethnicity *(the word* ethnic *comes from the Greek word for "nation") is based on cultural heritage, nationality characteristics, race, religion, and language.* Ethnicity involves descent from common ancestors, usually in a specifiable part of the world. Given the descent of individuals from common ancestors, people often make inferences about someone's ethnicity based on physical features believed to be typical of an ethnic group. For example, one of the downed American flyers in the Gulf War had features that would be considered "Arab." He was treated worse than the other prisoners of war, who had non-Arab features. This reminds us that ethnicity is a category that is often applied to people even if they don't want to be categorized that way and feel the inferences are wrong and unfair (Brislin, 1990, 2000).

Our American culture is becoming increasingly more diverse in terms of including more people of color. In 1980, ethnic minority groups made up 20 percent of all individuals under the age of 17 in the United States. By the year 2000, the percentage will rise to about 33 percent. This changing demographic tapestry promises not only the richness that diversity produces but also difficult challenges in extending the American dream to all ethnic minority individuals (McLoyd, 1998, 1999).

So far we have discussed two aspects of sociocultural influences—culture and ethnicity. A third important aspect is **gender,** *the sociocultural dimension of being female or male.* **Sex** *is the biological dimension of being female or male.* Few aspects of our existence are more central to our identity and to our social relationships than our sex and gender (Bonvillian, 1998). Our gender attitudes and behavior are changing, but how much? Is there a limit to how much society can determine what

Cross-Cultural Psychology
Diversity Resources
Women Pioneers

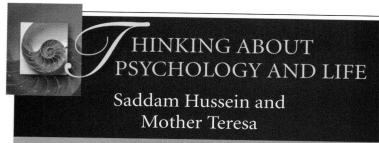

THINKING ABOUT PSYCHOLOGY AND LIFE
Saddam Hussein and Mother Teresa

WE HAVE EXAMINED seven different approaches in psychology. As a check on your understanding of these approaches and to stretch your thinking, explain how the seven approaches would differ in accounting for Iranian leader Saddam Hussein's inhumane behavior and Indian religious leader Mother Teresa's humanitarian efforts.

Saddam Hussein repeatedly has embarked on campaigns of violence against people in his own country and other Mideastern nations.

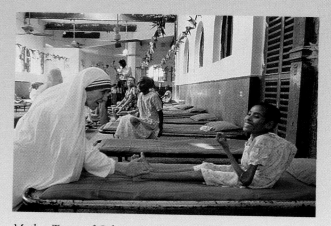

Mother Teresa of Calcutta, a Catholic nun, was a pillar of altruism in helping people in poverty, not just in India but around the world.

Psychology's Early Approaches

is appropriate behavior for females and males? A special concern on the part of many feminist writers is that in much of its history psychology has portrayed human behavior with a "male-dominant theme" (Crawford & Unger, 2000; Demark & Rabinowitz & Sechzer, 2000; Doyle & Paludi, 1998; Yoder, 1999).

The sociocultural approach is one of psychology's newest lenses for examining behavior and mental processes. As the future brings increasing contact between people from quite different backgrounds, the sociocultural approach will help to expand psychology's role as a relevant discipline in the twenty-first century.

Which Approach Is Best?
All of these approaches to psychology are in a sense correct. They are all valid ways of looking at human behavior, just as blueprints, floor plans, and photographs are all valid ways of looking at a house. Some approaches are better for some purposes. A floor plan, for instance, is more useful than a photograph for deciding how much lumber to buy, just as the neurobiological approach is more useful than the sociocultural approach for explaining how cells in the brain communicate with each other. And, in turn, the sociocultural approach is more useful than the neurobiological approach for understanding how to reduce prejudice and discrimination. But no single approach is "right" or "wrong."

Some psychologists adopt a particular approach, such as cognitive or behavioral or sociocultural; many others take a more eclectic approach. An **eclectic approach** *does not follow any one conceptual approach, but rather selects and uses whatever is considered best in each approach.* No single approach is infallible or capable of explaining all of psychology's rich and varied subject matter. Thus, the behavioral neuroscience approach informs us about the detailed workings of the brain and how they influence behavior, the cognitive approach provides guidance in how people make decisions, and the sociocultural approach describes strategies for communicating more effectively across cultures.

In our coverage of early and contemporary approaches, we have examined a number of approaches and individuals who were pioneers in various areas of psychology. For a glimpse of some of the main theorists and pioneers in psychology's history, see figure 1.2.

In presenting psychology's seven main approaches, we have encountered various themes that characterize the field of psychology. Next, we systematically explore these themes.

Psychology and Life: What Matters

What matters in psychology and life? There are few bigger questions we can tackle. We are going to describe ten things that do matter in psychology and life. These ten principles and themes also are woven through this book. You will discover that these

Wilhelm Wundt (1832–1920) **William James** (1842–1910)

Alfred Binet (1857–1911) **Ivan Pavlov** (1849–1936)

Ruth Howard (1900–) **B. F. Skinner** (1904–1990)

Erik Erikson (1902–1994) **Abraham Maslow** (1908–1970)

Carl Rogers (1902–1987) **Albert Bandura** (1925–)

Sandra Bem (1944–) **Eleanor Maccoby** (1917–)

1879: Wilhelm Wundt develops the first psychology laboratory at the University of Leipzig.

1890: William James publishes *Principles of Psychology*, which promotes functionalism.

1891: Mary Calkins establishes a laboratory for psychology at Wellesley.

1892: E. B. Titchener popularizes structuralism in the United States. G. Stanley Hall founds the American Psychological Association at Clark University.

1894: Margaret Washburn becomes the first woman to receive a Ph.D. in psychology.

1900: Sigmund Freud publishes *The Interpretation of Dreams*, reflecting his psychoanalytic view.

1905: Alfred Binet (with Theodore Simon) develops the first valid intelligence test to assess French schoolchildren.

1906: The Russian Ivan Pavlov publishes the results of his learning experiments with dogs.

1913: John Watson publishes his book on behaviorism, promoting the importance of environmental influences.

1934: Ruth Howard becomes the first African American woman to receive a Ph.D. in psychology.

1938: B. F. Skinner publishes *The Behavior of Organisms*, expanding the view of behaviorism.

1939: Mamie Phipps Clark and Kenneth Clark conduct research on African American children's self-conceptions and identity. Later, in 1971, Kenneth Clark becomes the first African American president of the American Psychological Association.

1945: Karen Horney criticizes Freud's psychoanalytic theory as male-biased and presents her sociocultural approach.

1950: Erik Erikson publishes *Childhood and Society*, a psychoanalytic revision of Freud's views.

1954: Abraham Maslow presents the humanistic view, emphasizing the positive potential of the individual.

1954: Gordon Allport writes his now classic book, *The Nature of Prejudice*.

1958: Herbert Simon presents his information-processing view.

1961: Carl Rogers publishes *On Becoming a Person*, highlighting the humanistic approach.

1961: Albert Bandura presents ideas about social learning theory, emphasizing the importance of imitation.

1964: Roger Sperry publishes his split-brain research, showing the importance of the brain hemispheres in behavior.

1969: John Berry, a Canadian psychologist, presents his ideas on the importance of cross-cultural research in psychology.

1974: Sandra Bem and Janet Spence develop tests to assess androgyny and promote the competence of females; Eleanor Maccoby (with Carol Jacklin) calls attention to the importance of sex and gender in understanding behavior and analyzing gender similarities and differences.

1977: Judith Rodin (with Ellen Langer) conducts research showing the powerful influence of perceived control over one's environment on behavior.

Mary Calkins (1863–1930) **G. Stanley Hall** (1844–1924)

Margaret Washburn (1871–1939) **John B. Watson** (1878–1958)

Mamie Clark (1917–1983) **Karen Horney** (1885–1952)

Gordon Allport (1897–1967) **Sigmund Freud** (1856–1939)

Roger Sperry (1913–1994) **John Berry** (1939–)

Judith Rodin (1944–) **Herbert Simon** (1916–)

*F*igure 1.2
Important Pioneers and Theorists in Psychology's History

principles and themes have relevance for understanding the academic discipline that studies mind and behavior (psychology) but also have applications to the real lives of people.

Biological Processes Matter

How strongly does your biological makeup influence your behavior? According to two of the approaches we discussed earlier—neurobiological and evolutionary psychology—biological processes have powerful influences on behavior. And they do. For example, when the visual areas of the brain are damaged, some aspects of visual experience disappear while others remain intact (Pinker, 1997, 1999). Individuals with such brain damage might see a complete world but pay attention only to half of it—they might eat food from the right side of the plate, shave only their right cheek, and draw a clock with all 12 numbers placed on the right half. Others lose their sensation of color but do not see the world as an artsy monochromatic film. Rather, surfaces appear as grimy and rat-colored, dulling their world. Yet others see changes in objects' positions but cannot see the objects move. The steam from a teapot does not flow but looks like an icicle. The cup does not gradually fill with tea. It is empty and then suddenly full. Others don't recognize the objects they see. They might copy a drawing of a tiger faithfully but identify it as a car. When they try to weed the garden, they pull out the roses. These faulty interpretations of the world are caused by an injury or a stroke that affects one or more of the thirty brain areas that make up the primate visual system. Some areas of this system specialize in form and color, others in where an object is, and yet others in how it moves. When you gaze at the world, you don't fathom all of the complex, inner workings of brain systems that are needed to perform behaviors you take for granted, like copying a drawing, perceiving an object as moving, and weeding a garden. The brain, after all, does nothing visible to you. But when injury and disease assault the brain, its powerful role in influencing behavior becomes apparent (Stoler & Hill, 1998). In psychology and life, *biological processes matter.*

Environmental Processes Matter

According to the behavioral approach we discussed earlier, environmental processes have powerful influences on behavior. Might the experiences you had when you were growing up have influenced the development of your brain and your behavior? Environmental experiences can contribute to a wiring, or rewiring, of the brain (Greenough, 1999; Nash, 1997). Repeated experiences especially contribute to this wiring or rewiring. For example, each time a baby tries to touch an attractive object or gazes intently at a face, tiny bursts of electricity shoot through the baby's brain, knitting together brain cells into circuits. And when Mark Rosenzweig (1969) randomly assigned animals to different environments to determine whether early experiences might alter the course of the brain's development, he found that they did. Animals in an enriched early environment lived in cages that offered stimulating experiences. They rotated wheels, climbed steps, pressed levers, and manipulated toys. The results were stunning. The brains of the "enriched" animals weighed more, had thicker layers, had more neural connections, and had higher levels of neurochemical activity than those of animals raised in standard cages or barren, isolated conditions. In psychology and life, *environmental experiences matter.*

Mental Processes Matter

How important is your mind in all that you do? We not only are biological and environmental beings, we also are mental beings. This concept is at the center of the cognitive approach we discussed earlier in the chapter. The universe inside

In neuroscientist Mark Rosenzweig's research, an "enriched" environment rewired the brains of rats by dramatically increasing their neural connections and neurochemical activity. In psychology and life, both biological and environmental processes matter. Can you think of other ways scientists might study how "enriched" environments might influence behavior?

your skull consists not only of a brain, but also of a mind whose mental processes allow you to remember, make decisions, plan, set goals, and be creative (Runko & Pritzker, 1999). Just as we take for granted the marvels of the brain's intricate workings, we also tend to gloss over the mind's remarkable adaptive and generative capacities that we use every day of our lives. Think about the following two mental feats that you are capable of (Hunt, 1982):

- *What is George Washington's phone number?* . . . You likely were quick to recognize that this question is absurd. But how did you know it was absurd without even considering the matter? Did you mentally search your memory phone book in a millisecond? Did you consult the encyclopedia of history in your mind? Whatever you did, it was fine mental performance!
- *ACORN is to OAK as INFANT is to* ——————. . . . Unless your mind was not focusing well, you knew at once that the blank should read *ADULT.* But how did you know? In brief, you compared the attributes of the first two capitalized words, inferred a rule that reflected their connection, and applied the rule to the third capitalized word *(INFANT).* Then you extrapolated to come up with the missing fourth word *(ADULT).*

To perform these two tasks, you had to use your memory and you had to think. As you read this section you thought about your mind and how it works. Twentieth-century French philosopher Albert Camus said that an intellectual is someone whose mind watches itself, but this is true of all human beings, more or less. An important dimension of psychology is the rigorous effort expended by many scientists to explore the inner workings of the human mind. In psychology and life, *mental processes matter.*

The Social World Matters

Take away people and what would your life be like? Imagine it. No one to talk with. No one to comfort you. Challenge you. Smile and cry with you. We are social beings

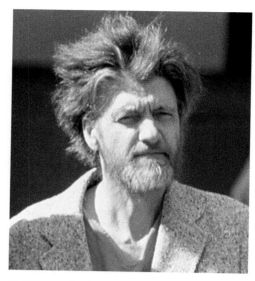

Ted Kaczynski, child genius, then math professor, who became the notorious Unabomber. Although intellectually talented, Kaczynski never fit in socially. Possibly if he had been able to "plug in" to a social network of peers and friends as he was growing up and as an adult, there would have been no Unabomber. Might a social skills training program when Kaczynski was growing up have prevented the Unabomber from developing?

who need other people to satisfy our wants and desires. Parents, teachers, peers, friends, and partners in close relationships play important roles in our socially connected lives (Collins & Laursen, 1999). How we treat others and they us, whether caring or hurting, stirs our minds and hearts. Most of us search for closeness, intimacy, and love. Some find these treasures, others discover they are elusive.

Consider the social deficiencies of the famed Unabomber, Ted Kaczynski (Waits & Shors, 1999). He sprinted through high school, not bothering with his junior year and making only passing efforts at social contact. When he reflected on his life, Kaczynski said that he was like a genius in a kid's body and stuck out like a sore thumb. Off to Harvard at 16, Ted was a loner in college. One of his Harvard roommates said that he had a special way of avoiding people by quickly shuffling by them and slamming the door behind him. After obtaining his Ph.D. in mathematics at the University of Michigan, Kaczynski became a professor at the University of California at Berkeley. His colleagues there remember him as hiding from the social world. He had no friends, no allies. He did no networking. After several years at Berkeley, Kaczynski resigned and moved to rural Montana, where he lived in a crude shack for 25 years. Residents there described him as a bearded eccentric. In 1996, the shy hermit was arrested and charged with being the notorious Unabomber, America's most wanted killer who sent sixteen mail bombs in 17 years that left twenty-three people wounded and maimed, and three people dead. One of the recipients of a Kaczynski bomb was University of Michigan psychologist James McConnell, whose writings on controlling people's lives by behaviorally engineering the environment had offended Kaczynski. In 1997, Kaczynski pled guilty to the Unabomber crimes. In psychology and life, *the social world matters*.

Culture Matters

How important for you is the culture in which you grew up, and the culture in which you now live your life? Earlier we indicated that one of psychology's newest approaches is the sociocultural approach, which has brought an increasing examination of culture's role in behavior. A change in cultural values and social policy took place in Zimbabwe in 1980 (Konner, 1991). At that time, fewer than 20 percent of the nation's children were enrolled in school and only a third had completed the seventh grade. Within 5 years, every child—2.3 million—was starting school and three of four had completed the 7-year course. The changing cultural values in Zimbabwe led to spending on education rising to 22 percent of the national budget, more than the defense and health-care budgets combined. Instead of working in the fields, Zimbabwe children now study science, mathematics, and the language arts. In a school at Tafara, children dug a fishpond in the shape of a world map and proceeded to study topics ranging from fish farming to geography to the control of water-borne diseases. They have no Cuisiniere rods or calculators; the children count with stones. There are no art supplies, but the children exercise their creative thinking by making compositions from mud and leaves.

Religion is also an important, but neglected, cultural area of study in psychology (Emmons, in press; Paloutzian, 2000). As nineteenth-century clergyman Henry Newman commented, religion can enlighten, terrify, and subdue. It can give faith, inspire resolutions, inflict remorse, and stir up wars. Religion also can inflame devotion, as it did in the 1990s when Branch Davidian leader David Koresh and Heaven's Gate leader Marshall Herff Appelwhite used religion to gain unwavering conformity in their followers. In adolescents, those with religious convictions are less likely to engage in sex than their less-religious counterparts (Thornton & Camburn, 1989). But when religious adolescents do have sex, they are less likely to use contraceptives. In psychology and life, *culture matters*.

Individual Variations Matter

How important is it to recognize that people are different from each other? Individuals play out their lives in different ways. No two people are exactly alike. Anyone who has lived with or been around another person for even a brief period of time knows this important principle. Roommates, parents and children, teachers and students, and friends and lovers soon find out that they are different from each other. One of psychology's important agendas is to chart not only the commonalities that we share with all others but also the unique ways we use our minds and the individual twists we put on our behavior (Stanovich, 1999). Your mix of genes and experiences cannot be duplicated. Even in these days of animal cloning and the potential for human cloning, unique experiences imprint every person's life.

With such a high divorce rate in the United States, psychologists are intrigued by what makes a successful marriage. In the recent study by John Gottman and his colleagues (1998), what were the best predictors of a successful marriage?

If we observed a group of seven people, we might find that each has a different set of skills, interests, and experiences (Gardner, 1993). One person excels at solving verbal problems and likes to do crossword puzzles, one loves math and reads computer magazines, one is good at creating mental maps of physical space and likes to draw buildings, one has great hand-eye coordination and excels at racquetball, one plays a musical instrument and likes to go to concerts, one has good self-evaluation skills and likes to write in a journal, and one is competent at "reading" other people and likes to help friends with their problems. Do you know anyone who is good at all of these things? At none of these things? Probably not. Our biological and experiential legacies interact to produce a unique composite of mind and behavior. In psychology and life, *individual variations matter.*

Science Matters

Does science matter in psychology and life? It sometimes is said that experience is the most important teacher. However, much of the knowledge we get from personal experience is based on our individual observations and interpretations. How do we know if these are accurate? Sometimes we make errors in sight, hearing, or perception. Chances are you can think of hundreds of situations in which you thought that other people read you the wrong way, just as they may have felt that you misread them. We bring our biases to situations and sometimes see only what we want to see. When we rely only on our own personal experiences, we aren't always totally objective because we sometimes base our judgments on a desire to protect our ego and self-esteem (McMillan, 2000).

As you read earlier in the chapter, psychology is a science. As a science, psychology can provide you with knowledge and understanding that is more objective than your personal interpretations. When asked about his personal thoughts on what it takes to make a good marriage, one man said "a wife who is attentive and listens to me." But in a recent scientific study of 130 newlywed couples over 6 years, John Gottman and his colleagues (1998) found that successful marriages are characterized by husbands who are flexible and often give in to what their wives want.* The autocrat husbands who failed to listen to their wives' complaints, greeting them with stonewalling, contempt, and belligerence, were doomed to have a failed marriage. However, wives were not completely off the hook in contributing to a successful marriage. When they couched their complaints in a gentle, soothing, sometimes even humorous, manner, their marriages were more successful than when they were belligerent. Gottman says that his research suggests there has to be a kind of gentleness in the way conflict is managed for marriages to work. Men have to be more accepting of a woman's position, and women have to be more sensitive in opening discussions. Scientific studies such as Gottman's can help correct our personal misinterpretations. In psychology and life, *science matters.*

*The inclusion of this research was encouraged by author John Santrock's wife, Mary Jo

Conceptual Diversity Matters

How varied are psychology's approaches? Earlier in this chapter we presented seven different approaches to psychology and concluded that all seven had some validity for examining and explaining behavior. Psychology is a field with considerable conceptual diversity. All of the seven grand approaches described in this chapter have made important contributions to psychology.

The diversity of approaches makes understanding psychology a challenging undertaking. Just when you think one approach provides the best explanation of behavior, another approach will crop up and make you rethink your earlier conclusion. To avoid frustration, remember that mind and behavior are very complex, and no single approach has been able to entirely explain them. Together, the varied conceptual approaches stimulate us to think about the complex landscape of mind and behavior and to search for more accurate understanding of it.

Psychology is characterized not only by grand approaches (like behavioral, cognitive, and behavioral neuroscience), but also by many "local" or "micro" approaches. Within the global cognitive approach are many specific approaches to studying memory, thinking, and creativity. For example, cognitive psychologists have proposed a number of competing theories about how people represent information in their memory, which we will discuss in chapter 7. This "micro" approach focuses on a specific aspect of mind and behavior, seeking precise explanations (Kuhn, 1998). As you read this book, you will come across many of these more focused views. Together the macro and micro approaches produce a more complete portrait of mind and behavior. In psychology and life, *conceptual diversity matters.*

Controversies Matter

How might psychology benefit from controversies? Psychology has advanced as a field because it does not accept simple explanations and because everyone does not agree with each other about why mind and behavior work the way they do. Rather, we have reached a more accurate understanding of mind and behavior because psychology is a field characterized by controversies.

What are some of psychology's controversies? In the area of gender, evolutionary psychologists argue that sex differences are large and biologically based. By contrast, sociocultural psychologists stress that sex differences are small or nonexistent in most areas and that when differences occur they are based on experience. Here is a brief sampling of other controversies in psychology:

- Whether memories of sexual abuse are real or imagined
- Whether intelligence can be increased
- Whether alcoholism is a biologically based disease or a learned behavior
- Whether it is best to treat depression with drugs or psychotherapy

As you read the remaining chapters of the book, you will come across many more controversies. In psychology and life, *controversies matter.*

Critical Thinking Matters

Are you a critical thinker? What does it mean to be a critical thinker? Understanding the complex nature of mind and behavior requires **critical thinking,** *which involves thinking reflectively and productively, and evaluating the evidence.* Thinking critically means asking yourself how you know something. Too often we have a tendency to recite, define, describe, state, and list rather than analyze, infer, connect, synthesize, criticize, create, evaluate, think, and rethink (Brooks & Brooks, 1993). Following is a brief sampling of some thinking strategies that can stimulate you to think reflectively and productively:

- *Be open-minded.* This involves exploring options and avoiding narrow thinking.

- *Be intellectually curious.* This includes wondering, probing, questioning, and inquiring, as well as recognizing problems and inconsistencies.
- *Be intellectually careful.* This consists of checking for inaccuracies and errors, being precise, and being organized.
- *Look for multiple determinants of behavior.* People have a tendency to explain things as having a single cause. After all, that's a lot easier than having to analyze the complexity of, say, mind and behavior and come up with multiple explanations. However, one of psychology's important lessons is that mind and behavior have multiple determinants. For example, if someone asked what causes a person to be a good critical thinker, the person might respond, "Being open-minded." However, that really is not a cause, but rather one of critical thinking's multiple dimensions. When another person is asked what causes critical thinking, the individual might respond, "Practice." Yet another person might say, "An inquiring, critical thinking mentor." Someone else might say, "A lifetime of education that stimulates wondering and probing." And someone might mention "good genes." Like all aspects of mind and behavior, critical thinking also has another dimension.
- *Think like a scientist.* A glimpse of how scientists think appeared earlier in this section. We said that science urges us to keep in mind that personal experiences and interpretations can be filled with errors and biases. Scientific thinkers examine what evidence is available about some aspect of mind and behavior, evaluate how strongly the data (information) supports their hunches, analyze disconfirming evidence, and carefully consider whether they have explored all of the possible factors and explanations (Stanovich, 1999). Critical thinking expert Diane Halpern (1996) underscores the importance of looking for biases in the way people think and behave. For example, a person raving about the remarkable effects of exercise on health might sell exercise videos on the side. In the next chapter, in our discussion of the scientific method, we will explore more systematically how to think like a scientist.

To read about some other areas in which people often fail to think critically, ranging from taking advice based on horoscopes to believing that eating a ground-up version of a tiger's sexual organ will increase the human male's sexual potency, see the Explorations in Psychology box. Also, because thinking critically is such an important aspect of psychology, several times in each chapter of this book you will be encouraged to think critically in Thinking About Psychology and Life boxes. In psychology and life, *thinking critically matters.*

Psychology's Careers and Areas of Specialization

Psychologists don't spend all of their time in a laboratory, white-smocked with clipboard in hand, observing rats and crunching numbers. Some psychologists spend their days seeing people with problems, others teach at universities and conduct research. Still others work in business and industry, designing more efficient criteria for hiring. In short, psychology is a field with many areas of specialization (figure 1.3).

Careers in Psychology You might already be wondering whether to major in psychology. Students who major in psychology often find that the subject matter is highly interesting. You already have encountered some of these interesting topics in this first chapter—including exploring the brain's role in behavior, figuring out ways to help children think critically, and analyzing why youth kill people. In the remaining chapters, you will encounter hundreds more of these truly fascinating inquiries in psychology.

Through the Eyes of Psychologists

Diane Halpern, *California State University, San Bernardino*

"Critical thinking is not a spectator sport. Research has shown that critical thinking skills must be practiced with a wide variety of problems in many different contexts to be learned and retained."

Being Skeptical

CRITICAL THINKING EXPERT Diane Halpern (in press) recently explained why she is concerned that so many people fail to use critical thinking. Approximately 75 percent of Americans read their horoscope and many of them believe that it is personally meant for them (Lister, 1992). Some phone their psychics and pay exorbitant amounts they cannot afford for advice that ranges from how to invest their money to whether or not a loved one should be disconnected from life-support systems. They spend large sums of money on remedies for which there is no evidence that they work or are safe to take. In a survey of college students, virtually 100 percent believed in at least one of the following (Messer & Griggs, 1989):

- channeling (the ability to enter a trance state and communicate with someone in another place and time, even centuries ago)
- clairvoyance (the ability to perceive remote events that are not visible to normal sight)
- precognition ("knowing" events before they occur)
- telepathy (the extrasensory transfer of thought from one person to another)
- psychic healing (performing miracle cures instantaneously through contact with a higher spiritual being)
- psychic surgery (a brand of faith healing where sleight of hand is relied on to achieve a miracle, such as removing dead or diseased tissue)
- crystal power (use of quartz crystals for healing)
- psychokinesis (being able to move objects without actually touching them)
- astral travel
- levitation
- the Bermuda Triangle mystery
- unidentified flying objects (UFOs)
- plant consciousness
- auras
- ghosts

If you believe in any of these phenomena, psychologists urge you to be more skeptical. Remember that thinking like a scientist means that you demand to see the evidence for such phenomena as channeling, crystal power, and plant consciousness. There is no scientific evidence for the existence of any of the above listed phenomena, only personal anecdotes and coincidences, and those do not meet science's criteria of objectivity and public verifiability.

If you still aren't convinced that these phenomena don't exist, at least critically examine the vague language used in horoscopes and the erroneous rationale that time of birth significantly predicts an individual's personality, future events, or anything else. When astrologers' predictions are successful, it is because they are so vague that they are virtually guaranteed to happen (for example, "Money is likely to be a concern for you this month" or

"A tragic plane crash will occur in the southern United States this winter"). When astrologers make more specific predictions (such as "An unidentified flying object will land on the field during the halftime of the ABC Monday Night Football game on October 8, 2001"), they never hold up.

When you think like a scientist, you will be skeptical of astrology, channeling, crystal power, and anything else that claims access to wondrous powers and supernatural forces (Ward & Grashial, 1995). When something sounds like it's too good to be true, think through the claims logically and demand to see the evidence. A failure to think critically and demand scientific evidence often underlies our purchase and use of highly touted, ineffective health-care products (Halpern, in press). For example, there is a widespread belief around the world today that a man who ingests the ground penis of a tiger will have more sexual potency. This belief is so pervasive that it has resulted in poaching of rare wild tigers and other endangered species. Males who believe that this works think like this: Tigers (presumably) have a great sex life; thus, eating a tiger's sexual organ will improve my sex life. You should be able to see what is wrong with this kind of thinking, especially in the absence of any evidence to support it.

Why should you be skeptical when you hear that eating a ground up penis of a tiger will increase the human male's sexual potency?

Why does the science of psychology urge you to be skeptical of astrology?

Not only will you gain considerable knowledge and understanding of mind and behavior by majoring in psychology, but majoring in psychology will equip you with a rich and diverse portfolio of skills that will serve you well in undertaking many different types of work, both practical and professional. A psychology major can help you improve your research skills, measurement and computing skills, problem-solving and critical thinking skills, and writing skills (Hayes, 1997). Integrating these skills, which span the arts and sciences, will provide you with unique qualifications. Even if you are not a psychology major or do not plan to major in psychology, this course and others in psychology can provide you with a richer, deeper understanding of many areas of life.

Psychology not only can give you a rich knowledge base and a great repertoire of skills, it also pays reasonably well (Sternberg, 1997). Psychologists earn well above the median salary in the United States. It is unlikely that you will live in a palatial mansion by majoring in psychology, but it is also unlikely that you will go broke. Although psychology is unlikely to make you fantastically wealthy, it will help you to improve peoples' lives, understand yourself and others, possibly advance the state of knowledge in the field, and have an enjoyable time while you are doing these things.

An undergraduate degree in psychology can provide you with access to a variety of jobs. For a list of some of the job possibilities in business, social/human services, and research, see figure 1.4. If you choose a career in psychology, you can greatly expand your opportunities (and your income) by getting a graduate degree, either a master's or a doctorate.

Where do psychologists work? Slightly more than one-third are teachers, researchers, or counselors at colleges or universities. Most other psychologists work in clinical and private practice settings (see figure 1.3).

Figure 1.3
Settings in Which Psychologists Work

More psychologists work in academic settings (34%), such as colleges and universities, than any other. However, clinical (24%) and private practice (22%) settings, both of which are contexts where many psychologists in the mental health professions work, combined make up almost half of the total settings.

Careers in Psychology

Areas of Specialization in Psychology

If you go to graduate school, you will be required to specialize in a particular area of psychology. Following is a list of some of the specializations: clinical and counseling; community; experimental; physiological psychology and neuroscience; developmental; social; personality; school and educational; industrial and organizational; cross-cultural; psychology of women; health; forensic; and sports. Sometimes the categories are not mutually exclusive. For example, some social psychologists are also experimental psychologists.

Clinical and counseling psychology *is the most widely practiced specialization in psychology: clinical and counseling psychologists diagnose and treat people with psychological problems.* The work of clinical psychologists often does not differ from that of counseling psychologists, although a counseling psychologist sometimes deals with people who have less serious problems. In many instances, counseling psychologists work with students, advising them about personal problems and career planning.

Clinical psychologists are different from psychiatrists. Typically a clinical psychologist has a doctoral degree in psychology, which requires 3 to 4 years of graduate work, plus 1 year of internship in a mental health facility. **Psychiatry** *is a branch of medicine practiced by physicians with a doctor of medicine (M.D.) degree who subsequently specialize in abnormal behavior and psychotherapy.* Clinical psychologists and psychiatrists both are interested in improving the lives of people with mental health problems. One important distinction is that psychiatrists can prescribe drugs, whereas clinical psychologists cannot (Friedman, 2000).

"Well, you don't look like an experimental psychologist to me."

Some Job Possibilities for Students with an Undergraduate Degree in Psychology

Following is a brief list of some job possibilities that students with an undergraduate degree in psychology may find available (Jalbert, 1996):

Business
- personnel administrator
- public relations
- sales representative
- admissions recruiter
- textbook representative
- advertising
- insurance agent
- management trainee
- retail sales management
- loan officer

Social/Human Services
- case worker
- youth counselor
- employment counselor
- fund-raising specialist
- alumni affairs coordinator
- mental health aide
- parent educator
- drug abuse counselor

Research
- research assistant
- trainee for product research companies
- marketing researcher
- grant and report writer
- information specialist/researcher
- research analyst
- statistical assistant

Figure 1.4
Some Job Possibilities for Students with an Undergraduate Degree in Psychology

Nonacademic Careers in Psychology

APA's Divisions

Community Psychology

Behavioral Neuroscience and Comparative Psychology

Community psychology *focuses on providing accessible care for people with psychological problems.* Community-based mental health centers are one means of providing such services as outreach programs to people in need, especially those who traditionally have been underserved by mental health professionals. Community psychologists view human behavior in terms of adaptation to resources and to one's situation. They work to create communities that are more supportive of residents by pinpointing needs, by providing needed services, and by teaching people how to gain access to resources already available (Kelly, 2000). Finally, community psychologists are also concerned about *prevention.* They try to prevent mental health problems by identifying high-risk groups and then intervening to provide appropriate services and by stimulating new opportunities in the community.

Experimental psychology *involves areas in which psychologists often conduct basic research and use an experimental strategy.* Among the main areas that experimental psychologists study are sensation and perception, cognitive processes (such as memory), learning, motivation, and emotion.

Behavioral neuroscience and comparative psychology *focus on biological processes, especially the brain's role in behavior.* Many of these scientists use animals in their research and investigate a range of topics from how the brain processes information to the effects of hormones on behavior (Dewsbury, 2000).

Developmental psychology *is concerned with how we become who we are, from conception to death.* In particular, developmental psychologists focus on the biological and environmental factors that contribute to human development. For many years the major emphasis was on child development. However, an increasing number of today's developmental psychologists show a strong interest in adult development and aging (Baltes, 2000). Their inquiries range across the biological, cognitive, and social domains of life.

Social psychology *deals with people's social interactions, relationships, social perceptions, and attitudes.* Social psychologists believe we can better understand mind and behavior if we know something about how people function in groups.

Personality psychology *focuses on the relatively enduring traits and characteristics of individuals.* Personality psychologists study such topics as self-concept, aggression, moral development, gender roles, and inner or outer directedness.

School and educational psychology *is concerned with children's learning and adjustment in school.* School psychologists work in elementary and secondary school systems, testing children, making recommendations about educational placement, and working on educational planning teams (Fagan, 2000). Educational psychologists work at colleges and universities, teach classes, and do research on teaching and learning.

Industrial/organizational psychology *deals with the workplace, focusing on both the workers and the organizations that employ them.* Industrial/organizational psychologists are concerned with training employees, improving working conditions, and developing criteria for selecting employees (Austin, 2000). For example, an organizational psychologist might recommend that a company adopt a new management structure that would increase communication between managers and staff. The background of industrial and organizational psychologists often includes training in social psychology.

Cross-cultural psychology *examines the role of culture in understanding behavior, thought, and emotion.* Cross-cultural psychologists compare the nature of psychological processes in different cultures, with a special interest in whether or not psychological phenomena are universal or culture specific (Berry, 2000). The International Association for Cross-Cultural Psychology promotes research on cross-cultural comparisons and awareness of culture's role in psychology.

The **psychology of women** *emphasizes the importance of promoting the research and study of women,* integrating this information about women with current psychological knowledge and beliefs, and applying the information to society and its institutions. The Division of the Psychology of Women in the American Psychological Association was formed in 1973.

Health psychology *is a multidimensional approach to health that emphasizes psychological factors, lifestyle, and the nature of the health-care delivery system.* Health psychologists may work in physical or mental health areas. Some are members of multidisciplinary teams that conduct research or provide clinical services (Weiss, 2000).

Forensic psychology *is the field of psychology that applies psychological concepts to the legal system.* Social and cognitive psychologists increasingly conduct research on topics related to psychology and law. And forensic psychologists are hired by legal teams to provide input about many aspects of a trial (Roesch, 2000).

Sport psychology *is the field of psychology that applies psychology's principles to improving sport performance and enjoying sport participation.* Sport psychology is a relatively new field but is rapidly gaining acceptance (Cox, 2000). At the 1996 Olympics, more than twenty sport psychologists worked with U.S. athletes and coaches.

In sum, the avenues an individual can follow as a psychologist are richly varied. We have only touched on this enormous variety in our description of psychology's main areas. For example, within each area numerous specializations are possible.

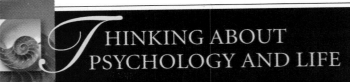

THINKING ABOUT PSYCHOLOGY AND LIFE

Which Areas of Psychology Interest You the Most?

PSYCHOLOGY has many diverse areas, ranging from exploring the brain's role in behavior to understanding how we develop as human beings to helping people with their psychological problems. Think about the areas of psychology described in the text. Which areas interest you the most? Go through the list of areas below and rank them from 1 (most interesting) to 11 (least interesting).

_____ Clinical and Counseling Psychology
_____ Community Psychology
_____ Experimental Psychology
_____ Physiological Psychology and Neuroscience
_____ Developmental Psychology
_____ Social Psychology
_____ Personality Psychology
_____ School and Educational Psychology
_____ Industrial/Organizational Psychology
_____ Cross-Cultural Psychology
_____ The Psychology of Women
_____ Health Psychology
_____ Forensic Psychology
_____ Sports Psychology

When you have finished studying this book and completed the course, you might want to return to this exercise to see if and how your rankings are different.

Educational Psychology

Health Psychology

Forensic Psychology

Sport Psychology

Psych Web

SUMMARY TABLE 1.1
Exploring Psychology

Concept	Processes/ Related Ideas	Characteristics/Description
Defining Psychology	Its Nature	Psychology is the scientific study of behavior and mental processes. Behavior is everything people do that can be directly observed. Mental processes are thoughts, feelings, and motives that each individual experiences. As a science, psychology uses systematic methods to observe, describe, predict, and explain behavior.
The Beginnings of Psychology as a Science	From Myth to Philosophy to Psychology	Myths gave way to the rational logic of philosophy, but the intellectual debate of philosophers did not yield much in the way of concrete, empirical answers. Psychology grew out of philosophy and biology.
	Early Contributors	Wundt created the first scientific laboratory of psychology in Leipzig, Germany. Titchener developed structuralism, which emphasized conscious thought and classification of the mind's structures. William James, the first psychologist in the United States, emphasized the functions of the mind in adapting to the environment. His view was called functionalism.
Early and Contemporary Approaches	Behavioral	Emphasizes the scientific study of behavior and its environmental determinants. Pavlov and Skinner are key figures. Social cognitive theory argues that thought processes modify environmental-behavior connections.
	Psychoanalytic	Stresses the unconscious aspects of mind, conflict between biological instincts and society's demands, and early childhood experiences. Freud and Erikson are key figures.
	Humanistic	Emphasizes a person's capacity for personal growth, freedom to choose one's destiny, and positive qualities. Rogers and Maslow are key figures.
	Cognitive	Places a premium on cognitive, or thought, processes. Information processing is the most widely adopted cognitive approach.
	Behavioral Neuroscience	Stresses that the brain and nervous system play important roles in understanding behavior and mental processes.
	Evolutionary Psychology	Emphasizes the importance of adaptation, reproduction, and "survival of the fittest" in explaining behavior.
	Sociocultural	Emphasizes that culture, ethnicity, and gender are important aspects of psychology.
	Which Approach Is Best?	No single theory offers all the answers. Each contributes to a better understanding of mental processes and behavior.
Psychology and Life: What Matters	Ten Themes	Biological processes, environmental processes, mental processes, the social world, culture, individual variations, science, conceptual diversity, controversies, and critical thinking all matter.
Psychology's Careers and Specializations	Careers in Psychology	Majoring in psychology can open up many career opportunities, and the field of psychology is highly interesting to many people. Majoring in psychology will not only provide you with considerable knowledge about mind and behavior, it also will help you improve in many skill areas. And careers in psychology pay reasonably well. A graduate degree will greatly expand your opportunities (and your income). Careers range from improving the lives of people with mental problems to teaching at a university and conducting research.
	Areas of Specialization	These include clinical and counseling; community; experimental; behavioral neuroscience and comparative psychology; developmental; social; personality; school and educational; industrial/organizational; cross-cultural; women's psychology; health psychology; forensic psychology; and sport psychology.

At this point we have explored a number of ideas about the field of psychology. A review of these ideas is presented in summary table 1.1. So far in this chapter, we have touched on psychology's role as a science on several occasions. Next we will more extensively explore psychology's scientific makeup.

Psychology's Scientific Approach

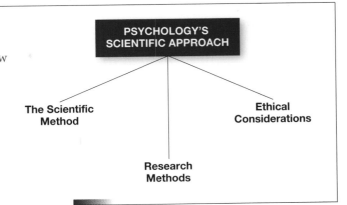

Can a discipline that studies why people are attracted to each other, how they reason about moral values, and the way ethnicity affects identity be equated with disciplines that examine gravity, the molecular structure of a compound, and the flow of blood in the circulatory system? Science is not defined by *what* it investigates but by *how* it investigates. Whether you study photosynthesis, butterflies, Saturn's moons, or why some people bite their fingernails more than others do, it is the way you study them that makes your approach scientific or not.

The Scientific Method

The scientific method is widely used by psychologists when they study behavior and mental processes. Scientific research is based on the **scientific method,** *an approach that can be used to discover accurate information. It includes these steps: Conceptualize a problem, collect data, draw conclusions, and revise research conclusions and theory.* We will apply the scientific method to aggressive behavior and violence to provide a common thread for their discussion and to help you understand them.

Conceptualize a Problem   The problem we have chosen is whether people become aggressive by observing other people's aggressive actions. Conceptualizing a problem might not seem like a difficult task. However, a common difficulty that many students (undergraduate and graduate) have is that they state the problem they want to study in vague, general terms. For example, a student might say, "I want to study aggression" or "I want to study why people become violent." That is a start, but it is important to go beyond a general description of a problem by narrowing and zeroing in on what you want to study. Do you want to study aggression's biological dimensions? environmental determinants? Do you want to study strategies for reducing aggression? For example, here is a specific problem that can be studied with regard to aggression's biological dimensions: What role does the hormone testosterone play in males' aggressive behavior? And here is a specific problem that can be studied in regard to strategies for reducing aggression: Does keeping children from watching aggression on TV decrease their aggressive behavior?

Operational Definition   In conceptualizing a problem, psychologists use an **operational definition,** *which consists of describing as precisely as possible the aspects of a problem and how it is to be studied in terms of observable events that can be measured.* By using operational definitions, psychologists eliminate some of the fuzziness and loose ends that easily creep into thinking about a problem and studying it. Operational definitions also make concepts public by being very specific about what observational measurements define them. An operational definition frees a concept from any particular individual's feelings and intuitions, allowing it to be studied by anyone who can conduct the measurable operations.

To see the importance of an operational definition, consider a concept like "depression." "Feeling sad" is not an operational definition of depression. Depression might be operationally defined as experiencing, for 2 weeks or longer, a major depressive episode, depressed characteristics such as lethargy and hopelessness, and impaired daily functioning. Further, for the definition to be operational, there would have to be clear ways to measure depression, such as through an interview, survey, or observations.

Albert Bandura examined aggression's many dimensions and possible determinants. He chose to focus on whether children learn to be aggressive from watching other people be aggressive (Bandura, 1965). In this first step in the scientific method,

Exploring Pseudoscience

Science and Research Methods

On Being a Scientist
Generating Research Ideas
Statistics Resources

Bandura identified a problem to study and used operational definitions to precisely describe aggression and how it was to be studied. Imitative aggression was operationally defined as observable physical and verbal behaviors shown by children as agreed upon by two independent judges. Bandura also operationally defined the procedure by which children observed a model in considerable detail. Following is an excerpt from one portion of the procedure, which clearly reveals how precise psychologists are when they conduct studies:

> The children were brought individually to a semi-darkened room. The experimenter informed the children that she had some business to attend to before they could proceed to the "surprise playroom," but that during the waiting period the child might watch a television program. After the child was seated, the experimenter walked over to the television console, ostensibly tuned in a program and then departed. A film of approximately 5 minutes duration depicting the model's responses was shown on a glass lenscreen in the television console by means of a rear projection arrangement, screened from the child's view by large panels. The televised form of presentation was utilized primarily because attending responses to televised stimuli are strongly conditioned in children and this procedure would therefore serve to enhance observation which is a necessary condition for imitative learning. (Bandura, 1965, p. 590)

Consider how much more precise this operational definition of the research procedure is than to just say, "The children will observe a model behave aggressively in a room" (which does not adequately operationally define the procedure).

Theory and Hypotheses   Theories might be used in conceptualizing a problem. A **theory** *is a coherent set of interrelated ideas that helps to make predictions and explain data.* A theory has **hypotheses,** *which are specific assumptions or predictions that can be tested to determine their accuracy.* Theories that have withstood the test of time have had a lot of hypotheses confirmed (Stanovich, 1998).

You might recall from chapter 1 our description of Bandura's social cognitive theory, a theory that emphasizes that both experiences and thoughts influence behavior. As part of his social cognitive theory, Bandura believes that observational learning is a key process. Bandura and others have conducted many research studies within this general theoretical framework. In his study of aggression, one of the hypotheses that Bandura (1965) tested was this: *Children who watch a model be either reinforced or given no consequence for being aggressive will be more likely to imitate the model than when the model is punished for being aggressive.* The reinforcement consisted of the model being given candy and soft drinks along with words of praise for a superb performance. The punishment consisted of another adult shaking a menacing finger at the aggressive model and saying, "Hey, you big bully. You quit picking on that clown. I won't tolerate it."

Collect Information (Data)   The second step in the scientific method is to collect data. Psychologists use research methods to collect data about the problem they are studying. Later in the chapter we will discuss many aspects of research methods, including how psychologists select the participants they want to study and how they design a study. In Bandura's study, the participants were young boys and girls who observed an adult model act aggressively and be reinforced, punished, or receive no consequences for the aggressive behavior. Bandura collected data about how aggressively the children acted after they watched the adult behave aggressively.

Draw Conclusions   The scientific method's third step is to draw conclusions. Once psychologists collect data, they use mathematical (statistical) procedures to understand what the data mean. Then they draw conclusions. In Bandura's study, the data that had been collected were statistically analyzed. Based on this analysis, Bandura concluded that children who saw adults be either reinforced or given no consequences for behaving aggressively are more likely to engage in aggressive actions themselves than are children who saw adults be punished for their aggressive actions (see figure 1.5).

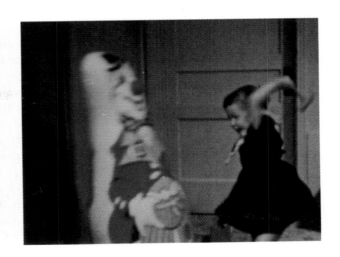

𝓕igure 1.5
Bandura's Study of Observational Learning

(Left) In Bandura's study, young children watched an adult act aggressively by punching a Bobo doll (a large plastic inflated toy with a clown-like appearance) and subsequently the adult was reinforced, punished, or given no consequences for the aggressive action. *(Right)* Subsequently, the children were more likely to imitate the adult's aggressive actions when the adult model was reinforced or given no consequences than when punished.

Revise Research Conclusions or Theory   The final step in the scientific method involves revising research conclusions in an area or theory. For example, psychologists have developed a number of theories about why people become aggressive. Data, such as those collected by Bandura, force psychologists to examine existing theories to see if they still hold up. For example, when Bandura conducted his research, the main theories of aggression were that aggression is a biological drive or occurs because it gets rewarded. Bandura's research, along with other similar studies, caused psychologists to recognize that aggression also occurs because of observational learning, not just because of a biological drive and reinforcement.

It is important to mention that a revision of theory usually occurs only after a number of studies produce similar results. In the case of observational learning's role in aggression, many researchers have found that when children watch people act aggressively, the children become more aggressive themselves (Coie & Dodge, 1998).

Research Methods

Researchers have to decide which research methods they will use. You will discover that this involves making quite a few decisions.

Observation   The fictional English detective Sherlock Holmes chided his assistant, Watson, "You see but you do not observe." What might Holmes have meant by this comment?

Exploring Observation   We look at things all of the time, but casually watching a friend cross the campus is not scientific observation. Unless you are a trained observer and practice your skills regularly, you might not know what to look for, you might not remember what you saw, what you are looking for might change from one moment to the next, and you might not communicate your observations effectively.

For observations to be effective, we have to know what we are looking for, whom we are observing, when and where we will observe, how the observations will be made, and in what form they will be recorded. That is, we need to observe in some *systematic* way (Zeren & Makosky, 1995). Consider aggression. Do we want to study verbal or physical aggression, or both? How will we know it when we see it? If one man punches another in the arm, will we mark that down as aggression? If both men are laughing and one punches the other in the arm, will we still count the punch as aggression? Do we want to study men, or women, or children, or all of these? Do we want to evaluate them in a university laboratory, at work, at play, in their homes, or at all of these locations? Do we want to audiotape or videotape their behavior, or both? A common way to record observations is to write them down, using shorthand or symbols; however, psychologists increasingly use tape recorders, video cameras, special coding sheets, and one-way mirrors to make observations more efficient.

Laboratory Observation   When we observe, we often need to *control* certain factors that determine behavior but are not the focus of our inquiry. For this reason much of psychology's research is conducted in a **laboratory,** *a controlled setting with many of the complex factors of the "real world" removed.* For example, Bandura's (1965) study of observational learning and aggression that we described earlier was conducted in a laboratory. By conducting his research in a laboratory with adults the child did not know, Bandura controlled when the child witnessed aggression, how much aggression the child saw, and what form the aggression took. Bandura could not have conducted his experiment as effectively if other factors, such as parents, siblings, friends, television, and a familiar room, had been present.

Laboratory research, however, does have some drawbacks. First, it is almost impossible to conduct research without the participants' knowing they are being studied. Second, the laboratory setting is unnatural and therefore can cause the par-

This researcher is using observation as part of a research study on infant development. Videotaped observation has allowed researchers to become increasingly precise in coding various behaviors because they can play the tape over and over to discover micro aspects of behavior.

ticipants to behave unnaturally. Research participants usually show less aggressive behavior in a laboratory than in a more familiar or natural setting, such as a park or at home. They also show less aggression when they are aware they are being observed than when they are unaware they are being observed. Third, people who are willing to come to a university laboratory are unlikely to represent groups from diverse cultural backgrounds. Those who are unfamiliar with university settings, and with the idea of "helping science," may be intimidated by the setting. Fourth, some aspects of mind and behavior are difficult if not impossible to examine in the laboratory. Certain types of stress are difficult (and unethical) to study in the laboratory. Alcohol, for instance, consistently increases aggression in an individual who is provoked. In 1985 at a soccer game in Brussels, Belgium, a riot broke out. The English fans, intoxicated by alcohol, aroused by the competition, and taunted by the Italian fans, attacked the Italians. As the Italians retreated, they were crushed against a wall—the death toll was 38. Recreating circumstances in a laboratory that even remotely resemble the Brussels soccer game is impossible and unethical.

Naturalistic Observation   Although laboratory research is a valuable tool for psychologists, naturalistic observation provides insight that we sometimes cannot achieve in the laboratory (Pellegrini, 1996). In **naturalistic observation,** *psychologists observe behavior in real-world settings and make no effort to manipulate or control the situation.* Psychologists conduct naturalistic observations at soccer games, day-care centers, college dormitories, rest rooms, corporations, shopping malls, restaurants, dances, and other places people live in and frequent. In contrast to Bandura's observations of aggression in a laboratory, some psychologists use naturalistic methods to observe the aggression of children in nursery schools, the aggression of marital partners at home, and the arguments and violence of people at sporting events and political protests (Mahoney, 1995).

Even though naturalistic observation can provide valuable information about how people behave in real-world settings, it has some drawbacks. As with laboratory observation, observers often have difficulty making their presence unobtrusive so they don't affect the participants. To combat the problem of participants' reacting to being observed, researchers usually observe long enough for people to become accustomed to being observed and to begin to behave more naturally. Also, naturalistic observation provides less control over the study's conditions than laboratory observation does.

Interviews and Questionnaires   Sometimes the best and quickest way to get information from people is to ask them for it. An **interview** involves asking questions to find out about a person's experiences and attitudes. Most interviews occur face-to-face, although they can take place over the telephone. Some interview questions are unstructured and open-ended, such as "Tell me about your aggressive tendencies" or "How violent would you say your marriage is?" Other interview questions are more structured and ask about more specific things. For example, a structured interview question might ask, "How many times have you and your marital partner argued in the last month: 0, 1–2, 3–5, 6–10, 10–30, every day?" One shortcoming of an interview is **social desirability,** *the tendency of participants to tell the interviewer what they think is socially acceptable or desirable rather than what they truly feel or think.* For example, a woman might not want to reveal the actual torment she has gone through because of her husband's abuse.

Questionnaires (or surveys) *are similar to structured interviews except that the respondents read the questions and mark their answers on paper instead of verbally responding to an interviewer.* A major advantage of questionnaires is that they can be given to large numbers of people easily (some now appear on the Internet). Good surveys have concrete, specific, and unambiguous questions. Social desirability is a problem for questionnaires just as it is for interviews (Krosnick, 1999).

"For crying out loud, gentlemen! That's us! Someone's installed the one-way mirror in backward!"

"Would you say Attila is doing an excellent job, a good job,
a fair job, or a poor job?"

Case Studies   A **case study** *is an in-depth look at a single individual; this method is used mainly by clinical psychologists when, for either practical or ethical reasons, the unique aspects of an individual's life cannot be duplicated.* A case study provides information about one person's fears, hopes, fantasies, traumatic experiences, upbringing, family relationships, health, or anything that helps the psychologist understand the person's mind and behavior.

Traumatic experiences have produced some truly fascinating case studies in psychology. Consider the following. A 26-year-old schoolteacher met a woman with whom he fell intensely in love. But several months after their love affair began, the schoolteacher became depressed, drank heavily, and talked about suicide. The suicidal ideas progressed to images of murder and suicide. His actions became bizarre. On one occasion he punctured the tires of his beloved's car. On another he stood on the side of the road where she passed frequently in her car, extending his hand in his pocket so she would think he was holding a gun. Only eight months after meeting her, the teacher shot her while he was a passenger in the car she was driving. Soon after the act, he ran to a telephone booth to call his priest. The girlfriend had died (Revitch & Schlesinger, 1978).

This case reveals how depressive moods and bizarre thinking can precede violent acts, such as murder. Other vivid case studies appear throughout this text, among them a woman with three personalities, each of which is unaware of the others, and a modern-day wild child named Genie, who lived in near total isolation during her childhood.

Case histories provide dramatic, in-depth portrayals of people's lives, but we must be cautious when generalizing from this information. The subject of a case study is unique, with a genetic makeup and experiences no one else shares. In addition, case studies involve judgments of unknown reliability. Psychologists who conduct case studies rarely check to see if other psychologists agree with their observations.

Standardized Tests

Standardized Tests   **Standardized tests** *require people to answer a series of written and/or oral questions, and they have two distinct features: (1) An individual's score is totaled to yield a single score, or set of scores, that reflects something about that individual; and (2) the individual's score is compared with the scores of a large group of similar people to determine how the individual responded relative to others.* Scores are often stated in terms of percentiles. For example, suppose you scored in the 92nd percentile on the SAT. This measure tells you that 92 percent of a large group of individuals who previously took the test received scores lower than yours. Among the most widely used standardized tests in psychology are the Stanford-Binet intelligence test and the Minnesota Multiphasic Personality Inventory (MMPI).

To continue our look at how psychologists use different methods to evaluate aggression, consider the MMPI, which includes a scale to assess an individual's delinquency and antisocial tendencies. The items on this scale ask you to respond whether or not you are rebellious, impulsive, and have trouble with authority figures. The 26-year-old teacher who murdered his girlfriend would have scored high on a number of the MMPI scales, including one designed to measure how strange and bizarre our thoughts and ideas are.

The main advantage of standardized tests is that they provide information about *individual differences* among people. But information obtained from standardized tests does not always predict behavior in nontest situations. Standardized tests are based on the belief that a person's behavior is consistent and stable. Although personality and intelligence, two of the primary targets of standardized tests, have some stability, they can vary, depending on the situation. For example, a person may perform poorly on a standardized intelligence test in an office setting but display a much higher level of intelligence at home where he or she is less anxious. This criticism is especially relevant for members of minority groups, some of whom have been inappropriately classified as mentally retarded on the basis of their scores on intelligence tests. And cross-cultural psychologists caution that while many psychological tests developed in Western cultures might work reasonably well in Western cultures, they might not always be appropriate in other cultures (Cushner & Brislin, 1995). For example, people in other cultures simply might not have had as much exposure to the information on the test.

Physiological Research   An additional method that psychologists use is physiological research. Research on the biological basis of behavior and technological advances continue to produce remarkable insights about mind and behavior. For example, researchers have found that electrical stimulation of certain areas of the brain turns docile, mild-mannered people into hostile, vicious attackers; and higher concentrations of some hormones have been associated with anger in adolescents (Tremblay & Schaal, 1995).

In a recent study of men who had a history of battering their wives, couples' bodies were monitored with electronic sensors during discussions about marital problems (Jacobsen & others, 1998). One type of these violent men (called "cobras" by the researchers) sounded and looked aggressive but were very calm physiologically. The other type of violent men (called "pit bulls" by the researchers) became internally aroused during discussions about marital problems, never letting up on their wives.

Because much physiological research cannot be carried out with humans, psychologists sometimes use animals. Animal studies permit researchers to control genetic background, diet, experiences during infancy, and countless other factors (Capaldi, 2000). In studying humans, psychologists treat these factors as random variation, or "noise," that can interfere with accurate results. In addition, animal researchers can investigate the effects of some treatments (brain implants, for example) that would be unethical with humans. Moreover, it is possible to track the entire life span of some animals over a relatively short period of time. Laboratory mice, for instance, have a life span of approximately 1 year.

With regard to aggression, we know that castration turns ferocious bulls into docile oxen by acting on the male hormone system. After a number of breedings of aggressive mice, researchers have created mice who are absolutely ferocious (Manning, 1989). Do these findings with animals apply to humans? Hormones and genes do influence human aggression, but the influence is less powerful than in animals. Because humans differ from animals in many ways, one disadvantage of research with animals is that the results might not apply to humans.

Correlational Research   In **correlational research,** *the goal is to describe the strength of the relation between two or more events or characteristics.* Correlational research is useful because the more strongly two events are correlated (related, or associated), the more effectively we can predict one from the other.

Continuing with our theme of applying research methods to aggression, let's examine the correlation between children's viewing of violence on TV and their aggressive behavior. In one study, long-term exposure to television violence was

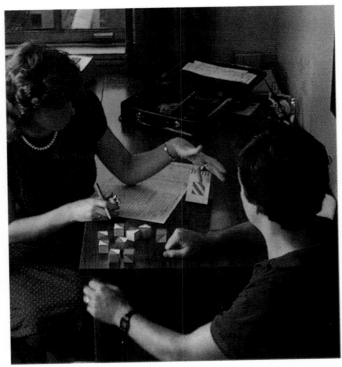

Standardized tests require individuals to answer a series of written or oral questions. The individual on the right is being given a standardized test of intelligence. Other than standardized tests, what other methods might be used to assess intelligence?

Physiological Research
Correlational Research Designs

Because some physiological research cannot be carried out with humans, psychologists might use animals in their research. Shown here are two previously peaceful monkeys in which the researcher has electrically stimulated a specific region of their brains (the limbic system). When their limbic system is electrically stimulated, they show rage. Can you think of other research topics that might be effectively studied with animals?

OBSERVED CORRELATION
As people make a lot of money, their self-esteem increases

Possible Explanations for this Observed Correlation

Making a Lot of Money	causes	High Self-Esteem
High Self-Esteem	causes	Making a Lot of Money
A third factor such as education, social upbringing, or genetic tendencies	causes both	Making a Lot of Money / High Self-Esteem

An observed correlation between two events cannot be used to conclude that one event causes the second event. Other possibilities are that the second event causes the first event or that a third, unknown event causes the correlation between the first two events.

Figure 1.6
Possible Explanations of Correlational Data

correlated with the likelihood of aggression in adolescent boys (Belson, 1978). Those who watched the most aggression on television were the most likely to commit a violent action, swear, be aggressive in sports, threaten violence toward another boy, write slogans on walls, or break windows.

Can we conclude from this study that television violence causes aggression? The answer is no. We only can say that watching violence on television is *associated* (or *related* or *correlated*) with acting aggressively. Remember this important research principle: *Correlation does not equal causation.* We cannot say that watching TV violence causes aggression in this study because it is possible that a third factor, such as genetic tendency, temperament, or inadequate parenting, underlies their association.

To ensure that you understand correlation, let's consider another example. People who make a lot of money have higher self-esteem than their counterparts who make less money (see figure 1.6). We mistakenly could interpret this to mean that making a lot of money causes high self-esteem. There are two other interpretations that we need to consider. First, it could be that developing high self-esteem causes people to make a lot of money. Second, a third factor, such as education, social upbringing, or genetic tendencies, could cause the correlation between making a lot of money and high self-esteem. Throughout this text you will read about numerous correlational research studies. Keep in mind how easy it is to assume causality when two events or characteristics merely are correlated.

Experimental Research   First we will describe how experimental research is conducted, and then we will discuss why researchers must be cautious when conducting such research.

How Experimental Research Is Conducted   **Experimental research** *allows psychologists to determine behavior's causes.* Psychologists accomplish this task by performing an **experiment,** *a carefully regulated procedure in which one or more factors believed to influence the behavior being studied are manipulated and all other factors are held constant.* If the behavior under study changes when a factor is manipulated, we say that the manipulated factor causes the behavior to change. Psychologists conduct experimental research to determine cause-and-effect relationships between events, something correlational research cannot do. *Cause* is the event being manipulated. *Effect* is the behavior that changes because of the manipulation. Nothing is manipulated in correlational research, but in experimental research the researchers actively change an event to see its effect on behavior.

Experiments involve at least one independent variable and one dependent variable. The **independent variable** *is the manipulated, influential, experimental factor.* The label *independent* is used because this variable can be changed independent of other factors to determine its effect on the dependent variable. Researchers have a vast array of options open to them in selecting an independent variable. In one experimental study, the researchers chose as the independent variable the amount and type of television violence that young children saw (Steuer, Applefield, & Smith, 1971). The **dependent variable** *is the factor that is measured in an experiment.* It can change as the independent variable is manipulated. The label dependent is used because this variable depends on what happens to the participants in the experiment. In the study of the relationship between television violence and aggression, the dependent variable was the children's aggressive behavior.

Experiments also involve one or more experimental groups and one or more control groups. An **experimental group** *is a group whose experience is manipulated.* In the study relating television violence and aggression, the experimental group was the children who saw television violence. A **control group** *is a comparison group that is treated in every way like the experimental group except for the manipulated factor.* The control group serves as a baseline against which the effects of the manipulated condition can be compared. In the study relating television violence and aggression, the control group was the group of children who did not see television violence.

Another important aspect of experimental research is **random assignment,** *which occurs when researchers assign participants to experimental and control groups by chance.* This practice reduces the likelihood that the experiment's results will be due to any preexisting differences between groups. For example, in the study relating television violence and aggression, random assignment decreased the probability that the two groups of children differed on such factors as aggressive tendencies, prior exposure to TV violence, intelligence, health, socioeconomic status, and so on.

To summarize the experimental research on television violence and aggression, young children were randomly assigned to one of two groups: one (the experimental group) watched television shows taken directly from violent Saturday-morning cartoon offerings on 11 different days; the second group (control group) watched television cartoon shows with all of the violence removed. The young children subsequently were observed during their play at preschool. The young children who saw the violent TV cartoon shows kicked, choked, and pushed their playmates more than their counterparts who saw the TV cartoon shows with the violence removed. Because this is experimental research, we can conclude that in this study TV violence *caused* an increase in the children's aggressive behavior (see figure 1.7).

Experimental Research Cautions   Although experimental research has considerable power to discover behavior's causes, such research must be done cautiously, with safeguards (Vadum & Rankin, 1998). Certain expectancies and biases on the part of experimenters and/or participants can tarnish results.

Experimenters can subtly influence their research participants, in many cases unknowingly. **Experimenter bias** *occurs when the experimenter's own expectations influence the outcome of the research.* In a classic study, Robert Rosenthal (1996) turned college students into experimenters. They were randomly assigned rats from the same litter. However, half of the students were told that their rats were "maze bright," while the other half were told that their rats were "maze dull." The students then conducted experiments to test their rats' ability to navigate mazes. The results were stunning. The so-called "maze-bright" rats were more successful than the "maze-dull" rats at running the mazes. The only explanation for the results is that the college students' expectations affected the performance of the rats. In subsequent studies, researchers have demonstrated that experimenter's expectations influence not only rodent behavior but human behavior as well (Rosenthal, 1994, 2000).

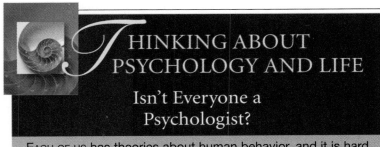

THINKING ABOUT PSYCHOLOGY AND LIFE

Isn't Everyone a Psychologist?

EACH OF US has theories about human behavior, and it is hard to imagine how we could get through life without them. In this sense, we are all psychologists. However, the theories of psychology that we carry around and the way we obtain support for our theories are often quite different from the way psychologists go about theorizing and collecting data about an issue or topic (Stanovich, 1998).

Think for a few moments about your views of human behavior. How did you arrive at them? Might at least some of them be biased? Now think about what you have read in this chapter about the science of psychology. How is our personal psychology different from scientific psychology? Which one is more likely to be accurate? Why? Although our personal psychology and scientific psychology are often different, in what ways might they be similar?

Experimental Research

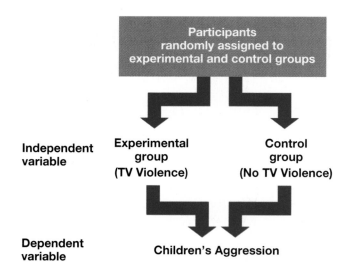

Participants randomly assigned to experimental and control groups

Independent variable → **Experimental group (TV Violence)**   **Control group (No TV Violence)**

Dependent variable → **Children's Aggression**

Figure 1.7
An Experimental Research Study:
The Effects of TV Violence on Young Children's Aggression

In this example of experimental research, young children were randomly assigned to one of two groups: the experimental group who saw TV violence and the control group who did not. The independent variable (which is always the manipulated variable) was the amount of violence the children saw. The dependent variable was the children's aggression shown at play. The researchers found that TV violence caused children's aggressive behavior to increase. We can use the word *cause* because this is an experimental study.

Research participant bias *reflects research participants' beliefs about how they are expected to behave.* Research participants routinely have expectations about what they are supposed to do and how they should behave. Imagine that researchers hypothesize that a particular new drug will decrease violent behavior. They randomly assign the participants to an experimental group (those who receive the drug) and a control group (those who do not). After 3 months, the experimental group shows less violent behavior than the control group. It seems as though we could conclude that the drug caused violent behavior to decrease. However, the effects might be due to the expectations of the participants in the experimental group, not to the drug itself. Possibly because they expected to be less violent, they were violent less often. The **placebo effect** *occurs when participants' expectations, rather than the experimental treatment, produce the desired outcome.*

How might this placebo effect be reduced? In studies like the one we just described, the researchers can give the control group a *placebo.* In this case, the placebo might be a sugar pill. The control group participants are not told that it is a placebo. Thus, both the experimental and the control groups think they are getting the drug. In any study, researchers try to minimize the participants' expectations or cancel them out across the groups by making them as identical as possible.

Might we be able to design an experiment in which neither the experimenter's nor the participants' expectancies affect the outcomes? Yes, and it is called a **double-blind experiment,** *in which neither the experimenter nor the participants are aware of which participants are in the experimental group and which are in the placebo control group until the results are calculated.* If the study of drug treatment for violence is conducted in a double-blind manner, the experimenter and the participants would be kept in the dark about which group is receiving the drug and which is getting the placebo. A double-blind study allows researchers to tease apart the actual effects of the independent variable from the experimenter's and the participants' enthusiasm for it.

Ethical Considerations

What are the ethics guidelines of the American Psychological Association? What ethical considerations are involved when research is conducted with animals?

Ethics Guidelines of the American Psychological Association

Psychologists increasingly recognize that considerable caution must be taken to ensure the well-being of the participants in a psychological study. Today colleges and universities have review boards that evaluate the ethical nature of research conducted at their institutions. Proposed research plans must pass the scrutiny of a research ethics committee before the research can be initiated. In addition, the American Psychological Association (APA) has developed ethics guidelines for its members.

The code of ethics adopted by the American Psychological Association instructs psychologists to protect their participants from mental and physical harm. The participants' best interests need to be kept foremost in the researcher's mind (Rosnow, 1995; Sieber, 2000). APA's guidelines include the requirement of **informed consent,** *which means that all participants must know what their participation will involve and any risks that might develop.* For example, research participants on dating should be told beforehand that a questionnaire might stimulate thoughts about issues in their relationship that they have not considered. Participants also should be informed that in some instances a discussion of the issues raised might improve their relationship, while in others it might worsen the relationship and even end it. Even after informed consent is given, participants retain the right to withdraw from the study at any time and for any reason.

Another important aspect of ethics in research is **confidentiality:** *researchers are responsible for keeping all of the data they gather on individuals completely confidential and, when possible, completely anonymous.*

Yet another responsibility of researchers is **debriefing,** *which consists of informing participants of the purpose and methods used in a study after the study has been completed.* In most cases it is possible to inform participants in a general manner about the purpose of the research beforehand without "giving away" the predicted results, which could create participants' expectations that the experimenter wants them to behave in a certain way. When this is not possible, participants must be debriefed after the research has been completed.

Deception is an ethical issue that psychologists debate extensively (Whitley, 1996; Yuille, 2000). In some circumstances, telling the participant beforehand what the research study is about substantially alters the participant's behavior and invalidates the researcher's data. For example, suppose a psychologist wants to know whether bystanders will report a theft. A mock theft is staged, and the psychologist observes which bystanders report it. Had the psychologist informed the bystanders beforehand that the study intended to discover the percentage of bystanders who will report a theft, the whole study would have been undermined. In all cases of deception, the psychologist must ensure that the deception will not harm the subject and that the subject will be told the complete nature of the study (debriefed) as soon as possible after the study is completed (Chastain & Landrum, 1999).

How Ethical Is Research with Animals?

For generations, some psychologists have used animals in their research, which has provided a better understanding of, and solutions for, many human problems. Neal Miller, a leading figure in contemporary psychology who has made important discoveries about the effects of biofeedback on health, listed the following areas where animal research has benefited humans (Miller, 1985):

- Psychotherapy and behavioral medicine
- Rehabilitation of neuromuscular disorders
- Understanding and alleviating effects of stress and pain
- Discovery and testing of drugs to treat anxiety and severe mental illness
- Knowledge about drug addiction and relapse

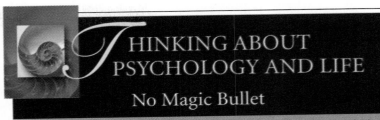

THINKING ABOUT PSYCHOLOGY AND LIFE

No Magic Bullet

IN OUR DESCRIPTION of experimental research, we concluded that TV violence caused young children's aggressive behavior to increase. It is easy to fall into the trap of thinking that TV violence is the *only* cause of children's aggression. That is not what the study's findings meant.

Always keep in mind one of psychology's most important lessons, which is highlighted in this chapter: Behavior has multiple determinants. Just because researchers find a causal connection between variable *A* and variable *B* does not mean that variable *A* is the only cause of variable *B*. That is, variable *A* is not a magic bullet that by itself brings about a change in variable B (Stanovich, 1998). Like other behaviors, children's aggressive behavior has multiple determinants, and TV violence is but one of them. Can you think of what some other determinants of children's aggression might be? Think about such factors as heredity, hormones, parenting, poverty, and the violence in society other than what is shown on TV. See if you can add to this list.

Let's consider another experimental study. In this study, the researchers find that when people are given a particular drug they become less depressed. Does that mean that too much or too little of a drug in people's brains causes depression? What might be some other causes of depression?

Psychologists' Ethical Principles

Observation	Interviews and Questionnaires	Case Studies	Standardized Tests	Physiological Research	Correlational Research	Experimental Research
Not an easy task, but researchers have observed that an individual's eyes move back and forth behind closed eyelids periodically during the night when dreams are occurring.	Individuals have been stimulated (shaken, yelled at, and splashed with water, for example) while they are asleep. When they awaken, they are interviewed about whether they experienced a dream related to these experiences (a dream about drowning, if they were splashed with water, for example).	Analysis of all that was said by one individual during an hour in which a dream was related. Assessment might take place periodically during the individual's life.	Psychologists have been ingenious at constructing psychological tests for many phenomena, but dreaming has not been one of them.	Measurement of the electrical activity of the brain indicates that the brain is more active and aroused when people are dreaming than when they are not dreaming. Animals have periods of REM sleep, but we can't say for certain whether or not they dream.	There have been many correlational studies of dreams. For example, researchers have studied whether dreams are related to age, gender, and a person's cultural experiences.	Fewer experimental than correlational studies of dreaming have been conducted. However, in experimental research, individuals in drug-induced states often report a different profile of dreaming than those not under the influence of drugs.

Figure 1.8
Psychology's Research Methods Applied to Dreaming

Ethical Guidelines in Animal Research

• Treatments to help premature infants gain weight so they can leave the hospital sooner
• Knowledge about memory used to alleviate deficits of memory in old age

How widespread is animal research in psychology? Only about 5 percent of APA members use animals in their research. Rats and mice are by far the most widely used, accounting for 90 percent of all psychological research with animals. How widespread is abuse to animals in psychological research? According to animal welfare and rights activists, it is extensive. It is true that researchers sometimes use procedures that would be unethical with humans, but they are guided by a stringent set of standards that address such matters as housing, feeding, and the psychological well-being of animals. Researchers are required to weigh the potential benefit of the research against the possible harm to the animal and to avoid inflicting unnecessary pain. Animal abuse simply is not as common as animal activist groups charge. However, stringent ethical guidelines must be followed when animals or humans are the subjects in psychological research (Herzog, 1995).

SUMMARY TABLE 1.2
Psychology's Scientific Approach

Concept	Processes/Related Ideas	Characteristics/Description
The Scientific Method	What Is the Scientific Method?	It is an approach that is used to discover accurate information about phenomena, including mind and behavior. It includes these steps: conceptualize a problem, collect information (data), draw conclusions, and revise research conclusions or theory.
	Conceptualize a Problem	This involves stating a problem to be studied in precise terms, an operational definition, a theory, and one or more hypotheses.
	Collect Data	Investigators choose from a wide variety of methods to collect data.
	Draw Conclusions	Psychologists use statistics to analyze data, which helps them to draw conclusions from research.
	Revise Research Conclusions and Theory	This often occurs when a number of studies produce similar results.
Research Methods	Observation	Observation is an important research method and can involve laboratory or naturalistic observation.
	Interviews and Questionnaires	Consist of asking questions to find out about a person's experiences; social desirability is a problem.
	Case Studies	An in-depth look at a single individual; caution needs to be exercised in generalizing to other people.
	Standardized Tests	Require people to answer a series of written or oral questions; an individual is given a score (or scores), which is compared to others' scores.
	Physiological Research	Provides insight about the biological dimensions of mind and behavior; animals often are used in this research.
	Correlational Research	The goal is to describe the strength of the relation between two or more events or characteristics. Correlation does not equal causation.
	Experimental Research	Allows psychologists to determine behavior's causes. This is accomplished by conducting an experiment, which involves examining the influence of at least one independent variable on one or more dependent variables. Experiments include the random assignment of participants to one or more experimental groups and one or more control groups. Experimental research cautions include experimenter bias, research participant bias. Placebo effects need to be considered.
Ethical Considerations	Guidelines of the American Psychological Association	Researchers must ensure the well-being of participants. The risk of physical and mental harm must be minimal. The American Psychological Association has precise ethics guidelines that include informed consent, confidentiality, and debriefing. Deception is an ethical issue that is debated by psychologists.
	How Ethical Is Research with Animals?	Controversy also swirls about the use of animals in psychological research, although abuse is not as widespread as some activists charge.

At this point we have studied many ideas about research methods. An overview of these methods is presented in summary table 1.2. In the next chapter, we continue our journey through psychology's many areas, turning our attention to mind and behavior's biological foundations ans neuroscience's fascinating exploration of the brain.

Overview

WE BEGAN THIS CHAPTER by exploring these aspects of psychology: Its definition, the beginnings of psychology as a science, early and contemporary approaches to psychology, what matters in psychology and life, and careers and areas of specialization. Our coverage of psychology's scientific approach focused on the scientific method, research methods, and ethical considerations.

You can obtain a detailed review of the chapter by again studying the two summary tables on pages 26 and 39.

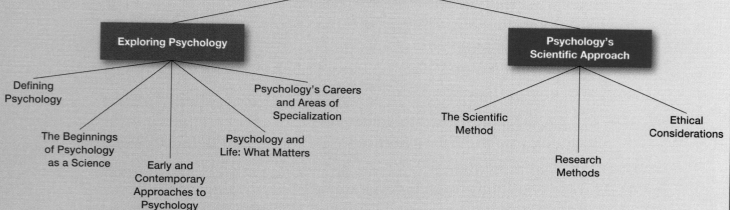

Key Terms

psychology 5
science 5
behavior 5
mental processes 5
natural selection 6
structuralism 7
functionalism 7
behavioral approach 8
social cognitive theory 8
psychoanalytic approach 10
humanistic approach 10
cognitive approach 11
information processing 11
behavioral neuroscience
   approach 11
evolutionary psychology
   approach 12
sociocultural approach 12

culture 12
ethnicity 13
gender 13
sex 13
eclectic approach 14
critical thinking 20
clinical and counseling
   psychology 23
psychiatry 23
community psychology 24
experimental psychology 24
behavioral neuroscience and
   comparative psychology 24
developmental psychology 24
social psychology 25
personality psychology 25
school and educational
   psychology 25

industrial/organizational
   psychology 25
cross-cultural psychology 25
psychology of women 25
health psychology 25
forensic psychology 25
sport psychology 25
scientific method 27
operational definition 27
theory 28
hypotheses 28
laboratory 30
naturalistic observation 31
interview 31
social desirability 31
questionnaires (surveys) 31
case study 32
standardized tests 32

correlational research 33
experimental research 34
experiment 34
independent variable 34
dependent variable 35
experimental group 35
control group 35
random assignment 35
experimenter bias 35
research participant bias 36
placebo effect 36
double-blind experiment 36
informed consent 37
confidentiality 37
debriefing 37

Key People

Taking It to the Net

1. The American Psychological Association requires that clinical psychologists have either a PhD or PsyD. Although both study clinical issues and techniques, PhD programs are generally more research oriented, while PsyD programs are more applied. Are you interested in research? Do you think it is important for a clinician to be involved in research in psychology? What kinds of things do researchers in clinical psychology study?

2. The behavioral approach to psychology emphasizes observable behavior and its environmental determinants (i.e., the cause and effect of behavior we can see). In contrast, the cognitive approach emphasizes mental processes (i.e., our thoughts and ideas about ourselves and the world around us). Some psychologists have in turn combined these two approaches to employ a cognitive-behavioral approach to therapy. Explain how the two branches of psychology can be combined to explain and treat abnormal behavior such as anxiety. Do you think that cognitive-behavioral therapy is a viable approach?

3. The American Psychological Association (APA) has strict ethical guidelines for research on human subjects. How do you think these issues apply to research on animals? Can you justify the use of animals in medical and psychological research? What about in cosmetic research? Think about your answers on both a subjective level and a more personal level (e.g., would you turn down medical procedures for yourself or a loved one because they were developed at the expense of animals?).

Connect to http://www.mhhe.com/psychology/santrock to find the answers!

Chapter 2

CHAPTER OUTLINE

Biological Foundations and Neuroscience

> "*Swiftly the brain becomes an enchanted loom, where millions of flashing shuttles weave a dissolving pattern—always a meaningful pattern—though never an abiding one.*"
>
> Sir Charles Sherrington
> *English Physiologist, 20th Century*

Images of Psychology and Life
The Jim and Jim Twins

Jim Springer and Jim Lewis are identical twins. They were separated at the age of 4 weeks and didn't see one another again until they were 39 years old. Even so, they share uncanny similarities that read more like fiction than fact. For example, they have both worked as a part-time deputy sheriff, have vacationed in Florida, have driven Chevrolets, have had dogs named Toy, and have married and divorced women named Betty. In addition, one twin named his son James Allan, and the other named his son James Alan. Both like math but not spelling, and both enjoy carpentry and mechanical drawing. They have chewed their fingernails down to the nubs and have almost identical drinking and smoking habits. Both have had hemorrhoids, put on ten pounds at about the same time, and first suffered headaches at the age of 18. They also have similar sleep patterns.

Jim and Jim have some differences as well. One wears his hair over his forehead, whereas the other wears it slicked back with sideburns. One expresses himself better verbally; the other is more proficient in writing. For the most part, however, they are more alike than different.

The Jim and Jim twins were part of the Minnesota Study of Twins Reared Apart, directed by Thomas Bouchard and his colleagues (1996). The researchers brought

Preview

ORGANISMS ARE NOT like billiard balls, moved by simple external forces to predictable positions. Biological foundations and environmental experiences work together to make us who we are. Of the biological structures that have evolved, none is more important than the three-pound universe inside of your skull—the brain. Much of this chapter focuses on the brain's role in behavior and mental processes. These are some of the questions we will explore in this chapter:

- How do nature and nurture interact to influence people's behavior?
- What is the field of neuroscience all about?
- What happens to people's behavior when the connections between the brain's two hemispheres are severed?
- What techniques do scientists use to "see inside" the brain?

The Jim twins: how coincidental? Springer, right, and Lewis were unaware of each other for 40 years.

---

identical (genetically identical because they come from the same fertilized egg) and fraternal (genetically dissimilar because they come from different fertilized eggs) twins from all over the world to Minneapolis to investigate the psychological aspects of the twins' lives. For example, the twins were interviewed and asked more than 15,000 questions about their family and childhood environment, personal interests, vocational orientation, values, and aesthetic judgments. Detailed medical histories were obtained, including information about their smoking, diet, and exercise habits. The researchers also took chest X rays, and gave heart stress tests, as well as EEGs (brain-wave tests). The twins were also given a number of personality, ability, and intelligence tests (Bouchard & others, 1981).

Critics of conclusions drawn about the genetic basis of behavior in the Minnesota twins study point out that some of the separated twins had been together several months prior to their adoption, that some twins had been reunited prior to their testing (in some cases a number of years earlier), that adoption agencies often place twins in similar homes, and that even strangers who spend several hours together and start comparing their lives are likely to come up with coincidental similarities (Adler, 1991). Still, even in the face of such criticism, the Minnesota study demonstrates the interest scientists have shown in the genetic basis of behavior.

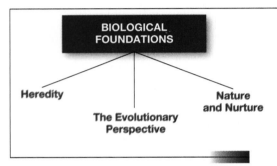

Biological Foundations

In the words of twentieth-century French essayist Antoine de Saint-Éxupéry, "The seed of the cedar will become cedar, the seed of the bramble can only become bramble." An English proverb says, "That which comes of a cat will catch mice." Why does the bramble become only bramble? Why does the cat catch mice? No matter what the species, there must be a mechanism used to pass the message of inheritance from one generation to the next. That mechanism is heredity.

Heredity

You began life as a single cell, a fertilized human egg, weighing about one-twenty-millionth of an ounce. From this single cell, you developed into a human being made of trillions of cells. The nucleus of each human cell contains 46 **chromosomes,** *which are threadlike structures that come in 23 pairs, one member of each pair coming from each parent.* Chromosomes contain the remarkable genetic substance **deoxyribonucleic acid,** or **DNA,** *a complex molecule that contains genetic information* (see figure 2.1). **Genes,** *the units of hereditary information, are short segments of chromosomes, composed of DNA.* Genes act like blueprints for cells to reproduce themselves and manufacture the proteins that maintain life. Chromosomes, DNA, and genes can be mysterious.

Although we have a long way to go before we unravel all the mysteries about the way genes work, some aspects of heritability are well understood. Every person has two genes for each characteristic governed by heredity. When genes combine to determine our characteristics, some genes are dominant over others. According to the **dominant-recessive genes principle,** *if one gene of a pair is dominant and one is recessive, the dominant gene exerts its effect, overriding the potential influence of the recessive gene.* A recessive gene exerts its influence only if both genes of a pair are recessive. If you inherit a recessive gene from only one parent, you may never know you carry the gene. In the world of dominant-recessive genes, brown eyes, farsightedness, and dimples rule over blue eyes, nearsightedness, and freckles. If you inherit a recessive gene for a trait from both of your parents, you will show the trait. That's why two brown-eyed parents can have a blue-eyed child: Each parent would have a dominant gene for brown eyes and a recessive gene for blue eyes. Since dominant genes override recessive genes, the parents have brown eyes. However, the child can inherit a recessive gene for blue eyes from each parent. With no dominant gene to override them, the recessive genes make the child's eyes blue.

Another aspect of understanding heredity involves the distinction between genotype and phenotype. **Genotype** *is the person's genetic heritage, the actual genetic material.* However, not all of this genetic material is apparent in a person's observed and measurable characteristics. **Phenotype** *is the way an individual's genotype is expressed in observable, measurable characteristics.* Phenotypes include physical characteristics (such as height, weight, and eye color) and psychological characteristics (such as intelligence and personality).

For each genotype, a range of phenotypes can be expressed. Imagine that we could identify all of the genes that would make a person introverted (shy) or extraverted (outgoing). Would measured introversion–extraversion be predictable from knowledge of specific genes? The answer is no, because even if the genetic model were adequate, introversion–extraversion is a characteristic that is influenced not only by heredity but also by experiences. For example, parents can guide a shy child to become more social.

The Human Genome Project (a genome is a complete set of genes), begun in the late 1970s, has as its goal the construction of the first detailed map of every human gene. Genetic engineers hope to use the knowledge derived from the project to reverse the course of many natural diseases. Recently, they have isolated the genes for Huntington's disease, Lou Gehrig's disease, the so-called bubble-boy disease, and a common form of colon cancer, among others.

The simple model of genes developed by Gregor Mendel at the beginning of the twentieth century with garden peas—in which the color of a flower is determined by a single gene—is almost never seen in human DNA. For example, a complex gene like the one that causes cystic fibrosis can go wrong in a vast number of locations. So far scientists already have identified 350 sites where the cystic fibrosis gene is disconfigured.

When 80,000 genes from one parent combine at conception with the 80,000 genes of the other parent, the number of possible combinations—in the trillions—is staggering. No wonder scientists are struck by the complexity of genetic transmission (Hartwell & others, 2000).

Figure 2.1
The Remarkable Substance
Known as DNA

Landmarks in the History of Genetics
Human Genome Project
Heredity Resources

Cynthia Cushall is evidence of the positive results of gene mapping. Three years after receiving gene therapy treatments, Cynthia no longer has to live in a plastic bubble to be protected from infection. What might the future hold for gene mapping?

Evolution
Evolutionary Psychology
Handbook of Evolutionary Psychology

The Evolutionary Perspective

Humans are relative newcomers to Earth. If we consider evolution in terms of a calendar year, humans arrived on the planet late in December (Sagan, 1980). Despite our brief existence, we have established ourselves as the most dominant species. As our earliest ancestors left the forests to form hunting societies on the grassy savannas, their thinking and behavior changed. How did these changes in thinking and behavior come about?

Natural Selection   Over time entire species can change through **natural selection,** *the evolutionary process that favors genes that code for design features most likely to lead to reproduction and survival.* Also known as "the survival of the fittest," natural selection lies at the heart of Charles Darwin's theory of evolution (Volpe & Rosenbaum, 2000). Darwin, a nineteenth-century naturalist, sailed to South America to study a multitude of plant and animal species in their natural surroundings. He observed that most organisms reproduce at rates that should result in overpopulation, yet somehow populations remain nearly constant.

Darwin reasoned that each new generation must engage in an intense, constant struggle for food, water, and other resources. In the course of this struggle, many of the young would die. Those who survive would be those who were better adapted to their environment. The survivors would reproduce and, in turn, pass on some of their characteristics to the next generation. Over the course of many generations, the organisms with the characteristics needed for survival (speed and sharp claws in predators or thick fur in Arctic animals, for instance) would make up an increasingly larger percentage of the population. Over many, many generations, this process could modify the entire population (Fancher, 2000; Mader, 2000). If environmental conditions were to change, however, other characteristics might be needed and would move the process in a different direction. Darwin published his observations and thoughts in *On the Origin of Species* (1859).

Over a million species have been classified, from bacteria to blue whales, with many varieties of beetles in between. The work of evolution produced the quills of porcupines and the extended period of parental care human beings give their offspring.

Generally, evolution proceeds at a very slow pace. The lines that led to the emergence of human beings and the great apes diverged about 14 million years ago. Modern humans, *Homo sapiens,* came into existence only about 50,000 years ago, and civilization as we know it began about 10,000 years ago. No sweeping evolutionary changes in humans have occurred since then—for example, our brains haven't become 10 times bigger, we haven't developed a third eye in the back of our heads, and we haven't learned to fly.

Evolutionary Psychology   In chapter 1, we introduced evolutionary psychology as psychology's newest approach. The **evolutionary psychology approach** *emphasizes the importance of adaptation, reproduction, and "survival of the fittest" in explaining behavior.* ◀ P. 12.

David Buss (1995, 2000) recently described the basic principles of evolutionary psychology. In evolutionary psychology, mechanisms (both psychological and physiological) are the product of evolution by selection. These mechanisms owe their existence to the successful solution to an adaptive problem that humans faced in ancestral environments. The adaptive problems are numerous, and they are all related to successful survival and reproduction, with reproduction being the engine that drives evolution, and survival being important because it aids reproduction.

Evolutionary psychologists believe that their approach provides an umbrella for unifying the diverse fields of psychology. Not all psychologists agree. Some argue that it is unlikely that one approach can unify the diverse, complex field of psychology

Through the Eyes of Psychologists

William Greenough,

University of Illinois

"The interaction of heredity and environment is so extensive that to ask which is more important, nature or nurture, is like asking which is more important to a rectangle, height or width."

(Graziano, 1995). Others stress that evolutionary approaches do not account for cultural diversity (Paludi, 1998).

Nature and Nurture

Although genes play a role in human behavior, they alone do not determine who we are. Genes exist within the context of a complex environment and are necessary for an organism to exist. Biologists who study even the simplest animals agree it is virtually impossible to separate the effects of an animal's genes from the effects of its environment (Lewis, 1999). **Environment** *refers to all of the surrounding conditions and influences that affect the development of living things.* Environment includes the food we eat, the air we breathe, and the many different physical and social contexts we experience—the cities and towns we live in; our relationships with our parents, peers, and teachers; and our continuing interactions at work, at home, and at play. The term **nurture** *is often used to describe an organism's environmental experiences.* The term **nature** *is often used to describe an organism's biological inheritance.* The interaction of nature and nurture, genes and environment, influences every aspect of mind and behavior to a degree. Neither factor operates alone (Brown, 1995; Mader, 2000; Wahlsten, 2000).

In sum, both genes and environment are necessary for a person even to exist. Without genes, there is no person; without environment, there is no person (Scarr & Weinberg, 1980). Heredity and environment operate together—or cooperate—to produce a person's intelligence, temperament, height, weight, ability to pitch a baseball, read, and so on (Gottlieb, Wahlsten, & Lickliter, 1998). If an attractive, popular, intelligent girl is elected president of her senior class in high school, is her success due to heredity or to environment? Of course, the answer is both.

The relative contributions of heredity and environment are not additive, as in such-and-such a percentage of nature, such-and-such a percentage of experience (Johnson, 2000; Tamarin, 1999). That's the old view. Nor is it accurate to say that

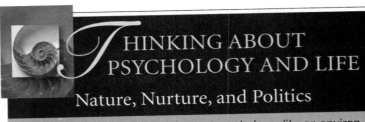

THINKING ABOUT PSYCHOLOGY AND LIFE

Nature, Nurture, and Politics

MIGHT A PERSON'S VIEWS on how strongly heredity or environment influences behavior be a lens for knowing their political leanings? Spend a few minutes thinking about this question. What is your view on how strongly heredity influences behavior? on how strongly environment influences behavior? What are your political leanings?

The more powerful heredity is, the less potent are such human qualities as free will, capacity to choose, and a sense of responsibility for these choices. That is, people tend to think that if it's in your genes, you are not accountable. This kind of thinking allows alcoholics to think that they are helpless victims of their biology rather than willful agents with control over their bodies. Genetic determinism can free families of responsibility, yet lock them in their suffering.

At the political level, biological determinism now colors all sorts of debates on issues such as health care, juvenile justice, and welfare reform. The effort to dismantle social programs is fueled by the belief that government interventions (the nurturing side of the nature-nurture debate) don't work very well and by the attitude that society can't make up for every citizen's bad luck. Conservative politicians take this stance, while liberal politicians are more likely to believe that environment makes a big difference in people's behavior. Political liberals are more likely to favor programs like Project Head Start and day care, which reflect environmental changes to improve the lives of children. As Northeastern University psychologist Leon Kamin notes, one of the simplest ways to find out someone's political leanings is to ask them where they stand on the nature-nurture issue (Herbert, 1997). Try this out with several of your friends.

Behavior Genetics

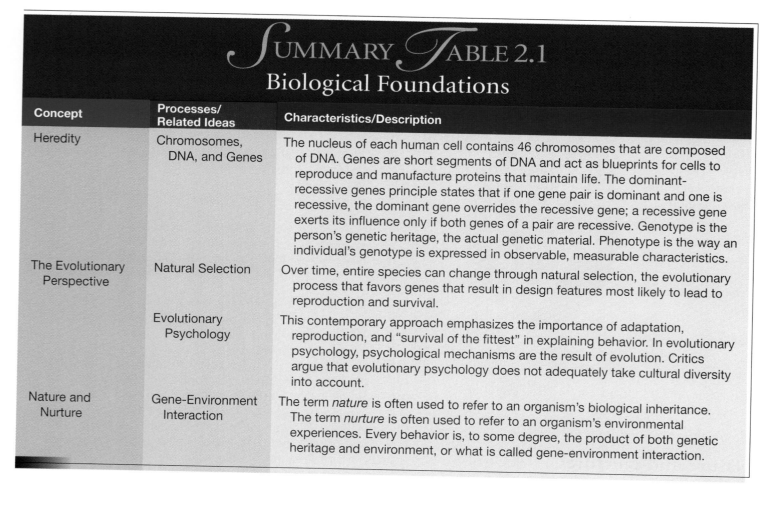

SUMMARY TABLE 2.1
Biological Foundations

Concept	Processes/Related Ideas	Characteristics/Description
Heredity	Chromosomes, DNA, and Genes	The nucleus of each human cell contains 46 chromosomes that are composed of DNA. Genes are short segments of DNA and act as blueprints for cells to reproduce and manufacture proteins that maintain life. The dominant-recessive genes principle states that if one gene pair is dominant and one is recessive, the dominant gene overrides the recessive gene; a recessive gene exerts its influence only if both genes of a pair are recessive. Genotype is the person's genetic heritage, the actual genetic material. Phenotype is the way an individual's genotype is expressed in observable, measurable characteristics.
The Evolutionary Perspective	Natural Selection	Over time, entire species can change through natural selection, the evolutionary process that favors genes that result in design features most likely to lead to reproduction and survival.
	Evolutionary Psychology	This contemporary approach emphasizes the importance of adaptation, reproduction, and "survival of the fittest" in explaining behavior. In evolutionary psychology, psychological mechanisms are the result of evolution. Critics argue that evolutionary psychology does not adequately take cultural diversity into account.
Nature and Nurture	Gene-Environment Interaction	The term *nature* is often used to refer to an organism's biological inheritance. The term *nurture* is often used to refer to an organism's environmental experiences. Every behavior is, to some degree, the product of both genetic heritage and environment, or what is called gene-environment interaction.

full genetic expression happens once, around conception or birth, after which we take our genetic legacy into the world to see how far it gets us. Genes produce proteins throughout the life span, in many different environments. Or they don't produce these proteins, depending on how harsh or nourishing those environments are (Greenough, 2000).

At this point, we have discussed some important ideas about heredity, evolution, and nature and nurture. A summary of these ideas is presented in summary table 2.1. Of all the aspects of human behavior that have evolved, none helps us adapt to our world more than the brain does. To its knowns and unknowns we now turn.

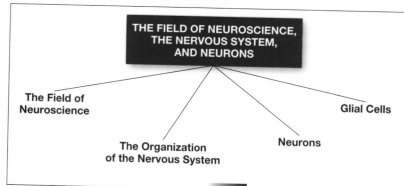

The Field of Neuroscience, the Nervous System, and Neurons

With "wiring" more complex than any computer, the human brain is the most complicated organization of matter we know of. Let's explore the field that studies this complex three-pound universe within our skulls.

The Field of Neuroscience

The **nervous system** *is the body's electrochemical communication circuitry, made up of billions of neurons.* The nervous system's central command system, the brain, controls all of your thoughts and movements. It weighs about three pounds and is slightly

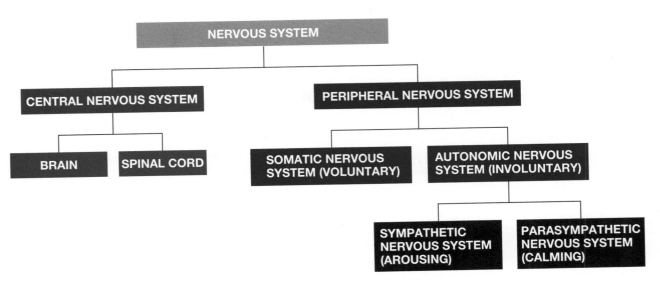

ℱigure 2.2
Major Divisions of the Human Nervous System

larger than a grapefruit. With its "crinkled" outer layer, it looks like a large, shelled walnut. Inside, the brain has the consistency of undercooked custard or a ripe avocado. **Neurons,** *or nerve cells, are the nervous system's basic units.* Highly organized, your nervous system is continuously at work processing information about everything you do, whether you are taking out the garbage, spotting a loved one across a crowded room, or preparing a speech (Conlan & others, 1999; Foote, 2000).

Not long ago the disciplines that studied the nervous system were virtually isolated from each other. Neuroanatomy studied the neuron's physical structure, neurophysiology investigated how neurons function, neurochemistry analyzed the neuron's chemical activity, and physiological psychology (which is now called behavioral neuroscience or biological psychology) focused on the nervous system's connections with behavior (Beatty, 1995). Such designations continue today, but these once-disparate disciplines increasingly overlap (Rosenzweig, 2000; Thalman, 1999). Today **neuroscience** *is the umbrella term for the multidisciplinary study of the nervous system.* ◀‖ P. 11. The Society for Neuroscience, the professional society for all types of neuroscientists, was founded in 1970 with 600 charter members and has grown to more than 25,000 members today.

The Organization of the Nervous System

When Emerson said, "The world was built in order and the atoms march in tune," he must have had the human nervous system in mind. This truly elegant system is highly ordered and organized. It is at work processing information in everything we do, whether stumbling across a tiger in the jungle or stretching out for a lazy nap on a hammock. The human nervous system is made up of bundles of nerve cells.

The nervous system is divided into two parts: the central nervous system and the peripheral nervous system. The **central nervous system (CNS)** *is made up of the brain and spinal cord.* More than 99 percent of all neurons (nerve cells) in our body are located in the CNS. The **peripheral nervous system** *is the network of nerves that connects the brain and spinal cord to other parts of the body.* The peripheral nervous system brings information to and from the brain and spinal cord and carries out the commands of the CNS to execute various muscular and glandular activities. Figure 2.2 displays the hierarchical organization of the nervous system's major divisions.

The two major divisions of the peripheral nervous system are the somatic nervous system and the autonomic nervous system. The **somatic nervous system** *consists of sensory nerves, which convey information from the skin and muscles to the CNS*

Neuroscience
Internet Neuroscience Resources
Exploring Neuroscience

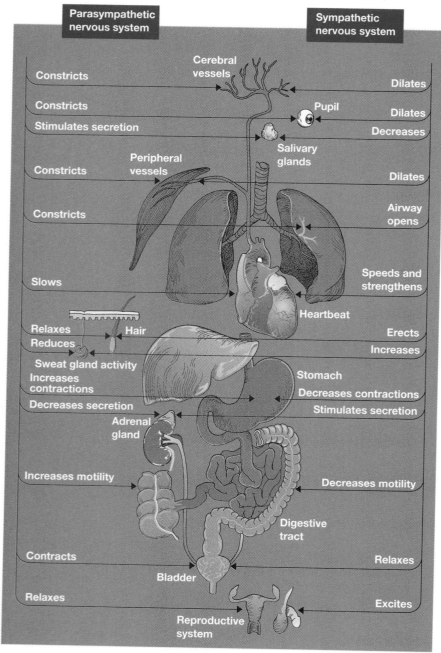

Parasympathetic nervous system

- Constricts — Cerebral vessels
- Constricts — Pupil
- Stimulates secretion — Salivary glands
- Constricts — Peripheral vessels
- Constricts
- Slows — Heartbeat
- Relaxes — Hair
- Reduces — Sweat gland activity
- Increases contractions — Stomach
- Decreases secretion
- Adrenal gland
- Increases motility — Digestive tract
- Contracts — Bladder
- Relaxes — Reproductive system

Sympathetic nervous system

- Dilates
- Dilates — Pupil
- Decreases — Salivary glands
- Dilates
- Airway opens
- Speeds and strengthens — Heartbeat
- Erects — Hair
- Increases — Sweat gland activity
- Decreases contractions — Stomach
- Stimulates secretion
- Decreases motility — Digestive tract
- Relaxes — Bladder
- Excites — Reproductive system

*F*igure 2.3
Autonomic Nervous System

Parasympathetic and sympathetic divisions. The sympathetic system is at work when we are aroused; the parasympathetic system is at work when we are calm. Both systems influence most organs. For example, the sympathetic system speeds and strengthens heartbeat; the parasympathetic system slows heartbeat.

Neural Processes

Neurons: Our Internal Galaxy

about such matters as pain and temperature, and motor nerves, which inform muscles when to act. The **autonomic nervous system** *takes messages to and from the body's internal organs, monitoring such processes as breathing, heart rate, and digestion.* It too is divided into two parts, the **sympathetic nervous system,** *the division of the autonomic nervous system that arouses the body,* and the **parasympathetic nervous system,** *the division of the autonomic nervous system that calms the body* (see figure 2.3).

To get a better feel for how the human nervous system works, imagine that you are preparing to give a speech in a class. As you go over your notes one last time, your peripheral nervous system carries information about the notes to your central nervous system. Your central nervous system processes the marks on the paper, interpreting the words as you memorize key points and plan ways to keep the audience interested. After studying the notes several minutes longer, you scribble a joke midway through them. Your peripheral nervous system is at work again, conveying to the muscles in your arm and hand the information from your brain that enables you to make the marks on the paper. The information transmitted from your eyes to your brain and from your brain to your hand is being handled by the somatic nervous system. This is your first speech in a while, so you are a little uptight. As you think about getting up in front of the class, your stomach feels queasy and your heart begins to thump. This is the sympathetic division of the autonomic nervous system functioning as you become aroused. You regain your confidence after reminding yourself that you know the speech cold. As you relax, the parasympathetic division of the autonomic nervous system is working.

Neurons

So far we have described the nervous system's major divisions. But there is much more to the intriguing story of how the nervous system processes information. Let's go inside the huge nervous system and find out more about the cells, chemicals, and electrical impulses that are the nuts and bolts of this operation.

Neuron Pathways Remember from earlier in the chapter that neuron is the name given to a nerve cell, which is the nerve system's basic unit. Information flows into the brain, within the brain, and out of the brain along specialized neurons known as afferent nerves, interneurons, and efferent nerves. **Afferent nerves,** *or sensory nerves, carry information to the brain.* The word *afferent* comes from the Latin word meaning "bring to." **Efferent nerves,** *or motor nerves, carry the brain's output.* The word *efferent* is derived from the Latin word meaning "bring forth."

To see how afferent and efferent nerves work, let's consider a well-known reflex, the knee jerk. When your knee jerks in response to a tap just below your kneecap, afferent cells transmit information directly to efferent cells, so the information processing is quick and simple.

The information involving the knee jerk is processed at the spinal cord and does not require the brain's participation. More complex information processing is accomplished by passing the information through systems of **interneurons,** *central nervous system neurons that mediate sensory input and motor output.* Interneurons make up most of the brain. For example, as you read the notes for your speech, the afferent input from your eye is transmitted to your brain, then passed through many interneuron systems, which translate (process) the patterns of black and white into neural codes for letters, words, associations, and meanings. Some of the information is stored in the interneuron systems for future associations and, if you read aloud, some is output as efferent messages to your lips and tongue.

Your gift of speech is possible because human interneuron systems are organized in ways that permit language processing. Although the neurons in a canary's brain are exactly the same as those in a frog's brain, frogs croak and canaries sing because the neurons are organized differently in the two brains. The interneurons in the frog's vocalization system are connected in such a way that they produce croaking, whereas the canary's produce singing. This is why the study of brain organization—the anatomy and fine structure of the brain—is so important. Brain organization is the key to understanding all of the complex and wondrous things that brains do. We'll tackle the brain's anatomy later; first, let's examine neurons in greater detail.

The Structure of the Neuron

Neuron is a neuroscientist's label for nerve cell. Neurons handle information processing in the nervous system at the cellular level. There are about 100 billion neurons in the human brain. The average neuron is as complex as a small computer, and has as many as 15,000 physical connections with other cells. At times the brain may be "lit up" with as many as a quadrillion connections.

The three basic parts of the neuron are the cell body, the dendrites, and the axon (see figure 2.4). The neuron's **cell body** *contains the nucleus, which directs the manufacture of the substances the neuron uses for its growth and maintenance.* Most neurons are created very early in life and will not be replaced if they are destroyed, although their shape, size, and connections can change throughout the life span.

The **dendrite** *is the receiving part of the neuron, serving the important function of collecting information and orienting it toward the cell body.* Most nerve cells have a number of dendrites. Although there are many dendrites radiating from the cell body of the neuron, there is only one axon. The **axon** *is the part of the neuron that carries information away from the cell body to other cells.* The axon is much thinner and longer than a dendrite and looks like an ultrathin cylindrical tube. The axon of a single neuron may extend all the way from the top of the brain to the base of the spinal cord, a distance of over three feet. A **myelin sheath,** *a layer of fat cells that insulates the axon, encases most axons.* Not only does the myelin sheath serve as insulation for the nerve cell, it also helps the nerve impulse to travel faster. The myelin sheath developed as brains evolved and became larger, which made it necessary for information to travel over long distances in the nervous system. This is similar to the appearance of freeways and turnpikes as cities grew. The newly developed roadways keep the fast-moving long-distance traffic from getting tangled up with slow-moving traffic.

The Nerve Impulse

Neurons send information down the axon as brief impulses, or waves, of electricity. Perhaps in a movie you have seen a telegraph operator sending a series of single clicks down a telegraph wire to the next station. That is what neurons do. To send information to other neurons, they send a series of single, electrical clicks down their axons. By changing the rate and timing of the clicks,

ℱigure 2.4
The Neuron

The cell body receives information from the dendrites of other neurons *(top)*. Information leaves the cell body and travels to other neurons, muscles, or glands through the axon *(bottom)*. A myelin sheath covers most axons and speeds information transmission. As it ends, the axon branches out. An actual neuron is shown in the large photograph. Notice the branching dendrites at the top and the cell body at the bottom left.

the neuron can vary the nature of the message it sends. As you reach to turn this page, hundreds of such clicks will stream down the axons in your arm to tell your muscles just when to flex and how vigorously.

The wave of electrical charge that sweeps down the axon abides by the **all-or-none principle,** *which means that once the electrical impulse reaches a certain level of intensity, it fires and moves all the way down the axon, remaining at the same strength throughout its travel.* The electrical impulse traveling down an axon is much like a fuse to a firecracker. It doesn't matter whether a match or blowtorch is used to light the fuse; as long as a certain minimal intensity has been reached, the spark travels quickly and at the same level of strength down the fuse until it reaches the firecracker.

To understand how a neuron, which is a living cell, creates and sends electrical signals, we need to examine this cell and the fluids in which it floats. A neuron is a balloonlike bag filled with one kind of fluid and surrounded by a slightly different kind of fluid. A piece of this balloon-like bag is stretched and pulled to form a long, hollow tube, which is the axon. The axon tube is very thin; a few dozen in a bundle would be about the thickness of human hair.

To see how this fluid-filled "balloon" called a neuron creates electrical signals, we must look at two things: the particles that float in the fluids and the actual wall of the cell, the membrane. The important particles in the fluids are the elements sodium and chloride (which we get from common table salt—sodium chloride) and potassium. **Ions** *are electrically charged particles.* The neuron creates electrical signals by moving these charged ions back and forth through its membrane; the waves of electricity that are created sweep along the membrane (Armstrong, 1999).

How does the neuron move these ions? It's really fairly simple; the membrane, the wall of the "balloon," is covered with hundreds of thousands of small doors or gates that open and close to let the ions pass in or out to the cell. Normally, when resting or not sending information, the membrane gates for sodium are closed, and those for potassium and chloride are partly open. Therefore, the membrane is in what is called a semipermeable state, and the ions separate; sodium is kept outside, lots of potassium ends up inside, and most of the chloride goes outside. Because the ions are separated, a charge is present along the membrane of the cell (see figure 2.5). **Resting potential** *is the stable, negative charge of an inactive neuron.* That potential, by the way, is about one-fourteenth of a volt, so fourteen neurons could make a one-volt battery. The electric eel's 8,400 cells could generate 600 volts.

When the neuron gets enough excitatory input to cause it to send a message, the sodium gates at the base of the axon open briefly, then shut again. While those gates are open, sodium rushes into the axon, carrying an electrical charge, and that charge causes the next group of gates on the axon to flip open briefly. And so it goes all the way down the axon, just like a long row of cabinet doors opening and closing in sequence. After the sodium gates close, potassium ions flow out of the cell and bring the membrane charge back to the resting condition. **Action potential** *is the brief wave of electrical charge that sweeps down the axon* (see figure 2.6).

Synapses and Neurotransmitters
What happens once the neural impulse reaches the end of the axon? Neurons themselves do not touch each other directly, but they manage to communicate. The story of the connection between one neuron and another is one of the most intriguing and highly researched areas of contemporary neuroscience. **Synapses** *are tiny gaps between neurons.* Most synapses are between the axon of one neuron and the dendrites or cell body of another neuron.

How does information get across this gap to the next neuron? The end of an axon branches out into a number of fibers that end in structures called terminal buttons. Neurotransmitters are found in the tiny synaptic vesicles (chambers)

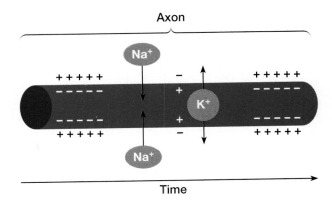

Figure 2.5
Movement of Sodium and Potassium Ions Down the Axon and the Action Potential
Electrical/chemical changes in the neuron produce an action potential. The sodium and potassium ions are shown moving down the axon. As the nerve impulse moves down the axon, electrical stimulation of the membrane makes it more permeable to sodium ions (Na^+). Sodium rushes into the axon, carrying a positive electrical charge, and that charge causes the next group of gates on the axon to flip open briefly. So it goes, all the way down the axon. After the sodium gates close, potassium ions (K^+) flow out of the cell, and the neuron returns to its resting state with a slight negative charge.

Action Potential

Action potential

Resting potential

Stimulation

Return to resting potential

Voltage (millivolts)

+40

0

-70

Time

$\mathscr{F}$igure 2.6
Action Potential

The action potential is shown on this graph in terms of its electrical voltage. The action potential is the positive charge in the cell generated by the influx of sodium (Na^+) ions. In the example shown here, the wave of electrical charge reaches about 40 millivolts. After the sodium gates close, potassium ions (K^+) flow out of the cell and bring the voltage back to its resting potential.

Neurotransmitters

located in the terminal buttons. **Neurotransmitters** *are chemical substances that carry information across the synaptic gap to the next neuron.* The molecules of these chemical substances wait for a nerve impulse to come down through the axon. Once the nerve impulse reaches the terminal buttons, the electrical signal causes these miniature springlike molecules to contract, pulling the vesicles out to the edge of the terminal buttons. At the edge, the vesicles burst open, and the neurotransmitter molecules spew forth into the gap between the two neurons. In the synaptic gap, the neurotransmitter molecules bump about in random motion, and some land on receptor sites in the next neuron, where they fit like small keys in equally small locks. The key in the lock, in turn, opens a "door" and electrical signals begin to sweep through the next neuron. Think of the synapse as a river that cuts two sections of a road in two. When a truck gets to the river via the road on one side of the river, it crosses the water by ferry and rolls right onto the second section of road to continue its journey. Similarly, a message in the brain is "ferried" across the synapse by a neurotransmitter, which pours out of the end of the cell just as the message approaches the synapse. Synapses and neurotransmitters might sound mysterious; to help turn your mystification into understanding, turn to figure 2.7.

More than fifty neurotransmitters, each with a unique chemical makeup, have been discovered, and the list will probably grow to a hundred or more in the near future (Johnson, 2000). Most creatures that have been studied, from snails to whales, use the same neurotransmitter molecules that our own brains use. And many animal venoms, such as that of the black widow, actually are neurotransmitter-like substances that disturb neurotransmission.

What are some of these neurotransmitters and how are they related to our behavior? **GABA,** *gamma aminobutyric acid, is a neurotransmitter that inhibits the firing of neurons and is found throughout the central nervous system.* It is believed to be the neurotransmitter in as many as one-third of the brain's synaptic connections. GABA is important in the brain because it keeps many neurons from firing. This inhibition helps to control the preciseness of the signal being carried from one neuron to the next. Low levels of GABA are linked with anxiety. Valium and other antianxiety drugs increase GABA's inhibitory effects.

Acetylcholine (ACh) *is a neurotransmitter that usually stimulates the firing of neurons and is involved in the action of muscles, learning, and memory.* The venom of the black widow spider causes ACh to gush through the synapses between the spinal cord and skeletal muscles, producing violent spasms. The drug curare, found on the tips of some South American Indians' poison darts, blocks some receptors for ACh, paralyzing muscles.

Norepinephrine *is a neurotransmitter that usually inhibits the firing of neurons in the central nervous system, but excites the heart muscles, intestines, and urogenital tract. It is involved in the control of alertness and wakefulness.* Too little norepinephrine also is associated with depression; too much with agitated, manic states.

Dopamine *is a neurotransmitter that is mainly inhibitory. It is involved in the control of voluntary movement.* Low levels of dopamine are associated with Parkinson's disease; high levels are associated with schizophrenia, a severe mental disorder.

Serotonin *is a neurotransmitter that is primarily inhibitory. It is involved in the regulation of sleep and depression.* The antidepressant drug Prozac works by restricting the movement of serotonin across synapses.

Endorphins *are natural opiates that mainly stimulate the firing of neurons. They increase pleasure and reduce pain.* As early as the fourth century B.C. the Greeks used the wild poppy to induce euphoria. However, it was not until more than 2,000 years later that the magical formula behind opium's addictive action was discovered. In the early 1970s, scientists found that opium plugs into a sophisticated system of natural opiates that lie deep within the brain's pathways (Pert, 1999; Pert & Snyder, 1973).

igure 2.7
How Synapses and Neurotransmitters Work

(a) When an axon reaches its destination, it branches out into a number of fibers that end in terminal buttons. There is a tiny gap between these terminal buttons at the tip of the axon terminal and the next neuron. (b) When it reaches the terminal buttons, the neural impulse releases tiny chemical molecules that are stored in synaptic vesicles in the knobs. These chemical substances are called neurotransmitters. They bump around in the synaptic gap between the sending and receiving neurons. Some of them land on receptor sites in the next neuron, where the neural impulse continues its travel. (c) Neurotransmitter molecules fit like small keys in equally small locks, once they reach the receptor site in the receiving neuron. The key in the lock opens the "door," and the neural impulse begins its travel through the second neuron.

The system involves neurotransmitters called endorphins, which shield the body from pain and elevate feelings of pleasure. A long-distance runner, a woman giving birth, and a person in shock after a car wreck all have elevated levels of endorphins. Figure 2.8 summarizes information about the six neurotransmitters we have discussed.

In the description of neurotransmitters, we indicated that the actions of some neurotransmitters stimulate, or excite, neurons to fire whereas those of other neurotransmitters inhibit neurons from firing. Some neurotransmitters are both excitatory and inhibitory, depending on what the information-processing job is. As the neurotransmitter moves across the synaptic gap to the receiving neuron, its molecules

Neurotransmitter	Description/Functions
GABA	Inhibits firing of neurons; low levels linked with anxiety; Valium and other antianxiety drugs increase GABA's inhibitory effects
Acetylcholine (Ach)	Usually stimulates firing of neurons; involved in action of muscles, learning, and memory
Norepinephrine	Usually inhibits firing of neurons; involved in control of alertness and wakefulness; too little is associated with depression, too much with agitated, manic states
Dopamine	Mainly inhibitory; involved in control of voluntary movement; low levels associated with Parkinson's disease; high levels associated with schizophrenia
Serotonin	Mainly inhibitory; involved in the regulation of sleep and depression; the antidepressant Prozac works by blocking the reabsorption and removal of serotonin from synapses
Endorphins	Natural opiates that mainly stimulate firing of neurons; involved in pleasure and pain

*F*igure 2.8
Description and Functions of Neurotransmitters

Drugs, the Brain, and Behavior

might spread out or be confined to a small space. The molecules might come in rapid sequence or be spaced out. The receiving neuron must integrate all of this information and decide whether or not to fire.

Another important point is that most drugs that influence behavior do so mainly by influencing neurotransmitters (Shier, Butler, & Lewis, 2000). Drugs can mimic or increase the effects of a neurotransmitter, or they can block those effects. An **agonist** *is a drug that mimics or increases a neurotransmitter's effects.* For example, the drug morphine mimics the action of endorphins by stimulating receptors in the brain involved with pleasure and pain. An **antagonist** *is a drug that can block a neurotransmitter's effects.* As we mentioned earlier, the antidepressant Prozac can block the effects of serotonin.

So far in our discussion of the brain's cells, we have focused on neurons. As we see next, another type of cell also is present in the brain.

Glial Cells

The Spanish neuroanatomist Santiago Ramón y Cajal discovered that the brain is made up of two types of cells—neurons, or nerve cells, and **glial cells,** *non-neuron cells that provide supportive and nutritive functions.* Somewhat amazingly, there are many more glial cells in the nervous system than there are neurons. Ramón y Cajal used advances in microscope techniques to discover the glial cells early in the twentieth century. He described the cells as looking like glue between the nerve cells.

Unfortunately, we do not know as much about glial cells as we do about neurons. We do know that glial cells do not have axons or dendrites, and they are not specialized to send or receive information. They probably function as physical supports for neurons. They seem to regulate the internal environment of the brain, especially the fluid surrounding neurons, and provide nutrition for neurons. For example, neurons placed in a solution containing glial cells grow more rapidly and prolifically than neurons floating in the same solution without glial cells (Kennedy & Folk-Seang, 1986). The myelin sheath that covers most axons is made up of glial cells.

SUMMARY TABLE 2.2
The Field of Neuroscience, the Nervous System, and Neurons

Concept	Processes/ Related Ideas	Characteristics/Description
The Field of Neuroscience	Its Nature	The nervous system is the body's electrochemical circuitry, made up of billions of neurons. Neurons, or nerve cells, are the nervous system's basic units *Neuroscience* is the umbrella term for the multidisciplinary study of the nervous system.
The Organization of the Nervous System	Central Nervous System	The central nervous system consists of the brain and spinal cord; it contains more than 99 percent of all neurons.
	Peripheral Nervous System	The peripheral nervous system is a network of nerves that connect the brain and spinal cord to other parts of the body. Two major divisions are the somatic nervous system and the autonomic nervous system. The autonomic nervous system is divided into the sympathetic and parasympathetic systems.
Neurons	Neuron Pathways	Afferent nerves (sensory nerves) carry input to the brain; efferent nerves (motor nerves) carry output away from the brain; interneurons do most of the information processing within the brain.
	Structure of the Neuron	The three basic parts of the neuron are the cell body, dendrite, and axon. The myelin sheath speeds information transmission.
	The Nerve Impulse	Neurons send information in the form of brief impulses, or "waves," of electricity. These waves are called the action potential and operate according to the all-or-none principle.
	Synapses and Neurotransmitters	Synapses are gaps between neurons. The neural impulse reaches the axon terminal and stimulates the release of neurotransmitters from tiny vesicles. These carry information to the next neuron, fitting like keys in locks. Important neurotransmitters include GABA, acetylcholine, norepinephrine, serotonin, and endorphins. Some neurotransmitters are excitatory, others are inhibitory. Agonists are drugs that mimic or increase a neurotransmitter's effects. Antagonists are drugs that block a neurotransmitter's effects.
Glial Cells	Their Nature	They provide support for neurons and are thought to be involved in the regulation and nutrition of neurons.

At this point we have discussed a number of ideas about the field of neuroscience, the nervous system, and neurons. An overview of these ideas is presented in summary table 2.2.

Brain Structure and Function

Most of the information we have covered about the brain has been about one or two cells. Earlier we indicated that about 99 percent of all neurons in the nervous system are located in the brain and the spinal cord. Neurons do not simply float in the brain. Connected in precise ways, they compose the various structures of the brain (Smock, 1999).

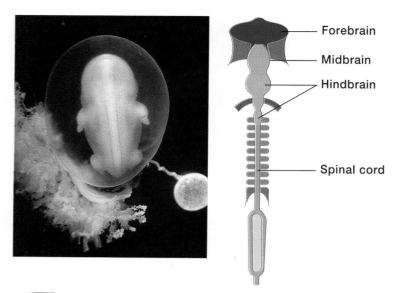

Forebrain
Midbrain
Hindbrain
Spinal cord

*F*igure 2.9
Embryological Development of the Nervous System

In this photograph you can see the primitive, tubular appearance of the nervous system at 6 weeks in the human embryo. The drawing shows the major brain regions and spinal cord as they appear early in the development of a human embryo.

Brain and Mind

Embryological Development and Levels in the Brain

As a human embryo develops inside the womb, the nervous system begins as a long, hollow tube on the embryo's back. At three weeks or so after conception, the brain forms into a large mass of neurons and loses its tubular appearance.

The elongated tube changes shape and develops into three major divisions: the hindbrain, which is the portion of the brain adjacent to the spinal cord; the midbrain, which is above the hindbrain; and the forebrain, which is the highest region of the brain (O'Rahilly & Muller, 1999) (see figure 2.9).

Hindbrain   The **hindbrain,** *located at the skull's rear, is the lowest portion of the brain. The three main parts of the hindbrain are the medulla, cerebellum, and pons.* Figure 2.10 shows the location of these brain structures as well as some of the forebrain's main structures. The **medulla** *begins where the spinal cord enters the skull. It helps to control our breathing and regulates a portion of reflexes that allow us to maintain an upright posture.* The **cerebellum** *extends from the rear of the hindbrain and is located just above the medulla. It consists of two rounded structures thought to play important roles in motor behavior.* Leg and arm movements are coordinated at the cerebellum, for example. When we play golf, practice the piano, or perfect our moves on the dance floor, the cerebellum is hard at work. If a higher portion of the brain commands us to write the number 7, it is the cerebellum that integrates the muscular activities required to do so. If the cerebellum becomes damaged, our movement becomes uncoordinated and jerky. The **pons** *is a bridge in the hindbrain that contains several clusters of fibers involved in sleep and arousal.*

Midbrain   The **midbrain,** *located between the hindbrain and forebrain, is an area where many nerve-fiber systems ascend and descend to connect the higher and lower portions of the brain.* In particular, the midbrain relays information between the brain and the eyes and ears. The ability to attend to an object visually, for example, is linked to one bundle of neurons in the midbrain. Parkinson's disease, a deterioration of movement that produces rigidity and tremors in the elderly, damages a section near the bottom of the midbrain.

Two systems in the midbrain are of special interest. One is the **reticular formation** (see figure 2.11), *a diffuse collection of neurons involved in stereotyped patterns of behavior such as walking, sleeping, or turning to attend to a sudden noise.* The other system consists of small groups of neurons that use the special neurotransmitters serotonin, dopamine, and norepinephrine. These three groups contain relatively few cells, but they send their axons to a remarkable variety of brain regions, perhaps explaining their involvement in high-level, integrative functions (Shier, Butler, & Lewis, 1999).

It is not the hindbrain or midbrain that separates humans from animals, however. In humans, it is the forebrain that becomes enlarged and specialized.

Forebrain   You try to understand what all of these terms and parts of the brain mean. You talk with friends and plan a party for this weekend. You remember it has been 6 months since you went to the dentist. You are confident you will do well on the next exam in this course. All of these experiences and millions more would not be possible without the **forebrain,** *the highest region of the human brain. Among its most important structures are the limbic system, amygdala, hippocampus, thalamus, basal ganglia, hypothalamus, and neocortex,* each of which we will discuss in turn.

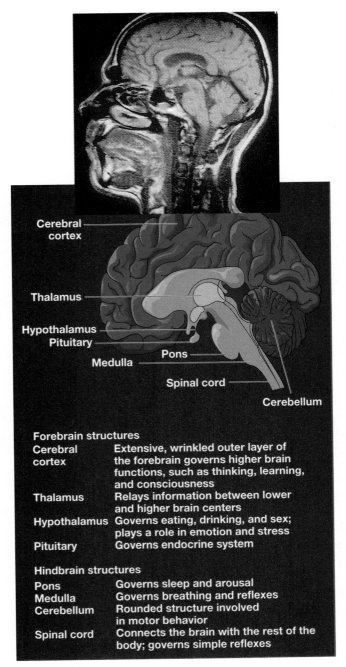

Forebrain structures

Cerebral cortex	Extensive, wrinkled outer layer of the forebrain governs higher brain functions, such as thinking, learning, and consciousness
Thalamus	Relays information between lower and higher brain centers
Hypothalamus	Governs eating, drinking, and sex; plays a role in emotion and stress
Pituitary	Governs endocrine system

Hindbrain structures

Pons	Governs sleep and arousal
Medulla	Governs breathing and reflexes
Cerebellum	Rounded structure involved in motor behavior
Spinal cord	Connects the brain with the rest of the body; governs simple reflexes

*F*igure 2.10
Structure and Regions in an Actual
Image of the Human Brain

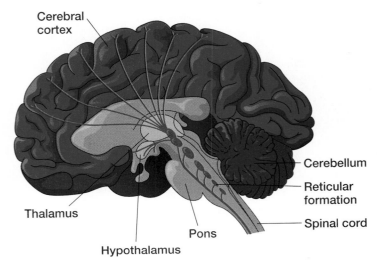

*F*igure 2.11
The Reticular Formation
The reticular formation is a network of nerve fibers that runs through the brain stem. The arrows shown radiating from the brain stem are drawn to show the connections of the reticular formation to the higher portions of the brain in the neocortex. The reticular formation is involved in arousal and attention.

Limbic System   The **limbic system,** *a loosely connected network of structures under the cerebral cortex, plays important roles in both memory and emotion.* Its two principal structures are the amygdala and hippocampus (see figure 2.12).

The **amygdala** *(from the Latin for "almond" shape) is a limbic system structure located within the base of the temporal lobe. It is involved in the discrimination of objects that are important in the organism's survival (such as appropriate food, mates, and social rivals) and in emotion (through its many connections with higher and lower portions of the brain)* (LeDoux, 1999). Neurons in the amygdala often fire selectively at the sight of such stimuli, and lesions in the amygdala can cause animals to attempt to eat, fight, or mate with inappropriate objects such as chairs.

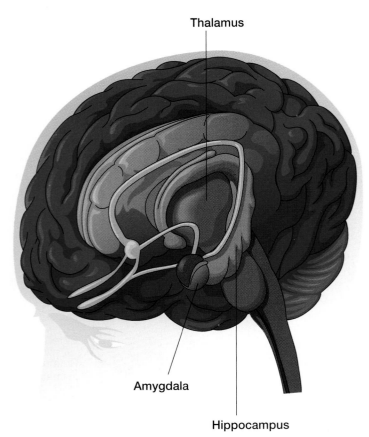

Thalamus

Amygdala

Hippocampus

𝓕igure 2.12
The Limbic System
The two main structures of the limbic system are the amygdala, which is involved in the discrimination of objects that are important for the organism's survival and in emotion; and the hippocampus, which is involved in memory.

The **hippocampus** *is a limbic system structure that has a special role in the storage of memories.* Individuals suffering extensive hippocampal damage simply cannot retain any new conscious memories after the damage (Thompson, 2000). It is fairly certain, though, that memories are not stored "in" the limbic system. Instead, the limbic system seems to control what parts of all the information passing through the cortex should be "printed" into durable, lasting neural traces in the cortex (Gluck, 1996).

Thalamus The **thalamus** *is a forebrain structure that sits at the top of the brain stem in the central core of the brain. It serves as a very important relay station, functioning much like a telephone switchboard.* While one area of the thalamus works to orient information from the sense receptors (hearing, seeing, and so on), another region seems to be involved in sleep and wakefulness, having ties with the reticular formation (see figure 2.11 for the location of the thalamus).

Basal Ganglia The **basal ganglia** *are forebrain structures essential to starting and stopping voluntary movements.* Individuals with damage to basal ganglia suffer from either unwanted movement (such as constant writhing or jerking of limbs) or too little movement (as in the slow and deliberate movements of those with Parkinson's disease).

Hypothalamus The **hypothalamus,** *much smaller than the thalamus and about the size of a kidney bean, is a forebrain structure located just below the thalamus. The hypothalamus monitors three enjoyable activities—eating, drinking, and sex; it helps direct the endocrine system through the pituitary gland; and it is involved in emotion, stress, and reward.* Perhaps the best way to describe the function of the hypothalamus is in terms of a regulator. It is sensitive to changes in the blood and neural input, and it responds by influencing the secretion of hormones and neural outputs. For example, if the temperature of circulating blood near the hypothalamus is increased by just 1 or 2 degrees, certain cells in the hypothalamus start increasing their rate of firing. As a result, a chain of events is set in motion. Increased circulation through the skin and sweat glands occurs immediately to release this heat from the body. The cooled blood circulating to the hypothalamus slows down the activity of some of the neurons there, stopping the process when the temperature is just right—37.1 degrees Centigrade. These temperature-sensitive neurons function like a finely tuned thermostat in returning the body to a balanced state.

The hypothalamus also is involved in emotional states and stress, playing an important role as an integrative location for handling stress. Much of this integration is accomplished through the hypothalamus' action on the pituitary gland, located just below it. If certain areas of the hypothalamus are electrically stimulated, a feeling of pleasure results. In a classic experiment, James Olds and Peter Milner (1954) implanted an electrode in the hypothalamus of a rat's brain. When the rat ran to a corner of an enclosed area, a mild electric current was delivered to its hypothalamus. The researchers thought the electric current was punishment for the rat and would cause it to avoid the corner. Much to their surprise, the rat kept returning to the corner. Olds and Milner believed they had discovered a pleasure center in the hypothalamus.

Olds (1958) conducted further experiments and found that rats would press bars until they dropped over from exhaustion just to continue to receive a mild electric shock to their hypothalamus. One rat pressed a bar more than 2,000 times an hour for a period of 24 hours to receive the stimulus to its hypothalamus (see figure 2.13). Today researchers agree that the hypothalamus is involved in pleasurable feelings, but that other areas of the brain, such as the limbic system and a bundle of fibers in the forebrain, are important in the link between brain and pleasure as well.

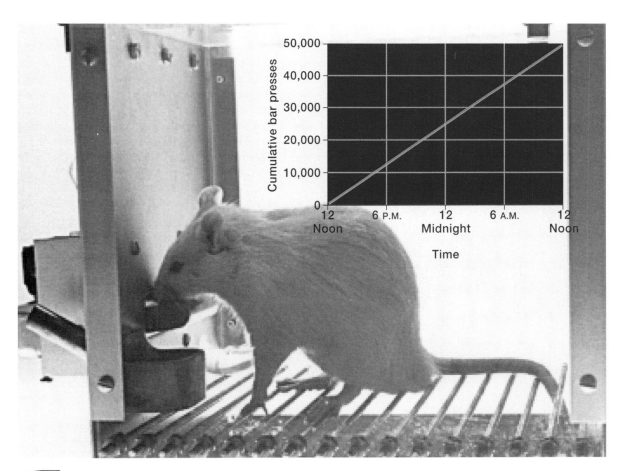

ℱigure 2.13
Results of the Experiment by Olds (1958) on the Role of the Hypothalamus in Pleasure

The graphed results for one rat show that it pressed the bar more than 2,000 times an hour for a period of 24 hours to receive the stimulus to its hypothalamus. One of the rats in Olds and Milner's experiments is shown pressing the bar to receive stimulation to its hypothalamus.

The Olds studies have implications for drug addiction. In the Olds studies, the rat pressed the bar mainly because of a positive reinforcing effect (pleasure), not because it wanted to avoid or escape a negative withdrawal effect (pain). Cocaine users talk about the drug's ability to heighten pleasure in food, in sex, and in a variety of activities, highlighting the reward aspects of the drug (Restak, 1988).

Neocortex

The Neocortex

The **neocortex** *is a region of the forebrain that is the most recently developed part of the brain in the evolutionary scheme.* The neural tissue that comprises the neocortex is the largest part of the brain in volume (about 80 percent) and covers the lower portions of the brain almost like a large cap. Let's look at the neocortex in more detail.

The wrinkled surface of the neocortex is divided into two halves (see figure 2.14). These two halves are called hemispheres, and each is divided into four lobes—frontal, parietal, temporal, and occipital (see figure 2.15). The **occipital lobe,** *the portion of the neocortex at the back of the head, is involved in visual functioning.* The **temporal lobe,** *the portion of the neocortex just above the ears, is involved in hearing.* The **frontal lobe,** *the portion of the neocortex behind the forehead, is involved in the control of voluntary muscles, intelligence, and personality.* Figure 2.16 describes a fascinating case that illustrates how damage to the frontal lobe can significantly alter personality. The **parietal lobe,** *the portion of the neocortex at the top of the head and toward the rear, is involved in bodily sensation.*

In the same way that the different lobes of the neocortex are associated with different processes, different regions of the lobes have different jobs. Scientists have determined this primarily through topographic mapping.

Projection maps are widely used topographical maps made by stimulating areas of the brain and detecting the resulting behavior or by recording the electrical activity of the neocortex during certain behaviors. Wilder Penfield (1947), a neurosurgeon at the Montreal Neurological Institute, worked with a number of patients who had a severe form of epilepsy. Penfield often performed surgery to remove portions of the epileptic patients' brains, but he was concerned that removing a portion of the brain

*F*igure 2.14
The Human Brain's Two Hemispheres
The two halves (hemispheres) of the human brain can be seen clearly in this photograph.

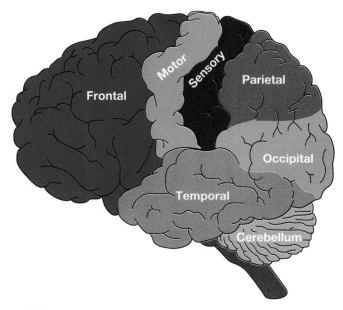

*F*igure 2.15
The Brain's Four Lobes
Shown here are the locations of the brain's four lobes: occipital, temporal, frontal, and parietal.

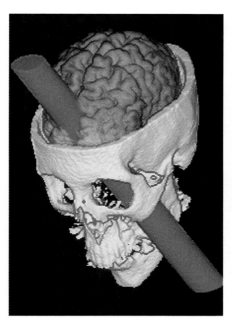

Phineas T. Gage, a 25-year-old foreman who worked for the Rutland and Burlington Railroad in Vermont, met with an interesting experience on September 13, 1848. Phineas and several co-workers were using blasting powder to construct a roadbed. The crew drilled holes in the rock and gravel, poured in the blasting powder, and then tamped down the powder with an iron rod. While Phineas was still tamping it down, the powder blew up, driving the iron rod up through the left side of his face and out through the top of his head. Though the wound in his skull healed in a matter of weeks, Phineas became a different person. He had been a mild-mannered, hardworking, emotionally calm individual prior to the accident, well liked by all who knew him. Afterward, he became obstinate, moody, irresponsible, selfish, and incapable of participating in any planned activities. The location of damage was the frontal lobe and it significantly altered Phineas's personality.

$\mathscr{F}$igure 2.16
The Injury to Phineas T. Gage

might impair some of the individuals' functions. Penfield's solution was to map the cortex during surgery by stimulating different cortical areas and observing the responses of the patients, who were given a local anesthetic so they would remain awake during the operation. He found that, when he stimulated certain sensory and motor areas of the brain, different parts of a patient's body moved (see figure 2.17). For both sensory and motor areas, there is a point-to-point relation between a part of the body and a location on the neocortex (see figure 2.18). The face and hands are given proportionally more space than other body parts. Because the face and hands are capable of finer perceptions and movements than are other body areas, they need more neocortex representation.

The point-to-point mapping of sensory fields onto the cortex's surface is the basis of our orderly and accurate perception of the world (Fox, 1996). When something touches your lip, for example, your brain knows what body part has been touched (your lip) because the nerve pathways from your lip are the only pathways that project to the lip region of the sensory cortex. This arrangement is analogous to the private hot line that connects Washington and Moscow. If the red phone rings in the president's office in Washington, the call must be from Moscow, because Moscow is the only city that is connected to the other end of the hot line. In the sensory cortex, every small region has its own neural hot line bringing in information directly from the corresponding part of the sensory field. In our telephone analogy, it would be as if the president (the cortex) had hundreds of telephones, each one connected to the capital city of a different country. Which phone was ringing would indicate which country (which part of the sensory field) had a message to convey.

One familiar example of what happens when these neural hot lines get connected the wrong way is seen in Siamese cats. Many Siamese cats have a genetic defect that causes the pathways from the eyes to connect to the wrong parts of the visual cortex during development. The result is that these cats spend their lives looking at things cross-eyed in an effort to "straighten out" the visual image of their visual cortex.

$\mathscr{F}$igure 2.17
Penfield's Research

Penfield stimulated specific locations with a very thin electric probe. When he stimulated a specific area, the patient opened his mouth, sneezed, and began chewing.

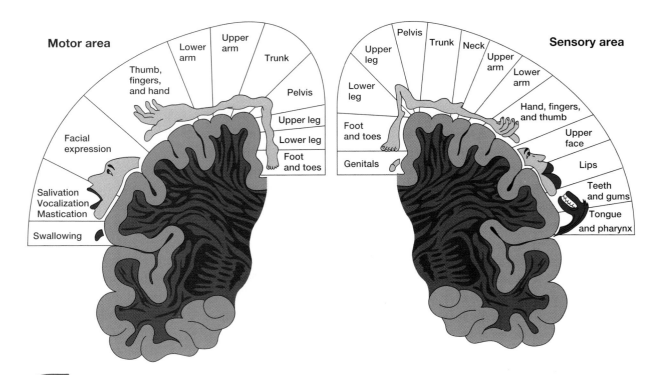

Motor area

Lower arm
Upper arm
Trunk
Thumb, fingers, and hand
Pelvis
Facial expression
Upper leg
Lower leg
Foot and toes
Salivation Vocalization Mastication
Swallowing

Pelvis
Trunk
Neck
Upper leg
Upper arm
Lower leg
Lower arm
Foot and toes
Hand, fingers, and thumb
Genitals
Upper face
Lips
Teeth and gums
Tongue and pharynx

Sensory area

Figure 2.18
Disproportionate Representation of Body Parts in the Motor and Sensory Areas of the Cortex

As can be seen in this drawing, the amount of cortex allotted to a body part is not proportionate to the body part's size. Instead, the brain has more space for body parts that require precision and control. Thus, the thumb, fingers, and hand require more brain tissue than do the upper leg and upper arm.

So far our description of the neocortex has focused on sensory and motor areas, but more than 75 percent of the neocortex is made up of areas called the association cortex. The **association cortex** *(or association areas) is the region of the neocortex involved in our highest intellectual functions, such as thinking and problem solving.* The neurons in the association cortex communicate with each other and with neurons in the motor area of the cortex.

Of special interest is the finding that damage to a specific part of the association cortex often does not result in a specific loss of function. With the exception of language areas (which are localized), loss of function seems to depend more on the extent of damage to the association areas than to the specific location of the damage. By observing brain-damaged individuals and using the mapping technique, scientists have found that the association cortex is involved in linguistic and perceptual functioning. The largest portion of association areas is located in the frontal lobe, directly under the forehead. Damage to this area does not lead to sensory or motor loss. Indeed, it is this area that may be most directly related to thinking and problem solving. Early experimentation even referred to the frontal lobe as the center of intelligence, but research suggests that frontal lobe damage may not result in a lowering of intelligence. Planning and judgment are characteristics often associated with the frontal lobe. Personality also may be linked with the frontal lobe. Recall the misfortune of Phineas Gage, whose personality radically changed after he experienced frontal lobe damage.

One of the truly fascinating areas of inquiry in contemporary neuroscience concerns the nature of cortical column function in the association cortex. Neuroscientist Vernon Mountcastle (1986) has speculated that individual columns of neurons in the association cortex might carry out specific functions such as planning new skeletal movements and shifting attention to new things. The coming decades likely will witness expansions on these themes. Imagine the behavioral result if some individuals had a genetic miswiring of association cortex columns similar to the miswiring of visual columns that occurs in some Siamese cats.

You have learned that the neocortex is divided into two hemispheres. The fascinating story of information processing in the neocortex involves lobes, maps, and columns, but it could not be completely told without knowing more about how the two sides, or hemispheres, of the brain work.

The Cerebral Hemispheres and Split-Brain Research

At the beginning of our discussion of the cerebral cortex, we indicated that it is divided into two halves—left and right (see figure 2.17). Might these hemispheres have different functions? In 1861, French surgeon Paul Broca saw a patient who had received an injury to the left side of his brain about 30 years earlier. The injury was to a precise area of the left hemisphere. The patient became known as Tan because *Tan* was the only word he could speak. Tan suffered from *aphasia,* a language disorder associated with brain damage. Tan died several days after Broca evaluated him and an autopsy revealed the location of the damage. Today we refer to this region of the brain as *Broca's area* and we know it plays an important role in the production of speech. Another area of the brain's left hemisphere that has an important role in language is called *Wernicke's area,* which if damaged causes problems in comprehending language. Figure 2.19 shows the locations of Broca's area and Wernicke's area.

Today, there continues to be considerable interest in the degree to which the brain's left hemisphere or right hemisphere is involved in various aspects of thinking, feeling, and behavior (Carlson, 1999). For many years scientists speculated that the **corpus callosum,** *a large bundle of axons that connects the brain's two hemispheres,* had something to do with relaying information between the two sides. Roger Sperry (1974) confirmed this in an experiment in which he cut the corpus callosum in cats. He also severed certain nerves leading from the eyes to the brain. After the operation, Sperry trained the cats to solve a series of visual problems with one eye blindfolded. After the cat learned the task, say with only its left eye uncovered, its other eye was blindfolded and the animal was tested again. The "split-brain" cat behaved as if it had never learned the task. It seems that the memory was stored only in the left hemisphere, which could no longer directly communicate with the right hemisphere.

Further evidence of the corpus callosum's function has come from experiments with patients who have severe, even life-threatening, forms of epilepsy. Epilepsy is caused by electrical "brainstorms" that flash uncontrollably across the corpus callosum. W. J. is one of the most famous cases. Neurosurgeons severed the corpus callosum of an epileptic patient now known as W. J. in a final attempt to reduce his unbearable seizures. Sperry (1968) examined W. J. and found that the corpus callosum functions the same in humans as in animals—cutting the corpus callosum seemed to leave the patient with "two separate minds" that learned and operated independently.

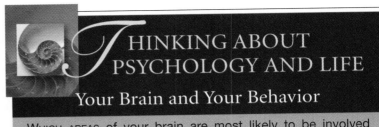

THINKING ABOUT PSYCHOLOGY AND LIFE
Your Brain and Your Behavior

WHICH AREAS of your brain are most likely to be involved when you do the following?

• Fall asleep
• Think critically
• Yell at someone
• Shoot a basketball
• Look at a painting
• Get hungry
• Say a word correctly

Aphasia
Corpus Callosum

Broca's area

Wernicke's area

Figure 2.19
Broca's Area and Wernicke's Area

Broca's area is located in the brain's left hemisphere and it is involved in the control of speech. Individuals with damage to Broca's area have problems in saying words correctly. Also shown is Wernicke's area, a portion of the left hemisphere that is involved in understanding language. Individuals with damage to this area cannot comprehend words; that is, they hear the words but don't know what they mean.

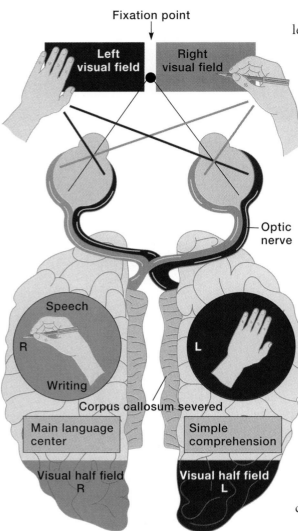

Figure 2.20
Visual Information in the Split Brain

In a split-brain patient, information from the visual field's left side projects only to the right hemisphere. Information from the visual field's right side projects only to the left hemisphere. Because of these projections, stimuli can be presented to only one of a split-brain patient's hemispheres.

The right hemisphere, it turns out, receives information only from the left side of the body, and the left hemisphere receives information only from the right side of the body. When you hold an object in your left hand, for example, only the right hemisphere of your brain detects the object. When you hold an object in your right hand, only the left hemisphere of the brain detects the object (see figure 2.20). Because you have a normal corpus callosum, both hemispheres receive this information.

The most extensive research on the brain's two hemispheres involves language. A common misconception is that virtually all language processing is carried out in the brain's left hemisphere. Speech and grammar can be localized to the left hemisphere in most people. However, understanding such aspects of language as appropriate use of language in different contexts, metaphor, and much of humor involves the right hemisphere.

Speculation continues about the brain's hemispheric specialization—the notion that the two hemispheres function in different ways and that some psychological processes are restricted almost exclusively to one hemisphere or the other (Levy, 2000; Saravi, 1993). In fact, people commonly use the phrases *left-brained* and *right-brained* to say which hemisphere is dominant. Explorations in Psychology addresses the nature of hemispheric specialization and separates fact from fantasy regarding a number of related myths.

Integration of Function in the Brain

How do all of the various brain regions cooperate to produce the wondrous complexity of thought and behavior that characterize humans? Part of the answer to this question, such as how the brain solves a murder mystery or writes a poetic essay, is beyond the grasp of neuroscience. Still, we can get a sense of integrative brain function by considering something like the act of escaping from a burning building. Gall and his phrenologists might have argued that such behavior was controlled by an "escaping from danger" center in the brain. Let's compare that view with a more contemporary one.

Imagine you are sitting at your desk writing letters when fire breaks out behind you. The sound of crackling flames is relayed from your ear, through the thalamus, to your auditory cortex, and on to the auditory association cortex. At each stage, the stimulus energy has been processed to extract information, and at some stage, probably at the association cortex level, the sounds are finally matched with something like a neural memory representing previous sounds of fires you have heard. The association "fire" sets new machinery in motion. Your attention (guided in part by the reticular formation) swings to the auditory signal being held in your association cortex, and simultaneously (again guided by reticular systems) your head turns toward the noise. Now your visual association cortex reports in: "Objects matching flames are present." In other association regions, the visual and auditory reports are synthesized ("We have things that look and sound like fire"), and neural associations representing potential actions ("flee") are activated. However, firing the neurons that code the plan to flee will not get you out of the chair. The basal ganglia must become engaged, and from there the commands will arise to set the brain stem, motor cortex, and cerebellum to the task of actually transporting you out of the room.

Which part of your brain did you use to escape? Virtually all systems had a role; each was quite specific, and together they generated the behavior. By the way, you would probably remember an event such as a fire in your room. That is because your

EXPLORATIONS IN PSYCHOLOGY
Left-Brain, Right-Brain Myths

TO MOST SCIENTISTS, the concept of the brain as split into two tidy halves—one being the source of creativity, the other the source of logical thinking—is simplistic. Jerre Levy (2000), a neuroscientist at the University of Chicago, points out that no complex function—music, art, reading, or whatever—can be assigned to one single hemisphere or the other. Complex thinking in normal people involves communication between both sides of the brain.

How did the left-brain, right-brain myth get started? It had its origin in Roger Sperry's classic studies of split-brain patients. Remember that Sperry examined people whose corpus callosum had been severed and found that after surgery the two sides of the brain learned and operated independently. As his findings made their way into the media, the complexity of Sperry's findings became oversimplified. Media reports indicated that when you worked on a novel, your left hemisphere was busy while your right was silent. Switch to creating an oil painting and your right brain is working while your left is quiet. People became either right-brained (and artistic) or left-brained (and logical). An example of the either/or oversimplification of the brain's left and right hemispheres is shown in the *Newsweek* drawing of how the brain divides its work (see figure 2.A).

Roger Sperry did discover that the left hemisphere is superior in the kind of logic used to prove geometric theorems. But in the logic of everyday life, our problems involve integrating information and drawing conclusions. In these instances, the right brain's functions are crucial. In virtually all activities, there is an interplay between the brain's two hemispheres (Hoptman & Davidson, 1994). For example, in reading, the left hemisphere comprehends syntax and grammar, which the right does not. However, the right brain is better at understanding a story's intonation and emotion. The same is true for music and art. Pop psychology assigns both to the right brain. In some musical skills, such

Neuroscientist Jerre Levy has conducted extensive research on the nature of hemispheric function in the brain. What conclusions does she reach about left brain-right brain functioning?

as recognizing chords, the right hemisphere is better. In others, such as distinguishing which of two sounds came first, the left hemisphere takes over. Enjoying or creating music requires the use of both hemispheres.

Another offshoot of the left-brain, right-brain hoopla is speculation that more right-brain activities and exercises should be incorporated into our nation's schools (Edwards, 1979). In schools that rely heavily on rote learning to instruct students, children probably would benefit from exercises in intuitive thought and holistic thinking. But this deficiency in school curricula has *nothing at all* to do with left-brain, right-brain specialization.

Further evidence of the brain's hemispheric flexibility and resilience involves 13-year-old Brandi Binder (Nash, 1997). She developed such a severe case of epilepsy that surgeons at UCLA had to remove the right side of her cortex when she was 6. Binder lost virtually all of the control she had established over muscles on the left side of her body, the side controlled by the right side of the brain. Yet today, after years of therapy ranging from leg lifts to math to music training, Binder is an A student. She loves music, math, and art, which usually are associated with the right side of the brain. Her recuperation is not 100 percent. For example, she never has regained the use of her left arm. However, her recovery is remarkable and shows that if there is a way to compensate, the brain will find it.

There is so much more to understanding brain function and organization than to characterize people as right- or left-brained. After all, we are trying to understand the most complex piece of matter in the known universe.

HOW THE BRAIN DIVIDES ITS WORK

Figure 2.A
Stereotyped Myths About Left Brain, Right Brain
Is left-brain, right-brain specialization all-or-none, as this drawing implies? No. © *Roy Doty/Newsweek*

Brandi Binder is evidence of the brain's hemispheric flexibility and resilience. Despite having the right side of her cortex removed because of a severe case of epilepsy, Brandi engages in many activities often portrayed as only "right-brain" activities. She loves music, math, and art, and is shown here working on one of her paintings.

Concept	Processes/Related Ideas	Characteristics/Description
Embryological Development and Levels in the Brain	Embryological Development	A neural tube develops into the hindbrain (lowest level), midbrain (middle level), and forebrain (highest level).
	Hindbrain	The hindbrain is located at the skull's rear and has three main structures: medulla (helps to control breathing and regulates reflexes that allow an upright position), cerebellum (involved in motor behavior), and pons (bridge involved in sleep and arousal).
	Midbrain	The midbrain is located between the hindbrain and the forebrain. It is an area where many fibers ascend and descend to connect higher and lower areas of the brain. There are two main systems in the midbrain: The reticular formation is involved in stereotyped patterns of behavior such as walking, sleeping, or turning toward a sudden noise. The other system consists of small groups of neurons that use special neurotransmitters.
	Forebrain	The forebrain is the highest region of the human brain. Its structures include the limbic system (involved in memory and emotion), amygdala (involved in discrimination of objects and emotion), hippocampus (involved in storage of memories), thalamus (important relay station), basal ganglia (involved in starting and stopping voluntary movements), hypothalamus (monitors eating, drinking and sex; helps direct the endocrine system through links with the pituitary gland; and is involved in emotions, stress, and reward), and the neocortex.
Neocortex	Its Nature	The neocortex is the region of forebrain that is divided into two hemispheres, each of which is divided into four lobes—occipital lobe, which is involved in visual functioning; temporal lobe, which is involved in hearing; frontal lobe, which is involved in the control of voluntary muscles; and parietal lobe, which is involved in bodily sensation. Projection maps have helped scientists determine the neocortex's role in different behaviors. The neocortex can be divided into sensory, motor, and association areas.
The Cerebral Hemispheres and Split-Brain Research	Their Nature	Broca's area (production of speech) and Wernicke's area (comprehension of language) are located in the brain's left hemisphere. The corpus callosum is a bundle of axons that connects the brain's two hemispheres. Pioneered by Sperry, split-brain research involves severing the corpus callosum. In normal individuals, the two hemispheres work together to process information. A number of myths have developed that exaggerate left-brain and right-brain functions.
Integration of Function in the Brain	Its Nature	Most psychological functions do not involve a single structure in the brain, but rather, the integration of information by a number of structures.

limbic circuitry would have likely issued the "start print" command when the significant association "fire" was first triggered. The next time the sounds of crackling flames reach your auditory association cortex, the associations triggered will include those of this most recent escape. In sum, there is considerable integration of function in the brain (Gevins, 1999).

At this point we have studied a number of ideas about structure and function in the brain. An overview of these ideas is presented in summary table 2.3.

Exploring the Brain

Other topics important for understanding the brain include these: What is the nature of brain damage, plasticity, and repair? What techniques can be used to study the brain? How do the brain and endocrine system work?

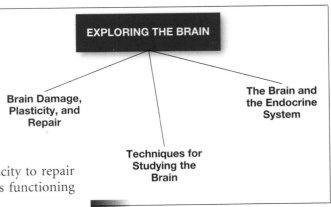

Brain Damage, Plasticity, and Repair

If the brain is damaged through injury or illness, does it have the capacity to repair itself? Are there external ways we can restore some or all of the brain's functioning after it has been damaged?

The Brain's Plasticity and Capacity for Repair   Brain damage can produce horrific effects, including paralysis, sensory loss, memory loss, and personality deterioration. When such damage occurs, can the brain recover some or all of its functions? Recovery from brain damage varies considerably (Garraghty, 1996).

Plasticity *is the brain's capacity to modify and reorganize itself following damage.* In one study, researchers surgically removed part of the monkey's somatosensory cortex. Later the somatosensory cortical map shifted to intact adjacent parts of the parietal lobes, restoring the body's ability to experience sensations (Fox, 1984).

The human brain shows the most plasticity in young children before the functions of the cortical regions become entirely fixed (Kolb, 1989). For example, if the speech areas in an infant's left hemisphere are damaged, the right hemisphere assumes much of this language function. However, after age 5, permanent damage to the left hemisphere can permanently disrupt language ability.

Brain Disorders
Repairing the Damaged Brain

A key factor in recovery is whether some, or all, of the neurons in an affected area are just damaged or completely destroyed (Black, 1999; Carlson, 1999). If the neurons are not completely destroyed, brain function often becomes restored over time. Unlike some fish and amphibians who can regenerate neurons, our central nervous system cannot. Once a human neuron is lost, it is gone forever.

Even though new neurons can't be regenerated in humans, other repair mechanisms exist (Azar, 1996). They include:

- *Collateral sprouting,* in which the axons of some healthy neurons adjacent to damaged cells grow new branches.
- *Substitution of function,* in which the damaged region's function is taken over by another area, or areas, of the brain. This is what happened in the example of the right hemisphere taking over the speech function of the damaged left hemisphere in infants.

Brain Tissue Implants   The brain's capacity to repair itself may restore some lost functions following damage, but not in all cases. In recent years, considerable excitement has been generated about **brain grafts,** *which involve implanting healthy tissue into damaged brains.* The potential success of brain grafts is much better when brain tissue from the fetal stage (an early stage in prenatal development) is used. The neurons of the fetus are still growing and have a much higher probability of making connections with other neurons than do the neurons of

Actress Patricia Neal suffered a stroke when she was 39 years of age. The stroke paralyzed one of her legs and left her unable to read, write, or speak. However, an intensive rehabilitation program and the human brain's plasticity allowed her to recover her functioning to the point where she resumed her career as an actress 4 years later. What is the nature of the human brain's plasticity and capacity for repair?

adults. In a number of studies, researchers have damaged part of a rat's (or some other animal's) brain, waited until the animal recovered as much as possible by itself, and assessed its behavioral deficits. Then they took the corresponding area of a fetal rat's brain and transplanted it into the damaged brain of the adult rat. In these studies, the rats that received the brain transplants demonstrated considerable behavioral recovery (Dunnett, 1989).

Might such brain grafts be successful with humans suffering from brain damage? One problem is finding donors. Aborted fetuses are a possibility, but they raise ethical issues. Another possibility has been attempted with individuals who have Parkinson's disease, a neurological disorder that affects about a million people in the United States. Parkinson's disease impairs coordinated movement to the point that just walking across a room can be a major ordeal. Brain grafters have tried to substitute adrenal gland tissue for brain tissue. Why adrenal gland tissue? Parkinson's disease damages neurons in an area of the brain that secretes the neurotransmitter dopamine. Adrenal gland cells produce dopamine. Early reports of adrenal gland transplants in Parkinson's patients were promising, but the long-term effects have been less so (Lewin, 1988).

The potential for brain grafts also exists for individuals with Alzheimer's disease, which is characterized by a progressive decline in intellectual functioning. Brain destruction in Alzheimer's disease involves the degeneration of neurons that function in memory. Such degenerative changes can be reversed in rats (Gage & Bjorklund, 1986). However, as yet no success with brain grafts with Alzheimer's patients has been reported. Nonetheless, the future holds promise that such grafts may someday be possible in humans.

Techniques for Studying the Brain

Earlier we discussed research by Wilder Penfield and James Olds in which electrodes were inserted into living brains in order to study brain functions. Neuroscientists no longer have to perform surgery on living patients or cadavers to study the brain. Sophisticated techniques allow researchers to "look inside" the brain while it is at work. Let's examine some of these fascinating techniques.

High-powered microscopes are widely used in neuroscience research. Neurons are stained with the salts of various heavy metals such as silver and lead. These stains coat only a small portion of any group of neurons. The stains allow neuroscientists to view and study every part of a neuron in microscopic detail.

Also widely used, the **electroencephalograph (EEG)** *records the electrical activity of the brain*. Electrodes placed on the scalp detect brain-wave activity, which is recorded on a chart known as an electroencephalogram (see figure 2.21). This device has been used to assess brain damage, epilepsy, and other problems.

Not every recording of brain activity is made with electrodes. In single-unit recording, a portrayal of a single neuron's electrical activity, a thin wire or needle is inserted in or near an individual neuron (Seidemann & others, 1996). The wire or needle transmits the neuron's electrical activity to an amplifier, which allows researchers to gather information about the activity.

For years X rays have been used to determine damage inside or outside our bodies, both in the brain and in other locations. But a single X ray of the brain is hard

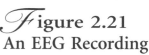

Figure 2.21
An EEG Recording
The electroencephalograph (EEG) is widely used in sleep research. It has led to some major breakthroughs in understanding sleep by showing how the brain's electrical activity changes during sleep.

Generating words

Seeing words

Hearing words

Speaking words

ℱigure 2.22
PET Scan
This PET scan of the left brain's hemisphere contrasts the different areas used in aspects of language activity: Generating words, hearing words, seeing words, and speaking words.

to interpret because it shows the three-dimensional nature of the brain's interior in a two-dimensional image. **Computer-assisted axial tomography (CAT scan)** *is three-dimensional imaging obtained from X rays of the head that are assembled into a composite image by computer.* The CAT scan provides valuable information about the location of damage due to a stroke, language disorder, or loss of memory.

Positron-emission tomography (PET scan) *measures the amount of glucose in various areas of the brain, then sends this information to a computer.* Because glucose levels vary with the levels of activity throughout the brain, tracing the amounts of glucose generates a picture of activity level throughout the brain (Fiez & others, 1996). Figure 2.22 shows PET scans of people's brain activity while they are hearing, seeing, speaking, and thinking.

Another technique is **magnetic resonance imaging (MRI),** *which involves creating a magnetic field around a person's body and using radio waves to construct images of the person's brain tissues and biochemical activities.* MRI provides very clear pictures of the brain's interior, does not require injecting the brain with a substance, and does not pose a problem of radiation overexposure (Toga, 1998; Toga & Mazziota, 1999).

At this point we have discussed many different aspects of the brain and techniques for studying it. One more important aspect of the body's biological makeup deserves further attention—the endocrine system.

Neuroimaging
MRI

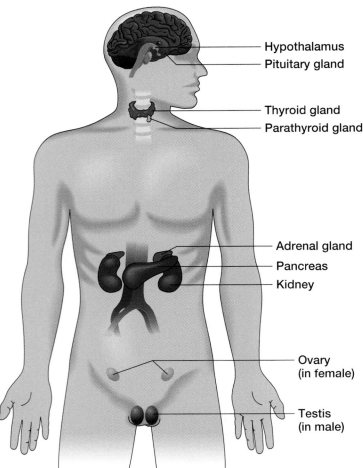

Hypothalamus
Pituitary gland

Thyroid gland
Parathyroid gland

Adrenal gland
Pancreas
Kidney

Ovary
(in female)

Testis
(in male)

The Brain and the Endocrine System

Recall that the autonomic nervous system involves connections with internal organs, regulating processes like respiration, heart rate, and digestion. The autonomic nervous system acts on the endocrine glands to produce a number of important physiological reactions to strong emotions such as rage and fear.

The **endocrine glands** *are a set of glands that release their chemical products directly into the bloodstream. Hormones are chemical messengers manufactured by the endocrine glands.* Hormones travel more slowly than nerve impulses. The bloodstream conveys hormones to all parts of the body, and the membrane of every cell has receptors for one or more hormones.

The endocrine glands consist of the hypothalamus and the pituitary gland at the base of the brain, the thyroid and parathyroid glands at the front of the neck, the adrenal glands just above the kidneys, the pancreas in the abdomen, and the ovaries in the female's pelvis and the testes in the male's scrotum (see figure 2.23). Other hormones are produced as well, including several in the gastrointestinal tract that control digestion. In much the same way that the brain's control of muscular activity is constantly monitored and altered to suit the information received by the brain, the action of the endocrine glands is continuously monitored and changed by the nervous, hormonal, and chemical information sent to them (Mader, 1999; McEwen, 2000).

The **pituitary gland** *is an important endocrine gland that sits at the base of the skull and is about the size of a pea; the pituitary gland controls growth and regulates other glands* (see figure 2.24). The anterior (front) part of the pituitary is known as the master gland, because almost all of its hormones direct the activity of target glands elsewhere in the body. For example, follicle-stimulating

Figure 2.23
The Major Endocrine Glands
The pituitary gland releases hormones that regulate the hormone secretions of the other glands. The pituitary gland is itself regulated by the hypothalamus.

Figure 2.24
The Pituitary Gland
The pituitary gland, which hangs by a short stalk from the hypothalamus, regulates the hormone production of many of the body's endocrine glands. Here it is enlarged 30 times.

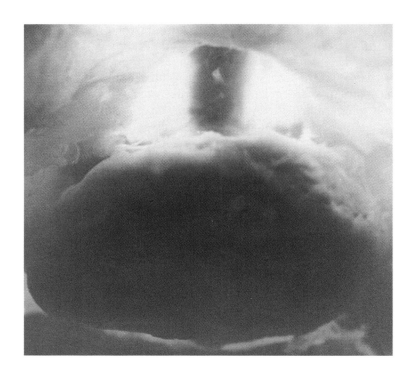

SUMMARY TABLE 2.4
Exploring the Brain

Concept	Processes/ Related Ideas	Characteristics/Description
Brain Damage, Plasticity, and Repair	The Brain's Plasticity and Capacity for Repair	Recovery from brain damage varies considerably. Plasticity is the brain's capacity for modification and reorganization following damage. If neurons in the central nervous system are destroyed, they cannot be regenerated. Plasticity is greater in young children than in adults. Collateral sprouting and substitution of function are two mechanisms of repair in the brain.
	Brain Tissue Implants	Brain grafts involve implanting healthy tissue into damaged brains. The most successful brain grafts involve the use of fetal brain tissue, but this procedure raises ethical issues. The potential for brain grafts exists for individuals with Parkinson's disease and with Alzheimer's disease. Brain grafts have been much more successful with animals than with humans.
Techniques for Studying the Brain	Their Nature	Among the most widely used techniques are high-powered microscopes, the electroencephalograph, single-unit recordings, the CAT scan, the PET scan, and magnetic resonance imaging (MRI).
The Brain and Endocrine System	Linkages	The autonomic nervous system acts on the endocrine glands to produce a number of physiological reactions to strong emotions such as rage and fear. The endocrine glands discharge their chemical products into the bloodstream. These chemical products, called hormones, can travel to all parts of the body. The pituitary gland and the adrenal glands are important parts of the endocrine system.

hormone (FSH) produced by the pituitary monitors the level of sex hormones in the ovaries of females and testes of males. Though most pituitary hormones influence a specific organ, growth hormone (GH) acts on all tissues to produce growth during childhood and adolescence. Dwarfs have too little of this hormone, giants too much.

The **adrenal glands** *play an important role in our moods, our energy level, and our ability to cope with stress.* Each adrenal gland secretes epinephrine (also called adrenaline) and norepinephrine (also called noradrenaline). While most hormones travel rather slowly, epinephrine and norepinephrine do their work quickly. Epinephrine helps a person get ready for an emergency by acting on smooth muscles, the heart, stomach, intestines, and sweat glands. Epinephrine also stimulates the reticular formation, which in turn arouses the sympathetic nervous system, and this system subsequently excites the adrenal glands to produce more epinephrine. Norepinephrine also alerts the individual for emergency situations by interacting with the pituitary and the liver. You may remember that norepinephrine also functions as a neurotransmitter when released by neurons. In the case of the adrenal glands, norepinephrine is released as a hormone. In both instances, norepinephrine conveys information—in the first instance to neurons, in the second to glands (Raven & Johnson, 1999).

At this point we have studied a number of ideas about exploring the brain. An overview of these ideas is presented in summary table 2.4. In the next chapter, we will examine sensation and perception, including the brain's role in the visual and auditory senses.

Overview

Overview

We began this chapter by exploring these aspects of biological foundations: heredity, evolution, and nature/nurture. Next, we studied neuroscience, the nervous system, and neurons. This included examining what the field of neuroscience is about, the organization of the nervous system, neurons, and glial cells. Our coverage of brain structure and function focused on embryological development and levels in the brain, the neocortex, cerebral hemispheres and split-brain research, and integration of function in the brain. In the final section of the chapter we explored these aspects of the brain: brain damage, plasticity, and repair, techniques for studying the brain, and the brain and endocrine system.

Don't forget that you can obtain a more detailed overview of the chapter by again studying the four summary tables on pages 48, 57, 68, and 73.

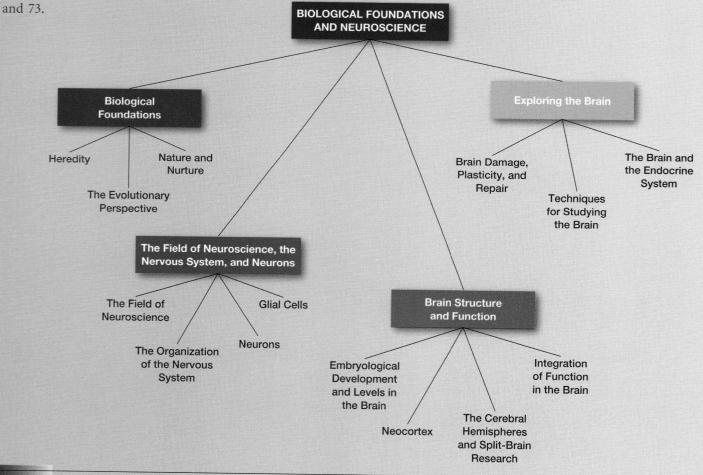

Key Terms

chromosomes 44
deoxyribonucleic acid (DNA) 44
genes 44
dominant-recessive genes principle 44
genotype 45
phenotype 45
natural selection 46
evolutionary psychology approach 46
environment 47
nurture 47
nature 47
nervous system 48
neurons 49
neuroscience 49
central nervous system (CNS) 49
peripheral nervous system 49
somatic nervous system 49

autonomic nervous system 50
sympathetic nervous system 50
parasympathetic nervous system 50
afferent nerves 50
efferent nerves 50
interneurons 51
cell body 51
dendrite 51
axon 51
myelin sheath 51
all-or-none principle 53
ions 53
resting potential 53
action potential 53
synapses 53
neurotransmitters 54
GABA 54
acetylcholine (ACh) 54
norepinephrine 54

dopamine 54
serotonin 54
endorphins 54
agonist 56
antagonist 56
glial cells 56
hindbrain 58
medulla 58
cerebellum 58
pons 58
midbrain 58
reticular formation 58
forebrain 58
limbic system 59
amygdala 59
hippocampus 60
thalamus 60
basal ganglia 60
hypothalamus 60
neocortex 62
occipital lobe 62

temporal lobe 62
frontal lobe 62
parietal lobe 62
association cortex (association areas) 64
corpus callosum 65
plasticity 69
brain graft 69
electroencephalograph (EEG) 70
computer-assisted axial tomography (CAT scan) 71
positron-emission tomography (PET scan) 71
magnetic resonance imaging (MRI) 71
endocrine glands 72
pituitary gland 72
adrenal glands 73

Key People

Thomas Bouchard 43
Charles Darwin 46
David Buss 46

Santiago Ramón y Cajal 56
James Olds and Peter Milner 61

Wilder Penfield 62
Paul Broca 65
Roger Sperry 65

Jerre Levy 67

Taking It to the Net

1. Have you ever seen a picture of the brain? Brain-imaging techniques have developed rapidly over the past half century. New technology has allowed us to see the brain in an entirely new way. Keeping in mind that each tool allows us to derive different information, describe the major imaging techniques, giving examples of when each would be employed. Which technique gives a color representation of the brain? Why is color used?

2. Prozac, a popular antidepressant drug, is a selective serotonin re-uptake inhibitor (SSRI). Other popular SSRIs include Zoloft and Paxil. They alleviate symptoms of depression by affecting the re-uptake of serotonin in the brain. Using the information provided at the web site listed below, explain the process of reuptake and how SSRIs inhibit the process of normal reuptake. What can you infer about the causal nature of depression? Do you think that is the only cause of depressive symptoms?

3. You probably have heard at one time or another that you are a "left-brained" or "right-brained" person. These expressions usually are used to describe your personality in terms of what we know about brain laterality. Can we, in fact, be left- or right-brained? What does that mean? Furthermore, what percentage of your brain do you actually use? Do you think you can learn to use more of your brain?

Connect to http://www.mhhe.com/psychology/santrock to find the answers!

Chapter 3

CHAPTER OUTLINE

Sensation and Perception

"*The setting sun, and music at close, As the last taste of sweets, is sweetest last, Writ in remembrance more than things long past.*"

William Shakespeare
English Playwright, (1564–1616)

Images of Psychology and Life
The Man Who Mistook His Wife for a Hat

Preview

EACH OF US has a number of sensory and perceptual systems to detect, process, and interpret what we experience in our environment. Sensing and perceiving involve a complex and sophisticated visual system, an auditory system that is an elaborate engineering marvel compacted into a space the size of an Oreo cookie, and other processes that inform us about soft caresses and excruciating pain, sweet and sour tastes, floral and peppermint odors, and whether our world is upside down or right side up.

These are some of the questions we will explore in this chapter:

- How close does an approaching bumblebee have to be before you can hear it buzzing?
- What factors are involved in an air traffic controller's detection of a plane where it is not supposed to be?
- How do we see, hear, touch, feel pain, taste, and smell?
- How do artists use perceptual cues to portray depth in their paintings?
- Why do you see illusions?
- Can some people actually perceive the world through something other than normal sensory pathways; that is, do they have extrasensory perception?

DR. P. WAS a distinguished musician, being an accomplished singer and teacher. However, he began to have difficulty in perceiving his world. It was his music students who first recognized his problem. Sometimes he would fail to recognize students he had known for a long time. However, the moment the students spoke, Dr. P. knew who they were by their voices. Becoming aware that something was wrong with the way he was seeing his world, Dr. P. went to see an ophthalmologist. Following a careful examination, Dr. P. was told there was nothing wrong with his eyes, but that he should see a neurologist.

Dr. P. was referred to a neurologist, Oliver Sacks (1985), who wrote about him in a book, *The Man Who Mistook His Wife for a Hat.* Dr. P. saw nothing as familiar, even confusing his wife for a hat. When shown a glove, Dr. P. said it was a container of some sort, maybe a change-purse. Visually, he was lost in a world of lifeless abstractions.

What would it be like to live in Dr. P.'s world, surrounded by a visual world that can never be put together into coherent objects and events? In Dr. P.'s case, damage to his brain interfered with his ability to integrate into meaningful wholes what his eyes saw. That is, his eyes adequately detected visual information in the world, but his brain failed to accurately interpret the sensory information. The eyes are just the beginning of visual perception (Hoffman, 1998). By themselves, our eyes provide little more than a faithful image of the world. It is only when we consider both what the eyes see and the brain interprets that we can fully understand how we visually perceive our world.

Detecting and Perceiving the World

How can sensation and perception be defined? How do we detect the sensory world?

Defining Sensation and Perception

How do you know the color of grass, that a smell is sweet, that a sound is a sigh, and that the lights around the shore are dim? You know these things because of your *senses*. All outside information comes into us through our senses. Without vision, hearing, touch, taste, smell, and other senses, your brain would be isolated from the world: you would live in a dark silence—a tasteless, colorless, feelingless void.

Sensation *is the process of detecting and encoding stimulus energy in the world.* Stimuli emit physical energy—light, sound, and heat, for example. The sense organs detect this energy and then transform it into a code that can be transmitted to the brain. The first step in "sensing" the world is the work of receptor cells, which respond to certain forms of energy. The retina of the eye is sensitive to light, and special cells in the ear are sensitive to sound, for example. This physical energy is transformed into electrical impulses; the information carried by these electrical impulses travels through nerve fibers that connect the sense organs with the central nervous system. Once in the brain, information about the external world travels to the appropriate area of the cerebral cortex (Halliday, 1998).

Perception *is the brain's process of organizing and interpreting sensory information to give it meaning.* The retinas of our eyes record a fast-moving silver object in the sky, but they do not "see" a passenger jet: our eardrum vibrates in a particular way, but it does not "hear" a Beethoven symphony. Organizing and interpreting what is sensed—"seeing" and "hearing" meaningful patterns in sensory information—is perception.

In our everyday lives, the two processes of sensation and perception are virtually inseparable. When the brain receives information, for example, it automatically interprets and responds to the information. Because of this, most contemporary psychologists refer to sensation and perception as a unified information-processing system (Goldstein, 1999).

Psychophysics
Perception & Psychophysics

Thresholds

How close does an approaching bumblebee have to be before you can hear its buzzing? How far away does a brewing coffeepot have to be for you to detect the smell of coffee? How different does the percentage of fat have to be for you to taste a difference between the "low-fat" and "regular" versions of your favorite ice cream?

Questions like those just posed are answered by **psychophysics**, *the field that studies links between the physical properties of stimuli and a person's experience of them* (Galanter, 2000). For example, an experiment in psychophysics might examine the relation between the rate at which a light flashes and a participant's ability to see individual flashes.

Absolute Threshold   A basic problem for any sensory system is its ability to detect varying degrees of energy in the environment. This energy can take the form of light, sound, chemical, or mechanical stimulation. How much of a stimulus is necessary for you to see, hear, taste, smell, or feel something? One way to address these questions is to assume that each of us has an **absolute threshold,** *or minimum amount of energy that we can detect.* When a stimulus has less energy than this absolute threshold, we cannot detect its presence; when the stimulus has more energy than the absolute threshold, we can detect the stimulus. An experiment with a wristwatch or a clock will help you understand the principle of absolute threshold. Find a wristwatch or clock that ticks; put it on a table and walk far enough across the room so that you no longer hear the ticking. Then gradually move toward the wristwatch or clock. At some point you will begin to hear the ticking. Hold your position and notice that occasionally the ticking fades and you may have to move forward to reach the threshold; at other times it may become loud and you can move backward.

In this experiment, if you measure your absolute threshold several times, you likely will record several different distances for detecting the stimulus. For example, the first time you try it, you might hear the ticking at 25 feet from the clock. But you probably won't hear it every time at 25 feet. Maybe you hear it only 38 percent of the time at this distance but hear it 50 percent of the time at 20 feet away and 65 percent of the time at 15 feet. Also, people have different thresholds because some people have better hearing than others and some people have better vision than others. Figure 3.1 shows one person's measured absolute threshold for detecting a clock's ticking sound. Measured absolute threshold has been arbitrarily decided by psychologists to be the point at which the individual detects the stimulus 50 percent of the time—in this case 20 feet away. Using the same clock, another person might have a measured absolute threshold of 26 feet, and yet another at 18 feet. The approximate absolute thresholds of five different senses are listed in table 3.1.

Under ideal circumstances, our senses have very low absolute thresholds, and so we can be remarkably good at detecting small amounts of stimulus energy. You can demonstrate this to yourself by using a sharp pencil point to carefully lift a single hair on your forearm. You will probably be surprised to realize that for most of us this tiny bit of pressure on the skin is easily detectable. You might also be surprised to learn in table 3.1 that the human eye can see a candle flame at 30 miles on a dark, clear night. But our environment seldom gives us ideal conditions to detect stimuli. If the night is cloudy and the air is polluted, for example, you would have to be much closer to see the flicker of a candle flame. And other lights on the horizon—car or house lights—might hinder your ability to detect the candle's flame. **Noise** *is the term given to irrelevant and competing stimuli.* For example, suppose someone speaks to you from the doorway of the room where you are sitting. You might fail to respond because your roommate is talking on the phone and a CD player is blaring out your favorite song. We usually think of noise as being auditory, but the psychological meaning of the term noise also involves other senses. The pollution, cloudiness, car lights, and house lights are forms of visual noise that hamper your ability to see a candle flame from a great distance.

We have discussed sensations that are above an individual's threshold of awareness, but what about the possibility that we experience the sensory world at levels below our conscious detection? To learn more about this controversial possibility, turn to Explorations in Psychology.

Difference Threshold   In addition to studying the amount of stimulation required for a stimulus to be detected, psychologists investigate the degree of difference that

*F*igure 3.1
Measuring Absolute Threshold

Absolute threshold is the minimum amount of energy we can detect. To measure a person's absolute threshold, psychologists have arbitrarily decided to use the criterion of detecting the stimulus 50 percent of the time. In the graph shown here, the person's measured absolute threshold for detecting the ticking clock is at a distance of 20 feet.

Research on Subliminal Perception

*T*ABLE 3.1
Approximate Absolute Thresholds for Five Senses

Vision	A candle flame at 30 miles on a dark, clear night
Hearing	A ticking watch at 20 feet under quiet conditions
Taste	A teaspoon of sugar in 2 gallons of water
Smell	One drop of perfume diffused throughout three rooms
Touch	The wing of a fly falling on your cheek from a distance of 1 centimeter

Adapted from Galanter, 1962

EXPLORATIONS IN PSYCHOLOGY
Analyzing Subliminal Perception

SUBLIMINAL PERCEPTION fascinates us. After all, aren't you curious about whether you can be influenced by messages you are not even aware of?

An experiment by Carol Fowler and her colleagues (1981) provides some evidence that we process information from our sensory world at a level beneath our awareness. In this experiment, words were shown on a screen so rapidly that the subjects could not tell what they were seeing. Subsequently, the subjects were shown two words (such as *hotel* and *book*) and asked which was most like the subliminally presented word *(lodge)*. Somewhat amazingly, the subjects answered most questions correctly. A possible explanation for these results is that sensory information too faint to be recognized consciously may be picked up by sensory receptors and transmitted to the brain at a level beneath conscious awareness.

More recently, researchers have verified these findings that people's performance is affected by stimuli that are too faint to be recognized at a conscious level (Greenwald & others, 1996).

An area involving subliminal perception that has generated considerable controversy is whether subliminal messages are embedded in rock music. Some rock groups allegedly have inserted satanic messages played backward in their records and tapes. According to this theory, when the record is played normally (forward), the messages cannot be consciously perceived, but they influence our behavior in a subliminal way. Researchers have been unable to find any evidence whatsoever that these and other backward satanic messages exist or, if they do, that they influence our behavior (McIver, 1988). Even if we were to take a very clearly recorded sentence and play it backward, no one could tell what it said. Investigators have found that people's perceptions of whether or not these messages exist is largely a function of what they expect to hear. In one experiment, when told beforehand that a message of satanic quality would influence them, participants were more likely to hear the message. With no such expectation, participants did not hear the message (Vokey & Read, 1985). And in a recent study, individuals failed to perceptually detect any information in subliminal self-help auditory tapes (Moore, 1995).

Mötley Crue's Shout at the Devil *album has been one of the targets of groups who believe that backward messages are embedded in songs. The protesters say that this album has the phrase* Backward mask where are you, oh. Lost in error, Satan. *However, researchers have been unable to find any evidence whatsoever that these and other satanic messages are encoded in the music or that, if they are, they can influence behavior.*

What can we make of the claims of subliminal perception enthusiasts and the research conducted by experimental psychologists? First, weak sensory stimuli can be registered by sensory receptors and is possibly encoded in the brain at a level beneath conscious awareness. Second, no evidence supports the claims of advertisers and rock music critics that such sensory registry and neural encoding have any substantial impact on our thoughts and behavior. Rather, evidence suggests that we are influenced extensively by those sounds and views we are consciously aware of and can attend to efficiently (Smith & Rogers, 1994).

must exist between two stimuli before this difference is detected. This **difference threshold**, *or just noticeable difference (jnd), is the smallest difference in stimulation required to discriminate one stimulus from another 50 percent of the time.* An artist might detect the difference between two similar shades of color. A tailor might determine a difference in the texture of two fabrics by feeling them. How different must the colors and textures be for these people to determine the difference? Just as the absolute threshold is determined by a 50 percent detection rate, the difference threshold is the point at which a person reports that two stimuli are different 50 percent of the time.

An important aspect of difference thresholds is that the threshold increases with the magnitude of the stimulus. You may notice when your roommate turns up the volume on the stereo by even a small amount when the music is playing softly. But if he or she turns the volume up an equal amount when the music is playing very loudly, you may not notice. More than 150 years ago, E. H. Weber, a German psychologist, noticed that, regardless of their magnitude, two stimuli must differ by a constant proportion to be detected. **Weber's law** *is the principle that two stimuli must differ by a constant minimum percentage (rather than a constant amount) to be perceived as different.* Weber's law generally holds true. For example, we add 1 candle to 60 candles and notice a difference in the brightness of the candles; we add 1 candle to 120 candles and do not notice a difference. We discover, though, that adding 2 candles to 120 candles does produce a difference in brightness. Adding 2 candles to 120 candles is the same proportionately as adding 1 candle to 60 candles. The exact proportion varies with the stimulus involved. For example, a change in a tone's pitch of 3 percent can be detected, but in taste a 20 percent change is required for a person to detect a difference, and in smell a 25 percent change is required.

Signal Detection Theory

Signal detection theory *is the theory that sensitivity to sensory stimuli depends on a variety of factors besides the physical intensity of the stimulus and the sensory abilities of the observer.* These factors include individual and contextual variations such as fatigue, expectancy, and the urgency of the moment. Let's consider the case of two air traffic controllers with exactly the same sensory ability to detect blips on a radar screen. One is monitoring the radar screen while working overtime late into the night and is feeling fatigued. The other is watching the screen in the morning after having a good night's sleep. The fatigued radar operator fails to see a blip indicating that a small private plane is flying too close to a large passenger jet, and the two collide. However, in a similar situation, the well-rested controller detects a private plane intruding in the air space of a large passenger jet and contacts the small private plane's pilot, who then changes course. Consider also the circumstance of two individuals at a dentist's office. One begins to "feel" pain the instant the drill touches the tooth's surface, the other doesn't "feel" pain until the dentist drills deep into a cavity.

At this point you should have a basic understanding of sensation and perception, the thresholds of sensory awareness, and signal detection theory. An overview of these ideas is presented in summary table 3.1. Now let's turn our attention to each of the senses, beginning with the sense we know the most about: vision.

Through the Eyes of Psychologists

Alice O'Toole, *University of Texas at Dallas*

"How the brain organizes and interprets sensory information to give it meaning is a little miracle that scientists are still trying to solve."

SUMMARY TABLE 3.1
Detecting and Perceiving the World

Concept	Processes/Related Ideas	Characteristics/Description
Defining Sensation and Perception	Their Nature	Sensation is the process of detecting and encoding stimulus energy in the world. Perception is the process of organizing and interpreting sensory information. Most contemporary psychologists refer to sensation and perception as a unified information-processing system.
Thresholds	Absolute Threshold	Psychophysics is the field that studies links between the physical properties of stimuli and a person's experience of them. A basic problem for any sensory system is to detect varying degrees of energy in the environment. One way to cope with this problem is to assume that each of us has an absolute threshold, or minimum amount of energy we can detect.
	Difference Threshold	The difference threshold, or just noticeable difference (jnd), is the smallest difference in stimulation required to discriminate one stimulus from another 50 percent of the time. Weber's law is the principle that two stimuli must differ by a constant minimum percentage (rather than a constant amount) to be perceived as different. Weber's law generally holds true.
Signal Detection Theory	Its Nature	This is the theory that sensitivity to sensory stimuli depends on a variety of factors besides the physical intensity of the stimulus and the sensory abilities of the observer. These factors include individual and contextual variations.

The First Steps of Visual Perception

The Visual System

We see a world of shapes and sizes—some stationary, others moving, some in black and white, others in color. But how do we see all of this? What is the machinery that enables us to experience this marvelous landscape?

The Visual Stimulus and the Eye

To understand our sense of vision, we need to know some basic facts about light, the energy that makes vision possible. **Light** *is a form of electromagnetic energy that can be described in terms of wavelengths.* Waves of light are much like the waves formed when a pebble is tossed into a lake. The **wavelength** *is the distance from the peak of one wave to the peak of the next.* Visible light's wavelengths range from about 400 to 700 nanometers (a nanometer is one-billionth of a meter and is abbreviated nm). The difference between visible light and other forms of electromagnetic energy is its wavelength. Outside the range of visible light are longer radio and infrared radiation waves, and shorter ultraviolet and X rays (see figure 3.2). These other wavelengths continually bombard us, but we do not see them. Why do we see only the narrow band of the electromagnetic spectrum between 400 and 700 nanometers? The most likely answer is that our visual system evolved in the sun's light. Thus, our visual system is able to perceive the spectrum of energy emitted by the sun. By the time sunlight reaches the earth's surface, it is strongest in the 400 to 700 nanometer range.

The purpose of the eye is not unlike that of a camera: to get the best possible "picture" of the world. A good picture is one that is in focus, is not too dark or too light, and has good contrast between the dark and light parts. Each of several

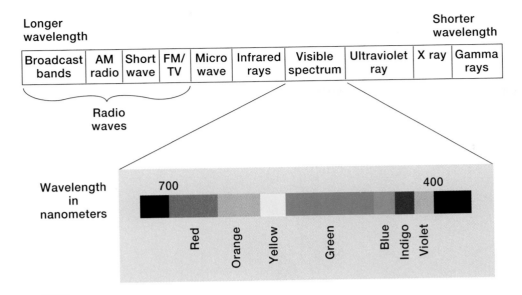

Figure 3.2
The Electromagnetic Spectrum and Visible Light
Visible light is only a narrow band in the electromagnetic spectrum. Visible light wavelengths range from about 400 to 700 nanometers. X rays are much shorter, and radio waves are much longer.

structures in the eye plays an important role in this process. By looking closely at your eyes in the mirror, you notice three parts—the sclera, iris, and pupil (figure 3.3). The **sclera** *is the white outer part of the eye that helps to maintain the shape of the eye and to protect it from injury.* The **iris** *is the colored part of the eye,* which can range from light blue to dark brown. The **pupil,** *which appears black, is the opening in the center of the iris.* The iris contains muscles that function to control the size of the pupil and, hence, the amount of light that gets into the eye. This allows the eye to function optimally under different conditions of illumination, which can range in the course of a normal day from the darkest of basements to the brightest of summer sunshine. To get a good "picture" of the world, the amount of light that enters the eye needs to be adjustable. In this sense, the pupil acts like the aperture of a camera, opening to let in more light when it is needed and closing to let in less light when there is too much.

You can demonstrate changes in the size of your own pupil by looking at your eyes in the mirror and turning the room lights up and down. (You obviously need to try this in a room with sufficient light to see your eyes even when the lights are turned all the way down.) As you turn down the room light, the pupil will begin to enlarge to let in more light; as you turn the room lights back up, the pupil opening will shrink to let in less light.

If the eye is to act like a camera, in addition to having the right amount of light, the image has to be in focus at the back of the eye. Two structures serve this purpose: the **cornea,** *which is a clear membrane just in front of the eye,* and the **lens of the eye,** *which is a transparent and somewhat flexible ball-like entity filled with a gelatinous material.* The function of both of these structures is to bend the light falling on the surface of the eye just enough to focus it at the back of the eye. The curved surface of the cornea does most of this bending, while the lens "fine-tunes" the focus as needed. When you are looking at far-away objects, the lens has a relatively flat shape. This is because the light reaching the eye from far-away objects is parallel and the bending power of the cornea is sufficient to keep things in focus. The light reaching the eye from objects that are close, however, is more scattered and so more bending of the light is required to achieve focus. This focusing is done by a process called

Seeing, Hearing, and Smelling the World

Figure 3.3
Main Structures of the Eye

Retina

Sclera

Retinal blood vessels

Optic nerve

Blind spot

Fovea

Lens

Iris

Pupil

Cornea

accommodation, *in which the lens changes its curvature.* Without this fine-tuning ability, it would be difficult to focus on objects that are close to us, like needlework or reading. As we get older, the lens of our eye begins to lose its flexibility and, hence, its ability to change from its normal flattened shape to the rounder shape needed to bring close objects into focus. This is why many people with normal vision throughout their young adult life require reading glasses when they get older.

The parts of the eye that we have discussed so far work together to get the best possible picture of the world. All of this effort, however, would be for naught without a method for keeping or "recording" the images we take of the world. In a camera, film serves just such a purpose. Film is made of a material that responds to light. Likewise, the **retina** *is the light-sensitive surface in the back of the eye that houses light receptors called rods and cones.* Making an analogy between the film of a camera and the retina, however, vastly underestimates the complexity and elegance of the retina's design. Even after decades of intense study, the full marvel of this structure is far from understood.

Because the retina is so important to vision, we need to study its makeup more closely. **Transduction** *involves the conversion of one form of energy into another.* In sensation, this consists of converting stimulus energy into neural impulses. There are two kinds of receptors in the retina—rods and cones—and they turn the electromagnetic energy of light into a form of energy that can be processed by the nervous system. **Rods** *are receptors in the retina that are sensitive to light but are not very useful for color vision.* Thus, they function well under low illumination; as you might expect, they are hard at work at night. **Cones** *are the receptors that we use for color perception.* Like the rods, cones are light sensitive. However, they require a larger amount of light than the rods do to respond, and so they operate best in daylight or under high illumination.

The rods and cones in the retina are receptors that transduce light into neural impulses by means of a photochemical reaction (Blake, 2000). The breakdown of the

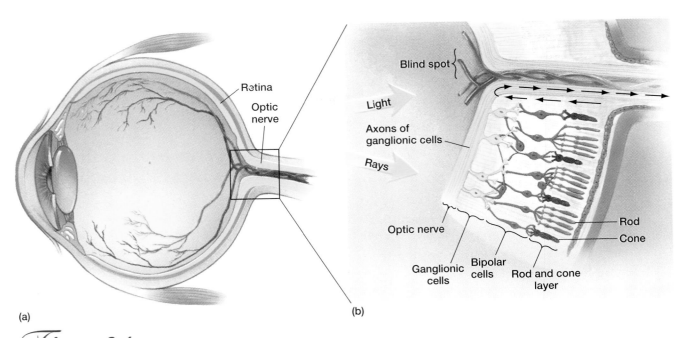

(a)   (b)

*F*igure 3.4
Direction of Light in the Retina

(a) Light passes through the cornea, pupil, and lens. Then it falls on the retina, a light-sensitive surface. *(b)* In the retina, light first triggers a photochemical reaction in the rods and cones. Next, the bipolar cells are activated, which in turn activate the ganglion cells. Then light information is transmitted into the optic nerve, which carries information to the brain. The arrows indicate the sequence in which light information moves in the retina.

chemicals produces a neural impulse that is first transmitted to the bipolar cells and then moves down to the ganglion cells (see figure 3.4). The nerve impulse then passes along the axons of the ganglion cells, which make up the optic nerve.

Rods and cones are involved in different aspects of vision and differ both in how they respond to light and in their distribution on the surface of the retina. The most important part of the retina is the **fovea,** *which is a minute area in the center of the retina where vision is at its best.* The fovea is able to resolve much finer detail than any other part of the retina and contains only cones. The fovea is vitally important to many visual tasks (try reading out of the corner of your eye!). By contrast, rods are found almost everywhere on the retina except in the fovea. As their name suggests, rods are long and cylindrical. Since they require little light to respond, they work best under conditions of low illumination. Because of this light sensitivity and the rods' location on the retina, we are able to detect fainter spots of light on the peripheral retina than at the fovea. It has been known for centuries that if you want to see a very faint star, you should gaze slightly to the right or left of the star.

Finally, there is one place on the retina that contains neither rods nor cones. Not surprisingly, this area is called the **blind spot;** *it is the place on the retina where the optic nerve leaves the eye on its way to the brain.* We cannot see anything that reaches only this part of the retina. To experience your blind spot, see figure 3.5.

*F*igure 3.5
The Eye's Blind Spot

There is a normal blind spot in your eye, a small area where the optic nerve leads to the brain. To find your blind spot, hold this book at arm's length, cover your left eye, and stare at the red pepper on the left with your right eye. Move the book slowly toward you until the yellow pepper disappears. To find the blind spot in your left eye, cover your right eye, concentrate on the yellow pepper, and adjust the book until the red pepper disappears.

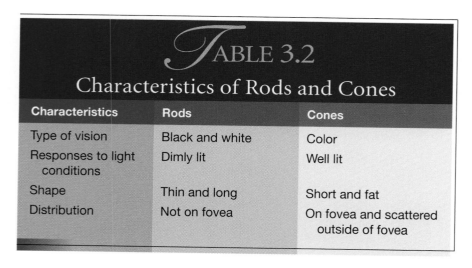

TABLE 3.2
Characteristics of Rods and Cones

Characteristics	Rods	Cones
Type of vision	Black and white	Color
Responses to light conditions	Dimly lit	Well lit
Shape	Thin and long	Short and fat
Distribution	Not on fovea	On fovea and scattered outside of fovea

A summary of some of the main characteristics of rods and cones is presented in table 3.2. So far we have studied the importance of light and structures of the eyes. The journey of vision now leads us to the brain and how it processes visual information.

From Eye to Brain and Neural-Visual Processing

The optic nerve leads out of the eye toward the brain carrying information about light. Stimuli in the left visual field are registered in the right half of the retina in both eyes, and stimuli in the right visual field were registered in the left half of the retina in both eyes. At the point called the *optic chiasm* the optic nerve fibers divide, and approximately half of the nerve fibers cross over the midline of the brain. The visual information originating in the right halves of the two retinae is then transmitted to the left side of the occipital lobe in the back of the brain; the visual information originating in the left halves of the retinae is transmitted to the right side of the occipital lobe ◀▥ P. 62. What all of these crossings mean is that what we see in the left side of our visual field ends up in the right side of our brain, and what we see in the right visual field ends up in the left side of our brain (see figure 3.6).

The visual cortex in the occipital lobe combines information from both eyes and is responsible for higher levels of visual processing (Farah, 1999). **Feature detectors** *are neurons in the brain's visual system that respond to particular lines or other features of a stimulus* ◀▥ P. 51. David Hubel and Torsten Wiesel (1965) won a Nobel Prize for their research on feature detectors. By recording the activity of a *single* neuron in a cat while it looked at patterns that varied in size, shape, color, and movement, the researchers found that the visual cortex has neurons that are individually sensitive to different types of lines and angles. For example, one neuron might show a sudden burst of activity when stimulated by lines of a particular angle; another neuron might fire only when moving stimuli appear; yet another neuron might be stimulated when the object in the visual field has a combination of certain angles, sizes, and shapes. Figure 3.7 illustrates Hubel and Wiesel's research on feature detectors in monkeys.

Hubel and Wiesel's discovery led to a revolutionary idea. While we are perceiving a unified scene, the brain is dissecting the view into many parts, each of which triggers a different set of neurons. One set of neurons responds to color and form, another only to motion. The challenge today is figuring out how the brain, once it has broken the sensory landscape into pieces, stitches them back together again (Brownlee, 1997; Mountcastle, 1998).

Sensory Adaptation

Turning out the lights in your bedroom at night, you stumble across the room to your bed, completely blind to the objects around you. Gradually, the objects in your room reappear and become more and more clear. The ability of the visual system to adjust to the darkened room is an example of the principle of **sensory adaptation**—*a change in the responsiveness of the sensory system based on the average level of surrounding stimulation.* You have experienced sensory adaptation countless times in your life—adapting to the temperature of a shower, to the water in an initially "freezing" swimming pool, or to the smell of the Thanksgiving dinner that is wonderful to the arriving guests but almost undetectable to the cook who slaved over it all day. These are examples of sensory adaptation. While all senses adapt to prolonged stimulation, we will take up this topic using vision as an example since you have just learned about the mechanisms involved in adapting to light.

Let's return to our example of adapting to the dark. When you turn out the lights, everything is black. Conversely, when you step out into the bright sunshine after spending some time in a dark basement, your eyes are flooded with light and everything appears light. When we talked about the purpose of the eye, we said that the eye needs to get a good picture of the world. Good pictures have sharp contrasts between dark and light parts. We have already seen that the pupil serves an important function in adjusting the amount of light that gets into the eye and therefore helping to preserve the contrast between dark and light in our picture. Additionally, structures throughout the visual system also adapt. You may have noticed that the change in the size of the pupil as you dim or brighten the lights happens very quickly. You also may have noticed that when you turn out the lights in your bedroom, the contrast between dark and light continues to improve for nearly 20 minutes. This is because both the rods and the cones in the visual system adapt or adjust their response rates on the basis of the average light level of the surrounding room. This adaptation takes longer than the pupil adjustment. All of these mechanisms allow the visual system to preserve the contrast in the images it takes of the world over an extremely large range of background illumination conditions. The price we pay for our ability to adapt to the mean light level is *time*. Driving out of a dark tunnel under a mountain into the glistening and blinding reflection of the sun off the snow reminds us that our ability to adapt does have a price.

Color Vision

We spend a lot of time thinking about color—the color of the car we want to buy, the color we are going to paint the walls of our room, the color of the clothes we wear. We can change our hair color or even the color of our eyes to make us look more attractive.

What Is Color?   The human eye registers light wavelengths between 400 and 700 nm, which we see as different colors of light. This is what was shown in figure 3.2. However, lightwaves themselves have no color. The sensations of color reside in the visual system of the observer. So, if we talk about red light, we refer to the wavelengths of light that evoke the sensation of red. Objects appear a certain color to us because they reflect specific wavelengths of light to our eyes. These wavelengths are split apart into a spectrum of colors when the light passes through a prism, as in the formation of a rainbow. We can remember the colors of the light spectrum by thinking of an imaginary man named ROY G. BIV, for the colors red, orange, yellow, green, blue, indigo, and violet.

If you go into a paint store and ask for some red paint, the salesperson will probably ask you what kind of paint you want—such as dark or light, pinkish or more crimson, pastel or deep, and so on. These variations in the shade of red are due to differences in their hue, saturation, and brightness.

A color's **hue** *is based on its wavelength.* As shown in figure 3.2, the longest wavelengths seen by the human eye (about 700 nm) appear as red, the shortest (about 400 nm) appear as violet. A color's **saturation** *is based on its purity.* The purity of a color is determined by the amount of white light added

Left visual field

Right visual field

Processing at retina

Optic nerve

Optic chiasm

Visual cortex in occipital lobe

ℱigure 3.6
Visual Pathways to and Through the Brain

Light from each side of the visual field falls on the opposite side of each eye's retina. Visual information then travels along the optic nerve to the optic chiasm, where most of the visual information crosses over to the other side of the brain. From there visual information goes to the occipital lobe at the rear of the brain. What all of the crossings mean is that what we see in the left side of our visual field (in this figure, the woman) ends up in the right side of our brain, and what we see in the right visual field (the man) ends up in the left side of our brain.

to a single wavelength of color. The color tree shown in figure 3.8 can help us understand saturation. Colors that are very pure have no white light. They are located outside of the color tree. As we move toward the color tree's interior, notice how the saturation of color changes. The closer we get to the tree's center, the more white light has been added to the single wavelength of a particular color. That is, the deep colors at the edge fade into the more pastel colors toward the center. When saturation is added to hue, we see a much larger range of colors—pink and crimson as well as basic red, for example. However, another dimension also is involved in color—brightness. A color's **brightness** *is based on its intensity*. White has the most brightness, black the least.

Theories of Color Vision

The study of human color vision using psychological methods has a long and distinguished history. A full century before the methods existed to study the anatomical and neurophysiological basis of color perception, psychological studies had discovered many of these basic principles of our color vision system. These studies resulted in two main theories, each of which turned out to be correct.

The first color vision theory we discuss is based on what you just learned about the three kinds of cone receptors in the retina. The **trichromatic theory** *states that color perception is based on the existence of three types of receptors that are maximally sensitive to different, but overlapping, ranges of wavelengths*. The trichromatic theory of color vision was proposed by Thomas Young in 1802 and extended by Hermann von Helmholtz in 1852. The theory is based on the results of experiments on human color-matching abilities. These experiments show that a person with normal vision can match any color in the spectrum by combining three other wavelengths. In this type of experiment, individuals are given a light of a single wavelength and are asked to combine three other single-wavelength lights to match the first light. They can do this by changing the relative intensities of the three lights until the color of the combination light is indistinguishable from the color of the first light. Young and Helmholtz reasoned that if the combination of any three wavelengths in different intensities is indistinguishable from any single pure wavelength, the visual system must be basing its perception of color on the relative responses of three receptor systems.

Further convincing support for the trichromatic theory is found in the study of defective color vision, or what is commonly referred to as color-blindness. The term *color blind* is

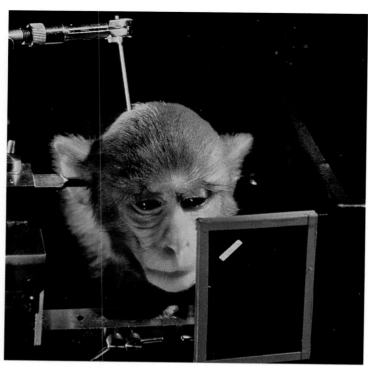

ℱigure 3.7
Hubel and Wiesel's Research on Visual Information Processing

This photograph shows an electrode inserted into a monkey's neuron at a location in the visual system. Various light stimuli are projected onto a screen in front of the animal's eyes.

ℱigure 3.8
A Color Tree Showing Color's Three Dimensions: Hue, Saturation, and Brightness

Hue is represented around the color tree, saturation horizontally, and brightness vertically.

somewhat misleading because it suggests that a color-blind person cannot see color at all. Complete color blindness is rare; most people who are color blind, the vast majority of whom are men, can see some colors but not others. The nature of color blindness depends on which of the three kinds of cones is inoperative. The three different cone systems are green, red, and blue. For example, in the most common form of color blindness, the green cone system malfunctions in some way. Green is indistinguishable from certain combinations of blue and red. Color-matching experiments performed by people with this form of color blindness show that they need only two other colors to match a pure color and hence have dichromatic color perception. **Dichromats** *are people with only two kinds of cones.* **Trichromats** *are people with normal color vision, having three kinds of cone receptors.*

The German physiologist Ewald Hering was not completely satisfied with the trichromatic theory of color vision. Hering observed that some colors cannot exist together whereas others can. For example, it is easy to imagine a greenish-blue or a reddish-yellow, but nearly impossible to imagine a reddish-green or a bluish-yellow. Hering also observed that trichromatic theory could not adequately explain **afterimages,** *sensations that remain after a stimulus is removed.* See figure 3.9 to experience an afterimage. Color afterimages are common and they involve complementary colors. Such information led Hering to propose that the visual system treats colors as complementary pairs: red-green and blue-yellow. One example of afterimages that many people are familiar with occurs after prolonged exposure to a computer terminal screen with green lettering, such as those used in many businesses. After working with a computer like this all day, it is not unusual for white objects and walls to appear reddish. Conversely, if you look at red long enough, eventually a green afterimage will appear; if you look at yellow long enough, eventually a blue afterimage will appear.

Hering's view is called **opponent-process theory,** *which states that cells in the visual system respond to red-green and blue-yellow colors; a given cell might be excited by red and inhibited by green, while another cell might be excited by yellow and inhibited by blue.* Researchers have found that opponent-process theory does explain afterimages (Hurvich & Jameson, 1969; Jameson & Hurvich, 1989). If you stare at red, for instance, your red-green system seems to "tire," and when you look away, it rebounds and gives you a green afterimage. Also, if you mix equal amounts of opponent colors, such as blue and yellow, you see gray; figure 3.10 illustrates this principle.

We have seen that the trichromatic theory of color perception is correct in that we do in fact have three kinds of cone receptors like those predicted by Young and Helmholtz. Then how can the opponent-process theory also be correct? The answer is

*F*igure 3.9
Negative Afterimage—Complementary Colors

If you gaze steadily at the dot in the colored panel on the left for a few moments, then shift your gaze to the gray box on the right, you will see the original hues change into their complementary colors. The blue appears as yellow, the red as green, the green as red, and the yellow as blue. This pairing of colors has to do with the fact that color receptors in the eye are apparently sensitive as pairs; when one color is turned off (when you stop staring at the panel), the other color in the receptor is briefly "turned on." The afterimage effect is especially noticeable when you spend time painting walls or objects in bright colors.

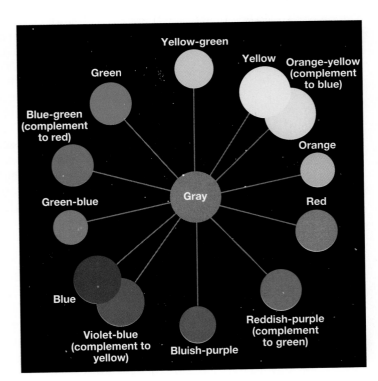

*F*igure 3.10
Color Wheel

Colors opposite each other produce the neutral gray in the center when they are mixed. For instance, blue-green is the complement of red.

Summary Table 3.2
The Visual System

Concept	Processes/Related Ideas	Characteristics/Description
The Visual Stimulus and the Eye	Their Nature	Light is a form of electromagnetic energy that can be described in terms of wavelengths. The wavelength is the distance from the peak of one wave of light to the next. The receptors in the human eye are sensitive to wavelengths from 400 to 700 nm. Key parts of the eye are sclera, iris, pupil, and cornea. The lens and the cornea bend the light falling on the surface of the eye just enough to focus it on the back of the eye. The retina is the light-sensitive surface in the back of the eye, consisting of light receptors called rods (which function well under low illumination), cones (which function in color vision), and different neurons.
From Eye to Brain and Neural-Visual Processing	The Nature of Transmission	The optic nerve transmits neural impulses to the brain. Because of crossovers of nerve fibers, what we see in the left visual field is registered in the right side of the brain and vice versa. Visual information reaches the occipital lobe of the brain, where it is further integrated. Hubel and Wiesel discovered that neurons in the visual cortex can detect features of our visual world such as line, angle, and size.
Sensory Adaptation	Its Nature	Sensory adaptation involves weakened sensory response after prolonged stimulation.
Color Vision	What Is Color?	Objects appear in color because they reflect certain wavelengths of light between 400 and 700 nm. Important properties of color are hue (based on wavelength content), saturation (based on purity), and brightness (based on intensity).
	Theories of Color Vision	Scientists have found support for two theories. The trichromatic theory states that color perception is based on the existence of three types of receptors, which are maximally sensitive to different, but overlapping, ranges of wavelengths. This theory is also called the Young-Helmholtz theory and emphasizes the colors of red, green, and blue. The trichromatic theory explains color blindness but not afterimages. The opponent-process theory does explain afterimages. The opponent-process theory, developed by Hering, states that cells in the visual system respond to red-green and blue-yellow colors. Researchers have found that the red, blue, and green cones are connected to the retinal ganglion cells in such a way that the three-color code is translated into the opponent-process code. Thus, both theories are right—the eye and the brain use both methods to code colors.

Color Vision
Color Blindness

that the red, blue, and green cones in the retina are connected to retinal ganglion cells in such a way that the three-color code is immediately translated into the opponent-process code. For example, a green cone might inhibit and a red cone might excite a particular ganglion cell. Thus, *both* the trichromatic and opponent-process theory are correct—the eye and the brain use both methods to code colors.

Our discussion of theories of color vision illustrates an important feature of psychology that we described in chapter 1. Science often progresses when conflicting ideas are posed and investigated. In many instances, as with color vision, a compromise solution may work best.

Our tour of the visual system has been extensive—you have read about the light spectrum, the structures of the eye, neural-visual processing, and the marvels of color vision. To help you remember the main themes of the visual system, see summary table 3.2. Next you will study the second most researched sensory system—hearing.

The Auditory System

Just as light provides us with information about the environment, so does sound. Think about what life would be like without music, the rushing sound of ocean waves, or the gentle voice of someone you love. Sounds in the world tell us about the approach of a person behind us, an approaching car, the force of the wind outside, the mischief of a 2-year-old, and, perhaps most importantly, the kinds of information that we transmit through language and song.

The Nature of Sound and How We Experience It

At a rock concert you may have felt the throbbing pulse of loud sounds or sensed that the air around you was vibrating. Bass instruments are especially effective at creating mechanical pulsations, even causing the floor or a seat to vibrate on occasion. When a bass is played loudly we can sense air molecules being pushed forward in waves from the speaker. **Sounds,** *or sound waves, are vibrations in the air that are processed by our auditory (or hearing) system.*

**Auditory Perception
Sound Waves**

Remember that we described light waves as being much like the waves fanned when a pebble is tossed into a lake, with concentric circles moving outward from where the pebble entered the water. Sound waves are similar. They vary in wavelength, which determines the **frequency** *of the sound wave or the number of cycles (or full wavelengths) that pass through a point in a given time* (see figure 3.11). **Pitch** *is the perceptual interpretation of the frequency of sound.* High-frequency sounds are perceived as having a high pitch, low-frequency sounds are perceived as having a low pitch. A soprano voice sounds high-pitched, a bass voice sounds low-pitched. As with the wavelength of light, human sensitivity is limited to a range of sound frequencies. It is common knowledge that dogs, for example, can hear higher frequencies than can humans.

Sound waves vary not only in frequency but also in amplitude. The sound wave's **amplitude** *is measured in decibels (dB), the amount of pressure produced by a sound wave relative to a standard;* the typical standard is the weakest sound the human ear can detect. Thus, zero decibels would be the softest noise detectable by humans.

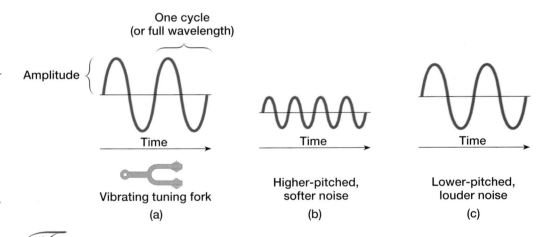

Figure 3.11
Frequency and Amplitude of Sound Waves

(a) A tuning fork is an instrument with two prongs that produces a tone when struck. You may have seen one in a music classroom or science laboratory. The vibrations of the tuning fork cause air molecules to vibrate like a musical instrument, producing a sound-wave pattern like the one shown. *(b)* Wavelength determines the frequency of the sound wave, which is the number of cycles, or full wavelengths, that can pass through a point in a given time. In the tuning fork example, two cycles (full wavelengths) have occurred in the time frame shown. In the sound waves shown here, four cycles have occurred in this time frame, so this sound wave has a higher frequency than the sound wave with the tuning fork; hence, it has a higher pitch. *(c)* The amplitude of the sound wave is the change in pressure created by the sound wave and is reflected in the sound wave's height. This sound wave has a smaller amplitude than the sound wave shown with the tuning fork; thus, it does not sound as loud.

Noise rated at 80 decibels or higher, if heard for prolonged periods of time, can cause permanent hearing loss. A quiet library is about 40 decibels, a car horn about 90 decibels, a rock band at close range 120 decibels, and a rocket launching 180 decibels. Noise levels have risen in recent years (Staples, 1996). **Loudness** *is the perception of a sound wave's amplitude.* In general, the higher the amplitude of the sound wave, the louder the sound is perceived to be. In the world of amplitude, this means that air is moving rapidly for loud sounds and slowly for soft sounds.

So far we have been describing a single sound wave with just one frequency. This is similar to the single wavelength or pure colored light we just discussed in the context of color matching. Most sounds, however, including those of speech and music, are complex sounds. **Complex sounds** *are those in which numerous frequencies of sound blend together.* **Timbre** *is the tone color or perceptual quality of a sound.* Timbre differences are what make the difference between a trumpet and a trombone playing the same note, and are also responsible for the quality differences we hear between human voices.

Structures and Functions of the Ear

What happens to sound waves once they reach your ear? How do various structures of the ear transform sound waves of expanded and compressed air so they can be understood by the brain as sound? The function of the ear is analogous to the function of the eye. The ear serves the purpose of transmitting a high-fidelity version of sounds in the world to the brain for analysis and interpretation. Just as an image needs to be in focus and sufficiently bright for the brain to interpret it, a sound needs to be transmitted in a way that preserves information about its location (think how confusing life would be if you could hear sounds without being able to determine where they are coming from!); its frequency, which helps us distinguish the voice of a child from that of an adult; and its timbre, which allows us to identify the voice of a friend on the telephone.

The ear is divided into the *outer ear, middle ear,* and *inner ear* (the major structures of the ear are shown in figure 3.12). The **outer ear** *consists of the pinna and the external auditory canal.* The pinna is the outer visible part of the ear (elephants have very large ones). Its shape helps us to localize sounds by making the sound different in front of us than behind us. The pinnae of many animals such as dogs are movable and serve a more important role in sound localization than do the pinnae of humans. Dogs will prick up their ears toward the direction of a faint and interesting sound.

After passing the pinna, sound waves are then funneled through the external auditory canal to the middle ear. The **middle ear** *has four main parts: eardrum, hammer, anvil, and stirrup.* The eardrum is the first structure that sound touches in the middle ear. The eardrum is a membrane that vibrates in response to a sound. The vibrations are then transmitted to the three smallest bones in the human body—the hammer, anvil, and stirrup. The middle ear bones translate the sound waves in air into sound waves in water (lymph) so they can be processed further in the inner ear. Most of us know that sound travels far more easily in air than in water. When we are swimming underwater, loud shouts from the side of the pool are barely detectable to us. Sound waves entering the ear travel in air up until they reach the inner ear, at which point they will begin to be transmitted through body fluids. At this border between air and fluid, sounds meet the same kind of resistance that shouts directed at an underwater swimmer meet when they hit the surface of the water. The hammer, anvil, and stirrup form a connected chain of bones that act like a lever to amplify the sound waves before they reach the liquid-filled inner ear.

The main parts of the **inner ear** *are the oval window, cochlea, and the organ of Corti.* The stirrup is connected to the oval window, which is a membrane like the eardrum and transmits the waves to the cochlea. The **cochlea** *is a long tubular fluid-filled structure that is coiled up like a snail.* The **basilar membrane** *is housed inside the cochlea and runs its entire length.* The **organ of Corti,** *also running the length of the*

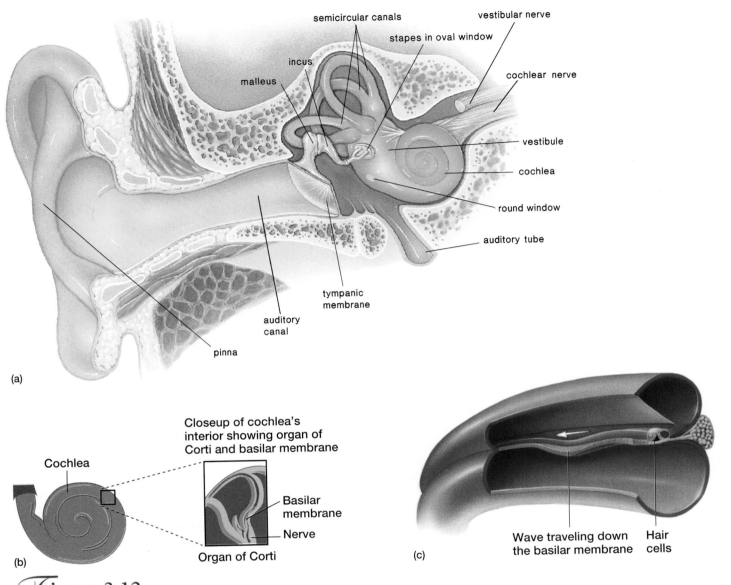

Figure 3.12
Major Structures of the Human Ear and the Transmission of Sound Waves

(a) The main structures of the external, middle, and inner ear. (b) This closeup of the cochlea's interior shows the organ of Corti and the basilar membrane. (c) This enlarged drawing was made by unwinding the snail-like structure of the cochlea and cutting it open. The sound wave is shown traveling down the membrane and stimulating hair cells.

cochlea, sits on the basilar membrane and contains the ear's sensory receptors, which change the energy of the sound waves into nerve impulses that can be processed by the brain. Hairlike sensory receptors in the organ of Corti are stimulated by vibrations of the basilar membrane. Sound waves traveling in the fluid of the inner ear cause these hairlike receptors to move. The movement generates nerve impulses, which vary with the frequency and extent of the membrane's vibrations. These nerve impulses are interpreted as sound by the brain.

Theories of Hearing

One of the auditory system's mysteries is how the inner ear registers the frequency of sound (Warren, 1999). Two theories have been proposed to explain this mystery: place theory and frequency theory. **Place theory** *is a theory of hearing which states* *that each frequency produces vibrations at a particular spot on the basilar membrane.* Georg von Békésy won a Nobel Prize in 1961 for his research on the basilar membrane. Von Békésy (1960) studied the effects of vibration applied at the oval window on the basilar membrane of human cadavers. Through a microscope, he saw that this stimulation produced a traveling wave on the basilar membrane. A traveling wave is like the ripples that appear in a pond when you throw in a stone. However, since the cochlea is a long tube, the ripples can travel in only one direction, from the end of the cochlea where the oval window is placed to the far tip of the cochlea. High-frequency vibrations create traveling waves that maximally displace (or move) the area of the basilar membrane next to the oval window; low-frequency vibrations maximally displace areas of the membrane closer to the tip of the cochlea.

Place theory adequately explains high-frequency sounds but fares poorly with low-frequency sounds. A high-frequency sound stimulates a very precise area on the basilar membrane. By contrast, a low-frequency sound causes a large part of the basilar membrane to be displaced, so it is hard to localize the "maximal displacement" of the basilar membrane. Because humans can hear low-frequency sounds better than can be predicted by looking at the precision of the basilar membrane's response to these sounds, some other factors must be involved. **Frequency theory** *states that the perception of a sound's frequency is due to how often the auditory nerve fires.* Higher-frequency sounds cause the auditory nerve to fire more often than do lower-frequency sounds. One problem with frequency theory is that a single neuron has a maximum firing rate of about 1,000 times per second. Because of this limitation, frequency theory cannot be applied to tones with frequencies that would require a neuron to fire more than 1,000 times per second.

To deal with this limitation, a modification of place theory called the **volley principle** *states that neural cells can fire neural impulses in rapid succession, producing a volley of impulses.* This alternate rapid neural firing attains a combined frequency above 1,000 times a second. Thus, frequency theory better explains the perception of low-frequency sounds and place theory provides a better explanation of high-frequency sounds. Both theories may be correct with sounds of low and high frequencies signaled with different neural coding schemes.

Neural-Auditory Processing

As we saw in the visual system, once energy from the environment is picked up by our receptors, it must be transmitted to the brain for processing and interpretation. An image on the retina does not a Picasso make—likewise, a pattern of receptor responses in the cochlea does not a symphony make! In the retina, we saw that the responses of the rod and cone receptors feed into ganglion cells in the retina and leave the eye via the optic nerve. In the auditory system, the **auditory nerve** *carries neural impulses to the brain's auditory areas* ◀▥ P. 62. Auditory information moves up the auditory pathway in a more complex manner than does visual information in the visual pathway. Many synapses occur in the ascending auditory pathway, with some fibers crossing over the midline and others proceeding directly to the hemisphere on the same side as the ear of reception. The auditory nerve extends from the cochlea to the brain stem, with some fibers crossing over the midline. The cortical destination of most of these fibers is the temporal lobes of the brain (beneath the temples of the head) (Wickesberg, 2000).

Now that we have described the visual and auditory systems in some detail, we turn to a number of other sensory systems—the skin senses, the chemical senses (smell and taste), and the kinesthetic and vestibular senses. As you can tell, we have more than the traditional five senses of sight, hearing, taste, touch, and smell.

Other Senses

In addition to our visual and auditory senses, we also have other senses that detect information in the environment. They include the skin senses, the chemical senses, and the kinesthetic and vestibular senses.

The Skin Senses

We know when a friend has a fever by putting our hand to her head; we know how to find our way to the light switch in a darkened room by groping along the wall; and we know whether or not a pair of shoes is too tight by the way the shoes touch different parts of our feet when we walk. Many of us think of our skin as a canvas rather than a sense. We color it with cosmetics, dyes, and tattoos. But the skin is our largest sensory system, draped over the body with receptors for touch, temperature, and pain. These three kinds of receptors form the cutaneous senses. A large variety of important information comes to us through our ability to detect touch.

Touch   Touch is one of the senses that we most often take for granted. As we saw in the earlier discussion on detection, our ability to respond to touch is astounding. Raising a single hair on your forearm with the sharp point of a pencil should be enough to convince you of this. What do we detect when we feel "touch"? What kind of energy does our sense of touch pick up from our external environment? In vision, we detect electromagnetic energy or light. In audition, we detect the vibrations of air or soundwaves pressing against our eardrum. In touch, we detect mechanical energy, or pressure against the skin. The lifting of a single hair causes pressure on the skin around the shaft of hair. This tiny bit of mechanical pressure at the base of the hair is sufficient for us to detect the "touch" of the pencil point! More commonly, we detect the mechanical energy of the pressure of a car seat against our buttocks, or the pressure of a pencil in our hands. Is this kind of energy so different than the kind of energy we detect in vision or audition? Sometimes the only difference is one of intensity—the sound of a rock band playing softly is auditory stimulus, but at the high volumes that make a concert hall reverberate, such an auditory stimulus is *felt* as mechanical energy pressing against your skin.

Just as our visual system is more sensitive to images on the fovea than to images in the peripheral retina, our sensitivity to touch is not equally good across all areas of the skin. As you might expect, human toolmakers need to have excellent touch discrimination in their hands, but much less touch discrimination in other parts of the body such as the torso or legs. What this amounts to is having more space in the brain to analyze touch signals coming from the hands than from the legs.

Temperature   Beyond the need to sense physical pressure on the skin, we need to detect temperature, even in the absence of direct contact with the skin. **Thermoreceptors,** *which are located under the skin, respond to increases and decreases in temperature.* Thermoreceptors not only serve a general function of sensing temperature changes at or near our skin, but also provide input to keep our body's temperature regulation at 98.6 degrees Fahrenheit. Thermoreceptors come in two types: warm and cold (warm thermoreceptors respond to the warming of the skin, and cold thermoreceptors respond to the cooling of the skin).

Pain   When contact with the skin takes the form of a sharp pinch, our sensation of mechanical pressure changes from touch to pain. When a pot handle is so

Pain

hot that it burns your hand, your sensation of temperature becomes one of pain. Many kinds of stimuli can cause pain. Intense stimulation of any one of the senses can produce pain—too much light, very loud sounds, very spicy food, for example. Our ability to sense pain is vital for our survival as a species. **Pain** *is the sensation that warns us that damage to our bodies is occurring.* It functions as a quick-acting system that tells the motor systems of the brain that they must act to minimize or eliminate this damage. A hand touching a hot stove must be pulled away; ears should be covered up when one walks by a loud pavement drill; chili should be buffered with some crackers.

Pain receptors are dispersed widely throughout the body (Beatty, 1995). Although all pain receptors are anatomically similar, they differ in the type of physical stimuli to which they most readily respond. Mechanical pain receptors respond mainly to pressure, such as when a sharp object is encountered. Heat pain receptors respond primarily to strong heat that is capable of burning the tissue in which they are embedded. Other pain receptors have a mixed function, responding to both types of painful stimuli. Many pain receptors are chemically sensitive, responding to a range of pain-producing substances.

While we have seen that all sensations are affected by factors such as motivation, expectation, and other related decision factors, the sensation of pain is especially susceptible to these factors (Philips & Rachman, 1996). Cultural and ethnic contexts, also, can greatly determine the degree to which an individual experiences pain. For example, one pain researcher described a ritual performed in India in which a chosen person travels from town to town delivering blessings to the children and the crops while suspended from metal hooks embedded in his back (Melzak, 1973). The chosen person apparently reports no sensation of pain and appears to be in ecstasy.

One theory of pain perception that offers insight into how cognitive and emotional factors might exert such dramatic influences on the experience of pain was developed by Ronald Melzak and Patricia Wall (1965, 1983). They proposed **gate-control theory,** *which states that the spinal column contains a neural gate that can be opened (allowing the perception of pain) or closed (blocking the perception of pain).* In this account, the brain can send signals downward to the spinal cord to close the gate, and hence suppress the sensation of pain (see figure 3.13). The gate-control theory has also been proposed as an explanation for the effects of **acupuncture,** *a technique in which thin needles are inserted at specific points in the body to produce various effects, such as local anesthesia.* The gate-control theory of pain assumes that the presence of acupuncture needles somehow manages to shut the pain gate, inhibiting the experience of pain. Gate-control theory may also explain the fact that gentle pressure on the skin, such as lightly rubbing the skin, seems to inhibit the pain signal.

The Chemical Senses

We've seen that the information impinging on our senses comes in many diverse forms: electromagnetic energy in vision, soundwaves in audition, and mechanical pressure and temperature in the cutaneous senses. The last two senses we will study are responsible for processing chemicals in our environment. With the sense of smell we detect airborne chemicals, and with taste we detect chemicals that have been dissolved in saliva. Taste and smell are frequently stimulated simultaneously. We sometimes only realize the strong links between the two senses when a nasty cold and nasal congestion seem to take the pleasure out of eating. Our favorite foods become "tasteless" without the smells that characterize them. Despite this link, we will see that our senses of taste and smell have lives and functions all their own.

Taste and Smell

Taste   What would life be with no sense of taste? For anyone who has tried to diet, "not worth living" is an all-too-often way of responding. The thought of

Neurotransmitters

Information from brain
(hypnosis, excitement)

Gate cell

Pain cell

Pain information
from periphery
of body, such
as thumb

Neurons
in spinal
cord

Inhibition, blocking
of neural impulse

Information from other
peripheral areas of body
(as when acupuncture is performed)

Cross-section of spinal cord

Figure 3.13
Gate-Control Theory of Pain

In the case of hitting your thumb with a hammer, pain signals initially go through the spinal cord and then to the brain. Gate-control theory states that pain information can be blocked in the spinal cord. Pain pathways from the periphery of the body (thumb, foot, etc.) make a synaptic connection in the spinal cord and then ascend to the brain. Interneurons can inhibit transmission through these pathways, as shown in the drawing on the right. When a strong peripheral stimulus (as applied during acupuncture) comes into the spinal cord, this can turn on the interneuron and close the gate in the pain pathway. Also, when a signal comes down from the brain (during hypnosis or the excitement of athletic competition), it, too, can turn on the interneuron and close the gate. The gate is not a physical structure that actually opens and shuts; rather, the gate is the inhibition of neural impulses. Neurotransmitters (the tiny circles in the synapse between the pain cell and the gate cell) are involved in gate control, but much is yet to be known about their identity.

giving up a favorite taste, such as chocolate or butter, can be a very depressing thought. We use our sense of taste to select food and to regulate food intake. While it is not so easy to see or smell mold on a blueberry, a small taste is enough to prompt you to sense that the fruit is no longer fit for consumption. Beyond that, the pleasure associated with the taste of food depends on many aspects of our body's need for a particular food (Bartoshuk & Beauchamp, 1994). The taste of devil's food cake can be very pleasurable when we are hungry yet almost revolting after eating a banana split.

It is not the prettiest sight you've ever seen, but try this anyway. Take a drink of milk and allow it to coat your tongue. Then go to a mirror, stick out your tongue, and look carefully at its surface. You should be able to see rounded bumps above the surface of your tongue. Those bumps, called **papillae**, *contain your taste buds, which are the receptors for your taste.* About 10,000 of these taste buds are located on your tongue. As in all of the other sensory systems we have discussed, the information picked up by these receptors is transmitted to the brain for analysis and response (spitting something out, for example) when it is necessary.

Many animals have a stronger sense of smell than humans do. Dogs especially have a powerful olfactory sense. Watson, a Labrador retriever, has reliably pawed his owner 45 minutes before her epileptic seizures begin, giving her time to move to a safe place. How does the Labrador do this? The best hypothesis is that the dog smells the chemical changes known to precede epileptic seizures.

Olfaction

The taste qualities we respond to can be categorized as sweet, sour, bitter, and salty. Though all areas of the tongue can detect each of the four tastes, different regions of the tongue are more sensitive to one taste than another. The tip of the tongue is the most sensitive to sweet; the rear of the tongue is the most sensitive to bitter; just behind the area for sweet is the area most sensitive for salt; and just behind that is the most sensitive area for sour. While the tastes we experience can be categorized along these dimensions, our tasting ability goes far beyond them. Most of us pride ourselves on being able to discriminate different brands of ice cream; caffeinated and decaffeinated soda, coffee, and tea; and the many variations of product substitutes that are supposed to be better for us than the standard high-cholesterol, high-sugar, and high-fat culinary pleasures. Think of the remarkable range of tastes that you have which are generated by variations and combinations of the four basic taste qualities (sweet, sour, bitter, and salty).

Smell   A good way to begin our discussion of smell is to consider the many functions it serves. It is often easier to understand the importance of smell when we think about animals with more sophisticated senses of smell than our own. A dog, for example, can use its sense of smell to find its way back from a lone stroll, distinguish friend from foe, or even (with some practice!) detect illegal drugs concealed in a suitcase. In fact, dogs can detect odors in concentrations 100 times lower than those detectable by humans. In comparison to the nasal feats of the average dog, we might be tempted to believe that the sense of smell has outlived its usefulness in humans. What do we use smell for? For one, humans need the sense of smell to decide what to eat. We can distinguish rotten food from fresh food, and remember (all too well) which foods have made us ill in the past. The smell of a food that has previously made us ill is often, by itself, enough to make us feel nauseous. Second, while tracking is a function of smell that we often associate only with animals, humans are competent odor trackers. We can follow the smell of gas to a leak, the smell of smoke to a fire, or the smell of a hot apple pie to a windowsill.

What physical equipment do we use to process odor information? Just as the eyes scan the visual field for objects of interest, and the pinnae prick up to direct attention to sounds of interest, the nose is not a passive instrument. We actively sniff when we are trying to track down the source of a fire, or of a burned-out fluorescent light. The receptor cells for smell are located in the roof of the nasal cavity (see figure 3.14), so sniffing has the effect of maximizing the chances of detecting an odor (Doty, 2000; Doty & Muller-Schwarze, 1992). The **olfactory epithelium,** *located at the top of the nasal cavity, contains a sheet of receptor cells for smell.* These receptor sites are covered with millions of minute hairlike antennae that project through the mucus in the top of the nasal cavity and make contact with air on its way to the throat and lungs.

How good are you at identifying smells? Without practice, most people do a rather poor job of identifying odors. But the human olfactory sense can be

Olfactory bulb

Olfactory nerve

Nasal passage

Receptor cells located in the olfactory epithelium of the upper nasal passage

Figure 3.14
The Olfactory Sense
Airborne molecules of an odor reach tiny receptor cells in the roof of the nasal cavity. The receptor cells form a mucous-covered membrane called the olfactory epithelium. Then the olfactory nerve carries information about the odor to the brain for further processing.

improved. Perfumers, as perfume testers are called, can identify between 100 and 200 different fragrances.

The Kinesthetic and Vestibular Senses

You know the difference between walking and running and between lying down and sitting up. To perform even the simplest acts of motor coordination, like reaching out to take a book off a library shelf or getting up out of a chair, the brain must be constantly receiving and coordinating information from every part of the body. Your body has two kinds of senses that provide information about your movement and orientation in space: the **kinesthetic senses** *provide information about movement, posture, and orientation*, and the **vestibular sense** *provides information about balance and movement*.

No specific organ contains the kinesthetic senses. Instead, they are embedded in muscle fibers and joints. As we stretch and move, these receptors signal the state of the muscle. Kinesthesia is a sense that you often don't even notice until it is gone. Try walking when your leg "is asleep," or smiling (never mind talking) when you've just come from a dentist's office and you are still under the effects of novocaine. Perhaps the sophistication of kinesthesis can be best appreciated when we think in terms of memory. Even a mediocre typist can bang out twenty words per minute—but how many of us could write down the order of the letters on a keyboard without looking? We say that our fingers remember the positions of the keys. Typing is a skill that relies on very coordinated sensitivity to the orientation, position, and movements of our fingers. Likewise, the complicated movements a pitcher uses to throw a ball cannot be written down or communicated easily using language. They involve nearly every muscle and joint in the body.

The vestibular sense tells us whether our head (and hence usually our body) is tilted, moving, slowing down, or speeding up. It works in concert with the kinesthetic senses to coordinate our proprioceptive feedback, which is information about the position of our limbs and body parts in relation to other body parts. Consider the combination of sensory abilities involved in the motion of ice hockey players skating down the ice with the puck cradled and pushed forward with the hockey stick. The hockey players are responding simultaneously to a multitude of sensations including those produced by the slickness of the ice, the position of the puck, the speed and momentum of the forward progression, and the requirements of the play to turn and to track the other players on the ice.

The **semicircular canals,** *located in the inner ear, contain the sensory receptors that detect head motion that is caused when we tilt or move our heads and/or bodies* (see figure 3.15). These canals consist of three fluid-filled circular tubes that lie in the three planes of the body—right-left, front-back, and up-down.

As you move your head, the fluid of the semicircular canals flows in different directions and at different speeds (depending upon the force of the head movement). Our perception of head movement and position is determined by the movements of these receptor cells. This ingenious system of using the motion of fluid in tubes to sense head position is not unlike the system we learned about in audition. In audition, though, the fluid movement in the cochlear is caused by the pressure sound exerts on the oval window, whereas in the vestibular sense the movements we sense are real movements of the head and body.

The combination of kinesthetic and vestibular senses is supplemented by information from vision. This simple principle has made many an amusement park and large-screen movie theater profitable. When films are shown on screens that are large enough to fill our visual field, such as those found in many theme parks, the motion you perceive on the screen can make you feel like you are moving. This is the same principle that causes motorists to slam on the brakes in their tiny little sports car when the big truck next to them starts to move forward. When everything in our visual field is moving, it is generally because we are moving.

At this point we have discussed a number of ideas about the auditory, skin, chemical, kinesthetic, and vestibular senses. A summary of these ideas is presented in summary table 3.3.

Our eyes take in the light reflecting off of objects around us. However, our brain pays attention to only part of the scene. For example, when you are looking for a pen on a messy desk, you scan the surface without noticing the papers scattered across it. Next, we examine such aspects of perception, beginning with attention.

*F*igure 3.15
The Semicircular Canals and Vestibular Sense

This is a photograph of the semicircular canals located in the ear. The semicircular canals play an important role in the vestibular sense. The three canals are roughly perpendicular to each other in the three planes of space. Any angle of head rotation is registered by hair cells in one or more semicircular canals in both ears.

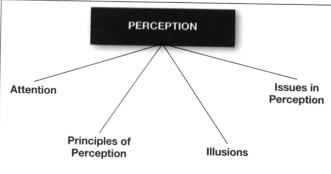

Perception

Earlier in this chapter we said that perception is the brain's process of organizing and interpreting sensory information to give it meaning ◄||||| P. 78. When perception goes to work, sensory receptors have received energy from stimuli in the external world and sensory organs have processed and transformed the information so it can be transmitted to the brain. Perception is a creation of the brain; it is based on input extracted from sensory organs, such as the eye, ear, and nose. But perception goes beyond this input. The brain uses information previously extracted as a basis for making educated guesses, or interpretations, about the state of the outside world.

Attention

The world holds a lot of information to perceive. Right now you are perceiving the letters and words that make up this sentence. Now look around the setting where you are and pick out something to look at other than this book. After that curl up the

Summary Table 3.3
The Auditory System and Other Senses

Concept	Processes/ Related Ideas	Characteristics/Description
The Auditory System	The Nature of Sound and How We Experience It	Sounds or sound waves are vibrations in the air that are processed by the auditory (or hearing) system. Sound waves vary in wavelength, which determines the frequency of the sound wave or the number of cycles (or full wavelengths) that pass through a point in a given time. Pitch is the perceptual interpretation of the frequency of sound. Amplitude is measured in decibels (dB), the amount of pressure produced by a sound wave relative to a standard. Loudness is the perception of a sound wave's amplitude. Complex sounds are those in which numerous frequencies of sound blend together. We experience the particular combination of frequencies in a sound as the quality or timbre of a sound.
	Structures and Functions of the Ear	The ear serves the function of transmitting a high-fidelity version of sounds in the world to the brain for analysis and interpretation. The ear is divided into the outer ear, middle ear, and inner ear. The outer ear consists of the pinna and the external auditory canal. The middle ear consists of the eardrum, hammer, anvil, and stirrup. The main parts of the inner ear are the oval window, cochlea, and the organ of Corti. The basilar membrane, located inside the cochlea, is where vibrations are changed into nerve impulses.
	Theories of Hearing	Place theory states that each frequency produces vibrations at a particular spot on the basilar membrane. Frequency theory states that the perception of a sound's frequency is due to how often the auditory nerve fires. Volley theory is a modification of place theory, stating that high frequencies can be signaled by teams of neurons that fire at different offset times to create an overall firing rate that could signal a very high frequency. Frequency theory is better at explaining lower-frequency sounds, volley and place theories higher-frequency sounds.
	Neural-Auditory Processing	Information about sound is carried from the cochlea to the brain by the auditory nerve. Information is integrated in the temporal lobe.
Other Senses	The Skin Senses	The skin senses consist of the senses of touch, temperature, and pain. In touch, we detect mechanical energy, or pressure against the skin. Thermoreceptors, which are located under the skin, respond to increases and decreases in temperature. Pain is the sensation that warns us that damage to our bodies is occurring. Gate-control theory states that the spinal column contains a neural gate that can be opened (allowing the perception of pain) or closed (blocking the perception of pain). Gate-control theory has been proposed as one explanation of acupuncture, a technique in which thin needles are inserted at specific points in the body to produce various effects, including local anesthesia. Gate-control theory does not completely explain how we experience pain.
	The Chemical Senses	The chemical senses consist of taste and smell. We use our sense of taste to select food and to regulate food intake. Papillae are rounded bumps above the surface of the tongue that contain taste buds, the receptors for taste. The taste qualities we can respond to are classified as sweet, sour, bitter, and salty. The functions of smell include guiding our decisions about what to eat, tracking, and communication. The olfactory epithelium, located at the top of the nasal cavity, contains a sheet of receptor cells for smell.
	The Kinesthetic and Vestibular Senses	The kinesthetic senses provide information about movement, posture, and orientation, while the vestibular sense provides information about balance and movement. The semicircular canals, located in the inner ear, contain the sensory receptors that detect head motion that is caused when we tilt or move our heads and/or bodies.

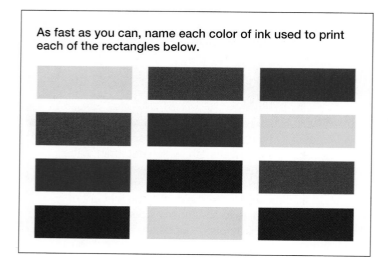

As fast as you can, name each color of ink used to print each of the rectangles below.

Now, as fast as you can, name the color of ink used to print each word shown below, *ignoring what each word says.*

GREEN   BLUE   RED

RED   GREEN   BLUE

YELLOW   RED   YELLOW

BLUE   YELLOW   GREEN

Figure 3.16
The Stroop Effect

Before reading further, make sure you have read the instructions above and completed the tasks. You probably had little or no difficulty in naming the colors of the rectangles in the left set. However, you likely stumbled more when you were asked to name the color of ink used to print each word in the right set. This demonstration of automaticity in perception is called the Stroop effect.

toes on your right foot. In each of these circumstances, you engaged in **selective attention,** *which involves focusing on a specific aspect of experience while ignoring others.* The cocktail party effect, the ability to attend selectively to one voice among many, is an example of selective attention.

Not only is attention selective, it also is *shiftable.* If the telephone rings while you are studying, you shift your attention from studying to the telephone. If you go to an art museum, you look at one painting, then another, then others, moving your attention from one painting to the next. And as you look at each painting, you shift your vision from one part of the painting to another, seeking to understand it better.

Why do we pay attention to some aspects of our experience and block out others? What you attend to is influenced by your motivation and interests. Art is one of my interests, so I will be more likely to attend to an advertisement for an art show than someone who has no interest in art. A person who is interested in sports is more likely to attend to an announcement that a basketball game will be on TV tonight than someone who is not interested in sports. There also are several features of stimuli that cause people to attend to them. Novel stimuli (those that are different or unusual) often attract our attention. If a Ferrari convertible whizzes by, you are more likely to notice it than if it were a Ford. Size, color, and movement also influence our attention. Objects that are large, vividly colored, or moving are more likely to grab our attention than objects that are small, dull-colored, or stationary.

Highly practiced and familiar stimuli, such as your own name or where you are from, often are perceived so automatically it is almost impossible to ignore them. The **Stroop effect** *is an example of automatic perception in which it is difficult to name the colors in which words are printed when the actual words refer to different colors.* To experience the Stroop effect, see figure 3.16. In most instances, the highly practiced and almost automatic perception of word meaning makes reading easier. However, this same automaticity makes it hard to ignore the meaning of the colors (such as blue) when they are printed in a different color (such as orange)

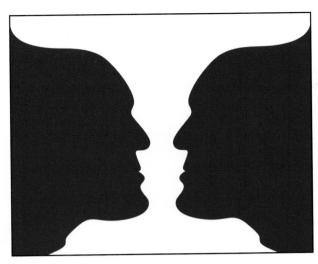

𝒻igure 3.17
Reversible Figure-Ground Pattern
Either a goblet or a pair of silhouetted faces in profile is seen.

𝒻igure 3.18
Sophisticated Use of the Figure-Ground Relationship in Escher's Woodcut *Relativity* **(1938)**

(Besner & Stolz, 1999). Thus, the Stroop effect represents a failure of selective attention.

Although attention plays an important role in perception, what we ultimately see, or interpret, also depends on a number of important principles of perception that involve specific characteristics of sensory stimuli.

Principles of Perception

Principles of perception include those involving shape perception, depth perception, motion perception, and perceptual constancy.

Shape Perception   Think about the world you see and its shapes—buildings against the sky, boats on the horizon, letters on this page. We see these shapes because they are marked off from the rest of what we see by **contour,** *a location at which a sudden change of brightness occurs.* Think about the letters on this page again. As you look at the page, you see letters, which are shapes, in a field or background, the white page. The **figure-ground relationship** *is the principle by which we organize the perceptual field into stimuli that stand out (figure) and those that are left over (ground).* Some figure-ground relationships, though, are highly ambiguous, and it is difficult to tell what is figure and what is ground. A well-known ambiguous figure-ground relationship is shown in figure 3.17.

As you look at the figure, your perception is likely to shift between seeing two faces or seeing a single goblet. Another example of figure-ground ambiguity is found in the work of artist M. C. Escher, which keeps us from favoring one figure over another seemingly because spatial location and depth cues are not provided (see figure 3.18).

One group of psychologists—the Gestalt psychologists—has been especially intrigued by how we perceive shapes. According to **Gestalt psychology,** *people naturally organize their perceptions according to certain patterns; Gestalt is a German word that*

THINKING ABOUT PSYCHOLOGY AND LIFE
Counting Aces of Spades

PLACE YOUR HAND over the bottom set of cards. Now as quickly as you can count how many aces of spades you see in the top set.

Now place your hand over the top set of cards. Quickly count the number of aces of spades in the set of 12 cards below.

Most people report that they see 2–3 aces of spades in the top set of 12 cards. However, if you look closely, there are 5. Two of the aces of spades are black and three are red. When people look at the bottom set of 12 cards they are more likely to count 5 aces of spades. Why the difference in what we perceive? The answer lies in our perceptual expectations: We expect the aces of spades to be black because that is how they are presented in a regular deck of cards. We don't expect them to be colored red, so it is easy to skip right over the red-colored ones. Interestingly, young children are more accurate at this task than adults. Why? Because they have not built up the perceptual expectation that aces of spades are black.

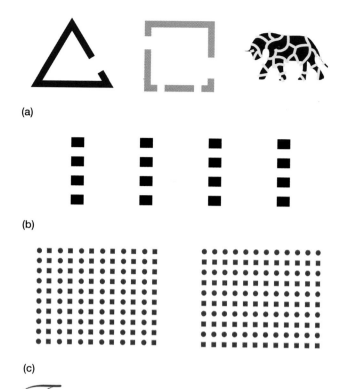

(a)

(b)

(c)

Figure 3.19
Gestalt Principles of Closure, Proximity, and Similarity

(a) Closure: When we see disconnected or incomplete figures, we fill in the spaces and see them as complete figures. (b) Proximity: When we see objects that are near each other, they tend to be seen as a unit. You are likely to perceive the grouping as 4 columns of 4 squares, not 1 set of 16 squares. (c) Similarity: When we see objects that are similar to each other, they tend to be seen as a unit. In this display, you are likely to see vertical columns of circles and squares in the left box but horizontal rows of circles and squares in the right box.

means "configuration" or "form." One of Gestalt psychology's main principles is that the whole is not equal to the sum of its parts. For example, when you watch a movie, the "motion" you see in the film cannot be found in the film itself; if you examine it, you see only separate frames at a rate of many per second. When you watch the film you perceive a whole that is very different from the separate individual pictures that are the whole's parts.

The figure-ground relationship just described is another Gestalt principle. Three other Gestalt principles are closure, proximity, and similarity. The principle of *closure* states that when individuals see a disconnected or incomplete figure, they fill in the spaces and see it as a complete figure (see figure 3.19a). The principle of *proximity* states that when individuals see objects closer to each other, they tend to group them together (see figure 3.19b). The principle of *similarity* states that the more similar objects are, the more likely we are to group them together (see figure 3.19c).

Depth Perception   The images of the world we see appear on our retinas in two-dimensional form, yet we see a three-dimensional world. **Depth perception** *is the ability to perceive objects three-dimensionally.* Look at the setting where you are. You don't see it as flat. You see some objects farther away, some closer. Some objects overlap each other. The scene and objects that you are looking at have depth. How do you see depth? To see a world of depth, we use two kinds of information, or cues—binocular and monocular. We have two eyes, which view the world from slightly different places. **Binocular cues** *are depth cues that are based on the combination of the images on the left and right eyes and on the way the two eyes work together.* **Monocular cues** *are depth cues that can be extracted from the image in one eye, either the left or the right eye.*

Because we have two eyes, we get two views of the world, one from each eye. The pictures are slightly different because the eyes are in slightly different positions. Try holding your hand about 10 inches from your face. Alternately close and open your left and right eyes, so that only one eye is open at a time. The image of your left hand will appear to jump back and forth. This is because the image of your hand is in a slightly different place on the left and right retinas. The **disparity,** *or difference of the image in the two eyes,* is the binocular cue the brain uses to determine the depth or distance of an object. Both images are combined in the brain, and the disparities between the images of objects in the two eyes gives us information about the three-dimensionality of the world (Schneider, Moraglia, & Speranza, in press).

In addition to having an indication of the depth of objects from the difference between the two-eye images, our perception of depth also makes use of a number of monocular cues, or cues available from a single-eye image. These are powerful cues and under normal circumstances can provide a very compelling impression of depth. Try closing one eye—your perception of the world still retains many of its three-dimensional qualities. Some examples of monocular cues are as follows:

1. *Aerial perspective.* Pollution and water vapor in the air scatter light waves, giving distant objects a hazy appearance.
2. *Familiar size.* This cue to the depth and distance of objects is based on what we have learned from experience about the standard sizes of objects. We know how large oranges tend to be, so we can tell something about how far away an orange is likely to be by the size of its image on the retina.
3. *Height in the field of view.* All other things being equal, objects that are higher in a picture are seen as farther away.
4. *Linear perspective.* This cue is based on the fact that objects farther away take up less space on the retina. As an object recedes into the distance, parallel lines in the scene appear to converge.
5. *Overlap.* An object that partially conceals or overlaps another object is perceived as closer.
6. *Shading.* This cue involves changes in perception due to the position of the light and the position of the viewer. Consider an egg under a desk lamp. If you walk around the desk, you will get different shading patterns on the egg.
7. *Size in the field of view.* All other things being equal, objects that are smaller are seen to be farther away.
8. *Texture gradient.* Texture becomes more dense and finer, the farther away it is from the viewer (see figure 3.20).

The Joy of Visual Perception
Stereoscopic Imagery
Vision and Art

Figure 3.20
Texture Gradient

The gradients of texture create an impression of depth on a flat surface.

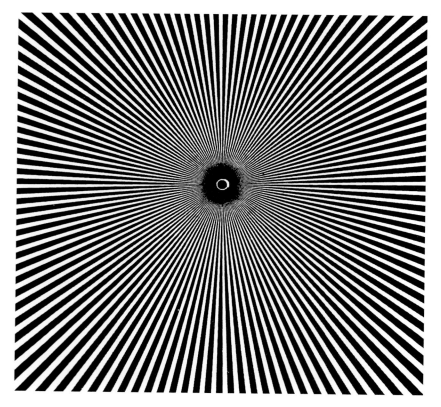

$\mathcal{F}$igure 3.21
Movement Aftereffects

This is an example of a geometric pattern that produces afterimages in which motion can be perceived. If the center of the pattern is fixated for approximately 10 seconds and then the afterimage is projected on a plain white surface, rotary motion is usually perceived.

Movement Aftereffects

Depth perception is especially intriguing to artists. They face a problem because the real world is three-dimensional and they have to paint on a two-dimensional canvas. Artists often use monocular cues to give the feeling of depth to their paintings. Indeed, monocular cues have become so widely used by artists that they have also been called *pictorial cues.*

Motion Perception   During the course of each day, we perceive objects that move—other people, cars, planes, animals. Why are we able to perceive motion? First, we have neurons that are specialized to detect motion. Second, feedback from our body tells us whether we are moving or someone or an object is moving. For example, you move your eye muscles as you watch a ball coming toward you. Third, the environment we see is rich in cues that give us information about movement. For example, when we run, we can tell that the background is moving.

Psychologists are interested in both real movement and **apparent movement,** *which occurs when an object is stationary but we perceive it to be moving.* An example of apparent movement can be experienced at Disneyland. Bell Telephone mounted nine cameras on an airplane to obtain nine different perspectives on a number of sights around the United States; the films are shown at a Disneyland attraction. The motion pictures are shown on nine screens that surround the viewers, who stand in the middle of the room, a setting that simulates the view from an airplane. Viewers are warned to hold the handrail because perceived movement is so realistic it is easy to fall while experiencing the "movement."

Two forms of apparent motion are stroboscopic motion and movement aftereffects. **Stroboscopic motion** *is the illusion of movement created when a rapid stimulation of different parts of the retina occurs—motion pictures are a form of stroboscopic motion.* **Movement aftereffects** *happen when we watch continuous movement and then look at another surface, which then appears to move in the opposite direction.* Figure 3.21 provides an opportunity to experience movement aftereffects.

Perceptual Constancy   Retinal images are constantly changing as we experience our world. Even though the stimuli that fall on the retinas of our eyes change as we move closer or farther away from objects, or look at objects from different orientations and in light or dark settings, we perceive objects as constant and unchanging. We experience three types of perceptual constancies: size constancy, shape constancy, and brightness constancy. **Size constancy** *is the recognition that an object remains the same size even though the retinal image of the object changes* (see figure 3.22). **Shape constancy** *is the recognition that an object remains the same shape even though its orientation to us changes.* Look around the room in which you are reading this book. You probably see objects of various shapes—chairs and tables, for example. If you walk around the room, you will see these objects from different sides and angles. Even though the retinal image of the object changes as you walk, you still perceive the objects as being the same shape (see figure 3.23). **Brightness constancy** *is the recognition that an object retains the* *same degree of brightness even though different amounts of light fall on it.* For example, regardless of whether you are reading this book indoors or outdoors, the white pages and the black print do not look any different to you in terms of their whiteness or blackness.

How are we able to resolve the discrepancy between a retinal image of an object and its actual size, shape, and brightness? Experience is important. For example, no matter how far away you are from your car, you know how large it is. Not only is familiarity important in size constancy, but so are binocular and monocular distance cues ◄|||| P. 105. Even if we have never previously seen an object, these cues provide us with information about an object's size. Many visual illusions are influenced by our perception of size constancy.

Illusions

Our perceptual interpretations are usually correct. For example, on the basis of a change in color or texture, we can conclude that a dog is on the rug. On the basis of a continuous increase in size, we conclude that a train is coming toward us. Sometimes, though, the interpretations or inferences are wrong, with the result being an illusion that is a misperception (Gregory, 2000).

A **visual illusion** *occurs when two objects produce exactly the same retinal image but are perceived as different images.* Illusions are incorrect, but they are not abnormal. They can provide insight into how our perceptual processes work (Nakamizo, Ono, & Medin, 1999; Rinkenauer, Mattes, & Ulrich, 1999). More than two hundred different types of illusions have been discovered; we will study six.

One of the most famous is the Müller-Lyer illusion, illustrated in figure 3.24. The two lines are exactly the same length, although *b* looks longer than *a*. Another illusion is the horizontal-vertical illusion in which a vertical line looks longer than a horizontal line even though the two are equal (see figure 3.25). In the Ponzo illusion (see figure 3.26), the top line looks much longer than the bottom line.

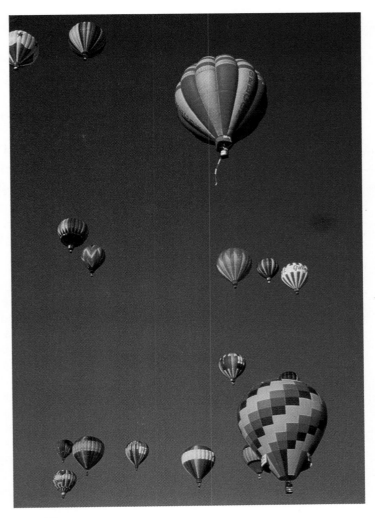

𝓕igure 3.22
Size Constancy

Even though our retinal image of the hot air balloons changes, we still perceive the different balloons as being approximately the same size. This illustrates the principle of size constancy.

𝓕igure 3.23
Shape Constancy

The various projected images from an opening door are quite different, yet you perceive a rectangular door.

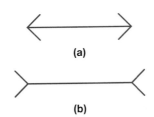

(a)

(b)

𝓕igure 3.24
Müller-Lyer Illusion

The two lines are exactly the same length, although *(b)* looks longer than *(a)*.

© *Sidney Harris*

$\mathcal{F}$igure 3.25
**The Horizontal-
Vertical Illusion**
The vertical line looks longer
than the horizontal line, but they
are the same length.

$\mathcal{F}$igure 3.26
Ponzo Illusion
The top line looks much longer
than the bottom line, but they
are equal in length.

Why do these illusions trick us? One reason is that we mistakenly use certain cues for maintaining size constancy. For example, in the Ponzo illusion we see the upper line as being farther away (remember that objects higher in a picture are perceived as being farther away). The Müller-Lyer illusion, though, is not so easily explained. We might make our judgments about the lines by comparing incorrect parts of the figures. For example, when people were shown the Müller-Lyer illusion with the wings painted a different color than the horizontal lines, the illusion was greatly reduced (Coren & Girus, 1972). Shortly we also will discuss how cultural experiences influence an individual's perception of the Müller-Lyer illusion.

Another well-known illusion is the moon illusion (see figure 3.27). The moon is 2,000 miles in diameter and 289,000 miles away. Because both the moon's size and its distance from us are beyond our own experience, we have difficulty judging just how far away it really is. When the moon is high in the sky, directly above us, little information is present to help us judge its distance—no texture gradients or stereoscopic cues exist, for example. But when the moon is on the horizon, we can judge its distance in relation to familiar objects—trees and buildings, for example—which makes it appear farther away. The result is that we estimate the size of the moon as much larger when it is on the horizon than when it is overhead.

The devil's tuning fork is another fascinating illusion. Look at figure 3.28 for about 30 seconds, then close the book. Now try to draw the tuning fork. You undoubtedly found this a difficult, if not impossible, task. Why? Because the figure's depth cues are ambiguous, you had problems correctly interpreting it.

**Visual Illusions
Exploring Visual Illusions**

Extrasensory Perception

Our eyes, ears, mouth, nose, and skin provide us with sensory information about the external world. Our perceptions are based on our interpretation of this sensory information. Some people, though, claim they can perceive the world through something other than normal sensory pathways. **Extrasensory perception (ESP)** *is perception that occurs without the use of any known sensory process.* Most psychologists do not believe in ESP; however, a few of them investigate it.

Extrasensory experiences fall into three main categories. The first is **telepathy,** *which involves the transfer of thought from one person to another.* For example, this skill is supposedly possessed by people who can "read" another person's mind. If two people are playing cards and one person can tell what cards the other person picked

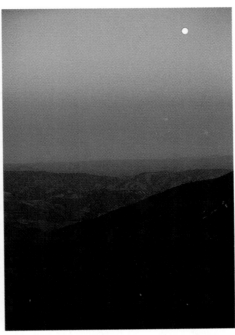

$\mathscr{F}$**igure 3.27**
Moon Illusion
When the moon is on the horizon, it looks much larger than when it is high in the sky, directly above us. Why does the moon look so much larger on the horizon?

up, telepathy is taking place (see figure 3.29). **Precognition** *involves "knowing" events before they happen.* For example, a fortune-teller might claim to see into the future and tell you what will happen to you in the coming year. Or an astrologer might predict that a major earthquake will take place in Los Angeles in June of next year. **Clairvoyance** *involves the ability to perceive remote events that are not in sight.* For example, a person at a movie theatre senses a burglar breaking into his house at that moment. **Psychokinesis,** closely associated with ESP, *is the mind-over-matter phenomenon of being able to move objects without touching them, such as mentally getting a chair to rise off the floor or shattering a glass merely by staring at it.*

One of the most famous claims of ESP involved Uri Geller, a psychic who supposedly performed mind-boggling feats. Observers saw Geller correctly predict the number on a die rolled in a closed box eight out of eight times, reproduce drawings that were hidden in sealed envelopes, bend forks without touching them, and start broken watches. While he had worked as a magician, Geller claimed his supernatural powers were created by energy sent from another universe. Careful investigation of Geller's feats revealed they were nothing more than a magician's tricks. For example, in the case of the die, Geller was allowed to shake the box and open it himself, giving him an opportunity to manipulate the die (Randi, 1980).

Through their astonishing stage performances, many psychics are very convincing. They seemingly are able to levitate tables, communicate with spirits, and read an audience member's mind. Many psychics, like Uri Geller, are also magicians who have the ability to perform sleight-of-hand maneuvers and dramatic manipulations that go unnoticed by most human eyes. One magician's personal goal, though, is to expose the hoaxes of the psychics. James Randi (1980) has investigated a number of psychics' claims and publicized their failures.

Not only have magicians such as Randi investigated psychics' claims, but scientists have also examined ESP in experimental contexts. Some ESP enthusiasts believe

$\mathscr{F}$**igure 3.28**
Devil's Tuning Fork

𝓕igure 3.29
An Experimental Situation Involving an Attempt to Demonstrate Telepathy

At the top *(blue insert)*, a person in one room tries to "send" a message through thought to a person (the subject) in another room. The sender selects a card and then attempts to relay the information mentally to the subject. The subject then selects a card, and it is compared to the one previously chosen by the sender to see if the cards match. If the mind-to-mind communication occurs beyond levels of chance, then it would be argued that telepathy has taken place.

the phenomena are more likely to occur when a subject is totally relaxed and deprived of sensory input. In this kind of ESP experiment, the subject lies down and half a Ping-Pong ball is placed over each eye, affixed with cotton and tape. An experimenter watches through a one-way mirror from an adjacent room, listening to and recording the subject's statements. At an agreed-upon time someone from another location concentrates on the message to be sent mind to mind.

Carl Sargent (1987) has used this procedure in a number of telepathy experiments and reported a great deal of ESP success. In one experiment, Sargent has a "sender" mentally transmit an image of one of four pictures selected from one of 27 randomly selected sets of four pictures. Immediately afterward, the experimenter and the subject examined a duplicate set of four pictures and together judged and ranked their degree of correspondence with the subject's recorded impression. Experimental psychologist Susan Blackmore (1987) was skeptical about Sargent's success in ESP experiments, so she visited his laboratory at Cambridge University in England and observed a number of his telepathy sessions. With the subject shown four pictures, the success rate expected by chance was 25 percent (one of four pictures). In the experimental sessions observed by Blackmore, the subjects' hit rate was 50 percent, far exceeding chance.

Sargent supposedly invokes a number of elaborate procedures to protect randomization, experimenter bias, unbiased selection by the subject, and so on. Blackmore was still skeptical, finding some disturbing flaws in the way Sargent's experiments were conducted. In some sessions, he did the randomization of the picture himself,

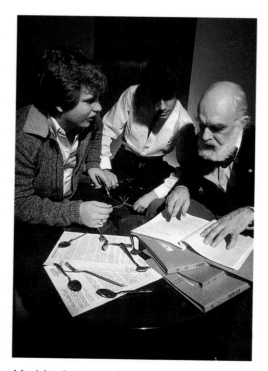

Magician James Randi (right) has investigated a large number of psychics' claims. No one has yet won Randi's standing offer of $10,000 to anyone whose psychic claims withstand his analysis.

SUMMARY TABLE 3.4
Perception

Concept	Processes/ Related Ideas	Characteristics/Description
Attention	Its Nature	Selective attention involves focusing on a specific aspect of experience while ignoring others. Not only is attention selective, it also is shiftable. Attention is influenced by a person's motivation and interests, as well as characteristics of stimuli, such as novelty. The Stroop effect is an example of automatic perception in which it is difficult to say words for colors that are printed in a different color.
Principles of Perception	Shape Perception	Shape is perceived because it is marked off by contour. Gestalt psychologists developed a number of principles of perceptual organization, a fundamental one being that the whole is not equal to the sum of its parts.
	Depth Perception	Depth perception is our ability to perceive objects as three-dimensional. To see a world of depth, we use binocular cues, such as retinal disparity and convergence, and monocular cues (also called pictorial cues), such as linear perspective, texture gradient, relative size, interposition, shadowing, and aerial perspective.
	Motion Perception	Motion perception focuses on both real movement and apparent movement. Stroboscopic motion and movement aftereffects are two prominent forms of apparent movement.
	Perceptual Constancy	This concept includes size, shape, and brightness constancy. Experience with objects and distance cues help us to see objects as unchanging.
Illusions	Their Nature	Illusions occur when two objects produce exactly the same retinal image but are perceived as different images. Among the more than 200 different illusions are the Müller-Lyer illusion and the moon illusion. Perceptual constancies and cultural experiences are among the factors thought to be responsible for illusions.
Extrasensory Perception	Its Nature	Extrasensory perception is perception that does not occur through normal sensory channels. Three main forms are telepathy, precognition, and clairvoyance. Psychokinesis is a closely related phenomenon. The claims of ESP enthusiasts have not held up to scientific scrutiny.

putting himself where he could manipulate the ordering of the pictures. In other sessions, he came in while the subject was judging the pictures and "pushed" the subject toward the picture that had been "transmitted" by the "sender."

No one has been able to replicate the high hit rates in Sargent's experiments. Proponents of ESP, such as Sargent, claim they have demonstrated the existence of ESP, but critics, such as Blackmore, demand to see or experience the same phenomena themselves. Replication is one of the hallmarks of scientific investigation, yet replication has been a major thorn in the side of ESP researchers. ESP phenomena have not been reproducible when rigorous experimental standards are applied (Bates, 1995; Hines, 1988) ◀▥ P. 34.

At this point, we have discussed a number of ideas about perception. To help you sort out the main concepts in this discussion, turn to summary table 3.4.

Extrasensory Perception
James Randi

Overview

Overview

WE BEGAN THIS CHAPTER by evaluating how people detect and perceive the world; we defined sensation and perception and also discussed thresholds and signal detection theory. Next we read about the visual sense—the visual stimulus and the eye, from eye to brain and neural-visual processing; and the auditory system—the nature of sound and how we experience it, structures and functions of the ear, theories of hearing, and neural-auditory processing. We also learned about the skin, chemical, kinesthetic, and vestibular senses. Our coverage of perception focused on attention, principles of perception, illusions, and extrasensory perception. Don't forget that you can obtain a more detailed overview of the chapter by again studying the four summary tables on pages 82, 90, 101, and 111.

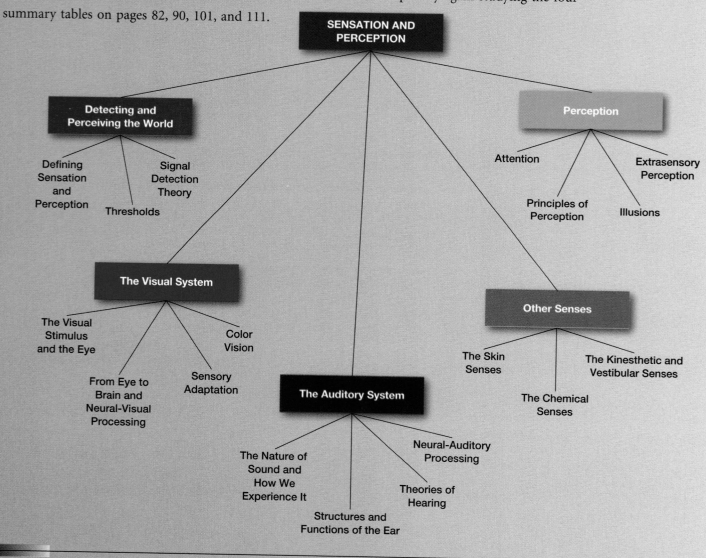

Key Terms

sensation 78
perception 78
psychophysics 78
absolute threshold 78
noise 79
difference threshold 81
Weber's law 81
signal detection theory 81
light 82
wavelength 82
sclera 83
iris 83
pupil 83
cornea 83
lens of the eye 83
accommodation 84
retina 84
transduction 84
rods 84
cones 84
fovea 85
blind spot 85

feature detectors 86
sensory adaptation 86
hue 87
saturation 87
brightness 88
trichromatic theory 88
dichromats 89
trichromats 89
afterimages 89
opponent-process theory 89
sounds 91
frequency 91
pitch 91
amplitude 91
loudness 92
complex sounds 92
timbre 92
outer ear 92
middle ear 92
inner ear 92
cochlea 92
basilar membrane 92

organ of Corti 92
place theory 93
frequency theory 94
volley principle 94
auditory nerve 94
thermoreceptors 95
pain 96
gate-control theory 96
acupuncture 96
papillae 97
olfactory epithelium 98
kinesthetic sense 99
vestibular sense 99
semicircular canals 100
selective attention 102
Stroop effect 102
contour 103
figure-ground relationship 103
Gestalt psychology 103
depth perception 105
binocular cues 105

monocular cues 105
disparity 105
apparent movement 106
stroboscopic motion 106
movement aftereffects 106
size constancy 106
shape constancy 106
brightness constancy 106
visual illusion 107
extrasensory perception (ESP) 108
telepathy 108
precognition 109
clairvoyance 109
psychokinesis 109

Key People

Oliver Sacks 77
E. H. Weber 81
David Hubel and Torsten Wiesel 86

Thomas Young and Hermann von Helmholtz 88
Ewald Hering 89
Georg von Békésy 94

Ronald Melzak and Patricia Wall 96
James Randi 109

Taking It to the Net

1. Noise-induced hearing loss (NIHL) is an extremely widespread, yet underreported, problem. Sounds that are loud enough to damage sensitive inner-ear structures can produce hearing loss that is not reversible by any available medical or surgical treatment. We are inundated with sounds throughout the day that reduce our normal hearing capabilities. What ear structures are affected by loud noise, and at what level does noise become dangerous? Give examples of dangerous noise that you are exposed to on a daily basis and what you can do to reduce the risk of NIHL.

2. Have you ever seen a visual illusion? A visual illusion occurs when two discrete objects produce identical retinal images, but are perceived as being different. They occur because we rely on certain visual cues to explain visual stimuli, and when the cues are deliberately used to deceive us, we perceive images as being different. One such illusion is the Hering illusion. Explain the phenomenon of the Hering illusion. What do you see? Why do you see that? What occurs in your visual system that could account for this illusion?

3. One important aspect of driving automobiles is being aware of your driving "blind spot." It can obstruct your view and/or cause you to miss seeing another car or person. A similar effect occurs in our actual eyes. A certain spot on our eyes is completely without the ability to see. Where is the blind spot in the human eye, and why does it exist? Give your answer in terms of both the biological structures of the eye and subjective perceptual experience. How does your eye react when stimuli in and surrounding the blind spot are altered? Does it accommodate for these changes?

Connect to http://www.mhhe.com/psychology/santrock to find the answers!

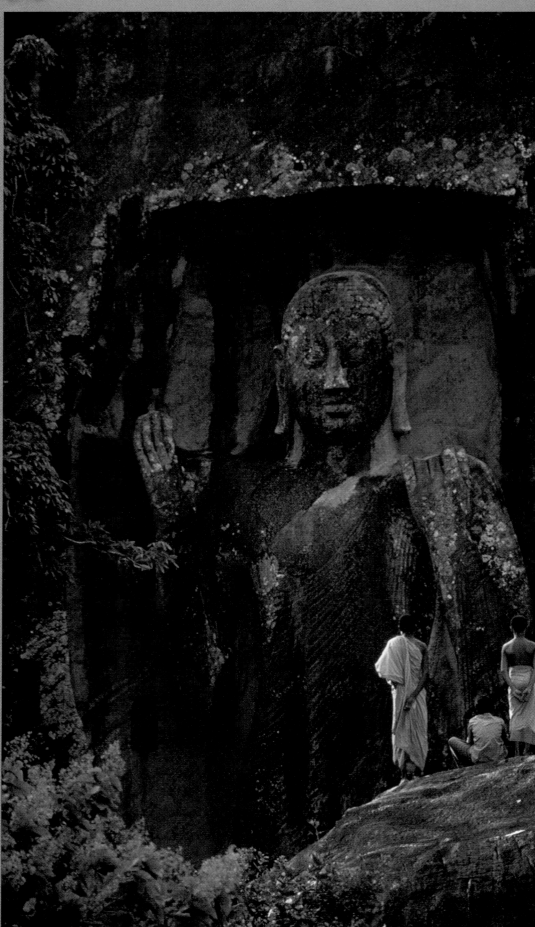

Chapter 4

CHAPTER OUTLINE

States of Consciousness

Images of Psychology and Life
Colin Kemp's Tragic Night Terror

"The ultimate gift of conscious life is a sense of mystery that encompasses it."

Lewis Mumford
American Cultural Historian, 20th Century

Preview

MOST OF US take for granted our nightly sojourn in the realm of sleep. But as you will see shortly, the experiences of one man, Colin Kemp, stimulate us to wonder about the nature of sleep and states of consciousness. These are some of the questions we will explore in this chapter:

• What are some different states of consciousness we experience?
• Why do we sleep? How much sleep do we need? What happens when we are deprived of sleep?
• Can you influence what you dream about?
• Can everyone be hypnotized?
• Why do people take psychoactive drugs?
• What are some strategies for preventing and treating drug abuse?

IT WAS AUGUST 1985, and Colin Kemp, a 33-year-old salesman in Caterham, England, went to sleep as usual. About 2 hours later, he was confronted by two soldiers in his bedroom. They started to chase him. One soldier had a knife, the other a gun. Kemp ran away from them as fast as he could, but he wasn't fast enough. Kemp wrestled with the knife-wielding soldier. The other soldier aimed his gun at Kemp's head. Kemp tripped him, gripped his neck, and began choking him, but he slipped away. He turned, aimed the gun at Kemp, and fired. Kemp awoke in a state of panic, sweat pouring down his head. In a frenzy of terror, he turned to his wife, who was lying next to him in bed. She was dead. Kemp had strangled her, not the soldier.

A trial was held 9 months later. Kemp said he was asleep when he killed his wife, pleading not guilty to the murder charge because he had intended to kill the solider, not his wife. Psychiatrists testified on Kemp's behalf, instructing the jury that Kemp was having a night terror at the time he killed his wife. *Night terrors* are characterized by sudden arousal from sleep and intense fear, usually accompanied by a number of physiological reactions such as rapid heart rate and breathing, loud screams, heavy perspiration, and physical movement. In most instances, the individual has little or no memory of what happened during the night terror.

Kemp experienced night terrors on two occasions prior to the fatal event. Both times he was being chased during his sleep. In one of the night terrors, he punched at his wife. She awakened and asked what was happening. The second time he kicked her in the back. Strangling someone to death is a much more elaborate and sustained activity than kicking an individual in the back. Is it possible that an action like Kemp's—strangling someone to death—could actually take place during sleep? The jury apparently thought so. They acquitted Kemp.

They viewed his act as an unconscious one. That is, the jury concluded that Kemp was not aware of what he was doing (Restak, 1988). One final note: Be aware that night terrors rarely lead to such extreme behavior as Colin Kemp's.

The Nature of Consciousness

Internet Resources on Consciousness

What Is Consciousness?

For much of the twentieth century, psychologists shunned the slippery, subjective trappings of consciousness that intrigued their predecessors in the late nineteenth century. Instead, they focused on overt behaviors and the rewards and punishments that determined those behaviors (Skinner, 1938; Watson, 1913). Recently, though, the study of consciousness has gained widespread respectability in psychology (Baars, 1999; Nelson, 1996). For the first time in many decades, psychologists from many different fields are interested in consciousness, including its relation to unconsciousness (Cohen & Schooler, 1996; Farthing, 2000; Grossenbacher, 1999; Schacter, 1999).

As we go through our lives, we process information at different levels of awareness. We are aware of some of the processing, unaware of other processing.

Although there is still disagreement about the nature of consciousness, we can define **consciousness** *as awareness of both external and internal stimuli or events*. The external events include what you attend to as you go through your day—the comment your best friend just made about your new hairstyle, the car in front of you that just swerved to miss a dog, the music you are listening to on your Walkman, for example. Internal events include your awareness of your sensations—my headache just returned, I'm breathing too fast, my stomach's rumbling—as well as your thoughts and feelings—I'm really having trouble in biology this semester, I'm anxious about the exam next week, I'm happy Marsha is coming with me to the game tonight.

The contents of our awareness may change from one moment to the next, since information can move rapidly in and out of consciousness. Many years ago, William James (1890/1950) described the mind as a **stream of consciousness**—*a continuous flow of changing sensations, images, thoughts, and feelings*. Our minds race from one topic to the next—from thinking about the person who is approaching us, to how well we feel, to what we are going to do tomorrow, to where we are going for lunch.

While William James was interested in charting the shifting nature of our stream of consciousness, remember that Sigmund Freud (1900/1953) believed that most of our thoughts are unconscious. **Unconscious thought**, *according to Freud, is a reservoir of unacceptable wishes, feelings, and thoughts that are beyond conscious awareness*. Unconscious thought has nothing to do with being unconscious after being knocked out by a blow on the head in a boxing match, being anesthetized, or falling into a coma.

According to Freud, unconscious thoughts are too laden with anxiety and other negative emotions for consciousness to admit them. For example, a young man who is nervous around women breaks into a cold sweat as a woman approaches him. He is unconscious that his fear of women springs from the cold, punitive way his mother treated him when he was a child. Freud believed that one of psychotherapy's main goals was to bring unconscious thoughts into conscious awareness so they can be addressed and dealt with.

Freud accurately recognized the complexity of consciousness. It is not simply a matter of being aware or unaware. Consciousness comes in different forms and levels. Sometimes consciousness is highly focused and alert, at other times it is more passive. Even sleep, once thought to be completely passive and unconscious, is now known to have active and at least minimally conscious properties. **Controlled processes** *represent the most alert states of consciousness, in which individuals actively focus their efforts toward a goal*. Controlled processes require focused attention and interfere with other ongoing activities. Consider Anne, who is learning how to use her new personal computer. She is completely absorbed in reading the tutorial manual that accompanies the computer—she doesn't hear her roommate humming to herself or the song on the radio. This state of focused awareness is what is meant by controlled processes.

Once Anne learns how to use the software, maneuvers on the computer keyboard become almost automatic; that is, she doesn't have to concentrate so hard on how to perform each of the steps required to get the computer to do something. Two weeks ago she had to stop and concentrate on which keys to press to move a paragraph from one page to another. Now her fingers fly across the computer keyboard when she needs to move a block of material. This kind of consciousness involves automatic processes. **Automatic processes** *are forms of consciousness that require minimal attention and do not interfere with other ongoing activities.* Automatic processes require less conscious effort than controlled processes. When we are awake, our automatic behaviors should be thought of as lower in awareness than controlled processes, rather than not conscious at all. Since Anne pushed the right keys at the right time on her computer keyboard, she apparently was aware of what she was doing, at some level.

"If you ask me, all three of us are in different states of awareness."

Daydreaming *is another form of consciousness that involves a low level of conscious effort.* Daydreaming lies somewhere between active consciousness and dreaming while we are asleep. It is a little like dreaming when we are awake. Daydreams usually start spontaneously when what we are doing requires less than our full attention. Mind-wandering is probably the most obvious type of daydreaming. We regularly take brief side trips into our own private kingdoms of imagery and memory even as we read, listen, or work. When we daydream we often drift off into a world of fantasy. We imagine ourselves on dates, at parties, on television, at faraway places, at another time in our lives. Sometimes our daydreams are about ordinary, everyday events, such as paying the rent, getting our hair done, or dealing with someone at work. This semi-automatic thought flow can be useful. As you daydream while you shave, iron a pair of pants, or walk to the store, you may be making plans or solving a problem. Daydreams can remind us of important things ahead. Daydreaming keeps our minds active while helping us to cope, to create, and to fantasize.

When we sleep and dream, our level of awareness is lower than when we daydream, but remember that we no longer think of being asleep as the complete absence of consciousness. Sleep and dreams, though, are at very low levels of consciousness. How is sleep different from being in a coma? Sleep differs from being in a coma in that it is periodic, natural, and reversible.

So far the states of consciousness we have described are normal, everyday occurrences in each of our lives. An **altered state of consciousness** *occurs when a person is in a mental state that noticeably differs from normal awareness.* Drugs, meditation, traumas, fatigue, hypnosis, and sensory deprivation produce altered states of consciousness. Whether a state of consciousness is described as normal or altered depends on how the word *normal* is defined. Someone who drinks a caffeinated soda to increase their alertness, for instance, is considered to be in a normal state of consciousness. But someone who takes a drug that induces hallucinations, such as LSD, is considered to be in an altered state of consciousness.

As you can see, our states of consciousness are many, varied, and complex (Rose, 1999). A summary of some of the main forms of consciousness and their level of awareness or unawareness is presented in figure 4.1. Now we turn our attention to the fascinating world of sleep and dreams.

HIGH-LEVEL AWARENESS	Controlled processes	High level of awareness, focused attention required		This student is using controlled processes that require focused concentration.
LOWER-LEVEL AWARENESS	Automatic processes	Awareness, but minimal attention required		This woman is an experienced computer operator. Her maneuvers with the keyboard are automatic, requiring minimal awareness.
	Daydreaming	Low level of awareness and conscious effort, somewhere between active consciousness and dreaming while asleep		Our daydreams often start spontaneously when what we are doing requires less than our full attention.
	Altered states of consciousness	A mental state noticeably different from normal awareness; produced by drugs, trauma, fatigue, hypnosis, meditation, and sensory deprivation		Shown here is a woman being hypnotized.
	Sleep and dreams	No longer thought of as the absence of consciousness, but they are at very low levels of consciousness		All of us dream while we sleep, but some of us dream more than others.
NO AWARENESS	Unconscious mind (Freudian)	Reservoir of unacceptable wishes, feelings, and memories, often with sexual and aggressive overtones, that are too anxiety provoking to be admitted to consciousness		The woman shown lying on the couch is undergoing psychoanalytic therapy to reveal her unconscious thoughts.
	Unconscious (non-Freudian)	Being knocked unconscious by a blow or when we are anesthetized; deep prolonged unconsciousness characterizes individuals who go into a coma as the result of injury, disease, or poison		Unconsciousness can result from an injury, such as a blow to the head.

Figure 4.1
Forms of Consciousness and Levels of Awareness

Sleep

Each night something lures us from work, from play, and from our loved ones into a solitary state. It is sleep, which claims about one-third of the time in our lives, more than any other pursuit. This alluring realm of mental escapades we enter each night has intrigued philosophers and scientists for centuries. Those who investigated sleep were primarily interested in its role as a springboard for dreams. We no longer regard sleep as the complete absence of consciousness. Now we know that sleep involves much more.

The Nature of Sleep

Jet Lag and Circadian Rhythms

Why Do We Sleep?

There are two main theories about why we sleep—repair theory and ecological theory. **Repair theory** *holds that sleep restores, replenishes, and rebuilds our brains and bodies, which somehow are worn out or used up by the day's waking activities.* This idea fits with the feeling of being "worn out" before we sleep and "restored" when we wake. Aristotle proposed a repair theory of sleep centuries ago, and most experts today believe in some version of repair (Dement, 1999; Hirshkowitz, Moore, & Minhoto, 1997; Webb, 2000).

Ecological theory *is a relatively recent view of why we sleep. This evolutionary-based approach argues that the main purpose of sleep is to prevent animals from wasting their energy and harming themselves during those parts of the day or night to which they have not adapted.* For example, it was not adaptive for our ancestors to fumble around in the dark, risking accidents or attack by large predators such as lions and tigers. So, like the chimpanzees who slept safely in treetops, our ancestors presumably hid and slept through the night.

In today's world, ecological factors still are important for animals in the wild. With good hiding places, small prey animals (such as mice and rabbits) sleep regularly and safely all through the daylight hours. By contrast, large animals that cannot hide, such as horses and cows, show scanty and irregular sleep patterns. Thus, body weight and danger of attack are important factors in determining how much sleep animals get. The total sleep of different animals ranges from slightly less than 3 to almost 20 hours of every 24-hour period (Webb, 1993) (see figure 4.2).

Both repair theory and ecological theory have merit. Repair theory accounts for the results of sleep deprivation. That is, not getting enough sleep makes us sleepy and getting sleep helps us to recover. Ecological theory explains the wide range of sleep and timing of sleep in animals. Possibly sleep originally was important for keeping humans out of harm's way but since has evolved to allow for restoration.

Sleep and Circadian Rhythms

We are unaware of most of our body's rhythms—for example, the rise and fall of hormones in the bloodstream, accelerated and decelerated cycles of brain activity, highs and lows in body temperature. Some rhythms are *circadian* (from the Latin words *circa* meaning "about" and *dies* meaning "day"). A **circadian rhythm** *is a daily behavioral or physiological cycle; an example is the 24-hour sleep/wake cycle.*

One circumstance in which the circadian rhythm of the human sleep/wake cycle may become desynchronized is when we take a long cross-country or transoceanic flight. If you fly from Los Angeles to New York and then go to bed at 11 P.M. eastern standard time, you may have trouble falling asleep because your body is still on Pacific time. Even if you sleep for 8 hours that night, you may find it hard to wake up at 7 A.M. eastern time, because your body

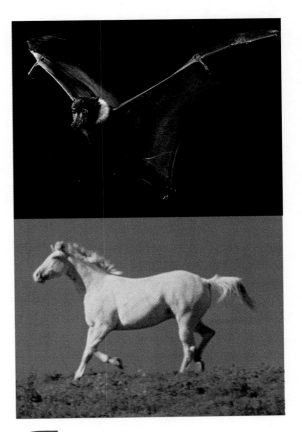

$\mathcal{F}$igure 4.2

From Bats to Horses: The Wide Range of Sleep in Animals

Animal	Hours of Sleep Per 24-Hour Period
Bat	19.9
Armadillo	18.5
Cat	14.5
Fox	9.8
Rhesus monkey	9.6
Rabbit	8.4
Human	8.0
Cow	3.9
Sheep	3.8
Horse	2.9

Sleep researchers are recording Randy Gardner's (he's the person doing the pushups) behavior during his 264-hour period of sleep deprivation. Most people who try to stay up even one night have difficulty remaining awake from 3 to 6 A.M. Why shouldn't you follow Gardner's sleep deprivation example?

thinks it is 4 A.M. If you stay in New York for several days, your body will adjust to the new schedule.

The phase shift that occurred when you flew from Los Angeles to New York means your body time is out of phase, or synchronization, with clock time. When jet lag occurs, it is the result of two or more body rhythms being out of sync. You usually go to bed when your body temperature begins to drop, but, in your new location, you may be trying to go to bed when it is rising. When you wake up in the morning, your adrenal glands release large doses of cortisol. In your new geographical location, the glands may be releasing this chemical just as you are getting ready for bed at night.

Another circumstance in which circadian rhythms may become desynchronized is when shift workers change their work hours. A number of near-accidents in air travel have been associated with pilots who have not yet become synchronized to their new shift and are not working as efficiently as usual. Shift rotation might have been one of the causes of the nuclear accident at Three Mile Island (Moore-Ede, Sulzman, & Fuller, 1982). The team of workers monitoring the nuclear plant when the incident took place had been placed on night shift just after a 6-week period of constant shift rotation.

Not all shift workers are affected equally (Monk, 1993). A small proportion actually prefer shift work. People over 50, those who require more than 9 hours of sleep a night, and those with a tendency to be "morning types" (get up early, go to bed early) are the most adversely affected by shift work.

For those who are shift workers, what can help them adjust to their schedule? Use of daylight levels of artificial illumination at work on the night shift and precise specification of 8 hours of total darkness at home from 9 A.M. to 5 P.M. can dramatically speed up the realignment of circadian rhythms (Czeilser & others, 1990). Although sleeping pills can improve daytime sleep, they don't affect circadian realignment and their long-term use is not recommended.

As researchers became intrigued by the role of biological rhythms, they naturally were curious about what happens when an individual is completely isolated from clocks, calendars, night, the moon, the sun, and all indices of time. A number of experiments have focused on such isolation experiences (Kales, 1970; Siffre, 1975).

French scientist Michel Siffre entered Midnight Cave near Del Rio, Texas, on February 14, 1972. A small nylon tent deep within the cave was Siffre's home for 6 months. Because Siffre could not see or sense the sun rising and setting in the cave, he began to live by biological cycles instead of by days. When Siffre wanted to go to sleep, he called the support crew outside and told them to turn off the lights in the cave. Just before he went to sleep, he attached electrodes to his scalp so his sleep cycles could be recorded. When he woke up, he called the support crew and asked them to turn on the cave's lights.

Siffre referred to each one of his sleep/wake cycles as a day. Siffre's days closely resembled a 24-hour cycle throughout the 6 months in the cave, although they were slightly longer and more varied toward the end of the 6 months. Near the end of his stay in the cave, occasionally Siffre's days were very long, but most still averaged about 28 hours.

After 6 months, Siffre misjudged which month it was. It was August, but he thought it was only July. On day 151 of Siffre's cave experience, the caveman made this entry into a diary:

> Gerard tells me it is August 10 . . . and the experiment is concluded; I am confused; I believed it to be mid-July. Then, as the truth sinks in, comes a flood of relief.

Siffre's comments about life in the cave reflect the cave's eeriness and the confusion such experiences create:

> You live following your mind . . . you have not the alternance of day and night . . . It's all in your brain . . . no sound, nothing . . . darkness completely.

The photograph shows the interior of the cave where Michel Siffre lived for six months. What were Siffre's sleep/wake cycles like?

Interestingly, the natural circadian rhythm of most animals, including humans, is 25 to 26 hours, but our internal clocks easily adapt to the 24-hour rhythms (light, sounds, warmth) of the turning earth. When we are isolated from environmental cues, our sleep/wake cycles continue to be rather constant but typically longer than 24 hours, as the experience of Michel Siffre showed.

Sleep Deprivation and Sleep Needs

How long can people go without sleep and still function? One 17-year-old high school student, Randy Gardner, went without sleep for 264 hours (about 11 days), the longest observed period of total sleep deprivation. He did it as part of a science fair project (Dement, 1978). Carefully monitored by sleep researchers, Randy did suffer some hallucinations, speech problems, and movement problems. However, on the last night Gardner played arcade games with sleep researcher William Dement and consistently beat him. Randy recovered fully after a 14 hour 40 minute restorative sleep. Randy's story is exceptional in that he was able to maintain a high level of physical activity and received national TV coverage, which helped him stay awake. Even then, he almost fell asleep several nights, but his observers would not let him close his eyes. In more normal circumstances, individuals have far more difficulty staying awake all night, especially between 3:00 and 6:00 A.M.

Although Randy Gardner was able to go about 11 days without sleep, the following discussion should convince you that even getting 60 to 90 minutes less sleep than you need each night can harm your ability to optimally perform the next day. As we also will see, it doesn't take very long for sleep deprivation to play havoc with our lives.

In the view of sleep researcher James Maas (1998), at least 50 percent of the American population is sleep deprived and a similar proportion report trouble sleeping on any given night. He argues that our quality of life, if not life itself, is jeopardized by sleep deprivation. With adequate sleep, you give yourself the opportunity to perform at peak level the next day.

On-Line Circadian Rhythm Experiment
Biological Clocks and Rhythms

The average American gets just under 7 hours of sleep a night (National Commission on Sleep Disorders Research, 1993). An increasing number of sleep researchers believe people need to deposit at least 8 hours of sleep in their nightly sleep debt account to stay fully alert and optimize their performance the next day (Maas, 1998). A sleep debt can build quickly, not unlike finance charges on an unpaid bank balance, when you are burning the candle at both ends. Consider a medical technician who tried to get by on about 4 hours of sleep a night—ironically, at a sleep disorders center—so she could take care of her infant daughter during the day. Before long, she developed heart palpitations, dizziness, a fear of driving, and wide mood swings from being up 20 hours a day.

Some sleep researchers now argue that our performance can be optimized by sleeping more than 8 hours a day. At one sleep disorders research center, the alertness of 8-hour sleepers who claimed to be well-rested increased when they added 2 more hours to their nightly sleep total (Roehrs & Roth, 1998).

Why are we getting too little sleep? Work pressures, school pressures, family obligations, and social obligations often lead to long hours of wakefulness and irregular sleep/wake schedules. Not having enough hours to do all we want to in a day, we cheat on our sleep. Most people need to get about 60 to 90 minutes more sleep each day than they presently get.

Stages of Sleep

Stages of sleep correspond to massive electrophysical changes throughout the brain, as the fast, irregular, and low-amplitude activity of wakefulness is replaced by the regular, slow, high-amplitude waves of deep sleep. The invention of the electroencephalograph (EEG) led to some major breakthroughs in understanding sleep by revealing how the brain's electrical activity changes during sleep ◀|||| P. 70. Figure 4.3 shows the EEG patterns for various sleep stages.

Through the Eyes of Psychologists

James Maas, *Cornell University*

"Sleep plays a major role in preparing the body and brain for an alert, productive, psychologically, and physiologically healthy tomorrow."

Alpha waves *make up the EEG pattern of individuals who are awake but relaxed.* As your breathing slows and your brain waves slow further, you enter the somewhat irregular wave pattern of stage 1 sleep. **Sleep spindles** *are brief bursts of higher-frequency waves that periodically occur during stage 2 sleep.* Stage 2 lasts up to 20 minutes. Beginning in stage 3 and increasingly in stage 4, **delta waves,** *which are large, slow brain waves associated with deep sleep, appear.* Together, stages 3 and 4 are often referred to as "deep sleep." The sleeper who awakens during deep sleep often appears confused, and it is during stage 4 sleep that sleepwalking, sleeptalking, and bed-wetting most often occur.

After about 90 minutes of sleep, much of which is spent in stages 3 and 4, the sleeper moves restlessly and drifts up through the sleep stages toward wakefulness. But instead of reentering stage 1, the person enters a different form of sleep called "rapid eye movement" (REM) sleep. **REM sleep** *is a periodic, active stage of sleep during which dreaming occurs.* During REM sleep, the EEG pattern shows fast waves similar to those of relaxed wakefulness and the sleeper's eyeballs move up and down and from left to right (see figure 4.4).

A person who is awakened during REM sleep is more likely to report having dreamed than when awakened at any other stage. Even people who claim they rarely dream frequently report dreaming when they are awakened during REM sleep. The longer the period of REM sleep, the more likely a person

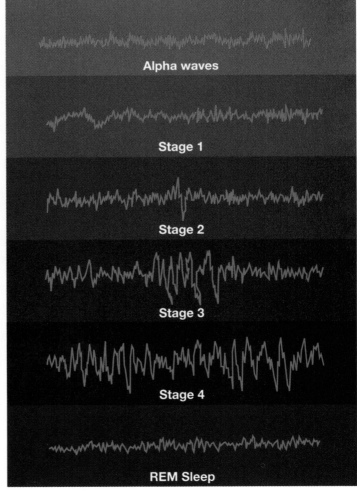

Figure 4.3
Stages of Sleep and EEG Recordings of Brain Waves

Note: Above: An individual being monitored in a sleep experiment. Right: EEG recordings of brain waves in different stages of sleep.

Figure 4.4
REM Sleep
During REM sleep, our eyes move rapidly as if we were observing the images we see moving in our dreams.

Figure 4.5
The Changing Rhythms of Sleep
During a typical night's sleep, REM sleep (shown in red) increases during the latter part of the night. Stages 3 and 4 dominate sleep early in the night but decrease dramatically toward the end of a night's sleep.

will report dreaming. Dreams do occur during slow-wave or non-REM sleep, but the frequency of dreams in the other stages is relatively low.

So far we have described a normal cycle of sleep, which consists of four stages, plus REM sleep. There are several important points to remember about the nature of these stages (see figure 4.5). One of these cycles lasts about 90 minutes and recurs several times during the night. The amount of deep sleep (stage 4) is much greater in the first half of a night's sleep than in the second half. The majority of REM sleep takes place during the latter part of a night's sleep, when the REM period becomes progressively longer. The night's first REM period might last for only 10 minutes, the final REM period for as long as an hour.

The amount of REM sleep changes over the life span. As indicated in figure 4.6, the percentage of total sleep made up of REM sleep is especially large in early infancy (almost 8 hours). Elderly adults engage in less than 1 hour of REM sleep a night. Figure 4.6 also reveals how the amount of total sleep changes from approximately 16 hours at the beginning of infancy to less than 6 hours in old age.

These dramatic developmental changes in REM sleep raise questions about its function. For young infants, REM sleep might play a role in stimulating the brain and contributing to its growth. Remember from chapter 1 that an enriched environment contributes to brain growth. Because most of a young infant's time is spent in sleep, REM sleep could be nature's way of stimulating the brain.

REM sleep also might contribute to memory. Researchers have presented individuals with unique phrases before they go to bed (Empson & Clarke, 1970). When they are awakened just before they begin REM sleep, they remember less the next morning than when they are awakened during the other sleep stages.

Through the Eyes of Psychologists
Mary Carskadon,
Brown University

"Of particular importance is the education of people of all ages about healthy approaches to sleep behavior."

The Neural Basis of Sleep

For many years researchers thought sleep occurred in the absence of enough sensory stimulation to keep the brain awake. Without stimuli, the brain was believed to just "slow down," producing sleep. But researchers realized that sleep comes and goes without any obvious change in the amount of environmental stimulation. Theorists suggested we might have an internal "activating system" in the reticular formation that keeps the brain activated, or awake, all day (Hobson & McCarley, 1977). According to this theory, "fatigue" of the so-called activating system, or an accumulation of some "sleep toxin" that chemically depressed the activating system, induced sleep.

The contemporary view of sleep is radically different. As you have learned, the brain does not "stop" during sleep, but instead carries out complex processes that produce both REM and non-REM sleep behaviors. In fact, at the cellular level, many neurons fire faster during sleep than in a waking state.

The puzzle is not completely solved, but some of the major pieces of the brain's machinery involved in sleep have been identified. Non-REM sleep, for example, requires the participation of neurons in both the forebrain and the medulla. REM sleep is a period of especially intense brain activity, also requiring the cooperation of a number of brain systems. To read further about the brain's role in sleep and in learning, turn to Explorations in Psychology.

Sleep Disorders

Sleep Disorders

A 1995 Gallup poll found that 49 percent of American adults were suffering from sleep disorders, a 15 percent increase from 1991. Why the increase in sleep disorders? The most plausible reasons are the increasingly frantic pace of work, work pressures, and an aging population (sleep disorders are more common in the elderly) (Aldrich, 1999). Somewhat amazingly, 95 percent of individuals with sleep disorders go undiagnosed and untreated, many of them struggling through the day feeling unmotivated and exhausted (National Commission on Sleep Disorders Research, 1993).

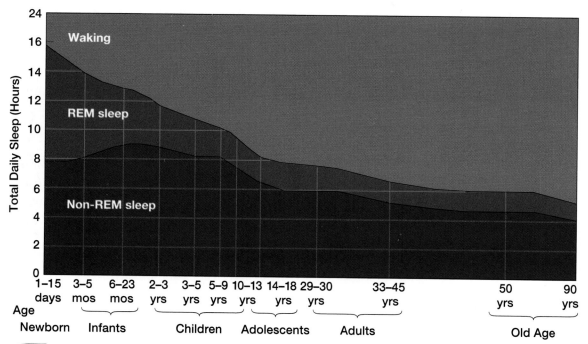

$\mathcal{F}$igure 4.6
Sleep Across the Human Life Span

EXPLORATIONS IN PSYCHOLOGY
Can We Learn While We Are Asleep?

KING HENRY IV OF FRANCE once said, "Great eaters and great sleepers are incapable of anything else that's great." But King Henry had not seen the recent sleep research that raises the possibility that learning might take place while we are asleep.

Two recent studies, one on rats and one on college students, demonstrated the value of sleep in strengthening memories from the previous day. To remember where you have been or learn a new skill, sleep seems to help.

In one of the studies, researchers fitted rats with recording devices that detected simultaneous firings of nerve cells in the hippocampus, a brain structure involved in remembering a new place (Wilson & McNaughton, 1994). When the rats were allowed to explore new locations, different hippocampus cells fired electrical impulses. The researchers found that the nerve cells most likely to fire together during sleep were the ones that fired together during daytime exploration. Apparently, the rat's brain uses sleep as an opportunity to strengthen memories from the previous day's activities.

This type of memory—of places, events, or facts—is called *declarative memory.* Neuroscientists have documented that the hippocampus plays an important role in declarative memory. Another type of memory, *procedural memory,* which involves learning skills or habits, like driving a car, does not seem to be based in the hippocampus. Rather, such repetition of tasks trains the brain's outer layer of "thinking" nerve cells to perform the job more automatically.

Researchers had thought that sleep strengthens declarative memory, but they saw no reason why sleep should improve procedural memory. However, in one recent study the results suggested otherwise (Karni & others, 1994). College students were trained to recognize subtle differences in visual patterns: to identify the shape of a figure in a pattern. They improved their performance with practice, and performed the task better after a good night's sleep than at the end of the previous day's practice session, suggesting that their brains were doing

something during sleep to enhance the newly learned skill. Actually, earlier research had shown that performance improves after an 8- to 10-hour lag, even if the lag is during the day and the performers are awake during it. The new study documented that the improvement also occurs during sleep.

In this chapter, we have learned that all sleep is not alike—for example, some is slow-wave sleep, other involves REM sleep. Might one phase of sleep enhance learning more than others? In the learning-task sleep study, the researchers monitored the students' brain waves to detect when REM sleep was occurring and rang a bell anytime they began to drift off into REM sleep (Karni & others, 1994). In another trial, the bell went off only during slow-wave sleep.

Apart from the obvious results—such as the students' being a little testy the next day from having their sleep interrupted—some interesting findings emerged in their ability to tell the shape of a pattern. If slow-wave sleep was disrupted, the students still scored better on the tasks than they had the previous day. But if REM sleep was disrupted, the sleep did the students no good and their skill was not improved. Thus, something about REM sleep might hold a key to strengthening this type of memory. Old skills, in which memories are presumably already strong enough, were not diminished by REM sleep deprivation in this study. So, presumably, REM sleep facilitates the learning of new skills (Siegfried, 1994).

But what about material that is presented to individuals during sleep? Could you possibly enhance your performance on tests or learn a foreign language by being presented with information while you are sleeping? The research evidence suggests that sleep learning is ineffective when measured in terms of an individual's ability to consciously remember material presented during sleep (Druckman & Bjork, 1994). So playing back a tape recording of your professor's lecture while you are sleeping will not improve your knowledge of the material.

Sometimes the symptoms of sleep disorders are bizarre and sufferers might not understand their own actions (Maas, 1998). They might be afraid of the stigma associated with their behavior and be unwilling to admit they have a problem. Following are some real-life experiences of individuals with sleep disorders (American Sleep Disorders Association, 1998):

—A sleeping woman who awakened to find herself in a grocery store aisle wheeling a cart filled with 56 boxes of cornflakes
—An air traffic controller whose only way to keep from falling asleep at work was to stand up all night and never sit down

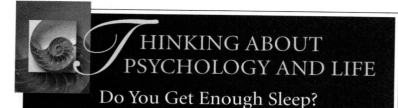

THINKING ABOUT PSYCHOLOGY AND LIFE

Do You Get Enough Sleep?

MANY COLLEGE STUDENTS don't get enough sleep. In a national poll of college freshmen, more than 80 percent said they stayed up all night at least once during the year (Sax & others, 1995). To evaluate whether you are sleep deprived, answer the following questions yes or no.

Yes   No

____ ____ I need an alarm clock to wake up at the appropriate time.
____ ____ It's a struggle for me to get out of bed in the morning.
____ ____ I feel tired, irritable, and stressed out during the week.
____ ____ I have trouble concentrating.
____ ____ I have trouble remembering.
____ ____ I feel slow with critical thinking, problem solving, and being creative.
____ ____ I often fall asleep watching TV.
____ ____ I often fall asleep in boring meetings or lectures in warm rooms.
____ ____ I often fall asleep after heavy meals or after low doses of alcohol.
____ ____ I often fall asleep within five minutes of getting into bed.
____ ____ I often feel drowsy while driving.
____ ____ I often sleep extra hours on weekend mornings.
____ ____ I often need a nap to get through the day.
____ ____ I have dark circles around my eyes.

According to psychologist James Maas (1998), who developed this quiz, if you responded yes to three or more of these items you probably aren't getting enough sleep. Later in the chapter we will describe some good strategies for reducing insomnia that will help you get the sleep you need to optimize your performance the next day and be healthy.

—A man in the back of a moving trailer who sleepwalked out the back door and was killed on the highway

At first glance, these experiences may seem humorous but sleep disorders can cause a great deal of suffering and even death as it did for the sleepwalker.

Insomnia   **Insomnia** *is a common sleep problem; put simply, it is the inability to sleep.* Insomnia can involve a problem in falling asleep, waking up during the night, or waking up too early (Davies, 1999). As many as one in five Americans has insomnia. It is more common among women, older adults, thin people, depressed or stressed people, and people who are poor (Devries, 1998).

We spend large sums of money, especially for drugs, trying to sleep better (Graber, Garber, & Govin, 1999). Many sleep experts now believe that physicians have been too quick to prescribe sedatives for insomniacs. Sedatives reduce the amount of time a person spends in stage 4 and REM sleep, and can disrupt the restfulness of sleep. There is some danger of overdose, and over time sedatives lose their effectiveness, requiring ever greater dosages to achieve the same effect. Sedatives and nonprescription sleeping pills should be used with caution and only for short-term sleep problems.

If possible, you should avoid taking sleeping pills for insomnia, because they often lead to fragmented sleep and tolerance. Also, when a person stops using them after several nights, bad dreams and even more insomnia are likely to appear. Sleep experts say they can be used on a temporary basis for short-term insomnia, such as jet lag, the loss of a loved one, or anticipation of a stressful event, such as giving a speech. However, sleeping pills should never be used for chronic insomnia, which lasts 6 months or more.

Recently, there has been considerable interest in the hormone *melatonin* for reducing insomnia. Melatonin is naturally secreted by the brain's pineal gland in response to darkness. Not only has melatonin been touted as an antidote for insomnia, it also has been promoted as an anti-aging remedy. Research on melatonin's role in inducing sleep and slowing aging is in its early phases with no definitive conclusions reached as yet. One of the potential risks of melatonin is its irregular quality in health-food stores.

Some good strategies for reducing insomnia are shown in figure 4.7.

Sleepwalking and Sleeptalking   **Somnambulism** *is the formal term for sleepwalking, which occurs during the deepest stages of sleep.* For many years experts believed somnambulists were acting out their dreams. But somnambulism occurs during stages 3 and 4, early in the night, the time when a person is least likely to dream (Chambers, 2000). Sleepwalking is most common in children, although some adults also sleepwalk. Most children outgrow the problem without having to seek professional help. Except for the danger of accidents while wandering about in the dark, there is nothing really abnormal about sleepwalking. It is safe to awaken sleepwalkers, and it's probably a good idea since they might harm themselves as they roam through the night (Swanson, 1999).

The most effective treatment for sleepwalking is to institute safety measures, such as erecting gates and locking all doors and windows. Hypnosis, which we will discuss later in the chapter, might be helpful with adults (Mindell, 1996).

Another quirky night behavior is sleeptalking. Most sleeptalkers are young adults, but sleeptalkers come in all ages. If you interrogated a sleeptalker, could you find out what he did last Thursday night? Probably not (Perlis, 2000). Although he may speak to you and make fairly coherent statements, the sleeptalker is soundly asleep. Most likely the sleeptalker will mumble some response to your question, but don't count on its accuracy.

Nightmares and Night Terrors

A **nightmare** *is a frightening dream that awakens the sleeper from REM sleep.* The nightmare's content invariably involves some danger— the dreamer is chased, robbed, raped, murdered, or thrown off a cliff. Nightmares are common. Most of us have had them, especially when we were young children. Nightmares peak at 3 to 6 years of age and then decline, although the average college student experiences 4 to 8 nightmares a year and the average adult 25 years and older has 1 or 2 a year (Hartmann, 1993). When people report an increase in the number of nightmares they have, or worsening nightmares, they often are associated with an increase in stress in their lives (such as loss of a relationship, conflict, or some type of negative event).

At the beginning of this chapter, we described the tragic night terror of Colin Kemp. Remember that a **night terror** *is characterized by sudden arousal from sleep and intense fear, usually accompanied by a number of physiological reactions such as rapid heart rate and breathing, loud screams, heavy perspiration, and physical movement.* Night terrors (also called sleep terrors) are less common than nightmares. Unlike nightmares, night terrors occur in slow-wave, non-REM sleep. As many as 6 percent of children have night terrors, with the peak at 5 to 7 years of age and a decrease thereafter. For both nightmares and night terrors, try to awaken and provide soothing reassurance to the person. Children usually do not remember their night terrors in the morning.

Treatment for nightmares and night terrors in adults often involves the use of anxiety reduction techniques, such as relaxation and imagery. We will describe how these techniques are carried out in chapter 5 ("Learning") and chapter 12 ("Therapies").

Narcolepsy

Narcolepsy *is the overpowering urge to fall asleep.* The urge is so strong that the person may fall asleep while talking or standing up. Narcoleptics immediately enter REM sleep rather than moving through the first four sleep stages. Researchers suspect that narcolepsy is inherited, because it runs in families. Treatment of narcolepsy often involves counseling to discover potential causes of the excessive sleepiness. Short-term use of stimulant medications sometimes is an effective treatment of daytime sleepiness.

Sleep Apnea

Sleep apnea *is a sleep disorder in which individuals stop breathing because the windpipe fails to open or brain processes involved in respiration fail to work properly.* Individuals with sleep apnea experience numerous brief awakenings during the night so they can breathe better, although they are not usually aware of their awakened state. During the day these people may feel sleepy because they were deprived of sleep at night. This disorder is most common among infants and people over the age of 65 (Cartwright, 2000).

Thirty million Americans suffer from sleep apnea, a temporary cessation of breathing during sleep that is potentially life-threatening, especially if it occurs when the individual has taken a sleeping pill or had too much alcohol. Being overweight also is a risk factor for sleep apnea (Culebras, 1996).

1. Reduce stress as much as possible
2. Exercise regularly (but not just before you go to bed)
3. Keep mentally stimulated during the day
4. Become a good time manager
5. Eat a proper diet
6. Stop smoking
7. Reduce caffeine intake
8. Avoid alcohol, especially near bedtime
9. Take a warm bath before bed
10. Maintain a relaxing atmosphere in the bedroom
11. Clear your mind at bedtime
12. Before going to bed, engage in a relaxation technique such as listening to a tape designed for relaxation
13. Learn to value sleep
14. If necessary, contact the health service at your college or university for advice about your sleeping problem

Figure 4.7
Strategies for Reducing Insomnia

Sleep Apnea

$\mathcal{S}$UMMARY $\mathcal{T}$ABLE 4.1
States of Consciousness and Sleep

Concept	Processes/ Related Ideas	Characteristics/Description
States of Consciousness	Their Nature	Consciousness is awareness of both external and internal stimuli and events. Consciousness is a rich, complex landscape of the mind, consisting of processes at varying levels of awareness. Among the many forms of consciousness are controlled processes, automatic processes, daydreaming, altered states of consciousness, sleep and dreams, unconscious thought (Freudian), and unconsciousness (non-Freudian, such as an anesthetized state).
Sleep	Why Do We Sleep?	We sleep for restoration and repair (repair theory) and to keep us from wasting energy and risking harm during the time of day or night to which we are not adapted (ecological theory).
	Sleep and Circadian Rhythms	A circadian rhythm is a cycle of about 24 hours. The human sleep/wake cycle is an important circadian rhythm. This cycle can become desynchronized. Individuals isolated in caves for months continue to approximate a 24-hour cycle, although at times the cycle is slightly longer.
	Sleep Deprivation and Sleep Needs	Individuals have gone without sleep as long as 11 days and, after a restorative sleep, seem to show no serious ill effects. In more normal circumstances, individuals have more difficulty staying awake all night, especially from 3 to 6 A.M. The average American gets just under 7 hours of sleep a night. An increasing number of sleep researchers believe that 8 hours or more are needed to function optimally the next day. Sleep debts can build quickly and jeopardize health and well-being.
	Stages of Sleep	Different stages of sleep are measured by the electroencephalograph (EEG), which measures the brain's electrical activity. Alpha waves occur when we are in a relaxed state. When we sleep we move from light sleep in stage 1 to deep sleep in stage 4 (delta waves). Then we go directly into REM sleep, where dreams occur. Each night we go through a number of these sleep cycles. REM sleep peaks in early infancy and then declines. REM sleep may be involved in the brain's growth and memory.
	The Neural Basis of Sleep	Early views emphasized environmental stimulation and subsequently an internal activating system in the reticular formation. The contemporary view states that the brain is actively engaged in producing sleep behaviors, and different neurotransmitters are involved.
	Sleep Disorders	Among the most prominent are insomnia, sleepwalking and sleeptalking, nightmares and night terrors, narcolepsy, and sleep apnea.

Treatment of sleep apnea includes surgery to remove the airway obstruction, weight loss for individuals in which obesity plays a role, position restriction for individuals in which the apnea occurs only in certain positions, avoidance of alcohol and other depressant drugs, nasal decongestants, anti-inflammatory agents, and other pharmacological agents.

At this point we have discussed many ideas about states of consciousness and sleep. An overview of these ideas is presented in summary table 4.1. We've toured the fascinating world of sleep and seen that dreams usually occur during REM sleep. Let's now explore the fascinating world of dreams in greater detail.

Dreams

Ever since the dawn of language, dreams have been imbued with historical, personal, and religious significance. As early as 5000 B.C. Babylonians recorded and interpreted their dreams on clay tablets. Egyptians built temples in honor of Serapis, the god of dreams. People occasionally slept in these temples in the hope that Serapis would appear in their dreams and either heal them or tell them what to do to be healed. Dreams are described at length in more than seventy passages in the Bible, and in many primitive cultures dreams are an extension of reality. For example, there is an account of an African chief who dreamed that he had visited England. On awakening, he ordered a wardrobe of European clothes. As he walked through the village in his new wardrobe, he was congratulated for having made the trip. Similarly, Cherokee Indians who dreamed of being bitten by a snake were treated for the snakebite.

Today, we still try to figure out what dreams mean. Much of the interest stems from psychoanalysts who have probed the unconscious mind to understand the symbolic content of dreams. Although we do have concrete information regarding sleep stages, there is little scientific data to explain why we dream or what the dreams mean ◀▥ P. 38.

DREAMS

The Interpretation of Dreams   More About Dreams

The Interpretation of Dreams

Many of us dismiss the nightly excursion into the world of dreams as a second-rate mental activity, unworthy of our rational selves. By focusing only on the less mysterious waking world, we deny ourselves the opportunity of chance encounters with distant friends, remote places, dead relatives, gods, and demons. But what, if anything, do our dreams really mean? Let's now explore three approaches that attempt to explain the nature of dreaming.

Dream Analysis

Freud's Theory   In Freud's (1900) theory, the reason we dream is **wish fulfillment,** *an unconscious attempt to fulfill needs (especially for sex and aggression) that cannot be expressed, or go ungratified during waking hours.* For example, people who are sexually inhibited while awake would likely have dreams with erotic content. Those who have strong aggressive tendencies but hold anger in while awake likely would have dreams filled with violence and hostility. Freud also stressed that dreams often contain memories of infancy and childhood experiences, especially events associated with parents. And he said our dreams frequently contain information from the day or two preceding the dream. In his view, many of our dreams reflect combinations of these distant early experiences with our parents and more recent daily events (Antrobus, 2000). Freud believed that the task of dream interpretation is a difficult one because we successfully disguise wish fulfillment when we dream. Note that the term *wish fulfillment* does not mean that all dreams reflect hopes; some reflect fears.

Freud distinguished between a dream's manifest and latent content. **Manifest content** *is the dream's surface content, which contains dream symbols that distort and disguise the dream's true meaning.* **Latent content** *is the dream's hidden content, its unconscious meaning.* For example, in Freud's view, a person might have a dream that included snakes and neckties. The snakes and neckties are the dream's manifest content. Another person might have a dream about a king or a president. However, Freud said that such dreams are symbols for underlying latent content (in these cases the snakes and neckties symbolize a male's genitals and the king or president symbolized a father or the therapist). Freud thought that once the therapist understood a client's symbolism, the nature of the dream then could be interpreted.

A final point to be made about Freud's dream theory involves its scientific merit. Researchers have found it extremely difficult to devise appropriate methods to even attempt to verify his dream theory.

Cognitive Theory

The **cognitive theory of dreaming** *proposes that dreaming can best be understood by relying on the same cognitive concepts that are used in studying the waking mind.* That is, dreaming involves processing information, memory, and possibly problem solving. Unlike in Freud's theory, in the cognitive theory of dreaming there is no search for the hidden, symbolic content of dreams (Foulkes, 1993, 1999).

Rather than being an arena in which to play out our unsatisfied needs, dreams might be a mental realm where we can solve problems and think creatively. For example, the Scottish author Robert Louis Stevenson (1850–1894) claimed he got the idea for Dr. Jekyll and Mr. Hyde in a dream. Elias Howe, attempting to invent a machine that sewed, reportedly dreamed he was captured by savages carrying spears with holes in their tips. Upon waking, Howe realized he should place the hole for the thread at the end of the needle, not the middle. Dreams may spark such gifts of inspiration because, in unique and creative ways, they weave together current experiences with the past.

Activation-Synthesis Theory

Activation-synthesis theory *states that dreams are powered by the spontaneous firing of neurons.* Dreams reflect the brain's efforts to make sense out of or find meaning in the neural activity that takes place during sleep. In this view, the brain's activity involves a great deal of random activity. Dreams are an attempt to make sense of this chaos (Hobson, 2000; McCarley, 1989). The sudden, uncoordinated eye movements of REM sleep make the dreamworld move in odd ways; for instance, it might include magic carpets over an undulating landscape. Dreams tend to truncate, dissolve, or shift suddenly in midstream. Freud explained this as the dreamer's attempt to elude the unpleasant and the taboo. In activation-synthesis theory, this shifting is due to normal cycles of neural activation (Hobson, 1999). One group of cells simply runs its course, another set is activated and a new dream landscape emerges. In sum, in the activation-synthesis view, dreams are merely a glitzy side show, not the main act (Hooper & Teresi, 1993).

More About Dreams

**The Study of Dreams
Exploring Dreams**

The world of dreams raises some intriguing questions. Let's explore four of these.

Do People Dream in Color?

Some people say they dream only in black and white, but virtually everyone's dreams contain color. However, we often forget the color by the time we awaken and recall the dream. Some people claim that certain colors have fixed meanings in their dreams—white for purity, red for passion, green for vitality, black for evil or death, for example. However, no evidence has been found to support this belief. Red may stand for passion in one dream, danger in another, and anger in yet another dream.

Do Animals Dream?

It is impossible to say for certain whether or not animals dream; we know they have periods of REM sleep, so it is possible that they do. But dogs' twitching and howling during sleep, for instance, should not be taken as evidence that they necessarily are dreaming.

Do Males and Females Dream About Different Things?

According to extensive assessments of what males and females dream about, the dreams of males are more likely than those of females to include content about males, aggression, torso/anatomy, sexuality, and dreamer-involved success (Domhoff & Schneider, 1998). The dream content of females is more likely to include females, friends, and victimization. In these surveys, about 80 percent of the dreams of both males and females have negative emotions present.

Why Can't We Remember All of Our Dreams?

Everyone dreams, but some of us remember our dreams better than others. It's not surprising that no one remembers all their dreams, since dreaming occurs at such a low level of consciousness. Psychoanalytic theory suggests we forget most of our dreams because they are threatening, but there is no evidence to support this belief. We remember our

Summary Table 4.2
Dreams

Concept	Processes/Related Ideas	Characteristics/Description
The Interpretation of Dreams	Freud's Theory	Freud's psychoanalytic theory states that dreams are the unconscious wish fulfillment of needs unmet during waking states. Freud believed that dreams often involve a combination of early childhood experiences and daily residue. He stressed that dreams have rich, symbolic content and distinguished between a dream's manifest content and latent content. Researchers have found it extremely difficult to devise appropriate methods to even attempt to verify Freud's dream theory.
	Cognitive Theory	Cognitive theory proposes that dreaming can best be understood by relying on the same cognitive concepts that are used in studying the waking mind. That is, dreaming involves processing information, memory, and possibly problem solving.
	Activation-Synthesis Theory	This theory states that dreams are powered by the spontaneous firing of neurons. Dreams reflect the brain's efforts to make sense out of or find meaning in the neural activity that takes place during sleep.
More About Dreams	Do People Dream in Color?	Virtually everyone's dreams contain color. Colors don't have fixed meanings in dreams.
	Do Animals Dream?	It is impossible to say whether animals dream or not, although they do have periods of REM sleep.
	Do Females and Males Dream About Different Things?	Males' dreams have more content about males, aggression, torso/anatomy, sexuality, and dreamer-involved success. Females' dreams are more likely to be about females, friends, and victimization.
	Why Can't We Remember All of Our Dreams?	We can't remember them because dreaming occurs at such a low level of consciousness. We remember our dreams best when we are awakened during or just after a dream.

dreams best when we are awakened during or just after a dream. Similarly, the dreams we have just before we awaken are the ones we are most likely to remember. People whose sleep cycles have long periods between their last REM stage and awakening are more likely to report they don't dream at all or rarely remember their dreams.

At this point we have studied a number of ideas about dreaming. An overview of these ideas is presented in summary table 4.2. Next, we will turn our attention to hypnosis.

Hypnosis

A young cancer patient is about to undergo a painful bone marrow transplant procedure. A man directs the boy's attention, asking him to breathe with him and listen carefully. The boy becomes absorbed in a pleasant fantasy—he is riding a motorcycle over a huge pizza, dodging anchovies and maneuvering around chunks of mozzarella. Minutes later the procedure is over. The boy is relaxed and feels good about his self-control. The doctor successfully used hypnosis as a technique to help the young cancer patient control pain.

Definition and History

Hypnosis *is a psychological state of altered attention and awareness in which the individual is unusually receptive to suggestions.* Hypnosis has been used since the beginning of recorded history. It has been associated with religious ceremonies, magic, the supernatural, and many erroneous theories. Today hypnosis is recognized as a legitimate process in psychology and medicine, although much is yet to be learned about how it works (Chaves, 2000; Kirsch & Linn, 1998).

In the eighteenth century the Austrian physician Friedrich Anton Mesmer cured his patients by passing magnets over their bodies. Mesmer said the problems were cured by "animal magnetism," an intangible force that passes from therapist to patient. In reality, the cures were due to some form of hypnotic suggestion. Mesmer's claims were investigated by a committee appointed by the French Academy of Science. The committee agreed that Mesmer's treatment was effective; however, they disputed his theoretical claims about animal magnetism and prohibited him from practicing in Paris. Mesmer's theory of animal magnetism was called mesmerism, and even today we use the term *mesmerized* to mean hypnotized or enthralled.

The Hypnotic State: Features and Individual Differences

There are four requirements for hypnosis to succeed. First, distractions are minimized and the person to be hypnotized is made comfortable. Second, the person is told to concentrate on something specific, such as an imagined scene or the ticking of a watch. Third, the individual is told what to expect in the hypnotic state (such as relaxation or a pleasant floating sensation). Fourth, the hypnotist suggests certain events or feelings that he knows will occur or observes occurring (such as "Your eyes are getting tired"). When the suggested effects occur, the individual interprets them as being caused by the hypnotist's suggestions and accepts them as an indication that something is happening. This increases the person's expectations that the hypnotism will make things happen in the future and makes him even more suggestible.

Do you think you could be hypnotized? What about your friends—are they more or less likely to be influenced by hypnosis than you? For as long as hypnosis has been studied, about 200 years, we've known that some people are more easily hypnotized than others. In fact, about 10 to 20 percent of the population are very susceptible to hypnosis, 10 percent or less cannot be hypnotized at all, and the remainder fall somewhere in between (Hilgard, 1965). There is no simple way to tell whether you can be hypnotized. But if you have the capacity to immerse yourself in imaginative activities—listening to a favorite piece of music or reading a novel, for example—you are a likely candidate. People susceptible to hypnosis become completely absorbed in what they are doing, removing the boundaries between themselves and what they are experiencing in their environment.

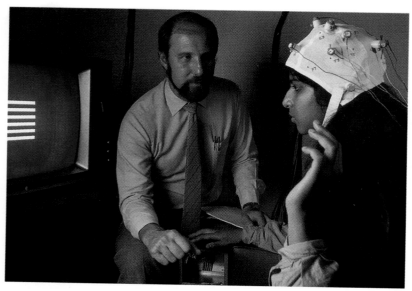

In special process theory, hypnotic responses, elicited by suggestions, are involuntary. In the situation shown here, the brain activity of a hypnotized individual is being monitored.

Theories of Hypnosis

Ever since Anton Mesmer proposed his theory of "animal magnetism," psychologists have been trying to figure out why hypnosis works. Contemporary theorists are divided on their answers to the following question: Is hypnosis a special cognitive state, or is it simply a form of learned social behavior?

Special Process Theory

Ernest Hilgard (1977) proposed the **special process theory,** *which states that hypnotic behavior involves a special cognitive state that is different than nonhypnotic behavior.* Hypnotic responses are involuntary and involve a hidden observer. The hidden observer allows the person to be fully aware of what is happening yet maintain passive involvement. Hilgard discovered this dual involvement during a classroom demonstration in which he hypnotized a student. Hilgard induced deafness in the student and showed that the person was completely unresponsive to any sounds around him—conversation, noise, taunts. Then a student from the class asked if the hypnotized individual was really as unresponsive to sounds as he seemed. Hilgard, being a flexible teacher, asked the person to raise a finger if a part of him could still hear. To the surprise of Hilgard and the rest of the class, the student raised his finger, suggesting a divided consciousness in which a part of the student's mind was passively aware of what was happening.

Nonstate Theory

A second theory of hypnosis is **nonstate theory,** *which proposes that individuals who become hypnotized are under the social influence of the hypnotist.* They are carrying out the social role of being a good hypnotic subject and letting the hypnotist direct their imaginative thinking. In this view, hypnotized individuals might appear to surrender their voluntary control to conform to situational demands (Spanos, 1996). However, according to nonstate theory, they are not partitioned into a divided consciousness of actor and observer like Hilgard suggested.

What are some different theories about hypnosis? What are some applications of hypnosis?

The special process and nonstate theories are not necessarily incompatible. Perhaps both divided consciousness (special process theory) and social influence (nonstate theory) are involved in many instances of hypnosis (Kihlstrom & McConkey, 1990).

Applications of Hypnosis

Hypnosis is widely used in psychotherapy, medicine and dentistry, criminal investigation, and sports. Hypnosis has been used in psychotherapy to treat alcoholism, somnambulism, suicidal tendencies, overeating, and smoking. One of the least effective, but most common, applications of hypnosis is to help people stop overeating and quit smoking. Hypnotists direct their patient to stop these behaviors, but dramatic results rarely are achieved unless the patient is already highly motivated to change. The most effective use of hypnosis is as an adjunct to different forms of psychotherapy.

A long history of research and practice clearly has demonstrated that hypnosis can reduce the experience of pain (Crasilneck, 1995). However, not everyone is hypnotizable enough to experience this effect. The effectiveness of hypnosis in increasing muscular strength and endurance, as well as sensory thresholds, has not been demonstrated (Druckman & Bjork, 1994).

At this point we have studied a number of ideas about hypnosis. An overview of these ideas is presented in summary table 4.3.

In our discussion of hypnosis, we have seen that, in the special process view, hypnosis alters the person's state of consciousness. Next we will see that ever since the dawn of human history people have used drugs to alter consciousness, to "get high."

Hypnosis
Hypnosis Applications

Summary Table 4.3
Hypnosis

Concept	Processes/Related Ideas	Characteristics/Description
Definition and History	Their Nature	Hypnosis is a psychological state of altered consciousness in which the subject is unusually receptive to suggestion. The history of hypnosis began with Friedrich Anton Mesmer and his belief in animal magnetism.
The Hypnotic State: Features and Individual Differences	Their Nature	Hypnosis involves reducing distracting stimuli and making the subject comfortable, getting the individual to concentrate, and suggesting what is to be experienced in the hypnotic state. About 10 to 20 percent of the population is highly susceptible to hypnosis, about 10 percent cannot be hypnotized at all, and the remainder fall in between. People who have the ability to immerse themselves in imaginative activities are good candidates for hypnosis.
Theories of Hypnosis	Special Process Theory	Hilgard proposed the special process theory, which states that hypnotic behavior involves a special cognitive state that is different than nonhypnotic behavior. Hypnotic responses are involuntary and involve a hidden observer.
	Nonstate Theory	According to nonstate theory, individuals who become hypnotized are under the social influence of the hypnotist. They are carrying out the social role of being a good hypnotic subject and letting the hypnotist direct their imaginative thinking.
Applications	Their Nature	Hypnosis has been widely applied, with mixed results, to a variety of circumstances, including psychotherapy, medicine, dentistry, criminal trials, and sports.

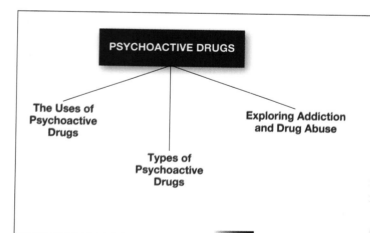

Psychoactive Drugs

During one phase of his medical career, Sigmund Freud experimented with therapeutic uses of cocaine. He was searching for possible medical applications, such as a painkiller for eye surgery. He soon found that the drug induced ecstasy. He even wrote to his fiancée and told her how just a small dose of cocaine produced lofty, wonderful sensations. As it became apparent that some people became psychologically addicted to cocaine, and after several died from overdoses, Freud quit using the drug. Cocaine is just one of many drugs taken to alter consciousness.

The Uses of Psychoactive Drugs

Psychoactive drugs *act on the nervous system to alter our state of consciousness, modify our perceptions, and change our moods.* Ever since the ancients first sat entranced in front of the communal fire, humans have searched for substances they hoped would produce pleasurable sensations and alter their state of consciousness. Among the substances that alter consciousness are alcohol, hemp and cactus plants, mushrooms, poppies, and tobacco, an herb that has been smoked and sniffed for more than 400 centuries.

Human beings are attracted to psychoactive substances because they help them adapt to an ever-changing environment. Smoking, drinking, and taking drugs reduce tension and frustration, relieve boredom and fatigue, and in some cases help us escape from the harsh realities of the world (Hales, 1999). Psychoactive drugs provide us with pleasure by giving us inner peace, joy, relaxation, kaleidoscopic perceptions, surges of exhilaration, and prolonged heightened sensation. They may be useful in helping us to get along in our world. For example, amphetamines can keep us awake all night so we can study for an exam. We might also take drugs because we are curious about their effects, in some cases because of sensationalistic accounts in the media. We might wonder if the drugs described can provide us with unique, profound experiences. We also take drugs for social reasons, hoping they will make us feel more at ease and happier in our interactions and relationships with others.

The use of psychoactive drugs for such personal gratification and temporary adaptation, however, can carry a high price tag: drug dependence, personal and social disorganization, and a predisposition to serious and sometimes fatal diseases (Goldberg, 2000). What was initially intended as enjoyment and adaptation can eventually turn into sorrow and maladaptation. For example, drinking may initially help people relax and forget about their worries. But then they may begin to drink more and more, until the drinking becomes an addiction that destroys relationships and careers, and leads to physical and psychological damage, including permanent liver damage and major depression. As a person continues to take a psychoactive drug, the body develops a **tolerance,** *which means that a greater amount of the drug is needed to produce the same effect.* The first time someone takes 5 milligrams of Valium, for example, the drug will make them feel very relaxed. But after taking the pill every day for 6 months, the person may need to take 10 milligrams to achieve the same calming effect.

Physical dependence *is the physical need for a drug that is accompanied by unpleasant withdrawal symptoms when the drug is discontinued.* **Psychological dependence** *is the strong desire and craving to repeat the use of a drug because of various emotional reasons, such as a feeling of well-being and reduction of stress.* Both physical and psychological dependence mean that the psychoactive drug is playing a powerful role in the person's life (Avis, 1999).

Types of Psychoactive Drugs

Three main types of psychoactive drugs are depressants, stimulants, and hallucinogens.

Depressants   **Depressants** *are psychoactive drugs that slow down mental and physical activity.* Among the most widely used depressants are alcohol, barbiturates, tranquilizers, and opiates.

Alcohol   We do not always think of alcohol as a drug, but it is an extremely powerful one. Alcohol acts upon the body primarily as a depressant and slows down the brain's activities. This might seem surprising, since people who normally tend to be inhibited may begin to talk, dance, or socialize after a few drinks, but people "loosen up" after one or two drinks because the areas in the brain involved in controlling inhibition and judgment *slow down.* As people drink more, their inhibitions become even further reduced and their judgments become increasingly impaired. Activities requiring intellectual functioning and skill, such as driving, become impaired as more alcohol is consumed. Eventually the drinker becomes drowsy and falls asleep. With extreme intoxication, a person may even lapse into a coma and die. Each of these effects varies with how the person's body metabolizes alcohol, body weight, the amount of alcohol consumed, and whether previous drinking has led to tolerance (Clayton, 1999).

Alcohol is the most widely used drug in our society. A 1992 Gallup poll revealed that 64 percent of American adults drank beer, wine, or liquor at least occasionally—down from 71 percent in the late 1970s. More than 13 million people in the United States call themselves alcoholics. Alcoholism is the third leading killer in the United

The Pleasure System, Drugs, and Society

Clearinghouse for Drug Information

Drugs and Behavior Links

Alcohol and the Brain

States. Each year approximately 25,000 people are killed, and 1.5 million injured, by drunk drivers. More than 60 percent of homicides involve the use of alcohol by either the offender or the victim, while 65 percent of aggressive sexual acts against women involve the use of alcohol by the offender. Alcohol costs the United States more than $40 billion each year in health costs, lost productivity, accidents, and crimes.

A special concern is the high rate of alcohol use by adolescents and college students in the United States (Dimeff & others, 1999). In the 1990s, drug use by young adolescents has increased considerably, and alcohol is the substance they abuse the most.

Almost half of U.S. college students say they binge drink (that is, have had 5 or more drinks in a row at least once in the last two weeks) (Johnston, O'Malley, & Bachmann, 1998). Can binge drinking have negative effects on students' lives? In a national survey on 140 campuses, binge-drinking students were 11 times more likely to fall behind in school and twice as likely to have unprotected sex than college students who did not drink (Wechsler & others, 1994).

Alcoholism *is a disorder that involves long-term, repeated, uncontrolled, compulsive, and excessive use of alcoholic beverages that impair the drinker's health and social relationships.* If you struggle to manage alcohol use, chances are good that you are not the only person in your family who had this problem. Family studies consistently find a high frequency of alcoholism in the first-degree relatives of alcoholics (Hannigan & others, 1999).

Alcohol Self-Evaluation

Alcoholism

In one review of research on family alcoholism, when the father was an alcoholic, both sons and daughters had increased rates of alcoholism; when the mother was an alcoholic, increased rates of alcoholism occurred only for daughters (Pollock & others, 1987). Twin studies of alcoholism have revealed a modest influence of heredity (Sher, 1991), while adoption studies document the contribution of biological relatives' alcoholism to alcoholism in male adoptees (Sher, 1993). Research along these lines has persuaded many psychologists that heredity plays an important role in alcoholism (Goodwin, 1998). However, the precise genetic mechanism has not yet been identified.

Although the family, twin, and adoption studies reveal a genetic influence on alcoholism, they also indicate that environmental factors play an important role. For example, family studies indicate that many alcoholics do not have close relatives who are alcoholics (Sher, 1993). Adoption studies suggest that heredity and environment interact for at least one form of alcoholism (environmentally dependent susceptibility), and some alcoholics do not have alcoholic biological parents. The large cultural variations in alcohol use also underscore that the environment plays an important role in alcoholism. Like other behaviors and problems, alcoholism is multiply determined and has multiple pathways of development (Sobell & Sobell, 1993). Later in the chapter, we will explore the prevention and treatment of alcoholism in our discussion of addiction and drug abuse.

Barbiturates   **Barbiturates,** *such as Nembutal and Seconal, are depressant drugs that are used to induce sleep.* In heavy dosages, they can lead to impaired memory and decision making. When combined with alcohol (for instance, sleeping pills taken after a night of binge drinking), the result can be lethal. Barbiturates by themselves also can produce death in heavy dosages, which makes them the drug most often chosen in suicide attempts. Abrupt withdrawal from barbiturates can produce seizures.

Tranquilizers   **Tranquilizers,** *such as Valium and Xanax, are depressant drugs that reduce anxiety and induce relaxation.* Unlike barbiturates, which often are given to induce sleep, tranquilizers are usually given to calm an anxious, nervous individual. Tranquilizers are among the most widely used drugs in the United States and can produce withdrawal symptoms when individuals stop taking them.

Opiates   **Opiates,** *which consist of opium and its derivatives, depress the central nervous system's activity.* The most common opiate drugs—morphine and heroin—

affect synapses in the brain that use endorphins as their neurotransmitter. When these drugs leave the brain, the affected synapses become understimulated. For several hours after taking an opiate, a person feels euphoric and relieved of pain and has an increased appetite for food and sex. Morphine is sometimes used medically as a painkiller. But the opiates are among the most physically addictive drugs, leading to craving and painful withdrawal when the drug becomes unavailable.

Recently, another hazardous consequence of opiate addiction has surfaced: AIDS. Most heroin addicts inject the drug intravenously. When they share their needles, blood from the needles can be passed on. When this blood comes from someone with AIDS, the virus can spread from the infected user to the uninfected user.

Stimulants

Stimulants *are psychoactive drugs that increase the central nervous system's activity.* The most widely used stimulants are caffeine, nicotine (in cigarettes), amphetamines, and cocaine. Coffee, tea, and caffeinated soft drinks are mild stimulants. We will discuss amphetamines, cocaine, and caffeine here but save nicotine for later.

Amphetamines

Amphetamines are widely prescribed, often in the form of diet pills. They are also called "pep pills" and "uppers." Amphetamines increase the release of the neurotransmitter dopamine, which increases the user's activity level and pleasurable feelings.

Cocaine

Cocaine comes from the coca plant, native to Bolivia and Peru. For centuries Bolivians and Peruvians have chewed on the plant to increase their stamina. Today cocaine is either snorted or injected in the form of crystals or powder. The effect is a rush of euphoria, which eventually wears off, followed by depression, lethargy, insomnia, and irritability. Cocaine can trigger a heart attack, stroke, or brain seizure.

When animals and humans chew coca leaves, small amounts of cocaine gradually enter the bloodstream, without any apparent adverse effects. However, when extracted cocaine is sniffed, smoked, or injected, it enters the bloodstream very rapidly, producing a rush of euphoric feelings that lasts for about 15 to 30 minutes. Because the rush depletes the supply of the neurotransmitters dopamine and norepinephrine in the brain, an agitated, depressed mood usually follows as the drug's effects decline.

Crack *is an intensified form of cocaine, consisting of chips of pure cocaine that are usually smoked.* Crack is believed to be one of the most addictive substances known, being much more addictive than heroin, barbiturates, and alcohol. Emergency-room admissions related to crack have soared from less than 600 cases in 1985 to more than 15,000 a year in the early 1990s.

Treatments for cocaine addiction have not been very successful. Cocaine's addictive properties are so strong that 6 months after treatment, more than 50 percent of cocaine abusers return to the drug. Experts on drug abuse believe the best approach to reduce cocaine addiction is through prevention programs.

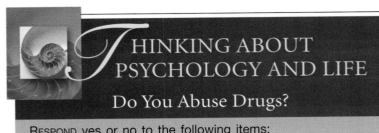

THINKING ABOUT PSYCHOLOGY AND LIFE

Do You Abuse Drugs?

RESPOND yes or no to the following items:

Yes	No	
_____	_____	I have gotten into problems because of using drugs.
_____	_____	Using alcohol or other drugs has made my college life unhappy at times.
_____	_____	Drinking alcohol or taking other drugs has been a factor in my losing a job.
_____	_____	Drinking alcohol or taking other drugs has interfered with my studying for exams.
_____	_____	Drinking alcohol or taking drugs has jeopardized my academic performance.
_____	_____	My ambition is not as strong since I've been drinking a lot or taking drugs.
_____	_____	Drinking or taking drugs has caused me to have difficulty sleeping.
_____	_____	I have felt remorse after drinking or taking drugs.
_____	_____	I crave a drink or other drugs at a definite time of the day.
_____	_____	I want a drink or another drug the next morning.
_____	_____	I have had a complete or partial loss of memory as a result of drinking or using other drugs.
_____	_____	Drinking or using other drugs is affecting my reputation.
_____	_____	I have been in the hospital or another institution because of my drinking or taking drugs.

College students who responded yes to items similar to these on the Rutgers Collegiate Abuse Screening Test were more likely to be substance abusers than those who answered no. If you responded yes to just 1 of the 13 items on this screening test, consider going to your college health or counseling center for further screening.

The Opiates

Cocaine

Effects of Cocaine on the Brain

Caffeine   Often overlooked as a drug, caffeine is the most widely used psychoactive drug in the world. Caffeine is a stimulant and a natural component of various plants that are the sources of coffee, tea, and cola-flavored soft drinks. Caffeine also is present in chocolate and many nonprescribed medications. The stimulating effects of caffeine are often perceived as beneficial, but some people experience unpleasant effects. *Caffeinism* is the term given to overindulgence of caffeine. It is characterized by mood changes, anxiety, disruption of sleep, and possibly other problems. Caffeinism often develops in individuals who consume 5 to 7 cups of coffee (500–700 mgs of caffeine) each day. Frequent symptoms of caffeinism are insomnia, irritability, headaches, ringing in the ears, dry mouth, increased blood pressure, and digestive problems.

Caffeine activates the pleasure centers of the brain, so it is not surprising that it is difficult to "kick the caffeine habit." When individuals remove caffeine from their diet, they typically initially incur headaches, lethargy, apathy, and concentration difficulties. These symptoms of withdrawal are usually mild and tolerable and subside after a brief period of time.

Hallucinogenic Drugs
Marijuana

Hallucinogens   **Hallucinogens** *are psychoactive drugs that modify a person's perceptual experience and produce visual images that are not real.* Hallucinogens are also called "psychedelic" (meaning "mind-altering") drugs. Marijuana has a milder hallucinogenic effect, LSD a stronger one.

Marijuana   Marijuana is the dried leaves and flowers of the hemp plant *Cannabis sativa*, which originated in central Asia but is now grown in most parts of the world. The plant's dried resin is known as hashish. The active ingredient in marijuana is THC, which stands for the chemical delta-9-tetrahydrocannabinol. This ingredient does not resemble the chemicals of other psychoactive drugs and does not affect a specific neurotransmitter. Rather, marijuana disrupts the membranes of neurons and affects the functioning of a variety of neurotransmitters and hormones.

The physical effects of marijuana include increases in pulse rate and blood pressure, reddening of the eyes, coughing, and dryness of the mouth. Psychological effects include a mixture of excitatory, depressive, and mildly hallucinatory characteristics, making it difficult to classify the drug. Marijuana can trigger spontaneous unrelated ideas, distorted perceptions of time and place, increased sensitivity to sounds and colors, and erratic verbal behavior. Marijuana can also impair attention and memory. When used daily in large amounts, marijuana can also alter sperm count and change hormonal cycles; it might be involved in some birth defects. Marijuana use declined during the 1980s, but an upsurge in its use has occurred in the 1990s (Johnston, O'Malley, & Bachman, 1998). Possible medical uses of marijuana include treating glaucoma, chemotherapy-caused nausea and vomiting, and AIDS-related weight loss (Avis, 1999).

LSD   LSD (lysergic acid diethylamide) is a hallucinogen that even in low doses produces striking perceptual changes. Objects change their shape and glow. Colors become kaleidoscopic, fabulous images unfold as users close their eyes. Designs swirl, colors shimmer, bizarre scenes appear. Sometimes the images are pleasurable; sometimes they are grotesque. LSD can influence the user's perception of time. Time often seems to slow down dramatically, so that brief glances at objects are experienced as deep, penetrating, and lengthy examinations, and minutes often seem to be hours or days.

LSD's effects on the body can include dizziness, nausea, and tremors. LSD acts primarily on the neurotransmitter serotonin in the brain, though it can affect dopamine as well. Emotional and cognitive effects may include rapid mood swings or impaired attention and memory. LSD was popular in the late 1960s and early 1970s, but its popularity dropped after its unpredictable effects became well publicized. However, a recent increase in LSD use by high school and college students has been reported (Johnston, O'Malley, & Bachman, 1998).

Exploring Addiction and Drug Abuse

Let's further examine drugs and their effects on behavior by studying addiction and then turn to the prevention and treatment of drug abuse.

Addictions
Drug Abuse Links

Addiction   Addiction *is a pattern of behavior characterized by an overwhelming involvement with using a drug and securing its supply.* This can occur despite adverse consequences associated with the use of the drug. There is a strong tendency to relapse after quitting or withdrawal. Withdrawal symptoms consist of significant changes in physical functioning and behavior. Depending on the drug, these symptoms might include insomnia, tremors, nausea, vomiting, cramps, elevation of heart rate and blood pressure, convulsions, anxiety, and depression when a physically dependent person stops taking the drug. Experts on drug abuse use the term *addiction* to describe either a physical or psychological dependence on the drug or both (Carroll, 1999; Pinger & others, 1998).

Controversy continues about whether addictions are diseases (Ray & Ksir, 1999). The **disease model of addiction** *describes addictions as biologically based, lifelong diseases that involve a loss of control over behavior and require medical and/or spiritual treatment for recovery.* In the disease model, addiction is either inherited or bred into a person early in life. Current or recent problems or relationships are not believed to be causes of the disease. Once involved in the disease, you can never completely rid yourself of it, according to this model. The disease model has been strongly promoted and supported by the medical profession and Alcoholics Anonymous (AA) (Humphreys, 2000).

Critics of the disease approach argue that the disease approach is not the best one because the biological mechanisms that might account for addictive behavior have not been identified, it keeps people from developing self-control, it stigmatizes people with labels such as *addict* and *alcoholic*—in some cases for life, it dispenses a rigid program of therapy rather than advocating more flexible approaches, and addiction is not necessarily life-long (Grabowski, 1999). Two critics of the disease model, Stanton Peele and Archie Brodsky (1991), believe that addiction is a habitual response and a source of gratification or security. They say that an addiction can involve *any* attachment or sensations that grow to such proportions that they impair the person's life—including drugs, food, gambling, shopping, love, and sex. In this view, the "hook" of the addiction—what keeps people coming back to it—is that it provides people with feelings and gratifying sensations they are not able to get in other ways. Peele and Brodsky believe that understanding addiction requires that it be placed in the proper context, as part of people's lives, their personalities, their relationships, their environments, and their perspectives. They call their model the "life-process" model. In sum, the **life-process model of addiction** *argues that addiction is not a disease but rather a habitual response and a source of gratification or security that can be understood only in the context of social relationships and experiences.*

Each of these views of addiction—the disease model and the nondisease, life-process model—has its supporters.

Prevention and Treatment of Drug Abuse   Prevention of drug abuse is an admirable goal. Let's explore some strategies for accomplishing this and examine treatment programs for drug abuse.

Prevention programs have focused on three goals: primary, secondary, and tertiary prevention, with the greatest emphasis being targeted at primary and tertiary prevention. **Primary prevention** *is prevention that attempts to stop people from taking drugs by helping them to not start.* Primary prevention programs are increasingly being initiated with elementary school children. The most recent primary prevention models are based on the belief that early prevention works best, especially through the influence of respected role models who advocate abstinence from drugs and through peer pressure (Pentz, 1993).

Secondary prevention *is an attempt to minimize the harm caused by drug use with a high-risk population or with a group that is involved in experimental or occasional use.* In high schools, secondary prevention often involves attempts to reduce alcohol or tobacco use. Recognizing that a majority of high school students drink at least occasionally, secondary prevention programs focus on the hazardous consequences of drinking and driving. Other secondary prevention programs include crisis counseling and drug-abuse counseling for individuals whose drug use has gone beyond experimental or occasional use.

Tertiary prevention *consists of treatment for people who abuse drugs. Tertiary prevention programs include medical treatment, residential facilities, and rehabilitation.*

Two factors stand out when the successful components of drug-abuse prevention are analyzed: intensive individualized attention and community-wide, multiagency collaboration (Dryfoos, 1990). Children who grow up in families in which they are given considerable nurturance and support are less likely to become drug abusers than are children who are neglected and not given adequate support and attention from their parents (Brook & others, 1990). When high-risk children or adolescents become attached to a responsible adult who gives them attention and responds to their needs, their risk status declines. In one successful substance-abuse program, a student assistance counselor was available full-time for individual counseling and referral for treatment.

The basic philosophy of community-wide programs is that a number of different programs have to be in place (Price, 2000). The Midwestern Prevention Program developed by Mary Ann Pentz (1993) implemented a community-wide health promotion campaign that used local media, community education, and parent programs in concert with a substance-abuse curriculum in the schools. An evaluation of the program after 18 months and again after 4 years in use revealed significantly lower rates of alcohol and marijuana use by adolescents than their counterparts in areas of the city where the program was not in operation.

The importance of prevention and early intervention is underscored when the percentage of individuals who recover from alcoholism is examined (Sales, 1999). Despite occasional positive claims that you will see in the media, the stunning reality is that no single inpatient, outpatient, counseling, self-help, or drug treatment has been shown to reduce relapse rates for alcoholism over the long term (Seligman, 1993; Seligman & Rosenhan, 1998). When researchers evaluate the effects of drug treatment programs over the short term, such as 6 months, they often find positive results, with about two-thirds of individuals still abstinent for this long after treatment. However, an analysis of more than 100 long-term studies on thousands of alcoholics revealed that no one treatment was better than the others and that no one type of treatment was superior to no treatment at all (Emrick, 1982; Goodwin, 1988; Seligman, 1993).

About one-third of alcoholics recover whether they are in a treatment program or not. This figure was found by George Vaillant (1983, 1992) in a long-term study of 700 individuals over 50 years and has consistently been found by other researchers as well. Vaillant describes the "one-third rule" for alcoholism: by age 65, one-third are dead or in terrible shape, one-third are abstinent or drinking socially, and one-third are still trying to beat their addiction. In his extensive research, Vaillant did reveal that a positive outcome and recovery from alcoholism are predicted by certain factors: (1) a strong negative experience related to drinking, such as a serious medical emergency or condition; (2) finding a substitute dependency to compete with alcohol abuse, such as meditation, exercise, or overeating (which of course has its own negative health consequences); (3) having new social supports (such as a concerned, helpful employer or a new marriage); and (4) joining an inspirational group, such as a religious organization or AA.

At this point we have discussed many ideas about psychoactive drugs. An overview of these ideas is presented in summary table 4.4. One topic we evaluated in this chapter was whether people can learn while they are sleeping. In the next chapter, we focus our attention exclusively on the topic of learning.

SUMMARY TABLE 4.4
Psychoactive Drugs

Concept	Processes/ Related Ideas	Characteristics/Description
The Uses of Psychoactive Drugs	Their Nature	Psychoactive drugs act on the central nervous system to alter states of consciousness, modify perceptions, and alter mood. They have been used since the beginning of recorded history for pleasure, utility, curiosity, and social reasons. Tolerance means that a greater amount of a drug is needed to produce the same effect. Physical dependence is the physical need for the drug that is accompanied by unpleasant withdrawal symptoms when the drug is discontinued. Psychological dependence is the strong desire and craving to repeat the use of a drug for various emotional reasons, such as a feeling of well-being and reduction of stress the drug produces.
Types of Psychoactive Drugs	Depressants	Depressants are psychoactive drugs that slow down mental and physical activity. Depressants include alcohol, barbiturates, tranquilizers, and opiates. Alcohol is the most widely used drug in America and the third leading killer. Special concerns are the high use of alcohol by adolescents and college students. Alcoholism is a disorder that involves long-term repeated, uncontrolled, compulsive, and excessive use of alcoholic beverages that impairs the drinker's health and social relationships. Both nature and nurture are involved in alcoholism. Barbiturates are depressant drugs that are used medically to induce sleep. Tranquilizers are depressant drugs that reduce anxiety and induce relaxation. Opiates, which consist of opium and its derivatives, depress the central nervous system's activity. The most common opiate drugs are morphine and heroin.
	Stimulants	Stimulants are psychoactive drugs that increase central nervous system activity. The most widely used stimulants are caffeine, nicotine, amphetamines, and cocaine. Cocaine provides a euphoric rush that is followed by depression, lethargy, insomnia, and irritability. Cocaine can even trigger a heart attack, stroke, or brain seizure. Crack is an intensified form of cocaine and is believed to be one of the most addictive drugs. Treatments for cocaine addiction have not been very successful. Caffeine also is a stimulant and might be the most widely used psychoactive drug in the world. A special concern is caffeinism, an overindulgence that is associated with a variety of psychological and physical problems.
	Hallucinogens	Hallucinogens are psychoactive drugs that modify perceptual experiences and produce visual images that are not real. Marijuana and LSD are hallucinogens. Marijuana produces a mixture of excitatory, depressive, and mildly hallucinatory psychological effects. LSD is a stronger hallucinogen than marijuana. Both marijuana use and LSD use have increased in the 1990s.
Exploring Addiction and Drug Abuse	Addiction	Addiction is a pattern of behavior characterized by an overwhelming involvement with using a drug and securing its supply. Two views of addiction are the disease model and the life-process model.
	Prevention and Treatment of Drug Abuse	Three forms of prevention/treatment are primary, secondary, and tertiary. Successful drug-abuse programs for children and youth have two significant components: (1) intensive individualized attention, and (2) community-wide, multiagency collaboration. Analyses of treatment programs for alcoholics over the short term show some positive results but over the long term reveal that no one treatment program is better than others and that no one treatment is superior to no treatment at all. About one-third of alcoholics recover with no treatment. However, Vaillant's research did reveal some factors that predict a positive outcome and recovery from alcoholism.

Overview

Overview

WE BEGAN THIS CHAPTER by discussing the nature of consciousness. Then we examined these aspects of sleep: why we sleep, sleep and circadian rhythms, sleep deprivation and sleep needs, the neural basis of sleep, and sleep disorders. We also studied the interpretation of dreams and many other aspects of dreams. Our coverage of hypnosis focused on its definition and history, the hypnotic state (features and individual differences), theories of hypnosis, and applications. We evaluated these aspects of psychoactive drugs: their uses, their types, and addiction and drug abuse.

Don't forget that you can obtain a more detailed overview of the chapter by again studying the four summary tables on pages 128, 131, 134, and 141.

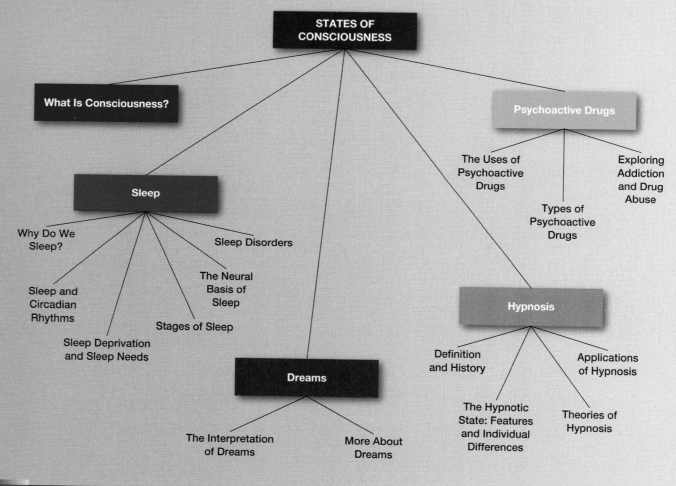

Key Terms

consciousness 116
stream of consciousness 116
unconscious thought 116
controlled processes 116
automatic processes 117
daydreaming 117
altered states of consciousness 117
repair theory 119
ecological theory 119
circadian rhythm 119
alpha waves 122
sleep spindles 122

delta waves 122
REM sleep 122
insomnia 126
somnambulism 126
nightmare 127
night terror 127
narcolepsy 127
sleep apnea 127
wish fulfillment 129
manifest content 129
latent content 129
cognitive theory of dreaming 130

activation-synthesis theory 130
hypnosis 132
special process theory 133
nonstate theory 133
psychoactive drugs 134
tolerance 135
physical dependence 135
psychological dependence 135
depressants 135
alcoholism 136
barbiturates 136
tranquilizers 136

opiates 136
stimulants 137
crack 137
hallucinogens 138
addiction 139
disease model of addiction 139
life-process model of addiction 139
primary prevention 139
secondary prevention 140
tertiary prevention 140

Key People

William James 116
Sigmund Freud 116

James Maas 122
Ernest Hilgard 132

Taking It to the Net

1. Do you require a lot of sleep, or can you function well with only a few hours sleep? Many of your friends probably differ greatly in the amount of sleep they need. Generally, however, we all need around the same amount of sleep to remain healthy. How much do you think we need? What happens to you if you don't get enough sleep? You may try to "catch up on your sleep," but does this really work? Explain the notion of sleep debt and how it relates to you.
2. Many college students travel home during Thanksgiving and Christmas break. If you have traveled long distances, you might have experienced jet lag. Jet lag can play interesting tricks on your mind, confusing you and making you tired. Explain why traveling long distances results in jet lag. How do you achieve it and what can you do to prevent it?
3. You have probably seen or heard things in the media about hypnotism. Maybe you have seen a hypnotist at your college, making students do strange and humorous things while under a trance. Do you think everyone can be hypnotized? You might also know that hypnosis has been used in psychotherapy for a variety of clinical applications. How does hypnosis work? Can memory be improved with hypnosis?

Connect to http://www.mhhe.com/psychology/santrock to find the answers!

Chapter 5

CHAPTER OUTLINE

Learning

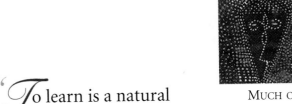

Images of Psychology and Life
"Sesame Street" Around the World

> "To learn is a natural pleasure."

Aristotle
Greek Philosopher, 4th Century B.C.

Preview

THE ABILITY TO LEARN is a remarkable and enchanting gift. When we think about learning, we might come up with an image of someone sitting at a desk and studying a book. Studying does involve learning, but learning is much more than just studying. You will see in this chapter that learning applies to many areas of acquiring new behaviors, skills, and knowledge. These are some of the questions we will explore:

- What is learning?
- How do people learn to fear things?
- How would you go about teaching a pigeon to play table tennis or guide a missile?
- Why is punishment often not a good choice when you want to change behavior?
- What are some good strategies for improving self-control?
- How much do we learn by observing others do something?
- What roles do biology and culture play in learning?

MUCH OF WHAT WE DO results from what we have *learned*. If you had grown up in another part of the world, you would speak a different language, would like different foods and clothing, and would behave in ways characteristic of that culture. Why? Because the content of your *learning* experiences in that culture would have been different.

One way we learn is by watching what other people do and say. This kind of learning is called *observational learning*. Observational learning has changed dramatically in the twentieth century because of the introduction and pervasive use of television, which has touched virtually every American's life. Television has been called a lot of names, not all of them good—the "one-eyed monster" and the "boob tube," for example. Television has been accused of interfering with children's learning; critics say television lures children from schoolwork and books, and makes them passive learners. Rarely does television require active responses from its observers.

Television can also contribute to children's learning. For example, it can introduce children to worlds that are different from the one they live in. *Sesame Street* was specifically designed to improve children's cognitive and social skills (Wright, 1995). Almost half of America's 2- to 5-year-olds watch it regularly (Condry, 1989). Highly successful at teaching kids, *Sesame Street* uses fast-paced action, sound effects, music, and humorous characters to grab the attention of its young audience.

In Spain, children watch "Barrio Sesamo"—the Spanish version of Sesame Street. *The bakery is Barrio Sesamo's central meeting place. The residents include two full-size puppets. Espinete, a special friend of the children, is a hedgehog who tries to get the cast members to play games whenever possible. Don Pimpon (shown above) is a shaggy old codger, at times a bit absentminded, who has traveled extensively and entertains with stories of his adventures.* How is observational learning involved in Sesame Street?

With their eyes "glued" to the screen, young children learn basic academic skills like letter and number recognition.

When "Sesame Street" first appeared in 1969, its creators had no idea that this "street" would lead to locations as distant as Kuwait, Israel, Latin America, and the Philippines. Since "Sesame Street" first aired in the United States, it has been televised in eighty-four countries and thirteen foreign-language versions have been produced. "Barrio Sesamo" is shown in seventeen South and Central American countries, as well as Puerto Rico. It emphasizes learning about the diversity of cultures and lifestyles in South America. "Rechov Sumsum" is shown in Israel; it especially encourages children to learn how people from different ethnic and religious backgrounds can live in harmony. When children in the Netherlands watch "Sesamstraat," they learn about the concept of school, and a 7-foot-tall blue bird named Pino who is always eager to learn.

Learning Theories and Applications

What Is Learning?

In learning how to use a computer, you might make some mistakes along the way, but at some point you will get the knack of how to use it. You will change from being someone who could not operate a computer to being one who can. Learning anything new involves change. Once you have learned to use a computer, the skill usually does not leave you. Once you learn how to drive a car, you do not have to go through the process again at a later time. Learning involves a relatively permanent influence on behavior. You learned how to use a computer through experience with the machine. Through experience you also learned that you have to study to do well on a test, that when you go to a rock concert there is usually a warm-up act, and that a field goal in American football scores three points. Putting these pieces together, we arrive at a definition of **learning**: *a relatively permanent change in behavior that occurs through experience.*

Psychologists explain our many experiences with a few basic learning processes. We respond to things that happen to us, we act and experience consequences for our behavior, and we observe what others say and do. These three aspects of experiences form the three main types of learning we will study in this chapter—classical conditioning (responding), operant conditioning (acting), and observational learning (observing). As we study the nature of learning, you will discover that early approaches investigated the way experience and behavior are connected without referring to cognitive or mental processes. In recent years, cognitive processes have assumed a more important role in learning. We will discuss more recent cognitive approaches to learning later in the chapter, but first we will examine classical conditioning.

Classical Conditioning

It is a nice spring day. A father takes his baby out for a walk. The baby reaches over to touch a pink flower and is badly stung by the bumblebee sitting on the petals. The next day, the baby's mother brings home some pink flowers. She removes a flower from the arrangement and takes it over for her baby to smell. The baby cries loudly as soon as she sees the pink flower. The baby's panic at the sight of the pink flower

Chapter 5 • Learning 147

illustrates the learning process of **classical conditioning,** *in which a neutral stimulus becomes associated with a meaningful stimulus and acquires the capacity to elicit a similar response.*

Pavlovian Conditioning

In the early 1900s, the Russian physiologist Ivan Pavlov investigated the way the body digests food ◄▥ P. 8. As part of his experiments, he routinely placed meat powder in a dog's mouth, causing the dog to salivate. Pavlov began to notice that the meat powder was not the only stimulus that caused the dog to salivate. The dog salivated in response to a number of stimuli associated with the food, such as the sight of the food dish, the sight of the individual who brought the food into the room, and the sound of the door closing when the food arrived. Pavlov recognized that the dog's association of these sights and sounds with the food was an important type of learning, which came to be called classical conditioning.

Pavlov wanted to know *why* the dog salivated to various sights and sounds before eating the meat powder. He observed that the dog's behavior included both learned and unlearned components. The "unlearned" part of classical conditioning is based on the fact that some stimuli automatically produce certain responses apart from any prior learning; in other words they are inborn or innate. **Reflexes** *are automatic stimulus-response connections.* They include salivation in response to food, nausea in response to bad food, shivering in response to low temperature, coughing in response to the throat being clogged, pupil constriction in response to light, and withdrawal in response to blows or burns. An **unconditioned stimulus (US)** *is a stimulus that produces a response without prior learning; food was the US in Pavlov's experiments.* An **unconditioned response (UR)** *is an unlearned response that is automatically elicited by the US.* In Pavlov's

If a bee stings this young girl while she is holding a pink flower, how would classical conditioning explain her panic at the sight of pink flowers in the future?

Pavlov (the white-bearded gentleman in the center) is shown demonstrating the nature of classical conditioning to students at the Military Medical Academy in Russia. © *The Granger Collection, New York*

experiments, the saliva that flowed from the dog's mouth in response to food was the UR. In the case of the baby and the flower, the baby's learning and experience did not cause her to cry when the bee stung her. Her crying was unlearned and occurred automatically. The bee's sting was the US and the crying was the UR.

In classical conditioning, the **conditioned stimulus (CS)** *is a previously neutral stimulus that eventually elicits the conditioned response after being associated with the unconditioned stimulus.* The **conditioned response (CR)** *is the learned response to the conditioned stimulus that occurs after CS-US pairing* (Pavlov, 1927). In studying a dog's response to various stimuli associated with meat powder, Pavlov rang a bell before giving meat powder to the dog. Until then, ringing the bell did not have a particular effect on the dog, except perhaps to wake the dog from a nap. The bell was a neutral stimulus. But the dog began to associate the sound of the bell with the food and salivated when it heard the bell. The bell had become a conditioned (learned) stimulus (CS) and the salivation a conditioned response (CR). Before conditioning (or learning), the bell and the food were not related. After their association, the conditioned stimulus (the bell) produced a conditioned response (salivation). For the unhappy baby, the flower was the baby's bell, or CS, and crying was the CR after the sting (US) and the flower (CS) were paired.

Classical conditioning is a form of **associative learning,** *which involves learning that two events are related or linked.* In classical conditioning, the learned association involves the link between two stimuli (CS and US). A summary of how classical conditioning works is shown in figure 5.1.

Classical Conditioning

Temporal Contiguity and Contingency

The interval between the CS and the US is one of the most important aspects of classical conditioning (DeCola & Fanselow, 1995; Weidemann, Georgilas, & Kehoe, 1999). It is important because it defines the **contiguity,** *or degree of association,* of the stimuli. Conditioned responses develop when the interval between the CS and US is very short, as in a matter of seconds. In many instances optimal spacing is a fraction of a second (Kimble, 1961). In Pavlov's work, if the bell rang 20 minutes after the presentation of the food, the dog probably would not associate the bell with the food.

Robert Rescorla (1966, 1988) believes that for classical conditioning to take place, it is important to have not only temporal contiguity in the CS-US connection, but also contingency. **Contingency (in classical conditioning)** *involves the predictability of the occurrence of one stimulus from the presence of another.* For example, a flash of lightning usually is followed by the sound of thunder. Thus, if you see lightning, you might put your hands over your ears or lean away in anticipation of the thunder.

Extinction, Generalization, and Discrimination

Pavlov rang the bell repeatedly in a single session and did not give the dog any food. Eventually the dog stopped salivating. This result is **extinction,** *which in classical conditioning is the weakening of the conditioned response in the absence of the unconditioned stimulus.* Without continued association with the unconditioned stimulus (US), the conditioned stimulus (CS) loses its power to elicit the conditioned response (CR). Over time, after her bee sting, the baby encountered many pink flowers and was not stung by a bee. Consequently, her fear of pink flowers subsided and eventually disappeared. The pink flower (CS) lost its capacity to elicit fear (CR) when the flower was no longer associated with bee stings (US) and the pain and fear they cause (UR).

Extinction is not always the end of the conditioned response. The day after Pavlov extinguished the conditioned salivation at the sound of a bell, he took the dog to the laboratory and rang the bell, still not giving the dog any meat powder. The dog salivated, indicating that an extinguished response can spontaneously recur. **Spontaneous recovery** *is the process in classical conditioning by which a conditioned response can recur after a time delay without further conditioning.* In the case of the baby, even

𝓕igure 5.1
Pavlov's Classical Conditioning

In one experiment, Pavlov presented a neutral stimulus (tone) just before an unconditioned stimulus (food). The neutral stimulus became a conditioned stimulus by being paired with the unconditioned stimulus. Subsequently, the conditioned stimulus (tone) by itself was able to elicit the dog's salivation.

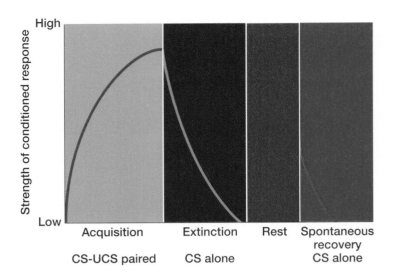

Figure 5.2
The Strength of a Classically Conditioned Response During Acquisition, Extinction, and Spontaneous Recovery

During acquisition the conditioned stimulus and unconditioned stimulus are associated. As seen in the graph, when this occurs, the strength of the conditioned response increases. During extinction the conditioned stimulus is presented alone, and, as can be seen, this results in a decrease of the conditioned response. After a rest period, spontaneous recovery appears, although the strength of the conditioned response is not nearly as great at this point as it was after a number of CS–US pairings. When the CS is presented alone again after spontaneous recovery, the response is extinguished rapidly.

though she saw many pink flowers after her first painful encounter and was not "stung" by them, she showed some signs of fear from time to time. Over time her conditioned fear (CR) to pink flowers (CS) diminished; she showed less tendency to recover her fear of pink flowers spontaneously, especially since she did not experience further painful stings (US). Figure 5.2 shows the sequence of acquisition, extinction, and spontaneous recovery. Spontaneous recovery can occur several times, but as long as the conditioned stimulus is presented alone, spontaneous recovery becomes weaker and eventually ceases to occur.

After many conditioning trials, Pavlov found that the dog salivated in response not only to the tone from the tuning fork, but to other sounds, such as a whistle. Pavlov did not pair these sounds with the unconditioned stimulus of the food. He discovered that the more similar the noise was to the original sound of the tone, the stronger was the dog's salivary flow. In the example of conditioned fear of pink flowers, the baby not only cried at the sight of pink flowers, but she also learned to cry at the sight of red and orange flowers. **Generalization** *in classical conditioning is the tendency of a new stimulus that is similar to the original conditioned stimulus to elicit a response that is similar to the conditioned response.*

Stimulus generalization is not always beneficial. For example, the cat that generalizes from a minnow to a piranha has a major problem; therefore it is important to discriminate between stimuli. **Discrimination** *in classical conditioning is the process of learning to respond to certain stimuli and not to respond to others.* To produce discrimination, Pavlov gave food to the dog only after ringing the bell and not after any other sounds. In this way, the dog learned to distinguish between the bell and other sounds. Similarly, the baby did not cry at the sight of blue flowers, thus discriminating between them and pink flowers.

How Classical Conditioning Works: Pavlov and the Contemporary Perspective

Stimulus substitution *was Pavlov's theory of how classical conditioning works; it states that the nervous system is structured in such a way that the CS and US bond together and eventually the CS substitutes for the US.* However, if the CS substitutes for the US, the two stimuli should produce similar responses. This does not always happen. Using a shock as a US often elicits flinching and jumping, whereas a light (CS) paired with a shock may cause the organism to be immobile, for example.

Information theory *is one contemporary explanation of why classical conditioning works; it stresses that the key to understanding classical conditioning focuses on the information an organism gets from the situation.* Some years ago, E. C. Tolman (1932) said the information value of the CS is important in telling the organism what will follow. In Tolman's words, the organism uses the CS as a sign or expectation that a US will follow. Tolman's belief that the information the CS provides is the key to understanding classical conditioning was a forerunner of contemporary thinking.

In one contemporary view of classical conditioning, an organism is seen as an information seeker using logical and perceptual relations among events, along with preconceptions, to form a representation of the world (Rescorla, 1988, 1996). The contemporary view still recognizes contiguity between the CS and US as important in classical conditioning, but it emphasizes that what is important about the CS-US connection is the information the stimuli give the organism (Kohn & Kalat, 1995; LoLordo, 2000).

A classic experiment conducted by Leon Kamin (1968) illustrates the importance of an organism's history and the information provided by a conditioned stimulus in classical conditioning. A rat was conditioned by repeatedly pairing a tone (CS) and a shock (US), until the tone alone produced a strong conditioned response (fear). The tone continued to be paired with the shock, but a light (a second CS) was turned on each time the tone was sounded. Even though the light (a CS) and the shock (US) were repeatedly paired, the rat showed no conditioning to the light. The light by itself produced no CR. Conditioning to the light was blocked, almost as if the rat had not attended to it. The rat apparently used the tone as a signal to predict that a shock would be forthcoming; it did not need to learn information about the light's pairing with the shock, because that information was redundant with the information already learned in the pairing of the tone and the shock. In this experiment, conditioning was governed not by the contiguity of the CS and US but, rather, by the rat's history and the information it received. Contemporary classical conditioning researchers are exploring further the role of information in an organism's learning (Domjan, 1996; Fanselow, DeCola, & Young, 1993).

Classical Conditioning in Humans

Since Pavlov's experiments, individuals have been conditioned to respond to the sound of a buzzer, a glimpse of light, a puff of air, or the touch of a hand (Woodruff-Pak, 1999). Classical conditioning has a great deal of survival value for the individual (Vernoy, 1995). Because of classical conditioning, we jerk our hands away before they are burned by fire. Classical conditioning also is at work when a tranquil scene—such as an empty beach with waves lapping onto the sand—is described and the harried executive relaxes as if she were actually lying on that beach.

You will note that their ability to comprehend, assess and process information increases dramatically when Professor Podhertz throws in the cat.

Reprinted by permission of Leo Cullum

*T*hrough the Eyes of Psychologists

Robert Rescorla, *University of Pennsylvania*

"Classical conditioning is now described as the learning of relations among events so as to allow the organism to represent its environment."

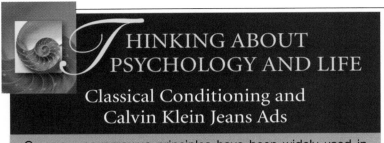

A **phobia** *is an irrational fear.* Classical conditioning provides an explanation of these and other fears. The famous behaviorist John Watson conducted an investigation to demonstrate classical conditioning's role in phobias. A little boy named Albert was shown a white laboratory rat to see if he was afraid of it. He was not. As Albert played with the rat a loud noise was sounded behind his head. As you might imagine, the noise caused little Albert to cry. After only seven pairings of the loud noise with the white rat, Albert began to fear the rat even when the noise was not sounded. Albert's fear was generalized to a rabbit, a dog, and a sealskin coat.

Today we could not ethically conduct such an experiment. Especially noteworthy is the fact that Watson and his associate did not remove Albert's fear of rats, so presumably this phobia remained with him after the experiment (Watson & Raynor, 1920). The experiment with little Albert was conducted in the early part of the twentieth century when there was less concern about the ethical aspects of research. As we saw in chapter 1 ("Psychology's Scientific Approach"), today psychologists must adhere to strict ethical guidelines when they conduct research. Today, the little Albert study would not be approved under the ethical guidelines of the American Psychological Association.

Watson was right about how many of our fears can be learned through classical conditioning. We might develop a fear of the dentist because of a painful experience, fear driving after having been in an automobile accident, and fear dogs after having been bitten by one.

If we can produce fears by classical conditioning, we should be able to eliminate them using conditioning procedures. **Counterconditioning** *is a classical conditioning procedure for weakening a CR by associating the fear-provoking stimulus with a new response incompatible with the fear.* Though Watson did not eliminate little Albert's fear of white rats, an associate of Watson's, Mary Cover Jones (1924), did eliminate the fears of a 3-year-old boy named Peter. Peter had many of the same fears as Albert; however, Peter's fears were not produced by Jones. Among Peter's fears were white rats, fur coats, frogs, fish, and mechanical toys. To eliminate these fears, a rabbit was brought into Peter's view but kept far enough away that it would not upset him. At the same time the rabbit was brought into view, Peter was fed crackers and milk. On each successive day the rabbit was moved closer to Peter as he ate crackers and milk. Eventually Peter reached the point where he would eat the food with one hand and pet the rabbit with the other. The feeling of pleasure produced by the crackers and milk was incompatible with the rabbit's feeling of fear, and fear was extinguished through counterconditioning.

Some of the behaviors we associate with health problems or mental disorders can involve classical conditioning. Certain physical complaints—asthma, headaches, ulcers, and high blood pressure, for example—can partly be the products of classical conditioning. We usually say that such health problems are caused by stress, but often what happened is that certain stimuli, such as a boss's critical attitude or a wife's threat of divorce, are conditioned stimuli for physiological responses. Over time, the frequent presence of the physiological responses may produce a health problem or disorder. A boss's persistent criticism may cause an employee to develop muscle tension, headaches, or high blood pressure. Anything associated with the boss, such as work itself, can then trigger stress in the employee (see figure 5.3).

Classical conditioning is not restricted to unpleasant emotions. Among the things in our life that produce pleasure because they have become conditioned might

In 1920, 9-month-old Albert was conditioned to fear a white rat by pairing the rat with a loud noise. When little Albert was subsequently presented with other stimuli similar to the white rat, such as the rabbit shown here with little Albert, he was afraid of them, too. This illustrates the principle of stimulus generalization in classical conditioning. What are some other examples of generalization in classical conditioning?
Courtesy of Professor Benjamin Harris

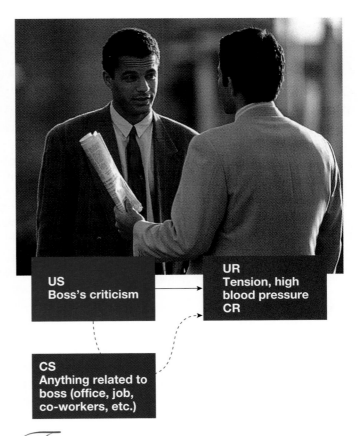

ℱigure 5.3
Classical Conditioning: Boss's Criticism and High Blood Pressure

be the sight of a rainbow, a sunny day, or a favorite song. If you have a positive romantic experience, the location where that experience took place can become a conditioned stimulus. This is the result of the pairing of a place (CS) with the event (US). Sometimes, though, classical conditioning involves an experience that is both pleasant and deviant from the norm. Consider a fetishist who becomes sexually aroused by the sight and touch of certain clothing, such as undergarments or shoes. The fetish may have developed when the fetish object (undergarment, shoe) was associated with sexual arousal, especially when the individual was young. The fetish object becomes a conditioned stimulus that can produce sexual arousal by itself (Chance, 1979).

Evaluating Classical Conditioning

Pavlov described learning in terms of classical conditioning. While classical conditioning helps us to learn about our environment, we learn about our world in other ways, too. Classical conditioning describes the organism as *responding* to the environment, a view that fails to capture the active nature of the organism and its influence on the environment. Next, we study a major form of learning that places more emphasis on the organism's *activity* in the environment—operant conditioning.

Before turning to that discussion, however, let's review the main themes of classical conditioning. Summary table 5.1 will help you with this review and will provide information about the basic nature of learning.

SUMMARY TABLE 5.1
The Nature of Learning and Classical Conditioning

Concept	Processes/Related Ideas	Characteristics/Description
What Is Learning?	Its Nature	Learning is a relatively permanent change in behavior due to experience. How we respond to the environment (classical conditioning), how we act in the environment (operant conditioning), and how we observe the environment (observational learning) are the most important ways in which we experience. Early approaches emphasized connections between environment and behavior; many contemporary approaches stress that cognitive factors mediate environment-behavior connections.
Classical Conditioning	Pavlovian Conditioning	Pavlov discovered that an organism learns the association between an unconditioned stimulus (US) and a conditioned stimulus (CS). The US automatically produces the UR (unconditioned response). After conditioning (CS-US pairing), the CS elicits the CR (conditioned response) by itself. Generalization, discrimination, and extinction also are involved. Classical conditioning is a form of associative learning, which involves learning that two events are related or linked. In classical conditioning, the learned association involves the link between two stimuli (CS and US).
	Temporal Contiguity and Contingency	Pavlov argued that for classical conditioning to take place, the CS–US connection has to have temporal contiguity. Rescorla believes the CS–US connection also has to involve contingency in that one stimulus has to be able to predict the presence of the other stimulus.
	How Classical Conditioning Works: Pavlov and the Contemporary Perspective	Pavlov explained classical conditioning in terms of stimulus substitution but one modern explanation is based on information theory.
	Classical Conditioning in Humans	Classical conditioning has survival value for humans, as when we develop a fear of hazardous conditions. Irrational fears are explained by classical conditioning. Counterconditioning has been used to eliminate fears.
	Evaluating Classical Conditioning	Classical conditioning is important in explaining the way learning in animals occurs. It is not the only way humans learn and fails to capture the active nature of an organism in the environment.

Operant Conditioning

We have discussed one major type of learning—classical conditioning. Now let's explore a second major type—operant conditioning.

What Operant Conditioning Is

Classical conditioning excels at explaining how neutral stimuli become associated with unlearned, involuntary responses, but it is not as effective in explaining voluntary behaviors, such as studying hard for a test, playing slot machines in Las Vegas, or teaching a pigeon to play Ping-Pong. Operant conditioning is usually better than

Classical Conditioning

Stimulus 1 (CS)	Stimulus 2 (US)

Note: A child associates going to a doctor's office (stimulus 1) with getting a painful injection (stimulus 2).

Operant Conditioning

Response	Consequences

5.9   5.8   5.8

Note: Performing well in skating in a competition (response) becomes associated with getting high marks (consequences).

Figure 5.4
Associative Learning: Comparing Classical and Operant Conditioning

classical conditioning at explaining voluntary behavior. The concept of operant conditioning was developed by the American psychologist B. F. Skinner (1938) ◀▥ P. 8. **Operant conditioning** *(or instrumental conditioning) is a form of learning in which the consequences of behavior produce changes in the probability of the behavior's occurrence.* Skinner chose the term *operant* to describe the behavior of the organism— the behavior operates on the environment, and the environment in turn operates on the behavior.

When we described classical conditioning earlier, we said that it is a form of associative learning. Operant conditioning also is a form of associative learning. However, in classical conditioning the association is between two stimuli, whereas in operant conditioning the association is between a response and its consequences (see figure 5.4). For example, in operant conditioning, performing a great skating routine in competition (response) is likely to result in a high score from the judges (consequences). Recall also that we said classical conditioning involves a contingency between the organism's response and its consequences. For example, a simple operant might be pressing a lever that leads to the delivery of food; the delivery of food is contingent on pressing the lever.

Operant Conditioning

Thorndike's Law of Effect

Although B. F. Skinner has emerged as the primary figure in operant conditioning, E. L. Thorndike's experiments established the power of consequences in determining voluntary behavior. At about the same time Ivan Pavlov was conducting classical conditioning experiments with salivating dogs, American psychologist E. L. Thorndike was studying cats in puzzle boxes. Thorndike put a hungry cat inside a box and a piece of fish outside. To escape from the box, the cat had to learn how to open the latch inside the box. At first the cat made a number of ineffective responses. It clawed or bit at the bars and thrust its paw through the openings. Eventually the cat accidentally stepped on the treadle that released the door bolt. When the cat returned to the box, it went through the same random activity until it

(a)

(b)

$\mathscr{F}$igure 5.5
Thorndike's Puzzle Box and the Law of Effect

(a) A box typical of the puzzle boxes Thorndike used in his experiments with cats to study the law of effect. Stepping on the treadle released the door bolt. A weight attached to the door then pulled the door open and allowed the cat to escape. *(b)* One cat's learning curve over 24 separate trials. Notice how the cat learned to escape much more quickly after about 5 trials, learning the consequences of its behavior.

stepped on the treadle once more. On subsequent trials, the cat made fewer and fewer random movements, until it immediately clawed the treadle to open the door (see figure 5.5). The **law of effect,** *developed by Thorndike, states that behaviors followed by positive outcomes are strengthened, whereas behaviors followed by negative outcomes are weakened.*

The key question for Thorndike was how the correct stimulus-response bond strengthens and eventually dominates incorrect stimulus-response bonds. According to Thorndike, the correct S-R association strengthens and the incorrect association weakens because of the *consequences* of the organism's actions. Thorndike's view is called *S-R theory* because the organism's behavior is due to a connection between a stimulus and a response. As we see next, Skinner's operant conditioning approach expanded Thorndike's basic ideas.

Skinner's Operant Conditioning

Earlier we indicated that Skinner described operant conditioning as a form of learning in which the consequences of behavior lead to changes in the probability of that behavior's occurrence. The consequences—reinforcement or punishment—are contingent on the organism's behavior. First we will tackle reinforcement, then we will discuss punishment.

Positive and Negative Reinforcement   *Reinforcement* means "to strengthen." In **positive reinforcement,** *the frequency of a response increases because it is followed by a rewarding stimulus.* For example, if someone you meet smiles at you and the two of you talk for some time, the smile has reinforced your talking. Similarly, complimenting someone you are attracted to might make that person more receptive to your advances and increase the probability that you will get to know the person better. The same principle of positive reinforcement is at work when an animal trainer teaches a dog to "shake hands" by giving it a piece of food when it lifts its paw.

Conversely, in **negative reinforcement** *the frequency of a response increases because it is followed by the removal of an aversive (unpleasant) stimulus.* For example,

B. F. Skinner
Positive Reinforcement
Skinner on Audio

your father nags at you to clean out the garage. He keeps nagging. Finally you get tired of the nagging and clean out the garage. Your response (cleaning out the garage) removed the unpleasant stimulus (nagging). Taking an aspirin works the same way. Taking aspirin is reinforced when this behavior is followed by a reduction of pain.

To understand the distinction between positive and negative reinforcement, remember that "positive" and "negative" don't have anything to do with "good" and "bad." And just keep remembering that they are procedures in which something is given (positive reinforcement) and something is removed (negative reinforcement). Figure 5.6 provides another example to further help you understand the distinction between positive and negative reinforcement.

Mechanisms of Learning Are the Same in All Species

One of Skinner's basic beliefs was that the mechanisms of learning are the same for all species. This belief led him to an extensive study of animals in the hope that the basic mechanisms of learning could be understood with organisms more simple than humans.

For example, during World War II, Skinner constructed a rather strange project—a pigeon-guided missile. A pigeon in the warhead of the missile operated the flaps on the missile and guided it home by pecking at an image of a target. How could this possibly work? When the missile was in flight, the pigeon pecked the moving image on a screen. This produced corrective signals to keep the missile on its course. The pigeons did their job well in trial runs, but top Navy officials just could not accept pigeons piloting their missiles in a war. Skinner, however, congratulated himself on the degree of control he was able to exercise over the pigeons (see figure 5.7).

Following the pigeon experiment, Skinner (1948) wrote *Walden Two*, a novel in which he presented his ideas about building a scientifically managed society. Skinner envisioned a utopian society that could be engineered through behavioral control. Skinner viewed existing societies as poorly managed because people believe in myths

"Once it became clear to me that, by responding correctly to certain stimuli, I could get all the bananas I wanted, getting this job was a pushover."

𝓕igure 5.6
Positive and Negative Reinforcement

*F*igure 5.7
Skinner's Pigeon-Guided Missile

Skinner wanted to assist the military by using pigeons' tracking behavior. A gold electrode covered the tip of the pigeons' beaks. Contact with the screen on which the image of the target was projected sent a signal informing the missile's control mechanism of the target's location. A few grains of food occasionally given to the pigeons maintained their tracking behavior.

Skinner Box

What are some ways shaping can be used in learning?

such as free will. He pointed out that humans are no more free than pigeons are; denying that our behavior is controlled by environmental forces is to ignore science and reality, he argued. Skinner believed that in the long run we would be much happier when we recognized such truths, especially his concept that we could live a prosperous life under the control of positive reinforcement.

Skinner and other behaviorists have made every effort to study organisms under precisely controlled conditions so that the connection between the operant and the specific consequences could be examined in minute detail. One of the ways in which Skinner achieved such control was the development in the 1930s of the Skinner box (see figure 5.8). A device in the box would deliver food pellets into a tray at random. After a rat became accustomed to the box, Skinner installed a lever and observed the rat's behavior. As the hungry rat explored the box, it occasionally pressed the lever and a food pellet would be dispensed. Soon after, the rat learned that the consequences of pressing the lever were positive—it would be fed. Further control was achieved by soundproofing the box to ensure that the experimenter was the only influence on the organism. In many experiments the responses were mechanically recorded and the food (the stimulus) was dispensed automatically. Such precautions were designed to avoid human error.

Time Interval   As with classical conditioning, learning is more efficient in operant conditioning when the interval between response and reinforcement is a few seconds rather than minutes or hours. An especially important distinction to remember is that learning is more efficient under *immediate* rather than delayed consequences (Holland, 1996).

Shaping   When a behavior takes time to occur, the learning process in operant conditioning can be shortened if an *approximation* of the desired behavior is rewarded. **Shaping** *is the process of rewarding approximations of desired behavior.* In one situation, parents used shaping to toilet train their 2-year-old son. The parents knew all too well that the grunting sound the child made signaled he was about to fill his diaper. In the first week they gave him candy if they heard the sound within 20 feet of the bathroom. The second week he was given candy only if he grunted within 10 feet of the bathroom, the third week only if he was in the bathroom, and the fourth week, he had to use the toilet to get the candy (Fischer & Gochros, 1975). It worked!

Primary and Secondary Reinforcement   Positive reinforcement can be classified as primary reinforcement or secondary reinforcement, which focuses on a distinction between inborn, unlearned, and learned aspects of behavior. **Primary reinforcement** *involves the use of reinforcers that are innately satisfying; that is, they do not take any learning on the organism's part to make them pleasurable.* Food, water, and sexual satisfaction are primary reinforcers.

Secondary reinforcement *acquires its positive value through experience; secondary reinforcers are learned or conditioned reinforcers.* Hundreds of secondary reinforcers characterize our lives. For example, secondary reinforcers include such social situations as getting a pat on the back, praise, and eye contact. One popular story in psychology focuses on the use of eye contact as a secondary reinforcer to shape the behavior of a famous university professor, an expert on operant conditioning. Some students decided to train the professor to lecture from one corner of the classroom. They used eye contact as a reinforcer and began reinforcing successive approximations to the desired response. Each time the professor moved toward the appropriate corner, the students would look at him. If he moved in another direction, they looked away. By gradually rewarding successive approximations to the desired response, the students were able to get the professor to deliver his lecture from just one corner of the classroom. The well-known operant conditioning expert denies that this shaping ever took place. Whether it did or not, the story provides an excellent example of how secondary reinforcers can be used to shape behavior in real-life circumstances (Chance, 1979).

Another example also helps to understand the importance of secondary reinforcement in our everyday lives. When a student is given $25 for an A on her report card, the $25 is a secondary reinforcer. It is not innate, and it increases the likelihood the student will work to get another A in the future. Money is often referred to as a *token reinforcer.* When an object can be exchanged for some other reinforcer, the object may have reinforcing value itself, so it is called a token reinforcer. Gift certificates and poker chips are other token reinforcers.

Schedules of Reinforcement   Most of the examples of reinforcement we have discussed so far have involved **continuous reinforcement,** *in which a response is reinforced every time it occurs.* When continuous reinforcement occurs, organisms learn rapidly. However, when reinforcement stops, extinction also takes place quickly. If a pay telephone we tend to use starts "eating" our coins and not giving us a dial tone, we quickly stop putting in more coins. However, several weeks later, we might try it again hoping it now works properly (which illustrates spontaneous recovery).

Partial reinforcement *involves a response being reinforced only a portion of the time.* Most of life's experiences involve partial reinforcement, not continuous reinforcement. A golfer does not win every tournament she enters; a chess whiz does not win every match he plays; a student is not patted on the back each time she solves a problem. **Schedules of reinforcement** *are "timetables" that determine when a response will be reinforced.* The four main schedules of reinforcement are fixed-ratio, variable-ratio, fixed-interval, and variable-interval.

A **fixed-ratio schedule** *reinforces a behavior after a set number of responses.* For example, if you are playing the slot machines in Atlantic City and they are on a fixed-ratio schedule, you might get $5 back every 20 times you put money in the machine. It wouldn't take long to figure out that if you watched someone else play the machine 18 or 19 times, not get any money back, and then walk away, you should step up, insert your coin, and get back $5. Fixed-ratio schedules often are used in business to increase production. For example, a salesperson might be required to sell a specific number of items to get a commission. One characteristic of fixed-ratio schedules is that performance often drops off just after reinforcement.

Consequently, slot machines are on a **variable-ratio schedule,** *a timetable in which responses are rewarded an average number of times, but on an unpredictable basis.* For example, a slot machine might pay off at an average of every twentieth time, but unlike the fixed-ratio schedule, the gambler does not know when this payoff will be. The slot machine might pay off twice in a row and then not again until after 58 coins have been inserted. This averages out to a reward for every 20 responses, but when the reward will be given is unpredictable. Variable-ratio schedules produce high, steady rates of responding that are more resistant to extinction than the other three schedules.

The remaining two reinforcement schedules are determined by *time elapsed* since the last behavior was rewarded. A **fixed-interval schedule** *reinforces the first appropriate response after a fixed amount of time has elapsed.* For example, you might get a reward the first time you put money in a slot machine after every 10-minute period has elapsed. The behavior of politicians campaigning for reelection often reflects a fixed-interval schedule of reinforcement. After they have been elected, they reduce their campaigning and then don't pick it up again heavily until just before the next election (which can be 2 to 4 years later). On a fixed-interval schedule, few responses are made until the time approaches that the behavior likely will be reinforced (in the example just mentioned, getting reelected), then the rate of responding picks up rapidly.

Figure 5.8

B. F. Skinner conducting an operant conditioning study in his behavioral laboratory.

Slot machines are on a variable-ratio schedule of reinforcement. What does this mean?

Schedules of Reinforcement

A **variable-interval schedule** *is a timetable in which a response is reinforced after a variable amount of time has elapsed.* On this schedule, the slot machines might reward you after 10 minutes, then after 2 minutes, then after 18 minutes, and so on. Pop quizzes are on a variable interval schedule. So is fishing—you don't know if the fish will bite in the next minute, in a half hour, in an hour, or at all. Because it is difficult to predict when a reward will come, behavior is slow and consistent on a variable-interval schedule.

Figure 5.9 shows how the different schedules of reinforcement result in different rates of responding.

Extinction, Generalization, and Discrimination   Remember from our discussion of classical conditioning that extinction, generalization, and discrimination are important principles. They also are important principles in operant conditioning.

Extinction   **Extinction** *in operant conditioning occurs when a previously reinforced response is no longer reinforced and there is a decreased tendency to perform the response.* Spontaneous recovery also characterizes the operant form of extinction. For example, a factory worker gets a monthly bonus for producing more than her quota. Then, as a part of economic tightening, the company decides that it can no longer afford the bonuses. When bonuses were given, the worker's productivity was above quota every month; once the bonus was removed, performance decreased.

Generalization   **Generalization** *in operant conditioning means giving the same response to similar stimuli.* For example, in one study pigeons were reinforced for pecking at a disc of a particular color (Guttman & Kalish, 1956). Stimulus generalization was tested by presenting the pigeons with discs of varying colors. As shown in figure 5.10, the pigeons were most likely to peck at the disc closest in color to the original. An example from everyday life involves a student who has great success in dating people who dress very neatly and not so good results with people who dress sloppily. The student subsequently seeks dates with people who dress neatly, the neater the better, and avoids dating sloppy dressers, especially the sloppiest.

Discrimination   **Discrimination** *in operant conditioning means responding to stimuli that signal that a behavior will or will not be reinforced.* For example, you might look at two street signs, both made of metal, both the same color, and both with words on them. However, one sign says "Enter at your own risk" and the other reads "Please walk this way." The words serve as discriminative stimuli because the sign that says "Please walk this way" indicates that you will be rewarded for doing so. However, the sign that says "Enter at your own risk" suggests that the consequences may not be positive if you walk past it. As another example, consider that football players are far more likely to tackle people in a football stadium than in a church. Further, they tackle people with certain colors on a uniform (the opposing team's rather than their own). They also don't tackle certain other people in uniforms, such as cheerleaders, referees, and police officers.

Punishment   Let's explore what punishment is and why one type of punishment usually is not recommended by psychologists.

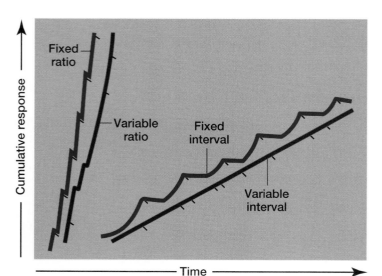

$\mathscr{F}$**igure 5.9**
Schedules of Reinforcement and Different Patterns of Responding

In this figure, each hash mark indicates the delivery of reinforcement. Notice on the fixed-interval schedule the dropoff in responding after each response; on the variable-interval schedule the high, steady rate of responding; on the fixed-interval schedule the immediate dropoff in responding after reinforcement and the increase in responding just before reinforcement (which results in a scallop-shaped curve); and on the variable-interval schedule the slow, steady rate of responding.

Exploring What Punishment Is   Punishment *refers to a conse-quence that decreases the likelihood a behavior will occur.* For example, a child plays with an attractive matchbox and gets burned when one of the matches is lit. In the future, the child is less likely to play with matches. Figure 5.11 provides another illustration of punishment in which a student interrupts the teacher, the teacher verbally reprimands the student, and the student subsequently stops interrupting the teacher.

Punishment differs from reinforcement in the following way. In punishment, a behavior is weakened. In reinforcement, a behavior is strengthened. Recall also that we distinguished between positive rein-forcement (a response increases because it is followed by a rewarding stimulus) and negative reinforcement (a response increases because it is followed by the removal of an aversive stimulus). So punishment is not the same as negative reinforcement. In punishment, a response de-creases because of its consequences; in negative reinforcement, a re-sponse increases because of its consequences.

The following example should further help you distinguish between negative reinforcement and punishment. When an alcoholic consumes liquor to alleviate uncomfortable withdrawal symptoms, the probability that that person will use alcohol in the future is increased. The reduction of the withdrawal symptoms was a negative reinforcer for drinking. But if an inebriated alcoholic is seriously injured in a car wreck and subse-quently quits drinking as much, punishment was involved because a be-havior (drinking) was decreased.

The positive–negative distinction also can be applied to punishment, although it is not used as widely as in reinforcement. In **positive pun-ishment,** *a behavior decreases when it is followed by an unpleasant stimu-lus.* In **negative punishment,** *a behavior decreases when a positive stimulus is removed from it.* Figure 5.12 compares positive reinforcement, negative reinforcement, positive punishment, and negative punishment.

Time-out *is a form of negative punishment in which a child is removed from a positive reinforcement.* It generally is recommended over presenting an aversive stim-ulus (positive reinforcement) as typically is done when punishment is administered. If a child is behaving in disruptive ways in the classroom, the teacher might put the child in a chair in the corner of the room facing away from the class or take the child to a time-out room.

Positive Punishment Often Is Not a Good Choice   Many people asso-ciate punishment with yelling at children or spanking them. However, remember that to satisfy a formal definition of punishment, the consequences have to decrease the behavior. All too often, though, aversive stimuli don't do what they are intended to do—namely, decrease an unwanted behavior (Edwards, 1999). Some people turn too

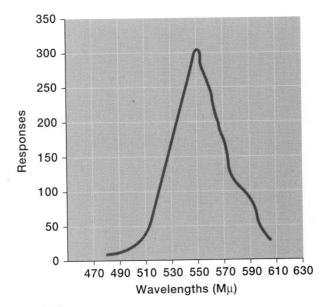

𝒯igure 5.10
Stimulus Generalization

In the experiment by Guttman and Kalish (1956), pigeons initially pecked a disc of a particular color (in this graph, a color with a wavelength of 550 Mµ) after they had been reinforced for this wavelength. Subse-quently, when the pigeons were presented discs of colors with varying wavelengths, they were more likely to peck discs that were similar to the original disc.

𝒯igure 5.11
Punishment

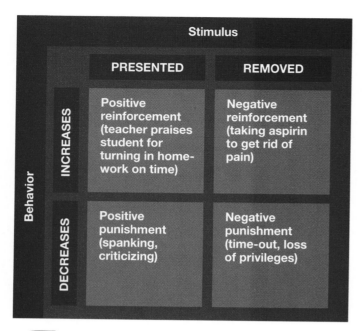

Figure 5.12
Positive Reinforcement, Negative Reinforcement, Positive Punishment, and Negative Punishment

quickly to aversive stimuli when trying to change a child's behavior. They might do this because they were harshly disciplined when they were growing up and they are just repeating how their parents dealt with them, or because they have developed a style of handling stress by yelling or screaming, feel they can effectively exercise power over their smaller charges, or are unaware of how positive reinforcement or other techniques, such as a time-out, can be used to improve children's behavior.

In one study, when parents spanked their children it increased their children's antisocial behavior, such as cheating, telling lies, being mean to others, bullying, getting into fights, and being disobedient (Strauss, Sugarman, & Giles-Sims, 1997). In a national sample of 807 mothers of children 6 to 9 years old, 44 percent of the mothers spanked their children. The mothers reported that the week prior to being interviewed, they spanked them an average of 2.1 times. The more the mothers spanked their children, the more likely the children were to engage in antisocial behavior 2 years later.

Why do most psychologists usually recommend positive reinforcement or a time-out over using aversive stimuli that are involved in punishment? The reasons include the following (Santrock, in press):

• When intense punishment like yelling, screaming, or spanking is used, the adult is presenting children with an out-of-control model for handling stressful situations. The children might imitate this aggressive, out-of-control model.
• Punishment can instill fear, rage, or avoidance in children. Skinner's biggest concern was that punishment teaches organisms to avoid something. For example, a student who has a punitive teacher might dislike the teacher and not want to come to school.
• When children are punished, they can be so aroused and anxious that they can't concentrate clearly on their work for a long time after the punishment is given.
• Punishment tells people what not to do rather than what to do. When an adult makes a punishing statement such as "No, that's not right," they should always accompany it with positive feedback, such as "but why don't you try this."
• Punishment can be abusive. When parents discipline their children, they might not intend to be abusive but become so aroused when they are punishing the child that they become abusive (Adams, 1998).
• And, as mentioned earlier, what is intended as punishing can turn out to be reinforcing. In school, a child might learn that misbehaving will not only bring the teacher's attention but put the child in the limelight with classmates as well.

Applications of Operant Conditioning

A preschool child repeatedly throws his glasses and breaks them. A high school student and her parents have intense arguments. A college student is deeply depressed. An elderly woman is incontinent. Operant conditioning procedures have helped people such as these to adapt more successfully and cope more effectively with their problems (Hersen & Miller, 1996; Luiselli & Cameron, 1998; Pierce & Epling, 1999). **Applied behavior analysis (behavior modification)** *is the application of operant conditioning principles to change human behavior.* Consequences for behavior are established to ensure that more-adaptive actions are reinforced and less-adaptive ones are not (Baldwin & Baldwin, 1999; Kohlenberg, Tsai, & Kohlenberg, 1996). Advocates of behavior modification believe that many emotional and behavior problems are caused by inadequate (or inappropriate) response consequences (Alberto & Trautman,

1999; Adams, 2000). The child who throws down his glasses and breaks them may be receiving too much attention from his teacher and peers for his behavior; they unwittingly reinforce an unacceptable behavior. In this instance, the parents and teachers would be instructed to divert attention from the destructive behavior and transfer it to a more constructive behavior, such as working quietly or playing cooperatively with peers (Harris, Wolf, & Baer, 1964).

Consider another circumstance. Barbara and her parents were on a collision course. Things got so bad that her parents decided to see a clinical psychologist. The psychologist, who had a behavioral orientation, talked with each family member, trying to get them to pinpoint the problem. The psychologist got the family to sign a behavioral contract that spelled out what everyone needed to do to reduce the conflict. Barbara agreed to (1) be home before 11 p.m. on weeknights; (2) look for a part-time job so she could begin to pay for some of her activities; and (3) refrain from calling her parents insulting names. Her parents agreed to (1) talk to Barbara in a low tone of voice rather than yell if they were angry; (2) refrain from criticizing teenagers, especially Barbara's friends; and (3) give Barbara a small sum of money each week for gas, makeup, and socializing, but only until she found a job.

Also consider Sam, a 19-year-old college student, who has been deeply depressed lately. His girlfriend broke off their relationship of 2 years, and his grades have been dropping. He decides to go to a psychologist who has a behavioral orientation. The psychologist enrolls him in the Coping with Depression course developed by Peter Lewinsohn (1987). Sam learns to monitor his daily moods and increase his ratio of positive to negative life events. The psychologist trains Sam to develop more efficient coping skills and gets Sam to agree to a behavioral contract, just as the psychologist did with Barbara and her parents.

Mary is an elderly woman who lives in a nursing home. In recent months she has become incontinent and is increasingly dependent on the staff for help with her daily activities. The behavioral treatment designed for Mary's problem involves teaching her to monitor her behavior and schedule going to the toilet. She is also required to do pelvic exercises. The program for decreasing Mary's dependence requires that the staff attend more to her independent behavior when it occurs and remove attention from dependent behavior whenever possible. Such strategies with the elderly have been effective in reducing problems with incontinence and dependence.

Behavior modification is used to teach couples to communicate more effectively, to encourage fathers to engage in more competent caregiving with their infants, to train autistic children's interpersonal skills, to help individuals lose weight, and to reduce an individual's fear of social situations. Another effective use of behavior modification is to improve an individual's self-control (Logue, 1995). Information about how this is accomplished is described in Explorations in Psychology.

Behavior modification not only is effective in therapy, but it has also been applied to the world of computers to promote better instruction. Some years ago, Skinner developed a machine to help teachers instruct students. The teaching machine engaged the student in a learning activity, paced the material at the student's rate, tested the student's knowledge of the material, and provided immediate feedback about correct and incorrect answers. Skinner hoped that the machine would revolutionize learning in schools, but the revolution never took place.

Today the idea behind Skinner's teaching machine is applied to computers, which help teachers instruct students. Research comparisons of computer-assisted instruction with traditional teacher-based instruction suggest that, in some areas, such as drill and practice on math problems, computer-assisted instruction can produce superior results (Kulik, Kulik, & Bangert-Drowns, 1985).

By now you should have a good feel for how operant conditioning works. A summary of the main themes of operant conditioning is presented in summary table 5.2.

Through the Eyes of Psychologists

B. F. Skinner, *Behaviorist*

"The effective management of human behavior is jeopardized when we appeal to feelings and ideas in the explanation of behavior. In doing so, we neglect useful environmental contingencies."

Applied Behavior Analysis
Walden "U"

EXPLORATIONS IN PSYCHOLOGY
Using Behavior Modification to Improve Self-Control

CHANCES ARE EACH OF US could stand to change something about our lives. What would you like to change? What would you like to be able to control more effectively in your life? To answer these questions, you first have to specify your problem in a concrete way. For Al, this is easy—he is overweight and wants to lose 30 pounds. Stated even more precisely, he wants to consume about 1,000 fewer calories per day than he uses to give him a weight loss of about 2 pounds per week. Some problems are more difficult to specify, such as "wasting time," "having a bad attitude toward school," "having a poor relationship with —— ," or "being too nervous and worrying a lot." These types of problems have been called "fuzzies" because of their abstract nature (Mager, 1972). It is important to "unfuzzify" these abstract problems and make them more specific and concrete. Problems can be made more precise by writing out your goal and listing the things that would give you clear evidence that you have reached your goal.

A second important step in a self-control program is to make a *commitment* to change (Martin & Pear, 1999). Both a commitment to change and a knowledge of change techniques have been shown to help college students become more effective self-managers of their smoking, eating, studying, and relationship problems. Building a commitment to change requires you to do things that increase the likelihood you will stick to your project. First, tell others about your commitment to change—they will remind you to stick to your program. Second, rearrange your environment to provide frequent reminders of your goal, making sure the reminders are associated with the positive benefits of reaching your goal. Third, put in a lot of time and energy in planning your project. Make a list of statements about your project, such as "I've put a lot of time into this project; I am certainly not going to waste all of this effort now." Fourth, because you will invariably face temptations to backslide or quit your project, plan ahead for ways you can deal with temptation, tailoring these plans to your problem.

A third major step in developing a self-control program is to collect data about your behavior. This is especially important in decreasing excessive behaviors such as overeating and frequent smoking. One of the reasons for tracking your behavior is that it provides a reference point for evaluating your progress. When recording the frequency of a problem during initial observations, you should examine the immediate consequences that could be maintaining the problem (Martin & Pear, 1999).

A fourth major step in developing self-control is to design a self-control program. Many good self-control programs involve setting long-term and short-term goals, and developing a plan for how to reach the goals. Good self-control problems also usually include some type of self-talk, self-instruction, or self-reinforcement. For example, a person whose goal is to jog 30 minutes a day 5 days a week might say, "I'll never make it. It just won't work." This person can benefit by saying something like, "I know it's going to be tough, but I can make it." Also, individuals can engage in self-reinforcing statements or treat themselves. This might involve saying something like, "Way to go. You are up to 30 minutes three times a week. You are on your way." Or they might treat themselves to something like a movie, a new piece of clothing, or a new CD.

A fifth important aspect of improving your self-control is to make it last. One strategy is to establish specific dates for postchecks and to plan a course of action if your postchecks are not favorable. For instance, if your self-control program involves weight reduction, you might want to weigh yourself once a week. If your weight increases to a certain level, then you immediately go back on your self-control program.

Another strategy is to establish a buddy system by finding a friend or someone with a similar problem. The two of you set mutual maintenance goals. Once a month, get together and check each other's behavior. If your goals have been maintained, get together and celebrate in an agreed-upon way. Table 5.A summarizes the main steps in the self-control program we have described.

For other ideas on how to establish an effective self-control program tailored to your needs, you might want to contact the counseling center at your college or university.

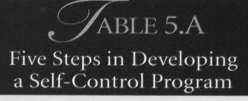

TABLE 5.A
Five Steps in Developing a Self-Control Program

1. Define the problem
2. Commit to change
3. Collect data about yourself
4. Design a self-control program
5. Make the program last—maintenance

Concept	Processes/ Related Ideas	Characteristics/Description
What Operant Conditioning Is	Its Nature	Operant conditioning (or instrumental conditioning) is a form of associative learning in which the consequences of behavior produce changes in the probability of the behavior's occurrence.
	How It Differs from Classical Conditioning	In classical conditioning, the association is between two stimuli, but in operant conditioning the association is between a response and its consequence. Operant conditioning mainly involves voluntary behavior, while classical conditioning primarily involves involuntary behavior.
Thorndike's Law of Effect	Its Nature	It states that behaviors followed by a positive outcome are strengthened, whereas those followed by a negative outcome are weakened. Thorndike's view is referred to as S-R learning.
Skinner's Operant Conditioning	Positive and Negative Reinforcement	In positive reinforcement, the frequency of response is strengthened because it is followed by a rewarding stimulus. In negative reinforcement the frequency of a response increases because the response is followed by the removal of an aversive (unpleasant) stimulus.
	Mechanisms of Learning Are the Same in All Species	This belief led Skinner to extensively study animals in the hope that basic mechanisms of learning could be understood with organisms more simple than humans. Skinner and other behaviorists made every effort to study organisms under precisely controlled conditions, which led to the creation of the Skinner box. Skinner presented his ideas for a scientifically managed society in *Walden Two.*
	Time Interval	Immediate consequences are more effective than delayed consequences.
	Shaping	Shaping is the process of rewarding approximations of the desired behavior.
	Primary and Secondary Reinforcement	Primary reinforcement refers to innate reinforcers (food, water, sex): secondary reinforcement refers to reinforcers that acquire positive value through experience (money, smiles).
	Schedules of Reinforcement	Continuous reinforcement involves a response being reinforced every time it occurs. Partial reinforcement involves a response being reinforced only a portion of the time, which leads to greater resistance to extinction than continuous reinforcement. Four schedules of partial reinforcement are fixed-ratio, variable-ratio, fixed-interval, and variable-interval.
	Extinction, Generalization, and Discrimination	Extinction is a decrease in the tendency to perform the response brought about by unreinforced consequences of that response. Generalization means giving the same response to similar stimuli. Discrimination is the process of responding in the presence of one stimulus that is reinforced but not in the presence of another stimulus that is not reinforced.
	Punishment	Punishment refers to a consequence that decreases the likelihood that a behavior will occur. Punishment differs from reinforcement because in punishment a behavior is weakened, in reinforcement a behavior is strengthened. Just like reinforcement, punishment can be classified as positive or negative. In positive punishment, a behavior decreases when it is followed by a negative stimulus. In negative punishment, a behavior decreases when a positive stimulus is removed from it. Many psychologists think that positive reinforcement and negative punishment (time-out) are better choices than positive punishment.
Applications of Operant Conditioning	Their Nature	This refers to the use of learning principles to change maladaptive or abnormal behavior; applications focus on changing behavior by following it with reinforcement. Behavior modification is used widely to reduce maladaptive behavior. Among its applications are controlling aggressive behavior, reducing conflicts between parents and adolescents, coping with depression, helping elderly individuals function more independently, teaching by computer-assisted instruction, and improving self-control.

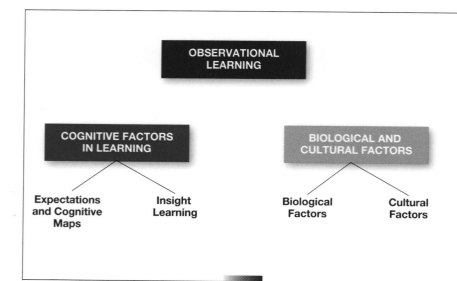

OBSERVATIONAL LEARNING

COGNITIVE FACTORS IN LEARNING

Expectations and Cognitive Maps

Insight Learning

BIOLOGICAL AND CULTURAL FACTORS

Biological Factors

Cultural Factors

Bandura's Theory

Observational Learning

Would it make sense to teach a 15-year-old boy how to drive by either classical conditioning or operant conditioning procedures? Driving a car is a voluntary behavior, so classical conditioning doesn't really apply. In terms of operant conditioning, we would ask him to drive down the road and then reward his positive behaviors. Not many of us would want to be on the road, though, when some of his disastrous mistakes occur. Albert Bandura (1986, 1994) believes that if we learned only in such a trial-and-error fashion, it would be exceedingly tedious and at times hazardous ◀▥ P. 8. Instead, many of our complex behaviors are the result of exposure to competent models who display appropriate behavior in solving problems and coping with their world (Striefel, 1998).

We initially encountered Bandura's ideas in chapter 1, where we briefly introduced his social cognitive theory, and in chapter 1, where we used his classic Bobo doll study of observational learning to demonstrate the steps in the scientific method. Let's now further explore his view of observational learning.

Observational learning, *also called imitation or modeling, is learning that occurs when a person observes and imitates someone's behavior.* The capacity to learn behavior patterns by observation eliminates tedious trial-and-error learning. In many instances observational learning takes less time than operant conditioning.

Bandura (1986) described four main processes that are involved in observational learning: attention, retention, motor reproduction, and reinforcement. For observational learning to take place, the first process that has to occur is *attention* (which we initially discussed in chapter 3 because of its important role in perception). That is, before people can reproduce a model's actions, they must attend to what the model is saying or doing. You might not hear what a friend says if the stereo is blaring, or you might miss the teacher's analysis of a problem if you are admiring someone sitting in the next row. Imagine you decide to take a class to improve your artistic skills. You need to attend to the instructor's words and hand movements. Attention to the model is influenced by a host of characteristics. For example, warm, powerful, atypical people command more attention than do cold, weak, typical people.

The next important process is *retention.* To reproduce a model's actions, you must code the information and keep it in memory so that it can be retrieved. A simple verbal description or a vivid image of what the model did assists retention. Memory is such an important cognitive process that the next chapter is devoted exclusively to it. In the example of taking a class to improve your art skills, you will need to remember what the instructor said and did in modeling good drawing skills.

Another process involved in observational learning is *motor reproduction.* People might attend to a model and code in memory what they have seen, but because of limitations in motor development they might not be able to reproduce the model's action. Thirteen-year-olds might see Michael Jordan do a reverse two-handed dunk but be unable to reproduce the pro's actions. In the example of taking an art class to improve your art skills, you will need good motor reproduction skills to carry out what the instructor said to do.

A final process in Bandura's conception of observational learning involves *reinforcement,* or incentive conditions. On many occasions we may attend to what a model says or does, retain the information in memory, and possess the motor capabilities to perform the action, but we might fail to repeat the behavior because of inadequate reinforcement. This was demonstrated in one of Bandura's (1965) studies in which children who had seen a model punished for aggression reproduced the model's aggression only when they were offered an incentive to do so ◀▥ P. 28. In the example of taking an art class, the instructor chooses one of your art pieces that you made during the class for display. This reinforcement encourages you to keep drawing and take another art skills class.

A summary of Bandura's model of observational learning is shown in figure 5.13.

Bandura views observational learning as an information-processing activity. As a person observes, information about the world is transformed into cognitive representations that serve as guides for action. As we see next, interest in the cognitive factors of learning has increased dramatically in recent years.

Cognitive Factors in Learning

In our excursion through learning we have had little to say about cognitive processes, except in our description of observational learning. In the operant conditioning view of Skinner and the classical conditioning view of Pavlov, no room is given to the possibility that cognitive factors such as memory, thinking, planning, or expectations might be important in learning. Skinnerians point out that they do not deny the existence of thinking processes, but since they cannot be observed they may interfere with the discovery of important environmental conditions that govern behavior.

Many contemporary psychologists, including behavioral revisionists who recognize that cognition should not have been ignored in classical and operant conditioning, believe that learning involves much more than environment-behavior connections. Let's explore these cognitive factors in learning: expectations, cognitive maps, and insight.

Expectations and Cognitive Maps

E. C. Tolman says that when classical and operant conditioning occur the organism acquires certain expectations. In classical conditioning the young boy fears the rabbit because he expects it will hurt him. In operant conditioning a woman works hard all week because she expects to be paid on Friday.

In his paper "Cognitive Maps in Rats and Men," Tolman (1948) articulated his belief that organisms select information from the environment and construct a cognitive map of their experiences. A **cognitive map** *is an organism's mental representation of the structure of physical space.* In Tolman's maze experiments, rats developed mental awareness of physical space and the elements in it. They used these cognitive maps to find where the food was located.

Tolman's idea of cognitive maps is alive and well today (Klatzky, 2000). When we move around in our environment, we develop a cognitive map of where things are located, on both small and large scales. We have a cognitive map of where rooms

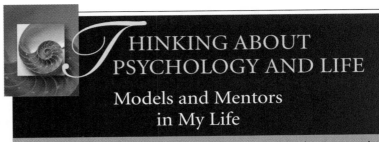

Thinking About Psychology and Life

Models and Mentors in My Life

HAVING POSITIVE ROLE MODELS and mentors to observe and learn from can make important contributions to whether individuals develop optimally and reach their full potential. A mentor is someone you look up to and respect, who serves as a competent model, and who is willing to work with you to help you achieve your goals. The role models and mentors could be your parents, teachers, an older peer, someone in the community. Spend a few minutes and think about the role models and mentors you have had in your life, including now. Do you remember any specific instances in which you watched them do or say something that had a lasting impact on you and you later modeled this behavior? List the most important role models and mentors in your life, then describe what you learned from them and how they helped your learning.

Role Models and Mentors	What I Learned from Them and How They Helped My Learning
1. _____	_____
	_____
	_____
	_____
2. _____	_____
	_____
	_____
3. _____	_____
	_____
	_____
4. _____	_____
	_____
	_____

A mentor can be very beneficial to students. If you currently don't have a mentor, think about the people at your college or university, or people in the community, you respect and look up to. Consider asking one of these people to be a mentor for you.

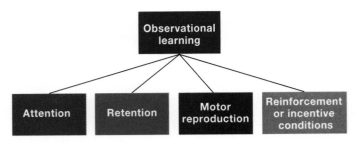

Figure 5.13
Bandura's Model of Observational Learning

Bandura argues that observational learning consists of four main processes: attention, retention, motor reproduction, and reinforcement or incentive conditions. Consider a circumstance involving learning to ski. You need to attend to the instructor's words and demonstrations. You need to remember what the instructor did and her tips for avoiding disasters. You also need the motor abilities to reproduce what the instructor has shown you, and praise from the instructor after you have completed a few moves on the slopes should improve your motivation to continue skiing.

are located in our house or apartment, and we have a cognitive map of where we are located in the United States, for example. A popular tradition is to draw a cognitive map reflecting our perception of the city or state in which we live, relative to the rest of the United States. Texans, for example, usually draw the state of Texas as about three-fourths the size of the entire United States. In Manhattan, "The City" is often drawn about nine-tenths the size of the United States. Of course, such cognitive maps deliberately distort the physical world, reflecting the perceivers' egocentric interest in their city or state.

Tolman was not the only psychologist in the first half of the twentieth century who believed that cognitive factors play an important role in learning. So did Gestalt psychologist Wolfgang Kohler.

Insight Learning

Wolfgang Kohler, a German psychologist, spent 4 months in the Canary Islands during World War I observing the behavior of apes. While there he conducted two fascinating experiments. One is called the "stick problem," the other the "box problem." Though these two experiments are basically the same, the solutions to the problems are different. In both situations, the ape discovers that it cannot reach an alluring piece of fruit, either because the fruit is too high or it is outside of the ape's cage and beyond its reach. To solve the stick problem, the ape has to insert a small stick inside a larger stick to reach the fruit. To master the box problem, the ape must stack several boxes to reach the fruit (see figure 5.14).

According to Kohler (1925), solving these problems does not involve trial and error or mere connections between stimuli and responses. Rather, when the ape realizes that his customary actions are not going to get the fruit, he often sits for a period of time and appears to ponder how to solve the problem. Then he quickly gets up, as if he had a sudden flash of insight, piles the boxes on top of one another, and gets the fruit. **Insight learning** *is a form of problem solving in which the organism develops a sudden insight or understanding of a problem's solution.*

Biological and Cultural Factors in Learning

Albert Einstein had many special talents. He combined enormous creativity with great analytic ability to develop some of this century's most important insights about the nature of matter and the universe. Genes obviously provided Einstein extraordinary intellectual skills to think and reason on a very high plane, but cultural factors also undoubtedly contributed to Einstein's genius. Einstein received an excellent, rigorous European education, and later in the United States he experienced the freedom and support believed to be important in creative exploration. Would Einstein have been able to fully develop his intellectual skills and make such brilliant insights if he had grown up in a Third World country? Unlikely. Quite clearly both biological *and* cultural factors contribute to learning.

Biological Factors

We can't breathe under water, fish can't play table tennis, and cows can't solve math problems. The structure of an organism's body permits certain kinds of learning and inhibits others (Chance, 1999). For example, chimpanzees cannot learn to speak

English because they lack the necessary vocal equipment. Some of us cannot solve difficult calculus problems, others of us can, and the differences do not all seem to be the result of experiences.

Instinctive Drift   An example of biological influences on learning is **instinctive drift,** *the tendency of animals to revert to instinctive behavior that interferes with learning.* Consider the situation of Keller and Marion Breland (1961), students of B. F. Skinner, who used operant conditioning to train animals to perform at fairs, conventions, and in television advertisements. They used Skinner's techniques of shaping, chaining, and discrimination to teach pigs to cart large wooden nickels to a piggy bank and deposit them. They also trained raccoons to pick up a coin and place it in a metal tray. Although the pigs and raccoons, as well as other animals such as chickens, performed well at most of the tasks (raccoons became adept basketball players, for example—see figure 5.15), some of the animals began acting strangely. Instead of picking up the large wooden nickel and carrying it to the piggy bank, the pigs would drop the nickel on the ground, shove it with their snouts, toss it in the air, and then repeat these actions. The raccoons began to hold onto their coin rather than dropping it into the metal container. When two coins were introduced, the raccoons rubbed them together in a miserly fashion. Somehow these behaviors overwhelmed the strength of the reinforcement that was given at the end of the day. Why were the pigs and the raccoons misbehaving? The pigs were rooting, an instinct which is used to uncover edible roots. The raccoons engaged in an instinctive food-washing response. Their instinctive drift interfered with learning.

Preparedness and Taste Aversion   Some animals learn readily in one situation but have difficulty learning in slightly different circumstances. The difficulty might result not from some aspect of the learning situation but from the organism's predisposition (Seligman, 1970). **Preparedness** *is the species-specific biological predisposition to learn in certain ways but not others.*

*𝓕*igure 5.14
Kohler's Box Problem Involving Insight Learning
Sultan, one of Kohler's brightest chimps, is faced with the problem of reaching a cluster of bananas overhead. Suddenly he solves the problem by stacking boxes on top of one another to reach the bananas. Kohler called this type of problem solving "insight learning."

Much of the evidence for preparedness comes from research on taste aversion (Garcia, 1989). Consider this situation: A psychologist went to dinner with his wife and ordered filet mignon with Bérnaise sauce, his favorite dish. Afterward they went to the opera. Several hours later, he became very ill with stomach pains and nausea. Several weeks later, he tried to eat Bérnaise sauce but couldn't bear it. The psychologist's experience involves *taste aversion,* another biological constraint on learning.

If an organism ingests a substance that poisons but does not kill it, the organism often develops considerable distaste for that substance. Rats that experience low levels of radiation after eating show a strong aversion to the food they were eating when the radiation made them ill. This aversion has been shown to last for as long as 32 days. Such long-term effects cannot be accounted for by classical conditioning, which would argue that a single pairing of the conditioned and unconditioned stimuli would not last that long (Garcia, Ervin, & Koelling, 1966). Radiation and chemical treatment of cancer often produces nausea in patients, and the resulting pattern of aversions often resembles those shown by laboratory animals.

Knowledge about taste aversion has been applied to balancing the ecological worlds of animals. For example, the livestock of farmers and ranchers may be threatened by wolves or coyotes. Instead of killing the pests or predators, the farmers feed them poisoned meat of their prey (cattle, sheep). The wolves and coyotes, poisoned but not killed, develop a taste aversion for cattle or sheep and, hence, are less of a threat to the farmers and ranchers. In this way, ranchers, farmers, cattle, sheep, wolves, and coyotes can live in a semblance of ecological balance.

Cultural Factors

In traditional views of learning, concepts such as culture have been given little or no attention. The behavioral orientation that dominated American psychology for much of the twentieth century does focus on the cultural contexts of learning, but the organisms in those contexts have often been animals. When humans have been the subjects, there has been little or no interest in the cultural context.

How does culture influence learning? Most psychologists agree that the principles of classical conditioning, operant conditioning, and observational learning are universal and are powerful learning processes in every culture. However, culture can influence the *degree* to which these learning processes are used, and it often determines the *content* of learning ◀▥ P. 12. For example, punishment is a universal learning process, but as we see next, its use and type show considerable sociocultural variation.

When behaviorism began its influential reign in the United States between 1910 and 1930, child-rearing experts regarded the infant as capable of being shaped into almost any child. Desirable social behavior could be achieved if the child's antisocial behaviors were always punished and never indulged, and if positive behaviors were carefully conditioned and rewarded in a highly controlled and structured child-rearing regimen. The famous behaviorist John Watson (1928) authored a publication, *Infant Care,* that was the official government booklet for parents. This booklet advocated never letting children suck their thumb, and, if necessary, restraining the child by tying her hands to the crib at night and painting her fingers with foul-tasting liquids. Parents were advised to let infants "cry themselves out" rather than reinforce this unacceptable behavior by picking them up to rock and soothe them.

However, from the 1930s to 1960s, a more permissive attitude prevailed and parents were advised to be concerned with the feelings and capacities of the child. Since the 1960s there has been a continued emphasis on the role of parental love in children's socialization, but experts now advise parents to play a less permissive and more active role in shaping children's behavior. Experts stress that parents should set limits and make authoritative decisions in areas where the child is not capable of reasonable judgment. However, they should listen and adapt to the child's point of view, should explain their restrictions and discipline, but not discipline the child in a hostile, punitive manner.

Most child-rearing experts in the United States today do not advocate the physical punishment of children, but the United States does not have a law that prohibits parents from spanking their children. In 1979 Sweden passed a law forbidding parents from using physical punishment, including spanking and slapping, when disciplining their children (Ziegert, 1983). Physical punishment of children is treated as a punishable offense, just like any other attack on a person. The law is especially designed to curb child abuse. Sweden is the only industrial country in the world to pass such a law.

The United States probably could not pass this type of law. Many Americans would view such a law as totalitarian, and the law would likely stimulate protest from civil libertarians and others. An important factor in Sweden's "antispanking" law is its attitude toward rule of law. The United States enforces laws through punishment, but Sweden takes a softer approach, encouraging respect for law through education designed to change attitudes and behavior. When people, often teachers or doctors, suspect that a parent has spanked a child, they often will report the incident because

𝒻igure 5.15
Instinctive Drift
This raccoon's skill in using its hands made it an excellent basketball player, but because of instinctive drift, the raccoon had a much more difficult time taking money to the bank.

SUMMARY TABLE 5.3
Observational Learning, Cognitive Factors, and Biological and Cultural Factors in Learning

Concept	Processes/Related Ideas	Characteristics/Description
Observational Learning	Its Nature	Occurs when an individual observes someone else's behavior. Also called imitation or modeling. It is important to distinguish between what is learned and whether it is performed.
	Processes	Bandura believes that observational learning involves attention, retention, motor reproduction, and reinforcement or incentive conditions.
Cognitive Factors in Learning	Expectations and Cognitive Maps	Tolman reinterpreted classical and operant conditioning in terms of expectations. We construct cognitive maps of our experiences that guide our behavior; psychologists still study the nature of cognitive maps.
	Insight Learning	Kohler, like Tolman, was dissatisfied with the S-R view of learning. He believed that organisms reflect and suddenly gain insight into how a problem should be solved.
Biological and Cultural Factors in Learning	Biological Factors	Biological factors restrict what an organism can learn from experience. These constraints include physical instinctive drift, preparedness, and taste aversion.
	Cultural Factors	While most psychologists agree that the principles of classical conditioning, operant conditioning, and observational learning are universal, cultural customs can influence the degree to which these learning processes are used and culture often determines the content of learning.

they know that the state will try to provide the parent with emotional and educational support rather than assessing a fine or sending the parent to jail. Accompanying the antispanking law was a parenting guide—*Can One Manage to Raise Children Without Spanking or Slapping?*—that was widely available at day-care centers, preschool programs, physicians' offices, and other similar locations. The publication includes advice about why physical punishment is not a good strategy for disciplining children, along with specific information about better ways to handle children's problems.

The content of learning is also influenced by culture (Cole & Cole, 1996). We cannot learn about something we do not experience. The 4-year-old who grows up among the Bushmen of the Kalahari desert is unlikely to learn about taking baths or pouring water from one glass into another. Similarly, a child growing up in Chicago is unlikely to be skilled at tracking animals or finding water-bearing roots in the desert. Learning often requires practice, and certain behaviors are practiced much more often in some cultures than others. In Bali many children are skilled dancers by the age of 6, while Norwegian children are much more likely to be good skiers and skaters by that age. Children growing up in a Mexican village famous for its pottery may work with clay day after day, while children in a nearby village famous for its woven rugs and sweaters rarely become experts at making clay pots.

Since our last review, we have studied a number of ideas about observational learning, cognitive factors in learning, and biological/cultural factors in learning. A summary of these ideas is presented in summary table 5.3.

In this chapter, we studied some important cognitive factors in learning, such as expectations. We devote the entire next chapter to a very important cognitive process: memory.

Overview

Overview

WE BEGAN THIS CHAPTER by defining learning and then turned our attention to three main forms of learning: classical conditioning, operant conditioning, and observational learning. Our coverage of classical conditioning focused on Pavlovian conditioning, temporal contiguity and contingency, extinction, generalization, and discrimination, how classical conditioning works (Pavlov and the contemporary perspective), classical conditioning in humans, and an evaluation of classical conditioning. Our discussion of operant conditioning involved describing what it is, Thorndike's law of effect, many aspects of Skinner's operant conditioning, and applications of operant conditioning. We also studied observational learning. Next, we examined these cognitive factors in learning: expectations, cognitive maps, and insight learning. At the end of the chapter, we explored biological and cultural factors in learning.

Don't forget that you can obtain a more detailed overview of the chapter by again studying the three summary tables on pages 154, 165, and 171.

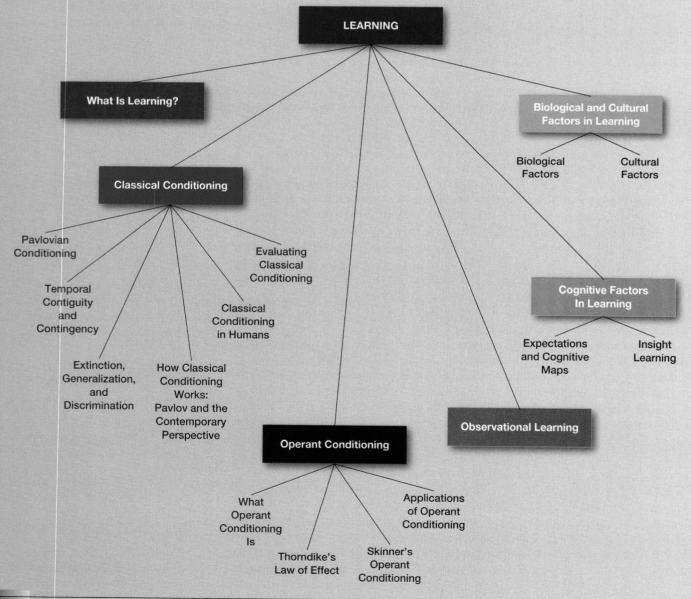

Key Terms

learning 146
classical conditioning 147
reflexes 147
unconditioned stimulus (US) 147
unconditioned response (UR) 147
conditioned stimulus (CS) 148
conditioned response (CR) 148
associative learning 148
contiguity 148
contingency (in classical conditioning) 148

extinction (in classical conditioning) 148
spontaneous recovery 148
generalization (in classical conditioning) 150
discrimination (in classical conditioning) 150
stimulus substitution 151
information theory 151
phobia 152
counterconditioning 152
operant conditioning 155
law of effect 156
positive reinforcement 156
negative reinforcement 156

shaping 158
primary reinforcement 158
secondary reinforcement 158
continuous reinforcement 159
partial reinforcement 159
schedules of reinforcement 159
fixed-ratio schedule 159
variable-ratio schedule 159
fixed-interval schedule 159
variable-interval schedule 160
extinction (in operant conditioning) 160
generalization (in operant conditioning) 160

discrimination (in operant conditioning) 160
punishment 161
positive punishment 161
negative punishment 161
time-out 161
applied behavior analysis (behavior modification) 162
observational learning 166
cognitive map 167
insight learning 168
instinctive drift 169
preparedness 169

Key People

Ivan Pavlov 147
Robert Rescorla 148
E. C. Tolman 151

Leon Kamin 151
John Watson 152
Mary Cover Jones 152

B. F. Skinner 155, 163
E. L. Thorndike 155
Albert Bandura 166

Wolfgang Kohler 168

Taking It to the Net

1. Many colleges now offer online courses, available over the Internet. They use a method of learning called programmed instruction. Information is presented in steps, requiring the student to first complete one task before moving on to more difficult material. After each step, the student is given feedback on her work and a letter grade. This programmed instruction model adheres to a specific type of learning. Can you name it and identify its components? Do you think this is an effective way of learning? What are some criticisms of this type of learning?

2. Consider a summer job in which you are required to canvass for a window-cleaning company. You are given a territory to cover and asked to knock on people's doors to sign them up for window cleaning. You receive no base pay, but earn a significant amount in commission. Therefore, the more people you sign up for the service, the more you get paid. Moreover, your boss gives extra bonuses after every 10 people you sign up. Your boss is using the concept of reinforcement, and a specific schedule of reinforcement in particular. Which schedule of reinforcement is being used? Do you think that you will work harder this way than if you are paid a smaller amount every two weeks? Explain.

3. *Clockwork Orange*, a film by Stanley Kubrick, popularized the idea of behavior modification. The main character is a teenage thug whose violent acts lead to his eventual imprisonment. In prison, he opts to get a sentence reduction by undergoing intense behavior modification. This behavior modification resulted in rapid rehabilitation and his eventual release from prison. Describe the behavior modification process and what it cost him. Do you think this is an effective method of rehabilitation? Explain your answer.

Connect to http://www.mhhe.com/psychology/santrock to find the answers!

Chapter 6

CHAPTER OUTLINE

Memory

Images of Psychology and Life
M. K. and the Russian, S.

> " $\mathcal{I}$ come into the fields and spacious palaces of my memory, where are treasures of countless images of things of every manner. "
>
> St. Augustine
> *Christian Church Father, 5th Century*

THERE ARE FEW moments when we are not steeped in memory. Memory can quietly stir, or spin off, with each step we take, each thought we think, each word we utter. Memory is the web of private images in which past and present are interwoven. It anchors the self in continuity. These are some of the questions we will explore in this chapter:

- How do memories get encoded, stored, and retrieved?
- What is the brain's role in memory?
- What are people most likely to remember about their lives?
- What role do emotional experiences play in memory?
- Why do we forget?
- What are some good memory and study strategies?

HOW IMPORTANT is memory to us? Consider the unfortunate case of M. K., a high school teacher who at the age of 43 was stricken with an acute episode of encephalitis (an inflammation of the brain caused by a virus, which, unless quickly treated, can cause serious brain damage). Within hours he lost access to almost all the memories he had formed during the previous 5 years. Worse still, he had virtually no memory of anything that happened to him after the onset of the encephalitis. Since the illness began, M. K. has learned a few names and a few major events over the years, and he can get around the hospital. M. K.'s tragic circumstance, in which a microscopic viral agent rendered him memoryless, conveys the emptiness of a life without memory.

The power of memory is also revealed in another, very different case. A Russian known only by the initial S. could remember a list of seventy items without making an error, and he had no difficulty recalling the list backward. S. once was asked to remember the following formula:

$$N \cdot \sqrt{d^2 \cdot \frac{85}{VX}} \cdot 3\sqrt{\frac{276^2 \cdot 86x}{n^2 V \cdot \pi 264}} \quad n^2 b$$
$$= sv \frac{1624}{32^2} \cdot r^2 s$$

S. studied the formula for 7 minutes and then reported how he memorized it. The following portion of his response reveals how he made up stories to aid his memory:

> Neiman (N) came out and jabbed at the ground with his cane ($\cdot$). He looked up at a tall tree, which resembled the square-root sign ($\sqrt{}$), and thought to himself: "No wonder this tree has withered and begun to expose its roots. After all, it was here when I built these two houses" (d^2). Once again he poked his cane ($\cdot$). Then he said: "The houses are old, I'll have to get rid of them; the sale will bring in far more money." He had originally invested $85,000 in them (85).

S.'s complete story was four times this length. It must have been a powerful one, because 15 years later with no advance notice he recalled the formula perfectly.

Envious as we might be of S.'s remarkable memory, especially when taking college exams, S. suffered from it. He had to devise techniques for forgetting because he remembered virtually everything, no matter how trivial. He once commented that each word called up images, which collided with one another—the result sometimes was chaos. Forgetting was M. K.'s curse, but it was S.'s salvation.

The Nature of Memory

Just what is memory? How necessary is it for our everyday functioning?

What Is Memory?

Memory *is the retention of information over time*. Psychologists study how information is initially placed or encoded into memory, how it is retained or stored after being encoded, and how it is found or retrieved for a certain purpose later ◀▥ P. 11.

Exploring Memory

Except for the annoying moments when memory fails or someone we know is afflicted with memory loss, most of us don't think much about how virtually everything we do or say depends on how smoothly our memory systems operate (Schacter, 1996, 1999, 2000). Take a moment and think about how important memory is in carrying out the simple task of meeting a friend at a restaurant. To begin with, you have to remember your friend's name and phone number. You have to bring to mind all of the information needed to execute the phone call. You have to use your memory of voices to determine whether the person answering the phone is your friend. To carry on the phone conversation with your friend, you have to access a vast dictionary of words, sounds, meanings, and syntax stored in your memory. At some point, you will have to sort through your memory of visits to restaurants, or recommendations of new ones, to decide on which restaurant is a good choice. You have to recall details of how to get to the restaurant. You also have to remember what else is going on in your life so that you don't plan to meet your friend when you have something else scheduled.

We rely on our memory systems to carry out similar feats every day of our lives. Human memory systems truly are remarkable when you think of how much information we put into our memory and how much we must retrieve to perform all of life's activities.

Human memory also has its imperfections, as we have all experienced. It is not unusual to find two people arguing about something that happened or didn't happen, each intensely confident that his or her memory is accurate and the other person remembers the circumstance inaccurately. Each of us also has had the frustrating experience of trying to remember someone's name or a place but not quite being able to retrieve it.

Among the other imperfections of memory that surface are the stunning, high-profile disagreements in our nation's courtrooms and political arenas. In the trials of O. J. Simpson, Timothy McVeigh, and others, one person remembers something one way while someone else remembers it another way. In Watergate, the Iran Contra Affair, and recent accusations of sexual misconduct against President Clinton, the main players often paint a different portrait of events and circumstances from their memories. An important point about memory is that we don't just coldly store and retrieve bits of data in a computer-like fashion (Schacter, 1996, 1999, 2000). In the early scientific study of memory, the subjective experience of memory was considered inappropriate subject matter for psychology. However, today, many scientists who study memory recognize its subjective nature and investigate how people reconstruct their own versions of the past. They recognize that the mind can distort, invent, and forget. And they know that emotions color memories. Clearly, we don't store judgment-free memories of reality.

Thus, the contemporary story of memory is about its phenomenal abilities, on the one hand, and its numerous limitations, on the other. In this chapter, we will

**Memory and Cognition
Exploring Memory**

$\mathcal{F}$igure 6.1
Processing Information in Memory
As you read about the many aspects of memory in this chapter, it
should help you to think about the organization of memory in
terms of these three main activities.

profile these memory skills, as well as the ways memories can fail us. The next three
sections of the chapter focus on encoding, storage, and retrieval. Although there are
many complex dimensions to memory, thinking about memory in terms of these
three domains should help you to understand it better (see figure 6.1). That is, for
memory to work, we have to take information in, store it or represent it in some
manner, and then retrieve it for some purpose later.

Encoding *involves how information gets into memory.* **Storage** *consists of the retention of information over time.* And **retrieval** *takes place when information is taken
out of storage.* Let's now explore each of these important memory activities in greater
detail.

Memory Encoding

In everyday experiences, encoding has much in common with learning. When you
are listening to a lecture, watching a movie, listening to music, or talking with a
friend, you are encoding information into memory. Some information gets into
memory virtually automatically, while getting other information in takes effort. Let's
examine some of encoding's processes that require effort. These include our rehearsal
of information, how deeply we process it, how extensively we elaborate it, our use of
mental imagery, and how effectively we organize what we need to remember.

Rehearsal

Rehearsal *is the conscious repetition of information that increases the length of time
that information stays in memory.* To understand what we mean by rehearsal, imagine that you are looking up a phone number. If you can directly reach for the telephone, you probably won't have much trouble dialing the number, because the entire
combined action of looking up the number and dialing it can take place in a brief
amount of time. But what if the telephone is not right by the phone book? Perhaps
the phone book is in the kitchen and you want to talk privately on the extension in
the bedroom. You probably will *rehearse* the number as you walk from the kitchen
to the bedroom. Most of us experience a kind of "inner voice" that repeats the number again and again until we finally dial it. If someone or something interrupts our
rehearsal, we might lose the information.

Rehearsal works best when we need to remember a list of numbers or items for
a brief time period. When we have to remember information for long periods of time,

SHALLOW PROCESSING	Physical and perceptual features are analyzed.	The lines, angles, and contour that make up the physical appearance of an object, such as a car, are detected.
INTERMEDIATE PROCESSING	Stimulus is recognized and labeled.	The object is recognized as a car.
DEEP PROCESSING	Semantic, meaningful, symbolic characteristics are used.	Associations connected with car are brought to mind—you think about the Porsche or Ferrari you hope to buy or the fun you and friends had on spring break when you drove a car to the beach.

Depth of processing (vertical axis label, arrow pointing downward)

Figure 6.2
Depth of Processing
According to the levels of processing theory of memory, deep processing of stimuli produces better memory of them.

as when we are studying for a test coming up next week, tomorrow, or even an hour from now, other strategies usually work better than rehearsal. A main reason rehearsal does not work well for retaining information over the long term is that rehearsal often involves just rotely repeating information without imparting any meaning to it. Remembering information over the long term works better when we add meaning to it. As we see next, memory also usually works better when we process it at a deep level and elaborate it.

Deep Processing

Following the discovery that rehearsal is not an efficient way to remember information over the long term, Fergus Craik and Robert Lockhart (1972) proposed that people process information at different levels. Their theory, **levels of processing theory,** *states that memory is on a continuum from shallow to deep, with deeper processing producing better memory.* The sensory or physical features of stimuli are analyzed first at a *shallow* level. This might involve detecting the lines, angles, and contours of a printed word's letters, or a spoken word's frequency, duration, and loudness. At an *intermediate* level of processing, the stimulus is recognized and given a label. For example, a four-legged, barking object is identified as a dog. Then, at the *deepest* level, information is processed semantically, in terms of its meaning. For example, if you saw the word *boat,* at the shallow level you might notice the shapes of the letters, at the intermediate level you might think of characteristics of the word (such as it rhymes with *coat*), and at deepest level you might think about the kind of boat you would like to own and the last time you went fishing. Figure 6.2 depicts the levels of processing theory of memory. A number of studies have shown that people's memories improve when they make associations to stimuli, as opposed to attending just to their physical aspects. In other words, you're more likely to remember something when you process information at a deep, rather than a shallow, level.

Elaboration

Cognitive psychologists soon recognized, however, that there is more to a good memory than just depth of processing. Within deep processing, the more extensive the processing, the better the memory (Craik, 2000; Craik & Tulving, 1975). **Elaboration** *is the extensiveness of processing at any given depth in memory.* For example, rather than memorizing the definition of *memory,* you would do better to learn the concept of memory by coming up with some examples of how information enters your mind, how it is stored, and how you can retrieve it. Thinking of examples of a concept is a good way to understand it. Self-reference is another effective way to elaborate information. For example, if the word *win* is on a list of words to remember, you might think of the last time you won a bicycle race, or if the word *cook* appears, you might imagine the last time you cooked dinner. In general, deep elaboration—elaborate processing of meaningful information—is an excellent way to remember.

One reason elaboration produces good memory is that it adds to the *distinctiveness* of the "memory codes" (Ellis, 1987). To remember a piece of information, such as a name, an experience, or a fact about geography, you need to search for the code that contains this information among the mass of codes contained in long-term memory. The search process is easier if the memory code is somehow unique (Hunt & Kelly, 1996). The situation is not unlike searching for a friend at a crowded airport. If your friend is 6 feet tall and has flaming red hair, it will be easier to find him or her in the crowd. Similarly, highly distinctive memory codes can be more easily differentiated. Also, as encoding becomes more elaborate, more information is stored. And as more information is stored, the more likely it is that this highly distinctive code will be easy to differentiate from other memory codes. For example, if you witness a bank robbery and observe that the getaway car is a red 1987 or 1988 Pontiac with tinted windows and spinners on the wheels, your memory of the car is more distinctive than that of a person who notices only that the getaway car is red.

Imagery

How many windows are in your apartment or house? If you live in a dorm room with only one or two windows, this question might be too easy. If so, how many windows are in your parents' apartment or house? Few of us have ever memorized this information, but many of us believe we can come up with a good answer, especially if we use imagery to "reconstruct" each room. We take a mental walk through the house, counting windows as we go.

Imagery

For many years psychologists ignored the role of imagery in memory because it was believed to be too mentalistic by behaviorists. But the studies of Allan Paivio (1971, 1986) documented how imagery can improve memory. Paivio argued that memory is stored in one of two ways: as a verbal code or as an image code. For example, a picture can be remembered by a label (verbal code) or by a mental image. Paivio thinks that the image code, which is highly detailed and distinctive, produces better memory. The *dual-code hypothesis* claims that memory for images is better because the memory for the concept (image) is stored both as an imaginal code *and* as a verbal code, thus providing two potential avenues by which information can be retrieved.

Although imagery is widely accepted as an important aspect of memory, there is controversy over whether we have separate codes for words and images. More about imagery appears later in the chapter when we discuss strategies for improving memory. For now, just keep in mind that if you need to remember a list of things, forming mental images will help you out (Katz, 2000; Shepard, 1996).

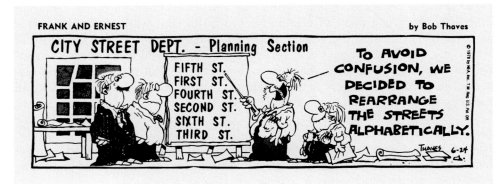

FRANK & ERNEST reprinted by permission of United Features Syndicate, Inc.

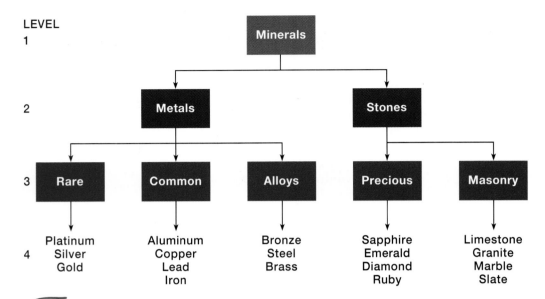

LEVEL
1

2

3

4

Figure 6.3
The Power of Organization in Memory

Memory works best when it is organized. In a 1969 study by Gordon Bower and his colleagues, participants remembered the words better when they were presented in a hierarchical format from general to specific (like the format shown above) than when the words were presented in a random arrangement.

Organization

Recall the 12 months of the year as quickly as you can. How long did it take you? What was the order of your recall? The answers to these questions probably are "four to six seconds," and "natural order" (January, February, March, etc.). Now try to remember the months in alphabetical order. Did you make any errors? How long did it take you? There is a clear distinction between recalling the months naturally and alphabetically. This demonstration makes it easy to see that your memory for the months of the year is organized. Indeed, one of memory's most distinctive features is its organization. Researchers have found that if people simply are encouraged to organize material, their memory of the material improves, even if no warning is given that their memory will be tested (Mandler, 1980).

In many instances we remember information better when we organize it hierarchically (Bruning, Schraw, & Ronning, 1999). A *hierarchy* is a system in which items are organized from general to specific classes. Gordon Bower and his colleagues (1969) showed the importance of hierarchical organization in memory. Participants who were presented words in hierarchies remembered them better than those who were given the words in random groupings (see figure 6.3).

Chunking *is another beneficial organizational memory strategy that involves grouping or "packing" information into higher-order units that can be remembered as single units.* Chunking is a form of elaborative processing and works by making large amounts of information more manageable. For example, consider this simple list of words: *hot, city, book, forget, tomorrow,* and *smile.* Try to hold these words in memory for a moment, then write them down. If you recalled all seven words, you succeeded in holding 34 letters in your memory. Now try to hold the following in memory for a moment and then write it down:

O LDH ARO LDAN DYO UNGB EN

How did you do? As presented above, this string of letters is very difficult to remember. However, if you chunk the letters to form the words "Old Harold and Young Ben," they become much easier to remember.

In summary, to encode something in memory more effectively you can rehearse

Summary Table 6.1
The Nature of Memory and Encoding

Concept	Processes/ Related Ideas	Characteristics/Description
The Nature of Memory	What Is Memory?	Memory is the retention of information over time. Psychologists study how information is initially placed or encoded into memory, how it is retained or stored after being encoded, and how it is found or retrieved for a certain purpose later.
	Exploring Memory	We often take for granted how smoothly our memory systems work. Human memory is remarkable and allows us to carry out many feats every day of our lives. However, human memory also has its imperfections. Although there are many complex dimensions to memory, thinking about memory in terms of encoding (getting information into memory), storage (retaining information over time), and retrieval (taking memory out of storage) should help you understand it better.
Encoding	Rehearsal	Rehearsal is the conscious repetition of information that increases the length of time that information stays in memory. Rehearsal works best when we need to remember a list of numbers or items for a brief time. Many psychologists believe that when people want to remember information for longer time frames, other encoding strategies work better, especially when they impart meaning to what is to be remembered.
	Deep Processing	The levels of processing theory states that memory processing occurs on a continuum from shallow to deep, with deeper processing producing better memory.
	Elaboration	The more elaboration involved, the better memory is. Elaboration is the extensiveness of processing at any given depth of memory.
	Imagery	Memory is stored either as a verbal code or as an image code. Paivio believes that the image code produces better memory because it often is detailed and distinctive.
	Organization	Memory works best when it is organized. Two ways to do this are hierarchical organization and chunking.

it, process it at a deep level, elaborate it, form imagery, organize it, and/or chunk it. At this point we have discussed a number of ideas about the nature of memory and encoding. An overview of these ideas is presented in summary table 6.1. Next, we turn our attention to how memory is stored.

Memory Storage

After we encode information, we need to retain or store the information. The three main stores of memory—sensory memory, working (or short-term) memory, and long-term memory—vary according to time. Let's explore these stores as well as other dimensions of retaining information.

Memory's Time Frames

We remember some information for less than a second, some for half a minute, and other information for minutes, hours, years, even a lifetime. Because memory often functions differently across these varied time intervals, we

ℱigure 6.4
Three Memory Stores that Vary According to How Long Memory Is Retained

can distinguish among different types of memory partly on the basis of their differing time frames. The three types of memory that vary according to their time frames are *sensory memory,* with time frames of a fraction of a second to several seconds; *working memory* (also often called short-term memory), with time frames of up to 30 seconds; and *long-term memory,* with time frames of up to a lifetime (see figure 6.4).

A Theory of Memory's Three Time Frames   An early popular theory of memory was formulated by Richard Atkinson and Richard Shiffrin (1968). The **Atkinson-Shiffrin theory** *states that memory involves a sequence of three stages: sensory memory, short-term (working) memory, and long-term memory* (see figure 6.5). As we have seen, much information makes it no further than the sensory memories of sounds and sights. This information is retained only for a brief instant. However, some information, especially that to which we pay attention, is transferred to short-term memory, where it can be retained for about 30 seconds (or longer with the aid of rehearsal). Atkinson and Shiffrin claimed that the longer information is retained in short-term memory through the use of rehearsal, the greater chance it has of getting into long-term memory. Notice in figure 6.5 that retrieval is used to search long-term memory and bring information back into short-term memory.

Some contemporary experts on memory, such as Alan Baddeley, believe that Atkinson and Shiffrin's theory is too simplified (Baddeley, 1993, 1998; Bartlett, 1998). They believe that memory doesn't always work in a neatly packaged three-stage sequence like Atkinson and Shiffrin proposed. They think that memory is far more complex and dynamic than this. For example, these contemporary experts believe that working memory uses long-term memory's contents in more flexible ways than simply retrieving information from it (Murdock, 1999). We will further discuss Baddeley's view of working memory shortly, but first we need to study sensory memory.

Sensory Memory   **Sensory memory** *holds information from the world in its original sensory form for only an instant, not much longer than the brief time it is exposed to the visual, auditory, and other senses.* Sensory memory is very rich and

ℱigure 6.5
Atkinson and Shiffrin's Theory of Memory
In this model, sensory input goes into sensory memory. Through the process of attention, information moves into short-term memory, where it remains for 30 seconds or less, unless it is rehearsed. Then, the information goes into long-term memory storage; from here it can be retrieved for some purpose later.

detailed, but the information in it is very quickly lost unless certain processes are engaged in that transfer it into working or long-term memory (Crowder, 2000).

Think about all the sights and sounds you encounter as you walk to class on a typical morning. Literally thousands of stimuli come into your fields of vision and hearing—cracks in the sidewalk, chirping birds, a noisy motorcycle, the blue sky, faces of hundreds of people. We do not process all of these stimuli, but we do process a number of them. In general, you process many more stimuli at the sensory level than you consciously notice. Sensory memory retains this information from your senses, including a large portion of what you think you ignore. But sensory memory does not retain the information very long. **Echoic memory** *(from the word* echo*) is the name given to auditory sensory memory in which information is retained for up to several seconds.* **Iconic memory** *(from the word* icon, *which means "image") is the name given to visual sensory memory in which information is retained only for about 1/4 second (see figure 6.6). The sensory memory for other senses, such as smell and touch, has received little attention.*

Type of sensory register	
Auditory	Visual
Up to several seconds	About 1/4 second

Figure 6.6
Auditory and Visual Sensory Memory
If you hear this bird's call while walking through the woods, your auditory sensory memory holds the information for several seconds. If you see the bird, your visual sensory memory holds the information for only about one-quarter of a second.

L H V
R F Z
D T C

Figure 6.7
Sperling's Sensory Memory Experiment
This array of stimuli is similar to those flashed for about 1/20 of a second to the participants in Sperling's study.

The first scientific research on sensory memory focused on iconic memory. In George Sperling's (1960) classic study, participants were presented with patterns of stimuli such as those in figure 6.7. As you look at the letters, you have no trouble recognizing them. But Sperling flashed the letters on a screen for only very brief intervals, about 1/20 second. After a pattern was flashed on the screen, the subjects could report only 4 or 5 letters. With such short exposure, reporting all 9 letters was impossible.

Some of the participants in Sperling's study reported feeling that, for an instant, they could *see* all 9 letters within a briefly flashed pattern. But they ran into trouble when they tried to *name* all the letters they had initially *seen*. One hypothesis to explain this experience is that all 9 letters were initially processed as far as iconic sensory memory. This is why all 9 letters were *seen*. However, forgetting was so rapid that the participants could name only a handful of letters before they were lost from sensory memory.

Sperling decided to test this hypothesis. He reasoned that if all 9 letters were actually processed in sensory memory, they should all be available for a brief time. To test this possibility, Sperling sounded a low, medium, or high tone just after a pattern of letters was shown. The participants were told that the tone was a signal to report only the letters from the bottom, middle, or top row, respectively. Under these conditions, the participants performed much better, suggesting a brief memory for most or all of the letters in the display.

Working or Short-Term Memory
Working memory, *also sometimes called short-term memory, is a limited-capacity memory system in which information is*

Sensory Memory
Short-Term Memory

𝓕igure 6.8
A Theory of Working Memory

In Baddeley's theory of working memory the two subsystems—the visuospatial scratchpad and the articulatory loop—help the executive do its job. The visuospatial scratchpad involves our spatial imagery skills, the articulatory loop our language skills.

𝓣hrough the Eyes of Psychologists

Alan Baddeley, *MRC Applied Psychology Unit, Cambridge, England*

"The concept of working memory provides a coherent framework for exploring the role of human memory in many aspects of cognition both within the laboratory and in the world outside."

retained for as long as 30 seconds, unless the information is rehearsed, in which case it can be retained longer. Compared to sensory memory, working memory is limited in capacity but can store information for a relatively longer duration. Its limited capacity was examined by George Miller (1956) in a classic paper with a catchy title, "The Magical Number Seven, Plus or Minus Two." Miller pointed out that on many tasks individuals are limited in how much information they can keep track of without external aids. Usually the limit is in the range of 7 ± 2 items. The most widely cited example of the 7 ± 2 capacity phenomenon involves **memory span,** which is the number of digits an individual can report back in order after a single presentation of them. Most college students can remember lists of 8 or 9 digits without making any errors. Longer lists, however, pose problems because they exceed your working memory capacity. If you rely on simple working memory to retain longer lists of items you probably will make errors.

As we saw earlier in the chapter, by chunking information we can remember much more than 7 ± 2 units of information. For example, we saw that when 34 letters were chunked into 7 words they could be handled in our short-term memory. Thus, although short-term memory has limited capacity, chunking helps us to make the most of it.

Information stored in working memory lasts half a minute or less without rehearsal. However, if rehearsal is not interrupted, information can be retained indefinitely. Our rehearsal is often verbal, giving the impression of an inner voice, but it can also be visual or spatial, giving the impression of a private inner eye. One way to use your visualization skills is to maintain the appearance of an object or scene for a period of time after you have viewed it. People who are unusually good at this task are said to have *eidetic imagery,* or a photographic memory. All of us can do this to some degree, but a small number of individuals may be so good at maintaining an image they literally "see" the page of a textbook as they try to remember information during a test. However, eidetic imagery is so rare it has been difficult to study; some psychologists even doubt its existence (Gray & Gummerman, 1975).

Rehearsal is an important aspect of working memory, but there is much more we need to know about this type of memory. Working memory is a kind of mental "workbench" that lets us manipulate and assemble information when we make decisions, solve problems, and comprehend written and spoken language (Klatsky, 1984).

One theory of how working memory functions was proposed by British psychologist Alan Baddeley, (1990, 1995) (see figure 6.8). In this theory, working memory consists of a general "executive" and two subsystems that help the executive do its job. One of the subsystems is the articulatory loop, which is specialized to process language information. This is where rehearsal occurs. The other subsystem is the visuospatial scratchpad, which includes some of our spatial imagery skills, such as visualizing an object or a scene.

The concept of working memory can help us understand how brain damage influences cognitive skills. For example, some types of amnesiacs perform well on working memory tasks, but show gross deficits in learning new information in long-term memory tasks. Another group of patients have normal long-term memory abilities, yet do very poorly on working memory tasks. One such patient had good long-term memory despite having a memory span of only two digits (Baddeley, 1992)! Working memory deficits also are involved in Alzheimer's disease—a progressive, irreversible brain disorder in older adults. Baddeley and his colleagues (in press) believe the central executive of the working memory model is the culprit, because Alzheimer's patients have great difficulty coordinating different mental activities, one of the central executive's functions.

Long-Term Memory   **Long-term memory** *is a relatively permanent type of memory that holds huge amounts of information for a long period of time.* In one study, people remembered the names and faces of their high school classmates with considerable accuracy for at least 25 years (Bahrick,

Bahrick, & Whitlinger, 1975). The storehouse of long-term memory is indeed staggering. John von Neumann, a distinguished computer scientist, put the size at 2.8×10^{20} (280 quintillion) bits, which in practical terms means that our storage capacity is virtually unlimited. Von Neumann assumed we never forget anything, but even considering that we do forget things, we can hold several billion times more information than a large computer. Even more impressive is the efficiency with which we retrieve information. It usually takes only a moment to search through this vast storehouse to find the information we want. Who discovered America? What was the name of your first date? When were you born? Who developed the first psychology laboratory? You can, of course, answer these questions instantly.

Memory's Contents

Just as different types of memory can be distinguished by how long they last—time frames of memory—memories within each time frame can be distinguished by their *content.* As we discussed earlier, the contents of sensory memory consist of memory for audition (echoic memory) and vision (iconic memory). Similarly, we learned that the contents of working memory vary according to at least two kinds of content—the articulatory loop, which holds information about speech, and the visuospatial scratchpad, which holds mental images. Therefore, it should be no surprise that the contents of long-term memory can also be differentiated.

Figure 6.9 shows a three-level organization of long-term memory's contents. In this hierarchical organization, memory is divided into the subtypes of declarative (explicit) memory and nondeclarative (implicit) memory. Declarative memory can be subdivided further into episodic and semantic memory. Let's now examine each of these categories.

Figure 6.9
Classification of Long-Term Memory's Contents

Declarative and Nondeclarative Memory   **Declarative memory** *is the conscious recollection of information, such as specific facts or events, and, at least in humans, information that can be verbally communicated.* Because of its conscious and verbalizable nature, declarative memory has been called "explicit memory." Examples of declarative (or explicit) memory include recounting the events of a movie you have seen and describing a basic principle of psychology to someone. However, you do not need to be talking to be using declarative memory. Simply sitting and consciously reflecting about Einstein's theory of relativity, or the date you had last weekend, involves declarative memory.

Nondeclarative memory *is memory in which behavior is affected by prior experience without that experience being consciously recollected.* Because nondeclarative memory cannot be verbalized or consciously recollected, at least not in the form of specific events or facts, it also is called "implicit memory" (Schacter, 2000). Examples of nondeclarative (implicit) memory include the skills of playing tennis, riding a bicycle, and typing. Another example of nondeclarative memory is getting a song you heard playing on the speakers in the supermarket stuck in your head without ever having consciously attended to what music was playing while you were busy shopping.

To further illustrate the distinction between declarative (explicit) and nondeclarative (implicit) memory, imagine you are at Wimbledon. Martina Hingis moves gracefully for a wide forehand, finishes her follow-through, runs quickly back to the center of the court, pushes off for a short ball, and volleys the ball for a winner. If we asked her about this rapid sequence of movements, she probably would have difficulty explaining each move. In contrast, if we asked her who her toughest opponent is, she might quickly respond, "Monica Seles." In the first instance, she was unable to verbally describe exactly what she had done. In the second, she had no problem answering our question.

Endel Tulving

Episodic and Semantic Memory   Canadian cognitive psychologist Endel Tulving (1972, 2000) has been the foremost advocate of distinguishing between two subtypes of declarative memory: episodic and semantic. **Episodic memory** *is the retention of information about the where and when of life's happenings.* For example, episodic memory includes what it was like when your younger brother or sister was born, what happened on your first date, what you were doing when you heard of Princess Diana's death, and what you had for breakfast this morning. Episodic memory involves autobiographical episodes and we will return to this idea later in this chapter.

Semantic memory *is a person's knowledge about the world.* This includes a person's fields of expertise, general academic knowledge of the sort learned in school and everyday knowledge about meanings of words, famous individuals, important places, and common things. For example, semantic memory is involved in a person's knowledge of chess, knowledge of geometry, and knowledge of who Nelson Mandela and Mahatma Ghandi are. An important aspect of semantic memory is that it appears to be independent of an individual's personal identity with the past. You can access a fact—such as that Lima is the capital of Peru—and not have the foggiest notion of when and where you learned it.

Several examples help to clarify the distinction between episodic and semantic memory. Your memory of your first day on campus involves episodic memory. Your memory of the information you need to know to do well on your next psychology test involves semantic memory.

Consider also that in a certain type of amnesiac state, a person might forget entirely who she is—her name, family, career, and all other personal information about herself—yet she can talk and demonstrate general knowledge about the world. Her episodic memory is impaired, but her semantic memory is functioning. An especially dramatic case of this type, a young man named K. C., was reported by Endel Tulving (1989). After suffering a motorcycle accident, K. C. lost virtually all use of his episodic memory. The loss was so profound that he was unable to consciously recollect a single thing that had ever happened to him. At the same time, K. C.'s semantic memory was sufficiently preserved that he could learn about his past as a set of facts, just as he would learn about another person's life. He could report, for example, that the saddest day of his life was when his brother died of drowning about 10 years before. This sounds as if K. C. had episodic memory, but further questioning revealed that he had no conscious memory of the drowning event. He simply knew about the drowning because he was able to recall—apparently through use of his semantic memory—what he had been told about his brother by other members of his family.

Some aspects of the episodic/semantic distinction are summarized in figure 6.10. Although the distinctions listed have attracted considerable attention, they remain controversial. One criticism is that many cases of declarative memory are neither purely episodic nor purely semantic but fall in a gray area in between. Consider your memory for what you studied last night. You probably added knowledge to your semantic memory—that was, after all, the reason you were studying. You probably remember where you were studying, as well as when you started and about when you stopped. You probably also can remember some minor occurrences, such as a burst of loud laughter from the room next door or the coffee you spilled on the desk. Is episodic or semantic memory involved here? Tulving (1983, 2000) argues that semantic and episodic systems often work together in forming new memories. In such cases, the memory that ultimately is formed might consist of an autobiographical episode *and* semantic information.

Characteristic	Episodic Memory	Semantic Memory
Units	Events, episodes	Facts, ideas, concepts
Organization	Temporal	Conceptual
Affect	More important	Less important
Retrieval process	Deliberate (effortful)	Automatic
Retrieval report	"I remember"	"I know"
Education	Irrelevant	Relevant
Intelligence	Irrelevant	Relevant
Legal testimony	Admissible in court	Inadmissible in court

Figure 6.10
Some Characteristics That Differentiate Episodic and Semantic Memory

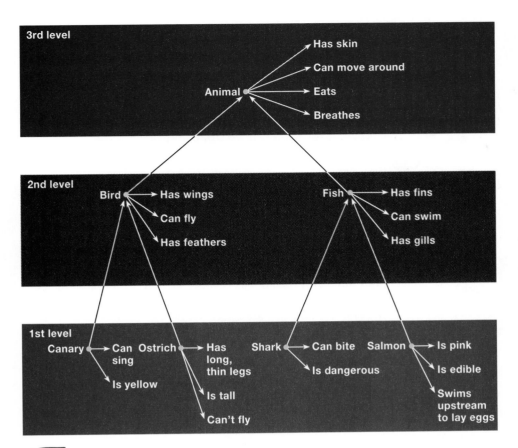

*F*igure 6.11
The Hierarchical Organization of Memory with Nodes (Branching Points) at Three Levels in the Hierarchy

Notice how the information becomes more detailed and specific as you move through the levels of the hierarchy in this model. Some psychologists have challenged this representation as too "clean" to portray the true complexity of our representation processes.

Representing Memory

We have seen that memory has three stores that vary by duration and that memory's contents can be differentiated into different categories. Another important aspect of memory storage is to understand how information is represented in memory. We will examine two main kinds of theories of this representation: network theories and schema theories.

Network Theories   One of the first network theories claimed that our memories can be envisioned as a complex network of nodes that stand for labels or concepts (see figure 6.11). The network was assumed to be hierarchically arranged with more-concrete concepts (canary, for example) nestled under more-abstract concepts (bird). More recently, cognitive psychologists realized that such hierarchical networks were too simple to describe the way human cognition actually works (Shanks, 1991). For example, people take longer to answer the true-or-false statement "An ostrich is a bird" than they do to answer the statement "A canary is a bird." Memory researchers now envision the network as more irregular and distorted: a *typical* bird, such as a canary, is closer to the node or center of the category *bird* than is the atypical ostrich. Figure 6.12 shows an example of the revised model, which allows for the typicality of information while retaining the original notion of node and network.

   We add new material to this network by placing it in the middle of the appropriate region. The new material is gradually tied in—by meaningful connections—to the appropriate nodes in the surrounding network. That is why if you cram for a test, you will not remember the information over the long term. The new material is not woven into the long-term web. In contrast, discussing the material or incorporating it into a research paper interweaves it and connects it to other knowledge you have. These multiple connections increase the probability that you will be able to retrieve the information many months or even years later. The concept of multiple connections fits with our description of the importance of elaboration in memory that we discussed earlier in the chapter.

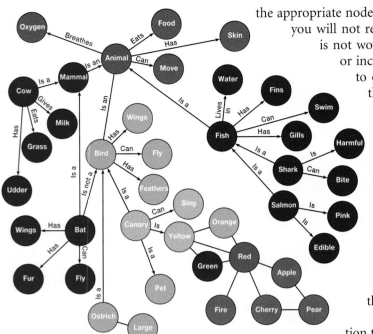

Figure 6.12
Revision of the Hierarchical Network View of How Information Is Organized in Long-Term Memory

Schema Theories   Long-term memory has been compared to a library. Your memory stores information just as a library stores books. We retrieve information in a fashion similar to the process we use to locate and check out a book. But the process of retrieving information from long-term memory is not as precise as the library analogy suggests. When we search through our long-term memory storehouse we don't always find the *exact* "book" we want, or we might find the book we want but discover that only several pages are intact. We have to *reconstruct* the rest.

When we reconstruct information, we often fit it into information that already exists in our mind. A **schema** *is a concept or framework that already exists in a person's mind and that organizes and interprets information.* Schemas from prior encounters with the environment influence the way we encode, make inferences about, and retrieve information (Jou, Shanteau, & Harris, 1996). Unlike network theories, which assume that retrieval involves specific facts, schema theory claims that long-term memory search is not very exact. We seldom find precisely what we want, or at least not all of what we want; hence, we have to reconstruct the rest. Our schemas support this reconstruction process, helping us fill in the gaps between our fragmented memories.

The schema theory of memory began with Sir Frederick Bartlett's (1932) studies of how people remember stories. Bartlett was concerned about how a person's background determines what they encode and remember about stories. Bartlett chose stories that sounded strange and were difficult to understand. He reasoned that a person's background, which is encoded in schemas, would reveal itself in the person's reconstruction (modification and distortion) of the story's content. For example, one of Bartlett's stories was called "War of the Ghosts," an English translation of an American Indian folktale. The story contained events that were completely foreign to the experiences of the middle- and upper-income British research participants. The participants in Bartlett's study read the story twice then waited 15 minutes, at which time they were asked to write down the tale the best they could remember it.

What interested Bartlett was how differently the participants might reconstruct this and other stories from the original versions. The British participants used their general schemas for daily experiences, and their schemas for adventurous ghost stories in particular, to reconstruct "War of the Ghosts." Familiar details from the story that "fit into" the participant's schemas were successfully recalled. But details that departed from the person's schemas were often extensively distorted. For example, the "something black" that came out of the Indian's mouth became blood in one reconstruction and condensed air in another. For one individual the two young men were hunting beavers rather than seals. Another person said the death at the end was due to a fever (this wasn't in the story).

There has been a flurry of interest in reconstructive memory, especially in the way people recall stories, give eyewitness testimony, remember their past, and recall conversations (Greene, 1999; Howe, 1995; Thompson & others, 1998). To learn more about the nature of reconstructive memory in eyewitness testimony turn to Explorations in Psychology.

*T*hrough the Eyes of Psychologists
Daniel Schacter, *Harvard University*

"Memory is a central part of the brain's attempt to make sense of experience and tell coherent stories about it. Yet our stories are built from many different ingredients: snippets of what actually happened, thoughts about what might have happened, and beliefs that guide us as we attempt to remember."

EXPLORATIONS IN PSYCHOLOGY
Memory Construction and Eyewitness Testimony

EYEWITNESS TESTIMONIES may contain errors (Schacter, 1995). When eyewitness testimony is inaccurate, the wrong person may go to jail (or even be put to death), or a person who committed a crime might not be prosecuted. Estimates are that between 2,000 and 10,000 people are wrongfully convicted each year in the United States because of faulty eyewitness testimony (Cutler & Penrod, 1995).

In the O. J. Simpson murder trial, many people were puzzled when Simpson's housekeeper testified that his infamous white Bronco had not moved from its spot all evening, yet his limousine driver testified that he did not remember seeing the car when he arrived late that evening. This was only one of many variations that occurred across different witnesses in the high-profile Simpson trial and that regularly occur in other trials. Much of the interest in eyewitness testimony focuses on distortion, bias, and inaccuracy in memory (Loftus, 1993a).

Memory fades over time. That's why the amount of time that has passed between an incident and a person's recollection of it is a critical factor in eyewitness testimony. In one study, people were able to identify pictures with 100 percent accuracy after a 2-hour time lapse. However, 4 months later they achieved an accuracy of only 57 percent; chance alone accounts for 50 percent accuracy (Shepard, 1967).

Unlike a videotape, memory can be altered by new information. In one study, students were shown a film of an automobile accident (Loftus, 1975). Some of the students were asked how fast the white sports car was going when it passed a barn. Other students were asked the same question without any mention of a barn. In fact, there was no barn in the film. However, 17 percent of the students who heard the question that included the barn mentioned it in their answer; only 3 percent of those whose question did not include the barn mentioned that they saw it. New information, then, can add or even replace existing information in memory.

Studies have shown that people of one ethnic group are less likely to recognize individual differences among people of another ethnic group. Latino eyewitnesses, for example, may have trouble distinguishing among several Asian suspects. This makes identifying individuals from a police lineup or photographs an unreliable tool. In one investigation, clerks in small stores were asked to identify photographs of customers who had shopped there two hours earlier (Brigham & others, 1982). Only 33 percent of the customers were correctly identified. In another experiment, a mugging was shown on a television news program. Immediately after, a lineup of six suspects was broadcast and viewers were asked to phone in and identify which of the six individuals they thought committed the robbery. Of the 2,000 callers, more than 1,800 identified the wrong person. In addition, even though the rob-

O. J. Simpson's white Bronco grabbed the country's attention when it was televised live as he drove it along a Los Angeles freeway and he threatened suicide. Later, in the Simpson murder trial, different witnesses gave varying testimony about whether the Bronco had ever moved from its spot during the evening when Nicole Brown Simpson had been murdered. Possibly someone was lying, but it also is possible that witnesses reconstructed their memories honestly but differently.

Identification of individuals from police lineups or photographs is not always reliable. People from one ethnic group often have difficulty recognizing differences among people of another ethnic group.

ber was White, one-third of the viewers identified an African American or Latino suspect as the criminal.

In sum, the problems with eyewitness testimony underscore how our memory often is not flawless. Like other memories, eyewitness memories are constructed and the constructions don't always match what actually happened.

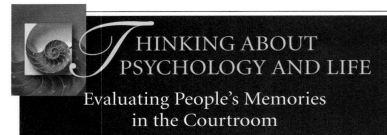

THINKING ABOUT PSYCHOLOGY AND LIFE

Evaluating People's Memories in the Courtroom

GET TOGETHER with several other students and go to the local courthouse. Observe part of a trial in a criminal court, domestic court, or even traffic court. Listen carefully to what the witnesses are saying. Were their memories likely to be completely accurate? What possible memory biases were at work in their descriptions of what they said took place? Do you think the trial might have had a different outcome if the jurors were aware that memory is often unreliable? If you can't make it to a courthouse, try watching part of a television trial to complete this exercise (Halpern, 1997). Some episodes from the television shows "Court TV" or "People's Court" could serve the purpose of this exercise. Or you might try attending an on-campus judicial hearing.

Eyewitness Memory

*T*hrough the Eyes of Psychologists

Elizabeth Loftus, *University of Washington*

"After a century of studying eyewitness identification, there is still much to learn."

We have schemas not only for stories but also for scenes or spatial layouts (a beach, a bathroom), as well as for common events (going to a restaurant, playing football, writing a term paper). A **script** *is a schema for an event* (Schank & Abelson, 1977). Scripts often have information about physical features, people, and typical occurrences. This kind of information is helpful when people need to figure out what is happening around them. For example, if you are enjoying your after-dinner coffee in a restaurant and a man in a tuxedo comes over and puts a piece of paper on the table, your script tells you that the man probably is a waiter who has just given you the check.

So far in our coverage of memory storage we have studied the three time frames of storage, the differentiated content in storage, and how information is represented in storage. Next, we discuss where in the brain memories are stored.

The Neurobiological Basis of Memory

Yet another important aspect of memory storage is the brain's role in the retention of memory (Haberlandt, 1999; Thompson, 2000). That is, where in the brain are memories stored?

Karl Lashley (1950) spent a lifetime looking for a location in the brain where memories are stored. He trained rats to discover the correct pathway in a maze and then cut out a portion of the animals' brains and retested their memory of the maze pathway. After experimenting with thousands of rats, Lashley found that the loss of various cortical areas did not affect rats' ability to remember the maze's path. Lashley concluded that memories are not stored in a specific location in the brain.

Many neuroscientists believe that memory is located in discrete sets or circuits of neurons ◀‖‖ P. 51. Brain researcher Larry Squire (1990), for example, says that most memories are probably clustered in groups of about 1,000 neurons. He points out that memory is distributed throughout the brain in the sense that no specific memory center exists. Many parts of the brain and nervous system participate in the memory of a particular event. Yet memory is localized in the sense that a limited number of brain systems and pathways are involved, and each probably contributes in different ways (Lynch, 1990).

Single neurons, of course, are at work in memory. Researchers who measure the electrical activity of single cells have found that some respond to faces, others to eye or hair color, for example. But for you to recognize your Uncle

"Why? You cross the road because it's in the script—that's why!"

Albert, individual neurons that provide information about hair color, size, and other characteristics must act together.

Ironically, some of the answers to the complex questions about the neural mechanics of memory come from studies on a very simple experimental animal—the inelegant sea slug. Eric Kandel and James Schwartz (1982) chose this large snail-without-a-shell because of the simple architecture of its nervous system, which consists of only about 10,000 neurons.

The sea slug can hardly be called a quick learner or an animal with a good memory, but it is equipped with a reliable reflex. When anything touches the gill on its back, it quickly withdraws it. First the researchers habituated the sea slug to having its gill prodded. After a while, it ignored the prod and stopped withdrawing its gill. Next the researchers applied an electric shock to its tail when they touched the gill. After many rounds of the shock-accompanied prod, the sea slug violently withdrew its gill at the slightest touch. The researchers found that the sea slug remembered this message for hours or even weeks.

More important than the discovery that sea slugs had memories was the finding that memory seems to be written in chemicals. Shocking the sea slug's gill releases the neurotransmitter serotonin at the synapses, and this chemical release basically provides a reminder that the gill was shocked. This "memory" informs the nerve cell to send out chemical commands to retract the gill the next time it is touched. If nature builds complexity out of simplicity, then the mechanism used by the sea slug may work in the human brain as well. Chemicals, then, may be the ink with which memories are written.

While some neuroscientists are unveiling the cellular basis of memory, others are examining the broadscale architecture of memory in the brain. Neuroscientists have found that the hippocampus, part of the limbic system, and the thalamus are involved in declarative memory (Mishkin & Appenzeller, 1987). The amygdala, also part of the limbic system, is critical for emotional memories. The cerebellum is involved in the implicit memory required to perform skills. Figure 6.13 shows the location of these structures in the brain.

Researchers also are using brain imaging techniques to reveal which areas of the brain are active when individuals are engaging in various memory activities P. 73. Using such memory imaging techniques as PET (positron emission tomograph, which depicts the activity of different brain regions by showing each area's consumption of sugar glucose), they have shown that:

- Deep encoding is specifically associated with activity in the brain's frontal lobe (Kapur & others, 1994)
- The parietal lobe is involved in the articulatory loop of working memory
- The temporal lobe is linked with priming of structurally visible objects, whereas the hippocampus is associated with the episodic recognition of these objects (Zola, 1996).

As neuroscientists discover the identity of memory circuits in the brain, might we reach a point at which the psychological study of memory becomes unimportant? That's unlikely. First, we are far from working out all of the complexities of the neurochemical underpinnings in human memory. And second, even if we are successful in unraveling the neurochemical mystery of memory, each person's private kingdom of memories will remain intact.

At this point we have explored many aspects of memory storage. An overview of these ideas is presented in summary table 6.2. Now that we have studied how

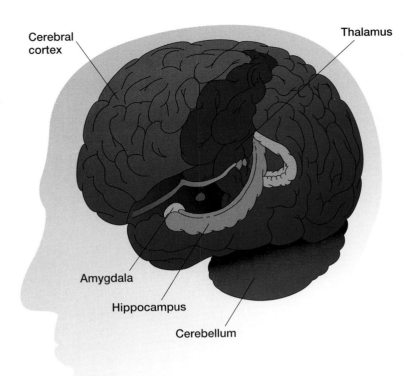

Figure 6.13
Some Important Brain Structures That Are Involved in Memory
This drawing with some of the cerebral cortex stripped away lets you look into the brain's interior and see the location of four brain structures that play important roles in memory: hippocampus, thalamus, amygdala, and cerebellum.

Brain Imaging

SUMMARY TABLE 6.2
Memory Storage

Concept	Processes/ Related Ideas	Characteristics/Description
Memory's Time Frame	A Theory of Memory's Three Time Frames	The Atkinson-Shiffrin theory states that memory occurs in a three-stage sequence: sensory memory to short-term (working) memory to long-term memory. Some contemporary experts believe this theory is too simplified, and that memory is more dynamic and complex than the theory implies.
	Sensory Memory	Sensory memory holds information from the world in its original form for only an instant, not much longer than the brief time it is exposed to the visual, auditory, and other senses. Visual sensory memory (iconic memory) retains information for about 1/4 second, auditory sensory memory (echoic memory) for several seconds. Sperling's classic study revealed that people have fleeting iconic memory.
	Working or Short-Term Memory	Working memory, also sometimes called short-term memory, is a limited-capacity memory system in which information is retained for as long as 30 seconds, unless the information is rehearsed, in which case it can be retained longer. According to George Miller, short-term memory's limitation is 7 ± 2 bits of information. In Baddeley's theory of working memory, an executive plus two subsystems—the phonological loop (language, rehearsal) and the visuospatial scratchpad (imagery)—are involved.
	Long-Term Memory	Long-term memory is a relatively permanent type of memory that holds huge amounts of information for a long period of time.
Memory's Contents	Declarative and Nondeclarative Memory	Memory can be divided into declarative (explicit) and nondeclarative (implicit) memory. Declarative memory can be further subdivided into episodic and semantic memory. Declarative (explicit) memory is the conscious recollection of information, such as facts and events, and, at least in humans, information that can be verbally communicated. Nondeclarative (implicit) memory refers to knowledge in the form of skills, habits, and cognitive operations that cannot be consciously remembered, at least in the form of events or facts. This makes implicit memory difficult, if not impossible, to communicate.
	Episodic and Semantic Memory	Episodic memory is the retention of information about the where and when of life's happenings. Semantic memory is a person's knowledge about the world.
Representing Memory	Network Theories	Early network theories stressed that memories consist of a complex network of nodes that are hierarchically arranged. More-recent network theories stress the role of meaningful nodes in the surrounding network.
	Schema Theories	A schema is a concept or framework that already exists in a person's mind and that organizes and interprets information. Schema theory claims that long-term memory is not very exact and that we construct our past. There has been a flurry of interest in reconstructive memory in recent years, especially in the way people recall stories, give eyewitness testimony, remember their past, and recall conversations. Schemas for events are called scripts.
	The Neurobiological Basis of Memory	A main neurobiological issue regarding memory is the extent to which memory is localized or distributed. Single neurons are involved in memory, but some neuroscientists believe that most memories are stored in circuits of about 1,000 neurons. There is no specific memory center in the brain, but the hippocampus and thalamus are involved in declarative memory, the amygdala is critical for emotional memories, and the cerebellum is involved in the implicit memory required to perform skills.

information gets into the brain (encoding) and how it is retained (storage), we need to learn about how we get information out of memory storage.

Memory Retrieval and Forgetting

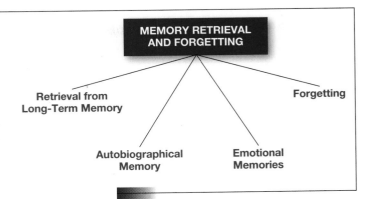

Have you ever forgotten where you parked your car, your mother's birthday, or to meet a friend to study? Have you ever sat in a class taking an exam, unable to remember the answer to a question but remembering where on a page of your textbook a relevant, elusive concept was located?

Retrieval from Long-Term Memory

To retrieve something from your mental "data bank," you search your store of memory to find the relevant information. Let's explore several concepts related to retrieval.

Tip-of-the-Tongue Phenomenon   One glitch in retrieving information that we're all familiar with is the **tip-of-the-tongue phenomenon, or TOT state.** *It is a type of "effortful retrieval" that occurs when people are confident they know something but just can't quite seem to pull it out of memory* (Beattie & Coughlan, 1999; Brown & Nix, 1996). People in a TOT state usually can successfully retrieve characteristics of the word such as the first letter and the number of syllables but not retrieve the word itself.

In one study of the TOT state, participants were shown photographs of famous people and asked to say their names (Yarmey, 1973). The researcher found that people tended to use two strategies to try to retrieve the name of a person they thought they knew. One strategy was to pinpoint the person's profession. For example, one participant correctly identified the famous person as an artist but the artist's name, *Picasso,* remained elusive. Another retrieval strategy was to repeat initial letters or syllables—such as *Monetti, Mona, Magett, Spaghetti,* and *Bogette* in the attempt to identify Liza Minelli.

The TOT state arises because a person can retrieve some of the desired information but not all of it (Schacter, 1996). For example, when a person asks someone the identity of an individual who is standing next to Barbara at a college social event, the person might not be able to recall Bill's name but might remember what he looks like and that his name begins with a *B*. A person's familiarity with a retrieval cue can induce a strong—sometimes spurious—feeling of knowing. For example, when the person cues the individual next to him about who is standing next to Barbara, the individual's familiarity with Bill might make him feel like he can easily retrieve Bill's name, but he might not be able to do so.

Serial Position Effect   Understanding how retrieval works also requires knowledge of the **serial position effect**—*that recall is superior for items at the beginning and at the end of a list.* If someone gave you the directions "Left on Mockingbird, right on Central, right on Stemmons, left on Balboa, and right on Parkside," you probably would remember "Left on Mockingbird" and "right on Parkside" more easily than the turns and streets in the middle. The **primacy effect** *refers to superior recall for items at the beginning of a list.* The **recency effect** *refers to superior recall for items at the end of the list.* Together with the relatively low recall of items from the middle of the list, this pattern makes up the serial position effect. See figure 6.14 for a typical serial position

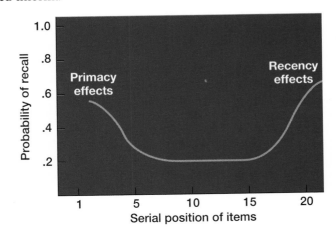

$\mathcal{F}$igure 6.14
The Serial Position Effect

When a person is asked to memorize a list of words, the words memorized last usually are recalled best, those at the beginning next best, and those in the middle least efficiently.

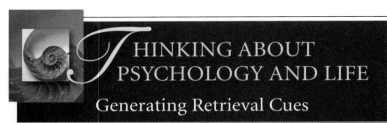

THINKING ABOUT PSYCHOLOGY AND LIFE
Generating Retrieval Cues

WE CAN LEARN to generate retrieval cues (Halpern, 1996). For example, memory researcher Elizabeth Loftus (1980) described the situation of going to a supermarket without a shopping list and forgetting what you were going to buy. She recommended going through different categories such as meats, dairy, cleaning supplies, desserts, and so on, then using these categories as retrieval cues for remembering your intended purchases.

To see how you can use categories to generate retrieval cues, write down the names of as many of your classmates from the middle or junior high school you attended as you can remember. When you run out of names, think about different locations and activities, such as math class, student council, eating lunch, basketball team, and so on. Did this help you to remember more of your classmates?

effect that shows a weaker primacy effect and a stronger recency effect. One application of primacy and recency effects is the advice to job candidates to try to be the first or last candidate interviewed.

How can primacy and recency effects be explained? The first few items in the list are easily remembered because they are rehearsed more often than later items (Atkinson & Shiffrin, 1968). Working memory is relatively empty when they enter, so there is little competition for rehearsal time. And since they get more rehearsal, they stay in working memory longer, and are more likely to be successfully encoded into long-term memory. In contrast, many items from the middle of the list drop out of working memory before being encoded into long-term memory. The last several items are remembered for different reasons. First, at the time these items are recalled, they might still be in working memory. Second, even if these items are not in working memory, their relative recency, compared to other list items, makes them easier to recall. For example, if you are a sports fan, try remembering football games you have seen at the end of the football season, or baseball games you have seen at the end of the baseball season. You probably will find that the more recent games are easier to remember than less recent games. This represents a recency effect that extends far beyond the time span of working memory.

Retrieval Cues and the Retrieval Task Two other factors involved in retrieval are (a) the nature of the cues that can prompt your memory, and (b) the retrieval task that you set for yourself. If effective cues for what you are trying to remember do not seem to be available, you need to create them—a process that takes place in working memory. For example, if you have a "block" about remembering a new friend's name, you might go through the alphabet, generating names that begin with each letter. If you manage to stumble across the right name, you'll probably recognize it.

While cues help, your success in retrieving information also depends on the task you set for yourself. For instance, if you're simply trying to decide if something seems familiar, retrieval is probably a snap. Let's say you see a short, dark-haired woman walking toward you. You quickly decide she's someone who lives in the next dorm. But remembering her name or a precise detail, such as when you met her, can be harder. Such findings have implications for police investigations: A witness might be certain she has previously seen a face, yet she might have a hard time deciding if it was at the scene of the crime or in a mugshot.

The two factors just discussed—the presence or absence of good cues, and the retrieval task required—are involved in an important memory distinction: recall versus recognition memory. **Recall** *is a memory measure in which the individual must retrieve previously learned information, as on an essay test.* **Recognition** *is a memory measure in which the individual only has to identify ("recognize") learned items, as on multiple-choice tests.* Most college students prefer multiple-choice tests because they're easier than essay tests or fill-in-the blank tests. Recall tests, such as fill-in-the-blank tests, have poor retrieval cues. You are told to try to recall a certain class of information ("Discuss the factors that caused World War II"). In multiple-choice "recognition" tests, you merely judge whether a stimulus is familiar or not (Does it match something you experienced in the past?).

You probably have heard some people say that they are terrible at remembering names but they never forget a face. If you have made that claim yourself, try to actually recall a face. It's not so easy. Law enforcement officers know that

Memory Exercises

*F*igure 6.15
Remembering Faces

At left is the FBI artist's sketch of Ted Kaczynski. At right is a photograph of Kaczynski. The FBI widely circulated the artist's sketch, which was based on bits and pieces of observations people had made of the infamous Unabomber, in the hope that someone would recognize the Unabomber if they saw him. Would you have been able to recognize Kaczynski from the artist's sketch of him? Probably not. Although most people say they are very good at remembering faces, they usually are not as good as they think they are.

witnesses often do a very poor job of describing a suspect, so in many cases they bring in an artist to reconstruct the suspect's face (see figure 6.15). Recalling faces is difficult. If you think you remember faces rather than names, it is probably because you are better at recognition than at recall.

Another consideration in understanding retrieval is the **encoding specificity principle,** *which states that associations formed at the time of encoding or learning tend to be effective retrieval cues.* For example, imagine that you have met someone whose occupation is tennis professional. If you encode that information along with such words as *racket, ball,* and *serve,* those words can be used as retrieval cues in trying to remember what the person's occupation is. Encoding specificity is compatible with our earlier discussion of elaboration. Recall that the more elaboration you use in encoding information, the better your memory of the information will be. Encoding specificity and elaboration reveal how interdependent encoding and retrieval are.

Retrieval also benefits from **priming,** *which involves activating particular connections or associations in memory.* In many cases, these associations are unconscious. Because the associations primarily are unconscious, priming has been categorized under nondeclarative or implicit memory (Kirsner & others, 1998).

In everyday life, priming likely is involved in unintentional acts of plagiarism (Schacter, 1996). For example, you propose an idea to a friend, who seems unimpressed by it or even rejects it outright. Weeks or months later, the friend excitedly describes your idea as if he had just come up with it himself. When you call your friend's attention to the fact that "his" idea is really "your" idea, you likely will face either heated denial or a sheepish apology born of a sudden dose of explicit memory.

Another practical example of priming involves those times when you are wandering the grocery store unable to remember one of the items you were supposed to

Level	Label	Description
Level 1	Life time periods	Long segments of time measured in years and even decades
Level 2	General events	Extended composite episodes that are measured in days, weeks, or months
Level 3	Event-specific knowledge	Individual episodes that are measured in seconds, minutes, or hours

Figure 6.16
The Three-Level Hierarchical Structure of Autobiographical Memory

Flashbulb Memories

buy. As you walk down the aisle you hear two people talking about fruit and this triggers your memory that you were supposed to buy raspberries. That is, hearing "fruit" primes your memory for raspberries.

Autobiographical Memory

Our retrieval of information from long-term memory can involve personal memories. **Autobiographical memory** *is a person's recollections of his or her life experiences.* Autobiographical memory is a form of episodic memory, which we discussed earlier in the chapter. Whereas autobiographical memories are complex and can seem like they contain unending strings of stories and snapshots, researchers have found that these memories can be categorized (Schacter, 1996). For example, based on their research, Martin Conway and David Rubin (1993) sketch a structure of autobiographical memory that has three levels (see figure 6.16). The first level consists of *life time periods* (long segments of life that are measured in years and even decades); for example, you might remember something about your life in high school. The middle level in the hierarchy is made up of *general events* (these are extended composite episodes that are measured in days, weeks, or months); for example, you might remember a trip you took with your friends after you graduated from high school. The lowest level in the hierarchy is comprised of *event-specific knowledge* (individual episodes that are measured in seconds, minutes, or hours); for example, on your post-graduation trip, you might remember the exhilarating time you had when you took your first bungee-jump. When people tell their life stories, all three levels of information are usually present and intertwined.

We stitch together complex mixtures of personal knowledge about our past to form our life story (Thompson & others, 1998). In most autobiographical memories there are some doses of reality and some doses of myth. Dan McAdams (1993) argues that these biographies of the self that connect the past and the present provide a set of memories that form the core of our personal identity. He says that our autobiographical memories are less about facts and more about meanings. They provide an embellished telling of the past. As people reconstruct their past in telling their autobiographical memories, their histories are made.

Emotional Memories

When we remember our life experiences, the memories are often wrapped in emotion. Let's begin our tour of emotional memories by examining flashbulb memories.

Flashbulb Memories   **Flashbulb memories** *are memories of emotionally significant events that people often recall with more accuracy and vivid imagery than everyday events.* Perhaps you can remember where you were when you first heard of the bombing of the Oklahoma federal building in 1995 or when Princess Diana died in 1997. I still have a vivid image of where I was when I heard President Kennedy had been shot in

Do you have a flashbulb memory for (left) the bombing of the Oklahoma federal building in 1995? (right) Princess Diana's death in 1997? What is the nature of flashbulb memories?

1963—I was watching the University of Miami (Florida) football team play in the Orange Bowl. An intriguing dimension of flashbulb memories is that several decades later people often remember where they were and what was going on in their lives at the time of such an event. These memories seem to be part of an adaptive system that fixes in memory the details that accompany important events so they can be interpreted at a later time. As we see next, the vast majority of flashbulb memories are of a personal nature rather than of nationally prominent events.

One study examined the types of events involved in flashbulb memories (Rubin & Kozin, 1984). College students were asked to report the three most vivid memories in their lives. Virtually all of these memories were of a personal nature rather than of nationally significant events or circumstances. The memories tended to center around an injury or accident, sports, members of the opposite sex, animals, deaths, the first week of college, and vacations. Students also answered questions about their memories of events that were most likely to produce flashbulb memories. Figure 6.17 shows which types of events more than 50 percent of the students said were of "flashbulb" quality.

Event	Percentage
A car accident you were in or witnessed	85
When you first met your roommate at Duke	82
The night of your high school graduation	81
The night of your senior prom (if you went or not)	78
An early romantic experience	77
A time you had to speak in front of an audience	72
When you got your admissions letter from Duke	65
Your first date—the moment you met him/her	57

The numbers refer to the percentages of college students who said these events triggered memories of "flashbulb" quality.

Figure 6.17
College Students' Flashbulb Memories

Most people are confident about the accuracy of their flashbulb memories. Just how accurate are our flashbulb memories? Some flashbulb memories are accurate but most probably are not as photographically etched in our brain as we think. Some flashbulb memories deteriorate and change over time. However, flashbulb memories are far more durable and accurate than memories of day-to-day happenings. One reason that flashbulb memories are so durable is that they are often discussed and thought about in the days, weeks, and even years following an event. That was the case in President Kennedy's death, and it certainly has been and will be the case in Princess Diana's death. However, its not just the discussion and rehearsal of information that make flashbulb memories so long-lasting. The emotions triggered by flashbulb events also are involved in their durability. Thus, if you have a flashbulb memory of Princess Diana's death, the emotional arousal you experienced when you heard about it also likely contributed to the flashbulb memory.

Earlier we indicated that the vast majority of flashbulb memories are of a personal nature. Some of these involve emotionally uplifting experiences, as when a person remembers the positive emotional experience of high school graduation night. Other events might be at the opposite end of the emotional spectrum and involve personal trauma. What are the memories of those episodes in our lives like that involve personal trauma?

Personal Trauma   In 1890, William James said that an experience can be so arousing emotionally as to almost leave a scar on the brain's tissue. Personal traumas that people experience are candidates for the type of emotionally arousing experience James was referring to. Some psychologists argue that memory for emotionally traumatic events is accurately retained, possibly forever, in considerable detail (Langer, 1991). There is good evidence that memory for traumatic events is usually more accurate than memory for ordinary events (Schacter, 1996). Consider the traumatic experience of children who were kidnapped at gunpoint on a school bus in Chowchilla, California, then buried underground for 16 hours before escaping. The children had the classic signs of traumatic memory—detailed and vivid recollections. However, when a child psychiatrist interviewed them 4 or 5 years after the chilling episode, she noted some striking errors and distortions in half of the children (Terr, 1988).

Memory under Stress

EXPLORATIONS IN PSYCHOLOGY
Repressed Memories, Child Abuse, and Reality

THERE HAS BEEN a dramatic increase in reported memories of childhood sexual abuse that were allegedly repressed for many years. With recent changes in legislation, people with recently discovered memories are suing alleged perpetrators for events that occurred 20, 30, even 40 or more years earlier.

In 1991, popular actress Roseanne was on the cover of *People* magazine. She reported that her mother had been abusing her from the time Roseanne was an infant until she was 6 or 7 years of age, but that she had become aware of the abuse only recently during therapy. Other highly publicized cases of repressed memories of child abuse coming into awareness during therapy dot the pages of popular magazines and self-help books.

There is little doubt that actual childhood abuse is tragically common. Memory experts such as Elizabeth Loftus (1993b) and others (Kutchinsky, 1992) don't dispute that child abuse is a serious problem. What they take issue with is the way therapists get their clients to recall abuse. Therapists might help their clients to reconstruct a memory that is not real. Some clients who originally claimed they were abused later have recanted their accusations, blaming their abuse report on the therapist's leading inquiries.

Few research studies offer convincing evidence about the extent to which repression of abuse actually occurs. At present, there are no satisfactory methods that can help us discover the answer. Although Loftus has demon-

Roseanne said that her mother abused her from the time she was an infant until she was 6 or 7 years old. Why have many psychologists questioned some of the reports of activation of repressed memories, such as Roseanne's?

strated the ease with which memories can be implanted in unsuspecting individuals, her critics say that her research might not accurately capture the actual trauma that occurs in abuse episodes.

Therapists and their clients are left with the chilling possibility that not all abuse memories recovered in therapy are real. In the absence of corroboration, some recollections might be authentic and others might not be.

According to Loftus (1993b), psychotherapists, counselors, social service agencies, and law enforcement personnel need to be careful about probing for horrors on the other side of some amnesiac barrier. They should be cautious in their interpretation of uncorroborated repressed memories that return later. Clarification, compassion, and gentle confrontation along with a demonstration of empathy are techniques that can be used to help individuals in their painful struggle to come to grips with their personal truths.

There is a final tragic risk involved in suggestive probing and uncritical acceptance of all allegations made by clients. These activities increase the probability that society in general will disbelieve the actual cases of child abuse that deserve extensive attention and evaluation. In general, any careless or uncritical acceptance of unreplicated findings in psychology, especially when they have a colorful element that attracts media attention, harms public attitudes toward the contributions of psychological research (Bruck & Ceci 1999; Ceci, 2000).

How can a traumatic memory be so vivid and detailed, yet at the same time have inaccuracies? A number of factors can be involved. Some children might have made perceptual errors at the time of encoding information because the episode was so shocking. Others might have distorted the information and recalled the episode as being less traumatic then it actually was, in order to reduce their anxiety about what happened. Others, in discussing the traumatic event with various people, might have incorporated bits and pieces of these persons' recollections of what happened into their own version of the event (Ceci, 2000).

In sum, memories of real-life traumas are usually more accurate and long-lasting than everyday events. However, memories of traumas are subject to some deterioration and distortion. In traumatic memories, the central part of the memory is almost always effectively remembered. Where distortion often arises is in the details of the traumatic episode.

Some cases of memory for personal trauma involve a mental disorder called *post-traumatic stress disorder*, which includes severe anxiety symptoms that can immediately follow the trauma or be delayed by months or even years until onset. This mental disorder can emerge as a consequence of exposure to any of several traumatic events, such as war, severe abuse (as in rape), and accidental disasters (such as a plane crash). The symptoms of this disorder can include "flashbacks" in which the individual relives the traumatic event in nightmares, or in an awake but dissociative-like state. They also can include difficulties with memory and concentration. We will have more to say about post-traumatic stress disorder in chapter 11 ("Abnormal Psychology").

Stress-related hormones likely play a role in memories that involve personal trauma. The release of stress-related hormones, which are signaled by the amgydala (see figure 6.13), likely account for some of the extraordinary longevity and vividness of emotional or traumatic experiences (Schacter, 1996).

Repressed Memories
The emotional blows of personal trauma can produce distortions of memory or vivid reenactments of the event in memory. In the case of post-traumatic stress disorder, the event might be pushed beneath awareness only to reappear in vivid flashbacks months or even years later. Repression takes place when something shocking happens and the mind pushes all memory of the occurrence into some inaccessible part of the unconscious mind. At some later point, the memory might emerge in consciousness, as in the case of post-traumatic stress disorder.

In psychoanalytic theory, which we initially discussed in chapter 1, repression's main function is to protect the individual from threatening information. Repression doesn't erase a memory, it just makes it extremely difficult to remember consciously. To read further about repressed memories, see Explorations in Psychology. We will have much more to say about repressed memories in our discussion of psychoanalytic theories in chapter 10 ("Personality") and chapter 12 ("Therapies").

Mood-Congruent Memory
Another aspect of emotional memories involves **mood-congruent memory,** *which means that people tend to remember information better when their mood is similar at encoding and retrieval.* Researchers have found that when people are in sad moods they are more likely to remember negative experiences, like failure and rejection, and that when they are in happy moods they are more likely to remember positive experiences, like success and acceptance (Mineka & Nugent, 1995). Unfortunately, for people who are depressed this means that they are likely to recall negative experiences, which only perpetuates their depression.

Now that we have studied many aspects of how we retrieve information, especially in the form of autobiographical and emotional memories, we turn our attention to why we forget.

Forgetting

Why do we forget? One of psychology's pioneers had some thoughts about this.

Ebbinghaus' Pioneering Research on Forgetting
Hermann Ebbinghaus (1850–1909) was the first individual to conduct scientific research on forgetting. In 1885, Ebbinghaus studied his own forgetting. He invented *nonsense syllables,* meaningless materials that are uncontaminated by prior learning. Examples of these consonant-vowel-consonant nonsense syllables include: *zeq, xid, lek, vut,* and *riy.* Ebbinghaus memorized a list of thirteen such nonsense syllables and then

Repressed Memories
False and Recovered Memories

Hermann Ebbinghaus (1850–1909) was the first psychologist to conduct scientific research on forgetting. What was the nature of this research?

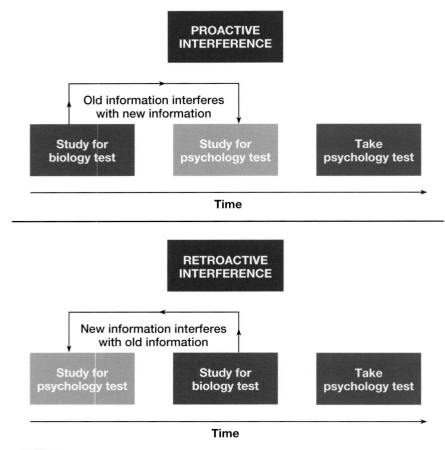

assessed how many of them he could remember. Even just one day later, he could only recall a few of the syllables. Ebbinghaus concluded that the most forgetting takes place soon after we learn something.

If we forget so quickly, why put effort into learning something? Fortunately, researchers have demonstrated that forgetting is not so extensive as Ebbinghaus envisioned (Baddeley, 1992). Ebbinghaus studied meaningless nonsense syllables. When we memorize more meaningful material, such as poetry, history, or the type of material in this text, forgetting is not so rapid and extensive. Let's now turn to how we actually retrieve information from our long-term memory.

Interference and Decay   Interference and decay have been proposed as two reasons people forget. **Interference theory** *states that we forget not because memories are actually lost from storage, but because other information gets in the way of what we want to remember.*

There are two kinds of interference: proactive and retroactive. **Proactive interference** *occurs when material that was learned earlier disrupts the recall of material learned later.* Remember that *pro-* means "forward in time." For example, suppose you had a good friend 10 years ago named *Mary,* and last night you met someone at a party named *Marie.* You might find yourself calling your new friend *Mary* because the old information *(Mary)* interferes with retrieval of new information *(Marie).* **Retroactive interference** *occurs when material learned later disrupts retrieval of information learned earlier.* Remember that *retro-* means "backward in time." Suppose you have become friends with *Marie* (and finally have gotten her name straight). If you find yourself sending a letter to your old friend *Mary,* you might address it to *Marie* because the new information *(Marie)* interferes with the old information *(Mary)* (see figure 6.18).

Figure 6.18
Proactive and Retroactive Interference
Pro- means "forward"; in proactive interference, old information has a forward influence by getting in the way of new material learned. *Retro-* means "backward"; in retroactive interference, new information has a backward influence by getting in the way of material learned earlier.

Proactive and retroactive interference *both* might be explained by cue-dependent forgetting. The reason *Mary* interferes with *Marie,* and the name *Marie* interferes with the name *Mary,* might be that the cue you are using to remember does not distinguish between the two memories. For example, if the cue you were using was "my good friend," it might evoke both names. This could result in retrieving the wrong name, or in a kind of blocking in which each name interferes with the other and neither comes to mind. Memory researchers have shown that retrieval cues (like *friend* in our example) can become overloaded, and when that happens we are likely to forget or to retrieve incorrectly.

Although interference is involved in forgetting, it is not the whole story. **Decay theory** *states that when something new is learned, a neurochemical "memory trace" is formed, but over time this trace tends to disintegrate.* Decay theory suggests that the passage of time always increases forgetting. However, there is one circumstance in which older memories can be stronger than more recent ones. Older memories are sometimes more resistant to shocks or physical assaults on the brain than recent memories.

Alabama businesswoman Patsy Cannon was in a car crash in 1986. Her injury was so severe that it left her with retrograde amnesia, and she had to relearn virtually everything she used to know. Patsy didn't even recognize her own daughter. The photograph on the left shows Patsy in 1986 just prior to the car crash. Today (right photo) Patsy works as an advocate for individuals with brain injury.

Amnesia   Consider the case of H. M. At the age of 27, H. M. underwent surgery to stop his epileptic seizures and emerged with his intelligence and most of his mental abilities intact, but the part of his brain that was responsible for laying down new memories (the hippocampus) was damaged beyond repair. This damage resulted in **amnesia,** *the loss of memory.* Although some types of amnesia clear up over time, H. M.'s amnesia endured. In the years following surgery, H. M.'s memory showed no improvement. The amnesia suffered by H. M. was anterograde in nature. **Anterograde amnesia** *is a memory disorder that affects the retention of new information or events.* What was learned before the onset of the condition is not affected. For example, H. M. could identify his friends, recall their names, and even tell stories about them—but only if he had known them before surgery. People who met H. M. after surgery remained virtual strangers, even if they spent thousands of hours with him. The vast majority of H. M.'s postsurgical experiences were never encoded in his long-term memory. Oddly enough, H. M.'s short-term memory remained unchanged, and as indicated earlier, his overall intelligence, which was above average, remained intact.

Amnesia also occurs in a second form, known as **retrograde amnesia,** *which involves memory loss for a segment of the past but not for new events.* It is much more common than anterograde amnesia, and frequently occurs when the brain is assaulted by an electrical shock or a physical blow—such as a head injury to a football player. The key difference from anterograde amnesia is that the forgotten information is *old* (prior to the event that caused the amnesia), and the person's ability to acquire new memories is not affected (Hamann, 2000).

At this point we have studied many ideas about retrieval and forgetting. A summary of these ideas is presented in summary table 6.3. Next, we focus on another important dimension of memory—how we can improve it.

Amnesia
Exploring Amnesia

SUMMARY TABLE 6.3
Memory Retrieval and Forgetting

Concept	Processes/Related Ideas	Characteristics/Description
Retrieval from Long-Term Memory	Tip-of-the-Tongue Phenomenon	This occurs when we can't quite pull something out of memory. The implication is that without good retrieval cues, information stored in memory is hard to find.
	Serial Position Effect	This influences retrieval, which is superior for items at the beginning of a list (primacy effect) and at the end of a list (recency effect).
	Retrieval Cues and the Retrieval Task	A key factor that makes retrieval effortful is the absence of effective cues. A second factor is the nature of the retrieval task, which, along with the presence or absence of retrieval cues, distinguishes recall and recognition memory. The encoding specificity principle states that associations formed at the time of encoding or learning tend to be effective retrieval cues. Retrieval also benefits from priming, which involves activating particular connections or associations in memory. In many cases, the associations are unconscious.
Autobiographical Memory	Its Nature	This refers to a person's recollections of his or her life experiences. Autobiographical memory has three levels: (1) life time periods, (2) general events, and (3) event-specific knowledge. Biographies of the self can connect the past and the present to form a portrait of our identity.
Emotional Memories	Flashbulb Memories	These are memories of emotionally significant events that people often recall with considerable accuracy and vivid imagery. Although flashbulb memories typically are more vivid and durable than memories for everyday events, they are subject to some deterioration and change.
	Personal Trauma	Memory for personal traumas also is usually more accurate than memory for ordinary events, but it too is subject to some distortion and inaccuracy. People tend to remember the core information about a personal trauma but might distort some of the details. Some cases of personal trauma result in post-traumatic stress disorder. The release of stress-related hormones, which are signaled by the amygdala, likely accounts for some of the extraordinary longevity and vividness of emotional or traumatic experiences.
	Repressed Memories	Personal trauma can cause individuals to repress emotionally laden information so that it is not accessible to the awareness of their conscious mind. Repression doesn't erase a memory, it just makes it extremely difficult to remember consciously.
	Mood-Congruent Memory	This principle states that people tend to remember information better when their mood is similar during encoding and retrieval.
Forgetting	Ebbinghaus' Pioneering Research on Forgetting	In 1885, Hermann Ebbinghaus tested his own memory of nonsense syllables. He discovered that his forgetting was rapid and extensive. However, researchers have found that we forget less than Ebbinghaus envisioned, especially when we learn meaningful material.
	Interference and Decay	Interference and decay have been proposed as two reasons people forget. Interference theory states that we forget not because memories are actually lost from storage but because other information gets in the way of what we want to remember. In proactive interference, material that was learned earlier disrupts the recall of material learned later. In retroactive interference, material learned later disrupts the retrieval of information that was learned earlier. Decay theory argues that when something new is learned, a memory trace is formed but, as time passes, this trace tends to deteriorate.
	Amnesia	Amnesia involves extreme memory deficits and comes in two forms. Anterograde amnesia is a memory disorder that prevents the retention of new information and events. Retrograde amnesia is a memory disorder that involves memory loss for a segment of the past but not for new events.

Memory and Study Strategies

Using the right memory and study strategies can help you improve your academic performance. Let's explore some of these strategies.

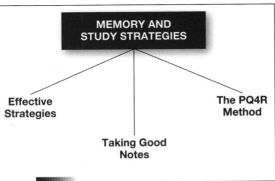

Effective Strategies

Effective memory and study strategies include paying attention, understanding the material, organizing, using mnemonics, asking yourself questions, spreading out and consolidating learning, cognitively monitoring your progress, and managing your time effectively.

Memory Strategies

Memory Techniques

Pay Attention and Minimize Distraction   Paying attention helps you remember something. If you want to remember something, give it your undivided attention. Monitor how well you pay attention. If you find yourself getting distracted, say to yourself a cue word or phrase like "Focus" or "Zero in" to increase your attention.

Understand the Material Rather Than Rotely Memorize It   You will remember information over the long term if you understand it rather than just rotely rehearse and memorize it. Rehearsal works well for encoding information into short-term memory, but when you need to retrieve the information from long-term memory it is much less efficient. So, for most information, understand it, give it meaning, elaborate on it, and personalize it.

Organize What You Put Into Memory   You will remember information better if you organize it hierarchically. Arrange information, rework material, and give it a structure to help you remember it.

Use Mnemonic Strategies   **Mnemonics** *are specific memory aids for remembering information.* Mnemonic strategies can involve imagery and/or words. Following are three types of mnemonics:

- The **method of loci** *is a mnemonic strategy in which you develop images of items to be remembered and store them in familiar locations (which is what "loci" means).* Rooms of houses or stores on a street are common locations used in this memory strategy. For example, if you need to remember a list of concepts, you can mentally place them in the rooms of a house you are familiar with, such as entry foyer, living room, dining room, kitchen, and so on. Then, when you need to retrieve the information, you imagine the house, mentally go through the rooms, and retrieve the concepts.
- *Acronyms* (creating a word from the first letters of items to be remembered) also can be used as a mnemonic strategy. For example, *Homes* can be used for remembering the Great Lakes: *Huron, Ontario, Michigan, Erie,* and *Superior.* Do you recall the acronym we used in chapter 3 to remember the colors in the light spectrum? It was an imaginary man named *ROY G. BIV* (*R*ed, *O*range, *Y*ellow, *G*reen, *B*lue, *I*ndigo, and *V*iolet).
- The **keyword method** *is a mnemonic strategy in which vivid imagery is attached to important words.* For example, when students need to remember that Annapolis is the capital of Maryland, they might connect vivid images of Annapolis and Maryland (such as two apples getting married) (see figure 6.19).

*F*igure 6.19
The Keyword Method

To help children remember the state capitals, the keyword method was used. A special component of the keyword method is the use of mental imagery, which was stimulated by presenting the children with a vivid visual image, such as two apples being married. The strategy is to help the children associate *apple* with Annapolis and *marry* with Maryland.

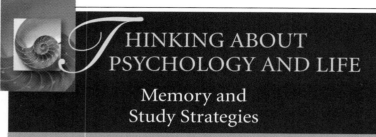

THINKING ABOUT PSYCHOLOGY AND LIFE

Memory and Study Strategies

CANDIDLY RESPOND to the following items about your own memory and study strategies. Rate yourself 1 = never, 2 = some, 3 = moderate, 4 = almost always, and 5 = always. Then total your points.

	1	2	3	4	5
1. I'm good at focusing my attention and minimizing distractions.					
2. I study for understanding rather than rotely memorizing material.					
3. I organize information hierarchically as part of my memory strategies.					
4. I use mnemonic strategies when I have to memorize lists or specific facts.					
5. I ask myself questions about what I have read or about class activities.					
6. I spread out my studying and consolidate my learning.					
7. I cognitively monitor what I read and study.					
8. I am a good time manager and planner.					
9. I have a good note-taking system.					
10. I regularly review my notes.					
11. I use the PQ4R or a similar study system.					

TOTAL: _____

If you scored 50 to 55 points, you likely use good memory and study strategies. If you scored 45 to 49 points, you likely have some reasonably good memory and study strategies. If you scored below 45, spend some time working on improving your memory and study strategies. Most colleges and universities have a study skills center where specialists can help you.

Many experts on memory and study skills recommend that mnemonics be used mainly when you need to remember a list of items or specific facts. However, in most cases, memory for understanding is preferred over rote memorization.

Ask Yourself Questions

When you ask yourself questions about what you have read or an activity in class, you expand the number of associations you make with the information you need to retrieve. This self-questioning strategy can help you to remember. As you read, periodically stop and ask yourself questions, such as "What is the meaning of what I just read?" "Why is this important?" and "What is an example of the concept I just read?"

Spread Out and Consolidate Your Learning

Regularly review what you learn. You will benefit by distributing your learning over a longer period rather than cramming for a test at the last minute. Cramming tends to produce short-term memory that is processed in a shallow rather than a deep manner. A final, concentrated tune-up before the test instead of struggling to learn everything at the last minute is desirable (Halonen & Santrock, 1999).

Cognitively Monitor Your Progress

Cognitive monitoring involves taking stock of your progress in an activity such as reading or studying. For example, you might make sure that you summarize what you have read and restudy those parts of the material that were unclear. Also, if you are writing a paper for a course you will want to cognitively monitor your progress in terms of having the right resources to draw on, as well as having enough time to write a first draft and revise it one or more times.

Be a Good Time Manager and Planner

Managing your time effectively and planning out the necessary time to study will give you the hours you need to do well academically. How many hours a week do you spend studying for each hour you are in class? Study skills experts report that students who make high grades typically spend a minimum of two, and in many cases three, hours studying out of class for every hour they are in class. That means if you are in class 15 hours, you should be managing your time to study 30 to 45 hours outside of class each week if you want to make high grades.

Taking Good Notes

Taking good notes either from a lecture or a text benefits your memory. Don't write down everything the instructor says. It is impossible to do this anyway and it can prevent you from getting the big picture of what the instructor is communicating. Some good note-taking strategies include these:

- *Summarizing.* In this method, you listen for a few minutes and then write down the main idea that the instructor is trying to get across in that time frame. Then you listen for several more minutes and write down another idea, and so on.

SUMMARY TABLE 6.4
Memory and Study Strategies

Concept	Processes/Related Ideas	Characteristics/Description
Effective Strategies	Memory and Study Strategies	These include paying attention and minimizing distraction, understanding the material rather than rotely memorizing it, organizing what you put into memory, using mnemonic strategies, asking yourself questions, spreading out and consolidating your learning, engaging in cognitive monitoring, as well as being a good time manager and planner.
Taking Good Notes	Its Nature	Don't take down everything the instructor says. Use a systematic strategy such as summarizing, outlining, concept maps, or the Cornell method. Get into the habit of reviewing your notes periodically.
The PQ4R Method	Its Nature	This system involves: Preview, Question, Read, Reflect, Recite, and Review.

- *Outlining.* You can outline what the instructor is saying, along the lines of how every chapter in this book is organized with "A"-level heads being the main topics, "B"-level heads as subtopics under the "A" heads, and "C"-level heads under the "B" heads.
- *Concept maps.* You can draw concept maps of what an instructor is saying, much like the concept maps you have studied at the end of each chapter in this book. The concept maps are similar to outlines but visually portray information in a spider-like format.
- *The Cornell Method.* Yet another note-taking strategy is the Cornell Method. It involves dividing an 8 1/2 × 11 sheet of paper into two columns by drawing a line down the page about 1/4 to 1/3 of the way from the left edge. You write your notes on the right 2/3 to 3/4 of the page. When you review your notes, you can then make notations and comments about the notes on the left side, which personalizes them for better understanding and retrieval.
- An excellent strategy is to get into the habit of reviewing your notes periodically rather than waiting to study them at the last minute before a test. Take a few minutes to review your notes just after a lecture if possible. This helps you to fill in information you might have missed but is still in your memory. And this strategy helps you to consolidate your learning.

The PQ4R Method

Various systems have been developed to help students remember information that they are studying. One of the earliest systems was called *SQ3R,* which stands for *Survey, Question, Read, Recite,* and *Review.* A more recently developed system is called **PQ4R,** *which stands for Preview, Question, Read, Reflect, Recite, and Review.* Thus, the PQ4R system adds an additional step to the SQ3R system: Reflect. This system can benefit you by getting you to meaningfully organize information, ask questions about it, reflect on it and think about it, and review it.

At this point we have discussed many ideas about memory and study strategies. An overview of these strategies is presented in summary table 6.4. In the next chapter, we continue our exploration of psychology's cognitive areas by studying thinking and language.

"You simply associate each number with a word, such as 'lipoprotein' and 3,467,009."

Reprinted by permission of Sidney Harris

Overview *Overview*

WE BEGAN THIS CHAPTER by examining the nature of memory, evaluating what memory is, and exploring memory's remarkable abilities and imperfections. Our coverage of memory encoding focused on rehearsal, deep processing, elaboration, imagery, and organization. We studied these aspects of memory storage: time frames, contents, representation, and neurological basis. We read about memory retrieval and forgetting, including ideas on retrieval from long-term memory, autobiographical memory, emotional memories, and forgetting. We discussed these dimensions of memory and study strategies: effective strategies, taking good notes, and the PQ4R method.

Don't forget that you can obtain a more detailed view of the chapter material by again studying the four summary tables on pages 181, 192, 202, and 205.

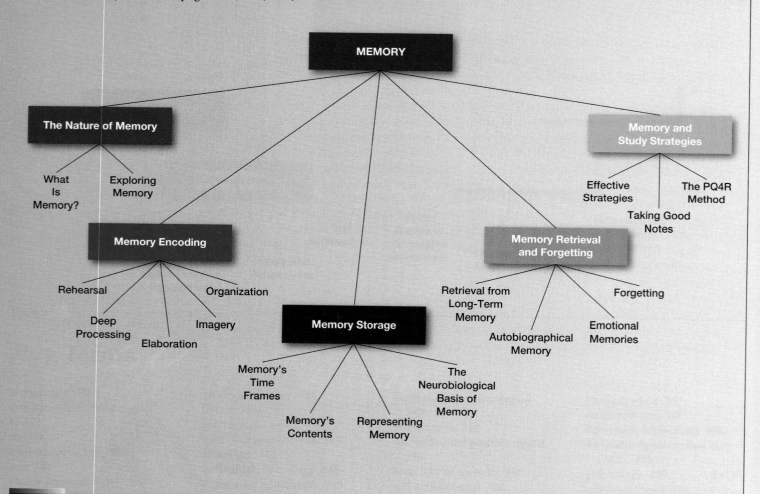

Key Terms

memory 176
encoding 177
storage 177
retrieval 177
rehearsal 177
levels of processing theory
    178
elaboration 178
chunking 180
Atkinson-Shiffrin theory 182
sensory memory 182
echoic memory 183

iconic memory 183
working memory 183
memory span 184
long-term memory 184
declarative memory 185
nondeclarative memory 185
episodic memory 186
semantic memory 186
schema 188
script 190
tip-of-the-tongue (TOT)
    phenomenon 193

serial position effect 193
primacy effect 193
recency effect 193
recall 194
recognition 194
encoding specificity principle
    195
priming 195
autobiographical memory 196
flashbulb memories 196
mood-congruent memory 199
interference theory 200

proactive interference 200
retroactive interference 200
decay theory 200
amnesia 201
anterograde amnesia 201
retrograde amnesia 201
mnemonics 203
method of loci 203
keyword method 203
cognitive monitoring 204
PQ4R 205

Key People

Fergus Craik and Robert
    Lockhart 178
Allan Paivio 179
Gordon Bower 180
Richard Atkinson and Richard
    Shiffrin 182

George Sperling 183
George Miller 184
Alan Baddeley 184
Endel Tulving 186
Sir Frederick Bartlett 188

Karl Lashley 190
Larry Squire 190
Eric Kandel and James
    Schwartz 191

Elizabeth Loftus 198
Hermann Ebbinghaus 199

Taking It to the Net

1. Have you ever used a rhyme or acronym to remember something for a test? These memory
techniques are called mnemonics and they can
be used to remember many different things. To illustrate the
power of mnemonics, complete the rhyme, "Thirty days hath
September, April, June, and November . . ." Do you think items
learned with mnemonics are more enduring than items learned
without such techniques? Describe the fundamental principles
underlying the use of mnemonics.

2. Imagine you have just started a new job as a server in a restaurant. On your first day, you meet all of your friendly co-workers.
Unfortunately, there are so many names you must remember, you
begin to feel overwhelmed. Between the busboys, the cooks, the
hostess, and the other servers, there are more than twenty names
to remember. So, being a keen psychology student, you apply

your knowledge of memory techniques to name/face recognition.
Explain how you tackle this problem and what methods you use.

3. In the popular media, amnesia is most often associated with some
kind of head injury. For instance, after a car accident, someone
might forget the events leading up to the accident. They might
even forget personal information, such as their name, the date, or
their children's names. However, amnesia can occur as a result of
events other than head injury. Stress, for instance, can lead to amnesia. Can you explain the process of how stress affects memory?
What about trauma? Why do some trauma victims remember detailed events of the traumatic event while others recall nothing?

Connect to http://www.mhhe.com/psychology/santrock to find the
answers!

Chapter 7

Thinking, Language, and Intelligence

Preview

THIS CHAPTER BUILDS on our earlier discussions of perception (chapter 3), consciousness (chapter 4), learning (chapter 5), and memory (chapter 6), each of which introduced important dimensions of cognitive psychology. We are now ready to explore how we think and use language and the concept of intelligence, which also are central topics in cognitive psychology. These are some of the questions we will explore in this chapter:

- What are some obstacles to solving problems?
- What are some good strategies for thinking critically and making decisions?
- What is language and how does it develop?
- Do animals have language?
- Do we have a single intelligence or multiple intelligences?
- How can people become more creative?

Images of Psychology and Life
The Human Versus Big Blue, Cog, and CYC

WHEN THE RUSSIAN chess champion Gary Kasparov faced off against an IBM computer named "Big Blue" in a celebrated chess match, he wasn't just after fame and money. By his own account, he was playing for me, you, and every member of the human species. He was trying, as he said, to "help defend our dignity."

Kasparov has competed against Big Blue on several occasions. In 1996, he barely escaped defeat. In 1997, he was not so fortunate. The computer won two games to one, with two matches ending in draws. Even Kasparov acknowledged that the computer had played a "humanlike" game.

Can machines like Big Blue actually "think" (Wright, 1996)? No one doubts Big Blue's chess skills, but at issue is whether it is a *thinking machine*. It uses "brute force" by computing zillions of calculations to arrive at decisions. On the topic of brute force, one organizer of an exclusively human chess tournament commented that you don't invite forklifts to weight-lifting competitions. Although relying on an almost

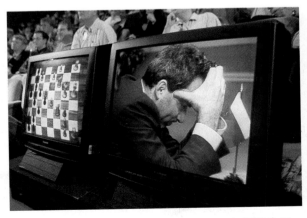

The Russian chess champion Gary Kasparov tied IBM's Big Blue in 1996, but in 1997, Big Blue (with its computing power doubled) sent Kasparov down to defeat.

With eight Macintosh-type processors for a brain, Cog tries to learn the way human infants do. Can machines like this actually "think?"

endless number of mechanical rules, Big Blue also used some chess programs that sized up the state of play and reasoned strategically from there.

Rodney Brooks, a professor at MIT, built a computer and nicknamed it "Cog" (Dibbell, 1996). It is a vaguely person-shaped concoction of metal, plastic, and silicon, with cameras where eyes should be and eight 32-bit microprocessors for a brain. Brooks is trying to get Cog to learn about the world the way human babies do, programming and reprogramming itself through interactions with people and objects around it. One of Brooks' goals is to someday have a conversation with Cog about nothing in particular.

Douglas Lenant, who works at an artificial intelligence systems firm in Austin, Texas, has similar hopes for his brainchild, a sprawling data-rich computer program called CYC (as in enCYClopedic). While Brooks tries to get Cog to teach itself about the world, Lenant has already programmed more than a million rules into CYC. He types these into CYC's memory one assertion ("Bread is food," "You're wet when you sweat") at a time. He doesn't want to have to do this spoon-feeding forever. Ultimately, he hopes CYC will digest an encyclopedia whole and ask questions about whatever it doesn't understand.

The effort to build machines that think is more than four decades old now. Lenant's ideas represent one strategy in this effort, Brooks' another. Cog is a member of the bottom-up school. Inspired more by biological structures than by logical ones, the bottom-uppers don't bother trying to enter the rules of thought into their intelligent machines. Rather, they try to generate thought by building lots of small, simple programs and encouraging them to interact. There's no one place in Cog that you can point to as the seat of intelligence. Brooks says, "There's no there, there."

Lenant's approach follows the belief that symbolic knowledge makes the mind go round. That is, if you enter into the machine the logical structures through which we understand the world, you are on the road to recreating intelligence.

At present, neither Cog nor CYC has reached its creator's goal of mimicking human thinking. However, with the dramatic increase in machines' abilities, some researchers in this area believe that such efforts will lead to the creation of an intelligence that not only is different from our own, but more intelligent.

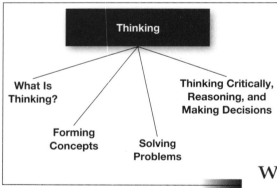

Thinking

In earlier chapters, we studied how people perceive information (chapter 3, "Sensation and Perception") and how information is encoded, stored, and retrieved (chapter 6, "Memory"). Here we will study how we use this information when we think. To understand thinking, we will explore what it is, how concepts are formed, how problems can be solved, and different types of thinking, reasoning, and decision making.

What Is Thinking?

Thinking *involves mentally manipulating information, as when we form concepts, solve problems, reason, and make decisions.* We begin our tour of thinking by seeing why concepts are important and how they are formed.

Forming Concepts

Regardless of the kind of thinking we engage in, our thinking is fueled by **concepts,** *which are mental categories used to group objects, events, and characteristics.*

We have a special ability for creating categories to help us make sense of information in our world. We know that apples and oranges are fruits, but that they have different tastes and colors. We know that Porsches and Ford Escorts are automobiles, but also know that they differ in cost, speed, and prestige. How do we know these things? The answer lies in our ability to group them on the basis of their features. For example, Porsches and Ford Escorts have such things as an engine, four wheels, and a steering wheel, and provide transportation. By such features we know that they are both automobiles. In other words, we have a *concept* of what an automobile is.

Why are concepts important? If we did not have concepts, each object and event in our world would be unique to us. We would not be able to draw any kind of generalization. Concepts allow us to relate experiences and objects. Basketball, ice hockey, and track are sports. The concept of *sport* gives us a way to compare these activities.

Concepts grease the wheels of memory, making it more efficient so we don't have to "reinvent the wheel" each time we come across a piece of information. For example, we don't have to relearn what the Dow Jones Industrial Average is each time we pick up a newspaper. We already have the concept. Concepts also provide clues about how to react to an object or experience. For example, if we see a bowl of pretzels, our concept of food lets us know it is okay to eat them. Concepts allow us to associate classes of objects or events.

Although psychologists have learned much about concept formation, some believe that the research has been too artificial. Eleanor Rosch (1973) argues that real-life concepts are less precise than those used in many psychology experiments. She says that real-life concepts often have "fuzzy boundaries." That is, it's not always clear exactly what features are critical to a concept. Consider the concept "cup." A little thought might suggest that cups (1) are concrete objects, (2) are concave, (3) can hold solids and liquids, (4) have handles, and (5) can be used to drink hot liquids. However, what about the cups in Chinese restaurants that don't have handles? And what about the poor-quality paper cups that conduct too much heat to be used for hot drinks? Although such objects lack certain "critical features" of cups, we still call them cups.

Rosch also believes that in considering how people think about concepts, prototypes (items that are typical of a category) often are involved. In **prototype matching,** *people decide whether an item is a member of a category by comparing it with the most typical item(s) of the category.* The more similar the item is to the prototype, the more likely a person will say it belongs in the category; the less similar, the more likely the person will judge that it doesn't belong in the category. For example, think of your concept of a football player: perhaps big and muscular like an offensive lineman. But some football players, such as many field goal kickers, are not so big and muscular. Thus, an offensive lineman is a more prototypical example of a football player than a field goal kicker is. When we consider whether someone belongs in the category of "football player," we are more likely to use "offensive lineman" as the prototype than "field goal kicker." Nonetheless, members of a conceptual category can vary greatly and still have qualities that make them a member of that category (see figure 7.1).

Figure 7.1
When Is a Cup a "Cup"?

Which of these would you describe as the prototype for the concept "cup"? In one study, participants were most likely to choose number 5 (Labov, 1973). Some participants called number 4 a bowl and number 9 a vase because they were so different from the prototype.

Solving Problems

We face many problems in the course of our everyday lives. These include trying to figure out the fastest way to get across town, planning how to get enough money to buy a CD player, working a jigsaw puzzle, or estimating how much we owe in taxes. **Problem solving** *is an attempt to find an appropriate way of attaining a goal when the goal is not readily available.* Whatever the problem, we want to come up with the fastest and best solution possible. Next, we examine some steps in solving problems.

Steps in Solving Problems
Efforts have been made to specify the steps that individuals go through to effectively solve problems (Bransford & Stein, 1993). Four such steps are (1) find and frame problems, (2) develop good problem-solving strategies, (3) evaluate solutions, (4) rethink and redefine problems and solutions over time.

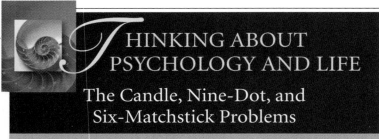

THINKING ABOUT PSYCHOLOGY AND LIFE

The Candle, Nine-Dot, and Six-Matchstick Problems

The following three problems are often used to illustrate the concept of fixation in problem solving.

The Candle Problem
The problem here is how to mount a candle on a wall so that it won't drip wax on a table or floor while it is burning. How would you solve this problem?

The Nine-Dot Problem
Take out a piece of paper and copy the following arrangement of dots:

Without lifting your pencil, connect the dots using only four straight lines.

The Six-Matchstick Problem
The problem posed is: Given six matchsticks of equal length, arrange them to make four equilateral triangles, the sides of which are one stick long.

Solutions to the problems are presented at the end of the chapter.

---

(1) Find and Frame Problems   Before a problem can be solved, it has to be recognized. Identifying a key problem to solve is an important first step in problem solving (Mayer, 1999). Unfortunately, our society all too often discourages people from identifying problems. Many businesses, government agencies, and schools reprimand or fire employees who identify problems in the workplace. For example, increased incidences of cancer from asbestos might have been avoided if problems identified by employees had been acknowledged and acted on by people in authority. The pressure to ignore problems is so strong that Congress finally passed a bill that provides protection for employees who are brave enough to persist in their fight to have the problems they identify recognized. It became known as the Whistle-Blower Protection Act.

Finding and framing problems often involves asking questions in creative ways (Goleman, Kaufman, & Ray, 1993). Bill Bowerman (inventor of Nike shoes) asked, "What happens if I pour rubber over an iron?" Fred Smith (founder of Federal Express) asked, "Why can't there be reliable overnight mail service?" Godfrey Hounsfield (inventor of the CAT scan) asked, "Why can't we see in three dimensions what is inside the human body without cutting it open?" Masaru Ibuka (honorary chairman of Sony) asked, "Why don't we remove the recording function and speaker and put headphones on the player?"

Many of these questions were ridiculed at first. Other shoe companies thought Bowerman's waffle shoe was a "really stupid idea." Fred Smith proposed the idea of Federal Express during his days as a student at Yale and got a C on the paper. Godfrey Hounsfield was told that the CAT scan was impractical. And Masaru Ibuka was told, "A player without speakers—you must be crazy!"

(2) Develop Good Problem-Solving Strategies   Once you find a problem and clearly define it, you need to develop strategies for solving it (Reed, 2000). Among the effective strategies are setting subgoals, using algorithms, and utilizing heuristics.

Subgoaling *involves setting intermediate goals that put you in a better position of reaching the final goal or solution.* People might not effectively solve a problem because they don't generate subproblems or subgoals. Let's return to the problem of writing a paper for a psychology course. What might be some subgoaling strategies? One might be locating the right books and research journals on the problem you have decided to study. At the same time you are searching for the right books and journals, you will likely benefit from establishing some subgoals in terms of what you need to accomplish along the way to your goal of a polished psychology paper. If the paper is due in two months, you might set a subgoal of a first draft of the paper two weeks before it is due, another subgoal of completing reading for the paper a month before it is due, and yet another subgoal of starting library research tomorrow.

Notice that in establishing the subgoals, we worked backward. Working backward in establishing subgoals is a good strategy. You first create a subgoal that is closest to the final goal and then work backward to the subgoal that is closest to the beginning of the problem-solving effort.

Algorithms *are strategies that guarantee a solution to a problem.* Algorithms come in different forms, such as using a formula, following a set of directions, or *trying out all possible solutions.* We often use algorithms in solving math problems by applying formulas, and when we follow the instructions to put something together, like a lawn chair or a table.

In some cases an algorithmic strategy might take a long time. Consider a person who is working a crossword puzzle. She comes across c_nt_ _ker_ _ _ and looks to see what hint is given. It says, "Ill-tempered and quarrelsome." An algorithm for finding the correct word exists. She could try every possible alphabet combination in the six blank spaces and then check through a dictionary to see which one is correct. However, not many people would want to go through the more than 1 million steps in this algorithmic effort. Clearly, the algorithmic strategy of trying out all possible solutions should be applied to problems with a small number of possible solutions.

Instead of using an algorithm to solve this type of problem, most crossword-puzzle enthusiasts use **heuristics,** *which are strategies or rules of thumb that suggest a solution to a problem but do not guarantee an answer.* Thus, we know that certain combinations of letters are more likely to work than others. For example, in our attempt to find the correct word in the crossword puzzle, we know we need a vowel between c and n, so b, q, and a lot of other letters won't work. We also know that combinations of letters like *an* are acceptable between the *t* and *k*. We also know that it helps to sound out some words at this point. We come up with "contank" and "can-tank." Then we get it: *cantankerous.*

In the real world, we are much more likely to face problems in which it is wise to use heuristics rather than algorithms. Heuristics help us narrow down the possible solutions to find the one that works.

Heuristics

(3) Evaluate Solutions   Once we think we have solved a problem, we really won't know how effective our solution is until we find out if it actually works. It helps to have in mind a clear criterion for the effectiveness of the solution. For example, what will your criterion be for your psychology paper? Will it be simply getting it completed? receiving positive feedback on the paper? getting an A? having the instructor say that it is one of the best papers on the topic she has read?

(4) Rethink and Redefine Problems and Solutions over Time   An important final step in problem solving is to continually rethink and redefine problems (Bereiter & Scardamalia, 1993). People who are good at problem solving are more motivated to improve on their past performances and to make original contributions. Thus, you can examine the paper after it is returned by your instructor and use the feedback to think about ways to improve it. Sony continues to try to improve its Walkman, striving to make it lighter, smaller, and better sounding.

Obstacles to Solving Problems   Obstacles include becoming fixated and not being adequately motivated.

Becoming Fixated   It is easy to fall into the trap of becoming fixated on a particular strategy for solving a problem. **Fixation** *involves using a prior strategy and failing to look at a problem from a fresh, new perspective.* **Functional fixedness** *is one type of fixation in which individuals fail to solve a problem because they are fixated on a thing's usual functions.* If you have ever used a shoe to hammer a nail, you have overcome functional fixedness to solve a problem.

An example of a problem that requires overcoming functional fixedness is the Maier String Problem (Maier, 1931) (see figure 7.2). The problem is to figure out how to tie two strings together when they can't be reached at the same time, and you must stand in one spot. If you hold one and then move it toward the other you cannot reach the second one. It seems as though you are stuck, but there is a pair of pliers on a table. Can you solve the problem?

The solution is to use the pliers as a weight, tying them to the end of one of the strings (see figure 7.3). Swing this string back and forth like a pendulum and grasp the stationary string. Your past experience with pliers makes this a difficult problem to solve. To solve the problem, you need to find a unique use for the pliers, in this case as a weight to create a pendulum.

Each of us occasionally gets into the mental rut of solving problems by using a particular strategy. A **mental set** *is a type of fixation in which an individual tries to solve a problem in a particular way that has worked in the past.* I (your author) had a mental set about using a typewriter rather than a computer to write my books. I felt comfortable with a typewriter and never lost any sections I had written. It took a long time to break out of this mental set. Once I did, the problem goal of finishing a book became much easier. You might feel the same about some aspects of technology. A good strategy is to keep an open mind about such technological changes and monitor whether your mental set is keeping you from trying out new technology.

Lacking Motivation and Persistence   Individuals might have great problem-solving skills, but it hardly matters what talents they have if they are not motivated to use them (Sternberg & Spear-Swerling, 1996). It is especially important to be internally motivated to solve a problem and persist with effort at finding a solution. Some people give up too easily when they encounter a problem.

Thinking Critically, Reasoning, and Making Decisions

Aside from forming concepts and solving problems, other aspects of thinking include thinking critically, reasoning effectively, and making good decisions.

Thinking Critically   In chapter 1, we defined **critical thinking** *as thinking reflectively and productively and evaluating the evidence.* People who think critically grasp the deeper meaning of ideas, keep an open mind about different approaches and perspectives, and decide for themselves what to believe or do (Gardner, 1999; Runco, 1999). Critical thinking currently is of considerable interest to both psychologists and educators ◀▥ P. 20. However, critical thinking is not an entirely new idea. Educator John Dewey (1933) was working with a similar idea when he advocated teaching students to "think reflectively." Today, educators at all levels embrace the idea that an important outcome of education is to have students who think critically.

Jacqueline and Martin Brooks (1993) lament that so few schools teach students to think critically and develop a deep understanding of concepts. For example, many high school students read *Hamlet* but don't think deeply about it, never transforming their prior notions of power, greed, and relationships. Deep understanding occurs when people are stimulated to rethink their prior ideas.

In Brooks and Brooks' view, schools spend too much time on getting students to give a single correct answer in an imitative way rather than encouraging students to expand their thinking by coming up with new ideas and rethinking earlier conclusions. As we indicated in chapter 1, they believe that too often teachers ask students to recite, define, describe, state, and list rather than to analyze, infer, connect, synthesize,

*F*igure 7.2
Maier String Problem
How can you tie the two strings together if you cannot reach them both at the same time?

*F*igure 7.3
Solution to the Maier String Problem
Use the pliers as a weight to create a pendulum motion that brings the second string closer.

The Critical Thinking Community
Critical Thinking Links
Schools for Thinking
Mindfulness

criticize, create, evaluate, think, and rethink. Too often we are inclined to stay on the surface of problems rather than stretch our minds and become deeply engaged in meaningful thinking (Bruning, Schraw, & Ronning, 1999).

Ellen Langer (1989, 1997; Moldoveanu & Langer, 1999) studies mindless behavior and encourages people to be more mindful. One of her favorite examples of mindless behavior involves the time she used a new credit card in a department store. The clerk noticed that she had not signed it and handed it to her to sign on the back. After passing the credit card through the machine, the clerk handed her a receipt to sign. Then the clerk held up the receipt Langer had signed and compared the signatures!

Langer's concept of mindfulness is similar to the way we described critical thinking earlier. She says that a mindful person (1) continues to create new ideas, (2) is open to new information, and (3) is aware of more than one perspective. By contrast, a mindless person is entrapped in old ideas, engages in automatic behavior, and operates from a single perspective. Langer believes that asking good questions is an important ingredient of mindful thinking.

Reasoning   What is reasoning? **Reasoning** *is the mental activity of transforming information to reach conclusions.* Reasoning is either inductive or deductive.

Inductive reasoning *involves reasoning from the specific to the general.* That is, it consists of drawing conclusions about all members of a category based on observing only some members. For example, imagine that you are a student in a literature class. You read a few of Shakespeare's plays. In this case, your inductive reasoning is being tapped. Now imagine that you learn a concept in psychology and are asked whether it applies to other domains, such as business or biology. Your inductive reasoning also is being challenged here.

Analogies draw on inductive reasoning. An **analogy** *is a type of formal reasoning that involves four parts, with the relation between the first two parts being the same as the relation between the last two.* For example, solve this analogy: Beethoven is to music as Picasso is to _____. To answer correctly ("art"), you had to induce the relation between Beethoven and music (the former created the latter) and apply this to Picasso (what did he create?).

THINKING ABOUT PSYCHOLOGY AND LIFE
Seeking Multiple Explanations

GOOD CRITICAL THINKERS often seek multiple or alternative explanations of something. They avoid believing something is due to a single cause. For example, consider 19-year-old Tom, a Native American. He dropped out of college midway through his first year. Suppose you heard someone say, "Tom quit college because he wasn't smart enough to do college work."

- Is this statement a valid judgment or an unfortunate stereotype?
- Generate at least three other reasons Tom might have quit college.
- Speculate about how you can find out for certain which factors are responsible.

"For God's sake, think! Why is he being so nice to you?"

© *The New Yorker Collection. 1998 Sam Gross from cartoonbank.com. All Rights Reserved.*

Through the Eyes of Psychologists
Ellen Langer, *Harvard University*

"I didn't want to be thought of as mindless so I changed the name of what I was studying from mindlessness to mindfulness."

(a)   (b)

Figure 7.4
Use of Analogy in Problem Solving

The benzene ring (a) is one of the most important structures in organic chemistry. It was discovered by Wilhelm Kekulé after he imagined how its structure might be analogous to a snake biting its tail (b).

Analogies can be helpful in solving problems, especially when they are visually represented (Mumford & Porter, 1999). Benjamin Franklin noticed that a pointed object drew a stronger spark than a blunt object when both were in the vicinity of an electrified body. Originally he believed this was an unimportant observation, but then, he realized that pointed rods of iron could be used to attract lightning, thus deflecting it from buildings and ships. Wilhelm Kukelé discovered the ringlike structure of the benzene molecule in organic chemistry only after he visualized a snake biting its tail and saw the analogy to the structure of the benzene molecule (see figure 7.4). In many ways, analogies make the strange familiar and the familiar strange.

In contrast to inductive reasoning, **deductive reasoning** *is reasoning from the general to the specific.* The British detective Sherlock Holmes was a master at deductive reasoning, always deducing the right solution. When solving a case, he sorted through a number of clues to zero in on the one correct solution to a murder.

When you solve puzzles or riddles, you are engaging in deductive reasoning. When you learn about a general rule and then understand how it applies in some situations but not others you are engaging in deductive reasoning. When psychologists, other scientists, Sherlock Holmes, and you use theories and intuitions to make predictions, then evaluate these predictions by making further observations, deductive reasoning is at work.

Making Decisions   Think of all the decisions you have to make in your life. Should I major in biology, psychology, or business? Should I go to graduate school right after college or get a job first? Should I establish myself in a career before settling down to have a family? Should I buy a house or rent? **Decision making** *involves evaluating alternatives and making choices among them.* In reasoning, people use established rules to draw conclusions. In contrast, when we make decisions, such rules aren't established and we don't know the consequences of the decisions (Tversky & Fox, 1995). Some of the information might be missing, and we might not trust all of the information we have (Matlin, 1998).

In one type of decision-making research, investigators study how people weigh the costs and benefits of various outcomes. They especially focus on whether people actually choose the outcome with the highest expected value (Smyth & others, 1994). In choosing a college, you might have made up a list of pluses and minuses of going to different colleges (related to such factors as cost, quality of education, social life, and so on), then made a decision based on how the colleges fared on these criteria. In making your decision, you might have weighed some of these factors more heavily than others (such as cost three points, quality of education two points, and social life one point).

In other instances when researchers study how people make decisions, they examine biases and flaws in decision making. In many cases, our decision-making strategies are well adapted to deal with a variety of problems (Nisbett & Ross, 1980). However, there are a number of biases and flaws that we are prone to make (Stanovich, 1999). Let's explore some of these.

Confirmation Bias   **Confirmation bias** *is the tendency to search for and use information that supports our ideas rather than refutes them.* Thus, in solving a problem, I might have an initial hypothesis that something is going to work. I test out the hypothesis and find out that it is right some of the time. I conclude that my hypothesis was right rather than exploring the fact that it did not work some of the time. It is easy to detect the confirmation bias in the way that many people think. Consider politicians. They often accept news that supports their views and dismiss evidence that runs counter to their views. Consider also physicians who misdiagnose a patient because one or two symptoms fit with previous successful diagnoses they have made. In their desire to confirm their diagnosis, they ignore symptoms that don't fit their diagnosis. Our decisions can become further biased because we tend to seek out and listen to people whose views confirm our own and tend to avoid acquaintances who have dissenting views.

Belief Perseverance   Closely related to confirmation bias, **belief perseverance** *is the tendency to hold on to a belief in the face of contradictory evidence.* People have a difficult time letting go of an idea or strategy once they have embraced it.

Consider Madonna (see figure 7.5). We have a hard time thinking of her in a maternal role because of the belief perseverance that she is a wild, fun-loving rock star.

Overconfidence Bias   **Overconfidence bias** *is the tendency to have more confidence in our judgments and decisions than we should based on the relative frequency of correct answers.* People are overconfident about how long people with a fatal disease will live, which businesses will go bankrupt, which psychiatric inpatients have serious mental disorders, whether a defendant is guilty in a court trial, and which students will do well in graduate school (Kahneman & Tversky, 1995). People consistently have more faith in their judgments than predictions based on statistically objective measures indicate they should. For example, in one study, college students were asked to make predictions about themselves in the coming academic year (Vallone & others, 1990). They were asked to predict whether they would drop any courses, vote in an election, and break up with their girlfriend or boyfriend. Then they were asked to rate how confident they were in their predictions. At the end of the year, the accuracy of their predictions was examined. The results: The students were overconfident about what they thought would happen to them. For example, they were more likely to drop a class, not vote in an election, and break up with a girlfriend or a boyfriend than they had predicted.

Hindsight Bias   People not only are overconfident about what they predict will happen in the future (overconfidence bias), they also tend to be overconfident about circumstances that already have happened. **Hindsight bias** *is our tendency to falsely report, after the fact, that we accurately predicted an event.* In the case of Madonna having a baby, many people predicted she would never have one. However, after she had the baby, some of these same people said that they knew all along she would become a mother. As I write this, baseball season is getting ready to begin. Lots of people in different cities are predicting that their teams are going to make it to the World Series. Come October, many of the same people will say, "I told you they weren't going to have a good season."

Availability Heuristic   Earlier in the chapter we described heuristics as rules of thumb that suggest a solution but do not ensure it will work. We will consider two heuristics that can produce flawed thinking: the availability heuristic and the representative heuristic. When we use the **availability heuristic** *we make a judgment about the probability of an event by recalling the frequency of the event's past occurrences.* When an event has recently occurred, we especially tend to overestimate its future occurrence. The media contribute to this prediction error by vividly exposing us to tornados, murders, diseases, and accidents. For example, if you saw a train wreck on television yesterday, you are more likely to estimate that train wrecks are more prevalent than if you had not seen the wreck.

Representativeness Heuristic   The **representativeness heuristic** *suggests that we make decisions based on how well something matches a prototype—that is, the most common or representative example.* Consider the following description of an individual's dinner companion: skilled at carpentry, proficient at wrestling, owns a pet snake, knows how to repair motorcycles, and has a police record. What is the probability that this person is a male? Most likely the description fits your prototype of a male more than a female, so you might estimate that there is a 9 in 10 chance the dinner companion is a male.

In this example, your prototype served you well because there are far more men than women in the population who fit the description. Sometimes, however, our prototypes do not take into account the frequency of events in the entire population. For example, would you say the probability is greater that the dinner companion is a

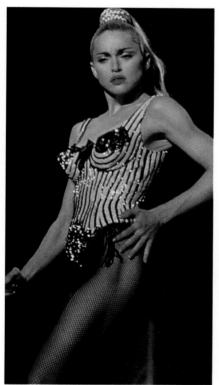

$\mathcal{F}$**igure 7.5**
Belief Perseverance

Belief perseverance is a common bias that infiltrates our judgments. How is belief perseverance involved in thinking it improbable that Madonna would have become a mother?

Summary Table 7.1
Thinking

Concept	Processes/ Related Ideas	Characteristics/Description
Thinking	What Is Thinking?	Thinking involves mentally manipulating information, as when we form concepts, solve problems, and engage in judgment and decision making.
	Forming Concepts	Concepts are mental categories used to group similar objects, events, and characteristics. Concepts help us to generalize, improve our memory, and keep us from constantly having to learn. Many real-life concepts have fuzzy boundaries. In forming concepts, people frequently use prototype matching.
	Solving Problems	Problem solving is an attempt to find an appropriate way of attaining a goal when the goal is not readily available. Four steps in solving problems are (1) find and frame problems, (2) develop good problem-solving strategies, (3) evaluate solutions, and (4) rethink and redefine problems and solutions over time. Finding and framing problems is an often-overlooked dimension of problem solving. Among effective strategies for solving problems are subgoaling (setting intermediate goals that put you in a better position to reach your goal), algorithms (strategies that guarantee a solution), and heuristics (strategies or rules of thumb that suggest a solution to a problem but do not guarantee an answer). Obstacles to solving problems include being fixated and not being adequately motivated. Being fixated means focusing on prior strategies and failing to look at a problem from a fresh, new perspective. Functional fixedness is a type of fixation in which individuals fail to solve a problem because they are fixated on a thing's usual functions. A mental set is a type of fixation in which an individual tries to solve a problem in a particular way that has worked in the past.
	Critical Thinking	Critical thinking involves thinking reflectively and productively, and evaluating the evidence. Some critics argue that schools do not do a good job of guiding students to think critically. Langer says that too many people engage in mindless behavior, and she encourages us to be more mindful.
	Reasoning	Reasoning is the mental activity of transforming information to reach conclusions. Inductive reasoning involves reasoning from the specific to the general. That is, it consists of drawing conclusions about all members of a category based on observing only some of them. Analogies draw on inductive reasoning. Deductive reasoning is reasoning from the general to the specific.
	Decision Making	Decision making involves evaluating alternatives and making choices among them. One type of decision-making research studies how people weigh costs and benefits of various outcomes. Another type studies people's biases and flaws in making decisions.
	Biases and Flaws	These biases and flaws involve confirmation bias (tendency to search for and use information that supports our ideas rather than refutes them), belief perseverance (tendency to hold on to a belief in the face of contradictory evidence), overconfidence bias (tendency to have more confidence in our judgments than we should, based on the relative frequency of correct answers), hindsight bias (tendency after the fact to falsely claim to have predicted an event), availability heuristic (making a judgment about the probability of an event by recalling the frequency of the event's past occurrences), and representativeness heuristic (making decisions based on how well something matches a prototype—that is, the most common representative or example).

member of a motorcycle gang or a salesman? You would probably say there is a much greater chance that he is a member of a motorcycle gang, in which case you would be wrong. Why? Although only a very small percentage of the millions of the world's salesmen fit the description of the dinner companion, the total number represented by this percentage is greater than the total of motorcycle gang members who fit this description. Let's assume there are 10,000 members of motorcycle gangs in the world versus 100 million salesmen. Even if 1 of every 100 motorcycle gang members fits our description, there would be only 100 of them. If just 1 of every 100,000 salesmen fits our description, their number would total 1,000. So the probability is 10 times greater that the dinner companion is a salesman than a member of a motorcycle gang. Our lives involve many such instances in which we judge probabilities based on representativeness and fail to consider the population from which a sample is drawn.

At this point we have studied many ideas about thinking. A review of these ideas is presented in summary table 7.1. Next, we will turn our attention to language, which provides us with a unique system for communicating our thoughts.

Language

In 1799, a nude boy was observed running through the woods in France. The boy was captured when he was 11 years old. He was called the Wild Boy of Aveyron and was believed to have lived in the woods alone for 6 years (Lane, 1976). When found, he made no effort to communicate. Even after a number of years, he never learned to communicate effectively. Sadly, a modern-day wild child named Genie was discovered in Los Angeles in 1970. Despite intensive intervention, Genie never acquired more than a primitive form of language. Both cases raise questions about the contribution of biology and environment to language, topics we will explore in depth later. First, though, we need to find out what language is.

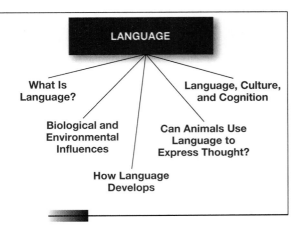

What Is Language?

To explore what language is, we will first define it, then examine its rule systems.

Defining Language   **Language** *is a form of communication, whether spoken, written, or signed, that is based on a system of symbols.* Think how important language is in our everyday lives. We need language to speak with others, listen to others, read, and write. Our language enables us to describe past events in detail and to plan for the future. Language lets us pass down information from one generation to the next and create a rich cultural heritage.

All human languages have some common characteristics. These include infinite generativity and organizational rules. **Infinite generativity** *is the ability to produce an endless number of meaningful sentences using a finite set of words and rules.* This quality makes language a highly creative enterprise (Carroll, 1999). Language is characterized by a number or organizational rules than include phonology, morphology, syntax, and semantics, which we will discuss next.

Exploring Language

Rule Systems   Language is made up of basic sounds, or phonemes (Lahari, 1999). **Phonology** *refers to a language's sound system.* Phonological rules ensure that certain sound sequences occur (for example, *sp*, *ba*, or *ar*) and others do not (for example, *zx*, or *qp*). A good example of a phoneme in the English language is /k/, the sound represented by the letter *k* in the word *ski* and the letter *c* in the word *cat*. Although the /k/ sound is slightly different in these two words, the variation is not distinguished, and the /k/ sound is described as a single phoneme. In some languages, such as Arabic, this kind of variation represents separate phonemes.

"If you don't mind my asking, how much does a sentence diagrammer pull down a year?"

© 1981 Thaves. Reprinted with permission.

Morphology *refers to word formation.* Every word in the English language is made up of one or more morphemes. Some words consist of a single morpheme (for example, *help*), whereas others are made up of more than one morpheme (for example, *helper,* which has two morphemes, *help + er,* with the morpheme *-er* meaning "one who," in this case "one who helps"). However, not all morphemes are words (for example, *pre-, -tion,* and *-ing*). Just as the rules that govern phonemes ensure that certain sound sequences occur, the rules that govern morphemes ensure that certain strings of sounds occur in particular sequences.

Syntax *involves the ways words are combined to form acceptable phrases and sentences.* If someone says to you, "Bob slugged Tom" or "Bob was slugged by Tom," you know who did the slugging and who was slugged in each case because you share the same syntactic understanding of sentence structure. You also understand that the sentence "You didn't stay, did you?" is a grammatical sentence but that "You didn't stay, didn't you?" is unacceptable and ambiguous.

Semantics *refers to the meaning of words and sentences.* Every word has a set of semantic features (Garrod & Pickering, 1999). *Girl* and *woman,* for example, share many of the same semantic features as the word *female,* but differ semantically in regard to age. Words have semantic restrictions on how they can be used in sentences. The sentence *The bicycle talked the boy into buying a candy bar* is syntactically correct but semantically incorrect. The sentence violates our semantic knowledge that bicycles do not talk.

Biological and Environmental Influences

Is the ability to generate rules for language and then use them to create an infinite number of words the product of biological factors and evolution? Or is language learned and influenced by the environment?

Biological Influences   Estimates vary as to how long ago humans acquired language—about 100,000 years ago. In evolutionary time, then, language is a very recent acquisition. A number of experts believe that biological evolution undeniably shaped humans into linguistic creatures (Chomsky, 1957). The brain, nervous system, and vocal apparatus of our predecessors changed over hundreds of thousands of years (Tallal, 2000). Physically equipped to do so, *Homo sapiens* went beyond grunting and shrieking to develop abstract speech. Language clearly gave humans an enormous edge over other animals and increased the chances of survival (Pinker, 1994) ◀▥ P. 12.

The famous linguist Noam Chomsky (1975) argues that language has strong biological underpinnings. In Chomsky's view, humans are biologically prewired to learn language at a certain time and in a certain way. Chomsky and many other language experts stress that the strongest evidence for language's biological basis resides in the fact that children all over the world acquire language milestones at about the same time developmentally and in about the same order, despite vast variations in the language input they receive from the environment. For example, in some cultures adults never talk to infants under 1 year of age, yet these infants still acquire language. Also, there is no convincing way to explain how quickly children learn language other than biological factors (Locke, 1999; Maratsos, 1999).

Environmental Influences   Behaviorists have advocated the view that language is primarily determined by environmental influences. For example, the famous behaviorist B. F. Skinner (1957) said that language is just another behavior, like sitting, walking, or running ◀▥ P. 155. He argued that all behaviors, including language, are learned through reinforcement. Albert Bandura (1977) later emphasized that language is learned through imitation ◀▥ P. 166.

In the wild, chimps communicate through calls, gestures, and expressions, which evolutionary psychologists believe might be the roots of true language.

However, virtually all language experts today agree that reinforcement and imitation cannot explain children's language development. Many of children's sentences are novel in the sense that they have not previously heard them. Thus, a child might hear the sentence, "The plate fell on the floor" and then say "My mirror fell on the blanket" after the child drops the mirror on the blanket. Reinforcement (smiles, hugs, pats on the back, corrective feedback) and imitation (modeling of words and syntax) simply cannot explain this utterance.

Roger Brown (1973) spent long hours observing parents and their young children, searching for evidence that parents reinforce their children for speaking grammatically. He found that parents sometimes smiled and praised their children for sentences they liked, but that they also reinforced lots of ungrammatical sentences as well. Brown concluded that no evidence exists that reinforcement is responsible for the development of children's language rule systems.

Although reinforcement and imitation are not responsible for children's development of language rule systems, it is important that children interact with language-skilled people (Gleason, 2000; Snow, 1999; Tracy, in press). The Wild Boy of Aveyron and Genie were not around such people when they were young children, and it clearly harmed their language development.

In one study, researchers observed the language environments of children from middle-income professional and welfare backgrounds, then examined the children's language development (Hart & Risley, 1995). All of the children developed normally in terms of learning to talk and acquiring all of the forms of English and basic vocabulary. However, there were enormous differences in the sheer amount of language the children were exposed to and the level of the children's language development. For example, in a typical hour, the middle-income professional parents spent almost twice as much time communicating with their children as the welfare parents did. The children from the middle-income professional families heard about 2,100 words an hour, their child counterparts in welfare families only 600 words an hour. The researchers estimated that by 4 years of age, the average welfare family child would have 13 million fewer words of cumulative language experience than the child in the average middle-income professional family. Amazingly, some of the 3-year-old children from middle-class professional families had a recorded vocabulary that exceeded the recorded vocabulary of some of the welfare parents!

Thus, in the real world of learning language, children are neither exclusively biological linguists nor exclusively socially driven language experts (Ratner, 1993). As with all areas of psychology we have studied, it is important to take an interactionist view of how children learn language. That is, children are biologically prepared to learn language but benefit enormously from being bathed in a competent language environment from an early age (Pan & Snow, 1999; Snow, 1998).

MIT linguist Noam Chomsky was one of the early architects of the view that children's language development cannot be explained by environmental input. In Chomsky's view, language has strong biological underpinnings, with children biologically prewired to learn language at a certain time and in a certain way.

Talking to Babies
Child Language

How Language Develops

Most individuals in the United States acquire a vocabulary of nearly 50,000 words in a language by the time they are adults. How does this development take place?

Early Development   Before babies ever say their first words, at the age of 10 to 13 months, they babble. Babbling—endlessly repeating sounds and syllables such as *bababa or dadada*—begins at about the age of 3 to 6 months and is determined by biological readiness, not reinforcement or the ability to hear (Locke, 1993). Even deaf babies babble for a time (Lenneberg, Rebelsky, & Nichols, 1965). Babbling probably allows the baby to exercise its vocal cords and helps develop articulation.

A child's first words name important people (*dada*), familiar animals (*kitty*), vehicles (*car*), toys (*ball*), food (*milk*), body parts (*eye*), clothes (*hat*), household items (*clock*), and greetings (*bye*). These were babies' first words 50 years ago, and they are babies' first words today (Clark, 1983).

Around the world, young children learn to speak in two-word utterances, in most cases at about 18 to 24 months of age. What implications does this have for the biological basis of language?

By the time children reach the age of 18 to 24 months, they usually utter two-word statements (Clark, 2000). They quickly grasp the importance of expressing concepts and the role that language plays in communicating with others (Schafer, 1999). To convey meaning in two-word statements, the child relies heavily on gesture, tone, and context. Children can communicate a wealth of meaning with two words; for instance:

Identification: See doggie.
Location: Book there.
Repetition: More milk.
Nonexistence: Allgone thing.
Negation: Not wolf.
Possession: My candy.
Attribution: Big car.
Agent-action: Mama walk.
Action-direct-object: Hit you.
Action-indirect-object: Give papa.
Action-instrument: Cut knife.
Question: Where ball? (Slobin, 1972)

These examples are from children whose first languages were English, German, Russian, Finnish, Turkish, and Samoan. Although these two-word sentences omit many parts of speech, they are remarkably succinct in conveying many messages. In fact, a child's first combination of words has this economical quality in every language. **Telegraphic speech** *is the use of short and precise words to communicate; it is characteristic of young children's two- or three-word combinations.* When we send a telegram, we try to be short and precise, excluding any unnecessary words. As a result, articles, auxiliary verbs, and other connectives usually are omitted. Of course, telegraphic speech is not limited to two-word phrases. "Mommy give ice cream" or "Mommy give Tommy ice cream" also are examples of telegraphic speech. As children leave the two-word stage, they move rather quickly into three-, four-, and five-word combinations.

As we have just seen, language unfolds in a sequence. At every point in development, the child's linguistic interaction with parents and others obeys certain rules (de Villiers & de Villiers, 1999; Goldin-Meadow, 2000; MacWhinney, 1999). The concept of morphological rules was examined in a classic study by Jean Berko (1958). She presented preschool and first-grade children with cards such as the one shown in figure 7.6. The children were asked to look at the card while the experimenter read the words on it aloud. Then the children were asked to supply the missing word. This might sound easy, but Berko was interested not only in their ability to say the missing word but to say it correctly (with the ending that was dictated by the morphological rules). Thus, *wugs* is the correct response for the card in figure 7.6. Although the children's responses were not always completely accurate, they were much better than chance. What makes Berko's study so impressive is that the words were fictional, created solely for the purpose of the study. Thus, the children could not have based their answers on remembering past instances of hearing the words. Instead, they were forced to rely on *rules*, and their performance suggested that they did so successfully. Now that we have explored some aspects of early language development, let's examine an important question in this area.

This is a wug.

Now there is another one. There are two of them. There are two _____.

*F*igure 7.6
Stimuli in Berko's Classic Study of Children's Understanding of Morphological Rules

In Jean Berko's (1958) study, young children were presented cards such as this one with a "wug" on it. Then the children were asked to supply the missing word and say it correctly. "Wugs" is the correct response here.

Is There a Critical Period for Learning Language?
A **critical period** *is a period when there is learning readiness; beyond this period learning is difficult or impossible.* Almost all children learn one or more languages during their early years of development, so it is difficult to determine whether there is a critical period for language development. In the 1960s, Eric Lenneberg (1967) proposed a

biological theory of language acquisition. He said that language is a maturational process and that there is a critical period between about 18 months of age and puberty during which a first language must be acquired. Central to Lenneberg's thesis is the idea that language develops rapidly and with ease during the preschool years as a result of maturation. Lenneberg provided support for the critical-period concept from studies of several atypical populations, including children and adults with damage in the left hemisphere of the brain, deaf children, and children with mental retardation (Tager-Flusberg, 1994, 1999). The children's brains had plasticity, and the children recovered their language skills but the adults did not. Lenneberg believed that adults had already passed the critical period during which plasticity of brain functioning allows reassignment and relearning of language skills.

The stunted language development of a modern "wild child" also supports the idea of a critical period for language acquisition. In 1970, a California social worker made a routine visit to the home of a partially blind woman who had applied for public assistance. The social worker discovered that the woman and her husband kept their 13-year-old daughter, Genie, locked away from the world. Kept in almost total isolation during her childhood, Genie could not speak or stand erect. She was forced to sit naked all day on a child's potty seat, restrained by a harness her father had made—she could move only her hands and feet. At night she was placed in a kind of straitjacket and caged in a crib with wire mesh sides and a cover. Whenever Genie made a noise, her father beat her. He never communicated with her in words but growled and barked at her.

Genie spent a number of years in extensive rehabilitation programs, such as speech and physical therapy (Curtiss, 1977; Rymer, 1993). She eventually learned to walk upright with a jerky motion and to use the toilet. Genie also learned to recognize many words and to speak in rudimentary sentences. At first she spoke in one-word utterances. Later she was able to string together two-word combinations such as "big teeth," "little marble," and "two hand." Consistent with the language development of most children, three-word combinations followed—for example, "small two cup." Unlike normal children, however, Genie did not learn how to ask questions and she doesn't understand grammar. Genie is not able to distinguish between pronouns or passive and active verbs. Four years after she began stringing words together, her speech still sounded like a garbled telegram. And as an adult she speaks in short, mangled sentences, such as "Father hit leg," "Big wood," and "Genie hurt."

Can Animals Use Language to Express Thought?

Many animal species do have complex and ingenious ways to signal danger and to communicate about basic needs such as food and sex. For example, in one species of firefly the female has learned to imitate the flashing signal of another species to lure the aliens into her territory. Then she eats them. But is this language in the human sense? And what about the animals who are our closest relatives, the great apes?

Chimpanzees and *Homo sapiens* have 98 percent of their genetic material in common. Chimpanzee behavior includes hunting, toolmaking, embracing, back patting, kissing, and holding hands. Do animals this closely related to us have language? Can we teach human language to them?

Some researchers believe apes can learn language. One celebrity in this field is a chimp named Washoe, who was adopted when she was about 10 months old (Gardner & Gardner, 1971). Since apes do not have the vocal apparatus to speak, the researchers tried to teach Washoe

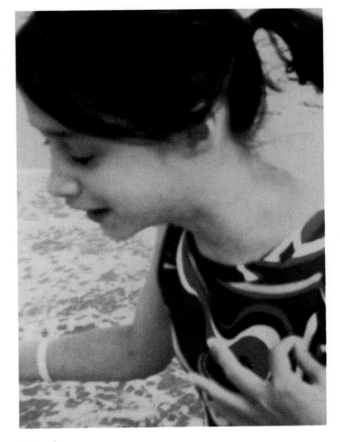

Genie

What were Genie's experiences like? What implications do they have for language acquisition?

"*Remember, don't talk sex, politics, or religion.*"

Reprinted courtesy of Omni Magazine © 1982.

Animal Communication

the American Sign Language, which is one of the sign languages of the deaf. Washoe used sign language during everyday activities, such as meals, play, and car rides. In 2 years, Washoe learned 38 different signs, and by the age of 5 she had a vocabulary of 160 signs. Washoe learned how to put signs together in novel ways, such as *You drink* and *You me tickle.* A number of other efforts to teach language to chimps have had similar results (Premack, 1986).

The debate about chimpanzees' ability to use language focuses on two key issues: Can apes understand the meaning of symbols—that is, can they comprehend that one thing stands for another? And can apes learn syntax—that is, can they learn the kinds of mechanics and rules that give human language its creative productivity? The first of these issues may have been settled by Sue Savage-Rumbaugh and her colleagues (1993). These researchers found strong evidence that the chimps Sherman and Austin can understand symbols. For example, if Sherman or Austin is sitting in a room, and a symbol for an object is displayed on a screen, he will go into another room, find the object, and bring it back. If the object is not there, he will come back empty-handed (Cowley, 1988). Austin and Sherman can play a game in which one chimp points to a symbol for food (such as M&Ms), and the other chimp selects the food from a tray, then they both eat it. These observations are clear evidence that chimps can understand symbols (see figure 7.7).

Recent evidence concerning chimps' syntactic ability has come from study of rare pygmy chimpanzees *(Pan paniscus),* also known as "bonobos." These chimps are friendlier and brighter than their cousins, and show some remarkable language abilities. For example, star pupil Kanzi is very good at understanding spoken English and has been shown to comprehend over 600 sentences, such as *Can you make the bunny eat the sweet potato?* (Savage-Rumbaugh, Shanker, & Taylor, 1998). Kanzi also produces fairly complex sentences using a response board hooked to a speech synthesizer.

The debate over whether or not animals can use language to express thoughts is far from resolved. Researchers agree that animals can communicate with each other and that some can manipulate language-like symbols with syntax that resembles that of young children (Rumbaugh, 2000). At the same time, it is clear that their language abilities do not show the same degree of generativity and complexity as adult human language.

Language, Culture, and Cognition

Take a moment and reflect on several questions. Did the culture in which you grew up influence your language? Does language influence the way you think? Does thinking influence the nature of your language?

Language and Culture   Linguist Benjamin Whorf (1956) argued that language actually determines the way we think. Whorf and his student Edward Sapir were specialists in Native American languages, and they were fascinated by the possibility that speakers of different languages might view the world differently as the result of the languages they speak. Whorf's **linguistic relativity hypothesis** *states that language determines the structure of thinking and shapes our basic ideas.* The Inuit in Alaska, for instance, have a dozen or more words to describe the various textures, colors, and physical states of snow. Hopi Indians have no words for past and future. And Arabs have 6,000 words for aspects of the camel.

Our cultural experiences for a particular concept shape a catalog of names that can be either rich or poor. An example of a name-rich concept in America is the "automobile" (we use terms like *coupe, convertible, minivan, station wagon,* and many others, not to mention various makes and models). The *automobile* part of your mental library of names is the product of many years of experience with automobiles. You probably will see and think about them in finer gradations than people who live in the jungles of South America or an isolated island in the Pacific Ocean. In this way, language acts as a window that filters the amount and nature of information that is passed on for further processing.

Critics of Whorf's theory say that words merely reflect, rather than cause, the way we think. The Inuits' adaptability and livelihood in Alaska depend on their capacity to recognize various conditions of snow and ice. A professional skier who is not Inuit might also know numerous words for snow, far more than the average person; and a person who doesn't know the words for the different types of snow might still be able to perceive these differences.

Eleanor Rosch (1973) found just that. She studied the effect of language on color perception among the Dani in New Guinea. The Dani have only two words for color—one that approximately means "white" and one that approximately means "black." If the linguistic relativity hypothesis were correct, the Dani would lack the ability to tell the difference between colors such as green, blue, red, yellow, and purple. But Rosch found that the Dani perceived colors just as we perceive them. As we know, color perception is biologically determined by receptors in the retinas in the eyes. Even though Whorf's linguistic relativity hypothesis missed the mark, researchers agree that although language does not determine thought, it can influence it.

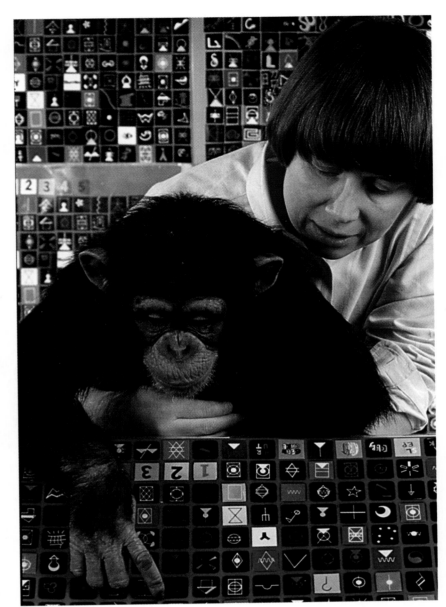

$\mathscr{F}$igure 7.7
Chimps and Symbols

Sue Savage-Rumbaugh and her colleagues at the Yerkes Primate Center and Georgia State University have studied the basic question of whether chimps understand symbols. Their research suggests that the answer to this question is yes.

Language and Cognition   What about our memory and problem solving? What role does language play in these important cognitive activities? Memory is stored not only in terms of sounds and images, but also in words. When words are stored in memory, their processing often is deep and their retrieval more effortful.

Language helps us think, make inferences, tackle difficult decisions, and solve problems (Lycan, 1999). Language can be thought of as a tool for representing ideas. Some psychologists have argued that we cannot think without language, a proposition that has produced heated controversy. Is thought dependent on language, or is

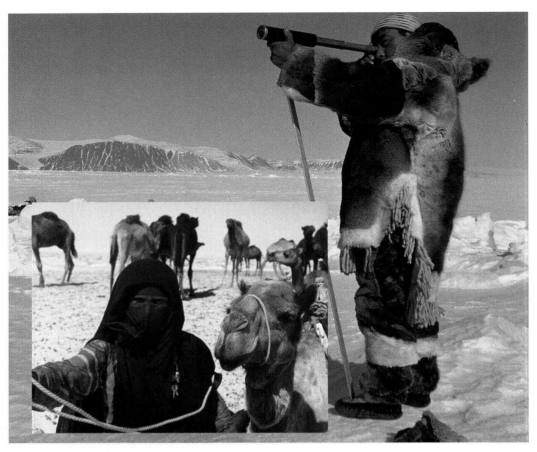

The linguistic relativity hypothesis states that our cultural experiences for a particular concept shape a catalog of names that can be either rich or poor. Consider how different your mental library of names for camel *might be if you had extensive experience with camels in a desert world and how different your mental library of names for* snow *might be if you lived in an arctic world of ice and cold. Despite its intriguing appeal, the linguistic relativity concept is controversial and many psychologists do not believe it plays a pivotal role in shaping thought.*

language dependent on thought? Language does provide a medium for representing abstract ideas. Our language rules are more sophisticated than thought at an earlier point in our development, suggesting that language is not always dependent on thought (Bruner, 1964).

Cognition also might be an important foundation for language (Gupta & Dell, 1999). Evidence that cognition is separate from language comes from studies of deaf children. On a variety of thinking and problem-solving tasks, deaf children perform at the same level as children of the same age who have no hearing problems. Some of the deaf children in these studies do not even have command of written or sign language (Furth, 1971).

So, thought can direct language, and language can direct thought (Jenkins, 1969). Language is virtually an unbounded symbol system, capable of expressing most thoughts, and language is the way we humans communicate most of our thoughts to each other. We do not always think in words, but undoubtedly our thinking would be greatly impoverished without them.

At this point we have studied many ideas about language. A review of these ideas is presented in summary table 7.2. So far in this chapter, we have explored thinking and language. Next, we will continue our examination of cognitive psychology's domains by studying the concept of intelligence.

SUMMARY TABLE 7.2
Language

Concept	Processes/ Related Ideas	Characteristics/Description
What Is Language?	Defining Language	Language is a form of communication, whether spoken, written, or signed, that is based on a system of symbols. All human languages have some common characteristics. These include infinite generativity (the ability to produce an endless number of meaningful sentences using a finite set of words and rules) and organizational rules.
	Rule Systems	Language's organizational rules include phonology (the sound system of a language), morphology (the rules for combining morphemes, which are meaningful strings of sounds that contain no smaller meaningful parts), syntax (the ways words are combined to form acceptable phrases and sentences), and semantics (the meaning of words and sentences).
Biological and Environmental Influences	Biological Influences	A number of experts believe that biological evolution shaped humans into linguistic creatures. The famous linguist Noam Chomsky and others argue that the strongest evidence for language's biological basis resides in the fact that children all over the world acquire language milestones at about the same time developmentally and in about the same order, despite vast variations in the language input they receive from the environment.
	Environmental Influences	Behaviorists, such as Skinner and Bandura, have advocated that language is primarily determined by environmental influences, especially reinforcement and imitation, but the evidence suggests that reinforcement and imitation are not responsible for the development of children's language rule systems. However, it is important for children to interact with language-skilled people. Children are biologically prepared to learn language but benefit enormously from being bathed in a competent language environment from early in development.
How Language Develops	Early Development	Before babies say their first words, they babble. At 10 to 13 months, infants say their first words. Infants' early speech is telegraphic.
	Is There a Critical Period for Learning Language?	A critical period is a period when there is learning readiness; beyond this period learning is difficult or impossible. The stunted growth of children such as Genie supports the critical period notion. However, this concept is still controversial.
Can Animals Use Language to Express Thought?	The Nature of the Issue	Animals clearly can communicate, and chimps have been taught to use symbols. Whether animals have the same language abilities as humans continues to be debated.
Language, Culture, and Cognition	Language and Culture	Whorf's linguistic relativity hypothesis states that language determines the structure of thinking and shapes our basic ideas. Whorf's ideas are controversial.
	Language and Cognition	Thoughts and ideas are associated with words and ideas. Different languages also promote different ways of thinking. Language does not completely determine thought but does influence it. Language is important in many cognitive activities, such as memory and thinking. Cognitive activities also influence language.

Mental Measurements Yearbook

Psychological Tests

Intelligence

The concept of intelligence is broad and there is controversy over what intelligence is, as well as a number of other controversies such as whether intelligence tests are sometimes misused. Twentieth-century English novelist Aldous Huxley said that children are remarkable for their intelligence. What do people mean when they use the term *intelligence*?

What Is Intelligence?

Intelligence is one of our most prized possessions, yet it is a concept that even the most intelligent people have not been able to agree on. Unlike such characteristics as height, weight, and age, intelligence cannot be directly measured. We can't peel back a person's scalp and observe the intelligence going on inside. We only can evaluate a person's intelligence *indirectly* by studying the intelligent acts that people generate. For the most part, intelligence tests have been relied on to provide an estimate of a person's intelligence (Kail & Pellegrino, 1985).

Some experts describe intelligence as having verbal ability and problem-solving skills. Others describe it as the ability to adapt to and learn from life's everyday experiences. Combining these ideas, we arrive at a definition of **intelligence** *as verbal ability, problem-solving skills, and the ability to adapt to and learn from life's everyday experiences.*

The primary components of intelligence are very close to the mental processes (thinking and language) that we discussed earlier in this chapter. The differences in how we described thinking and language and how we will discuss intelligence lie in the concepts of individual differences and assessment. **Individual differences** *are the stable, consistent ways in which people are different from each other* ◀▥ P. 18. In terms of assessment, intelligence tests are designed to tell us whether a person can reason better than others who have taken the test. The two main areas of individual differences in psychology that have been emphasized the most are intelligence and personality. We will explore these aspects of personality in chapter 10.

Intelligence Tests

At some point in your life you probably have taken an intelligence test. Psychologist Robert Sternberg (1997) remembers his early experiences with intelligence tests. Sternberg eventually overcame his anxieties about IQ tests. He not only began performing better on them but when he was 13 he devised his own intelligence test and began using it to assess classmates—that is, until the school principal found out and scolded him. Sternberg became so fascinated by intelligence that he made its study one of his lifelong pursuits. Later in the chapter we will discuss his approach to intelligence. To begin, though, we need to explore how tests are constructed and evaluated, then examine the most widely used tests of intelligence.

How Tests Are Constructed and Evaluated   Tests have become commonplace in today's world as psychologists have sought more precise measurement of psychology's concepts (Wright, 1999). Any good test must meet three criteria—it must be reliable, it must be valid, and it must be standardized. We will consider each of these criteria.

Reliability   If a test that measures a characteristic is a stable and consistent test, scores should not significantly fluctuate because of chance factors, such as how much sleep you get the night before the test, who the examiner is, the temperature in the room where you take the test, and so on. **Reliability** *is the extent to which a test yields a consistent, reproducible measure of performance.* Reliability can be measured in several ways. **Test-retest reliability** *is the extent to which a test yields the same measure* *of performance when an individual is given the same test on two different occasions.* Thus, if we gave an intelligence test to a group of high school students today and then gave them the same test in 6 months, the test would be considered reliable if those who scored high on the test today generally score high on the test in 6 months. One limitation of test-retest reliability is that individuals sometimes do better the second time they take the test because they are familiar with it.

Alternative forms reliability *involves giving alternate forms of the same test on two different occasions.* The test items on the two forms of the test are similar but not identical. This strategy eliminates the chance of individuals performing better due to familiarity with the items, but it does not eliminate an individual's familiarity with the procedures and strategies involved in the testing. One difficulty with alternate forms reliability is creating two truly parallel alternative forms.

A third method of measuring reliability is **split-half reliability,** *which involves dividing the items into two halves, such as the first half of the test and second half of the test.* Individuals' scores on the two halves of the test are compared to determine how consistently they performed. When split-half reliability is high, we say that a test is *internally consistent.* For example, if we gave an intelligence test in which vocabulary items made up the first half of the test and logical reasoning items made up the second half, to be internally consistent individuals' scores would have to be similar on each half of the test. Sometimes psychologists compare individuals' scores on odd-numbered and even-numbered items as another means of establishing the internal consistency of a test.

Reliability and Validity

Validity   A test may consistently measure an attribute, such as intelligence or personality, but this consistency does not ensure that we are measuring the attribute we want to measure (Embretson, 1999). A test of intelligence might actually measure something else, such as anxiety. The test might consistently measure how anxious you are and, thus, have high reliability but not measure your intelligence, which it purports to measure. **Validity** *is the extent to which a test measures what it is intended to measure.*

Like reliability, there are a number of methods to measure validity. One method is **content validity,** *which refers to the test's ability to test a broad range of the content that is to be measured.* For example, a final test in this class, if it is over the entire book, should sample items from each of the chapters rather than just two or three chapters. If an intelligence test purports to measure both verbal ability and problem-solving ability, the items should include a liberal sampling of items that reflects both of these domains. The test would not have high content validity if it asked you to define several vocabulary items but did not require you to reason logically in solving a number of problems.

One of the most important methods of measuring validity is **criterion validity,** *which is the test's ability to predict an individual's performance when assessed by other measures, or criteria, of the attribute.* For example, a psychologist might validate an intelligence test by asking the employers of the individuals who took the intelligence test how intelligent they are at work. The employers' perceptions would be another criterion for measuring intelligence. It is not unusual for the validation of an intelligence test to be another intelligence test. When the scores on the two measures overlap substantially, we say the test has high criterion validity. Of course, we may use more than one other measure to establish criterion validity. We might give the individuals a second intelligence test, get their employers' perceptions of their intelligence, and observe their behavior in real-life problem-solving situations ourselves.

Criterion validity can follow one of two courses, concurrent or predictive. **Concurrent validity** *is a form of criterion validity that assesses the relation of a test's scores to a criterion that is presently available (concurrent).* For example, a test might assess children's intelligence. Concurrent validity might be established by analyzing how the scores on the intelligence test correspond to the children's grades in school at this time.

Predictive validity *is a form of criterion validity that assesses the relation of a test's scores to an individual's performance at a point in the future.* For example, scores on an

Figure 7.8
Links Between Reliability and Validity
A test that is valid is reliable, but a test that is reliable is not necessarily valid. This is illustrated by the dart-throwing analogy. All three darts might land far away from the bull's-eye but land in about the same place (reliability or consistency). To be valid, though, all three darts have to hit the bull's-eye (which also means they have to be reliable, or consistent).

intelligence test might be used to predict whether the individual will be successful in college. Likewise, the SAT test is used for a similar purpose. Tests might also be developed to determine success as a police officer or pilot. Individuals take the test and then are evaluated *later* to see if they are indeed able to perform effectively in these jobs.

In considering reliability and validity, a test that is valid is reliable, but a test that is reliable is not necessarily valid. People can respond consistently on a test but the test might not be measuring what it purports to measure. To understand this, imagine that you have three darts to throw. If all three fall close together, you have reliability. However you have validity only if all three hit the bull's-eye (see figure 7.8).

Standardization Good tests are not only reliable and valid, they are standardized as well (Hopkins, 1998) ◀ P. 32. **Standardization** *involves developing uniform procedures for administering and scoring a test, as well as creating norms for the test.* Uniform testing procedures require that the testing environment be as similar as possible for all individuals. Without standardization, it is difficult to compare scores across individuals. If individuals take the SAT in a room where loud music is playing, they are disadvantaged compared to others who take the test in a quiet room. The test directions and the amount of time allowed to complete the test should be the same, for example. **Norms** *are established standards of performance for a test. Norms are created by giving the test to a large group of individuals representative of the population for whom the test is intended. This allows the test constructor to determine the distribution of test scores.* Norms inform us which scores are considered high, low, or average. For example, suppose you receive a score of 120 on an intelligence test; that number alone has little meaning. The score takes on meaning when we compare it with the other scores. If only 20 percent of the standardized group scored above 120, then we can interpret your score as high rather than low or average. Many tests of intelligence are designed for individuals from diverse groups. So that the tests are applicable to such different groups, many of them have norms—established standards of performance for individuals of different ages, socioeconomic statuses, and ethnic groups (Popham, 1999).

Standardization of tests requires that uniform procedures be followed. What are some examples of these uniform procedures?

The Binet Tests and the Wechsler Scales

Intelligence tests can be administered to people on an individual basis or in a group. The two most widely used individual tests of intelligence are the Binet tests and Wechsler scales.

The Binet Tests In 1904 the French Ministry of Education asked psychologist Alfred Binet to devise a method that would determine which students did not profit from typical school instruction. School officials wanted to reduce overcrowding by placing those who did not benefit from regular classroom teaching in special schools. Binet and his student Theophile Simon developed an intelligence test to meet this request. The test is referred to as the 1905 Scale and consisted of 30 items ranging from the ability to touch one's nose or ear when asked to the ability to draw designs from memory and define abstract concepts.

Binet developed the concept of **mental age (MA),** *which is an individual's level of mental development relative to others.* Binet reasoned that a mentally retarded child would perform

like a normal child of a younger age. He developed norms for intelligence by testing 50 nonretarded children from the ages of 3 to 11. Children suspected of mental retardation were given the test and their performance was compared with children of the same chronological age in the normal sample. Average mental age (MA) scores correspond to chronological age (CA), which is age from birth. A bright child has an MA considerably above CA; a dull child has an MA considerably below CA.

The term **intelligence quotient (IQ)** *was devised in 1912 by William Stern. IQ consists of an individual's mental age divided by chronological age multiplied by 100:*

$$IQ = \frac{MA}{CA} \times 100$$

If mental age is the same as chronological age, then the individual's IQ is 100; if mental age is above chronological age, the IQ is more than 100; if mental age is below chronological age, the IQ is less than 100. Scores noticeably above 100 are considered above average; those considerably below are considered below average. For example, a 6-year-old child with a mental age of 8 would have an IQ of 133, whereas a 6-year-old child with a mental age of 5 would have an IQ of 83.

Over the years, extensive effort has been expended to standardize the Binet test, which has been given to thousands of children and adults of different ages selected at random from different parts of the United States. By administering the test to large numbers of individuals and recording the results, it has been found that intelligence measured by the Binet approximates a normal distribution (see figure 7.9). A **normal distribution** *is symmetrical, with a majority of cases falling in the middle of the possible range of scores and few scores appearing toward the extremes of the range.*

The Binet test has been revised many times to incorporate advances in the understanding of intelligence and intelligence testing. The many revisions are called the Stanford-Binet tests (Stanford University is where the revisions were done). Many of the revisions were carried out by Lewis Terman, who applied Stern's IQ concept to

Alfred Binet (1857–1911)
Alfred Binet constructed the first intelligence test after being asked to create a measure to determine which children could benefit from instruction in France's schools and which could not. Binet's 1905 scale measured more complex mental processes than Galton's and Cattell's tests.

Alfred Binet

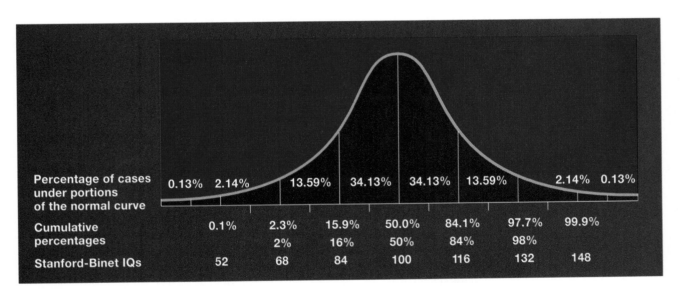

$\mathcal{F}$igure 7.9
The Normal Curve and Stanford-Binet IQ Scores
The distribution of IQ scores approximates a normal curve. Most of the population falls in the middle range of scores. Notice that extremely high and extremely low scores are very rare. Slightly more than two-thirds of the scores fall between 84 and 116. Only about 1 in 50 individuals has an IQ of more than 132 and only about 1 in 50 individuals has an IQ of less than 68.

The Binet Test

the test, developed extensive norms, and provided detailed, clear instructions for each problem on the test.

The current Stanford-Binet is given to individuals from the age of 2 through adulthood. It includes a wide variety of items, some requiring verbal responses, others nonverbal responses. For example, items that characterize a 6-year-old's performance on the test include the verbal ability to define at least six words, such as *orange* and *envelope,* and the nonverbal ability to trace a path through a maze. Items that reflect the average adult's intelligence include defining such words as *disproportionate* and *regard,* explaining a proverb, and comparing idleness and laziness.

The fourth edition of the Stanford-Binet was published in 1985. One important addition to this version is the analysis of the individual's responses in terms of four content areas: verbal reasoning, quantitative reasoning, abstract/visual reasoning, and short-term memory. A general composite score also is obtained to reflect overall intelligence. The Stanford-Binet continues to be one of the most widely used individual tests of intelligence (Naglieri, 2000).

The Wechsler Scales   Besides the Stanford-Binet, the other most widely used intelligence tests are the Wechsler scales, developed by David Wechsler. They include the Wechsler Adult Intelligence Scale–Revised (WAIS-R); the Wechsler Intelligence Scale for Children–III (WISC-III), to test children between the ages of 6 and 16; and the Wechsler Preschool and Primary Scale of Intelligence (WPPSI), to test children from the ages of 4 to 6½.

The Wechsler scales not only provide an overall IQ score but the items are grouped according to eleven subscales, six of which are verbal and five of which are nonverbal. This allows the examiner to obtain separate verbal and nonverbal IQ scores and to see quickly the areas of mental performance in which the individual is below average, average, or above average. The inclusion of a number of nonverbal subscales makes the Wechsler test more representative of verbal and nonverbal intelligence; the Binet test includes some nonverbal items but not as many as the Wechsler scales. Several of the Wechsler subscales are shown in figure 7.10.

Do We Have a Single Intelligence or Multiple Intelligences?

Is it more accurate to describe intelligence as a general ability, or is intelligence made up of a number of specific abilities?

Early Views   The concept of mental age and IQ fits in the camp of viewing intelligence as a general ability. So although the early Binet tests tapped some different cognitive skills (such as memory and comprehension), individuals' performance on these skills was lumped together to describe their general intellectual ability. The Wechsler scales provide an indication of a person's general ability and skills in a number of specific areas.

Long before David Wechsler analyzed intelligence in terms of general and specific abilities (giving the individual an overall IQ but also providing information about specific subcomponents of intelligence), Charles Spearman (1927) proposed that intelligence has two factors. **Two-factor theory** *is Spearman's theory that individuals have both general intelligence, which he called* g, *and a number of specific intelligences, which he called* s. Spearman believed that these two factors accounted for a person's performance on an intelligence test.

However, some researchers abandoned the idea of a general intelligence and searched for specific factors only. **Multiple-factor theory** *is L.L. Thurstone's (1938) theory that intelligence consists of seven primary mental abilities: verbal comprehension,*

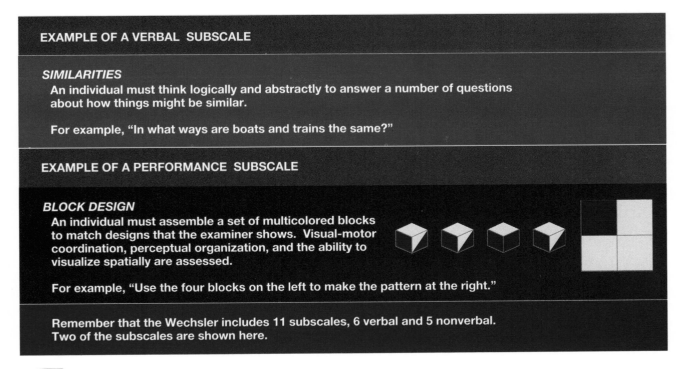

EXAMPLE OF A VERBAL SUBSCALE

SIMILARITIES
An individual must think logically and abstractly to answer a number of questions about how things might be similar.

For example, "In what ways are boats and trains the same?"

EXAMPLE OF A PERFORMANCE SUBSCALE

BLOCK DESIGN
An individual must assemble a set of multicolored blocks to match designs that the examiner shows. Visual-motor coordination, perceptual organization, and the ability to visualize spatially are assessed.

For example, "Use the four blocks on the left to make the pattern at the right."

Remember that the Wechsler includes 11 subscales, 6 verbal and 5 nonverbal. Two of the subscales are shown here.

*F*igure 7.10
Sample Subscales of the Wechsler Adult Intelligence Scale–Revised

Simulated items from the Wechsler Adult Intelligence Scale–Revised. Copyright © 1981, 1955 by The Psychological Corporation. All rights reserved.

number ability, word fluency, spatial visualization, associative memory, reasoning, and perceptual speed.

Contemporary Approaches   Two contemporary approaches that emphasize our multiple intellectual abilities have been proposed by Howard Gardner and Robert Sternberg.

Gardner's Eight Frames of Mind   Howard Gardner (1983, 1993) believes there are eight types of intelligence. They are described below along with the types of individuals in which they are reflected as strengths (Campbell, Campbell, & Dickinson, 1999):

- *Verbal skills:* Ability to think in words and to use language to express meaning (authors, journalists, speakers)
- *Mathematical skills:* Ability to carry out mathematical operations (scientists, engineers, accountants)
- *Spatial skills:* Ability to think in three-dimensional ways (architects, artists, sailors)
- *Bodily-kinesthetic skills:* Ability to manipulate objects and be physically skilled (surgeons, craftspeople, dancers, athletes)
- *Musical skills:* Possessing a sensitivity to pitch, melody, rhythm, and tone (composers, musicians, and sensitive listeners)
- *Interpersonal skills:* Ability to understand and effectively interact with others (successful teachers, mental health professionals)
- Intrapersonal skills: Ability to understand one's self and effectively direct one's life (theologians, psychologists)

Interview with Howard Gardner

Multiple Intelligences

*T*hrough the Eyes of Psychologists

Howard Gardner, *Harvard University*

"If by 2013 [the 30th anniversary of the publication of Gardner's Frames of Mind] there is a wider acceptance of the notion that intelligence deserves to be pluralized, I will be pleased."

Through the Eyes of Psychologists

Robert J. Sternberg,
Yale University

"*My view of intelligence is quite different from the conventional one. Successful intelligence, as I view it, involves analytical, creative, and practical aspects.*"

Sternberg's Theory

"You're wise, but you lack tree smarts."

• *Naturalist skills:* Ability to observe patterns in nature and understand natural and human-made systems (farmers, botanists, ecologists, landscapers)

Gardner says that the different forms of intelligence can be destroyed by brain damage, that each involves unique cognitive skills, and that each shows up in unique ways in both the gifted and idiot savants (individuals with mental retardation but have an exceptional talent in a particular domain, such as drawing, music, or computing).

Sternberg's Triarchic Theory   While Gardner believes there are eight types of intelligence, Robert J. Sternberg (1986) thinks there are three. **Triarchic theory** *is Sternberg's theory that intelligence consists of componential intelligence, experiential intelligence, and contextual intelligence.* Consider Ann, who scores high on traditional intelligence tests such as the Stanford-Binet and is a star analytical thinker. Consider Todd, who does not have the best test scores but has an insightful and creative mind. And consider Art, a street-smart person who has learned to deal in practical ways with his world, although his scores on traditional IQ tests are low.

Sternberg calls Ann's analytical thinking and abstract reasoning "componential intelligence"; it is the closest to what we call intelligence in this chapter and what is commonly measured by intelligence tests. Todd's insightful and creative thinking is called "experiential intelligence" by Sternberg. And Art's street smarts and practical know-how is called "contextual intelligence" by Sternberg.

In Sternberg's view of componential intelligence, the basic unit in intelligence is a component, simply defined as a basic unit of information processing. Sternberg believes such components include the ability to acquire or store information; to retain or retrieve information; to transfer information; to plan, make decisions, and solve problems; and to translate our thoughts into performance.

The second part of Sternberg's model focuses on experience. According to Sternberg, intellectual people have the ability to solve new problems quickly, but they also learn how to solve familiar problems in an automatic, rote way so their minds are free to handle other problems that require insight and creativity.

The third part of the model involves practical intelligence—such as how to get out of trouble, how to replace a fuse, and how to get along with people. Sternberg describes this practical or contextual intelligence as all of the important information about getting along in the real world that you are not taught in school. He believes contextual intelligence is sometimes more important than the "book knowledge" that is often taught in school.

Sternberg (1999) believes that few tasks are purely analytic, creative, or practical. Most tasks require some combination of these skills. For example, when students write a book report, they might (1) analyze the book's main themes, (2) generate new ideas about how the book could have been written better, and (3) think about how the book's themes can be applied to people's lives. Sternberg argues that what is important in teaching is to balance instruction related to all three types of intelligence. That is, students should be given opportunities to learn through analytical, creative, and practical thinking, in addition to the conventional strategy of having students memorize material.

Evaluating the Multiple Intelligences Approach
Gardner's and Sternberg's approaches have much to offer. They have stimulated us to think more broadly about what

makes up people's intelligence. And they have motivated educators to develop programs that instruct students in different domains. However, some critics say that classifying such domains as musical skills (in Gardner's approach) is off base. They ask whether there are possibly other skills domains that Gardner has left out. For example, there are outstanding chess players, prizefighters, writers, politicians, lawyers, ministers, and poets. Yet we don't refer to chess intelligence, prizefighter intelligence, and so on. Other critics say that the research base to support the three intelligences of Sternberg and the eight intelligences of Gardner as the best way to characterize intelligence has not yet been developed.

Controversies and Issues in Intelligence

We have seen that intelligence is a complex and slippery concept with many competing definitions, theories, and tests. It is not surprising, therefore, that attempts to understand the nature of intelligence have been filled with controversy. Three controversies that currently share the spotlight are the following: (1) the degree to which intelligence is due to heredity or to environment, (2) the extent of ethnic differences and the role of culture in intelligence, and (3) the use and misuse of intelligence tests.

The Heredity-Environment Controversy
Arthur Jensen (1969) sparked lively and, at times, hostile debate when he stated his theory that intelligence is primarily inherited and that environment and culture play only a minimal role in intelligence ◀▥ P. 44. In one of his most provocative statements, Jensen claimed that genetics account for clear-cut differences in the average intelligence between races, nationalities, and social classes. When Jensen published an article in the *Harvard Educational Review* stating that lower intelligence probably was the reason that African Americans do not perform as well in school as Whites, he was called naive and racist. He received hate mail by the bushel, and police had to escort him to his classes at the University of California at Berkeley.

Jensen reviewed the research on intelligence, much of which involved comparisons of identical and fraternal twins. Identical twins have exactly the same genetic makeup. If intelligence is genetically determined, Jensen reasoned, identical twins' IQs should be similar. Fraternal twins and ordinary siblings are less similar genetically, so their IQs should be less similar. Jensen found support for his argument.

The studies on intelligence in identical twins that Jensen examined showed an average correlation of .82, a very high positive association. Investigations of fraternal twins, however, produced an average correlation of .50, a moderately high positive correlation. Note the substantial difference of .32. To show that genetic factors are more important than environmental factors, Jensen compared identical twins reared together with those reared apart. The correlation for those reared together was .89, and for those reared apart it was .78, a difference of .11. Jensen argued that if environmental factors were more important than genetic factors, siblings reared apart, who experienced different environments, should have IQs that differed more than .11.

Jensen (1998) places heredity's influence on intelligence at about 80 percent and is such an advocate of heredity's power that he thinks we can breed for intelligence. Just such an effort is being made today at the Repository for Germinal Choice. To read about the "Nobel Prize sperm bank" (called that because it houses the sperm of several Nobel Prize winners as well as others), see Explorations in Psychology.

The most recent controversy about heredity and intelligence focuses on the book *The Bell Curve: Intelligence and Class Structure in American Life* (1994) by Richard Herrnstein and Charles Murray. The authors argued that America is rapidly

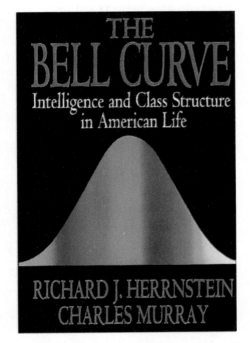

Herrnstein and Murray's (1994) book, The Bell Curve, *advocates a strong role for heredity in intelligence and that a large portion of underclass individuals, especially African Americans, are doomed because of their heredity.* What are some of the criticisms that have been leveled at Herrnstein and Murray?

EXPLORATIONS IN PSYCHOLOGY
The Repository for Germinal Choice

DORAN (A NAME FROM the Greek word meaning "gift") learned all of the elements of speech by 2 years of age. An intelligence test showed that, at the age of 1, his mental age was 4. Doran was the second child born through the sperm bank. The sperm bank was founded by Robert Graham in Escondido, California, with the intent of producing geniuses. Graham collected the sperm of Nobel Prize–winning scientists and offered it free of charge to intelligent women of good stock, whose husbands were infertile.

One of the contributors to the sperm bank is physicist William Shockley, who shared the Nobel Prize in 1956 for inventing the transistor. During the 1960s and 1970s, Shockley received his share of criticism for preaching the genetic basis of intelligence. Two other Nobel Prize winners have donated their sperm to the bank, but Shockley is the only one who has been identified.

Are the progeny prodigies? It may be too early to tell. Except for Doran, little has been revealed about the children. Doran's genetic father was labeled "28 Red" in the sperm bank (the color apparently has no meaning). He is listed in the sperm bank's catalog as handsome, blond, and athletic, with a math SAT score of 800 and several prizes for his classical music performances. One of his few drawbacks is that he passed along to Doran an almost one-in-three chance of developing hemorrhoids. Doran's mother says that her genetic contribution goes back to the royal court of Norway and to the poet William Blake.

The odds are not high that a sperm bank will yield that special combination of factors required to produce a creative genius. George Bernard Shaw, who believed that the influence of heredity on intelligence is strong, once told a story about a beautiful woman who wrote him saying that, with her body and his brain, they could produce marvelous offspring. Shaw responded by saying that unfortunately the offspring might get his body and her brain.

Not surprisingly, the Nobel Prize sperm bank is heavily criticized. Some say that brighter does not mean better. They also say that IQ is not a good indicator of social competence or human contribution to the world. Other critics say that intelligence is an elusive concept to measure and that it cannot reliably be reproduced, as the sperm bank is trying to do. Visions of the German gene program of the 1930s and 1940s are created. The German Nazis believed that certain traits were superior; they tried to breed children with such traits and killed people without them.

Although Graham's Repository of Germinal Choice (as the Nobel Prize sperm bank is formally called) is strongly criticized, consider its possible contributions. The repository does provide a social service for couples who cannot conceive a child, and individuals who go to the sperm bank probably provide an enriched environment for the offspring (Garelik, 1985).

Where do you stand on this controversial topic of breeding for intelligence? Do you think it is unethical? Can you see where it might bring hope for once childless parents?

Doran, conceived using sperm from the Repository for Germinal Choice

Dr. Robert Graham in the room that houses the sperm of Nobel Prize winners. What do you think about Graham's breeding for geniuses?

evolving a huge underclass that consists of intellectually deprived individuals whose cognitive abilities will never match the future needs of most employers. They believe that this underclass, a large proportion of which is African American, may be doomed by their shortcomings to welfare dependency, poverty, crime, and lives devoid of any hope of ever reaching the American dream.

Why do Herrnstein and Murray call their book *The Bell Curve*? A bell curve is the shape of a normal distribution graph (see figure 7.9). The normal distribution graph is used to represent large numbers of people who are sorted according to some shared characteristic, such as weight, exposure to asbestos, taste in clothes, or IQ.

Herrnstein and Murray often refer to bell curves to make a point: that predictions about any individual based exclusively on the person's IQ are virtually useless. Weak correlations between intelligence and job success have predictive value only when they are applied to large groups of people. Within such large groups, say Herrnstein and Murray, the pervasive influence of IQ on human society becomes apparent. Significant criticisms have been leveled at Jensen's work as well as *The Bell Curve*. Experts on intelligence generally agree that African Americans score lower than Whites on IQ tests. However, many of these experts raise serious questions about the ability of IQ tests to accurately measure a person's intelligence. For instance, it has been argued that the tests are culturally biased against African Americans and Latinos. In 1971, the Supreme Court endorsed such criticisms and ruled that tests of general intelligence, in contrast to tests that solely measure fitness for a particular job, are discriminatory and cannot be administered as a condition of employment. Cognitive psychologist Robert J. Sternberg (1994) said that using one index—IQ—for a basis of policy judgment is not only irresponsible, it is dangerous. Another criticism is that most investigations of heredity and environment do not include environments that differ radically. Thus, it is not surprising that many genetic studies show environment to be a fairly weak influence on intelligence (Fraser, 1995).

Today, most researchers agree that heredity does not determine intelligence to the extent Jensen and Herrnstein and Murray envisioned (Ceci, 1996). For most people, this means that modifying their environment can change their IQ scores considerably (Campbell & Ramey, 1993). It also means that programs designed to enrich a person's environment can have a considerable impact, improving school achievement and the acquisition of skills needed for employability. While genetic endowment may always influence a person's intellectual ability, the environmental influences and opportunities we provide children and adults do make a difference.

In a study that was described initially in our coverage of environmental influences on language earlier in this chapter, researchers went into homes and observed how extensively parents from welfare and middle-income professional families talked and communicated with their young children (Hart & Risley, 1995) ◀▥ P. 221. They found that the middle-income professional parents were much more likely to talk and communicate with their young children than the welfare parents were. And how much the parents talked and communicated with their children in the first three years of their lives was correlated with the children's Stanford-Binet IQ scores at age 3 (the more they talked and communicated with their children, the higher the children's IQs were).

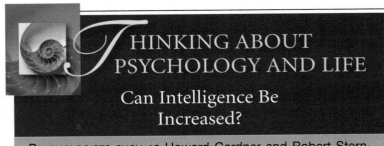

THINKING ABOUT PSYCHOLOGY AND LIFE

Can Intelligence Be Increased?

PSYCHOLOGISTS SUCH AS Howard Gardner and Robert Sternberg believe that intelligence can be increased considerably. Other psychologists such as Arthur Jensen contend that intelligence has such a strong hereditary basis that programs designed to increase intelligence are likely to have little success.

Which side do you come down on? Can intelligence be increased substantially through stimulating mental exercises and environmental experiences? Or is intelligence so strongly influenced by heredity that any efforts to increase intelligence are likely to fail? To read further about this issue, see a book to which a number of experts including Gardner, Sternberg, and Jensen contributed articles—*Intelligence, Heredity, and Environment* (1997), edited by Sternberg and Elena Grigorenko.

The Bell Curve

As measured by the Stanford-Binet intelligence test, American children seem to be getting smarter. Scores of a group tested in 1932 fell along a bell-shaped curve with half below 100 and half above. Studies show that if children took that same test today, half would score above 120 on the 1932 scale. Very few of them would score in the "intellectually deficient" end, on the left side, and about one-fourth would rank in the "very superior" range.

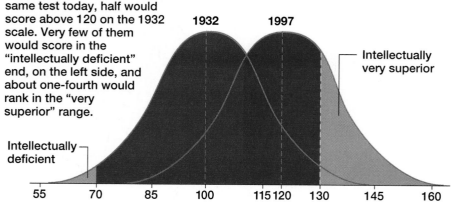

Figure 7.11
The Increase in IQ Scores from 1932 to 1997

Keep in mind, though, that environmental influences are complex (Neisser & others, 1996; Okagaki, 2000). Growing up with all the "advantages," for example, does not necessarily guarantee success. Children from wealthy families may have easy access to excellent schools, books, travel, and tutoring, but they may take such opportunities for granted and fail to develop the motivation to learn and to achieve. In the same way, "poor" or "disadvantaged" does not automatically equal "doomed."

Researchers increasingly are interested in manipulating the early environment of children who are at risk for impoverished intelligence (Blair & Ramey, 1996) ◀‖‖ P. 16. The emphasis is on prevention rather than remediation. Many low-income parents have difficulty providing an intellectually stimulating environment for their children. Programs that educate parents to be more sensitive caregivers and train them to be better teachers, as well as support services, such as high quality Head Start programs, can make a difference in a child's intellectual development. The current trend is to conduct two-generation poverty interventions by working to improve the quality of life and skills of parents, as well as providing the child with an enriched environment (McLoyd, 1998).

Another argument for the importance of environment in intelligence involves the increasing scores of IQ tests around the world (Flynn, 1999). Scores on these tests have been increasing so fast that a high percentage of people regarded as having average intelligence at the turn of century would be considered below average in intelligence today (Hall, 1998) (see figure 7.11). If a representative sample of people today took the Stanford-Binet test used in 1932, about one-fourth would be defined as having very superior intelligence, a label usually accorded to fewer than 3 percent of the population. Because the increase has taken place in a relatively short period of time, it can't be due to heredity, but rather may be due to such environmental factors as the explosion in information people are exposed to as well as a much greater percentage of the population experiencing more education.

Culture and Ethnicity
Are there cultural and ethnic differences in intelligence? Are standard intelligence tests biased? If so, can we develop tests that are culturally fair?

Cultural and Ethnic Comparisons   In the United States, children from African American and Latino families score below children from White families on standardized intelligence tests. On the average, African American schoolchildren score 10 to 15 points lower on standardized intelligence tests than White American schoolchildren do (Lynn, 1996). We are talking about average scores, though. Estimates also indicate that 15 to 25 percent of all African American schoolchildren score higher than half of all White schoolchildren do, and many Whites score lower than most African Americans. This is because the distribution of scores for African Americans and Whites overlap.

How extensively are ethnic differences in intelligence influenced by heredity and environment? There is no evidence to support a genetic interpretation (Neisser & others, 1996). For example, as African Americans have gained social, economic, and educational opportunities, the gap between African American and White children on standardized intelligence tests has begun to narrow. Also, when children from

Cultural Bias and Testing

disadvantaged African American families are adopted into more-advantaged middle-class families, their scores on intelligence tests more closely resemble national averages for middle-class children than for lower-class children (Scarr & Weinberg, 1983).

Cultural Bias and Culture-Fair Tests   Many of the early intelligence tests were culturally biased, favoring people who were from urban rather than rural environments, middle-class rather than lower-class, and White rather than African American (Miller-Jones, 1989). For example, a question on an early test asked what should be done if you find a 3-year-old child in the street. The correct answer was "call the police." But children from inner-city families who perceive the police as adversaries are unlikely to choose this answer. Similarly, children from rural areas might not choose this answer if there is no police force nearby. Such questions clearly do not measure the knowledge necessary to adapt to one's environment or to be "intelligent" in an inner-city neighborhood or in rural America (Scarr, 1984). Also, members of minority groups often do not speak English or may speak nonstandard English. Consequently, they may be at a disadvantage in trying to understand verbal questions that are framed in standard English, even if the content of the test is appropriate (Gibbs & Huang, 1989).

Cultures also vary in the way they define intelligence (Rogoff, 1990; Serpell, 2000) ◀▥ P. 18. Most European Americans, for example, think of intelligence in terms of technical skills, but people in Kenya consider responsible participation in family and social life an integral part of intelligence. Similarly, an intelligent person in Uganda is someone who knows what to do and then follows through with appropriate action. Intelligence to the Iatmul people of Papua, New Guinea, involves the ability to remember the names of 10,000 to 20,000 clans, and the islanders in the widely dispersed Caroline Islands incorporate the talent of navigating by the stars in their definition of intelligence.

Another example of possible cultural bias in intelligence tests can be seen in the life of Gregory Ochoa. When Gregory was a high school student, he and his classmates took an IQ test. When Gregory looked at the test questions, he understood only a few words, since he did not speak English very well and spoke Spanish at home. Several weeks later, Gregory was placed in a special class for mentally retarded students. Many of the students in the class, it turns out, had last names such as Ramirez and Gonzales. Gregory lost interest in school, dropped out, and eventually joined the Navy. In the Navy, Gregory took high school courses and earned enough credits to attend college later. He graduated from San Jose City College as an honor student, continued his education, and became a professor of social work at the University of Washington in Seattle.

As a result of such cases, researchers have tried to develop tests that accurately reflect a person's intelligence. **Culture-fair tests** *are intelligence tests that are intended to not be culturally biased.* Two types of culture-fair tests have been devised. The first includes questions that are familiar to people from all socioeconomic and ethnic backgrounds. For example, a child might be asked how a bird and a dog are different, on the assumption that virtually all children are familiar with birds and dogs. The second type of culture-fair test removes all verbal questions. Figure 7.12 shows a sample question from the Raven Progressive Matrices Test. Even though tests such as the Raven Progressive Matrices are designed to be culture-fair, people with more education still score higher than those with less education do.

"You can't build a hut, you don't know how to find edible roots and you know nothing about predicting the weather. In other words, you do terribly *on our I.Q. test."*
Reprinted by permission of Sidney Harris

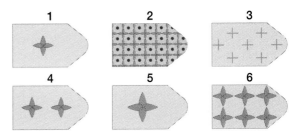

𝒻igure 7.12
Sample Item from the Raven Progressive Matrices Test
Individuals are presented with a matrix arrangement of symbols, such as the one at the top of this figure and must then complete the matrix by selecting the appropriate missing symbol from a group of symbols.

"How are her scores?"

One test that takes into account the socioeconomic background of children is the SOMPA, which stands for System of Multicultural Pluralistic Assessment (Mercer & Lewis, 1978). This test can be given to children from 5 to 11 years of age, and was especially designed for children from low-income families. Instead of relying on a single test, SOMPA is based on information from four different areas of the child's life: (1) verbal and nonverbal intelligence, assessed by the WISC-III; (2) social and economic background, obtained through a one-hour parent interview; (3) social adjustment to school, determined through a questionnaire that parents complete; and (4) physical health, assessed by a medical examination.

Why is it so hard to create culture-fair tests? Most tests tend to reflect what the dominant culture thinks is important (Sax, 1997). If tests have time limits, that will bias the test against groups not concerned with time. If languages differ, the same words might have different meanings for different language groups. Even pictures can produce bias because some cultures have less experience with drawings and photographs (Anastasi & Urbina, 1996). Even within the same culture, different groups could have different attitudes, values, and motivation, and this could affect their performance on intelligence tests. Items that ask why buildings should be made of brick are biased against children who have little or no experience with brick houses. Questions about railroads, furnaces, seasons of the year, distances between cities, and so on can be biased against groups who have less experience than others with these circumstances.

The Use and Misuse of Intelligence Tests

Psychological tests are tools. Like all tools, their effectiveness depends on the knowledge, skill, and integrity of the user. A hammer can be used to build a beautiful kitchen cabinet or it can be used as a weapon of assault. Like a hammer, psychological tests can be used for positive purposes or they can be badly abused. It is important for both the test constructor and the test examiner to be familiar with the current state of scientific knowledge about intelligence and intelligence tests.

Even though they have limitations, tests of intelligence are among psychology's most widely used tools. To be effective, though, intelligence tests must be viewed realistically. They should not be thought of as unchanging indicators of intelligence. They should be used in conjunction with other information about an individual, not relied on as the sole indicator of intelligence. For example, an intelligence test should not solely determine whether a child is placed in a special education or gifted class. The child's developmental history, medical background, performance in school, social competencies, and family experiences should be taken into account too.

The single number provided by many IQ tests can easily lead to stereotypes and expectations about an individual (Rosnow & Rosenthal, 1996). Many people do not know how to interpret the results of intelligence tests, and sweeping generalizations are too often made on the basis of an IQ score. For example, imagine that you are a teacher in the teacher's lounge the day after school has started in the fall. You mention a student—Johnny Jones—and a fellow teacher remarks that she had Johnny in class last year; she comments that he was a real dunce and points out that his IQ is 78. You cannot help but remember this information, and it might lead to thoughts that Johnny Jones is not very bright so it is useless to spend much time teaching him. In this way, IQ scores are misused and stereotypes are formed (Rosenthal & Jacobsen, 1968).

Ability tests can help a teacher group together children who function at roughly the same level in math or reading so they can be taught the same concepts together. However, when children are placed in tracks, such as "advanced," "intermediate," and "low," extreme caution needs to be taken. Periodic assessment of the groups is needed, especially with the "low" group. Ability tests measure *current* performance, and maturational changes or enriched environmental experiences may advance in a child's intelligence, requiring that she be moved to a higher group.

Despite their limitations, when used judiciously by a competent examiner, intelligence tests provide valuable information about individuals. There are not many alternatives to these tests. Subjective judgments about individuals simply reintroduce the bias the tests were designed to eliminate.

Creativity

Howard Gardner (1993) believes that, like intelligence, creativity is domain specific. Keep this important idea in mind as you read about creativity.

What Is Creativity?
Creativity *is the ability to think about something in novel and unusual ways and come up with unique solutions to problems.* Thus, intelligence and creativity are not the same thing (Michael, 1999). This was recognized in Sternberg's account of intelligence and also by J. P. Guilford (1967). He distinguished between **convergent thinking,** *which produces one correct answer and is characterized by the kind of thinking required on conventional intelligence tests,* and **divergent thinking,** *which produces many answers to the same question and is more characteristic of creativity.* For example, a typical item on a conventional intelligence test is, "How many quarters will you get in return for 60 dimes?" By contrast, the following question has many possible answers. What image comes to mind when you hear the phrase "sitting alone in a dark room" or "Can you think of some unique uses for a paper clip?"

Are intelligence and creativity related? Although most creative people are quite intelligent, the reverse is not necessarily true. Many highly intelligent people (as measured by high scores on conventional tests of intelligence) are not very creative. And, if Sternberg had his way, creative thinking would become part of a broader definition of intelligence.

Steps in the Creative Process
The creative process has often been described as a five-step sequence:

1. *Preparation.* You become immersed in a problem or an issue that interests you and arouses your curiosity.
2. *Incubation.* You churn ideas around in your head. This is the point at which you are likely to make some unusual connections in your thinking.
3. *Insight.* At this point, you experience the "Aha!" moment when all pieces of the puzzle seem to fit together.
4. *Evaluation.* Now you must decide whether the idea is valuable and worth pursuing. Is the idea really novel or is it obvious?
5. *Elaboration.* This final step often covers the longest span of time and the hardest work. This is what the famous twentieth-century American inventory Thomas Edison was talking about when he said that creativity is 1 percent inspiration and 99 percent perspiration.

Mihaly Csikszentmihalyi (pronounced ME-high CHICK-sent-me-high-ee) (1996) believes that the five-step sequence provides a helpful framework for thinking about how creative ideas are formed and developed. However, he argues that in reality creative people don't always go through the steps in a linear sequence. For example, elaboration is often interrupted by periods of incubation. Many fresh insights also may appear during incubation, evaluation, and elaboration. And in terms of a time frame, insight might last for years or it might only take a few hours

Through the Eyes of Psychologists

Mihaly Csikszentmihalyi,
University of Chicago

"*A genuinely creative accomplishment is almost never the result of a sudden insight, a lightbulb flashing in the dark, but comes after years of hard work.*"

(Csikszentmihalyi, 2000). Sometimes the creative idea consists of one deep insight, at others a series of small ones.

Living a More Creative Life   Csikszentmihalyi (1996) interviewed ninety leading figures in art, business, government, education, and science to learn how creativity works. He discovered that creative people regularly engage in challenges that absorb them. Based on his interviews with some of the most creative people in the world, he concluded that the first step toward a more creative life is to cultivate your curiosity and interest. Here are his recommendations for doing this:

- *Try to be surprised by something every day.* Maybe it is something you see, hear, or read about. Become absorbed in a lecture or a book. Be open to what the world is telling you. Life is a stream of experiences. Swim widely and deeply in it, and your life will be richer.
- *Try to surprise at least one person every day.* In a lot of things you do, you have to be predictable and patterned. Do something different for a change. Ask a question you normally would not ask. Invite someone to go to a show or a museum you never have visited.
- *Write down each day what surprised you and how you surprised others.* Most creative people keep a diary, notes, or lab records to ensure that their experience is not fleeting or forgotten. Start with a specific task. Each evening record the most surprising event that occurred that day and your most surprising action. After a few days, reread your notes and reflect on your past experiences. After a few weeks, you might see a pattern of interest emerging in your notes, one that might suggest an area you can explore in greater depth.
- *When something sparks your interest, follow it.* Usually when something captures your attention, it is short-lived—an idea, a song, a flower. Too often we are too busy to explore the idea, song, or flower further. Or we think these areas are none of our business because we are not experts about them. Yet the world is our business. We can't know which part of it is best suited to our interests until we make a serious effort to learn as much about as many aspects of it as possible.
- *Wake up in the morning with a specific goal to look forward to.* Creative people wake up eager to start the day. Why? Not necessarily because they are cheerful, enthusiastic types but because they know that there is something meaningful to accomplish each day, and they can't wait to get started.
- *Take charge of your schedule.* Figure out which time of the day is your most creative time. Some of us are more creative late at night, others early in the morning. Carve out some time for yourself when your creative energy is at its best.
- *Spend time in settings that stimulate your creativity.* In Csikszentimihalyi's (1996) research, he gave people an electronic pager and beeped them randomly at different times of the day. When he asked them how they felt, they reported the highest levels of creativity when walking, driving, or swimming. I (your author) do my most creative thinking when I'm jogging. These activities are semi-automatic in that they take a certain amount of attention while leaving some time free to make connections among ideas. Another setting in which highly creative people report coming up with novel ideas is the sort of half-asleep, half-awake state we are in when we are deeply relaxed or barely awake.

Csikszentmihalyi
Harvard Project Zero

At this point we have discussed a number of ideas about intelligence. A review of these ideas is presented in summary table 7.3. In the next chapter, we will turn our attention to how we develop through the life span. Included in our exploration of human development will be ideas about how we develop intellectually.

SUMMARY TABLE 7.3
Intelligence

Concept	Processes/ Related Ideas	Characteristics/Description
What Is Intelligence?	Its Nature	Intelligence involves verbal ability, problem-solving skills, and the ability to adapt to and learn from life's everyday experiences. Interest in intelligence has focused on individual differences (the stable, consistent way people are different from each other) and assessment.
Intelligence Tests	How Tests Are Constructed and Evaluated	A good test is reliable, valid, and standardized. Reliability is how consistently an individual performs on a test. Three forms of reliability are test-retest, alternate forms, and split-half. Validity is the extent to which a test measures what it is intended to measure. Validity can be assessed in terms of content validity and criterion validity. Criterion validity involves either concurrent or predictive validity. Standardization focuses on uniform procedures for administering and scoring a test; it also involves norms.
	The Binet Tests and the Wechsler Scales	Alfred Binet developed the first intelligence test, known as the 1905 Scale. He created the concept of mental age, whereas William Stern developed the concept of IQ. The Binet has been standardized and revised a number of times. The many revisions are called the Stanford-Binet. The test scores approximate a normal distribution and assess more complex cognitive abilities than Galton's and Cattell's did. The Stanford-Binet is given to individuals from the age of 2 through adulthood. Besides the Binet, the other most widely used individual tests of intelligence are the Wechsler scales, created by David Wechsler. These tests provide an overall IQ, verbal and performance IQs, and information about eleven subtests.
Do We Have a Single Intelligence or Multiple Intelligences?	Early Views	The concept of mental age and IQ fits in the camp of viewing intelligence as a general ability. The Wechsler scales assess general intelligence and skills in specific areas. Spearman proposed the two-factor theory, which says people have a general ability (g) and specific abilities (s). Thurstone abandoned the idea of general intelligence. His multiple-factor theory proposed seven primary mental abilities.
	Contemporary Approaches	Gardner argues that intelligence consists of eight frames of mind (verbal, math, spatial, movement, music, insight about self, insight about others, and naturalist). There currently is considerable interest in applying his ideas to education. Sternberg proposed the triarchic theory, according to which intelligence comes in three forms: componential, experiential, and practical. There is much to offer in these views, although their research base has not been adequately developed.
Controversies and Issues in Intelligence	Their Nature	These are among the main controversies in intelligence: The heredity-environment controversy, culture and ethnicity issues (such as cultural bias and culture-fair tests), and the use and misuse of intelligence tests.
Creativity	Its Nature	Creativity is the ability to think about something in novel and unusual ways and come up with unique solutions to problems. Guilford distinguished between convergent and divergent thinking. We studied 5 steps in the creative process and living a more creative life.

Overview

WE BEGAN THIS CHAPTER by exploring these aspects of thinking: forming concepts, solving problems, thinking critically, reasoning, and making decisions. Our coverage of language focused on what it is, biological and environmental influences, how language develops, whether animals can use language to express thought, and language, culture, and cognition. We also studied these aspects of intelligence: What it is, intelligence tests, whether we have a single intelligence or multiple intelligences, controversies and issues in intelligences, and creativity. Don't forget that you can obtain a detailed review of the chapter by again studying the three summary tables on pages 218, 227, and 243.

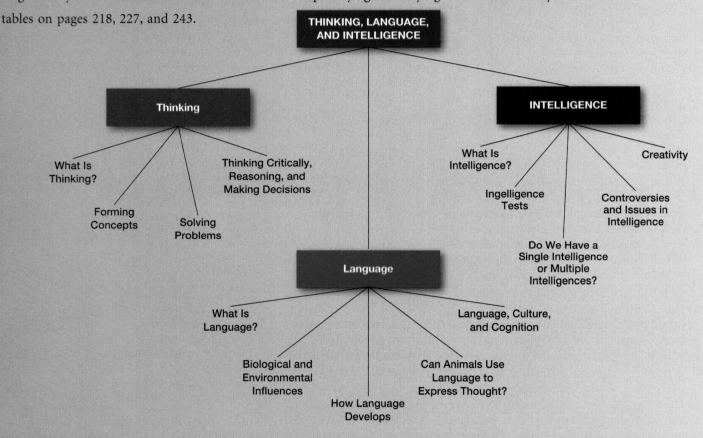

Key Terms

thinking 210
concepts 210
prototype matching 211
problem solving 211
subgoaling 212
algorithms 213
heuristics 213
fixation 213
functional fixedness 213
mental set 214
critical thinking 214

reasoning 215
inductive reasoning 215
analogy 215
deductive reasoning 216
decision making 216
confirmation bias 216
belief perseverance 217
overconfidence bias 217
hindsight bias 217
availability heuristic 217
representativeness heuristic 217

language 219
infinite generativity 219
phonology 219
morphology 220
syntax 220
semantics 220
telegraphic speech 222
critical period 222
linguistic relativity hypothesis 225
intelligence 228

individual differences 228
reliability 228
test-retest reliability 228
alternative forms reliability 229
split-half reliability 229
validity 229
content validity 229
criterion validity 229
concurrent validity 229
predictive validity 229
standardization 230

Key People

Taking It to the Net

1. Heuristics are rules of thumb that suggest a solution but do not ensure it will work. They help us narrow down possible solutions to problems. Often, however, heuristics are obstacles in solving problems because we are fixed on relying on these heuristics. Some problems require us to ignore heuristics in order to adequately solve them. Optical illusions often trick us into using heuristics that don't work. Explain how optical illusions are affected by these heuristic biases. How do you think this might relate to problems in your everyday life?

2. Have you ever heard of animals that are taught to communicate? One famous example is Washoe, a chimpanzee who was taught to use sign language. Washoe has used more than 1,000 taught signs in American Sign Language (Ameslan). Interestingly, she has since formed more than 200 signs that she was never taught. Why do you think psychologists want to teach chimps to communicate? What sorts of things can we learn from chimps who have language abilities?

3. Eric Clapton's albums have sold millions of copies over the last 20 years. His fans believe that he possesses incredible guitar skills and the ability to score beautiful music. Some psychologists have deemed his abilities a type of intelligence. Do you think musical intelligence is really a distinct type of intelligence? Explain your answer in terms of the definition of intelligence and the special abilities it takes to be musically gifted.

Connect to http://www.mhhe.com/psychology/santrock to find the answers!

Solutions to Problems in Thinking About Psychology and Life

The Candle Problem

The solution requires a unique perception of the function of the box in which the matches came. It can become a candleholder when tacked to the wall.

The Six-Matchsticks Problem

Nothing in the instructions said that the solution had to be two-dimensional.

The Nine-Dot Problem

Most people have difficulty with this problem because they try to draw the lines within the boundaries of the dots. Notice that by extending the lines beyond the dots, the problem can be solved.

Chapter 8

Human Development

Images of Psychology and Life
Jessica Dubroff, Child Pilot

"*In* every child who is born, Under no matter what circumstances, And of no matter what parents, The potentiality of the human race Is born again."

James Agee
American Writer, 20th Century

Preview

AS THE TWENTY-FIRST century approaches, children's well-being is one of our most important concerns. Development does not end with childhood, though, and intriguing questions are being raised about how much people can continue to change even when they are old. These are some of the questions we will explore in this chapter:

• What does it mean to "develop"?
• Is there a best age to be?
• How does the way children think change as they develop?
• How important is attachment to a caregiver in infancy?
• Is there a best way to parent children?
• What are some key aspects of adolescent development?
• Why do people age?
• Does everyone go through a midlife crisis?
• How can people age successfully?

THINK FOR A MOMENT about how your parents reared you. Were they permissive or controlling? Warm or cold? Later in the chapter we will examine styles of parenting based on such characteristics, but for now to encourage you to think about parenting, let's examine the tragic story of Jessica Dubroff.

In 1996, Jessica Dubroff took off in cold rain and died when her single-engine Cessna nosedived into a highway. Seven-year-old Jessica was only 4 feet, 2 inches tall and weighed just 55 pounds. What was she doing flying an airplane, especially in quest of being the youngest person ever to fly across the continent?

Jessica had been urged on by overzealous parents, by media drawn to a natural human-interest story, and by a Federal Aviation Administration that looked the other way. Jessica's feet did not even reach the rudder pedals. Overnight Jessica's death resulted in her becoming the poster child of parental and media exploitation. Some thought she had been granted too much freedom and had not been allowed to be a child.

Jessica's parents seemed determined to give their daughter independence from the beginning. She was delivered in a birthing tub without the benefit of a doctor or midwife. Her parents' philosophy was that real life is the best tutor, experience the best preparation for life. As a result, they kept Jessica and her brother (age 9) and sister (age 3) at home without filing a home-schooling plan with local authorities. Jessica had no dolls, only tools. Instead of studying grammar, she did chores and sought what her mother called "mastery." Jessica had few, if any, boundaries. Parenting mainly consisted of cheerleading.

Jessica became interested in flying after her parents gave her an airplane ride for her sixth birthday, only 23 months before her fatal crash. Her father admitted that the cross-country flight was his idea, but claimed that he had presented it to Jessica as a choice. The father became her press agent, courting TV, radio, and newspapers to publicize her flight.

After the crash, TV viewers were treated to a spectacle almost as disturbing as the accident itself. Jessica's mother said that if she had it to do over again, she would have done nothing differently. She also commented that she did everything she could to give Jessica freedom and choice. Developmental psychologists would counter that children should be given freedom and choice, but within the bounds of responsibility (Stengel, 1996).

Jessica's story is rare and tragic. However, the dangers of overachieving, of growing up too soon, of intensely focusing on a single activity, often show up in many different ways. The child actor grows up without an education. The adolescent tennis star mysteriously drops off the circuit to become a teenager. The young figure skater plots to club an opponent. Child athletes might ruin their bodies: ballerinas develop anorexia, teenage football players take steroids. Too many children have lives that are overscheduled, moving from one lesson to the next. They are being robbed of the time to develop coping skills that they need to deal with life's realities.

A vicious cycle has been set in motion. Parents who live vicariously through their children produce children who grow up feeling they have missed out on childhood, a time when play and its unstructured freedom should be prominent. Children should be allowed to have a well-rounded life, one that is not focused on achievement in a single domain.

We've been talking about Jessica Dubroff's development as a child. Let's now explore just what we mean by the term *development*.

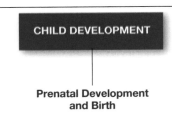

What Is Development?

As children, each of us traveled some common paths. Each of us—Leonardo da Vinci, Joan of Arc, George Washington, Martin Luther King, Jr., myself, and you—walked at about the age of 1, talked at about the age of 2, engaged in fantasy play as a young child, and became more independent as an adolescent. Yet we are also unique. No one else in the world, for example, has the same set of fingerprints as you. Researchers who study child development are intrigued by children's universal characteristics as well as by their idiosyncrasies.

When we speak of **development,** *we mean a pattern of movement or change that begins at conception and continues throughout the life span.* Most development involves growth, although it also consists of decay (as in death). The pattern of change is complex because it is the product of several processes—biological, cognitive, and socioemotional.

Biological, Cognitive, and Socioemotional Processes

Biological processes *involve changes in an individual's physical nature.* Genes inherited from parents, the development of the brain, height and weight gains, motor skills, and the hormonal changes of puberty all reflect the role of biological processes in development.

Cognitive processes *involve changes in an individual's thought, intelligence, and language.* The tasks of watching a colorful mobile swinging above a crib, putting together a two-word sentence, memorizing a poem, solving a math problem, and imagining what it would be like to be a movie star all reflect the role of cognitive processes in children's development.

Socioemotional processes *involve changes in an individual's relationships with other people, changes in emotions, and changes in personality.* An infant's smile in response to her mother's touch, a young boy's aggressive attack on a playmate, a girl's development of assertiveness, and an adolescent's joy at the senior prom all reflect the role of socioemotional processes in children's development.

Remember as you read about biological, cognitive, and socioemotional processes that they are intricately interwoven. You will read about how socioemotional processes shape cognitive processes, how cognitive processes promote or restrict socioemotional processes, and how biological processes influence cognitive processes. Although it is helpful to study the various processes involved in children's development in separate sections of the chapter, keep in mind that you are studying the development of an integrated human child in whom mind and body are interdependent (see figure 8.1).

Periods of Development

For the purposes of organization and understanding, we commonly describe development in terms of periods. The most widely used classification of developmental periods involves the following sequence: prenatal period, infancy, early childhood, middle and late childhood, adolescence, early adulthood, middle adulthood, and late adulthood. Approximate age ranges are placed on the periods to provide a general idea of when a period first appears and when it ends.

The **prenatal period** *is the time from conception to birth.* It is a time of tremendous growth—from a single cell to an organism complete with a brain and behavioral capabilities, produced in approximately a 9-month period.

Infancy *is the developmental period that extends from birth to 18 or 24 months.* Infancy is a time of extreme dependence on adults. Many psychological activities are just beginning—language, symbolic thought, sensorimotor coordination, and social learning, for example.

Early childhood *is the developmental period that extends from the end of infancy to about 5 or 6 years; sometimes the period is called the preschool years.* During this time, young children learn to become more self-sufficient and to care for themselves, develop school readiness skills (following instructions, identifying letters), and spend many hours in play and with peers. First grade typically marks the end of this period.

Middle and late childhood *is the developmental period that extends from about 6 to 11 years of age, approximately corresponding to the elementary school years; sometimes the period is called the elementary school years.* Children master the fundamental skills of reading, writing, and arithmetic, and they are formally exposed to the larger world and its culture. Achievement becomes a more central theme of the child's world, and self-control increases.

Adolescence *is the developmental period of transition from childhood to early adulthood, entered approximately at 10 to 12 years of age and ending at 18 to 21 years of age.* Adolescence begins with rapid physical changes—dramatic gains in height and weight; changes in body contour; and the development of sexual characteristics such as enlargement of the breasts, development of pubic and facial hair, and deepening of the voice. At this point in development, the pursuit of independence and an identity are prominent. Thought is more logical, abstract, and idealistic. More and more time is spent outside of the family during this period.

Early adulthood *is the developmental period that begins in the late teens or early twenties and lasts through the thirties.* It is a time of establishing personal and economic independence; a time of career development; and for many a time of selecting a mate, learning to live with someone in an intimate way, starting a family, and rearing children.

Middle adulthood *is the developmental period that begins at approximately 35 to 45 years of age and extends into the sixties.* It is a time of expanding personal and social involvement and responsibility; of assisting the next generation in becoming competent, mature individuals; and of reaching and maintaining satisfaction in one's career.

Figure 8.1
Changes in Development Are the Result of Biological, Cognitive, and Socioemotional Processes

These processes are interwoven as individuals develop.

Children's Issues
National Institute of Child Health and Human Development

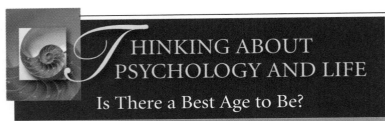

Thinking About Psychology and Life

Is There a Best Age to Be?

MIGHT PEOPLE BE HAPPIER in one developmental period than others? Consider adolescence, early adulthood, middle adulthood, and late adulthood. Do you think most people are happier in one of these periods than others? For example, when people are 15, 30, 50, and 70 might we find differences in whether people are happier at one of these ages than others? One woman in the psychology class I teach spent about 10 minutes expounding on why 28 years of age is the best age to be. Essentially her argument was that at 28 a person is old enough to have experienced enough things in life to show maturity yet still be physically healthy and strong enough to fully enjoy life. Of course, many other students did not agree and asked her questions, such as, "If you are only 30 yourself, how do you know 28 is the best age to be?" and "Aren't there factors in many people's lives that might make a different age be best for them?"

Researchers have found no differences in how happy people are at different ages (Ingelhart & Rabier, 1996; Stock & others, 1993). Think some more about the different periods. Doesn't every period of the human life span have its highs and lows, hills and valleys? Get together with several other students and discuss what some of these uplifting and down-turning characteristics of different periods are.

Children and Poverty

Late adulthood *is the developmental period that begins in the sixties or seventies and lasts until death.* It is a time of adjustment to decreasing strength and health, life review, retirement, and adjustment to new social roles.

In our description of the life span's periods, we placed approximate age bands on the periods; however, one expert on life-span development, Bernice Neugarten (1980), believes that we rapidly are becoming an age-irrelevant society. She says we are already familiar with the 28-year-old mayor, the 35-year-old grandmother, the 65-year-old father of a preschooler, the 55-year-old widow who starts a business, and the 70-year-old student. Neugarten says that she has had difficulty clustering adults into age brackets that are characterized by particular issues. She stresses that choices and dilemmas do not spring forth at 10-year intervals, and decisions are not made and then left behind as if they were merely beads on a chain. Neugarten argues that most adulthood themes appear and reappear throughout the human life span. The issues of intimacy and freedom can haunt couples throughout their relationship. Feeling the pressure of time, reformulating goals, and coping with success and failure are not the exclusive property of adults of any age.

Developmental Issues

Three important developmental issues focus on nature and nurture, continuity and discontinuity, and early and later experience.

Nature and Nurture

In chapter 2 ("Biological Foundations and Neuroscience"), we stressed that one of psychology's most important issues is the extent to which behavior is influenced by nature (heredity) or nurture (environment) ◀▥ P. 47. The nature-nurture issue is especially applicable to human development because it addresses the roles of heredity and environment in determining how we develop as human beings.

Some developmentalists emphasize the power of heredity in development. They argue that although the range of environments can be vast, the genetic blueprint produces some common developmental changes. We walk before we talk, speak one word before two words, grow rapidly in infancy and less so in early childhood, experience a rush of sexual hormones in adolescence, reach the peak of physical strength in late adolescence and early adulthood, then experience some decline. The nature proponents acknowledge that extreme environments—those that are psychologically barren or hostile—can depress development, but they believe that basic growth tendencies are genetically wired into humans.

By contrast, other developmentalists emphasize the importance of experiences in life-span development. Experiences run the gamut from the individual's biological environment (nutrition, medical care, drugs, and physical accidents) to the social environment (family, peers, schools, community, media, and culture).

Continuity and Discontinuity

Think for a moment about who you are. Did you become this person gradually, like the slow, cumulative growth of a seedling into a giant oak? Or did you experience sudden, distinct changes in your development, the way a caterpillar changes into a butterfly? For the most part, developmental psychologists who emphasize experience have described development as a gradual, continuous process; those who emphasize maturation have described development as a series of distinct stages.

The view that stresses **continuity of development** *argues that development involves gradual, cumulative change from conception to death.* A child's first word, while seemingly an abrupt, discrete event, is actually the result of months of growth and practice. Similarly, while puberty might seem to happen overnight, it is actually a gradual process that occurs over several years.

The view that stresses **discontinuity of development** *argues that development involves distinct stages in the life span.* In this view, each of us passes through a sequence of stages that are qualitatively, rather than quantitatively, different. As a caterpillar changes into a butterfly, it does not become more caterpillar; it becomes a different kind of organism. Its development is discontinuous. Similarly, a child who earlier could think only in concrete terms becomes capable of thinking abstractly about the world. This is a qualitative, discontinuous change in development, not a continuous, quantitative change.

"If you ask me, he's come too far too fast."

© The New Yorker Collection *1988 Lee Lorenz from cartoonbank.com. All Rights Reserved.*

Early and Later Experience

The early-later experience issue has a long history and continues to be hotly debated among developmentalists (Cairns, 1998) ◀ IIII P. 16. Some believe that unless infants experience warm, nurturant caregiving in the first year or so of life, their development will never be optimal (Bowlby, 1989). Plato was sure that infants who were rocked frequently became better athletes. Nineteenth-century New England ministers told parents in Sunday sermons that the way they handled their infants would determine their children's future character. The emphasis on the importance of early experience rests on the belief that each life is an unbroken trail on which a psychological quality can be traced back to its origin (Kagan, 1992).

The early-experience doctrine contrasts with the later-experience view that, rather than a statuelike permanence after change in infancy, development continues to be like the ebb and flow of a river. The later-experience advocates argue that children are malleable throughout development and that later sensitive caregiving is just as important as earlier sensitive caregiving (Lewis, 1997). A number of life-span developmentalists, who focus on the entire life span rather than only on child development, stress that too little attention has been given to later experiences in development (Baltes, Lindenberger, & Staudinger, 1998). They argue that early experiences are important contributors to development, but no more important than later experiences.

Conclusions About Developmental Issues

Most developmentalists do not take extreme positions on developmental issues. Development is not all nature or all nurture, not all continuity or all discontinuity, and not all early or later experience (Lerner, 1998; Santrock, 1999). Both nature and nurture, continuity and discontinuity, early experience and later experience characterize our development through the human life span. Regarding the nature-nurture issue, the key to development is the *interaction* of nature and nurture rather than either factor alone. For instance, an individual's cognitive development is the result of heredity-environment interaction, not heredity or environment alone.

Child Development

Many special things have taken place in your life since you were born. But imagine . . . at one time you were a microscopic organism floating around in a sea of fluid in your mother's womb. As nineteenth-century American poet, essayist Samuel Taylor remarked, "The history of man for nine months preceding his birth is probably far more interesting and contains more stunning events than all the years that follow it."

Reproductive Health Resources

Prenatal Development and Birth

Within a matter of hours after fertilization, a human egg divides, becomes a system of cells, and continues this mapping of cells at an astonishing rate. In a mere 9 months, there is a squalling bundle of energy that has its grandmother's nose, its father's eyes, and its mother's abundant hair.

(a)

(b)

(c)

ℱigure 8.2
Embryonic Period

(a) Embryo at 4 weeks. At about 4 weeks, an embryo is about 0.2 inches in length. The head, eyes, and ears begin to show. The head and neck are half the body length; the shoulders will be located where the whitish arm buds are attached.
(b) Embryo at 8 weeks. At 8 weeks and 4 centimeters (1.6 inches), the developing individual is no longer an embryo, but a fetus. Everything that will be found in the fully developed human being has now begun to form. The fetal stage is a period of growth and perfection of detail. The heart has been beating for a month, and the muscles have just begun their first exercises. *(c)* Fetus at 4½ months. At 4½ months, the fetus is about 18 cm (just over 7 inches). When the thumb comes close to the mouth, the head may turn, and lips and tongue begin their sucking motions—a reflex for survival.

The Visible Embryo

The Course of Prenatal Development   **Conception** *occurs when a single sperm cell from the male penetrates the female's ovum (egg). This process also is called fertilization.* A **zygote** *is a fertilized egg.* It receives one-half of its chromosomes from the mother, the other half from the father. The zygote begins as a single cell. After 1 week and many cell divisions, the zygote is made up of 100 to 150 cells. By the end of 2 weeks, the mass of cells attaches to the uterine wall. The **germinal period** *is these first 2 weeks after conception.*

During the **embryonic period,** *weeks 3 through 8 after conception, some remarkable developments unfold (see figure 8.2). Before most women even know they are pregnant, the rate of cell differentiation intensifies, support systems for the cells form, and the beginnings of organs appear.* In the third week the neural tube that eventually becomes the spinal cord is forming. At about 21 days, eyes begin to appear, and by 24 days the cells of the heart begin to differentiate. During the fourth week, arm and leg buds emerge. At 5 to 8 weeks, arms and legs become more differentiated, the face starts to form, and the intestinal tract appears. All of this is happening in an organism that by 8 weeks weighs only ⅓₀ ounce and is just over 1 inch long.

The **fetal period** *begins 2 months after conception and lasts, on the average, for 7 months. Growth and development continue their dramatic course, and organs mature to* *the point where life can be sustained outside the womb.* At 4 months after conception, the fetus is about 6 inches long and weighs 4 to 7 ounces. Prenatal reflexes become more apparent, and the mother feels the fetus move for the first time. At 6 months after conception, the eyes and eyelids are completely formed, a fine layer of hair covers the fetus, the grasping reflex appears, and irregular breathing begins. By 7 to 9 months, the fetus is much longer and weighs considerably more. In addition, the functioning of various organs steps up.

As these massive changes take place during prenatal development, some pregnant women tiptoe about in the belief that everything they do has a direct effect on the unborn child. Others behave more casually, assuming their experiences have little impact. The truth lies somewhere between these extremes. Although it floats in a comfortable, well-protected environment, the fetus is not totally immune to the larger environment surrounding the mother (Kopp, 1984).

A **teratogen** *(the word comes from the Greek word* tera, *meaning "monster") is any agent that causes a birth defect.* Rarely do specific teratogens, such as drugs, link up with specific birth defects, such as leg malformation, but the drug thalidomide is an exception. During the late 1950s, several hundred women took thalidomide early in pregnancy to prevent morning sickness and insomnia. Tragically, babies born to these mothers had arms and legs that had not developed beyond stumps.

The importance of women's health to the health of their offspring is nowhere better exemplified than when the mother is infected with human immunodeficiency virus (HIV), the virus that is believed to be the cause of acquired immune deficiency syndrome (AIDS). As the number of women infected with HIV increases, more newborns are born infected with HIV (Temoshok, 1998).

AIDS is currently the sixth leading cause of death for children 1 to 4 years of age in the United States. Between 15 to 30 percent of infants born to women infected with HIV become infected with the virus. This results in approximately 1,500 to 2,000 children born with HIV annually in the United States. Treatment can considerably reduce the rate of HIV transmission from an infected woman to her baby (Committee on Pediatric AIDS, 1998).

There are three ways a mother with HIV can infect her offspring: (1) during pregnancy, through the placenta (a life-support system of tissues); (2) during delivery, through contact with maternal blood and other fluids; and (3) after birth, through breast-feeding. HIV and AIDS will be discussed further in chapter 13, "Health Psychology."

Heavy drinking by pregnant women can also have devastating effects on offspring (Abel, 1984; Toth, Conner, & Streissguth, 1999). **Fetal alcohol syndrome (FAS)** *is a cluster of abnormalities that occur in children born to mothers who are heavy drinkers.* These abnormalities include a small head (microencephaly) and defective limbs, face, and heart. Most of these children are also below average in intelligence. Recently concern has increased about the well-being of the fetus when pregnant women drink even small amounts of alcohol. In summary, a woman who is pregnant or anticipates becoming pregnant should not drink any alcohol (Streissguth, 1997).

**Fetal Alcohol Syndrome
Touch Research Institute**

Pregnant women also should not smoke. Fetal and neonatal deaths, and preterm birth, are higher among smoking mothers. Studies of whether smoking during pregnancy increases cancer risk in children are inconclusive and long-term studies into adulthood have not been conducted. However, in one recent study, urine samples from 22 of 31 newborns of smoking mothers showed substantial amounts of one of the strongest carcinogens (NNK) in tobacco smoke; the urine samples of newborns whose mothers did not smoke did not contain the carcinogen (Hecht, 1998). In another study, prenatal exposure to cigarette smoking was related to poorer language and cognitive skills at 4 years of age (Fried & Watkinson, 1990).

Birth and the Newborn   The newborn is on a threshold between two worlds. In the womb the fetus exists in a dark, free-floating, low-gravity environment with a relatively warm, constant temperature. At birth, the newborn must quickly adapt to light, gravity, cold, and a buzzing array of changing stimuli.

EXPLORATIONS IN PSYCHOLOGY
The Power of Touch and Massage in Development

THERE HAS BEEN great interest recently in the roles of touch and massage in improving the growth, health, and well-being of infants and children. This interest has especially been stimulated by a number of research investigations by Tiffany Field (1995), director of the Touch Research Institute at the University of Miami School of Medicine. In one study, 40 preterm infants who had just been released from an intensive care unit and placed in a transitional nursery were studied (Field, Scafidi, & Schanberg, 1987). Twenty of the preterm babies were given special stimulation with massage and exercise for three 15-minute periods at the beginning of 3 consecutive hours every morning for 10 weekdays. For example, each infant was placed on its stomach and gently stroked. The massage began with the head and neck and moved downward to the feet. It also moved from the shoulders down to the hands. The infant was then rolled over. Each arm and leg was flexed and extended; then both legs were flexed and extended. Next, the massage was repeated.

The massaged and exercised preterm babies gained 47 percent more weight than their preterm counterparts who were not massaged and exercised, even though both groups had the same number of feedings per day and averaged the same intake of formula. The increased activity of the massaged, exercised infants would seem to work against weight gain. However, similar findings have been

Shown here is Dr. Tiffany Field massaging a newborn infant. Dr. Field's research has clearly demonstrated the power of massage in improving the developmental outcome of at-risk infants. Under her direction the Touch Research Institute in Miami, Florida, was recently developed to investigate the role of touch in a number of domains of health and well-being.

discovered with animals. The increased activity may increase gastrointestinal and metabolic efficiency. The massaged infants were more active and alert, and they performed better on developmental tests. Also, their hospital stays were about 6 days shorter than those of the nonmassaged, nonexercised group, which saved about $3,000 per preterm infant. Field has recently replicated these findings with preterm infants.

In another study, Field (1992) gave the same kind of massage (firm stroking with the palms of the hands) to preterm infants who had been exposed to cocaine in utero. The infants also showed significant weight gain and improved scores on developmental tests. Currently, Field is using massage therapy with HIV-exposed preterm infants with the hope that their immune system functioning will be improved. Others she has targeted include infants of depressed mothers, infants with colic, infants and children with sleep problems, as well as children who have diabetes, asthma, and juvenile arthritis.

Field also reports that touch has been helpful with children and adolescents who have touch aversions, such as children who have been sexually abused, autistic children, and adolescents with eating disorders. Field also is studying the amount of touch a child normally receives during school activities. She hopes that positive forms of touch will return to school systems, where touching has been outlawed because of potential sexual-abuse lawsuits.

A full-term infant has grown in the womb for the full 38 to 42 weeks between conception and delivery. A **preterm infant** *is an infant born prior to 38 weeks after conception.* Whether a preterm infant will have developmental problems is a complex issue. Very small preterm infants are more likely than their larger counterparts to have developmental problems. Also, preterm infants who grow up in conditions of poverty are more likely to have developmental problems than are those who live in higher socioeconomic conditions. Indeed, many larger preterm infants from middle- and high-income families do not have developmental problems. Nonetheless, more preterm infants than full-term babies have learning disorders (Kopp, 1984).

Researchers are continuing to unveil new ideas for improving the lives of preterm infants. One increasingly used technique is to regularly massage and gently exercise preterm infants. This technique is described in Explorations in Psychology.

SUMMARY TABLE 8.1
What Development Is;
Prenatal Development and Birth

Concept	Processes/ Related Ideas	Characteristics/Description
What Is Development?	Biological, Cognitive, and Socioemotional Processes	Biological processes involve changes in a person's physical nature. Cognitive processes involve changes in a person's thought, intelligence, and language. Socioemotional processes involve changes in a person's relationships with other people, changes in emotions, and changes in personality.
	Periods of Development	The developmental periods are: prenatal (conception to birth), infancy (birth to 18/24 months), early childhood (3–5 years), middle and late childhood (6–11 years), adolescence (10–12 to 18–21 years), early adulthood (twenties and thirties), middle adulthood (35–45 to 60s), and late adulthood (60s–70s to death). The interaction of biological, cognitive, and socioemotional processes produces the periods of development. Neugarten argues that we are moving toward a society in which age is a weaker predictor of development in adulthood.
	Developmental Issues	Three main developmental issues focus on (1) nature and nurture, (2) continuity and discontinuity, and (3) early and later experience. Most developmentalists do not take extreme positions on these issues.
Prenatal Development and Birth	The Course of Prenatal Development	Conception occurs when a single sperm cell from the male penetrates the female's egg. This process is called fertilization. A zygote is a fertilized egg. Prenatal development is divided into three periods: germinal (first 2 weeks after conception), embryonic (weeks 3 through 8 after conception), and fetal (begins 2 months after conception and lasts for approximately 7 months). A teratogen is any nongenetic agent that causes a birth defect. HIV can be transmitted from pregnant mothers to their offspring. Fetal alcohol syndrome is a cluster of abnormalities that occur in children born to mothers who are heavy drinkers. Even when pregnant women drink only small amounts of alcohol, it can affect the fetus' well-being. Thus, if women anticipate they are going to become pregnant or are pregnant, they should not drink alcohol. Smoking by pregnant mothers also has adverse effects on their offspring.
	Birth and the Newborn	A full-term infant has grown in the womb for 38 to 42 weeks. A preterm infant is born prior to 38 weeks after conception. Whether preterm infants have problems is a complex issue. Massage therapy has been effectively used with preterm infants.

At this point we have studied a number of ideas about what development is, as well as prenatal development and birth. An overview of these ideas is presented in summary table 8.1. Next, we continue our exploration of development by examining children's physical development.

Physical Development

At no other time in a person's life will there be so many changes occurring so fast as during the first few years. During infancy, we change from virtually immobile, helpless beings to insatiably curious, talking creatures who toddle as fast as our legs can carry us.

Infancy   The newborn is not an empty-headed organism. It comes into the world already equipped with several genetically "wired" reflexes. For example, the

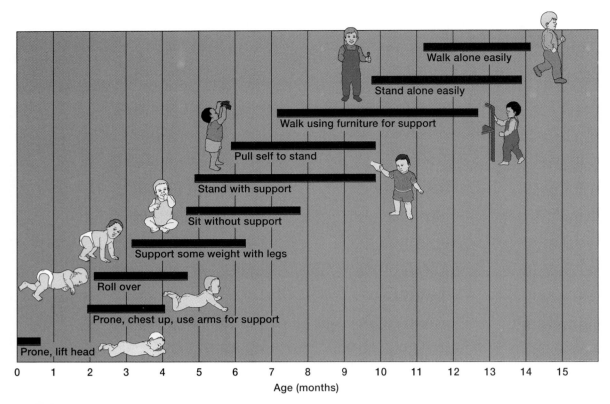

Figure 8.3
Developmental Accomplishments in Gross Motor Skills During the First 15 Months

Zero to Three

newborn has no fear of water, naturally holding its breath and contracting its throat to keep water out. Some of the reflexes we possess as newborns persist throughout our lives—coughing, blinking, and yawning, for example. Others disappear in the months following birth as higher brain functions mature and we develop voluntary control over many behaviors. Among the reflexes that weaken or disappear by 6 or 7 months of age are grasping (when the infant's palms are touched, the infant grasps tightly), sucking (when an object touches the infant's mouth, the infant automatically begins sucking), stepping (when the infant is held above a surface and its feet lowered to touch the surface, the infant moves its feet as if to walk), and startle (when sudden stimulation occurs, such as hearing a loud noise or being dropped, the infant startles, arches its back, and throws back its head, flings out its arms and legs and then rapidly closes them to the center of its body).

The infant's physical development in the first 2 years of life is dramatic. At birth, the newborn (neonate) has a gigantic head (relative to the rest of the body) that flops around uncontrollably. In the span of 12 months, the infant becomes capable of sitting anywhere, standing, stooping, climbing, and often walking. During the second year, growth decelerates, but rapid increases in such activities as running and climbing take place. Figure 8.3 shows the average ages at which infants accomplish various motor milestones.

As an infant walks, talks, runs, shakes a rattle, smiles, and frowns, changes in its brain are occurring. Consider that the infant began life as a single cell and 9 months later was born with a brain and nervous system that contained approximately 100 billion nerve cells. Indeed, at birth the infant has virtually all of the nerve cells (neurons) it is going to have in its entire life. However, at birth and in early infancy, neurons have only minimal connections.

As the infant ages from birth to 2 years, the interconnection of neurons increases dramatically as the dendrites (the receiving parts) of the neurons branch out (see figure 8.4).

Figure 8.4
The Development of Dendritic Spreading
Note the increase in connections among neurons over the course of the first 2 years of life.

Childhood   By their third birthday, children are full of new tricks such as climbing, skipping, and jumping. They are beginning to be able to make their body do what they want it to do, giving them a greater sense of self-control.

Catching, throwing, kicking, balancing, rolling, cutting, stacking, snapping, pushing, dancing, and swimming—preschool children perform these special feats and many, many more. As twentieth-century Welsh poet Dylan Thomas put it, "All the sun long they were running." The growth rate slows down in early childhood. Otherwise, we would be a species of giants. The growth and development of the brain underlie the young child's improvement in motor skills, reflected in activities such as the ability to hold a pencil and make increasingly efficient marks with it. A child's brain is closer to full growth than the rest of its body, attaining 75 percent of its adult weight by the age of 3 and 90 percent by age 5.

In middle and late childhood, motor development is much smoother and more coordinated than in early childhood. While a preschool child can zip, cut, latch, and dance, an elementary school child can zip, cut, latch, and dance more efficiently and with more flair. Physical activities are essential for children to refine their developing skills. Child development experts believe children should be *active,* rather than passive, and should be able to plan and select many of their own activities. An ideal elementary school, for example, would include a gym and a safe, elaborate outdoor play area where students can participate in a variety of games and sports; a classroom with a fully equipped publishing center, complete with materials for writing, typing, illustrating, and binding student-made books; and a science area with animals and plants for observation and books to study. Children also need to "just" play. Education experts recognize that spontaneous play provides additional opportunities for children to learn. Schools that offer children many opportunities to engage in a wide range of self-initiated activities, such as the ideal school we just described, considerably enhance their students' physical development.

At this point, we have discussed a number of ideas about what development is, the prenatal period and birth, and children's physical development. In the school atmosphere just described, in which children's education involves many opportunities

Child Development
Children's Education

for physical and self-initiated activities, not only is physical development enhanced, so is cognitive development, the topic to which we now turn.

Cognitive Development

Jean Piaget, the famous Swiss developmental psychologist, was a meticulous observer of his three children—Lucienne, Jacqueline, and Laurent. His books on cognitive development are filled with these observations. The following provide a glimpse of Piaget's observations of his children's cognitive development in infancy (Piaget, 1952).

- Toward the end of her fourth month, Lucienne is lying in her crib. Piaget hangs a doll over her feet. Lucienne thrusts her feet at the doll and makes it move. Afterward she looks at her motionless foot for a second, then kicks at the doll again. She has no visual control of her foot because her movements are the same whether she only looks at the doll or whether it is placed over her head. By contrast, she has tactile control of her foot because when she tries to kick the doll and misses, she slows her foot movements to improve her aim.
- At 11 months, while seated, Jacqueline shakes a little bell. She then pauses abruptly so she can delicately place the bell in front of her right foot; then she kicks the bell hard. Unable to recapture it, she grasps a ball and places it in the same location where the bell was. She gives the ball a firm kick.

For Piaget, such observations reflect the infant's cognitive development.

Piaget's Theory of Cognitive Development   Piaget (1896–1980) changed the way we think about children's minds. When Piaget's ideas were imported to the United States in the 1960s, there was no theory available that explained how children's minds change as they age. Prior to Piaget, American psychologists had to choose from behaviorism, which emphasized that children receive information from the environment, or the IQ testing approach, which emphasized individual differences in children's intelligence. American psychologists embraced Piaget's view that children *actively construct* their cognitive world and that they go through a series of stages in doing this.

In actively constructing their cognitive world, children use schemas. In chapter 6, "Memory," we defined a **schema** *as a concept or framework that already exists in a person's mind which organizes and interprets information.* In our discussion of memory we indicated that schemas help us to understand how people don't remember the past exactly but rather reconstruct it. Piaget's interest in schemas wasn't in terms of how people reconstruct the past but rather how they use schemas to organize and make sense out of their current experience.

Piaget (1952) said that two processes are responsible for how people use and adapt their schemas: assimilation and accommodation. **Assimilation** *occurs when individuals incorporate new information into existing knowledge.* That is, in assimilation people assimilate the environment to a schema. **Accommodation** *occurs when individuals adjust to new information.* That is, people accommodate their schemas to the environment. Consider this circumstance to see how assimilation and accommodation work: A young infant lunges at a rattle and tries to grasp it but is unable to pick it up. In this instance the infant has assimilated the rattle into the reaching schema of objects to be picked up. Over the course of several months and repeated attempts, the infant refines its movements and is able to pick up the rattle (accommodation). Consider how newborns reflexively suck everything that touches their lips. By sucking different objects, infants learn about the nature of these objects—their taste, texture, shape, and so on (assimilation). After several months of experience, though, they construct their understanding of the world differently. Some objects, such as fingers and the mother's breast, can be sucked, whereas others, such as fuzzy blankets, should not be (accommodation).

Infant Cognition

Piaget also believed that we go through four stages in understanding the world (see figure 8.5). Each of the stages is age-related and consists of distinct ways of thinking. Remember, it is the *different* way of understanding the world that makes one stage more advanced than another. Knowing *more* information does not make the child's thinking more advanced, in Piaget's view. This is what Piaget meant when he said that the child's cognition is *qualitatively* different in one stage compared to another. Let's now examine Piaget's four stages.

The Sensorimotor Stage   The **sensorimotor stage,** *which lasts from birth to about 2 years of age, is the first Piagetian stage. In this stage, infants construct an understanding of the world by coordinating sensory experiences (such as seeing and hearing) with physical (motor) actions—hence the term sensorimotor.* It is non-symbolic through much of its duration and object permanence is an important accomplishment. At the beginning of this stage, newborns have little more than reflexive patterns with which to work. By the end of the stage, 2-year-olds show complex sensorimotor patterns and are beginning to use symbols in their thinking.

We live in a world of objects. Imagine yourself as a 5-month-old infant and how

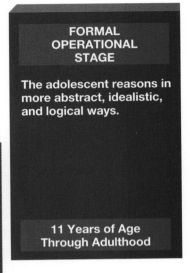

FORMAL OPERATIONAL STAGE

The adolescent reasons in more abstract, idealistic, and logical ways.

11 Years of Age Through Adulthood

CONCRETE OPERATIONAL STAGE

The child can now reason logically about concrete events and classify objects into different sets.

7 to 11 Years of Age

PREOPERATIONAL STAGE

The child begins to represent the world with words and images. These words and images reflect increased symbolic thinking and go beyond the connection of sensory information and physical action.

2 to 7 Years of Age

SENSORIMOTOR STAGE

The infant constructs an understanding of the world by coordinating sensory experiences with physical actions. An infant progresses from reflexive, instinctual action at birth to the beginning of symbolic thought toward the end of the stage.

Birth to 2 Years of Age

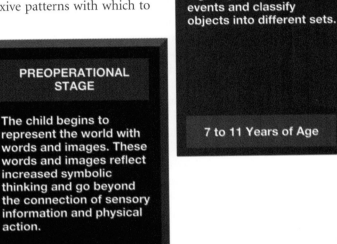

*F*igure 8.5
Piaget's Four Stages of Cognitive Development

you might experience the world. You are in a playpen filled with toys. One of the toys, a monkey, falls out of your grasp and rolls behind a larger toy, a hippopotamus. Would you know the monkey is behind the hippopotamus, or would you think it is completely gone? Piaget believed that "out of sight" literally was "out of mind" for young infants. At 5 months of age, you would not have reached for the monkey when it fell behind the hippopotamus. By 8 months of age, though, infants begin to understand that out of sight is not out of mind. At this point, you probably would have reached behind the hippopotamus to search for the monkey, coordinating your senses with your movements.

Object permanence *is Piaget's term for one of the infant's most important accomplishments: understanding that objects and events continue to exist even when they cannot directly be seen, heard, or touched.* The most common way to study object

Jean Piaget, the famous Swiss developmental psychologist, changed the way we think about the development of children's minds.

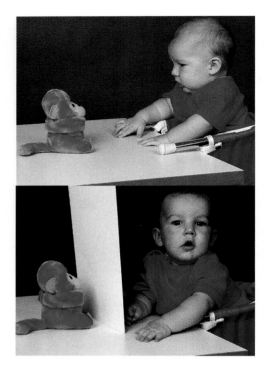

Figure 8.6
Object Permanence
Piaget thought that object permanence was one of infancy's landmark cognitive accomplishments. For this 5-month-old boy, "out of sight" is literally out of mind. The infant looks at the toy monkey *(top),* but when his view of the toy is blocked *(bottom),* he does not search for it. Eventually, he will search for the hidden toy monkey, reflecting the presence of object permanence.

permanence is to show an infant an interesting toy and then cover the toy with a sheet or a blanket. If infants understand that the toy still exists, they try to uncover it (see figure 8.6). Object permanence continues to develop throughout the sensorimotor period. For example, when infants initially understand that objects exist even when out of sight, they only briefly look for them. By the end of the sensorimotor stage, infants engage in a more prolonged and sophisticated search for an object.

In sum, we have seen that sensorimotor thought involves the ability to organize and coordinate sensations with physical movements, is nonsymbolic throughout its duration, and includes the development of object permanence. Next, we examine the second Piagetian cognitive stage.

The Preoperational Stage   The **preoperational stage** *is Piaget's second stage of cognitive development. Lasting from approximately 2 to 7 years of age, it is more symbolic than sensorimotor thought, does not involve operational thought, is egocentric, and is intuitive rather than logical.*

Preschool children begin to represent their world with words, images, and drawings. Symbolic thoughts go beyond simple connections of sensorimotor information and physical action.

While preschool children can symbolically represent the world, they still cannot perform operations. **Operations,** *in Piaget's theory, are mental representations that are reversible.* Preschool children have difficulty understanding that reversing an action brings about the original conditions from which the action began. The following two examples will help you to understand Piaget's concept of reversibility. The preschool child may know that $4 + 2 = 6$ but not understand that the reverse, $6 - 2 = 4$, is true. Or let's say a preschooler walks to his friend's house each day but always gets a ride home. If you asked him to walk home one day he would probably reply that he didn't know the way since he had never walked home before.

A well-known test of whether a child can think "operationally" is to present a child with two identical beakers, A and B, filled with liquid to the same height (see figure 8.7). Next to them is a third beaker, C. Beaker C is tall and thin, while beakers A and B are wide and short. The liquid is poured from B into C, and the child is asked whether the amounts in A and C are the same. The 4-year-old child invariably says that the amount of liquid in the tall, thin beaker (C) is greater than that in the short, fat beaker (A). The 8-year-old child consistently says the amounts are the same. The 4-year-old child, a preoperational thinker, cannot mentally reverse the pouring action; that is, she cannot imagine the liquid going back from container C to container B. Piaget said that children such as this 4-year-old girl have not grasped the concept of **conservation,** *a belief in the permanence of certain attributes of objects or situations in spite of superficial changes.*

The child's thought in the preoperational stage also is egocentric. By **egocentrism,** *Piaget meant the inability to distinguish between one's own perspective and someone else's perspective.* Piaget and Barbel Inhelder (1969) initially studied young children's egocentrism by devising the three mountains task (see figure 8.8). The child walks around the model of the mountains and becomes familiar with what the mountains look like from different perspectives. The child can see that different objects are on the mountains as well. The child is then seated on one side of the table on which the mountains are placed. The experimenter takes a doll and moves it to different locations around the table, at each location asking the child to select one photo from a series of photos that most accurately reflects the view the doll is seeing. Children in the preoperational stage often pick the photo that shows the view they have rather than the view the doll has.

Piaget also called preoperational thought *intuitive,* because when he asked children why they knew something, they often did not give logical answers, but offered personal insights or guesses instead. Yet, as Piaget observed, young children seem so sure that they know something, even though they do not use logical reasoning to arrive at the answer. Young children also have an insatiable desire to know their world, and they ask a lot of questions:

"Why does a lady have to be married to have a baby?"
"Who was the mother when everybody was the baby?"
"Why do leaves fall?"
"Why does the sun shine?"

In sum, we have seen that preoperational thought is more symbolic than sensorimotor thought, is characterized by an inability to perform operations, is egocentric, and is intuitive rather than logical. Next, we explore the third Piagetian cognitive stage.

The Concrete Operational Stage   The **concrete operational stage** *is Piaget's third stage of cognitive development, which occurs from 7 to 11 years of age. Concrete operational thought involves using operations, and logical reasoning replaces intuitive reasoning, but only in concrete situations. It is characterized by a lack of abstract thinking, but classification skills are present.*

Earlier we described the beaker task that was too difficult for a preoperational child. Another well-known task to demonstrate operational thinking involves showing a child two identical balls of clay (see figure 8.9). The experimenter rolls one ball into a long, thin shape. The other is retained in its original ball shape. Then the child is asked if there is more clay in the ball or in the long, thin piece of clay. By the time children reach 7 to 8 years of age, most answer that the amount of clay is the same. To solve this problem correctly, children have to imagine that the clay ball is rolled out into a long, thin strip and then returned to its original round shape—imagination that involves a reversible mental action. Concrete operations allow the child to coordinate several characteristics rather than focusing on a single property of an object. In the clay example, the preoperational child is likely to focus on height *or* width. The child who has reached the stage of concrete operational thought coordinates information about both dimensions.

Many of the concrete operations identified by Piaget focus on the way children think about the properties of objects. One important skill at this stage of reasoning is the ability to classify or divide things into different sets or subsets and to consider their interrelations. Figure 8.10 shows an example of children's classification skills.

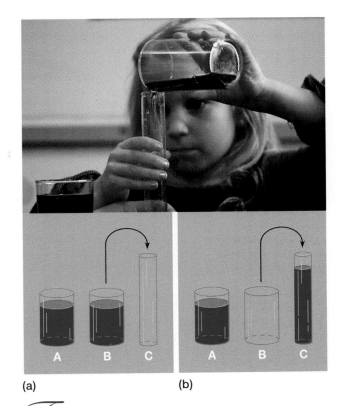

(a)   (b)

𝓕igure 8.7
Piaget's Conservation Task
The beaker test is a well-known Piagetian test to determine whether a child can think operationally—that is, can mentally reverse actions and show conservation of the substance. (a) Two identical beakers are presented to the child. Then, the experimenter pours the liquid from B into C, which is taller and thinner than A or B. (b) The child is asked if these beakers (A and C) have the same amount of liquid. The preoperational child says no. When asked to point to the beaker that has more liquid, the preoperational child points to the tall, thin beaker.

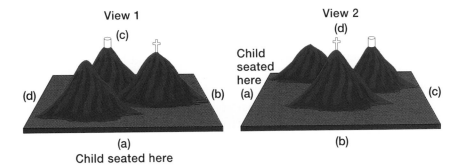

𝓕igure 8.8
The Three Mountains Task
View 1 shows the child's perspective from where he or she is sitting. View 2 is an example of the photograph the child would be shown mixed in with others from different perspectives. To correctly identify this view, the child has to take the perspective of a person sitting at spot (b). Invariably, a preschool child who thinks in a preoperational way cannot perform this task. When asked what a view of the mountains looks like from position (b), the child selects a photograph taken from location (a), the child's view at the time.

Initial presentation	Manipulation	Preoperational child's answer	Concrete operational child's answer
Two identical balls of clay are shown to the child. The child agrees that they are equal.	The experimenter changes the shape of one of the balls and asks the child whether they still contain equal amounts of clay.	No, the longer one has more.	Yes, they still have equal amounts.

Figure 8.9
Preoperational and Concrete Operational Children: The Clay Example

In sum, we have seen that concrete operational thought involves operational thinking, logical reasoning in concrete but not abstract contexts, and classification skill. Next, we examine the fourth Piagetian cognitive stage.

The Formal Operational Stage   The **formal operational stage** *is Piaget's fourth and final stage of cognitive development, entered at 11 to 15 years of age and continuing through the adult years. It is more abstract, idealistic, and logical than concrete operational thought.* Unlike elementary school children, adolescents are no longer limited to actual concrete experience as the anchor of thought. They can conceive make-believe situations, hypothetical possibilities, or purely abstract propositions. Thought also becomes more idealistic. Adolescents often compare themselves and others to ideal standards. And they think about what an ideal world would be like, wondering if they couldn't carve out a better world than the one the adult generation has handed to them.

At the same time adolescents think more abstractly and idealistically, they also think more logically. Adolescents begin to think more like a scientist thinks, devising plans to solve problems and systematically testing solutions. This type of problem solving has an imposing name. **Hypothetical-deductive reasoning** *is Piaget's name for adolescents' ability to develop hypotheses, or best hunches, about ways to solve problems, such as an algebraic equation.* They then systematically deduce, or conclude, which is the best path to follow to solve the problem. By contrast, children are more likely to solve problems in a trial-and-error fashion.

In sum, we have seen that formal operational thought is abstract, idealistic, and logical. Now that we have learned about Piaget's stages, let's evaluate the current status of his ideas in developmental psychology.

Evaluating Piaget   We have read about Freud in abnormal psychology, Skinner in learning, and Piaget in cognitive development. Freud altered the way we think about people's problems, and Skinner changed the way we look at how people learn. Likewise, Piaget completely opened up a new way of looking at how children's minds develop. All three are giants in their fields.

We owe to Piaget a long list of masterful concepts that have enduring power and fascination (Scholnick, 1999; Vidal, 2000). These include the concepts of schemas, assimilation, accommodation, cognitive stages, object permanence, egocentrism, and conservation. We also owe to Piaget the currently accepted

Through the Eyes of Psychologists
John Flavell, *Stanford University*

"We owe to Piaget the present field of cognitive development with its image of the developing child, who through its own active and creative commerce with its environment, builds an orderly succession of cognitive structures enroute to intellectual maturity."

vision of children as active constructive thinkers who manufacture their own development.

But just as Freud's and Skinner's views have been criticized, so have Piaget's (Lutz & Sternberg, 1999; Pascual-Leone & Johnson, 1999). Some cognitive abilities emerge earlier than Piaget thought. For example, Renee Baillargeon (1997) has documented that infants as young as 4 months of age know that objects continue to exist even when hidden (which Piaget did not think was possible until 8 months of age). Memory and other forms of symbolic activity occur by at least the first half of the first year (much earlier than Piaget thought possible) (Mandler, 1998).

Formal operational thought does not emerge as consistently in early adolescence as Piaget envisioned. Many adolescents and even adults do not reason as logically as Piaget proposed. Thus, infants are more cognitively competent than Piaget thought, adolescents and adults less competent.

Piaget was interested in examining the species-general ways that all people go through cognitive stages, and he showed little interest in individual variations in people's thinking. Not surprisingly, he has been criticized for ignoring individual differences in thinking.

Information-processing psychologists argue that Piaget's view places too much emphasis on grand stages and not enough on smaller, precise steps in solving problems. Information-processing psychologists believe that children's minds can be best understood by focusing more on strategies and skills, as well as how fast and efficiently people process information (Siegler, 1998).

Piaget also did not think that culture and education play important roles in children's cognitive development. However, researchers have found that the age at which children acquire conservation skills is related to some extent with whether their culture provides relevant practice (Cole, 1999; Cole & Cole, 2000). The Russian psychologist Lev Vygotsky (1962) recognized that cognitive development does not occur in a sociocultural vacuum. In Vygotsky's view, the goal of cognitive development is to learn the skills that will allow you to be competent in your culture. To do this, he says that it is important to be guided and assisted by skilled members of the culture, much like being a cognitive apprentice (Rogoff, 1998). Vygotsky's view has become increasingly popular in education because of its emphasis on collaborative learning through interaction with skilled others.

In sum, today children's cognitive development is approached from plural points of view. Yet even though some of his ideas have been modified, Piaget still stands head and shoulders above all others in this field. It was his masterpiece that let us see how, as they develop, children's minds change in orderly, sequential ways (Scholnick & others, 1999).

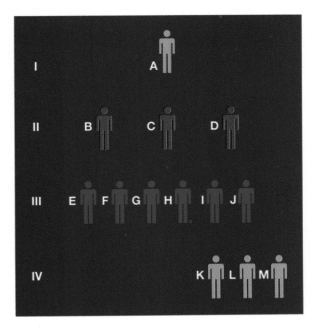

𝒻igure 8.10
Classification Involving a Family Tree

One way to determine if children possess classification skills is to see if they can understand a family tree of four generations (Furth & Wachs, 1975). This family tree suggests that the grandfather (A) has three sons (B, C, & D), each of whom has two sons (E through J), and that one of these sons (J) has three sons (K, L, & M). A child who comprehends this classification system can move up and down a level (vertically), across a level (horizontally), and up and down and across a level (obliquely) within the system. A child who thinks in a concrete operational way understands that person J can, at the same time, be father, brother, and grandson, for example. A preoperational child cannot perform this classification and says that a father cannot fulfill these other roles.

Socioemotional Development

As children grow and develop, they are socialized by and socialize others—parents, siblings, peers, teachers, and others. Their small world widens as they grow older. We will begin this section by studying Erik Erikson's theory of how we develop socio-emotionally.

Erikson's Theory of Socioemotional Development
Erik Erikson (1902–1994) spent his childhood and adolescence in Europe. After working as a psychoanalyst under Freud's direction, he came to the United States and taught at Harvard University. While he accepted some of Freud's beliefs, he disagreed with others. For example, while Freud argued that *psychosexual stages* are the key to understanding development, Erikson said that *psychosocial stages* are the key. In addition, while Freud stressed that personality is shaped in the first 5 years of life, Erikson emphasized lifelong development. In Erikson's (1968) view, people pass through eight

Erikson's Theory

Figure 8.11
Erikson's Eight Life-Span Stages

	Erikson's stages	Developmental period
	Integrity versus despair	Late adulthood (60s–)
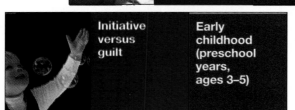	Generativity versus stagnation	Middle adulthood (40s, 50s)
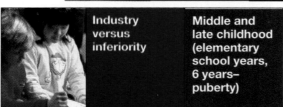	Intimacy versus isolation	Early adulthood (20s, 30s)
	Identity versus identity confusion	Adolescence (10 to 20 years)
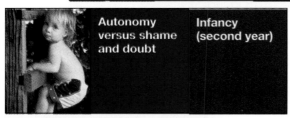	Industry versus inferiority	Middle and late childhood (elementary school years, 6 years–puberty)
	Initiative versus guilt	Early childhood (preschool years, ages 3–5)
	Autonomy versus shame and doubt	Infancy (second year)
	Trust versus mistrust	Infancy (first year)

stages in their journey through the human life span. The first four stages take place in childhood, the last four in adolescence and adulthood (see figure 8.11).

Each stage represents a developmental task or crisis that must be negotiated. For Erikson, the developmental task can be a turning point of increased vulnerability or enhanced potential. The more successfully people resolve the issues, the more competent they are likely to become.

Trust Versus Mistrust   **Trust versus mistrust** *is Erikson's first psychosocial stage, which occurs during the first year of life.* Trust is built when a baby's basic needs—such as comfort, food, and warmth—are met. If infants' needs are not met by responsive, sensitive caregivers, the result is mistrust. Trust in infancy sets the stage for a lifelong expectation that the world will be a good and pleasant place to live.

Autonomy Versus Shame and Doubt   **Autonomy versus shame and doubt** *is Erikson's second stage, which occurs from 1 to 3 years of age.* The positive side of the stage involves developing a sense of independence and autonomy, the negative side a sense of shame and doubt. In seeking autonomy, toddlers assert their will. If they are restrained too much or punished too harshly, they are not likely to develop this sense of independence.

Initiative Versus Guilt   *Initiative versus guilt is Erikson's third stage, which occurs from 3 to 5 years of age.* Asked to assume more responsibility for themselves, children develop initiative. If children are irresponsible or made to feel anxious, they might develop too much guilt. During the preschool years, children's social worlds widen and they are challenged to develop purposeful behavior and cope with these challenges. Erikson believed that young children are resilient. He said that most guilt is quickly compensated for by a sense of accomplishment.

Industry Versus Inferiority   *Industry versus inferiority is Erikson's fourth stage, which occurs from 6 years of age until puberty.* Industry is achieved by mastering knowledge and intellectual skills. When children don't attain this mastery, they can feel inferior. Erikson believed that at the end of early childhood's period of expansive imagination, children are ready to turn their energy to learning academic skills. If they don't, they might develop a sense of being incompetent and unproductive.

Identity Versus Identity Confusion   *Identity versus identity confusion is Erikson's fifth stage, which occurs during the adolescent years.* At this time individuals are faced with finding out who they are, what they are all about, and where they are going in life. If they don't adequately explore their identity, they emerge from this stage with a sense of identity confusion. Adolescents are confronted with many new roles and adult statuses, such as vocational and romantic. Parents need to allow adolescents to explore many different roles and paths within a particular role. If parents push an identity on adolescents without letting them adequately explore various roles and if a positive future path is not defined, identity confusion reigns.

Intimacy Versus Isolation   *Intimacy versus isolation is Erikson's sixth stage, which is experienced in the twenties and thirties (early adulthood).* At this time, individuals face the developmental task of forming intimate relationships with others. If they do not find intimacy in relationships with a partner and/or friends, they can develop a sense of social isolation. Erikson eloquently described intimacy as finding yourself yet losing yourself in another person.

Generativity Versus Stagnation   *Generativity versus stagnation is Erikson's seventh stage, which occurs in the forties and fifties (middle adulthood).* A chief concern is to assist the younger generation in developing and leading useful lives. This is what Erikson meant by generativity. The feeling of having done little or nothing for the next generation is what is meant by stagnation.

Integrity Versus Despair   *Integrity versus despair is Erikson's eighth and final stage, which individuals experience from the sixties on (late adulthood).* In late adulthood, people review their lives. If the retrospective glances reveal a life well spent, the person feels a sense of satisfaction—integrity is achieved. If the retrospective glances are negative, the person may feel a sense of despair.

Erikson did not believe that the proper solution to a stage is always completely positive. Some exposure or commitment to the negative side of a developmental task can be inevitable. For example, you can't trust all people under all circumstances and survive. Nonetheless, positive resolutions to a stage should dominate for optimal development to take place.

Evaluating Erikson's Theory   At a time when it was believed that most development takes place in childhood, Erikson charted how development is lifelong. His insights also helped to move us away from Freud's focus on sexuality and toward understanding the importance of successfully resolving different socioemotional tasks at different points in our lives. Erikson's ideas changed the way we think about some periods of development (Marcia, 1999). For example, Erikson encouraged us to look at adolescents not just as sexual beings, but as individuals seeking to find out who they are and searching to find their niche in the world. He informed us to not just think of middle-aged individuals as being in a state of decline but rather as having the important developmental task of contributing to the next generation.

Just as Piaget's theory has been criticized, so has Erikson's. Critics argue that the research base for Erikson's entire theory has not been developed. However, research on specific stages—such as identity versus identity confusion, as well as generativity versus stagnation—reveal that these are important developmental tasks at these points in our lives. Critics also say that Erikson's attempt to capture each stage with a single concept sometimes leaves out other important developmental tasks. For example, regarding early adulthood Erikson focused on intimacy versus isolation. However, another important developmental task in early adulthood involves careers and work, which were underplayed by Erikson.

However, such criticisms cannot tarnish Erikson's monumental contributions. He, along with Piaget, is a twentieth-century giant in developmental psychology.

Attachment   Erikson (1968) believes that the caregiver's responsive and sensitive behavior toward the infant during its first year provides an important foundation for later development. A number of contemporary developmental psychologists who study the process of "attachment" during infancy agree. Attachment usually refers to a strong relationship between two people in which each person does a number of things to continue the relationship. Many types of people are attached: relatives, lovers, a teacher and a student. In the language of developmental psychology, **attachment** *is the close emotional bond between the infant and its caregiver.*

Theories about infant attachment abound. Freud believed that the infant becomes attached to the person or object that provides oral satisfaction. For most infants, this is the mother, since she is most likely to feed the infant.

But researchers have questioned the importance of feeding in attachment. Harry Harlow and Robert Zimmerman (1959) evaluated whether feeding or contact comfort was more important to infant attachment. The researchers separated infant monkeys from their mothers at birth and placed them in cages where they had access to two artificial "mothers." One of the mothers was made of wire, the other of cloth. Half of the infant monkeys were fed by the wire mother, half by the cloth mother. The infant monkeys nestled close to the cloth mother and spent little time on the wire one, even when it was the wire mother that gave milk. This study clearly demonstrates that contact comfort, not feeding, is the crucial element in the attachment process (see figure 8.12).

In a famous study, Konrad Lorenz (1965) illustrated attachment behavior in geese. Lorenz separated the eggs laid by one goose into two groups. He returned one group to the goose to be hatched; the other group was hatched in an incubator. The goslings in the first group performed as predicted; they followed their mother as soon as they hatched. But those in the second group, who first saw Lorenz after hatching, followed him everywhere as if he were their mother. Lorenz marked the goslings and then placed both groups under a box. Mother goose and "mother" Lorenz stood aside as the box was lifted. Each group of goslings went directly to its "mother" (see figure 8.13). Lorenz called this process **imprinting,** *the tendency of an infant animal to form an attachment to the first moving object it sees and/or hears.*

For goslings, the critical period for imprinting is the first 36 hours after birth. There also appears to be a longer, more flexible "sensitive" period for attachment in human infants. A number of developmental psychologists believe that attachment to the caregiver in humans during the *first year* provides an important foundation for later development. This view has been especially emphasized by John Bowlby (1969, 1989) and Mary Ainsworth (1979). Bowlby believes the infant and the mother instinctively form an attachment. He believes the newborn is innately equipped to elicit the mother's attachment behavior; it cries, clings, smiles, and coos. Later the infant crawls, walks, and follows the mother. The infant's goal is to keep the mother nearby.

Figure 8.12
Harlow's Classic "Contact Comfort" Study

Regardless of whether they were fed by a wire mother or by a cloth mother, the infant monkeys overwhelmingly preferred to be in contact with the cloth mother, demonstrating the importance of contact comfort in attachment.

*F*igure 8.13
Konrad Lorenz, a Pioneering Student of Animal Behavior, Is Followed Through the Water by Three Imprinted Greylag Geese
Lorenz described imprinting as rapid, innate learning within a critical period that involves attachment to the first moving object seen. For goslings, the critical period is the first 36 hours after birth.

Research on attachment supports Bowlby's view that the infant's attachment to its caregiver intensifies at about 6 to 7 months (Schaffer & Emerson, 1964).

Some babies have a more positive attachment experience than others (Levy, 1999). Ainsworth (1979) believes that the difference depends on how sensitive the caregiver is to the infant's signals. Ainsworth says that in **secure attachment** *infants use the caregiver, usually the mother, as a secure base from which to explore the environment.* Infants who are securely attached are more likely to have mothers who are more sensitive, accepting, and expressive of affection toward them than those who are insecurely attached (Main, 2000; Waters & others, 1995).

The securely attached infant moves freely away from the mother but also keeps tabs on her location by periodically glancing at her. The securely attached infant responds positively to being picked up by others, and when put back down, happily moves away to play. An insecurely attached infant, in contrast, avoids the mother or is ambivalent toward her. The insecurely attached infant fears strangers and is upset by minor, everyday sensations.

Not all developmentalists believe that a secure attachment in infancy is the only path to competence in life. Some developmentalists believe that too much emphasis is placed on the importance of the attachment bond in infancy. Jerome Kagan (1998), for example, believes that infants are highly resilient and adaptive. He argues that they are evolutionarily equipped to stay on a positive developmental course even in the face of wide variations in parenting. Kagan and others stress that genetic and temperament characteristics play more important roles in a child's social competence than the attachment theorists, such as Bowlby, Ainsworth, and Sroufe, are willing to acknowledge. For example, infants may have inherited a low tolerance for stress; this, rather than an insecure attachment bond, may be responsible for their inability to get along with peers.

Another criticism of attachment theory is that it ignores the diversity of socializing agents and contexts that exist in an infant's world (Lamb, 2000; Thompson, 1991, 1998). In some cultures, infants show attachments to many people. In the African Hausa culture, both grandmothers and siblings provide a significant amount of care to infants (Harkness & Super, 1995). Infants in agricultural societies tend to form attachments to older siblings who are assigned a major responsibility for younger siblings' care. The attachments formed by infants in group care in Israeli kibbutzim provide another challenge to the singular attachment thesis.

Researchers recognize the importance of competent, nurturant caregivers in an infant's development. At issue, though, is whether or not secure attachment, especially to a single caregiver, is critical (Rosen & Burke, 1999).

Attachment

Parenting

Through the Eyes of Psychologists

Mary Ainsworth,
University of Virginia

"It is an essential ground plan of the human species for an infant to become attached to a caregiver."

Temperament   As we mentioned, Jerome Kagan (1998) and others believe that temperament is an important dimension of development. **Temperament** *refers to an individual's behavioral style and characteristic way of responding.* A widely debated issue involves what the basic types of temperament are. Psychiatrists Alexander Chess and Stella Thomas (1977) believe that there are three basic types or clusters:

- *Easy child,* who generally is in a positive mood, quickly establishes regular routines in infancy, and adapts easily to new experiences
- *Difficult child,* who tends to react negatively and cry frequently, engages in irregular daily routines, and is slow to accept new experiences
- *Slow-to-warm-up child,* who has a low activity level, is somewhat negative, shows low adaptability, and displays a low intensity of mood

Other researchers argue that the basic factors in temperament are *emotionality* (tendency to be distressed), *sociability* (tendency to prefer the company of others to being alone), and *activity level* (tempo and vigor of movement) (Buss & Plomin, 1987).

Many parents don't become believers in temperament's importance until they have their second child (Rothbart & Bates, 1998). Parents typically view the firstborn child's behavior as due to the way they have socialized the child. However, management strategies that worked with the first child might not be as effective with the second child. Such differences in children's temperament, which appear very early in their lives, support the belief that "nature" as well as "nurture" influence development.

Good parenting involves paying attention to and respecting the child's individuality (Sanson & Rothbart, 1995). Temperament is an important dimension of this individuality (Thompson, 1999). Next, we explore further what is involved in good parenting.

Parenting   Even though many children spend a great deal of time in child-care situations away from the home, parents are still the main caregivers for the vast majority of the world's children. And parents have always wondered what is the best way to rear their children. "Spare the rod and spoil the child." "Children are to be seen and not heard." There was a time when parents took those adages seriously. But our attitudes toward children—and parenting techniques—have changed.

Parenting Styles   At the beginning of the chapter we raised the issue of what the best way to parent is when we discussed Jessica Dubroff's tragic story. Diana Baumrind (1971, 1991) believes parents interact with their children in one of four basic ways. She classifies parenting styles as authoritarian, authoritative, neglectful, and indulgent.

Authoritarian parenting *is a restrictive, punitive style in which the parent exhorts the child to follow the parent's directions and to respect work and effort.* The authoritarian parent firmly limits and controls the child with little verbal exchange. Authoritarian parenting is associated with children's social incompetence. In a difference of opinion about how to do something, for example, the authoritarian parent might say, "You do it my way or else. . . .There will be no discussion!" Children of authoritarian parents often are anxious about social comparison, fail to initiate activity, and have poor communication skills.

Authoritative parenting *encourages children to be independent but still places limits and controls on their behavior. Extensive verbal give-and-take is allowed and parents are warm and nurturant toward the child.* Authoritative parenting is associated with children's social competence. An authoritative parent might put his arm around the child in a comforting way and say, "You know you should not have done that; let's talk about how you can handle the situation better next time." Children whose parents are authoritative tend to be socially competent, self-reliant, and socially responsible.

Neglectful parenting *is a style in which parents are uninvolved in their child's life.* This style is associated with the child's social incompetence, especially a lack of self-control. This type of parent cannot give an affirmative answer to the question, "It's 10 P.M. Do you know where your child is?" Children have a strong need for their parents to care about them. Children whose parents are neglectful might develop a sense that other aspects of the parents' lives are more important than they are. Children whose parents are neglectful tend to show poor self-control and do not handle independence well.

Indulgent parenting *is a style in which parents are involved with their children but place few demands on them.* Indulgent parenting is associated with children's social incompetence, especially a lack of self-control. Such parents let their children do what they want, and the result is the children never learn to control their own behavior and always expect to get their way. Some parents deliberately rear their children in this way because they believe the combination of warm involvement with few restraints will produce a creative, confident child. One boy whose parents deliberately reared him in an indulgent manner moved his parents out of their bedroom suite and took it over for himself. He is almost 18 years old and still has not learned to control his behavior; when he can't get something he wants, he throws temper tantrums. As you might expect, he is not very popular with his peers. Children whose parents are indulgent never learn respect for others and have difficulty controlling their behavior.

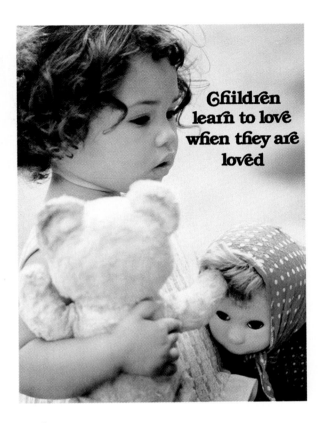

Children learn to love when they are loved

There is more to understanding parent-child relationships than parenting style (Crouter & others, 1999; Lamb & others, 1999). For many years the socialization of children was viewed as a straightforward, one-way matter of indoctrination—telling small children about the use of spoons and potties, the importance of saying thank you, and not killing the baby brother. The basic philosophy was that children had to be trained to fit into the social world, so their behavior had to be shaped into that of a mature adult. The young child is not like the inanimate blob of clay the sculptor forms into a polished statue. **Reciprocal socialization** *is the process by which children socialize parents just as parents socialize children.* For example, children's smiles usually elicit positive overtures by parents. However, when children are difficult and aggressive, their parents are more likely to punish them. As another example of reciprocal socialization, consider adolescents. They lay guilt trips on parents, just as parents lay guilt trips on them.

A recent controversy about parenting focuses on the nature–nurture issue P. 47. In a provocative book, *The Nurture Assumption,* Judith Harris (1998) argued that what parents do does not make a difference in their children's behavior. Spank them. Hug them. Read to them. Ignore them. Harris says it won't influence how they turn out. She argues that children's genes and peers are far more important than parents in children's development.

Harris is right that genes matter and she is right that peers matter, but she is wrong that parents don't matter. There is a huge parenting research literature with many research studies documenting the importance of parents in children's development. For example, many studies reveal that when parents abuse their children, the children have problems in regulating their emotions, becoming securely attached to others, developing competent peer relations, and adapting to school. They also develop anxiety and depression disorders (Cicchetti & Toth, 1998; Rogosch & others, 1995). Child development expert T. Berry Brazelton (1998) commented, "*The Nurture Assumption* is so disturbing it devalues what parents are trying to do. . . . Parents might say, 'If I don't matter, why should I bother?' That's terrifying and it's coming when children need a stronger home base."

Parenting and Genes

The Mother's and Father's Roles   What do you think of when you hear the word *motherhood*? If you are like most people, you associate motherhood with a

EXPLORATIONS IN PSYCHOLOGY
Child Care in the United States

AS INCREASING NUMBERS of women enter and remain in the workforce after pregnancy, and more of them are single parents, more families are relying on nonmaternal care for their infants and young children (Appelbaum & others, 1999; NICHD Early Child Care Research Network, 1997, in press; Peth-Pierce, 1998). In 1975, less than 40 percent of mothers with children under age 6 worked outside the home. Today, almost two-thirds do. Most mothers return to work in their child's first 3 to 5 months of life, so their children spend much of their early lives in a variety of child-care arrangements.

Some child development experts argue that child care, especially as it is constituted in the United States, poses risks for infants because healthy development requires caregiving by a single person. Yet others say that children can thrive in child care of high quality and that they are harmed only when the quality is poor.

Aware of the growing use of child care, the National Institute of Child Health and Human Development (NICHD) set out to develop a comprehensive, longitudinal study (a study that follows the same individuals over time, usually several years or more) that focuses on the child-care experiences of children and their development. The study began in 1991, and data were collected on a diverse sample of almost 1,400 children and their families at ten locations across the United States. Researchers are assessing children over 7 years of their lives, using multiple methods (trained observers, interviews, questionnaires, and testing) and measuring many facets of children's development (physical health, cognitive development, and socioemotional development).

Following are some of the results of this extensive study to date:

- Infants from low-income families were more likely to receive low-quality child care than were their higher-income counterparts. Quality of care was based on such characteristics as group size, child-adult ratio, physical environment, caregiver characteristics (such as formal education, specialized training, and child-care experience), and caregiver behavior (such as sensitivity to children).

- Child care in and of itself neither adversely affected nor promoted the security of infants' attachments to their mothers. Certain child-care conditions, in combinations with certain home environments, did increase the probability that infants would be insecurely attached to their mothers. Infants who received either poor-quality care or more than ten hours per week of care, or were in more than one setting in the first 15 months of life, were more likely to be insecurely attached, but only if their mothers were less sensitive in responding to them.

- Child-care quality, especially sensitive and responsive attention from caregivers, was linked with fewer child problems. The higher the quality of child care (more positive language stimulation and interaction between the child and the provider) over the first three years of life, the greater the child's language and cognitive abilities. No cognitive benefits were found for children in the exclusive care of their mother.

number of positive images, such as warmth, selflessness, dutifulness, and tolerance (Matlin, 1993). And while most women expect that motherhood will be happy and fulfilling, the reality is that motherhood has been accorded relatively low prestige in our society (Hoffnung, 1984). When stacked up against money, power, and achievement, motherhood unfortunately doesn't fare too well, and mothers rarely receive the appreciation they warrant. When children don't succeed or they develop problems, our society has had a tendency to attribute the lack of success or the development of problems to a single source—mothers. One of psychology's most important lessons is that behavior is multiply determined. So it is with children's development—when development goes awry, mothers are not the single cause of the problems, even though our society stereotypes them in this way.

A special concern of many contemporary mothers is whether working full-time in a career will harm their children's development. There is no evidence that this is the case (Parke & Buriel, 1998). Nonetheless, when working mothers place their children in child care (nonmaternal care), they worry about whether it will harm their children. This is a legitimate concern because much child care in the United States is of poor quality. To read further about child care, see Explorations in Psychology.

Children's socioemotional development can significantly benefit from interaction with a caring, accessible, and dependable father who fosters a sense of trust and confidence (Lamb, 1998; Snarey, 1998). The father's positive family involvement assumes special importance in developing children's social competence, because he is often the only male the child encounters on a regular day-to-day basis.

Father-mother cooperation and mutual respect help the child develop positive attitudes toward both males and females (Biller, 1993). It is much easier for working parents to cope with changing family circumstances and day-care issues when the father and mother equitably share child-rearing responsibilities. Mothers feel less stress and have more positive attitudes toward their husbands when they are supportive partners.

At this point we have discussed many ideas about children's cognitive and socioemotional development. An overview of these ideas is presented in summary table 8.2. Next, we continue our journey through the human life span by focusing on adolescence.

Fathers and Children

Adolescence

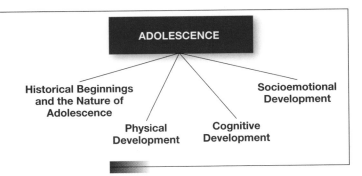

Twentieth-century poet-essayist Roger Allen once remarked, "In case you are worried about what's going to become of the younger generation, it's going to grow up and start worrying about the younger generation." Virtually every society has worried about its younger generation, but it was not until the beginning of the twentieth century that the scientific study of adolescence began.

Historical Beginnings and the Nature of Adolescence

In 1904, psychologist G. Stanley Hall wrote the first scientific book on adolescence. Hall referred to the adolescent years as a time of "storm and stress." **The storm-and-stress view** *is Hall's concept that adolescence is a turbulent time charged with conflict and mood swings.* Thoughts, feelings, and actions oscillate between conceit and humility, good and temptation, happiness and sadness. The adolescent may be nasty to a peer one moment and kind the next moment. At one time the adolescent may want to be alone, yet seconds later seek companionship.

Too often adolescents have been stereotyped as abnormal and deviant. In addition to Hall, Freud described adolescents as sexually driven and conflicted. Young people of every generation have seemed radical, unnerving, and different to adults—different in how they look, how they behave, and the music they enjoy. But it is an enormous error to confuse the adolescent's enthusiasm for trying on new identities and enjoying moderate amounts of outrageous behavior with hostility toward parents and society. Acting out and boundary testing are time-honored ways in which adolescents move toward accepting, rather than rejecting, parental and societal values.

It does little good, and can do considerable disservice, to think of adolescence as a time of rebellion, crisis, pathology, and deviation. It's far more accurate to view adolescence as a time of evaluation, a time of decision making, a time of commitment as young people carve out their place in the world (Santrock, 1998). How competent they will become often depends on their access to a range of legitimate opportunities and long-term support from adults who deeply care about them.

Our discussion underscores an important point about adolescents: They do not make up a homogeneous group (Hauser, 1999). The majority of adolescents negotiate the lengthy path to adult maturity successfully, but too large a group does not. Ethnic, cultural, gender, socioeconomic, age, and lifestyle differences influence the

Healthy Adolescents

SUMMARY TABLE 8.2
Children's Physical, Cognitive, and Socioemotional Development

Concept	Processes/ Related Ideas	Characteristics/Description
Physical Development	Infancy	The newborn comes into the world with some genetically equipped reflexes. The infant's physical development in the first two years is extensive. Neuronal interconnections increase dramatically in the first two years.
	Childhood	Children gain more self-control over their body in early childhood. The child's brain development continues and is reflected in improved motor skills. In middle and late childhood, motor development is smoother and more coordinated.
Cognitive Development	Piaget's Theory	Piaget changed forever the way we think about children's minds. Piaget argued that children actively construct an understanding of the world. Children use schemas to understand their world. Two processes are responsible for how people use and adapt their schemas: assimilation and accommodation. Piaget also believed that we go through four stages in understanding the world: sensorimotor stage (0–2 years; involves coordinating sensory experiences with physical motoric actions, is nonsymbolic through most of its duration, and object permanence is an important accomplishment); preoperational stage (2–7 years; is more symbolic than sensorimotor thought, does not involve operational thought, is egocentric, and is intuitive rather than logical); concrete operational (7–11 years; involves using operations, logical thought replaces intuitive thought but only in concrete situations, abstract thinking is absent, and classification skills are present); formal operational thought (entered at 11–15 years, extends through adult years; thinking is more abstract, idealistic, and logical).
	Evaluating Piaget	Piaget is one of developmental psychology's giants. He gave us the model of the child as an active, constructivist thinker and a masterful list of concepts. Like all major theories, his has been criticized. Information-processing psychologists think he placed too much emphasis on grand stages; Vygotsky said he underplayed culture.
Socioemotional Development	Erikson's Theory	Erikson's theory is a psychosocial theory, while Freud's theory is a psychosexual theory. Erikson said development is lifelong, Freud thought the key changes took place in the first 5 years of life. Erikson theorized that people go through eight stages: trust vs. mistrust (1st year), autonomy vs. shame and doubt (1–3 years), initiative vs. guilt (3–5 years), industry vs. inferiority (6–puberty), identity vs. identity confusion (adolescence), intimacy vs. isolation (early adulthood), generativity vs. stagnation (middle adulthood), and integrity vs. despair (late adulthood). Erikson's stages represent developmental tasks that are turning points in people's lives.
	Evaluating Erikson's Theory	Like Piaget, Erikson is one of developmental psychology's giants. His emphasis on lifelong developmental changes was a major contribution. His theory has been criticized for not having a research base to support the grand scheme of eight stages.
	Attachment	Attachment is the close emotional bond between an infant and a caregiver. Harlow demonstrated the importance of contact comfort in attachment, Lorenz the importance of familiarity in attachment through his work on imprinting. Bowlby and Ainsworth believe that attachment in the first year is necessary for optimal development. Ainsworth described secure attachment as having the caregiver as a secure base from which to explore the environment. Critics of secure attachment say that biological factors such as temperament and the wider social world are not given enough attention.
	Temperament	Temperament is a person's behavioral style and characteristic ways of responding. Chess and Thomas proposed that there are three basic temperament styles: easy, difficult, and slow to warm up, although other classifications have been made. It is important for parents to be sensitive to the child's individuality, and temperament is an aspect of that individuality.
	Parenting	Baumrind described four parenting styles: authoritarian, authoritative, neglectful, and indulgent, with authoritative parenting (a combination of warmth, verbal give-and-take, and some limit setting) as optimal. Understanding parenting also involves understanding reciprocal socialization, the mother's role, and the father's role.

actual life trajectory of every adolescent (Alsaker & Flammer, 1999). Different portrayals of adolescents emerge, depending on the particular group of adolescents being described (Brooks-Gunn, 1996). Later in our discussion of adolescence we will discuss at-risk youth, but first we need to explore some basic ideas about adolescents' physical, cognitive, and socioemotional development.

Physical Development

Imagine a toddler displaying all the features of puberty—a 3-year-old girl with fully developed breasts or a boy just slightly older with a deep male voice. We would see this by the year 2250 if the age of puberty were to continue to decrease at its present pace. Menarche (the first menstruation) has declined from 14.2 years in 1900 to about 12.45 years today. Age of menarche has been declining an average of about 4 months a decade for the last century. We are unlikely, though, to see pubescent toddlers in the future because what happened in the last century is special. That something special is a higher level of nutrition and health. A lower age of menarche is associated with higher standards of living (Petersen, 1979).

Menarche is one event that characterizes puberty, but there are others as well. **Puberty** *is a period of rapid skeletal and sexual maturation that occurs mainly in early adolescence.* However, it is not a single, sudden event. We know when a young person is going through puberty, but pinpointing its beginning and its end is difficult. Except for menarche, which occurs rather late in puberty, no single marker heralds puberty. For boys, the first whisker or first wet dream could mark its appearance, but both may go unnoticed.

Hormonal changes characterize pubertal development. Hormones are powerful chemical substances secreted by the endocrine glands and carried through the body in the bloodstream. The concentrations of certain hormones increase dramatically during puberty (Dorn & Chrousos, 1996; Petersen, 2000). **Testosterone** *is a hormone associated in boys with the development of genitals, an increase in height, and a change in voice.* **Estradiol** *is a hormone associated in girls with breast, uterine, and skeletal development.* In one study, testosterone levels doubled in girls but increased eighteen-fold in boys during puberty; similarly, estradiol doubled in boys but increased eightfold in girls (Nottelmann & others, 1987). These hormonal and body changes occur on the average about two years earlier in females (10½ years) than in males (12½ years) (see figure 8.14).

Adolescence is not best viewed as a time of crisis, rebellion, pathology, and deviation. Rather, a more accurate portrait is that adolescence is a time of evaluation, decision making, and commitment as youth seek to find out who they are and carve out a place for themselves in the world.

Biological Changes in Adolescence

Cognitive Development

As we noted earlier, cognitive development continues after the childhood years. Adolescents undergo some significant cognitive changes. We will briefly recap Piaget's view of adolescent cognitive development, then discuss adolescent egocentrism.

Piaget's Formal Operational Stage
Piaget said that adolescents enter a new stage of cognitive development from about 11 to 15 years of age, which he called the formal operational stage. Recall that Piaget believes that this stage is characterized by thought that is abstract, idealistic, and logical.

In actuality, not all adolescents are formal operational thinkers, at least not in terms of the logical thinking Piaget called *hypothetical-deductive reasoning*. For example, some adolescents still think at Piaget's concrete operational stage.

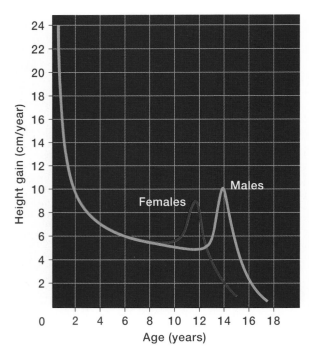

Figure 8.14
Pubertal Growth Spurt

On the average, the growth spurt that characterizes pubertal change occurs 2 years earlier for girls (age 10½) than for boys (age 12½).

Lawrence Kohlberg, a pioneer in constructing a cognitive developmental theory of how people morally reason.

Adolescent Egocentrism   Adolescent thought, especially in early adolescence, is also egocentric. **Adolescent egocentrism** *involves the belief that others are as preoccupied with the adolescent as she herself is, the belief that one is unique, and the belief that one is indestructible* (Elkind, 1978). Attention-getting behavior, so common in adolescence, reflects egocentrism and the desire to be onstage, noticed, and visible. Imagine the eighth-grade boy who feels as if all eyes are riveted on his tiny facial blemish. Imagine also the sense of uniqueness felt by the following adolescent girl: "My mother has no idea about how much pain I'm going through. She has never been hurt like I have. Why did Bob break up with me?" And imagine the sense of indestructibility of two adolescent males drag racing down a city street. This sense of indestructibility may lead to drug use and suicide attempts.

Moral Development   Another aspect of cognitive development that changes during adolescence is reasoning about moral issues.

Kohlberg's Theory   Lawrence Kohlberg (1986) created eleven stories and asked children, adolescents, and adults some questions about the stories. One of the stories goes like this:

> In Europe a woman was near death from a special kind of cancer. There was one drug that the doctors thought might save her. It was a form of radium that a druggist in the same town had recently discovered. The drug was expensive to make, but the druggist was charging ten times what the drug cost him to make. He paid $200 for the radium and charged $2,000 for a small dose of the drug. The sick woman's husband, Heinz, went to everyone he knew to borrow the money, but he could get together only $1,000. He told the druggist that his wife was dying and asked him to sell it cheaper or let him pay later. But the druggist said, "No. I discovered the drug, and I am going to make money from it." Desperate, Heinz broke into the man's store to steal the drug for his wife. (Kohlberg, 1969)

After reading the story, the interviewee answers a series of questions about the moral dilemma. Should Heinz have done that? Was it right or wrong? Why? Is it a husband's duty to steal the drug for his wife if he can get it in no other way? Would a good husband do it? Did the druggist have the right to charge that much when there was no law actually setting a limit on the price? Why?

Based on the answers people gave to questions about this and other moral dilemmas, Kohlberg proposed that individuals go through three levels of moral development, each characterized by two stages (see figure 8.15). A key concept in understanding moral development, especially Kohlberg's theory, is **internalization,** *the developmental change from behavior that is externally controlled to behavior that is controlled by internal, self-generated standards and principles.*

The **preconventional level** *is Kohlberg's lowest level of moral thinking, in which the individual shows no internalization of moral values.* Moral thinking is based on punishments (stage 1) or rewards (stage 2) that come from the external world. In regard to the Heinz and the druggist story, at stage 1 an individual might say that Heinz should not steal the drug because he might get caught and sent to jail. At stage 2, the person might say he should not steal the drug because the druggist needs to make a profit on the drug.

The **conventional level** *is Kohlberg's second level of moral thinking, in which the individual has an intermediate level of internalization.* The individual abides by certain standards (internal), such as parents (stage 3) or society's laws (stage 4). At stage 3, an individual might say that Heinz should steal the drug for his wife because that is what society expects a good husband would do. At stage 4, the person might say that it is natural for Heinz to want to save his wife but that it still is always wrong to steal.

LEVEL 3
Postconventional Level
Full Internalization

Stage 5
Community Rights Versus Individual Rights

The person understands that values and laws are relative and that standards can vary from one person to another. The person recognizes that laws are important for society but knows that laws can be changed. The person believes that some values, such as freedom, are more important than the law.

Stage 6
Universal Ethical Principles

The person has developed moral judgments that are based on universal human rights. When faced with a dilemma between law and conscience, a personal, individualized conscience is followed.

LEVEL 2
Conventional Level
Intermediate Internalization

Stage 3
Interpersonal Norms

The person values trust, caring, and loyalty to others as the basis of moral judgments. Children often adopt their parents' moral standards at this stage, seeking to be thought of as a "good girl" or "good boy."

Stage 4
Social System Morality

Moral judgments are based on understanding and the social order, law, justice, and duty.

LEVEL 1
Preconventional Level
No Internalization

Stage 1
Punishment and Obedience Orientation

Children obey because adults tell them to obey. People base their moral decisions on fear of punishment.

Stage 2
Individualism and Purpose

Moral thinking is based on rewards and self-interest. Children obey when it is in their best interest to obey. What is right is what feels good and what is rewarding.

*F*igure 8.15
Kohlberg's Three Levels and Six Stages of Moral Development

The **postconventional level** *is Kohlberg's highest level of moral thinking. Moral development is completely internalized and not based on others' standards.* The individual recognizes alternative moral courses, explores the options, and then develops a personal moral code. The code is among the principles generally accepted by the community (stage 5) or it is more individualized (stage 6). At stage 5, a person might say that the law was not set up for these circumstances, so Heinz can steal the drug. It is not really right, but he is justified in doing it. At stage 6, the individual evaluates alternatives, but recognizes that Heinz's wife's life is more important than a law.

Kohlberg believed these levels and stages occur in a sequence and are age-related. Some evidence for the sequence of Kohlberg's stages has been found, although few people reach stage 6 (Colby & others, 1983). Children are often in stages 1 and 2, although in the later elementary school years they may be in stage 3. Most adolescents are at stages 3 or 4.

Kohlberg believed that advances in moral development take place because of the maturation of thought (especially Piaget's stages), opportunities for role-taking, and

Kohlberg's Theory

Carol Gilligan with some of the students she has interviewed about the importance of relationships in a female's development. According to Gilligan (center), the sense of relationships and connectedness is at the heart of a female's development.

Gilligan's Care Perspective

discussing moral issues with a person who reasons at a stage just above your own. In Kohlberg's view, parents contribute little to children's moral thinking because parent-child relationships are often too power-oriented.

Evaluating Kohlberg's Theory   Kohlberg's ideas stimulated considerable interest in the field of moral development. His provocative view continues to stimulate considerable research about how people think about moral issues (Narvaez & others, 1999; Thoma & Rest, 1999).

Kohlberg's theory also has its share of critics. One criticism is that moral reasons can always be a shelter for immoral behavior. When bank embezzlers and presidents are asked about their moral reasoning, what they say might be at Kohlberg's advanced stages, but their actual behavior might be filled with cheating, lying, and stealing. The cheaters, liars, and thieves might know what is right and what is wrong, but still *do* what is wrong.

A second major criticism of Kohlberg's view is that it does not adequately reflect relationships and concerns for others. The **justice perspective** *is a theory of moral development that focuses on the rights of the individual; individuals stand alone and independently make moral decisions. Kohlberg's theory is a justice perspective.* By contrast, the **care perspective** *is Carol Gilligan's (1982) theory of moral development that sees people in terms of their connectedness with others and focuses on interpersonal communication, relationships with others, and concern for others.* According to Gilligan, Kohlberg greatly underplayed the care perspective in moral development. She believes this may have happened because he was a male, most of his research was with males rather than females, and he used male responses as a model for his theory.

Gilligan (1996, 1998) also believes that girls reach a critical juncture in their development when they reach adolescence. Gilligan says that at the edge of adolescence, at about 11 or 12 years of age, girls become aware that their intense interest in intimacy is not prized by the male-dominated culture, even though society values females as caring and altruistic. The dilemma, says Gilligan, is that girls are presented with a choice that makes them appear either selfish (if they become independent and self-sufficient) or selfless (if they remain responsive to others). Gilligan states that as young adolescent girls experience this dilemma, they increasingly "silence" their distinctive voice. They become less confident and more tentative in offering their opinions, which often persists into adulthood. Some researchers believe this self-doubt and ambivalence too often translate into depression and eating disorders among adolescent girls.

Socioemotional Development

Who are you and where are you headed in life? This is a central question in identity and the adolescent's socioemotional development. It also is a question that continues to be important in the college years and throughout adult development as well.

Identity Development   Recall from our earlier discussion that identity versus identity confusion is the fifth stage in Erikson's eight-stage life-span theory, occurring during the adolescent years. During adolescence, individuals enter what Erikson calls a "psychological moratorium"—a gap between the security of childhood and the autonomy of adulthood. In their search for identity, adolescents experiment with different roles. Those who successfully explore a number of alternatives emerge with a new sense of self that is both refreshing and acceptable; those who do not successfully resolve the identity crisis are confused, suffering what Erikson calls identity confusion. This confusion takes one of two courses: Individuals withdraw, isolating themselves from peers and family, or they lose themselves in the crowd. Adolescents want to decide freely for themselves such matters as what careers they will pursue, whether they will go to college, and whether they will marry. In other words, they want to free themselves from the shackles of their parents and other adults and make their own choices. At the same time, many adolescents have a deep fear of making the wrong decision and of failing. But as adolescents pursue their identity and their thoughts become more abstract and logical, they reason in more sophisticated ways. They are better able to judge what is morally right and wrong and become capable decision makers.

Identity is a self-portrait composed of many pieces, including these:

- The career and work path a person wants to follow (vocational/career identity)
- Whether a person is conservative, liberal, or a middle-of-the-roader (political identity)
- A person's spiritual beliefs (religious identity)
- Whether a person is single, married, divorced, and so on (relationship identity)
- The extent to which the person is motivated to achieve and is intellectual (achievement, intellectual identity)
- Whether a person is heterosexual, homosexual, or bisexual (sexual identity)
- Which part of the world or country a person is from and how intensely the person identifies with his/her cultural heritage (cultural/ethnic identity)
- The kinds of things a person likes to do, which can include sports, music, hobbies, and so on (interest)
- The individual's personality characteristics (such as being introverted or extraverted, anxious or calm, friendly or hostile, and so on) (personality)
- The individual's body image (physical identity)

Is an identity something that is cast in stone once you achieve it? No, people's lives can change and so can their identities. College plays an important role in many people's identity development because it is a setting where exploration and different views are encouraged (Santrock & Halonen, 1999).

At-Risk Youth
Adolescence is best viewed as a time of decision making and commitment rather than a time of crisis and pathology. However, a large subset of adolescents are at risk because their likelihood of becoming productive adults is limited. Four areas of special concern regarding a large portion of at-risk youth are delinquency, substance abuse, unprotected sex and adolescent pregnancy, and school-related problems (Dryfoos, 1990). Estimates are that as many as 25 percent of youth have three or more of these problems.

In an analysis of successful programs focused on at-risk youth, Joy Dryfoos (1990) found that two approaches had the widest application: providing individual attention to at-risk children and adolescents, and developing broad community-wide interventions. In successful programs, at-risk youth are attached to a responsible adult who pays attention to the adolescent's specific needs. For example, in substance abuse programs, a student assistance counselor might be available full-time for individual counseling. In delinquency prevention, a family worker might give "intensive" support to a predelinquent and the family so they will make the necessary changes to avoid repeated delinquent acts.

"Do you have any idea who I am?"

© The New Yorker Collection 1988 *Edward Koren from cartoonbank.com. All Rights Reserved.*

Identity Development

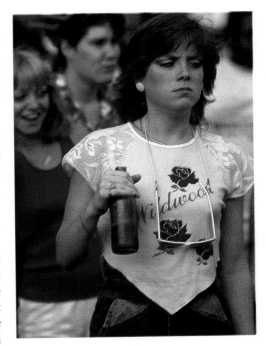

What characterizes the most successful programs for intervening in adolescents' problems?

SUMMARY TABLE 8.3
Adolescence

Concept	Processes/ Related Ideas	Characteristics/Description
Historical Beginnings and the Nature of Adolescence	Historical Beginnings	G. Stanley Hall is the father of the scientific study of adolescence. In the early 1900s, he proposed the storm-and-stress view.
	Nature of Adolescence	Adolescence is a transition between childhood and adulthood that is best viewed as a time of evaluation, decision making, and commitment rather than as a time of rebellion, crisis, and pathology. Different portrayals of adolescence emerge, depending on the particular group of adolescents being described.
Physical Development	Its Nature	Puberty is a rapid change to maturation occurring mainly in early adolescence. Puberty has been occurring earlier in recent years. Puberty occurs roughly 2 years earlier for girls (10½) than for boys (12½).
Cognitive Development	Revisiting Piaget	Piaget argued that formal operational thought appears at 11 to 15 years of age. At this point, thought becomes more abstract, idealistic, and logical. However, not all adolescents are formal operational thinkers.
	Adolescent Egocentrism	This involves the belief that others are as preoccupied with you as you yourself are. It also involves the belief that you are unique and indestructible.
	Moral Development	Kohlberg proposed three levels (each with two stages) of moral development, which vary in the degree to which moral behavior is internalized: preconventional, conventional, and post conventional. Critics of Kohlberg's theory argue that moral thoughts do not always predict moral action. Gilligan also stresses that the theory is a justice perspective. She promotes a care perspective of morality and argues that early adolescence is a critical juncture in the development of females.
Socioemotional Development	Identity Development	Identity versus identity confusion is Erikson's fifth stage, which occurs during adolescence. Adolescents are in a psychological moratorium between childhood dependency and adult independence. The college years are an important time for identity changes.
	At-Risk Youth	Four problems characterize at-risk youth more than any others: substance abuse, delinquency, unprotected sex and adolescent pregnancy, and school-related problems. Many at-risk youth have more than one of these problems. Two approaches have had the best success in intervening in adolescent programs: (1) individual attention and (2) community-wide collaboration.

Helping Adolescents

Treating Adolescent Problems

The basic concept of community-wide programs is that, to improve the lives of at-risk youth, a number of programs and services need to be in place (O'Donnell & others, 1999). For example, a substance abuse program might involve a community-wide health promotion that uses local media and community education in conjunction with a substance abuse prevention curriculum in the schools. A delinquency program might consist of a neighborhood development program that includes local residents in neighborhood councils who work with schools, police, courts, gang leaders, and the media.

At this point, we have discussed a number of ideas about adolescence. An overview of these ideas is presented in summary table 8.3. Next, we turn our attention to adult development and aging.

Adult Development and Aging

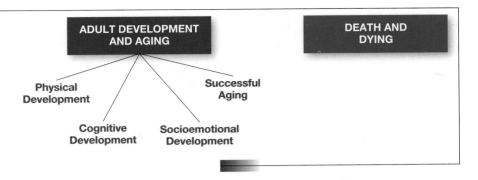

Just as physical, cognitive, and socioemotional changes take place in the child and adolescent years, so too do they occur in the adult years. We will examine changes in the early, middle, and late adulthood years. Use this discussion as a springboard for thinking about your own development as an adult as well as for understanding your aging parents and grandparents.

Physical Development

**Adult Development and Aging
Menopause**

Actress Bette Midler said that after 30 a body has a mind of its own. And comedian Bob Hope once remarked that middle age is when your age starts to show around your middle. How do we age physically as we go through the adult years?

Early and Middle Adulthood   Not only do we reach our peak performance during early adulthood, but we also are the healthiest then. Few young adults have chronic health problems. They have fewer colds and respiratory problems than they had as children. However, young adults rarely recognize that bad eating habits, heavy drinking, and smoking in early adulthood can impair their health as they age. Despite warnings on packages and in advertisements that cigarettes are hazardous to health, individuals actually increase their use of cigarettes as they enter early adulthood (Johnston, Bachman, & O'Malley, 1989). They also increase their use of alcohol, marijuana, amphetamines, barbiturates, and hallucinogens.

As we enter middle adulthood, we are more acutely concerned about our health status. We experience a general decline in physical fitness throughout middle adulthood and some deterioration in health. The three greatest health concerns at this age are heart disease, cancer, and weight. Cancer related to smoking often surfaces for the first time in middle adulthood.

Because U.S. culture stresses a youthful appearance, physical deterioration—graying hair, wrinkling skin, and a sagging body—in middle adulthood is difficult to handle. Many middle-aged adults dye their hair and join weight reduction programs; some even undergo cosmetic surgery to look young. In one study, middle-aged women focused more attention on their facial attractiveness than did the older or younger women. Middle-aged women also perceived that the signs of aging had a more detrimental effect on their appearance (Novak, 1977).

For women, middle age also means that menopause will occur. **Menopause** *is the time in middle age, usually in the late forties or early fifties, when a woman's menstrual periods cease completely.* The average age at which women have their last period is 52. A small percentage of women—10 percent—undergo menopause before 40. There is a dramatic decline in the production of estrogen by the ovaries. Estrogen decline produces some uncomfortable symptoms in some menopausal women—"hot flashes," nausea, fatigue, and rapid heartbeat, for example. Some menopausal women report depression and irritability, but in some instances these feelings are related to other circumstances in the women's life, such as becoming divorced, losing a job, caring for a sick parent, and so on (Dickson, 1990).

Research investigations reveal that menopause does not produce psychological problems or physical problems for the majority of

What are some physical changes that women go through as they age?

Species (common name)	Maximum life span (years)
Human	120
Galápagos turtle	100+
Indian elephant	70
Chinese alligator	52
Golden eagle	46
Gorilla	39
Common toad	36
Domestic cat	27
Domestic dog	20
Vampire bat	13
House mouse	3

Figure 8.16
Maximum Recorded Life Spans of Various Species

Aging Research

women (McKinlay & McKinlay, 1984). Although menopause overall is not the negative experience for most women it was once thought to be, the loss of fertility is an important marker for women—it means that they have to make final decisions about having children. Women in their thirties who have never had children sometimes speak about being "up against the biological clock" because they cannot postpone much longer questions about having children.

Estrogen replacement therapy increasingly is recommended for women who are making the transition to menopause (Stefanick, 1999). The American Geriatrics Association's recent recommendations include these (Bidikov & Meier, 1997):

- All middle-aged women should consider estrogen replacement therapy because it can reduce the risk of osteoporosis (loss of bone tissue), coronary disease, and menopausal symptoms such as hot flashes and sweating. However, the risk of estrogen replacement therapy can outweigh its benefits for women who are at risk for breast cancer.
- Women should actively participate in decision-making about using estrogen replacement therapy.

Do men go through anything like the menopause that women experience? Men do experience sex-related hormone declines in their fifties and sixties but they are usually not as precipitous as women's estrogen decline (Lemme, 1999).

Late Adulthood and Aging   The rhythm and meaning of human development eventually wend their way to late adulthood. To begin, we will explore the distinction between life span and life expectancy.

Life Span and Life Expectancy   We are no longer a youthful society. The concept of a period called "late adulthood" is a recent one—until the twentieth century, most individuals died before they were 65.

Developmentalists distinguish between life span and life expectancy. **Life span** *is the upper boundary of a species' life, the maximum number of years an individual can live.* The maximum number years human beings can live is about 120 years. As can be seen in figure 8.16, *Homo sapiens* is believed to have one of the longest, if not the longest, life spans.

Life expectancy *is the number of years that will probably be lived by the average person born in a particular year.* Improvements in medicine, nutrition, exercise, and lifestyle have increased our life expectancy an average of 30 additional years since 1900! (see figure 8.17). The life expectancy of individuals born today in the United States is 77 years (80 for women, 73 for men). One in three women born today is expected to live to be 100 or more years of age. The world's population of individuals 65 years of age and older doubled from 1950 to 1990, and the fastest growing segment of the population is the 85 years and over group. Thus, life expectancy has increased dramatically, but life span does not seem to have increased since the beginning of recorded history.

Time Period	Average Life Expectancy (in years)
Prehistoric times	18
Ancient Greece	20
Middle Ages, England	33
1620, Massachusetts Bay Colony	35
19th century, England	41
1900, USA	47
1915, USA	54
1954, USA	70
1998, USA	77

Figure 8.17
Human Life Expectancy at Birth from Prehistoric to Contemporary Times

Biological Theories of Aging   Even if we are remarkably healthy through our adult lives, we begin to age at some point. What are some of the biological explanations of aging?

There are many of these theories, but two that especially merit attention are the cellular clock theory and the free-radical theory. Both of these theories look within the body's cells in an effort to unlock the mysteries of aging. The **cellular clock theory** *is Leonard Hayflick's (1977) view that cells can divide a maximum number of about 100 times, and that as we age, our cells become increasingly less capable of dividing.* Hayflick found that cells extracted from older adults, in their fifties to seventies, divided fewer than 100 times. Based on the way cells divide, Hayflick places the upper limit of the human life span at about 120 years. Thus, we rarely age to the end of our life span potential.

More recently in the 1990s, scientists have added an extension to the cellular clock theory. Hayflick didn't know why cells die. The answer may lie at the tip of chromosomes. Telomeres are DNA sequences that cap chromosomes, protecting them. Each time a cell divides, the telomeres of the daughter cells become shorter and shorter. After about 100 replications, the telomeres are dramatically reduced and the cell no longer can reproduce.

A second biological theory of aging is **free-radical theory,** *which states that people age because inside their cells unstable oxygen molecules known as free radicals are produced. These molecules ricochet around in the cells, damaging DNA and other cellular structures.* As the free radicals bounce around inside of cells, their damage can lead to a range of disorders, including cancer and arthritis.

A number of other biological theories of aging have been proposed. Theorized causes of aging range from a decline in the immune system's functioning to deficiencies in hormones (Whitbourne, 2000).

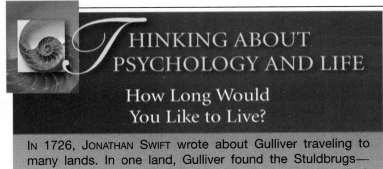

THINKING ABOUT PSYCHOLOGY AND LIFE

How Long Would You Like to Live?

IN 1726, JONATHAN SWIFT wrote about Gulliver traveling to many lands. In one land, Gulliver found the Stuldbrugs—people who were immortal. Even though they never died, they continued to age, becoming blind, crippled, immobile, in constant pain, and begging for their death. Gulliver's world was a world of science fiction, but it raises interesting issues about how long we would like to live and what we want our lives to be like when we become old. How long would you like to live? Why? Describe the oldest person you know. What is he or she like?

Alzheimer's disease   **Alzheimer's disease** *is a progressive, irreversible brain disorder that is characterized by gradual deterioration of memory, reasoning, language, and eventually physical functioning.* Approximately 2.5 million people over the age of 65 have this disease. One deficiency in the brains of individuals with Alzheimer's is in the important neurotransmitter acetylcholine (which we discussed in chapter 2, "Biological Foundations and Neuroscience") ◀|||| P. 54. Acetylcholine is involved in memory. Tacrine (its trade name is Cognex) is the main drug used to treat Alzheimer's today and it works by blocking chemicals that ordinarily cut acetylcholine apart.

Tacrine preserves a diminishing supply of acetylcholine for a while, but it does not attack the root cause of acetylcholine deficiency. Scientists now believe that Alzheimer's disease is the result of a complex unraveling of neural structure and function that involves many different cellular dimensions (Davis, 1999). Some clues are beginning to emerge that may help researchers eventually solve the Alzheimer puzzle. One clue is the possible role of free radicals, the unstable oxygen molecules we just discussed. But something that occurs earlier likely causes the oxidative damage to the free radicals. One candidate is a protein called "amyloid-beta," which might do its damage by activating immune system cells. Another possibility is that mutations in various genes cause abnormalities in the protein.

As we just mentioned, individuals with Alzheimer's have deficits in memory and thinking. Next, we explore the developmental course of such cognitive processes in adulthood.

Cognitive Development

Think back to when you were an adolescent, maybe taking an algebra class or writing a paper. How have you changed cognitively since then?

Early and Middle Adulthood   Piaget did not believe that you have changed at all cognitively since you were a young adolescent. He does not even think that a Ph.D. in physics thinks any differently than a formal operational thinking young adolescent. Piaget recognized that the physicist has more knowledge in a specific domain—physics. However, Piaget said that the way the physicist thinks is the same as a formal operational thinking adolescent. The physicist and the young adolescent both use logical thought to develop alternatives for solving a problem, then they deduce the correct solution from the options.

Frenchwoman Jeanne Louise Calment pushed the upper boundary of the human life span, dying in 1997 at the age of 122. Greater ages have been claimed, but scientists say that the human life span is approximately 120 years of age. However, as genetic engineering continues to make progress, the possibility of altering cellular functioning to increase the human life span is raised. Some biologists even have brought up the possibility that in the future humans might live to be 400 years of age! What kinds of ethical issues are involved in genetically engineering cellular functioning to increase the human life span?

(Left) Former president Ronald Reagan was diagnosed with Alzheimer's at the age of 83.
(Right) Actress Rita Hayworth died of Alzheimer's at age 68—her struggle focused attention on the disease.

Alzheimer's Disease

Was Piaget right? He was right for some adolescents and some adults, but not for all. As we saw earlier, some adolescents are not formal operational thinkers and many adults never become formal operational thinkers.

Other psychologists believe that the absolute nature of adolescent logic and youth's buoyant optimism diminish in early adulthood (Labouvie-Vief, 1986). They argue that competent young adults are less caught up in idealism and tend to think logically and to adapt to life as circumstances demand. Less clear is whether our mental skills, especially memory, actually decline with age.

Putting together the pieces of the research puzzle, memory appears to decline more often when long-term rather than short-term memory is involved. For example, middle-aged individuals can remember a phone number they heard 30 seconds ago, but they probably won't remember the number as efficiently the next day. Memory is also more likely to decline when organization and imagery are not used. In addition, memory tends to decline when the information to be recalled is recently acquired or when the information is not used often. For example, middle-aged adults probably won't remember the rules to a new game after only a lesson or two, and they are unlikely to know the new fall television schedule after its first week. And finally, memory tends to decline if recall rather than recognition is required. Middle-aged individuals can more efficiently select a phone number they heard yesterday if they are shown a list of phone numbers (recognition) rather than having to simply recall the number off the tops of their heads. Memory in middle adulthood also declines if the individual's health is poor (Rybash, Roodin, & Hoyer, 1999).

Late Adulthood and Aging
At age 70, John Rock introduced the birth control pill. And at age 76, Anna Mary Roberston, better known as Grandma Moses, took up painting and became internationally famous. And when Pablo Casals reached 95 years of age, a reporter called him the greatest cellist who ever lived but wondered why he still practiced 6 hours a day. Casals replied, "Because I feel like I am making progress."

The issue of intellectual decline through the adult years is a provocative one. David Wechsler (1972) whose intelligence scales you read about in chapter 7, concluded that intelligence peaks in early adulthood and then begins a continual decline until we die. But the issue of intellectual decline is more complex than Wechsler envisioned. Remember also from chapter 7 that many contemporary psychologists believe that intelligence comes in different forms ◀▥ P. 233. One of the most consistent findings is that when speed of processing information is involved, older adults do more poorly than their younger counterparts (Salthouse, 1994, 2000). They also tend to do more poorly on memory tasks than younger adults.

However, might there be some aspects of cognition that actually improve with age? One candidate is **wisdom** *which involves expert knowledge about the practical aspects of life.* Nonetheless, while wisdom may increase with age because of the buildup of life experiences we have, not every older person has wisdom (Baltes, Lindenberger, & Staudinger, 1998). Individual variations characterize all aspects of our cognitive life (Belsky, 1999).

Even for those aspects of cognitive aging that decline, such as memory, the possibility is raised that through education and training elderly adults can improve their cognitive skills (Luszcz & Bryan, 1999; Parke, Nisbett, & Hedden, 1999). Researchers have demonstrated that by using such memory strategies as organization and chunking, as well as mnemonics, older adults' memory can improve (Baltes, 1993; Willis & Schaie, 1994). However, while cognitive improvement is possible in older adults, many aging experts believe that older adults lose some of the plasticity they had earlier in development.

Older adults might not be as quick with their thoughts as younger adults, but wisdom may be an entirely different matter. This elderly woman shares the wisdom of her experiences with a classroom of children.

Socioemotional Development

As both Sigmund Freud and the nineteenth-century Russian novelist Leo Tolstoy observed, adulthood's two most important themes are work and love. As we discuss socioemotional development in the adult years, you will see that indeed work and love are two of adulthood's most important domains.

Exploring Aging Issues

Early and Middle Adulthood   Careers, work, and lifestyles are among the themes of early and middle adulthood for many people.

Careers and Work   Earning a living, choosing an occupation, and developing a career are important themes for people in their twenties and thirties. A few people seem to have known what they wanted to be ever since they were a child. But for many of us, choosing an occupation involves exploring a number of options during college and even beyond.

It is a good idea to keep up with the occupational outlook of various fields. An excellent resource is *The Occupational Outlook Handbook,* which is revised every 2 years. According to the most recent edition of the handbook (1998–1999), service-producing industries will account for the most new jobs, with business, health, and education services projected to account for 70 percent of the job growth through 2005. Jobs that require the most education and training will be the fastest growing and highest paying.

What are the most important skills that today's job applicants need? In a national survey of companies that employ college graduates, communication skills, interpersonal skills, and teamwork skills were at the top of the list (Collins, 1996) (see figure 8.18). All of these skills focus on communicating effectively.

Career interests continue to be an important dimension of life for many middle-aged adults. Midlife is a time when many people examine their career, evaluate what they have accomplished, and look to the future and see that they have a limited amount of time to accomplish what they want. However, many people reach the highest satisfaction in their careers during middle age and only about 10 percent of Americans change careers at midlife. A recent concern of some middle-aged adults is the downsizing and early retirement programs of many companies.

Lifestyles   Should I get married? If I wait any longer, will it be too late? Will I get left out? Should I stay single or is it too lonely a life? If I get married, do I want to have children? How will it affect my marriage? These are questions that many young adults ask themselves as they try to figure out what they want their life to be about.

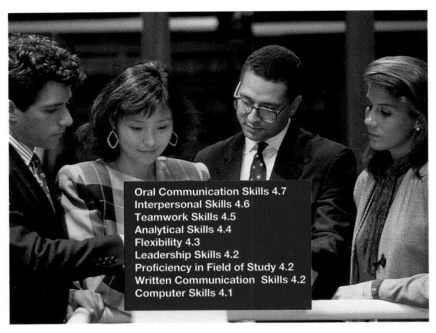

*F*igure 8.18
The Skills That Employers Want a Job Candidate to Have

In a national survey of employers, the skills that employers want a job candidate to have were rated on a scale of 1 (extremely unimportant) to 5 (extremely important) (Collins, 1996). Notice how important communication skills—oral, interpersonal, teamwork—are to today's employers.

Until about 1930, the goal of a stable marriage was accepted as a legitimate endpoint of adult development. In the last 60 years, however, we have seen the emergence of the desire for personal fulfillment—both inside and outside a marriage—as a force that can compete with marriage's stability. The changing norm of male-female equality in marriage has produced relationships that are more fragile and intense than they were earlier in the twentieth century. More adults are remaining single longer in the 1990s, and the average duration of a marriage in the United States currently is just over 9 years. The divorce rate, which increased astronomically in the 1970s, has finally begun to slow down, although it still remains alarmingly high. Even with adults remaining single for longer and divorce a frequent occurrence, Americans still show a strong preference for marriage—the proportion of women who never marry has remained at about 7 percent throughout the twentieth century, for example (Hernandez, 1988).

We often have idealistic expectations of marriage, which helps to explain our nation's high divorce rate and dissatisfaction in marriage (Notarius, 1996). We expect our spouse to simultaneously be a lover, a friend, a confidant, a counselor, a career person, and a parent. Many myths about marriage contribute to these unrealistic expectations.

Many myths also are associated with being single, ranging from "the swinging single" to "the desperately lonely, suicidal single." Most singles are somewhere between these two extremes. The pluses of being single include time to make decisions about one's life, time to develop personal resources to meet goals, freedom to make autonomous decisions and pursue one's own schedule and interests, opportunities to explore new places and try out new things, and privacy. Common

"Your son has made a career choice, Mildred. He's going to win the lottery and travel a lot."

© 1985; Reprinted courtesy of Bunny Hoest.

problems of single adults include a lack of intimate relationships with others, loneliness, and finding a niche in a marriage-oriented society. Some single adults would rather remain single; others would rather be married.

Stage Theories of Adult Development   Psychologists have proposed different theories about adult development. Most theories address themes of work and love, career and intimacy. One set of theories proposes that adult development unfolds in stages ◀▦ P. 249.

Recall from our discussion of Erikson's theory earlier in the chapter that his eight stages of the human life span include one stage for early adulthood and one for middle adulthood. Erikson's early adulthood stage is intimacy versus isolation. Intimacy involves developing close, loving relationships, and isolation involves the lonely feelings of not having a positive relationship with a partner and/or friends.

Erikson's middle adulthood stage is generativity versus stagnation. At this point in development, Erikson believes, it is important to contribute something meaningful to the next generation (generativity). If they do not, people in middle adulthood are left with a feeling of stagnation.

In *The Seasons of a Man's Life,* Daniel Levinson (1978) also described adult development as a series of stages. He extensively interviewed middle-aged male hourly workers, academic biologists, business executives, and novelists and concluded that developmental tasks must be mastered at a number of different points in adulthood (see figure 8.19).

In early adulthood, the two major tasks are exploring the possibilities for adult living and developing a stable life structure. The twenties represent the novice phase of adult development. By the end of a boy's teens, a transition from dependence to independence should occur. This transition is marked by a dream—an image of the kind of life the young man wants, especially in terms of marriage and a career. The novice phase is a time of experimenting and testing the dream in the real world.

Men actually determine their goals by the age of 28 to 33. During the thirties, a man usually works to develop his family life and career. In the late thirties, he enters a phase of becoming his own man (or BOOM, becoming one's own man, as Levinson calls it). By age 40, he reaches a stable point in his career; outgrows his earlier, more tenuous status as an adult; and now looks forward to the kind of life he will lead as a middle-aged adult.

In Levinson's view, the change to middle adulthood lasts about 5 years and requires that adults come to grips with four major conflicts that have existed since adolescence: (1) being young versus being old; (2) being destructive versus being constructive; (3) being masculine versus being feminine; and (4) being attached to others versus being separated from them. The success of the midlife transition depends on how effectively they can reduce these polarities and accept each of them as a part of their being. Levinson's original subjects were all males, but more recently he reported that these midlife issues hold for females as well (Levinson, 1978).

Erikson and Levinson emphasize that we go through a number of stages of adult development. In evaluating these theories, keep in mind they are based mainly on clinical observations rather than highly controlled research studies. Also, the perspectives tend to describe the stages as crises, especially in the case of Levinson's emphasis on a midlife crisis. Research on middle-aged adults reveals that few adults experience midlife in the tumultuous way described by Levinson. Individuals vary extensively in how they cope with and perceive midlife (Vaillant, 1977). In a recent large-scale study of 3,032 Americans 25–74 years of age, a special focus was midlife development (Brim & others, 1999). The portrait of midlife was mainly positive, with only about 10 percent described as in a midlife crisis. Middle-aged individuals (40–65 years old) had lower anxiety levels and worried less than people under 40. The middle-aged individuals did

Era of late adulthood:
60–?

Late adult transition: Age 60–65

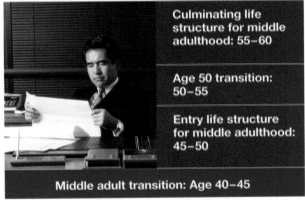

Culminating life structure for middle adulthood: 55–60

Age 50 transition: 50–55

Entry life structure for middle adulthood: 45–50

Middle adult transition: Age 40–45

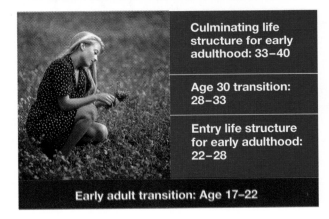

Culminating life structure for early adulthood: 33–40

Age 30 transition: 28–33

Entry life structure for early adulthood: 22–28

Early adult transition: Age 17–22

𝓕igure 8.19
Levinson's Periods of Adult Development

Middle Age Issues

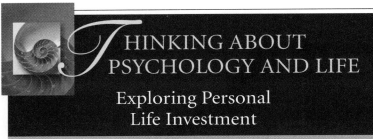

THINKING ABOUT PSYCHOLOGY AND LIFE

Exploring Personal Life Investment

TAKE A FEW MINUTES and evaluate yourself in terms of the domains of personal life investment described in figure 8.20. Rank-order the following from most important (1) to least important (7) in terms of your personal life investment—that is, how important they are in your life.

Domain	Ranking
work	_____
family	_____
friends	_____
independence	_____
cognitive fitness	_____
health	_____
thinking about life	_____

Now that you have thought about which of these domains is most important for you at your age, find at least one person from two age ranges other than your own in figure 8.20 and ask them to rank the domains in terms of their personal life investment. The age ranges are 25–34, 35–54, 55–65, 70–84, and 85–105. How do the other individuals' rankings of personal life investment compare with yours? Are your rankings and the rankings of the individuals of different ages the same as or different from those listed in figure 8.20? If you are a traditional-age college student (approximately 18–22), your age isn't represented in the adult life span study. Does your ranking of personal life investment match up with the 25- to 34-year-old age group? Regardless of your age, are there domains not listed above that are more important to you?

report more negative life events than people under 40, but they showed considerable resiliency and good coping skills in the face of the stressors. The midlife individuals generally had few illnesses, but had poor physical fitness.

Rather than emphasizing that most people go through a midlife *crisis*, what actually happens is that most people experience a midlife *consciousness* (Santrock, 1999). That is, during middle age people do become aware of the young–old polarity and the shrinking time left in their lives. They do think about their role in contributing to the next generation. They do contemplate the meaning of life. But for most people, midlife consciousness does not become tumultuous and take on crisis proportions.

Life Events, Cohort Effects, and Social Clocks
Life events rather than stages may be responsible for changes in our adult lives. Events such as marriage, divorce, the death of a spouse, a job promotion, and being fired from a job involve varying degrees of stress and influence our development as adults (Holmes & Rahe, 1967). However, we also need to know about the many factors that mediate the influence of life events on adult development—physical health, intelligence, personality, family support, and income, for example (Hultsch & Plemons, 1979). In addition, we need to know how a person perceives the life events and how he or she copes with the stress involved. For instance, one person may perceive a divorce as highly stressful, whereas another person may perceive the same life event as a challenge. We also need to consider the person's life stage and circumstances. Divorce may be more stressful for an individual in his fifties who has been married for many years, for example, than for someone in her twenties who has been married only a few years. Individuals may cope with divorce more effectively at the beginning of the twenty-first century than people did at the beginning of the twentieth century because divorce has become more commonplace and accepted in today's society.

An increasing number of developmental psychologists stress that changing social expectations influence how different **cohorts**—*groups of individuals born in the same year or time period*—move through the life cycle. For example, people born during the Depression may have a different outlook on life than those born during the optimistic 1950s.

Bernice Neugarten (1980) believes that the social environment of a particular age group can alter its "social clock"—the timetable according to which individuals are expected to accomplish life's tasks, such as getting married, having children, and establishing themselves in a career. Social clocks act as guides for our lives. People who are somehow "out of sync" with these social clocks find their lives more stressful than those who are on schedule, says Neugarten. One study found that between the late 1950s and the late 1970s there was a dramatic decline in adults' beliefs that there is a "right age" for major life events and achievements (Passuth, Maines, & Neugarten, 1984).

Late Adulthood and Aging   Although we are in the evening of our lives in late adulthood, we were not meant to live out our remaining years passively (Hilleras & others, 1999). **Activity theory** *states that the more active and involved older people are, the more satisfied they are and the more likely it is that they will stay healthy.* Researchers have found that older people who go to church, attend meetings, take trips, and exercise are happier than those who simply sit at home.

Social Aspects of Aging

Another aspect of understanding in late adulthood is life review. The nineteenth-century Danish philosopher Søren Kierkegaard said, "Life is lived forward, but understood backward." This is truer of late adulthood than of any other life-span period. Kierkegaard's words reflect Erikson's final stage of integrity versus despair, which is a time of looking back to evaluate what we have done with our lives. Recall from earlier in the chapter that the retrospective glances can be positive (integrity) or negative (despair).

Successful Aging

For too long, adult development and aging were looked at as processes of continual decline from early adulthood through the end of late adulthood (Baltes, 2000; Smith & Baltes, 1999). Though some decline is inevitable as we age, many experts on aging believe that it is important to conceptualize aging more in terms of "success" than "decline." The good news about aging is that with a proper diet, exercise, mental stimulation, good social relationships and support, and the absence of disease, many of our abilities decline very slowly (Antonucci, 2000). Leading an active rather than a passive life helps to slow aging. However, it is important to recognize that successful aging requires effort. Engaging in a regular exercise program requires effort for people of any age. So does practicing effective coping skills.

*F*igure 8.20
Degree of Personal Life Investment at Different Points in Life
Shown here are the top four domains of personal life investment at different points in life. The highest degree of investment is listed at the top (for example, work was the highest personal investment from 25 to 34 years of age, family from 35 to 84, and health from 85 to 105).

In thinking about successful aging through the adult years, an interesting question focuses on the personal life investments of people at different points in their lives. One recent study examined these personal life investments (Staudinger, 1996). As can be seen in figure 8.20, personal life investment varied somewhat, depending on the ages of the individuals. Work was most important for ages 25 to 34, then family became most important for ages 35 to 84. However, from age 85 to 105, health became the most important personal life investment. Clearly, successful aging for much of our adult life focuses on how effective we are at work, how loving our relationships are

(a)

(b)

Figure 8.21
Cultural Variations Regarding Death

(a) A New Orleans street funeral is in progress. (b) A deceased person's belongings are left on a mountainside in Tibet.

in our family, how good our friendships are, how healthy we are, and how cognitively fit we are.

Death and Dying

"I'd like to know what this show is all about before it's out," wrote the twentieth-century Dutch poet and inventor Piet Hein. Death may come at any time, but it is during late adulthood that we realize our days are literally numbered. Societies throughout history have had philosophical or religious beliefs about death (Petrinovich, 1996). And most have some form of ritual to mark the passing from life to death. Some cultures hold a ceremonial meal accompanied by festivities. In others, mourners wear a black armband. Figure 8.21 shows two rituals that reveal cultural variations in dealing with death.

In most cultures, death is not viewed as the end of existence—although the biological body dies, the spirit lives on. This belief is held by many Americans. Reincarnation, the belief that the soul is reborn in a new human body, is an important aspect of Hindu and Buddhist religions. Cultures often differ in their perception of death and their reaction to death. In the Gond culture of India, death is believed to be caused by magic and demons; Gonds react to death with anger. In the Tanala culture of Madagascar, death is thought to be caused by natural forces. The members of the Tanala culture peacefully react to death.

Elisabeth Kübler-Ross (1974) says that we go through five stages in facing death: denial and isolation, anger, bargaining, depression, and acceptance. Initially, the individual responds, "No, it can't be me. It's not possible." But denial is only a temporary defense. When the individual recognizes that denial no longer can be maintained, she often becomes angry and resentful. Now the individual's question becomes, "Why me?" Anger often is displaced onto physicians, nurses, family members, and even God. In the third stage, the dying person develops the hope that death can somehow be postponed or delayed. The individual now says, "Yes, me, but. . . ." The dying person bargains and negotiates, often with God, offering a reformed life dedicated to God and the service of others for a few more months of life.

As the dying individual comes to accept the certainty of her death, she often enters a period of preparatory grief, becoming silent, refusing visitors, and spending much of the time crying or grieving. This behavior is a normal effort to disconnect the self from all love objects. Kübler-Ross describes the final stage, characterized by peace and acceptance of one's fate, as the end of the struggle, the final resting stage before death.

Not everyone goes through the stages in the sequence Kübler-Ross proposed. Indeed, Kübler-Ross herself says she has been misread, pointing out that she never believed every individual copes with death in a specific sequence. But she does maintain that the optimal way to cope with death is through the stages she has outlined.

But some individuals struggle until the very end, angrily hanging onto their lives. They follow the encouragement of Dylan Thomas: "Do not go gentle into that good night. Old age should burn and rave at close of day . . . rage, rage against the dying of the light." In these instances, acceptance of death never comes. People die in different ways and experience different feelings and emotions in the process: hope, fear, curiosity, envy, apathy, relief, even anticipation. They often move rapidly from one mood to another and in some instances two moods may be present simultaneously.

Those left behind after the death of an intimate partner suffer profound grief and often endure financial loss, loneliness, increased physical illness, and increased psychological disorders including depression (DeSpelder & Strickland, 1999). But how they cope with the crisis varies considerably. Widows outnumber widowers by

Death and Dying

SUMMARY TABLE 8.4
Adult Development and Aging; Death and Dying

Concept	Processes/ Related Ideas	Characteristics/Description
Adult Development and Aging	Physical Development	The peak of our physical skills usually comes in early adulthood, when it becomes easy to develop bad health habits. In middle adulthood, most individuals experience a decline in physical skills, some deterioration in health, and an increased interest in health matters. Menopause is a midlife biological marker for women, but it does not produce physical or psychological problems for most women. Human life expectancy has increased dramatically, but the human life span has remained virtually unchanged for centuries. Two biological theories of aging that focus on cellular functioning are cellular clock theory and free-radical theory. Based on the rate at which cells divide, the upper limit of the human life span is about 120 years. Alzheimer's disease is a progressive, irreversible brain disorder. Today, scientists believe Alzheimer's involves a complex unraveling of neural structure and function.
	Cognitive Development	An ongoing issue is how much intellectual decline takes place as people age, and when the decline takes place. In evaluating this issue it is important to consider which aspect of intelligence is being examined. For example, speed of processing and memory do decline as aging progresses, but wisdom likely increases. Even when decline takes place, cognitive strategies can be used to reduce the decline. There is less plasticity in cognitive functioning among older than younger adults, but there is some plasticity.
	Socioemotional Development	Careers and work are important dimensions of early adulthood. Adults must choose the type of lifestyle they want to follow—single, married, or divorced, for example. One set of adult personality theories proposes that adult development unfolds in stages (Erikson, Levinson). The midlife crisis is not as pervasive as Levinson proposed. However, most middle-aged adults experience a midlife consciousness that involves awareness of the young–old polarity and the shrinking amount of time left in life, generativity, and the meaning of life. Life events, cohort effects, and social clocks also are involved in understanding adult development. Everything we know about late adulthood suggests that an active lifestyle is preferable to disengagement. Erikson believes that the final issue in the life span to be negotiated is integrity versus despair, which involves a life review. For too long, adult development and aging were looked at as processes of continual decline. Today, more emphasis is given to successful aging.
Death and Dying	Their Nature	Death can come at any point in the life span, but in late adulthood we know it is near. Most societies have rituals that deal with death, although cultures vary in their orientation toward death. Kübler-Ross proposed five stages of coping with death, although they don't always occur in the sequence she proposed.

the ratio of 5 to 1 because women live longer than men, because women tend to marry men older than themselves, and because a widowed man is more likely to re-marry. Widowed women are probably the poorest group in America, despite the myth of huge insurance settlements. Many are also lonely, and the poorer and less educated they are, the lonelier they tend to be. The bereaved are at increased risk for many health problems, including death. For both widows and widowers, social support helps them to adjust to the death of a spouse.

At this point we have discussed many ideas about adult development and aging, as well as death and dying. An overview of these ideas is presented in summary table 8.4. In this chapter we indicated that successful aging requires motivation and effort. In the next chapter, we will examine the topic of motivation, as well as emotion.

Bereavement and Grief

Overview

Overview

Overview

WE BEGAN THIS CHAPTER by examining what development is, including its biological, cognitive, and socioemotional processes, periods of development, and developmental issues. Our coverage of child development focused on prenatal development and birth, physical development, cognitive development, and socioemotional development. In studying adolescence, we evaluated its historical beginnings and nature, as well as physical, cognitive, and socioemotional changes. We also explored adult development and aging, including physical development, cognitive development, socioemotional development, and successful aging. And we read about death and dying.

Don't forget that you can obtain a more detailed overview of the chapter by again studying the four summary tables on pages 255, 272, 278, and 289.

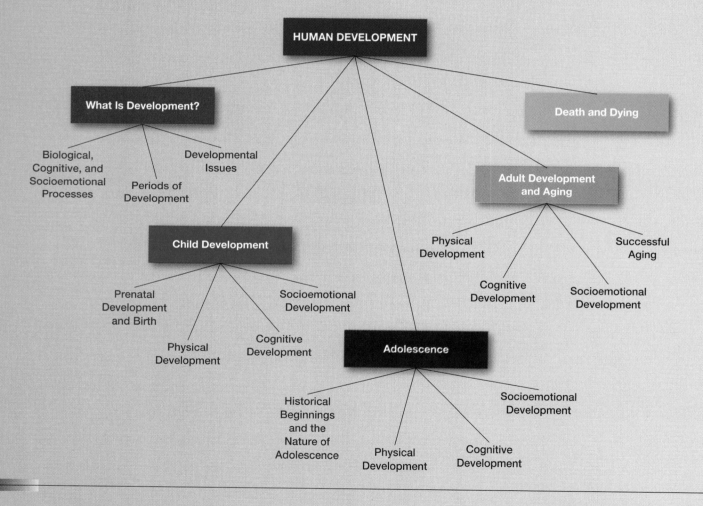

Key Terms

Key People

Taking It to the Net

1. Imagine you are playing with your 5-year-old cousin. You give her one quarter and she seems very pleased. Then, you playfully ask her if she wants to trade that quarter for three shiny new pennies. She looks at the quarter in her hand, looks at your hand, and gleefully says, "yes!" You ask her why, and she replies, "Because three is more than one." At what stage of cognitive development, according to Piaget, is your cousin right now? How do you know? What are some of the other common ways of thinking at this stage?

2. Early childhood care and development is essential to both individual children and society as a whole. This involves providing programs to communities, parents, and the children themselves. From a very early age (birth to age 8), children need to be supported in the development of their cognitive, social, and physical abilities. Children's development can be facilitated by instituting programs in communities throughout the world. Clearly the children benefit from such support, but how do you think society gains from early childhood intervention?

3. Although we usually associate development with the childhood years, key changes also occur in our aging years. As your grandparents will undoubtedly tell you, aging facilitates cognitive, physical, and social changes. One aspect of aging involves changes in our immune system. How is this system affected by aging? Why does this change occur? Explain the repercussions of such a change in our immune system.

Connect to http://www.mhhe.com/psychology/santrock to find the answers!

Motivation and Emotion

"No bird soars too high if he soars with his own wings."

William Blake
English Poet, 19th Century

Images of Psychology and Life
Terry Fox's Marathon Run

A young Canadian, Terry Fox, attempted one of the greatest long-distance runs in history. Averaging almost a marathon (26.2 miles) a day for five months, he ran 3,359 miles across Canada. What makes his feat truly remarkable is that Terry Fox had lost his leg to cancer and completed his grueling run with the aid of a prosthetic limb.

What motivated Terry Fox to complete his run? When he was hospitalized with cancer, he decided that if he survived he would do something to generate funds for cancer research. Many people feel overwhelmed by a cancer diagnosis and resign themselves to a lesser quality of life while they wait for the disease to run its course. Terry Fox, though, found a compelling reason to live. He concluded that his purpose in life was to go beyond himself and make a positive difference in the world. He felt renewed by his second chance.

Terry encountered unforeseen hurdles on his long run: severe headwinds, heavy rain, snow, and icy roads. These challenges took a toll. After his first month of running, he was only averaging eight miles a day, far less than he needed to accomplish if he was to finish his run before the worst of Canadian winter set in. Yet he managed to reach down inside himself to muster more motivation and energy to succeed. He kept going, picking up his pace in the second month to the point that he was back on track to reach his goal.

Terry Fox's accomplishments are all the more impressive when we consider that prior to his cancer diagnosis, he only was an average athlete and had a shy, introverted personality. Once his motivation had kicked in, he completed one of the most meaningful runs in history. He learned to shed some of his shyness and began to give impassioned

Terry Fox completed one of the greatest long-distance runs in history. What was his motivation?

Preview

WHEN YOU ARE MOTIVATED badly enough to get something, you will expend the energy and effort to get it. In this chapter, we will explore many aspects of motivation, evaluating why people do what they do, and emotion, examining our world of affect and feelings. Both motivation and emotion can regulate or modulate our behavior. For example, if you have a strong motivation to achieve, you might spend long hours studying and working. And your feelings of pride likewise can help to keep you on a path to achievement. These are some of the questions we will evaluate in this chapter:

• Are some needs more important to people than others?
• What explains why we get hungry? Is dieting harmful or beneficial?
• Why are people sexually motivated? What causes people to have a motivation for homosexual behavior?
• What are some good strategies for getting motivated to achieve?
• What happens to our bodies when we experience emotion?
• Can lie detectors accurately determine if people are lying?
• How do people express their emotions?
• Do women and men experience emotions differently?

speeches to thousands of people in an effort to persuade them to donate to cancer research. Terry's contributions go far beyond the funds he raised. His example stands as a testimonial to what motivation can accomplish even in the face of great adversity.

Motivation and Emotion

Some Ideas About the "Whys" of Behavior

Why do we do what we do? Let's explore this central question in motivation.

Defining Motivation

We are all motivated, just motivated to do different things. Thus, some students are motivated to watch television, others to study for an exam. **Motivation** *involves the question of why people behave, think, and feel the way they do. Motivated behavior is energized, directed, and sustained.*

If you are hungry, you will probably put this book down and go to the refrigerator. If you are sexually motivated and have a part- ner, you might ask that person to engage in sexual behavior with you. If you are sex- ually motivated and don't have a partner, you might flirt with someone who attracts you. If you are motivated to achieve, you might stay in the library until midnight studying. When you are motivated, your behavior is energized and directed: you go to the refrigerator, to a party, to the library. Hunger, sex, and achievement are three important motivational areas of our lives—each of which we discuss in this chapter.

Motivations differ not only in kind, such as an individual's being motivated to eat rather than have sex, but also in intensity. We can speak of an individual as being more or less hungry, or more or less motivated to have sex. Let's now turn our attention to dif- ferent ways psychologists conceptualize motivation, beginning with biological influences.

Biological Influences

Biological influences on motivation have been proposed in the form of instincts, needs and drives, and physiological factors such as brain processes and hormones. You also will see that ethology and evolutionary psychology propose biological views of motivation.

Instincts   An **instinct** *is an innate (unlearned), biological pattern of behavior that is assumed to be universal throughout a species.* Influenced by Darwin's evolutionary theory, American psychologist William McDougall (1908) argued that all behavior involves instincts. In particular, he said that we have instincts for acquisitiveness, cu- riosity, pugnacity, gregariousness, and self-assertion. At about the same time, Sig- mund Freud (1917) argued that behavior is instinctually based. He believed that sex and aggression were especially powerful in motivating behavior ◀▥ P. 9.

It was not long before a number of psychologists had crafted laundry lists of in- stincts, some lists running into the thousands. However, it soon became apparent that what the early instinct theorists were doing was naming a behavior rather than ex- plaining it. If we say that people have an instinct for sex, or for curiosity, or for ac- quisitiveness, these behaviors are not being explained, only named.

Although the early instinct approach of merely labeling behaviors as instincts landed in psychology's dust heap many years ago, the idea that some motivation is unlearned is still alive and well today. It is widely accepted that instinctive behavior is common in nonhuman species, and in chapter 8, "Human Development," we saw that human infants come into the world equipped with some unlearned instincts such as sucking. Most attachment theorists also believe that infants have an unlearned instinct for orienting toward a caregiver ◀▥ P. 266.

Needs and Drives

If you do not have an instinct for sex, maybe you have a need or a drive for it. A **drive** *is an aroused state that occurs because of a physiological need.* A **need** *is a deprivation that energizes the drive to eliminate or reduce the deprivation.* You might have a need for water, for food, or for sex. The need for food, for example, arouses your hunger drive. This motivates you to do something—to go out for a hamburger, for example—to reduce the drive and satisfy the need. As a drive becomes stronger, we are motivated to reduce it. This explanation is known as *drive reduction theory.*

Usually, but not always, needs and drives are closely associated in time. For example, when your body needs food, your hunger drive will probably be aroused. An hour after you have eaten a hamburger, you might still be hungry (thus, you need food), but your hunger drive might have subsided. From this example you can sense that drive pertains to a psychological state; need involves a physiological state.

The goal of drive reduction is **homeostasis,** *the body's tendency to maintain an equilibrium, or a steady state.* Literally hundreds of biological states in our bodies must be maintained within a certain range: temperature, blood-sugar level, potassium and sodium levels, oxygen, and so on. When you dive into an icy swimming pool, your body heats up. When you walk out of an air-conditioned room into the heat of a summer day, your body begins to cool down. These changes occur automatically in an attempt to restore your body to its optimal state of functioning.

Homeostasis is achieved in our bodies much like a thermostat in a house keeps the temperature constant. For example, assume that the thermostat in your house is set at 68 degrees. The furnace heats the house until a temperature of 68 degrees is reached, then the furnace shuts off. Without a source of heat, the temperature in the house eventually falls below 68 degrees. The thermostat detects this and turns the furnace back on again. The cycle is repeated so that the temperature is maintained within narrow limits. Today homeostasis is used to explain both physiological and psychological imbalances.

What is the status of drive reduction theory today? It has not been completely discarded, but most psychologists believe it does not provide a comprehensive framework for understanding motivation. Drive reduction theory states that people are motivated to reduce a drive. However, people often behave in ways that increase rather than reduce a drive. For example, they might skip meals in an effort to lose weight, which can increase their hunger drive rather than reduce it. Consider also people who seek stimulation and thrills, such as going bungee-jumping or riding a roller coaster. Instead of reducing a drive, they appear to be increasing their level of stimulation. In one study, monkeys

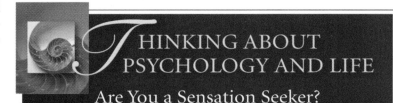

THINKING ABOUT PSYCHOLOGY AND LIFE
Are You a Sensation Seeker?

SENSATION SEEKING is defined as the motivation for varied, novel, and complex sensations and experiences (Zuckerman, 1979). High sensation seekers take physical and social risks just for the sake of the experiences. By responding to the items below you can get a sense of your motivation for sensation seeking.

For each of the following items, decide which of the two choices best describes your likes and feelings. If neither choice applies, choose the one that *most* describes you. Answer all of the items.

1. a. I like the tumult of sounds in a busy city.
   b. I prefer the peace and quiet of the country.
2. a. I dislike the sensations one gets when flying.
   b. I enjoy many of the rides in amusement parks.
3. a. I would like a job that would require a lot of traveling.
   b. I would prefer a job in one location.
4. a. I often wish I could be a mountain climber.
   b. I can't understand people who risk their necks climbing mountains.
5. a. I get bored seeing the same old faces.
   b. I like the comfortable familiarity of everyday friends.
6. a. I like to explore a strange city or section of town by myself, even if it means getting lost.
   b. I prefer a guide when I am in a place I don't know well.
7. a. I find people who disagree with my beliefs more stimulating than people who agree with me.
   b. I don't like to argue with people whose beliefs are sharply divergent from mine, since such arguments are never resolved.
8. a. I prefer more subdued colors in decoration.
   b. I like to decorate with bright colors.
9. a. When I have nothing to do or look at for any length of time, I get very restless.
   b. I often enjoy just relaxing and doing nothing.
10. a. Most people spend entirely too much money on life insurance.
    b. Life insurance is something that no one can afford to be without.
11. a. I don't like to drink coffee because it overstimulates me and keeps me awake.
    b. I like to drink coffee because of the lift it gives me.
12. a. The worst social sin is to be rude.
    b. The worst social sin is to be a bore.
13. a. The most important goal of life is to live it to the fullest and experience as much of it as you can.
    b. The most important goal of life is to find peace and happiness.
14. a. If I were a salesperson, I would prefer working on commission if I had a chance to make more money than I could on a salary.
    b. If I were a salesperson, I would prefer a straight salary rather than the risk of making little or nothing on a commission basis.
15. a. I like sharp or spicy foods.
    b. I prefer foods with a minimum of seasoning.

Count one point for sensation seeking for each of the following: 1a, 2b, 3a, 4a, 5a, 6a, 7a, 8b, 9a, 10a, 11b, 12b, 13a, 14a, 15a. If you answered 11 or more items this way, you probably have a strong motivation for sensation seeking. If you answered 5 items or less this way, you probably have a weak motive for sensation seeking. If you responded this way 6 to 10 times, you probably are in the average range of sensation seekers. The older one gets, the more sensation seeking scores go down.

solved simple problems just for the opportunity to watch a toy train (Butler, 1953). And a series of experiments suggested that college students could not tolerate sensory deprivation for more than 2 to 3 days, even though they were being paid for their participation (Bexton, Heron, & Scott, 1954). Also when people are curious and seek information, drive reduction does not seem to be involved.

Ethology and Evolutionary Psychology   Although psychologists rejected the biological concept of instinct many years ago, biology's role in motivation continues to be strong. Recall from chapter 8, "Human Development," that Konrad Lorenz (1965) conducted a classic study in which goslings became attached to Lorenz because he was the first moving object they saw shortly after they were born ◀▥ P. 266. Lorenz interpreted the goslings' behavior as evidence of rapid innate learning within a critical time period. Lorenz's field is **ethology,** *the study of the biological basis of behavior in natural habitats.* Ethology emerged as an important theory because of the work of European zoologists such as Lorenz in the 1930s, who argued that behaviorism had gone too far in promoting environmental experiences in motivation.

In chapter 1, we also discussed the theory in psychology that currently is receiving the most attention for its emphasis on the biological and evolutionary basis of behavior: evolutionary psychology ◀▥ P. 46. According to evolutionary psychologists such as David Buss (1995), to understand motivation it is necessary to examine its evolutionary ties. Evolutionary psychologists argue that explaining the motivation for sex, aggression, achievement, and other behaviors is rooted in our evolutionary past. Thus, if a species is highly competitive, it is because such competitiveness provided an advantage and was passed down through the genes from generation to generation.

Physiological Processes   Our body's physiological makeup (such as brain processes and hormones) also represents another important aspect of biology's role in motivation (Stricker, 2000). We will discuss these physiological mechanisms shortly when we explore hunger. In sum, although the concept of instinct did not survive, the views of ethologists and evolutionary psychologists, as well as physiological mechanisms, underscore biology's influence on motivation.

Cognitive Influences

The contemporary view of motivation also emphasizes the importance of cognitive factors (Petri, 1996). Consider your motivation to do well in this class. Your confidence in your ability to do well and your expectation for success may help you to relax, concentrate better, and study more effectively. If you think too much about not doing well in the class and fear that you will fail, you can become too anxious and not perform as well. Your ability to consciously control your behavior and resist the temptation to party too much and avoid studying will improve your achievement, as will your ability to use your information-processing abilities of attention, memory, and problem solving as you study for and take tests ◀▥ P. 11.

Psychologists continue to debate the role of conscious versus unconscious thought in understanding motivation. Freud's legacy to contemporary psychoanalytic theory is the belief that we are largely unaware of why we behave the way we do. Psychoanalytic theorists argue that few of us know why we love someone, why we eat so much, why we are so aggressive, or why we are so shy. Although some cognitive psychologists have begun to study the role of the unconscious mind, for the most part they emphasize that human beings are rational and aware of their motivation. Humanistic theorists like Maslow (whose view we will explore shortly) also stress our ability to examine our lives and become aware of what motivates us.

Behavioral/Social/Cultural Influences

Environmental influences on motivation focus on the behavioral concept of incentives, as well as social/cultural influences.

Incentives   So far we have been discussing internal factors that motivate behavior (such as needs, drives, and thoughts). But aren't external factors also involved in motivation? Isn't external motivation at work when a person is not hungry but sees a familiar fast-food place and becomes motivated to go in and buy a hamburger?

External factors were added to motivation when psychologists developed the concept of **incentives,** *positive or negative stimuli or events that motivate behavior.* Incentives are motivation's external pull. The prospect of a lucrative income of $100,000+ is a positive incentive for going to medical school and becoming a doctor. The threat of an intruder is a negative incentive for purchasing a security system for a home.

Internal and external factors can work in tandem in motivating behavior. Think of internal factors as like a "push" from inside to motivate behavior and external factors as like a "pull" from outside to motivate behavior. You might be more likely to go into a fast-food restaurant and buy some food if you are hungry (the internal push) and you see the familiar sign for it (the external pull).

Social/Cultural Influences   As is true of much human behavior, environmental and sociocultural influences play an important role in motivation. Even "biological" motives have environmental and sociocultural underpinnings. Why does the same meal—say, steak, baked potato, and salad—satisfy our hunger so much more when we are seated near someone we love in a candle lit room than in a noisy school cafeteria, for example? And consider the social motive of achievement. To fully understand achievement, we need to evaluate how parents and children interact, explore how peers compare one another, and examine the people we look up to as models of success, along with the standards for achievement in different cultures.

We have explored a number of different perspectives on motivation that consider biological, cognitive, and behavioral/social/cultural factors. Next, we turn our attention to a perspective that attempts to provide an integrative organization of various motives.

The Hierarchy of Motives

Is getting an A in this class more important than eating? If the person of your dreams told you that you were marvelous, would that motivate you to throw yourself in front of a car for the person's safety? According to Abraham Maslow (1954, 1971), our basic "needs" must be satisfied before our "higher" needs can be. Maslow's **hierarchy of motives** *states that individuals' main needs are satisfied in the following sequence: physiological, safety, love and belongingness, esteem, and self-actualization* (see figure 9.1). According to this hierarchy, people are motivated to satisfy their need for food before they are motivated to achieve, and their motivation for safety needs to be satisfied before their need for love.

Maslow's Hierarchy of Motives

Self-actualization

Esteem

Love and belongingness

Safety

Physiological

Figure 9.1
Maslow's Hierarchy of Motives
Abraham Maslow developed the hierarchy of human motives to show how we have to satisfy certain basic needs before we can satisfy higher needs.

It is the need for self-actualization that Maslow has described in the greatest detail. **Self-actualization,** *the highest and most elusive of Maslow's needs, is the motivation to develop one's full potential as a human being.* According to Maslow, self-actualization is possible only after the other needs in the hierarchy are met. Maslow cautions that most people stop maturing after they have developed a high level of esteem and thus do not become self-actualized. Many of Maslow's writings focus on how people can reach the elusive motivational state of self-actualization. We will have more to say about self-actualization in the next chapter, "Personality."

The idea that human motives are hierarchically arranged is an appealing one. Maslow's theory stimulates us to think about the ordering of motives in our own lives. However, the ordering of the needs is somewhat subjective. Some people might seek greatness in a career to achieve self-esteem, while putting on hold their needs for love and belongingness.

Self-Actualization

Issues in Motivation

In our discussion of motivation's biological, cognitive, and behavioral/social/cultural underpinnings, we have encountered three important issues: (1) To what degree are we motivated by innate, unlearned, biological factors as opposed to learned, sociocultural, experientially based factors? (2) To what degree are we aware of what motivates us—that is, to what extent is our motivation conscious? (3) To what degree are we internally or externally motivated? These are issues that researchers continue to wrangle with and debate.

Keep in mind that, although we separated the biological, cognitive, and behavioral/social/cultural underpinnings of motivation for the purpose of organization and clarification, in reality they are often interrelated. For example, in the study of social cognition, psychologists call attention to how contextual/social factors interact with thinking to determine our motivation. Thus, a person's achievement motivation might be influenced by both the person's optimistic outlook (cognitive) and their relationship with an outstanding mentor (social).

At this point we have studied a number of basic ideas about the whys of behavior. An overview of these ideas is presented in summary table 9.1. Now we will turn our attention to some specific areas of motivation: hunger, sex, and achievement. These areas of motivation were chosen because they represent diverse aspects of motivation in our lives and reflect varying degrees of biological, cognitive, and behavioral/social/cultural influences. First, we will study hunger, which has strong biological underpinnings. Second, we will study sex, a bridge between biological and social motives. And third, we will evaluate the cognitive/social motive of achievement.

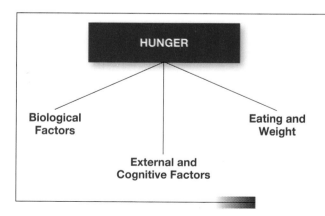

Hunger

Imagine that you live in the Bayambang area of the Philippines. You are very poor and have little food to eat. Hunger continuously gnaws at everyone in your village. Now imagine yourself as the typical American, eating not only breakfast, lunch, and dinner, but snacking along the way—and maybe even raiding the refrigerator at midnight.

Food is an important aspect of life in any culture. Whether we have very little or large amounts of food available to us, hunger influences our behavior. What mechanisms explain why we get hungry?

SUMMARY TABLE 9.1
Some Ideas About the "Whys" of Behavior

Concept	Processes/ Related Ideas	Characteristics/Description
Defining Motivation	Its Nature	Motivation involves the question of why people think, feel, and behave the way they do. Motivated behavior is energized, directed, and sustained.
Biological Influences	Instinct	An instinct is an innate (unlearned) biological pattern of behavior that is assumed to be universal throughout a species. The concept of instinct was popularized by McDougall at the beginning of the twentieth century. The idea that some of our motivation is unlearned and involves physiological factors is still present today.
	Needs and Drives	A drive is an arousal state that occurs because of a physiological need. A need is a deprivation that energizes the drive to eliminate or reduce the deprivation. Drive reduction theory was proposed as an explanation for motivation with the goal of drive reduction being homeostasis, the body's tendency to maintain an equilibrium. The concept of homeostasis is used to explain both physiological and psychological imbalances.
	Ethology and Evolutionary Psychology	Lorenz's ideas came from the field of ethology, the study of the biological basis of behavior in natural habitats. Ethologists argue that rapid innate learning often takes place in a critical period. Evolutionary psychologists also emphasize the biological and evolutionary basis of motivation.
	Physiological Processes	Motivation's biological basis also involves physiological processes such as brain processes and hormones.
Cognitive Influences	Their Nature	The contemporary view of motivation also emphasizes cognitive factors, including such information-processing abilities as attention, memory, and problem solving. Psychologists continue to debate the role of conscious versus unconscious thought in understanding motivation.
Behavioral/Social/ Cultural Factors	Incentives	These are positive or negative external stimuli that motivate an individual's behavior.
	Social/Cultural Influences	These environmental factors also influence motivation. The role of behavioral, social, and cultural factors raises an important issue about motivation: Is behavior internally or externally motivated?
The Hierarchy of Motives	Maslow's view	According to Maslow's hierarchy of motives, our main needs are satisfied in this sequence: physiological, safety, love and belongingness, esteem, cognitive, aesthetic, and self-actualization. Maslow gave the most attention to self-actualization, the motivation to develop to one's full potential.
Issues in Motivation	Their Nature	Three important issues focus on (1) whether motivation is based on innate, unlearned, biological factors or learned, sociocultural, experiential factors; (2) to what degree we are aware of what motivates us; and (3) to what degree we are internally or externally motivated.

Biological Factors

You are sitting in class and it is 2 P.M. You were so busy today that you skipped lunch. As the professor lectures, your stomach starts to growl. For many of us, a growling stomach is one of the main signs that we are hungry. Psychologists have wondered for many years about the role of peripheral factors—such as the stomach, liver, and blood chemistry—in hunger.

Peripheral Factors   In 1912, Walter Cannon and A. L. Washburn conducted an experiment that revealed a close association between stomach contractions

$\mathscr{F}$igure 9.2
Cannon and Washburn's Classic Experiment on Hunger

In this experiment, the researchers demonstrated that stomach contractions, which were detected by the stomach balloon, accompany a person's hunger feelings, which were indicated by pressing the key.

and hunger (see figure 9.2). As part of the procedure, a partially inflated balloon was passed through a tube inserted in Washburn's mouth and pushed down into his stomach. A machine that measures air pressure was connected to the balloon to monitor Washburn's stomach contractions. Every time Washburn reported hunger pangs, his stomach was also contracting. This finding, which was confirmed in subsequent experiments with other volunteers, led the two to believe that gastric activity was *the* basis for hunger.

Stomach signals are not the only factors that affect hunger. People whose stomachs have been surgically removed still get hunger pangs. Stomach contractions can be a signal for hunger, but the stomach also can send signals that stop hunger. We all know that a full stomach can decrease our appetite. In fact, the stomach actually tells the brain not only how full it is, but also how much nutrient is in the stomach load. That is why a stomach full of rich food stops your hunger faster than a stomach full of water. The same stomach hormone that helps start the digestion of food (called cholecystokinin, or CCK) reaches your brain through the bloodstream and signals you to stop eating.

Blood sugar (glucose) is an important factor in hunger, probably because the brain is critically dependent on sugar for energy. One set of sugar receptors is located in the brain itself, and these receptors trigger hunger when sugar levels get too low. Another set of sugar receptors is in the liver, which is the organ that stores excess sugar and releases it into the blood when needed. The sugar receptors in the liver signal the brain via the vagus nerve, and this signal also can make you hungry. Another important factor in blood-sugar control is the hormone insulin, which causes excess sugar in the blood to be stored in cells as fats and carbohydrates. Insulin injections cause profound hunger because they lower blood sugar drastically.

Psychologist Judith Rodin (1984) has further clarified the role of insulin and glucose in understanding hunger and eating behavior. She pointed out that when we eat complex carbohydrates such as cereals, bread, and pasta, insulin levels go up but then fall off gradually. When we consume simple sugars like candy bars and Cokes, insulin levels rise and then fall off sharply—the all-too-familiar "sugar low." Glucose levels in the blood are also affected by these complex carbohydrates and simple sugars in similar ways. The consequence is that we are more likely to eat within the next several hours after eating simple sugars than after eating complex carbohydrates. And the food we eat at one meal often influences how much we will eat at our next meal. So consuming doughnuts and candy bars, in addition to providing no nutritional value, sets up an ongoing sequence of what and how much we probably will crave the next time we eat.

Brain Processes   In chapter 2, "Biological Foundations and Neuroscience," we described the role of the hypothalamus in regulating important body functions, including hunger ◀||||| P. 60. More specifically, activity in two areas of the hypothalamus contributes to our understanding of hunger (see figure 9.3). The *lateral hypo-*

Ventromedial
hypothalamus

Lateral hypothalamus

Figure 9.3
The Hypothalamus and Hunger

The hypothalamus plays an important role in regulating various body functions, one of which is hunger. More specifically, the lateral hypothalamus is involved in stimulating hunger and the ventromedial hypothalamus functions in restricting eating.

thalamus is involved in stimulating eating. When it is electrically stimulated in a well-fed animal, the animal begins to eat. And if this area of the hypothalamus is destroyed, even a starving animal will show no interest in food. The *ventromedial hypothalamus* is involved in reducing hunger and restricting eating. When this area of an animal's brain is stimulated, the animal stops eating. When the area is destroyed, the animal eats profusely and quickly becomes obese (see figure 9.4).

Today, neuroscientists believe that while the lateral and ventromedial hypothalamus play roles in hunger, there is much more to the brain's role in determining hunger than these on/off centers in the hypothalamus. They are exploring how neurotransmitters (recall from chapter 2 that these are chemical messengers that convey information from neuron to neuron) and neural circuits (clusters of neurons that often involve different parts of the brain) function in hunger ◀▥ P. 54.

Your internal physiological world is very much involved in whether or not you are hungry. But some external and cognitive factors are also involved.

External and Cognitive Factors

Might external cues stimulate hunger? Might the cognitive factor of self-control be involved in hunger?

External Cues   Psychologists are interested in how environmental cues might stimulate hunger. You may know someone who seems literally incapable of walking past an ice cream shop without stopping to eat a huge hot fudge sundae. Stanley Schachter (1971) believes that one of the main differences between obese and normal weight individuals is their attention to environmental cues for signals of when to eat. From this perspective, people of normal weight attend to internal cues for signals of when to eat—for example, when blood sugar level is low, hunger pangs are sensed in the stomach. In

Figure 9.4
The Ventromedial Hypothalamus (VMH) and Obesity in Rats

(top) A rat gained three times its normal body weight after a lesion was made in its VMH. *(bottom)* This graph displays the weight gain by a group of rats in which lesions were made in the VMH (hyperphagic) and by a group of rats in which no lesions were made (control). Notice how quickly the hyperphagic rats gained weight but that, after about 1 month, they virtually stopped gaining weight.

contrast, an obese person responds to external cues as signals of when to eat—how the food tastes, looks, and smells, for example. One problem that is left unresolved by Schachter's view is that not all people who have this special sensitivity to such cues are overweight (Rodin, 1984). Alternative perspectives have sought to integrate what we know about the importance of physiology and external cues in understanding obesity.

Self-Control   Rodin (1984) points out that not too long ago we believed that obesity was caused by such factors as unhappiness or responding to external food cues. According to Rodin, a number of biological, cognitive, and social factors are more important. We already discussed some important biological factors, including the roles of complex carbohydrates and simple sugars in insulin and glucose levels. In regard to external cues, Rodin says that while obese persons are more responsive to external food cues than normal-weight persons are, there are individuals at all weight levels who respond more to external than to internal stimuli. Many persons who respond to external cues also have the conscious ability to control their behavior and keep environmental food cues from externally controlling their eating patterns.

Eating and Weight

So far in our coverage of the hunger motive, we have explored some important factors that motivate a person to eat. In this section we examine other factors that influence the motivation to eat. In some cases, this motivation involves obesity and the ability of overweight individuals to become motivated to take off pounds and maintain the weight loss. In others, the motivation focuses on the motivation of individuals who are not overweight to be extremely thin.

Obesity
Heredity and Obesity

Obesity   Obesity is a serious and pervasive problem. Let's explore its pervasiveness and costs, as well as the roles that heredity, set point and metabolism, and environmental factors play in its development.

Pervasiveness and Costs   Approximately one-third of the American population are overweight enough to be at increased health risk, and the prevalence of obesity has risen 8 percent in the 1990s (Friedman & Brownell, 1998). Obesity often becomes more common with increased age, especially among women.

   The health care costs linked to obesity are estimated to be $46 billion per year. Obesity is associated with increased risk of hypertension, diabetes, and cardiovascular disease (Agras, 2000).

Heredity   Until recently, the genetic component of obesity had been underestimated by scientists. Some individuals do inherit a tendency to be overweight. Only 10 percent of children who do not have obese parents become obese themselves, whereas 40 percent of children who become obese have one obese parent and 70 percent of children who become obese have two obese parents. Researchers also have documented that animals can be inbred to have a propensity for obesity (Blundell, 1984). Further, identical human twins have similar weights, even when they are reared apart. Estimates of the variance in body mass that can be explained by heredity range from 25 to 70 percent.

Set Point and Metabolism   The amount of stored fat in your body is an important factor in your **set point,** *the weight maintained when no effort is made to gain or lose weight.* Fat is stored in what are called adipose cells. When these cells are filled, you do not get hungry. When people gain weight—because of genetic predisposition, childhood eating patterns, or adult overeating—the number of their fat cells increases, and they might not be able to get rid of them. A normal-weight individual has 30 to 40 billion fat cells. An obese individual has 80 to 120 billion fat cells. Some scientists have proposed that these fat cells can shrink but might not go away.

Another factor in weight is **basal metabolism rate (BMR),** *the minimal amount of energy an individual uses in a resting state.* BMR varies with age and sex. Rates decline precipitously during adolescence and then more gradually in adulthood; they also are slightly higher for males than females (see figure 9.5). Many people gradually increase their weight over many years. To some degree the weight gain can be due to a declining basal metabolism rate.

Environmental Factors

The human gustatory system and taste preferences developed at a time when reliable food sources were scarce. Our earliest ancestors probably developed a preference for sweets, because ripe fruit, which is a concentrated source of sugar (and calories), was so accessible. Today many people still have a "sweet tooth," but unlike our ancestors' ripe fruit that contained sugar *plus* vitamins and minerals, the soft drinks and candy bars we snack on today often fill us with empty calories.

Strong evidence of the environment's influence on weight is the doubling of the rate of obesity in the United States since 1900. This dramatic increase in obesity likely is due to greater availability of food (especially food high in fat), energy-saving devices, and declining physical activity. Obesity is six times more prevalent among women with low incomes than among women with high incomes. Americans also are more obese than Europeans and people in many other areas of the world.

Dieting

Let's explore the diet scene in America, restrained eating, whether diets work, the role of exercise in losing weight, and the potential harm and benefits of dieting.

The Diet Scene

Many divergent interests are involved in the topic of dieting. These include the public, health professionals, policy makers, the media, and the powerful diet and food industries. On one side are the societal norms that promote a very lean, aesthetic body. This ideal is supported by $30 billion a year in sales of diet books, programs, videos, foods, and pills. On the other side are health professionals and a growing minority of the press. Although they recognize the alarmingly high rate of obesity, they are frustrated by high relapse rates and the obsession with excessive thinness that can lead to chronic dieting and serious health risks (Brownell & Rodin, 1994).

Restrained Eating

One area related to dieting that psychologists have studied is restrained eating. Too many people live their lives as one big, long diet, interrupted by occasional hot fudge sundaes or chocolate chip cookies. **Restrained eaters** *are individuals who chronically restrict their food intake to control their weight.* Restrained eaters are often on diets, are very conscious of what they eat, and tend to feel guilty after splurging on sweets. An interesting characteristic of restrained eaters is that when they stop dieting, they tend to binge eat—that is, eat large quantities of food in a short time (McFarlane, Polivy, & Herman, 1998).

Do Diets Work?

Although many Americans regularly embark on a diet, few are successful in keeping weight off long-term. Some critics argue that all

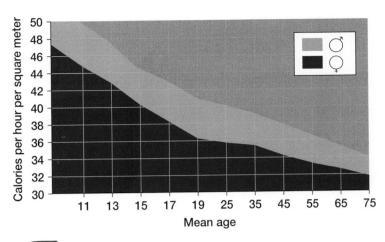

Figure 9.5
Changes in Basal Metabolism Rate with Age
BMR varies with age and sex. Rates are usually higher for males and decline proportionately with age for both sexes.

Why People Are Getting Fatter

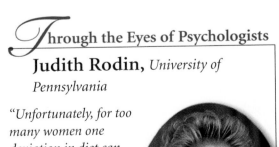

Through the Eyes of Psychologists
Judith Rodin, *University of Pennsylvania*

"Unfortunately, for too many women one deviation in diet can spell the difference between confidence and despair."

Anorexia nervosa has become an increasing problem for adolescent girls and young adult women. What are some possible causes of anorexia nervosa?

Anorexia Nervosa

diets fail (Wooley & Garner, 1991). However, the weight of the evidence is that some individuals who go on diets do lose weight and maintain the loss (Brownell & Cohen, 1995). How often this occurs and whether some diet programs work better than others are still open questions.

Exercise   What we do know about losing weight is that the most effective programs include an exercise component. Exercise not only burns up calories, but continues to elevate the person's metabolic rate for several hours *after* the exercise. Also, exercise lowers a person's set point for weight, which makes it easier to maintain a lower weight (Bennett & Gurin, 1982).

Dieting: Harm or Benefit?   Dieting is a pervasive concern of many Americans, but the population is not uniform and many people who are on diets should not be. A 10 percent reduction in body weight might produce striking benefits for an older, obese, hypertensive man but be unhealthy for a female college student who is not overweight. The pressure to be thin, and thus diet, is greatest among young women, yet they do not have the highest risk of obesity.

Even when diets do produce weight loss, they can place the dieter at risk for other health problems. One main concern focuses on weight cycling (commonly called "yo-yo dieting"), in which the person is in a recurring cycle of dieting and weight gain (Wadden & others, 1996). Researchers have found a link between frequent changes in weight and chronic disease (Brownell & Rodin, 1994). Also, liquid diets and other very-low-calorie strategies are related to gall bladder damage.

With these problems in mind, when overweight people diet and maintain their weight loss, they do become less depressed and reduce their risk for a number of health-impairing disorders (Christensen, 1996). Next, we will explore problems that occur at the other end of the weight spectrum—when people get so thin it impairs their health.

Anorexia Nervosa and Bulimia   **Anorexia nervosa** *is an eating disorder that involves the relentless pursuit of thinness through starvation.* Anorexia nervosa can eventually lead to death, as it did for popular singer Karen Carpenter in 1983.

Most anorexics are White adolescent or young adult females from well-educated, middle- and upper-income families. They distort their body image, perceiving themselves as overweight (Mussell & Mitchell, 1998). Numerous causes of anorexia have been proposed. One is the current fashion image of thinness, reflected in the saying "You can't be too rich or too thin." Many anorexics grow up in families with high achievement demands. Unable to meet these high expectations and control their grades, they turn to something they can control: their weight. As we see next, while anorexics control their eating by restricting it, most bulimics often cannot.

Bulimia *is an eating disorder in which the individual consistently follows a binge-and-purge eating pattern.* The bulimic goes on an eating binge and then purges by self-induced vomiting or using a laxative. Sometimes the binges alternate with fasting, at other times with normal eating. Like anorexia nervosa, bulimia is primarily a female disorder. Bulimia has become prevalent among traditional-age college women.

Bulimia can produce gastric and chemical imbalances in the body. Depression is common among bulimics. Many of the same causes proposed for anorexia nervosa also are offered for bulimia (Fairburn, 1995).

At this point, we have evaluated many aspects of hunger. An overview of these ideas is presented in summary table 9.2. Next, we will continue our coverage of motivation by examining our motivation for sex.

SUMMARY TABLE 9.2
Hunger

Concept	Processes/ Related Ideas	Characteristics/Discussions
Biological Factors	Peripheral Factors	Interest in the stomach's role in hunger was stimulated by Cannon's classic research, although stomach signals aren't the only factors that affect hunger. Blood sugar (glucose) is an important factor, probably because the brain is critically dependent on sugar for energy. Rodin helped clarify the role of insulin and glucose in understanding hunger and eating.
	Brain Processes	The hypothalamus plays an important role in regulating hunger. The lateral hypothalamus is involved in stimulating eating, the ventromedial hypothalamus in restricting eating. Today, neuroscientists are exploring the roles that neurotransmitters and neural circuits play in hunger.
External and Cognitive Factors	Their Nature	Schachter's research suggested that environmental cues are involved in the control of eating. However, not all people equally sensitive to external cues are overweight. Rodin argues that self-control is an important cognitive factor in understanding eating behavior.
Eating and Weight	Obesity	Obesity is a serious and pervasive problem, with about one-third of the American population overweight enough to be at increased health risk. Heredity, set point, and basal metabolism are biological factors involved in obesity. Environmental factors also influence eating behavior. Our culture has changed from when our early ancestors ate natural fruits to the empty calories of many sweets today. The dramatic increase in obesity in the twentieth century underscores the importance of environmental factors in obesity as increasing numbers of people eat high-fat foods and lead more sedentary lives.
	Dieting	Many divergent interests are involved in the topic of dieting. One area related to dieting that is studied by psychologists is restrained eating. Most diets don't work, although some people do lose weight when they diet and maintain the loss. Exercise is an important component of a competent weight-loss program. Many people, especially females in their teens and early twenties, who go on a diet don't need to lose weight. The pressure to be thin can lead to harmful effects for people who are not overweight. However, when overweight people diet and maintain their weight loss, it has health benefits.
	Anorexia Nervosa and Bulimia	Anorexia nervosa is an eating disorder that involves relentless pursuit of thinness through starvation. Bulimia is an eating disorder that involves a binge-and-purge eating pattern. Both disorders are common among young college women. They are serious health disorders and even can lead to death.

Sexuality

We do not need sex for everyday survival, the way we need food and water, but we do need it for the survival of the species.

Biological, Cognitive, Sensory/ Perceptual, and Cultural Factors

Our sexual motivation is fueled by many complex factors, including biological, cognitive, sensory/perceptual, and cultural.

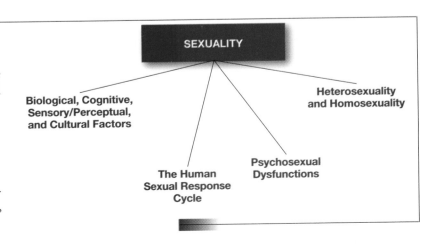

Biological Factors   Sex hormones are powerful chemicals that are controlled by the master gland in the brain, the pituitary ◄‖‖‖ P. 62. The two main classes of sex hormones are estrogens and androgens. **Estrogens,** *the most important of which is estradiol, influence the development of female physical sex characteristics and help to regulate the menstrual cycle.* Estrogens are produced by the ovaries. **Androgens,** *the most important of which is testosterone, promote the development of male genitals and secondary sex characteristics.* They influence sexual motivation in both sexes. Androgens are produced by the adrenal glands in males and females, and by the testes in males.

The secretion of sex hormones is regulated by a feedback system. The pituitary gland monitors hormone levels, but it is regulated by the hypothalamus. The pituitary gland sends out a signal to the testes or ovaries to manufacture the hormone. Then the pituitary gland, through interaction with the hypothalamus, detects when an optimal hormone level is reached and maintains this level.

The importance of the hypothalamus in sexual activity has been shown by electrically stimulating or surgically removing it. Electrical stimulation of certain hypothalamic areas increases sexual behavior; surgical removal of areas of the hypothalamus produces sexual inhibition. Electrical stimulation of the hypothalamus in a male can lead to as many as twenty ejaculations in 1 hour. The limbic system, which runs through the hypothalamus, also seems to be involved in sexual behavior. Its electrical stimulation can produce penile erection in males and orgasm in females.

In higher animals, the temporal lobes of the neocortex play an important role in moderating sexual arousal and directing it to an appropriate goal object ◄‖‖‖ P. 72. For example, temporal lobe damage in male cats impairs the animals' ability to select an appropriate partner. Male cats with temporal lobe damage try to copulate with everything in sight: teddy bears, chairs, even researchers. Temporal lobe damage in humans also has been associated with changes in sexual activity.

As we move from the lower to the higher animals, the role of hormones is less clear, especially in females (Crooks & Bauer, 1999). For human males, higher androgen levels are associated with sexual motivation and orgasm frequency (Booth, Johnson, & Granger, 1999; Knussman, Christiansen, & Couwenbergs, 1986; Udry & others, 1985). Nonetheless, sexual behavior is so individualized in humans that it is difficult to specify the effects of hormones.

Cognitive and Sensory/Perceptual Factors   From our experiences, we know that our cognitive world plays an important role in our sexuality (Crooks & Bauer, 1999). Thoughts and images are extensively involved in our sexual lives. We might be sexually attracted to someone but understand that it is important to inhibit our sexual urges until the relationship has time to develop and we get to know the person better. We have the cognitive capacity to think about the importance of not raping or inflicting sexual harm on others. We also have the cognitive capacity to generate sexual images. For example, some individuals become sexually aroused by generating erotic images and even reach orgasm while they are having fantasy images of sex (Whipple, Ogden, & Komisaruk, 1992).

Cognitive interpretation of sexual activity also involves our perception of the individual with whom we are having sex and his or her perception of us. We imbue our sexual acts with such perceptions as these: Is he loyal to me? What is our future relationship going to be like? How important is sex to her? What if she gets pregnant? Amid the wash of hormones in sexual activity is the cognitive ability to control, reason about, and try to make sense of the activity.

Not only are cognitive factors involved in sexual behavior, so are sensory/perceptual factors. The sensory system of touch usually predominates during sexual intimacy, but vision also plays an important role for some individuals ◄‖‖‖ P. 95. And we will see that smell has been proposed as a potential influence on sexual behavior, as have various foods and substances ◄‖‖‖ P. 98.

Men and women vary in how much touch and visual stimulation arouse their sexual motivation. In general, women are more aroused by touch, men by what they

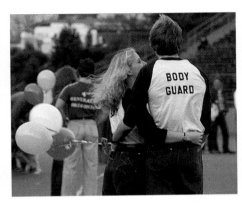

Sexual behavior has its magnificent moments throughout the animal kingdom. Insects mate in midair, peacocks display their plumage, and male elephant seals have prolific sex lives. Experience plays a more important role in human sexual behavior. We can talk about sex with each other, read about it in magazines, and watch it on television and the movie screen.

see. This might explain why erotic magazines and X-rated movies are directed more toward males than toward females (Money, 1986). Women are more aroused by tender, loving touches that are coupled with verbal expressions of love than men are. Moreover, men are more likely to quickly become sexually aroused, whereas women's sexual arousal tends to build more gradually.

Might smell also be involved in sexual interest? **Pheromones** *are odorous substances released by animals that are powerful attractants.* Pheromones are involved when male guinea pigs are attracted by the urine of ovulating females. They are at work when all the male cats in a neighborhood know that a female cat is in heat. Several years ago Jovan developed a fragrance they claimed would attract men to women who wore it. The company advertised that the perfume contained a pheromone derived from human sweat. It was designed to lure human males just as pheromones attract male guinea pigs and cats. The fragrance was not the smashing success the perfumery anticipated, indicating there is far more to sexual attraction in humans than smell.

Various foods and substances also have been proposed as having a dramatic impact on sexual arousal. **Aphrodisiacs** *are substances that supposedly arouse a person's sexual desire and increase their capacity for sexual activity.* Recall from chapter 1 that we urged you to be skeptical about claims of how eating a ground up version of a tiger's penis will increase the male's sexual potency ◀|||| P. 22. Some foods, such as oysters, bananas, celery, tomatoes, and potatoes, are touted as aphrodisiacs. As with a tiger's genital parts, we urge your skepticism about these foods; they do not influence sexual behavior. A substance referred to as "Spanish fly" also has been promoted as a powerful aphrodisiac. This is not an effective sexual stimulant and can cause genital inflammation, tissue damage, and even death.

Pheromones

Cultural Factors   Sexual motivation also is influenced by cultural factors. The range of sexual values across cultures is substantial ◀▥ P. 18. Some cultures consider sexual pleasures to be "normal" or "desirable," other cultures view sexual pleasures as "weird" or "abnormal" (Caron, 1998). Consider the people who live on the small island of Ines Beag off the coast of Ireland. They are among the most sexually repressed people in the world. They know nothing about tongue kissing or hand stimulation of the penis, and nudity is detested. For both females and males, premarital sex is out of the question. Men avoid most sexual experiences because they believe that sexual intercourse reduces their energy level and is bad for their health.

Under these repressive conditions, sexual intercourse occurs only at night and takes place as quickly as possible as the husband opens his nightclothes under the covers and the wife raises her nightgown. As you might suspect, female orgasm is rare in this culture (Messinger, 1971).

By contrast, consider the Mangaian culture in the South Pacific. In Mangaia, young boys are taught about masturbation and are encouraged to engage in it as much as they like. At age 13, the boys undergo a ritual that initiates them into sexual manhood. First their elders instruct them about sexual strategies, including how to aid their female partner in having orgasms. Then, 2 weeks later, the boy has intercourse with an experienced woman who helps him hold back ejaculation until she can achieve orgasm with him. By the end of adolescence, Mangaians have sex virtually every day. Mangaian women report a high frequency of orgasm.

As reflected in the behavior of the people in these two different cultures, our sexual motivation is influenced by **sexual scripts.** *These are stereotyped patterns of expectancies for how people should sexually behave.* Two well-known sexual scripts are the traditional religious script and the romantic script. In the **traditional religious script,** *sex is accepted only within marriage.* Extramarital sex is taboo, especially for women. Sex means reproduction and sometimes affection. In the **romantic script,** *sex is synonymous with love.* If we develop a relationship with someone and fall in love, it is acceptable to have sex with the person whether we are married or not.

You probably are familiar with some sex differences in sexual scripts. Females tend to link sexual intercourse with love more than males do, and males are more likely to emphasize sexual conquest. Some sexual scripts involve a double standard, such as that it is okay for male adolescents to have sex but not females; and if the female gets pregnant, it's her fault for not using contraception.

$\mathscr{F}$igure 9.6
Male and Female Sexual Response Patterns

(a) This diagram shows the excitement, plateau, orgasm, and resolution phases of the human male sexual response pattern. Notice that males enter a refractory period, which lasts from several minutes up to a day, in which they cannot have another orgasm. *(b)* This diagram shows the excitement, plateau, orgasm, and resolution phases of the human female sexual response pattern. Notice that female sexual responses follow one of three basic patterns. Pattern A somewhat resembles the male pattern, except that pattern A includes the possibility of multiple orgasm (the second peak in pattern A) without falling below the plateau level. Pattern B represents nonorgasmic arousal. Pattern C represents intense female orgasm, which resembles the male pattern in its intensity and rapid resolution.

The Human Sexual Response Cycle

How do humans respond physiologically during sexual activity? To answer this question, gynecologist William Masters and his colleague Virginia Johnson (1966) carefully observed and measured the physiological responses of 382 female and 312 male volunteers as they masturbated or had sexual intercourse. The **human sexual response pattern** *consists of four phases—excitement, plateau, orgasm, and resolution—as identified by Masters and Johnson* (see figure 9.6). The *excitement phase* begins erotic responsiveness; it lasts from several minutes to several hours, depending on the nature of the sex play involved. Engorgement of blood vessels and increased blood flow in genital areas and muscle tension characterize the excitement phase. The most obvious signs of response in this phase are lubrication of the vagina and partial erection of the penis.

The second phase of the human sexual response, called the *plateau phase,* is a continuation and heightening of the arousal begun in the excitement phase. The increases in breathing, pulse rate, and blood pressure that occurred during the excitement phase become more intense, penile erection and vaginal lubrication are more complete, and orgasm is closer.

The third phase of the human sexual response cycle is *orgasm*. How long does orgasm last? Some individuals sense that time is standing still when it takes place, but orgasm lasts for only about 3 to 15 seconds. Orgasm involves an explosive discharge of neuromuscular tension and an intense pleasurable feeling. However, orgasms are not all exactly alike. For example, females show three different patterns in the orgasm phase, as shown in figure 9.6: (a) multiple orgasms, (b) no orgasm, and (c) excitement rapidly leading to orgasm, bypassing the plateau phase; the third pattern most clearly corresponds to the male pattern in intensity and resolution.

Following orgasm, the individual enters the *resolution phase* in which blood vessels return to their normal state. One difference between males and females in this phase is that females may be stimulated to orgasm again without delay. Males enter a refractory period, lasting anywhere from several minutes to an entire day, in which they cannot have another orgasm. The length of the refractory period increases as men age.

Psychosexual Dysfunctions

Myths about females and males would have us believe that many women are uninterested in sexual pleasure and most men can hardly get enough. However, men and women have similar desires for sexual pleasure, and both sexes can experience psychological problems that interfere with the attainment of sexual pleasure. **Psychosexual dysfunctions** *are disorders that involve impairments in the sexual response pattern, either in the desire for gratification or in the inability to achieve it.* In disorders associated with the desire phase, both men and women show little or no sexual drive or interest. In disorders associated with the excitement phase, men may not be able to maintain an erection (McKinlay, 1999). In disorders associated with the orgasmic phase, both women and men reach orgasm too quickly or not at all. Premature ejaculation in men occurs when the time between the beginning of sexual stimulation and ejaculation is unsatisfactorily brief. Many women do not routinely experience orgasm in sexual intercourse, a pattern so common it can hardly be called dysfunctional. Inhibited male orgasm does occur, but it is much less common than inhibited female orgasm.

The treatment of psychosexual dysfunctions has undergone nothing short of a revolution in recent years (LoPiccolo, 2000). Once thought of as extremely difficult therapeutic challenges, most cases of psychosexual dysfunction now yield to techniques tailored to improve sexual functioning (Bhugra & de Silva, 1998; Crooks & Bauer, 1999).

Attempts to treat psychosexual dysfunctions through traditional forms of psychotherapy, as if the dysfunctions were personality disorders, have not been very successful; however, new treatments that focus directly on each sexual dysfunction have reached success rates of 90 percent or more (McConaghy, 1993). For example, the success rate of a treatment that encourages women to enjoy their bodies and engage in self-stimulation to orgasm, with a vibrator if necessary, approaches 100 percent (Anderson, 1983). Some of these women subsequently transfer their newly developed sexual responsiveness to interactions with partners.

Recently, the most attention in helping individuals with a sexual dysfunction has focused on Viagra, a drug designed to conquer impotence. Its success rate is in the range of 60 to 80 percent, and its prescription rate has outpaced such popular drugs as Prozac (antidepressant) and Rogaine (baldness remedy) in first-year comparisons (Padma-Nathan, 1999). Viagra also is being taken by some women to improve their sexual satisfaction. However, Viagra is not an aphrodisiac; it won't work in the absence of desire. The possible downside of Viagra involves headaches in 1 of 10 men, seeing blue (because the eyes contain an enzyme similar to the one on which Viagra works in the penis, about 3 percent of users develop temporary

Psychosexual Dysfunction in Men
Psychosexual Dysfunction in Women
Viagra

© 1998 Jack Ziegler from cartoonbank.com. All Rights Reserved.

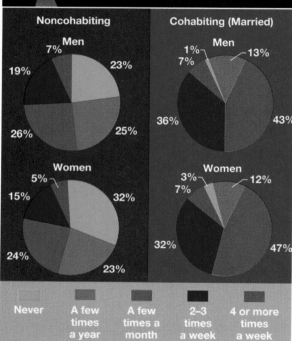

ℱigure 9.7
The Sex in America Survey

Percentages show noncohabiting and cohabiting (married) males' and females' responses to the question "How often have you had sex in the past year?"

Human Sexuality

vision problems ranging from blurred vision to a blue or green halo effect), and blackouts (Viagra can trigger a sudden drop in blood pressure). Also, scientists do not know the long-term effects of taking the drug, although in short-term trials it appears to be a relatively safe drug.

Heterosexuality and Homosexuality

Now we turn our attention to our sexual orientation and various aspects of heterosexuality and homosexuality.

Heterosexual Attitudes and Behavior   Describing sexual practices in America has always been challenging. Alfred Kinsey and his colleagues (1948) shocked the nation by reporting that his survey of American sexual practices revealed that, among other observations, half of American men had engaged in extramarital affairs. However, Kinsey's results were not representative, because he recruited volunteers wherever he could find them, including hitchhikers who passed through town, fraternity men, and even mental patients. Despite the study's flaws, the Kinsey data were widely circulated and many people felt that they must be leading a more conservative sexual life than others.

Subsequent large-scale magazine surveys confirmed the trend toward permissive sexuality (for example, a *Playboy* magazine poll of its readers) (Hunt, 1974). In these surveys, Americans were portrayed as engaging in virtually unending copulation. However, most magazine polls are skewed because of the background of the readers who complete the surveys. For example, surveys in *Playboy* and *Cosmopolitan* might appeal to subscribers who want to use the survey to brag about their sexual exploits.

Not until 1994 were more accurate data obtained from a well-designed, comprehensive study of American sexual patterns. Robert Michael and his colleagues (1994) interviewed nearly 3,500 people from 18 to 50 years of age who were randomly selected, a sharp contrast from earlier samples that were based on unrepresentative groups of volunteers.

Some of the key findings from the 1994 survey (see figure 9.7):

- Americans tend to fall into three categories: One-third have sex twice a week or more, one-third a few times a month, and one-third a few times a year or not at all.
- Married couples have sex the most and also are the most likely to have orgasms when they do. Figure 9.7 portrays the frequency of sex for married and noncohabitating individuals in the past year.
- Most Americans do not engage in kinky sexual acts. When asked about their favorite sexual acts, the vast majority (96 percent) said that vaginal sex was "very" or "somewhat" appealing. Oral sex was in third place, after an activity that many have not labeled a sexual act—watching a partner undress.
- Adultery is clearly the exception rather than the rule. Nearly 75 percent of the married men and 85 percent of the married women indicated that they have never been unfaithful.
- Men think about sex far more than women do—54 percent of the men said they think about it every day or several times a day, whereas 67 percent of the women said they think about it only a few times a week or a few times a month.

In sum, one of the most powerful messages in the 1994 survey was that Americans' sexual lives are more conservative than previously believed. Although 17 percent of the men and 3 percent of the women said they have had sex with at least 21 partners, the overall impression from the survey was that sexual behavior is ruled by

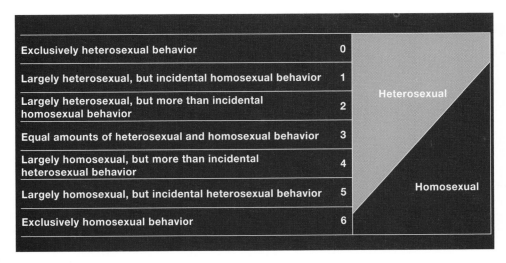

Exclusively heterosexual behavior	0
Largely heterosexual, but incidental homosexual behavior	1
Largely heterosexual, but more than incidental homosexual behavior	2
Equal amounts of heterosexual and homosexual behavior	3
Largely homosexual, but more than incidental heterosexual behavior	4
Largely homosexual, but incidental heterosexual behavior	5
Exclusively homosexual behavior	6

*𝓕*igure 9.8
The Continuum of Sexual Orientation

The continuum ranges from exclusive heterosexuality, which Kinsey and associates (1948) rated as 0, to exclusive homosexuality (6). People who are about equally attracted to both sexes (ratings 2 to 4) are bisexual.

marriage and monogamy for most Americans. To read further about the sexual landscape in America and some of its myths, see Explorations in Psychology.

Homosexual Attitudes and Behavior   Until the end of the nineteenth century, it was generally believed that people were either heterosexual or homosexual. Today, it is more accepted to view sexual orientation along a continuum from exclusive heterosexuality to exclusive homosexuality rather than as an either/or proposition. Kinsey and his associates (Kinsey, Pomeroy, & Martin, 1948) described this continuum on a scale ranging from 0 (exclusive heterosexuality) to 6 (signifying exclusive homosexuality) (see figure 9.8). Some individuals are also **bisexual,** *being sexually attracted to people of both sexes.* In Kinsey's research, approximately 1 percent of individuals reported being bisexual (1.2 percent of males and 0.7 percent of females) and about 2 to 5 percent of individuals reported being homosexual (4.7 percent of males and 1.8 percent of females). In the recent Sex in America survey, only 2.7 percent of the men and 1.3 percent of the women reported that they had had homosexual sex in the past year (Michael & others, 1994).

Why are some individuals homosexual and others heterosexual? Speculation about this question has been extensive, but no firm answers are available. Homosexuals and heterosexuals have similar physiological responses during sexual arousal and seem to be aroused by the same types of tactile stimulation. Investigators find no differences between homosexuals and heterosexuals in a wide range of attitudes, behaviors, and adjustments (Bell, Weinberg, & Mammersmith, 1981). Homosexuality once was classified as a mental disorder, but both the American Psychiatric Association and the American Psychological Association discontinued this classification as a mental disorder in the 1970s.

Recently, researchers have explored the possible biological basis of homosexuality (D'Augelli, 2000; Gladue, 1994). The results of hormone studies have been inconsistent. If male homosexuals are given male sex hormones (androgens), their sexual orientation doesn't change. Their sexual desire merely increases. A very early prenatal critical period might influence sexual orientation. In the second to fifth months after conception, exposure of the fetus to hormone levels characteristic of females might cause the individual (male or female) to become attracted to males (Ellis & Ames, 1987). If this critical-period hypothesis turns out to be correct, it would explain why clinicians have found that sexual orientation is difficult, if not impossible, to modify.

American Sexual Behavior
Homosexuality

EXPLORATIONS IN PSYCHOLOGY
America's Sexual Landscape and Its Myths

ACCORDING TO sexuality expert Bernie Zilbergeld (1992), dramatic changes in the sexual landscape have taken place in the last decade—from changing expectations of women to new definitions of masculinity, from the fear of disease to the renewed focus on long-term relationships. Sexuality's many myths have led to unrealistic expectations for our sexual lives. One man commented that he had learned so much misinformation about sex as a child that it was taking him the rest of his life to unlearn it. In middle age, he still can't believe how much stress he caused himself when he was younger and wishes he could apologize to the women who knew him in his earlier years. Among the sexual myths, according to Zilbergeld, are the myths that men need a large penis to satisfy a woman; that male and female orgasm are absolutely necessary for sexual satisfaction; that intercourse is the only real sexual act; that good sex has to be spontaneous (without planning or talking); and that when men have any questions, doubts, or problems in sex, it is virtually a crime.

Too often people conceive of sex as a performance skill like race car driving or swimming. However, sex is best conceptualized as a form of communication within a relationship. Indeed, caring couples with good communication skills can usually survive most sexual problems, but uncaring couples with poor communication skills often do not have lasting relationships even if their sexual experiences are adequate or even good.

Although the majority of us manage to develop a mature sexuality, for most individuals there are some periods of vulnerability and confusion along the way. Many individuals have an almost insatiable curiosity about sexuality. Some wonder and worry about their sexual attractiveness, their ability to satisfy their sexual partner, and whether they will experience the ultimate sexual fantasy. Often our worries about our sexuality are fueled by media stereotypes about sexual potency and superhuman sexual exploits.

With regard to anatomical structures, neuroscientist Simon LeVay (1991) found that an area of the hypothalamus that governs sexual behavior is twice as large (about the size of a grain of sand) in heterosexual males as in homosexual males. This area was found to be about the same size in homosexual males and heterosexual females. Critics of this research point out that many of the homosexuals in the study had AIDS and suggest that their brains could have been altered by the disease.

An individual's sexual orientation—homosexual, heterosexual, or bisexual—is most likely determined by a combination of genetic, hormonal, cognitive, and environmental factors (Baldwin & Baldwin, 1998). Most experts on homosexuality believe that no one factor alone causes homosexuality and that the relative weight of each factor can vary from one individual to the next. In effect, no one knows exactly why some individuals are homosexual. Scientists have a clearer picture of what does not cause homosexuality. For example, children raised by gay or lesbian parents or couples are no more likely to be homosexual than are children raised by heterosexual parents (Patterson, 1995). There also is no evidence that male homosexuality is caused by a dominant mother or a weak father, or that female homosexuality is caused by girls choosing male role models.

How can gays and lesbians adapt to a world in which they are a minority? According to psychologist Laura Brown (1989), gays and lesbians experience life as a minority in a dominant, majority culture. For lesbian women and gay men, developing a *bicultural identity* creates new ways of defining themselves. Brown believes that gays and lesbians adapt best when they don't define themselves in polarities, such as trying to live in an encapsulated gay or lesbian world completely divorced from the majority culture or completely accepting the dictates and bias of the majority culture. Balancing the demands of the two cultures—the minority gay/lesbian

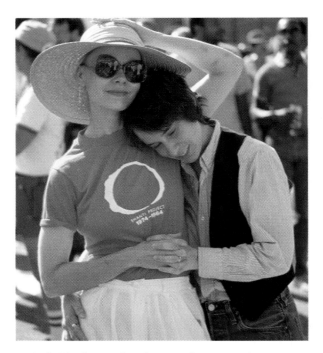

An individual's sexual preference—heterosexual, homosexual, or bisexual—is most likely determined by a mix of genetic, hormonal, cognitive, and environmental factors.

SUMMARY TABLE 9.3
Sexuality

Concept	Processes/ Related Ideas	Characteristics/Discussions
Biological, Cognitive, Sensory/ Perceptual, and Cultural Factors	Biological Factors	Sex hormones are powerful chemicals that are controlled by the master gland in the brain, the pituitary. The two main classes of sex hormones are estrogens, the most important of which is estradiol, and androgens, the most important of which is testosterone. As we move from the lower to the higher animals, the role of hormones becomes less clear, especially in females.
	Cognitive and Sensory/ Perceptual Factors	Humans' thoughts and images are involved in their sexual lives. So are sensory/ perceptual factors. Females tend to be more sexually aroused by touch, males by visual stimulation. Pheromones are involved in sexual attraction in many nonhuman animals, but their role in humans has not been documented. Many "aphrodisiacs" have been proposed as sexual stimulants, but there is no clear evidence that anything we eat, drink, or inject has aphrodisiac qualities.
	Cultural Factors	Sexual motivation is also influenced by cultural factors, and sexual values vary extensively across cultures. Sexual scripts, such as traditional religious and romantic, influence sexual behavior.
The Human Sexual Response Cycle	Its Nature	Masters and Johnson mapped out the human sexual response cycle, which consists of four phases: excitement, plateau, orgasm, and resolution.
Psychosexual Dysfunctions	Their Nature	Psychosexual dysfunctions involve impairments in the sexual response cycle. Significant advancements in treating these dysfunctions have occurred in recent years.
Heterosexuality and Homosexuality	Heterosexual Attitudes and Behavior	Describing sexual practices in America always has been challenging. The 1994 Sex in America Survey was a major improvement over the earlier surveys by Kinsey and Hunt. In the 1994 survey, Americans' sexual lives were portrayed as being more conservative than in the earlier surveys.
	Homosexual Attitudes and Behavior	It generally is accepted to view sexual orientation along a continuum from exclusively heterosexual to exclusively homosexual. An individual's sexual orientation likely is the result of a combination of genetic, hormonal, cognitive, and environmental factors.

culture and the majority heterosexual culture—can often lead to more effective coping for homosexuals, says Brown.

At this point we have discussed a number of ideas about sexuality. An overview of these ideas is presented in summary table 9.3. Next, we continue our journey through different topics in motivation as we explore the motivation to be competent and to achieve.

Achievement Motivation

In our discussion of sexual motivation, we described biological, cognitive, and social aspects of the motivation. With achievement, we move away from biological factors and focus more on cognitive and social factors. Some people are highly motivated to succeed and spend considerable effort striving to excel. Others are not as motivated to succeed and don't work as hard to achieve. These two types of individuals vary in their achievement motivation.

Motivation and Learning

Need for Achievement

Need for achievement *is the desire to accomplish something, to reach a standard of excellence, and to expend effort to excel.* Borrowing from Henry Murray's (1938) theory and measurement of personality, psychologist David McClelland (1955) assessed achievement by showing individuals ambiguous pictures that were likely to stimulate achievement-related responses. The individuals were asked to tell a story about the picture, and their comments were scored according to how strongly they reflected achievement. Researchers have found that individuals whose stories reflect high achievement motivation have a stronger hope for success than fear of failure, are moderate rather than high- or low-risk takers, and persist with effort when tasks become difficult (Atkinson & Raynor, 1974).

McClelland (1978) also wondered if you could boost achievement behavior by increasing achievement motivation. To find out, he trained the businessmen in a village in India to become more achievement oriented, encouraging them to increase their hope for success, reduce their fear of failure, take moderate risks, and persist with a great deal of effort when tasks become difficult. Compared to village businessmen in a nearby town, the village businessmen who were trained by McClelland started more new businesses and employed more new people in the 2 years after the training.

Person/Cognitive Factors

In chapter 1, we explored Albert Bandura's social cognitive theory ◀▥ P. 8. Recall that Bandura believes that person/cognitive factors are an important aspect of understanding behavior. Let's examine what some of these person/cognitive factors are in understanding achievement, beginning with intrinsic/extrinsic motivation.

Intrinsic and Extrinsic Motivation   Earlier in this chapter we mentioned that whether motivation is internal (intrinsic) or external (extrinsic) is a key aspect of understanding motivation. This is especially true in the area of achievement.

Almost every boss, parent, or teacher has wondered whether or not to offer a reward to someone who does well (extrinsic motivation), or whether to let the individual's internal, self-determined motivation operate (intrinsic motivation). If someone is producing shoddy work, seems bored, or has a negative attitude, offering incentives may improve his or her motivation. But there are times when external rewards can diminish achievement motivation. One study showed that,

Calvin and Hobbes   by Bill Watterson

of students who already had a strong interest in art, those who did not expect a reward spent more time drawing than did their counterparts who knew they would be rewarded for drawing (Lepper, Greene, & Nisbett, 1973). The problem with using a reward as an incentive is that individuals may perceive that the reward is what caused their achievement behavior rather than their own motivation to be competent.

Many psychologists believe intrinsic motivation has more positive outcomes than extrinsic motivation (Deci & Ryan, 1994; Harackiewicz, 1998). They argue that intrinsic motivation is more likely to produce competent behavior and mastery. Especially important is the view that self-determination (which is intrinsic) produces a sense of personal control that benefits the individual. Some psychologists, though, stress that many highly successful individuals are intrinsically motivated (have a high personal standard of achievement and emphasize personal effort) and extrinsically motivated (are highly competitive). However, extrinsic motivation (being competitive, frequently comparing yourself with others, and seeking external rewards) by itself usually is not recommended.

Next, our attention shifts to attribution. As you read about attribution, you will see that intrinsic and extrinsic motivation are often one set of causes that individuals look to as they attempt to explain their behavior.

Intrinsic Motivation
Motivating Students

Attribution

Attribution theory *states that individuals are motivated to discover the underlying causes of behavior as part of the effort to make sense out of the behavior.* In a way, attribution theorists say, people are like intuitive scientists, seeking the cause behind what happens.

The reasons individuals behave the way they do can be classified in a number of ways, but one basic distinction stands out above all others—the distinction between internal causes, such as the actor's personality traits or motives, and external causes, which are environmental, situational factors such as rewards or task difficulty (Heider, 1958). If college students do not do well on a test, do they attribute it to the teacher's plotting against them and making the test too difficult (external cause) or to their not studying hard enough (internal cause)? The answer to such a question influences how people feel about themselves. If students believe that their performance is the teacher's fault, they will not feel as bad as when they do poorly because they do not spend enough time studying.

An extremely important aspect of internal causes for achievement is *effort*. Unlike many causes of success, effort is under a person's control and amenable to change. The importance of effort in achievement is recognized even by children. In one study, third- to sixth-grade students felt that effort was the most effective strategy for good school performance (Skinner, Wellborn, & Connell, 1990).

Goal-Setting, Planning, and Monitoring

Goal-setting, planning, and self-monitoring are critical aspects of achievement. Goal-setting and planning often work in concert. Goals help individuals to reach their dreams, increase their self-discipline, and maintain interest.

Currently, there is considerable interest in studying people's self-generated goals (Schultheiss & Brunstein, 1999). Some examples of these goals are "personal projects," "life tasks," and "personal strivings." Personal projects can range from trivial pursuits (such as letting a bad haircut grow out) to life goals (such as becoming a good parent). Life tasks are problems individuals currently are working on. They usually focus on normal life transitions such as going to college, getting married, and entering an occupation. Many college students say that their life tasks revolve around academic achievement and social concerns (Cantor & Langston, 1989). Personal strivings represent what a person is typically trying to do. For example, someone might say that she typically tries to do well in school.

Researchers have found that individuals' achievement improves when they set goals that are specific, proximal, and challenging (Bandura, 1997; Schunk, 1996).

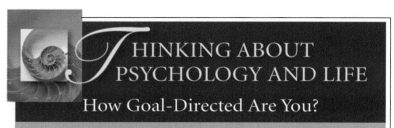

THINKING ABOUT PSYCHOLOGY AND LIFE
How Goal-Directed Are You?

To EVALUATE HOW goal-directed you are, consider how much each of the following statements is like you or not like you:

- I set long-term and short-term goals.
- I set challenging goals that are neither too easy nor beyond my reach.
- I am good at managing my time and setting priorities to make sure I get the most important things done.
- I regularly do "to do" lists and successfully get most of these items done.
- I set deadlines and consistently meet them.
- I regularly monitor how well I'm progressing toward my goals and make changes in my behavior if necessary.
- When I am under pressure, I still plan my days and weeks in a clear, logical manner.
- I set task-involved, mastery goals rather than ego-involved or work-involved goals.

If most of your answers were that these descriptions characterize you then you likely are a goal-directed individual. If these statements do not characterize you, consider ways that you can become more goal-directed.

A fuzzy, nonspecific goal is "I want to be successful." A more concrete, specific goal is "I want to have a 3.5 average at the end of the semester." You can set long-term (distal) and short-term (proximal) goals. It is okay to set long-term goals, such as "I want to be a clinical psychologist," but if you do, make sure that you also create short-term goals, which are steps along the way. "Getting an A on the next psychology test" is an example of a short-term, proximal goal. So is "Doing all of my studying for this class by 4 P.M. Sunday." David McNally (1990), author of *Even Eagles Need a Push,* advises that when individuals set goals and plan, they should remind themselves to live their lives one day at a time. Make your commitments in bite-size chunks. A house is built one brick at a time, a cathedral one stone at a time. The artist paints one stroke at a time. You also should work in small increments.

Another good strategy is to set challenging goals. A challenging goal is a commitment to self-improvement. Strong interest and involvement in activities are sparked by challenges. Goals that are easy to reach generate little interest or effort. However, unrealistically high goals can bring failure and diminish self-confidence.

Achievement motivation researcher John Nicholls and his colleagues (Nicholls, 1979; Nicholls & others, 1990) distinguish among ego-involved goals, task-involved goals, and work-avoidant goals. Individuals with ego-involved goals strive to maximize favorable evaluations and minimize unfavorable ones. Thus, ego-involved individuals focus on how smart they will look and their ability to outperform others. By contrast, individuals who have task-involved goals focus more on mastering tasks. They concentrate on how well they can do the task and what they can learn. Individuals with work-avoidant goals try to exert as little effort as possible on a task. A good achievement strategy is to develop task-involved, mastery goals rather than ego-involved or work-avoidant goals.

Planning how to reach a goal and monitoring progress toward the goal are critical aspects of achievement (Eccles, Wigfield, & Schiefele, 1998). Researchers have found that high-achieving individuals monitor their own learning and systematically evaluate their progress toward their goal more than low-achieving individuals do (Zimmerman, Bonner, & Kovach, 1996).

Cultural, Ethnic, and Socioeconomic Variations in Achievement

People in the United States are often more achievement-oriented than people in many other countries. One study of 104 societies revealed that parents in nonindustrialized countries placed a lower value on their children's achievement and independence and a higher value on obedience and cooperation than did the parents in industrialized countries (Barry, Child, & Bacon, 1959). In comparisons between Anglo-American children and Mexican and Latino children, the Anglo-American children were more competitive and less cooperative. For example, one study found that Anglo-American children were more likely to keep other children from gaining when they could not realize those gains themselves (Kagan & Madsen, 1972). Another study showed that Mexican children were more family-oriented whereas Anglo-American children tend to be more concerned about themselves (Holtzmann, 1982).

UCLA psychologist Sandra Graham is shown here talking with a group of young boys about motivation. Dr. Graham has conducted important research showing that middle-class African American children—like their White counterparts—have high achievement expectations and attribute their failures to lack of effort rather than to lack of luck.

SUMMARY TABLE 9.4
Achievement

Concept	Processes/ Related Ideas	Characteristics/Discussions
Need for Achievement	Its Nature	Early interest focused on the need for achievement, defined as the desire to accomplish something, to reach a standard of excellence, and to expend an effort to excel.
Person/Cognitive Factors	Intrinsic/Extrinsic Motivation	Motivation can be described as intrinsic (internal) or extrinsic (external). Many psychologists believe it is important to emphasize intrinsic motivation, although some successful individuals are both intrinsically and extrinsically motivated.
	Attribution	Attribution theory states that people are motivated to discover the underlying causes of behavior as part of their effort to make sense out of the behavior. The main emphasis in attribution theory has focused on internal causes, especially effort, or external causes.
	Goal Setting, Planning, and Monitoring	These are critical aspects of achievement. Self-generated goals focus on such areas as personal projects, life tasks, and personal strivings. High achievers often set specific, proximal, and challenging goals. They are also likely to set task-involved, mastery goals rather than ego-involved or work-avoidant goals.
Cultural, Ethnic, and Socioeconomic Variations	Their Nature	Individuals in the United States are more achievement oriented than individuals in many other countries. A special concern is the achievement of individuals from various ethnic minority groups. Too often differences have become interpreted as "deficits" by middle-income, White standards. When researchers study both ethnicity and socioeconomic status in the same study, socioeconomic status is often a much better achievement predictor. Middle-income individuals fare better than their low-income counterparts in many achievement settings.

Until recently, researchers studying achievement focused almost exclusively on White males, and when achievement in ethnic minority groups has been studied, the cultural differences have too often been viewed against standards of achievements for White males. As a result, many researchers have reached the conclusion that ethnic minorities are somehow deficient when it comes to achievement (Gibbs & Huang, 1989).

In addition, most studies on ethnic minorities do not take into account socioeconomic status. Socioeconomic status (also called SES) is determined by a combination of occupation, education, and income. When both ethnicity and socioeconomic status are taken into account in the same study, socioeconomic status tends to be a far better predictor of achievement than is ethnicity (Graham, 1986). For example, middle-SES individuals, regardless of their ethnic background, have higher aspirations and expectations than their low-SES counterparts do. Sandra Graham (1986) has found that middle-SES African American children do not fit the stereotypes of either deviant or special populations. They, like their middle-SES White counterparts, have high expectations for their own achievement and understand that failure is often due to lack of effort rather than to luck.

At this point we have studied a number of ideas about achievement. An overview of these ideas is presented in summary table 9.4. Next, we continue our exploration of motivation and emotion, turning to the topic of emotion.

Exploring Emotion
Emotion Research
The Autonomic Nervous System

Emotion

Motivation and emotion are closely linked. Think about sex, which often is associated with joy; about aggression, which usually is associated with anger; and about achievement, which is associated with pride, joy, and anxiety. The terms *motivation* and *emotion* both come from the Latin word *movere*, which means "to move." Both motivation and emotion spur us into action.

Just as with motivation, there are different kinds and intensities of emotions (Brehm, 1999). Not only can a person be motivated to eat rather than have sex, but be more or less hungry, or more or less interested in having sex. Similarly, a person can be happy or angry, and can be fairly happy or ecstatic, annoyed or fuming.

Defining Emotion

Defining emotion is difficult because it is not easy to tell when a person is in an emotional state. Are you in an emotional state when your heart beats fast, your palms sweat, and your stomach churns? Or are you in an emotional state when you think about how much you are in love with someone? Or when you smile or grimace? The body, the mind, and the face play important roles in understanding emotion. Psychologists debate how critical each is in determining whether we are in an emotional state. For our purposes, we will define **emotion** *as feeling, or affect, that can involve physiological arousal (a fast heartbeat, for example), conscious experience (thinking about being in love with someone, for example), and behavioral expression (a smile or grimace, for example).* Psychologists debate which of these components is the most important aspect of emotion and how they mix to produce emotional experiences (Cacioppo & Gardner, 1999; Keltner, 2000).

Biological Dimensions

To further explore emotion, let's begin by examining the biological dimensions of emotion with a special focus on the first component of emotion we described: arousal.

Arousal   As you drive down a highway, the fog thickens. Suddenly you see a pile of cars in front of you. Your mind temporarily freezes, your muscles tighten, your stomach becomes queasy, and your heart feels like it is going to pound out of your chest. You immediately slam on the brakes and try to veer away from the pile of cars. Tires screech, windshield glass flies, and metal smashes. Then all is quiet. After a few short seconds you realize you are alive. You find that you can walk out of the car. Your fear turns to joy, as you sense your luck in not being hurt. In a couple of seconds, the joy turns to anger. You loudly ask who caused the accident.

The Autonomic Nervous System   As you moved through the emotions of fear, joy, and anger, your body changed. Recall from chapter 2, "Biological Foundations and Neuroscience," that the **autonomic nervous system (ANS)** *takes messages to and from the body's internal organs, monitoring such processes as breathing, heart rate, and digestion* ◀▥ P. 50. *The ANS is divided into the sympathetic (SNS) and parasympathetic (PNS) nervous systems* (see figure 9.9).

The **sympathetic nervous system** *is involved in the body's arousal being responsible for quick responses to a stressor, which sometimes is referred to as the fight-or-flight response.* The SNS immediately causes an increase in blood pressure, a faster heart rate, more rapid breathing for greater oxygen intake, and more efficient blood flow to the brain and major muscle groups. All of these changes prepare us for action. At the same time the body stops digesting food, because this is not necessary for immediate action (which could explain why just before an exam, students usually are not hungry).

The **parasympathetic nervous system** *calms the body. Whereas the sympathetic nervous system prepares the individual for fighting or running away, the parasympathetic system promotes relaxation and healing.* When the PNS is activated, heart rate and blood pressure drop, stomach activity and food digestion increase, and breathing slows.

The sympathetic and parasympathetic nervous systems are important in understanding people's emotions. Some emotions are more activating than others. For example, when we are angry, our body becomes prepared for fighting and fleeing. Not surprisingly, anger is associated with elevated SNS activity such as heightened blood pressure and heart rate. Similarly, states of happiness and contentment generally are associated with lower SNS activation.

You have been asked to think about your emotional states in the face of an automobile crash and a college exam. Now put yourself in the situation of lying to someone. Because body changes predictably accompany emotional states, it was reasoned that a machine might be able to determine if a person is lying. The **polygraph** *is a machine used by examiners to try to determine if someone is lying; it monitors changes in the body— heart rate, breathing, and electrodermal response (an index detecting skin resistance to passage of a weak electric current)— thought to be influenced by emotional states.* To read further about the polygraph, see Explorations in Psychology.

Arousal and Performance   Early in this century, two psychologists described the role of arousal in performance. What is now known as the **Yerkes-Dodson law** *states that performance is best under conditions of moderate rather than low or high arousal.* At the low end of arousal you might be too lethargic to perform tasks well; at the high end you may not be able to concentrate. Think about how aroused you were the last time you took a test. If your arousal was too high, your performance probably suffered. If it was too low, you may not have worked fast enough to finish the test. Also think about performance in sports. Being too aroused usually harms athletes' performance. For example, a thumping heart and rapid breathing have been present on many golfers' missed putts and basketball players' failed free-throw attempts. However, if these athletes' arousal is too low they may not concentrate well on the task at hand.

Moderate arousal often serves us best in tackling life's tasks, but there are times when low or high arousal produces optimal performance. For well-learned or simple tasks (signing your name, pushing a button on request), optimal arousal can be quite high. By contrast, when learning a task or doing something complex (such as solving an algebraic equation), much lower arousal is preferred. Figure 9.10 projects how arousal might influence easy, moderate, and difficult tasks. As tasks become more difficult, the ability to be alert and attentive, but relaxed, is critical to optimal performance.

Sympathetic Nervous System		Parasympathetic Nervous System
Increases	Blood Flow to Brain	Decreases
Dilate	Pupils of Eyes	Constrict
Faster	Breathing Rate	Slower
Faster	Heartbeat	Slower
Increases	Skin Perspiration	Decreases
Decreases	Digestive Activity	Increases
Increases; stress hormones released	Adrenal Gland Activity	Decreases; stress hormones inhibited

Figure 9.9
Autonomic Nervous System

Polygraph Skepticism

Figure 9.10
Arousal and Performance
The Yerkes-Dodson law states that optimal performance occurs under moderate arousal. However, for new or difficult tasks, low arousal may be best; for well-learned, easy tasks, high arousal can facilitate performance.

EXPLORATIONS IN PSYCHOLOGY
Evaluating Lie Detectors

IN A TYPICAL POLYGRAPH TEST, an individual is asked a number of neutral questions and several key, not so neutral, questions. If the individual's heart rate, breathing, and electrodermal response increase substantially when the key questions are asked, the individual is assumed to be lying.

The polygraph has been widely used, especially in business, to screen new employees for honesty and to reveal employee theft. Following President Reagan's directive in 1983, the government increased their use of the polygraph to discover which individuals were leaking information to the media. Congressional hearings followed and psychologists were called to testify about the polygraph's effectiveness (Saxe, Dougherty, & Cross, 1985). Testimony focused on how a standard lie detector situation does not exist. Inferring truth or deception based on physiological assessment of emotions requires a number of strategies. The complexity of the lie detector situation was brought out in testimony. Although the degree of arousal to a series of questions is measured through simple physiological changes, no unique physiological response to deception has been revealed (Lykken, 1987). Heart rate and breathing can increase for reasons other than lying, making interpretation of the physiological indicators of arousal complex.

Accurately identifying truth or deception rests on the skill of the examiner and the skill of the individual being examined. There are simple things people can do to avoid being detected of lying such as moving their body, taking drugs, and using various cognitive strategies or biofeedback techniques. Tensing your muscles, biting your tongue, squeezing your toes, and shifting your position in the chair can affect the polygraph's accuracy—examiners detect only about 50 to 75 percent of the countermeasures. Drugs, such as tranquilizers that have a calming effect on the individual, are more difficult to detect unless a test is conducted to reveal their use. Sometimes, though, the mere presence of the polygraph and the subject's belief it is accurate at detecting deception triggers confession. Police may use the polygraph in this way to get a criminal to confess. In such cases, the polygraph has served a positive purpose, but in too many instances it has been misused and misrepresented. Experts argue that the polygraph errs just under 50 percent of the time, especially because it cannot distinguish between such feelings as anxiety and guilt (Iacono & Lykken, 1997). The testimony of psychologists that lie detectors are not always accurate led to the Employee Polygraph Protection Act of 1988, which restricts most nongovernment polygraph testing. Most courts also do not accept the results of polygraph testing. However, some psychologists still defend the polygraph's use, saying that polygraph results are about as sound as other, admissible forms of evidence such as hair fiber analysis (Honts, 1998). The majority of psychologists, though, argue against the polygraph's use because of its inability to tell who's lying and who isn't (Iacono & Lykken, 1997; Saxe, 1998).

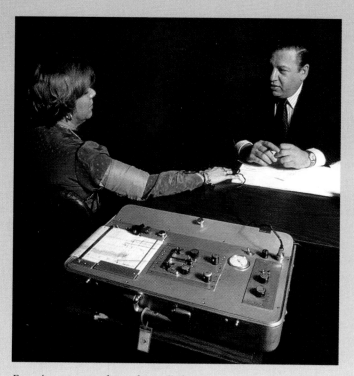

Examiners use a polygraph to tell if someone is lying; it monitors changes in the body believed to be influenced by emotional states. Controversy has swirled about the polygraph's use. Because of the polygraph's inaccuracy, Congress passed the Employee Polygraph Protection Act of 1988, restricting the use of the polygraph in nongovernment settings.

James-Lange and Cannon-Bard Theories

Psychologists have developed a number of theories about the role of arousal in emotion. Imagine that you and your date are enjoying a picnic in the country. As you prepare to eat, a bull runs across the field toward you. Why are you afraid? Two well-known theories of emotion that involve physiological processes provide answers to this question.

Common sense tells you that you are trembling and running away from the bull because you are afraid. But William James (1890/1950) and Carl Lange (1922) said emotion works in the opposite way. The **James-Lange theory** *suggests that emotion results from physiological states triggered by stimuli in the environment. Emotion occurs after physiological reactions.* You see the bull scratching his hoof, and you begin to run away. The aroused body then sends sensory messages to the brain, at which point emotion is perceived. According to this theory, you do not run away because you are afraid, rather you are afraid because you are running away. In other words, you perceive a stimulus in the environment, your body responds, and you interpret the body's reaction as emotion. In one of James' own examples, you perceive you have lost your fortune, you cry, and then interpret the crying as feeling sad. This goes against the commonsense sequence of losing your fortune, feeling sorry, and then crying.

Walter Cannon (1927) objected to the James-Lange theory. To understand his objection, imagine the bull and the picnic once again. Seeing the bull scratching its hooves causes the hypothalamus of your brain to do two things simultaneously: first, it stimulates your autonomic nervous system to produce the physiological changes involved in emotion (increased heart rate, rapid breathing); second, it sends messages to your cerebral cortex where the experience of emotion is perceived. Philip Bard (1934) supported this theory, and so the theory became known as the **Cannon-Bard theory,** *the theory that emotion and physiological reactions occur simultaneously. In the Cannon-Bard theory, the body plays a less important role than in the James-Lange theory.* Figure 9.11 shows how the James-Lange and Cannon-Bard theories differ.

Neural Circuits and Neurotransmitters

Going beyond the early theories of emotion, contemporary emotion researchers are interested in more precisely charting the neural circuitry of emotions, especially specific emotions such as fear, and discovering the role of neurotransmitters in emotion.

In terms of neural circuits, in chapter 2, "Biological Foundations and Neuroscience," we described the amygdala as an almond-shaped part of the limbic system at the base of each of the brain's temporal lobes (see figure 9.12) ◀▥▥ P. 52. It houses circuits that color our experience with emotion. The amygdala not only receives simple signals (such as loud noises) from the brain's lower stations but also abstract, complex information from the brain's highest levels in the cerebral cortex. The amygdala

Figure 9.11
James-Lange and Cannon-Bard Theories

Thalamus

Amygdala

Hippocampus

*F*igure 9.12
Important Structures in the Brain's Emotion Circuitry

The amygdala plays an important role in emotion through its many connections to other areas of the brain. For example, it has reciprocal connections with the cerebral cortex's frontal lobes, which are involved in abstract, complex information processing. In the specific emotion of fear, information is processed in the thalamus and then either is transmitted to the cerebral cortex and on to the amygdala or is directly transmitted to the amygdala.

The Emotional Brain

Psychophysiology and Emotion

in turn sends signals to many other parts of the brain, including the decision-making circuitry of the cerebral cortex's frontal lobes (Pinker, 1997).

The neural pathway of one emotion—fear—has been mapped well (Izard, Schultz, & Levinson, 1998). When an organism perceives an external stimulus (such as the raging bull), the neural message is transmitted to the thalamus (see figure 9.12). From there, the information moves along one of two pathways: (1) to the cerebral cortex where more extensive information processing takes place or (2) directly to the amygdala. The direct route from the thalamus to the amygdala does not require higher cortical processing. The direct route is rapid, automatic, and unconscious.

Thus, the amygdala appears to be an important structure in the neural circuitry of emotion through its many connections with other areas of the brain.

In addition to charting the main brain structures involved in neural pathways of emotions, researchers also are intrigued by the roles that neurotransmitters play in these pathways. Endorphins and dopamine might be involved in positive emotions such as happiness, and norepinephrine might function in regulating arousal (Panskepp, 1993; White & Milner, 1992) ◀▥ P. 54.

Much of what we have said about emotion has focused on its physiological basis. While physiological factors play important roles in emotion, cognitive processes are at work as well.

Cognitive Dimensions

Does emotion depend on the tides of the mind? Are we happy only when we think we are happy? Cognitive theories of emotion share an important point: emotion always has a cognitive component (Cornelius, 1996). Thinking is said to be responsible for feelings of love and hate, joy and sadness. While giving cognitive processes the main credit for emotion, the cognitive theories also recognize the role of the brain and body in emotion. That is, the hypothalamus and autonomic nervous system make connections with the peripheral areas of the body when emotion is experienced. According to cognitive theorists, body and thought are involved in emotion (Oatley, 2000).

The Two-Factor Theory of Emotion Stanley Schachter and Jerome Singer (1962) developed a theory of emotion that gave cognition a stronger role in emotion. The **two-factor theory of emotion** *is Schachter and Singer's theory that emotion is determined by two main factors: physiological arousal and cognitive labeling* (see figure 9.13). They argue that we look to the external world for an explanation of why we are aroused. We interpret the external cues present and label the emotion. For example, if you feel good after someone has made a pleasant comment to you, you might label the emotion "happy." If you feel bad after you have done something wrong, you may label the feeling "guilty."

To test their theory of emotion, Schachter and Singer (1962) injected subjects with epinephrine, a drug that produces high arousal. After volunteer subjects were given the drug, they observed someone else behave in either a euphoric way (shooting papers at a wastebasket) or an angry way (stomping out of the room). As predicted, the euphoric and angry behavior influenced the subjects' cognitive interpretation of their own arousal. When they were with a happy person, they rated themselves as happy; when they were with an angry person, they said they were angry. But this effect was found only when the subjects were not told about the true effects of the injection. When subjects were told that the drug would increase their heart rate and make them jittery, they said the reason for their own arousal was the drug, not the other person's behavior.

Psychologists have had difficulty replicating the Schachter and Singer experiment but, in general, research supports the belief that misinterpreted arousal intensifies emotional experiences (Leventhal & Tomarken, 1986). An intriguing study substantiates this belief. It went like this: An attractive woman approached men while they were crossing the Capilano River Bridge in British Columbia. Only those without a female companion were approached. The woman asked the men to make up a brief story for a project she was doing on creativity (Dutton & Aron, 1974). By the way, the Capilano River Bridge sways precariously more than 200 feet above rapids and rocks (see figure 9.14). The female interviewer made the same request of other men crossing a much safer, lower bridge. The men on the Capilano River Bridge told more sexually oriented stories and rated the female interviewer more attractive than did men on the lower, less frightening bridge.

The Primacy Debate: Cognition or Emotion?
Richard Lazarus (1991) believes cognitive activity is a precondition for emotion. He says we cognitively appraise ourselves and our social circumstances. These appraisals, which include values, goals, commitments, beliefs, and expectations, determine our emotions. People may feel happy because they have a deep religious commitment, angry because they did not get the raise they anticipated, or fearful because they expect to fail an exam.

Robert Zajonc (1984) disagrees with Lazarus. Emotions are primary, he says, and our thoughts are a result of them. Who is right? Both likely are correct. Lazarus refers mainly to a cluster of related events that occur over a period of time, whereas Zajonc describes single events or a simple preference for one stimulus over another. Lazarus speaks about love over the course of months and years, a sense of value to the community, and plans for retirement; Zajonc talks about a car accident, an encounter with a snake, and liking ice cream better than spinach. Some of our emotional reactions are virtually instantaneous and probably don't involve cognitive appraisal, such as a shriek on detecting a snake. Other emotional circumstances, especially those that occur over a long period of time, such as a depressed mood or anger toward a friend, are more likely to involve cognitive appraisal.

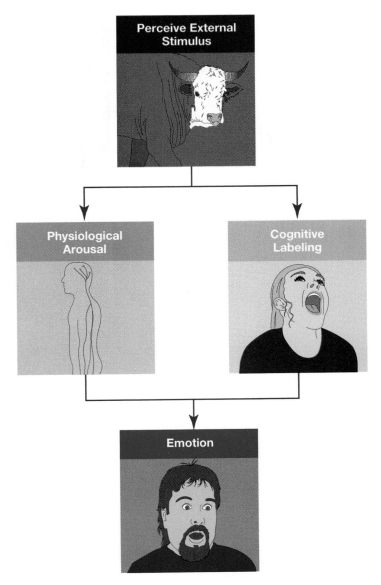

𝓕igure 9.13
Schachter and Singer's Two-Factor Theory of Emotion

Behavioral Dimensions

Remember that our definition of emotion includes not only physiological and cognitive components, but also a behavioral component. The behavioral component can be verbal or nonverbal. Verbally, a person might show their love for someone by professing it verbally or display their anger by saying some nasty things. Nonverbally, a person might smile, frown, show a fearful expression, droop their head, or slump their posture.

The most interest in the behavioral dimension of emotion has focused on the nonverbal behavior of facial expressions. Emotion researchers have been intrigued by people's ability to detect the emotion a person is experiencing on the basis of his or her facial expression. In a typical research study, individuals will be shown photographs like those in figure 9.15. In the research of Paul Ekman and his colleagues

$\mathcal{F}$igure 9.14
Capilano River Bridge Experiment: Misinterpreted Arousal Intensifies Emotional Experiences

The precarious Capilano River Bridge in British Columbia is shown at left; the experiment is shown in progress at right. An attractive woman approached men while they were crossing the 200-foot-high bridge; she asked them to make up a story to help her out. She also made the same request on a lower, much safer bridge. The men on the Capilano River Bridge told sexier stories, probably because they were aroused by the fear or excitement of being up so high on a swaying bridge. Apparently they interpreted their arousal as sexual attraction for the female interviewer.

Emotion Research Resources

(Ekman & Friesen, 1984; Ekman & O'Sullivan, 1991), participants are usually able to identify these six basic emotions: happiness, anger, sadness, surprise, disgust, and fear.

Might our facial expressions not only reflect our emotions but also influence them? The **facial feedback hypothesis** *states that facial expressions can influence emotions as well as reflect them. In this view, facial muscles send signals to the brain, which help individuals recognize the emotion they are experiencing.* For example, we feel happier when we smile and sadder when we frown.

Support for the facial feedback hypothesis was found in an experiment by Ekman and his colleagues (1983). In this study, professional actors moved their facial muscles in very precise ways, such as raising their eyebrows and pulling them together, raising their upper eyelids, and stretching their lips horizontally back to their ears (you might want to try this out yourself). They were asked to hold their expression for 10 seconds, during which time the researchers measured their heart rate and body temperature. When they moved facial muscles in the way we described, they showed a rise in heart rate and a steady body temperature, physiological reactions that characterize fear. When the actors made an angry expression with their face (eyes have a penetrating stare, brows are drawn together and downward, and lips are pressed together or opened and pushed forward), their heart rate and body temperature both increased. The concept involved in the facial feedback hypothesis might sound familiar. It provides support for the James-Lange theory of emotion we discussed earlier—namely, that emotional experiences can be generated by changes in and awareness of our own bodily states.

Are the facial expressions that are associated with different emotions largely innate or do they vary considerably across cultures?

Sociocultural Dimensions

Culture and the Expression of Emotion

In *The Expression of the Emotions in Man and Animals,* Charles Darwin (1872/1965) argued that the facial expressions of human beings are innate, not learned; are the same in all cultures around the world; and evolved from the emotions of animals. Darwin compared the similarity of human snarls of anger with the growls of dogs and the hisses of cats. He compared the giggling of chimpanzees when they are tickled under their arms with human laughter.

Today psychologists still believe that emotions, especially facial expressions of emotion, have strong biological ties. For example, children who are blind from birth and have never observed the smile or frown on another person's face, still smile or frown in the same way that children with normal vision do.

How does culture influence the expression of emotions? What role does gender play in emotion?

The universality of facial expressions and the ability of people from different cultures to accurately label the emotion that lies behind the facial expression has been extensively researched. Psychologist Paul Ekman's (1980, 1996) careful observations reveal that our many faces of emotion do not vary significantly from one culture to another. For example, Ekman and his colleague photographed people expressing emotions such as happiness, fear, surprise, disgust, and grief. They found that when they showed the photographs to other people from the United States, Chile, Japan, Brazil, and Borneo (an Indonesian island in the western Pacific Ocean), each person tended to label the same faces with the same emotions (Ekman & Friesen, 1968). In another study the focus was on the way the Fore tribe, an isolated Stone Age culture in New Guinea, matched descriptions of emotions with facial expressions (Ekman & Friesen, 1971). Before Ekman's visit, most of the Fore had never seen a Caucasian face. Ekman showed them photographs of American faces expressing emotions such as fear, happiness, anger, and surprise. Then he read stories about people in emotional situations. The Fore were able to match the descriptions of emotions with the facial expressions in the photographs. The similarity of facial expressions of emotions by persons in New Guinea and the United States is shown in figure 9.16.

While facial expressions of basic emotions appear to be universal across cultures, display rules for emotion are not culturally universal. **Display rules** *are sociocultural standards that determine when, where, and how emotions should be expressed.* For example, while happiness is a universally expressed emotion, when, where, and how it is displayed may vary from one culture to another. The same is true for other emotions such as fear, sadness, and anger. For example, members of the Utku culture in Alaska discourage anger by cultivating acceptance and by dissociating themselves from any display of anger. If a trip is hampered by an unexpected snowstorm, the Utku do not become frustrated, but accept the presence of the snowstorm and build an igloo. Most of us would not act as mildly in the face of subzero weather and barriers to our travel.

In addition to facial expressions, emotions are also expressed in many other nonverbal signals of body movement, posture, and gesture (Russell, 1999). Some basic

Figure 9.15
Recognizing Emotions in Facial Expressions
Before reading further, look at the six photographs and determine the emotion reflected in each of the six faces. They are: *(top row across)* happiness, anger, sadness; *(bottom row across)* surprise, disgust, fear.

Paul Ekman's Research
Cultural Contexts and Emotion

Figure 9.16
Emotional Expressions in the United States and New Guinea

At left are two females from the United States; on the right are two males from the Fore tribe in New Guinea. Notice the similarity in their expressions of disgust and happiness. Psychologists believe that the facial expression of emotion is virtually the same in all cultures.

Nonverbal Communication of Emotions

nonverbal signals appear to be universal indicators of certain emotions, just as facial expressions are. For example, when people are depressed it shows not only in their sad facial expression, but also in their slow body movement, downturned head, and slumped posture.

Many nonverbal signals of emotion, though, vary from one culture to another (Cohen & Borsoi, 1996). For example, male-to-male kissing is commonplace in some cultures, such as Yemen (in the Middle East), but uncommon in other cultures, such as the United States. And the "thumb up" sign, which in most cultures means either everything is OK or the desire to hitch a ride, is an insult in Greece, similar to a raised third finger in the United States.

Gender Influences　Unless you've been isolated on a mountaintop away from people, television, magazines, and newspapers, you probably know the master stereotype about gender and emotion: She is emotional, he is not. This stereotype is a powerful and pervasive image in our culture (Shields, 1991).

Is this stereotype supported when researchers study the nature of emotional experiences in females and males? Researchers have found that females and males are often more alike in the way they experience emotion than the master stereotype would lead us to believe. Females and males often use the same facial expressions, adopt the same language, and describe their emotional experiences similarly when they keep diaries about their life experiences. Thus, the master stereotype that females are emotional and males are not is simply that—a stereotype. Thus, for many emotional experiences, researchers do not find differences between females and males—both sexes are equally likely to experience love, jealousy, anxiety in new social situations, be angry when they are insulted, grieve when close relationships end, and be embarrassed when they make mistakes in public (Tavris & Wade, 1984).

When we go beyond the master stereotype and consider some specific emotional experiences, the context in which emotion is displayed, and certain beliefs about emotion, gender does matter in understanding emotion (Brannon, 1999; Shields, 1991). Consider anger. Men are more likely to show anger toward strangers, especially other men, when they

In the Middle Eastern country of Yemen, male-to-male kissing is commonplace, but in the United States it is very uncommon.

feel they have been challenged, and men are more likely to turn their anger into aggressive action than women are.

Differences between females and males regarding emotion are more likely to occur in contexts that highlight social roles and relationships. For example, females are more likely than males to give accounts of emotion that include interpersonal relationships. And females are more likely to express fear and sadness than males, especially when communicating with their friends and family.

Classifying Emotions

Emotions are complex and varied. For example, there are more than 200 words for emotions in the English language. One way of classifying emotions is the wheel model.

The Wheel Model   A number of psychologists have classified the emotions we experience by placing them on a wheel. One such model was proposed by Robert Plutchik (1980) (see figure 9.17). He believes emotions have four dimensions: (1) They are positive or negative, (2) they are primary or mixed, (3) many are polar opposites, and (4) they vary in intensity. Ecstasy and enthusiasm are positive emotions; grief and anger are negative emotions. For example, think about your ecstasy when you get an unexpected A on a test, or your enthusiasm about the football game this weekend—these are positive emotions. In contrast, think about negative emotions, such as your grief when someone close to you dies or your anger when someone verbally attacks you. Positive emotions enhance our self-esteem; negative emotions lower our self-esteem. Positive emotions improve our relationships with others; negative emotions depress the quality of those relationships.

Plutchik also believes that emotions are like colors. Every color of the spectrum can be produced by mixing the primary colors. Possibly some emotions are primary, and if mixed together, they combine to form all other emotions. Happiness, disgust, surprise, sadness, anger, and fear are candidates for primary emotions. For example, combining sadness and surprise gives disappointment. Jealousy is composed of love and anger. Plutchik developed the emotion wheel to show how primary emotions work. Mixtures of primary emotions adjacent to each other combine to produce other emotions. Some emotions are opposites—love and remorse, optimism and disappointment.

To illustrate how positive emotions are involved in our lives, we will explore the nature of happiness. Then, to illustrate negative emotions in our lives, we will examine anger.

A Positive Emotion: Happiness   It was not until 1973 that *Psychological Abstracts*, the major source of psychological research summaries, included *happiness* as an index term. The recent interest in happiness focuses on positive ways we experience our lives, including cognitive judgments of our well-being (Parducci, 1996). That is, psychologists want to know what makes you happy and how you perceive your happiness. Many years ago, French philosopher Jean-Jacques Rousseau described the subjective nature of happiness this way: "Happiness is a good bank account, a good cook, and a good digestion."

In a recent review of research on happiness, being a good cook and having a good digestion were not on the list of factors that contribute to our happiness, but the following were (Diener & Diener, 1998; Diener & others, 1999):

- Psychological and personality characteristics: high levels of self-esteem, optimism, extroversion, and personal control
- A supportive network of close relationships
- A culture that offers positive interpretations of most daily events
- Being engaged by work and leisure
- A faith that embodies social support, purpose, and hope

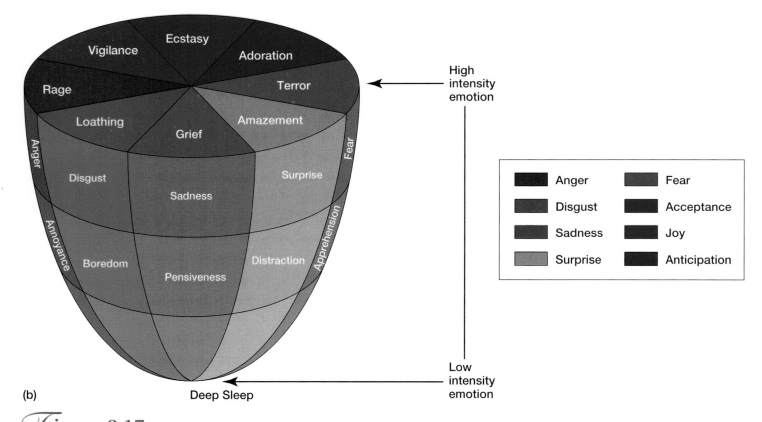

𝒯igure 9.17
Plutchik's Classification of Emotions

(a) Plutchik theorized that people experience the eight basic emotions represented in the colored part of the drawing (such as joy and sadness), as well as some combination of these (such as love being a combination of joy and acceptance). *(b)* The bottom drawing illustrates how changes in intensity can modify each of the eight basic emotions. For example, notice how anger, when experienced intensely, becomes rage.

Some factors that many people believe are involved in happiness (such as age and gender) are not.

But what about Rousseau's "good bank account"? Can we buy happiness? One study tried to find out if lottery winners are happier than people who have not received a landslide of money (Brickman, Coates, & Janoff-Bulman, 1978). Twenty-two major lottery winners were compared with twenty-two people living in the same area of the city. The general happiness of the two groups did not differ when they were asked about the past, present, and the future. The people who hadn't won a lottery actually were happier doing life's mundane things such as watching television, buying clothes, and talking with a friend.

Winning a lottery does not appear to be the key to happiness. What is important, though, is having enough money to buy life's necessities. Extremely wealthy people are not happier than people who can purchase the necessities. People in wealthy countries are not happier than people in poor countries. The message is clear: If you believe money buys happiness, think again (Diener, 1984).

Psychologist Ed Diener (1984) agrees that intense positive emotions—such as winning a lottery or getting a date with the person of your dreams—do not add much to a person's general sense of well-being in part because they are rare, and because they can decrease the positive emotion and increase the negative emotion we feel in other circumstances. According to Diener, happiness boils down to the frequency of positive emotions and the infrequency of negative emotions. Diener's view flies in the face of common sense; you would think that frequent, intense positive emotions and minimal nonintense negative emotions produce the most happiness. But the common-sense view fails to consider that intense positive moments can diminish the sensation of future positive events. For example, if you shoot par in a round of golf, you will be overwhelmed with happiness at the time you perform this feat, but if you play golf a week later and do well but not great, the previous emotional high can diminish your positive emotion the next week. It is the rare, if nonexistent, human being who experiences intense positive emotions and infrequent negative emotions week after week after week.

A Negative Emotion: Anger

Anger is a powerful emotion. It has a strong impact not only on our social relationships, but also on the person experiencing the emotion (Norcross & Kobayashi, 1999). We can easily recount obvious examples of anger that often harm not only others but the angry individual as well—unrestrained and recurrent violence toward others, verbal and physical abuse of children, perpetual bitterness, the tendency to carry a "chip on the shoulder" in which a person overinterprets others' actions as demeaning, and the inability to inhibit the expression of anger.

What makes people angry? People often get angry when they feel they are not being treated fairly or when their expectations are violated. One researcher asked people to remember or keep records of their anger experiences (Averill, 1983). Most of the people said they became at least mildly angry several times a week; some said they became mildly angry several times a day. In many instances, the people said they got angry because they perceived that a friend or a loved one performed a misdeed. They especially got angry when they perceived the other person's behavior as unjustified, avoidable, and willful (Zillman, 1998).

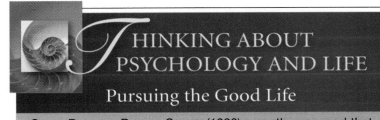

THINKING ABOUT PSYCHOLOGY AND LIFE
Pursuing the Good Life

CAROL RYFF AND BURTON SINGER (1998) recently proposed that living the good life primarily involves positive health. Furthermore, they argued that positive psychological health is most likely to be achieved by (1) leading a life of purpose, (2) having quality connections with others, (3) having positive self-regard, and (4) having mastery.

What do you think? What would your list of items be for living the good life? What about the subjective well-being of happiness? And what about intelligence and wisdom? Might they be important dimensions of living the good life? Some people might value intelligence and wisdom higher than happiness in living the good life (King & Pennebaker, 1998). The nineteenth-century English philosopher John Stuart Mill once said that it is better to be a dissatisfied human being than a satisfied pig. Better to be Socrates dissatisfied than a fool satisfied? Also, might there be a problem in measuring the good life?

Through the Eyes of Psychologists

Ed Diener, *University of Illinois, and*
Mary Beth Diener, *University of Kentucky*

"Often, what leads to happiness at the moment may not be the same as what produces long-term happiness."

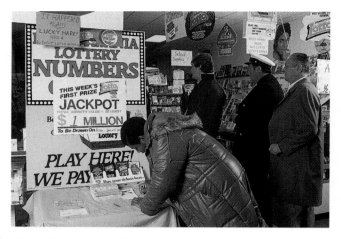

How might winning the lottery affect your happiness?

Anger

Emotional Intelligence

"My life is O.K., but it's no jeans ad."

Doesn't getting angry sometimes make us feel better and possibly help us cope better with our challenging lives? For example, Mark Twain once remarked, "When angry, count four; when very angry, swear." **Catharsis** *is the release of anger or aggressive energy by directly or vicariously engaging in anger or aggression; the catharsis hypothesis states that behaving angrily or watching others behave angrily reduces subsequent anger.*

Psychoanalytic theory promotes catharsis as an important way to reduce anger, arguing that people have a natural, biological tendency to display anger ◀▥ P. 9. From this perspective, taking out your anger on a friend or a loved one should reduce your subsequent tendency to display anger; so should heavy doses of anger on television and the anger we see in football, hockey, professional wrestling, and other aspects of our culture. Why? Because such experiences release pent-up anger.

Social cognitive theory argues strongly against this view ◀▥ P. 8. This theory states that by acting angrily, people often are rewarded for their anger, and that by watching others display anger, people learn how to be angry themselves. Which view is right? Research on catharsis suggests that acting angrily does not have any long-term power in reducing anger. If the catharsis hypothesis were correct, war should have a cathartic effect in reducing anger and aggression, but a study of wars in 110 countries since 1900 showed that warfare actually stimulated domestic violence (Archer & Gartner, 1976). Compared with nations that remained at peace, postwar nations had an increase in homicide rates. As psychologist Carol Tavris (1989) says in her book *Anger: The Misunderstood Emotion,* one of the main results of the ventilation approach to anger is to raise the noise level of our society, not to reduce anger or solve our problems. Individuals who are the most prone to anger get angrier, not less angry. Ventilating anger often follows this cycle: a precipitating event, an angry outburst, shouted recriminations, screaming or crying, a furious peak (sometimes accompanied by physical assault), exhaustion, and a sullen apology or just sullenness.

Every person gets angry at one time or another. How can we control our anger so it does not become destructive? Tavris (1989) makes the following recommendations:

1. When your anger starts to boil and your body is getting aroused, work on lowering the arousal by waiting. Emotional arousal will usually simmer down if you just wait long enough.
2. Cope with the anger in ways that involve neither being chronically angry over every little bothersome annoyance nor passively sulking, which simply rehearses your reasons for being angry.
3. Form a self-help group with others who have been through similar experiences with anger. The other people will likely know what you are feeling and together you might come up with some good solutions to anger problems.
4. Take action to help others, which can put your own miseries in perspective, as exemplified in the actions of the women who organized Mothers Against Drunk Drivers or any number of people who work to change conditions so that others will not suffer what they did.
5. Seek ways of breaking out of your usual perspective. Some people have been rehearsing their "story" for years, repeating over and over the reasons for their anger. Retelling the story from other participants' points of view often helps individuals to find routes to empathy.

At this point we have studied a number of ideas about emotion. An overview of these ideas is presented in summary table 9.5. Emotional self-awareness is an important aspect of being emotionally intelligent and earlier in the chapter we said that the degree to which we are aware of what motivates us is an important aspect of motivation. In the next chapter, you also will see that the unconscious-conscious dimension is a key aspect of understanding personality as well.

SUMMARY TABLE 9.5
Emotion

Concept	Processes/ Related Ideas	Characteristics/Discussions
Defining Emotion	Its Nature	Emotion is feeling or affect that can involve (1) physiological arousal, (2) conscious experience, and (3) behavioral expression. Psychologists debate which of these ingredients is the most important and how they mix to produce emotion.
Biological Dimensions	Arousal	The autonomic nervous system and its two subsystems (sympathetic, which arouses the body, and parasympathetic, which calms the body) are involved in emotion. The polygraph is based on detecting changes in people's emotions, but it can be flawed.
	James-Lange and Cannon-Bard Theories	The James-Lange theory states that emotion results from physiological states triggered by environmental stimuli: Emotion follows physiological reactions. The Cannon-Bard theory states that emotion and physiological reactions occur simultaneously.
	Neural Circuits and Neurotransmitters	In contemporary biological views of emotion, neural circuitry and neurotransmitters are increasingly being highlighted. The amygdala especially plays an important role in this circuitry. The neural pathway of fear has been charted.
Cognitive Dimensions	The Two-Factor Theory	The two-factor theory of emotion is Schachter and Singer's theory that emotion is determined by two main factors: (1) physiological arousal and (2) cognitive labeling.
	The Primacy Debate: Cognition or Emotion?	Lazarus believes cognition always directs emotion, whereas Zajonc argues that emotions are dominant. Both probably are right.
Behavioral Dimensions	Their Nature	Emotion has not only a physiological and cognitive component, but also a behavioral component. The most interest in the behavioral component has focused on facial expressions. Ekman and his colleagues have found that individuals can identify six basic emotions from facial expressions. The facial feedback hypothesis states that facial expressions can influence emotions as well as reflect them, and Ekman's research supports this hypothesis.
Sociocultural Dimensions	Culture	Most psychologists believe that facial expressions of basic emotions are the same across cultures. However, display rules, which involve nonverbal signals of body movement, posture, and gesture, vary across cultures.
	Gender	The master stereotype of gender and emotion is that she is emotional, he is not. When we go beyond the master stereotype and consider specific aspects of emotional experiences and the contexts in which emotion is displayed, gender matters in understanding emotion. Gender differences in emotion are most likely to occur in contexts that highlight social roles and relationships.
Classifying Emotions	The Wheel Model	Plutchik's wheel model portrays emotions in terms of four dimensions: (1) positive or negative, (2) primary or mixed, (3) polar opposites, and (4) intensity.
	A Positive Emotion: Happiness	Happiness involves such psychological and personality factors as high self-esteem, optimism, extraversion, and personal control; a supportive network of close relationships; a culture that offers positive interpretations of most daily events; being engaged by work and leisure; and a faith that embodies social support, purpose, and hope.
	A Negative Emotion: Anger	Anger has a strong impact on our social relationships. Catharsis is generally considered to not be a good strategy for dealing with anger.

Overview

TO LEARN ABOUT MOTIVATION, we studied some ideas behind the whys of behavior: defining motivation, biological influences, cognitive influences, behavioral/social/ cultural influences, the hierarchy of motives, and issues in motivation. Our coverage of hunger focused on biological factors, external and cognitive factors, as well as eating and weight. We studied these aspects of sexuality: biological, cognitive, sensory/perceptual, and cultural factors, the human sexual response cycle, psychosexual dysfunctions, as well as heterosexuality and homosexuality. We also examined many aspects of achievement motivation, including the need for achievement, person/cognitive factors, and cultural, ethnic, and socioeconomic variations in achievement. And we evaluated these aspects of emotion: defining emotion, biological dimensions, cognitive dimensions, behavioral dimensions, sociocultural dimensions, and classifying emotions.

Don't forget that you can obtain a more detailed overview of the chapter by again studying the five summary tables on pages 299, 305, 313, 317, and 331.

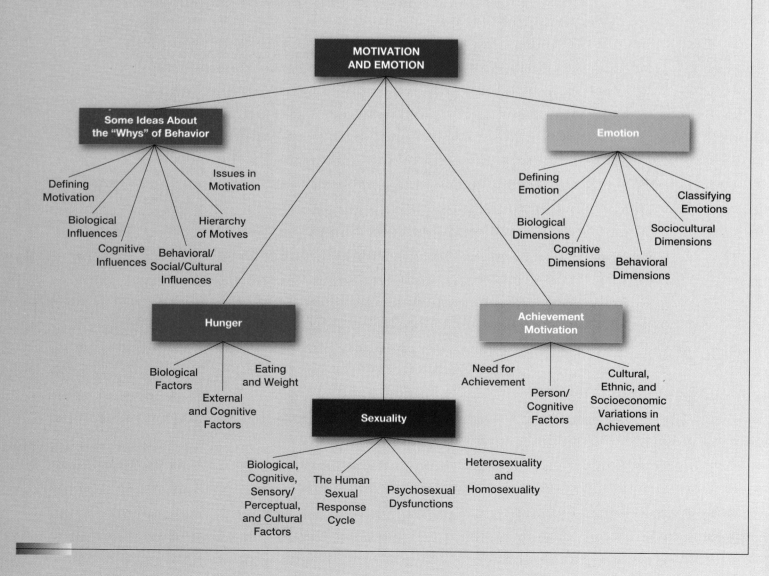

McGraw-Hill Online Learning Center Test

1. Psychology is best defined as the

- ○ A. study of perception and memory.
- ○ B. investigation of the human psyche.
- ○ C. scientific study of conscious and unconscious processes.
- ○ D. scientific study of behavior and mental processes.

2. As you read the definition of psychology you begin to think about examples. Of the following, which one is the best example of behavior?

- ○ A. planning your weekend activities
- ○ B. adding two numbers in your head
- ○ C. a two-year-old boy coloring a picture
- ○ D. thinking about this question

3. A team of researchers wants to study aggressive behavior in adolescents. The researchers plan to use observations to describe, make predictions about, and explain adolescents' aggressive behavior. Which of the following best describes what these researchers are doing?

- ○ A. They are trying to define mental processes.
- ○ B. They are identifying environmental determinants of behavior.
- ○ C. They are studying peer pressure.
- ○ D. They are following the scientific method.

4. The definition of psychology is made up of several parts. Which part refers to "thoughts, feelings, and motives"?

- ○ A. scientific study
- ○ B. behavior
- ○ C. contexts
- ○ D. mental processes

5. What is the main difference between philosophers and psychologists?

    ○ A. the types of questions they ask about human behavior
    ○ B. the causes they presume for human behavior
    ○ C. the debate of the question how people acquire knowledge
    ○ D. the methods they use for obtaining evidence

6. The British naturalist Charles Darwin is best known for his suggestion that

    ○ A. organisms that are best adapted to their environment survive and pass on their characteristics to their offspring
    ○ B. consciousness experience is made up of structure
    ○ C. psychology should focus only on observable behavior not the mind
    ○ D. people have freedom to choose their own destiny

7. A structuralist would have been most interested in studying

    ○ A. the unconscious.
    ○ B. dreams.
    ○ C. conscious thought.
    ○ D. behavior.

8. The mind's content is to Titchener as the mind's function is to

    ○ A. Wundt.
    ○ B. James.
    ○ C. Watson.
    ○ D. Darwin.

9. Structuralism is to _____ as functionalism is to _____ .

    ○ A. Wundt; Titchener
    ○ B. Skinner; Wundt
    ○ C. James; Bandura

Key Terms

motivation 294
instinct 294
drive 295
need 295
homeostasis 295
ethology 296
incentives 297
hierarchy of motives 297
self-actualization 298
set point 302
basal metabolism rate (BMR) 303

restrained eaters 303
anorexia nervosa 304
bulimia 304
estrogens 306
androgens 306
pheromones 307
aphrodisiacs 307
sexual scripts 308
traditional religious script 308
romantic script 308
human sexual response pattern 308

psychosexual dysfunctions 309
bisexual 311
need for achievement 314
attribution theory 315
emotion 318
autonomic nervous system (ANS) 318
sympathetic nervous system 318
parasympathetic nervous system 319

polygraph 319
Yerkes-Dodson law 319
James-Lange theory 321
Cannon-Bard theory 321
two-factor theory of emotion 322
facial feedback hypothesis 324
display rules 325
catharsis 330

Key People

William McDougall 294
Konrad Lorenz 296
Abraham Maslow 297
Walter Cannon and A. L. Washburn 299
Judith Rodin 300

Stanley Schachter 301
William Masters and Virginia Johnson 308
Alfred Kinsey 310
David McClelland 314
Sandra Graham 317

William James and Carl Lange 321
Stanley Schachter and Jerome Singer 322
Richard Lazarus 323
Robert Zajonc 323

Paul Ekman 323
Robert Plutchik 327
Ed Diener 329

Taking It to the Net

1. Do you know someone who is always angry? Do you know someone who has a bad temper? Emotions are complex phenomena that affect the way we think and the way we behave. Consider, for example, a time when you have been really angry. Chances are, your anger altered the way you behaved, the thoughts you thought, and the things you said. Is emotion inherited? Why do you suppose some people are angrier than others? Explain.

2. Anorexia nervosa is an eating disorder that involves the relentless pursuit of thinness through starvation. Serious nutritional repercussions result from not eating. Hair falls out, teeth turn yellow and fall out, and bones become brittle and break easily. Ultimately, there comes a time when major organs are undernourished and the health of the person with anorexia is at serious risk. Anorexia nervosa is clearly a medical condition, but it is also a psychiatric disorder. Explain some of the psychological theories of anorexia nervosa. According to the *Diagnostic and Statistical Manual,* fourth edition *(DSM-IV),* what are the diagnostic criteria for anorexia nervosa?

3. Have you ever noticed that some people are really good at reading other people's emotions? They can look at you and know exactly how you are feeling. This is one component of emotional intelligence, a concept that has received considerable public interest recently. Some psychologists believe that emotional intelligence is a better predictor for success in business than IQ. What are the other components of emotional intelligence, and can it be improved? Why do you think it is called emotional *intelligence?*

Connect to http://www.mhhe.com/psychology/santrock to find the answers!

Chapter 10

Personality

Images of Psychology and Life
Everyday Descriptions of Personality

"*E*very person cries out to be read differently."

Simone Weil
French Philosopher, 20th Century

Preview

How do the images of personality we use in our everyday conversations about people correspond to the way psychologists describe personality? The images suggest that personality is a property of the individual that is related to how the individual functions in the world. These are some of the questions we will explore in this chapter:

• What is personality?
• How do the psychoanalytic perspectives portray personality? Is some of our personality unconscious? Is it tied to early experiences in our family?
• How do the humanistic perspectives describe personality? How important is the self in personality?
• What do the behavioral and social cognitive perspectives say are the key aspects of understanding personality?
• What is the trait perspective on personality? How much can our personality traits be modified by situations?
• What are some ways personality can be assessed?
• How do the main theoretical perspectives on personality stack up against each other on some key issues?

"She has a great personality."
"He has no personality."
"She is a personality."
"She has her mother's personality."

These statements reflect our everyday use of the term personality. You probably have used similar statements to describe someone you have known or known about. Let's look further at each of these statements (Peterson, 1988).

"She has a great personality." This statement is a positive evaluation. When you say this about a woman, it means you like something about her that does not involve looks, possessions, or status. There is something about her that makes you feel good when you are around her. Maybe it's the way she behaves, her attitude, her flair, her values, or even some of her quirks.

"He has no personality." This statement also is an evaluation, but it is a negative one. You do not really like this guy, but you might not dislike him either, unless you happen to be his college roommate or he is your boss. He makes your day boring. He has nothing unique that stamps him as very different from others: no passion, no weird hobby or unusual ability, and not much desire except just to go through life unnoticed. He can take or leave Mexican food or Geraldo Rivera, he has no mismatched socks. He is almost like a piece of furniture.

Many celebrities, such as Whoopi Goldberg, are called "personalities." They are well known not just for what they do, but also for how they do it. Whoopi Goldberg's outgoing personality is a property of Whoopi Goldberg and is related to how she functions in the world. Of course, it is not just celebrities who have a personality. Each of us has a personality that is our property and is related to how we function in the world.

"She is a personality." Andy Warhol once said that in the future everyone will be famous for 15 minutes. Then it will be someone else's turn. Some of us make *People* magazine; most of us don't. People write about celebrities so noncelebrities can read about them. Many celebrities have unique personalities and we call them "personalities." Madonna, Whoopi Goldberg, and Robin Williams are celebrities we think of as personalities. They are well known not just for what they do, but for how they do it. They play a role in our culture that becomes identified with the personality they bring to the role.

"She has her mother's personality." Many statements about personality focus on distinctive characteristics, what makes us different from others in some way.

Personality is also used to make comparisons among individuals, describing common characteristics and similarities. Most of us have talked about the way certain people remind us of someone else we have known. They may have similar mannerisms. She holds grudges just like her mother does, for example. They may have similar temperaments. She is the life of the party and loves to be around people, just like her father. Many people look at their family members and see certain similar personality characteristics. For example, someone may say, "My brother is an introvert just like my cousin Robert." Or "My sister has my grandmother's personality—she has a stubborn streak a mile long."

Personality

Journal of Personality and Social Psychology

What Is Personality?

Think about yourself for a moment. What are you *really* like? Are you outgoing or shy? Aggressive or calm? Intellectual or nonintellectual? Considerate or uncaring? Try to come up with seven or eight of these traits that reflect the way you respond to your world. In compiling this list, you chose personality characteristics that you probably feel are an enduring part of your makeup as a person. For example, if you said that you are an outgoing person, wouldn't you also say that you were outgoing a year ago and that you will probably be an outgoing person 1 year, 5 years, and 10 years from now? Most of us believe that we do have some enduring personality characteristics.

Now that you have thought about yourself in terms of your characteristics, think for a moment about how you would define personality. It's not that easy. Personality is one of those concepts that we think we know what it is but when we try to express what it is verbally it can be quite difficult. Our definition of personality includes enduring characteristics and adaptation: **Personality** *consists of enduring, distinctive thoughts, emotions, and behaviors that characterize the way an individual adapts to the world.*

We will be discussing a number of theoretical perspectives on personality. They ask why individuals react to the same situation in different ways. For example, *why* is Sam so talkative and gregarious, and Al so shy and quiet when they meet someone for the first time? *Why* is Gretchen so confident and Mary so insecure about upcoming job interviews? Some theorists believe that biological and genetic factors are responsible; others argue that life experiences are more important. Some theorists claim that the way we think about ourselves is the key to understanding personality, while others stress that the way we behave toward each other is more important (Friedman & Schustack, 1999).

The diversity of theories makes understanding personality a challenging undertaking (Maddi, 1996). Just when you think one theory has the correct explanation of personality, another theory will crop up and make you rethink your earlier conclusion. To keep from getting frustrated, remember that personality is a complex, multifaceted topic and no single theory has been able to account for all its aspects. Each theory has contributed an important piece to the personality puzzle. In fact, much of the information is *complementary* rather than contradictory. Together they let us see the total landscape of personality in all its richness (Feist & Feist, 1998).

Perspectives on Personality

The field of personality includes a number of theoretical perspectives. The main perspectives we will discuss are these: psychoanalytic, behavioral and social learning, humanistic, and trait theory and trait-situation interaction.

Psychoanalytic Perspectives

Initially we will describe some common characteristics of the psychoanalytic perspectives, then turn to Freud's theory of personality, next discuss other important psychoanalytic theories, and finally evaluate the psychoanalytic perspectives.

Defining the Psychoanalytic Perspectives **Psychoanalytic perspectives** *view personality as primarily unconscious (that is, beyond awareness) and as occurring in stages* ◀▥ P. 9. *Most psychoanalytic perspectives emphasize that early experiences with parents play an important role in sculpting personality.* Psychoanalytic theorists believe that behavior is merely a surface characteristic and that to truly understand someone's personality we have to explore the symbolic meanings of behavior and the deep inner workings of the mind. These characteristics are highlighted by the original architect of psychoanalytic theory: Sigmund Freud.

Freud's Theory   Loved and hated, respected and despised, Sigmund Freud, whether right or wrong in his views, has been one of the most influential thinkers of the twentieth century. Freud was a medical doctor who specialized in neurology. He developed his ideas about psychoanalytic theory from his work with psychiatric patients. He was born in Austria in 1856, and he died in London at the age of 83. Freud spent most of his life in Vienna, but he left the city near the end of his career to escape Nazi anti-Semitism.

As an eldest child, Freud was regarded as a genius by his brothers and sisters and doted on by his mother. Later we will see that one aspect of Freud's theory emphasizes a young boy's sexual attraction for his mother; it is possible that this aspect of his theory was derived from his own romantic attachment to his mother, who was beautiful and some 20 years younger than Freud's father.

In Freud's view, much more of our mind is unconscious than conscious. He envisioned our mind as a huge iceberg, with the massive part below the surface of the water being the unconscious part. Freud said that each of our lives is filled with tension and conflict; to reduce this tension and conflict we keep information locked in our unconscious mind. For Freud, the unconscious mind held the key to understanding behavior. Freud believed that even trivial behaviors have special significance when the unconscious forces behind them are revealed. A twitch, a doodle, a joke, a smile, each may have an unconscious reason for appearing. They often slip into our lives without our awareness. For example, Barbara is kissing and hugging Tom, whom she is to marry in several weeks. She says, "Oh, *Jeff*, I love you so much." Tom pushes her away and says, "Why did you call me Jeff? I thought you didn't think about him anymore. We need to have a talk!" You probably can think of times when these so-called *Freudian slips* tumbled out of your own mouth.

Freud also believed that dreams hold important clues to our behavior ◀▥ P. 129. He said dreams are unconscious representations of the conflict and tension in our everyday lives. Since the conflict and tension are too painful to handle consciously, they come out in our dreams. Much of the dream content is disguised in symbolism, requiring extensive analysis and probing to be understood.

Sigmund Freud (1856–1939), the architect of psychoanalytic theory.

Psychoanalytic Theory
The Structure of the Unconscious

"Good morning beheaded—uh, I mean beloved."

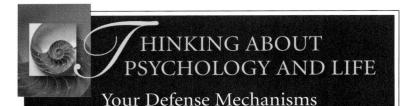

THINKING ABOUT PSYCHOLOGY AND LIFE
Your Defense Mechanisms

WE ALL USE defense mechanisms at one time or another in our lives. Some of us use them more than others. Examine figure 10.2 again to be sure you understand what the different defense mechanisms are like. For each of the following defense mechanisms, think about how you have used it in your life. If you don't think you have used it, in what future situations might you use it?

Repression
Rationalization
Displacement
Sublimation
Projection
Reaction Formation
Denial
Regression

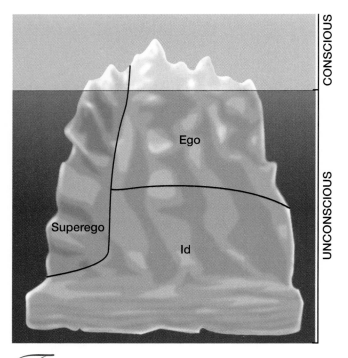

$\mathscr{F}$igure 10.1
The Conscious and Unconscious Mind: The Iceberg Analogy

The analogy of the conscious and unconscious mind to an iceberg is often used to illustrate how much of the mind is unconscious in Freud's theory. The conscious mind is the part of the iceberg above water, the unconscious mind the part below water. Notice that the id is totally unconscious, while the ego and superego can operate at either the conscious or the unconscious level.

The Structure of Personality   Freud (1917) believed that personality has three structures: the id, the ego, and the superego.

The **id** *is the Freudian structure of personality that consists of instincts, which are the individual's reservoir of psychic energy.* In Freud's view, the id is unconscious; it has no contact with reality. The id works according to the pleasure principle. The **pleasure principle** *is the Freudian concept that the id always seeks pleasure and avoids pain.*

It would be a dangerous and scary world if our personalities were all id. As young children mature, they learn they cannot slug other children in the face. They also learn they have to use the toilet instead of their diaper. As children experience the demands and constraints of reality, a new structure of personality is formed—the **ego**, *the Freudian structure of personality that deals with the demands of reality.* According to Freud, the ego abides by the **reality principle**: *It tries to bring the individual pleasure within the norms of society.* Few of us are cold-blooded killers or wild wheeler-dealers; we consider obstacles to our satisfaction that exist in our world. We recognize that our sexual and aggressive impulses cannot go unrestrained. The ego helps us to test reality, to see how far we can go without getting into trouble and hurting ourselves.

While the id is completely unconscious, the ego is partly conscious. It houses our higher mental functions—reasoning, problem solving, and decision making, for example. For this reason, the ego is referred to as the executive branch of the personality; like an executive in a company, it makes the rational decisions that help the company succeed.

The id and ego have no morality. They do not consider whether something is right or wrong. The **superego** *is the Freudian structure of personality that is the moral branch of personality.* The superego considers whether something is right or wrong. The superego is what we often refer to as our "conscience." Like the id, the superego does not consider reality; it doesn't deal with what is realistic, only with whether the id's sexual and aggressive impulses can be satisfied in moral terms. You probably are beginning to sense that both the id and the superego make life rough for the ego. Your ego might say, "I will have sex only occasionally and be sure to use an effective form of birth control." But your id is saying, "I want to be satisfied; sex feels so good." And your superego is at work too, "I feel guilty about having sex."

Remember that Freud considered personality to be like an iceberg; most of our personality exists below the level of awareness, just as the massive part of an iceberg is beneath the surface of the water. Figure 10.1 illustrates this analogy and how extensive the unconscious part of our mind is in Freud's view.

Defense Mechanisms   In addition to describing personality in terms of three structures (id, ego, and superego), Freud also said that defense mechanisms are important in understanding how personality works. The ego calls on a number of strategies to resolve the conflict between its demands for reality, the wishes of the id, and the constraints of the superego. **Defense mechanisms** *are the ego's protective methods for reducing anxiety by unconsciously distorting reality.* In Freud's view,

Defense Mechanism	How It Works	Example
Repression	The master defense mechanism; the ego pushes unacceptable impulses out of awareness, back into the unconscious mind.	A young girl was sexually abused by her uncle. As an adult, she can't remember anything about the traumatic experience.
Rationalization	The ego replaces a less acceptable motive with a more acceptable one.	A college student does not get into the fraternity of his choice. He says that if he would have tried harder he could have gotten in.
Displacement	The ego shifts unacceptable feelings from one object to another, more acceptable object.	A woman can't take her anger out on her boss so she goes home and takes it out on her husband.
Sublimation	The ego replaces an unacceptable impulse with a socially acceptable one.	A man with strong sexual urges becomes an artist who paints nudes.
Projection	The ego attributes personal shortcomings, problems, and faults to others.	A man who has a strong desire to have an extramarital affair accuses his wife of flirting with other men.
Reaction Formation	The ego transforms an unacceptable motive into its opposite.	A woman who fears her sexual urges becomes a religious zealot.
Denial	The ego refuses to acknowledge anxiety-producing realities.	A man won't acknowledge that he has cancer even though a team of doctors has diagnosed his cancer.
Regression	The ego seeks the security of an earlier developmental period in the face of stress.	A woman returns home to mother every time she and her husband have a big argument.

Figure 10.2
Defense Mechanisms

the conflicting demands of the personality structures produce anxiety. For example, when the ego blocks the pleasurable pursuits of the id, a person feels inner anxiety. This diffuse, distressed state develops when the ego senses that the id is going to cause some harm. The anxiety alerts the ego to resolve the conflict by means of defense mechanisms.

Repression *is the most powerful and pervasive defense mechanism, according to Freud; it works to push unacceptable id impulses out of awareness and back into the unconscious mind.* Repression is the foundation from which all other defense mechanisms work; the goal of every psychological defense is to *repress* or push threatening impulses out of awareness. Freud said that our early childhood experiences, many of which he believed were sexually laden, are too threatening and stressful for us to deal with consciously. We reduce the anxiety of this conflict through repression.

Among the other defense mechanisms we use to protect the ego and reduce anxiety are rationalization, displacement, sublimation, projection, reaction formation, denial, and regression. Figure 10.2 describes the defense mechanisms and gives an example of each.

Two final points about defense mechanisms need to be understood. First, they are unconscious; we are not aware we are calling on them to protect our ego and

Defense Mechanisms

reduce anxiety. Second, when used in moderation or on a temporary basis, defense mechanisms are not necessarily unhealthy. For example, defense mechanisms such as denial can help a person cope with impending death. For the most part, though, we should not let defense mechanisms dominate our behavior and prevent us from facing life's demands.

The Development of Personality As Freud listened to, probed, and analyzed his patients, he became convinced that their prob-

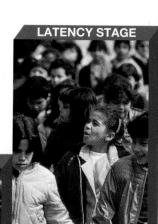

GENITAL STAGE

Adolescence
and Adulthood

LATENCY STAGE

6 Years–Puberty

lems were the result of experiences early in life. Freud believed that we go through five stages of psychosexual development, and that at each stage of development we experience pleasure in one part of the body more than in others. **Erogenous zones,** *according to Freud, are parts of the body that have especially strong pleasure-giving qualities at particular stages of development.*

Freud thought that our adult personality is determined by the way we resolve conflicts between these early sources of pleasure—the mouth, the anus, and then the genitals—and the demands of reality. When these conflicts are not resolved, the individual may become fixated at a particular stage of development. **Fixation** *is the psychoanalytic defense mechanism that occurs when the individual remains locked in an earlier developmental stage because needs are under- or overgratified.* For example, a parent might wean a child too early, be too strict in toilet training the child, punish the child for masturbation, or "smother" the child with too much attention. We will return to the idea of fixation and how it may show up in an adult's personality, but first we need to learn more about the early stages of personality development. Figure 10.3 illustrates the five Freudian stages.

Oral stage *is the term Freud used to describe development during the first 18 months of life, in which the infant's pleasure centers on the mouth.* Chewing, sucking, and biting are chief sources of pleasure. These actions reduce tension in the infant.

The **anal stage** *is Freud's second stage of development, occurring between 1½ and 3 years of age, in which the child's greatest pleasure involves the anus or the eliminative functions associated with it.* In Freud's view, the exercise of anal muscles reduces tension.

The **phallic stage,** *Freud's third stage of development, occurs between the ages of 3 and 6. Its name comes from the Latin word* phallus, *which means "penis." During the phallic stage, pleasure focuses on the genitals as the child discovers that self-stimulation is enjoyable.*

PHALLIC STAGE

3–6 Years

ANAL STAGE

1½–3 Years

ORAL STAGE

0–1½ Years

Figure 10.3
Freudian Stages

EXPLORATIONS IN PSYCHOLOGY
Freud's Oedipus Complex: Cultural and Gender Biases

THE OEDIPUS COMPLEX was one of Freud's most influential concepts relating early psychosexual relationships to later personality development. Freud developed this aspect of his theory during the Victorian era of the late 1800s when sexual interests, especially the female's, were repressed.

According to Freud, the phallic stage begins for a girl when she realizes she has no penis. He also believed that she recognizes the superiority of the penis to her anatomy, and thus develops *penis envy*. Blaming her mother for her lack of a penis, the girl renounces her love for her mother and becomes intensely attached to her father. Since her desire for having a penis can never be satisfied directly, Freud speculated that the young girl yearns for a penis substitute, a baby (especially a male baby). This female version of the Oedipus complex is sometimes referred to as the *Electra complex*. Freud believed that the Electra complex is never fully resolved but merely dissipates over time as the girl begins to identify with her mother and take on similar values and feminine behavior. As a result, Freud assumed that women do not develop as strong a conscience (superego) as do men.

Many psychologists believe Freud placed far too much emphasis on anatomy's role in personality development. Freud concluded, for example, that boys are likely to de-

velop a dominant, powerful personality because they have a penis; without a penis, girls are predisposed to become submissive and weak. In basing his view of male/female differences in personality development on anatomical differences, Freud ignored the enormous impact of culture and experience.

More than half a century ago, the English anthropologist Bronislaw Malinowski (1927) observed the family dynamics of the Trobriand Islanders of the Western Pacific and found that the Oedipus complex is not universal. In the Trobriand Islands, the biological father is not the head of the household; that disciplinarian role is reserved for the mother's brother. In Freud's view, this family constellation would not alter the Oedipus complex; the young boy should still vie for his mother's love and perceive his father as the hated rival, but Malinowski found no such conflict between fathers and sons in the Trobriand Islanders. He did observe, however, that young boys feared the authoritarian, maternal uncle and directed negative feelings toward him. Malinowski's finding undermined Freud's Oedipus complex because it showed that the sexual relations within the family did not always create conflict and fear for a child.

In Freud's view the phallic stage has a special importance in personality development because this period triggers the Oedipus complex. This name comes from Greek mythology, in which Oedipus, the son of the King of Thebes, unwittingly killed his father and married his mother. The **Oedipus complex** *is the young child's development of an intense desire to replace the parent of the same sex and enjoy the affections of the opposite-sex parent.* As discussed in Explorations in Psychology, the Oedipus complex was not as universal as Freud believed; his concept was heavily influenced by the sociohistorical, cultural setting of turn-of-the-century Vienna.

At about 5 to 6 years of age, children recognize that their same-sex parent might punish them for their incestuous wishes. To reduce this conflict, the child identifies with the same-sex parent, striving to be like him or her. If the conflict is not resolved, though, the individual may become fixated at the phallic stage. Figure 10.4 illustrates some possible links between adult personality characteristics and fixation, sublimation, and reaction formation involving the phallic stage, as well as the oral and anal stage.

The **latency stage** *is the fourth Freudian stage of development, occurring approximately between 6 years of age and puberty; the child represses all interest in sexuality and develops social and intellectual skills.* This activity channels much of the child's energy into emotionally safe areas and aids the child in forgetting the highly stressful conflicts of the phallic stage.

The **genital stage** *is the fifth and final Freudian stage of development, occurring from puberty on. The genital stage is the time of sexual reawakening; the source of*

THE FAR SIDE   By GARY LARSON

"So Mr. Fenton. . . . Let's begin with your mother."

Stage	Adult Extensions (Fixations)	Sublimations	Reaction Formations
Oral	Smoking, eating, kissing, oral hygiene, drinking, chewing gum	Seeking knowledge, humor, wit, sarcasm, being a food or wine expert	Speech purist, food faddist, prohibitionist, dislike of milk
Anal	Notable interest in one's bowel movements, love of bathroom humor, extreme messiness	Interest in painting or sculpture, being overly giving, great interest in statistics	Extreme disgust with feces, fear of dirt, prudishness, irritability
Phallic	Heavy reliance on masturbation, flirtatiousness, expressions of virility	Interest in poetry, love of love, interest in acting, striving for success	Puritanical attitude toward sex, excessive modesty

Figure 10.4
Possible Links Between Adult Personality Characteristics and Fixation at Oral, Anal, and Phallic Stages

The Oedipus Complex
Horney's Theory

sexual pleasure now becomes someone outside of the family. Freud believed that unresolved conflicts with parents reemerged during adolescence. Once resolved, Freud believed, the individual would become capable of developing a mature love relationship and functioning independently as an adult.

Psychoanalytic Dissenters and Revisionists
Because Freud was among the first theorists to explore many new and uncharted regions of personality, some of his ideas have needed to be updated, others revised, and some have been tossed out altogether. In particular, Freud's critics have said his ideas about sexuality, early experience, social factors, and the unconscious mind were misguided (Adler, 1927; Erikson, 1968; Fromm, 1947; Horney, 1945; Jung, 1917; Kohut, 1977; Rapaport, 1967; Sullivan, 1953). The critics stressed the following:

• Sexuality is not the pervasive underlying force behind personality that Freud believed it to be.
• The first 5 years of life are not as powerful in shaping adult personality as Freud thought; later experiences deserve more attention.
• The ego and conscious thought processes play more dominant roles in our personality than Freud gave them credit for; we are not wed forever to the id and its instinctual, unconscious clutches. The ego has a separate line of development from the id; viewed in this way, achievement, thinking, and reasoning are not always tied to sexual impulses as Freud thought.
• Sociocultural factors are much more important than Freud believed. Freud placed more emphasis on the biological basis of personality by stressing the id's dominance.

Let's examine three theories by dissenters and revisionists of Freud's theory in greater detail—Horney's, Jung's, and Adler's theories.

Horney's Sociocultural Approach
Karen Horney (1885–1952) rejected the classical psychoanalytic concept that "anatomy is destiny" in favor of an approach that emphasized the importance of sociocultural factors in development. She cautioned that ideas such as "penis envy" were only hypotheses. She insisted that these hypotheses should be supported with observable data before they were accepted as fact.

Horney pointed out that previous research about how women function was limited by the fact that those who described women, who influenced and represented the culture, and who determined the standards for suitable growth and development were men. She countered the notion of penis envy with the hypothesis that both sexes envy the attributes of the other, with men coveting women's reproductive capacities.

Karen Horney (1885–1952) developed the first feminist criticism of Freud's theory. Horney's view emphasizes women's positive qualities and self-evaluation.

She also argued that women who feel penis envy are desirous only of the status that men have in most societies.

Horney also believed that the need for security, not for sex or aggression, was the prime motive in human existence. Horney reasoned that when an individual's needs for security are met they should be able to develop their capacities to the fullest extent. She also suggested that people usually develop one of three strategies in their effort to cope with anxiety. First, individuals might *move toward* people, seeking love and support. Second, individuals might *move away* from people, becoming more independent. And third, individuals might *move against* people, becoming competitive and domineering. The secure individual uses these three ways of coping in moderation and balance, while the insecure individual often uses one or more of these strategies in an exaggerated fashion, becoming too dependent, too independent, or too aggressive.

Psychologists are still revamping psychoanalytic theory. Nancy Chodorow's (1978, 1989) feminist revision of psychoanalytic theory, for example, emphasizes that many more women than men define themselves in terms of their relationships, that many men use denial as a defense mechanism in regard to their relationships with others, and that emotions tend to be more salient to women's lives.

Through the Eyes of Psychologists

Nancy Chodorow, *University of California, Berkeley*

"The selves of women and men tend to be constructed differently—women's more in relationships, men's more in denials of self-other connections."

Jung's Analytical Psychology   Freud's contemporary Carl Jung (1875–1961) shared an interest in the unconscious, but he believed Freud underplayed the unconscious mind's role in our personality. Jung believed that the roots of personality go back to the dawn of human existence. The **collective unconscious** *is the impersonal, deepest layer of the unconscious mind, shared by all human beings because of their common ancestral past.* These common experiences have made a deep, permanent impression on the human mind (Harris, 1996). **Archetype** *is the name Jung gave to the emotionally laden ideas and images in the collective unconscious that have rich and symbolic meaning.* Jung believed that these archetypes emerge in art, religion, and dreams. He used archetypes to help people understand themselves.

Two common archetypes are *anima* (woman) and *animus* (man). Jung believed each of us has a passive "feminine" side and an assertive "masculine" side. We also have an archetype for self, which often is expressed in art. For example, the mandala, a figure within a circle, has been used so often Jung took it to represent the self (see figure 10.5). Another archetype is the shadow, our darker self. The shadow is evil and immoral. The shadow appears in many evil and immoral figures—Satan, Dracula, Mr. Hyde (of Jekyll and Hyde), and Darth Vader (of the *Star Wars* films) (Peterson, 1988) (see figure 10.6).

Jung's Theory
Jungian Links
Adler's Theory

Adler's Individual Psychology   Alfred Adler (1870–1937) was another of Freud's contemporaries. In Adler's **individual psychology,** *people are motivated by purposes and goals, being creators of their own lives.* They are seen as responsible for their own lives. Unlike Freud, who believed in the power of the unconscious mind, Adler argued that people have the ability to consciously monitor their lives. He also believed that social factors are more important in shaping personality than sexual motivation (Silverman & Corsini, 1984).

Adler thought that everyone strives for superiority. Adler's concept of **striving for superiority** *emphasizes the human motivation to adapt, improve, and master the environment.* Striving for superiority is our response to feelings of inferiority that we all experience as infants and young children when we interact with people who are bigger and more powerful. We strive to overcome these feelings of inferiority because they are uncomfortable. **Compensation** *is Adler's term for the individual's attempt to overcome imagined or real inferiorities or weaknesses by developing one's abilities.* Adler believed that compensation was normal, and he said we often make up for a weakness in one ability by excelling in a different ability. For example, one person may be a

Swiss psychoanalytic theorist Carl Jung developed the concepts of the collective unconscious and archetypes.

mediocre student but compensate for this by excelling in athletics. **Overcompensation** *is Adler's term for the individual's attempt to deny rather than acknowledge a real situation, or the exaggerated effort to conceal a weakness.* Adler described two patterns of overcompensation. **Inferiority complex** *is the name Adler gave to exaggerated feelings of inadequacy.* **Superiority complex** *is his concept for exaggerated self-importance designed to mask feelings of inferiority.*

In summary, Adler's theory emphasized that people are striving toward a positive being and that they create their own goals. Their adaptation is enhanced by developing social interests and reducing feelings of inferiority. Like Jung, Adler has a number of disciples today.

Evaluating of the Psychoanalytic Perspectives

Although psychoanalytic theories have diverged, they do share some core principles. Psychoanalytic theorists assert that our personality is determined both by current experiences and those from early in life. Two basic principles of psychoanalytic theory have withstood the test of time: early experiences do shape our personality, and personality can be better understood by examining it developmentally.

Another belief that continues to receive considerable attention is that we mentally transform environmental experiences. Psychologists also recognize that the mind is not all consciousness; unconscious motives lie behind some of our puzzling behavior. Psychoanalytic theorists' emphasis on conflict and anxiety leads us to consider the dark side of our existence, not just its bright side. Adjustment is not always an easy task, and the individual's inner world often conflicts with the outer demands of reality. And finally, psychoanalytic theories continue to force psychologists to study more than the experimental, laboratory topics of sensation, perception, and learning; personality and adjustment are rightful and important topics of psychological inquiry as well.

However, the main concepts of psychoanalytic theories have been difficult to test; they are largely matters of inference and interpretation. Researchers have not, for example, successfully investigated such key concepts as repression in the laboratory.

Much of the data used to support psychoanalytic theories have come from clinicians' subjective evaluations of clients; in such cases, it is easy for the clinician to see what she expects because of the theory she holds. Other data come from patients' recollections of the distant past (especially those from early childhood) and are of unknown accuracy. And psychoanalytic theories place too much weight on these early experiences within the family to shape personality. We retain the capacity for change and adaptation throughout our lives.

Some psychologists object that Freud overemphasized the importance of sexuality in understanding personality, and that Freud and Jung placed too much faith in the unconscious mind's ability to control behavior. Others object that the psychoanalytic perspectives provide a model of the person that is too negative and pessimistic. We are not born into the world with only a bundle of sexual and aggressive instincts. The demands of reality do not always conflict with our biological needs.

Many psychoanalytic theories of personality have a male bias, especially Freud's. Although Horney's theory helped to correct this bias, psychoanalytic theory continues to be revised today.

You now should have a sense of what personality is and the themes of psychoanalytic theories. A summary of these ideas is presented in summary table 10.1. Next we will discuss a view of personality *very* different from the psychoanalytic theories.

Figure 10.5
The Mandala as an Archetype of the Self

In his exploration of mythology, Carl Jung found that the self is often symbolized by a mandala, which is named for the Sanskrit word that means "circle." Jung believed that the mandala represents the self's unity.

Contemporary Psychoanalytic Views

Figure 10.6
Star Wars Characters as Archetypes of Good and Evil

In *Star Wars,* Ben Kenobi represented the archetype of good and Darth Vader the archetype of evil.

SUMMARY TABLE 10.1
The Nature of Personality, and Psychoanalytic Perspectives

Concept	Processes/ Related Ideas	Characteristics/Description
What Is Personality?	Its Nature	Personality involves our enduring thoughts, emotions, and behaviors that characterize the way we adapt to the world. A key question is why different individuals respond to the same situation in different ways.
Psychoanalytic Perspectives	Defining the Psychoanalytic Perspectives	They view personality as primarily unconscious and as occurring in stages. Most psychoanalytic perspectives emphasize the importance of early experiences with parents in sculpting personality.
	Freud's Theory	Freud was one of the most influential thinkers of the twentieth century. He believed that most of the mind is unconscious, and that personality has three structures: id, ego, and superego. The id is the reservoir of psychic energy that tries to satisfy our basic needs. It is unconscious and operates according to the pleasure principle. The ego tries to provide us with pleasure by operating within the boundaries of reality. The superego is the moral branch of personality. The conflicting demands of these personality structures produce anxiety. Defense mechanisms protect the ego and reduce this anxiety. Repression is the master defense mechanism. Defense mechanisms are unconscious. Freud was convinced that problems develop because of childhood experiences. He said we go through five psychosexual stages: oral, anal, phallic, latency, and genital. If our needs are under- or overgratified at a particular stage, we can become fixated at that stage. During the phallic stage, the Oedipus complex is a major source of conflict.
	Psychoanalytic Dissenters and Revisionists	They criticized Freud for placing too much emphasis on sexuality and the first five years of life. They argued that Freud gave too little power to the ego, conscious thought, and sociocultural factors. Karen Horney believed that Freud did not emphasize sociocultural factors enough and that his theory has a masculine bias. Horney said the need for security, not sex or aggression, is our most important need. Carl Jung thought Freud underplayed the unconscious mind's role. He developed the concept of the collective unconscious and placed special emphasis on archetypes. Alfred Adler's theory is called individual psychology. It stresses that people are striving toward a positive being and that they create their own goals. Adler placed more emphasis on social motivation than Freud did.
	Evaluating the Psychoanalytic Perspectives	Strengths are an emphasis on the past, personality's developmental course, mental representation of the environment, unconscious mind, emphasis on conflict, and influence on psychology as a discipline. Weaknesses include the difficulty of testing the main concepts, the lack of an empirical data base and overreliance on reports from the past, too much emphasis on sexuality and the unconscious mind, a negative view of human nature, too much power given to early experience, and a male bias.

PERSPECTIVES ON PERSONALITY

Behavioral and Social Cognitive Perspectives → Humanistic Perspectives

Behavioral and Social Cognitive Perspectives

Tom is engaged to marry Ann. Both have warm, friendly personalities, and they enjoy being with each other. Psychoanalytic theorists would say that their personalities are derived from long-standing relationships with their parents, especially their early childhood experiences. They also would argue that the reason for their attraction is unconscious; they are unaware of how their biological heritage and early life experiences have been carried forward to influence their adult personalities.

Behaviorists and social learning theorists would observe Tom and Ann and see something quite different. They would examine their experiences, especially their most recent ones, to understand the reason for Tom and Ann's attraction to one another. Tom would be described as rewarding Ann's behavior, and vice versa, for example. No reference would be made to unconscious thoughts, the Oedipus complex, defense mechanisms, and so on.

Defining the Behavioral and Social Cognitive Perspectives

The **behavioral and social cognitive perspectives** *emphasize the importance of studying environmental experiences and people's observable behavior to understand their personality. Social cognitive theory emphasizes person/cognitive factors in personality.*

At about the same time as Freud was interpreting his patients' unconscious minds through recollections of their childhood experiences, John B. Watson and Ivan Pavlov were conducting detailed observations of behavior under controlled laboratory conditions. Recall from chapter 5, "Learning," that Pavlov believed organisms learn through classical conditioning. Out of the behavioral tradition grew the belief that personality is observable behavior, learned through experiences with the environment. The two main versions of the behavioral and social cognitive perspectives are (1) behaviorism and (2) social cognitive theory.

Skinner's Behaviorism
In chapter 5, we described B. F. Skinner's approach to learning called *operant conditioning* ◀|||| P. 154. Skinner concluded that personality is the individual's *behavior,* which is determined by the *external environment.* Skinner believed we do not have to resort to biological or cognitive processes to explain personality (behavior). Some psychologists say that including Skinner among personality theorists is like inviting a wolf to a party of lambs because he took the "person" out of personality (Phares, 1984).

Behaviorists counter that you cannot pinpoint where personality is or how it is determined. In Skinner's view, personality simply consists of the collection of the person's observed, overt behaviors; it does not include internal traits or thoughts. For example, observations of Sam reveal that his behavior is shy, achievement-oriented, and caring. In short, these behaviors *are* his personality. According to Skinner, Sam is this way because the rewards and punishments in Sam's environment have shaped him into a shy, achievement-oriented, and caring person. Because of interactions with family members, friends, teachers, and others, Sam has *learned* to behave in this fashion.

Behaviorists who support Skinner's view would say that Sam's shy, achievement-oriented, and caring behavior may not be consistent and enduring. For example, Sam is uninhibited on Saturday night with friends at a bar, unmotivated to excel in English class, and occasionally nasty to his sister. In addition, Skinnerians believe that consistency in behavior comes from consistency in environmental experiences. If Sam's shy, achievement-oriented, and caring behavior is consistently rewarded, his pattern of behavior likely will be consistent. However, Skinner stressed that our behavior

𝒯hrough the Eyes of Psychologists

Walter Mischel, *Columbia University*

"Personality psychology is a field of great breadth, overlapping the neighboring areas of human development, abnormal behavior, emotion, cognition, learning, and social relations."

always has the capacity for change if new experiences are encountered. The issue of consistency in personality is an important one. We will return to it on several occasions later in the chapter.

Since behaviorists believe that personality is learned and often changes according to environmental experiences and situations, it follows that by rearranging experiences and situations the individual's personality can be changed. For the behaviorist, shy behavior can be changed into outgoing behavior; aggressive behavior can be shaped into docile behavior; and lethargic, boring behavior can be shaped into enthusiastic, interesting behavior.

Social Cognitive Theory   Some psychologists believe the behaviorists basically are right when they say that personality is learned and influenced strongly by environmental experiences. But they think Skinner went too far in declaring that characteristics of the person or cognitive factors are unimportant in understanding personality. **Social cognitive theory** *states that behavior, environment, and person/cognitive factors are important in understanding personality* ◀▥ P. 8.

Albert Bandura (1986, 1997, 1998) and Walter Mischel (1973, 1995) are the architects of social cognitive theory's contemporary version, which initially was labeled *cognitive social learning theory* by Mischel (1973). Bandura says that behavior, environment, and person/cognitive factors interact in a reciprocal manner (see figure 10.7). Thus, in Bandura's view, the environment can determine a person's behavior (which matches up with Skinner's view), but there is much more to consider. The person can act to change the environment. Person/cognitive factors can influence a person's behavior and vice versa. Person/cognitive factors include self-efficacy (a belief that one can master a situation and produce positive outcomes), plans, and thinking skills.

Remember from chapter 5, "Learning," that Bandura believes observational learning is a key aspect of how we learn. Through observational learning we form ideas about the behavior of others and then possibly adopt this behavior ourselves. For example, a young boy might observe his father's aggressive outbursts and hostile exchanges with people; when the boy is with his peers, he interacts in a highly aggressive way, showing the same characteristics as his father's behavior. Or a young executive adopts the dominant and sarcastic style of her boss. When this young woman interacts with one of her subordinates, she says, "I need this work immediately if not sooner; you are so far behind you think you are ahead!" Social cognitive theorists believe we acquire a wide range of such behaviors, thoughts, and feelings through observing others' behavior; these observations form an important part of our personality.

Social cognitive theorists also differ from the behavioral view of Skinner by emphasizing that we can regulate and control our own behavior, despite our changing environment (Metcalfe & Mischel, 1999). For example, another young executive who observed her boss behave in a dominant and sarcastic manner toward employees found the behavior distasteful and went out of her way to be encouraging and supportive of her subordinates. Someone tries to persuade you to join a particular social club on campus and makes you an enticing offer. You reflect about the offer, consider your interests and beliefs, and make the decision not to join. Your *cognition* (your thoughts) leads you to control your behavior and resist environmental influence in this instance.

Like the behavioral approach of Skinner, the social cognitive view emphasizes the importance of empirical research in studying personality. This research has focused on the processes that explain personality—the social and cognitive factors that influence what we are like as people. One process that Walter Mischel believes is important in understanding an individual's personality is delay of gratification, which is the ability to defer immediate satisfaction for a more desirable future outcome. For example, when you are in school you resist the temptation to slack off and have a

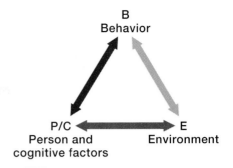

𝓕igure 10.7
Bandura's Social Cognitive Theory
Bandura's social cognitive theory emphasizes reciprocal influences of behavior, environment, and person/cognitive factors.

Bandura's Theory

Albert Bandura (above) and Walter Mischel are the architects of contemporary social cognitive theory.

good time now so you will be rewarded with good grades later. Again, the point is that we are capable of controlling our behavior rather than always being influenced by others.

Evaluating the Behavioral and Social Learning Perspectives

The behavioral and social cognitive theories emphasize that environmental experiences and situational influences determine personality. These approaches have fostered a scientific climate for understanding personality that highlights the observation of behavior. Social cognitive theory emphasizes both environmental influences and cognitive processes in explaining personality. This theory also suggests that people have the ability to control their environment.

Critics of both the behavioral and social learning perspectives take issue with several aspects of both theorists. The behavioral view is criticized for ignoring the importance of cognition in personality and placing too much importance on the role of environmental experiences. Both approaches have been described as being too concerned with change and situational influences on personality and not paying adequate tribute to the enduring qualities of personality. Both views are said to ignore the role biology plays in personality. Both are labeled reductionistic, which means they try to explain the complex concept of personality in terms of one or two factors. The critics charge that the behavioral and social cognitive views are too mechanical, missing the most exciting, rich dimensions of personality. This latter criticism—that the creative, spontaneous, human dimensions of personality are missing from the behavioral and social cognitive perspectives—has been made on numerous occasions by humanists, whose perspective we consider next.

Humanistic Perspectives

Association for Humanistic Psychology
Rogers' Theory

Remember our example of the engaged couple, Tom and Ann, who were described as having warm, friendly personalities? Humanistic psychologists would say that Tom and Ann's warm, friendly personalities are a reflection of their inner self. They would emphasize that a key to understanding their attraction is their positive perception of each other. Tom and Ann are not viewed as controlling each other or each other's behavior. Rather, they have determined their own course of action and each has freely chosen to marry. No recourse to biological instincts or unconscious thoughts as reasons for their attraction occurs in the humanistic perspectives.

Defining the Humanistic Perspectives

The **humanistic perspectives** *stress the person's capacity for personal growth, freedom to choose one's own destiny, and positive qualities* P. 10. Humanistic psychologists believe each of us has the ability to cope with stress, control our lives, and achieve what we desire. Each of us has the ability to break through and understand ourselves and our world; we can burst the cocoon and become a butterfly, say the humanists.

You probably sense that the humanistic perspectives provide stark contrasts to the psychoanalytic perspectives, which are based on conflict, destructive drives, and little faith in human nature, and to the behavioral perspective, which, at its extreme, seems to reduce human beings to mere puppets on the strings of rewards and punishments. Carl Rogers and Abraham Maslow were the leading architects of the humanistic perspective.

Rogers' Approach

Like Freud, Rogers (1902–1987) began his inquiry about human nature with people who were troubled. In the knotted, anxious, defensive verbal stream of his clients, Rogers (1961) examined the conditioned, controlling world that kept them from having positive self-concepts and reaching their full potential as human beings.

Our Conditioned, Controlling World   Rogers believed that most people have considerable difficulty accepting their own true feelings, which are innately positive. As we grow up, people who are central to our lives condition us to move away from these positive feelings. Our parents, siblings, teachers, and peers place constraints and contingencies on our behavior; too often we hear people say things like "Don't do that," "You didn't do that right," and "How can you be so stupid?" When we don't do something right, we often get punished. And parents may even threaten to take away their love. **Conditional positive regard** *is Rogers' term for love and praise being withheld unless the individual conforms to parental or social standards.* The result is lower self-esteem.

These constraints and negative feedback continue during our adult lives. The result tends to be that our relationships either carry the dark cloud of conflict or we conform to what others want. As we struggle to live up to society's standards, we distort and devalue our true self. And we might even completely lose our sense of self by mirroring what others want.

The Self   Through the individual's experiences with the world, a self emerges—this is the "I" or "me" of our existence. Rogers did not believe that all aspects of the self are conscious, but he did believe they are all accessible to consciousness. The self is a whole, consisting of one's self-perceptions (how attractive I am, how well I get along with others, how good an athlete I am) and the values we attach to these perceptions (good/bad, worthy/unworthy, for example). **Self-concept** *is a central theme in Rogers' and other humanists' views; self-concept refers to individuals' overall perceptions of their abilities, behavior, and personality.* In Rogers' view, a person who has an inaccurate self-concept is likely to be maladjusted.

In discussing self-concept, Rogers distinguished between the real self—that is, the self as it really is as a result of our experiences—and the ideal self, which is the self we would like to be. The greater the discrepancy between the real self and the ideal self, said Rogers, the more maladjusted we will be. To improve our adjustment, we can develop more positive perceptions of our real self, not worry so much about what others want, and increase our positive experiences in the world.

Unconditional Positive Regard, Empathy, and Genuineness   Rogers stressed that we can help a person develop a more positive self-concept through unconditional positive regard, empathy, and genuineness. Rogers said that we need to be accepted by others, regardless of what we do. **Unconditional positive regard** *is Rogers' term for accepting, valuing, and being positive toward another person regardless of the person's behavior.* Rogers recognized that when a person's behavior is below acceptable standards, inappropriate, or even obnoxious, the person still needs the respect, comfort, and love of others. Rogers strongly believed that unconditional positive regard elevates the person's self-worth. However, Rogers (1974) distinguished between unconditional positive regard directed at the individual as a person of worth and dignity and directed at the individual's behavior. For example, a therapist who adopts Rogers' view might say, "I don't like your behavior, but I accept you, value you, and care about you as a person."

Rogers also said we can help other people develop a more positive self-concept if we are *empathic* and *genuine*. Being empathic means being a sensitive listener and understanding another's true feelings. Being genuine means being open with our feelings and dropping our pretenses and facades. For Rogers, unconditional positive regard, empathy, and genuineness are three key ingredients of human relations. We can use these techniques to get other people to feel good about themselves and the techniques also help us to get along better with others.

The Fully Functioning Person   Rogers (1980) stressed the importance of becoming a fully functioning person—someone who is open to experience, is not very defensive, is aware of and sensitive to the self and the external world, and for the most part has a harmonious relationship with others. A discrepancy between our

Through the Eyes of Psychologists

Carl Rogers, *(1902–1987)*

"In becoming a person, individuals drop one after another of their defensive masks with which they have faced life."

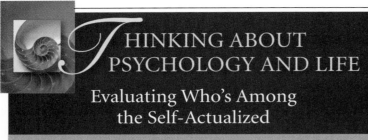

THINKING ABOUT PSYCHOLOGY AND LIFE
Evaluating Who's Among the Self-Actualized

THE FOLLOWING INDIVIDUALS were among the people identified as self-actualized by Maslow: Pablo Casals (cellist), Albert Einstein (physicist), Ralph Waldo Emerson (writer), William James (psychologist), Thomas Jefferson (politician), Abraham Lincoln (politician), Eleanor Roosevelt (humanitarian, diplomat), and Albert Schweitzer (humanitarian).

Maslow made up his list about three decades ago. Not all of his examples of self-actualized individuals were included here but there were considerably more men than women on the complete list. Most of the individuals also were from Western cultures. With Maslow's description of self-actualization in mind (including the characteristics of self-actualized individuals listed in figure 10.8), get together with some other students and brainstorm about who you would add to Maslow's list of self-actualized persons. For starters, consider Mahatma Gandhi (Indian political and spiritual leader) and Martin Luther King (clergyman, civil rights activist) (Endler, 1995), two individuals who were described as self-actualized by Maslow.

Abraham Maslow

*T*hrough the Eyes of Psychologists

Abraham Maslow, *(1908–1970)*

"Self-actualizing stresses full humanness."

real self and our ideal self may occur; others may try to control us; and our world may have too little unconditional positive regard. But Rogers believed that we are highly resilient and capable of becoming a fully functioning person.

Humans' self-actualizing tendencies are reflected in Rogers' comparison of a person with a plant he once observed on the northern California coastline. As Rogers looked out at the waves furiously beating against the jagged rocks and shooting mountains of ocean spray into the air, he noticed the breakers pounding against a tiny sea palm tree 2 or 3 feet tall. The waves crashed against it, bending its slender trunk and whipping its leaves in a torrent of spray. Yet the moment the wave passed, the plant became erect, tough, and resilient once again. The plant took this incessant pounding hour after hour, week after week, possibly even year after year, all the time nourishing itself, maintaining its position, and growing. In this tiny tree, Rogers saw the tenacity of the human spirit and the ability of a living thing to push into a hostile environment and not only hold its own, but adapt, develop, and become itself. So it is with each of us, Rogers said.

Rogers believed that a person's basic tendencies are to actualize, maintain, and enhance life. He thought that the tendency for fulfillment—toward actualizing one's essential nature and attaining potential—is inborn in every person.

Maslow's Approach   Recall from chapter 9, "Motivation and Emotion," that another psychologist, Abraham Maslow (1908–1970), believed that self-actualization is the highest form of motivation ◀▥ P. 287. He also believed it is an important aspect of personality. Maslow was one of the most powerful figures in psychology's humanistic movement. He called the humanistic approach the "third force" in psychology—that is, an important alternative to the psychoanalytic and behavioral forces. Maslow pointed out that psychoanalytic theories place too much emphasis on disturbed individuals and their conflicts. Behaviorists ignore the person all together, he said.

Remember that Maslow (1954, 1971) believes our "basic" needs must be satisfied before our "higher" needs can be. According to Maslow's concept of **hierarchy of motives,** *individuals' needs must be satisfied in this sequence: physiological, safety, love and belongingness, esteem, and self-actualization.* Also recall that it is **self-actualization,** *the motivation to develop one's full potential as a human being, that Maslow focused on the most. He believed self-actualization is the highest human need and that most people have difficulty reaching this level in their lives.* Figure 10.8 describes the main characteristics that Maslow attributes to a self-actualized individual.

Self-Esteem   Interest in the self led to the belief that self-esteem is an important aspect of personality. **Self-esteem** *is the evaluative and affective dimension of self-concept. Self-esteem is also referred to as self-worth.*

Following are some of the issues and findings involving research on self-esteem (Baumeister, 1997):

• Does self-esteem fluctuate from day to day or remain stable? Most research studies have found it to be stable at least across a month or so of time (Baumeister, 1991). Self-esteem can change, especially in response to transitions in life (such as graduating from high school or going to college) and to life events (such as getting a job or losing a job).

Maslow's Characteristics of Self-Actualized Individuals

Realistic orientation
Self-acceptance and acceptance of others and the natural world as they are
Spontaneity

Problem-centered rather than self-centered
Air of detachment and need for privacy
Autonomous and independent

Fresh rather than stereotyped appreciation of people and things
Generally have had profound mystical or spiritual, though not necessarily religious, experiences
Identification with humankind and a strong social interest

Tendency to have strong intimate relationships with a few special, loved people rather than superficial relationships with many people
Democratic values and attitudes
No confusion of means with ends
Philosophical rather than hostile sense of humor

High degree of creativity
Resistance to cultural conformity
Transcendence of environment rather than always coping with it

Figure 10.8
Maslow's Characteristics of Self-Actualized Individuals

- Is self-esteem something very general or does it consist of a number of independent self-evaluations in different areas? That is, is it more appropriate to think of people having high or low self-esteem overall, or high or low self-esteem in specific areas of their lives, such as high in social, low in cognitive (academic)? Current thinking about this issue has evolved toward the conclusion that people do have a general level of self-esteem but still can have fluctuating levels of self-esteem in particular domains of their lives. (Fleming & Courtney, 1984).
- Low self-esteem is linked with depression (Harter, 1998). The failure to live up to one's standards is especially implicated in the connection between low self-esteem and depression.

An important point needs to be made about much of the research on self-esteem: It is correlational rather than experimental. Remember from our discussion in chapter 1, "What Is Psychology?," that correlation does not equal causation ◀▐▐▐ P. 34. Thus, if a correlational study finds an association between self-esteem and depression, depression could just as well cause self-esteem as much as self-esteem causes depression.

A topic of considerable interest is what can be done to increase the self-esteem of individuals with low self-esteem. Researchers have found that four main strategies help to improve self-esteem (Bednar, Wells, & Peterson, 1995; Harter, 1998): (1) identifying the causes of self-esteem, (2) experiencing emotional support and approval, (3) achieving, and (4) coping (see figure 10.9). The emphasis on experiencing emotional support and approval meshes with Carl Rogers' emphasis on unconditional positive regard that we discussed earlier in this chapter. Some psychologists argue that the most effective ways to improve self-esteem are to improve the person's achievement and coping skills. Rogers believes that when a person's

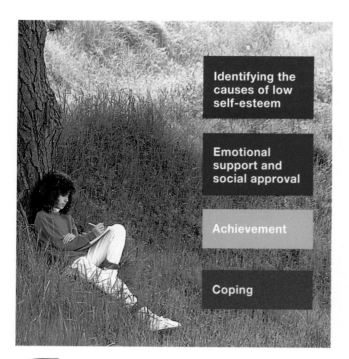

achievement and coping skills improve, the individual's self-esteem is likely to follow suit.

Evaluating the Humanistic Perspectives

The humanistic perspectives made psychologists aware that the way we perceive ourselves and the world around us are key elements of personality. Humanistic psychologists also reminded us that we need to consider the whole person and the positive bent of human nature. Their emphasis on conscious experience has given us the view that personality contains a well of "potential" that can be developed to its fullest.

A weakness of the humanistic perspective is that it is difficult to test. Self-actualization, for example, is not clearly defined. Psychologists are not certain how to study this concept empirically. Some humanists even scorn the experimental approach, preferring clinical interpretation as a data base. Verification of humanistic concepts has come mainly from clinical experiences rather than controlled, experimental studies. Some critics believe humanistic psychologists are too optimistic about human nature, overestimating the freedom and rationality of humans. And some critics say the humanists encourage self-love and narcissism.

We have seen that the behavioral and social cognitive perspectives, and the humanistic perspectives, take different paths to understanding personality. An overview of the main ideas in these perspectives is presented in summary table 10.2. Next we turn our attention to a fourth set of personality perspectives, the trait perspectives.

Figure 10.9
Four Main Strategies for Improving Self-Esteem

Personality Traits

Trait Perspectives

Through the ages we have used an infinite variety of traits to describe ourselves and one another. More than 2,000 years ago Theophrastus described the stingy man, the liar, and the flatterer. A magazine article takes a modern swipe at the stingy man:

Could a miser be lurking beneath the sensuous flesh and persuasive charm? Well, don't expect sapphires from him, if he

- itemizes who owes what when you're out Dutch-treat rather than splitting the bill
- washes plastic party cups to reuse them
- steams uncanceled stamps from letters
- reshapes bent paper clips
- has a dozen recipes for chicken wings
- cuts his own hair
- wants rolls and butter included in his doggie bag. (*Cosmopolitan*, September 1976, p. 148)

Think about yourself and your friends. How would you describe yourself? You might say that you're outgoing and sociable and that, in contrast, one of your friends is shy and quiet. You might refer to yourself as emotionally stable and describe one of your other friends as a bit skittish. Part of our everyday existence involves describing ourselves and others in terms of traits.

Trait Theories
Trait theories *state that personality consists of broad dispositions, called traits, that tend to lead to characteristic responses.* In other words, people can be described in terms of the basic ways they behave, such as whether they are outgoing and friendly or whether they are dominant and assertive. People who have a strong tendency to behave in these ways are described as high on the traits; those

SUMMARY TABLE 10.2
The Behavioral and Social Cognitive Perspectives, and the Humanistic Perspectives

Concept	Processes/ Related Ideas	Characteristics/Description
Behavioral and Social Cognitive Perspectives	Defining the Behavioral and Social Cognitive Perspectives	They emphasize the importance of studying environmental experiences and a person's observable behavior to understand that person's personality. The contemporary version of social cognitive theory emphasizes person/cognitive factors in personality.
	Skinner's Behaviorism	This view emphasizes that cognition is unimportant in personality; personality is observed behavior, which is influenced by the rewards and punishments in the environment. Personality often varies according to the situation.
	Social Cognitive Theory	This theory, whose main architects are Bandura and Mischel, states that behavior, environment, and person/cognitive factors are important in understanding personality. In Bandura's view, these factors can reciprocally interact.
	Evaluating the Behavioral and Social Cognitive Perspectives	Strengths of both perspectives include emphases on environmental determinants and a scientific climate for investigating personality, as well as a focus on cognitive processes and self-control in the social cognitive approach. The behavioral view has been criticized for taking the "person" out of personality and for ignoring cognition. These approaches have not given adequate attention to enduring individual differences, to biological factors, and to personality as a whole.
Humanistic Perspectives	Defining the Humanistic Perspectives	They stress the person's capacity for personal growth and freedom, ability to choose one's own destiny, and positive qualities.
	Rogers' Approach	Each of us is a victim of conditional positive regard. The result is that the real self is not valued. The self is the core of personality; it includes both the real and ideal self. Rogers said we can help others develop a more positive self-concept in three ways: unconditional positive regard, empathy, and genuineness. Rogers also stressed that each of us has the innate, inner capacity to become a fully functioning person.
	Maslow's Approach	Maslow called the humanistic movement the "third force" in psychology. Maslow developed the hierarchy of needs concept with self-actualization being the highest human need.
	Self-Esteem	Self-esteem is the evaluative and affective dimension of the self. Self-esteem also is referred to as self-worth. Four main strategies for increasing self-esteem are (1) identifying the causes of low self-esteem, (2) emotional support and approval, (3) achievement, (4) coping.
	Evaluating the Humanistic Perspectives	They sensitized us to the importance of subjective experience, consciousness, self-conception, the whole person, and our innate, positive nature. Weaknesses focus on the absence of an empirical orientation, a tendency to be too optimistic, and an inclination to encourage self-love.

who have a weak tendency to behave in these ways are described as low on the traits. While trait theorists sometimes differ on which traits make up personality, they all agree that traits are the fundamental building blocks of personality (Cloninger, 1996; Matthews & Dreary, 1998).

Figure 10.10
Eysenck's Dimensions of Personality

Eysenck believed that for people without a psychological disorder, personality consists of two basic dimensions: (1) introversion–extraversion and (2) stability–instability. He thought that a third dimension—psychoticism—was needed to describe the personality of individuals with a psychological disorder.

**Eysenck's View
The Big Five**

Allport's View of Traits   Gordon Allport (1897–1967) believed that each individual has a unique set of personality traits. He argued that if a person's traits could be determined, it would be possible to predict the individual's behavior in various circumstances.

In going through an unabridged dictionary, Allport (1937) identified more than 4,500 personality traits. To impose some organization on the vast number of trait terms that might be used to describe an individual's personality, Allport grouped personality traits into three main categories: Central, secondary and cardinal.

Cardinal traits *are the most powerful and pervasive traits. When they are present, they dominate an individual's personality.* However, according to Allport, few people actually possess cardinal traits. We might think of some famous individuals as having these (Hitler's power, Mother Teresa's altruism). But most people aren't characterized by just one or two traits (unlike the way we think about Hitler or Mother Teresa). **Central traits** *are a limited number of traits (Allport believed most people have about 6 to 12 of these) that are usually adequate to describe most people's personalities.* For an example, an individual's personality might be described as friendly, calm, kind, and humorous. **Secondary traits** *are limited in frequency and least important in understanding an individual's personality.* They include particular attitudes and preferences, such as the type of food or music a person likes.

Eysenck's Dimensions of Personality   Hans Eysenck (1967) also tackled the task of determining the basic traits of personality. He gave personality tests to large numbers of people and analyzed each person's responses. Eysenck said that three main dimensions were needed to explain personality: (1) introversion–extraversion, (2) stable–unstable (known as the *neuroticism* dimension), and (3) psychoticism.

In terms of the introversion–extraversion dimension, an introverted person is quiet, unsociable, passive, and careful; an extraverted person is active, optimistic, sociable, and outgoing. In terms of the stable–unstable dimension, a stable person is calm, even-tempered, carefree, and has leadership possibilities; an unstable person is moody, anxious, restless, and touchy. Figure 10.10 shows these two basic dimensions in Eysenck's view. Eysenck believed that various combinations of these dimensions result in certain personality traits. For example, a person who is extraverted and unstable is likely to be impulsive. The third dimension, psychoticism, reflects the degree to which people are in contact with reality, control their impulses, and are cruel or caring toward others.

The Big Five Factors   Considerable interest continues to be generated in determining what the key factors of personality really are (Saucier & Ostendorf, 1999). In a number of areas, you have seen that psychologists are interested in pinning down the number and identity of factors involved in a concept. For example, in chapter 7, "Thinking, Language, and Intelligence," we saw that Sternberg thinks intelligence is made up of three main factors and Gardner believes it is made up of seven.

The **big five factors of personality** *consists of emotional stability (neuroticism), extraversion, openness to experience, agreeableness, and conscientiousness* (see figure 10.11). A number of research studies point toward these factors as important dimensions of personality (Costa & McRae, 1995, 1998; David & Suls, 1999; Hogan, 1987; McNulty, 2000).

Research on the big five factors includes the extent to which the factors appear in personality profiles in different cultures, how stable the factors are over time, and the role the factors might play in predicting physical and mental health.

Do the five factors show up in the assessment of personality in cultures around the world? There is increasing evidence that they do (Ozer & Reise, 1994). Researchers have found that some version of the five factors appears in people in countries as diverse as Canada, Finland, Poland, China, and Japan (Paunonen & others, 1992).

Using their five-factor personality test, Paul Costa and Robert McRae (1995) studied approximately a thousand college-educated men and women aged 20 to 96, assessing the same individuals over a period of many years. Data collection began in the 1950s to the mid-1960s and is ongoing. Costa and McRae concluded that considerable stability occurs in the five personality factors—emotional stability, extraversion, openness, agreeableness, and conscientiousness.

The notion that personality characteristics might influence vulnerability to illness and illness progression continues to attract widespread research attention. Much of this research, though, is conducted without reference to a unified framework of personality. The big five trait structure offers the potential for such a unified framework.

In one study, Costa and McRae's big five personality test, along with representative personality scales from health psychology (such as scales for personal control and self-esteem, optimism and hope, negative affectivity, and emotional control) were administered to two samples of male military recruits (Marshall & others, 1994). Variations in many of the health-related personality scales could be moderately explained by the big five factors. In health psychology research, neuroticism and extraversion have been given disproportionate attention (not surprisingly, given the prominence of these factors in theories of arousal and stress). The factors of conscientiousness and openness to experience have especially been neglected in research on personality's role in health and illness. Later in the chapter we will examine the tests that have been developed to assess the big five factors.

Research has generally supported the concept of the big five "general" traits, but some personality researchers believe they might not end up being the final list of supertraits. For example, some support has been found for two additional factors: excellent–ordinary and evil–decent, so the big five could become the big seven (Almagor, Tellegen, & Waller, 1995; Benet & Waller, 1995).

The Attack on Traits   In his landmark book *Personality and Assessment* Walter Mischel (1968) criticized the trait view of personality as well as the psychoanalytic approach, both of which emphasize the internal organization of personality. Rather than viewing personality as consisting of broad, internal traits that are consistent across situations and time, Mischel said that personality often changes according to a given situation.

Mischel reviewed an array of studies and concluded that trait measures do a poor job of predicting actual behavior. For example, let's say Anne is described as an aggressive person. But when we observe her behavior we find that she is more or less aggressive depending on the situation—she might be aggressive with her boyfriend but almost submissive with her new boss. Mischel's view was called **situationism,** *which means that personality often varies considerably from one context to another.* Mischel's argument was an important one, but as we see next, many psychologists were not willing to abandon altogether the trait concept.

Trait-Situation Interaction   Today, most psychologists in the field of personality are interactionists, including Mischel. They believe both trait (person) and situation variables are necessary to understand personality (Ackerman, Kyllonen,

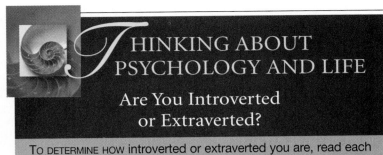

THINKING ABOUT PSYCHOLOGY AND LIFE
Are You Introverted or Extraverted?

To determine how introverted or extraverted you are, read each of the following 20 questions and answer either *yes* (if it is generally true for you) or *no* (if it is not generally true for you).

	Yes	No
1. Do you often long for excitement?		
2. Are you usually carefree?		
3. Do you stop and think things over before doing anything?		
4. Would you do almost anything for a dare?		
5. Do you often do things on the spur of the moment?		
6. Generally, do you prefer reading to meeting people?		
7. Do you prefer to have few but special friends?		
8. When people shout at you do you shout back?		
9. Do other people think of you as very lively?		
10. Are you mostly quiet when you are with people?		
11. If there is something you want to know about, would you rather look it up in a book than talk to someone about it?		
12. Do you like the kind of work that you need to pay close attention to?		
13. Do you hate being with a crowd who plays jokes on one another?		
14. Do you like doing things in which you have to act quickly?		
15. Are you slow and unhurried in the way you move?		
16. Do you like talking to people so much that you never miss a chance of talking to a stranger?		
17. Would you be unhappy if you could not see lots of people most of the time?		
18. Do you find it hard to enjoy yourself at a lively party?		
19. Would you say that you were fairly self-confident?		
20. Do you like playing pranks on others?		

To arrive at your score for extraversion, give one point for each of the following items answered *yes:* #1, 2, 4, 5, 8. 9, 14, 16, 17, 19, and 20. Then give yourself one point for each of the following items answered *no:* #3, 6, 7, 10, 11, 12, 13, 15, 18. Add up all the points to arrive at a total score.

Your total score should be between 0 and 20. If your scores are very high (15–20), you are the "life of the party." You clearly prefer being with others to being alone. If your scores are very low (1–5), you are a loner. You find greater pleasure in solitary activities. If you are somewhere in between (6–14), you are flexible in how you prefer to spend your time. You can take pleasure in the company of others (especially if your score is in the higher range) but still manage to appreciate solitude.

Emotional Stability	Extraversion	Openness	Agreeableness	Conscientiousness
• Calm or anxious	• Sociable or retiring	• Imaginative or practical	• Softhearted or ruthless	• Organized or disorganized
• Secure or insecure	• Fun-loving or somber	• Interested in variety or routine	• Trusting or suspicious	• Careful or careless
• Self-satisfied or self-pitying	• Affectionate or reserved	• Independent or conforming	• Helpful or uncooperative	• Disciplined or impulsive

Figure 10.11
The Big Five Factors of Personality

& Roberts, 1999; Edwards & Rothbard, 1999). They also agree that the degree of consistency in personality depends on the kind of persons, situations, and behaviors sampled (Pervin, 1993; Mischel, 1995).

Suppose you want to assess the happiness of Bob, an introvert, and Jane, an extravert. According to trait-situation interaction theory, we cannot predict who will be happier unless we know something about the situations they are in. Imagine you get the opportunity to observe them in two situations, at a party and in a library.

One outcome of the trait-situation controversy is that the link between traits and situations has been more precisely specified (Walsh, 1995). For example, researchers have found that (1) the narrower and more limited a trait is, the more likely it will predict behavior; (2) some people are consistent on some traits and other people are consistent on other traits; and (3) personality traits exert a stronger influence on an individual's behavior when situational influences are less powerful.

Cross-cultural psychologists go several steps farther. They believe that considering both the immediate setting *and* the broader cultural context leads to a better understanding of the situation's role in the way personality is expressed (Katigbak, Church, & Akamine, 1996). For example, cross-cultural psychologists investigating certain aspects of personality and religion would observe a person's behavior in a chapel and put it in the context of social conventions regarding who should be in church, when, with whom, and how the person is expected to behave.

At this point, we have studied a number of ideas about the trait perspectives. An overview of these ideas is presented in summary table 10.3. Now that we have explored the main theoretical perspectives in personality, we will turn our attention to another important aspect of studying personality: how it can be assessed.

Personality Assessment

"This line running this way indicates that you are a gregarious person, someone who really enjoys being around people. This division over here suggests that you are a risk taker; I bet you like to do things that are adventurous sometimes." These are the words you might hear from a palmist. Palmistry purports to "read" an individual's personality by interpreting the irregularities and folds in the skin of the hand. Each of these signs is interpreted in a precise manner. For example, a large mound of Saturn, the portion of the palm directly below the third joint of the middle finger, ostensibly relates to wisdom, good fortune, and prudence.

Summary Table 10.3
Trait Perspectives

Concept	Processes/Related Ideas	Characteristics/Description
Trait Theories	Their Nature	Trait theories emphasize that personality involves the organization of traits within the individual. These traits are assumed to be essentially stable over time and across situations.
	Allport's View of Traits	Allport believed that each individual has a unique set of personality traits. He grouped personality traits into three main categories: cardinal, central, and secondary.
	Eysenck's Dimensions of Personality	Eysenck said that the basic dimensions of personality are (1) introversion–extraversion, (2) stability–instability (neuroticism), and (3) psychoticism.
	The Big Five Factors	There is much current interest in the big five factors in personality: emotional stability, extraversion, openness to experience, agreeableness, and conscientiousness.
	The Attack on Traits	Mischel's (1968) *Personality and Assessment* ushered in an attack on trait theory. Basically, the argument was that personality varies across situations more than trait theorists acknowledged.
Trait-Situation Interaction	Its Nature	Today most personality psychologists are interactionists. They believe that personality is determined by a combination of traits or person factors and the situation. Cross-cultural psychologists believe the situation involves both the immediate setting and the broader cultural context.

While palmists claim to provide a complete assessment of personality through reading lines in the hand, researchers debunk palmistry as quackery. Researchers argue that palmists give no reasonable explanation for their inferences about personality, and point out that the hand's characteristics can change through age and even exercise.

Even so, palmists manage to stay in business. They do so, in part, because they are keen observers—they respond to such cues as voice, general demeanor, and dress, which are more relevant signs of personality than the lines and folds on a person's palm. Palmists also are experts at offering general, trivial statements such as, "Although you usually are affectionate with others, sometimes you don't get along with people." This statement falls into the category of the **Barnum effect:** *If you make your predictions broad enough, any person can fit the description.* The effect was named after circus owner P. T. Barnum.

Some Themes in Personality Assessment

In contrast to palmists, psychologists use a number of scientifically developed tests and methods to evaluate personality (Walsh & Betz, 1995). And they assess personality for different reasons. Clinical and school psychologists assess personality to better understand an individual's psychological problems; they hope the assessment will improve their diagnosis and treatment of the individual. Industrial psychologists and vocational counselors assess personality to aid the individual's selection of a career. And research psychologists assess personality to investigate the theories and dimensions of personality we have discussed so far in this chapter. For example, if a psychologist wants to investigate self-concept, some measure of self-concept is needed.

Before we describe some specific personality tests, two more important points need to be made about the nature of personality assessment. First, the kinds of tests chosen by psychologists frequently depend on the psychologist's theoretical bent. And

Assessment Journals

second, most personality tests are designed to assess stable, enduring characteristics, free of situational influence (Hy & Loevinger, 1996).

Projective Tests

A **projective test** *presents individuals with an ambiguous stimulus and then asks them to describe it or tell a story about it. Projective tests are based on the assumption that the ambiguity of the stimulus allows individuals to project into it their feelings, desires, needs, and attitudes.* The test is especially designed to elicit the individual's unconscious feelings and conflicts, providing an assessment that goes deeper than the surface of personality (Auerbach, 1999; Handler, 1999). Projective tests attempt to get inside of your mind to discover how you really feel and think, going beyond the way you overtly present yourself.

The Rorschach Inkblot Test
The **Rorschach inkblot test,** *developed in 1921 by the Swiss psychiatrist Hermann Rorschach, is a widely used projective test; it uses an individual's perception of inkblots to determine his or her personality.* The test consists of ten cards, half in black and white and half in color, which are shown to the individual one at a time (see figure 10.12). The person taking the Rorschach test is asked to describe what he or she sees in each of the inkblots. For example, an individual may say, "That looks like two people fighting." After the individual has responded to all ten inkblots, the examiner presents each of the inkblots again and inquires about the individual's earlier response. For example, the examiner might ask, "*Where* did you see the two people fighting?" and "*What* about the inkblot made the two people look like they were fighting?" Besides recording the responses, the examiner notes the individual's mannerisms, gestures, and attitudes.

How useful is the Rorschach in assessing personality? The answer to this question depends on one's perspective. From a scientific perspective, researchers are skeptical about the Rorschach (Feshbach & Weiner, 1996). Their disenchantment stems from the failure of the Rorschach to meet the criteria of reliability and validity. If the Rorschach were reliable, two different scorers should agree on the personality characteristics of the individual. If the Rorschach were valid, the individual's personality should predict behavior outside of the testing situation; that is, it should predict whether an individual will attempt suicide, become severely depressed, cope successfully with stress, or get along well with others. Conclusions based on research evidence suggest that the Rorschach does not meet these criteria of reliability and validity ◄⃞⃥ P. 218. This has led to serious reservations about the Rorschach's use in diagnosis and clinical practice.

Yet the Rorschach continues to enjoy widespread use in clinical circles; some clinicians swear by the Rorschach, saying it is better than any other measure at getting at the true, underlying core of the individual's personality (Sloan & others, 1996). They are not especially bothered by the Rorschach's low reliability and validity, pointing out that this is so because of the extensive freedom of response encouraged by the test. It is this freedom of response that makes the Rorschach such a rich clinical tool, say its advocates. In one survey, Rorschach-based testimony was legally challenged in only 6 of nearly 8,000 court cases (Weiner, Exner, & Sciara, 1996).

The Rorschach controversy continues (Baity & Hilsenroth, 1999; Hilsenroth, 2000; Murstein & Mathes, 1996). And it probably will not subside in the near future. Research psychologists will continue to criticize the low reliability and validity of the Rorschach; many clinicians will continue to say that the Rorschach is a valuable clinical tool, providing insights about the unconscious mind that no other personality test can.

Other Projective Tests
The **Thematic Apperception Test (TAT),** *which was developed by Henry Murray and Christina Morgan in the 1930s, is an ambiguous projective test designed to elicit stories that reveal something about an individual's personality.* The TAT consists of a series of pictures, each on an individual card (see figure 10.13). The person taking the TAT is asked to tell a story about each of the pictures, including events leading up to the situation described, the characters' thoughts and feelings, and how the situation turns out. It is assumed that the person projects her own unconscious feelings and thoughts into the story she tells. In

Figure 10.12
Type of Stimulus Used in the Rorschach Inkblot Test

The Rorschach

"Rorschach! What's to become of you?"
Reprinted by permission of Sidney Harris

addition to being used as a projective test in clinical practice, the TAT is used in research of achievement motivation (Cramer, 1999). Several of the TAT cards stimulate the telling of achievement-related stories, which enables the researcher to determine the person's need for achievement (McClelland & others, 1953).

Many other projective tests are used in clinical assessment. One test asks the individual to complete a sentence (for example "I often feel . . ." "I would like to . . ."); another test asks the individual to draw a person; and another test presents a word, such as *fear* or *happy,* and asks the individual to say the first thing that comes to mind. Like the Rorschach, these projective tests have their detractors and advocates; the detractors often criticize the tests' low reliability and validity, and the advocates describe the tests' abilities to reveal the underlying nature of the individual's personality better than more straightforward tests. Recently, another projective measure has generated considerable controversy—**graphology,** *the use of handwriting analysis to determine an individual's personality.* To read further about graphology and its lack of scientific status, turn to Explorations in Psychology.

Self-Report Tests

Unlike projective techniques derived from psychoanalytic perspectives, self-report tests, which are derived from the trait perspectives, do not attempt to assess an individual's hidden, unconscious personality. Rather, **self-report tests,** *also called objective tests or inventories, directly ask people whether items (usually true/false or agree/disagree) describe their personality traits or not.* For example, self-report personality tests include items such as:

- I am easily embarrassed.
- I love to go to parties.
- I like to watch cartoons on TV.

Self-report tests are questionnaires that include a large number of statements or questions like these. You respond with a limited number of choices (yes or no; true or false; agree or disagree). How do psychologists construct self-report tests of personality?

Constructing Self-Report Tests   Many of the early personality tests were based on **face validity,** *which is an assumption that the content of the test items is a good indicator of the individual's personality.* For example, if I developed a test item that asks you to respond whether or not you are introverted, and you answer, "I enjoy being with people," I accept your response as a straightforward indication that you are not introverted. Tests based on face validity assume that you are responding honestly and nondefensively, giving the examiner an accurate portrayal of your personality.

But not everyone is honest, especially when it concerns their own personality. Even if the individual basically is honest, he may be giving socially desirable answers. When motivated by **social desirability,** *individuals say what they think the interviewer wants to hear or what they think will make them look better.* For example, if I am basically a lazy person, I might not want you to know this, and I may try to present myself in a more positive way; therefore, I would respond negatively to the following item: "I fritter away time too much." Because of such responses psychologists realized they needed to go beyond face validity in constructing personality tests; they accomplished this by developing empirically keyed tests.

An **empirically keyed test** *relies on its items to predict some criterion.* Unlike tests based on face validity, in which the content of the items is supposed to be a good indicator of what the individual's personality is like, empirically keyed tests make no assumptions about the nature of the items. Imagine we want to develop a test that will determine whether or not applicants for a position as a police officer are likely to be competent at the job. We might ask a large number of questions of police officers, some of whom have excellent job records, others who have not performed as well. We would then use the questions that differentiate between competent and incompetent police officers on our test to screen job applicants. If the item, "I enjoyed reading poetry" predicts success as a police officer, then we would include it on the

$\mathcal{F}$igure 10.13
Picture from the Thematic Apperception Test (TAT)

EXPLORATIONS IN PSYCHOLOGY
Being Skeptical About Graphology

CAN THE ANALYSIS of a person's handwriting provide insight into her personality? Examine the writing in figure 10.A to see the kinds of interpretations graphologists make. At least 3,000 firms in the United States use graphology when hiring individuals. In other countries, such as Israel and Japan, the use of graphological analysis in hiring is even more widespread. One survey found that 85 percent of all European firms use graphology as part of their employee-selection process (Levy, 1979). The managing editor of the journal *United States Banker* commented, "Graphoanalysis [graphology] reveals capabilities and aptitudes in an individual, many of which the applicant may not be aware of" (Van Deventer, 1983). Given the recent popularity of handwriting analysis in business hiring, it is important to examine whether it really does reveal anything about an individual's personality characteristics (Hines, 1988).

The growing research literature on graphology is almost universally negative (Furnham, 1988; Nevo, 1986). One investigation typifies these negative results (Ben-Shakhar & others, 1986). Three professional graphologists agreed to rate handwriting samples from 52 bank employees. The graphologists were asked to assess the employees' competence at their jobs and the nature of their relationships with co-workers. The samples consisted of brief autobiographical essays and responses to a short biographical questionnaire. The researchers also used information from the samples, such as the employees' ages and job interests, the quality of their essays, and the attractiveness of their handwriting to make assessments about the employees' competence. The researchers' predictions and the graphologists' ratings were compared with the ratings by the employees' supervisors. The graphologists did no better than the researchers at matching the supervisors' ratings. A battery of personality tests were better at matching the supervisors' ratings. In a second study, five graphologists did no better than chance when asked to predict the occupations of 40 successful professional men based on several pages of their handwriting.

If the research investigation of graphological claims is so negative, why is graphology so widely used and accepted? Graphological analysis has a mysterious, powerful ring to it. People are easily impressed by confident, so-called experts and assume they know what they are talking about. Positive, unscientific reports of graphologists' abilities appear frequently in magazines and business commentaries. People are fascinated by graphology and want to believe that their handwriting, because it is highly individual, reveals something about themselves. Also, graphologists' predictions, like those of palmists and astrologers, are usually very general and difficult to disprove.

1. Level of emotional responsiveness

Withdrawal   **Objectiveness**   **Intensity**

The backward slant at left indicates withdrawal, the vertical slant in the middle indicates objectiveness, and the forward slant on the right indicates intensity.

2. Social responsiveness

Repression   **Lack of inhibition**

Note the tight loops of the m and n on the left, which indicate repression, and the spread loops of the m and n on the right, which indicate a lack of inhibition.

3. Approach to achievement

Lack of self-confidence   **Strong willpower**

Note the low t-bar on the left, which indicates a lack of self-confidence, and the high t-bar on the right, which indicates strong willpower.

Figure 10.A
Some Graphological Interpretations

test even though it seems unrelated to police work. Next, we examine the most widely used empirically keyed personality test.

The Minnesota Multiphasic Personality Inventory (MMPI)

The **Minnesota Multiphasic Personality Inventory (MMPI)** *is the most widely used and researched self-report personality test.* The MMPI initially was constructed to assess "abnormal" personality tendencies and improve the diagnosis of individuals with a mental disorder. A thousand statements were given to both mental patients and apparently normal people. How often individuals agreed with each item was calculated; only the items that clearly differentiated the psychiatric patients from the normal individuals were retained. For example, a statement might be included on the depression scale of the MMPI if patients diagnosed with a depressive disorder agreed with the statement significantly more than did normal individuals. For example, a statement with little face validity, such as "I sometimes tease animals," might be included on the depression scale, or any other scale, of the MMPI.

The MMPI eventually was streamlined to 550 items, each of which can be answered true, false, or cannot say. The items vary widely in content and include such statements as the following:

- I like to read magazines.
- I never have trouble falling asleep.
- People are out to get me.

A person's answers are grouped according to ten clinical categories, or scales, that measure problems such as depression, psychopathic deviation, schizophrenia, and social introversion.

The MMPI includes four validity scales in addition to the ten clinical scales. The validity scales were designed to indicate whether an individual is lying, careless, defensive, or evasive when answering the test items. For example, if the individual responds "false" to a number of items, such as "I get angry sometimes," it would be interpreted that she is trying to make herself look better than she really is. The rationale for the lie scale is that each of us gets angry at least some of the time, so the individual who responds "false" to many such items is faking her responses.

For the first time in its approximately 40-year history, the MMPI was revised in 1989. The revision is called the MMPI-2. It has a number of new items (for a total of 567 items), but the 10 clinical scales were retained as were several of the validity scales (such as the lie scale). New content scales were added to the MMPI-2. These include substance abuse, eating disorders, anger, self-esteem, family problems, and inability to function in a job.

The MMPI-2 continues to be widely used around the world to assess personality and predict outcomes (Butcher, 1999; Butcher, Lim, & Nezami, 1998). It has been so popular that it has been translated into more than 20 languages. Not only is it used by clinical psychologists to assess a person's mental health, it also is used to predict which individuals will make the best job candidates or which career an individual should pursue.

One trend is the increased use of computers to score the MMPI-2 (Finger & Ones, 1999; Iverson & Barton, 1999). Some critics argue that too often this has meant untrained individuals have been tempted to use the test in ways that it was not validated for.

Assessing the Big Five Factors   Earlier in the chapter we indicated that there is considerable interest in the big five factors in personality: emotional stability, extraversion, openness, agreeableness, and conscientiousness. Paul Costa and Robert McRae (1992) constructed a test, the *Neuroticism Extraversion Openness Personality Inventory, Revised* (or *NEO-PI-R* for short), to assess the big five factors. The test also evaluates six subdimensions that make up the five main factors. Costa and McRae believe that the test can improve the diagnosis of personality disorders and help therapists understand how therapy might influence different types of clients. For instance, individuals who score high on the extraversion factor might prefer group over individual psychotherapy, whereas introverts might do better in individual psychotherapy.

Another measure that is used to assess the big five factors is the Hogan Personality Inventory (HPI) created by Robert Hogan (1986). One way the HPI and the NEO-PI-R are used is to attempt to predict job success. Researchers have found that the HPI effectively predicts such job performance criteria as supervisor ratings and training course success (Wiggins & Trapnell, 1997).

**Journal of Personality Assessment
MMPI-2**

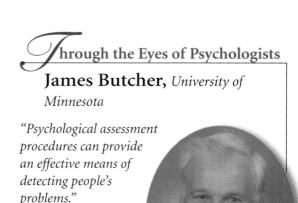
Through the Eyes of Psychologists
James Butcher, *University of Minnesota*
"Psychological assessment procedures can provide an effective means of detecting people's problems."

Exploring Personality Tests

Journal of Personality

Evaluating Self-Report Tests   Adherents of the trait approach have strong faith in the utility of self-report tests. They point out that self-report tests have produced a better understanding of the nature of an individual's personality traits than can be derived from, for example, projective tests. However, some critics (especially psychoanalysts) believe the self-report measures do not get at the underlying core of personality and its unconscious determinants. Other critics (especially behaviorists) believe the self-report tests do not adequately capture the situational variation in personality and the ways personality changes as the individual interacts with the environment.

Behavioral and Cognitive Assessment

Behavioral assessment attempts to obtain more objective information about an individual's personality by observing the individual's behavior directly ◀IIII P. 29. Instead of removing situational influences from personality as projective tests and self-report measures do, behavioral assessment assumes that personality cannot be evaluated apart from the environment. Behavior modification is an attempt to apply learning principles to change maladaptive behavior. Behavioral assessment of personality emerged from this tradition. For example, recall that the observer often will make baseline observations of the frequency of the individual's behaviors. This might be accomplished under controlled laboratory conditions or in more naturalistic circumstances. The therapist then will modify some aspect of the environment, such as getting parents and the child's teacher to stop giving the child attention when he engages in the aggressive behavior. After a specified period of time, the therapist will observe the child again to determine if the changes in the environment were effective in reducing the child's maladaptive behavior.

Sometimes, though, direct observations are impractical. What does a psychologist with a behavioral orientation then do to assess personality? She might ask individuals to make their own assessments of behavior, encouraging them to be sensitive to the circumstances that produced the behavior and the outcomes or consequences of the behavior. For example, a therapist might want to know the course of marital conflict in the everyday experiences of a couple. Figure 10.14 shows a spouse observation checklist that couples can use to record their partner's behavior.

The influence of social cognitive theory has increased the use of cognitive assessment in personality evaluation. The strategy is to discover what thoughts underlie the individual's behavior; that is, how do individuals think about their problems? What kinds of thoughts precede maladaptive behavior, occur during its manifestation, and follow it? Cognitive processes such as expectations, planning, and memory are assessed, possibly by interviewing the individual or asking him or her to complete a questionnaire. For example, an interview might include questions that address whether the individual overexaggerates his faults and condemns himself more than is warranted. A questionnaire might ask a person what her thoughts are after an upsetting event or it might assess the way she thinks during tension-filled moments.

It has been some time since we considered the different theoretical approaches to personality. Next, to conclude the chapter, we return to those theories and compare their orientation on a number of important issues involving personality.

Comparing Perspectives on Personality

Three important issues in personality are the degree to which it is innate or learned (biologically or experientially based); the degree to which it is conscious or unconscious; and the degree to which it is internally or externally determined.

1. *Innate versus learned.* Is personality due more to heredity and biological factors or more to learning and environmental experiences? ◀IIII P. 37. Are individuals conceited and self-centered because they inherited the tendency to be conceited and self-centered from their parents, or did they learn to be that way through experiences with other conceited, self-centered individuals? Freud's theory has a strong biogenetic foundation, although many psychoanalytic revisionists argued

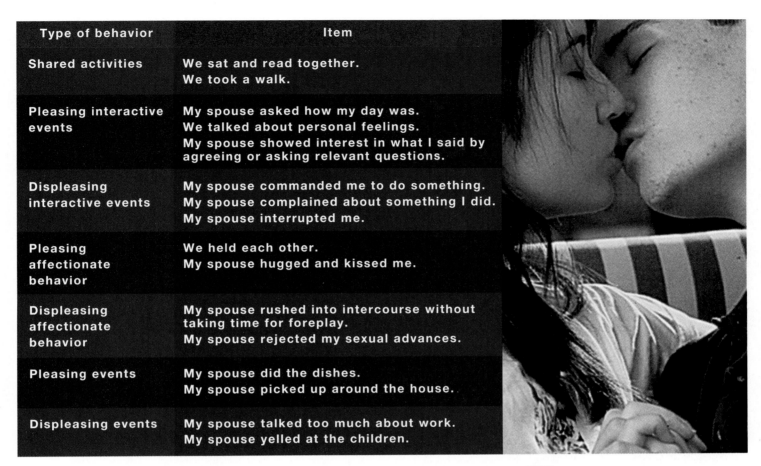

Type of behavior	Item
Shared activities	We sat and read together. We took a walk.
Pleasing interactive events	My spouse asked how my day was. We talked about personal feelings. My spouse showed interest in what I said by agreeing or asking relevant questions.
Displeasing interactive events	My spouse commanded me to do something. My spouse complained about something I did. My spouse interrupted me.
Pleasing affectionate behavior	We held each other. My spouse hugged and kissed me.
Displeasing affectionate behavior	My spouse rushed into intercourse without taking time for foreplay. My spouse rejected my sexual advances.
Pleasing events	My spouse did the dishes. My spouse picked up around the house.
Displeasing events	My spouse talked too much about work. My spouse yelled at the children.

Figure 10.14
Items from the Spouse Observation Checklist

Couples are instructed to complete a more extensive checklist for fifteen consecutive evenings. Spouses record their partner's behavior, and they make daily ratings of their overall satisfaction with the spouse's behavior.

that he underestimated the power of environmental experiences and culture in determining personality. Behaviorism and humanism both endorse environment as a powerful determinant of personality, Skinner being the strongest advocate of environment's influence. However, humanistic theorists do believe that people have the innate ability to become self-actualized. Trait theorists vary in their emphasis on heredity and environment; Eysenck stressed the biological basis of personality, while Allport weighted biology and environment more equally.

2. *Conscious versus unconscious.* Is personality due more to conscious factors or more to unconscious factors? How aware are individuals that they are conceited and self-centered? How aware are they of the reasons they became conceited and self-centered? Freud and Jung were the strongest advocates of the unconscious mind's role in personality. Freud stressed that our deeply repressed experiences in infancy and early childhood determine what our personalities are like as adults, for example. Most psychoanalytic theorists argue that we are largely unaware of how our individual personalities developed. Skinner argues that neither unconscious nor conscious thoughts are important in determining personality, although social cognitive theorists Bandura and Mischel stress that cognitive factors mediate the environment's influence on personality. The humanists, such as Rogers and Maslow, stress the conscious aspects of personality, especially in the form of self-perception. Trait theorists pay little attention to the conscious/unconscious issue.

3. *Internal versus external determinants.* Is personality due more to an inner disposition or more to outer situations? Are individuals conceited and self-centered because of something inside themselves, a characteristic they have and carry around with them, or are they conceited and self-centered because of the situations they are in and the way they are influenced by people around them? Psychoanalytic theorists emphasize the internal dimensions of personality (Freud's internal structures of id, ego, and superego, for example). Trait theorists also stress internal determinants through

| | PERSONALITY THEORY | | | |
ISSUE	Psychoanalytic Perspectives	Behavioral and Social Cognitive Perspectives	Humanistic Perspectives	Trait Perspectives
Innate versus learned	Strong emphasis on biological foundations by Freud. Adler, Sullivan, and Erikson gave social experiences and culture more importance than Freud.	Skinner said personality is behavior that is environmentally determined. Social cognitive theorists also emphasize environmental experiences.	Humanistic theorists emphasize that personality is influenced by experience and can be changed.	Eysenck stresses personality's biological basis; Allport gave attention to both heredity and environment.
Conscious versus unconscious	Strong emphasis on unconscious thought, especially Freud and Jung	Skinner didn't think conscious or unconscious thought was important in personality. Bandura and Mischel emphasize cognitive process.	Stress conscious aspects of personality, especially self-concept, self-perception	Pay little attention to this issue
Internal versus external determinants	Emphasize internal determinants, personality structures	Emphasize external situational determinants of personality. Bandura and Mischel emphasize internal and external determinants, especially self-control.	Emphasize internal determinants of self-concept and self-determination	Stress internal, person variables
Personality measurement	Clinical interviews, unstructured personality tests, and psychohistorical analysis of lives	Observation, especially laboratory observation	Self-report measures and interviews. Clinical judgment more important than scientific measurement is view of many humanists.	Self-report tests such as MMPI–2

Sigmund Freud   B.F. Skinner   Carl Rogers   Gordon Allport

𝓕igure 10.15
Comparing Perspectives on Personality

SUMMARY TABLE 10.4
Personality Assessment and Comparing Perspectives on Personality

Concept	Processes/ Related Ideas	Characteristics/Description
Personality Assessment	Some Themes	Psychologists use a wide variety of tests and measures to assess personality. These measures often are tied to psychologists' theoretical orientations. Personality tests basically were designed to measure stable, enduring aspects of personality.
	Projective Tests	A projective test involves presenting individuals with an ambiguous stimulus and then asking them to describe it or tell a story about it. Projective tests are based on the assumption that the ambiguity of the stimulus allows individuals to project their personality into it. Projective tests are designed to assess the unconscious aspects of personality. The Rorschach inkblot test is a widely used projective test; its effectiveness is controversial. The Thematic Apperception Test (TAT) is another projective test.
	Self-Report Tests	Self-report tests assess your personality traits by asking you what they are. In constructing self-report tests, we discussed face validity and the problem of socially desirable responses. Empirically keyed tests rely on their items to predict some criterion. The Minnesota Multiphasic Personality Inventory (MMPI) is the most widely used and researched self-report personality test. The MMPI-2 (a revision that appeared in 1989) has a number of new items but preserves the 10 clinical scales and some validity scales. Some items were deleted from the original MMPI and some new content scales were added. Two tests that have been created to assess the big five personality factors are the NEO-PI-R and the HPI. Self-report tests mesh with the trait theoretical approach to personality. As with other types of personality assessment, some criticisms of the self-report tests have been made.
	Behavioral and Cognitive Assessment	Behavioral assessment tries to obtain more objective information about personality through observation of behavior and its environmental ties. Cognitive assessment is increasingly being used.
Comparing Perspectives on Personality	Some Issues and Measures	Three important issues addressed by perspectives on personality are the degree to which personality is innate versus learned, conscious versus unconscious, and internally versus externally determined. Different perspectives on personality advocate the use of particular assessment strategies. We examined how psychoanalytic, behavioral/social cognitive, humanistic, and trait perspectives address these issues and which assessment strategies they support.

their belief in the importance of self-concept and self-determination. By contrast, behaviorists emphasize personality's external, situational determinants, although social cognitive theorists examine both external and internal determinants.

A summary of comparisons of personality perspectives on these three important issues—innate versus learned, conscious versus unconscious, and internal versus external determination—is presented in figure 10.15, along with a comparison of the methods advocated by theorists.

At this point we have discussed a number of ideas about personality assessment and comparing personality perspectives. An overview of these ideas is presented in summary table 10.4. In this chapter we discussed the normal aspects of personality. In the next chapter, we will explore abnormal psychology, including some personality disorders.

Society for Personality and Social Psychology

Overview

WE BEGAN THIS CHAPTER by exploring what personality is. Our coverage of perspectives included many ideas about the psychoanalytic perspectives, behavioral and social cognitive perspectives, humanistic perspectives, and trait perspectives. We examined these dimensions of personality assessment: its themes, projective tests, and self-report tests, as well as behavioral and cognitive assessment. And we compared the main perspectives on personality on some important issues and described the types of methods they use to assess personality.

Remember that you can obtain a more detailed overview of the chapter by again studying the four summary tables on pages 345, 353, 357, and 365.

Key Terms

personality 336
psychoanalytic perspectives 337
id 338
pleasure principle 338
ego 338
reality principle 338
superego 338
defense mechanisms 338
repression 339
erogenous zones 340
fixation 340
oral stage 340
anal stage 340
phallic stage 340

Oedipus complex 341
latency stage 341
genital stage 341
collective unconscious 343
archetype 343
individual psychology 343
striving for superiority 343
compensation 343
overcompensation 344
inferiority complex 344
superiority complex 344
behavioral and social cognitive perspectives 346
social cognitive theory 347
humanistic perspectives 348

conditional positive regard 349
self-concept 349
unconditional positive regard 349
hierarchy of motives 350
self-actualization 350
self-esteem 350
trait theories 352
cardinal traits 354
central traits 354
secondary traits 354
big five factors of personality 354
situationism 355

Barnum effect 357
projective test 358
Rorschach inkblot test 358
Thematic Apperception Test (TAT) 358
graphology 359
self-report tests 359
face validity 359
social desirability 359
empirically keyed test 359
Minnesota Multiphasic Personality Inventory (MMPI) 360

Key People

Taking It to the Net

1. Imagine a boy who has extreme anger, rage, and fantasies of violence. He generally keeps his emotions to himself and rarely shows how angry he is. Moreover, he is embarrassed by his violent fantasies and hasn't told anyone about them. Instead, he plays football and focuses all of his emotions into the sport. Fortunately, he winds up being very good at football, and ends up playing professionally. Describe the defense mechanisms that he has used to reduce his anxiety about his emotions. Is this an effective strategy?

2. Consider a famous experiment by Albert Bandura. Three groups of children watched an adult in a playroom behave aggressively (e.g., hit, kick, yell) toward a large plastic doll. The film had three different endings. One group of children saw the adult praised for his or her behavior; a second group saw the adult being told that he or she must go sit down in a corner and not play with the toys; a third group (the control group) saw a film with the adult simply walking out of the room. The children were then left in the room to play with the plastic doll in any way they chose. What do you think happened? Do you think there were differences between boys and girls? Explain.

3. Personality tests are often a good way to learn more about yourself. They are also used to predict how people will act in a given situation. For example, a personality assessment might show that you are very introverted (i.e., reserved, somber, unsociable). It is therefore reasonable to predict that in a party atmosphere, you would not want all of the attention directed at you. Because of this predictive value, some employers have used personality tests in their hiring process. What do you think of this practice? How would you feel if you were not accepted for a job on the basis of a personality assessment? Consider also the benefits of learning what jobs suit your personality.

Connect to http://www.mhhe.com/psychology/santrock to find the answers!

Chapter 11

Abnormal Psychology

"*He* raves; his words are loose as heaps of sand, and scattered from sense. So high he's mounted on his airy throne, that now the wind has got into his head, and turns his brain to frenzy."

John Dryden
English Poet, 17th Century

Preview

MENTAL DISORDERS **know no social and economic boundaries. They find their way into the lives of the rich and famous and the poor and unknown. These are some of the questions we will explore in this chapter:**

• **How can you tell if someone has a mental disorder?**
• **What is involved in the insanity defense in courtrooms?**
• **What causes abnormal behavior?**
• **How many people have mental disorders?**
• **How are mental disorders classified?**
• **What are some of the main types of mental disorders?**

Images of Psychology and Life
Showering Seven Times a Day, Looking at a Bleak Future, and Avoiding Breathing on People

THIRTY-YEAR-OLD RUTH has a long-standing feeling of contamination that compels her to carry out numerous cleansing activities each day (Leon, 1990). She becomes intensely uncomfortable when she notices any dirt on her or in her immediate environment. Whenever she detects the presence of even the smallest bit of dirt, she thoroughly washes her hands and arms. If she finds any dirt in her apartment, she feels compelled to scrub it from top to bottom, then shower in a rigidly specific manner. She also feels contaminated after using the bathroom, doing housework, or cooking, again feeling compelled to wash herself after these activities. Currently, she is washing her hands at least 3 to 4 times an hour, showering 6 to 7 times a day, and thoroughly cleaning her apartment at least twice a day. She reports that her life is very restricted because most of the time she feels driven to carry out these cleansing activities.

Thirty-year-old Janet has been divorced for about a year. She is raising her three children and recently resumed her college education on a part-time basis (Oltmanns, Neale, & Davison, 1986). Her return to college didn't last very long, however. One of her children, 2-year-old Adam, was having sleep-related problems, so she began spending considerable time with him. Janet's mood had become depressed when her husband asked for a divorce because he had fallen in love with a younger woman. She felt sad, discouraged, and lonely. The feeling became more severe just prior to her recent withdrawal from college. She has bouts of crying, in some cases for long periods of time. Nothing seems to cheer her up, she doesn't have any interest in her friends, and she sees her children as more burdensome than ever. From her current situation, the future looks bleak.

Twenty-seven-year-old Jim is an unemployed, single man who says that what really bothers him is that he has a special power (Gorenstein, 1997). He says that he

369

can influence other people, even endanger them, with the way he breathes. He believes he has to go to great lengths to avoid people so that he won't put them in jeopardy. He currently has isolated himself from others by secluding himself in a room at his parents' house. Jim doesn't like avoiding the world, but feels he has no other choice. Jim explains that it is like having God's power but with none of the desire or wisdom to use it. He only comes out of his room for occasional meals, bathroom visits, and church services. He doesn't want his power to fall into malevolent hands, which he sees as another reason for not appearing in public.

Each of these three individuals has a mental disorder. Ruth has an obsessive-compulsive disorder, Janet has a depressive disorder, and Jim has schizophrenia. We will discuss these and many other disorders in this chapter's coverage of the fascinating landscape of abnormal psychology.

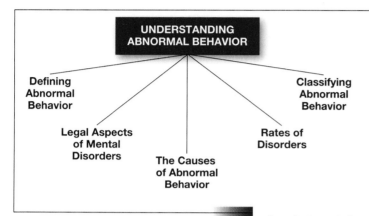

Understanding Abnormal Behavior

Many people live their lives in mental suffering and desperation. Abnormal psychology is concerned with these problems of adaptation.

Defining Abnormal Behavior

In thinking about how to define abnormal behavior, consider the three individuals you just read about: Ruth, who washes her hands 3 to 4 times an hour, showers 6 to 7 times a day, and cleans her apartment at least twice a day; Janet, who has severe feelings of depression; and Jim, who has isolated himself from the world because he believes his breath can influence, even endanger, others. Would you agree that their behavior is abnormal? If so, what do you base your judgment on?

Abnormal behavior is one of those concepts that is not easy to define. The line between what is normal and what is abnormal is not always clear-cut and easy to specify. Nonetheless, the following definition specifies several criteria that can help us think about what abnormal behavior is. **Abnormal behavior** is *behavior that is deviant, maladaptive, or personally distressful.*

There are three criteria in our definition of abnormal behavior: (1) deviance, (2) maladaptiveness, and (3) personal distress. Only one of these criteria needs to be met for the classification of abnormal behavior, but two or three may be present.

Abnormal behavior is *deviant.* Let's again consider Ruth's compulsive behavior. Is it deviant? One way that abnormal behavior has been described is to refer to it as *atypical.* However, people like Albert Einstein and Barbara Walters are atypical, but we don't usually categorize them as abnormal because of their extraordinary intellectual power and interviewing skills, respectively. However, when atypical behavior deviates from what is acceptable in a culture, it often is considered abnormal. Ruth's compulsive behavior deviates from acceptable norms. Normal people don't wash their hands 3 to 4 times an hour, take seven showers a day, and clean their apartment at least twice a day.

Abnormal behavior is *maladaptive.* Maladaptive behavior interferes with a person's ability to function effectively in the world. Jim's belief that his breath has powerful, even harmful, effects on others keeps him isolated from society and prevents him from functioning in the everyday world.

Abnormal behavior involves *personal distress.* Ruth is distressed about how driven she is to stay clean and keep her immediate environment clean. Janet also is distressed about her life and looks at the future as extremely bleak.

A number of myths and misconceptions about abnormal behavior exist. Figure 11.1 describes some of these myths and misconceptions.

Legal Aspects of Mental Disorders

The legal status of the mentally disordered raises a number of controversial issues, including these: What is involved in committing disordered and dangerous individuals to mental institutions? What is the status of using the insanity defense for capital crimes?

The behavior of some mentally disordered individuals is so severe and extreme that they are a threat to themselves and/or to others, and they may need protective confinement. Being mentally disordered in itself is not adequate grounds for placing individuals in a mental institution against their will. While procedures vary somewhat from state to state, certain conditions usually need to be met before a person can be formally committed to a mental institution: Individuals must either be dangerous to themselves or to other people. Determining whether a mentally disordered individual is dangerous is not easy even for mental health professionals. Nonetheless, there are times when professionals have to make "dangerousness" judgments (Slobogin, 1996). Recent court decisions held mental health professionals liable when unconfined clients they were treating caused harm to others. Therapists are required to warn potential victims if their patients threaten to kill someone.

Insanity is a legal term, not a psychological term. The **insanity defense** *requires that the defendant be wholly or partially irrational when the crime took place, and that the irrationality affected his or her behavior.* When the insanity defense is successful, the defendant is said to be "not guilty by reason of insanity." The modern insanity defense standard, which is now used in all federal courts, was enacted in 1984. An insanity defense requires only that the defendant was unable to appreciate the nature and quality or wrongfulness of his or her acts.

Controversy swirls about the insanity defense because of concerns that sane criminals will use this plea to avoid prosecution or reduce the severity of their sentence. Recently, in the Unabomber case, Ted Kaczynski's lawyers included the insanity defense in representing their client. This became part of the plea bargain that reduced Kaczynski's sentence from death to life imprisonment.

Revisions and reforms of the insanity defense have taken place (Wrightsman, Nietzel, & Fortune, 1998). Since 1976, about one-fourth of states have passed laws that allow juries to reach a verdict of "guilty but mentally ill." The intent is for such defendants to begin their sentence in a mental hospital and then be transferred to a prison when treatment is completed. In reality, for the most part this has been a bogus promise because the majority of defendants found guilty but mentally ill go straight to prison. To read further about the insanity defense, see Explorations in Psychology.

The insanity defense is not used very often and when it is, it is not usually successful. Media attention on high-profile cases leads us to believe that the insanity defense is used far more than it actually is.

Myth/ Misconception	Fact
Abnormal behavior is always bizarre.	The behavior of many people who are diagnosed as having a mental disorder often cannot be distinguished from that of "normal" people. In some cases, like Jim's belief in the power of his breath, abnormal behavior is bizarre. However, in the case of Janet's depression, her behavior would not be considered bizarre.
Normal and abnormal behavior are different in kind.	Few, if any, types of behavior displayed by individuals with a mental disorder are unique to them. Abnormal behavior often consists of a poor fit between the behavior and the situation in which it is enacted.
People with a mental disorder are dangerous.	With the exception of a few people, such as those with an antisocial personality disorder (which we will discuss later in the chapter), most people with a mental disorder are not dangerous.
Once people have a mental disorder, they will never get rid of it.	Most people can be successfully treated for a mental disorder.

Figure 11.1
Some Myths and Misconceptions About Abnormal Behavior

**Legal Aspects of Mental Disorders
The Insanity Defense**

EXPLORATIONS IN PSYCHOLOGY
Jack Ruby, Sirhan Sirhan, Jeffrey Dahmer, Ed Gein, John Hinckley, and Lorena Bobbitt

FOLLOWING ARE some famous cases in which the insanity plea failed, and some in which it succeeded (Wrightsman, Nietzel, & Fortune, 1998).

Famous Cases in Which the Insanity Defense Plea Failed

Among the murder defendants who pleaded insanity as a defense but were convicted in spite of these pleas were Jack Ruby, whom millions saw kill Lee Harvey Oswald, President John F. Kennedy's alleged assassin, on television; and Sirhan Sirhan, charged with Robert F. Kennedy's assassination.

A more recent example involves Jeffrey Dahmer. In 1991, a man in handcuffs dashed out of Dahmer's bizarrely cluttered Milwaukee apartment and called the police, stammering that someone had just tried to kill him. At least 17 other victims had not gotten away. Dahmer killed his first victim in 1978 with a barbell. He dismembered the 17 victims' bodies, hoarded them, and then ate the parts of them he "liked" the most. Dahmer's lawyers said, "This is not an evil man, this is a mentally sick man." The prosecution argued that Dahmer knew what he was doing all the time. The jury ruled 10–2 that Dahmer was sane. He was sentenced to life in prison and while there was beaten to death by a fellow prisoner.

Famous Cases in Which the Insanity Defense Plea Succeeded

Ed Gein, another serial killer from Wisconsin, was acquitted by reason of insanity on charges involving the murder of two women in the 1950s in the Plainfield, Wisconsin, area. Gein admitted to other heinous crimes, including robbing bodies from graves. He later made the corpse parts into ornaments and clothes that he wore to reenact the image of his dead mother. Gein was the real-life inspiration for several Hollywood films, including *Psycho* and *Silence of the Lambs*. Gein was committed to a mental institution, where he remained until his death in 1984.

John Hinckley, Jr., is the single case that stimulated much of the legislative revision of the insanity plea. As seen live on television, Hinckley shot President Ronald Reagan. Hinckley's attorneys argued that Hinckley was insane, and the jury agreed. Hinckley was sent to a mental institution where he resides today. On several occasions, he has requested to be released from the institution but the requests have been denied.

In 1994, Lorena Bobbitt waited for her husband to go to sleep and then she cut off his penis, drove away from the house, and threw it out the car window. Her attorneys claimed that she had suffered years of physical and mental abuse from her husband, John. Bobbitt was ruled "guilty but insane." She spent several weeks at a mental hospital, then was released.

The Causes of Abnormal Behavior

What causes people to become abnormal—to behave in deviant, maladaptive, and personally distressful ways? The causes include biological, psychological, and sociocultural factors, as well as a possible combination of these factors.

Biological Factors   In the biological approach to mental disorders, it is believed that a malfunctioning of the person's body is responsible for the disorders. Today, scientists who adopt a biological approach to mental disorders often focus on brain processes, such as neurotransmitters, and genetic factors as the causes of abnormal behavior ◀ P. 54. In the biological approach, drug therapy is frequently used to treat abnormal behavior (Hales & Yudofsky, 1999).

The biological approach is evident in the **medical model,** *which describes mental disorders as medical diseases with a biological origin.* From the perspective of the medical model, abnormalities are called mental *illnesses,* the individuals afflicted are *patients in mental hospitals,* and they are treated by *doctors.*

Psychological Factors   Among the psychological factors that have been proposed as contributors to abnormal behavior are distorted thoughts, emotional turmoil, inappropriate learning, and troubled relationships. When we examine some of the main mental disorders later in the chapter, such as the mood disorders and schizophrenic disorders, we will further explore these psychological factors.

Many of the theories of personality we discussed in chapter 10 address abnormal as well as normal aspects of behavior. Recall that psychoanalytic theorists often attribute psychological problems to stressful early experiences with parents. Remember that social learning theorists believe that behavior, whether normal or abnormal, is learned through social experiences with others. And recall that humanistic theorists believe that inadequate emotional support from others and low self-esteem are especially implicated in people's problems.

In the next chapter, "Therapies," we will extensively examine the theories of personality—psychoanalytic, behavioral/social learning, and humanistic—in terms of how to help people with a mental disorder.

Sociocultural Factors   Most experts on abnormal behavior agree that many psychological disorders are universal, appearing in most cultures (Al-Issa, 1982). However, the frequency and intensity of abnormal behavior varies across cultures with variations related to social, economic, technological, and religious aspects of cultures (Draguns, 1990). Some disorders, though, are culture-related, as indicated in figure 11.2.

Sociocultural factors that influence mental disorders include socioeconomic status and neighborhood quality (Brown & Adler, 1998). People from low-income, minority neighborhoods have the highest rates of mental disorders. When socioeconomic status and ethnicity are examined for their roles in mental disorders, socioeconomic status plays a much stronger role. Thus, the living conditions of poverty create stressful circumstances that can contribute to whether a person has a mental disorder (Grizenko, 1998).

Gender is another sociocultural factor that is associated with the presence of certain mental disorders (Greenglass, 1998; Paludi, 1998). Women tend to be diagnosed as having internalized disorders. In particular, women are more likely than men to suffer from anxiety disorders and depression, which have symptoms that are turned inward (internalized). Conversely, men are socialized to direct their energy toward

On January 16, 1996, multimillionaire John Dupont (above), a 58-year-old heir to the Dupont chemical fortune, pulled out a gun and killed Olympic Gold Medal wrestler David Schultz, who lived in a home on Dupont's estate and was one of several wrestlers training at Dupont's state-of-the art wrestling facility. No one disputes that Dupont killed Schultz. Dupont's lawyers argued that he was so incapacitated by the mental disorder schizophrenia that he could not be held accountable for the murder. Prosecutors claimed he was an eccentric man driven by envy and anger who knew exactly what he was doing. After a week's deliberation, the jury concluded that Dupont was mentally ill but also guilty of third-degree murder.

Disorder	Culture	Description/Characteristics
Amok	Malaysia, Philippines, Africa	This disorder involves sudden, uncontrolled outbursts of anger in which the person may injure or kill someone. Amok is often found in males who are emotionally withdrawn before the onset of the disorder. After the attack on someone, the individual feels exhausted and depressed, and does not remember the rage and attack.
Anorexia Nervosa	Western cultures, especially the United States	This eating disorder involves a relentless pursuit of thinness through starvation, and can eventually lead to death.
Windigo	Algonquin Indian hunters	This disorder involves a fear of being bewitched. The hunter becomes anxious and agitated, worrying he will be turned into a cannibal with a craving for human flesh.

*F*igure 11.2
Some Culture-Related Disorders

the external world (that is, to externalize their feelings). They more often have externalized disorders that involve aggression and substance abuse. We will have more to say about gender differences shortly in our discussion of rates of mental disorders and later in the chapter when we study depression.

An Interactionist Approach: Biopsychosocial   When considering an individual's behavior, whether normal or abnormal, biological as well as psychological/sociocultural factors may be involved. Abnormal behavior can be influenced by biological factors (such as brain processes and heredity), psychological factors (such as emotional turmoil and distorted thoughts), and sociocultural factors (such as poverty). These factors can interact to produce abnormal behavior. Sometimes this interactionist approach is called "biopsychosocial" (Evans, 1999).

Rates of Disorders

How prevalent are mental disorders in the United States today? Nearly 20,000 individuals were randomly selected from five different regions of the United States and asked whether they had experienced a mental disorder in their lifetime and whether they currently were suffering from one (Robins & Regier, 1991). Almost one-third (32 percent) of the respondents said that they had experienced one or more mental disorders in their lifetime, and 20 percent said they currently had an active disorder.

You might be surprised that this many individuals have had a mental disorder or currently have one. However, the figures include individuals both in institutions and in the community. They also include individuals who have a substance abuse disorder (alcohol or other drugs) (17 percent). As we describe a number of mental disorders shortly, we will mention the percentage of individuals in this national study who reported that they experienced the particular disorder.

Surprisingly, only one-third of the individuals in this study who said they currently had a mental disorder had received treatment for it in the previous 6 months.

Classifying Abnormal Behavior

Ever since human history began, people have suffered from diseases, sadness, and bizarre behavior. And for almost as long, healers have tried to treat and cure them. The classification of mental disorders goes back to the ancient Egyptians and Greeks, and has its roots in biology and medicine.

The first classification of mental disorders in the United States, based on the census data of 1840, used one category for all mental disorders. This one category included both the mentally retarded and the insane.

In the twentieth century, the American Psychiatric Association (APA) developed the first major classification of mental disorders in the United States. The *Diagnostic and Statistical Manual of Mental Disorders (DSM),* first published in 1952, included better definitions of mental disorders than previous classification efforts. A revised edition, the *DSM-II,* with more systematic assistance from expert diagnosticians, appeared in 1968. The APA published a third edition, the *DSM-III,* in 1980, and a revision of that manual, the *DSM-III-R,* in 1987. Published in 1994, the current *DSM-IV* emphasizes refined empirical support of diagnostic categories.

The revisions of the *DSM* underscore that (1) classifying mental disorders is not an easy task and (2) clinicians are making an ongoing, conscientious effort to achieve a clearer, more accurate categorization of mental disorders.

Before we discuss the system most widely used to classify mental disorders, we will explore the benefits of classifying mental disorders. First, a classification system gives professionals a shorthand system for communicating with each other. For example, if one psychologist says in a case review that her client has a panic disorder and another psychologist says that his client has schizophrenia, the two psychologists understand which disorders these clients have been diagnosed as having. Second, a classification system can help clinicians make predictions about disorders; it provides information about the likelihood that a disorder will occur, which individuals are most susceptible to the disorder, progress of the disorder once it appears, and the prognosis for effective treatment (Meehl, 1986).

Continuing changes in the *DSM* reflect advancements in knowledge about the classification of mental disorders (Hales & others, 1999). On the basis of research and clinical experience, the *DSM-IV* added, dropped, or revised categories, sometimes generating controversy among the diagnosticians who rely on the classification system.

For example, the *DSM-III* dropped two important categories that have some historical importance: the categories of neurosis and psychosis. The term **neurotic** *referred to conditions that are personally distressful but the individual has not lost contact with reality.* Individuals who are extremely anxious, troubled, and unhappy may still be able to carry out their everyday functions and have a clear perception of reality; these individuals would be referred to by some people as "neurotic."

The term **psychotic** *referred to severe mental disorders in which the individual has lost contact with reality.* The thinking and perception of psychotic individuals are so distorted that they live in a world far removed from others. Psychotic individuals might hear voices that are not present or think they are famous individuals, such as Jesus Christ or Napoleon. Although the *DSM* classification system still mentions the terms *neurotic* and *psychotic,* most psychologists believe they are too broad and ill-defined to be used as effective diagnostic labels.

The **DSM-IV** (Diagnostic and Statistical Manual of Mental Disorders, *fourth edition) is the most recent major classification of mental disorders; it contains eighteen major classifications and describes more than 200 specific disorders.*

One feature of the *DSM-IV* is its **multiaxial system,** *which classifies individuals on the basis of five dimensions, or "axes," that include the individual's history and highest level of functioning in the last year.* This system ensures that the individual will not merely be assigned to a mental disorder category, but instead will be characterized in terms of a number of clinical factors (Gelder, Mayou, & Geddes, 1999). Figure 11.3 describes the multiaxial system.

What are some of the changes in the *DSM-IV?* The more than 200 mental health professionals who contributed to the development of the *DSM-IV* were a much more diverse group than their predecessors, who were mainly White male psychiatrists. More women, ethnic minorities, and nonpsychiatrists, such as clinical psychologists, were involved in the construction of the *DSM-IV,* and greater attention was given to gender- and ethnicity-related diagnosis. For example, the *DSM-IV* contains an appendix entitled "Guidelines for Cultural Formation and Glossary of Culture-Related Syndromes" (Nathan, 1994). Also, the *DSM-IV* is accompanied by a number of sourcebooks that present the empirical base of the *DSM-IV* (Francis & Ross, 1996). In previous versions of the *DSM,* the reasons for diagnostic changes were not always explicit, so the evidence that led to their formulation was never available for public evaluation.

The most controversial aspect of the *DSM-IV* continues to be an issue that has been present since the publication of the *DSM-I* in 1952. Although more nonpsychiatrists than in previous editions were responsible for drafting the *DSM-IV,* it still reflects a medical, or disease, model (Clark, Watson, & Reynolds, 1995; Nathan & Langenbucher, 1999). Classifying individuals based on their symptoms and using medical terminology continues the dominance of the psychiatric tradition of thinking

Axis	Description
I	The primary classification or diagnosis of the disorder (for example, fear of people). This axis includes all disorders except the personality disorders and mental retardation.
II	Personality disorders, long-standing problems in relating to others (for example, a person with long-standing antisocial personality disorder) and mental retardation.
III	General medical conditions that might be relevant in understanding the mental disorder (for example, an individual's history of disease, such as a cardiovascular problem)
IV	Psychosocial stressors in the individual's recent past that might have contributed to the mental problem (for example, divorce, death of a parent, or loss of job)
V	The individual's current level of functioning and highest level of functioning in the last year. For example, does the individual have a history of poor work and relationship patterns, or have there been times in the recent past when the individual performed effectively at work and enjoyed positive interpersonal relationships? If functioning has been high at some point in the past, prognosis for recovery is improved.

*F*igure 11.3
The *DSM-IV* Multiaxial System

These are brief descriptions of the five axes in the *DSM-IV* classification of mental disorders.

DSM-IV

SUMMARY TABLE 11.1
Understanding Abnormal Behavior

Concept	Processes/ Related Ideas	Characteristics/Discussions
Defining Abnormal Behavior	Its Nature	Abnormal behavior is behavior that is deviant, maladaptive, or personally distressful. Only one of these criteria needs to be present for the classification of abnormal behavior, but two or all three can be present. We described some myths and misconceptions about abnormal behavior, and we indicated that there often is a thin line between what is normal and what is abnormal.
Legal Aspects of Mental Disorders		Individuals with a mental disorder must be dangerous either to themselves or to others for formal commitment to a mental institution. *Insanity* is a legal term, not a psychological term. The insanity defense requires that the defendant be wholly or partially irrational when the crime took place, and that the irrationality affected his or her behavior. Controversy swirls about the insanity defense.
The Causes of Abnormal Behavior	Biological Factors	In the biological approach, the malfunctioning of the person's body is responsible for abnormal behavior. Today, the biological factors of brain processes and heredity are emphasized. In the biological approach, drug therapy is often used to treat abnormal behavior. The biological approach is evident in the medical model, which describes mental disorders as medical diseases with biological origins.
	Psychological Factors	Psychological factors include emotional turmoil, inappropriate learning, distorted thoughts, and inadequate relationships as determinants of abnormal behavior. Theories of personality—psychoanalytic, behavioral/social learning, and humanistic—specify psychological factors in abnormal behavior.
	Sociocultural Factors	Sociocultural factors in abnormal behavior include cultural bias, poverty and low socioeconomic conditions, as well as gender.
	An Interactionist Approach	This proposes that abnormal behavior might result from an interaction of biological, psychological, and sociocultural factors. Sometimes this approach is called "biopsychosocial."
Rates of Disorders	Their Nature	In a large national study, almost one-third of the individuals reported that they had experienced a mental disorder in their lifetime and 20 percent said they currently were suffering from one. These figures might seem surprisingly high, but they include people in institutions and the community, and they include individuals with a substance-abuse disorder (17 percent).
Classifying Abnormal Behavior	Its Nature	*DSM* stands for *Diagnostic and Statistical Manual of Mental Disorders.* The *DSM-II* included the categories of *neurotic* and *psychotic* behavior, although most psychologists today believe the terms are too broad and ill-defined to be effective diagnostic categories. Mental disorder classification systems have advantages and disadvantages. The most recent version of the *DSM—DSM-IV*—was published in 1994. One of its features is a multiaxial system. *DSM-IV* continues to be controversial, with one of the main criticisms by psychologists being its perpetuation of the medical model of mental disorders.

about mental disorders in terms of illness and disease. This strategy implies an internal cause that is more or less independent of external or environmental factors (Adams & Cassidy, 1993). Thus, even though researchers have begun to illuminate the complex interaction of genetic, neurobiological, cognitive, and environmental factors in the *DSM* disorders, the *DSM-IV* continues to espouse the medical/disease model of mental disorders (Sarbin & Keen, 1998).

The *DSM-IV* is also controversial because it continues to label as mental disorders what are often thought of as everyday problems. For example, under learning or academic skills disorders, the *DSM-IV* includes the categories of reading disorder, mathematics disorder, and disorder of written expression. Under substance-related disorders, the *DSM-IV* includes the category of caffeine-use disorders. We don't usually think of these problems as mental disorders, but including them implies that such "normal behavior" should be treated as mental disorders. The developers of the *DSM* system argue that mental health providers have been treating many problems not included in earlier editions of *DSM* and that the classification system should be more comprehensive. One practical reason for including everyday problems in living in the *DSM-IV* is to help more individuals get their health insurance companies to pay for professional help. Most health insurance companies reimburse their clients only for disorders listed in the *DSM-IV* system.

Another criticism of the *DSM-IV,* and indeed of this type of classification system in general, is that the system focuses strictly on pathology and problems, with a bias toward finding something wrong with anyone who becomes the object of diagnostic study (Allen, 1998).

Because labels can become self-fulfilling prophecies, emphasizing strengths as well as weaknesses might help to destigmatize labels such as *paranoid schizophrenic* or *ex-mental patient.* It would also help to provide clues to treatment that promote mental competence rather than working only to reduce mental distress.

Although psychologists usually go along with the *DSM-IV,* psychiatrists are more satisfied with it. Even though the *DSM-IV* has its critics, it is still the most comprehensive classification system available.

At this point, we have discussed a number of ideas about what abnormal behavior is, what causes abnormal behavior, and how abnormal behavior can be classified. A summary of these ideas is presented in summary table 11.1. Now we turn our attention to the specific diagnostic categories of mental disorders.

National Institute of Mental Health
Mental Health Net
Mental Health Disorders

Categories of Mental Disorders

This cognitive map gives you a picture of the topics we will be discussing before we get to the next summary table. It outlines the first three of six main categories of diagnosis in the *DSM-IV* that we will explore in this chapter. Figure 11.4 gives you an overall picture of eight prominent categories of mental disorders—the six we will evaluate in this chapter, plus two that we have examined in previous chapters—substance-related disorders (chapter 4) and eating disorders (chapter 9). Let's now begin our coverage of categories of mental disorders with anxiety disorders.

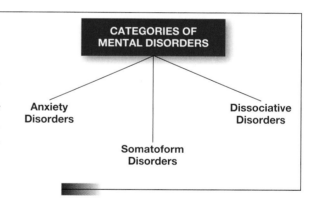

Anxiety Disorders

To explore the anxiety disorders, we will describe their general characteristics, then turn to five main types of anxiety disorders. Anxiety is a diffuse, vague, highly unpleasant feeling of fear and apprehension. People with high levels of anxiety worry a lot. **Anxiety disorders** *are psychological disorders that include the following main features: motor tension (jumpiness, trembling, inability to relax); hyperactivity (dizziness, a racing heart, or, possibly, perspiration); and apprehensive expectations and thoughts.*

Anxiety Disorders

Generalized Anxiety Disorder
Anna, who is 27 years old, had just arrived for her visit with the psychologist. She seemed very nervous and was wringing her hands, crossing and uncrossing her legs, and playing nervously with strands of her hair. She said her stomach felt like it was in knots, that her hands were cold, and that her neck muscles were so tight they hurt. She said that lately arguments with her husband had escalated. In recent weeks, Anna indicated she felt more and more nervous throughout the day as if something bad were about to happen. If the doorbell sounded or the phone rang, her heart beat rapidly and her breathing quickened. When she was around people she had a difficult time speaking. She began to isolate

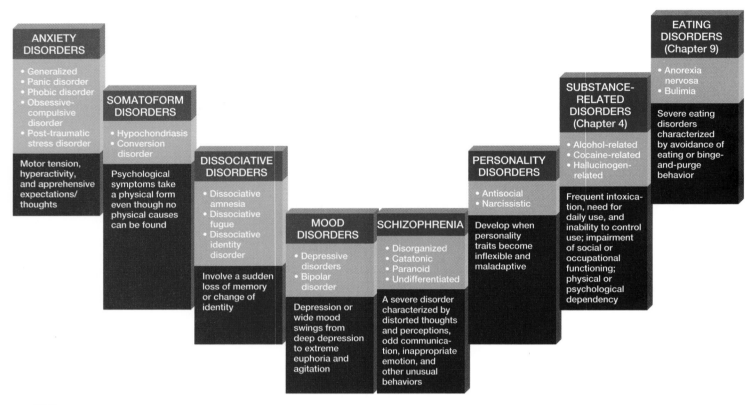

*F*igure 11.4
Some Prominent Categories of Mental Disorders in the *DSM-IV*

Panic Disorder

herself. Her husband became impatient with Anna, so she decided to see a psychologist (Goodstein & Calhoun, 1982).

Anna has a **generalized anxiety disorder,** *an anxiety disorder that consists of persistent anxiety for at least a month; the individual with a generalized anxiety disorder is unable to specify the reasons for the anxiety.* People with generalized anxiety disorder are nervous most of the time. In the national study of the prevalence of mental disorders, almost 4 percent of the individuals said they had ever experienced an anxiety disorder (Robins & Regier, 1991).

Panic Disorder   **Panic disorder** *is an anxiety disorder marked by the recurrent sudden onset of intense apprehension or terror.* The individual often has a feeling of impending doom but may not feel anxious all the time. Anxiety attacks often strike without warning and produce severe palpitations, extreme shortness of breath, chest pains, trembling, sweating, dizziness, and a feeling of helplessness (Craske, 2000). Victims are seized by fear that they will die, go crazy, or do something they cannot control (Asnis & van Praag, 1995).

What are some psychosocial and biological factors involved in panic disorder? In many instances, a stressful life event has occurred in the last six months, most often a threatened or actual separation from a loved one or a change in job. Biological factors in panic disorder also have been explored (McNally, 1998). For example, in a panic attack an overreaction to lactic acid (which is produced by the body when it is under stress) occurs.

Mrs. Reiss is a 48-year-old woman who is afraid to go out alone, a fear she has had for six years but which has intensified in the last two years (Greenberg, Szmulker, & Tantum, 1986). The first signs of her fear appeared after an argument with her husband. After the argument, she went to the mailbox to get the mail and began to feel very anxious and dizzy. It was a struggle to get back to the house. Her fear lessened for several years, but reappeared even more intensely after she learned that her sister had cancer. Her fear continued to escalate after arguments with her husband. She became increasingly apprehensive about going outside alone. When she did try to leave, her heart would pound, she would perspire, and she would begin to tremble. After only briefly being outside, she would quickly go back into her house.

Mrs. Reiss had developed **agoraphobia,** *an anxiety disorder characterized by an intense fear of entering crowded, public places, of traveling away from home, especially by public transportation, of feeling confined or trapped, and of being separated from a place or person associated with safety.* In the *DSM-IV,* a panic attack can be classified as with or without agoraphobia (Thorpe, 1998). Agoraphobia causes some people to remain housebound. It usually first appears in early adulthood, with 2.5 percent of individuals in the United States classified as having the disorder. Females are more likely than males to have the disorder.

Phobic Disorders   Agnes is an unmarried 30-year-old who had been unable to go higher than the second floor of any building for more than a year. When she tried to overcome her fear of heights by going up to the third, fourth, or fifth floor, she became overwhelmed by anxiety. She remembers how it all began. One evening she was working alone and was seized by an urge to jump out of an eighth-story window. She was so frightened by her impulse that she hid behind a file cabinet for more than 2 hours until she calmed down enough to gather her belongings and go home. As she reached the first floor of the building, her heart was pounding and she was perspiring heavily. After several months she gave up her position and became a lower-paid salesperson so she could work on the bottom floor of the store (Cameron, 1963).

A **phobic disorder,** *commonly called phobia, is an anxiety disorder in which the individual has an irrational, overwhelming, persistent fear of a particular object or situation.* Individuals with generalized anxiety disorder cannot pinpoint the cause of their nervous feelings; individuals with phobias can. A fear becomes a phobia when a situation is so dreaded that an individual goes to almost any length to avoid it. For example, Agnes quit her job to avoid being in high places. Some phobias are more debilitating than others. An individual with a fear of automobiles has a more difficult time functioning in our society than a person with a fear of snakes, for example. In the national study of the prevalence of mental disorders, almost 4 percent of the individuals said they had ever experienced an anxiety disorder (Robins & Regier, 1991).

Phobias come in many forms. Some of the most common phobias involve social situations, dogs, height, dirt, flying, and snakes. Figure 11.5 labels and describes a number of phobias.

Social phobia is an intense fear of being humiliated or embarrassed in social situations. Individuals with this phobia are afraid that they will say or do the wrong thing. As a consequence, they might avoid speaking up in a conversation, giving a speech, going out to eat, or attending a party. Their intense fear of such contexts can severely restrict their social life and increase their loneliness (Schneider & others, 1992).

Why do people develop phobias? Different theoretical perspectives provide different explanations. Psychoanalytic theorists, for example, say phobias develop as defense mechanisms to ward off threatening or unacceptable impulses—Agnes hid behind a file cabinet because she feared she would jump out of an eighth-story window. Learning theorists, however,

Edvard Munch's The Scream. *Many experts interpret Munch's painting as an expression of the terror brought on by a panic attack.*

Agoraphobia

Acrophobia	Fear of high places
Aerophobia	Fear of flying
Ailurophobia	Fear of cats
Algophobia	Fear of pain
Amaxophobia	Fear of vehicles, driving
Arachnophobia	Fear of spiders
Astrapophobia	Fear of lightning
Cynophobia	Fear of dogs
Gamophobia	Fear of marriage
Hydrophobia	Fear of water
Melissophobia	Fear of bees
Mysophobia	Fear of dirt
Nyctophobia	Fear of darkness
Ophidiophobia	Fear of nonpoisonous snakes
Thanatophobia	Fear of death
Xenophobia	Fear of strangers

Figure 11.5
Phobias
This is only a partial listing of phobias.

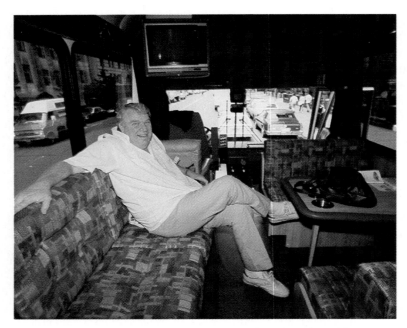

Popular professional football announcer John Madden has a fear of flying. Because of his phobia about flying, Madden crisscrosses the United States from week to week during football season in his "Maddencruiser" bus.

Obsessive-Compulsive Disorder
Post-Traumatic Stress Disorder

Jack Nicholson portrayed an individual with obsessive-compulsive disorder in the movie As Good As It Gets.

explain phobias differently; they say phobias are learned fears. In Agnes' case, she may have fallen from a high place when she was a little girl. As a result, she associates falling with pain and now fears high places. Or she may have heard about or seen other people who were afraid of high places. These last two examples are classical conditioning and observational learning explanations for Agnes' phobia.

Neuroscientists are finding that biological factors, such as greater blood flow and metabolism in the right side of the brain than in the left hemisphere, may also be involved in phobias. First-generation relatives of individuals suffering from agoraphobia and panic attacks have high rates of these disorders themselves, suggesting a possible genetic predisposition for phobias (d'Ansia, 1989). Others have found that identical twins reared apart sometimes develop the same phobias; one pair independently became claustrophobic, for example (Eckert, Heston, & Bouchard, 1981).

Obsessive-Compulsive Disorder

At the beginning of this chapter you read about 30-year-old Ruth who has an obsessive-compulsive disorder. Twenty-seven-year-old Bob also has this disorder. As a young adult, he found himself ensnared in an exacting ritual in which he would remove his clothes in a prearranged sequence, then scrub every inch of his body from head to toe. He dresses himself in an order precisely the opposite to that in which he takes off his clothes. If he deviates from this order, he feels compelled to start the sequence all over again. Sometimes Bob performs the cleansing ritual four or five times a day, and even though he is aware the ritual is absurd, he simply can't stop performing it (Meyer & Osborne, 1982).

Obsessive-compulsive disorder (OCD) *is an anxiety disorder in which the individual has anxiety-provoking thoughts that will not go away (obsession) and/or urges to perform repetitive, ritualistic behaviors to prevent or produce some future situation (compulsion).* Individuals with OCD repeat and rehearse normal doubts and daily routines, sometimes hundreds of times a day. (Frost & Steketee, 1998). In the national study of the prevalence of mental disorders, almost 3 percent of individuals said they had ever experienced an obsessive-compulsive disorder (Robins & Regier, 1991).

The most common compulsions are excessive checking, cleansing, and counting. For example, a young man feels he has to check his apartment for gas leaks and make sure the windows are locked. His behavior is not compulsive if he does this once, but if he goes back to check five or six times and then constantly worries that he might not have checked carefully enough once he has left the house, his behavior is compulsive. Most individuals do not enjoy their ritualistic behavior but feel anxious when they do not carry it out.

Positron emission tomography (PET) and other new brain-imaging techniques indicate a neurological basis for OCD. Irregularities in neurotransmitter systems, especially serotonin and dopamine, seem to be involved. And there may be a genetic basis for the disorder since OCD runs in families.

Post-Traumatic Stress Disorder

Post-traumatic stress disorder *is a mental disorder that develops through exposure to a traumatic event, such as war; severely oppressive* *situations, such as the Holocaust; severe abuse, as in rape; natural disasters, such as floods and tornados; and accidental disasters, such as plane crashes.* The disorder is characterized by anxiety symptoms that may immediately follow the trauma or be delayed by months or even years until onset (Ford, 1999; Ursano & others, 1999). The symptoms vary, but can include the following:

- "Flashbacks" in which the individual relives the event
- Constricted ability to feel emotions, often reported as feeling numb, resulting in an inability to experience happiness, sexual desire, or enjoyable interpersonal relationships
- Excessive arousal, resulting in an exaggerated startle response, or inability to sleep
- Difficulties with memory and concentration
- Feelings of apprehension, including nervous tremors
- Impulsive outbursts of behavior such as aggressiveness, or sudden changes in lifestyle

"He always times '60 Minutes.'"

Not every individual exposed to the same disaster develops post-traumatic stress disorder, which overloads the individual's usual coping abilities (Brewin & others, 1999; Fruehi, 2000; Jaycox & Foa, 1998). For example, it is estimated that 15 to 20 percent of Vietnam veterans experienced post-traumatic stress disorder. Vietnam veterans who had some autonomy and decision-making authority, such as Green Berets, were less likely to develop the disorder than soldiers who had no control over where they would be sent or when, and who had no option but to follow orders. Preparation for a trauma also makes a difference in whether an individual will develop the disorder. For example, emergency workers who are trained to cope with traumatic circumstances usually do not develop post-traumatic stress disorder. Some experts consider sexual abuse and assault victims to be the single largest group of post-traumatic stress disorder sufferers (Koss & Boeschen, 1998).

Somatoform Disorders

"Look, I am having trouble breathing. You don't believe me. Nobody believes me. There are times when I can't stop coughing. I'm losing weight. I know I have cancer. My father died of cancer when I was twelve." Herb has been to six cancer specialists in the last 2 years; none can find anything wrong with him. Each doctor has taken X rays and conducted excessive laboratory tests, but Herb's test results do not indicate any illnesses. Might some psychological factors be responsible for Herb's sense that he is physically ailing?

Somatoform disorders *are mental disorders in which psychological symptoms take a physical, or somatic, form even though no physical causes can be found.* Although these symptoms are not caused physically, they are highly distressing for the individual; the symptoms are real or believed, not faked. Two examples of somatoform disorders are hypochondriasis and conversion disorder.

Hypochondriasis   Individuals with hypochondriasis overreact to a missed heartbeat, shortness of breath, or a slight chest pain, fearing that something is wrong with them. **Hypochondriasis** *is a somatoform disorder in which the individual has a pervasive fear of illness and disease.* At the first indication of something amiss in their bodies, individuals with hypochondriasis call a doctor. When a physical examination reveals no problems, hypochondriacs usually do not believe the doctor. They often change doctors, moving from one to another searching for a diagnosis that matches their own. Most individuals with hypochondriasis are pill enthusiasts whose medicine chests spill over with bottles of drugs that they hope will cure their imagined maladies.

Hypochondriasis is a difficult category to diagnose accurately. It is quite rare for it to occur without other mental disorders, such as depression.

Hypochondriasis

(a)   (b)

ℱigure 11.6
Glove Anesthesia

A patient who complains of numbness in the hand might be diagnosed as suffering from conversion disorder if the area of the hand affected showed that a disorder of the nervous system was not responsible. The skin areas served by nerves in the arm are shown in *(a)*. The glove anesthesia shown in *(b)* could not result from damage to these nerves.

Dissociative Disorders

Conversion Disorder   **Conversion disorder** *is a somatoform disorder in which the individual experiences specific physical symptoms even though no physiological problems can be found.* Conversion disorder received its name from psychoanalytic theory, which stressed that anxiety was "converted" into a specific physical symptom. The individual with hypochondriasis has no physical disability; the individual with a conversion disorder does have some loss of motor or sensory ability. Individuals with a conversion disorder might be unable to speak, might faint, or they even might be deaf or blind.

Conversion disorder was more common in Freud's time than today. Freud was especially interested in this disorder, in which physical symptoms made no neurological sense. For example, with *glove anesthesia* individuals report that their entire hand is numb from the tip of their fingers to a cutoff point at the wrist. As shown in figure 11.6, if these individuals were experiencing true physiological numbness, their symptoms would be very different. Like hypochondriasis, conversion disorder often appears in conjunction with other mental disorders. During long-term evaluation, conversion disorder turns out to be another mental or physical disorder.

Dissociative Disorders

Our exploration of dissociative disorders focuses on their basic nature and then turns to some specific dissociative disorders.

Dissociative disorders *are psychological disorders that involve a sudden loss of memory or change in identity.* Under extreme stress or shock, the individual's conscious awareness becomes dissociated (separated or split) from previous memories and thoughts. Three kinds of dissociative disorders are dissociative amnesia, dissociative fugue, and dissociative identity.

Dissociative Amnesia and Fugue   Amnesia is the inability to recall important events ◀ ▥ P. 191. Amnesia can be caused by an injury to the head, for example. But **dissociative amnesia** *is a dissociative disorder involving memory loss caused by extensive psychological stress.* For example, an individual showed up at a hospital and said he did not know who he was. After several days in the hospital, he awoke one morning and demanded to be released. Eventually he remembered that he had been involved in an automobile accident in which a pedestrian had been killed. The extreme stress of the accident and the fear that he might be held responsible triggered the amnesia.

Dissociative fugue *("fugue" means flight) is a dissociative disorder in which the individual not only develops amnesia, but also unexpectedly travels away from home and assumes a new identity.* For example, one day a woman named Barbara vanished without a trace. Two weeks later, looking more like a teenager—with her hair in a ponytail and wearing bobby socks—than a 31-year-old woman, Barbara was picked up by police in a nearby city. When her husband came to see her, Barbara asked, "Who are you?" She could not remember anything about the last 2 weeks of her life. During psychotherapy, she gradually began to recall her past. She had left home with enough money to buy a bus ticket to the town where she grew up as a child. She spent days walking the streets and standing near a building where her father had worked. Later she went to a motel with a man; according to the motel manager, she entertained a series of men over a 3-day period (Goldstein & Palmer, 1975).

Dissociative Identity Disorder   **Dissociative identity disorder (DID),** *formerly called multiple personality disorder, is the most dramatic but least common dissociative disorder; individuals suffering from this disorder have two or more distinct personalities or selves, like the fictional Dr. Jekyll and Mr. Hyde of Robert Louis Stevenson's short story.* Each personality has its own memories, behaviors, and relationships; one personality dominates the individual at one point, another personality will take over at another time. The shift from one personality to the other usually occurs under distress.

ℱigure 11.7
The Three Faces of Eve

Chris Sizemore, the subject of the book *The Three Faces of Eve,* is shown here with a work she painted, entitled *Three Faces in One.*

One of the most famous cases of dissociative identity disorder involves the "three faces of Eve" (Thigpen & Cleckley, 1957). Eve White was the original dominant personality. She had no knowledge of her second personality, Eve Black, although Eve Black had been alternating with Eve White for a number of years. Eve White was bland, quiet, and serious—a rather dull personality. By contrast, Eve Black was carefree, mischievous, and uninhibited. She would "come out" at the most inappropriate times, leaving Eve White with hangovers, bills, and a reputation in local bars that she could not explain. During treatment, a third personality, Jane, emerged. More mature than the other two, Jane seemed to have developed as a result of therapy. Figure 11.7 provides a portrayal of the three faces of Eve.

In some cases, therapists have been blamed for creating a second or third personality. At one point, Eve said that her therapist created one of her personalities.

A summary of research on dissociative identity disorder suggests that the disorder is characterized by an inordinately high rate of sexual or physical abuse during early childhood (Ludolph, 1982). Sexual abuse occurred in 56 percent of the reported cases, for example. Note, though, that the majority of individuals who have been sexually abused do not develop this disorder. Mothers tend to be rejecting and depressed; fathers distant, alcoholic, and abusive. Remember that while fascinating, dissociative identity disorder is rare. Until the 1980s approximately 300 cases had ever been reported (Suinn, 1984). In the last decade, hundreds more have been labeled "dissociative identity disorder," although some argue that the increase represents a diagnostic fad. Others believe that it is not so rare, but has been frequently misdiagnosed as schizophrenia. Improved techniques for assessing the physiological changes that occur when individuals change personalities increase the likelihood that more accurate rates can be determined.

At this point, we have considered three major types of mental disorders—anxiety, somatoform, and dissociative. An overview of the main ideas about these disorders is presented in summary table 11.2. Next, we turn to the final three main categories of mental disorders we will discuss in this chapter (mood, schizophrenic, and personality), beginning with the mood disorders.

SUMMARY TABLE 11.2
The Anxiety, Somatoform, and Dissociative Disorders

Concept	Processes/ Related Ideas	Characteristics/Description
Anxiety Disorders	Their Nature	Anxiety is a diffuse, vague, highly unpleasant feeling of fear and apprehension. The main features of anxiety disorders are motor tension, hyperactivity, and apprehensive expectations and thoughts.
	Generalized Anxiety Disorder	This disorder consists of persistent anxiety for at least 1 month without being able to specify the reason for the anxiety.
	Panic Disorder	Recurrent panic attacks marked by the sudden onset of intense apprehension or terror characterize a panic disorder. Panic disorder can occur with or without agoraphobia.
	Phobic Disorders	Commonly called phobias, they involve an irrational, overwhelming, persistent fear of a particular object or situation. Phobias come in many forms. Psychoanalytic and learning explanations of phobias have been given. Biological factors also have been implicated, with individuals possibly having a genetic predisposition to develop a phobia.
	Obsessive-Compulsive Disorder	Recurrent obsessions or compulsions characterize these disorders. Obsessions are anxiety-provoking thoughts that won't go away. Compulsions are urges to perform repetitive, ritualistic behaviors that usually occur to prevent or produce a future situation.
	Post-Traumatic Stress Disorder	This disorder develops through exposure to a traumatic event, such as war; severely oppressive situations, such as the Holocaust; severe abuse, such as rape; natural disasters; and accidental disasters. Anxiety symptoms may immediately follow the trauma, or be delayed months or even years until onset.
Somatoform Disorders	Their Nature	Psychological symptoms take a physical, or somatic, form, even though no physical cause can be found.
	Hypochondriasis	This disorder involves a pervasive fear of illness and disease. It rarely occurs alone; depression often accompanies hypochondriasis.
	Conversion Disorder	This disorder occurs when an individual experiences specific symptoms even though no physiological problems can be found. Conversion disorder received its name from psychoanalytic theory, which stressed that anxiety was "converted" into a specific physical symptom. Some loss of motor or sensory ability occurs. The disorder was more common in Freud's time than today.
Dissociative Disorders	Their Nature	Dissociative disorders occur when a person has a sudden loss of memory or change in identity. Under extreme stress or shock, conscious awareness becomes dissociated (separated or split) from previous memories and thoughts.
	Dissociative Amnesia and Fugue	Dissociative amnesia involves memory loss caused by extensive psychological stress. Dissociative fugue also involves a loss of memory, but individuals unexpectedly travel away from home or work, assume a new identity, and do not remember their old one.
	Dissociative Identity Disorder	Formerly called multiple personality disorder, this disorder involves the presence of two or more distinct personalities in the same individual. The disorder is rare.

Mood Disorders

Our coverage of the mood disorders focuses on their basic nature, depressive disorders, bipolar disorder, and causes of mood disorders. The **mood disorders** *are psychological disorders characterized by wide emotional swings, ranging from deep depression to extreme euphoria and agitation.* Depression can occur alone, as in the depressive disorders, or it can alternate with mania (an overexcited, unrealistically optimistic state), as in bipolar disorder. In the national study of the prevalence of mental disorders, almost eight percent of the individuals reported that they had ever experienced a mood disorder (Robins & Regier, 1991).

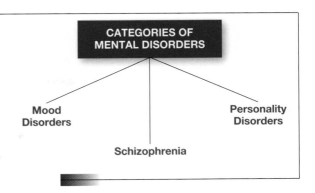

Depressive Disorders   The **depressive disorders** *are mood disorders in which the individual suffers depression without ever experiencing mania.* The severity of the depressive disorders varies with some individuals experiencing what is classified as major depressive disorder while others are given the diagnosis of dysthymic disorder (more chronic depression with fewer symptoms than major depression) (Coyne, 2000).

The Depressive Disorders
Major Depressive Disorder

In **major depressive disorder** *the individual experiences a major depressive episode and depressed characteristics, such as lethargy and hopelessness, for at least two weeks or longer.* The individual's daily functioning becomes impaired. Nine symptoms define a major depressive episode (and of the nine, at least five must be present during a 2-week period):

1. Depressed mood most of the day
2. Reduced interest or pleasure in all or most activities
3. Significant weight loss or gain, or significant decrease or interest in appetite
4. Trouble sleeping or sleeping too much
5. Psychomotor agitation or retardation
6. Fatigue or loss of energy
7. Feeling worthless or guilty in an excessive or inappropriate manner
8. Problems in thinking, concentrating, or making decisions
9. Recurrent thoughts of death and suicide

Consider Peter, who had been depressed for several months. Nothing cheered him up. His depression began when the girl he wanted to marry decided marriage was not for her, at least not with Peter. Peter's emotional state deteriorated to the point where he didn't leave his room for days at a time, he kept the shades drawn and the room dark, and he could hardly get out of bed in the morning. When he managed to leave his room, he had trouble maintaining a conversation and he felt exhausted most of the time. By the time Peter finally contacted his college counseling center, he had gone from being mildly depressed to being in the grips of major depression.

Dysthymic disorder *is generally more chronic and has fewer symptoms than major depressive disorder.* The individual has a depressed mood for most days for at least 2 years as an adult or at least 1 year as a child or adolescent. To be classified as having dysthymic disorder, a major depressive episode must not have occurred and the 2-year period of depression must not have been broken by a normal mood lasting more than 2 months. Two or more of these six symptoms must be present: poor appetite or overeating, sleep problems, low energy or fatigue, low self-esteem, poor concentration or difficulty making decisions, and feelings of hopelessness (Munoz, 1998).

Although most people don't spiral into major depression as Peter did, everyone feels "blue" sometimes. In our stress-filled world, people often use the term *depression* to describe brief bouts of normal sadness or discontent over life's problems. Perhaps you haven't done well in a class or things aren't working out in your love life. You feel down in the dumps and say you are depressed. In most instances, though, your depression won't last as long or be as intense as Peter's; after a few hours, days,

This painting by Vincent Van Gogh, Portrait of Dr. Gatchet, *reflects the extreme melancholy that characterizes the depressive disorders.*

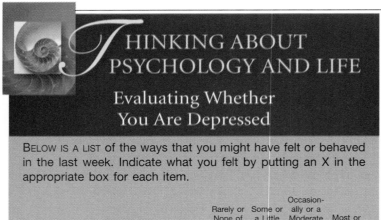

Evaluating Whether You Are Depressed

BELOW IS A LIST of the ways that you might have felt or behaved in the last week. Indicate what you felt by putting an X in the appropriate box for each item.

During the past week:	Rarely or None of the Time (Less Than 1 Day)	Some or a Little of the Time (1–2 Days)	Occasionally or a Moderate Amount of the Time (3–4 Days)	Most or All of the Time (5–7 Days)
1. I was bothered by things that usually don't bother me.	☐	☐	☐	☐
2. I did not feel like eating; my appetite was poor.	☐	☐	☐	☐
3. I felt that I could not shake off the blues even with help from my family and friends.	☐	☐	☐	☐
4. I felt that I was just as good as other people.	☐	☐	☐	☐
5. I had trouble keeping my mind on what I was doing.	☐	☐	☐	☐
6. I felt depressed.	☐	☐	☐	☐
7. I felt that everything I did was an effort.	☐	☐	☐	☐
8. I felt hopeful about the future.	☐	☐	☐	☐
9. I thought my life had been a failure.	☐	☐	☐	☐
10. I felt fearful.	☐	☐	☐	☐
11. My sleep was restless.	☐	☐	☐	☐
12. I was happy.	☐	☐	☐	☐
13. I talked less than usual.	☐	☐	☐	☐
14. I felt lonely.	☐	☐	☐	☐
15. People were unfriendly.	☐	☐	☐	☐
16. I enjoyed life.	☐	☐	☐	☐
17. I had crying spells.	☐	☐	☐	☐
18. I felt sad.	☐	☐	☐	☐
19. I felt that people disliked me.	☐	☐	☐	☐
20. I could not get going.	☐	☐	☐	☐

For items 4, 8, 12, and 16, give yourself a 3 each time you checked rarely or none, 2 each time you checked some or little, 1 each time you checked occasionally or moderate, and a 0 each time you checked most or all of the time. For the remaining items, give yourself a 0 each time you checked rarely or none, 1 each time you checked some or a little, 2 each time you checked occasionally or moderate, and 3 each time you checked most or all of the time. Total up your score for all 20 items.

If your score is around 7, then you are like the average male in terms of how much depression you have experienced in the last week. If your score is around 8 or 9 your score is similar to the average female. Scores less than the average for either males or females indicate that depression probably has not been a problem for you during the past week. If your score is 16 or more and you are bothered by your feelings, you might benefit from professional help.

Keep in mind, though, that self-diagnosis is not always accurate and to adequately diagnose anyone, the professional judgment of a qualified clinician is required.

or weeks, you snap out of your gloomy state and begin to cope more effectively with your problems. Nonetheless, depression is so widespread that it has been called the "common cold" of mental disorders; more than 250,000 individuals are hospitalized every year for the disorder. Students, professors, corporate executives, laborers—no one is immune to depression, not even F. Scott Fitzgerald, Ernest Hemingway, Virginia Woolf, Abraham Lincoln, or Winston Churchill—each of whom experienced depression.

After years of depression, Hemingway eventually took his own life. To read about suicide, including some helpful strategies for communicating with someone who is considering suicide, see Explorations in Psychology.

The inadequate care that results from a lack of understanding or a misunderstanding of depression is tragic. Given the existing range of psychological and pharmacological treatments available today, those individuals who go untreated suffer needlessly.

Bipolar Disorder   Although she had experienced extreme mood swings since she was a child, Mrs. M. was first admitted to a mental hospital at the age of 38. At 33, shortly before the birth of her first child, she became very depressed. One month after the baby was born she became agitated and euphoric. Mrs. M. signed a year's lease on an apartment, bought furniture, and piled up debts. Several years later other manic and depressive mood swings occurred. In one of her excitatory moods, Mrs. M. swore loudly and created a disturbance at a club where she was not a member. Several days later she began divorce proceedings. On the day prior to her admission to the mental hospital, she went on a spending spree and bought 57 hats. Several weeks later, she became despondent, saying "I have no energy. My brain doesn't work right. I have let my family down. I don't have anything to live for." In a subsequent manic bout, Mrs. M. pursued a romantic relationship with her doctor (Kolb, 1973).

Bipolar disorder *is a mood disorder that is characterized by extreme mood swings that include one or more episodes of mania (an overexcited, unrealistically optimistic state)* (Coryell & others, 1999). *Bipolar* means that the person may experience depression and mania. Most bipolar individuals experience multiple cycles of depression interspersed with mania. Less than 10 percent of bipolar individuals tend to experience manic-type episodes and not depression.

A manic episode is like the flip side of a depressive episode (DeBattista, Solvason, & Schatzberg, 1998). Instead of feeling depressed, the person feels euphoric and on top of the world. However, as the manic episode unfolds the person can experience panic and eventually depression. Instead of feeling fatigued as many depressed individuals do, when individuals experience mania they have tremendous energy and might sleep very little. There is often an impulsivity when individuals are in a manic state that can get them in trouble in business and legal transactions. For example, they might spend their life

EXPLORATIONS IN PSYCHOLOGY
Suicide

THE RATE OF SUICIDE has tripled since the 1950s in the United States. Each year about 25,000 people take their own lives. After about the age of 15, the suicide rate begins to rise rapidly (Weissman & others, 1999). Suicide accounts for 12 percent of the mortality in the adolescent and young adult age group. Men are about three times more likely than women to succeed at committing suicide. This may be due to their choice of method for attempting it—shooting themselves, for example. By contrast, females more often select methods, such as sleeping pills, which do not immediately cause death. Although males successfully commit suicide more frequently, females attempt it more often (Maris, 1998).

Estimates indicate that 6 to 10 suicide attempts occur for every successful suicide in the general population. For adolescents, the figure is as high as 50 attempts for every life taken. As many as 2 in every 3 college students have thought about suicide on at least one occasion.

There is no simple answer to why people commit suicide. Biological factors appear to be involved. Suicide, as with major depressive disorder, tends to run in families. Immediate and highly stressful circumstances, such as the loss of a spouse or a job, flunking out of school, or an unwanted pregnancy, can lead people, especially those who are genetically predisposed, to attempt suicide. Also, drug-related suicide attempts are more common now than in the past.

However, earlier experiences, such as a long-standing history of family instability and unhappiness, can also play a role in attempted suicides. Studies of gifted men and women found several predictors of suicide, such as anxiety, conspicuous instability in work and relationships, depression, and alcoholism (Shneidman, 1971; Tomlinson-Keasey, Warren, & Elliot, 1986).

Substance abuse and having a terminal illness are related to suicidal thoughts and behavior. Also, in high-pressure cultures, such as Japan and the United States, suicide rates are much higher than in less achievement oriented cultures.

Psychologists do not have the complete answers for detecting suicide impulses or for preventing them. However, psychologists believe that the most effective intervention for preventing suicide comes from those who have had special training. For some valuable suggestions for communicating with someone you think may be contemplating suicide, see table 11.A.

TABLE 11.A
What To Do and What Not To Do When Someone Is Threatening Suicide

What To Do	What Not To Do
1. Ask direct, straightforward questions in a calm manner. For example: "Are you thinking about hurting yourself?" Be a good listener.	1. Don't ignore the warning signs.
2. Take the suicide threat very seriously. Ask questions about the person's feelings, relationships, and thoughts about the type of method to be used. If a gun, pills, rope, or other means is mentioned and a specific plan has been developed, the situation is dangerous. Stay with the person until help arrives.	2. Don't refuse to talk about suicide if the person wants to talk about it. 3. Don't react with horror, disapproval, or repulsion. 4. Don't offer false reassurances ("Everything will be all right") or make judgments ("You should be thankful for . . .").
3. Listen and be supportive. Emphasize that unbearable pain can be survived.	5. Don't abandon the person after the crisis seems to have passed or after professional counseling has begun.
4. Encourage the person to get professional help and assist him or her in getting this help. If the person is willing, take the person to a mental health facility or hospital.	

Suicide

Bipolar Disorder

Bipolar Disorder Resources

savings on a foolish business venture. By definition in the *DSM-IV* classification, manic episodes must last 1 week. They average 8 to 16 weeks. Individuals with bipolar disorder can have manic and depressive episodes that occur four or more times a year, but they usually are separated by 6 months to a year.

Causes of Mood Disorders
Causes of mood disorders, such as Peter's depression and Mrs. M.'s bipolar disorder, are biological as well as psychosocial.

Biological Causes   Biological explanations of mood disorders involve heredity and brain processes, especially neurotransmitters (DeBattista, Solvason, & Schatzberg, 1998). Depressive and bipolar disorders tend to run in families, although the family link is stronger for bipolar disorder than depressive disorders. One of the greatest risks for developing a mood disorder is having a biological parent who suffers from a mood disorder. For example, in bipolar disorder, the rate of the disorder in first degree relatives is 10 to 20 times higher than in the general population.

Abnormalities in what are called monoamine neurotransmitters, such as serotonin, norepinephrine, and dopamine, have been implicated in mood disorders (Meyers & others, 1999) P. 54. Mood disorders also are associated with neuroendocrine abnormalities, such as higher levels of the stress hormone cortisol.

Psychosocial Causes   Psychosocial factors that may be involved in the mood disorders have been proposed by psychoanalytic theorists such as Freud P. 337. Cognitive and sociocultural explanations also have been proposed.

Freud (1917) believed that depression was a turning inward of aggressive instincts. He theorized that the child's early attachment to a love object (usually the mother) contains a mixture of love and hate. When the child loses the love object or her dependency needs are frustrated, feelings of loss coexist with anger. Since the child cannot openly accept such angry feelings toward the individual she loves, the hostility is turned inward and experienced as depression. The unresolved mixture of anger and love is carried forward to adolescence and adulthood, where loss can bring back these early feelings of abandonment.

The British psychiatrist John Bowlby (1989) agrees with Freud that childhood experiences are an important determinant of depression in adulthood P. 256. He believes a combination of an insecure attachment to the mother, a lack of love and affection as a child, and the actual loss of a parent during childhood gives rise to a negative cognitive set, or schema. The schema built up during childhood causes the individual to interpret later losses as yet other failures in one's effort to establish enduring and close positive relationships.

The cognitive approach provides another perspective on mood disorders. Individuals who are depressed rarely think positive thoughts. They interpret their lives in self-defeating ways and have negative expectations about the future (Bradley, 1996). Psychologist Aaron Beck (1967) believes such negative thoughts reflect schemas that shape the depressed individual's experiences. These habitual negative thoughts magnify and expand a depressed person's negative experiences (Teasdale & others, 1995). The depressed person might overgeneralize about a minor occurrence and think that he is worthless because a work assignment was turned in late, his son was arrested for shoplifting, or a friend made a negative comment about his hair. An individual might be given a work evaluation that shows a deficiency in one area and magnify the significance of the evaluation. Catastrophic thinking, such as expecting to be fired and not being able to find another job, might ensue. The accumulation of such cognitive distortions can lead to depression.

Learned helplessness *occurs when individuals are exposed to aversive stimulation, such as prolonged stress or pain, over which they have no control. The inability to avoid such aversive stimulation produces an apathetic state of*

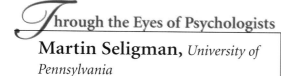

Martin Seligman, *University of Pennsylvania*

"In learned helplessness, people expect bad events to occur and believe there is nothing they can do to prevent them from occurring."

helplessness. Martin Seligman (1975) argued that learned helplessness is one reason some individuals become depressed. When individuals encounter stress and pain over which they have no control, they eventually feel helpless and depressed. Some researchers believe that the hopelessness characteristic of learned helplessness is often the result of a person's extremely negative, self-blaming attributions (Metalsky & others, 1993).

Seligman's (1989) belief is that the reason so many young American adults are prone to depression is our society's emphasis on self, independence, and individualism, coupled with an erosion of connectedness to others, family, and religion, which has spawned a widespread sense of hopelessness. Depressive disorders are found in virtually all cultures in the world, but their incidence, intensity, and components vary across cultures. A major difference in depression between Western and many non-Western cultures is the absence of guilt and self-deprecation in the non-Western cultures (Draguns, 1990).

Earlier in this chapter we mentioned that women run a far greater risk of depression than men—at a ratio of 2:1. Studies have shown that depression is especially high among single women who are the head of household and among young married women who work at unsatisfying, dead-end jobs (Russo, 1990). Such stressful circumstances, as well as others involving sexual abuse, sexual harassment, unwanted pregnancy, and powerlessness disproportionately affect women. These sociocultural factors can interact with biological and cognitive factors to increase women's rate of depression. However, in cultures where alcohol abuse and aggression are rare, such as the culturally homogeneous Amish community (a religious sect in Pennsylvania), the rate of depression for women and men is virtually equal.

Schizophrenia

Bob began to miss work. He spent his time watching his house from a rental car parked inconspicuously down the street and following his fellow employees as they left work to see where they went and what they did. He kept a little black book in which he scribbled cryptic notes. When he went to the water cooler at work, he pretended to drink but instead looked carefully around the room to observe if anyone looked guilty or frightened.

Bob's world seemed to be closing in on him. After an explosive scene at the office one day, he became very agitated. He left and never returned. By the time Bob arrived at home, he was in a rage. He could not sleep that night and the next day he kept his children home from school; all day he kept the shades pulled on every window. The next night he maintained his vigil. At 4 A.M., he armed himself and burst out of the house, firing shots in the air while daring his enemies to come out (McNeil, 1967).

Bob, like Jim who was described at the beginning of the chapter (recall that he believed his breath possessed a special power), has a schizophrenic disorder. Schizophrenia produces a bizarre set of symptoms and wreaks havoc on the individual's personality. **Schizophrenia** *is a severe psychological disorder characterized by distorted thoughts and perceptions, odd communication, inappropriate emotion, abnormal motor behavior, and social withdrawal.* The term *schizophrenia* comes from the Latin words *schizo*, meaning "split," and *phrenia*, meaning "mind." The individual's mind is split from reality, and personality loses its unity. Schizophrenia is not the same as multiple personality, which sometimes is called a "split personality." Schizophrenia involves the split of an individual's personality from reality, not the coexistence of several personalities within one individual.

In the national study of the prevalence of psychological disorders, 1.5 percent reported that they had ever experienced schizophrenia (Robins & Regier, 1991). Other surveys also suggest that about 1 in 100 Americans will be classified as having schizophrenia in their lifetime (Gottesman, 1989). Schizophrenia is a serious,

Schizophrenia

This painting is named Landscape *and it is by August Neter, a successful nineteenth-century electrical engineer until he developed schizophrenia in 1907. He lost interest in his work as an engineer as his mind became disorganized.*

debilitating mental disorder. About one-half of all mental hospital patients are individuals with schizophrenia. More now than in the past, individuals with schizophrenia live in society and return to mental hospitals periodically for treatment. Drug therapy is primarily responsible for fewer individuals with schizophrenia being hospitalized. About one-third of individuals with schizophrenia get better, about one-third get worse, and about one-third stay the same once they develop this severe mental disorder.

What are the symptoms of schizophrenia? Individuals with schizophrenia have *delusions,* or false beliefs. One individual might think he is Jesus Christ, another Napoleon, for example. The delusions are utterly implausible. One individual might think her thoughts are being broadcast over the radio, another might think that a double agent is controlling her every move. Individuals with schizophrenia also might hear, see, feel, smell, and taste things not there. These *hallucinations* often take the form of voices. An individual with schizophrenia might think that he hears two people talking about him. Or, on another occasion, he might say, "Hear that rumbling noise in the pipe. That is one of my men watching out for me."

Often individuals with schizophrenia do not make sense when they talk or write. For example, one individual with schizophrenia might say, "Well, Rocky, babe, help is out, happening, but where, when, up, top, side, over, you know, out of the way, that's it. Sign off." Such speech has no meaning. These incoherent, loose word associations are called "word salad."

The motor behavior of the individual with schizophrenia can be bizarre, sometimes taking the form of an odd appearance, pacing, statue-like postures, or strange mannerisms. Some individuals with schizophrenia withdraw from their social world. They become so insulated from others they seem totally absorbed in their interior thoughts.

Types of Schizophrenia   There are four main types of schizophrenia: disorganized, catatonic, paranoid, and undifferentiated.

Disorganized schizophrenia *is a type of schizophrenia in which an individual has delusions and hallucinations that have little or no recognizable meaning—hence, the label disorganized.* An individual with disorganized schizophrenia may withdraw from human contact and may regress to silly, childlike gestures and behavior. Many of these individuals were isolated or maladjusted during adolescence.

Catatonic schizophrenia *is a type of schizophrenia characterized by bizarre motor behavior, which sometimes takes the form of a completely immobile stupor* (see figure 11.8). Even in this stupor, individuals with catatonic schizophrenia are completely conscious of what is happening around them. In a catatonic state, the individual sometimes shows *waxy flexibility;* for example, if the person's arm is raised and then allowed to fall, the arm stays in the new position.

Paranoid schizophrenia *is a type of schizophrenia characterized by delusions of reference, grandeur, and persecution.* The delusions usually form a complex, elaborate system based on a complete misinterpretation of actual events. It is not unusual for the individual with paranoid schizophrenia to develop all three delusions in the following order. First, they sense they are special and have been singled out for attention (delusions of reference). Individuals with delusions of reference misinterpret chance events as being directly relevant to their own lives—a thunderstorm, for example, might be perceived as a personal message from God. Second, they believe that this special attention is the result of their admirable and special characteristics (delusions of grandeur). Individuals with delusions of grandeur think of themselves as exalted beings—the pope or the president, for example. Third, they think that others are so jealous and threatened by these characteristics that they spy and plot against them (delusions of persecution). Individuals with delusions of persecution often feel they are the target of a conspiracy—for example, recall Bob's situation described earlier.

Undifferentiated schizophrenia *is a type of schizophrenia characterized by disorganized behavior, hallucinations, delusions, and incoherence.* This category of schizophrenia is used when an individual's symptoms either don't meet the criteria for the other types or they meet the criteria for more than one of the other types.

Causes of Schizophrenia   As with mood disorders, possible causes of schizophrenia are found in biological and psychosocial factors.

Biological Factors   Biological factors that have been proposed to explain schizophrenia involve heredity and neurobiological factors. If you have a relative with schizophrenia, what are the chances you will develop schizophrenia? It depends on how closely you are related. As genetic similarity increases, so does a person's risk of becoming schizophrenic (Pritchard, 1996). As shown in figure 11.9, an identical twin of an individual with schizophrenia has a 46 percent chance of developing the disorder, a fraternal twin 14 percent, a sibling 10 percent, a nephew or niece 3 percent, and an unrelated individual in the general population 1 percent (Gottesman & Shields, 1982). Such data strongly suggest that genetic factors are involved in schizophrenia, although the precise nature of the genetic influence is unknown.

Many neuroscientists believe imbalances in brain chemistry, including deficits in brain metabolism, a malfunctioning dopamine system, and distorted cerebral blood

Figure 11.8
A Person with Catatonic Schizophrenia
Unusual motor behaviors are prominent symptoms in catatonic schizophrenia. Individuals may cease to move altogether, sometimes taking on bizarre postures.

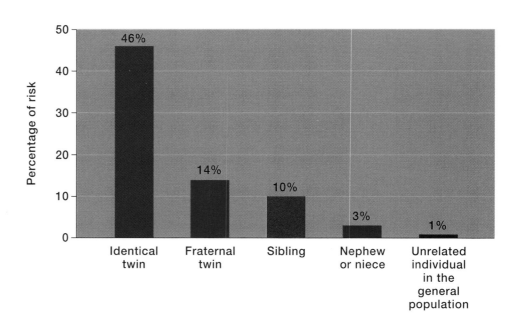

*F*igure 11.9
Lifetime Risk of Developing Schizophrenia, According to Genetic Relatedness
As your genetic relatedness to an individual with schizophrenia increases, so does your risk of becoming schizophrenic.

In the summer of 1998, 44-year-old Russell Weston, Jr., walked into the United States Capitol building and fired on a crowd, killing two policemen in a shootout. Almost a decade and a half earlier he had been diagnosed as having paranoid schizophrenia. He thought the CIA was spying on him via satellite dishes, and he was arrested by the Secret Service in 1996 for making threatening comments about President Clinton. The Secret Service concluded that he was a low-level threat. Several months later, a judge ordered him to be committed to a state mental hospital after he threatened someone in Montana, where he lived at the time.

His mental health situation began to improve because at the mental hospital he received medication for the first time. After about 2 months at the hospital, he was released with two weeks' worth of pills and prescriptions for more. He did not refill them.

Only a small percentage of individuals with schizophrenia are violent toward others. Individuals with schizophrenia who get no treatment are much more likely to harm themselves than others. About 15 percent of individuals with schizophrenia commit suicide. Some mental health experts fear that high-profile cases like Russell Weston's will stigmatize all individuals with schizophrenia, even those who never have committed a crime. Others hope it will bring attention to the problems of individuals with schizophrenia and help people to better understand them. They also hope it will encourage people who know individuals with schizophrenia to help them get treatment and medication, and stay on the medication.

flow, cause schizophrenia (Bertolino & others, 1999; Byrne & Davis, 1999; Goldberg, Berman, & Weinberger, 1995). Imaging techniques, such as the PET scan, clearly show deficits in brain metabolism 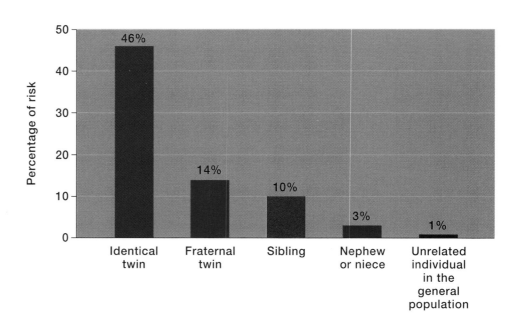 P. 71. Do these deficits cause the disorder, or are they simply symptoms of a disorder whose true origin lies deeper in the brain, in the genes, or in the environment? Whether cause or effect, information about neurobiological factors improves our knowledge of schizophrenia's nature. We do know that individuals with schizophrenia produce higher than normal levels of the neurotransmitter dopamine. They also have a reduced blood flow in the prefrontal cortex (Poole & others, 1999). For example, when scientists monitored the brains of individuals with schizophrenia as they performed a card-sorting task, blood did not adequately flow into the prefrontal region, where much of our advanced thinking takes place (Weinberger, Berman, & Zec, 1986).

Psychosocial Factors   Although contemporary theorists don't propose psychosocial factors as stand-alone causes of schizophrenia, stress is the psychosocial factor that is given the most attention in understanding schizophrenia. The **diathesis–stress view** argues that a combination of biogenetic disposition and stress causes schizophrenia (Meehl, 1962). The term *diathesis* means physical vulnerability or predisposition to a particular disorder. A defective gene makeup might produce schizophrenia only when the individual lives in a stressful environment. Advocates of the diathesis–stress view emphasize the importance of stress reduction and family support in treating schizophrenia.

Disorders of thought and emotion are common to schizophrenia in all cultures, but the type and incidence of schizophrenic disorders may vary from culture to culture. Individuals in poverty are more likely to have schizophrenia than people at higher socioeconomic levels. The link between schizophrenia and poverty is correlational, and contemporary theorists do not believe that poverty causes schizophrenia (Schiffman & Walker, 1998).

Odd/Eccentric Cluster

Paranoid	Lack of trust in others, suspicious. See themselves as morally correct yet vulnerable and envied.
Schizoid	Inability to form adequate social relationships. Shy, withdrawn behavior, difficulty expressing anger. Most are considered "cold" people.
Schizotypal	Many of the same features of the schizoid category also apply here. Some differences with the schizoid disorder are that the schizotypal disorder involves odd thinking patterns likely to have developed because of eccentric beliefs, more overt suspicion, and more overt hostility.

Dramatic/Emotionally Problematic Cluster

Histrionic	Seek attention and are over reactive. Responses are expressed more dramatically and intensely than is appropriate, hence the term *histrionic*. The disorder is much more common in women than in men.
Narcissistic	Unrealistic sense of self-importance, exhibitionistic attention seeking, inability to take criticism, interpersonal manipulation, and lack of empathy. These characteristics lead to substantial problems in interpersonal relationships.
Antisocial	Guiltless, law-breaking, exploitive, irresponsible, self-indulgent, and interpersonally intrusive. These individuals often resort to a life of crime and violence. The disorder is considerably more common in men than in women.
Borderline	Similar to schizotypal but borderline disorder does not involve behavior that is as consistently withdrawn and thinking that is as bizarre. These individuals are often emotionally unstable, impulsive, unpredictable in their behavior, irritable, and anxious. They also are prone to boredom.

Chronic Fearfulness/Avoidant Cluster

Avoidant	These individuals are shy and inhibited yet desire interpersonal relationships, which distinguishes them from the schizotypal or schizoid disorders. They often have low self-esteem and are extremely sensitive to rejection. This disorder is close to being an anxiety disorder but is not characterized by as much personal distress.
Dependent	These individuals lack self-confidence and don't express their own personality. They have a pervasive need to cling to stronger personalities, whom they allow to make a wide range of decisions for them. The disorder is far more common in women than in men.
Obsessive-compulsive	This disorder is often confused with the obsessive-compulsive disorder (which is an anxiety disorder), but there are significant differences between them. The obsessive-compulsive personality seldom becomes obsessed about issues. Obsessive-compulsive personality involves a lifestyle in which compulsive features are chronic and pervasive, but it does not involve a specific behavior such as persistent hand-washing. And the obsessive-compulsive personality does not become upset or distressed about his/her lifestyle. Individuals with obsessive-compulsive personality disorder are preoccupied with rules and duties, rarely express warmth or caring, are emotionally insensitive, and are oriented toward a lifestyle of productivity and efficiency.
Passive-aggressive	Pouting, procrastination, stubbornness, or intentional inefficiency designed to frustrate other people. A typical thought pattern is "I don't have to get there. Nobody can tell me what to do."

Figure 11.10
Three Clusters of Personality Disorders

Personality Disorders

We will explore the nature of personality disorders, in general, then examine antisocial personality disorder.

Personality disorders *are chronic, maladaptive cognitive-behavioral patterns that are thoroughly integrated into the individual's personality.* The patterns are often

Personality Disorders

Gary Gilmore was a classic case of antisocial personality disorder. As a young adolescent, Gilmore had low grades, was often truant, and stole from classmates. At 14, he was placed in a juvenile detention center for stealing a car. He was arrested on numerous occasions in high school and at 20 was sent to the state penitentiary for burglary and robbery. Several years later Gilmore was released, but it didn't take long for him to be put back in the penitentiary for other armed robberies. Subsequently released again, he moved in with a woman, but his drinking, carousing, and fighting caused her to kick him out. Later that year, he pulled into a gas station in Utah and ordered the attendant to hand over all of his cash, which the attendant did. Then Gilmore shot him twice in the head, killing him. The next morning, Gilmore walked into a hotel and shot the manager. Later Gilmore was caught and convicted of the two murders. He was executed in 1977.

Antisocial Personality Disorder

The Psychopath's Brain

recognizable by adolescence or earlier. Personality disorders usually are not as bizarre as schizophrenia and they don't have the intense, diffuse feelings of fear and apprehension that characterize the anxiety disorders.

Personality disorders are patterns of behavior, or lack of behavior, that are troublesome to others or whose pleasure sources are either harmful or illegal (Meyer, 1998). In the *DSM-IV,* the personality disorders are grouped into three clusters (see figure 11.10). The odd/eccentric cluster includes the paranoid, schizoid, and schizotypal disorders. The dramatic and emotionally problematic cluster consists of the histrionic, narcissistic, antisocial, and borderline disorders. The chronic fearfulness/avoidant cluster is made up of the avoidant, dependent, obsessive-compulsive, and passive-aggressive personality disorders. As you can see, some of the personality disorders have names that are similar to other disorders we have described in other categories earlier in the chapter, such as schizotypal personality disorder and schizophrenic disorders, as well as obsessive-compulsive personality disorder and obsessive-compulsive anxiety disorder. The schizotypal disorder is not as clearly bizarre as schizophrenia. Figure 11.10 lists a number of differences between obsessive-compulsive personality disorder and obsessive-compulsive anxiety disorder.

Antisocial personality disorder *is in the dramatic/emotionally problematic cluster. It is the most problematic disorder for society, because these individuals often resort to a life of crime and violence.* They are guiltless, exploitive, irresponsible, self-indulgent, and interpersonally intrusive. In the national study of the prevalence of psychological disorders, 2.6 percent of the individuals reported that they ever had experienced an antisocial personality disorder (Robins & Regier, 1991).

The following individual has an antisocial personality disorder (Carson, Butcher, & Mineka, 1998). Mark, 22 years old, is awaiting trial for car theft and armed robbery. He has a long history of arrests beginning at 9 years of age, when he was arrested for vandalism. He was expelled from high school for truancy and disruptive behavior. He ran away from home on numerous occasions. He has not held a job for more than a few days at a time, even though his charming manner enables him to obtain work rather easily. He is a loner with few friends and, although initially charming, he soon antagonizes the people he meets with his aggressive, self-oriented behavior. While Mark was awaiting trial, he skipped bail and left town.

People with antisocial personality disorder used to be called psychopaths or sociopaths. They regularly violate other people's rights. The disorder begins before the age of 15 and continues into adulthood. It is much more common in males than in females. These individuals represent a small percentage of the population but commit a disproportionately large percentage of violent and property crimes (Meyer, Wolverton, & Deitsch, 1998). The disorder is very difficult to treat. Also, most HMOs will not authorize treatment of antisocial personality disorder or any of the other personality disorders. We will say more about managed care issues in the next chapter.

Both biological and psychosocial explanations of antisocial personality disorder have been given (Widiger, 2000). In terms of biological factors, a genetic predisposition for the disorder may be present. For example, the disorder is more likely to appear in identical twins than in fraternal twins (Gottesman & Goldsmith, 1994).

In terms of psychosocial factors, inadequate socialization regularly appears in the history of individuals who develop antisocial personality disorder (Sutker & Allain, 1993). Parents of these children may be neglectful or inconsistent and punitive in their discipline. Individuals with this disorder are more likely to have at least one parent with antisocial personality traits than are their counterparts without the disorder. Thus, children growing up in these families presumably have many opportunities to observe and imitate parents who behave in exploitive, immoral ways. Further, the impulsive and aggressive behavior that characterize individuals with antisocial personality disorder suggests that they have not adequately learned to delay gratification (Sher & Trull, 1994).

SUMMARY TABLE 11.3
Mood Disorders, Schizophrenia, and Personality Disorders

Concept	Processes/ Related Ideas	Characteristics/Description
Mood Disorders	Their Nature	Mood disorders are psychological disorders characterized by wide emotional mood swings, ranging from deep depression to extreme euphoria and agitation. Depression can occur alone, as in the depressive disorders, or it can alternate with mania, as in bipolar disorder.
	Depressive Disorders	These are mood disorders in which the individual suffers depression without ever experiencing mania. In major depressive disorder, the individual experiences a major depressive episode and depressed characteristics, such as lethargy and hopelessness, for 2 weeks or longer. Dysthymic disorder is generally more chronic and has fewer symptoms than major depressive disorder.
	Bipolar Disorder	This is a mood disorder characterized by extreme mood swings that include one or more episodes of mania (an overexcited, unrealistic, optimistic state). "Bipolar" means the person may experience depression and mania. Less than 10 percent of bipolar individuals experience mania but not depression.
	Causes of Mood Disorders	Biological explanations include heredity and brain processes, especially the monoamine neurotransmitters. Psychosocial factors include those proposed by psychoanalytic theorists such as Freud, cognitive explanations such as Beck's emphasis on cognitive distortions, and Seligman's focus on the negative expectations of learned helplessness, as well as sociocultural factors such as gender (with women diagnosed with depression about twice as often as men).
Schizophrenia	Its Nature	This is a severe psychological disorder characterized by distorted thoughts and perceptions, odd communication, inappropriate emotion, abnormal motor behavior, and social withdrawal. The individual's mind is split from reality and personality loses its unity. About 1 in 100 Americans develops schizophrenia.
	Types of Schizophrenia	There are four main types of schizophrenia: disorganized, catatonic, paranoid, and differentiated.
	Causes of Schizophrenia	Biological factors include heredity and such neurobiological factors as too much of the neurotransmitter dopamine. Possible psychosocial factors include stress.
Personality Disorders	Their Nature	Personality disorders are chronic, maladaptive cognitive-behavioral patterns that are thoroughly integrated into the individual's personality. They are often recognizable by adolescence or earlier. In the *DSM-IV,* they are divided into three clusters: odd/eccentric, dramatic/emotionally problematic, and chronic fearfulness/avoidant.
	Antisocial Personality Disorder	This is in the dramatic/emotionally problematic cluster and is the most problematic personality disorder for society because these individuals often resort to a life of crime and violence. They are guiltless, exploitive, irresponsible, self-indulgent, and interpersonally intrusive.

At this point we have discussed a number of ideas about the mood disorders, schizophrenic disorders, and personality disorders. An overview of these ideas is presented in summary table 11.3. In the next chapter, we continue our exploration of abnormal psychology by examining the therapies used to treat people's mental disorders.

Overview

OUR COVERAGE OF ABNORMAL PSYCHOLOGY began by examining a number of ideas about understanding abnormal behavior. These ideas focused on defining abnormal behavior, legal aspects of mental disorders, the causes of abnormal behavior, rates of disorders, and classifying abnormal behavior. Our extensive discussion of categories of mental disorders emphasized six prominent categories: anxiety disorders, somatoform disorders, dissociative disorders, mood disorders, schizophrenia, and personality disorders.

Remember that you can obtain a more detailed overview of the chapter by again studying the three summary tables on pages 376, 384, and 395.

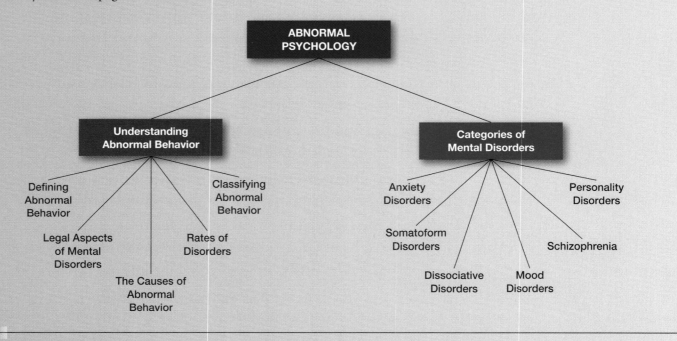

Key Terms

abnormal behavior 370
insanity defense 371
medical model 372
neurotic 375
psychotic 375
DSM-IV 375
multiaxial system 375
anxiety disorders 377
generalized anxiety disorder 378
panic disorder 378

agoraphobia 379
phobic disorder 379
obsessive-compulsive disorder (OCD) 380
post-traumatic stress disorder 380
somatoform disorders 381
hypochondriasis 381
conversion disorder 382
dissociative disorders 382
dissociative amnesia 382

dissociative fugue 382
dissociative identity disorder (DID) 382
mood disorders 385
depressive disorders 385
major depressive disorder 385
dysthymic disorder 385
bipolar disorder 386
learned helplessness 388
schizophrenia 389

disorganized schizophrenia 391
catatonic schizophrenia 391
paranoid schizophrenia 391
undifferentiated schizophrenia 391
diathesis–stress view 392
personality disorders 393
antisocial personality disorder 394

Key People

Sigmund Freud 388   John Bowlby 388   Martin Seligman 389

Taking It to the Net

1. Imagine you are sitting in a movie theater enjoying a film when all of the sudden your heart starts to race. You begin to tremble, sweat, and feel very dizzy. Because there are no explanations for this event, you think you are either having a heart attack or going crazy. In fact, you have just experienced a panic attack, the hallmark of panic disorder. What are the causes of panic disorder and what can be done about it? Can people with panic disorder lead normal lives? Explain.

2. Have you ever felt depressed? Chances are that you answered yes, but this might be because you are using a different meaning of the word. Where do you think the line is drawn between feeling "the blues" and clinical depression? To be clinically depressed, there are strict criteria that must be met. What are those criteria? How are they different from merely feeling "the blues"? What are some of the effective treatments for depression?

3. Seasonal affective disorder (SAD) is a disorder in which mood and behavior are affected by time of year. Therefore, during winter seasons, some people become very depressed, they eat more, have trouble sleeping, and feel lethargic. Interestingly, researchers have discovered that the symptoms can be alleviated by exposure to bright light for extended periods of time. So, people with SAD sit in front of a special bright light every day, and although the light is otherwise completely normal, their symptoms are alleviated. Why do you suppose that bright light helps these people? Would moving to a location with more sunlight also improve their moods? Explain.

Connect to http://www.mhhe.com/psychology/santrock to find the answers!

12

CHAPTER OUTLINE

Images of Psychology and Life
Should I End My Life Today?

MANY PEOPLE today seek therapy. Some, like Linda whom you will read about shortly, seek insight about their depression. Others may need help overcoming trauma, such as physical or sexual abuse in childhood. And others may be in the throes of conflict with a partner, in the immobilizing grip of fears such as agoraphobia, or immersed in the delusions of schizophrenia. Whatever the reason people seek therapy, there are many different approaches to help them—at last count more than 400. These are some of the questions that we will explore in this chapter:

- How were individuals with a mental disorder dealt with at different points in history?
- What are some approaches to psychotherapy?
- What is it like to go to a therapist with a particular approach?
- How effective is psychotherapy? Are some types of psychotherapy more effective with some mental disorders than others?
- What are biomedical therapies like? Which drugs are most effective in treating particular mental disorders?

LINDA TRIED HARD to listen to what Sally, her college roommate, was saying, but as soon as Sally said "Linda, do you think something is wrong with you? Should you go talk to someone?" the wind went right out of her and her thoughts began spinning wildly. She had known for a long time that she had been losing it, but she thought she was maintaining her outward image as the most together person in the dorm. For weeks her feelings of sadness and worthlessness had been getting worse. She could not see any hope for the future, and she fought valiantly just to keep going. Every morning she woke at 4 A.M. and just lay there wondering if this was the day she should just end it all. Now that Sally was telling her that the whole world could see her the way she saw herself, it seemed more hopeless than ever.

But Sally was now saying something about her own experience with an eating problem and how a psychologist at the health service had helped her. Sally? Problems? They didn't go together at all. Sally had always seemed so self-confident. Maybe Linda should go talk to the health service people. After all, if it didn't help, she could always kill herself tomorrow. Sally asked if she should make the call for her, and Linda agreed.

Three torturous hours later, Linda found herself in a comfortable office talking with a psychotherapist, Dr. Simmons. He told her that he was a clinical psychologist, was reassuring, and asked a lot of questions. She had been so afraid that he would just sit there and make her explain the unexplainable, but he seemed to know that would be the wrong strategy for her. As he talked, she could feel herself unwinding. After awhile she started to cry and continued to cry for what seemed like hours, although only 10 minutes had passed. Linda was amazed that Dr. Simmons just sat there quietly, yet somehow made her feel supported. He never asked what she was crying about. The fact was, she had absolutely no idea, and he seemed to understand that before she did. He said that people were very complicated, especially when they were going through difficult times, and it would take a little time to figure things out, but they would work through this together.

Dr. Simmons surprised her when he asked for her promise that she would stay alive while they took this journey. That seemed fair, as long as she could kill herself later. Linda was even more surprised at how relieved she felt when she agreed to his request.

Dr. Simmons said the next day or two would be very busy. He was scheduling her for some testing that would help both of them understand her better, and then they would decide together how they should proceed.

His voice echoed softly in her ear as she walked back to her room: "Linda, you would be amazed at how many college students go through something like you are experiencing now and go on to happy, productive lives." At first she could not identify the feeling that passed over her. It had been so long since she had felt anything like it, but as she got to her room she realized that she was feeling hopeful for the first time in months (Harmatz, 1997).

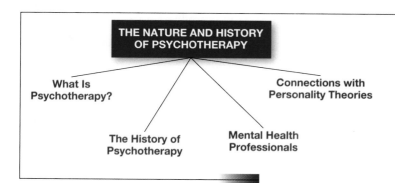

The Nature and History of Psychotherapy

To begin, we will explore what psychotherapy is, then turn to psychotherapy's intriguing history, which includes early efforts to cure people's psychological problems by cutting holes in their skulls. Then we will discuss the range of mental health professionals and describe the ties of different psychotherapy approaches to personality theories.

Psychotherapy

What Is Psychotherapy?

Psychotherapy *is the process used by mental health professionals to help individuals recognize, define, and overcome their psychological and interpersonal difficulties and improve their adjustment.* Psychotherapists use a number of strategies to accomplish these goals: talking, interpreting, listening, rewarding, and modeling, for example.

The History of Psychotherapy

To begin our exploration of therapies, let's trace the evolution of views and treatments from ancient times to the twentieth century. In this journey, you will see how views have changed from a focus on supernatural causes to natural causes.

Early History   In primitive societies, abnormal behavior was thought to be caused by evil spirits residing within the afflicted person. *Trephining,* which involved chipping a hole in the skull, was one early method of letting the evil spirit escape (see figure 12.1). The Greek physician Hippocrates, however, believed that mental problems and abnormal behavior were the result of brain damage or an imbalance of body fluids. In the fourth century B.C., Hippocrates prescribed rest, exercise, a bland diet, and abstinence from sex and alcohol as cures for depression.

Over time, Hippocrates' ideas were lost. In the Middle Ages, theories of "possession" by evil spirits or the devil again became popular. People who simply were "different" or who suffered from neurological disorders such as Tourette's syndrome or epilepsy were thought to be possessed or witches. *Exorcism,* a religious rite that involved prayer, starvation, beatings, and various forms of torture, was used to cast out evil spirits. The notion behind exorcism was to make the mentally disordered people so physically uncomfortable that no devil would want to stay in their bodies. If that didn't work, the only "cure" left was to get rid of the body altogether. Between the fourteenth and seventeenth centuries, 200,000 to 500,000 people thought to be witches were either hanged or burned at the stake.

*F*igure 12.1
Trephining

The technique of trephining involved chipping a hole in the skull through which an evil spirit, believed to be the source of the person's abnormal behavior, might escape. The fact that some people actually survived the operation is shown by this skull. The bone had had time to heal considerably before the individual died.

During the Renaissance, *asylums* (*asylum* means "sanctuary") were built to house the mentally disordered. Mentally disordered people were placed in an asylum to protect them from the exploitation they experienced on the streets. But the asylums were not much better; the mentally disordered often were chained to walls, caged, or fed sparingly.

Fortunately, Philippe Pinel (1745–1826), the head physician at a large asylum in Paris, initiated a significant change in the treatment of the mentally disordered. Pinel described them as ordinary people who could not reason well because of their serious personal problems. He believed that treating the mentally disordered like animals was not only inhumane but also hindered their recovery. Pinel convinced the French government to unchain large numbers of patients, some of whom had not been outside of the asylum for 30 to 40 years (see figure 12.2). He replaced the dungeons with bright rooms and spent long hours talking with patients, listening to their problems and giving advice.

Although Pinel's efforts led to reform, it was slow. Even as late as the nineteenth century in the United States, the mentally disordered were kept alongside criminals in prisons. Dorothea Dix, a nurse who had taken a position at a prison in the middle of the nineteenth century, was instrumental in getting the mentally disordered separated from criminals. She embarked on a state-to-state campaign to upgrade prisons and persuaded officials to use better judgment in deciding which individuals should be placed in prisons. State governments began building large asylums for the mentally disordered because of Dix's efforts, although the conditions in the asylums often were no better than in the prisons.

Mental Hospitals and Deinstitutionalization

In the first half of the twentieth century, severely mentally disordered individuals were usually institutionalized for life in large state mental hospitals (Lamb, 1998). In 1955, when the numbers of people in state hospitals reached their peak, more than 500,000 of the nation's 165 million people were housed there. By the mid-1990s, those figures had dropped to just over 70,000 individuals out of a total U.S. population of more than 250 million.

Deinstitutionalization *is the movement to transfer the treatment of mental disorders from inpatient mental hospitals to community-based facilities that stress outpatient care.* Why was deinstitutionalization possible? New drugs for treating the severely mentally disordered, especially individuals with schizophrenia, meant that large numbers of people could be released from mental institutions and treated in community-based facilities. As indicated in figure 12.3, controversy still characterizes the release of severely mentally disordered individuals from mental hospitals.

In 1963, Congress passed the Community Mental Health Center Act, which provided funds for establishing one facility for every 50,000 individuals in the nation. The centers were designed to meet two basic goals: (1) to provide community-based mental health services, and (2) to commit resources to help prevent mental disorders as well as treat them. Outpatient care is one of the important services that community health centers provide. Individuals can attend therapy sessions at the center and still keep their job and live with their family. Community mental health centers have successfully helped large numbers of people with psychological problems (Seidman & French, 1998). They especially have been important in reaching people in low-income neighborhoods who have mental health problems, many of whom otherwise would never have received psychological help (Price, 2000).

Figure 12.2
Pinel Unchaining Mentally Disordered Individuals

In this painting, Philippe Pinel is shown unchaining the inmates at La Bicêtre Hospital. Pinel's efforts led to widespread reform and more humane treatment of mentally disordered individuals.

Even after Pinel and others reformed mental institutions, some rather strange techniques were invented to control the most difficult mentally disordered individuals. This tranquilizing chair was used to calm mentally disordered individuals at the beginning of the nineteenth century. Fortunately, its use was soon abandoned.

$\mathcal{F}$igure 12.3
Deinstitutionalization: Ongoing Controversy

The increased use of drug therapy in mental institutions facilitated the transfer of many mental patients back to the community. The architects of deinstitutionalization believed that these individuals could be given medication to keep them stabilized until they could find continuing care. However, many residents of mental health institutions have no families or homes to go to and community mental health facilities are not adequately equipped to deal with the severe cases. Many individuals who are discharged from state mental hospitals join the ranks of "the homeless." Of course, though, not all homeless people are former mental patients. Controversy continues about whether individuals should be discharged so readily from state mental institutions, which usually struggle with underfunding and staff shortages.

Recent Development   Psychotherapy can be expensive. Even though reduced fees and in some cases free services can be arranged in public hospital and community mental health centers, many people who most need psychotherapy don't get it. Psychotherapists have been criticized for limiting their work to young, attractive, verbal, intelligent, and successful clients (YAVISes) rather than quiet, ugly, old, institutionalized, and different clients (called QUOIDs). Mental health professionals have become increasingly sensitive to this problem, but it still has not been completely solved.

The challenge of paying for psychotherapy has led to substantial changes in mental health care delivery in recent years (Berman, 2000; Pipes & Davenport, 1999). **Managed care** *consists of strategies for controlling health-care costs, including mental health treatment, and demands for accountability of treatment success.* This typically is accomplished by interjecting a managed care organization between the mental health client and the providers of mental health services. Managed care providers attempt to offer services at lower costs by limiting traditional services, using stringent review procedures, and using lower-cost brief treatment options (Villani & Sharfstein, 1999). Managed care emerged in the early 1980s and has grown dramatically (Hoge, 1998).

Criticisms of managed care abound and include these (Butcher, 1997; Giles & Marafiote, 1998; Lazarus, 1996; Roback & others, 1999):

- Managed care organizations are reluctant to provide for more than a few therapy sessions for a given patient
- Long-term psychotherapy has been eliminated except for a relatively few wealthy clients who can pay their own way
- Some managed care organizations are employing less well-trained therapists who work at lower fees

Managed Care
Mental Health Advocacy

Mental Health Professionals

Psychotherapy is practiced by a variety of mental health professionals, including clinical psychologists, psychiatrists, and counselors. You might recall from chapter 1 that psychiatrists have a medical degree. Clinical psychologists, by contrast, are trained in graduate programs in psychology. Figure 12.4 lists the main types of mental health professionals, their degrees, the years of education required, and the nature of their training.

Professional Type	Degree	Education Beyond Bachelor's Degree	Nature of Training
Clinical psychologist	Ph.D. or Psy.D	5–7 years	Includes both clinical and research training. Involves a 1-year internship in a psychiatric hospital or mental health facility. Recently some universities have developed Psy.D. programs, which lead to a professional degree with a stronger clinical than research emphasis. The Psy.D. training program takes about the same number of years as the clinical psychology Ph.D. program and also requires the equivalent of a 1-year internship.
Psychiatrist	M.D.	7–9 years	Four years of medical school, plus an internship and residency in psychiatry are required. A psychiatry residency involves supervision in therapies, including psychotherapy and biomedical therapy.
Counseling psychologist	M.A., Ph.D., Psy.D., or Ed.D.	3–7 years	Similar to clinical psychologist with emphasis on counseling and therapy. Some counseling psychologists specialize in vocational counseling. Some counselors complete master's degree training, others Ph.D. or Ed.D training, in graduate schools of psychology or education.
School psychologist	M.A., Ph.D., Psy.D., or Ed.D.	3–7 years	Training in graduate programs of education or psychology. Emphasis on psychological assessment and counseling practices involving students' school-related problems. Training is at the master's or doctoral level.
Social worker	M.S.W./D.S.W. or Ph.D.	2–5 years	Graduate work in a school of social work that includes specialized clinical training in mental health facilities.
Psychiatric nurse	R.N., M.A., or Ph.D.	0–5 years	Graduate work in a school of nursing with special emphasis on care of mentally disturbed individuals in hospital settings and mental health facilities.
Occupational therapist	B.S., M.A., or Ph.D.	0–5 years	Emphasis on occupational training with focus on physically or psychologically handicapped individuals. Stresses getting individuals back into the mainstream of work.
Pastoral counselor	None to Ph.D. or D.D. (Doctor of Divinity)	0–5 years	Requires ministerial background and training in psychology. An internship in a mental health facility as a chaplain is recommended.
Counselor	M.A. or M.Ed.	2 years	Graduate work in a department of psychology or department of education with specialized training in counseling techniques.

Figure 12.4
Main Types of Mental Health Professionals

Licensing and certification are two ways that society retains control over individuals who practice psychotherapy (Harmatz, 1997). Laws at the state level are used to license or certify such professionals. These laws vary in toughness from one state to another, but invariably they specify the training the mental health professional must have and provide for some assessment of the applicant's skill through formal examination. Licensing boards exist to protect the public from unscrupulous individuals who might use the title *psychologist* to offer treatment and collect payment without sufficient training to do so.

Licensing and certification require mental health practitioners to engage in ethical practices. Laws typically address the importance of doing no harm to clients, protecting the privacy of clients, and avoiding inappropriate relationships with clients. Violations of ethical codes can result in a loss of the license to practice psychotherapy (Wierzbicki, 1999).

Connections with Personality Theories

Many of the theories of personality we discussed in chapter 10 are foundations for some important approaches to psychotherapy. The psychoanalytic theories of Freud and his dissenters and revisionists underlie the psychodynamic therapies ◀|||| P. 337. The humanistic theories of Rogers and Maslow provide an important foundation for the humanistic therapies ◀|||| P. 348. The term **insight therapy** *characterizes both psychodynamic and humanistic therapies because their goal is to encourage insight and self-awareness.*

The behavioral and social learning theories of Skinner and Bandura, as well as Pavlov's classical conditioning (Chapter 5, "Learning"), stimulated the development of the behavior therapies ◀|||| P. 144. Other important approaches to psychotherapy we will discuss include cognitive therapy and group therapy.

At this point we have discussed many ideas about the nature and history of psychotherapy. An overview of these ideas is presented in summary table 12.1. Next, we will begin our evaluation of psychotherapies with the insight therapies, first examining psychodynamic therapies, and then turning to humanistic therapies.

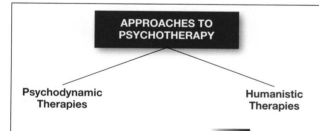

APPROACHES TO PSYCHOTHERAPY

Psychodynamic Therapies   Humanistic Therapies

Exploring Psychotherapies

Approaches to Psychotherapy

Our coverage of psychotherapies will focus on these main approaches: psychodynamic, humanistic, behavioral, cognitive, and group. Figure 12.5 provides an overview of these approaches. The cognitive map outlines the two main approaches that we will discuss before the next summary table. We begin our discussion of psychotherapies with the psychodynamic approaches because they are the oldest of the approaches.

Psychodynamic Therapies

Our study of psychodynamic therapies focuses on their basic nature, Freud's psychoanalysis, and contemporary psychodynamic therapies.

The **psychodynamic therapies** *stress the importance of the unconscious mind, extensive interpretation by the therapist, and the role of experiences in early childhood.* Many psychodynamic approaches have grown out of Freud's psychoanalytic theory of personality. Today some therapists with a psychodynamic perspective show allegiance to Freud, others do not (Watkins & Guarnaccia, 1999).

Freud's Psychoanalysis   Freud once said that if your give psychoanalysis your little finger, it will soon have your whole hand. As you read about the basic philosophy of psychoanalysis and its therapy techniques, you will see that Freud believed the therapist acts like a psychological detective, sometimes taking the smallest clue and using it as a springboard for understanding the individual's major problems. Let's see how one analyst approached an individual's problems.

SUMMARY TABLE 12.1
The Nature and History of Psychology

Concept	Processes/Related Ideas	Characteristics/Description
What Is Psychotherapy?	Its Nature	Psychotherapy is the process used by mental health professionals to help individuals recognize, define, and overcome their psychological difficulties and improve their adjustment.
The History of Psychotherapy	Early History	Many early treatments of mental disorders were inhumane. Asylums were built during the Renaissance. Pinel's efforts led to extensive reform. Dix's efforts helped to separate mentally disordered individuals from prisoners.
	Mental Hospitals and Deinstitutionalization	In 1955, the mental hospital population in the United States reached a peak. In the last half of the twentieth century this population dropped dramatically. Deinstitutionalization is the movement to transfer the treatment of mental disorders from inpatient mental hospitals to community-based facilities that stress outpatient care. Deinstitutionalization was possible because of advances made in drug therapy. Community mental health centers have successfully reached many people who otherwise might not have received help for their mental problems, especially individuals in low-income neighborhoods.
	Recent Developments	Psychotherapy can be expensive, and a special concern continues to be reaching people who are in the most need of psychotherapy. The challenge of paying for psychotherapy has led to substantial changes in mental health care delivery in recent years. Managed care consists of strategies for controlling health care costs, including mental health treatment, and demands for accountability of treatment success. Numerous criticisms of managed care have been made.
Mental Health Professionals	Who Are They?	They include clinical and counseling psychologists, psychiatrists, school psychologists, social workers, psychiatric nurses, occupational therapists, pastoral counselors, and counselors. These mental health professionals have different degrees, education, and training. Licensing and certification are two ways society retains control over individuals who practice psychotherapy.
Connections with Personality Theories	Their Nature	Many of the theories of personality—psychoanalytic, humanistic, and behavioral—serve as foundations for main approaches to psychotherapy. The term *insight therapy* characterizes both psychodynamic and humanistic therapies because their goal is to encourage insight and self-awareness.

Psychoanalysis

A 50-year-old business executive came to therapy because he felt depressed and anxious and these feelings wouldn't go away. Although he was perceived as being very successful by his family and business associates, he perceived himself to be weak and incompetent. Through many sessions, the psychoanalyst had begun to suspect that the man's feelings of failure stemmed from his childhood experiences with a punitive and critical father, who was even more successful than his son. The father never seemed to be satisfied with the son's efforts. Following is an exchange between the analyst and the businessman that occurred about one year into therapy (Davison & Neale, 1994, p. 533):

Client: "I don't really feel like talking today."
Analyst: Remains silent for several minutes, then says "Perhaps you would like to talk about why you don't feel like talking."
Client: "There you go again, making demands on me, insisting I do what I just don't feel up to doing. (Pause) Do I always have to talk here, when I don't feel like it? (Voice becomes angry and petulant) Can't you just get off my back? You don't really care how I feel."

PSYCHODYNAMIC	HUMANISTIC	BEHAVIOR	COGNITIVE	GROUP
• Freud's psychoanalysis • Contemporary psychodynamic therapies	• Person-centered therapy • Gestalt therapy	• Classical conditioning • Operant conditioning	• Cognitive-behavior • Rational-emotive • Beck's cognitive	• Family/couple • Self-help
Emphasize the unconscious mind, extensive interpretation by the therapist, and early child experiences	Emphasize self-understanding, personal growth, conscious thoughts, the present rather than past, and fulfillment	Emphasize principles of learning to reduce or eliminate maladaptive behavior	Emphasize that the individual's cognition or thoughts are the main source of abnormal behavior and mood; attempt to change the person's feelings and behaviors by changing cognitions	Emphasize solving people's mental problems through experiences in a group rather than an individual therapy session; focus is on interpersonal relationships

Figure 12.5
Overview of Main Psychotherapy Approaches

We will be discussing these five main psychotherapy approaches. For each, this figure lists several representatives of the approach and gives a brief description of the approach.

Analyst: "I wonder why you feel I don't care?"
Client: "Because you're always pressuring me to do what I feel I can't do."

This exchange was interpreted by the analyst as an expression of resentment by the client of his *father's* pressures that were put on him and had little to do with the analyst himself. The transfer of the client's feelings from the father to the analyst was regarded as significant by the analyst and was used in subsequent sessions to help the client overcome his fear of expressing anger toward his father.

Psychoanalysis *is Freud's therapeutic technique for analyzing an individual's un-conscious thought.* Freud believed that clients' current problems could be traced to childhood experiences, many of which involved conflicts about sexuality. He also recognized that the early experiences were not readily available to the individual's conscious mind. Only through extensive questioning, probing, and analyzing was Freud able to put the pieces of the person's personality together and help the individual become aware of how these early experiences were affecting present adult behavior.

To reach the shadowy world of the unconscious, psychoanalytic therapists often use the following therapeutic techniques: free association, catharsis, interpretation, dream analysis, analysis of transference, and analysis of resistance, each of which we discuss in turn.

One technique used by psychoanalysts is **free association,** *which consists of encouraging individuals to say aloud whatever comes to mind no matter how trivial or embarrassing.* When Freud detected a person resisting the spontaneous flow of thoughts, he probed further. He believed that the crux of the person's emotional problem probably lurked below this point of resistance. By encouraging people to talk freely, Freud thought, emotional feelings would emerge. **Catharsis** *is the psychoanalytic term for people's release of emotional tension when they relive an emotionally charged and conflicted experience.*

Interpretation plays an important role in psychoanalysis. As the therapist interprets free association and dreams, the person's statements and behavior are not taken at face value. To understand what is truly causing the person's conflicts, the therapist constantly

To encourage his patients to relax, Freud had them recline on the couch while he sat in the chair on the left, out of their view.

searches for symbolic, hidden meanings in what the individual says and does. From time to time the therapist suggests possible meanings of the person's statements and behavior. Explorations in Psychology provides an example of how a psychoanalyst used interpretation to improve a woman's understanding of her problems.

Dream analysis *is the psychotherapeutic technique used by psychoanalysts to interpret a person's dream.* Psychoanalysts believe dreams contain information about the individual's unconscious thoughts and conflicts ◀▥ P. 129. Freud distinguished between the dream's manifest and latent content. **Manifest content** *is the psychoanalytic term for the conscious, remembered aspects of a dream.* **Latent content** *is the psychoanalytic term for the unconscious, unremembered, symbolic aspects of a dream.* The psychoanalyst interprets the dream by analyzing the manifest content for disguised unconscious wishes and needs, especially those that are sexual and aggressive in nature. For some examples of the sexual symbols psychoanalysts use to interpret dreams, see figure 12.6. But even Freud cautioned against overinterpreting. As he once quipped, "Sometimes a cigar is just a cigar."

Freud believed transference was an inevitable and essential aspect of the analyst-patient relationship. **Transference** *is the psychoanalytic term for the person's relating to the analyst in ways that reproduce or relive important relationships in the individual's life.* A person might interact with an analyst as if the analyst were a parent or lover, for example. When transference dominates therapy, the person's comments may become directed toward the analyst's personal life. Transference is often difficult to overcome in psychotherapy. However, transference can be used therapeutically as a model of how individuals relate to important people in their lives (Boyer, 1999; Gelso & others, 1999).

Resistance *is the psychoanalytic term for the person's unconscious defense strategies that prevent the analyst from understanding the person's problems.* Resistance occurs because it is painful to bring conflicts into conscious awareness. By resisting therapy, individuals do not have to face their problems. Showing up late or missing sessions, arguing with the psychoanalyst, or faking free associations are examples of resistance. Some people go on endlessly about a trivial matter to avoid facing their conflicts. A major goal of the analyst is to break through this resistance (Strean, 1996).

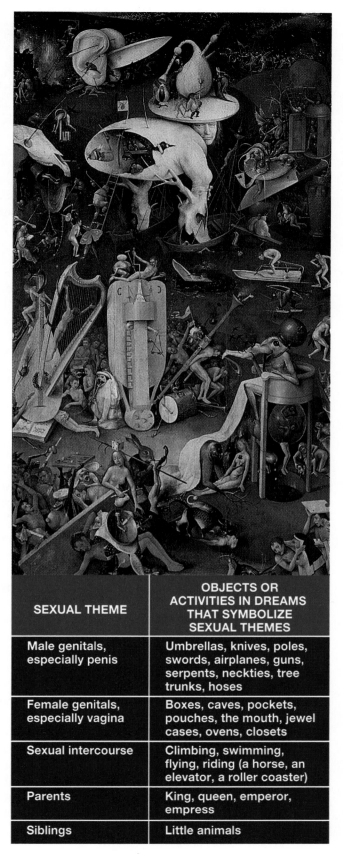

SEXUAL THEME	OBJECTS OR ACTIVITIES IN DREAMS THAT SYMBOLIZE SEXUAL THEMES
Male genitals, especially penis	Umbrellas, knives, poles, swords, airplanes, guns, serpents, neckties, tree trunks, hoses
Female genitals, especially vagina	Boxes, caves, pockets, pouches, the mouth, jewel cases, ovens, closets
Sexual intercourse	Climbing, swimming, flying, riding (a horse, an elevator, a roller coaster)
Parents	King, queen, emperor, empress
Siblings	Little animals

Figure 12.6
Freudian Interpretation of Sexual Symbolism in Dreams

EXPLORATIONS IN PSYCHOLOGY
Penetrating Mrs. A. H.'s Thoughts

MRS. A. H. BEGAN her session with a psychoanalyst by describing how her husband, a businessman, had been caught in a financial squeeze and had anxiously gone to the bank to raise additional funds. She was in a state of panic, even though there was a good probability her husband would be able to obtain a loan from the bank. The previous night she had had diarrhea and had dreamed that her two sisters were discussing her mother, saying that she seldom did all that she had promised to others. Mrs. A. H. then commented that her mother had been wealthy and could have provided all the money her husband needed. Her father could have too, she said, but he was hard to deal with. She went on to recall her mother's involvement with another man and the illness her mother had had when Mrs. A. H. was an infant. Her sisters, who were considerably older, had taken care of their mother, but Mrs. A. H. wondered why they criticized their mother, who had been briefly hospitalized. They tended to blame poor health habits for her illness. Mrs. A. H. also reviewed her adolescent years, during which her mother denied the impact of her absence. She thought her mother's attitude was rather bizarre.

The psychoanalytic session seemed to be prompted by the husband's financial crisis and the repercussions it had for Mrs. A. H.'s longings for her mother, who would rescue her and her husband; her rage at her mother for her absence and possible unfaithfulness; and some implied concerns regarding her husband's ability to handle the business situation. There was little in the session to suggest what unconscious thoughts were evoking the gastrointestinal symptoms.

However, this session is intriguing in the light of the next session that took place. In that session, Mrs. A. H. revealed she inadvertently had not mentioned an incident that had occurred prior to the previous session. One of her girlfriends had seen her husband having a drink with an attractive woman at a local restaurant. In this context, the psychoanalyst was able to gain more insight into what Mrs. A. H. had said in the previous session. In fact, she had used the past to conceal the present. She had used her mother as a screen to hide her most active and meaningful conflicts and unconscious fantasies about her husband. In the second session, her free associations related to fears of finding out that her husband was having an affair, to her dread of confronting him, and to her anxiety that others would be talking about his having an affair. The associations revealed her rage, her wishes to publicly humiliate him, and her death wishes toward him. The sister in the dream had also been suspected of having an affair. The bowel symptoms actually related to fantasies of defecating on and soiling her husband in an uncontrolled release of aggression, according to the analyst (Langs, 1978).

"Looking good!"

Contemporary Psychodynamic Therapies   Although the face of psychodynamic therapy has changed extensively since its inception almost a century ago, many contemporary psychodynamic therapists still probe a person's unconscious thoughts about early childhood experiences to provide clues to the person's current problems (Comarow & Chescheir, 1999). Many contemporary psychodynamic therapists also try to help individuals gain insight into their emotionally laden, repressed conflicts (Horowitz, 1998; Luborsky, 2000).

However, only a small percentage of contemporary psychodynamic therapists rigorously follow Freud's guidelines. Although many psychodynamic therapists still emphasize the importance of unconscious thought and early family experiences, they also accord more power to the conscious mind and current relationships in understanding a person's problems. Individuals rarely lie on a couch or see their therapist several times a week. Now people usually have weekly appointments and sit in a comfortable chair facing their therapist.

Contemporary psychodynamic approaches emphasize the development of the self in social contexts (Erikson, 1968; Horowitz, 1998; Kohut, 1977; St. Clair, 1996; Summers, 1999). In Heinz Kohut's view, early relationships with attachment figures, such as one's parents, are critical. As we develop we do not relinquish these attachments; we continue to need them. Kohut's prescription for therapy involves getting the person to identify and seek out appropriate relationships with others. He also wants individuals to develop more realistic appraisals of relationships. Kohut believes therapists need to interact with individuals in ways that are empathic and understanding. As we will see next, empathy and understanding are absolute cornerstones for humanistic therapists as they encourage individuals to further their sense of self.

Humanistic Therapies

To understand the humanistic therapies we will describe their basic nature, then turn to two representatives of this approach: person-centered therapy and Gestalt therapy.

The underlying philosophy of humanistic therapies is captured by the metaphor of how an acorn, if provided with appropriate conditions, will grow in positive ways, pushing naturally toward its actualization as an oak (Corey, 1996). In the **humanistic therapies,** *people are encouraged to understand themselves and to grow personally.* In contrast to the psychoanalytic therapies, the humanistic therapies emphasize conscious rather than unconscious thoughts, the present rather than the past, and growth and self-fulfillment rather than illness ◀▥ P. 348.

Person-Centered Therapy

Person-Centered Therapy

Therapist:	"Everything's lousy, huh? You feel lousy. (Silence of 39 seconds). Want to come in Friday at 12 at the usual time?"
Client:	(Yawns and mutters something unintelligible). (Silence of 48 seconds).
Therapist:	"Just kind of feel sunk way down deep in those lousy, lousy feelings, hm? Is that something like it?"
Client:	"No."
Therapist:	"No?" (Silence of 20 seconds).
Client:	"No. I'm just no good to anybody, never was, and never will be."
Therapist:	"Feeling that now, hm? That you're no good to yourself, no good to anybody. Just that you're completely worthless, huh? Those are really lousy feelings. Just feel that you're no good at all, hm?"

This is an excerpt from a therapy session conducted by a person-centered therapist with a young man who was depressed. The therapist was Carl Rogers (Meador & Rogers, 1979). Notice how Rogers unconditionally accepted the client's feelings. **Person-centered therapy** *is a form of humanistic therapy developed by Carl Rogers (1961, 1980) in which the therapist provides a warm, supportive atmosphere to improve the client's self-concept and encourage the client to gain insight about problems.* Rogers' therapy was initially called client-centered therapy, but he rechristened it person-centered therapy to underscore his deep belief that every person has the ability to grow. The relationship between the therapist and the person is an important aspect of Rogers' therapy. The therapist must enter into an intensely personal relationship with the client, not as a physician diagnosing a disease, but as one human being to another. Notice that Rogers referred to the "client" and then the "person" rather than the "patient."

You might recall from chapter 10, "Personality," that Rogers believed each of us grows up in a world filled with *conditions of worth,* the positive regard we received from others that has strings attached. We usually do not receive love and praise unless we conform to the standards and demands of others. This causes us to be unhappy and have low self-esteem. Rarely do we feel that we measure up to such standards or that we are as good as others expect us to be.

To free the person from worry about the society's demands, the therapist engages in **unconditional positive regard** *in which the therapist creates a warm and caring environment, never disapproving of the client.* Rogers believed this unconditional positive regard improves the person's self-esteem. The therapist's role is "nondirective," that is, he or she does not lead the client to any particular revelation. The therapist is there to listen sympathetically to the client's

*T*hrough the Eyes of Psychologists

Carl Rogers *(1902–1987)*

"People who enter psychotherapy are often asking: How can I discover my real self? How can I become what I deeply wish to become?"

problems and to encourage positive self-regard, independent self-appraisal, and decision making (Hill, 2000). Though person-centered therapists give approval of the person, they do not always approve of the person's behavior.

In addition to unconditional positive regard, Rogers also advocated the use of these techniques in person-centered therapy:

- *Genuineness,* which involves letting a client know the therapist's feelings and not hiding behind a facade.
- *Accurate empathy,* which focuses on the therapist's identification with the client. Rogers believed that therapists must sense what it is like to be the client at any moment in the client-therapist relationship.
- *Active listening,* which consists of giving total attention to what the person says and means. One way therapists improve active listening is to restate and support what the client has said and done.

Gestalt Therapy

Gestalt Therapy **Gestalt therapy** *is a humanistic therapy developed by Fritz Perls (1893–1970) in which the therapist questions and challenges clients to help clients become more aware of their feelings and face their problems.* Perls was trained in Europe as a Freudian psychoanalyst, but as his career developed, his ideas became different from Freud's. Perls (1969) agreed with Freud that psychological problems originate in unresolved past conflicts and that these conflicts need to be acknowl-

$\mathcal{S}$UMMARY $\mathcal{T}$ABLE 12.2
The Psychodynamic and Humanistic Therapies

Concept	Processes/ Related Ideas	Characteristics/Description
Psychodynamic Therapies	Its Nature	They stress the importance of the unconscious mind, early family experiences, and extensive interpretation by therapists.
	Freud's Psychoanalysis	Mental disorders are caused by unresolved unconscious; the conflicts originate in early childhood family experiences. A therapist's interpretation of free association, dreams, transference, and resistance provides tools for understanding a client's unconscious conflicts.
	Contemporary Psychodynamic Therapies	Although psychodynamic therapy has changed, many contemporary psychodynamic therapists still probe the unconscious mind for early family experiences that might provide clues to clients' current problems. The development of the self in social contexts is an important theme in Kohut's contemporary approach.
Humanistic Therapies	Their Nature	Clients are encouraged to understand themselves and to grow personally. The humanistic therapies emphasize conscious thoughts, the present, and growth and fulfillment.
	Person-Centered Therapy	This therapy was developed by Carl Rogers; a therapist provides a warm, supportive atmosphere to improve a client's self-concept and to encourage the client to gain insight into problems. The therapist replaces conditions of worth with unconditional positive regard and uses genuineness, accurate empathy, and active listening to raise the client's self-esteem.
	Gestalt Therapy	This therapy was developed by Fritz Perls. In this approach, therapists question and challenge clients to help them become more aware of their feelings and face their problems. Gestalt psychologists use a number of therapy techniques, including setting examples and role playing. Gestalt therapy's techniques are more directive than person-centered therapies.

edged and worked through. Also like Freud, Perls stressed that interpretation of dreams is an important aspect of therapy.

But in other ways, Perls and Freud were miles apart. Perls believed that unresolved conflicts should be brought to bear on the here and now of the individual's life. The therapist *pushes* clients into deciding whether they will continue to allow the past to control their future or whether they will choose *right now* what they want to be in the future. To this end, Perls *confronted* individuals and encouraged them to actively control their lives and be open about their feelings.

Gestalt therapists use a number of techniques to encourage individuals to be open about their feelings, to develop self-awareness, and to actively control their lives (Wertheimer, 2000). The therapist sets examples, encourages congruence between verbal and nonverbal behavior, and uses role playing. To demonstrate an important point to a client, the Gestalt therapist might exaggerate a client's characteristic. To stimulate change, the therapist often will openly confront the client.

Another technique used in Gestalt therapy is role playing, either by the client, the therapist, or both. For example, if an individual is bothered by conflict with her mother, the therapist might play the role of the mother and reopen the quarrel. The therapist might encourage the individual to act out her hostile feelings toward her mother by yelling, swearing, or kicking the couch, for example. In this way, Gestalt therapists hope to help individuals better manage their feelings instead of letting their feelings control them.

As you probably noticed, the Gestalt therapist is much more directive than the nondirective, person-centered therapist. By being more directive, the Gestalt therapist provides more interpretation and feedback. Nonetheless, both of these humanistic therapies encourage individuals to take responsibility for their feelings and actions, to truly be themselves, to understand themselves, to develop a sense of freedom, and to look at what they are doing with their lives.

At this point we have studied a number of ideas about the insight therapies—psychodynamic and humanistic. An overview of these ideas is presented in summary table 12.2. Now that we have explored the insight therapies, we turn our attention to therapies that take a very different approach to working with individuals to reduce their problems and improve their adjustment—the behavior therapies.

Frederick (Fritz) Perls was the founder of Gestalt therapy.

Behavior Therapies

Behavior therapies offer action-oriented strategies to help people change what they are doing. We will describe their basic nature, then turn to two main approaches: classical conditioning and operant conditioning.

Behavior therapies *use principles of learning to reduce or eliminate maladaptive behavior.* Behavior therapies are based on the behavioral and social cognitive theories of learning and personality ◀🔢 P. 346. Behavior therapists do not search for unconscious conflicts like psychodynamic therapists or encourage individuals to develop accurate perceptions of their feelings and self like humanistic therapists. Insight and self-awareness are not the keys to helping individuals develop more adaptive behavior patterns, say the behavior therapists.

Behavior therapists assume that the overt maladaptive symptoms are the problem (Adams, 2000; Sloan & Mizes, 1999). Individuals can become aware of why they are depressed and still be depressed, say the behavior therapists. The behavior therapist tries to eliminate the depressed symptoms or behaviors themselves rather than trying to get individuals to gain insight or awareness of why they are depressed (Lazarus, 1996).

The behavior therapies were initially based almost exclusively on the learning principles of classical and operant conditioning, but behavior therapies have become more diverse in recent years. As social cognitive theory grew in popularity, behavior therapists increasingly included observational learning, cognitive factors, and self-instruction in their efforts to help people with their problems (Maultsby & Wirga,

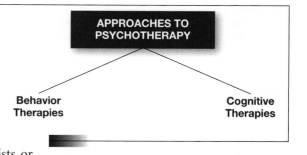

APPROACHES TO PSYCHOTHERAPY

Behavior Therapies

Cognitive Therapies

"Now relax.... Just like last week, I'm going to hold the cape up for the count of 10. ... When you start getting angry, I'll put it down."

1. On the way to the university on the day of an examination
2. In the process of answering an examination paper
3. Before the unopened doors of the examination room
4. Awaiting the distribution of examination papers
5. The examination paper lies face down before her
6. The night before an examination
7. One day before an examination
8. Two days before an examination
9. Three days before an examination
10. Four days before an examination
11. Five days before an examination
12. A week before an examination
13. Two weeks before an examination
14. A month before an examination

Figure 12.7
A Desensitization Hierarchy Involving Test Anxiety

In the above hierarchy, the individual begins with the least feared circumstance (a month before the exam) and moves through each of the circumstances until reaching the most feared circumstance (being on the way to the university the day of the examination). At each step of the way, the person replaces fear with deep relaxation and successful visualizations.

1998; Tracy, Sherry, & Albright, 1999). In self-instruction, therapists try to get people to change what they say to themselves. For now, though, let's focus on classical conditioning and operant conditioning.

Classical Conditioning Approaches   Some behaviors, especially fears, can be acquired or learned through classical conditioning ◀▥ P. 147. If such fears can be learned, possibly they can be unlearned as well. If an individual has learned to fear snakes or heights through classical conditioning, perhaps the individual can unlearn the fear.

The two main therapy techniques based on classical conditioning are systematic desensitization and aversive conditioning. **Systematic desensitization** is a *method of behavior therapy based on classical conditioning that treats anxiety by getting the person to associate deep relaxation with increasingly intense anxiety-producing situations* (Wolpe, 1963). Consider the common fear of giving a speech. Using systematic desensitization, the behavior therapist first asks the person which aspects of the feared situation—in this case, giving a speech—are the most and least frightening. Then, the behavior therapist arranges these circumstances in order from most to least frightening. An example of this type of desensitization hierarchy is shown in figure 12.7.

The next step is to teach individuals to relax. Clients are taught to recognize the presence of muscular contractions or tensions in various parts of their bodies and then how to contract and relax different muscles. Once individuals are relaxed, the therapist asks them to imagine the least fearful stimulus in the hierarchy. Subsequently, the therapist moves up the list of items from least to most fearful while clients remain relaxed. Eventually, individuals are able to imagine the most fearsome circumstance without being afraid—in our example, on the way to the university the day of the oral exam. In this manner, individuals learn to relax while thinking about the speech instead of feeling anxious.

Researchers have found that systematic desensitization is often an effective treatment for a number of phobias, such as fear of giving a speech, fear of heights, fear of flying, fear of dogs, and fear of snakes. If you were afraid of snakes, for instance, the therapist might initially have you watch someone handle a snake. Then the therapist would ask you to engage in increasingly more feared behaviors—you might first just go into the same room with the snake, next you would approach the snake, subsequently you'd touch the snake, and eventually you would play with the snake (Bandura, Blanchard, & Ritter, 1969). Figure 12.8 shows a desensitization treatment with individuals who were afraid of snakes.

The second main therapy technique that involves classical conditioning is **aversive conditioning,** *which consists of repeated pairings of the undesirable behavior with aversive stimuli to decrease the behavior's rewards.* Aversive conditioning is used to teach people to avoid such behaviors as smoking, eating, and drinking. Electric shocks, nausea-inducing substances, and verbal insults are some of the noxious stimuli used in aversive conditioning.

How could aversive conditioning be used to reduce a person's alcohol consumption? Every time a person drank an alcoholic beverage, he or she also would consume a mixture that induced nausea. In classical conditioning terminology, the alcoholic beverage is the conditioned stimulus and the nausea-inducing agent is the unconditioned stimulus. By repeatedly pairing alcohol with the nausea-inducing agent, alcohol becomes the conditioned stimulus that elicits nausea, the conditioned response. As a consequence, alcohol no longer is associated with something pleasant, but rather something highly unpleasant. Figure 12.9 illustrates how classical conditioning is the backbone of aversive conditioning.

Operant Conditioning Approaches   The basic philosophy of using operant conditioning as a therapy approach is that because maladaptive behavior patterns are learned, they can be unlearned. Therapy involves conducting a careful analysis of the person's environment to determine what factors need to be modified. Especially important is changing the consequences of the person's behavior to ensure that behavioral responses are followed by positive reinforcement.

Operant therapy's techniques focus on **behavior modification,** *the application of operant conditioning principles to change human behavior; its main goal is to replace unacceptable, maladaptive responses with acceptable, adaptive ones* ◀▥ P. 162. Consequences for behavior are established to ensure that acceptable actions are reinforced and unacceptable ones are not. Advocates of behavior modification believe that many emotional and behavioral problems are caused by inadequate (or inappropriate) response consequences (Stanley & Turner, 1995). Consider the circumstance in which Barbara and her parents are on a collision course. Things get so bad that her parents decide to see a clinical psychologist. The psychologist, who has a behavioral orientation, talks with each family member, trying to get them to pinpoint the problem. The psychologist gets the family to sign a behavioral contract that spells out what everyone needs to do to reduce the conflict. Barbara agrees to (1) be home before 11 P.M. on weeknights; (2) look for a part-time job so she can begin to pay for some of her activities; and (3) refrain from calling her parents insulting names. Her parents agree to (1) talk to Barbara in a low tone of voice rather than yell if they are angry; (2) refrain from criticizing young people, especially Barbara's friends; and (3) give Barbara a small sum of money each week for gas, makeup, and socializing, but only until she has found a job.

A **token economy** *is a behavior modification system in which behaviors are reinforced with tokens (such as poker chips) that later can be exchanged for desired rewards (such as candy, money, or going to a movie).* Token economies have been established in a number of classrooms, institutions for the mentally retarded, homes for delinquents, and mental hospitals with schizophrenics.

In some instances, behavior modification works, in others it does not. One person may become so wedded to the tokens that when they are removed, the positive behavior associated with the tokens may disappear. Yet another person might continue the positive behavior after the tokens are removed. Some critics object to behavior modification because they believe such extensive control of another person's behavior unethically infringes on the individual's rights. But as with the college student who could not study, maladaptive responses can be turned into adaptive ones through behavior modification.

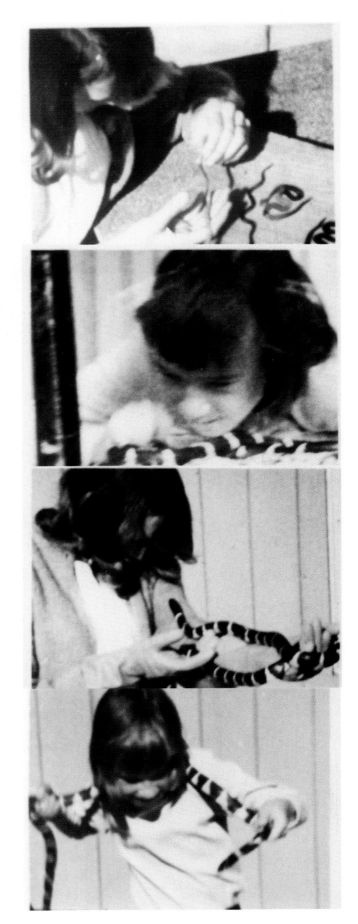

ℱigure 12.8
Systematic Desensitization

Systematic desensitization is often used to help eliminate phobias. In this systematic desensitization treatment, individuals have progressed from handling rubber snakes *(top)*, to peering at snakes in an aquarium *(second from top)*, to handling snakes with rubber gloves *(second from bottom)*, to handling live but harmless snakes *(bottom)*.

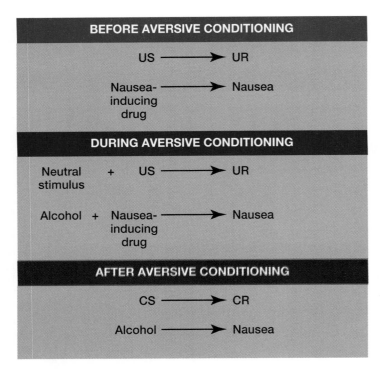

igure 12.9
Classical Conditioning: The Backbone of Aversive Conditioning

The above illustrations reveal how classical conditioning can provide a conditional aversion to alcohol. After the association of the drug with alcohol, the alcohol becomes a conditioned stimulus for nausea. Remember these abbreviations from chapter 5, "Learning": US (unconditioned stimulus), UR (unconditioned response), CS (conditioned stimulus), and CR (conditioned response).

Rational-Emotive Behavior Therapy
Beck's Cognitive Therapy

The behavior therapies have been used to treat a wide variety of problems. To read about the use of this approach in treating depression, see Explorations in Psychology.

Cognitive Therapies

To understand the cognitive therapies, we will discuss their basic nature and then turn to two main cognitive therapy approaches: (1) rational-emotive behavior therapy and (2) Beck's cognitive therapy.

D., a 21-year-old, single, undergraduate student, perceives himself as a failure in school and a failure to his parents. He is preoccupied with negative thoughts, dwells on his problems, and exaggerates his faults. Such thinking is common among depressed individuals, and suggests that cognitive therapy might be a viable approach to treat D.'s depression. The **cognitive therapies** *emphasize that the individual's cognitions or thoughts are the main source of abnormal behavior.* Cognitive therapies attempt to change the individual's feelings and behaviors by changing cognitions. Cognitive therapies differ from psychoanalytic therapies by focusing more on overt symptoms instead of deep-seated unconscious thoughts, by providing more structure to the individual's thoughts, and by being less concerned about the origin of the problem.

Rational-Emotive Behavior Therapy   **Rational-emotive behavior therapy** *is based on Albert Ellis' assertion that individuals become psychologically disordered because of their beliefs, especially those that are irrational and self-defeating.* Ellis (1962, 1996) says that we usually talk to ourselves when we experience stress; too often the statements are irrational, making them more harmful than helpful.

Ellis abbreviated the therapy process into the letters A, B, C, D, E (see figure 12.10). Therapy usually starts at C, the individual's upsetting emotional *C*onsequence; this might involve depression, anxiety, or a feeling of worthlessness. The individual often says that C was caused by A, the *A*ctivating Experience, such as a blowup in marital relations, loss of job, or failure in school. The therapist works with the individual to show that an intervening factor, B, the individual's *B*elief System, is actually responsible for why he moved from A to C. Then the therapist goes on to D, which stands for *D*isputation; at this point, the individual's irrational beliefs are disputed or contested by the therapist. Finally, E is reached, which stands for *E*ffects or outcomes of the rational-emotive behavior therapy, as when individuals put their changed beliefs to work. To learn more about Ellis' rational-emotive behavior therapy, read Explorations in Psychology.

Beck's Cognitive Therapy   Aaron Beck (1976, 1993) developed a form of cognitive therapy to treat psychological problems, especially depression. A basic assumption in Beck's therapy is that psychological problems like depression result when people think illogically about themselves, the world they live in, and the future. Beck's approach shares with Ellis' approach the idea that the goal of therapy should be to help people to recognize and discard self-defeating cognitions.

In the initial phases of therapy, individuals are taught to make connections between their patterns of thinking and their emotional responses. The therapist helps them to identify their own automatic thoughts and to keep records of their thought content and emotional reactions. With the therapist's assistance, they learn about logical errors in their thinking and to challenge the accuracy of these automatic

EXPLORATIONS IN PSYCHOLOGY
Contemporary Behavior Therapy and the Treatment of Depression—the Lewinsohn Approach

HENRY GREENE IS a 36-year-old lawyer who wrestled with depression for months before finally seeking psychotherapy. His initial complaints were physical—fitful sleep, often ending at 3 A.M., lack of appetite, weight loss of 15 pounds, and a disinterest in sex. Henry began to move more slowly and his voice became monotonous. He reached the point where he could barely cope with life. Henry finally let his guard down and confessed that, although he looked successful on the outside, he felt like a failure on the inside. He said he actually was a third-rate lawyer, husband, lover, and father—he felt he was bound to remain that way. Henry perceived life as a treadmill of duty and guilt; he felt exhausted and saw no reason to continue (Rosenfeld, 1985).

How would a contemporary behaviorist treat someone like Henry Greene? Peter Lewinsohn and his colleagues developed the "Coping with Depression Course" (Lewinsohn & others, 1984). A basic principle of the program is that feelings are caused by behavior. Therapists encourage people to increase the ratio of positive life events to negative life events to improve mood. To accomplish the desired ratio, most individuals require a variety of skill training exercises.

Someone like Henry Greene would first be assigned to monitor his moods, which would force him to pay attention to them. This information is used to determine which events are associated with which moods. Relaxation training would follow, because relaxation skills improve an individual's sense of well-being. Along with direct benefits of relaxation, clients experience an enhanced sense of self-efficacy by mastering a new skill.

The next step for Henry Greene would be to determine how his moods are associated with pleasant and unpleasant events in his life. Henry would be asked to fill out a "Pleasant Events Schedule" and an "Unpleasant Events Schedule." Each week, Henry would complete a graph showing the number of pleasant and unpleasant events, as well as his mood, for each day. Henry probably would see a close relation between unpleasant events and negative moods, and between pleasant events and positive moods. The therapist would encourage Henry to increase the time he spends in pleasant activities with the hope that more positive moods will follow. The outcome should be that Henry gains control over his moods.

Some people require individually tailored approaches. For example, some people need training in social skills to improve their social relationships. Others need more work in changing their thoughts. In Lewinsohn's approach, thoughts are treated as behaviors to be modified, for example, positive thoughts are reinforced or a specified period is set aside for "worry time."

The final stage in this approach is maintenance planning. Henry would be asked to identify the components of the behavioral therapy that were the most successful in changing his maladaptive behavior, once they have been identified, Henry would be encouraged to continue their use. He also would be required to develop emergency plans for those times when stress overwhelms him. Henry would continue to go to follow-up sessions for 6 months after his treatment.

Figure 12.10
A–E Steps in Ellis' Rational-Emotive Behavior Therapy

EXPLORATIONS IN PSYCHOLOGY
"My Work Is Boring and I Resent It"

THE FOLLOWING CASE illustrates the nature of rational-emotive behavior therapy. You will notice that this type of therapy is a forceful type of therapeutic persuasion.

Client: I know that I should do the inventory before it piles up to enormous proportions, but I just keep putting it off. To be honest, I guess it's because I resent it so much.

Therapist: But why do you resent it so much?

Client: It's boring; I just don't like it.

Therapist: So it's boring. That's a good reason for disliking this work, but is it an equally good reason for resenting it?

Client: Aren't the two the same thing?

Therapist: By no means. Dislike equals the sentence, "I don't enjoy this thing; therefore, I don't want to do it." That's a perfectly sane sentence in most instances, but resentment is the sentence, "*Because* I dislike doing this thing, I shouldn't *have* to do it," and that's invariably a very crazy sentence.

Client: Why is it so crazy to resent something that you don't like to do?

Therapist: There are several reasons. First of all, from a purely logical standpoint, it just makes no

sense at all to say to yourself, "Because I dislike doing this thing, I shouldn't *have* to do it." The second part of this sentence just doesn't follow in any way from the first part. Your reasoning goes something like this: "Because I dislike doing this thing, *other people* and the *universe* should be so considerate of me that they should never make me do what I dislike," but, of course, this doesn't make any sense. Why *should* other people and the universe be that considerate of you? It might be nice if they were, but why the devil *should* they be? In order for your reasoning to be true, the entire universe, and all the people in it, would really have to revolve around and be uniquely considerate of you. (Ellis, 1962)

The therapist has directly attacked the client's belief and forcefully told him that his thoughts are irrational. This represents an important distinction between cognitive therapists, such as Ellis, and behavioral or psychodynamic therapists. Behavioral and psychodynamic therapists might describe this client's behavior and attitudes as maladaptive and self-defeating, but Ellis points out that they are irrational and illogical as well.

Through the Eyes of Psychologists

Albert Ellis, *Clinical Psychologist, New York City*

"People largely control their own destinies by believing in and acting on the values or beliefs they hold."

thoughts. Their logical errors in thinking lead them to do the following (Carson, Butcher, & Mineka, 1996):

- Perceive the world as harmful while ignoring evidence to the contrary, such as still feeling worthless even though a friend has just told them how much other people like them
- Overgeneralize on the basis of limited examples, such as seeing themselves as worthless because one individual stopped dating them
- Magnify the importance of undesirable events, such as seeing the loss of a dating partner as the end of the world
- Engage in absolutistic thinking, such as exaggerating the importance of someone's mildly critical comment and perceiving it as proof of their inadequacy

As we mentioned earlier, Beck's and Ellis' cognitive therapies have some similarities. However, there also are some differences between them. Rational-emotive behavior therapy is very directive, persuasive, and confrontational. It also focuses on the therapist's teaching role. In contrast, Beck's cognitive therapy involves more of an open-ended dialogue between the therapist and the individual. The aim of this dialogue in Beck's approach is to get individuals to reflect on personal issues and discover their own misconceptions. Beck also encourages individuals to gather information about themselves and to try out unbiased experiments that reveal the inaccuracies of their beliefs.

SUMMARY TABLE 12.3
The Behavior and Cognitive Therapies

Concept	Processes/Related Ideas	Characteristics/Description
Behavior Therapies	Their Nature	They use principles of learning to reduce or eliminate maladaptive behavior. They are based on the behavioral and social cognitive theories of personality. Behavior therapies try to eliminate the symptoms of behaviors rather than get individuals to gain insight into their problems. Behavior therapists increasingly have used observational learning, cognitive factors, and self-instruction in their efforts to help people with their problems.
	Classical Conditioning Approaches	The two main therapy techniques based on classical conditioning are systematic desensitization and aversive conditioning. In systematic desensitization, anxiety is treated by getting the person to associate deep relaxation with increasingly intense anxiety-producing situations. In aversive conditioning, there are repeated pairings of the undesirable behavior with aversive stimuli to decrease the behavior's rewards.
	Operant Conditioning Approaches	In operant conditioning approaches to therapy, a careful analysis of the person's environment is conducted to determine which factors need to be modified. Behavior modification is the application of operant conditioning to change human behavior; its main goal is to replace unacceptable, maladaptive responses with acceptable, adaptive ones. A token economy is a behavior modification system in which behaviors are reinforced with tokens that later can be exchanged for desired rewards.
Cognitive Therapies	Their Nature	They emphasize that the individual's cognitions or thoughts are the main source of abnormal behavior. Cognitive therapies attempt to change the person's feelings and behaviors by changing cognitions.
	Rational-Emotive Behavior Therapy	Ellis' approach is based on the assertion that individuals become psychologically disordered because of their beliefs, especially those that are irrational and self-defeating.
	Beck's Cognitive Therapy	Especially used for depression, this involves initially getting people to make connections between their patterns of behavior and emotional responses. With the therapist's assistance, they learn about logical errors in their thinking, then how to challenge these mistakes in thinking. Ellis' approach is more directive, persuasive, and confrontational than Beck's; Beck's approach is more of an open-ended dialogue and he encourages people to gather information and conduct experiments to reveal the inaccuracies of their beliefs.

At this point we have discussed a number of ideas about the behavior therapies and the cognitive therapies. An overview of these ideas is presented in summary table 12.3. Next, we will consider yet another set of therapies—the group therapies.

Group Therapies

A major issue in therapy is how it can be structured to reach more people and at less cost. One way to address this problem is for the therapist to see clients in a group.

Nine people make their way into a room, each looking tentatively at the others. Although each person has met the therapist during a diagnostic

Because many psychological problems develop in the context of interpersonal relationships and group experiences—within one's family, marriage, or peer group—group therapy can be an important context for learning how to cope more effectively with these problems.

Group Therapies
Exploring Group Psychotherapy

interview, no one knows any of the other clients. Some of the people seem reluctant, others enthusiastic. All are willing to follow the therapist's recommendation that group therapy might help each of them learn to cope better with their problems. As they sit down and wait for the session to begin, one thinks, "Will they really understand me?" Another thinks, "Do the others have problems like mine?" Yet another thinks, "How can I stick my neck out with these people?"

Individual therapy is often expensive and time consuming. Freud believed that therapy is a long process and saw clients as often as three to five times a week for a number of years. Advocates of group therapy stress that individual therapy is limited because the client is seen outside the normal context of relationships, relationships that may hold the key to successful therapy (Gladding, 1995, 1999). Many psychological problems develop in the context of interpersonal relationships—within one's family, marriage, or peer group, for example. By seeing individuals in the context of these important groups, therapy may be more successful (Fuhrman & Burlingame, 1995; Morgan & Cummings, 1999).

Group therapy is diversified (Fuhriman, 2000). Psychodynamic, humanistic, behavior, or cognitive therapy is practiced by some therapists. Others use group approaches that are not based on the major psychotherapeutic perspectives. Six features make group therapy an attractive format (Yalom, 1975, 1995):

1. *Information.* The individual receives information about his problem from either the group leader or other group members.
2. *Universality.* Many individuals develop the sense that they are the only person who has such frightening and unacceptable impulses. In the group, individuals observe that others feel anguish and suffering as well.
3. *Altruism.* Group members support one another with advice and sympathy and learn that they have something to offer others.
4. *Corrective recapitulation of the family group.* A therapy group often resembles a family (and in family therapy the group *is* a family), with the leaders representing parents and the other members siblings. In this "new" family, old wounds may be healed and new, more positive "family" ties made.
5. *Development of social skills.* Corrective feedback from peers may correct flaws in the individual's interpersonal skills. A self-centered individual may see that he is self-centered if five other group members inform him about his self-centeredness; in individual therapy he may not believe the therapist.
6. *Interpersonal learning.* The group can serve as a training ground for practicing new behaviors and relationships. A hostile woman may learn that she can get along better with others by not behaving so aggressively, for example.

Family/Couple Therapy   "A friend loves you for your intelligence, a mistress for your charm, but your family's love is unreasoning; you were born into it and are of its flesh and blood. Nevertheless, it can irritate you more than any group of people in the world," commented the French biographer André Maurois. His statement suggests that the family may be the source of the individual's problems.

Family therapy *is group therapy with family members.* **Couple therapy** *is group therapy with married or unmarried couples whose major problem is their relationship.* These approaches stress that while one person may have some abnormal symptoms, the symptoms are a function of family or couple relationships (Capuzzi & Gross, 1999; Christensen & Heavy, 1999; Davis, 1996; Snyder, 2000). Psychodynamic, humanistic, or behavior therapies may be used in family or couple therapy, but the main form of family therapy is family systems therapy.

Four of the most widely used family therapy techniques are these:

1. *Validation.* The therapist expresses an understanding and acceptance of each family member's feelings and beliefs, and thus validates the person. When the therapist talks with each family member, she finds something positive to say.

2. *Reframing.* The therapist teaches families to reframe problems; problems are cast as a family problem, not an individual's problem. A delinquent adolescent boy's problems are reframed in terms of how each family member contributed to the situation. The father's lack of attention to his son and marital conflict may be involved, for example.

3. *Structural change.* The family systems therapist tries to *restructure* the coalitions in a family. In a mother-son coalition, the therapist might suggest that the father take a stronger disciplinarian role to relieve some of the burden from the mother. Restructuring might be as simple as suggesting that parents explore satisfying ways to be together; the therapist may recommend that once a week the parents go out for a quiet dinner together, for example.

4. *Detriangulation.* In some families, one member is the scapegoat for two other members who are in conflict but pretend not to be. For example, in the triangle of two parents and one child, the parents may insist that their marriage is fine but find themselves in subtle conflict over how to handle the child. The therapist tries to disentangle, or *detriangulate,* this situation by shifting attention away from the child to the conflict between the parents.

Family therapy has become increasingly popular in recent years. In family therapy, the assumption is that psychological adjustment is related to patterns of interaction within the family unit.

Family Therapy and Culture

Couples therapy proceeds in much the same way as family therapy. Conflict in marriages and in relationships between unmarried individuals frequently involves poor communication. In some instances, communication has broken down entirely. The therapist tries to improve the communication between the partners. In some cases, she will focus on the roles partners play: one may be "strong," the other "weak"; one may be "responsible," the other "spoiled," for example. Couples therapy addresses diverse problems such as jealousy, sexual messages, delayed childbearing, infidelity, gender roles, two-career families, divorce, and remarriage (Sullivan & Christensen, 1998).

Self-Help Support Groups
Self-help support groups *are voluntary organizations of individuals who get together on a regular basis to discuss topics of common interest.* The groups are not conducted by a professional therapist but rather by a paraprofessional or a member of the common interest group. A paraprofessional is someone who is taught by a professional to provide some mental health services, but who does not have formal mental health training. The group leader and members provide support to help individuals with their problems. Self-help support groups play an important role in our nation's mental health, with as many as 10 million people participating in such groups each year.

In addition to reaching so many people in need of help, these groups are important because they use community resources and are relatively inexpensive. They also serve people who are less likely to receive help otherwise, such as less-educated adults, individuals living in low-income circumstances, and homemakers.

Founded in 1930 by a reformed alcoholic, Alcoholics Anonymous (AA) is one of the best-known self-help groups. Mental health professionals often recommend AA for their alcoholic clients. Weight Watchers and TOPS (Take Off Pounds Sensibly) are also self-help groups. There are myriad self-help groups such as Parents Without Partners, lesbian and gay support groups, cocaine-abuse support groups, and child-abuse

Social Concerns

Tulsa Society for Depressed Women
Love Without Shame
Gamblers Anonymous
Phobia Society of Tulsa

Relocated Corporate Wives
Rebuilders: For Divorces
Sex Addicts: Anonymous
Rap Group and Caring and Coping
Partners of Vietnam Veterans

Eating/Weight Disorders

Movers and Shapers
Overeaters Anonymous

TOPS (Take Off Pounds Sensibly)

Alcohol/Substance Abuse

Students Against Drugs and Alcohol
Alcoholics Victorious
How to Cope with a Dependent Person
Adult Children of Alcoholic Parents

Alcoholics Anonymous
Teen Awareness Group
Cocaine Anonymous

Parenting

Single Working Mothers
Tulsa Adoptive Parents
Parents Without Partners
After Baby Comes

Happier Home Parents
Stepparents Group
Sooner Parents of Twins

Health

Resolve of Tulsa (an infertility group)
Group for Alzheimer's Caregivers
AIDS Support Program
ENCORE (for breast cancer patients)
Mended Hearts (for those who have had open-heart surgery)

SHHH (Self-Help for the Hard of Hearing)
Families of Children with Diabetes
Indian Health Care Resource Center
Families of Nursing Home Residents
LITHIUM Group (for those with bipolar disorder)

Figure 12.11
Examples of Self-Help Groups
A listing of self-help groups in a Tulsa, Oklahoma, Sunday newspaper included more than 200 entries. Among the wide variety of self-help groups listed were those above.

support groups. Figure 12.11 lists a sampling of the variety of self-help groups available in one city.

Self-help support groups also provide members with a sympathetic audience for confession, sharing, and emotional release. The social support, role modeling, and sharing of concrete strategies for solving problems that unfold in self-help groups add to their effectiveness. A woman who has been raped might not believe a male therapist who tells her that, with time, she will be able to put back together the pieces of her shattered life and work through much of the psychological pain. But the same message from another rape survivor—someone who has had to work through the same feelings of rage, fear, and violation—might be more believable.

Self-help support groups have broad, though not universal, appeal (Gottlieb, 1998). For people who tend to cope by seeking information and affiliation with similar peers, such groups can reduce stress and promote adjustment. However, as with any group therapy, there is the possibility that negative emotions will spread through the group, especially if the members face circumstances that deteriorate over time, such as terminal cancer patients. Group leaders who are sensitive to the spread of negative emotions can minimize such effects.

Is Psychotherapy Effective?

Do individuals who go through therapy get better? Are some approaches more effective than others? Or is the situation similar to that of the Dodo in *Alice's Adventures in Wonderland*? Dodo was asked to judge the winner of a race; he decided, "Everybody has won and all must have prizes." And how would we evaluate the effectiveness of psychotherapy? Would we take the client's word? The therapist's word? What would be our criteria for effectiveness? Would it be "feeling good," "adaptive behavior," "improved interpersonal relationships," "autonomous decision making," or "more positive self-concept," for example? During the last several decades an extensive amount of thought and research has addressed these questions.

**Society of Clinical Psychology
The Effectiveness of Psychotherapy**

Research on the Effectiveness of Psychotherapy   Four decades ago, Hans Eysenck (1952) came to the shocking conclusion that psychotherapy is ineffective. Eysenck analyzed 24 studies of psychotherapy and found that approximately two-thirds of the individuals with neurotic symptoms improved. Sounds impressive so far. But Eysenck also found that a similar percentage of neurotic individuals on waiting lists to see a psychotherapist also showed marked improvement even though they were not given any psychotherapy at all.

Eysenck's pronouncement prompted a flurry of research on psychotherapy's effectiveness (Kopta & others, 1999; Pilkonis, 1999; Pilkonis & Krause, 1999). Hundreds of studies on the outcome of psychotherapy have now been conducted (Dawes, 1998; Wampold & others, 1997). One strategy for analyzing these diverse studies is called **meta-analysis,** *in which the researcher statistically combines the results of many different studies.* In one meta-analysis of psychotherapy research, 475 studies were statistically combined (Smith, Glass, & Miller, 1980). Only those studies in which a therapy group had been compared with an untreated control group were compared. The results showed greater psychotherapy effectiveness than Eysenck's earlier results: On 88 percent of the measures, individuals who received therapy improved more than those who did not. This meta-analysis and others (Lipsey & Wilson, 1993) document that psychotherapy is effective in general, but they do not inform us about the specific ways in which different therapies might be effective.

People who are thinking about seeing a psychotherapist not only want to know whether psychotherapy in general is effective, but they also especially want to know which form of psychotherapy is most effective for their particular problem. Mary Lee Smith and her colleagues (Smith, Glass, & Miller, 1980) conducted a meta-analysis to compare types of psychotherapy. For example, behavior therapies were compared with insight therapies (psychodynamic, humanistic). Behavior and insight therapies were found to be superior to no treatment at all, but they did not differ from each other in effectiveness.

Research that evaluates the effectiveness of a psychotherapy usually includes a comparison group—either a control group of individuals who do not experience the therapy or a group that receives a different type of psychotherapy (Alloy, Jacobson, & Acocella, 1999) ◀▥ P. 34. When a control group is included, it often consists of individuals waiting to see a psychotherapist but who as yet have not been given therapy (this is called a *wait-list control group*). Why is it so important for psychotherapy research to include a control or comparison group? Because it gives us some idea of how many people in the study who experienced the targeted psychotherapy (such as cognitive therapy for depression) would have gotten better without the psychotherapy.

Let's examine one study that illustrates how control and comparison groups are used in psychotherapy research. The National Institute of Mental Health conducted an evaluation

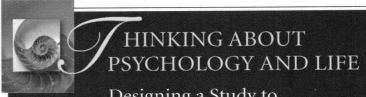

THINKING ABOUT PSYCHOLOGY AND LIFE

Designing a Study to Evaluate the Effectiveness of Psychotherapy

THERE IS A GREAT deal of interest among therapists in finding out the effectiveness of various psychotherapies. Based on what you have read about psychotherapy and psychotherapy research in this chapter, and what you learned in chapter 1, "What Is Psychology?" design a study to measure the effectiveness of psychotherapy. Describe which approach(es) of psychotherapy you will be evaluating, what you might use as a control group(s), how you would measure successful treatment, and how long the study would last (including follow-up data collection) (Zakrajsek, 1999).

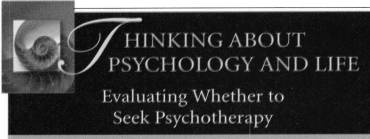

THINKING ABOUT PSYCHOLOGY AND LIFE

Evaluating Whether to Seek Psychotherapy

THERE ARE NO hard-and-fast rules about when people should go to a psychotherapist for help with their personal problems. However, to get a sense of whether you should see a psychotherapist evaluate whether you have recently experienced the following:

- I feel sad or blue a lot.
- My self-esteem is really low.
- I feel like other people are always out to get me.
- I feel so anxious that it is hard for me to function.
- I have trouble concentrating on my academic work.
- I don't do anything social and spend much of my spare time alone.
- I have a tendency to alienate people when I don't really want to.
- I'm frightened by things that I know should not be fear-provoking.
- I hear voices that tell me what I should do.
- I know I have problems, but I just don't feel I can talk with anyone about them.

If any of the above statements describe your life, consider talking over your concerns with a qualified therapist. Most colleges and universities have counseling or mental health services that are covered by your student fees. This is a good place to start in seeking mental health consultation.

of three types of treatment for depression (cognitive therapy; interpersonal therapy, which emphasized improving the individual's social relationships; and drug therapy) (Mervis, 1986). Two-hundred and forty individuals who were depressed were randomly assigned to the three psychotherapy conditions or a control group (who received a placebo medication along with supportive advice). A placebo is a medically inactive substance that mimics the appearance of the active drug. After 16 weeks in treatment, just over 50 percent of the individuals in each of the three psychotherapy groups were not depressed anymore. How did the people in the control group fare? Twenty-nine percent of them no longer were depressed after 16 weeks, a significantly lower percentage than in the psychotherapy groups.

Although no particular therapy was found to be best in this study, some therapies have been found to be more effective than others in treating some disorders (DeRubeis & Crits-Christoph, 1998; Howard, 2000). Behavior therapies have been most successful in treating specific behavioral problems, such as phobias and sexual dysfunctions (Bowers & Clum, 1988; Sanderson, 1995). Cognitive therapies have been most successful in treating depression and anxiety (Butler & others, 1991; Clark & others, 1994). Relaxation therapy also has been successful in treating anxiety disorders (Arnitz & van den Hout, 1996).

Common Themes in Psychotherapy

After carefully studying the nature of psychotherapy for more than 25 years, Jerome Frank (1982) concluded that effective psychotherapies have the common elements of expectations, mastery, and emotional arousal. By inspiring an expectation of help, the therapist motivates the client to continue coming to therapy (Jennings & Skovholt, 1999). These expectations are powerful morale builders and symptom relievers in themselves. The therapist also increases the client's sense of mastery and competence (Brammer & MacDonald, 1999; Hill & O'Brien, 1999). For example, clients begin to feel that they can cope effectively with their world. Therapy also arouses the individual's emotions, essential to motivating behavioral change, according to Frank.

The therapeutic relationship is another important ingredient in successful psychotherapy (Strupp, 1989, 1995). A relationship in which the client has confidence and trust in the therapist is essential to effective psychotherapy. In one study, the most common ingredient in the success of different psychotherapies was the therapist's supportiveness of the client (Wallerstein, 1989). The client and therapist engage in a "healing ritual," which requires the active participation of both the client and the therapist. As part of this ritual, the client gains hope and becomes less alienated. To read about guidelines for seeking professional help, turn to Explorations in Psychology.

Gender and Ethnicity

In the last several decades, psychologists have become sensitive to the concerns of gender and ethnicity in psychotherapy (Helms & Cook, 1999; Wisch & Mahalik, 1999). Let's explore the roles of gender and ethnicity in psychotherapy.

Gender One of the by-products of changing gender roles for women and men is evaluation of the goals of psychotherapy ◀▮▮▮ P. 13. Traditionally, the goal of psychotherapy has been autonomy or self-determination for the client. However, autonomy and self-determination are often more central characteristics of life for men than for women,

MARCIA FELT ANXIOUS most of the time. But what caused her the greatest difficulty was that she became so anxious during exams in her classes that she would nearly freeze. Her mind would go blank and she would begin to sweat and shake all over. It was such a problem that she was failing her classes. She told one of her professors that this was the problem with her grades. He told her that it sounded like she had a serious case of test anxiety, and that she should get some help. Marcia decided that she better take his advice and wanted to find a psychotherapist. How would she go about finding a therapist? Are certain professionals more qualified than others? How could she know that she was going to see someone who could help her, as opposed to a professional who would not be helpful, or perhaps even make things worse? These are only a few of the questions people commonly have when they seek to find a therapist.

When trying to find a therapist, Marcia could consider a psychologist, psychiatrist, social worker, counselor, or any number of other helping professionals. Each of these mental health professionals is qualified to provide psychotherapeutic services. They all practice from any one or combination of the therapeutic orientations discussed in this chapter. They may also see people on an individual, one to one basis, or in small groups, as in group therapy. The critical question is, of course, how does someone go about selecting a therapist to help them? This is not as easy a question as it may appear at first glance. We may face many of the same problems when we try to find a "good" medical doctor, accountant, or dentist; however, the way that most people go about finding these other professional services may not be the best way of selecting a therapist. Asking a friend for a good therapist ignores the fact that some approaches to therapy work better with some problems than others. Also, every therapeutic relationship is different, so one person's experience in therapy is not translatable to another person's. Below, we offer some general suggestions when looking for a therapist.

Identify the Professional's Credentials

Although all different types of mental health professionals may be competent, psychologists, psychiatrists, and social workers all differ in their approach to therapy based on differences in training: psychologists tend to be focused on the person's emotions and behaviors; psychiatrists are trained as medical doctors so their perspective is likely to involve physical aspects of psychological problems; and social workers will be inclined to take a person's entire family and social situation into account. Regardless of the exact profession, some minimal credentials should be considered important. All states have licensing regulations for professionals who provide public services. Thus, a therapist should be licensed or certified by a state in order to practice. In addition, in some cases it may be important for a professional to have some advanced, specialized training in a certain area. For example, if a person is seeking help with a specific problem, like drug abuse, alcohol abuse, or a sexual problem, the therapist should have some training in that area. You should ask about the professional's credentials either before or during a first visit.

When Starting Therapy, Give It Some Time Before Judging Its Usefulness

Making changes is very difficult. Expecting too much too soon can result in premature dissatisfaction and disappointment. Because a large part of therapy involves the development of a relationship with the therapist, it may take several meetings to really know if things are going well. One suggestion is to give it between four and six weekly meetings. If it does not seem like things are going the way you would like, it is a good idea to discuss your progress with the therapist and ask what you should expect with regard to making progress. Setting specific goals with specific time expectations can be helpful. If your goals are not being met, you should consider a new therapist.

Be a Thoughtful and Careful Consumer of Mental Health Services

Just as is true for when you seek any services, the more informed you are about the services provided, the better decision you can make about whether or not they are the right services for you. Calling around and asking specific questions about approaches and specializations is one way to become informed about the services offered by therapists. Consider how important it may be that the therapist is of your same or opposite sex, whether it is important that they have experience with your specific difficulty, as well as other specific characteristics. You may also want to learn more about their theoretical orientation to therapy as described in this chapter. Another way to find out more about the therapist is to ask these kinds of questions during your first visit. Most professionals are quite comfortable talking about their background and training. Your confidence and trust in the professional is an important part of how well therapy will work for you.

These general guidelines should be used when first looking for a therapist. Remember that people should continually evaluate their own progress throughout therapy and when they feel dissatisfied with how it is going, they should discuss this with their therapist. Remember that therapy is like other services: When dissatisfied, you can always look for another therapist. Don't think that just because one therapist has not been helpful none will be. All therapists and therapeutic relationships are different. Finding the right therapist is one of the most important factors in therapy success.

Greater attention has been paid to the roles of gender and ethnicity in psychotherapy in recent decades. Among the issues raised by this increased attention are these: (1) *What should the appropriate goals of psychotherapy be?* (2) *Does psychotherapy work best when there is an ethnic match between the therapist and the client?*

whose lives generally are more characterized by relatedness and connection with others. Thus, some psychologists believe that therapy goals should involve more emphasis on relatedness and connection with others, especially for women, or at a minimum an emphasis on both autonomy/self-determination and relatedness/connection to others (Worrell & Robinson, 1993).

Ethnicity   Many ethnic minority individuals prefer discussing problems with parents, friends, and relatives rather than with mental health professionals (Atkinson, Morten, & Sue, 1998; Gibson & Mitchell, 1999). Might therapy progress best when the therapist and the client are from the same ethnic background? Researchers have found that when there is an ethnic match between the therapist and client and when ethnic-specific services are provided, clients are less likely to drop out of therapy early and in many cases have better treatment outcomes (Orlinsky, Grawe, & Parks, 1994; Sue, 1977). Ethnic-specific services include culturally appropriate greetings and arrangements (for example, serving tea rather than coffee to Chinese American clients), providing flexible hours for treatment, and employing a bicultural/bilingual staff (Nystul, 1999).

Nonetheless, therapy can be effective when the therapist and client are from different ethnic backgrounds if the therapist has excellent clinical skills and is culturally sensitive (Atkinson, Morten, & Sue, 1998; Fischer, Jome, & Atkinson, 1998). Culturally skilled psychotherapists have good knowledge of the cultural groups they work with, understand sociopolitical influences, and have skills in working with culturally diverse groups.

So far we have discussed a variety of psychotherapies that can help individuals cope more effectively with stress and develop more adaptive behavior. In recent years considerable progress has also been made in biomedical therapies, which we now discuss.

Biomedical Therapies

Biomedical therapies *are treatments to reduce or eliminate the symptoms of psychological disorders by altering the way an individual's body functions.* Drug therapy is the most common form of biomedical therapy. Much less widely used biomedical therapies are electroconvulsive therapy and psychosurgery. Psychologists and other mental health professionals may provide psychotherapy in conjunction with the biomedical therapy administered by psychiatrists and medical doctors. Indeed, in many instances a combination of psychotherapy and medication is a desirable course of treatment.

Psychotherapeutic Drugs
Drug Therapy

Drug Therapy

Although medicine and herbs have long been used to alleviate symptoms of emotional distress, it was not until the twentieth century that drug treatments began to revolutionize mental health care. Psychotherapeutic drugs are used mainly in three diagnostic categories: anxiety, mood, and schizophrenia. Let's explore the effectiveness of drugs in these areas, beginning with drugs to treat anxiety.

Antianxiety Drugs   **Antianxiety drugs** *are commonly known as tranquilizers* ◀||||| P. 136. These drugs reduce anxiety by making individuals less excitable and more calm ◀||||| P. 377. Benzodiazepines are the antianxiety drugs that offer the greatest relief for anxiety symptoms. They work by binding to the receptor sites of neurotransmitters that become overactive during anxiety. The most frequently prescribed benzodiazepines include Xanax, Valium, and Librium.

Why are antianxiety drugs so widely used? Many individuals experience stress and/or anxiety. Family physicians or psychiatrists prescribe these drugs to improve people's ability to cope with their problems more effectively. The relaxed feelings brought on by antianxiety drugs bring welcome relief from high levels of anxiety and stress.

Antianxiety medications are controlled drugs that should be used only temporarily for symptomatic relief. In some instances they are overused and can become addictive.

Antidepressant Drugs   **Antidepressant drugs** *regulate mood* ◀‖‖‖ P. 385.
The three main classes of antidepressant drugs are tricyclics, such as Elavil; MAO inhibitors, such as Nardil; and SSRI drugs, such as Prozac (Gorman & Kent, 1999). The *tricyclics,* so called because of their three-ringed molecular structure, are believed to work by increasing the level of certain neurotransmitters, especially norepinephrine and serotonin (Evans, 1999; Feighner, 1999; Shelton, 2000). The tricyclics reduce the symptoms of depression in approximately 60 to 70 percent of cases. The tricyclics usually take 2 to 4 weeks to improve mood. They sometimes have adverse side effects, such as restlessness, faintness, and trembling.

The MAO (monamine oxidase) inhibitors are not as widely used as the tricyclics because they are more toxic. However, some individuals who do not respond to the tricyclics do respond to the MAO inhibitors.

The most prominent of the SSRI (selective serotonin reuptake inhibiting) antidepressant drugs is Prozac. SSRI drugs work mainly by interfering with the reabsorption of serotonin in the brain. Prozac is most frequently prescribed for dysthymic disorder. Zoloft and Paxil are other drugs in the SSRI category. The SSRI drugs not only are being used to treat mood disorders but they also are often effective for individuals with obsessive-compulsive disorder.

Lithium *is a drug that is widely used to treat bipolar disorder* (recall that this disorder involves wide mood swings of depression and mania). The amount of lithium that circulates in the bloodstream needs to be carefully monitored because its effective dosage is precariously close to toxic levels.

Antipsychotic Drugs   **Antipsychotic drugs** *are powerful drugs that diminish agitated behavior, reduce tension, decrease hallucinations and delusions, improve social behavior, and produce better sleep patterns in individuals who have a severe mental disorder, especially schizophrenia* ◀‖‖‖ P. 389. Before antipsychotic drugs were developed in the 1950s, few, if any, interventions brought relief from the torment of psychotic symptoms. Once the effectiveness of these medications was apparent, the medical community significantly reduced more intrusive interventions, such as brain surgery and electroconvulsive shock for schizophrenia (Grunberg, Klein, & Brown, 1998).

The *neuroleptics* are the most widely used class of antipsychotic drugs. The most widely accepted explanation for the effectiveness of the neuroleptics is their ability to block the dopamine system's action in the brain (Rebec, 1996; Zahn, 2000). Schizophrenics have too much of the neurochemical messenger dopamine. Numerous well-controlled investigations reveal that when used in sufficient doses, the neuroleptics reduce a variety of schizophrenic symptoms, at least in the short term (Friedman, Temporini, & Davis, 1999; Holcomb & others, 1996).

The neuroleptics do not cure schizophrenia, and they can have severe side effects. The neuroleptics treat the symptoms of schizophrenia, not its causes. If an individual with schizophrenia stops taking the drug, the symptoms return. Neuroleptic drugs have substantially reduced the length of hospital stays for individuals with schizophrenia. However, although these individuals are able to return to the community because drug therapy keeps their symptoms from reappearing, most have difficulty coping with the demands of society and most are chronically unemployed.

Tardive dyskinesia *is a major side effect of the neuroleptic drugs; it is a neurological disorder characterized by grotesque, involuntary movements of the facial muscles and*

Drug Treatment of Schizophrenia

mouth as well as extensive twitching of the neck, arms, and legs. As many as 20 percent of individuals with schizophrenia taking neuroleptics develop this disorder. Elderly women are especially vulnerable. Long-term neuroleptic therapy also is associated with increased depression and anxiety. Nonetheless, for the majority of schizophrenics, the benefits of neuroleptic treatment outweigh its risk and discomforts.

A new group of medications called "atypical antipsychotic medications" was introduced in the 1990s. The most widely used drug in this group is Clozaril, which shows promise for reducing schizophrenia's symptoms without the side effects of neuroleptics (Rosenheck & others, 1999). Clozaril produces its effects by blocking the reuptake of the neurotransmitter serotonin. However, for a small portion of individuals with schizophrenia, Clozaril has a toxic effect on white blood cells, which requires regular blood testing.

Strategies to increase the effectiveness of the antipsychotic drugs involve administering lower dosages over time, rather than a large initial dose, and combining drug therapy with psychotherapy. The small percentage of schizophrenics who are able to hold jobs suggests that drugs alone will not make them contributing members of society. They also need training in vocational, family, and social skills.

We have discussed a number of drugs that can be used for various mental disorders. A summary of these drugs, the disorders for which they are used, their effectiveness, and side effects are shown in figure 12.12. Notice that for some types of anxiety disorders, such as agoraphobia, MAO inhibitors (which are antidepressant drugs) might be used rather than antianxiety drugs.

At this point we have discussed not only drug therapy but a number of psychotherapy approaches to help people with mental disorders. This is a good time to reflect on all of these different therapies and compare their strategies. To help you do this, see figure 12.13.

The use of psychotherapeutic drugs is the most widely practiced biomedical therapy. However, as we see next, in extreme circumstances, electroconvulsive therapy and even psychosurgery might be used.

Electroconvulsive Therapy

Electroconvulsive Therapy

Electroconvulsive therapy (ECT), *commonly called "shock treatment," is used mainly to treat severely depressed individuals. The goal of ECT is to cause a seizure in the brain much like what happens spontaneously in some forms of epilepsy.* A small electric current lasting for one second or less passes through two electrodes placed on the individual's head. The current excites neural tissue, stimulating a seizure that lasts for approximately 1 minute.

ECT has been used for more than 40 years. In earlier years it often was used indiscriminately, sometimes even as a punishment for patients. ECT is still used with as many as 60,000 individuals a year, mainly to treat major depressive disorder. Adverse side effects can include memory loss and other cognitive impairment. Today ECT is given mainly to individuals who have not responded to drug therapy or psychotherapy. ECT sounds as if it would entail intolerable pain, but the manner in which it is administered today involves little discomfort. The patient is given anesthesia and muscle relaxants before the current is applied; this allows the individual to sleep through the procedure, minimizes convulsions, and reduces the risk of physical injury. The individual awakens shortly afterward with no conscious memory of the treatment.

How effective is electroconvulsive therapy? In one analysis of studies, its effectiveness in treating depression was compared with cognitive therapy and antidepressant drugs (Seligman, 1994). ECT was as effective as cognitive therapy or drug therapy, with about 4 of 5 individuals showing marked improvement in all three therapies. However, as with the other therapies, the relapse rate for ECT is moderate to high. The side effects for ECT are more severe than for drugs. Cognitive therapy shows no side effects. A positive aspect of ECT is that its effects appear in a matter of days, whereas the effects of antidepressant drugs can take weeks, and those for cognitive therapy months, to appear.

Mental Disorder	Drug	Effectiveness	Side Effects
EVERYDAY ANXIETY AND ANXIETY DISORDERS			
Everyday anxiety	Anti-anxiety drugs (tranquilizers); most frequently prescribed are the benzodiazepines (Xanax, Valium, and Lithium)	Substantial improvement short-term	Less powerful the longer people take them; may be addictive
Generalized anxiety disorder	Anti-anxiety drugs	Not very effective	Less powerful the longer people take them; may be addictive
Panic disorder	Anti-anxiety drugs	About half show improvement	Less powerful the longer people take them; may be addictive
Agoraphobia	Tricyclic drugs and MAO inhibitors	Majority show improvement	For tricyclics, restlessness, fainting, and trembling; for MAO inhibitors, toxicity
Specific phobias	Anti-anxiety drugs	Not very effective	Less powerful the longer people take them; can be addictive
MOOD DISORDERS			
Depressive disorders	Tricyclic drugs, MAO inhibitors, and SSRI drugs (Prozac)	Majority show moderate improvement	For tricyclics, cardiac problems, mania, confusion, memory loss, fatigue; for MAO inhibitors, toxicity; for SSRI drugs, nausea, nervousness, insomnia, and in a few cases possible suicidal thoughts
Bipolar disorder	Lithium	Large majority show substantial improvement	Toxicity
SCHIZOPHRENIC DISORDERS			
Schizophrenia	Neuroleptics; atypical antipsychotic medications (Clozaril)	Majority show partial improvement	For neuroleptics, irregular heartbeat, low blood pressure, uncontrolled fidgeting, tardive dyskinesia, and immobility of face in neuroleptics. These side effects are less extensive with Clozaril but Clozaril can have a toxic effect on white blood cells.

Figure 12.12
Drug Therapy for Mental Disorders

Psychosurgery

Psychosurgery *is a biomedical therapy that involves removal or destruction of brain tissue to improve the individual's psychological adjustment.* The effects of psychosurgery are irreversible. In the 1930s, Portuguese physician Egas Moniz developed a procedure known as a *prefrontal lobotomy.* In this procedure, a surgical instrument is inserted into the brain and rotated, severing fibers that connect the frontal lobe, important in higher thought processes, and the thalamus, important in emotion. Moniz theorized that by severing the connections between these brain structures the

Psychosurgery

Topic	Psychodynamic Therapies	Humanistic Therapies	Behavior Therapies	Cognitive Therapies	Group Therapies	Drug Therapies
Cause of problem	Client's problems are symptoms of deep-seated, unresolved unconscious conflicts.	Client is not functioning at an optimal level of development.	Client has learned maladaptive behavior patterns.	Client has developed inappropriate thoughts.	Diverse causes depending on type of group therapy.	Problems have a biological origin.
Therapy emphasis	Discover underlying unconscious conflicts and work with client to develop insight.	Develop awareness of inherent potential for growth.	Learn adaptive behavior patterns through changes in the environment or cognitive processes.	Change feelings and behaviors by changing cognitions.	Diverse depending on type of therapy but emphasis on group's role in changing person's behavior.	Change behaviors, thoughts, and feelings by administering psychotherapeutic drugs.
Nature of therapy and techniques	Psychoanalysis, including free association, dream analysis, resistance, and transference; therapist interprets heavily.	Person-centered therapy, including unconditional positive regard, genuineness, accurate empathy, and active listening; Gestalt therapy including confrontation to encourage honest expression of feelings; self-appreciation emphasized.	Observation of behavior and its controlling conditions; specific advice given about what should be done; therapies based on classical conditioning, operant conditioning.	Conversation with client designed to get him or her to change irrational and self-deflating beliefs.	Interaction with other people who have psychological problems. In family therapy, emphasis on changing patterns of interaction among family members.	Often used in conjunction with psychotherapy but emphasis is on the drug's ability to improve the person's symptoms.

*F*igure 12.13
Therapy Comparisons

symptoms of severe mental disorders could be alleviated. Prefrontal lobotomies were conducted on thousands of patients from the 1930s through the 1950s. Moniz was even awarded the Nobel Prize for his work. However, while some patients may have benefited from the lobotomies, many were left in vegetable-like states because of the massive assaults on their brains.

These crude lobotomies are no longer performed. Since the 1960s, psychosurgery has become more precise. When psychosurgery is now performed, a small lesion is made in the amygdala or another part of the limbic system. Today, only several hundred patients, who have severely debilitating conditions, undergo psychosurgery per year. It is used only as a last resort and with extreme caution.

At this point we have discussed many ideas about group therapies, the effectiveness of psychotherapy, and biomedical therapies. A review of these ideas is presented in summary table 12.4. In this chapter, we discovered that one approach to therapy involves group therapies. In the next chapter, we will study social psychology, including further information about how people behave in groups.

SUMMARY TABLE 12.4
Group Therapies; Effectiveness of Psychotherapies; and Biomedical Therapies

Concept	Processes/ Related Ideas	Characteristics/Description
Group Therapies	Their Nature	Group therapies emphasize that relationships can hold the key to successful therapy. Group therapy is diversified.
	Family/Couple Therapy	Family therapy is group therapy with family members. Couple therapy is group therapy with married or unmarried couples whose major problem is their relationship. Four widely used family therapy techniques are validation, reframing, structural change, and detriangulation.
	Self-Help Support Groups	These are voluntary organizations of individuals who get together on a regular basis to discuss topics of common interest. They are conducted without a professional therapist.
Is Psychotherapy Effective?	Research on Psychotherapy Effectiveness	Psychotherapy in general is effective. Behavior therapies are often most successful in treating specific behavior problems, such as phobias. Cognitive therapy is often effective in treating depression and anxiety.
	Common Themes	Common themes in successful therapies include positive expectations of help, increasing the client's sense of mastery, arousing the person's emotions, and developing confidence and trust in the therapist.
	Gender and Ethnicity	In recent years, psychologists have become more sensitive to gender and ethnicity issues in therapy. The issues raised include these: (1) What should be the appropriate goals of therapy (e.g., autonomy or relatedness, or both)? and (2) Does psychotherapy work best when there is a gender and/or ethnic match between the therapist and the client? In conducting therapy with people of a different ethnicity or gender, it is important to be a culturally sensitive therapist.
Biomedical Therapies	Their Nature	They are treatments to reduce or eliminate the symptoms of psychological disorders by altering the way the person's body functions. Drug therapy is the most common form. Much less used are electroconvulsive therapy and psychosurgery.
	Drug Therapy	Three major classes of psychotherapeutic drugs are (1) antianxiety drugs, (2) antidepressant drugs, and (3) antipsychotic drugs. Antianxiety drugs are commonly known as tranquilizers. Benzodiazepines are the most commonly used antianxiety drugs. Antidepressant drugs regulate mood. The three main classes are tricyclics, MAO inhibitors, and SSRI drugs. Lithium is often successfully used in the treatment of bipolar disorder. Antipsychotic drugs are powerful drugs that are used to treat people with severe mental disorders, especially schizophrenia. We described the effectiveness and side effects of various drug therapies.
	Electroconvulsive Therapy	This is commonly called "shock therapy" and is used mainly to treat severe depression when other strategies have not worked.
	Psychosurgery	This is an irreversible procedure in which brain tissue is destroyed in an attempt to improve adjustment. Today's psychosurgery, although rarely used, is more precise than the early prefrontal lobotomies.

Overview

Overview

WE BEGAN THIS CHAPTER by examining these aspects of the nature and history of psychotherapy: the nature of psychotherapy, the history of psychotherapy, mental health professionals, and connections with personality theories. Our coverage of psychotherapies focused on psychodynamic therapies, humanistic therapies, behavior therapies, cognitive therapies, and group therapies, as well as how effective psychotherapy is. We explored these aspects of biomedical therapies: drug therapy, electroconvulsive therapy, and psychosurgery.

Remember that you can obtain a more detailed overview of the chapter by again studying the four summary tables on pages 405, 410, 417, and 429.

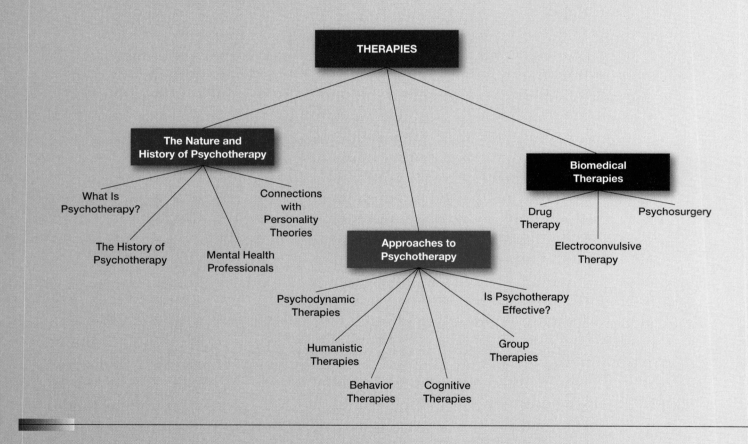

Key Terms

psychotherapy 400
deinstitutionalization 401
managed care 402
insight therapy 404
psychodynamic therapies 404
psychoanalysis 406
free association 406
catharsis 406
dream analysis 407
manifest content 407

latent content 407
transference 407
resistance 407
humanistic therapies 409
person-centered therapy 409
unconditional positive regard 409
Gestalt therapy 410
behavior therapies 411
systematic desensitization 412

aversive conditioning 412
behavior modification 413
token economy 413
cognitive therapies 414
rational-emotive behavior therapy 414
family therapy 418
couple therapy 418
self-help support groups 419
meta-analysis 421

biomedical therapies 424
antianxiety drugs 424
antidepressant drugs 425
lithium 425
antipsychotic drugs 425
tardive dyskinesia 425
electroconvulsive therapy (ECT) 426
psychosurgery 427

Key People

Phillipe Pinel 401
Dorothea Dix 401

Sigmund Freud 404
Carl Rogers 409

Frederick (Fritz) Perls 410
Albert Ellis 414

Aaron Beck 414
Egas Moniz 427

Taking It to the Net

1. "Battacca bats" are padded sticks that are used to hit chairs or sofas in psychotherapy. They are often used in couples therapy or therapy involving adolescents. The client is instructed to use the bats to safely express their anger. Clients often feel a sense of purging their anger after effectively using the battacca bats. Which type of psychotherapy uses battacca bats? What other tools are employed by this type of therapy?

2. Prefrontal lobotomies were prescribed for a variety of disorders. The lobotomy could be performed in the physician's office, without the need to be hospitalized. The physician simply jammed a sharp instrument behind the eye of the patient and severed the nearby neural fibers. The procedure was usually effective in reducing symptoms, but the side effects were devastating. In time,

the procedure became very unpopular, and few are performed today. Some types of psychosurgery are still performed, however, in spite of their drastic nature. What psychosurgery procedures are still being done? What disorders are treated by psychosurgery?

3. Freud's psychoanalysis is a therapeutic technique for analyzing an individual's unconscious thought. Freud used several techniques to uncover people's thoughts, including free association and dream analysis. Free association consists of encouraging people to say whatever comes to their mind, no matter what. Dream analysis involves interpreting a person's dreams to uncover any hidden fantasies or conflicts. We've all heard the term Freudian slip. Have you ever made a Freudian slip? What is it, and does it really tell people what you are unconsciously thinking? Explain.

Connect to http://www.mhhe.com/psychology/santrock to find the answers!

Chapter 13

"Man is a knot, a web, a mesh into which relationships are tied."

Antoine de St. Exupéry,
French Novelist, 20th Century

Preview

IN THE FOURTH CENTURY B.C., the Greek philosopher Aristotle once commented that humans are by nature social animals. The subfield of social psychology studies people's social thinking, influence, and relationships. Social psychology differs from the field of sociology in that social psychology focuses more on the individual as a social being while sociology places more emphasis on society at large. In our coverage of social psychology, these are among some of the questions we will explore:

• How do people think about their social world?
• Do people's attitudes predict their behavior?
• How much do people conform to what others are doing?
• Why do people join groups?
• Why are prejudice, stereotyping, and ethnocentrism so pervasive? How can interethnic relations be improved?
• Why are people aggressive? altruistic?
• What attracts us to others?

Images of Psychology and Life
The Reverend James Jones' Dark Side

WITH THE NOBLE INTENT of eliminating social injustice and improving interracial harmony, James W. Jones established a small church in Indiana in 1953. His congregation included a number of African Americans. He and his wife adopted seven children, including an African American, a Chinese, and a Korean. As a missionary for 2 years, Jones lived in Brazil, where he founded an orphanage and a mission. When he returned to the United States he changed the name of his church to the People's Temple Full Gospel.

Jones moved his church to northern California, where he increased his money-making efforts and community work. By the early 1970s, Jones had developed churches in the African American areas of San Francisco and Los Angeles. He was showered with accolades and his social programs were rated among the best in the country.

But Reverend Jones' dark side began to surface. As he stepped up fund-raising, he at first asked his congregation to make modest donations in the name of universal brotherhood and peace. Eventually he induced people to sell their homes and turn over all their money as a testament to their faith and loyalty. Rumors leaked that physical abuse, death threats, and attempts to gain the guardianship of children were meted out to members who were disobedient or tried to leave Jones' church. Jones was able to deflect public investigations through his tight rein on information and his respectability in the community.

By the early 1970s, Jones increasingly saw parallels between himself and Christ. He portrayed himself as a

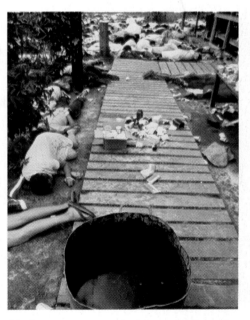

The Jonestown massacre, elaborately planned by People's Temple leader James Jones, reveals the macabre side of social thinking and influence.

Cults

On-line Articles about Cults

Cults and College Campuses

Heaven's Gate

messiah and required his congregation to call him "Father." Jones declared that everything he said was law. Jones was a charismatic leader and a master at getting members to conform to his wishes.

In 1977, shortly before an article exposing Jones' megalomania and repressive cruelty appeared in *New West* magazine, Jones' "flock" migrated en masse to Jonestown, Guyana. In Jonestown, the members of the People's Temple were isolated from their families and the world. They had been stripped of their possessions and individuality, and they were utterly obedient.

On November 17, 1978, United States Representative Leo Ryan and four of his aides, who were in Guyana to evaluate charges of abuse in the People's Temple, were gunned down by Jones' henchmen as they boarded a plane to leave the country. Jones convinced his congregation that hostile intruders were on their way to exterminate them in retaliation for the deaths at the airstrip.

The next day, Jones gathered before him more than 900 members of the People's Temple. It was time, he said, for them to die. Their death, the "martyr" Jones claimed, would be a revolutionary and positive act. Amidst few protests or acts of resistance, parents gave their children cyanide-laced Kool-Aid, drank it themselves, then lay down and waited to die.

The Jonestown massacre is but one of America's many experiences with cults (Galanter, 1999). David Koresh's Branch Davidians also met with a terrible end when their compound in Waco, Texas, went up in flames in 1993. And more recently, in 1997, Marshall Herff Applewhite convinced the members of his Heaven's Gate cult that the appearance of the Hale-Bopp comet meant that it was time for them to commit mass suicide so their spirits could escape their "mortal containers" and ascend to the "level above human." Like the Reverend James Jones and David Koresh, Marshall Herff Applewhite was a charismatic leader who gained enormous social influence over others.

Social Psychology

Social Thinking

Social psychologists are intrigued by how people think about the social world. Our exploration of social thinking focuses on attribution, social perception, and attitudes.

Attribution

You might remember that in chapter 9, "Motivation and Emotion," we introduced attribution theory in the context of achievement ◀ P. 305. We revisit attribution here and expand on its important contributions to understanding the ways people think about their social world.

Human beings are curious, seeking answers to all sorts of questions about their social world. We often ask and explore why something has happened or is happening. We might be curious about why someone is yelling at another person, why someone is in love with a particular person, or why someone got into a sorority or fraternity. Finding causal explanations for these and many other social circumstances is complex. We can observe people's behavior and listen to what they say, but to determine the cause of their behavior we have to make inferences from these observations.

Attribution theorists argue that we want to know why people do the things they do because the knowledge will enable us to cope more effectively with the situations that confront us (Alderman, 1999). Recall from chapter 9 that **attribution theory** *views people as motivated to discover the underlying causes of behavior as part of their effort to make sense of the behavior.* Thus, attributions are thoughts about why people behave the way they do. In a way, attribution theorists say people are a lot like detectives or scientists, seeking the reasons for human actions.

The Dimensions of Causality   Social psychologists have proposed a number of dimensions to describe the types of attributions people make (Jones,

1998). These dimensions reflect whether the cause is internal or external, stable or unstable, and controllable or uncontrollable.

Internal/External Causes   In our discussion of achievement in chapter 9, we indicated that an important attribution people make is whether the cause of achievement is due to external causes or internal causes ◀▥ P. 304. Fritz Heider (1958) argued that this internal/external explanation is the central issue in attribution. *Internal attributions* include all causes internal to the person, such as personality traits, intelligence, models, attitudes, and health. *External attributions* include all causes external to the person, such as social pressure, aspects of the social situation, money, the weather, and luck.

To think about how internal and external causes are involved in the attributions we make, consider this situation: Jason and Ashley have been dating for several months when Ashley breaks off the relationship. Jason wants to know why. Ashley says she is ending the relationship because of pressure from her parents, who want her to tone down her social life and study more (external attribution). But is that the true reason she is breaking off the relationship? Possibly Ashley is dumping Jason because she has grown tired of his introverted personality (internal cause).

Stable/Unstable Causes   In addition to internal and external causes, a second dimension involved in making attributions focuses on whether the cause is stable or unstable. This refers to whether an internal or external cause is relatively enduring and permanent or whether it is temporary. If Ashley infers that Jason's introverted personality is not going to change and that he is always going to be this way, a stable cause is present. On the other hand, if Ashley perceives that Jason just isn't putting enough effort forth but has the capability of being more outgoing, an unstable cause is involved. These are both examples of internal causes. What are some examples of stable and unstable external causes? If Ashley's parents never like anybody she dates, an external stable cause is present, but if they don't like Jason and approve of someone else Ashley dates, an external unstable cause is at work.

Controllable/Uncontrollable Causes   A third dimension of causality consists of whether a cause is controllable or uncontrollable (Weiner, 1986). We perceive that we can control some causes but that others are beyond our control. This dimension can coexist with any combination of internal/external and stable/unstable dimensions. We won't go through all of the combinations of these dimensions, but consider these to illustrate the nature of causes we can control and causes we can't control. An internal unstable cause like effort or mood is usually thought of as controllable. An external unstable cause like luck is generally seen as uncontrollable.

Bernard Weiner (1986) argues that there are emotional and motivational implications of differing attributions. Successful outcomes attributed to ourselves increase our self-esteem more than when such outcomes are attributed to external causes like easiness of a task or luck. Weiner especially believes that the attributions we make regarding controllability are of particular importance because personal responsibility is involved. Attributions of controllability for personal failure are linked with such emotions as guilt, shame, and humiliation. By contrast, attributions associated with uncontrollability for personal failure don't lead to such self-criticism. We also hold others responsible for failures attributed to controllable causes and might feel angry toward them. On the other hand, we might feel sympathy toward people whose failures are the result of circumstances beyond their control. For example, consider the situation in which a vase is accidentally knocked off a table and broken, in one instance by a child with a disability, in another by a drunken adult. The child with the disability is likely to elicit sympathy, the drunk anger.

Attributional Errors and Biases   So far what we have said about attribution suggests it is a logical, rational process. However, some common errors and biases infiltrate our attributions.

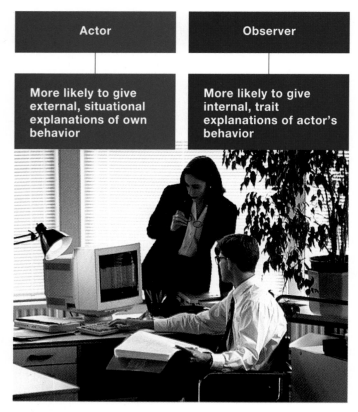

Actor	Observer
More likely to give external, situational explanations of own behavior	More likely to give internal, trait explanations of actor's behavior

Figure 13.1
The Fundamental Attribution Error

In this situation, the female supervisor is the observer and the male employee is the actor. If the employee has made an error in his work, how are the employee and his supervisor likely to differ in their explanations of his behavior, based on your knowledge of actor/observer differences and the fundamental attribution error?

Social Cognition

The Fundamental Attribution Error   In attribution, the person who acts, or the actor, produces the behavior to be explained. Then the onlooker, or the observer, offers a causal explanation of the actor's behavior or experience. Actors often explain their own behavior in terms of external causes. In contrast, observers frequently explain the actor's behavior in terms of internal causes. The **fundamental attribution error** *is that observers overestimate the importance of traits and underestimate the importance of situations when they seek explanations of an actor's behavior* (see figure 13.1).

The fundamental attribution error suggests that when most people encounter examples of social behavior, they have a tendency to explain the behavior in terms of the personalities of the people involved rather than the situation they are in (Aronson, Wilson, & Akert, 1997). For example, when we try to explain why people do repugnant or bizarre things, such as the people in Jonestown, Waco, or the Heaven's Gate cult who took their own lives and the lives of their children, the tendency is to describe them as flawed human beings. This emphasis on traits of victims without considering how they may have been overpowered by the social forces of the situation reflects the fundamental attribution error.

Because actors and observers often have different ideas about what causes behavior, many attributions are biased. Behavior is determined by a number of factors, so it is not surprising that our lives are full of squabbling and arguing about the causes of behavior (Harvey, 1995).

Self-Serving Bias   We tend to be self-enhancing (Sedikides & others, 1998). We often believe that we are more trustworthy, moral, and physically attractive than other people are. We also tend to believe that we are above-average teachers, managers, and leaders. One mechanism through which individuals maintain such exaggerated positive beliefs about themselves involves self-serving bias (Pittman, 1998).

When our self-esteem is threatened, we may depart from the fundamental attribution error and infuse our attributions with a different type of bias. **Self-serving bias** *involves attributing explanations for one's successes to internal factors and explanations for one's failures to external factors.* That is, we tend to take credit for our successes and blame our failures on others or the situation. In the case of Ashley breaking up with Jason, Jason might go along with Ashley's external explanation that she is doing it because of her parents. That's a lot easier for Jason to take than the internal attribution that he basically is a "hermit-like" introvert. As we indicated earlier, self-serving bias tends to rear its head when our self-esteem is threatened.

Social Perception

When we think about our social world and try to make sense of it, we not only make attributions but also engage in these social perceptions: We develop social impressions of others, gain self-knowledge by engaging in social comparison, and present ourselves to others in an attempt to influence their social perceptions of us.

Developing Impressions of Others   Our evaluations of people often fall into broad categories—good or bad, happy or sad, introvert or extravert, for example. If someone asked for your impression of your psychology professor, you might respond, "She is great." Then you might go on to describe your perception of her characteristics, for example, "She is charming, intelligent, witty, and sociable." From this description we can infer that you have a positive impression of her.

As we form impressions of others, we cognitively organize the information in two important ways. First, our impressions are *unified,* and second, our impressions are *integrated.* Traits, actions, appearance, and all of the other information we obtain about a person are closely connected in memory even though the information may have been obtained in an interrupted or random fashion. We might obtain some information today, more next week, some more in 2 months. During those 2 months, we interacted with many other people and developed impressions of them as well. Nonetheless, we usually perceive the information about a particular person as unified, as a continuous block of information (Brown, 1986).

Impressions are integrated, in the sense that we reach beyond the information we have, adding, manipulating, and modifying the information to form a whole impression (Asch, 1946). When we do not have much information about an individual, we stretch it to form a complete impression of that person. In Solomon Asch's original work (1946), participants were asked to think of a short list of traits for an individual. Asch then asked the participants to write character sketches based on a brief list of traits. The sketches included many different combinations of the traits and went far beyond the original list. **Implicit personality theory** *is the term given to the public's or a layperson's conception of how personality traits go together in an individual* (Bruner & Tagiuri, 1954). Implicit personality theory is reflected in this person's perception: "Because most of my friends who are extraverted also are optimistic, I assume all extraverted people are optimistic."

When we integrate information about people, we follow certain rules. We use some evaluative dimensions more than others. Norman Anderson (1974, 1989) thinks we use three dimensions more than any others to categorize people. The most common dimension is good/bad. Think for a moment about the people you know. Chances are you categorize each of them as either good or bad. Our tendency to categorize people as good or bad is so strong that Anderson calls this *the* evaluation dimension. Potency (strong/weak) and activity (active/passive) are two other dimensions we often use to categorize people (see figure 13.2).

You might recall our discussion of schemas from chapter 6, "Memory" ◀║║║ P. 178. A *schema* is a category we use to organize information. When we read a book, we do not remember every paragraph word for word; rather, we get the gist of what the author says and fit the

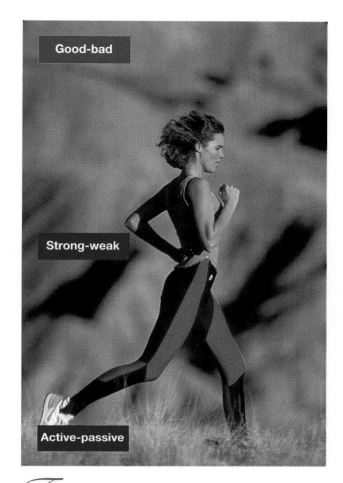

*F*igure 13.2
Developing Impressions of Others: Three Dimensions We Use to Categorize People
Look at the individual running. What is your impression of her? You probably will categorize her as good or bad, possibly as strong or weak, or as active or passive.

What is the prototype for a business executive? How well do these men fit the prototype?

information into existing categories in our mind. We "read" people in a similar way. We don't remember everything about what they are like and what they do, but we get the gist of their personality and behavior, and we fit the information about them into existing categories of memory. One set of categories has been given special attention: **prototypes** *are abstract categorizations of traits that describe a particular personality type.* Prototypes act as standards against which we match the individuals we evaluate. For example, a prototype for extraversion is being outgoing, talkative, and assertive.

We tend to simplify the task of understanding people by classifying them as members of groups or categories with which we are familiar. It takes more mental effort to consider a person's individual characteristics than it does to label her as a member of a particular group or category. Thus, when we categorize an individual, the categorization is often based on stereotypes.

We do not always respond to others on the basis of categories, however. Imagine that you meet a salesman. Based on the category-classification system, you would develop an impression of him based on the "salesman" category. Without seeking any additional information, you might perceive that person as pushy, self-serving, and materialistic; however, as you interact with him, you discover that he is actually interesting, modest, bright, and altruistic. You would then have to revise your impression and perceive him differently. When impressions are formed in this manner, a more individualized, or *individuated*, orientation in impression formation occurs.

The information available largely determines whether a category-based or an individuated-based impression formation will occur. When we discover information that is inconsistent with a category or when we simply become more personally involved with someone, we are more likely to take an individuated approach.

Our first encounter with someone also contributes to the impression we form. First impressions are often enduring. **Primacy effect** *is the term used to describe the enduring quality of initial impressions.* One reason for the primacy effect is that we pay less attention to subsequent information about the individual (Anderson, 1965). The next time you want to impress someone, a wise strategy is to make sure that you put your best foot forward in your first encounter.

Gaining Self-Knowledge from Our Perceptions of Others: Social Comparison

How many times have you asked yourself questions such as "Am I as smart as Jill?" "Is Bob better looking than I am?" or "Is my taste as good as Carmen's?" We gain self-knowledge from our own behavior; we also gain it from others through **social comparison,** *the process in which individuals evaluate their thoughts, feelings, behaviors, and abilities in relation to other people.* Social comparison helps individuals to evaluate themselves, tells them what their distinctive characteristics are, and aids them in building an identity.

Some years ago Leon Festinger (1954) proposed a theory of social comparison. He stressed that when no objective means is available to evaluate our opinions and abilities, we compare ourselves with others. Festinger believed that we are more likely to compare ourselves with others who are similar to us than dissimilar to us. He reasoned that if we compare ourselves with someone who is very different from us, we will not be able to obtain an accurate appraisal of our own behavior and thoughts. This means that we will develop more accurate self-perceptions if we compare ourselves with people in communities similar to where we grew up and live, with people who have similar family backgrounds, and with people of the same sex, for example. Social comparison theory has been extended and modified over the years and continues to provide an important rationale for why we affiliate with others and how we come to know ourselves (Gibbons, Benbow, & Gerrard, 1994; Gibbons & Buunk, 1999).

In contrast to Festinger's emphasis on the role of social comparison in evaluating one's abilities, recently researchers have focused more on the self-enhancing properties of downward comparisons (Wood, 1989). Individuals under threat (from negative feedback, low self-esteem, depression, and illness, for example) try to

PEOPLE

"Randall, my old college nemesis, I was hoping I'd find you here."

EXPLORATIONS IN PSYCHOLOGY
Impression Management and Job Interviewing

MOST OF US WANT to make a good impression the first time we meet someone. We especially want to make a good impression if the other person is interviewing us for a job. What nonverbal cues might we use to improve the likelihood that an interviewer will develop a favorable impression of us? People who are successful at impression management recognize that certain facial expressions, patterns of eye contact, and body postures or movements are part of the reason we are liked or disliked. For example, to improve the likelihood that an interviewer will have a favorable impression of you, you might smile often, lean forward, maintain a high degree of eye contact, and frequently nod your head in agreement with what the interviewer says.

Some people smile frequently, maintain good eye contact, and show a strong interest in what someone else is saying more naturally than others. Even if you don't normally behave this way when you are interacting with someone, you can make a conscious effort to control your nonverbal behavior. In general, researchers have found that individuals who use these impression management techniques receive more favorable ratings than individuals who do not (Riggio, 1986). These nonverbal cues, along with other impression management strategies such as behavioral matching, conforming to situational norms, and showing appreciation of others, apply to a number of social encounters in addition to interviews, including first dates and salesperson-customer situations. In one investigation, it was observed that individuals who were selected for engineering apprenticeships had smiled more, had maintained greater eye contact with the interviewer, and had nodded their heads affirmatively more during their interviews than had rejected applicants (Forbes & Jackson, 1980).

Is there a point, though, at which there can be too much of a good thing and we can overuse impression management? You *can* overdo it, using so many positive nonverbal cues that the other individual perceives you negatively and labels you as insincere. In one research investigation, the frequent use of positive nonverbal cues had favorable outcomes in a job interview situation only when the applicants also had competent qualification (Rasmussen, 1984).

In sum, using positive nonverbal cues can improve the way other people perceive you, but don't overdo it (Reece & Brandt, 1990).

improve their well-being by comparing themselves with someone less fortunate (Gibbons & McCoy, 1991).

Presenting Ourselves to Others to Influence Their Social Perceptions

How do you present yourself to others? Do you try to act naturally and be yourself, or do you deliberately change your behavior to get other people to have a more favorable impression of you? Let's explore two dimensions of presenting ourselves to others to influence their social perceptions: impression management and self-monitoring.

Impression Management   **Impression management** (also called **self-presentation**) *involves acting in a way to present an image of oneself as a certain sort of person, which might or might not be who one really is.* In most instances, we try to present ourselves to look better than we really are. We spend billions of dollars rearranging our faces, bodies, minds, and social skills, usually to make a favorable impression on others. We especially use self-presentational motives with people we are not familiar with and with people toward whom we have a sexual interest (Leary & others, 1994).

Nonverbal cues can often be used in successful impression management. To read about how nonverbal cues can get other people to perceive you positively, especially in a job interview, see Explorations in Psychology.

Keep in mind, though, that impression management techniques that work in one cultural setting may not work in another. In particular, appreciation and flattery are often culture bound. For example, in some Eastern European countries, if one person expresses great admiration for another's watch, courtesy dictates that the watch should be given to the admirer! In the Native American culture of the

THESE STATEMENTS CONCERN personal reactions to a number of situations. No two statements are exactly alike, so consider each statement carefully before answering. If a statement is true or mostly true as applied to you, check the T. If a statement is false or not usually true as applied to you, check the F.

	True	False
1. I find it hard to imitate the behavior of other people.		
2. I guess I put on a show to impress or entertain people.		
3. I would probably make a good actor.		
4. I sometimes appear to others to be experiencing deeper emotions than I actually am.		
5. In a group of people, I am rarely the center of attention.		
6. In different situations and with different people, I often act like very different persons.		
7. I can only argue for ideas I already believe.		
8. In order to get along and be liked, I tend to be what people expect me to be.		
9. I may deceive people by being friendly when I really dislike them.		
10. I'm not always the person I appear to be.		

Scoring: Give yourself one point for each of questions, 1, 5, and 7 that you answered F. Give yourself one point for each of the remaining questions that you answered T. Add up your points. If you are a good judge of yourself and scored 7 or above, you are probably a high-self-monitoring individual; 3 or below, you are probably a low-self-monitoring individual.

Attitudes

Sioux, it's considered courteous to open a conversation with a compliment.

Self-Monitoring Some people are more concerned about and aware of the impressions they make than others are (Snyder & Stukas, 1999). **Self-monitoring** *is individuals' attention to the impressions they make on others and the degree to which they fine-tune their performance accordingly.* Lawyers and actors are among the best self-monitors; salespeople, con artists, and politicians are not far behind. A former mayor of New York City, Fiorello LaGuardia, was so good at self-monitoring that, by watching silent films of his campaign speeches, it was possible to tell which ethnic group he was courting for votes.

Individuals who are very skilled at self-monitoring seek information about appropriate ways to present themselves and invest considerable time in trying to "read" and understand others (Simpson, 1995). In thinking about self-monitoring, keep in mind that overall it is neither good nor bad.

Attitudes

Social thinking involves not only attributions and social perceptions but also attitudes.

Attitudes *are beliefs or opinions about people, objects, and ideas.* We have attitudes about all sorts of things, such as "Most people are out for themselves," "Money is evil," and "Television has caused families to talk less with each other." We also live in a world where people try to influence others' attitudes, as when politicians try to get your vote and advertisers try to convince you that their product is the best.

Many strategies have been devised to change people's attitudes. Two such strategies are foot-in-the-door and door-in-the-face. In the **foot-in-the-door strategy,** *an individual presents a weaker point or makes a small request with which the listeners will probably comply in the beginning, saving the strongest point until the end.* In the words of social psychologist Robert Cialdini (1993), "Start small and build." For example, a sales pitch for a health spa might offer you 4 weeks' use of the facility for $10 and hope that, after the 4 weeks, you will pay $200 for a 1-year membership. In contrast, in the **door-in-the-face strategy,** *a communicator makes the strongest point or demand in the beginning, which the listeners probably will reject, then presents a weaker point or moderate "concessionary" demand toward the end.* For example, the salesperson for the health spa might initially offer you the 1-year membership for $200, which you turn down, then offer you a "bargain" 4-weeks-for-$10 package.

Do Attitudes Predict Behavior? Strategies such as the foot-in-the-door technique imply that changing people's attitudes will lead to changes in their behavior. However, in some cases individuals will say one thing and do another. For example, they might respond in a poll that they are going to vote for one candidate and then actually vote for another. In others, what they say is what they do. Studies over the course of the last half century indicate that under some conditions attitudes guide actions (Eagly & Chalkin, 1998).

Predicting behavior from attitudes is more reliable when the person's attitudes are strong (Petty & Krosnick, 1995). For example, most senators whose attitudes toward President Clinton are "highly favorable" are more likely to vote for his policies than their counterparts who only have "moderately favorable" attitudes toward him. Predicting behavior from attitudes also is more reliable when the person shows a strong awareness of his or her attitudes and when the person rehearses and practices them (Fazio & others, 1982). Furthermore, predicting behavior from attitudes is more reliable when the attitudes are relevant to the behavior. In many instances, the more specifically relevant the attitude is to the behavior, the better it will predict the behavior. For example, in one study, general attitudes toward birth control were virtually unrelated to the use of birth control pills in the next 2 years, but a more specific attitude toward taking birth control pills in the next 2 years showed a much higher correlation with actual use (Davidson & Jacard, 1979).

Can Behavior Predict Attitudes?   In examining attitudes, social psychologists have studied behavior's influence on attitudes, the role that cognitive dissonance plays in the connection between attitudes and behavior, and how perceiving our behavior influences our attitudes.

Behavior's Influence on Attitudes

"The actions of men are the best interpreters of their thoughts," asserted the seventeenth-century English philosopher John Locke. Does doing change your believing? If you quit drinking, will you have a more negative attitude toward drinking? If you take up an exercise program, are you more likely to extol the benefits of cardiovascular fitness when someone asks your attitude about exercise?

Ample evidence exists that changes in behavior sometimes precede changes in attitudes (Bandura, 1989). Social psychologists offer two main explanations of why behavior influences attitudes. The first view is that we have a strong need for cognitive consistency; consequently, we change our attitudes to make them more consistent with our behavior (Carkenord & Bullington, 1995). The second view is that our attitudes are not completely clear, so we observe our behavior and make inferences about it to determine what our attitudes should be. Let's consider these two views in more detail.

Cognitive Dissonance

Cognitive dissonance, *a concept developed by social psychologist Leon Festinger (1957), refers to an individual's motivation to reduce the discomfort (dissonance) caused by two inconsistent thoughts.* We might feel uneasy about a discrepancy that exists between our attitudes and our behavior. The absence of internal justification for the difference between what we believe and what we do creates dissonance (Harmon-Jones & Mills, 1999). We can engage in a variety of actions to reduce the dissonance. For example, most smokers believe it is unhealthy to smoke, yet can't seem to resist lighting up. This discrepancy between attitude and behavior creates discomfort. To reduce this dissonance, the smoker must either stop smoking or change his or her attitudes. "No one has proven smoking kills people" and "I'll have to die from something" are dissonance-reducing attitudes.

We often justify our behavior in our mind, as George Bernard Shaw did with his father's alcoholism: "If you cannot get rid of the family skeleton, you may as well make it dance." Shaw's justification helped him reduce the tension between his attitude about his father's drinking problems and its actual occurrence. Cognitive dissonance is about making our skeletons dance, about trying to reduce tension by cognitively justifying things that are unpleasant (Aronson, 1995).

We justify the negative things we do in life. We need to convince ourselves that we are decent, reasonable human beings. For example, when we have had a bad argument with someone, we often develop a negative attitude toward that person, which justifies the nasty things we said. We also have a strong need to justify the effort we put forth in life. We positively evaluate goals that require

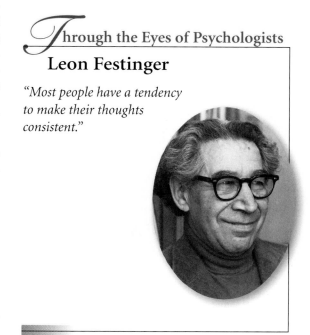

*T*hrough the Eyes of Psychologists

Leon Festinger

"Most people have a tendency to make their thoughts consistent."

considerable effort. Whether we reach the goals or not, we engage in the process of *effort justification*. The reasoning goes like this: if we work hard to attain a goal but then evaluate that goal in a negative way, dissonance would occur. If we put forth considerable effort, yet still do not reach the goal, how could we reduce the dissonance? We could convince ourselves that we did not work as hard as we actually did, or we could say that the goal was not all that important in the first place.

Our most intense justifications of our actions take place when our self-esteem is involved (Aronson, 1999; Aronson, Cohen, & Nails, 1999). If you do something cruel, then it follows that you have to perform some mental gymnastics to keep yourself from thinking you are a cruel person. The clearest results in the hundreds of research studies on cognitive dissonance occur when self-esteem is involved, and it is when individuals with the highest self-esteem act in cruel ways that the most dissonance results. What about individuals with low self-esteem? They probably experience less dissonance because acting in a cruel way is consistent with their attitudes toward themselves—attitudes that might entail such labels as *loser, jerk, zero,* or *bad guy.* Put another way, individuals who think of themselves as bad might do bad things because it keeps dissonance at a minimum.

Not all of our thoughts and behaviors are aimed at reducing dissonance, however. Some of us learn from our mistakes. There are times when we need to catch ourselves, look in the mirror, and say, "You blew it. Now what can you do to prevent that from happening again?" Eliot Aronson (1995) offers three suggestions that can keep our lives from being a treadmill of dissonance reduction:

1. Know your defensive and dissonance-reducing tendencies. Be able to sense them before you get in over your head.
2. Realize that behaving in stupid and cruel ways does not necessarily mean that you are a stupid and cruel person.
3. Develop enough strengths and competencies to be able to tolerate your mistakes without having to spend a lifetime rationalizing them away.

Self-Perception Theory　Not all social psychologists, however, are satisfied with cognitive dissonance as an explanation for the influence of behavior on attitudes. Daryl Bem (1967), for example, believes that the cognitive dissonance view relies too heavily on internal factors, which are difficult to measure. Bem argues that we should move away from such fuzzy and nebulous concepts as "cognitions" and "psychological discomfort" and replace them with more behavioral terminology. **Self-perception theory** *is Bem's theory about the connection between attitudes and behavior; it stresses that individuals make inferences about their attitudes by perceiving their behavior.* For example, consider the remark, "I am spending all of my time thinking about the test I have next week. I must be anxious." Or, "This is the third time I have gone to the student union in two days. I must be lonely." Bem believes we look to our own behavior when our attitudes are not completely clear. This means that when we have clear ideas about something, we are less likely to look to our behavior for clues about our attitudes; but if we feel more ambivalent about something or someone, our behavior is a good place to look to determine our attitude. Figure 13.3 provides a comparison of cognitive dissonance theories and self-perception theories.

Theory	Cognitive dissonance theory	Self-perception theory
Theorist	Festinger	Bem
Nature of theory	We are motivated toward consistency between attitude and behavior and away from inconsistency.	We make inferences about our attitudes by perceiving and examining our behavior and the context in which it occurs, which might involve inducements to behave in certain ways.
Example	"I hate my job. I need to develop a better attitude toward it, or I could quit and be a beach bum."	"I am spending all of my time thinking about how much I hate my job. I really must not like it."

Figure 13.3
Two Theories of the Connections Between Attitudes and Behavior

Which theory is right: the theory of cognitive dissonance or self-perception? Bem's self-perception theory is most compelling when people are not strongly committed to attitudinal positions before taking actions relevant to them (Aronson, Wilson, & Akert, 1997). Self-perception theory also has been more useful in understanding what happens to people's attitudes when they are offered an inducement to do something they would want to do anyway. The pattern of research on cognitive dissonance suggests that the heart of dissonance has to do with not wanting to feel cheap or stupid or guilty. Dissonance theory argues that individuals should avoid information inconsistent with their views. Early attempts to document this selective exposure failed, although more recently researchers have found that people will avoid unpleasant information only if (1) they think they cannot refute the uncomfortable argument, and (2) they are irrevocably committed to their way of thinking or behaving. In sum, cognitive dissonance theory and self-perception theory both have merit in explaining different dimensions of the connection between attitudes and behavior (Sabini, 1995).

At this point we have studied many ideas about social thinking. An overview of these ideas is presented in summary table 13.1. In our discussion of social thinking, we touched on the topic of social influence, such as how we present ourselves to others to influence their perception of us. Next, we will further explore many other aspects of social influence.

Social Influence

Social psychologists are interested in how our behavior is influenced by other people and groups. In this section, we will explore these aspects of social influence: conformity and obedience, group influence, and cultural and ethnic influences.

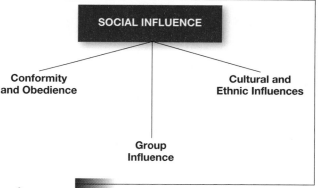

Conformity and Obedience

How extensively do people change their behavior so it will coincide more with what others are doing? How readily do people obey someone in authority? What factors influence whether people will resist such social influences?

Social Influence

Conformity   **Conformity** *involves a change in a person's behavior to coincide more with a group standard.* Conformity comes in many forms and affects many aspects of people's lives. Conformity is at work when a person takes up jogging because everyone else is doing it. Conformity also is present when an individual lets his hair grow short one year because it's fashionable and long next year because long hair has become vogue.

Conformity to rules and regulations results in people's engaging in a number of behaviors that make society run more smoothly. For example, consider what would happen if most people did not conform to rules such as these: stopping at red lights, driving on the correct side of the road, not punching others in the face, and going to school regularly. However, in the following experiments, researchers reveal how conformity pressures can sometimes make us act against our better judgment, which can lead to dramatic, unfortunate consequences.

Asch's Conformity Experiment   Put yourself in this situation: You are taken into a room where you see six other people seated around a table. A person in a white lab coat enters the room and announces that you are about to participate in an experiment on perceptual accuracy. The group is shown two cards, the first having only a single vertical line on it, the second card three vertical lines of varying length. You are told that the task is to determine which of the three lines on the second card is the same length as the line of the first card. You look at the cards and think, "What a snap. It's so obvious which is longest" (see figure 13.4 on p. 445).

SUMMARY TABLE 13.1
Social Thinking

Concept	Processes/Related Ideas	Characteristics/Description
Attribution	What Are Attributions?	Attributions are our thoughts about why people behave the way they do and about who or what is responsible for the outcome of the events. Attribution theory views people as motivated to discover the causes of behavior as part of their effort to make sense of the behavior.
	The Dimensions of Causality	These include internal/external, stable/unstable, and controllable/uncontrollable. There are motivational and emotional implications of differing attributions.
	Attributional Errors and Biases	The fundamental attribution error states that observers overestimate the importance of traits and underestimate the importance of situations when they seek explanations of an actor's behavior. When our self-esteem is threatened, we might depart from the fundamental attribution error and engage in a self-serving bias, which involves attributing explanations for one's success to internal causes and explanations for one's failures to external causes.
Social Perception	Developing Impressions of Others	Our impressions are unified and integrated. An individual's notion of how traits go together is called implicit personality theory. We have social schemas, or prototypes, that we use to evaluate others. We simplify our impressions by categorizing others. In some instances, though, we develop a more individuated approach to impressions. First impressions are important and influence impressions at a later point.
	Gaining Self-Knowledge from Our Perceptions of Others: Social Comparison	We evaluate ourselves by comparison with others. Festinger stresses that social comparison provides an important source of self-knowledge, especially when no other objective means is available. We are more likely to compare ourselves with similar others.
	Presenting Ourselves to Others to Influence Their Social Perceptions	Two dimensions of presenting ourselves to others to influence their social perceptions are impression management (self-presentation) and self-monitoring. Impression management involves acting in a way to present an image of oneself, which might or might not be who one is. Self-monitoring involves individuals' awareness of the impressions they make on others and the degree to which they fine-tune their performance accordingly.
Attitudes	What Are Attitudes?	Attitudes are beliefs or opinions about people, objects, and ideas. Two strategies for changing people's attitudes are foot-in-the-door and door-in-the-face.
	Do Attitudes Predict Behavior?	Under these conditions, predicting behavior from attitudes is likely to be more reliable: when the person's attitudes are strong, when the person is very aware of his or her attitudes and rehearses, and practices them, and when attitudes are specifically relevant to the behavior.
	Can Behavior Predict Attitudes?	Evidence exists that sometimes changes in behavior precede changes in attitude. Cognitive dissonance theory, developed by Festinger, argues that we have a strong need for cognitive consistency. We change our attitudes to make them more consistent with our behavior in order to reduce dissonance. In many cases, this involves justification of our actions. Justification is most intense when our self-esteem is involved. Not all of our thoughts are dissonance reducing. Bem developed a more behavioral approach called self-perception theory. It stresses the importance of making inferences about our own behavior, especially when our attitudes are not clear.

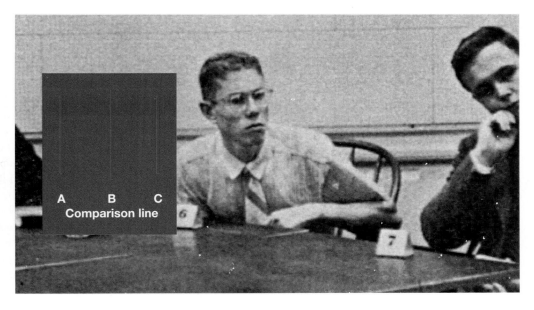

Figure 13.4
Asch's Conformity Experiment

The figures on the left show the stimulus materials for the Asch conformity experiment on group influence. The photograph shows the dilemma for one subject after five confederates of the experimenter chose the incorrect line.

The other people in the room are actually in league with the experimenter; they've been hired to perform in ways the experimenter dictates (of course, you are not aware of this). On the first several trials everyone agrees about which line matches the standard. Then on the fourth trial each of the others picks an incorrect line; you have a puzzled look on your face. As the last person to make a choice, you're in the dilemma of responding as your eyes tell you or conforming to what the others before you said. How do you think you would answer?

Solomon Asch conducted this classic experiment on conformity in 1951. He believed there would be little yielding to group pressure. To find out if this was so, Asch instructed the hired accomplices to give incorrect responses on 12 of the 18 trials. To his surprise, Asch found that the volunteer participants conformed to the incorrect answers 35 percent of the time. (Figure 13.4 shows the actual participants in Asch's experiment on conformity.) The pressure to conform is strong. Even in a clear-cut situation, such as the Asch experiment, we often conform to what others say and do. We don't want to be laughed at or have others be angry with us.

In a more recent test of group pressure and conformity, college students watched the third Bush-Clinton presidential debate and then rated the candidates' performances (Fein & others, 1993). Students were randomly assigned to one of three groups: (1) a 30-student group that included 10 confederates of the experimenter who openly supported Bush and criticized Clinton, (2) a 30-student group that included 10 confederates who cheered Clinton and put down Bush, and (3) a 30-student group with no confederates of the experimenter. The effects of the group pressure exerted by the confederates were powerful; even Bush supporters rated Clinton's performance more favorably when their group included pro-Clinton confederates of the experimenter.

Factors that Contribute to Conformity   Many factors influence whether an individual will conform or not (Cialdini & Trost, 1998). When people do conform, they usually do so because of either normative social influence or informational social influence. **Normative social influence** *is the influence that other people* *have on us because we seek their approval or avoid their disapproval.* When normative social influence is at work, we conform in order to be liked and accepted by others. So if a group is important to us, we might wear a particular kind of clothing, adopt a particular hairstyle, use some slang words, and show a certain set of attitudes that characterize the group's members.

Informational social influence *is the influence other people have on us because we want to be right.* Thus, while normative social influence causes people to conform because they want to be liked, informational social influence causes people to conform because they want to be right (Taylor, Peplau, & Sears, 1997). The tendency to conform based on informational social influence especially depends on two factors: how confident we are in our own independent judgment and how well-informed we perceive the group to be. Thus, if you don't know much about computers and three of your acquaintances who work in the computer industry say not to buy a particular brand of computer, you are likely to conform to their recommendation.

Let's explore some other factors involved in conforming or not conforming. In Asch's study with lines on cards, the group opinion was unanimous. When unanimity is broken, the group's power is lessened and individuals feel less pressure to conform. Also, if you do not have a prior commitment to an idea or action, you are more likely to be influenced by others. If you publicly commit to a course of action, conformity to another point of view is less likely.

Three other factors that contribute to conformity involve an individual's characteristics, the characteristics of the group members, and the culture in which people live. People with low self-esteem and doubts about their abilities are more likely to conform (Campbell, Tesser, & Fairey, 1986), and you are more likely to conform if the group members are experts, attractive to you, or similar to you in any way. In experiments conducted in fourteen countries, conformity rates were lower in individualistic cultures (like that of the United States) and higher in collectivistic cultures (like that of China) (Bond & Smith, 1994).

Obedience

Obedience   **Obedience** *is behavior that complies with the explicit demands of the individual in authority.* That is, we are obedient when someone demands that we do something and we do it. How is obedience different from conformity? In conformity, people change their thinking or behavior so that it will be more like others'. Explicit demands are not made to conform. However, such demands are present in obedience (Miller, 2000).

Obedient behavior sometimes can be destructive. The mass suicides at Jonestown described at the beginning of the chapter, the massacre of Vietnamese civilians at My Lai, and the Nazi crimes against Jews in World War II are other examples of destructive obedience. Karl Adolf Eichmann, for example, has been described as an ambitious functionary who believed that it was his duty to obey Hitler's orders. An average middle-class man with no identifiable criminal tendencies, Eichmann ordered the killing of 6 million Jews. The following experiment by Stanley Milgram provides insight into such obedience.

As part of an experiment in psychology, you are asked to deliver a series of painful electric shocks to another person. You are told that the purpose of the study is to determine the effects of punishment on memory. Your role is to be the "teacher" and punish the mistakes made by the "learner." Each time the learner makes a mistake your job is to increase the intensity of the shock by a certain amount.

You are introduced to the "learner," a nice 50-year-old man who mumbles something about having a heart condition. He is strapped to a chair in the next room; he communicates with you through an intercom. As the trials proceed, the "learner" quickly runs into trouble and is unable to give the correct answers. Should you shock him? The apparatus in front of you has thirty switches, ranging from 15 volts (light) to 450 volts (marked as dangerous, "severe shock XXX"). Before this part of the experiment began, you had been given a 75-volt shock to see how it feels. As you raise the intensity of the shock, the "learner" says he's in pain. At 150 volts, he demands to have the experiment stopped. At 180 volts, he cries out that he can't stand it

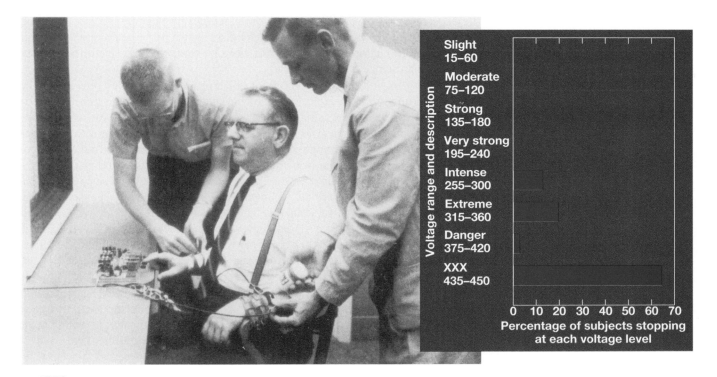

Voltage range and description	Percentage of subjects stopping at each voltage level
Slight 15–60	
Moderate 75–120	
Strong 135–180	
Very strong 195–240	
Intense 255–300	
Extreme 315–360	
Danger 375–420	
XXX 435–450	

Figure 13.5

Milgram Obedience Study

A 50-year-old man ("learner") is strapped into a chair. The experimenter makes it look as if a shock generator is being connected to his body through several electrodes. The chart at the right shows the percentage of subjects ("teachers") who stopped shocking the experimenter at each voltage level.

anymore. At 300 volts, he yells about his heart condition and pleads to be released. But if you hesitate in shocking the learner, the experimenter tells you that you have no choice, the experiment must continue.

The experiment just described is a classic one devised by Stanley Milgram (1963, 1974) to study obedience. As you might imagine, the "teachers" were uneasy about shocking the "learner." At 240 volts, one "teacher" responded, "240 volts delivered; aw, no. You mean I've got to keep going with that scale? No sir, I'm not going to kill that man—I'm not going to give him 450 volts!" (Milgram, 1965). At the very high voltage, the "learner" quit responding. When the "teacher" asked the experimenter what to do, he simply instructed the "teacher" to continue the experiment and told him that it was his obligation to complete the job. Figure 13.5 shows the results of the study and what the situation in the Milgram experiment was like. By the way, the 50-year-old man was in league with the experimenter. He was not being shocked at all. Of course, the "teachers" were completely unaware of this.

Forty psychiatrists were asked how they thought individuals would respond to this situation. The psychiatrists predicted that most would go no further than 150 volts, that less than 1 in 25 would go as far as 300 volts, and that only 1 in 1,000 would deliver the full 450 volts. The psychiatrists, it turns out, were way off the mark. The majority of the individuals obeyed the experimenter. In fact, almost two of every three delivered the full 450 volts.

In subsequent studies, Milgram set up a storefront in Bridgeport, Connecticut, and recruited volunteers through newspaper ads. Milgram wanted to create a more natural environment for the experiment and to use a wider cross section of volunteers. In these additional studies, close to two-thirds of the individuals still selected the highest level of shock for the "learner." In variations

Through the Eyes of Psychologists

Stanley Milgram *(1933–1984)*

"Most people do what they are told to do as long as they perceive that the command comes from a legitimate authority."

of the experiment, Milgram discovered some factors that encouraged disobedience: When an opportunity was given to see others disobey, when the authority figure was not perceived to be legitimate and was not close by, and when the victim was made to seem more human.

We're going to sidetrack for a moment and raise an important point about the Milgram experiments: How *ethical* were they? The volunteers in Milgram's experiment clearly felt anguish and some were very disturbed about "harming" another individual. After the experiment was completed, they were told that the "learner" was not actually shocked. Even though they were debriefed and told that they really had not shocked or harmed anyone, was the anguish imposed on them ethical?

Milgram argues that we have learned a great deal about human nature from the experiments. He claims that they tell us how far individuals will go in their obedience, even if it means being cruel to someone. The volunteers were interviewed later and more than four of every five said that they were glad they had participated in the study; none said they were sorry they participated. When Milgram conducted his studies on obedience, the ethical guidelines for research were not as stringent as they are today. The current ethical guidelines of the American Psychological Association stress that researchers should obtain informed consent from their volunteers. Deception should be used only for very important purposes. Individuals are supposed to feel as good about themselves when the experiment is over as they did when it began. Under today's guidelines, it is unlikely that the Milgram experiment would be conducted.

Resisting Social Influence   "If a man does not keep pace with his companions, perhaps it is because he hears a different drummer. Let him step to the music which he hears, however measured or far away." Thoreau's words suggest that some of us resist social influence. Most of us would prefer to think of ourselves as stepping to our own music, maybe even setting the rhythms for others, rather than trying to keep pace with our companions. However, a certain degree of conformity is required if society is to function at all. As we go through our lives we are both conformists and nonconformists. Sometimes we are overwhelmed by the persuasion and influence of others; in other circumstances we resist and gain personal control over our lives. It is important to remember that our relation to the social world is recip-

In 1989, Chinese students led a massive demonstration against the Chinese government in Beijing. The students resisted the government's social influence by putting together resources to challenge the Chinese authorities; however, the government eventually eliminated the protests, massacring hundreds.

rocal. Individuals may be trying to control us, but we can exert personal control over our actions and influence others in turn (Bandura, 1986).

If you believe someone in a position of authority is making an unjust request or asking you to do something wrong, what choice of action do you have?

- You can comply.
- You also can give the appearance of complying but secretly do otherwise.
- You can publicly dissent by showing doubts and disenchantment but still follow directives.
- You can openly disregard the orders and refuse to comply.
- You can challenge or confront the authority.
- You might get higher authorities to intervene or organize a group of people who agree with you to show the strength of your view.

Group Influence

A student joining a fraternity, a jury making a decision about a criminal case, a president of a company delegating authority, a prejudiced remark against a minority group, conflict among nations, and attempts to reach peace—all of these circumstances reflect our lives as members of groups. The smallest group (called a "dyad") consists of two people. Each of us belongs to many different groups. Some we choose, others we do not. We choose to belong to a club, but we are all born into a particular ethnic group, for example. Some of the important questions about group relations are these: Why do we join groups? What is the structure of groups? How do we perform and make decisions in groups? Why are some people leaders and others followers? How do groups deal with each other, especially ethnic groups?

Group Dynamics
Group Processes

Motivation for Group Behavior and the Structure of Groups

Why does one student join a study group? A church? An athletic team? A company? Groups satisfy our personal needs, reward us, provide information, raise our self-esteem, and give us an identity. We might join a group because we think it will be enjoyable and exciting and satisfy our need for affiliation and companionship. We might join a group because we will receive rewards, either material or psychological. By taking a job with a company we get paid to work for a group, but we also reap prestige and recognition. Groups are an important source of information. For example, as we listen to other members talk in a Weight Watchers group we learn about their strategies for losing weight. As we sit in the audience at a real estate seminar we learn how to buy property with no money down. The groups in which you are a member—your family, college, a club, a team—make you feel good, raise your self-esteem, and provide you with an identity.

Any group to which you belong has certain things in common with all other groups. **Norms** *are rules that apply to all members of a group.* A sorority may require each of its members to maintain a 3.00 grade point average. This is a norm. The city government requires each of its workers to wear socks. Mensa requires individuals to have a high IQ. The Polar Bear club says its members must complete a 15-minute swim in below-freezing temperatures. These, too, are norms.

Roles *are rules and expectations that govern certain positions in the group.* Roles define how people should behave in a particular position in the group. In a family, parents have certain roles, siblings have other roles, and a grandparent has yet another role. On a football team, many different roles must be fulfilled: center, guard, tackle, end, quarterback, running back, and wide receiver, for example, and that only covers the offense. Roles and norms, then, tell us what is expected of a particular group.

Group Performance

Do we perform better in a group or when alone? The very first experiment in social psychology examined this question. Norman Triplett (1898) found that bicyclists performed better when they raced against each other than when they raced alone against the clock. Triplett also built a "competition

Do you perform better as a member of a group or as an individual?

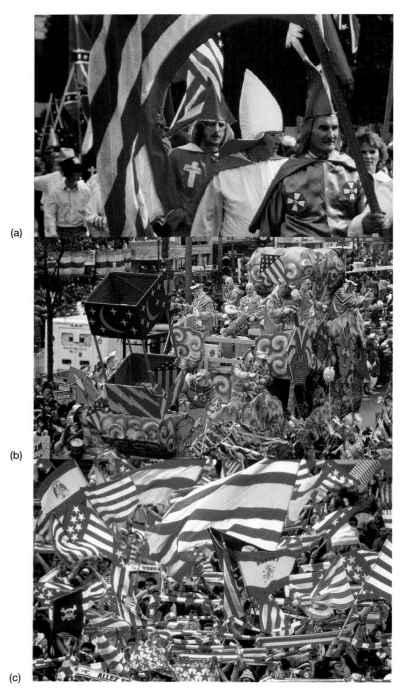

(a)

(b)

(c)

We can become deindividuated in groups. Examples of situations in which people can lose their individual identity include (a) at Ku Klux Klan rallies, (b) at Mardi Gras, and (c) in national patriotism crowds.

machine" made out of fishing reels. The machine allowed two individuals to turn the reels side by side. Observing 40 children, he discovered that those who reeled next to another child worked faster than those who reeled alone.

Since Triplett's work almost a century ago, many investigations of group versus individual performance have been conducted. Some studies reveal that we do better in groups, others that we are more productive when we work alone (Paulus, 1989). Is there any way we can make sense out of these contradictory findings?

Social facilitation *is the phenomenon that occurs when an individual's performance improves because of the presence of others.* Social facilitation occurs with well-learned tasks but not with new or difficult tasks. Robert Zajonc (1965) argued that the presence of other individuals arouses us. The arousal produces energy and facilitates our performance in groups. If our arousal is too high, however, we won't be able to learn new or difficult tasks efficiently. Social facilitation, then, improves our performance on well-learned tasks. For new or difficult tasks, we might be best advised to work things out on our own before trying them in a group. If you are good at basketball, you might perform better when others are watching, but, if you are just learning to play golf, you probably will fare better if you step up to the first tee when no one else is around. In one investigation, expert and poor pool players were observed in the student union at Virginia Polytechnic Institute (Michaels & others, 1982). When they were observed unobtrusively, the experts hit 71 percent of their shots, the poor players 36 percent; when four individuals walked up to observe their play, however, the experts improved, making 80 percent of their shots, whereas the poor players got worse, making only 25 percent of their shots.

Another factor in group performance is how closely our behavior is monitored. **Social loafing** *is each person's tendency to exert less effort in a group because of reduced monitoring.* The effect of social loafing is lowered group performance (Latané, 1981). Social loafing is common when a group of students is assigned a school project. The larger the group, the more likely a person can loaf without being detected. One way to decrease social loafing is for people to develop a sense of personal responsibility (Brickner, Harkins, & Ostrom, 1986). Another way is to provide a standard that allows the group to evaluate its performance.

Our behavior in groups also can become deindividuated (Dodd, 1995). **Deindividuation** *occurs when the presence of a group results in the loss of personal identity and a decrease in responsibility.* As early as 1895, Gustav LeBon observed that a group can foster uninhibited behavior, ranging from wild celebrations to mob activity. Ku Klux Klan violence, Mardi Gras wild times, and a mob rolling a car on spring break in Fort Lauderdale might be due to deindividuated behavior. One explanation of deindividuation is that groups give us anonymity. We may act in a disinhibited way because we believe that authority figures and victims are less likely to discover that we are the culprits.

Group Interaction and Decision Making
Many of the decisions we make take place in a group—juries, teams, families, clubs, school boards, the Senate, a class vote, for example (Davis, 1996; Levine & Moreland, 1998). What happens

when people put their minds to the task of making a group decision? How do they decide whether a criminal is guilty, a country should attack another, a family should stay home or go on vacation, or sex education should be part of a school curriculum? Three aspects of group decision making bear special mention: the risky shift and group polarization, groupthink, and majority-minority influence.

The Risky Shift and Group Polarization   When we make decisions in a group, do we take risks and stick our necks out or do we compromise our opinions and move toward the center? The **risky shift** *is the tendency for a group decision to be riskier than the average decision made by individual group members.* In one investigation, fictitious dilemmas were presented, and subjects were asked how much risk the characters in the dilemmas were willing to take (Stoner, 1961). When the individuals discussed the dilemmas as a group, they were more willing to say the characters would make risky decisions than when they were queried alone. Many studies have been conducted on this topic with similar results (Goethals & Demorest, 1995).

We do not always make riskier decisions in a group than when alone; however, hundreds of research studies show that being in a group does move us even more strongly in the direction of the position we initially held (Moscovici, 1985). The **group polarization effect** *is the solidification and further strengthening of a position as a consequence of group discussion.* A "hawk" in the Senate may listen to endless hours of committee discussion about nuclear disarmament; a Senate "dove" hears the same words. After 2 years on the committee, each is even more strongly committed to her position than before the deliberation began. Initially held views often become even more polarized because of group discussion.

Why does group polarization occur? It may take place because people hear more persuasive arguments as group members than they knew about previously; such arguments strengthen their position. It might also occur because of social comparison. We may find that our position is not as extreme as others, which may motivate us to take a stand at least as strong as the most extreme advocate of the position.

Groupthink   Sometimes groups make rational decisions and come up with the best solution to a problem. But not always. Group members, especially leaders, often seek to develop or maintain unanimity among group members (Whyte, 2000). **Groupthink** *involves impaired decision making and avoidance of realistic appraisal to maintain group harmony.* Groupthink evolves because members boost each other's ego and increase each other's self-esteem by seeking conformity, especially in the face of stress (Janis, 1972). Groupthink involves many heads, but only one group mind. This motivation for harmony and unanimity can result in disastrous decisions and policy recommendations. Examples of groupthink include the United States invasion of Cuba (the Bay of Pigs), escalation of the Vietnam war, failure to prepare for the invasion of Pearl Harbor, the Watergate coverup, Irangate, and the explosion of the space shuttle *Challenger.* In the case of the *Challenger,* NASA leaders went ahead with the launch of the space shuttle in 1985 despite engineers' objections that the freezing temperatures might damage the O-ring seals (which eventually failed during the launch and caused the rocket's explosion and death of all crew members aboard). Because of a string of successes in recent launches and overconfidence of higher-up NASA leaders, the engineers' objections were ignored in a disastrous groupthink decision.

In groupthink, leaders typically have a favored solution and promote it within the group. Members of the group also tend to be cohesive and isolate themselves from qualified outsiders who could influence their decisions (as the NASA leaders did when they isolated themselves from the engineers and ignored their judgments). Leaders can avoid groupthink by encouraging dissident opinions, by not presenting a favored plan at the outset, and by having several independent groups working on the same problem.

Leadership   "I am certainly not one of those who needs to be prodded. In fact, if anything, I am the prod," the British Prime Minister Winston Churchill once

Groupthink

"All those in favor say 'Aye.'"
"Aye."   "Aye."   "Aye."   "Aye."   "Aye."

© *The New Yorker Collection 1979 Henry Martin from cartoonbank.com. All Rights Reserved.*

(a)

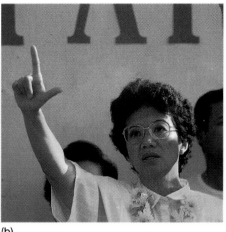

(b)

Certain individuals in the minority have played important roles in history. (a) Martin Luther King, Jr., helped African Americans gain important rights. (b) Corazon Aquino, who became president of the Philippines after defeating Ferdinand Marcos, toppled a corrupt political regime and reduced the suffering of many Philippine citizens.

Leadership

said of himself. What made Churchill a great leader? Was it a set of personality traits, the situation into which he was thrust, or some combination of the two?

The **great-person theory** *says that some individuals have certain traits that are best suited for leadership positions.* Leaders are commonly thought to be assertive, cooperative, decisive, dominant, energetic, self-confident, tolerant of stress, willing to assume responsibility, diplomatic and tactful, and persuasive. While we can list traits and skills possessed by leaders, a large number of research studies conclude that we cannot predict who will become a leader solely from the individual's personality characteristics.

Is it the situation, then, that produces leaders? The situational view of leadership argues that the needs of a group change from time to time. The individual who emerges as the leader in one particular circumstance will not necessarily be the individual who becomes the leader in another circumstance.

The **contingency model of leadership** *states that both personality characteristics and situational influences determine who will become a leader.* Leadership is viewed as a complex undertaking in which leaders influence their followers and followers influence their leaders (Fielder, 1978). In the contingency model, leaders follow one of two styles: They direct leadership either toward getting a task completed or toward members' relationships (helping members get along). Is one of these two styles superior? The contingency model emphasizes that the appropriate style of leadership depends on the situation. If a group is working under very favorable or very unfavorable conditions, a task-oriented leader is better, but if group conditions are more moderate, a relationship-oriented leader is better. Full tests of these ideas have not been made, but the concept that leadership is a function of both personality characteristics and situational influences is an important one.

Majority and Minority Influence   Think about the groups in which you have been a member. Who had the most influence, the majority or the minority? In most groups—whether a jury, family, or corporate meeting—the majority holds sway over the minority. The majority exerts both normative and informational pressure on the group. Its adherents set the group's norm; those who do not go along may be rejected or even given the boot. The majority also has a greater opportunity to provide information that will influence decision making.

In most cases the majority wins, but there are occasions when the minority has its day (Latané, 1996). How can the minority swing the majority? The minority cannot win through normative influence because it is outnumbered. It must do its work through *informational pressure.* If the minority presents its view consistently and confidently, then the majority is more likely to listen to the minority's views.

In group situations, some individuals are able to command the attention of others and thus have a better opportunity to shape and direct subsequent social outcomes. To achieve such a high social impact, they have to distinguish themselves in various ways from the rest of the group. They have to make themselves noticed by others—by the opinions they express, the jokes they tell, or their nonverbal style. They might be the first ones to raise a new idea, to disagree with a prevailing point of view, or to propose a creative alternative solution to a problem. People who have a strong social impact often are willing to be different.

(a)   (b)

Conflicts among ethnic and cultural groups are common in today's world. They include conflicts between (a) Israelis and Palestinians in the Middle East and (b) ethnic and cultural groups in the United States, spurred by incidences such as the beating of African American Rodney King by White police officers.

Certain individuals in a minority may play a crucial role. Individuals with a history of taking minority stands may trigger others to dissent, showing them that disagreement is possible and that it may be the best course. Such is the ground of some of history's greatest moments—when Lincoln spoke out against slavery, racism dominated and tore at the country; when Corazon Aquino became a candidate for president of the Philippines, few people thought Ferdinand Marcos could be beaten.

Cultural and Ethnic Influences

Membership in some groups, such as cultural and ethnic groups, can be especially intense. This intensity can generate conflicts and produce clashes between the groups. In chapter 1 ("What is Psychology?") we described the nature of sociocultural diversity ◄▥▥▥ P. 12. Here we focus on the prejudice, stereotyping, and ethnocentrism that often characterize cultural and ethnic groups, as well as ways to improve interethnic relations.

Conflicts among ethnic and cultural groups are rampant around the world today. Serbs and Croats act on centuries-old hatred related to geographic, familial, and political loyalties in the former country known as Yugoslavia. Israelis and Palestinians bicker and fight over territory in the Middle East, each claiming religious rights to disputed land. In Africa, the countries of Rwanda and Burundi are experiencing civil turmoil as new tribal chiefs try to craft a new social order favorable to their own rule. In Northern Ireland, clashes between Catholics and Protestants break out with almost clockwork regularity. And in the United States, ethnic clashes continue to appear as the outgrowth of such things as the widely televised videotape of White Los Angeles police officers beating Rodney King, an African American. Prejudice, stereotyping, and ethnocentrism can help us understand the intensity of such cultural and ethnic conflicts.

PeaceNet
Racism

Prejudice, Stereotyping, and Ethnocentrism   Understanding the antagonism that develops between groups requires knowledge about prejudice, stereotyping, and ethnocentrism. These factors are involved in discrimination against groups.

Prejudice   Prejudice is a worldwide phenomenon. Its dark side has appeared on many occasions in human history, including the ethnic and cultural clashes in today's world that we just mentioned. The population of North American Indians dropped from an estimated 3 million in the seventeenth century to about 600,000 today

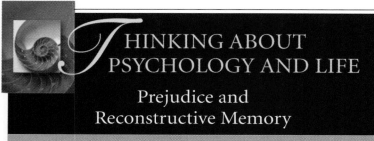

THINKING ABOUT PSYCHOLOGY AND LIFE

Prejudice and Reconstructive Memory

IN CHAPTER 6, "MEMORY," you read about the pioneering work of Sir Frederick Bartlett on reconstructive memory. Since Bartlett's research in the 1930s, hundreds of studies have shown that memory is reconstructive and that people often distort information to fit their assumptions and cultural expectations (Task Force on Diversity Issues, 1998). Our schemas influence what we recall about members of particular groups. In one early study on rumors, an initial description of a razor being held by a White workman was changed to the point at which the razor was being held by a well-dressed African American man (Allport & Postman, 1947).

How might people's prejudices influence what they remember about people? How might they influence what we see or hear about? How might this tendency to remember or forget things systematically help or hinder our encounters with others?

because of brutal slayings. More than 6 million Jews were murdered by the Nazis in the 1940s under the justification of "purifying" the European racial stock. Only a fraction of the world's Jews remain in Europe today.

Whites' racial prejudice against African Americans has characterized much of America's history. When Africans were imported into America as slaves, they were described as property and treated in subhuman ways. In the first half of the twentieth century, most African Americans still lived in the South and were still largely segregated by law—restaurants, movie theaters, and buses had separate areas for Whites and African Americans. Even with the downfall of segregation, much higher portions of African Americans than Whites live below the poverty line today.

African Americans and Native Americans are not the only ethnic minority groups that have been subjected to prejudice in the United States. Many Latinos also live below the poverty line and have low educational achievement and low-paying jobs. Historically, lesbians and gays have been subjected to considerable prejudice from the heterosexual majority. This prejudice has been so intense that most homosexuals stayed "in the closet" until recently, not revealing their sexual preferences for fear of prejudice and discrimination. In fact, virtually every social group has been the victim of prejudice at one time or another.

You probably are reasonably sure that you know what prejudice means. And, like most people, you probably don't think of yourself as prejudiced. In fact, each of us has prejudices and stereotypes. **Prejudice** *is an unjustified negative attitude toward an individual based on the individual's membership in a group.* The group against which the individual is prejudiced can be made up of people of a particular race, sex, age, religion, nation, or can have some other detectable difference (Jones, 1997).

Through the Eyes of Psychologists

James Jones, *University of Delaware*

"Prejudice narrows understanding by biasing our judgments and predetermining what will be discovered from exploring our environment."

Stereotyping   A **stereotype** *is a generalization about a group's characteristics that does not consider any variation from one individual to the next.* Think about your image of a dedicated accountant. Most of us would probably describe such a person as quiet, boring, unsocial, and so on. Rarely would we come up with a mental image of this person as extraverted, the life of the party, or artistic. Characterizing all accountants as boring is a clear example of a stereotype. Another stereotype is to describe all Italians as excitable. Researchers have found that we are less likely to detect variations among individuals who belong to "other" groups than those who belong to "our" group. For example, Whites are more likely to stereotype African Americans than other Whites during eye-witness identification (Brigham, 1986).

Stereotypes often are described as cognitive categories that people use when thinking about groups and individuals from these groups (Fiske, 1998; Steele, 1996). In this cognitive perspective, the perceiver's beliefs about social groups are biased. Some individuals also might engage in stereotyping without being aware of it (Greenwald & Banaji, 1995).

Ethnocentrism   **Ethnocentrism** *is the tendency to favor one's own group over other groups.* Ethnocentrism's positive side is that it fosters a sense of pride in our group that fulfills the human urge to attain and maintain a positive self-image. As we enter the new millennium, group pride has mushroomed. There's Black Pride and Gay Pride. The Scots grow more Scottish, the Irish more Irish.

There is something paradoxical, though, about such pride. Most members of a group will attest that the group does not discriminate against others. As African American activist Stokeley Carmichael said in 1966, "I'm for the Negro. I'm not against anything." Too often members of groups stress differences with others rather than solely emphasizing pride in their own group (Spencer, 2000).

However, in-group pride does not always reflect ethnocentrism. What might be occurring in some in-group/out-group considerations is in-group/out-group bias, the tendency to view members of one's own group as having heterogeneous and desirable qualities and to view the members of other groups as having homogeneous and undesirable qualities. Members of socioeconomical and/or sociopolitical minority groups (such as women, African Americans, Latinos, and gays and lesbians) often assert in-group pride as a necessary counter to the many overt and covert messages transmitted by society that denigrate them simply by virtue of their group membership (Crocker, Major, & Steele, 1998; Gaines & Reed, 1995).

Henry Tajfel (1978) proposed **social identity theory,** *which states that when individuals are assigned to a group, they invariably think of the group as an in-group for them.* This occurs because individuals want to have a positive self-image. Social

Group members often show considerable pride in their group identity, as reflected in (a) African Americans' celebration of Martin Luther King Day, (b) Mexican Americans' celebration of Cinco de Mayo, (c) Native Americans' celebration of their heritage, and (d) Polish Americans' celebration of their cultural background.

identity theory helps explain prejudice and conflict between groups. Tajfel is one of an increasingly small group of European Jews who survived World War II. His goal was to explain the extreme violence and prejudice his group experienced.

Self-image consists of both a personal identity and many different social identities. Tajfel argues that individuals can improve their self-image by enhancing either their personal or their social identity. Tajfel believes our social identity is especially important. When we compare the social identity of our group with the social identity of another group, we often maximize the distinctiveness of the two groups. Think about your social identity with your home town. Or imagine two fans of professional basketball teams, one of whom lives in Chicago and is a Chicago Bulls fan, the other of whom lives in Salt Lake City and is a Utah Jazz fan. When the Bulls won the 1998 NBA title, the Bulls fan's self-image was enhanced.

As these two fans talk with each other, they argue about the virtues of their teams, reinforcing the distinctiveness of their social identities with two different groups. As they strive to promote their social identities, it is not long before they intersperse proud, self-congratulatory remarks with nasty comments about the opposing team. In a capsule, the theme of the conversation has become, "My team is good and I am good. Your team is bad and you are bad." And so it goes with the sexes, ethnic groups, nations, social classes, religions, sororities, fraternities, and countless other groups. These comparisons often lead to competition and even to "legitimizing" discrimination against other groups.

Tajfel showed that for us to think in terms of "we" and "they," it doesn't take much. For example, he assigned one person to a particular group because she overestimated the number of dots on a screen. He assigned another person to a different group because he underestimated the number. Once assigned to the two groups, the members were asked to award money to other participants. Those eligible to receive the money were distinguished only by their membership in one of the two groups just described. Invariably, an individual acted favorably (awarded money) toward a member of his or her own group. It is no wonder, then, that if we favor our own group based on such trivial criteria that we will show intense in-group favoritism when differences are not so trivial (Hogg, 1996).

Improving Interethnic Relations

Martin Luther King once said, "I have a dream that my four little children will one day live in a nation where they will not be judged by the color of their skin but by the content of their character." How might we possibly reach the world Martin Luther King envisioned—a world without prejudice and racism? Researchers have consistently found that contact itself does not improve relations with people from other ethnic backgrounds (Brewer & Brown, 1998). What does improve interethnic relations?

Diversity

Superordinate Goals   Years ago social psychologist Muzafer Sherif and his colleagues (1961) fueled "we/they" competition between two groups of 11-year-old boys at a summer camp called Robbers Cave in Oklahoma. In the first week one group hardly knew the other group existed. One group became known as the Rattlers (a tough and cussing group whose shirts were emblazoned with a snake insignia) and the other was known as the Eagles.

Near the end of the first week each group learned of the other's existence. It took little time for "we/they" talk to surface ("They had better not be on our ball field." "Did you see the way one of them was sneaking around?"). Sherif, who disguised himself as a janitor so he could unobtrusively observe the Rattlers and Eagles, arranged for the two groups to compete in baseball, touch football, and tug-of-war. Counselors manipulated and judged events so the teams were close. Each team perceived the other to be unfair. Raids, burning the other group's flag, and fights resulted. The Rattlers and Eagles further derided one another, as they held their noses in the air as they passed each other. Rattlers described all Rattlers as brave, tough, and friendly, and called all Eagles sneaky and smart alecks. The Eagles reciprocated by labeling the Rattlers crybabies.

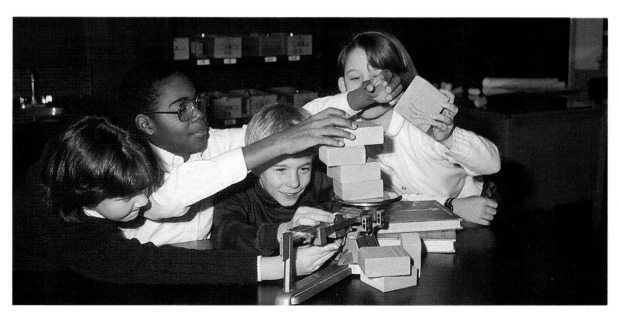

Eliot Aronson developed the concept of the jigsaw classroom to reduce ethnic conflict. How does the jigsaw classroom work?

After we/they competition transformed the Rattlers and Eagles into opposing "armies," Sherif devised ways to reduce hatred between the groups. He tried noncompetitive contact but that didn't work. Only when both groups were required to work cooperatively to solve a problem did the Rattlers and Eagles develop a positive relationship. Sherif created superordinate tasks that required the efforts of both groups: working together to repair the only water supply to the camp, pooling their money to rent a movie, and cooperating to pull the camp truck out of a ditch.

Might Sherif's idea—that of creating cooperation between groups rather than competition—be applied to ethnic groups? When the schools of Austin, Texas, were desegregated through extensive busing, increased racial tension among African Americans, Mexican Americans, and Whites resulted in violence in the schools. The superintendent consulted Eliot Aronson, a prominent social psychologist, who was at the University of Texas in Austin at the time. Aronson (1986) thought it was more important to prevent ethnic hostility than to control it. He observed a number of elementary school classrooms in Austin and saw how fierce the competition was between children of unequal status.

Aronson stressed that the reward structure of the classrooms needed to be changed from a setting of unequal competition to one of cooperation among equals, without making any curriculum changes. To accomplish this, he put together the *jigsaw classroom*. The jigsaw classroom works by creating a situation where all of the students have to pull together to get the "big picture." Let's say we have a class of 30 students, some White, some African American, and some Latino. The academic goal is to learn about the life of Joseph Pulitzer. The class might be broken up into five study groups of six students each, with the groups being as equal as possible in terms of ethnic composition and academic achievement level. Learning about Pulitzer's life becomes a class project divided into six parts, with one part given to each member of the six-person group. The components might be paragraphs from Pulitzer's biography, such as how the Pulitzer family came to the United States, Pulitzer's childhood, his early work, and so on. The parts are like the pieces of a jigsaw puzzle. They have to be put together to form the complete puzzle.

Each student has an allotted time to study her or his part. Then the group meets and each member tries to teach her or his part to the group. After an hour or so each student is tested on the life of Pulitzer. Each student must learn the entire lesson; learning depends on the cooperation and effort of other members. Aronson believes

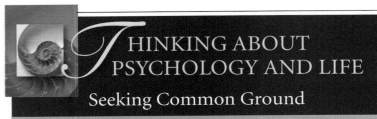

THINKING ABOUT PSYCHOLOGY AND LIFE
Seeking Common Ground

IDENTIFY SOMEONE WHO comes from a different cultural and ethnic background from you. It might be a classmate, someone who lives in your neighborhood, or someone in an interest group you attend. Ask him or her to sit down and talk with you for 15 minutes. Tell them this involves a requirement for a college class you are taking. Your conversation objective: Establish how similar you are in as many ways as you can.

that this type of learning increases students' interdependence through cooperatively teaching a common goal.

The strategy of emphasizing cooperation rather than competition and the jigsaw approach have been widely used in classrooms in the United States (Johnson & Johnson, 1999). A number of studies reveal that this type of cooperative learning is associated with increased self-esteem, better academic performance, friendships among classmates, and improved interethnic perceptions (Slavin, 1989).

It is not easy to get groups who do not like each other to cooperate. The air of distrust and hostility is hard to overcome. Creating superordinate goals that require cooperation of both groups is one viable strategy, as evidenced in Sherif's and Aronson's work. Other strategies involve disseminating positive information about the "other" and reducing the potential threat of each group.

Intimate Contact   We indicated earlier that contact by itself does not improve interethnic relations. However, one form of contact—intimate contact—can (Brislin, 1993). Intimate contact in this context does not mean sexual relations; rather it involves sharing one's personal worries, troubles, successes, failures, personal ambitions, and coping strategies. When people reveal personal information about themselves, they are more likely to be perceived as an individual rather than as a member of a category. And the sharing of personal information often produces the discovery that others previously considered as "them" or the out-group have many of the same feelings, hopes, and concerns, which can help to break down in-group/out-group, we/they barriers. Intimate contact may be more effective when the individuals involved are of relatively equal status (Devine, Evett, & Vasquez-Suson, 1996).

In one of the initial investigations of extensive interethnic contact, African American and White residents in an integrated housing project were studied (Deutsch & Collins, 1951). The residents lived in small apartments, and the housing project included shared facilities, such as laundry rooms and playgrounds for children, which allowed for interethnic contact. Whites found it more enjoyable to talk with African Americans than to stare at the walls while their laundry was being cleaned, and African American and White parents began to converse with each other as they watched their children play. The young African American and White children played with each other regardless of skin color. Initially the conversations focused on such nonintimate matters as the quality of the washing machines and the weather, but eventually they moved on to more personal matters. The Whites and the African Americans discovered that they shared a number of similar concerns, such as jobs and work, the quality of schools for their children, taxes, and so on. The African Americans' and Whites' revelation that they shared many of the same concerns and problems helped to diminish in-group/out-group thoughts and feelings. Sharing intimate information and becoming friendly with someone from another ethnic group helps to make people more tolerant and less prejudiced toward the other ethnic group.

At this point we have studied many ideas about social influence. An overview of these ideas is presented in summary table 13.2. Next, we continue our exploration of social psychology by examining some important aspects of social interaction and relationships.

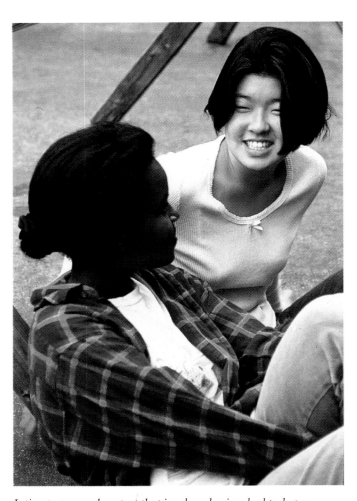

Intimate personal contact that involves sharing doubts, hopes, problems, ambitions, and much more is one way to improve interethnic relations.

SUMMARY TABLE 13.2
Social Influence

Concept	Processes/ Related Ideas	Characteristics/Description
Conformity and Obedience	Conformity	Conformity involves a change in a person's behavior to coincide more with a group standard. Asch's classic study on judgments of line length illustrated the power of conformity. Many factors influence whether we conform, including normative social influence and informational social influence.
	Obedience	Obedience is behavior that complies with the explicit demands of an individual in authority. Milgram's classic experiment demonstrated the power of obedience. Participants obeyed the experimenter's directions even though they thought they were hurting someone. Milgram's work raises the question of ethics in psychological experimentation.
	Resisting Social Influence	As we go through our lives we are both conformist and nonconformist, obedient and not obedient. Sometimes we are overwhelmed by persuasion. At other times, we exert personal control and resist such influence.
Group Influence	Motivation for Group Behavior and the Structure of Groups	Groups satisfy our personal needs, reward us, provide us with information, raise our self-esteem, and enhance our identity. Every group has norms and roles.
	Group Performance	Our performance in groups can be improved through social facilitation and lowered because of social loafing. In a group we can also experience deindividuation—a loss of personal identity and a decrease in responsibility.
	Group Interaction and Decision Making	The risky shift is the tendency for a group decision to be riskier than the average decision made by individual group members. The group polarization effect is the solidification and further strengthening of a position as a consequence of group discussion. Groupthink involves impaired decision making and avoidance of realistic appraisal to maintain harmony in the group. The majority usually gets its way in group influence, but occasionally the minority has its day.
	Leadership	Theories of group leadership include the great-person theory, the situational approach, and the person-situation view, known as the contingency model of leadership.
Cultural and Ethnic Influences	Prejudice, Stereotyping, and Ethnocentrism	Prejudice is an unjustified negative attitude toward an individual based on the individual's membership in a group. A stereotype is a generalization about a group's characteristics that does not consider any variation from one individual to the next. Ethnocentrism is the tendency to favor one's own group over other groups. One theory to explain prejudice and conflict is Tajfel's social identity theory, which states that when individuals are assigned to a group they invariably think of the group as an in-group for them. This occurs because they want to have a positive self-image.
	Improving Interethnic Relations	Contact, by itself, between ethnic groups does not decrease conflict and improve relations. One effective strategy is to develop a superordinate goal requiring the cooperation of both groups. Sherif found support for the superordinate goal strategy in his study of boys at a summer camp. Aronson showed its effectiveness in the jigsaw classroom. Another effective way to improve interethnic relations is for members of different ethnic groups to share intimate information.

Social Interaction and Relationships

Our social interactions and relationships bring us warm and cherished moments. They also can bring us experiences we would rather forget, moments that are charged with conflict and harm. Our exploration of social interactions and relationships focuses on aggression, altruism, and attraction, love, and relationships.

Violence

Aggression

The strength of aggression was captured vividly by Yoda in the movie *The Empire Strikes Back:* "Beware of the dark side. Anger, fear, aggression. Easily they flow. Once you start down the dark path, it will forever dominate your destiny and consume your will." Is this dark side biologically based or is it learned?

Biological Influences   The ancient Assyrian king Ashurbanipal delighted in beheading his enemies and blinding and mutilating his prisoners. Russian Czar Ivan the Terrible bludgeoned his own son and destroyed the second largest city in his empire, Novgorod, in the sixteenth century. In the twentieth century, 80 to 100 million people have been violently killed. In the 1970s, 4 million Cambodians were killed by their fellow Cambodians; murders in the United States take place at the rate of 20,000 per year, assaults at 700,000 per year. Rape and domestic abuse have increased dramatically (Walker, 1999); there are at least 200,000 reports of rape per year in the United States. Asked Shakespeare, "Is there any cause in nature that makes these hard hearts?"

Ethologists say that aggression is biologically based; certain stimuli act as *innate* releasers of an organism's responses (Lorenz, 1965; Tinbergen, 1969). For example, a male robin will attack another male when it sees a red patch on the other bird's breast. When the patch is removed, however, no attack takes place. Severe fighting and some intraspecies killing does occur in the animal kingdom, but most hostile encounters do not escalate to killing or even severe harm. Much of the fighting is ritualistic and involves threat displays. For example, elephant seals show approximately 65 threat displays for every fight that actually takes place (LeBoeuf & Peterson, 1969). The type of threat display varies from one species to the next: a cat arches its back, bares its teeth, and hisses; a chimpanzee stares, stomps the ground, and screams.

A basic theme of evolutionary theory is the survival of the fittest ◀||| P. 46. Early in human evolution, the most aggressive individuals were probably the survivors. Hunters and food gatherers had to kill animals and compete for the best food territories if they were to survive.

Freud argued that aggression is instinctive. He said we have a self-destructive urge he called the death instinct. He believed that the self-destructive nature of humans comes in conflict with their self-preserving life instinct; thus, the death instinct is redirected and aimed at others in the form of aggression. However, humans do not have an instinct to be killers or murderers. Most psychologists feel uneasy about the concept of instinct. For example, the instinct theorists would support their belief that humans have an instinct for aggression by referring to the behaviors to which it is related, such as the 80 to 100 million people killed in the twentieth century. However, to give a behavior such as aggression the label *instinct* is not to explain it. Rather than an instinct for aggression, what may have evolved is an aggressive capability wired into the human neuromuscular system. For example, children born deaf and blind still show aggressive patterns—foot stomping, teeth clenching, and fist-making—even though they have had no opportunity to observe these behaviors (Eibl-Eibesfeldt, 1977).

Genes are important in understanding the biological basis of aggression ◀||| P. 44. The selective breeding of animals provides evidence for the genetic basis of

(a)   (b)

Aggression is pervasive, both in today's world and in the past. (a) Russian Czar Ivan the Terrible bludgeoned his own son. (b) In the 1970s, 4 million Cambodians were killed by their fellow Cambodians.

aggression. After a number of breedings of aggressive animals with each other and docile animals with each other, vicious and timid strains of animals emerge. The vicious strains attack virtually anything in sight; the timid strains rarely fight, even when attacked. The genetic basis for aggression is more difficult to demonstrate with humans (Brennan, Mednick, & Kandel, 1991). Nonetheless, in one investigation of 573 sets of adult twins, identical twins had more similar aggressive tendencies than did fraternal twins (Rushton & others, 1986).

The brain is also involved in the biological processes of aggression (Niehoff, 1999). In 1966 Charles Whitman climbed to the top of the campus tower at the University of Texas at Austin. As he looked down on students walking to and from class, he pulled the trigger of a high-powered rifle and killed fifteen people. Then he took his own life. An autopsy revealed a tumor in the limbic system of Whitman's brain. In another instance, an electrode was implanted in the amygdala portion of a meek female mental patient's brain (which is part of the limbic system) ◀‖‖‖ P. 59. Immediately after electric current stimulated the amygdala, the mild-mannered woman became vicious. She yelled, snarled, and flailed around the room (King, 1961). We do not have a specific aggression center in the brain, but, when the lower, more primitive areas of the brain (such as the limbic system) are stimulated by fine electric currents, aggressive behavior often results (Herbert, 1988).

Alcohol is a drug that acts on the brain to cause a disinhibiting effect on many of our behaviors, especially those we might otherwise resist, such as violent aggression ◀‖‖‖ P. 135. Something said or done may provoke an individual under the influence of alcohol to unleash harsh words, throw a punch, or pull the trigger of a gun (Dougherty, Cherek, & Bennett, 1996). If not under the influence, the individual might not respond so violently to such words or actions. Aggression-prone individuals are more likely to drink and to become violent when they become intoxicated (Seto & Barbaree, 1995). People under the influence of alcohol commit almost one-half of all rapes and other violent crimes (Abbey, Ross, & McDuffie, 1993).

Hormones also play a part in aggression (Susman & others, 1996) ◀‖‖‖ P. 72. For example, Sam, a bull, was a terror. With hooves scratching, eyes glazed, and nostrils snorting, he roared across a field at an intruder. Barely escaping with his life, the intruder (who turned out to be a tractor salesman) filed a complaint against the bull's owner. The local sheriff convinced the owner it was time to do something about Sam. What was Sam's fate? He was castrated, which changed him from a simmering volcano into a docile ox. The castration reduced Sam's motivation to terrorize by acting on his male hormone system. Although humans are less sensitive to hormonal changes than animals are, violent criminals tend to be muscular young males with higher than average testosterone levels (Dabbs, 1992).

Environmental and Psychological Influences   In our exploration of environmental and psychological influences on aggression, we will discuss culture, frustrating and aversive circumstances, and reducing aggression.

Culture   In the past, hunters and food gatherers had to kill animals and compete for the best food territories to survive. However, as anthropologist Loren Eiseley commented, "The need is now for a gentler, a more tolerant people than those who won for us against the ice, the tiger, and the bear."

Some cultures are more violence prone than others (Bellesiles, 1999; Geen, 1998; Staub, 1996). The U.S. homicide rate does not compare well to rates for other countries (United Nations, 1992). The risk of being murdered in the United States is much higher than in many other countries—about four times as high as for Canadians and six times as high as for Europeans. Crime rates are higher in countries where there is a considerable gap between the rich and the poor and where fathers do not participate in child care (Triandis, 1994).

What in a culture promotes aggression in its members? Imagine yourself on a barren mountainside away from civilization in the country of Uganda. For about 2,000 years, your ancestors lived as nomadic hunters, but, early in this century, the government of Uganda turned your hunting grounds into a national park. Hunting is forbidden in the park, so you now are forced to farm its steep, barren mountain areas. Famine, crowding, and drought have led to tremendous upheaval in families and moral values. You were sent out on your own at the age of 6 with no life supports; you fight and maim others to obtain food and water. Love does not seem to exist at all in your culture (Turnbull, 1972). If you were placed in this circumstance of the Ik culture, would you be this callous and aggressive?

Frustrating and Aversive Circumstances   The world of the Ik involved many frustrating and aversive circumstances that produced pain and hunger. Frustration is the blocking of motivated behavior, as in situations in which an individual's attempt to reach a goal is prevented from taking place. Some years ago, John Dollard and his colleagues (1939) proposed that frustration triggers aggression. The **frustration-aggression hypothesis** *states that frustration always leads to aggression.* Not much later, psychologists acknowledged that, although aggression is one outcome of frustration, other responses are possible. Some individuals who experience frustration become passive, for example (Miller, 1941). Psychologists also later recognized that a broad range of aversive experiences can cause aggression; frustration is just one such experience. Others include physical pain, personal insults, and unpleasant events such as divorce. An individual's cognitive interpretation of an aversive circumstance influences whether the individual will respond aggressively (Baumeister, 1999; Berkowitz, 1990; Novaco, 1998).

Aversive circumstances can also involve the physical environment. For example, environmental psychologists have demonstrated how such factors as noise, weather, and crowding can stimulate aggression. Murder, rape, and assault increase when temperatures are the hottest (during the third quarter of the year), as well as in the hottest years and in the hottest cities (Anderson, 1989).

Our everyday encounters with other people also produce aversive experiences that can trigger aggressive responses (Schwartz, 1999). For example, when someone cuts into a line in front of us (such as at a ticket booth), we may respond aggressively toward that person (Milgram & others, 1986).

Whether we respond aggressively to aversive situations is determined by such psychological factors as expectations, equity, intentions, and responsibility (Berkowitz, 1990). With regard to *expectations,* you expect to be jostled on a crowded bus, but don't expect someone to run into you when there are only five or six people on the bus; thus, you might respond more aggressively. With regard to *equity*, if you perceive that an aversive experience is not equitable, or justified, you might also respond aggressively. For example, if you deserve a D in a class, you are less likely to say nasty things about the professor than if you perceive the grade to be unfair. With regard to *intentions*, if you think someone has intentionally tripped you, you are more likely to respond aggressively than if you think the individual's feet accidentally became tangled with yours. With regard to *responsibility*, when you perceive that other people are responsible for their aggressive actions, you are more likely to behave aggressively toward them. For example, when are you more likely to respond aggressively: when an 8-year-old child hits you with her shopping cart in a store, or when her assertive, healthy, 30-year-old mother does the same thing? You are likely to perceive that the mother is more responsible for her behavior, so you would probably respond more aggressively toward her.

Observational Learning and Reinforcement   Social learning theorists also believe that aggression is learned through the processes of reinforcement and observational learning. ◀▐▐▐ P. 166. Aggression is reinforced when it helps individuals attain money, attention, sex, power, or status. Aggression can also be learned by watching others behave aggressively (Bandura, 1989). One of the most frequent opportunities people have to observe aggression in our culture is to watch violence on television.

Violence is pictured as a way of life on many television shows. Evildoers kill and get killed; police and detectives violently uphold society's laws. Violence on television is portrayed unrealistically; viewers rarely see its lasting effects. In real life, an injured person may not recover for weeks, for months, or perhaps not at all, but on television recovery takes only 30 to 60 minutes.

The amount of aggression on television is a special problem for children. In the 1990s, children watched an average of 26 hours of television each week. Almost every day of their lives, children watch someone being stabbed, maimed, or slaughtered. What are the effects of television violence on children's aggression? Does television violence merely stimulate a child to go out and buy a Star Wars ray gun, or can it trigger an attack on a playmate and increase the likelihood that, when the child grows up, he will violently attack or murder someone?

Although some critics have argued that the effects of television violence do not warrant the conclusion that TV violence causes aggression (Freedman, 1984), many experts argue that TV violence can induce aggressive or antisocial behavior in children (Huston, Watson, & Kunkel, 1989; Singer & Singer, 1998). Of course, television violence is not the *only* cause of aggression. There is no *one* cause of any social behavior. Aggression, like all other social behaviors, has multiple determinants. Television violence does not affect adults in isolation from such other factors as aggressive tendencies, marital problems, and job stress. Likewise, the link between TV violence and aggression in children is influenced by children's aggressive tendencies and parental monitoring.

Many of the studies of television violence and aggression have been correlational in nature. As we have mentioned frequently, cause cannot be determined from correlational studies. However, as indicated in our discussion of research methods in chapter 1, some experimental studies have shown that watching television violence causes increased aggression, but mainly in children who are the most aggressive before they watch the violence (Friedrich & Stein, 1973; Steur, Applefield, & Smith, 1971).

Reducing Aggression   You might recall that in chapter 9, "Motivation and Emotion," we explored the negative emotion of anger, a powerful emotion that can generate aggression ◀▐▐▐ P. 319. We explored several strategies for reducing anger that apply to our evaluation of aggression here. Both psychoanalytic and ethological theorists believe that catharsis helps to reduce aggression. **Catharsis** *is the release of*

Calvin and Hobbes

Television and Aggression
Conflict and Violence
Prevention of Youth Violence

anger or aggressive energy by directly engaging in anger or aggression. The catharsis hypothesis states that behaving angrily or watching others behave angrily reduces subsequent anger or aggression.

Social learning theorists argue strongly against catharsis as a strategy for reducing aggression. They believe that by acting aggressively people often are rewarded for their aggression and that by watching others behave aggressively, people learn to be aggressive themselves. Researchers have found more support for the social learning view than for the psychoanalytic and ethological views on reducing aggression (Bandura, 1986, 1997). That is, decreasing rewards for aggression and observing fewer incidences of aggression are good candidates for reducing aggression. Parents' roles in children's lives also have been targeted for reducing aggression. Recommended parenting strategies include encouraging young children to develop empathy toward others and better monitoring of adolescents. For example, Gerald Patterson and his colleagues (1989) consistently have found that a lack of parental monitoring is related to juvenile delinquency. Another strategy that is being tried in many schools is to teach youths conflict management skills and have them serve as peer counselors.

Aggression and Gender   In a classic analysis of research studies, the following conclusions were reached about aggression and gender (Maccoby & Jacklin, 1974): (1) Males are more aggressive than females in all cultures; (2) males are more aggressive than females from early in life, with differences consistently appearing as early as 2 years of age; and (3) more aggression by males than females is found in animals as well as humans. These findings often have been interpreted as supporting the view that gender differences in aggression are biologically based.

What are some examples of gender differences in aggression? As children, boys are more likely to engage in rough-and-tumble play and get in more fights in which they are physically aggressive toward each other. As adolescents, males are more likely to be members of gangs and commit violent acts. As adults, males are more likely to murder or rape.

As we mentioned earlier, these gender differences in aggression often have been interpreted as having a biological basis. However, environment and culture also contribute to gender differences in aggression (Geen, 1998). In one cross-cultural study, both biological and cultural factors were at work in gender differences in aggression (Archer & McDaniel, 1995). Individuals in twelve different countries were asked to write stories in response to conflicts presented to them. In all twelve countries, males wrote stories with more violent themes than females did, suggesting a biological interpretation of gender differences in aggression. However, the degree of violence described varied considerably across the cultures, suggesting an environmental/cultural interpretation.

An important point needs to be made about gender differences in aggression, as well as other areas. When we say that males are more aggressive than females, it does not mean that all males are more aggressive than all females. In any given culture, some females will be more aggressive than some males.

Another important point about gender and aggression focuses on the type of aggression. Differences in aggression are much stronger for physical aggression than for verbal aggression (Eagly & Steffen, 1986). In one longitudinal study, no gender differences in verbal aggression were found in 8-year-old children (Björkqvist, Österman, & Lagerspetz, 1994). However, at age 18, females displayed more verbal aggression than males.

Altruism

Helping Others

Our exploration of altruism focuses on what altruism is, biological influences, environmental and psychological influences, and gender. **Altruism** *is an unselfish interest in helping someone else.* We often hear or read about acts of generosity and courage,

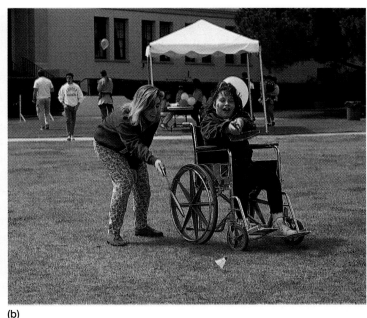

(a)   (b)

Examples of altruism: (a) Shown here is an example of animal altruism—a baboon plucking bugs from another baboon. Most acts of animal altruism involve kin. (b) A young woman assists a handicapped child.

such as rock concerts and fund raisers to help AIDS victims, the taxi driver who risks his life to save a woman in a dark alley, and volunteers who pull a baby from an abandoned well. You may have placed some of your hard-earned cash in the palm of a homeless person or perhaps cared for a wounded cat (Brehony, 1999). How do psychologists account for such acts of human altruism?

The Biological Basis of Altruism   Evolutionary psychologists emphasize that some types of altruism help to perpetuate our genes (Buss, 1995, 1999; Buss & Kendrick, 1998). An act in the biological realm is altruistic if it increases another's prospects for survival and having the opportunity to reproduce (Sober & Wilson, 1998).

Evolutionary psychologists believe that tremendous benefits can accrue to individuals who form cooperative reciprocal relationships (Trivers, 1971). By being good to someone now, individuals increase the likelihood that they will receive a benefit from the other person in the future. Through this reciprocal process, both gain something beyond what they could have by acting alone.

Evolutionary psychologists also stress that those who carry our genes— our children—have a special place in the domain of altruism P. 44. Natural selection favors parents who care for their children and improve their probability of surviving. A parent feeding its young is performing a biological altruistic act because the young's chance of survival is increased. So is a mother bird who performs a distraction ritual to lure predators away from the eggs in her nest. She is willing to sacrifice herself so that three or four of her young offspring will have the chance to survive, thus preserving her genes. Individuals also often show more empathy toward other relatives in relation to their genetic closeness. In the case of a natural disaster, people's uppermost concern is their family (Cunningham, 1986). In one study involving a hypothetical decision to help in life-or-death situations, college students chose to aid close kin over distant kin, the young over the old, and healthy over the sick, the wealthy over the poor, and the

Evolutionary Psychology

"All I'm saying is, giving a little something to the arts might help our image."

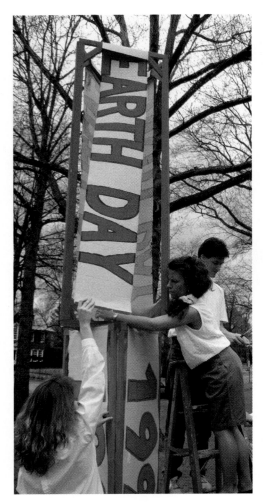

How strongly are today's college students interested in self-fulfillment versus helping others?

premenopausal woman over the postmenopausal woman (Burnstein, Crandall, & Kitayama, 1994). In this same study, when an everyday favor rather than a life-or-death situation was involved, the college students gave less weight to kinship and chose to help either the very young or the very old over those of intermediate age, the sick over the healthy, and the poor over the wealthy.

Environmental and Psychological Influences

Reciprocity and exchange are important aspects of altruism. Reciprocity, which encourages us to do unto others as we would have them do unto us, is present in every widely practiced religion in the world—Judaism, Christianity, Buddhism, and Islam, for example. Certain human sentiments are involved in reciprocity: Trust is probably the most important principle over the long run, guilt occurs if we do not reciprocate, and anger results if someone else does not reciprocate.

Not all altruism is motivated by reciprocity but this view alerts us to the importance of considering interactions between oneself and others to understand altruism. And not all seemingly altruistic behavior is unselfish. Some psychologists even argue that true altruism has never been demonstrated, while others argue that a distinction between altruism and egoism is possible (Cialdini & others, 1987). **Egoism** *involves giving to another person to ensure reciprocity; to gain self-esteem; to present oneself as powerful, competent, or caring; or to avoid social and self-censure for failing to live up to normative expectations.* By contrast, altruism occurs when someone gives to another person with the ultimate goal of benefiting that other person (Clark, 2000). Any benefits that come to the giver are unintended.

Describing individuals as having altruistic or egoistic motives implies that person variables are important in understanding altruistic behavior. Altruistic behavior is determined by both person and situational variables. A person's ability to empathize with the needy or to feel a sense of responsibility for another's welfare affects altruistic motivations. The stronger these personality dispositions, the less we would expect situational variables to influence whether giving, kindness, or helping occurs.

But as with any human behavior, characteristics of the situation influence the strength of altruistic motivation. Some of these characteristics include the degree of need shown by the other individual, the needy person's responsibility for his plight, the cost of assisting the needy person, and the extent to which reciprocity is expected (Batson, 1998).

One of the most widely studied aspects of altruism is bystander intervention. Why does one person help a stranger in distress while another won't lift a finger? It often depends on the circumstances. More than 30 years ago a young woman named Kitty Genovese cried out repeatedly as she was brutally murdered. She was attacked at about 3 A.M. in a respectable area of New York City. The murderer left and returned three times; he finally put an end to Kitty's life as she crawled to her apartment and screamed for help. It took the slayer about 30 minutes to kill Kitty. Thirty-eight neighbors watched the gory scene and heard Kitty Genovese's screams. No one helped or even called the police.

The **bystander effect** *is that individuals who observe an emergency help less when someone else is present than when they are alone.* The bystander effect helps to explain the apparent cold-blooded indifference to Kitty Genovese's murder. Social psychologists John Darley and Bibb Latané (1968) documented the bystander effect in a number of criminal and medical emergencies. Most of the bystander intervention studies show that when alone, a person will help 75 percent of the time, but when another bystander is present, the figure drops to 50 percent. Apparently the difference is due to the diffusion of responsibility among witnesses and our tendency to look to the behavior of others for clues about what to do. People may think that someone else will call the police or that since no one is helping, possibly the person does not need help.

Many other aspects of the situation influence whether the individual will intervene and come to the aid of the person in distress (Darley, 2000). Bystander intervention is less likely to occur in the following situations (Shotland, 1985): a situation is not clear;

$\mathscr{F}$igure 13.6
Changing Freshman Life Goals, 1968–1998

In the last three decades, a significant change has occurred in freshmen students' life goals. A far greater percentage of today's college freshmen state that a "very important" life goal is to be well-off financially, and far fewer state that developing a meaningful philosophy of life is a "very important" life goal.

the individuals struggling or fighting are married or related; a victim is perceived to be intoxicated; the person is thought to be from a different ethnic group; the intervention might lead to personal harm, or retaliation by the criminal. Also, helping requires considerable time, such as days in court testifying. When bystanders have no prior history of victimization themselves, have seen few crimes and intervention efforts, or have not had training in first aid, rescue, or police tactics, intervention is less likely to occur.

How altruistic are college students? Are they less altruistic than several decades ago? Over the past two decades, college students have shown an increased concern for personal well-being and a decreased concern for the well-being of others, especially the disadvantaged (Sax & others, 1998). As shown in figure 13.6, today's college freshmen are more strongly motivated to be well-off financially and less motivated to develop a meaningful philosophy of life than were their counterparts of 20 or 30 years ago.

However, there are some signs that today's college students are shifting toward a stronger interest in the welfare of our society. For example, between 1986 and 1995, there was a small increase in the percentage of college freshman who said they were strongly interested in participating in community action programs (19 percent in 1998 compared to 18 percent in 1986) and helping promote racial understanding (40 percent in 1998 compared to 27 percent in 1986) (Sax & others, 1998). For successful adjustment in adult life, it is important to seek self-fulfillment *and* have a strong commitment to others.

Altruism and Gender   The main areas in which gender and altruism have been investigated are helping and caring. Who is more helping and caring, females or males? You likely responded: females. However, as with most domains, it is a good idea to think about gender in context. Females are more likely to help when

Values of College Students
Volunteerism

the context involves nurturing, as when volunteering time to help a child with a personal problem. However, males are more likely to help in situations in which a perceived danger is present and they feel competent to help (Eagly & Crowley, 1986). For example, males are more likely than females to help a person who is stranded by the roadside with a flat tire. An automobile problem is an area in which many males feel a sense of competence. Males also are more likely than females to give a ride to a hitchhiker, because of the perceived danger in this situation.

In terms of caring, females have a stronger orientation than males toward caregiving. However, in the few cultures where boys and girls are placed in charge of caring for their younger siblings on a regular basis, girls and boys are similar in their tendencies to nurture (Whiting, 1989).

Attraction, Love, and Relationships

Social relationships involve more than aggression and altruism. Attraction, love, and close relationships also are important dimensions of our social relationships (Baumeister & Bratslavsky, 1999).

Relationships

Attraction   What attracts us to others and motivates us to spend more time with them? Does just being around someone increase the likelihood a relationship will develop? Do birds of a feather flock together; that is, are we likely to associate with those who are similar to us? How important is physical attraction in a relationship?

Familiarity and Similarity   Physical proximity does not guarantee that we will develop a positive relationship with another person. Familiarity can breed contempt, but familiarity is a condition that is necessary for a close relationship to develop. For the most part, friends and lovers have been around each other for a long time; they may have grown up together, gone to high school or college together, worked together, or gone to the same social events. Once we have been exposed to someone for a period of time, what is it that makes the relationship breed friendship and even love?

Birds of a feather do indeed flock together. One of the most powerful lessons generated by the study of close relationships is that we like to associate with people who are similar to us. Our friends, as well as our lovers, are much more like us than unlike us. We have similar attitudes, behavior, and characteristics, as well as clothes, intelligence, personality, other friends, values, lifestyle, physical attractiveness, and so on. In some limited cases and on some isolated characteristics, opposites may attract. An introvert may wish to be with an extravert, or someone with little money may wish to associate with someone who has a lot of money, for example. But overall we are attracted to individuals with similar rather than opposite characteristics. In one study, for example, the old adage "Misery loves company" was supported as depressed college students preferred to meet unhappy others while nondepressed college students preferred to meet happy others (Wenzlaff & Prohaska, 1989). The fact that individuals are attracted to each other on the basis of similar characteristics and attitudes is reflected in the questions that computer dating services ask their clients.

Consensual validation *provides an explanation of why people are attracted to others who are similar to them.* Our own attitudes and behavior are supported when someone else's attitudes and behavior are similar to ours—their attitudes and behavior validate ours. People tend to shy away from the unknown. We might tend, instead, to prefer people whose attitudes and behavior we can predict. And similarity implies that we will enjoy doing things with the other person, which often requires a partner who likes the same things and has similar attitudes. In one study, self-verifying evaluations were especially important in marriage (Swann, De La Ronde, & Hixon, 1994).

Physical Attraction   How important is *physical attraction* in a relationship? Many advertising agencies have us believe it is the most important factor in establishing and maintaining a relationship. However, heterosexual men and women differ on the importance they place on good looks when they seek an intimate partner. Women tend to rate as most important such traits as considerateness, honesty, dependability, kindness, and understanding; men prefer good looks, cooking skills, and frugality (Buss & Barnes, 1986).

Complicating research conclusions about the role of physical attraction in relationships is changing standards of what is deemed attractive. The criteria for beauty can differ, not just *across* cultures, but over time *within* cultures as well (Lamb & others, 1993). In the 1940s, the ideal female beauty in the United States was typified by the well-rounded figure of Marilyn Monroe. As a result of the American preoccupation with health, Monroe's 135 pound, 5-foot-5-inch physique is regarded as overweight by today's standards. In the 1980s and 1990s, the ideal physique for both men and women is neither pleasingly plump nor extremely slender.

The force of similarity also operates at a physical level. We usually seek out someone at our own level of attractiveness in both physical characteristics and social attributes. Most of us come away with a reasonably good chance of finding a "good match." Research indicates that this **matching hypothesis**—*that while we may prefer a more attractive person in the abstract, in the real world we end up choosing someone who is close to our own level of attractiveness*—holds up (Kalick & Hamilton, 1986).

Several additional points help to clarify the role of physical beauty and attraction in our close relationships. Much of the research has focused on initial or short-term encounters; researchers have not often evaluated attraction over the course of months and years. As relationships endure, physical attraction probably assumes less importance. Rocky Dennis, as portrayed in the movie *Mask,* is a case in point. His peers and even his mother initially wanted to avoid Rocky, whose face was severely distorted, but over the course of his childhood and adolescent years, the avoidance turned into attraction and love as people got to know him. As Rocky's story demonstrates, familiarity can overcome even severe initial negative reactions to a person.

Once attraction initiates a relationship, other opportunities exist to deepen the relationship to friendship and love.

Romantic Love

Romantic love *is also called passionate love or Eros; it has strong components of sexuality and infatuation, and it often predominates in the early part of a love relationship.* Poets, playwrights, and musicians through the ages have lauded the fiery passion of romantic love—and lamented the searing pain when it fails. Think for a moment about songs and books that hit the top of the charts. Chances are they're about love. Well-known love researcher Ellen Berscheid (1988) says that it is romantic love we mean when we say that we are "in love" with someone. It is romantic love she believes we need to understand if we are to learn what love is all about. Berscheid believes that sexual desire is the most important ingredient of romantic love.

In our culture, romantic love is the main reason we get married. In 1967, a famous study showed that men maintained that they would not get married if they were not "in love." Women either were undecided or said that they would get married even if they did not love their prospective husband (Kephart, 1967). In the 1980s, women and men tended to agree that they would not get married unless they were "in love." And more than half of today's men and women say that not being "in love" is sufficient reason to dissolve a marriage (Bersheid, Snyder, & Omoto, 1989).

Romantic love is especially important among college students. One study of unattached college men and women found that more than half identified a romantic partner, rather than a parent, sibling, or friend, as their closest relationship (Bersheid, Snyder, & Omoto, 1989). We are referring to romantic love when we say, "I am *in love,*" not just "I *love.*"

Romantic love includes a complex intermingling of different emotions—fear, anger, sexual desire, joy, and jealousy, for example. Obviously, some of these emotions are a source of anguish. One study found that

Eric Stoltz's portrayal of Rocky Dennis in the movie Mask. *Rocky was unloved and unwanted as a young child because of his grotesque features. As his mother and peers got to know him, they became much more attracted to him.*

Love

*T*hrough the Eyes of Psychologists

Ellen Berscheid, *University of Minnesota*

"To discuss romantic love without also prominently mentioning the role that sexual arousal and desire plays in it is very much like printing a recipe for tiger soup that leaves out the main ingredient."

Figure 13.7
Sternberg's Triangle of Love

Sternberg identified three dimensions that shape the experience we call love: passion, intimacy, and commitment. Various combinations of the three dimensions produce particular types of love.

Gender

romantic loves were more likely than friends to be the cause of depression (Berscheid & Fei, 1977).

Affectionate Love   Love is more than just passion. **Affectionate love,** *also called companionate love, is the type of love that occurs when individuals desire to have the other person near and have a deep, caring affection for the person.*

There is a growing belief that the early stages of love have more romantic ingredients, but as love matures, passion tends to give way to affection (Berscheid & Reis, 1998). Phillip Shaver (1986) describes the initial phase of romantic love as a time that is fueled by a mixture of sexual attraction and gratification, a reduced sense of loneliness, uncertainty about the security of developing another attachment, and excitement from exploring the novelty of another human being. With time, he says, sexual attraction wanes, attachment anxieties either lessen or produce conflict and withdrawal, novelty is replaced with familiarity, and lovers either find themselves securely attached in a deeply caring relationship or distressed—feeling bored, disappointed, lonely, or hostile, for example. In the latter case, one or both partners may eventually seek another close relationship.

When two lovers go beyond their preoccupation with novelty, unpredictability, and the urgency of sexual attraction, they are more likely to detect deficiencies in each other's caring. This may be the point in a relationship when women, who often are better caregivers than men, sense that the relationship has problems. Wives are almost twice as likely as husbands to initiate a divorce, for example (National Center for Health Statistics, 1989).

So far we have discussed two forms of love: romantic (or passionate) and affectionate (or companionate). Robert J. Sternberg (1988) described a third form of love, consummate love, which he said is the strongest, fullest type of love. Sternberg proposed the **triangular theory of love:** *that love includes three dimensions—passion, intimacy, and commitment* (see figure 13.7). Couples must share all three dimensions to experience consummate love.

Passion, as described earlier, is physical and sexual attraction to another. Intimacy is the emotional feelings of warmth, closeness, and sharing in a relationship. Commitment is our cognitive appraisal of the relationship and our intent to maintain the relationship even in the face of problems. If passion is the only ingredient (with intimacy and commitment low or absent), we are merely *infatuated.* This might happen in an affair or a fling in which there is little intimacy and even less commitment. A relationship marked by intimacy and commitment but low or lacking in passion is called *affectionate love,* a pattern often found among couples who have been married for many years. If passion and commitment are present but intimacy is not, Sternberg calls the relationship *fatuous love,* as when one person worships another from a distance.

A current interest in close relationships is the role that environmental changes play in them (Berscheid, in press). It is not enough to know a partner's vulnerabilities or strengths in a vacuum in predicting the relationship's future. We also need to know the nature of environments the relationship will face as it moves through time (Berscheid & Lopez, 1997). Some fragile relationships survive forever because they never encounter a relationship-toxic environment, but some strong relationships dissolve because of external forces they encounter, such as economic strains, job stress, and disapproval by others (Berscheid, 1999).

Relationships and Gender   Earlier we indicated that women are more strongly motivated caregivers than men and often are quicker to sense that a relationship has problems. As children, boys often define themselves apart from their caregivers and peers, while girls emphasize their social ties. You might recall our discussion of Carol Gilligan's care perspective in chapter 8, "Human Development." Gilligan believes that social relationships are more important to females than they are to males and that females are more sensitive in these social relationships ◄▥ P. 266. By contrast, she argues that males have a stronger individualistic, self orientation. Researchers have found that adult females often are caring, supporting, and empathic, while adult males are independent, self-reliant, and unexpressive (Brannon, 1999; Paludi, 1998).

Deborah Tannen (1990) analyzed the talk of women and men. She reported that a common complaint women have about their husbands is, "He doesn't listen to me anymore." Another is, "He doesn't talk to me anymore." Lack of communication, while high on women's list of reasons for divorce, is much less often mentioned by men.

Tannen distinguishes between rapport talk and report talk. **Rapport talk** *is the language of conversation. It is a way of establishing connections and negotiating relationships.* Women prefer to engage in rapport talk. Women enjoy private conversations more than men do, and it is men's lack of interest in rapport talk that bothers many women. By contrast, **report talk** *is talk designed to give information, which includes public speaking.* Men prefer to engage in report talk. Men hold center stage through such verbal performances as telling stories and jokes. They learn to use talk as a way of getting and keeping attention. Tannen and others (Nadien & Denmark, 1999; Snarey, 1998) argue that these gender differences are the result of girls and boys being socialized differently as they grow up. Mothers have participated far more in rearing children than fathers have and have modeled a stronger interest in relationships when interacting with their daughters than when interacting with their sons.

Tannen and others (Levant, 1995; Levant & Brooks, 1997) recommended that men develop a stronger interest in relationships and make women feel more comfortable in public speaking contexts. Tannen also recommends that women seek more report-talk opportunities, including speaking up in groups.

Not all of us have close relationships, and not all of us have experienced the passion, intimacy, and commitment of love. We have all heard that it is better to have loved and lost than never to have loved at all. However, as we see next, over many lives hangs the dark cloud of loneliness, something few people want to feel.

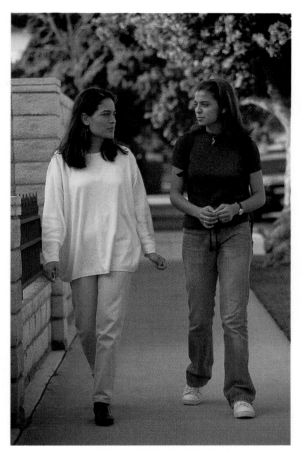

Many females show a stronger interest in relationships than many males do. What has been your experience with the gender differences in relationship orientation that we have discussed? If you are a female, do you have a strong interest in relationships? If you are a male, do you have less interest in relationships than most females you know?

Loneliness   Some of us are lonely. We might feel that no one knows us very well. We might feel isolated and sense that we do not have anyone we can turn to in time of need or stress. Our society's emphasis on self-fulfillment and achievement, the importance we attach to commitment in relationships, and a decline in stable close relationships are among the reasons loneliness is common today (de Jong-Gierveld, 1987). Researchers have found that married individuals are less lonely than their nonmarried counterparts (never married, divorced, or widowed) in studies conducted in more than twenty countries (Perlman & Peplau, 1998).

Loneliness is interwoven with how people pass through life transitions. One of those transitions is the first year of college. When students leave the familiar world of their hometown and family to enter college, they especially can feel lonely. Many college freshmen feel anxious about meeting new people and developing a new social life. As one student commented:

> My first year here at the university has been pretty lonely. I wasn't lonely at all in high school. I lived in a fairly small town—I knew everybody and everyone knew me. I was a member of several clubs and played on the basketball team. It's not that way at the university. It is a big place and I've felt like a stranger on so many occasions. I'm starting to get used to my life here and the last few months I've been making myself meet people and get to know them, but it has not been easy.

As this comment illustrates, freshmen rarely bring their popularity and social standing from high school into the college environment. There may be a dozen high school basketball stars, National Merit scholars, and former student council presidents in a single dormitory wing. Especially if students attend college away from home, they face the task of forming completely new social relationships.

One study found that 2 weeks after the school year began, 75 percent of 354 college freshmen felt lonely at least part of the time since arriving on campus (Cutrona, 1982). More than 40 percent said their loneliness was moderate to severe in intensity. Students who were the most optimistic and had the highest self-esteem were more likely to overcome their loneliness by the end of their freshman year. Loneliness is not reserved only for college freshmen, though. Upperclassmen are often lonely as well.

Lonely males and females attribute their loneliness to different sources, with men more likely to blame themselves, women more likely to blame external factors. Men are socialized to initiate relationships, whereas women are traditionally socialized to wait, then respond. Perhaps men blame themselves because they feel they should do something about their loneliness, while women wonder why no one calls.

How do you determine if you are lonely? Scales of loneliness ask you to respond to items like "I don't feel in tune with the people around me" and "I can find companionship when I want it." If you consistently respond that you never or rarely feel in tune with people around you and rarely or never can find companionship when you want it, you are likely to fall into the category of people who are described as moderately or intensely lonely (Russell, 1996).

If you are lonely, how can you become better connected with others? Following are some strategies:

- *Participate in activities that you can do with others.* Join organizations or volunteer your time for a cause you believe in. You likely will get to know others whose views are similar to yours. Going to just one social gathering can help you develop social contacts. When you go, introduce yourself to others and start a conversation. Another strategy is to sit next to new people in your classes or find someone to study with.
- *Be aware of the early warning signs of loneliness.* People often feel bored or alienated before loneliness becomes pervasive. Head off loneliness by becoming involved in new social activities.
- *Draw a diagram of your social network.* List whether the people in the diagram meet your social needs. If not, pencil in the people you would like to get to know.
- *Engage in positive behaviors when you meet new people.* You will improve your chances of developing enduring relationships if, when you meet new people, you are nice, considerate, honest, trustworthy, and cooperative. Have a positive attitude, be supportive of the other person, and make positive comments about him or her.
- *See a counselor or read a book on loneliness.* If you can't get rid of your loneliness on your own, you might want to contact the counseling services at your college. The counselor can talk with you about strategies for reducing your loneliness. You also might want to read a good book on loneliness. A good one is *Intimate Connections* by David Burns (1985), which is described at the end of this chapter in the "Resources" section.

At this point we have studied many ideas about social relationships. An overview of these ideas is presented in summary table 13.3.

You have arrived at the end of this book. You should be able to look back and say you learned a lot about human beings, both others and yourself. Many unanswered questions about human behavior remain, but psychology's quest to understand human behavior produces information we can use to make our life more enjoyable and humane. What could be more intriguing and important to all of us than psychology's mission of describing, explaining, and predicting the behavior of the human species?

SUMMARY TABLE 13.3
Social Interaction and Relationships

Concept	Processes/ Related Ideas	Characteristics/Discussion
Aggression	Biological Influences	We do not have an instinct for aggression, but biological factors are at work in aggression through genes, the brain, and hormones.
	Environmental and Psychological Influences	Aggression is more prevalent in some cultures than in others. Frustration is one of many aversive experiences that can cause aggression. An individual's cognitive interpretation of aversive circumstances determines whether the individual will respond aggressively. Aggression can be learned through reinforcement and observational learning. There is little support for the catharsis hypothesis. Various strategies have been proposed for reducing aggression, including increased parental involvement and monitoring of children and adolescents. Poverty and a sense of powerlessness can especially be involved in youth violence.
	Aggression and Gender	Males are more physically aggressive than females, and this difference often has been explained as biologically based. However, there are cultural variations in aggression. Gender differences in verbal aggression are less consistent than for physical aggression.
Altruism	What Is Altruism?	Altruism is an unselfish interest in helping someone else.
	Biological Basis	Evolutionary psychologists stress that altruism increases the prospects of survival as well as reproduction. Examples involve kin as well as when a parent cares for its young.
	Environmental and Psychological Influences	Reciprocity often is involved in altruism. The motivation can be altruistic or egoistic. Psychologists have studied both the person and situation variables in altruism. Extensive research has been conducted on bystander intervention.
	Altruism and Gender	In considering altruism and other areas of behavior, it is important to consider gender in context. Females are more likely to help in situations that are not dangerous and that involve caregiving. Males are more likely to help in situations where danger is perceived or where they feel competent.
Attraction, Love, and Relationships	Attraction	Familiarity precedes a close relationship. We like to associate with people who are similar to us. The principles of consensual validation and matching can explain this. Physical attraction is usually more important in the early part of a relationship, and criteria of physical attractiveness vary across cultures and historical time.
	Romantic Love	Also called passionate love, this love is involved when we say we are "in love." It includes passion, sexuality, and a mixture of emotions, not all of which are positive.
	Affectionate Love	Also called companionate love, this type of love usually becomes more important as relationships mature. Shaver proposed a developmental model of love and Sternberg a triarchic model of love (passion, intimacy, and commitment).
	Relationships and Gender	Females have a stronger interest in relationships than males do. Tannen distinguishes between rapport talk (females) and report talk (males).
	Loneliness	Loneliness often emerges when people make life transitions, so it is not surprising that loneliness is common among college freshmen. A number of strategies were described to help lonely individuals become more socially connected.

Overview *Overview*

WE BEGAN THIS CHAPTER on social psychology by examining these dimensions of social thinking: attribution, social perception, and attitudes. Our coverage of social influence focused on conformity and obedience, group influence, and cultural and ethnic influences. We also read about these aspects of social interaction and relationships: aggression, altruism, and attraction, love, and relationships.

Don't forget that you can obtain a more detailed overview of the chapter by again studying the summary tables on pages 444, 459, and 473.

Key Terms *Key Terms*

attribution theory 434
fundamental attribution error 436
self-serving bias 436
implicit personality theory 437
prototypes 438
primacy effect 438
social comparison 438
impression management (self-presentation) 439
self-monitoring 440
attitudes 440

foot-in-the-door strategy 440
door-in-the-face strategy 440
cognitive dissonance 441
self-perception theory 442
conformity 443
normative social influence 445
informational social influence 446
obedience 446
norms 449
roles 449
social facilitation 450
social loafing 450

deindividuation 450
risky shift 451
group polarization effect 451
groupthink 451
great-person theory 452
contingency model of leadership 452
prejudice 454
stereotype 454
ethnocentrism 454
social identity theory 455
frustration-aggression hypothesis 462

catharsis 463
altruism 464
egoism 466
bystander effect 466
consensual validation 468
matching hypothesis 469
romantic love 469
affectionate love 470
triangular theory of love 470
rapport talk 471
report talk 471

Key People

Taking It to the Net

1. In the early 1990s, an incident involving a child arsonist received tremendous press. Although children light fires all the time, this case was different. After careful questioning, the boy revealed that he was a regular viewer of MTV's *Beavis and Butthead,* a popular (and often violent) cartoon. Moreover, he told police that he had seen Beavis and Butthead light fires and burn down buildings. The boy merely imitated the behavior he saw on TV. Unfortunately, this event is not isolated. Between the local news and *Cops,* we are exposed to violence on television on a daily basis. Does viewing television violence necessarily lead people to become violent? What evidence supports this?

2. Imagine an old woman walking down the street in a small town on her way to the grocery store. Suddenly, a masked man grabs her purse and hits her, knocking her to the ground. Horrified, the old woman cries out for help. A young man runs to her aid and helps her to safety. Now, imagine the same scenario in downtown New York City. Would anyone come to her aid? Who is more likely to offer assistance: people in small towns, people in suburbs, or people in the inner city? Why do you think this is so?

3. Have you ever noticed that you don't usually laugh out loud at a funny movie when you see it on video alone, even though you are always laughing when you see a funny movie with your friends? Conversely, do you tend to cry more when you see a movie alone than with your friends? Do music groups sound better if the audience is more lively? Why do you think this is? Chances are that you are influenced by people around you, whether you realize it or not. Why do we experience things differently depending on who we are with? Explain the process of social influence and how you might be affected by it.

Connect to http://www.mhhe.com/psychology/santrock to find the answers!

Glossary

A

abnormal behavior Behavior that is deviant, maladaptive, or personally distressful. Only one of these criteria needs to be present for the classification of abnormal behavior, but two or all three can be present.   370

absolute threshold The minimum amount of energy that we can detect.   78

accommodation Adjustment of the eye lens to change its curvature.   258

accommodation An individual's adjustment to new information.   84

acetylcholine (ACh) A neurotransmitter that usually stimulates the firing of neurons and is involved in the action of muscles, learning, and memory.   54

action potential The brief wave of electrical charge that sweeps down the axon.   53

activation-synthesis view The view that dreams have no inherent meaning but, rather, reflect the brain's efforts to make sense out of or find meaning in the neural activity that takes place during REM sleep. In this view, the brain has considerable random activity during REM sleep, and dreams are an attempt to synthesize the chaos.   130

activity theory The theory that the more active and involved older people are, the more satisfied they will be with their lives and the more likely they will stay healthy.   286

acupuncture A technique in which thin needles are inserted at specific points in the body to produce various effects, such as local anesthesia.   96

addiction A pattern of behavior characterized by an overwhelming involvement with using a drug and securing its supply.   139

adolescence The transition from childhood to adulthood, which involves physical, cognitive, and socioemotional changes. In most cultures adolescence begins at about 10 to 13 years of age and ends at about 18 to 21 years of age.   249

adolescent egocentrism The adolescent's belief that others are as preoccupied with the adolescent as she is herself, that she is unique, and that she is indestructible.   274

adrenal glands Glands that play an important role in our moods, energy level, and ability to cope with stress; each adrenal gland secretes epinephrine (also called adrenaline) and norepinephrine (also called noradrenaline).   73

affectionate love Also called companionate love, this type of love occurs when individuals desire to have each other near and have a deep, caring affection for each other.   470

afferent nerves Sensory nerves that carry information to the brain.   50

afterimages Sensations that remain after a stimulus is removed.   89

agonist A drug that mimics or increases a neurotransmitter's effects.   56

agoraphobia An anxiety disorder characterized by an intense fear of entering crowded, public places, of traveling away from home, especially by public transportation, of feeling confined or trapped, and of being separated from a place or person associated with safety.   379

alcoholism A disorder that involves long-term, repeated, uncontrolled, compulsive, and excessive use of alcoholic beverages, impairing the drinker's health and interpersonal relationships.   136

algorithms Strategies that guarantee a solution to a problem.   213

all-or-none principle The principle that once the electrical impulse reaches a certain level of intensity, it fires and moves all the way down the axon, remaining at the same strength throughout its travel.   53

alpha waves Brain waves that make up the EEG pattern of a person who is awake but relaxed.   122

altered states of consciousness Mental states that noticeably differ from normal awareness. Drugs, meditation, fatigue, hypnosis, and sensory deprivation can produce altered states of consciousness.   117

alternate forms reliability Giving alternate forms of the same test on two different occasions.   229

altruism An unselfish interest in helping someone else.   464

Alzheimer's disease A progressive, irreversible brain disorder that is characterized by gradual deterioration of memory, reasoning, language, and eventually physical functioning.   281

amnesia Loss of memory.   201

amplitude The amount of pressure produced by a sound wave relative to a standard, measured in decibels (dB).   91

amygdala A limbic system structure located within the base of the temporal lobe; involved in the discrimination of objects and emotion.   59

anal stage Freud's second stage of development, occurring between 1½ and 3 years of age, in which the child's greatest pleasure involves the anus or the eliminative functions associated with it.   340

analogy A type of formal reasoning that involves four parts, relationship between the first two parts being the same as the relationship between the last two.   215

androgen A class of sex hormones, the most important of which is testosterone, that promotes the development of male genitals and male secondary sex characteristics. Androgens influence sexual motivation in both sexes and are produced by the adrenal glands in males and females, and in the testes in males.   306

anorexia nervosa An eating disorder that involves the relentless pursuit of thinness through starvation.   304

antagonist A drug that can block a neurotransmitter's effects.   56

anterograde amnesia A memory disorder that affects the retention of new information or events. What was learned before the onset of the condition is not affected.   201

antianxiety drugs Drugs that reduce anxiety by making the individual less excitable and more calm. Commonly known as tranquilizers.   424

antidepressant drugs Drugs that regulate mood. The three main classes of antidepressant drugs are tricyclics, such as Elavil; MAO inhibitors, such as Nardil; and SSRI drugs, such as Prozac.   425

antipsychotic drugs Powerful drugs that diminish agitated behavior, reduce tension, decrease hallucinations and delusions, improve social behavior, and produce better sleep patterns in individuals who have a severe mental disorder, especially schizophrenia.   425

antisocial personality disorder A disorder in the dramatic/emotionally problematic cluster of personality disorders. It is the most problematic because these individuals often resort to a life of crime and violence. They are guiltless, exploitive, irresponsible, self-indulgent, and interpersonally intrusive.   394

anxiety disorders Psychological disorders that include these main features: motor tension, hyperactivity, and apprehensive expectations and thoughts.   377

aphrodisiacs Substances that supposedly arouse a person's sexual desire and increase the capacity for sexual activity.   307

apparent movement Our perception of a stationary object as being in motion.   106

applied behavior analysis (behavior modification) The application of operant conditioning principles to change human behavior.   162

archetype The primordial influences in every individual's collective unconscious; Jung's psychoanalytic theory is often referred to as "depth psychology" because archetypes rest deep within the unconscious mind, far deeper than the Freudian personal unconscious.   343

assimilation The incorporation of new information into one's existing knowledge; Piagetian concept.   258

association cortex (association areas) The region of the neocortex involved in the highest intellectual functions, such as problem solving and thinking.   64

associative learning Learning that two events are related or linked.   148

Atkinson-Shiffrin theory The theory that memory involves a sequence of three stages: sensory memory, short-term (working) memory, and long-term memory.   182

attachment   A close emotional bond between the infant and its caregiver.   266

attitudes   Beliefs or opinions about people, objects, and ideas.   440

attribution theory   The theory that individuals are motivated to discover the underlying causes of behavior as part of an effort to make sense out of the behavior.   315, 434

auditory nerve   The nerve that carries neural impulses to the brain's auditory areas.   94

authoritarian parenting   A restrictive, punitive style in which the parent exhorts the child to follow the parent's directions and to respect work and effort. The authoritarian parent places firm limits and controls on the child and allows little verbal exchange. Authoritarian parenting is associated with children's social incompetence.   268

authoritative parenting   A style in which parents encourage children to be independent but still places limits and controls on their actions. Extensive verbal give-and-take is allowed, and parents are warm and nurturant toward the child. Authoritative parenting is associated with children's social competence.   268

autobiographical memory   A person's recollection of her or his life experiences.   196

automatic processes   Forms of consciousness that require minimal attention and do not interfere with other ongoing activities.   117

autonomic nervous system (ANS)   The system of nerves that takes messages to and from the body's internal organs, monitoring such processes as breathing, heart rate, and digestion.   50, 318

autonomy versus shame and doubt   Erikson's second stage, occurring from 1 to 3 years of age. The positive side of the stage involves developing a sense of independence and autonomy, the negative side a sense of shame and doubt.   264

availability heuristic   Judging the probability of an event by recalling the frequency of the event's past occurrences.   217

aversive conditioning   A behavior therapy based on classical conditioning in which there are repeated pairings of the undesirable behavior with aversive stimuli to decrease the behavior's rewards.   412

axon   The part of the neuron that carries information away from the cell body to other cells.   51

barbiturates   Depressant drugs, such as Nembutal and Seconal, that induce sleep or reduce anxiety.   136

Barnum effect   If you make your predictions broad enough, any person can fit the description.   357

basal ganglia   Forebrain structures essential to starting and stopping voluntary movements.   60

basal metabolism rate (BMR)   The minimal amount of energy a person uses in a resting state.   303

basilar membrane   A membrane housed inside the cochlea that runs its entire length.   92

behavior   Everything we do that can be directly observed.   5

behavior modification   The application of operant conditioning techniques to change human behavior. Its main goal is to replace unacceptable, maladaptive responses with acceptable, adaptive ones.   413

behavior therapies   Therapies that use principles of learning to reduce or eliminate maladaptive behavior.   411

behavioral and social cognitive perspectives   Perspectives that emphasize the importance of studying environmental experiences and peoples' observable behavior to understand personality. The contemporary version of social cognitive theory stresses the importance of person/cognitive factors in personality.   346

behavioral approach   An emphasis on the scientific study of observable behavioral responses and their environmental determinants.   8

behaviorial neuroscience and comparative psychology   This area focuses on biological processes, especially the brain's role in behavior.   24

behavioral neuroscience approach   An approach that emphasizes the importance of understanding the brain and nervous system if we are to understand behavior, thought, and emotion.   11

belief perseverance   The tendency to hold on to a belief in the face of contradictory evidence.   217

big five factors of personality   Emotional stability (neuroticism), extraversion, openness to experience, agreeableness, and conscientiousness.   354

binocular cues   Depth cues that are based on both eyes working together.   105

biological processes   Processes that involve changes in an individual's physical nature.   248

biomedical therapies   Treatments to reduce or eliminate the symptoms of psychological disorders by altering the way an individual's body functions. Drug therapy is the most common form; less common are electroconvulsive therapy and psychosurgery.   424

bipolar disorder   A mood disorder characterized by extreme mood swings that include one or more episodes of mania (an overexcited, unrealistically optimistic state). *Bipolar* means that the person may experience depression and mania.   386

bisexual   Being sexually attracted to people of both sexes.   311

blind spot   The area of the retina where the optic nerve leaves the eye on its way to the brain.   85

brain graft   The transplantation of healthy tissue into a damaged brain.   69

brightness   A characteristic of color based on its intensity.   88

brightness constancy   Recognition that an object retains the same degree of brightness even when different amounts of light fall on it.   106

bulimia   An eating disorder in which the individual consistently follows a binge-and-purge eating pattern.   304

bystander effect   Individuals who observe an emergency help less when someone else is present than when they are alone.   466

Cannon-Bard theory   The theory that emotions and physiological reactions occur simultaneously.   321

cardinal traits   In Allport's view, the most powerful and pervasive traits.   354

care perspective   In Carol Gilligan's theory of moral development, the care perspective focuses on people in terms of their connectedness with others, interpersonal communication, relationships with others, and concern for others.   276

case study   An in-depth look at a single individual, used mainly by clinical psychologists when, for ethical or practical reasons, the unique aspects of an individual's life cannot be duplicated.   32

catatonic schizophrenia   A type of schizophrenia characterized by bizarre motor behavior, which sometimes takes the form of a completely immobile stupor.   391

catharsis   The release of anger or aggressive energy by directly or vicariously engaging in anger or aggression; the catharsis hypothesis states that behaving angrily or aggressively reduces subsequent anger.   330, 406, 463

cell body   The part of the neuron that contains the nucleus, which directs the manufacture of the substances the neuron uses for its growth and maintenance.   51

cellular clock theory   Hayflick's view that cells can divide, at maximum, about 100 times, and that as we age, our cells become increasingly less capable of dividing.   280

central nervous system (CNS)   The brain and spinal cord.   49

central traits   In Allport's view, a limited number of traits that are adequate to describe most people's personalities. Most people have 6 to 12 of these traits.   354

cerebellum   A part of the brain that extends from the rear of the hindbrain, above the medulla. It consists of two rounded structures thought to play important roles in motor control.   58

chromosomes   Threadlike structures that come in 23 pairs, one member of each pair coming from each parent; chromosomes contain DNA.   44

chunking   A beneficial organizational strategy for memory that involves grouping or "packing" information into higher-order units that can be remembered as single units.   180

circadian rhythm   A daily behavioral or physiological cycle, an example being the 24-hour sleep/wake cycle.   119

clairvoyance   The ability to perceive remote events that are out of view.   109

classical conditioning   A form of learning in which a neutral stimulus becomes associated with a meaningful stimulus and acquires the capacity to elicit a similar response.   147

clinical and counseling psychology   The most widely practiced specialization in psychology; clinical and counseling psychologists diagnose and treat people with psychological problems.   23

cochlea   A long tubular fluid-filled structure in the inner ear that is coiled up like a snail.   92

cognitive approach   An emphasis on the mental processes involved in knowing: How we direct our attention, perceive, remember, think, and solve problems.   11

cognitive dissonance   A concept developed by social psychologist Leon Festinger that refers to an individual's motivation toward consistency and away from inconsistency.   441

cognitive map   An organism's mental representation of the structure of physical space.   167

cognitive monitoring   Taking stock of your progress in an activity such as reading or studying.   204

cognitive processes   Processes that involve changes in an individual's thought, intelligence, and language.   248

cognitive theory of dreaming   The theory that dreaming can be best understood by relying on the same cognitive concepts that are used in studying the waking mind. That is, dreaming involves processing information, memories, and possible problem solving.   130

cognitive therapies   Therapies that emphasize the individual's cognitions or thoughts as the main source of abnormal behavior. Cognitive therapists attempt to change the individual's feelings and behaviors by changing cognitions.   414

cohorts   Groups of individuals born in the same year or time period.   286

collective unconscious   According to Jung, the impersonal, deepest layer of the unconscious mind, which is shared by all human beings because of their common ancestral past.   343

community psychology   A branch of psychology that focuses on providing accessible care for people with psychological problems. Community-based mental health centers are one means of providing such services as outreach programs to people in need, especially those who traditionally have been underserved by mental health professionals.   24

compensation   Adler's term for the individual's attempt to overcome imagined or real inferiorities or weaknesses by developing one's abilities.   343

complex sounds   Sounds in which sound waves of numerous frequencies blend together.   92

computer-assisted axial tomography (CAT scan)   Three-dimensional imaging obtained from X rays of the head that are assembled into a composite image by computer.   71

conception   The penetration of an ovum (egg) by a sperm cell; also called fertilization.   252

concepts   Mental categories used to group similar objects, events, and characteristics.   210

concrete operational stage   Piaget's third cognitive stage, which lasts from about 7 to 11 years of age. This stage involves using operations, and operational thought replaces intuitive thought, but only in concrete situations. It is characterized by a lack of abstract thinking, but classification skills are present.   261

concurrent validity   A form of criterion validity that assesses the relation of a test's scores to a criterion that is presently available (concurrent).   229

conditional positive regard   Rogers' term for love and praise being withheld if the individual does not conform to parental or social standards.   349

conditioned response (CR)   The learned response to the conditioned stimulus that occurs after CS-US association.   148

conditioned stimulus (CS)   A previously neutral stimulus that elicits the conditioned response after being paired with the unconditioned stimulus.   148

cones   Receptors in the retina for color perception.   84

confidentiality   Researchers are responsible for keeping all of the data they collect completely confidential and, when possible, completely anonymous.   37

confirmation bias   The tendency to search for and use information that supports our ideas rather than refutes them.   216

conformity   Changing one's behavior to make it coincide more with a group standard.   443

consciousness   Awareness of both external and internal stimuli or events.   116

consensual validation   An explanation of why people are attracted to others who are similar to them: Our own attitudes and behavior are supported when someone else's attitudes and behavior are similar to ours—their attitudes and behavior validate ours.   468

conservation   A belief in the permanence of certain attributes of objects or situations in spite of superficial changes.   260

content validity   A test's ability to test a broad range of the content that is to be measured.   229

contiguity   The degree of association of stimuli.   148

contingency (in classical conditioning)   The predictability of the occurrence of one stimulus from the presence of another.   148

contingency model of leadership   The view that both personality characteristics and situational influences determine who will become a leader; leadership is viewed as a complex undertaking in which leaders influence their followers and followers influence their leaders.   452

continuity of development   The view that development involves gradual, cumulative change from conception to death.   251

continuous reinforcement   Reinforcement of a response every time it occurs.   159

contour   A location on a surface at which a sudden change of brightness occurs.   103

control group   A comparison group that is treated in every way like the experimental group except for the manipulated factor.   35

controlled processes   The most alert states of consciousness, in which individuals actively focus their efforts toward a goal.   116

conventional level   Kohlberg's second level of moral thinking, in which an individual shows an intermediate level of internalization. The individual abides by certain standards (internal), but they are the standards of others (external), such as parents' standards (stage 3) or society's laws (stage 4).   274

convergent thinking   Thinking that produces one correct answer; characteristic of the kind of thinking required on conventional intelligence tests.   241

conversion disorder   A somatoform disorder in which the individual experiences specific physical symptoms even though no physiological problems can be found. Conversion disorder received its name from psychoanalytic theory, which stressed that anxiety was "converted" into a specific physical symptom.   382

cornea   A clear membrane on the front surface of the eye. Its function is to bend the light falling on the surface of the eye just enough to focus it at the back of the eye.   83

corpus callosum   A large bundle of axons that connects the brain's two hemispheres.   65

correlational research   Research with the goal of describing the strength of the relation between two or more events or characteristics.   33

counterconditioning   A classical conditioning procedure for weakening a conditioned response of fear by associating the fear-provoking stimulus with a new response that is incompatible with the fear.   152

couple therapy   Group therapy with married or unmarried couples whose major problem is their relationship.   418

crack   An intensified form of cocaine; chips of pure cocaine that are usually smoked.   137

creativity   The ability to think about something in novel and unusual ways and come up with unique solutions to problems.   241

criterion validity   The test's ability to predict an individual's performance when assessed by other measures, or criteria, of an attribute.   229

critical period   A period when there is learning readiness; beyond this period learning is difficult or impossible.   222

critical thinking   Thinking reflectively and productively, and evaluating the evidence.   20, 214

cross-cultural psychology   An area of psychology that examines the role of culture in understanding behavior, thought, and emotion.   25

culture   The behavior patterns, beliefs, and other products of a particular group of people, such as the values, work patterns, music, dress, diet, and ceremonies that are passed on from generation to generation.   12

culture-fair tests   Intelligence tests that are intended to not be culturally biased.   239

daydreaming   A form of consciousness that involves a low level of conscious effort.   117

debriefing   Informing participants of the purpose and methods used in a study after the study has been completed.   37

decay theory   The theory that a neurochemical "memory trace" is formed when something new is learned, but that this trace tends to disintegrate.   200

decision making   Evaluating alternatives and making choices among them.   216

declarative memory   The conscious recollection of information, such as specific facts or events, and at least in humans, information that can be verbally communicated. Because of its conscious and verbalizable nature, declarative memory has been called "explicit memory."   185

deductive reasoning   Reasoning from the general to the specific.   216

defense mechanisms   The ego's protective methods for reducing anxiety by unconsciously distorting reality.   338

deindividuation   The loss of personal identity and a decrease in responsibility in the presence of a group.   450

deinstitutionalization   The movement to transfer the treatment of mental disorders from inpatient mental hospitals to community-based facilities that stress outpatient care.   401

delta waves   Large, slow brain waves associated with deep sleep.   122

dendrite   The receiving part of the neuron, serving the important function of collecting information and orienting it toward the cell body.   51

deoxyribonucleic acid (DNA)   A complex molecule that contains genetic information.   44

dependent variable   The factor that is measured in an experiment. It can change as the independent variable is manipulated. The label "dependent" is used because this variable depends on what happens to the participants in the experiment.   35

depressants   Psychoactive drugs that slow down mental and physical activity.   135

depressive disorders   Mood disorders in which the individual suffers depression without ever experiencing mania. The severity varies; some individuals experience a major depressive disorder others dysthymic disorder.   385

depth perception   The ability to perceive objects three-dimensionally.   105

development   The pattern of movement or change that begins at conception and continues through the life span.   248

developmental psychology   A branch of psychology concerned with how we become who we are, from conception to death.   24

diathesis-stress view   The view that a combination of biogenetic disposition and stress causes schizophrenia.   392

dichromats   People with only two kinds of cones.   89

difference threshold   The smallest difference in stimulation required to discriminate one stimulus from another 50 percent of the time. Also called the just noticeable difference (jnd).   81

discontinuity of development   The view that development involves distinct stages in the life span.   251

discrimination (in classical conditioning)   The process of learning to respond to certain stimuli and not to respond to others.   150

discrimination (in operant conditioning)   The tendency to respond only to those stimuli that are correlated with reinforcement.   160

disease model of addiction   The view that addictions are biologically based, lifelong diseases that involve a loss of control over behavior and require medical and/or spiritual treatment for recovery.   139

disorganized schizophrenia   A type of schizophrenia in which an individual has delusions and hallucinations with little or no recognizable meaning.   391

disparity   The difference between the images from the left and right eye that the brain uses as a binocular cue to determine the depth or distance of an object.   105

display rules   Sociocultural standards that determine when, where, and how emotions should be expressed.   325

dissociative amnesia   A dissociative disorder involving memory loss caused by extensive psychological stress.   382

dissociative disorders   Psychological disorders that involve a sudden loss of memory or change in identity. Under extreme stress or shock, the individual's conscious awareness becomes dissociated (separated or split) from previous memories and thoughts.   382

dissociative fugue   A dissociative disorder in which the individual not only develops amnesia but also unexpectedly travels away from home and assumes a new identity. *Fugue* means "flight."   382

dissociative identity disorder (DID)   The most dramatic but least common dissociative disorder. In this disorder, individuals have two or more distinct personalities or selves. Formerly called multiple personality disorder.   382

divergent thinking   Thinking that produces many answers to the same question and is more characteristic of creativity.   241

dominant-recessive genes principle   The principle that if one gene of a pair is dominant and the other is recessive, the dominant gene exerts its effect, overriding the potential influence of the recessive gene. A recessive gene exerts its influence only if both genes in the pair are recessive.   44

door-in-the-face strategy   The technique in which a communicator makes the strongest point or demand in the beginning, which listeners will probably reject, then presents a weaker point or moderate, "concessionary" demand toward the end.   440

dopamine   A neurotransmitter that usually is inhibitory and is involved in the control of voluntary movement. Low levels are found in Parkinson's disease, high levels in schizophrenia.   54

double-blind experiment   An experiment in which neither the experimenter nor the research participants are aware of which participants are in the experimental group and which are in the placebo control group until after the results are calculated.   36

dream analysis   A technique used by psychoanalysts to interpret a person's dream. Psychoanalysts believe dreams contain information about the unconscious mind's thoughts and contents.   407

drive   An aroused state that occurs because of a physiological need.   295

DSM-IV   *Diagnostic and Statistical Manual of Mental Disorders,* fourth edition. The most recent major classification of mental disorders, containing 18 major classifications and describing more than 200 specific disorders.   375

dysthymic disorder   A depressive disorder that generally is more chronic and has fewer symptoms than major depressive disorder. The individual has a depressed mood for most days for at least 2 years as an adult or at least 1 year as a child or adolescent.   385

E

early adulthood   The developmental period that begins in the late teens or early twenties and ends in the thirties. It is a time when individuals establish personal and economic independence, intensely pursue a career, and seek intimacy with one or more individuals.   249

early childhood   The developmental period that extends from the end of infancy to about 5 or 6 years; sometimes the period is called the preschool years.   249

echoic memory   Auditory sensory memory in which information is retained for up to several seconds.   183

eclectic approach   An approach that follows no one particular conceptual perspective; rather, it uses whatever is considered best in each approach.   14

ecological theory   The relatively recent view that sleep is evolution based. This theory argues that the main purpose of sleep is to prevent animals from wasting their energy and harming themselves during the parts of the day or night to which they have not adapted.   119

efferent nerves   Motor nerves that carry the brain's output.   50

ego   The Freudian structure of personality that deals with the demands of reality; the ego is called the executive branch of personality because it makes decisions based on rationality.   338

egocentrism   A salient feature of preoperational thought; the inability to distinguish between one's own perspective and someone else's perspective.   260

egoism   Giving to another to ensure reciprocity; to gain self-esteem; to appear powerful, competent, or caring; or to avoid social and self-censure for failing to live up to normative expectations.   446

elaboration   The extensiveness of processing at any given depth of memory.   178

electroconvulsive therapy (ECT)   This therapy used mainly to treat severely depressed individuals. The goal of ECT is to cause a seizure in the brain much like what happens spontaneously in some forms of epilepsy. Commonly called "shock treatment."   426

electroencephalograph (EEG)   A machine that records the electrical activity of the brain. Electrodes placed on an individual's scalp record brain-wave activity, which is reproduced on a chart known as an electroencephalogram.   70

embryonic period   The period of prenatal development that occurs from 3 to 8 weeks after conception. During the embryonic period, the rate of cell differentiation intensifies, support systems for the cells form, and the beginnings of organs appear.   252

emotion   Feeling or affect, that can involve physiological arousal (a fast heartbeat, for example), conscious experience (thinking about being in love with someone, for example), and behavioral expression (a smile or grimace, for example).   318

emotion-focused coping   Lazarus' term for responding to stress in an emotional manner, especially using defensive appraisal.   529

empirically keyed test   A test that relies on its items to predict a particular criterion; unlike tests based on face validity, empirically keyed tests make no assumptions about the nature of the items.   359

encoding   How information gets into memory.   177

encoding specificity principle   The principle that associations formed at the time of encoding or learning tend to be effective retrieval cues.   195

endocrine glands   Glands that release their chemical products, called hormones, directly into the bloodstream.   72

endorphins   Neurotransmitters that function as natural opiates which usually stimulate the firing of neurons; involved in pleasure and pain.   54

environment   All of the surrounding conditions and influences that affect the development of living things.   47

episodic memory   The retention of information about the where and when of life's happenings.   186

erogenous zones   According to Freud, parts of the body that have especially strong pleasure-giving qualities at particular stages of development.   340

estradiol   A hormone associated in girls with breast, uterine, and skeletal development.   273

estrogens   A class of sex hormones, the most important of which is estradiol, that influences the development of female physical characteristics and helps to regulate the menstrual cycle. Estrogens are produced by the ovaries.   306

ethnicity   A person's heritage based on cultural heritage, nationality characteristics, race, religion, and language.   13

ethnocentrism   The tendency to favor one's own group over other groups.   454

ethology   The study of the biological basis of behavior in natural habitats.   296

evolutionary psychology approach   Emphasizes the importance of adaptation, reproduction, and "survival of the fittest" in explaining behavior.   46

evolutionary psychology approach   Psychology's newest approach, emphasizing the importance of adaptation, reproduction, and "survival of the fittest" in explaining behavior.   12

experiment   A carefully regulated procedure in which one or more factors believed to influence the behavior being studied are manipulated and all other factors are held constant.   34

experimental group   A group whose experience is manipulated.   35

experimental psychology   Areas of psychology in which psychologists often conduct basic research and use an experimental strategy. These areas include sensation and perception, cognitive processes (such as memory), learning, motivation, and emotion.   24

experimental research   Research that allows psychologists to discover behavior's causes.   34

experimenter bias   The influence of the experimenter's own expectations on the outcome of the research.   35

extinction (in classical conditioning)   The weakening of the conditioned response in the absence of the unconditioned stimulus.   148

extinction (in operant conditioning)   A decrease in the tendency to perform a behavior that no longer receives either positive or negative reinforcement.   160

extrasensory perception (ESP)   Perception that occurs without the use of any known sensory process.   108

face validity   An assumption that the content of the test items is a good indicator of an individual's personality.   359

facial feedback hypothesis   The hypothesis that facial expressions can influence emotions as well as reflect them. In this view, facial muscles send signals to the brain, which helps individuals recognize the emotion they are experiencing.   324

family therapy   Group therapy with family members.   418

feature detectors   Neurons in the brain's visual system that respond to particular lines or other features of a stimulus.   86

fetal alcohol syndrome (FAS)   A cluster of abnormalities that appear in the offspring of mothers who drink alcohol heavily during pregnancy.   253

fetal period   The prenatal period of development that begins 2 months after conception and lasts for 7 months, on the average.   252

figure-ground relationship   The principle by which we organize the perceptual field into stimuli that stand out (figure) and those that are left over (ground).   103

fixation   Focusing only on a prior strategy and failing to look at a problem from a fresh, new perspective.   213

fixation   The psychoanalytic defense mechanism that occurs when the individual remains locked in an earlier developmental stage because needs are under- or overgratified.   340

fixed-interval schedule   Reinforcement of the first appropriate response after a fixed amount of time has elapsed.   159

fixed-ratio schedule   Reinforcement of a behavior after a set number of responses.   159

flashbulb memories   Memories of emotionally significant events that people often recall with more accuracy and vivid imagery than everyday events.   196

foot-in-the-door strategy   A strategy in which an individual presents a weaker point or makes a small request with which the listeners will probably comply in the beginning, saving the strongest point until the end.   440

forebrain   The highest region of the brain; among its important structures are the thalamus, the hypothalamus and endocrine system, the limbic system, and the cerebrum.   58

forensic psychology   The field of psychology that applies psychological concepts to the legal system.   25

formal operational stage   Piaget's fourth and final cognitive stage, which is entered at about 11 to 15 years of age and continues through adulthood. It involves abstract, idealistic, and logical thinking.   262

fovea   A minute area in the center of the retina where vision is at its best.   85

free association   The psychoanalytic technique of encouraging individuals to say aloud whatever comes to mind, no matter how trivial or embarrassing.   406

free-radical theory   The theory that people age because inside their cells unstable oxygen molecules known as free radicals are produced. These ricochet around the cells, damaging DNA and other cellular structures.   281

frequency   The number of cycles (or full wavelengths) that pass through a point in a given time.   91

frequency theory   The theory that the perception of a sound's frequency is due to how often the auditory nerve fires.   94

frontal lobe   A portion of the cerebral cortex that is behind the forehead and is involved in the control of voluntary muscles and in intelligence.   62

frustration-aggression hypothesis   The hypothesis that frustration always leads to aggression.   462

functional fixedness   A type of fixation in which individuals fail to solve a problem because they are fixated on a thing's usual functions.   213

functionalism   William James' theory that psychology's role is to study the functions of the mind and behavior in adapting to the environment.   7

fundamental attribution error   Observers' tendency to overestimate the importance of traits and underestimate the importance of situations when they seek explanations of an actor's behavior.   436

GABA   Gamma aminobutyric acid, a neurotransmitter that inhibits the firing of neurons and is found throughout the central nervous system.   54

gate-control theory   The theory that the spinal column contains a neural gate that can be opened (allowing the perception of pain) or closed (blocking the perception of pain).   96

gender   The sociocultural dimension of being female or male, especially how we learn to think and behave as females and males.   13

generalization (in classical conditioning) The tendency of a new stimulus that is similar to the original conditioned stimulus to elicit a response that is similar to the conditioned response. 150

generalization (in operant conditioning) Giving the same response to similar stimuli. 160

generalized anxiety disorder An anxiety disorder that consists of persistent anxiety for at least a month; the individual is unable to specify the reasons for the anxiety. 378

generativity versus stagnation Erikson's seventh stage, which occurs in middle adulthood. A chief concern is to assist the younger generation in developing and leading useful lives. The feeling of having done little or nothing for the next generation is what is meant by stagnation. 265

genes Short segments of chromosomes that are the units of hereditary information and are composed of DNA. 44

genital stage The fifth Freudian stage of development, occurring from puberty on; the genital stage is the time of sexual reawakening and the source of sexual pleasure now becomes someone outside of the family. 341

genotype The person's genetic heritage, the actual genetic material. 45

germinal period The period of prenatal development that takes place in the first 2 weeks after conception. It includes the creation of the zygote, continued cell division, and the attachment of the zygote to the uterine wall. 252

Gestalt psychology An approach that states that people naturally organize their perceptions according to certain patterns. *Gestalt* is a German word that means "configuration" or "form." One of Gestalt psychology's main principles is that the whole is not equal to the sum of its parts. 103

Gestalt therapy The humanistic therapy developed by Fritz Perls in which the therapist questions and challenges clients to help them become more aware of their feelings and face their problems. 410

glial cells Non-neuron cells that provide supportive and nutritive functions. 56

graphology The use of handwriting analysis to determine an individual's personality. 359

great-person theory The theory that some individuals have certain traits that are best suited for leadership positions. 452

group polarization effect The solidification and further strengthening of a position as a consequence of group discussion. 451

groupthink Impaired decision making and avoidance of realistic appraisal in order to maintain group harmony. 451

H

hallucinogens Psychoactive drugs that modify a person's perceptual experiences and produce hallucinatory visual images; hallucinogens are called psychedelic ("mind altering") drugs. 138

health psychology A multidimensional approach to health that emphasizes psychological factors, lifestyle, and the nature of the health-care delivery system. 25

heuristics Strategies or rules of thumb that can suggest a solution to a problem but do not guarantee a solution. 213

hierarchy of motives Maslow's view that we need to satisfy our main needs in this sequence: physiological, safety, love and belongingness, esteem, and self-actualization. 297, 350

hindbrain The lowest portion of the brain, located at the skull's rear. It consists of the spinal cord, lower brain stem (pons and medulla), and cerebellum. 58

hindsight bias Our tendency to falsely report, after the fact, that we accurately predicted an event. 217

hippocampus A limbic system structure that has a special role in the storage of memories. 60

homeostasis The body's tendency to maintain an equilibrium, or steady state. 295

hue A characteristic of color based on its wavelength content. 87

human sexual response cycle Consists of four phases: excitement, plateau, orgasm, and resolution. Identified by Masters and Johnson. 308

humanistic approach An emphasis on a person's capacity for personal growth, freedom to choose his or her own destiny, and positive qualities. 10

humanistic perspectives Perspectives that stress personal growth, choosing one's own destiny, and positive qualities. 348

humanistic therapies Therapies that encourage people to understand themselves and to grow personally. In contrast to the psychoanalytic therapies, the humanistic therapies emphasize conscious rather than unconscious thoughts, the present rather than the past, and growth and self-fulfillment rather than illness. 409

hypnosis A psychological state of altered attention and awareness in which the individual is unusually receptive to suggestions. 132

hypochondriasis A somatoform disorder in which the individual has a pervasive fear of illness and disease. 381

hypothalamus Located just below the thalamus, the hypothalamus monitors three enjoyable activities—eating, drinking, and sex. It also helps to direct the endocrine system through the pituitary gland, and is involved in emotion, stress, and reward. 60

hypotheses Specific assumptions or predictions that can be tested to determine their accuracy. 28

hypothetical-deductive reasoning Piaget's name for adolescents' cognitive ability to develop hypotheses, or best guesses, about how to solve problems, such as algebraic equations. 262

I

iconic memory Visual sensory memory in which information is retained for about 1/4 second. 183

id The Freudian structure of personality that consists of instincts, which are the individual's reservoir of psychic energy. 338

identity versus identity confusion Erikson's fifth stage, which occurs during adolescence. At this time, individuals are faced with finding out who they are, what they are all about, and where they are going in life. If they don't adequately explore their identity, they emerge from this stage with a sense of identity confusion. 265

implicit personality theory The public's conception of how personality traits go together in an individual. 437

impression management (also called self-presentation) Presenting an image of oneself as a certain sort of person, which might or might not be who one really is. 439

imprinting The tendency of an infant animal to form an attachment to the first moving object it sees or hears. 266

incentives Positive or negative stimuli that motivate an individual's behavior. 297

independent variable The manipulated, influential, experimental factor in an experiment. The label "independent" is used because this variable can be changed independent of other factors to determine its effect on the dependent variable. 34

individual differences The stable, consistent ways in which people are different from each other. 228

individual psychology The name Adler gave to his theory of psychology to emphasize the uniqueness of every individual. 343

inductive reasoning Reasoning from the specific to the general. That is, drawing conclusions about all members of a category based on observing only some members. 215

indulgent parenting A style of parenting in which parents are very involved with their children but place few demands or controls on them; it is associated with children's social incompetence, especially a lack of self-control. 269

industrial/organizational psychology A branch of psychology that deals with the workplace, focusing on both the workers and the organizations that employ them. 25

industry versus inferiority Erikson's fourth stage, which occurs from 6 years to puberty. Industry is achieved by mastering knowledge and intellectual skills. When children don't attain this mastery, they can feel inferior. 265

infancy The developmental period that extends from birth to 18 or 24 months of age. 249

inferiority complex Adler's name for exaggerated feelings of inadequacy. 344

infinite generativity The ability to produce an endless number of meaningful sentences using a finite set of words and rules. 219

information theory The contemporary explanation of how classical conditioning works: The key to understanding classical conditioning is the information the organism obtains from the situation. 151

informational social influence The influence other people have on us because we want to be right. 446

information-processing approach The most widely adopted cognitive approach. Information-processing psychologists study how individuals process information—how they attend to information, how they perceive it, how they store it, how they think about it, and how they retrieve it for further use. 11

informed consent Participants' consent based on knowing what their participation will involve and any risks that might develop. 37

initiative versus guilt Erikson's third stage, which occurs from 3 to 5 years of age. Asked to assume more responsibility for themselves, children develop initiative. If children are irresponsible or made to feel anxious, they may develop guilt. 265

inner ear The oval window, cochlea, and the organ of Corti. 92

insanity defense A defense that requires that the defendant have been wholly or partially irrational when the crime took place, and that the irrationality affected his or her behavior. 371

insight learning A form of problem solving in which an organism develops a sudden understanding of a problem's solution. 168

insight therapy A term for psychodynamic and humanistic therapies because their goal is to encourage insight and self-awareness. 404

insomnia A common sleep problem; the inability to sleep. 126

instinct An innate (unlearned), biological pattern of behavior that is assumed to be universal throughout the species. 294

instinctive drift The tendency of animals to revert to instinctive behavior that interferes with learning. 169

integrity versus despair Erikson's eighth and final stage, which occurs in late adulthood. At this point people review their lives. If their retrospective glances are positive, integrity results; if they are negative, despair is the outcome. 265

intelligence Verbal ability, problem-solving skills, and the ability to adapt to and learn from life's everyday experiences. 228

intellignece quotient (IQ) An individual's mental age divided by chronological age multiplied by 100 231

interference theory The theory that we forget, not because memories are actually lost from storage, but because other information gets in the way of what we want to remember. 200

internalization The developmental change from behavior that is externally controlled to behavior that is controlled by internal, self-generated standards and principles. 274

interneurons Central nervous system neurons that go between sensory input and motor output. Interneurons make up most of the brain. 51

interview Asking questions to find out about a person's experiences and attitudes. 31

intimacy versus isolation Erikson's sixth stage, which occurs in early adulthood. At this time, individuals face the developmental task of forming intimate relationships with others. If they don't find intimacy in relationships with a partner and/or friends, they may develop a sense of social isolation. 265

ions Electrically charged particles, including sodium (Na) chloride (Cl) and potassium (K). The neuron creates electrical signals by moving these charged ions back and forth through its membrane; the waves of electricity that are created sweep along the membrane. 53

iris The colored part of the eye, which can range from light blue to dark brown. 83

J

James-Lange theory The theory that emotion results from physiological changes triggered by stimuli in the environment: Emotion follows a physiological reaction. 321

justice perspective A theory of moral development that focuses on the rights of the individual; individuals independently make moral decisions. Kohlberg's theory is a justice perspective. 276

K

keyword method A mnemonic strategy in which vivid imagery is attached to important words. 203

kinesthetic sense The sense that provides information about movement, posture, and orientation. 99

L

laboratory A controlled setting with many of the complex factors of the "real world" removed. 30

language A form of communication, whether spoken, written, or signed, that is based on a system of symbols. 219

late adulthood The developmental stage that begins around 60 to 70 years of age and ends when an individual dies. It is a time of adjustment to decreased strength and health, retirement, reduced income, new social roles, and learning how to age successfully. 250

latency stage The fourth Freudian stage of development, occurring approximately between 6 years of age and puberty; the child represses all interest in sexuality and develops social and intellectual skills. 341

latent content A dream's hidden content, its unconscious meaning. 129, 407

law of effect Developed by Robert Thorndike, this law states that behaviors followed by positive outcomes are strengthened, whereas behaviors followed by negative outcomes are weakened. 156

learned helplessness A condition that occurs in individuals who are exposed to aversive stimulation over which they have no control. The inability to avoid such aversive stimulation produces an apathetic state of helplessness. 388

learning A relatively permanent change in behavior that occurs through experience. 146

lens of the eye A transparent and somewhat flexible ball-like entity at the front of the pupil, filled with a gelatinous material; its function is to bend the light falling on the surface of the eye just enough to focus it at the back of the eye. 83

levels of processing theory The theory that memory is processed on a continuum from shallow to deep, with deeper processing producing better memory. 178

life expectancy The number of years that will probably be lived by the average person born in a particular year. 280

life span The upper boundary of life for a species, the maximum number of years an individual of that species can live. 280

life-process model of addiction The view that addiction is not a disease but rather a habitual response and a source of gratification and security that can be understood only in the context of social relationships and experiences. 139

light A form of electromagnetic energy that can be described in terms of wavelengths. 82

limbic system A loosely connected network of structures under the cerebral cortex that plays an important role in both memory and emotion. 59

linguistic relativity hypothesis The hypothesis that language determines the structure of thinking and shapes our basic ideas. 225

lithium A drug that is widely used in treating bipolar disorder. 425

long-term memory A relatively permanent type of memory that holds huge amounts of information for a long period of time. 184

loudness The perception of a sound wave's amplitude. 92

M

magnetic resonance imaging (MRI) A technology in which a magnetic field is created around a person's body and radio waves are used to construct images of the person's brain tissues and biochemical activity. 71

major depressive disorder A depressive disorder in which the individual experiences a major depressive episode and depressed characteristics, such as lethargy and hopelessness, for at least 2 weeks. Daily functioning becomes impaired. 385

managed care Strategies for controlling health-care costs, including mental health treatments. 402

manifest content A dream's surface content, which contains dream symbols that distort and disguise the dream's true meaning. 129, 407

matching hypothesis The hypothesis that while we may prefer a more attractive person in the abstract, in the real world we end up choosing someone who is close to our own level of attractiveness. 469

medical model   A model that describes mental disorders as mental diseases with a biological origin.   372

medulla   The portion of the brain located where the spinal cord enters the skull. It helps control breathing and regulates a portion of the reflexes that allow us to maintain an upright posture.   58

memory   The retention of information over time. Psychologists study how information is initially encoded into memory, how it is retained or stored, and how it is found or retrieved for a certain purpose later.   176

memory span   The number of digits an individual can report back in order after a single presentation of them.   184

menopause   The time in middle age, usually in the late forties or early fifties, when a woman's menstrual periods cease completely.   279

mental age (MA)   An individual's level of mental development relative to others.   230

mental processes   The thoughts, feelings, and motives that each of us experiences privately but that cannot be observed directly.   5

mental set   A type of fixation in which an individual tries to solve a problem in a particular way that has worked in the past.   214

meta-analysis   A research technique that involves statistically combining the results of many different studies.   421

method of loci   A mnemonic strategy in which you develop an image of items to be remembered and store them in familiar locations *(loci)*.   203

midbrain   Located between the hindbrain and forebrain, this is an area where many nerve-fiber systems ascend and descend to connect lower and higher portions of the brain; in particular, the midbrain relays information between the brain and the eyes and ears.   58

middle adulthood   The developmental period that begins at about 35 to 45 years of age and ends at about 55 to 65 years of age. It is a time of expanding personal and social involvement, increased responsibility, adjustment to physical decline, and attainment and maintenance of career satisfaction.   249

middle and late childhood   The developmental period that extends from about 6 to 11 years of age, approximately corresponding to the elementary school years; sometimes the period is called the elementary school years.   249

middle ear   The section of the ear consisting primarily of the eardrum, hammer, anvil, and stirrup.   92

Minnesota Multiphasic Personality Inventory (MMPI)   The self-report personality test most widely used in clinical and research settings.   360

mnemonics   Specific memory aids for remembering information.   203

monocular cues   Depth cues based on each eye working independently.   105

mood-congruent memory   Memory is better when mood is similar during encoding and retrieval.   199

mood disorders   Psychological disorders characterized by wide mood swings, ranging from deep depression to extreme euphoria and agitation. Depression can occur alone, as in the depressive disorders, or it can alternate with mania, as in bipolar disorder.   385

morphology   The rules for word formation.   220

motivation   Why people behave, think, and feel the way they do. Motivated behavior is energized, directed, and sustained.   294

movement aftereffects   An illusion of movement that occurs when people watch continuous movement and then look at another surface, which then appears to move in the opposite direction.   106

multiaxial system   A feature of the DSM-IV system that classifies individuals on the basis of five dimensions, or "axes," that include the individual's history and highest level of functioning in the last year.   375

multiple-factor theory   L. L. Thurstone's theory that intelligence consists of seven primary mental abilities: verbal comprehension, number ability, word fluency, spatial visualization, associative memory, reasoning, and perceptual speed.   232

myelin sheath   A layer of fat cells that encases most axons; this sheath not only insulates the axon but also helps the nerve impulse travel faster.   51

N

narcolepsy   The overpowering urge to fall asleep.   127

natural selection   The evolutionary principle that the organisms that are best adapted to their environment are the most likely to survive, reproduce, and pass on their genes to their offspring.   6, 46

naturalistic observation   Observations of behavior in real-world settings with no effort made to manipulate or control the situation.   31

nature   An organism's biological inheritance.   47

need   A deprivation that energizes the drive to eliminate or reduce the deprivation.   295

need for achievement   The desire to accomplish something, to reach a standard of excellence, and to expend effort to excel.   314

negative punishment   The removal of a positive stimulus after a behavior, decreasing the likelihood that the behavior will occur again.   161

negative reinforcement   The frequency of a response increases because it is followed by the removal of an aversive (unpleasant) stimulus.   156

neglectful parenting   A style of parenting in which parents are very uninvolved in the child's life; it is associated with children's social incompetence, especially a lack of self-control.   269

neocortex   The most recently evolved part of the brain; covering the rest of the brain almost like a cap, it is the largest part of the brain and makes up about 80 percent of its volume.   62

nervous system   The body's electrochemical communication circuitry, made up of billions of neurons.   48

neurons   Nerve cells, the basic units of the nervous system.   49

neuroscience   The umbrella term for the multidisciplinary study of the nervous system.   49

neurotic   A term for mental disorders that are personally distressful but in which the individual does not lose contact with reality; the term is largely out of use because it is vague.   375

neurotransmitters   Chemical substances that carry information across the synaptic gap to the next neuron.   54

night terror   Sudden arousal from sleep, with intense fear, usually accompanied by a number of physiological reactions.   127

nightmare   A frightening dream that awakens the sleeper from REM sleep.   127

noise   Irrelevant and competing stimuli.   79

nondeclarative memory   Memory that is affected by prior experience without that experience being consciously recollected. Because nondeclarative memory cannot be verbalized or consciously recollected, at least not in the form of specific events or facts, it also is called "implicit memory."   185

nonstate theory   The theory that individuals who become hypnotized are under the social influence of the hypnotist, that they are carrying out the social role of being a good hypnotic subject and letting the hypnotist direct their imaginative thinking.   133

norepinephrine   A neurotransmitter that usually is inhibitory but excites the heart muscles, intestines, and urogenital tract; is involved in the control of alertness and wakefulness.   54

normal distribution   A symmetrical distribution with a majority of the cases falling in the middle of the possible range of scores and few scores appearing toward the extremes of the range.   231

normative social influence   The influence that other people have on us because we seek their approval or avoid their disapproval.   445

norms   Established standards of performance for a test. Norms are established by giving the test to a large group of individuals who are representative of the population for whom the test is intended. Norms allow the test constructor to determine the distribution of test scores, informing us which scores are considered high, low, or average.   230

norms   Rules that apply to the members of a group.   449

nurture   An organism's environmental experiences.   47

O

obedience   Behavior that complies with the explicit demands of the individual in authority.   446

object permanence   The Piagetian term for one of an infant's most important accomplishments: understanding that objects and events continue to exist even when they cannot directly be seen, heard, or touched.   259

observational learning   Learning that occurs when a person observes and imitates someone else's behavior; also called imitation or modeling.   166

obsessive-compulsive disorder (OCD)   An anxiety disorder in which the individual has anxiety-provoking thoughts that will not go away (obsession) and/or urges to perform repetitive, ritualistic behaviors to prevent or produce some future situation (compulsion).   380

occipital lobe   The portion of the cerebral cortex at the back of the head that is involved in vision.   62

Oedipus complex   Freud's idea that the young child develops an intense desire to replace the parent of the same sex and enjoy the affections of the opposite-sex parent.   341

olfactory epithelium   Tissue located at the top of the nasal cavity that contains a sheet of receptor cells for smell.   98

operant conditioning (instrumental conditioning)   A form of learning in which the consequences of behavior produce changes in the probability of the behavior's occurrence.   155

operational definition   A description that is as precise as possible about the aspects of a problem and how it is to be studied in terms of observable events that can be measured.   27

operations   In Piaget's theory, mental representations that are reversible; internalized sets of actions that allow the child to do mentally what was done physically before.   260

opiates   Opium and its derivatives; these depress the central nervous system's activity.   136

opponent-process theory   The theory that cells in the visual system respond to red-green and blue-yellow colors; a given cell might be excited by red and inhibited by green, while another cell might be excited by yellow and inhibited by blue.   89

oral stage   The term Freud used to describe development during the first 18 months of life, in which the infant's pleasure centers on the mouth.   340

organ of Corti   A tissue that runs the length of the cochlea and sits on the basilar membrane. It contains the ear's sensory receptors, which change the energy of sound waves into nerve impulses that can be processed by the brain.   92

outer ear   The pinna and the external auditory canal.   92

overcompensation   Adler's term for the individual's attempt to deny rather than acknowledge a real situation or the individual's exaggerated effort to conceal a weakness.   344

overconfidence bias   The tendency to have more confidence in our judgments and decisions than we should based on the relative frequency of our correct answers.   217

pain   The sensation that warns us that damage is occurring to our bodies.   96

panic disorder   An anxiety disorder marked by the recurrent sudden onset of intense apprehension or terror.   378

papillae   Bumps on the surface of the tongue that contain taste buds, the receptors for taste.   97

paranoid schizophrenia   A type of schizophrenia characterized by delusions of reference, grandeur, and persecution.   391

parasympathetic nervous system   The division of the autonomic nervous system that calms the body.   50, 319

parietal lobe   A portion of the cerebral cortex at the top of the head, and toward the rear, that is involved in processing bodily sensations.   62

partial reinforcement   Reinforcement of responses only a portion of the time they occur.   159

perception   The brain's process of organizing and interpreting sensory information to give it meaning.   78

peripheral nervous system   A network of nerves that connects the brain and spinal cord to other parts of the body. The peripheral nervous system takes information to and from the brain and spinal cord and carries out the commands of the CNS to execute various muscular and glandular activities.   49

personality   The enduring, distinctive thoughts, emotions, and behaviors that characterize the way an individual adapts to the world.   336

personality disorders   Chronic, maladaptive cognitive-behavioral patterns that are thoroughly integrated into the individual's personality.   393

personality psychology   An area that focuses on relatively enduring traits and characteristics of individuals.   25

person-centered therapy   A form of humanistic therapy developed by Carl Rogers in which the therapist provides a warm, supportive atmosphere to improve the client's self-concept and encourage the client to gain insight about problems.   409

phallic stage   Freud's third stage of development, which occurs between the ages of 3 and 6. Its name comes from the Latin word phallus, which means "penis." During the phallic stage, pleasure focuses on the genitals as the child discovers that self-stimulation is enjoyable.   340

phenotype   The way an individual's genotype is expressed in observable, measurable characteristics.   45

pheromones   Odorous substances released by animals that are powerful attractants in the lower animals but much less so in humans.   307

phobias   Irrational fears.   152

phobic disorder   An anxiety disorder in which the individual has an irrational, overwhelming, persistent fear of a particular object or situation; commonly called phobia.   379

phonology   A language's sound system.   219

physical dependence   The physical need for a drug that is accompanied by unpleasant withdrawal symptoms when the drug is discontinued.   135

pitch   The perceptual interpretation of a sound's frequency.   91

pituitary gland   An important endocrine gland that sits at the base of the skull and is about the size of a pea; it controls growth and regulates other glands.   72

place theory   The theory that each frequency of sound waves produces vibrations at a particular spot on the basilar membrane.   93

placebo effect   Production of the desired experimental outcome by participants' expectations rather than the experimental treatment.   36

plasticity   The brain's capacity to modify and reorganize itself following damage.   69

pleasure principle   The Freudian concept that the id always seeks pleasure and avoids pain.   338

polygraph   A machine used by examiners to determine if someone is lying; it monitors changes in the body—heart rate, breathing, and electrodermal response (an index that detects skin resistance to passage of a weak electric current)—thought to be influenced by emotional states.   319

pons   A bridge in the hindbrain that contains several clusters of fibers involved in sleep and arousal.   58

positive punishment   An unpleasant stimulus following a behavior which decreases the likelihood that that behavior will occur again.   161

positive reinforcement   The frequency of a response increases because it is followed by a rewarding stimulus.   156

positron-emission tomography (PET scan)   A technology in which the amount of specially treated glucose in various areas of the brain is measured and then analyzed by computer.   71

postconventional level   Kohlberg's highest level of moral thinking; moral development is completely internalized and not based on others' standards. An individual recognizes alternative moral courses, explores the options, and then develops a personal moral code. The code is among the principles generally accepted by the community (stage 5) or it is more individualized (stage 6).   275

post-traumatic stress disorder   A mental disorder that develops through exposure to a traumatic event, such as war; severely oppressive situations, such as the holocaust; severe abuse, as in rape; natural disasters, such as floods and tornados; and accidental disasters, such as plane crashes. Characterized by anxiety symptoms that might immediately follow the trauma or be delayed in onset by months or even years.   380

PQ4R   A study system that involves Preview, Question, Read, Reflect, Recite, and Review.   205

precognition   "Knowing" events before they occur.   109

preconventional level   Kohlberg's lowest level of moral thinking, in which an individual shows no internalization of moral values—moral thinking is based on punishments (stage 1) or rewards (stage 2) that come from the external world.   274

predictive validity   A form of criterion validity that assesses the relation of a test's scores to an individual's performance at a point in the future.   229

prejudice   An unjustified negative attitude toward an individual based on the individual's membership in a group.   454

prenatal period   The time from conception to birth.   249

preoperational stage   Piaget's second stage of cognitive development, which lasts from about 2 to 7 years of age. This stage is more symbolic than sensorimotor thought, does not involve operational thought, is egocentric, and is intuitive rather than logical.   260

preparedness   The species-specific biological predisposition to learn in certain ways but not in others.   169

preterm infant   An infant who is born prior to 38 weeks into the prenatal period; also called a premature infant.   254

primacy effect   Superior recall for items at the beginning of a list.   193

primacy effect   The enduring quality of initial impressions.   438

primary prevention   Prevention that attempts to stop people from taking drugs by helping them to not start.   139

primary reinforcement   The use of reinforcers that are innately satisfying (that is, they do not require any learning on the organism's part to make them pleasurable).   158

priming   Activating particular connections or associations in memory. These associations often are unconscious.   195

proactive interference   Material that was learned earlier disrupts the recall of material learned later.   200

problem solving   An attempt to find an appropriate way of attaining a goal when the goal is not readily available.   211

projective test   A test that presents individuals with an ambiguous stimulus and then asks them to describe it or tell a story about it. Projective tests are based on the assumption that the ambiguity of the stimulus allows individuals to project into it their feelings, desires, needs, and attitudes.   358

prototype matching   Deciding whether an item is a member of a category by comparing it with the most typical item(s) of the category.   211

prototypes   Abstract categorizations of traits that describe a particular personality type. Prototypes act as standards against which we match the individuals we evaluate.   438

psychiatry   A branch of medicine practiced by physicians with a doctor of medicine (M.D.) degree who subsequently specialize in abnormal behavior and psychotherapy.   23

psychoactive drugs   Drugs that act on the nervous system to alter states of consciousness, modify perceptions, and change moods.   134

psychoanalysis   Freud's therapeutic technique for analyzing an individual's unconscious thought.   406

psychoanalytic approach   An emphasis on the unconscious aspects of the mind, conflict between biological instincts and society's demands, and early family experiences.   10

psychoanalytic perspectives   Perspectives that view personality as primarily unconscious and as occurring in stages. Most psychoanalytic perspectives emphasize the role of early experiences in sculpting personality.   337

psychodynamic therapies   Therapies that stress the importance of the unconscious mind, extensive interpretation by the therapist, and the role of experiences in early childhood.   404

psychokinesis   Closely associated with ESP, the mind-over-matter phenomenon of being able to move objects without touching them, such as mentally getting a chair to rise off the floor or shattering a glass merely by staring at it.   109

psychological dependence   The strong craving to repeat the use of a drug in order to obtain its emotional effects, such as a feeling of well-being and a reduction of stress.   135

psychology   The scientific study of behavior and mental processes.   5

psychology of women   An area of psychology that emphasizes the importance of promoting the research and study of women, integrating this information about women with current psychological knowledge and beliefs, and applying the information to society and its institutions.   25

psychophysics   The field that studies links between the physical properties of stimuli and a person's experience of them.   78

psychosexual dysfunctions   Disorders that involve impairments in the sexual response pattern, either in the desire for gratification or in the ability to achieve it.   309

psychosurgery   A biomedical therapy that involves removal or destruction of brain tissue to improve the individual's psychological adjustment.   427

psychotherapy   The process used by mental health professionals to help individuals recognize, define, and overcome their psychological and interpersonal difficulties and improve their adjustment.   400

psychotic   A term for severe mental disorders in which the individual has lost contact with reality; the term is generally out of use because it is vague.   375

puberty   A period of rapid skeletal and sexual maturation that occurs in early adolescence.   273

punishment   A consequence that decreases the likelihood a behavior will occur.   161

pupil   The opening in the center of the iris; it appears black. The iris contains muscles that control the size of the pupil and, hence, the amount of light that enters the eye.   83

questionnaires (surveys)   A data collection method similar to structured interviews except that the respondents read the questions and mark their answers on paper rather than verbally responding to an interviewer.   31

random assignment   Assignment of participants to experimental and control groups by chance. This practice reduces the likelihood that the experiment's results will be due to any preexisting differences between groups.   35

rapport talk   The language of conversation. A way of establishing connections and negotiating relationships. Preferred by women.   471

rational-emotive behavior therapy   A cognitive therapy based on Albert Ellis' assertion that individuals invariably become psychologically disordered because of their beliefs, especially those that are irrational and self-defeating.   414

reality principle   The Freudian principle that the ego tries to bring the individual pleasure within the norms of society.   338

reasoning   The mental activity of transforming information to reach conclusions.   215

recall   A memory measure in which the individual must retrieve previously learned information, as on an essay test.   194

recency effect   Superior recall for items at the end of a list.   193

reciprocal socialization   Bidirectional socialization, in which children socialize their parents just as parents socialize their children.   269

recognition   A memory measure in which the individual only has to identify ("recognize") learned items, as on a multiple-choice test.   194

reflexes   Automatic stimulus-response connections that are "hardwired" into the brain.   147

rehearsal   The conscious repetition of information that increases the length of time that information stays in memory.   177

reliability   The extent to which a test yields a consistent, reproducible measure of performance.   228

REM sleep   A periodic, active stage of sleep during which dreaming occurs.   122

repair theory   The theory that sleep restores, replenishes, and rebuilds our brains and bodies, which are somehow worn out by the day's waking activities.   119

report talk   Talk designed to give information, as in public speaking. Preferred by men.   471

representativeness heuristic   Making decisions based on how well something matches a prototype—that is, the most common or representative example.   217

repression   The most powerful and pervasive defense mechanism, according to Freud; it works to push unacceptable id impulses out of awareness and back into the unconscious mind.   339

research participant bias   The influence of research participants' beliefs about how they are expected to behave.   36

resistance   The psychoanalytic term for the person's unconscious defense strategies that prevent the analyst from understanding the person's problems.   407

resting potential   The stable, negative charge of an inactive neuron.   53

restrained eaters   Individuals who chronically restrict their food intake to control their weight. Restrained eaters are often on diets, are very conscious of what they eat, and tend to feel guilty after splurging on sweets.   303

reticular formation   A diffuse collection of neurons involved in stereotyped patterns of behavior such as walking, sleeping, or turning to attend to a sudden noise.   58

retina   The light-sensitive surface at the back of the eye that houses light receptors called rods and cones.   84

retrieval   Bringing information out of memory storage.   177

retroactive interference   Material learned later disrupts retrieval of information learned earlier.   200

retrograde amnesia   Memory loss for a segment of the past but not for new events.   201

risky shift   The tendency for a group decision to be riskier, on the average, than decisions made by individual group members.   451

rods   The receptors in the retina that are exquisitely sensitive to light but are not very useful for color vision.   84

roles   Rules and expectations that govern certain positions in the group. Roles define how people should behave in a particular position in the group.   449

romantic love   Also called passionate love or eros, this type of love has strong components of sexuality and infatuation; it often predominates in the early part of a love relationship.   469

romantic script   Sex is synonymous with love. If we develop a relationship with someone and fall in love, it is acceptable to have sex with the person whether we are married or not.   308

Rorschach inkblot test   The most well known projective test, developed in 1921 by the Swiss psychiatrist Hermann Rorschach. It uses individuals' perceptions of inkblots to determine their personality.   358

saturation   A characteristic of color based on its purity.   87

schedules of reinforcement   Timetables that determine when a response will be reinforced.   159

schema   A concept or framework that already exists in a person's mind and that organizes and interprets information.   188, 258

schizophrenia   A severe psychological disorder characterized by distorted thoughts and perceptions, odd communication, inappropriate emotion, abnormal motor behavior, and social withdrawal. The individual's mind is split from reality and personality loses its unity.   389

school and educational psychology   An area of psychology that is concerned with children's learning and adjustment in school.   25

science   In psychology, the use of systematic methods to observe, describe, explain, and predict behavior.   5

scientific method   An approach used to discover accurate information about phenomena, including mind and behavior. It includes these steps: Identify a problem, collect information (data), draw conclusions, and revise theory.   27

sclera   The white outer part of the eye that helps maintain the shape of the eye and protect it from injury.   83

script   A schema for an event.   190

secondary prevention   Prevention that attempts to minimize the harm caused by drug use with a high-risk population or with a group that is involved in experimental or occasional use.   140

secondary reinforcement   Reinforcement that acquires its positive value through experience; secondary reinforcers are learned, or conditioned, reinforcers.   158

secondary traits   In Allport's view, traits that are limited in frequency and least important in describing an individual's personality.   354

secure attachment   Securely attached infants use the caregiver, usually the mother, as a secure base from which to explore the environment. Ainsworth believes that secure attachment in the first year of life provides an important foundation for psychological development later in life.   267

selective attention   Focusing on a specific aspect of experience while ignoring others.   102

self-actualization   The highest and most elusive human need, according to Maslow; the motivation to develop one's full potential as a human being.   298

self-actualization   The highest and most elusive of Maslow's needs; the motivation to develop one's full potential as a human being.   350

self-concept   A central theme in the views of Rogers and other humanists; individuals' overall perceptions of their abilities, behavior, and personality.   349

self-esteem   The evaluative and affective dimension of self-concept. Self-esteem is also referred to as self-worth.   350

self-help support groups   Voluntary organization of individuals who get together on a regular basis to discuss topics of common interest. The groups are not conducted by a professional therapist but rather by a paraprofessional or a member of the common interest group.   419

self-monitoring   Individuals' attention to the impressions they make on others and the degree to which they fine-tune their performance accordingly.   440

self-perception theory   Bem's theory of attitude-behavior connection; it stresses that individuals make inferences about their attitudes by perceiving their behavior.   442

self-report tests   Tests that involve directly asking people whether items (usually true-false or agree-disagree) describe their personality traits or not; also called objective tests or inventories.   359

self-serving bias   Attributing explanations for one's successes to internal factors and explanations for one's failures to external factors.   436

semantic memory   A person's knowledge about the world. This includes a person's field of expertise, general academic knowledge of the sort learned in school, and everyday knowledge about meanings of words, famous individuals, important places, and common things.   186

semantics   The meanings of words and sentences.   220

semicircular canals   Canals in the inner ear that contain the sensory receptors that detect head motion caused by tilting the head or other bodily motion.   100

sensation   The process of detecting and encoding stimulus energy in the world.   78

sensorimotor stage   The first Piagetian stage, which lasts from birth until about 2 years of age. In this stage, infants construct an understanding of the world by coordinating sensory experiences with physical motoric actions. This stage is nonsymbolic through much of its duration, and object permanence is an important accomplishment.   259

sensory adaptation   A change in the responsiveness of the sensory system based on the average level of surrounding stimulation.   86

sensory memory   A form of memory storage that holds information from the world in its original sensory form for only an instant, not much longer than the brief time it is exposed to the visual, auditory, and other senses.   182

serial position effect   Recall is superior for the items at the beginning of a list and the end of a list.   193

serotonin   A neurotransmitter that is mainly inhibitory and is involved in the regulation of sleep and depression.   54

set point   The weight maintained when no effort is made to gain or lose weight.   302

sex   The biological dimension of being female or male.   13

sexual scripts   Stereotyped patterns of expectancies for how people should sexually behave.   308

shape constancy   Recognition that an object remains the same shape even though its orientation to us changes.   106

shaping   The process of rewarding approximations of desired behavior.   158

signal detection theory   The theory that sensitivity to sensory stimuli depends on a variety of factors besides the physical intensity of the stimulus and the sensory abilities of the observer.   81

situationism   Mischel's view that personality often varies from one context to another.   355

size constancy   Recognition that an object remains the same size even though the retinal image of the object changes.   106

sleep apnea   A sleep disorder in which the sleeper stops breathing because the windpipe fails to open or brain processes involved in respiration fail to work properly.   127

sleep spindles   Brief bursts of higher-frequency waves that periodically occur during stage 2 sleep.   122

social cognitive theory   The theory that behavior is determined not only by environmental conditions, but also by how thought processes modify these experiences.   8, 347

social comparison   The process in which individuals evaluate their thoughts, feelings, behaviors, and abilities in relation to other people.   438

social desirability   The tendency of participants to tell the interviewer what they think is socially acceptable or desirable rather than what they truly feel or think.   31, 359

social facilitation   The phenomenon that occurs when an individual's performance improves because of the presence of others; occurs with well-learned tasks not with new or difficult tasks.   450

social identity theory   The theory that when individuals are assigned to a group, they invariably think of the group as an in-group for them. This occurs because individuals want to have a positive self-image. Social identity theory helps to explain prejudice and conflict between groups.   455

social loafing   Each person's tendency to exert less effort in a group because of reduced monitoring. The result is lowered group performance.   450

social psychology   An area that deals with people's social interactions, relationships, perceptions, and attitudes.   25

sociocultural approach   An approach that emphasizes the influences of culture, ethnicity, and gender, among other sociocultural factors, on behavior, thought, and emotion.   12

socioemotional processes   Processes that involve changes in an individual's relationships with other people, changes in emotions, and changes in personality.   248

somatic nervous system   The sensory nerves, which convey information from the skin and muscle to the CNS about such matters as pain and temperature, and the motor nerves, which tell muscles when to act.   49

somatoform disorders   Mental disorders in which psychological symptoms take a physical, or somatic, form even though no physical causes can be found.   381

somnambulism   The formal term for sleepwalking; somnambulism occurs during the deepest stages of sleep.   126

sounds   Vibrations of air that are processed by the auditory (hearing) system; also called sound waves.   91

special process theory   The theory that hypnotic behavior is different from nonhypnotic behavior, and that hypnotic responses are elicited by suggestion rather than being voluntary reactions.   133

split-half reliability   Dividing the items into two halves, such as the first half of the test and the second half of the test. Individuals' scores on the two halves are compared to determine how consistently they performed.   229

spontaneous recovery   The process in classical conditioning by which a conditioned response can appear again after a time delay without further conditioning.   148

sport psychology   The field of psychology that applies psychology's principles to improving sport performance and enjoying sport participation.   25

standardization   Developing uniform procedures for administering and scoring a test, as well as creating norms for the test.   230

standardized tests   Tests that require people to answer a series of written and/or oral questions. Standardized tests have two distinct features: (1) An individual's score is totaled to yield a single score, or set of scores, and (2) the individual's score is compared with the scores of a large group of similar people to determine how the individual responded relative to others.   32

stereotype   A generalization about a group's characteristics that does not consider any variation from one individual to another.   454

stimulants   Psychoactive drugs that increase the central nervous system's activity.   137

stimulus substitution   Pavlov's theory of how classical conditioning works: The nervous system is structured in such a way that the CS and US bond together and eventually the CS substitutes for the US.   151

storage   The retention of information over time.   177

storm-and-stress view   G. Stanley Hall's view that adolescence is a turbulent time charged with conflict and mood swings.   271

stream of consciousness   A continuous flow of changing sensations, images, thoughts, and feelings.   116

stress management programs   Programs that teach individuals how to appraise stressful events, how to develop skills for coping with stress, and how to put these skills into use.   535

striving for superiority   According to Jung, the human motivation to adapt, improve, and master the environment.   343

stroboscopic motion   The illusion of movement created by a rapid stimulation of different parts of the retina.   106

Stroop effect   An example of automatic perception in which it is difficult to name the colors that words are printed in when the actual words refer to different colors.   102

structuralism   The early theory of psychology developed by Titchener that emphasized the importance of conscious thought and classification of the mind's structures.   7

subgoaling   Setting intermediate goals that put you in a better position to reach a final goal or solution.   212

superego   The Freudian structure of personality that is the moral branch of personality. The superego takes into account whether something is right or wrong.   338

superiority complex   Adler's concept of exaggerated self-importance designed to mask feelings of inferiority.   344

sympathetic nervous system   The division of the autonomic nervous system that arouses the body.   50

sympathetic nervous system   The subdivision of the autonomic nervous system that is involved in the body's arousal, being responsible for quick responses to a stressor, which sometimes is referred to as the "fight-or-flight" response.   318

synapses   Tiny gaps between neurons. Most synapses are between the axon of one neuron and the dendrites or cell body of another neuron.   53

syntax   Rules for the ways words are combined to form acceptable phrases and sentences.   220

systematic desensitization   A method of behavior therapy based on classical conditioning that treats anxiety by getting the person to associate deep relaxation with increasingly intense anxiety-producing situations.   412

tardive dyskinesia   A major side effect of the neuroleptic drugs; a neurological disorder characterized by grotesque, involuntary movements of the facial muscles and mouth as well as extensive twitching of the neck, arms, and legs.   425

telegraphic speech   The use of short and precise words to communicate; it is characteristic of young children's two- and three-word combinations.   222

telepathy   The extrasensory transfer of thought from one person to another.   108

temperament   An individual's behavioral style and characteristic way of responding.   268

temporal lobe   A portion of the neocortex that is just above the ears and is involved in hearing.   62

teratogen   (The word comes from the Greek word *tera*, meaning "monster.") Any agent that causes a birth defect. The field of study that investigates the causes of birth defects is called teratology.   253

tertiary prevention   Treatment for people who abuse drugs.   140

testosterone   A hormone associated in boys with development of the genitals, an increase in height, and a change of voice.   273

test-retest reliability   The extent to which a test yields the same measure of performance when an individual is given the test on two different occasions.   228

thalamus   A portion of the brain that sits at the top of the brain stem in the central core of the brain. It serves as an important relay station, functioning much like a telephone switchboard between the diverse areas of the cortex and the reticular formation.   60

Thematic Apperception Test (TAT)   A projective test designed to elicit stories that reveal something about an individual's personality; developed by Henry Murray and Christina Morgan in the 1930s.   358

theory A coherent set of interrelated ideas that helps to make predictions and explain data. 28

thermoreceptors Receptors located under the skin that respond to changes in temperature. 95

thinking Mentally manipulating information, as when we form concepts, solve problems, reason, and make decisions. 210

timbre The tone color or perceptual quality of a sound. 92

time-out A form of negative punishment in which a child is removed from a positive reinforcement. 161

tip-of-the-tongue (TOT) phenomenon A type of "effortful retrieval" that occurs when people are confident they know something but just can't quite seem to pull it out of memory. 193

token economy A behavior modification system in which behaviors are reinforced with tokens (such as poker chips) that later can be exchanged for desired rewards (such as candy, money, or going to a movie). 413

tolerance The need for a greater amount of a drug to produce the same effect. 135

traditional religious script Sex is accepted only within marriage. Extramarital sex is taboo, especially for women. Sex means reproduction and sometimes affection. 308

trait theories Theories that propose that people have broad dispositions (traits) that are reflected in the basic ways they behave, such as whether they are outgoing and friendly or whether they are dominant and assertive. 352

tranquilizers Depressant drugs, such as Valium and Xanax, that reduce anxiety and induce relaxation. 136

transduction The conversion of one form of energy into another. In sensation, this consists of converting stimulus energy into neural impulses. 84

transference The psychoanalytic term for the person's relating to the analyst in ways that reproduce or relive important relationships in that person's life. 407

triangular theory of love Sternberg's view that love comes in three main dimensions: passion, intimacy, and commitment. 470

triarchic theory Sternberg's theory that intelligence consists of componential intelligence, experiential intelligence, and contextual intelligence. 234

trichromatic theory The theory that color perception is based on the existence of three types of receptors that are maximally sensitive to different, but overlapping, ranges of wavelengths. 88

trichromats People with normal color vision— they have three kinds of cone receptors. 89

trust versus mistrust Erikson's first psychosocial stage, which occurs in the first year of life. Trust is built when a baby's basic needs—such as comfort, food, and warmth—are met. If infants' needs are not met by responsive, sensitive caregivers, the result is mistrust. 264

two-factor theory Spearman's theory that individuals have both a general intelligence *(g)* and a number of specific intelligences *(s)*. 232

two-factor theory of emotion Schachter and Singer's theory that emotion is determined by physiological arousal and cognitive labeling. 322

U

unconditional positive regard Rogers' term for accepting, valuing, and being positive toward another person regardless of the person's behavior. 349, 409

unconditioned response (UR) An unlearned response that is automatically associated with the unconditioned stimulus. 147

unconditioned stimulus (US) A stimulus that produces a response without prior learning. 147

unconscious thought According to Freud, a reservoir of unacceptable wishes, feelings, and thoughts that we are not consciously aware of. 116

undifferentiated schizophrenia A type of schizophrenia characterized by disorganized behavior, hallucinations, delusions, and incoherence. 391

V

validity The extent to which a test measures what it is intended to measure. 229

variable-interval schedule Reinforcement of a response after a variable amount of time has elapsed. 160

variable-ratio schedule A timetable in which responses are rewarded an average number of times, but on an unpredictable basis. 159

vestibular sense The sense that provides information about balance and movement. 99

visual illusion Illusion that occurs when two objects produce exactly the same retinal image but are perceived as different images. 107

volley principle The principle that neural cells can fire neural impulses in rapid succession, producing a volley of impulses. This alternate rapid neural firing attains a combined frequency above 1,000 firings per second. 94

W

wavelength The distance from the peak of one wave to the peak of the next. 82

Weber's law This law states that the difference threshold is a constant percentage of the magnitude of the comparison stimulus rather than a constant amount. Weber's law generally holds true. 81

wisdom Expert knowledge about the practical aspects of life. 283

wish fulfillment In Freud's theory, the reason we dream. For Freud, dreaming is an unconscious attempt to fulfill needs (especially sex and aggression) that cannot be expressed or go ungratified during the waking hours. 129

working memory Also sometimes called short-term memory, working memory is a limited-capacity storage system in which information is retained for as long as 30 seconds, unless it is rehearsed, in which case it can be retained longer. 183

Y

Yerkes-Dodson law The law that performance is best under conditions of moderate rather than low or high arousal. 319

Z

zygote A single cell formed through fertilization. 252

A

Abbey, A., Ross, L.T., & McDuffie, D. (1993). Alcohol's role in sexual assault. In R.R. Watson (Eds.), *Drug and alcohol abuse reviews. Vol. 5: Addictive behaviors in women.* Totowa, NJ: Humana Press.

Abel, E.L. (1984). *Fetal alcohol syndrome and fetal alcohol effects.* New York: Plenum.

Ackerman, P.L., Kyllonen, P.C., & Roberts, R.D. (Eds.) (1999). *Learning and individual differences: Process, trait, and content determinants.* Washington, DC: American Psychological Association.

Adams, H. (2000). Behavior therapy. In A. Kazdin (Ed.), *Encyclopedia of psychology.* Washington, DC, & New York: American Psychological Association and Oxford U. Press.

Adams, H.E., & Cassidy, J.F. (1993). The classification of abnormal behavior: An overview. In P.B. Sutker & H.E. Adams (Eds.), *Comprehensive textbook of psychopathology* (2nd ed.). New York: Plenum Press.

Adams, R. (1998). *The abuses of punishment.* New York: St. Martin's Press.

Adler, A. (1927). *The theory and practice of individual psychology.* Fort Worth: Harcourt Brace.

Adler, T. (1991, January). Seeing double? Controversial twins study is widely reported, debated. *APA Monitor, 22,* 1, 8.

Agras, W.S. (2000). Eating disorders. In A. Kazdin (Ed.), *Encyclopedia of psychology.* Washington, DC, & New York: American Psychological Association and Oxford U. Press.

Aiken, L.R. (1996). *Assessment of intellectual functioning* (2nd ed.). New York: Plenum.

Ainsworth, M.D.S. (1979). Infant-mother attachment. *American Psychologists, 34,* 932–937.

Al-Issa, I. (1982). Does culture make a difference in psychopathology? In I. Al-Issa (Ed.), *Culture and psychopathology.* Baltimore: University Park Press.

Alberti, R., & Emmons, M. (1995). *Your perfect right* (7th ed.). San Luis Obispo, CA: Impact.

Alberto, P., & Troutman, A.C. (1999). *Applied behavior analysis for teachers.* Upper Saddle River, NJ: Merrill.

Alderman, M.K. (1999). *Motivation for achievement.* Mahwah, NJ: Erlbaum.

Aldrich, M.S. (1999). *Sleep medicine.* New York: Oxford University Press.

Allan, R., & Scheidt, S. (Eds.). (1996). *Heart and mind.* Washington, DC: American Psychological Association.

Allen, J.J.B. (1998). DSM-IV. In H.S. Friedman (Ed.), *Encyclopedia of mental health* (Vol. 2). San Diego: Academic Press.

Allison, K.R., Dwyer, J.J., & Mankin, S. (1999). Self-efficacy and participation in vigorous physical activity by high school students. *Health Education & Behavior, 26,* 12–24.

Alloy, L.B., Jacobson, N.S., & Acocella, J. (1999). *Abnormal psychology* (8th ed.). New York: McGraw-Hill.

Allport, G. H., & Postman, L. (1947). *The psychology of rumor.* New York: Holt.

Allport, G.W. (1937). *Personality: A psychological interpretation.* New York: Holt.

Almagor, M., Tellegen, A., & Waller, N.G. (1995). The big seven model: A cross-cultural replication and further exploration of the basic dimensions of natural language trait descriptors. *Journal of Personality and Social Psychology, 69,* 300–307.

Alsaker, F.D., & Flammer, A. (Eds.). (1999). *The adolescent experience.* Mahwah, NJ: Erlbaum.

Anastasi, A., & Urbina, S. (1996). *Psychological testing* (7th ed.). Upper Saddle River, NJ: Prentice-Hall.

Anderson, B.L. (1983). Primary orgasmic dysfunction: Diagnostic considerations and a review of treatment. *Psychological Bulletin, 93,* 105–136.

Anderson, B.L. (1998). Cancer. In H.S. Friedman (Ed.), *Encyclopedia of mental health* (Vol. 1). San Diego: Academic Press.

Anderson, B.L., Kiecolt-Glaser, J.K., & Glaser. R. (1994). A biobehavioral model of cancer stress and disease course. *American Psychologist, 49,* 389–404.

Anderson, C.A. (1989). Temperature and aggression. *Journal of Personality and Social Psychology, 106,* 74–96.

Anderson, N.H. (1965). Primacy effects in personality impression formation using a generalized order effect paradigm. *Journal of Personality and Social Psychology, 2,* 1–9.

Anderson, N.H. (1974). Cognitive algebra: Integration theory applied to social attribution. In L. Berkowitz (Ed.), *Advances in experimental social psychology* (Vol. 7). New York: Academic Press.

Anderson, N.H. (1989). Functional memory and on-line attribution. In J.N. Bassili (Ed.), *On-line cognition in person perception.* Mahwah, NJ: Erlbaum.

Antonnuci, T. (2000). Adulthood and aging: Social processes and development. In A. Kazdin (Ed.), *Encyclopedia of psychology.* Washington, DC, & New York: American Psychological Association and Oxford U. Press.

Antrobus, J.S. (2000). Dreams: Theories and research. In A. Kazdin (Ed.), *Encyclopedia of psychology.* Washington, DC, & New York: American Psychological Association and Oxford U. Press.

Applebaum, M.I., & others (1999, April). *Effect sizes from the NICHD study of early child care.* Paper presented at the meeting of the Society for Research in Child Development, Albuquerque.

Archer, D., & Gartner, R. (1976). Violent acts and violent times: A comparative approach in postwar homicide. *American Sociological Review, 41,* 937–963.

Archer, D., & McDaniel, P. (1995). Violence and gender: Differences and similarities across societies. In R.B. Ruback & N.A. Weiner (Eds.), *Interpersonal violent behaviors: Social and cultural aspects.* New York: Springer.

Armstrong, D.L., & Rossie, S. (Eds.)(1999). *Advances in second messenger and phosphoprotein research: Ion channel regulation.* San Diego: Academic Press.

Arnitz, A., & van den Hout, M.A. (1996). Psychological treatment of panic disorder without agoraphobia: Cognitive therapy versus applied relaxation. *Behaviour Research and Therapy, 34,* 113–121.

Arnoux, D. (1998, September). Description of teaching experiences prepared for John Santrock's text, *Educational Psychology.* New York: McGraw-Hill.

Aronson, E. (1986, August). *Teaching students things they think they already know all about: The case of prejudice and desegregation.* Paper presented at the meeting of the American Psychological Association, Washington, DC.

Aronson, E. (1995). *The social animal* (7th ed.). New York: W.H. Freeman.

Aronson, E. (1999). Self-affirmation theory. In E. Harmon-Jones & J. Mills (Eds.), *Cognitive dissonance.* Washington, DC: American Psychological Association.

Aronson, E., Wilson, T.D., & Akert, R.M. (1997). *Social psychology* (2nd ed.). New York: Longman.

Aronson, J., Cohen, G., & Nails, P.R. (1999). Unwanted consequences and the self: In search of the motivation for dissonance reduction. In E. Harmon-Jones & J. Mills (Eds.), *Cognitive dissonance.* Washington, DC: American Psychological Association.

Asch, S.E. (1946). Forming impressions of personality. *Journal of Personality and Social Psychology, 41,* 248–290.

Asch, S.E. (1951). Effects of group pressure on the modification and distortion of judgments. In H.S. Guetzkow (Ed.), *Groups, leadership, and men.* Pittsburgh: Carnegie University Press.

Asnis, G.M., & van Praag, H.M. (1995). *Panic disorder.* New York: Wiley.

Atkinson, D., Morten, G., & Sue, D. (1998). *Counseling American minorities* (5th ed.). New York: McGraw-Hill.

Atkinson, D.R., Morten, G., & Sue, D.W. (1998). *Counseling American minorities.* New York: McGraw-Hill.

Atkinson, J.W., & Raynor, I.O. (1974). *Motivation and achievement.* Washington, DC: Winston.

Atkinson, R.C., & Shiffrin, R.M. (1968). Human memory: A proposed system and its control processes. In K.W. Spence & J.T. Spence (Eds.), *The psychology of learning and motivation* (Vol. 2). San Diego: Academic Press.

Auerbach, J.S. (1999). Psychoanalysis and projective testing: A review of *The interpretation of psychological tests. Journal of Personality Assessment, 72,* 147–163.

Auerbach, S.M., & Gramling, S.E. (1998). *Stress management.* Upper Saddle River, NJ: Prentice-Hall.

Austin, J.T. (2000). Industrial/organizational psychology: History of the field. In A. Kazdin (Ed.), *Encylcopedia of psychology.* Washington, DC, & New York: American Psychological Association and Oxford U. Press.

Averill, J.R. (1983). Studies on anger and aggression: Implications for theories of emotion. *American Psychologist, 38,* 1145–1160.

Avis, M.H. (1999). *Drugs and life* (4th ed.). New York: McGraw-Hill.

Azar, B. (1996, January). Damaged area of brain can reorganize itself. *APA Monitor,* p. 19.

B

Baars, B. (1999). Psychology in a world of sentimental, self-knowing beings: A modest utopian fantasy. In R.L. Solso (Ed.), *Mind and brain sciences in the 21st century.* Cambridge, MA: MIT Press.

Baddeley, A. (1990). *Human memory.* Boston: Allyn & Bacon.

Baddeley, A. (1992). Working memory. *Science, 255,* 556–560.

Baddeley, A. (1993). Working memory and conscious awareness. In A.F. Collins, S.E. Gatherhole, M.A. Conway, & P.E. Morris (Eds.), *Theories of memory.* Mahwah, NJ: Erlbaum.

Baddeley, A. (1995). Applying the psychology of memory to clinical problems. In D. Hermann, C. McEvoy, C. Hertzog, P. Hertel, & M. Johnson (Eds.), *Basic and applied memory research* (Vol. 1). Mahwah, NJ: Erlbaum.

Baddeley, A. (1998). *Human memory* (Rev. ed.). Boston: Allyn & Bacon.

Bahrick, H.P., Bahrick, P.O., & Whitlinger, R.P. (1975). Fifty years of memory for names and faces: A cross-sectional approach. *Journal of Experimental Psychology: General, 104,* 54–75.

Baillargeon, R. (1997). The object concept revisited. In C.E. Granrud (Ed.), *Visual perception and cognition in infancy.* Mahwah, NJ: Erlbaum.

Baity, M.R., & Hilsenroth, M.J. (1999). Rorschach aggression variables: A study of reliability and validity. *Journal of Personality and Assessment, 72,* 93–110.

Balch, W.R., Myers, D.M., & Papotto, C. (1999). Dimensions of mood in mood-congruent memory. *Journal of Experimental Psychology: Learning, Memory, and Condition, 25,* 70–83.

Baldwin, J.D., & Baldwin, J.I. (1998). Sexual behavior. In H.S. Friedman (Ed.), *Encyclopedia of mental health* (Vol. 3). San Diego: Academic Press.

Baldwin, J.D., & Baldwin, J.I. (1999). *Behavior principles in everyday life* (3rd ed.). Upper Saddle River, NJ: Prentice-Hall.

Bales, J. (1988, December). Vincennes: Findings could have averted tragedy, scientists tell Hill panel. *APA Monitor,* pp. 10–11.

Baltes, P.B. (1993). The aging mind: Potentials and limits. *Gerontologist, 33,* 580–594.

Baltes, P.B. (2000). Life-span developmental theory. In A. Kazdin (Ed.), *Encyclopedia of psychology.* Washington, DC, & New York: American Psychological Association and Oxford U. Press.

Baltes, P.B., Lindenberger, U., & Staudinger, U.M. (1998). Life-span theory in developmental psychology. In W. Damon (Ed.), *Handbook of child psychology* (5th ed., Vol. 1), New York: Wiley.

Bandura, A. (1965). Influences of models' reinforcement contingencies on the acquisition of imitative responses. *Journal of Personality and Social Psychology, 1,* 589–596.

Bandura, A. (1977). *Social learning theory.* Upper Saddle River, NJ: Prentice-Hall.

Bandura, A. (1986). *Social foundations of thought and action.* Englewood Cliffs, NJ: Prentice-Hall.

Bandura, A. (1989). Social cognitive theory. In R. Vasta (Ed.), *Six theories of child development.* Greenwich, CT: JAI Press.

Bandura, A. (1994). Social cognitive theory of mass communication. In J. Bryant & D. Zillman (Eds.), *Media effects.* Mahwah, NJ: Erlbaum.

Bandura, A. (1997). *Self-efficacy.* New York: W.H. Freeman.

Bandura, A. (1998). Self-efficacy. In H.S. Friedman (Ed.), *Encyclopedia of mental health* (Vol. 3). San Diego: Academic Press.

Bandura, A. (1998, August). *Exercise of agency in accenting the positive.* Paper presented at the meeting of the American Psychological Association, San Francisco.

Bandura, A. (2000). Social cognitive theory. In A. Kazdin (Ed.), *Encyclopedia of psychology.* Washington, DC, & New York: American Psychological Association and Oxford U. Press.

Bandura, A., Blanchard, E.B., & Ritter, B. (1969). Relative efficacy of desensitization and modeling approaches for inducing behavioral, affective, and attitudinal changes. *Journal of Personality and Social Psychology, 13,* 173–199.

Bard, P. (1934). Emotion. In C. Murchison (Ed.), *Handbook of general psychology.* Worcester, MA: Clark University Press.

Barker, P. (1998). Family therapy. In H.S. Friedman (Ed.), *Encyclopedia of mental health* (Vol. 2). San Diego: Academic Press.

Barry, H., Child, I.L., & Bacon, M.K. (1959). Relation of child training to subsistence economy. *American Anthropologist, 61,* 51–63.

Bartlett, F.C. (1932). *Remembering.* Cambridge: Cambridge University Press.

Bartlett, J.C. (1998, March). *Personal communication.* Richardson, TX: University of Texas at Dallas, Program in Psychology.

Bartoshuk, L.M., & Beauchamp, G.K. (1994). Chemical senses. *Annual Review of Psychology* (Vol. 45). Palo Alto, CA: Annual Reviews.

Bates, J.A. (1995). Teaching hypothesis testing by debunking a demonstration of telepathy. In M.E. Ware & D.E. Johnson (Eds.), *Handbook of demonstrations and activities in the teaching of psychology* (Vol. 1). Washington, DC: American Psychological Association.

Batson, C.D. (1998). Altruism and prosocial behavior. In D.T. Gilbert, S.T. Fiske, & G. Lindzey (Eds.), *Handbook of social psychology* (4th ed., Vol. 2). New York: McGraw-Hill.

Baum, A., & Posluszny, D.M. (1999). Health psychology. *Annual Review of Psychology, 50.* Palo Alto, CA: Annual Reviews.

Baumeister, R.F. (1989). The optimal margin of illusion. *Journal of Social and Clinical Psychology, 8,* 176–189.

Baumeister, R.F. (1991). *Meanings of life.* New York: Guilford.

Baumeister, R.F. (1993). *Self-esteem: The puzzle of low self-regard.* New York: Plenum Press.

Baumeister, R.F. (1997). Identity, self-concept, and self-esteem. In R. Hogan, J. Johnson, & S. Briggs (Eds.), *Handbook of personality psychology.* San Diego: Academic Press.

Baumeister, R.F. (1999). *Evil: Inside human violence and cruelty.* New York: W.H. Freeman.

Baumeister, R.F., & Bratslavsky, E. (1999). Passion, intimacy, and time: Passionate love as a function of change in intimacy. *Personality and Social Psychology Review, 3,* 2–22.

Baumrind, D. (1971). Current patterns of parental authority. *Developmental Psychology Monographs, 4,* (1, Pt. 2).

Baumrind, D. (1991). Parenting styles and adolescent development. In J. Brooks-Gunn, R. Lerner, & A.C. Petersen (Eds.), *The encyclopedia of adolescence* (Vol. 2). New York: Garland.

Beattie, G., & Couglan, J. (1999). An experimental investigation of the role of iconic gestures in lexical access using the tip-of-the-toungue phenomenon. *British Journal of Psychology, 90,* 35–56.

Beatty, J. (1995). *Neuroscience.* New York: McGraw-Hill.

Beatty, J. (1995). *Principles of neuroscience.* New York: McGraw-Hill.

Beck, A. (1967). *Depression.* New York: Harper & Row.

Beck, A.T. (1976). *Cognitive therapies and the emotional disorders.* New York: International Universities Press.

Beck, A.T. (1993). Cognitive therapy: Past, present, and future. *Journal of Consulting and Clinical Psychology, 61,* 194–198.

Bednar, R.L., Wells, M.G., & Peterson, S.R. (1995). *Self-esteem* (2nd ed.). Washington, DC: American Psychological Association.

Bell, A.P., Weinberg, M.S., & Mamersmith, S.K. (1981). *Sexual preference.* New York: Simon & Schuster.

Bellesiles, M.A. (1999). *Lethal imagination.* New York: New York University Press.

Belsky, J.K. (1999). *The psychology of aging* (3rd ed.). Belmont, CA: Wadsworth.

Belson, W. (1978). *Television violence and the adolescent boy.* London: Saxon House.

Bem, D. (1967). Self-perception: An alternative explanation of cognitive dissonance phenomena. *Psychological Review, 74,* 183–200.

Ben-Shakhar, G., Bar-Hillel, M., Yoram, B., Ben-Abba, E., & Flug, A. (1986). Can graphology predict occupational success? Two empirical studies and some methodological ruminations. *Journal of Applied Psychology, 71,* 645–653.

Benet, V., & Waller, N.G. (1995). The big seven factor model of personality description: Evidence for its cross-cultural generality in a Spanish sample. *Journal of Personality and Social Psychology, 69,* 701–718.

Benjamin, L.T. (1999). Psychology's portrait gallery: Part III. *Contemporary Psychology, 44,* 27–28.

Bennett, M.E., & others (1993). Identifying young adult substance abusers. *Journal of Studies on Alcohol, 54,* 526.

Bennett, W.I., & Gurin, J. (1982). *The dieter's dilemma: Eating less and weighing more.* New York: Basic Books.

Bereiter, C., & Scardamalia, M. (1993). *Surpassing ourselves: An inquiry into the nature and implications of expertise.* Chicago: Open Court.

Berkman, L.F., & Syme, L.L. (1979). Social networks, host resistance, and mortality. *American Journal of Epidemiology, 109,* 186–204.

Berko, J. (1958). The child's learning of English morphology. *World, 14,* 150–157.

Berkowitz, L. (1990). On the formation and regulation of anger and aggression: A cognitive neoassociationistic analysis. *American Psychologist, 45,* 494–503.

Berman, W. (2000). Managed care. In A. Kazdin (Ed.), *Encyclopedia of psychology.* Washington, DC, & New York: American Psychological Association and Oxford U. Press.

Berry, J. (2000). Culture: Cultural foundations of human behavior. In A. Kazdin (Ed.), *Encyclopedia of psychology.* Washington, DC, & New York: American Psychological Association and Oxford U. Press.

Berry, J.W. (1980). Acculturation as varieties of adaptation. In A. Padilla (Ed.), *Acculturation: Theory, model, and some new findings.* Washington, DC: American Association for the Advancement of Science.

Berscheid, E. (1988). Some comments on love's anatomy: Or, whatever happened to old-fashioned lust? In R.J. Sternberg (Ed.), *Anatomy of love.* New Haven, CT: Yale University Press.

Berscheid, E. (1999). Integrating relationship knowledge. In W.A. Collins & B. Laursen (Eds.), *Relationships as developmental contexts.* Mahwah, NJ: Erlbaum.

Berscheid, E. (in press). The greening of relationship science. *American Psychologist.*

Berscheid, E., & Fei, J. (1977). Sexual jealousy and romantic love. In G. Clinton & G. Smith (Eds.), *Sexual jealousy.* Englewood Cliffs, NJ: Prentice-Hall.

Berscheid, E., & Lopez, J. (1997). A temporal model of relationship satisfaction and stability. In R.J. Sternberg (Ed.), *Satisfaction in close relationships.* New York: Guilford.

Berscheid, E., & Reis, H.T. (1998). Attraction and close relationships. In D.T. Gilbert, S.T. Fiske, & G. Lindzey (Eds.), *Handbook of social psychology* (4th ed., Vol. 2). New York: McGraw-Hill.

Berscheid, E., Snyder, M., & Omato, A.M. (1989). Issues in studying close relationships. In C. Hendrick (Ed.), *Close relationships.* Newbury Park, CA: Sage.

Bertolino, A., & others (1999). The relationship between dorsolateral prefrontal *N-Acetylasparate* measures and striatal dopamine activity in schizophrenia. *Biological Psychiatry, 45,* 660–667.

Besner, D., & Stolz, J.A. (1999). What kind of attention modulates the Stroop effect? *Psychonomic Bulletin & Review, 6,* 99–105.

Bexton, W.H., Heron, W., & Scott, T.H. (1954). Effects of decreased variation in the sensory environment. *Canadian Journal of Psychology, 8,* 70–76.

Bhugra, D., & de Silva, P. (1998). Sexual dysfunction therapy. In H.S. Friedman (Ed.), *Encyclopedia of mental health* (Vol. 3). San Diego: Academic Press.

Bidikov, I., & Meier, D.E. (1997). Clinical decision-making with the woman after menopause. *Geriatrics, 52,* (3), 28–35.

Biller, H. (1993). *Fathers and families.* Westport, CT: Auburn House.

Billings, A.G., Cronkite, R.C., & Moos, R.H. (1983). Social-environment factors in unipolar depression. *Journal of Abnormal Psychology, 92* 119–133.

Björkqvist, K., Österman, K., & Lagerspetz, K.M.J. (1994). Sex differences in covert aggression among adults. *Aggressive Behavior, 20,* 27–33.

Black, I.B. (1999). Plasticity. In M.S. Gazzaniga (Ed.), *The new cognitive neurosciences* (2nd ed.). Cambridge, MA: MIT Press.

Blackmore, S. (1987). A report of a visit to Carl Sargent's laboratory. *Journal of the Society for Psychical Research, 54,* 186–198.

Blair, C., & Ramey, C. (1996). Early intervention with low-birthweight infants: The path to second generation research. In M.J. Guralnick (Ed.), *The effectiveness of early interventions.* Baltimore: Paul H. Brookes.

Blake, R. (2000). Eye. In A. Kazdin (Ed.), *Encyclopedia of psychology.* Washington, DC, & New York: American Psychological Association and Oxford U. Press.

Blundell, J.E. (1984). Systems and interactions: An approach to the pharmacology of feeding. In A.J. Stunkdard & E. Stellar (Eds.), *Eating and its disorders.* New York: Raven Press.

Bond, R., & Smith, P.B. (1994). Culture and conformity: A meta-analysis of studies using the Asch-type perceptual judgment task. *British Psychological Society 1994 Proceedings, 9,* 297–308.

Bonvillain, N. (1998). *Women and men: Cultural constructs of gender* (2nd ed.). Upper Saddle River, NJ: Erlbaum.

Booth, A., Johnson, D.R., & Granger, D.A. (1999). Testosterone and men's health. *Journal of Behavioral Medicine, 22,* 1–12.

Bouchard, T.J., Heston, L., Eckert, E., Keyes, M., & Resnick, S. (1981). The Minnesota Study of Twins Reared Apart: Project description and sample results in the developmental domain. *Twin Research, 3,* 227–233.

Bouchard, T.J., Lykken, D.T., Tellegen, A., & McGue, M. (1996). Genes, drives, environment, and experience. In D. Lubinski & C. Benbow (Eds.), *Psychometrics and social issues concerning intellectual talent.* Baltimore: Johns Hopkins University Press.

Boudewyns, P.A. (1996). Post-traumatic stress syndrome. In M. Herson & P.M. Miller (Eds.), *Progress in behavior modification* (Vol. 30). Pacific Grove, CA: Brooks/Cole.

Bourne, E.J. (1995). *The anxiety and phobia workbook* (2nd ed.). Oakland, CA: New Harbinger.

Bower, G.H., Clark, M., Winzenz, D., & Lesgold, A. (1969). Hierarchical retrieval schemes in recall of categorized word lists. *Journal of Verbal Learning and Verbal Behavior, 3,* 323–343.

Bowers, T.G., & Clum, G.A. (1988). Relative contribution of specific and nonspecific treatment effects: Meta-analysis of placebo-controlled behavior therapy research. *Psychological Bulletin, 103,* 315–323.

Bowlby, J. (1969). *Attachment and loss* (Vol. 1). London: Hogarth Press.

Bowlby, J. (1989). *Secure and insecure attachment.* New York: Basic Books.

Boyer, L.B. (1999). *Countertransference and aggression.* Mahwah, NJ: Erlbaum.

Bradley, M.M. (1996). Gonna change my way of thinking. *Contemporary Psychology, 41,* 258–259.

Brammer, L.M., & MacDonald, G. (1999). *The helping relationship* (7th ed.). Boston: Allyn & Bacon.

Brannon, L. (1999). *Gender: Psychological perspectives* (2nd ed.). Boston: Allyn & Bacon.

Bransford, J.D., & Stein, B.S. (1993). *The IDEAL problem solver.* New York: W.H. Freeman.

Brazelton, T.B. (1998, September 7). Commentary. *Dallas Morning News,* p. C2.

Brehm, J.W. (1999). The intensity of emotion. *Personality and Social Psychology Review, 3,* 2–22.

Brehony, K.A. (1999). *Ordinary grace.* New York: Riverhead Books.

Breland, K., & Breland, M. (1961). The misbehavior of organisms. *American Psychologist, 16,* 681–684.

Brennan, P., Mednick, S., & Kandel, E. (1991). Congenital determinants of violent and property offencing. In D. Pepler & K. Rubin (Eds.), *The development and treatment of childhood aggression.* Mahwah, NJ: Erlbaum.

Brewer, J.B., Zuo, Z., Desmond, J.E., Glover, G.H., & Gabrieli, J.D.E. (1998). Making memories: Brain activity that predicts how well visual experience will be remembered. *Science, 281,* 1185–1187.

Brewer, M.B., & Brown, R.J. (1998). Intergroup relations. In D.T. Gilbert, S.T. Fiske, & G. Lindzey (Eds.), *Handbook of social psychology* (4th ed., Vol. 2). New York: McGraw-Hill.

Brewin, C.R., Andrews, B., Rose, S., & Kirk, M. (1999). Acute stress disorder and posttraumatic stress disorder in victims of violent crime. *The American Journal of Psychiatry, 156,* 360–366.

Brickman, P., Coates, D., & Janoff-Bulman, R.J. (1978). Lottery winners and accident victims: Is happiness relative? *Journal of Personality and Social Psychology, 36,* 917–927.

Brickner, M.A., Harkins, S.G., & Ostrom, T.M. (1986). Effects of personal involvement: Thought-provoking implications for social loafing. *Journal of Personality and Social Psychology, 51,* 763–769.

Brigham, J.C. (1986). Race and eyewitness identifications. In S. Worschel & W.G. Austin (Eds.), *Psychology of intergroup relations.* Chicago: Nelson-Hall.

Brigham, J.C., Maas, A., Snyder, L.D., & Spaulding, K. (1982). Accuracy of eyewitness identification in a field setting. *Journal of Personality and Social Psychology, 41,* 683–691.

Brim, O., & others (1999). *Midlife development in the United States.* New York: The McArthur Foundation.

Brislin, R. (1993). *Understanding culture's influence on behavior.* Fort Worth, TX: Harcourt Brace.

Brislin, R.C. (Ed.). (1990). *Applied cross-cultural psychology.* Newbury Park, CA: Sage.

Brislin, R.W. (2000). Cross-cultural training. In A. Kazdin (Ed.), *Encyclopedia of psychology.* Washington, DC, & New York: American Psychological Association and Oxford U. Press.

Brook, J.S., Brook, D.W., Gordon, A.S., Whiteman, M., & Cohen, P. (1990). The psychological etiology of adolescent drug use: A family interactional approach. *Genetic Psychology Monographs, 116,* no. 2.

Brooks, J.G., & Brooks, M.G. (1993). *The case for constructivist classrooms.* Alexandria, VA: Association for Supervision and Curriculum Development.

Brooks-Gunn, J. (1996, April). *The uniqueness of the early adolescent transition.* Paper presented at the meeting of the Society for Research on Adolescence, Boston.

Brown, A.L. (1997). Transforming schools into communities of thinking and learning about serious matters. *American Psychologist, 52,* 399–413.

Brown, A.L., & Campione, J.C. (1996). Psychological theory and the design of innovative learning environments. In L. Schauble & R. Glaser (Eds.), *Innovations in learning.* Mahwah, NJ: Erlbaum.

Brown, A.S., & Nix, L.A. (1996). Age-related changes in the tip-of-the-tongue experiences. *American Journal of Psychology, 109,* 79–92.

Brown, G., Bhrolchain, M., & Harris, T. (1975). Social class and psychiatric disturbance among women in an urban population. *Sociology, 9,* 225–254.

Brown, G.D. (1995). *Human evolution.* New York: McGraw-Hill.

Brown, H.D., & Adler, N.E. (1998). Socioeconomics status. In H.S. Friedman (Ed.), *Encyclopedia of mental health* (Vol. 3). San Diego: Academic Press.

Brown, L.S. (1989). New voices, new visions: Toward a lesbian/gay paradigm for psychology. *Psychology of Women Quarterly, 13,* 445–458.

Brown, R. (1973). *A first language: The early stages.* Cambridge, MA: Harvard University Press.

Brown, R. (1986). *Social psychology* (2nd ed.). New York: Free Press.

Brownell, K.A., & Rodin, J. (1994). The dieting maelstrom: Is it possible to lose weight? *American Psychologist, 9,* 781–791.

Brownell, K.D., & Cohen, L.R. (1995). Adherence to dietary regimens. *Behavioral Medicine, 20,* 226–242.

Brownlee, S. (1997, January 13). The senses. *US News & World Report,* pp. 51–59.

Bruck, M., & Ceci, S.J. (1999). The suggestibility of children's memory. *Annual Reviews of Psychology.* Palo Alto, CA: Annual Reviews, Inc.

Bruner, J. (1964). The concept of cognitive growth. *American Psychologist, 19,* 1–15.

Bruner, J.S., & Tagiuri, R. (1954). The perception of people. In G. Lindzey (Ed.), *Handbook of social psychology* (Vol. 2). Boston: Addison-Wesley.

Bruning, R.H., Schraw, G.J., & Ronning, R.R. (1999). *Cognitive psychology and instruction* (3rd ed.). Upper Saddle River, NJ: Erlbaum.

Burns, D. (1985). *Intimate connections.* New York: William Morrow.

Burnstein, E., Crandall, C., & Kitayama, S. (1994). Some neo-Darwinian decision rules for altruism: Weighing cues for inclusive fitness as a function of the biological importance of the decision. *Journal of Personality and Social Psychology, 67,* 773–789.

Buss, A.H., & Plomin, R. (1987). Commentary. In H.H. Goldsmith, A.H. Buss, R. Plomin, M.K. Rothbart, A. Thomas, A. Chess, R.R. Hinde, & R.B. McCall (Eds.). Roundtable: What is temperament? Four approaches. *Child Development, 58,* 505–529.

Buss, D. (1995). Evolutionary psychology: A new paradigm for psychological science. *Psychological Inquiry, 6,* 1–30.

Buss, D. (2000). Evolutionary psychology. In A. Kazdin (Ed.), *Encyclopedia of psychology.* Washington, DC, & New York: American Psychological Association and Oxford U. Press.

Buss, D.M. (1995). Psychological sex differences: Origins through sexual selection. *American Psychologist, 50,* 164–168.

Buss, D.M. (1999). Adaptive individual differences revisited. *Journal of Personality, 67,* 259–264.

Buss, D.M. (1999). *Evolutionary psychology: The new science of the mind.* Boston: Allyn & Bacon.

Buss, D.M. (2000). Evolutionary psychology. In A. Kazdin (Ed.), *Encyclopedia of psychology.* Washington, DC, & New York: American Psychological Association and Oxford U. Press.

Buss, D.M., & Barnes, M. (1986). Preferences in human mate selection. *Journal of Personality and Social Psychology, 50,* 559–570.

Buss, D.M., & Greiling, H. (1999). Adaptive individual differences. *Journal of Personality, 67,* 209–244.

Buss, D.M., & Kendrick, D.T. (1998). Evolutionary social psychology. In D.T. Gilbert, S.T. Fiske, & G. Lindzey (Eds.), *Handbook of social psychology* (4th ed., Vol. 2). New York: McGraw-Hill.

Butcher, J.N. (1997, August). *Psychological assessment, therapy, and managed care.* Paper presented at the meeting of the American Psychological Association, Chicago.

Butcher, J.N. (1999). *A beginner's guide to the MMPI-2.* Washington, DC: American Psychological Association.

Butcher, J.N., Lim, J., & Nezami, E. (1998). Objective study of abnormal personality in cross-cultural settings: The Minnesota Multiphasic Personality Inventory (MMPI-2). *Journal of Cross-Cultural Psychology, 29,* 189–211.

Butler, G., Fennell, M., Robson, P., & Gelder, M. (1991). Comparison of behavior therapy and cognitive behavior therapy in the treatment of generalized anxiety disorder. *Journal of Consulting and Clinical Psychology, 59,* 167–175.

Butler, R.A. (1953). Discrimination learning by rhesus monkeys to visual-exploration motivation. *Journal of Comparative and Physiological Psychology, 46,* 95–98.

Byne, W., & Davis, K.L. (1999). The role of the prefrontal cortex in the dopaminergic dysregulation of schizophrenia. *Biological Psychiatry, 45,* 657–659.

Cacioppo, J.T., & Gardner, W.L. (1999). Emotion. *Annual Reviews of Psychology.* Palo Alto: Annual Reviews.

Cairns, R.B. (1998). The making of developmental psychology. In W. Damon (Ed.), *Handbook of child psychology* (5th ed., Vol. 1), New York: Wiley.

Cameron, N. (1963). *Personality development and psychopathology.* Boston: Houghton Mifflin.

Campbell, F.A., & Ramey, C.T. (1993, March). *Mid-adolescent outcomes for high risk students: An examination of the continuing effects of early intervention.* Paper presented at the biennial meeting of the Society for Research in Child Development, New Orleans.

Campbell, J.D., Tesser, A., & Fairey, P.J. (1986). Conformity and attention to the stimulus: Some temporal and contextual dynamics. *Journal of Personality and Social Psychology, 51,* 315–324.

Campbell, L., Campbell, B., & Dickinson, D. (1999). *Teaching and learning through multiple intelligences* (2nd ed.). Boston: Allyn & Bacon.

Cannon, W.B. (1927). The James-Lange theory of emotions: A critical examination and an alternative theory. *American Journal of Psychology, 39,* 106–124.

Cannon, W.B., & Washburn, A.L. (1912). An explanation of hunger. *American Journal of Physiology, 29,* 444–454.

Cantor, N., & Langston, C.A. (1989). Ups and downs of life tasks in a life transition. In L.A. Pervin (Ed.), *Goal concepts in personality and social psychology.* Mahwah, NJ: Erlbaum.

Capaldi, E.J. (2000). Animal learning and behavior: Methods of study. In A. Kazdin (Ed.), *Encylcopedia of psychology.* Washington, DC, & New York: American Psychological Association and Oxford U. Press.

Capuzzi, D., & Gross, D.R. (1999). *Counseling and psychotherapy* (2nd ed.). Upper Saddle River, NJ: Prentice-Hall.

Carkenord, D.M., & Bullington, J. (1995). Bringing cognitive dissonance to the classroom. In M.E. Ware & D.E. Johnson (Eds.), *Demonstrations and activities in teaching of psychology* (Vol. 3). Mahwah, NJ: Erlbaum.

Carlson, N. (1999). *Foundations of physiological psychology* (4th ed.). Boston: Allyn & Bacon.

Caron, S.L. (1998). *Cross-cultural perspectives on human sexuality.* Boston: Allyn & Bacon.

Carroll, D.W. (1999). *Psychology of language* (3rd ed.). Belmont, CA: Wadsworth.

Carson, R.C., Butcher, J.N., & Mineka, S. (1998). *Abnormal psychology and life.* (10th ed.). New York: HarperCollins.

Cartwright, R. (2000). Sleep apnea. In A. Kazdin (Ed.), *Encyclopedia of psychology.* Washington, DC, & New York: American Psychological Association and Oxford U. Press.

Catania, C.A. (2000). Behavior analysis. In A. Kazdin (Ed.), *Encyclopedia of psychology.* Washington, DC, & New York: American Psychological Association and Oxford U. Press.

Ceci, S. (1996). Unpublished review of *Child Development* (8th ed.) by J.W. Santrock. New York: McGraw-Hill.

Ceci, S.J. (2000). Memory: Constructive processes. In A. Kazdin (Ed.), *Encyclopedia of psychology.* Washington, DC, & New York: American Psychological Association and Oxford U. Press.

Centers for Disease Control and Prevention (1998, June). *Combating complacency in HIV prevention.* Atlanta: Centers for Disease Control and Prevention.

Chambers, M.J. (2000). Sleepwalking. In A. Kazdin (Ed.), *Encyclopedia of psychology.* Washington, DC, & New York: American Psychological Association and Oxford U. Press.

Chance, P. (1979). *Learning and behavior.* Belmont, CA: Wadsworth.

Chance, P. (1999). *Learning and behavior* (4th ed.). Belmont, CA: Wadsworth.

Chang, E.C. (1996). Cultural differences in optimism, pessimism, and coping. *Journal of Counseling Psychology, 43,* 113–123.

Changeux, J., & Chavillion, J. (1995). *Origins of the human brain.* New York: Oxford University Press.

Chase-Landsdale, P.L., & Brooks-Gunn, J. (Eds.). (1996). *Escape from poverty.* New York: Cambridge University Press.

Chastain, G., & Landrum, R.E. (1999). *Protecting human subjects.* Washington, DC: American Psychological Association.

Chaves, J.F. (2000). Hypnosis. In A. Kazdin (Ed.), *Encyclopedia of psychology.* Washington, DC, & New York: American Psychological Association and Oxford U. Press.

Chess, S., & Thomas, A. (1977). Temperamental individuality from childhood to adolescence. *Journal of Child Psychiatry, 16,* 218–226.

Chodorow, N. (1978). *The reproduction of mothering.* Berkeley: University of California Press.

Chodorow, N. (1989). *Feminism and psychoanalytic theory.* New Haven, CT: Yale University Press.

Chomsky, N. (1975). *Reflections on language.* New York: Pantheon.

Christensen, L. (1996). *Diet-behavior relationships.* Washington, DC: American Psychological Association.

Christiansen, A. & Heavy, C.L. (1999). Intervention for couples. *Annual Review of Psychology, 50.* Palo Alto: CA. Annual Reviews.

Cialdini, R.B. (1993). *Influence: Science and practice* (3rd ed.). New York: HarperCollins.

Cialdini, R.B., & Trost, M.R. (1998). Social influence: Social norms, conformity, and compliance. In D.T. Gilbert, S.T. Fiske, & G. Lindzey (Eds.), *Handbook of social psychology* (4th ed., Vol. 2). New York: McGraw-Hill.

Cialdini, R.B., Schaller, M., Houlihan, D., Arps, K., Fultz, J., & Beaman, A.L. (1987). Empathy-based helping: Is it selflessly of selfishly motivated? *Journal of Personality and Social Psychology, 52,* 749–758.

Cicchetti, D., & Toth, S. (1998). Perspectives on research and practice in developmental psychopathology. In I.E. Sigel & K.A. Renninger (Eds.), *Handbook of child psychology* (5th ed., Vol. IV). New York: Wiley.

Clark, D.M., Salkovskis, P.M., Hackmann, A., Middelton, H., Anastasiades, P., & Gelder, M. (1994). A comparison of cognitive therapy, applied relaxation, and imipramine in the treatment of panic disorder. *British Journal of Psychiatry, 164,* 759–769.

Clark, E. (2000). Language acquisition. In A. Kazdin (Ed.), *Encyclopedia of psychology.* Washington, DC, & New York: American Psychological Association and Oxford U. Press.

Clark, E.V. (1983). Meanings and concepts. In P.H. Mussen (Ed.), *Handbook of child psychology* (4th ed., Vol. 2). New York: Wiley.

Clark, L.A., Watson, D., & Reynolds, S. (1995). Diagnosis and classification in psychopathology. *Annual Review of Psychology, 46.* Palo Alto, CA: Annual Reviews.

Clark, M. (2000). Altruism. In A. Kazdin (Ed.), *Encyclopedia of Psychology.* Washington, DC, & New York: American Psychological Association and Oxford U. Press.

Clark, N.M., & Dodge, J.A. (1999). Exploring self-efficacy as a predictor of disease management. *Health Education & Behavior, 26,* 72–89.

Clayton, L. (1999). *Alcohol drug dangers.* New York: Enslow Publications.

Cloninger, S.C. (1996). *Theories of personality* (2nd ed.). Upper Saddle River, NJ: Prentice-Hall.

Cochran, S.D., & Mays, V.M. (1990). Sex, lies, and HIV. *New England Journal of Medicine, 322,* 774–775.

Cohen, J.D., & Schooler, J.W. (Eds.) (1996). *Scientific approaches to consciousness.* Mahwah, NJ: Erlbaum.

Cohen, L.A. (1987, November). Diet and cancer. *Scientific American,* pp. 128–137.

Cohen, R.J., Swerdlik, M.E., & Phillips, S.M. (1996). *Psychological testing and assessment* (3rd ed.). Mountain View, CA: Mayfield.

Cohen, R.L., & Borsoi, D. (1996). The role of gestures in description-communication: A cross-sectional study of aging. *Journal of Nonverbal Behavior, 20,* 45–64.

Cohen, S., Doyle, W.J., Skoner, D.P., Rabin, B.S., & Gawaltney, J.M. (1997). Social ties and susceptibility to the common cold. *Journal of the American Medical Association, 277,* 1940–1944.

Cohen, S., Frank, E., Doyle, W., Skoner, D.P., Rabin, B.S., & Gwaltney, J.M. (1998). Types of stressors that increase susceptibility to the common cold in healthy adults. *Health Psychology, 17,* 214–223.

Coie, J.D., & Dodge, K. (1998). Aggression and antisocial behavior. In W. Damon (Ed.), *Handbook of child psychology* (5th ed., Vol. 3). New York: Wiley.

Colby, A., Kohlberg, L., Gibbs, J., & Lieberman, M. (1983). A longitudinal study of moral judgment. *Monographs of the Society for Research in Child Development* (Serial No. 201).

Cole, M. (1999). Culture in development. In M.H. Bornstein & M.E. Lamb (Eds.), *Developmental psychology: An advanced textbook* (4th ed.). Mahwah, NJ: Erlbaum.

Cole, M., & Cole, S.R. (2000). *The development of children* (4th ed.). New York: W.H. Freeman.

Cole, M., & Cole, S. (1997). *The development of children* (3rd ed.). New York: W.H. Freeman.

Cole, M., & Cole, S.R. (1996). *The development of children* (3rd ed.). New York: W.H. Freeman.

Coleman, J. (1995, March). *Adolescent sexual knowledge: Implications for health and health risks.* Paper presented at the meeting of the Society for Research in Child Development, Indianapolis.

Collins, M. (1996, Winter). The job outlook for '96 grads. *Journal of Career Planning.* 51–54.

Collins, W.A., & Laursen, B. (Eds.)(1999). *Relationships as developmental contexts.* Mahwah, NJ: Erlbaum.

Comarow, D.D., & Chescheir, M.W. (1999). *Talking about therapy.* Westport, CT: Greenwood.

Committee on Pediatric AIDS (1998). Surveillance of pediatric HIV infection. *Pediatrics, 101,* 315–319.

Condry, J.C. (1989). *The psychology of television.* Mahwah, NJ: Erlbaum.

Conlan, R., Hobson, J.A., Hyman, S., Kagan, J., & Conlan, R. (1999). *States of mind.* New York: Wiley.

Conway, M.A., & Rubin, D.C. (1993). The structure of autobiographical memory. In A.F. Collins, S.E. Gathercole, M.A. Conway, & P.E. Morris (Eds.), *Theories of memory.* Mahwah, NJ: Erlbaum.

Coren, S., & Girus, J.S. (1972). Illusion decrement in intersecting figures. *Psychonomic Science, 26,* 108–110.

Corey, G. (1996). *Theory and practice of counseling and psychotherapy* (5th ed.). Pacific Grove, CA: Brooks/Cole.

Cornelius, R.R. (1996). *The science of emotion.* Upper Saddle River, NJ: Prentice-Hall.

Cornell, D. (1998, April 6). Commentary. *Newsweek,* p. 24.

Coryell, W.H., & others (1999). Polarity sequence, depression, and chronicity in bipolar I disorder. *The Journal of Nervous and Mental Disease, 64,* 181–187.

Costa, P.T., & McRae, R.R. (1992). *Revised NEO personality inventory.* Odessa, FL: Psychological Assessment Resources.

Costa, P.T., & McCrae, R.R. (1995). Solid ground on the wetlands of personality: A reply to Black. *Psychological Bulletin, 117,* 216–220.

Costa, P.T., & McRae, R.R. (1998). Personality assessment. In H.S. Friedman (Ed.), *Encyclopedia of mental health* (Vol. 3). San Diego: Academic Press.

Cowley, G. (1988, May 23). The wisdom of animals. *Newsweek,* pp. 52–58.

Cowley, G. (1998, April 6). Why children turn violent. *Newsweek,* pp. 24–25.

Cox, R.H. (2000). Sport psychology. In A. Kazdin (Ed.), *Encyclopedia of psychology.* Washington, DC, & New York: American Psychological Association and Oxford U. Press.

Coyne, J. (2000). Mood disorders. In A. Kazdin (Ed.), *Encyclopedia of psychology.* Washington, DC, & New York: American Psychological Association and Oxford U. Press.

Cozby, F. (1991). *Juggling.* New York: Macmillan.

Craik, F.I.M. (2000). Memory: Coding processes. In A. Kazdin (Ed.), *Encyclopedia of psychology.* Washington, DC, & New York: American Psychological Association and Oxford U. Press.

Craik, F.I.M., & Lockhart, R.S. (1972). Levels of processing; A framework for memory research. *Journal of Verbal Learning and Verbal Behavior, 11,* 671–684.

Craik, F.I.M., & Tulving, E. (1975). Depth of processing and retention of words in episodic memory. *Journal of Experimental Psychology: General, 104,* 268–294.

Cramer, P. (1999). Future directions for the Thematic Apperception Test. *Journal of Personality Assessment, 72,* 74–92.

Crasilneck, H.B. (1995). The use of the Crasilneck bombardment technique in problems of intractible organic pain. *American Journal of Clinical Hypnosis, 37,* 255–266.

Craske, M. (2000). Panic disorder. In A. Kazdin (Ed.), *Encyclopedia of psychology.* Washington, DC, & New York: American Psychological Association and Oxford U. Press.

Crawford, M., & Unger, R. (2000). *Women and gender* (3rd ed.). Boston: McGraw-Hill.

Crocker, J., Major, B., & Steele, C. (1998). Social stigma. In D.T. Gilbert, S.T. Fiske, & G. Lindzey (Eds.), *Handbook of social psychology* (4th ed., Vol. 2). New York: McGraw-Hill.

Crooks R., & Bauer, K. (1999). *Our sexuality* (7th ed.). Belmont, CA: Wadsworth.

Crouter, A.C., Helms-Erikson, H., Updegraff, K., & McHale, S.M. (1999). Conditions underlying parents' knowledge about children's daily lives in middle childhood: Between- and within-family comparisons. *Child Development, 70,* 246–259.

Crowder, R. (2000). Sensory stores. In A. Kazdin (Ed.), *Encyclopedia of psychology.* Washington, DC, & New York: American Psychological Association and Oxford U. Press.

Csikszentmihalyi, M. (1996). *Creativity.* New York: HarperCollins.

Csikszentmihalyi, M. (2000). Creativity: An overview. In A. Kazdin (Ed.), *Encyclopedia of psychology.* Washington, DC, & New York: American Psychological Association and Oxford U. Press.

Culebras, A. (1996). *Clinical handbook of sleep disorders.* Boston: Butterworth-Heinemann.

Cuningham, M.R. (1986). Measuring the physical in physical attractiveness. *Journal of Personality and Social Psychology, 50,* 925–935.

Curtiss, S. (1977). *Genie.* New York: Academic Press.

Cushner, K., & Brislin, R.W. (1995). *Intercultural interactions* (2nd ed.). Newbury Park, CA: Sage.

Cutler, B.L., & Penrod, S.D. (1995). *Mistaken identities: The eyewitness, psychology, and the law.* New York: Cambridge University Press.

Cutrona, C.E. (1982). Transition to college: Loneliness and the process of social adjustment. In L.A. Peplau & D. Perlman (Eds.), *Loneliness.* New York: Wiley.

Czeisler, C.A., Johnson, M.P., Duffy, J.F., Brown, E.N., Ronda, J.M., & Kronauer, R.E. (1990). Exposure to bright light and darkness to treat physiologic maladaption to night work. *New England Journal of Medicine, 322,* 1253–1259.

D

Dabbs, J.M. (1992). Testosterone measurements in social and clinical psychology. *Journal of Social and Clinical Psychology, 11,* 302–321.

d'Ansia, G.I.D. (1989). Familial analysis of panic disorder and agoraphobia. *Journal of Affective Disorders, 17,* 1–8.

Darley, J. (2000). Bystander intervention. In A. Kazdin (Ed.), *Encyclopedia of psychology.* Washington, DC, & New York: American Psychological Association and Oxford U. Press.

Darley, J.M., & Latané, B. (1968). Bystander intervention in emergencies: Diffusion of responsi-

bility. *Journal of Personality and Social Psychology, 8,* 377–383.

Darwin, C. (1859). *On the origin of species.* London: John Murray.

Darwin, C. (1872/1965). *The expression of the emotions in man and animals.* Chicago: University of Chicago Press.

D'Augelli, A. (2000). Sexual orientation. In A. Kazdin (Ed.), *Encyclopedia of psychology.* Washington, DC, & New York: American Psychological Association and Oxford U. Press.

David, J.P., & Suls, J. (1999). Coping efforts in daily life: Role of big-five traits and problem appraisals. *Journal of Personality, 67,* 265–294.

Davidson, A.R., & Jacard, J.J. (1979). Variables that moderate the attitude-behavior relation: Results of a longitudinal survey. *Journal of Personality and Social Psychology, 37,* 1364–1376.

Davies, D. (1999). *Insomnia.* New York: Bantam.

Davis, J.H. (1996). Group decision making and quantitative judgments: A consensus model. In E.H. Witte & J.H. Davis (Eds.), *Understanding group behavior* (Vol. 1). Mahwah, NJ: Erlbaum.

Davis, K. (1996). *Families.* Pacific Grove, CA: Brooks/Cole.

Davis, K.L. (1999). Alzheimer's disease: Seeking new ways to preserve brain function. *Geriatrics, 54,* 42–47.

Davison, G. C., & Neale, J.M. (1994). *Abnormal psychology* (6th ed.). New York: Wiley.

Dawes, R.M. (1998). Standards for psychotherapy. In H.S. Friedman (Ed.), *Encyclopedia of mental health* (Vol. 3). San Diego: Academic Press.

de Jong-Gierveld, J. (1987). Developing and testing a model of loneliness. *Journal of Personality and Social Psychology. 53,* 119–128.

DeBattista, C., Solvason, H.B., & Schatzberg, A.F. (1998). Mood disorders. In H.S. Friedman (Ed.), *Encyclopedia of mental health* (Vol. 2). San Diego: Academic Press.

Deci, E., & Ryan, R. (1994). Promoting self-determined education. *Scandinavian Journal of Educational Research, 38,* 3–14.

DeCola, J.P., & Fanselow, M.S. (1995). Differential inflation with short and long CS-US intervals: Evidence of a nonassociative process in long delay taste avoidance. *Animal Learning & Behavior, 23,* 154–163.

Dement, W.C. (1978). *Some must watch while some must sleep.* New York: Norton.

Dement, W.C. (1999). *The promise of sleep.* New York: Delacourte Press.

Denmark, F., Rabinowitz, V.C., & Sechzer, J.A. (2000). *Engendering psychology.* Boston: Allyn & Bacon.

DeRubeis, R.J., & Crits-Cristoph, P. (1998). Empirically supported individual and group psychological treatments for adult mental disorders. *Journal of Consulting and Clinical Psychology, 66,* 37–52.

DeSpelder, L.A., & Strickland, A.L. (1999). *The last dance* (5th ed.). Mountain View, CA: Mayfield.

Deutsch, M., & Collins, M. (1951). *Interracial housing: A psychological evaluation of a social experiment.* Minneapolis: University of Minnesota Press.

deVilliers, J.G., & deVilliers, P.A. (1999). Language development. In M.H. Bornstein & M.E. Lamb

(Eds.), *Developmental psychology: An advanced textbook.* Mahwah, NJ: Erlbaum.

Devine, P.G., Evett, S.R., & Vasquez-Suson, K.A. (1996). Exploring the interpersonal dynamics of intergroup contact. In R.M. Sorrentino & E.T. Higgins (Eds.), *Handbook of motivation and cognition: The interpersonal context* (Vol. 3). New York: Guilford Press.

Devries, L.K. (1998). New York: Harold Shaw.

Dewey, J. (1993). *How we think.* Lexington, MA: D.C. Heath.

Dewsbury, D. (2000). Comparative psychology. In A. Kazdin (Ed.), *Encyclopedia of psychology.* Washington, DC, & New York: American Psychological Association and Oxford U. Press.

Dibbell, J. (1996, March 25). Technology. *Time,* pp. 57–58.

Dickson, G.L. (1990). A feminist post-structuralist analysis of the knowledge of menopause. *Advances in Nursing Science, 12,* 15–31.

Dickson, K.L., & Harris, S.D. (1999). *Instructor's manual for Santrock life-span development,* (7th ed.). New York: McGraw-Hill.

Diener, E. (1984). Subjective well-being. *Psychological Bulletin, 109,* 542–575.

Diener, E., & Diener, M.B. (1998). Happiness. In H.S. Friedman (Ed.), *Encyclopedia of mental health* (Vol. 2). San Diego: Academic Press.

Diener, E., Suh, E.M., Lucas, R.E., & Smith, H.L. (1999). Subjective well-being: Three decades of progress. *Psychological Bulletin, 125,* 276–301.

Dimeff, L.A. (Ed.)(1999). *Brief alcohol screening and intervention for college students.* New York: Guilford.

Dodd, D.K. (1995). Robbers in the classroom: A deindividuation exercise. In M.E. Ware & D.E. Johnson (Eds.), *Demonstrations and activities in teaching of psychology* (Vol. 3). Mahwah, NJ: Erlbaum.

Dohrenwend, B.S., & Shrout, P.E. (1985). "Hassles" in the conceptualization and measurement of life event stress variables. *American Psychologist, 40,* 780–785.

Dollard, J., Doob, L.W., Miller, N.E., Mowrer, O.H., & Sears, R.R. (1939). *Frustration and aggression.* New Haven, CT: Yale University Press.

Domhoff, G.W., & Schneider, A. (1997). New rationales and methods for quantitative dream research outside of the laboratory. *Sleep, 21,* 398–404.

Domjan, M.P. (1996). *Essentials of conditioning and learning.* Pacific Grove: CA: Brooks/Cole.

Dorn, L.D., & Chrousos, G.P. (1996, March). *Behavioral predictors of stress hormone responses.* Paper presented at the meeting of the Society for Research on Adolescence, Boston.

Doty, R.L. (2000). Smell. In A. Kazdin (Ed.), *Encyclopedia of psychology.* Washington, DC, & New York: American Psychological Association and Oxford U. Press.

Doty, R.L., & Muller-Schwarze, S.D. (1992). *Chemical signals in vertebrates.* New York: Plenum.

Dougherty, D.M., Cherek, D.R., & Bennett, R.H. (1996). The effects of alcohol on the aggressive responding of women. *Journal of Alcohol Studies, 57,* 178–186.

Doyle, J., & Paludi, M. (1998). *Sex and gender* (4th ed.). New York: McGraw-Hill.

Draguns, J.G. (1990). Applications of cross-cultural psychology in the field of mental health. In R.W. Brislin (Ed.), *Applied cross-cultural psychology.* Newbury Park, CA: Sage.

Druckman, D., & Bjork, R.A. (Eds.) (1994). *Learning, remembering, and believing.* Washington, DC: National Academy Press.

Dryfoos, J.G. (1990). *Adolescents at risk.* New York: Oxford University Press.

Dunnett, S.B. (1989). Neural transplantation: Normal brain function and repair after damage. *Psychologist, 1,* 4–8.

Dutton, D., & Aron, A. (1974). Some evidence for heightened sexual attraction under conditions of high anxiety. *Journal of Personality and Social Psychology, 30,* 510–517.

Eagly, A.H., & Chalken, S. (1998). Attitude structure and function. In D.T. Gilbert, S.T. Fiske, & G. Lindzey (Eds.), *Handbook of social psychology* (4th ed., Vol. 2). New York: McGraw-Hill.

Eagly, A.H., & Crowley, M. (1986). Gender and helping: A meta-analytic review of the social psychological literature. *Psychological Bulletin, 108,* 233–256.

Eagly, A.H., & Steffen, V.J. (1986). Gender and aggressive behavior: A meta-analytic review of the social psychological literature. *Psychological Bulletin, 111,* 3–22.

Ebata, A.T., & Moos, R.H. (1989, April). *Coping and adjustment in four groups of adolescents.* Paper presented at the meeting of the Society for Research in Child Development, Kansas City.

Eccles, J.S., Wigfield, A., & Schiefele, U. (1998). Motivation to succeed. In W. Damon (Ed.), *Handbook of child psychology* (Vol. 3). New York: Wiley.

Eckert, E.D., Heston, L.L., & Bouchard, T.J. (1981). MZ twins reared apart. In L. Gedda, P. Paris, & W.D. Nance (Eds.), *Twin research* (Vol. 1). New York: Alan Liss.

Edwards, B. (1979). *Drawing on the right side of the brain.* Los Angeles: Tarcher.

Edwards, C.D. (1999). *How to handle a hard-to-handle kid.* Los Angeles: Free Spirit Pub.

Edwards, J.R., & Rothbard, N.P. (1999). Work and family stress and well-being: An examination of person-environment fit in the work and family domains. *Organizational Behavior and Human Decision Processes, 77,* 85–129.

Eibl-Eibesfeldt, I. (1977). Evolution of destructive aggression. *Aggressive Behavior, 3,* 127–144.

Eissenberg, T., Stitzer, M.L., & Henningfield, J.E. (1999). Current issues in nicotine replacement. In D.F. Seidman & L.S. Covey (Eds.), *Helping the hard-core smoker.* Mahwah, NJ: Erlbaum.

Ekman, P. (1980). *The face of man.* New York: Garland.

Ekman, P. (1996). Lying and deception. In N.L. Stein, C. Brainerd, P.A. Ornstein, & B. Tversky (Eds.), *Memory for everyday emotional events.* Mahwah, NJ: Erlbaum.

Ekman, P., & Friesen, W.V. (1968). The repertoire of nonverbal behavior—Categories, origins, usage, and coding. *Semiotica, 1,* 49–98.

Ekman, P., & Friesen, W.V. (1971). Constants across cultures in the face and emotion. *Journal of Personality and Social Psychology, 17,* 124–129.

Ekman, P., & Friesen, W.V. (1984). *Unmasking the face.* Palo Alto, CA: Consulting Psychology Press.

Ekman, P., Levenson, R.W., & Friesen, W.V. (1983, September 16). Autonomic nervous system activity distinguishes among emotions. *Science, 223,* 1208–1210.

Ekman, P., & O'Sullivan, M. (1991). Facial expressions: Methods, means, and moues. In R.S. Feldman & B. Rime (Eds.), *Fundamentals of nonverbal behavior.* Cambridge: Cambridge University Press.

Elkind, D. (1978). Understanding the young adolescent. *Adolescence, 13,* 127–134.

Ellis, A. (1962). *Reason and emotion in psychotherapy.* New York: Lyle Stuart.

Ellis, A. (1996). A rational-emotive behavior therapist's perspective on Ruth. In G. Corey (Ed.), *Case approach to counseling and psychotherapy.* Pacific Grove, CA: Brooks/Cole.

Ellis, H.C. (1987). Recent developments in human memory. In V.P. Makosky (Ed.), *The G. Stanley Hall Lecture Series.* Washington, DC: American Psychological Association.

Ellis, L., & Ames, M.A. (1987). Neurohormonal functioning and sexual orientation. *Psychological Bulletin, 101,* 233–258.

Embretson, S.E. (1999). Issues in the measurement of cognitive abilities. In S.E. Embretson & S.L. Hershberger (Eds.), *The new rules of measurement.* Mahwah, NJ: Erlbaum.

Emmons, R.A. (in press). Religion in the psychology of personality: An introduction. *Journal of Personality.*

Empson, J.A.C., & Clarke, P.R.F. (1970). Rapid eye movements and remembering. *Nature, 227,* 287–288.

Emrick, D.C. (1982). Evaluation of alcoholism therapy methods. In E.M. Pattison & E. Kaufman (eds.), *Encyclopedic handbook of alcoholism.* New York: Gardner.

Endler, N.S. (1995). *Personality theories* (4th ed.). Fort Worth: Harcourt Brace.

Eppley, K.R., Abrams, A.I., & Shear, J. (1989). Differential effects of relaxation effects on trait anxiety. *Journal of Clinical Psychology, 45,* 957–974.

Erikson, E. (1968). *Identity: Youth and crisis.* New York: W.W. Norton.

Evans, D.L. (1999). Introduction: Assessing antidepressant effectiveness. *Journal of Clinical Psychology, 60, Supplement 4,* 3.

Evans, D.L., & others (1999). Depression in the medical setting: Biopsychosocial interactions and treatment considerations. *Journal of Clinical Psychology, 60, Supplement 4,* 40–56.

Eysenck, H.J. (1952). The effects of psychotherapy: An evaluation. *Journal of Consulting Psychology, 16,* 319–324.

Eysenck, H.J. (1967). *The biological basis of personality.* Springfield, IL: Charles C Thomas.

Faber, D., & Burns, J.W. (1996). Anger management style, degree of expressed anger, and gender influence on cardiovascular recovery from interpersonal harassment. *Journal of Behavioral Medicine, 19,* 55–72.

Fagan, T. (2000). School psychology. In A. Kazdin (Ed.), *Encyclopedia of psychology.* Washington, DC, & New York: American Psychological Association and Oxford U. Press.

Fairburn, C.G. (1995). *Overcoming binge eating.* New York: Guilford.

Fancher, R.E. (2000). Darwin, Charles. In A. Kazdin (Ed.), *Encyclopedia of psychology.* Washington, DC, & New York: American Psychological Association and Oxford U. Press.

Faneslow, M.S., DeCola, J.P., & Young, S.L. (1993). Mechanisms responsible for reduced contextual conditioning with masses unsignaled unconditioned stimuli. *Journal of Experimental Psychology: Animal Processes, 19,* 121–127.

Farah, M.J. (1999). *The cognitive neuroscience of vision.* Philadelphia: Blackwell.

Farthing, G.W. (2000). Consciousness and unconsciousness. In A. Kazdin (Ed.), *Encyclopedia of psychology.* Washington, DC, & New York: American Psychological Association and Oxford U. Press.

Fazio, R.H., Chen, J., McDonel, E.C., & Sherman, S.J. (1982). Attitude accessibility, attitude-behavior consistency, and the strength of the object-evaluation association. *Journal of Experimental Social Psychology, 18,* 339–357.

Feighner, J.P. (1999). Mechanisms of action of antidepressant medications. *Journal of Clinical Psychology, 60, Supplement 4,* 4–13.

Fein, S., Goethals, G.R., Kassin, S.M., & Cross, J. (1993, August). *Social influence and presidential debates.* Paper presented at the meeting of the American Psychological Association, Toronto.

Feist, J., & Feist, G.J. (1998). *Personality* (4th ed.). New York: McGraw-Hill.

Feshbach, S., & Weiner, B. (1996). *Personality* (4th ed.). Lexington, MA: Heath.

Festinger, L. (1954). A theory of social comparison processes. *Human Relations, 7,* 117–140.

Festinger, L. (1957). *A theory of cognitive dissonance.* Evanston, IL: Row Peterson.

Field, T.M. (1992, September). Stroking babies helps growth. *Brown University Child and Adolescent Behavior Letter,* pp. 1,6.

Field, T.M. (Ed.) (1995). *Touch in early development.* Mahwah, NJ: Erlbaum.

Field, T.M., Scafidi, F., & Schanberg, S. (1987). Massage of preterm newborns to improve growth and development. *Pediatric Nursing, 13,* 386–388.

Fielder, F.E. (1978). Contingency model and the leadership process. In L. Berkowitz (Ed.), *Advances in experimental social psychology* (Vol. 11). New York: Academic Press.

Fiez, J.A., Raife, E.A., Balota, D.A., Schwarz, J.P., Raichle, M.E., & Petersen, S.E. (1996). A positron emission tomography study of the short-term maintenance of verbal information. *The Journal of Neuroscience, 16,* 808–822.

Finger, M.S., & Ones, D.S. (1999). Psychosomatic equivalence of the computer and booklet forms of the MMPI: A meta-analysis. *Psychological Assessment, 11,* 58–66.

Fischer, A.R., Jome, L.R., & Atkinson, D.R. (1998). Reconceptualizing multicultural counseling: Universal healing conditions in a culturally specific context. *Counseling Psychologist, 26,* 525–588.

Fischer, J., & Gochros, H.L. (1975). *Planned behavior change.* New York: Free Press.

Fiske, S.T. (1998). Stereotyping, prejudice, and discrimination. In D.T. Gilbert, S.T. Fiske, & G. Lindzey (Eds.), *The handbook of social psychology* (4th ed., Vol. 2). New York: McGraw-Hill.

Fleming, J.S., & Courtney, B.E. (1984). The dimensionality of self-esteem. *Journal of Personality and Social Psychology, 46,* 404–421.

Flynn, J.R. (1999). Searching for justice: The discovery of IQ gains over time. *American Psychologist, 54,* 5–20.

Fogarty, R., & Bellanca, J. (1998). *Multiple intelligences.* Boston: Allyn & Bacon.

Folkman, S., & Lazarus, R.S. (1980). An analysis of coping in a middle-aged community sample. *Journal of Health and Social Behavior, 21,* 219–239.

Fomm, E. (1947). *Man for himself.* New York: Holt, Rinehart & Winston.

Foote, S.L. (2000). Neuroscience. In A. Kazdin (Ed.), *Encyclopedia of psychology.* Washington, DC, & New York: American Psychological Association and Oxford U. Press.

Forbes, R.J., & Jackson, P.R. (1980). Non-verbal behavior and the outcome of selection interviews. *Journal of Occupational Psychology, 53,* 65–72.

Ford, J.D. (1999). Disorders of extreme stress following war-zone military trauma: Associated features of posttraumatic stress disorder or comorbid but distinct syndromes? *Journal of Consulting and Clinical Psychology, 67,* 3–12.

Foulkes, D. (1993). Cognitive dream theory. In M.A. Carskadon (Ed.), *Encyclopedia of sleep and dreams.* New York: Macmillan.

Foulkes, D. (1999). *Children's dreaming and the development of consciousness.* Cambridge, MA: Harvard University Press.

Fowler, C.A., Wolford, G., Slade, R., & Tassinary, L. (1981). Lexical access without awareness. *Journal of Experimental Psychology: General, 110,* 341–362.

Fox, J.L. (1984). The brain's dynamic way of keeping in touch. *Science, 225,* 820–821.

Fox, S.I. (1996). *Human physiology* (5th ed.). New York: McGraw-Hill.

Francher, R.E. (2000). Darwin, Charles. In A. Kazdin. (Ed.), *Encyclopedia of psychology.* Washington, DC, & New York: American Psychological Association and Oxford U. Press.

Francis, A., & Ross, R. (1996). *DSM-IV case studies.* Washington, DC: American Psychiatric Association.

Frank, J.D. (1982). Therapeutic components shared by all psychotherapies. In J.H. Harvey & M.M. Parks (Eds.), *Psychotherapy research and behavior change.* Washington, DC: American Psychological Association.

Fraser, S. (Ed.). (1995). *The bell curve wars: Race, intelligence, and the future of America.* New York: Basic Books.

Freud, S. (1900/1953). The interpretation of dreams. In J. Strachey (Ed.), *The standard edition of the complete psychological works of Sigmund Freud.* New York: Washington Square Press.

Freud, S. (1917) *A general introduction to psychoanalysis.* New York: Washington Square Press.

Fried, P.A., & Watkinson, B. (1990). 36- and 48-month neurobehavioral follow-up of children prenatally exposed to marijuana, cigarettes, and alcohol. *Developmental and Behavioral Pediatrics, 11,* 49–58.

Friedman, D.K. (2000). Psychiatry. In A. Kazdin (Ed.), *Encyclopedia of psychology.* Washington, DC, & New York: American Psychological Association and Oxford U. Press.

Friedman, H.S., & Schustack, M.W. (1999). *Personality: Classic theories and modern research.* Boston: Allyn & Bacon.

Friedman, J.I., Temporini, H., & Davis, K.L. (1999). Pharmacologic strategies for augmenting cognitive performance in schizophrenia. *Biological Psychiatry, 45,* 1–16.

Friedman, M., & Rosenman, R. (1974). *Type A behavior and your heart.* New York: Knopf.

Friedman, M.A., & Brownell, K.A. (1998). Obesity. In H.S. Friedman (Ed.), *Encyclopedia of mental health* (Vol. 3). San Diego: Academic Press.

Friedman, R., Myers, P., & Benson, H. (1998). Meditation and the relaxation response. In H.S. Friedman (Ed.), *Encyclopedia of mental health* (Vol. 2). San Diego: Academic Press.

Friedrich, L.K., & Stein, A.H. (1973). Aggressive and prosocial TV programs and the natural behavior of preschool children. *Monographs of the Society for Research in Child Development, 38,* (4, Serial No. 151).

Frischoltz, E.Z. (1995, August.). *Discriminating hypnotic and nonhypnotic influences on human memory.* Paper presented at the meeting of the American Psychological Association, New York City.

Frost, R.O., & Steketee, G. (1998). Obsessive-compulsive disorder. In H.S. Friedman (Ed.), *Encyclopedia of mental health* (Vol. 3). San Diego: Academic Press.

Frueh, B.C. (2000). Posttraumatic stress disorder. In A. Kazdin (Ed.), *Encyclopedia of psychology.* Washington, DC, & New York: American Psychological Association and Oxford U. Press.

Fuhriman, A. (2000). Group therapy. In A. Kazdin (Ed.), *Encyclopedia of psychology.* Washington, DC, & New York: American Psychological Association and Oxford U. Press.

Fuhrman, A., & Burlingame, G.M. (1995). *Handbook of group psychotherapy.* New York: Wiley.

Furnham, A. (1988). Write and wrong: The validity of graphological analysis. *Skeptical Inquirer, 13,* 64–69.

Furth, H. (1971). Linguistic deficiency and thinking: Research with deaf subjects. *Psychological Bulletin, 75,* 52–58.

Furth, H.G., & Wachs, H. (1975). *Thinking goes to school.* New York: Oxford University Press.

Gage, F.H., & Bjorklund, A. (1986). Cholinergic septal grafts into the hippocampal formation improve spatial learning and memory in aged rats by an atropine-sensitive mechanism. *Journal of Neuroscience, 6,* 2837–2847.

Gaines, S.O., & Reed, E.S. (1995). Prejudice: From Allport to Dubois. *American Psychologist, 50,* 96–103.

Galanter, E. (1962). Contemporary psychophysics. In R. Brown (Ed.), *New directions in psychology.* New York: Holt, Rinehart, & Winston.

Galanter, E. (2000). Psychophysics. In A. Kazdin (Ed.), *Encyclopedia of psychology.* Washington, DC, & New York: American Psychological Association and Oxford U. Press.

Galanter, M. (1999). *Cults.* New York: Oxford University Press.

Garbarino, J. (1999). *Lost boys: Why our sons turn violent and what we can do to save them.* New York: Free Press.

Garcia, J. (1989). Food for Tolman: Cognition and cathexis in concert. In T. Archer & L. Nilsson (Eds.), *Aversion, avoidance, and anxiety.* Mahwah, NJ: Erlbaum.

Garcia, J., Ervin, F.E., & Koelling, R.A. (1966). Learning with prolonged delay of reinforcement. *Psychonomic Science, 5,* 121–122.

Gardner, B.T., & Gardner, R.A. (1971). Two-way communication with an infant chimpanzee. In A. Schreir & F. Stollnitz (Eds.), *Behavior of nonhuman primates* (Vol. 4). New York: Academic Press.

Gardner, H. (1983). *Frames of mind.* New York: Basic Books.

Gardner, H. (1993). *Multiple intelligences.* New York: Basic Books.

Gardner, H. (1999). *The disciplined mind.* New York: Simon & Schuster.

Garelik, G. (1985, October). Are the progeny progenies? *Discoverer, 6,* 45–47, 78–84.

Garmezy, N. (1985). Stress resistant children: The search for protective factors. In J.E. Stevenson (Ed.). Recent research in developmental psychopathology. *Journal of Child Psychology and Psychiatry Book Supplement, 4,* 213–233.

Garmezy, N. (1993). Children in poverty: Resilience despite risk. *Psychiatry, 56,* 127–136.

Garraghty, P.E. (1996, June). *Neuroplasticity: From mechanisms to behavior.* Paper presented at the meeting of the American Psychological Association, San Francisco.

Garrod, S., & Pickering, M. (Eds.) (1999). *Language processing.* Philadelphia: Psychology Press.

Geen, R.G. (1998). Aggression and antisocial behavior. In D.T. Gilbert, S.T. Fiske, & G. Lindzey (Eds.), *Handbook of social psychology* (4th ed., Vol. 2). New York: McGraw-Hill.

Gelder, M.G., Mayou, R., & Geddes, J. (1999). *Psychiatry* (2nd ed.). New York: Oxford University Press.

Gelso, C.J., Hill, C.E., Mohr, J.J., Rochlen, A.B., & Zack, J. (1999). Describing the face of transference. *Journal of Counseling Psychology, 46,* 257–267.

Gevins, A.S. (1999). What to do with your own personal brain scanner. In R.L. Solso (Ed.), *Mind and brain sciences in the 21st century*. Cambridge, MA: MIT Press.

Gibbons, F.X., Benbow, C.P., & Gerrard, M. (1994). From top dog to bottom half: Social comparison strategies in response to poor performance. *Journal of Personality and Social Psychology, 67*, 638–652.

Gibbons, F.X., & Buunk, B.P. (1999). Individual differences in social comparison: Development of a scale of social comparison orientation. *Journal of Personality and Social Psychology 76*, 129–142.

Gibbons, F.X., & McCoy, S.B. (1991). Self-esteem, similarity, and reactions to active versus passive downward comparison. *Journal of Personality and Social Psychology, 60*, 414–424.

Gibbs, J.T., & Huang, L.N. (1989). A conceptual framework for assessing and treating minority youth. In J.T. Gibbs & L.N. Huang (Eds.), *Children of color*. San Francisco: Jossey-Bass.

Gibbs, J.T., & Huang, L.N. (Eds.). (1989). *Children of color*. San Francisco: Jossey-Bass.

Gibson, R.L., & Mitchell, M.H. (1999). *Introduction to counseling and guidance* (5th ed.). Upper Saddle River, NJ: Prentice-Hall.

Giles, T.R., & Marafiote, R.A. (1998). Managed care and the practitioner. *Clinical Psychology and Practice, 5*, 41–50.

Gilligan, C. (1982). *In a different voice*. Cambridge, MA: Harvard University Press.

Gilligan, C. (1996). The centrality of relationships in psychological development. In G. Noam & K.W. Fischer (Eds.), *Development and vulnerability in close relationships*. Mahwah, NJ: Erlbaum.

Gilligan, C. (1998). *Minding women: Reshaping the educational realm*. Cambridge, MA: Harvard University Press.

Gladding, S.T. (1995). *Group work* (2nd ed.). Upper Saddle River, NJ: Prentice-Hall.

Gladding, S.T. (1999). *Family therapy* (2nd ed.). Upper Saddle River, NJ: Prentice-Hall.

Gladding, S.T. (1999). *Group work: A counseling specialty* (3rd ed.). Upper Saddle River, NJ: Prentice-Hall.

Gladue, B.A. (1994). The biopsychology of sexual orientation. *Current Directions in Psychological Science, 3*, 150–154.

Gleason, J.B. (2000). Language: An overview. In A. Kazdin (Ed.), *Encyclopedia of psychology*. Washington, DC, & New York: American Psychological Association and Oxford U. Press.

Goethals, G.R., & Demorest, A.P. (1995). The risky shift is a sure bet. In M.E. Ware & D.E. Johnson (Eds.), *Demonstrations and activities in teaching of psychology* (Vol. 3). Mahwah, NJ: Erlbaum.

Goldberg, R. (2000). *Clashing views on controversial issues in drugs and society* (4th ed.). New York: McGraw-Hill.

Goldberg, T.E., Berman, K.F., & Weinberger, D.R. (1995). Neuropsychology and neurophysiology of schizophrenia. *Current Opinions in Psychiatry, 8*, 34–40.

Goldenberg, I. (1996). *Family therapy* (4th ed.). Pacific Grove, CA: Brooks/Cole.

Goldin-Meadow, S. (2000). Language development, syntax, and communication. In A. Kazdin (Ed.), *Encyclopedia of psychology*. Washington, DC, & New York: American Psychological Association and Oxford U. Press.

Goldstein, E.B. (1999). *Sensation and perception* (5th ed.). Pacific Grove, CA: Brooks/Cole.

Goldstein, M.J., & Palmer, J.O. (1975). *The experience of anxiety*. New York: Oxford University Press.

Goleman, D., Kaufman, P., & Ray, M. (1993). *The creative mind*. New York: Plume.

Goleman, D., Kaufman, P., & Ray, M. (1993). *The creative spirit*. New York: Plume.

Goodstein. I.K., & Calhoun, J.F. (1982). *Understanding abnormal behavior*. Reading, MA: Addison-Wesley.

Goodwin, D.W. (1988). Alcoholism: Who gets better and who does not? In R.M. Rose & J. Barrett (eds.), *Alcoholism*. New York: Raven Press.

Gorenstein, E.E. (1997). *Case studies in abnormal psychology*. New York: Longman.

Gorman, J.M., & Kent, J. M. (1999). SSRIs and SNRIs: Broad spectrum of efficacy beyond major depression. *Journal of Clinical Psychology, 60*, Supplement 4, 33–39.

Gottesman, I.I. (1989). Vital statistics, demography, and schizophrenia. *Schizophrenia Bulletin, 15*, 5–8.

Gottesman, I.I., & Goldsmith, H.H. (1994). Developmental psychopathology of antisocial behavior. In C.A. Nelson (Ed.), *Threats to optimal development*. Mahwah, NJ: Erlbaum.

Gottesman, I.I., & Shields, J. (1982). *The schizophrenic puzzle*. New York: Cambridge University Press.

Gottlieb, B.H. (1998). Support groups. In H.S. Friedman (Ed.), *Encyclopedia of mental health* (Vol. 3). San Diego: Academic Press.

Gottlieb, G., Wahlsten, D., & Lickliter, R. (1998). The significance of biology for human development: A developmental psychobiological systems view. In W. Damon (Ed.), *Handbook of child psychology* (5th ed.). New York: Wiley.

Gottman, J.M., Coan, J., Carrere, S., & Swanson, C. (1998). Predicting marital happiness and stability from newlywed interactions. *Journal of Marriage and the Family, 60*, 5–22.

Graber, R., Garber, R., & Gouin, P. (1998). *How to get a good night sleep*. New York: Wiley.

Grabowski, J. (1999, January). Addicted to addictions? *APA Monitor*, p. 8.

Graham, S. (1986, August). *Can attribution theory tell us something about motivation in Blacks?* Paper presented at the meeting of the American Psychological Association, Washington, DC.

Gray, C.R., & Gummerman, K. (1975). The enigmatic eidetic image: A critical examination of methods, data, and theories. *Psychological Bulletin, 82*, 383–407.

Graziano, W.J. (1995). Evolutionary psychology: Old music, but now on CDs? *Psychological Inquiry, 6*, 41–44.

Greenberg, J.S., Bruess, C.E., & Mullen, K.D. (1992). *Sexuality* (3rd ed.). New York: McGraw-Hill.

Greenberg, M., Szmukler, G., & Tantam, D. (1986). *Making sense of psychiatric cases*. New York: Oxford University Press.

Greene, R.L. (1999). Applied memory research: How far from bankruptcy? *Contemporary Psychology, 44*, 29–31.

Greenglass, E.R. (1998). Gender differences in mental health. In H.S. Friedman (Ed.), *Encyclopedia of mental health* (Vol. 2). San Diego: Academic Press.

Greenough, W. (1999, April). *Experience, brain development, and links to mental retardation*. Paper presented at the meeting of the Society for Research in Child Development, Albuquerque.

Greenough, W.T. (2000). Brain development. In A. Kazdin (Ed.), *Encyclopedia of psychology*. Washington, DC, & New York: American Psychological Association and Oxford U. Press.

Greenwald, A.G., & Banaji, M.R. (1995). Implicit social cognition: Attitudes, self-esteem, and stereotypes. *Psychological Review, 102*, 4–27.

Greenwald, A.G., Draine, S.C., & Abrams, R.L. (1996). Three cognitive markers of unconscious semantic activation. *Science, 273*, 1699–1702.

Gregory, R. (2000). Visual illusions. In A. Kazdin (Ed.), *Encylcopedia of psychology*. Washington, DC, & New York: American Psychological Association and Oxford U. Press

Grizenko, N. (1998). Protective factors in development of psychopathology. In H.S. Friedman (Ed.), *Encyclopedia of mental health* (Vol. 3). San Diego: Academic Press.

Grossenbacher, P.G. (1999). *Finding consciousness in the brain*. New York: John Benjamins Pub.

Grunberg, N.E., Klein, L.C., & Brown, K.J. (1998). Psychopharmacology. In H.S. Friedman (Ed.), *Encyclopedia of mental health* (Vol. 3). San Diego: Academic Press.

Guilford, J.P. (1967). *The structure of intellect*. New York: McGraw-Hill.

Gupta, P., & Dell, G.S. (1999). The emergence of language from serial order and procedural memory. In B. MacWhinney (Ed.), *The emergence of language*. Mahwah, NJ: Erlbaum.

Guttman, N., & Kalish, H.I. (1956). Discriminability and stimulus generalization *Journal of Experimental Psychology, 51*, 79–88.

H

Haberlandt, K. (1999). *Human memory*. Boston: Allyn & Bacon.

Hales, D. (1999). *Invitation to health* (8th ed.). New York: McGraw-Hill.

Hales, R.E., Yudofsky, S.C. (Eds.) (1999). *Essentials of clinical psychiatry*. Washington, DC: American Psychiatric Pub.

Hales, R.E., Yudofsky, S.C., Talbott, J.A., & Pardes, H. (Eds.) (1999). *Textbook of psychiatry* (3rd ed.). Washington, DC: American Psychiatric Pub.

Hall, W. (1998, February 24). IQ scores are up, and psychologists wonder why. *Wall Street Journal*, pp. B11–12.

Halliday, T. (Ed.) (1998). *The senses and communication*. New York: Springer Verlag.

Halonen, J.A., & Santrock, J.W. (1999). *Psychology* (3rd ed.). New York: McGraw-Hill.

Halpern, D.F. (1996). *Thinking critically about critical thinking*. Mahwah, NJ: Erlbaum.

Halpern, D.F. (in press). Teaching and learning critical thinking: Lessons from cognitive psychology. *American Psychologist*.

Hamann, S.B. (2000). Amnesia. In A. Kazdin (Ed.), *Encyclopedia of psychology.* Washington, DC, & New York: American Psychological Association and Oxford U. Press.

Handler, L. (1999). Introduction to the special series on personality assessment: Classics in contemporary perspective. *Journal of Personality Assessment, 72,* 144–146.

Hannigan, J.H., Spear, L.P., Spear, N.E., & Goodlet, C.R. (Eds.)(1999). *Alcohol and alcoholism.* Mahwah, NJ: Erlbaum.

Harackiewicz, J.M. (1998). Intrinsic motivation and goals. In H.S. Friedman (Ed.), *Encyclopedia of mental health* (Vol. 2). San Diego: Academic Press.

Harkness, S., & Super, E.M. (1995). Culture and parenting. In M.H. Bornstein (Ed.), *Handbook of parenting* (Vol. 3). Hillsdale, NJ: Erlbaum.

Harlow, H.F., & Zimmerman, R.R. (1959). Affectional responses in the infant monkey. *Science, 130,* 421–432.

Harmatz, M. (1997). Introduction to clinical psychology. In Santrock, J.W. *Psychology* (5th ed.). New York: McGraw-Hill.

Harmon-Jones, E., & Mills, J. (Eds.) (1999). *Cognitive dissonance.* Washington, DC: American Psychological Association.

Harris, A.S. (1996). *Living with paradox: An introduction to Jungian Psychology.* Pacific Grove, CA: Brooks/Cole.

Harris, J.R. (1998). *The nurture assumption.* New York: Free Press.

Harris, R.F., Wolf, N.M., & Baer, D.M. (1964). Effects of adult social reinforcement on child behavior. *Young Children, 20,* 8–17.

Harrison, Y. (1999). *Sleep talking.* New York: Blanford.

Hart, B., & Risley, T.R. (1995). *Meaningful differences.* Baltimore: Paul H. Brookes.

Harter, S. (1998). The development of serf-representations. In W. Damon (Ed.), *Handbook of child psychology* (5th ed., Vol. 3). New York: Wiley.

Hartmann, E. (1993). Nightmares. In M.A. Carskadon (Ed.), *Encyclopedia of sleep and dreams.* New York: Macmillan.

Hartwell, L., Hood, L., Goldberg, M.L., Silver, L.M., Veres, R.C., & Reynolds, A. (2000). *Genetics: From genes to genomes.* New York: McGraw-Hill.

Harvey, J.H. (1995). *Odyssey of the heart.* New York: W.H. Freeman.

Hatcher, R., & others (1988). *Contraceptive technology, 1988–1989* (14th ed.). New York: Irvington.

Hauser, S.T. (1999). Understanding resilient outcomes: Adolescent lives across time and generations. *Journal of Research on Adolescence, 9,* 1–24.

Hayes, N. (1997, July). The distinctive skills of a psychology graduate. *APA Monitor,* p. 33.

Hayflick, L. (1997). The cellular basis for biological aging. In C.E. Finch & L. Hayflick (Eds.), *Handbook of the biology of aging.* New York: Van Nostrand.

Heider, F. (1958). Attitudes and cognitive organization. *Journal of Psychology, 21,* 107–122.

Heider, F. (1958). *The psychology of interpersonal relations.* New York: Wiley.

Helms, J.E., & Cook, D.A. (1999). *Using race and culture in counseling and psychotherapy.* Boston: Allyn & Bacon.

Herbert, J. (1988). The physiology of aggression. In J. Groebel & R. Hinde (Eds.), *Aggression and war: The biological and social bases.* New York: Cambridge University Press.

Herbert, W. (1997, April 21). Politics of biology. *U.S. News & World Report,* pp. 72–79.

Hernandez, D.J. (1988). Demographic trends and the living arrangements of children. In E.M. Hetherington & J.D. Arasteh (Eds.), *Impact of divorce, single-parenting, and stepparenting on children.* Mahwah, NJ: Erlbaum.

Herrnstein, R.J., & Murray, C. (1994). *The bell curve: Intelligence and class structure in American life.* New York: Macmillan.

Hersen, M., & Miller, P.M. (Eds.) (1996). *Progress in behavior modification* (Vol. 30). Pacific Grove: CA: Brooks/Cole.

Herzog, H.A. (1995). Discussing animal rights and animal research in the classroom. In M.E. Ware & D.E. Johnson (Eds.), *Demonstrations and activities in teaching of psychology* (Vol. 1). Mahwah, NJ: Erlbaum.

Hilgard, E.R. (1965). *Hypnotic suggestibility.* Ft. Worth, TX: Harcourt Brace.

Hilgard, E.R. (1977). *Divided consciousness: Multiple controls in human thought and action.* New York: Wiley.

Hill, C.E. (2000). Client-centered therapy. In A. Kazdin (Ed.), *Encyclopedia of psychology.* Washington, DC, & New York: American Psychological Association and Oxford U. Press.

Hill, C.E., & O'Brien, K.M. (1999). *Helping skills.* Washington, DC: American Psychological Association.

Hilleras, P., Jorm, A.F., Herlitz, A., & Winblad, B. (1999). Activity patterns in very old people. *Age and Aging, 28,* 147–152.

Hilsenroth, M. (2000). Rorschach test. In A. Kazdin (Ed.), *Encyclopedia of psychology.* Washington, DC, & New York: American Psychological Association and Oxford U. Press.

Hines, T. (1988). *Pseudoscience and the paranormal.* Buffalo, NY: Promethus Books.

Hobfoll, S.E. (1989). Conversation of resources: A new attempt at conceptualizing stress. *American Psychologist, 44,* 513–524.

Hobson, J.A. (1999). Dreams. In R. Conlan (Ed.), *States of mind.* New York: Wiley.

Hobson, J.A. (2000). Dreams: physiology. In A. Kazdin (Ed.), *Encyclopedia of psychology.* Washington, DC, & New York: American Psychological Association and Oxford U. Press.

Hobson, J.A., & McCarley, R.W. (1977). The brain as a dream state generator: An activation-synthesis hypothesis of the dream process. *American Journal of Psychiatry, 134,* 1335–1348.

Hofferth, S.L. (1990). Trends in adolescent sexual activity, contraception, and pregnancy in the United States. In J. Bancroft & J.M. Reinisch (Eds.), *Adolescence and puberty.* New York: Oxford University Press.

Hoffman, D.D. (1998). *Visual intelligence.* New York: Norton.

Hoffnung, M. (1984). Motherhood. In J. Freeman (Ed.), *Women* (3rd ed.). Palo Alto, CA: Mayfield.

Hogan, J. (1986). *Hogan Personality Inventory manual.* Minneapolis: National Computer Systems.

Hogan, R.T. (1987, August). *Conceptions of personality and the prediction of job performance.* Paper presented at the meeting of the American Psychological Association, New York City.

Hoge, M.A. (1998). Managed care. In H.S. Friedman (Ed.), *Encyclopedia of mental health* (Vol. 2). San Diego: Academic Press.

Hogg, M.A. (1996). Social identity, self-categorization, and the small group. In E.H. Witte & J.H. Davis (Eds.), *Understanding group behavior* (Vol. 2). Mahwah, NJ: Erlbaum.

Holcomb, H.H., Cascella, N.G., Thaker, G.K., Medoff, D.R., Dannals, R.F., & Tamminga, C.A. (1996). Functional sites of neuroleptic drug action in the human brain. *American Journal of Psychiatry, 153,* 41–49.

Holland, P.C. (1996). The effects of intertrial and feature-target intervals on operant serial feature-positive discrimination learning. *Animal Learning & Behavior, 24,* 411–428.

Holmes, D.S. (1988). The influence of meditation versus rest on physiological considerations In M. West (Ed.), *The psychology of meditation.* New York: Oxford University Press.

Holmes, T.H., & Rahe, R.H. (1967). The social readjustment rating scale. *Journal of Psychosomatic Research, 11,* 213–218.

Holtzmann, W. (1982). Cross-cultural comparisons of personality development in Mexico and the United States. In D. Wagner & H.W. Stevenson (Eds.), *Cultural perspectives on child development.* San Francisco: Jossey-Bass.

Honts, C. (1998, June). Commentary. *APA Monitor,* p. 30.

Hooper, J., & Teresi, D. (1993). *The 3-Pound Universe.* New York: Tarcher/Putnam.

Hopkins, K.D. (1998). *Educational and psychological measurement and evaluation* (8th Ed.). Boston: Allyn & Bacon.

Hoptman, M.J., & Davidson, R.J. (1994). How and why do the two cerebral hemispheres interact? *Psychological Bulletin, 116,* 195–219.

Horney, K. (1945). *Our inner conflicts.* New York: W.W. Norton.

Horowitz, M.J. (1998). Psychoanalysis. In H.S. Friedman (Ed.), *Encyclopedia of mental health* (Vol. 3). San Diego: Academic Press.

Howard, K.I. (2000). Psychotherapy: Research. In A. Kazdin (Ed.), *Encyclopedia of psychology.* Washington, DC, & New York: American Psychological Association and Oxford U. Press.

Howe, M.L. (1995, March). *Early memory development and the emergence of autobiographical memory.* Paper presented at the meeting of the Society for Research in Child Development, Indianapolis.

Hubel, D.H., & Wiesel, T.N. (1965). Receptive fields and functional architecture in two nonstriate areas (18 and 19) of the cat. *Journal of Neurophysiology, 28,* 229–289.

Hultsch, D.F., & Plemons, J.K. (1979). Life events and life-span development. In P.B. Baltes & O.G. Brim (Eds.), *Life-span development and behavior.* San Diego: Academic Press.

Humphreys, K.N. (2000). Alcoholics Anonymous. In A. Kazdin (Ed.), *Encyclopedia of psychology.* Washington, DC, & New York: American Psychological Association and Oxford U. Press.

Hunt, H. (1982). *The universe within.* New York: Simon & Schuster.

Hunt, M. (1974). *Sexual behavior in the 1970s.* Chicago: Playboy.

Hunt, R.R., & Kelly, R.E.S. (1996). Accessing the particular from the general: The power of distinctiveness in the context of organization. *Memory and Cognition, 24,* 217–225.

Hurvich, L.M., & Jameson, D. (1969). Human color perception. *American Scientist, 57,* 143–166.

Huston, A.C. (1995, August). *Children in poverty.* Paper presented at the meeting of the American Psychological Association, New York City.

Huston, A.C., Watkins, B.A., & Kunkel, D. (1989). Public policy and children's television. *American Psychologist, 44,* 424–433.

Hy, L., & Loevinger, J. (1996). *Measuring ego development.* Mahwah, NJ: Erlbaum.

Iacono, W.G., & Lykken, D.T. (1997). The validity of the lie detector: Two surveys of scientific opinion. *Journal of Applied Psychology, 82,* 426–433.

Iverson, G.L., & Barton, E. (1999). Interscorer reliability of the MMPI-2: Should TRIN and VRIN be computer scored? *Journal of Clinical Psychology, 55,* 65–70.

Izard, C.E., Schultz, D., & Levinson, K.L. (1998). Emotions and mental health. In H.S. Friedman (Ed.), *Encyclopedia of mental health* (Vol. 2). San Diego: Academic Press.

J

Jacobsen, N., & others (1998). *When men batter women.* New York: Simon & Schuster.

Jalbert, N.L. (1996, Summer). What can I do with a psychology major? *Psi Chi Newsletter, 22* (No. 3, pp. 1, 6.

James, W. (1890/1950). *Principles of psychology.* New York: Dover.

Jameson, D., & Hurvich, L.M. (1989). Essay concerning color constancy. *Annual Review of Psychology* (Vol. 40). Palo Alto, CA: Annual Reviews.

Janis, I. (1972). *Victims of groupthink: A psychological study of foreign-policy decisions and fiascos.* Boston: Houghton Mifflin.

Jausovec, N. (1999). Brain biology and brain functioning. In M.A. Runco & S. Pritzker (Eds.), *Encyclopedia of creativity.* San Diego: Academic Press.

Jaycox, L.H., & Foa, E.B. (1998). Post traumatic stress. In H.S. Friedman (Ed.), *Encyclopedia of mental health* (Vol. 2). San Diego: Academic Press.

Jenkins, J.J. (1969). Language and thought. In J.F. Voss (Ed.), *Approaches to thought.* Columbus, OH: Merrill.

Jennings, L., & Skovholt, T.M. (1999). The cognitive, emotional, and relational characteristics of master therapists. *Journal of Counseling Psychology, 46,* 3–11.

Jensen, A.R. (1969). How much can we boost IQ and scholastic achievement? *Harvard Educational Review, 39,* 1–123.

Jensen, A.R. (1998). *The g factor: The science of mental ability.* Westport, CT: Praeger.

Johnson, D.W., & Johnson, R.T. (1999). *Learning together and alone* (5th ed.). Boston: Allyn & Bacon.

Johnson, G.B. (2000). *The living world* (2nd ed.). New York: McGraw-Hill.

Johnson, L.D., O'Malley, P.M., & Bachman, J.G. (1998, December). *Report of the Monitoring the Future Project.* Ann Arbor, MI: University of Michigan, Institute for Social Research.

Johnston, L., Bachman, G., & O'Malley, P. (1989, February 24). *Teenage drug use continues decline* [News release]. Ann Arbor: University of Michigan, Institute for Social Research.

Johnston, L.D., O'Malley, P., & Bachman, J.G. (1997). *National survey results on drug use from The Monitoring the Future Study: Vol. II College Students.* Ann Arbor, MI: University of Michigan, Institute for Social Research.

Jones, E.E. (1998). Major developments in five decades of social psychology. In D.T. Gilbert, S.T. Fiske, & G. Lindzey (Eds.), *Handbook of social psychology* (4th ed., Vol. 1). New York: McGraw-Hill.

Jones, J.H. (1997). *Prejudice and racism* (2nd ed.). New York: McGraw-Hill.

Jones, M.C. (1924). A laboratory study of fear: The case of Peter. *Journal of Genetic Psychology, 31,* 308–315.

Jou, J., Shanteau, J., & Harris, R.J. (1996). An information processing view of framing effects: The role of causal schemas in decision making. *Memory and Cognition, 24,* 1–15.

Jung, C. (1917). *Analytic psychology.* New York: Moffat, Yard.

K

Kagan, J. (1992). Yesterday's premises, tomorrow's promises. *Developmental Psychology, 28,* 990–997.

Kagan, J. (1998). Biology and the child. In W. Damon (Ed.), *Handbook of child psychology* (5th ed., Vol. 3). New York: Wiley.

Kagan, S., & Madsen, M.C. (1972). Experimental analysis of cooperation and competition of Anglo-American and Mexican children. *Developmental Psychology, 6,* 49–59.

Kahneman, D., & Tversky, A. (1995). Conflict resolution: A cognitive perspective. In K. Arrow, R.H. Mnookin, L. Ross, A. Tversky, & R. Wilson (Eds.), *Barriers to conflict resolution.* New York: Norton.

Kail, R., & Pellegrino, J.W. (1985). *Human intelligence.* New York: W.H. Freeman.

Kales, A. (1970). Sleep patterns following 205 hours of sleep deprivation. *Psychosomatic Medicine, 32,* 189–200.

Kalichman, S. (1996). *Answering your questions about AIDS.* Washington, DC: American Psychological Association.

Kalick, S.M., & Hamilton, T.E. (1986). The matching hypothesis reexamined. *Journal of Personality and Social Psychology, 51,* 673–682.

Kamin, L.J. (1968). Attention-like processes in classical conditioning. In M.R. Jones (Ed.), *Miami Symposium on the prediction of behavior: Aversive stimuli.* Coral Gables, FL: University of Miami Press.

Kandel, E. R., & Schwartz, J.H. (1982). Molecular biology of learning: Modulation of transmitter release. *Science, 218,* 433–443.

Kanner, A.D., Coyne, J.C., Schaefer, C., & Lazarus, R.S. (1981). Comparisons of two modes of stress measurement: Daily hassles and uplifts versus major life events. *Journal of Behavioral Medicine, 4,* 1–39.

Kaplan, R.M., & Kerner, D.N. (1998). Behavioral medicine. In H.S. Friedman (Ed.), *Encyclopedia of mental health* (Vol. 1). San Diego: Academic Press.

Kapur, S., Craik, F.I.M., Tulving, E., Wilson, A.A., Houle, S., & Brown, G.M. (1994). Neuroanatomical correlates of encoding in episodic memory: Levels of processing effect. *Proceedings of the National Academy of Science of the United States, 91,* 2008–2111.

Karni, A., Tanne, D., Rubenstein, B.S., Askensay, J.J.M., & Sagi, D. (1994). Overnight improvement in a perceptual skill. *Science, 265,* 679–681.

Katigbak, M.S., Church, A.T., & Akamine, T.X. (1996). Cross-cultural generalizability of personality dimensions. *Journal of Personality and Social Psychology, 70,* 99–114.

Katz, A. (2000). Mental imagery. In A. Kazdin (Ed.), *Encyclopedia of psychology.* Washington, DC, & New York: American Psychological Association and Oxford U. Press.

Kavanaugh, D.J., & Wilson, P.H. (1989). Prediction of outcome with a group version of cognitive therapy for depression. *Behaviour Research and Therapy, 27,* 333–347.

Kelly, J.G. (2000). Community psychology: History of the field. In A. Kazdin (Ed.), *Encyclopedia of psychology.* Washington, DC, & New York: American Psychological Association and Oxford U. Press.

Keltner (2000). Emotion: An overview. In A. Kazdin (Ed.), *Encyclopedia of psychology.* Washington, DC, & New York: American Psychological Association and Oxford U. Press.

Kennedy, P.G.E., & Folk-Seang, J.F. (1986). Studies on the development, antigenic phenotype and function of human glial cells in tissue culture. *Brain, 109,* 1261–1277.

Kephart, W.M. (1967). Some correlates of romantic love. *Journal of Marriage and the Family, 29,* 470–474.

Kiecolt-Glaser, J.K., Dura, J.R., Specher, C.E., Trask, O.J., & Glaser, R. (1991). Spousal caregivers of dementia victims. *Psychosomatic Medicine, 53,* 345–362.

Kihlstrom, J.F., & McConkey, K.M. (1990). William James and hypnosis: A centennial reflection. *Psychological Science, 1,* 174–177.

King, H.E. (1961). Psychological effects of excitement of the limbic system. In D.E. Sheer (Ed.), *Electrical stimulation of the brain.* Austin: University of Texas Press.

King, L.A., & Pennebaker, J. (1998). *Unpublished manuscript, subjective well-being.* Dept. of Psychology, Southern Methodist U., Dallas, TX.

Kinsey, A.C., Pomeroy, W.B., & Martin, E.E. (1948). *Sexual behavior in the human male.* Philadelphia: W.B. Saunders.

Kirsch, I., & Lynn, S.J. (1998). Dissociation theories of hypnosis. *Psychological Bulletin, 123,* 100–115.

Kirsner, K., Speelman, C., Maybery, M., O'Brien-Malone, A., Anderson, M., & McLeod, C. (Eds.) (1998), *Implicit and explicit memory processes.* Mahwah, NJ: Erlbaum.

Klatzky, R.L. (1984). *Memory and awareness.* New York: W.H. Freeman.

Klatzky, R.L. (2000). Cognitive maps. In A. Kazdin (Ed.), *Encyclopedia of psychology.* Washington, DC, & New York: American Psychological Association and Oxford U. Press.

Knussmann, R., Christiansen, K., & Couwenbergs, C. (1986). Relations between sex hormone level and sexual behavior in men. *Archives of Sexual Behavior, 15,* 429–445.

Kobasa, S., Maddi, S., & Kahn, S. (1982). Hardiness and health: A prospective study. *Journal of Personality and Social Psychology, 42,* 168–177.

Kobasa, S., Maddi, S., Puccetti, M., & Zola, M. (1985). Relative effectiveness of hardiness, exercise, and social support as resources against illness. *Journal of Psychosomatic Research, 29,* 525–533.

Kohlberg, L. (1969). Stage and sequence: The cognitive-developmental approach to socialization. In D. Goslind (Ed.), *Handbook of socialization theory and research.* Chicago: Rand McNally.

Kohlberg, L. (1976). Moral stages and moralization: The cognitive-developmental approach. In T. Lickona (Ed.), *Moral development and behavior.* New York: Holt, Rinehart, & Winston.

Kohlberg, L. (1986). A current statement on some theoretical issues. In S. Modgil & C. Modgil (Eds.), *Lawrence Kohlberg.* Philadelphia: Falmer.

Kohlenberg, R.J., Tsai, M., & Kohlenberg, G.S. (1996). Functional analysis in behavioral therapy. In M. Hersen & P.M. Miller (Eds.), *Progress in behavior modification* (Vol. 30). Pacific Grove: CA: Brooks/Cole.

Kohler, W. (1925). *The mentality of apes.* New York: Harcourt Brace Jovanovich.

Kohn, A., & Kalat, J.W. (1995). Preparing for an important event: Demonstrating the modern view of classical conditioning. In M.E. Ware & D.E. Johnson (Eds.), *Demonstrations and activities in teaching psychology* (Vol. 2). Mahwah, NJ: Erlbaum.

Kohut, H. (1977). *Restoration of the self.* New York: International Universities Press.

Kolb, B. (1989). Brain development, plasticity, and behavior. *American Psychologist, 44,* 1203–1212.

Kolb, B., & Whishaw, I.Q. (1999). *Human neuropsychology* (4th ed.). New York: W.H. Freeman.

Kolb, L. (1973). *Modern clinical psychiatry* (8th ed.). Philadelphia: W.B. Saunders.

Konner, M. (1991). *Childhood: A multicultural view.* Boston: Little, Brown.

Kopp, C. (1984). *Baby steps.* New York: W.H. Freeman.

Kopta, S.M., Lueger, R.J., Saunders, S.M., & Howard, K.I. (1999). Individual psychotherapy outcome and process research. *Annual Reviews of Psychology.* Palo Alto: Annual Reviews, Inc.

Koss, M., & Boeschen, L. (1998). Rape. In H.S. Friedman (Ed.), *Encyclopedia of mental health* (Vol. 3). San Diego: Academic Press.

Kotlowitz, A. (1991). *There are no children here.* New York: Anchor Books.

Krosnick, J.A. (1999). Survey research. *Annual Reviews of Psychology.* Palo Alto, CA: Annual Reviews, Inc.

Kübler-Ross, E. (1974). *Questions and answers on death and dying.* New York: Macmillan.

Kuhn, D. (1998). Afterword to Volume 2. In W. Damon (Ed.), *Handbook of child psychology* (5th ed., Vol. 2). New York: Wiley.

Kuhn, D., Weinstock, M., & Flaton, R. (1994). How well do jurors reason? Competence dimensions of individual variation in a juror reasoning task. *Psychological Science, 5,* 289–296.

Kulik, J.A., Kulik, C.C., & Bangert-Drowns, R.L. (1985). Effectiveness of computer-based education in elementary schools. *Computers in Human Behavior, 1,* 59–74.

Kutchinsky, B. (1992). The child sexual abuse panic. *Norsisk Sexoligi, 10,* 30–42.

Labbe, E.E. (1998). Biofeedback. In H.S. Friedman (Ed.), *Encyclopedia of mental health* (Vol. 1). San Diego: Academic Press.

Labouvie-Vief, G. (1986, August). *Modes of knowing and life-span cognition.* Paper presented at the meeting of the American Psychological Association, Washington, DC.

Labov, W. (1973). The boundaries of words and their meanings. In C.N. Bailey & R.W. Shuy (Eds.), *New ways of analyzing variations in English.* Washington, DC: Georgetown University Press.

Lahari, A. (1999). On phonology and phonetics. In L.R. Wheeldon (Ed.), *Aspects of language production.* Philadelphia: Psychology Press.

Lamb, C.S., Jackson, L.A., Cassiday, P.B., & Priest, D.J. (1993). Body figure preferences of men and women: A comparison of two generations. *Sex Roles, 28,* 345–358.

Lamb, H.R. (1998). Mental hospitals and deinstitutionalization. In H.S. Friedman (Ed.), *Encyclopedia of mental health* (Vol. 2). San Diego: Academic Press.

Lamb, M. (1998). Nonparental child care. In W. Damon (Ed.), *Handbook of child psychology* (5th ed., Vol. 4). New York: Wiley.

Lamb, M.E. (2000). Attachment research. In A. Kazdin (Ed.), *Encyclopedia of psychology.* Washington, DC, & New York: American Psychological Association and Oxford U. Press.

Lamb, M.E., Hwang, C.P., Ketterlinus, R.D., & Fracasso, M.P. (1999). Parent-child relationships: Development in the context of the family. In M.H. Bornstein & M.E. Lamb (Eds.), *Developmental psychology: An advanced textbook* (4th ed.). Mahwah, NJ: Erlbaum.

Lane, H. (1976). *The wild boy of Aveyron.* Cambridge, MA: Harvard University Press.

Lange, C.G. (1922). *The emotions.* Baltimore: Williams & Wilkins.

Langer, E. (1989). *Mindfulness.* Reading, MA: Addison-Wesley.

Langer, E. (1997). *The power of mindful learning.* Reading, MA: Addison-Wesley.

Langer, L.L. (1991). *Holocaust testimonies: The ruins of memory.* New Haven: Yale University Press.

Langs, R. (1978). *Technique in transition.* New York: Jason Aronson.

Lashley, K. (1950). In search of the engram. In *Symposium of the Society for Experimental Biology* (Vol. 4). New York: Cambridge University Press.

Latané, B. (1981). The psychology of social impact. *American Psychologist, 36,* 343–356.

Latané, B. (1996). Strength from weakness: The fate of opinion minorities in spatially distributed groups. In E.H. Witte & J.H. Davis (Eds.), *Understanding group behavior* (Vol. 1). Mahwah, NJ: Erlbaum.

Lazarus, A.A. (1996). A multimodal behavior therapist's perspective on the truth. In G. Corey (Ed.), *Case approach to counseling and psychotherapy* (4th ed.). Pacific Grove, CA: Brooks/Cole.

Lazarus, R.S. (1991). On the primacy of cognition. *American Psychologist, 39,* 124–129.

Lazarus, R.S. (1993). Coping theory and research: Past, present, and future. *Psychosomatic Medicine, 55,* 234–247.

Leahey, T.H. (1997). *A history of psychology.* Upper Saddle River, NJ: Prentice-Hall.

Leary, M.R., Nezlek, J.B., Downs, D., Radford-Davenport, J., Martin, J., & McMullen, A. (1994). Self-presentation in everyday interactions. *Journal of Personality and Social Psychology, 67,* 664–673.

LeBoeuf, B.J., & Peterson, R.S. (1969). Social status and mating activity in elephant seals. *Science, 163,* 91–93.

Lebow, J.L., & Gurman, A.S. (1995). Research assessing couple and family therapy. *Annual Review of Psychology, 46,* Palo Alto, CA: Annual Reviews.

Lee, I., Hsieh, C., & Paffenbarger, O. (1995). Exercise intensity and longevity in men. *Journal of the American Medical Association, 273,* 1179–1184.

Leiter, M.P., & Maslach, C. (1998). Burnout. In H.S. Friedman (Ed.), *Encyclopedia of mental health* (Vol. 1). San Diego: Academic Press.

Leith, L.M. (1998). Exercise and mental health. In H.S. Friedman (Ed.), *Encyclopedia of mental health* (Vol. 2). San Diego: Academic Press.

Lemme, B.H. (1999). *Development in adulthood* (2nd ed.). Boston: Allyn & Bacon.

Lenneberg, E. (1967). *The biological foundations of language.* New York: Wiley.

Lenneberg, E.H., Rebelsky, F.G., & Nichols, I.A. (1965). The vocalization of infants born to deaf and hearing parents. *Human Development, 8,* 23–37.

Leon, G.R. (1990). *Case histories of psychopathology* (4th ed.). Boston: Allyn & Bacon.

Lepper, M., Greene, D., & Nisbett, R.E. (1973). Undermining children's intrinsic interest with extrinsic rewards. *Journal of Personality and Social Psychology, 28,* 129–137.

Lerner, R.M. (1989). Theories of human development: Contemporary perspectives. In W. Damon (Ed.), *Handbook of child psychology* (5th ed., Vol. 1), New York: Wiley.

Levant, R.F. (1995). *Masculinity Reconstructed: Changing rules of manhood.* New York: Dutton.

Levant, R.F., & Brooks, G.R. (1997). *Men and sex: New psychological perspectives.* New York: Wiley.

LeVay, S. (1991). A difference in the hypothalamic structure between heterosexual and homosexual men. *Science, 253,* 1034–1037.

Leventhal, H., & Tomarken, A.J. (1986). Emotion: Today's problems. *Annual Review of Psychology, 37,* 565–610.

Levine, J.H., & Moreland, R.H. (1998). Small groups. In D.T. Gilbert, S.T. Fiske, & G. Lindzey (Eds.), *Handbook of social psychology* (4th ed., Vol. 2). New York: McGraw-Hill.

Levinson, D. (1978). *The seasons of a man's life.* New York: Knopf.

Levy, J. (2000). Hemispheric functions. In A. Kazdin (Ed.), *Encyclopedia of psychology.* Washington, DC, & New York: American Psychological Association and Oxford U. Press.

Levy, L. (1979). Handwriting and hiring. *Dun's Review, 113,* 72–79.

Levy, S.M., Herberman, R.B., Lee, J., Whiteside, T., Kirckwood, J., & McFreeley, S. (1990). Estrogen receptor concentration and social factors as predictors of natural killer cell activity in early-stage breast cancer patients. *Natural Immunity and Cell Growth Regulation, 9,* 313–324.

Levy, T.M. (Ed.) (1999). *Handbook of attachment interventions.* San Diego: Academic Press.

Lewin, R. (1988). Brain graft puzzles. *Science, 240,* 879.

Lewinsohn, P. (1987). The Coping with Depression course. In R.F. Munoz (Ed.), *Depression prevention.* New York: Hemisphere.

Lewinsohn, P.M., Antonuccio, D.O., Steinmetz, J., & Teri, L. (1984). *The coping with depression course: A psychoeducational intervention for unipolar depression.* Eugene, OR: Castalia.

Lewis, J.R. (1999). *Cults in America.* New York: Abc-Clio.

Lewis, M. (1997). *Altering fate.* New York: Guilford.

Lewis, R. (1999). *Human genetics* (3rd ed.). New York: McGraw-Hill.

Lipsey, M.W., & Wilson, D.B. (1993). The efficacy of psychological, educational, and behavioral treatment: Confirmation from meta-analysis. *American Psychologist, 48,* 1181–1209.

Lister, P. (1992, July). A skeptic's guide to psychics. *Redbook,* pp. 103–105, 112–113.

Locke, J.L. (1993). *The child's path to spoken language.* Cambridge, MA: Harvard University Press.

Locke, J.L. (1999). Towards a biological science of language development. In M. Barrett (Ed.), *The development of language.* Philadelphia: Psychology Press.

Loehr, J. (1989, May). (Personal Communication). United States Tennis Association Training Camp, Saddlebrook, FL.

Loftus, E. (1980). *Memory.* Reading, MA: Addison-Wesley.

Loftus, E.F. (1975). Spreading activation within semantic categories. *Journal of Experimental Psychology, 104,* 234–240.

Loftus, E.F. (1980). *Memory.* Reading, MA: Addison-Wesley.

Loftus, E.F. (1993a). Psychologists in the eyewitness world. *American Psychologist, 48,* 550–552.

Loftus, E.F. (1993b). The reality of repressed memories. *American Psychologist, 48,* 518–537.

Logue, A.W. (1995). *Self-control.* Upper Saddle River, NJ: Prentice-Hall.

LoLordo, V.M. (2000). Classical conditioning. In A. Kazdin (Ed.), *Encyclopedia of psychology.* Washington, DC, & New York: American Psychological Association and Oxford U. Press.

Longo, D.A., Lent, R.W., & Brown, S.D. (1992). Social cognitive variables in the prediction of client motivation and attribution. *Journal of Counseling Psychology, 39,* 447–452.

LoPiccolo, J. (2000). Sexual dysfunctions. In A. Kazdin (Ed.), *Encyclopedia of psychology.* Washington, DC, & New York: American Psychological Association and Oxford U. Press.

Lorenz, K.Z. (1965). *Evolution and modification of behavior.* Chicago: University of Chicago Press.

Luborsky, L.B. (2000). Psychoanalytic psychotherapies. In A. Kazdin (Ed.), *Encyclopedia of psychology.* Washington, DC, & New York: American Psychological Association and Oxford U. Press.

Ludolph, P. (1982, August). *A reanalysis of the literature on multiple personality.* Paper presented at the meeting of the American Psychological Association, Washington, DC.

Luiselli, J.K., & Cameron, M.J. (1998). *Antecedent control: Approaches to behavioral support.* Baltimore: Paul H. Brookes.

Luszcz, M.A., & Bryan, J. (1999). Toward understanding age-related memory loss in late adulthood. *Gerontology, 45,* 2–9.

Lutz, D.J., & Sternberg, R.J. (1999). Cognitive development. In M.H. Bornstein & M.E. Lamb (Eds.), *Developmental psychology: An advanced textbook* (4th ed.). Mahwah, NJ: Erlbaum.

Lycan, W. (Ed.). (1999). *Mind and cognition.* Malden, MA: Blackwell.

Lykken, D.T. (1987). The probity of the polygraph. In S.M. Kassin & L.S. Wrightsman (Eds.), *The psychology of evidence and trial procedures.* Newbury Park, CA: Sage.

Lynch, G. (1990, June). *The many shapes of memory and the several forms of synaptic plasticity.* Paper presented at the meeting of the American Psychological Society, Dallas.

Lynn, R. (1996). Racial and ethnic differences in intelligence in the U.S. on the Differential Ability Scale. *Personality and Individual Differences, 20,* 271–273.

M

Maas, J. (1998). *Power sleep.* New York: Villard.

Maccoby, E.E., & Jacklin, C.N. (1974). *The psychology of sex differences.* Palo Alto, CA: Stanford University Press.

MacMillan, J.H. (2000). *Educational research* (3rd ed.). New York: Pearson.

MacWhinney, B. (Ed.) (1999). *The emergence of language.* Mahwah, NJ: Erlbaum.

Maddi, S. (1996). *Personality theories* (6th ed.). Pacific Grove, CA: Brooks/Cole.

Maddi, S. (1998). Hardiness. In H.S. Friedman (Ed.), *Encyclopedia of mental health* (Vol. 3). San Diego: Academic Press.

Mader, S. (1999). *Biology* (6th ed.). New York: McGraw-Hill.

Mader, S.S. (2000). *Inquiry into life* (9th ed.). New York: McGraw-Hill.

Mager, R.F. (1972). *Goals analysis.* Belmont, CA: Fearon.

Mahoney, G.J. (1995, March). *The maternal behavior rating scale.* Paper presented at the meeting of the Society for Research in Child Development, Indianapolis.

Maier, N.R.F. (1931). Reasoning in humans. *Journal of Comparative Psychology, 12,* 181–194.

Main, M. (2000). Attachment theory. In A. Kazdin (Ed.), *Encyclopedia of psychology.* Washington, DC, & New York: American Psychological Association and Oxford U. Press.

Malinowski, B. (1927). *Sex and repression in savage society.* New York: Humanities Press.

Mandler, G. (1980). Recognizing: The judgment of previous occurrence. *Psychological Review, 87,* 252–271.

Mandler, G. (1996). The situation of psychology: Landmarks and choice points. *American Journal of Psychology, 109,* 1–35.

Mandler, J.M. (1998). Representation. In W. Damon (Ed.), *Handbook of child psychology* (5th ed., Vol. 2). New York: Wiley.

Manning, A. (1989). The genetic basis of aggression. In J. Groebel & R.A. Hinde (Eds.), *Aggression and war: Their biological and social bases.* New York: Cambridge University Press.

Maratsos, M. (1999). Some aspects of innateness and complexity in grammar acquisition. In M. Barrett (Ed.), *The development of language.* Philadelphia: Psychology Press.

Marcia, J.E. (1999). Representational thought in ego identity, psychotherapy, and psychosocial developmental theory. In I.E. Sigel (Ed.), *Development of mental representation.* Mahwah, NJ: Erlbaum.

Maris, R.W. (1998). Suicide. In H.S. Friedman (Ed.), *Encyclopedia of mental health* (Vol. 3). San Diego: Academic Press.

Marshall, G.N., Wortman, C.B., Vickers, R.R., Kusulas, J.W., & Hervig, L.K. (1994). The five-factor model of personality as a framework for personality-health research. *Journal of Personality and Social Psychology, 67,* 278–286.

Martin, G., & Pear, J. (1999). *Behavior modification* (6th ed.). Upper Saddle River, NJ: Prentice-Hall.

Maslow, A. (1971). *The farther reaches of human nature.* New York: Viking.

Maslow, A.H. (1954). *Motivation and personality.* New York: Harper & Row.

Masters, W.H., & Johnson, V.E. (1966). *Human sexual response.* Boston: Little, Brown.

Matas, L., Arend, R.A., & Sroufe, L.A. (1978). Continuity in adaptation: Quality of attachment and later competence. *Child Development, 49,* 547–556.

Matlin, M. (1993). *The psychology of women* (2nd ed.). Fort Worth: Harcourt Brace.

Matlin, M.W. (1998). *Cognition* (4th ed.). Fort Worth: Harcourt Brace.

Matsumoto, D. (1996). *Culture and psychology.* Pacific Grove, CA: Brooks/Cole.

Matthews, G., & Dreary, I.J. (1998). *Personality traits.* Cambridge, Eng: Cambridge U. Press.

Maultsby, M.C., & Wirga, M. (1998). Behavior therapy. In H.S. Friedman (Ed.), *Encyclopedia of mental health* (Vol. 1). San Diego: Academic Press.

Mayer, R. (1999). Problem solving. In M.A. Runco & S. Pritzker (Eds.), *Encyclopedia of psychology*. San Diego: Academic Press.

McAdams, D.P. (1993). *The stories we live by*. New York: Morrow.

McCarley, R.W. (1989). The biology of dreaming sleep. In M.H. Drager, T. Roth, & W.C. Dement (Eds.), *Principles and practices of sleep medicine*. Ft. Worth, TX: Harcourt Brace.

McClelland, D.C. (1955). Some social consequences of achievement motivation. In M.R. Jones (Ed.), *Nebraska Symposium of Motivation*. Lincoln: University of Nebraska Press.

McClelland, D.C. (1978). Managing motivation to expand human freedom. *American Psychologist, 33*, 201–210.

McClelland, D.C., Atkinson, J.W., Clark, R., & Lowell, E.L. (1953). *The achievement motive*. New York: Appleton-Century-Crofts.

McConaghy, N. (1993). *Sexual behavior: Problems and management*. New York: Plenum Press.

McDougall, W. (1908). *Social psychology*. New York: G. Putnam & Sons.

McEwen, B.S. (2000). Endocrine systems. In A. Kazdin (Ed.), *Encyclopedia of psychology*. Washington, DC, & New York: American Psychological Association and Oxford U. Press.

McFarlane, T., Polivy, J., & Herman, C.P. (1998). Dieting. In H.S. Friedman (Ed.), *Encyclopedia of mental health* (Vol. 1). San Diego: Academic Press.

McIver, T. (1988). Backward masking and other backward thoughts about music. *Skeptical Inquirer, 13*, 50–63.

McKinlay, J.B. (1999, March). *Erectile dysfunction: The most overlooked biobehavioral marker of disease*. Paper presented at the meeting of the American Psychosomatic Association, Vancouver.

McKinlay, S.M., & McKinlay, J.B. (1984). *Health status and health care utilization by menopausal women*. Unpublished manuscript, Cambridge Research Center, American Institutes for Research, Cambridge, MA.

McKnight, C.C., Crosshite, F.J., Dossey, J.A., Kifer, E., Swafford, J.O., Travers, K.J., & Cooney, T.J. (1987). *The underachieving curriculum*. Champaign, IL: Stipes.

McLoyd, V.C. (1998). Children in poverty. In W. Damon (Ed.), *Handbook of child psychology* (5th ed., Vol. 4). New York: Wiley.

McLoyd, V.C. (1999). Cultural influences in a multicultural society. In A.S. Masten (Ed.), *Cultural processes in child development*. Mahwah, NJ: Erlbaum.

McLoyd, V.C. (1999). Cultural influences in a multicultural society: Conceptual and methodological issues. In A.S. Masten (Ed.), *Cultural processes in child development*. Mahwah, NJ: Erlbaum.

McMillan, J. (1996). *Classroom assessment*. Boston: Allyn & Bacon.

McNally, D. (1990). *Even eagles need a push*. New York: Dell.

McNally, R.J. (1998). Panic attacks. In H.S. Friedman (Ed.), *Encyclopedia of mental health* (Vol. 3). San Diego: Academic Press.

McNeil, E.B. (1967). *The quiet furies*. Englewood Cliffs, NJ: Prentice-Hall.

McNulty, J. (2000). Five-factor model of personality. In A. Kazdin (Ed.), *Encyclopedia of psychology*.

Washington, DC, & New York: American Psychological Association and Oxford U. Press.

Meador, B.D., & Rogers, C.R. (1979). Person-centered therapy. In R.J. Corsini, *Current psychotherapies* (2nd ed.). Itasca, IL: Peacock.

Meehl, P. (1962). Schizotonia, schizotypy, schizophrenia. *American Psychologist, 17*, 827–838.

Meehl, P.E. (1986). Diagnostic taxa as open concepts. In T. Millon & G.I. Klerman (Eds.), *Contemporary directions in psychopathology*. New York: Guilford.

Melzack, R. (1973). *The puzzle of pain*. New York: Basic Books.

Melzack, R., & Wall, P.D. (1965). Pain mechanisms: A new theory. *Science, 150*, 971–979.

Melzack, R., & Wall, P.D. (1983). *The challenge of pain*. New York: Basic Books.

Mercer, J.R., & Lewis, J.F. (1978). *System of multicultural pluralistic assessment*. New York: Psychological Corporation.

Mervis, J. (1996, July). NIMH data point way to effective treatment. *APA Monitor*, pp. 1, 13.

Messer, W.S., & Griggs, R.A. (1989). Student belief and involvement in the paranormal and performance in introductory psychology. *Teaching of Psychology, 16*, 187–191.

Messinger, J.C. (1971). Sex and repression in an Irish folk community. In D.S. Marshall & R.C. Suggs (Eds.), *Human sexual behavior*. New York: Basic Books.

Metalsky, G.I., Joiner, T.E., Hardin, T.S., & Abramson, L.Y. (1993). Depressive reactions to failure in a naturalistic setting. *Journal of Abnormal Psychology, 102*, 101–109.

Metcalfe, J., & Mischel, W. (1999). A hot/cool system analysis of delay of gratification: Dynamics of will power. *Psychological Review, 106*, 3–19.

Meyer, R.G. (1998). Personality disorders. In H.S. Friedman (Ed.), *Encyclopedia of mental health* (Vol. 2). San Diego: Academic Press.

Meyer, R.G., & Osborne, Y.V.H. (1982). *Case studies in abnormal behavior*. Boston: Allyn & Bacon.

Meyer, R.G., Wolverton, D., & Deitsch, S.E. (1998). Antisocial personality disorder. In H.S. Friedman (Ed.), *Encyclopedia of mental health* (Vol. 2). San Diego: Academic Press.

Meyers, B.S., & others (1999). Depression dopamine beta-hydroxylase activity in unipolar geriatric delusional depression. *Biological Psychiatry, 45*, 448–456.

Micael, R.T., Gagnon, J.H., Laumann, E.O., & Kolata, G. (1994). *Sex in America*. Boston, Little, Brown.

Michael, W. (1999). Guilford's view. In M.A. Runco & S. Pritzker (Eds.), *Encyclopedia of creativity*. San Diego: Academic Press.

Michaels, J.W., Bloomel, J.M., Brocato, R.M., Linkous, R.A., & Rowe, J.S. (1982). Social facilitation and inhibition in a natural setting. *Replications in Social Psychology, 2*, 21–24.

Milgram, S. (1963). Behavioral study of obedience. *Journal of Abnormal and Social Psychology, 67*, 171–178.

Milgram, S. (1965). Some conditions of obedience and disobedience to authority. *Human Relations, 18*, 56–76.

Milgram, S. (1974). *Obedience to authority*. New York: Harper & Row.

Milgram, S., Liberty, H.J., Toledo, R., & Wackenhut, J. (1986). Response to intrusion in waiting lines. *Journal of Personality and Social Psychology, 51*, 683–689.

Miller, A. (2000). Obedience. In A. Kazdin (Ed.), *Encyclopedia of psychology*. Washington, DC, & New York: American Psychological Association and Oxford U. Press.

Miller, G.A. (1956). The magical number seven, plus or minus two: Some limits on our capacity for information processing. *Psychological Review, 48*, 337–442.

Miller, N.E. (1941). The frustration-aggression hypothesis. *Psychological Review, 48*, 337–442.

Miller, N.E. (1959). Liberalization of basic S-R concepts: Extension to conflict behavior, motivation, and social learning. In S. Koch (Ed.), *Psychology: A study of science*. New York: McGraw-Hill.

Miller, N.E. (1969). Learning of visceral glandular responses. *Science, 163*, 434–445.

Miller, N.E. (1985). The value of behavioral research on animals. *American Psychologist, 40*, 432–440.

Miller-Jones, D. (1989). Culture and testing. *American Psychologist, 44*, 360–366.

Millis, R.M. (1998). Smoking. In H.S. Friedman (Ed.), *Encyclopedia of mental health* (Vol. 3). San Diego: Academic Press.

Mindell, J.A. (1996). Children and sleep. In M.R. Pressman & W.C. Orr (Eds.), *Understanding sleep*. Washington, DC: American Psychological Association.

Mineka, S., & Nugent, K. (1995). Mood-congruent memory biases in anxiety and depression. In D.L. Schacter, J.T. Coyle, G.D. Fischbach, M.M. Mesulam, & L.E. Sullivan (Eds.), *Memory distortion: How minds, brains, and societies reconstruct the past*. Cambridge, MA: Harvard University Press.

Mischel, W. (1968). *Personality and assessment*. New York: Wiley.

Mischel, W. (1973). Toward a cognitive social learning theory reformulation of personality. *Psychological Review, 80*, 252–283.

Mischel, W. (1995, August). *Cognitive-affective theory of person-environment psychology*. Paper presented at the meeting of the American Psychological Association, New York City.

Mishkin, M., & Appenzellar, T. (1987). The anatomy of memory. *Scientific American, 256*, 80–89.

Moldoveanu, M.C., & Langer, E. (1999). Mindfulness. In M.A. Runco & S. Pritzker (Eds.), *Encyclopedia of creativity*. San Diego: Academic Press.

Money, J. (1986). *Lovemaps: Clinical concepts of sexual/erotic health and pathology, paraphilia, and gender transposition in childhood, adolescence, and maturity*. New York: Irvington.

Monk, T.H. (1993). Shiftwork. In M.A. Carskadon (Ed.), *Encyclopedia of sleep and dreaming*. New York: Macmillan.

Moore, T.E. (1995). Subliminal self-help auditory tapes: An empirical test of perceptual consequences. *Canadian Journal of Behavioural Science, 27*, 9–20.

Moore-Ede, M.C., Sulzman, F.M., & Fuller, C.A. (1982). *The clocks that time us*. Cambridge, MA: Harvard University Press.

Morgan, T., & Cummings, A.L. (1999). Change experienced during group therapy of female survivors of childhood sexual abuse. *Journal of Consulting and Clinical Psychology, 67,* 28–36.

Moscovici, S. (1985). Social influence and conformity. In G. Lindzey & E. Aronson (Eds.), *Handbook of social psychology* (3rd ed., Vol. 2). New York: Random House.

Moses, J., Steptoe, A., Mathews, A., & Edwards, S. (1989). The effects of exercise training on mental well-being in a normal population: A controlled trial. *Journal of Psychosomatic Research, 33,* 47–61.

Mountcastle, V.B. (1986). *The parietal visual system and optic flow.* Paper presented at the meeting of the American Psychological Association, Washington, DC.

Mountcastle, V.B. (1998). *Perceptual neuroscience.* Cambridge, MA: Harvard University Press.

Mumford, M., & Porter, P.P. (1999). Analogies. In M.A. Runco & S. Pritzker (Eds.), *Encyclopedia of creativity.* San Diego: Academic Press.

Munoz, R.F. (1998). Depression—applied aspects. In H.S. Friedman (Ed.), *Encyclopedia of mental health* (Vol. 1). San Diego: Academic Press.

Murdock, B.B. (1999). The buffer 30 years later: Working memory in a theory of distributed associative model (TODAM). In C. Izawa (Ed.), *On human memory.* Mahwah, NJ: Erlbaum.

Murray, H.A. (1938). *Explorations in personality.* Cambridge, MA: Harvard University Press.

Murstein, B.I., & Mathes, S. (1996). Projection on projective techniques = pathology: The problem that is not being addressed. *Journal of Personality Assessment, 66,* 337–351.

Mussell, M.P., & Mitchell, J.E. (1998). Anorexia nervosa and bulimia nervosa. In H.S. Friedman (Ed.), *Encyclopedia of mental health* (Vol. 1). San Diego: Academic Press.

Nadien, M.B., & Denmark, F.L. (1999). *Females and autonomy: A life-span perspective.* Boston: Allyn & Bacon.

Naglieri, J.A. (2000). Stanford-Binet Intelligence Scale. In A. Kazdin (Ed.), *Encyclopedia of psychology.* Washington, DC, & New York: American Psychological Association and Oxford U. Press.

Nakamizo, S., Ono, H., & Ujuke, H. (1999). Subjective staircase: A multiple wallpaper illusion. *Perception & Psychophysics, 61,* 13–22.

Narvaez, D., Getz, I., Rest, J.R., & Thoma, S.J. (1999). Individual moral judgment and cultural ideologies. *Developmental Psychology, 3,* 478–488.

Nash, J.M. (1997, February 3). Fertile minds. *Time,* pp. 50–54.

Nathan, P.E. (1994). DSM-IV. *Journal of Clinical Psychology, 50,* 103–109.

Nathan, P.E., & Langenbucher, J.W. (1999). Psychopathology: Description and classification. *Annual Reviews of Psychology.* Palo Alto: Annual Reviews, Inc.

National Advisory Council on Economic Opportunity. (1980). *Critical choices for the 80s.* Washington, DC: U.S. Government Printing Office.

National Center for Health Statistics. (1989, June). *Statistics on marriage and divorce.* Washington, DC: U.S. Government Printing Office.

National Commission on Sleep Disorders Research. (1993, January). *Report of the National Commission on Sleep Disorders Research.* Report submitted to the United States Congress and to the Secretary of the U.S. Department of Health and Human Services.

Neisser, U., Boodoo, G., Bouchard, T.J., Boykin, A.W., Brody, N., Ceci, S.J., Halpern, D.F., Loehlin, J.C., Perloff, R., Sternberg, R.J., & Urbina, S. (1996). Intelligence: Knowns & unknowns. *American Psychologist, 51,* 77–101.

Nelson, T.O. (1996). Consciousness and metacognition. *American Psychologist, 51,* 102–116.

Neugarten, B.L. (1980). Must everything be a midlife crisis? *Annual Editions Human Development 80/81.* Guilford, CT: Dushkin.

Nevo, B. (1986). *Scientific aspects of graphology.* Springfield, IL: Charles C Thomas.

NICHD Early Child Care Research Network. (1997). Infant child care and attachment security. *Child Development, 68,* 860–879.

NICHD Early Child Care Research Network. (in press). Relations between family predictors and child outcomes: Are they weaker for children in child care? *Developmental Psychology.*

Nicholls, J.G. (1979). Development of perception of own attainment and causal attribution for success and failure in reading. *Journal of Educational Psychology, 71,* 94–99.

Nicholls, J.G., Cobb, P., Wood, T., Yackel, E., & Patashnick, M. (1990). Assessing students' theories of success in mathematics: Individual and classroom differences. *Journal for Research in Mathematics Education, 21,* 109–122.

Nickerson, R.S. (1999). Engineering psychology. In P.A. Hancock (Ed.), *Human performance and ergonomics.* San Diego: Academic Press.

Niehoff, D. (1999). *The biology of violence.* New York: The Free Press.

Nisbett, R.E., & Ross, L. (1980). *Human inference.* Upper Saddle River, NJ: Prentice-Hall.

Norcross, J.C., & Kobayashi, M. (1999). Treating anger in psychotherapy: Introduction and cases. *Journal of Clinical Psychology in Session, 55,* 275–282.

Norem, J.K., & Cantor, N. (1986). Anticipatory and post-hoc cushioning strategies: Optimism and defensive pessimism in risk "situations." *Cognitive Therapy Research, 10,* 347–362.

Notarius, C.I. (1996). Marriage: Will I be happy or sad? In N. Vanzetti & S. Duck (Eds.), *A lifetime of relationships.* Pacific Grove: CA: Brooks/Cole.

Nottelmann, E.D., Susman, E.J., Blue, J.H., Inoff-Germain, G., Dorn, L.D., Loriaux, D.L., Cutler, G.B., & Chrousos, G.P. (1987). Gonadal and adrenal hormone correlates of adjustment in early adolescence. In R.M. Lerner & T.T. Foch (Eds.), *Biological-psychological interactions in early adolescence.* Hillsdale, NJ: Erlbaum.

Novaco, R.W. (1998). Aggression. In H.S. Friedman (Ed.), *Encyclopedia of mental health* (Vol. 1). San Diego: Academic Press.

Novak, C.A. (1977). Does youthfulness equal attractiveness? In L.E. Troll, J. Israel, & D. Israel (Eds.), *Looking ahead: A woman's guide to the problems and joys of growing older.* Upper Saddle River, NJ: Prentice-Hall.

Nystul, M.S. (1999). *Introduction to counseling.* Boston: Allyn & Bacon.

Oatley, K. (2000). Emotion: Theories. In A. Kazdin (Ed.), *Encyclopedia of psychology.* Washington, DC, & New York: American Psychological Association and Oxford U. Press.

Occupational Outlook Handbook. (1998–1999). Washington, DC: U.S. Dept. of Labor, Bureau of Labor Statistics.

O'Donnell, L., & others (1999). Violence prevention and young adolescents' participation in community service. *Journal of Adolescent Health, 24,* 28–37.

Okagaki, L. (2000). Socialization of intelligence. In A. Kazdin (Ed.), *Encyclopedia of psychology.* Washington, DC, & New York: American Psychological Association and Oxford U. Press.

Olds, J.M. (1958). Self-stimulation experiments and differential reward systems. In H.H. Jasper, L.D. Proctor, R.S. Knighton, W.C. Noshay, & R.T. Costello (Eds.), *Reticular formation of the brain.* Boston: Little, Brown.

Olds, J.M., & Milner, P.M. (1954). Positive reinforcement produced by electrical stimulation of the septal area and other areas of the rat brain. *Journal of Comparative and Physiological Psychology, 47,* 419–427.

Olff, M. (1999). Stress, depression, and immunity. *Psychiatry Research, 85,* 7–16.

Oltmanns, T.F., Neale, J.M., & Davison, G.C. (1986). *Case studies in abnormal psychology* (2nd ed.). New York: Wiley.

O'Rahilly, R., & Muller, F. (1999). *The embryonic human brain.* New York: Wiley.

Orlinsky, D.E., Grawe, K., & Parks, B.K. (1994). Process and outcome in psychotherapy. In A.E. Bergin & S.L. Garfield (Eds.), *Handbook of psychotherapy and behavior change* (4th ed.). New York: Wiley.

Ozer, D.J., & Riese, S.P. (1994). Personality assessment. *Annual Review of Psychology, 45,* 357–388.

Padma-Nathan, H. (1999, March). *Oral drug therapy for erectile dysfunction: What have we learned from the Viagra experience?* Paper presented at the meeting of the American Psychosomatic Association, Vancouver.

Paffenbarger, O., Hyde, R.T., Wing, A.L., & Hsieh, C. (1986). Physical activity, all-cause mortality, and longevity of college alumni. *New England Journal of Medicine, 324,* 605–612.

Paivio, A. (1971). *Imagery and verbal processes.* New York: Holt, Rinehart & Winston.

Paivio, A. (1986). *Mental representations: A dual coding approach.* New York: Oxford University Press.

Paloutzian, R. (1996). *The psychology of religion* (2nd ed.). Boston: Allyn & Bacon.

Paloutzian, R. (2000). *Invitation to the psychology of religion* (3rd ed.). Boston: Allyn & Bacon.

Paludi, M.A. (1998). *The psychology of women.* Upper Saddle River, NJ: Prentice-Hall.

Pan, B.A., & Snow, C.E. (1999). The development of conversational and discourse skills. In M. Barrett (Ed.), *The development of language.* Philadelphia: Psychology Press.

Panskepp, J. (1993). Neurochemical control of moods and emotions: Amino acids to neuro-peptides. In M. Lewis & J.M. Haviland (Eds.), *Handbook of emotion.* New York: Guilford Press.

Parducci, A. (1996). *Happiness, pleasure, and judgment.* Hillsdale, NJ: Erlbaum.

Park, D.C., Nisbett, R., & Hedden, T. (1999). Aging, culture, and cognition. *Journal of Gerontology, 54B,* P75–P84.

Parke, R.D., & Buriel, R. (1998). Socialization in the family. In W. Damon (Ed.), *Handbook of child psychology* (5th ed., Vol. 3). New York: Wiley.

Pascual-Leone, J., & Johnson, J. (1999). A dialectical constructivist view of representation. In I.E. Sigel (Ed.), *Development of mental representation.* Mahwah, NJ: Erlbaum.

Passuth, P.M., Maines, D.R., & Neugarten, B.L. (1984). *Age norms and age constraints twenty years later.* Paper presented at the meeting of the Midwest Sociological Society, Chicago.

Patterson, C. (1995). Lesbian and gay parenthood. In M.H. Bornstein (Ed.), *Handbook of parenting* (Vol. 3). Mahwah, NJ: Erlbaum.

Patterson, G.R., Debaryshe, B.D., & Ramsey, E. (1989). A developmental perspective on antisocial behavior. *American Psychologist, 44,* 329–335.

Paulus, P.B. (1989). An overview and evaluation of group influence. In P.B. Paulus (Ed.), *Psychology of group influence.* Mahwah, NJ: Erlbaum.

Paunonen, S., Jackson, D., Trzebinski, J., & Forserling, F. (1992). Personality structures across cultures: A multimethod evaluation. *Journal of Personality and Social Psychology, 62,* 447–456.

Pavlov, I.P. (1927). *Conditioned reflexes* (G.V. Anrep, Trans.). New York: Dover.

Payne, L.R., Smith, P.O., Sturges, L.V., & Holleran, S.A. (1996). Reactivity to smoking cues: Mediating roles of nicotine and duration of deprivation. *Addictive Behaviors, 21,* 139–154.

Peele, S., & Brodsky, A. (1991). *The truth about addiction and recovery.* New York: Simon & Schuster.

Pellegrini, A.D. (1996). *Observing children in their natural worlds.* Mahwah, NJ: Erlbaum.

Penfield, W. (1947). Some observations in the cerebral cortex of man. *Proceedings of the Royal Society, 134,* 349.

Pennebaker, J. (1990). *Opening up.* New York: Avon.

Pentz, M.A. (1993). Comparative effects of community-based drug abuse prevention. In J.S. Baer, G.A. Marlatt, & R.J. McMahon (Eds.), *Addicitve behaviors across the life span.* Newbury Park, CA: Sage.

Perlis, M. (2000). Sleeptalking. In A. Kazdin (Ed.), *Encyclopedia of psychology.* Washington, DC, & New York: American Psychological Association and Oxford U. Press.

Perlman, D., & Peplau, L.A. (1998). Loneliness. In H.S. Friedman (Ed.), *Encyclopedia of mental health* (Vol. 2). San Diego: Academic Press.

Perls, E. (1969). *Gestalt therapy verbatim,* Lafayette, CA: Real People Press.

Pert, A.B., & Snyder, S.H. (1973). Opiate receptor: Demonstration in a nervous tissue. *Science, 179,* 1011.

Pert, C.B. (1999). *Molecules of emotion.* New York: Simon & Schuster.

Pervin, L.A. (1993). *Personality* (6th ed.). New York: Wiley.

Petersen, A. (1979, January). Can puberty come any faster? *Psychology Today,* pp. 45–56.

Petersen, A.C. (2000). Adolescence: Puberty and biological maturation. In A. Kazdin (Ed.), *Encyclopedia of psychology.* Washington, DC, & New York: American Psychological Association and Oxford U. Press.

Peterson, C., & Seligman, M.E.P. (1984). Casual explanations as a risk factor for depression. *Psychological Review, 91,* 347–374.

Peterson, C., & Seligman, M.E.P., & Vaillant, G.E. (1986). *Explanatory style as a risk factor for physical illness.* Unpublished manuscript, Dept. of Psychology, University of Michigan, Ann Arbor.

Peth-Pierce, R. (1998). *The NICHD Study of early child care.* Washington, DC: National Institute of Child Health Development.

Petri, H.L. (1996). *Motivation.* Pacific Grove: CA: Brooks/Cole.

Petrinovich, L. (1996). *Living and dying well.* New York: Plenum.

Petty, R.E., & Krosnick, J.A. (Eds.). *Attitude strength: Antecedents and consequents.* Mahwah, NJ: Erlbaum.

Phares, E.J. (1984). *Personality.* Columbus, OH: Merrill.

Philips, H.C., & Rachman, S. (1996). *The psychological management of chronic pain* (2nd ed.). New York: Springer.

Piaget, J. (1952). *The origins of intelligence in children.* New York: Oxford University Press.

Piaget, J., & Inhelder, B. (1969). *The child's conception of space* (F.J. Langdon & J.L. Lunzer, Trans.). New York: W.W. Norton.

Pierce, W.D., & Epling, W.F. (1999). *Behavior analysis and learning* (2nd ed.). Upper Saddle River, NJ: Prentice-Hall.

Pilkonis, P.A. (1999). Introduction: Paradigms for psychotherapy outcome research. *Journal of Clinical Psychology, 55,* 145–146.

Pilkonis, P.A., & Krause, M.S. (1999). Summary: Paradigms for psychotherapy outcome research. *Journal of Clinical Psychology, 55,* 201–206.

Pillow, D.R., Zautra, A.J., & Sandler, I. (1996). Major life events and minor stressors. *Journal of Personality and Social Psychology, 70,* 381–394.

Pinger, R.R., Payne, W.A., Hahn, D.B., & Hahn, E.J. (1998). *Drugs* (3rd ed.). New York: McGraw-Hill.

Pinker, S. (1994). *The language instinct.* New York: HarperCollins.

Pinker, S. (1997). *How the mind works.* New York: Norton.

Pinker, S. (1999). *How the mind works.* New York: Norton.

Pipes, R.B., & Davenport, D.S. (1999). *Introduction to psychotherapy* (2nd ed.) Boston: Allyn & Bacon.

Pittman, T.S. (1998). Motivation. In D.T. Gilbert, S.T. Fiske, & G. Lindzey (Eds.), *Handbook of social psychology* (4th ed., Vol. 1). New York: McGraw-Hill.

Plutchik, R. (1980). *Emotion: A psychoevolutionary synthesis.* New York: Harper & Row.

Pollock, V.E., Schneider, L.S., Gabrielli, W.F., & Goodwin, D.W. (1987). Sex of parent and sex of offspring in the transmission of alcoholism: A meta-analysis. *Journal of Nervous and Mental Disease, 173,* 668–673.

Poole, J.H., Ober, B.A., Shenaut, G.K., & Vinogradov, S. (1999). Independent frontal-system deficits in schizophrenia. *Psychiatry Research, 85,* 161–176.

Popham, W.J. (1999). *Classroom assessment.* Boston: Allyn & Bacon.

Premack, D. (1986). *Gavagi! The future history of the ape language controversy.* Cambridge, MA: MIT Press.

Price, R.H. (2000). Community psychology: Prevention and intervention. In A. Kazdin (Ed.), *Encyclopedia of psychology.* Washington, DC, & New York: American Psychological Association and Oxford U. Press.

Price, R.H. (2000). Prevention and intervention. In A. Kazdin (Ed.), *Encyclopedia of psychology.* Washington, DC, & New York: American Psychological Association and Oxford U. Press.

Pritchard, D.J. (1996). Genetic analysis of schizophrenia. *Annual of Human Genetics, 60,* 105–123.

Proctor, R.A. (1999). Artificial intelligence. In M.A. Runco & S. Pritzker (Eds.), *Encyclopedia of creativity.* San Diego: Academic Press.

Qualls, P.J., & Sheehan, P.W. (1981). Electromyograph biofeedback as a relaxation technique: A critical appraisal and reassessment. *Psychological Bulletin, 90,* 21–42.

Raikkonen, K., Matthews K.A., Flory, J.D., Owens, J.F., & Gump, B.B. (1999). Effects of optimism, pessimism, and trait anxiety on ambulatory blood pressure and mood during everyday life. *Journal of Personality and Social Psychology, 76,* 104–113.

Raikkonen, K., Matthews, K.A., Flory, J.D., & Owens, J.F. (1999). Effects of hostility on ambulatory blood pressure and mood during daily living in healthy adults. *Health Psychology, 18,* 44–53.

Randi, J. (1980). *Flim-flam!* New York: Lippincott.

Rapaport, D. (1967). On the psychoanalytic theory of thinking. In M.M. Gill (Ed.), *The collected papers of David Rapaport.* New York: Basic Books.

Rasmussen, K.G. (1984). Nonverbal behavior, verbal behavior, resume credentials, and selection interview outcomes. *Journal of Applied Psychology, 69,* 551–556.

Ratner, N.B. (1993). Learning to speak. *Science, 262,* 260.

Raven, P.H., & Johnson, G.B. (1999). *Biology* (5th ed.). New York: McGraw-Hill.

Ray, O.S., & Ksir, C. (1999). *Drugs, society, and human behavior* (8th ed.). New York: McGraw-Hill.

Rebec, G.V. (1996, June). *Neurochemical and behavioral insights into mechanisms of action of stimulant drugs.* Paper presented at the meeting of the American Psychological Society, San Francisco.

Redd, W.H. (1995). Behavioral research in cancer as a model for health psychology. *Health Psychology, 14,* 99–100.

Reece, B.L., & Brandt, R. (1990). *Effective human relations in organizations* (4th ed.). Boston: Houghton Mifflin.

Reed, S. (2000). Problem solving. In A. Kazdin (Ed.), *Encyclopedia of psychology.* Washington, DC, & New York: American Psychological Association and Oxford U. Press.

Reinisch, J.M. (1990). *The Kinsey Institute new report on sex: What you must know to be sexually literate.* New York: St. Martin's Press.

Rescorla, R.A. (1966). Predictability and number of pairings in Pavlovian fear conditioning. *Psychonomic Science, 4,* 383–384.

Rescorla, R.A. (1988). Pavlovian conditioning: It's not what you think it is. *American Psychologist, 43,* 151–160.

Rescorla, R.A. (1996). Spontaneous recovery after training with multiple outcomes. *Animal Learning & Behavior, 24,* 11–18.

Restak, R.M. (1988). *The mind.* New York: Bantam.

Revitch, E., & Schlesinger, L.B. (1978). Murder: Evaluation, classification, and prediction. In I.L. Kutash, S.B. Kutash, & O.B. Schlesinger (Eds.), *Violence.* San Francisco: Jossey-Bass.

Riggio, R.E. (1986). Assessment of basic social skills. *Journal of Personality and Social Psychology, 51,* 649–660.

Rinkenauer, G., Mattes, S., & Ulrich, R. (1999). The surface-weight illusion. *Perception & Psychophysics, 61,* 23–30.

Roback, H.W., Barton, D., Castelnuovo-Tedesco, P., Gay, V., Havens, L., & Nash, J. (1999). A symposium on psychotherapy in the age of managed care. *American Journal of Psychotherapy, 53,* 1–16.

Roberts, D., Anderson, B.L., & Lubaroff, A. (1994). *Stress and immunity at cancer diagnosis.* Unpublished manuscript, Dept. of Psychology, Ohio State University, Columbus.

Robins, L. & Regier, D. (Eds.). (1991). *Psychiatric disorders in America.* New York: Free Press.

Rodin, J. (1984, December). Interview: A sense of control. *Psychology Today,* pp. 38–45.

Rodrigues, M.S., & Cohen, S. (1998). Social support. In H.S. Friedman (Ed.), *Encyclopedia of mental health* (Vol. 3). San Diego: Academic Press.

Roehrs, T., & Roth, T. (1998). Reported in Maas, J. (1998). *Power sleep.* New York: Villard, p. 44.

Roesch, R.M. (2000). Forensic psychology. In A. Kazdin (Ed.), *Encyclopedia of psychology.* Washington, DC, & New York: American Psychological Association and Oxford U. Press.

Roffwarg, H.P., Muzio, J.N., & Dement, W.C. (1966). Ontogenetic development of human sleep-dream cycle. *Science, 152,* 604–609.

Rogers, C.R. (1961). *On becoming a person.* Boston: Houghton Mifflin.

Rogers, C.R. (1974). In retrospect: Forty-six years. *American Psychologist, 29,* 115–123.

Rogers, C.R. (1980). *A way of being.* Boston: Houghton Mifflin.

Rogoff, B. (1990). *Apprenticeship in thinking.* New York: Oxford University Press.

Rogoff, B. (1998). Cognition as a collaborative process. In W. Damon (Ed.), *Handbook of child psychology* (5th ed., Vol. 2), New York: Wiley.

Rogosch, F.A., Cicchetti, D., Shields, A., & Toth, S.L. (1995). Parenting dysfunction in child maltreatment. In M.H. Bornstein (Ed.), *Handbook of parenting* (Vol. 4). Hillsdale, NJ: Erlbaum.

Rosch, E. (1973). On the internal structure of perceptual and semantic categories. In T.E. Mooer (Ed.), *Cognition and the acquisition of language.* San Diego: Academic Press.

Rose, S. (Ed.). (1999). *From brains to consciousness?* Princeton, NJ: Princeton University Press.

Rosen, K.S., & Burke, P.B. (1999). Multiple attachment relationships within families. *Developmental Psychology, 35,* 436–444.

Rosenfeld, A.H. (1985, June). Depression: Dispelling despair. *Psychology Today.* pp. 28–34.

Rosenheck, R., & others (1999). Impact of Clozapine on negative symptoms and on the deficit syndrome in refractory schizophrenia. *The American Journal of Psychiatry, 156,* 88–96.

Rosenthal, R. (1966). *Experimenter effects in behavioral research.* New York: Appleton-Century-Crofts.

Rosenthal, R. (1994). Interpersonal expectancy effects: A 30-year-perspective. *Current Dimensions in Psychological Science, 3,* 176–179.

Rosenthal, R. (2000). Expectancy effects. In A. Kazdin (Ed.), *Encyclopedia of psychology.* Washington, DC, & New York: American Psychological Association and Oxford U. Press.

Rosenthal, R., & Jacobsen, L. (1968). *Pygmalion in the classroom.* Fort Worth: Harcourt Brace.

Rosenzweig, M. (1969). Effects of heredity and environment on brain chemistry, brain anatomy, and learning ability in the rat. In M. Monosevitz, G. Lindzey, & D.D. Theissen (Eds.), *Behavioral genetics.* New York: Appleton-Century-Crofts.

Rosenzweig, M.R. (2000). Biological psychology. In A. Kazdin (Ed.), *Encyclopedia of psychology.* Washington, DC, & New York: American Psychological Association and Oxford U. Press.

Rosnow, R.L. (1995). Teaching research ethics through role-playing and discussion. In M.E. Ware & D.E. Johnson (Eds.), *Demonstrations and activities in teaching psychology* (Vol. 1). Mahwah, NJ: Erlbaum.

Rosnow, R.L., & Rosenthal, R. (1996). *Beginning behavioral research* (2nd ed.). Upper Saddle River, NJ: Prentice-Hall.

Rothbart, M.K., & Bates, J.E. (1988). Temperament. In W. Damon (Ed.), *Handbook of child psychology* (5th ed., Vol. 3). New York: Wiley.

Rubin, D.C., & Kozin, M. (1984). Vivid memories. *Cognition, 16,* 81–95.

Rumbaugh, D. (2000). Nonhuman intelligence. In A. Kazdin (Ed.), *Encyclopedia of psychology.* Washington, DC, & New York: American Psychological Association and Oxford U. Press.

Runco, M. (1999). Critical thinking. In M.A. Runco & S. Pritzker (Eds.), *Encyclopedia of creativity.* San Diego: Academic Press.

Runko, M.A., & Pritzker, S. (Eds.) (1999). *Encyclopedia of creativity.* San Diego: Academic Press.

Rushton, J.P., Fulker, D.W., Neal, M.C., Nias, D.K.B., & Eysenck, H.J. (1986). Altruism and aggression: The heritability of individual differences. *Journal of Personality and Social Psychology, 50,* 1192–1198.

Russell, D.W. (1996). UCLA Loneliness Scale (Version 3): Reliability, validity, and factor structure. *Journal of Personality, Assessment, 66,* 20–43.

Russell, J.A. (1999). Emotion communicates. *Contemporary Psychology, 44,* 26–27.

Russo, N.F. (1990). Overview: Forging research priorities for women's health. *American Psychologist, 45,* 373–386.

Ryan-Finn, K.D., Cause, A.M., & Grove, K. (1995, March). *Children and adolescents of color: Where are you? Selection, recruitment, and retention in developmental research.* Paper presented at the meeting of the Society for Research in Child Development, Indianapolis.

Rybash, J.M., Roodin, P.A., & Hoyer, W.J. (1999). *Adult development and aging* (4th ed.). New York: McGraw-Hill.

Ryff, C.D., & Singer, B. (1998). Middle age and well-being. In H.S. Friedman (Ed.), *Encyclopedia of mental health* (Vol. 2). San Diego: Academic Press.

Rymer, R. (1993). *Genie.* New York: HarperCollins.

S

Sabini, J. (1995). *Social psychology* (2nd ed.). New York: Norton.

Sacks, O. (1985). *The man who mistook his wife for a hat.* New York: Summit Books.

Sagan, C. (1980). *Cosmos.* New York: Random House.

Sales, P. (1999). *Alcohol abuse.* New York: Ixia Publications.

Salovey, P., Rotman, A.J., & Rodin, J. (1998). Health behavior. In D.T. Gilbert, S.T. Fiske, & G. Lindzey (Eds.), *The handbook of social psychology* (Vol. 2). New York: McGraw-Hill.

Salthouse, T. (1994). The nature of influence of speed on adult differences in cognition. *Developmental Psychology, 30,* 240–259.

Salthouse, T. (2000). Adulthood and aging: Cognitive processes and development. In A. Kazdin (Ed.), *Encyclopedia of psychology.* Washington, DC, & New York: American Psychological Association and Oxford U. Press.

Sanderson, W.C. (1995, March). Which therapies are proven effective? *APA Monitor,* p. 4.

Sandler, D.P., Comstock, G.W., Helsing, K.J., & Shore, D.L. (1989). Deaths from all causes in nonsmokers who lived with smokers. *American Journal of Public Health, 79,* 163–167.

Sanson, A., & Rothbart, M.K. (1995). Child temperament and parenting. In M.H. Bornstein (Ed.), *Handbook of parenting* (Vol. 4). Hillsdale, NJ: Erlbaum.

Santrock, J.W. (1998). *Adolescence* (7th ed.). New York: McGraw-Hill.

Santrock, J.W. (1999). *Life-span development* (7th ed.). New York: McGraw-Hill.

Santrock, J.W., & Halonen, J.S. (1999). *Your guide to college success.* Belmont, CA: Wadsworth.

Sapon-Shevin, M. (1999). *Because we can change the world.* Boston: Allyn & Bacon.

Saravi, R.D. (1993). The right hemisphere: An esoteric closet? *Skeptical Inquirer, 17,* 380–387.

Sarbin, T.R., & Keen, E. (1998). Classifying mental disorders. In H.S. Friedman (Ed.), *Encyclopedia of mental health* (Vol. 1). San Diego: Academic Press.

Sargent, C. (1987). Skeptical fairytales from Bristol. *Journal of the Society for Psychical Research, 54,* 166–185.

Saucier, G., & Ostendorf, F. (1999). Hierarchical subcomponents of the big five personality factors: A cross-language replication. *Journal of Personality and Social Psychology, 76,* 613–627.

Savage-Rumbaugh, E.S., Murphy, J., Sevcik, R.A., Brakke, K.E., Williams, S.L., & Rumbaugh, D.M. (1993). Language comprehension in ape and child. *Monographs of the Society for Research in Child Development,* Serial No. 233 (Vol. 58, Nos. 3–4).

Savage-Rumbaugh, S., Shanker, S., & Taylor, T. (1998). *Apes, language, and mind.* New York: Oxford U. Press.

Sax, G. (1997). *Principles of educational and psychology measurement* (4th ed.). Belmont, CA: Wadsworth.

Sax, L.J., Astin, A.W., Korn, W.S., & Manoney, K.M. (1995). *The American college freshman: National norms for fall, 1995.* Los Angeles: UCLA, Higher Education Research Institute.

Sax, L.J., Astin, A.W., Korn, W.S., & Mahoney, K. M. (1998). *The American freshman: National norms for fall 1998.* Los Angeles: American Council on Education, UCLA.

Saxe, L. (1998, June). Commentary. *APA Monitor,* p. 30.

Saxe, L., Dougherty, D., & Cross, T. (1985). The validity of polygraph testing. *American Psychologist, 40,* 355–366.

Scarr, S. (1984, May). Interview. *Psychology Today,* pp. 59–63.

Scarr, S., & Weinberg, R.A. (1980). Calling all camps! The war is over. *American Sociological Review, 45,* 859–865.

Scarr, S., & Weinberg, R.A. (1983). The Minnesota adoption studies: Genetic differences and malleability. *Child Development, 54,* 182–203.

Schachter, S., & Singer, J.E. (1962). Cognitive, social, and physiological determinants of emotional state. *Psychological Review, 69,* 379–399.

Schacter, D.L. (1995). Memory distortion. In D.L. Schacter, J.T. Coyle, G.D. Gisbach, M.M. Mesulam, & L.E. Sullivan (Eds.), *Memory distortion.* Cambridge, MA: Harvard University Press.

Schacter, D.L. (1996). *Searching for memory.* New York: Basic Books.

Schacter, D.L. (1999). Consciousness. In M.S. Gazzaniga (Ed.), *The new cognitive neurosciences* (2nd ed.). Cambridge, MA: MIT Press.

Schacter, D.L. (1999). The seven sins of memory: Insights from psychology and cognitive neuroscience. *American Psychologist, 54,* 182–203.

Schacter, D.L. (2000). Memory systems. In A. Kazdin (Ed.), *Encyclopedia of psychology.* Wash-ington, DC, & New York: American Psychological Association and Oxford U. Press.

Schacter, S. (1971). Some extraordinary facts about obese humans and rats. *American Psychologist, 26,* 129–144.

Schafer, G. (1999). Early speech perception and word learning. In M. Barrett (Ed.), *The development of language.* Philadelphia: Psychology Press.

Schaffer, H.R., & Emerson, P.E. (1964). The development of social attachments in infancy. *Monographs of the Society for Research in Child Development, 29,* (3, Serial No. 94).

Schank, R., & Abelson, R. (1977). *Scripts, plans, goals, and understanding.* Mahwah, NJ: Erlbaum.

Schiffman, J., & Walker, E. (1998). Schizophrenia. In H.S. Friedman (Ed.), *Encyclopedia of mental health* (Vol. 2). San Diego: Academic Press.

Schliefer, S.J. (1999). Psychoneuroimmunology. *Psychiatry Research, 85,* 3–6.

Schneider, B.A., Moraglia, G., & Speranza, F. (in press). Binocular vision enhances phase discrimination by filtering the background. *Perception & Psychophysics.*

Schneider, F.R., Johnson, J., Hornig, C.D., Olibowitz, M.R., & Weissman, M.M. (1992). Social phobia: Comorbidity and morbidity in an epidemiologic sample. *Archives of General Psychiatry, 49,* 278–288.

Scholnick, E.K. (1999). Piaget's legacy: Heirs to the house that Jean built. In E.K. Scholnick, K. Nelson, S.A. Gelman, & Miller, P.H. (Eds.), *Conceptual development: Piaget's legacy.* Mahwah, NJ: Erlbaum.

Scholnick, E.K., Nelson, K., Gelman, S.A., & Miller, P.H. (Eds.). (1999). *Conceptual development: Piaget's legacy.* Mahwah, NJ: Erlbaum.

Schultheiss, O.C., & Brunstein, J.C. (1999). Goal imagery: Bridging the gap between implicit motives and explicit goals. *Journal of Personality, 67,* 1–38.

Schunk, D.H. (1996). *Learning theories* (2nd ed.). Upper Saddle River, NJ: Prentice-Hall.

Schwartz, T. (1999). *Kids and guns.* New York: Franklin Watts.

Sedikides, C., Campbell, W.K., Reeder, G.D., & Elliot, A.J. (1998). The self-serving bias in relational context. *Journal of Personality and Social Psychology, 74,* 378–386.

Seffge-Krenke, I. (1995). *Stress, coping, and relationships in adolescence.* Mahwah, NJ: Erlbaum.

Seidemann, E., Meilijson, I., Abeles, M., Bergman, H., & Vaadia, E. (1996). Simultaneously recorded single units in the frontal cortex go through sequences of discrete and stable states in monkeys performing a delayed localization task. *The Journal of Neuroscience, 16,* 752–768.

Seidman, D.F., Rosecan, J., & Role, L. (1999). Biological and clinical perspectives on nicotine addiction. In D. F. Seidman & L.S. Covey (Eds.), *Helping the hard-core smoker.* Mahwah, NJ: Erlbaum.

Seidman, E., & French, S.E. (1998). Community mental health. In H.S. Friedman (Ed.), *Encyclopedia of mental health* (Vol. 1). San Diego: Academic Press.

Seligman, M.E.P. (1970). On the generality of the laws of learning. *Psychological Review, 77,* 406–418.

Seligman, M.E.P. (1975). *Helplessness: On depression, development, and death.* San Francisco: W.H. Freeman.

Seligman, M.E.P. (1990). *Learned optimism.* New York: Knopf.

Seligman, M.E.P. (1993). *What you can change and what you can't.* New York: Knopf.

Seligman, M.E.P. Why is there so much depression today? In *The G. Stanley Hall Lecture Series.* Washington, DC: American Psychological Association.

Seligmen, M.E.P. (1994). *What you can change and what you can't.* New York: Knopf.

Seligman, M.E.P., & Rosenhan, D.L. (1998). *Abnormality.* New York: Norton.

Selye, H. (1974). *Stress without distress.* Philadelphia: W.B. Saunders.

Selye, H. (1983). The stress concept: Past, present, and future. In C.I. Cooper (Ed.), *Stress research.* New York: Wiley.

Serpell, R. (2000). Culture and intelligence. In A. Kazdin (Ed.), *Encyclopedia of psychology.* Washington, DC, & New York: American Psychological Association and Oxford U. Press.

Servaes, P., Vignerhoets, A., Vreugdenhil, G., Keuning, J.J., & Broekhuijsen, A.M. (1999). Inhibition of emotional expression in breast cancer patients. *Behavioral Medicine, 25,* 26–34.

Seto, M.C., & Barbaree, H.E. (1995). The role of alcohol in sexual aggression. *Clinical Psychology Review, 15,* 545–566.

Shanks, D.R. (1991). Categorization by a connectionist network. *Journal of Experimental Psychology: Learning, Memory, and Cognition, 17,* 433–443.

Shaver, P. (1986, August). *Being lonely, falling in love: Perspectives from attachment theory.* Paper presented at the meeting of the American Psychological Association, Washington, DC.

Shelton, R.C. (2000). Antidepressants. In A. Kazdin (Ed.), *Encyclopedia of psychology.* Washington, DC, & New York: American Psychological Association and Oxford U. Press.

Shepard, R.N. (1967). Recognition memory for words, sentences, and pictures. *Journal of Verbal Learning and Verbal Behavior, 6,* 156–163.

Shepard, R.N. (1996, August). *The eye's mind and the mind's eye.* Paper presented at the meeting of the American Psychological Association, Toronto.

Sher, K.J. (1991). *Children of alcoholics: A critical appraisal of theory and research.* Chicago: University of Chicago Press.

Sher, K.J. (1993). Children of alcoholics and the intergenerational transmission of alcoholism: A biopsychological perspective. In J.S. Baer, G.A. Marlatt, & R.J. McMahon (Eds.), *Addicitve behaviors across the life span.* Newbury Park, CA: Sage.

Sher, K.J., & Trull, J.J. (1994). Personality and disinhibitory psychopathology: Alcoholism and antisocial personality disorder. *Journal of Abnormal Psychology, 103,* 92–102.

Sherif, M., Harvey, O.J., White, B.J., Hood, W.R., & Sherif, C.W. (1961). *Intergroup cooperation and competition: The Robbers Cave experiment.* Norman: University of Oklahoma Press.

Sherwood, A., Light, K.C., & Blumenthal, J.A. (1989). Effects of aerobic exercise training on hemodynamic responses during psychosocial stress in normotensive and borderline hypertensive

Type A men: A preliminary report. *Psychosomatic Medicine, 51,* 123–136.

Shields, S.A. (1991). Gender in the psychology of emotion. In K.T. Strongman (Ed.), *International Review of Studies of Emotion* (Vol. 1). New York: Wiley.

Shier, D., Butler, J., & Lewis, R. (1999). *Hole's human anatomy and physiology.* New York: McGraw-Hill.

Shier, D., Butler, J., & Lewis, R. (1999). *Human anatomy and physiology* (8th ed.). New York: McGraw-Hill.

Shneidman, E.S. (1971). Suicide among the gifted. *Suicide and Life-Threatening Behavior, 1,* 23–45.

Shotland, R.L. (1985, June). When bystanders just stand by. *Psychology Today.* pp. 50–55.

Showers, C. (1986). *The motivational consequences of negative thinking.* Paper presented at the meeting of the American Psychological Association, Washington, DC.

Sieber, J.E. (2000). Ethics: Ethics in research. In A. Kazdin (Ed.), *Encyclopedia of psychology.* Washington, DC, & New York: American Psychological Association and Oxford U. Press.

Siegfried, T. (1994, August 1). Ability to learn while asleep not just in a scientist's dreams. *Dallas Morning News,* p. 7D.

Siegler, R.S. (1998). *Children's thinking* (3rd ed.). Upper Saddle River, NJ: Erlbaum.

Siffre, M. (1975). Six months alone in a cave. *National Geographic, 147,* 426–435.

Silverman, N.N., & Corsini, R.J. (1984). Is it true what they say about Adler's individual psychology? *Teaching of Psychology, 11,* 188–189.

Simon, H.A. (1969). *The sciences of the artificial.* Cambridge, MA: MIT Press.

Simon, H.A. (1996). Putting the story together. *Contemporary Psychology, 41,* 12–14.

Simpson, J.A. (1995). Self-monitoring and commitment to dating relationships: A classroom demonstration. In M.E. Ware & D.E. Johnson (Eds.), *Demonstrations and activities in teaching of introductory psychology.* Mahwah, NJ: Erlbaum.

Singer, D.G., & Singer, J.L. (1998). Television viewing. In H.S. Friedman (Ed.), *Encyclopedia of mental health* (Vol. 3). San Diego: Academic Press.

Skinner, B.F. (1938). *The behavior of organisms: An experimental analysis.* New York: Appelton-Century-Crofts.

Skinner, B.F. (1948). *Walden Two.* New York: Macmillan.

Skinner, B.F. (1957). *Verbal behavior.* New York: Appleton-Century-Crofts.

Skinner, E.A., Wellborn, J.G., & Connell, J.P. (1990). What it takes to do well in school and whether I've got it. *Journal of Educational Psychology, 82,* 22–32.

Slavin, R. (1989). Cooperative learning and student achievement. In R. Slavin (Ed.), *School and classroom organization.* Mahwah, NJ: Erlbaum.

Sloan, D.M., & Mizes, J.S. (1999). Foundations of behavior therapy in the contemporary health-care context. *Clinical Psychology Review, 19,* 255–274.

Sloan, P., Arsenault, L., Hilsenroth, M., & Harvill, L. (1996). Rorschach measures of post-traumatic stress in Persian Gulf War veterans: A three-year follow-up study. *Journal of Personality Assessment, 66,* 54–64.

Slobin, D. (1972, July). Children and language: They learn the same way around the world. *Psychology Today,* 71–76.

Slobogin, C. (1996). A jurisprudence of dangerousness as a criterion in the criminal process. In B.D. Sales & D.W. Shuman (Eds.), *Law, mental health, and mental disorder.* Pacific Grove, CA: Brooks/Cole.

Smith, J., & Baltes, P.B. (1999). Life-span perspectives on development. In M.H. Bornstein & M.E. Lamb (Eds.), *Developmental psychology: An advanced textbook* (4th ed.). Mahwah, NJ: Erlbaum.

Smith, K.H., & Rogers, M. (1994). Effectiveness of subliminal messages in television commercials. *Journal of Applied Psychology, 79,* 866–874.

Smith, M.L., Glass, G.N., & Miller, R.L. (1980). *The benefit of psychotherapy.* Baltimore: Johns Hopkins University Press.

Smock, T.K. (1999). *Physiological psychology: A neuroscience approach.* Upper Saddle River, NJ: Prentice-Hall.

Smyth, M.M., Collins, A.F., Morris, P.E., & Levy, P. (1994). *Cognition in action* (2nd ed.). Hove, Great Britain: Erlbaum.

Snarey, J. (1998). Fathers. In H.S. Friedman (Ed.), *Encyclopedia of mental health* (Vol. 2). San Diego: Academic Press.

Snow, C. (1999). Social perspectives on the emergence of language. In B. MacWhinney (Ed.), *The emergence of language.* Mahwah, NJ: Erlbaum.

Snow, C.E. (1998). Social perspectives on the emergence of language. In B. MacWhinney (Ed.), *The emergence of language.* Mahwah, NJ: Erlbaum.

Snyder, D.K. (2000). Couples therapy. In A. Kazdin (Ed.), *Encyclopedia of psychology.* Washington, DC, & New York: American Psychological Association and Oxford U. Press.

Snyder, M., & Stukas, A.A. (1999). Interpersonal processes: The interplay of cognitive, motivational, and behavioral activities in social interaction. Palo Alto: Annual Reviews, Inc.

Sobell, M.B., & Sobell, M. (1993). Treatment for problem drinkers: A public health priority. In J.S. Baer, G.A. Marlatt, & R.J. McMahon (Eds.), *Addictve behaviors across the life span.* Newbury Park, CA: Sage.

Sober, E., & Wilson, D.S. (1998). *Unto others: The evolution of unselfish behavior.* Cambridge, MA: Harvard University Press.

Solomon, B., Powell, K., & Gardner, H. (1999). Multiple intelligences. In M.A. Runco & S. Pritzker (Eds.), *Encyclopedia of creativity.* San Diego: Academic Press.

Solso, R.L. (2000). Cognitive psychology: A history of the field. In A. Kazdin (Ed.), *Encyclopedia of psychology.* Washington, DC, & New York: American Psychological Association and Oxford U. Press.

Spanos, N.P. (1996). *Multiple identities and false memories: A social cognitive perspective.* Washington, DC: American Psychological Association.

Spearman, C.E. (1927). *The abilities of man.* New York: Macmillan.

Spencer, M.B. (2000). Ethnocentrism. In A. Kazdin (Ed.), *Encyclopedia of psychology.* Washington, DC, & New York: American Psychological Association and Oxford U. Press.

Sperling, G. (1960). The information available in brief presentations. *Psychological Monographs, 74* (Whole No. 11).

Sperry, R.W. (1964). The great cerebral commissure. *Scientific American, 210,* 42–52.

Sperry, R.W. (1968). Hemisphere deconnection and unity in conscious awareness. *American Psychologist, 23,* 723–733.

Sperry, R.W. (1974). Lateral specialization in surgically separated hemispheres. In F.O. Schmitt & F.G. Worden (Eds.), *The neurosciences: Third study program.* Cambridge, MA: MIT Press.

Squire, L. (1990, June). *Memory and brain systems.* Paper presented at the meeting of the American Psychological Society, Dallas.

St. Clair, M. (1996). *Object relations and self psychology.* Pacific Grove, CA: Brooks/Cole.

Stanley, M.A., & Turner, S.M. (1995). Current status of pharmacological and behavioral treatment of obsessive-compulsive disorder. *Behavior Therapy, 26,* 163–177.

Stanovich, K. (1998). *How to think straight about psychology* (5th ed.). New York: Longman.

Stanovich, K.E. (1999). *Who is rational? Individual differences in reasoning.* Mahwah, NJ: Erlbaum.

Staples, S.L. (1996). Human response to environmental noise. *American Psychologist, 51,* 143–150.

Staub, E. (1996). Cultural-societal roots of violence. *American Psychologist, 51,* 117–132.

Staudinger, U.M. (1996). Psychologische prodktivitat und selbstentfaltung im alter. In M.M. Baltes & L. Montada (Eds.), *Produktives leben im alter.* Berlin: Campus.

Steele, C.M. (1996, August). *A burden of suspicion: The role of stereotypes in shaping intellectual identity.* Paper presented at the meeting of the American Psychological Association, Toronto.

Stefanick, M.L. (1999). Estrogen, progesterons, and cardiovascular risk. *Journal of Reproductive Medicine, 44,* 221–226.

Stengel, R. (1996, April 22). Fly till I die. *Time,* pp. 34–40.

Sternberg, E.M., & Gold, P.W. (1996). The mind-body interaction in disease. *Mysteries of the mind.* New York: Scientific American.

Sternberg, R.A. (Ed.) (1997). *Career paths in psychology.* Washington, DC: American Psychological Association.

Sternberg, R.J. (1986). *Intelligence applied.* Fort Worth: Harcourt Brace.

Sternberg, R.J. (1988). *The triangle of love.* New York: Basic Books.

Sternberg, R.J. (1994, December). Commentary. *APA Monitor,* p. 22.

Sternberg, R.J. (1997). *Successful intelligence.* New York: Simon & Schuster.

Sternberg, R.J. (1999). Intelligence. In M.A. Runco & S. Pritzker (Eds.), *Encyclopedia of creativity.* San Diego: Academic Press.

Sternberg, R.J., & Grigorenko, E. (Eds.). (1997). *Intelligence, heredity, and environment.* New York: Cambridge University Press.

Sternberg, R.J., & Spear-Swirling, P. (1996). Washington, DC: American Psychological Association.

Steuer, F.B., Applefield, J.M., & Smith, R. (1971). Televised aggression and interpersonal aggression of preschool children. *Journal of Experimental Child Psychology, 11,* 442–447.

Stoler, D.R., & Hill, B.A. (1998). *Coping with mild brain injury.* New York: Avery.

Stoner, J. (1961). *A comparison of individual and group decisions, including risk.* Unpublished master's thesis, School of Industrial Management, MIT.

Strauss, M.S., Sugarman, D.B., & Giles-Sims, J. (1997). Spanking by parents and subsequent antisocial behavior in children. *Archives of Pediatric and Adolescent Medicine, 151,* 761–767.

Strean, H.S. (1996). Resistance viewed from different perspectives. *American Journal of Psychotherapy, 50,* 29–31.

Streissguth, A. (1997). *Fetal alcohol syndrome: A guide for families and communities.* Baltimore, Paul H. Brookes.

Stricker, E.M. (2000). Motivation: Physiological aspects. In A. Kazdin (Ed.), *Encyclopedia of psychology.* Washington, DC, & New York: American Psychological Association and Oxford U. Press.

Striefel, S. (1998). *How to teach through modeling and imitation.* Austin, TX: ProEd.

Strupp, H.H. (1989). Psychotherapy. *American Psychologist, 44,* 717–724.

Strupp, H.H. (1995). The psychotherapist's skills revised. *Clinical Psychology: Science and Practice, 2,* 70–74.

Sue, D.W., Ivey, A., & Peterson, P. (1996). *A theory of multicultural counseling and therapy.* Pacific Grove, CA: Brooks/Cole.

Sue, S. (1977). Community mental health services to minority groups: Some optimism, some pessimism. *American Psychologist, 32,* 616–624.

Sue, S. (1997, August). *In search of cultural competence in psychotherapy and counseling.* Paper presented at the meeting of the American Psychological Association, Chicago.

Suinn, R.M. (1984). *Fundamentals of abnormal psychology.* Chicago: Nelson-Hall.

Sullivan, H.S. (1953). *The interpersonal theory of psychiatry.* New York: W.W. Norton.

Sullivan, K.T., & Christensen, A. (1998). In H.S. Friedman (Ed.), *Encyclopedia of mental health* (Vol. 1). San Diego: Academic Press.

Suls, J., & Swain, A. (1998). Type A–Type B personalities. In H.S. Friedman (Ed.), *Encyclopedia of mental health* (Vol. 3). San Diego: Academic Press.

Summers, F.L. (1999). *Transcending the self.* Hillsdale, NJ: The Analytic Press.

Susman, E.J., Worrall, B.K., Murowchick, E., Frobose, C.A., & Schwab, J.E. (1996). Experience and neuroendocrine parameters of development: Aggressive behaviors and competencies. In D.M. Stoff & R.B. Cairns (Eds.), *Aggression and violence.* Mahwah, NJ: Erlbaum.

Sutker, P.B., & Allain, A.N. (1993). Behavior and personality assessment in men labeled adaptive sociopaths. *Journal of Behavioral Assessment, 5,* 65–79.

Swann, W.B., De La Ronde, C., & Hixon, J.G. (1994). Authenticity and positive strivings in marriage and courtship. *Journal of Personality and Social Psychology, 66,* 857–869.

Swanson, J. (Ed.)(1999). *Sleep disorders sourcebook.* New York: Omnigraphics, Inc.

Tager-Flusberg, H. (1999). Language development in atypical children. In M. Barrett (Ed.), *The development of language.* Philadelphia: Psychology Press.

Tager-Flusberg, H. (Ed.). (1994). *Constraints on language acquisition.* Mahwah, NJ: Erlbaum.

Tajfel, H. (1978). The achievement of group differentiation. In H. Tajfel (Ed.), *Differentiation between social groups.* London: Academic Press.

Tallal, P. (2000). Language and brain systems. In A. Kazdin (Ed.), *Encyclopedia of psychology.* Washington, DC, & New York: American Psychological Association and Oxford U. Press.

Tamarin, R.H. (1999). *Principles of genetics* (6th ed.). New York: McGraw-Hill.

Tannen, D. (1990). *You just don't understand!* New York: Ballantine.

Task force on diversity issues. (1998, January). Talking about prejudice can be a powerful teaching tool. *APA Monitor,* p. 32.

Tavris, C. (1989). *Anger: The misunderstood emotion* (2nd ed.). New York: Touchstone.

Tavris, C., & Wade, C. (1984). The longest war: Sex differences in perspective (2nd ed.). Fort Worth: Harcourt Brace.

Taylor, S.E. (1998). Positive illusions. In H.S. Friedman (Ed.), *Encyclopedia of mental health* (Vol. 3). San Diego: Academic Press.

Taylor, S.E. (1999). *Health psychology* (4th ed.). New York: McGraw-Hill.

Taylor, S.E., & Brown, J.D. (1994). Positive illusions and well-being revisited: Separating fact from fiction. *Psychological Bulletin, 116,* 21–27.

Taylor, S.E., Peplau, L.A., & Sears, D.O. (1997). *Social psychology* (8th ed.). Upper Saddle River, NJ: Prentice-Hall.

Teachman, J.D., & Polonko, K.A. (1990). Cohabitation and marital stability in the United States. *Social Forces, 69,* 207–220.

Teasdale, J.D., Taylor, M.J., Cooper, Z., Hayhurst, H., & Paykel, E.S. (1995). Depressive thinking. *Journal of Abnormal Psychology, 104,* 500–507.

Temoshok, L. (1998). HIV/AIDS. In H.S. Friedman (Ed.), *Encyclopedia of mental health* (Vol. 2). San Diego: Academic Press.

Terman, L. (1925). *Genetic studies of genius* (Vol. 1). Stanford, CA: Stanford University Press.

Terr, L.C. (1988). What happens to early memories of trauma? *Journal of the American Academy of Child and Adolescent Psychiatry, 27,* 96–104.

Thalman, R.H. (1999). *Basic concepts in neuroscience.* New York: McGraw-Hill.

Thayer, J.F., Rossy, I., Sollers, J., Friedman, B. H., & Allen, M.T. (1996, March). *Relationships among heart period variability and cardiodynamic measures vary as a function of fitness.* Paper presented at the meeting of the American Psychosomatic Society, Williamsburg, VA.

Thigpen, C.H., & Cleckley, H.M. (1957). *Three faces of Eve.* New York: McGraw-Hill.

Thoma, S.J., & Rest, J.R. (1999). The relationship between moral decision making and patterns of consolidation and transition in moral judgment development. *Developmental Psychology, 35,* 323–334.

Thomas, C.B. (1983). *Stress and coping.* Unpublished manuscript, Johns Hopkins University, Baltimore.

Thompson, C.P., Hermann, D.J., Read, D., Bruce, D., Payne, D.G., & Toglia, M.P. (1998). *Autobiographical memory.* Mahwah, NJ: Erlbaum.

Thompson, C.P., Hermann, D.J., Read, D., Bruce, D., Payne, D.G., & Toglia, M.P. (1998). *Eyewitness memory.* Mahwah, NJ: Erlbaum.

Thompson, R. (1999). The individual child: Temperament, emotion, self, and personality. In M.H. Bornstein & M.E. Lamb (Eds.), *Developmental psychology: An advanced textbook* (4th ed.). Mahwah, NJ: Erlbaum.

Thompson, R.A. (1991). Emotional regulation and emotional development. *Educational Psychology Review, 3,* 269–307.

Thompson, R.A. (1998). Early social development. In W. Damon (Ed.), *Handbook of child psychology* (5th ed., Vol. 3). New York: Wiley.

Thompson, R.A. (2000). Memory: brain systems. In A. Kazdin (Ed.), *Encyclopedia of psychology.* Washington, DC, & New York: American Psychological Association and Oxford U. Press.

Thompson, R.F. (2000). Memory: Brain systems. In A. Kazdin (Ed.), *Encyclopedia of psychology.* Washington, DC, & New York: American Psychological Association and Oxford U. Press.

Thorpe, G.L. (1998). Agoraphobia. In H.S. Friedman (Ed.), *Encyclopedia of mental health* (Vol. 1). San Diego: Academic Press.

Thorton, A., & Camburn, D. (1989). Religious participation and sexual behavior and attitudes. *Journal of Marriage and the Family, 49,* 117–128.

Thurstone, L.L. (1938). *Primary mental abilities.* Chicago: University of Chicago Press.

Tinbergen, N. (1969). *The study of instinct.* New York: Oxford University Press.

Toga, A.W. (Ed.)(1998). *Brain warping.* San Diego: Academic Press.

Toga, A.W., & Mazziota, J.C. (Eds.). *Brain mapping.* New York: Morgan Kaufman.

Tolan, P., Miller, L., & Thomas, P. (1988). Perception and experience of two types of social stress and self-image among adolescents. *Journal of Youth and Adolescence, 17,* 147–163.

Tolman, E.C. (1932). *Purposive behavior in animals and man.* New York: Appleton-Century-Crofts.

Tolman, E.C. (1948). Cognitive maps in rats and men. *Psychological Review, 55,* 189–208.

Tomlinson-Keasey, C., Warren, L.W., & Elliott, J.F. (1986). Suicide among gifted women. *Journal of Abnormal Psychology, 95,* 123–130.

Toth, S.K., Connor, P.D., & Streissguth, A.P. (1999, April). *Psychiatric/behavioral and learning and memory problems in young adults with fetal alcohol syndrome and fetal alcohol effects.* Paper presented at the meeting of the Society for Research in Child Development, Albuquerque.

Tracey, T.J., Sherry, P., & Albright, J.M. (1999). The interpersonal process of cognitive-behavioral therapy. *Journal of Counseling Psychology, 46,* 80–91.

Tracy, K. (Ed.). (in press). Language and social interaction at the turn of the century. *Research on Language and Social Interaction.*

Tremblay, R.E., & Schaal, B. (1995, March). *Testosterone levels of physically active boys.* Paper presented at the meeting of the Society for Research in Child Development, Indianapolis.

Triandis, H.C. (1994). *Culture and social behavior.* New York: McGraw-Hill.

Triandis, H.C. (2000). Cross-cultural psychology: A history of the field. In A. Kazdin (Ed.), *Encyclopedia of psychology.* Washington, DC, & New York: American Psychological Association and Oxford U. Press.

Triplett, N. (1898). The dynamogenic factors in peacemaking and competition. *American Journal of Psychology, 9,* 507–533.

Trivers, R. (1971). The evolution of reciprocal altruism. *Quarterly Review of Biology, 46,* 35–57.

Tulving, E. (1972). Episodic and semantic memory. In E. Tulving & W. Donaldson (Eds.), *Origins of memory.* San Diego: Academic Press.

Tulving, E. (1983). *Elements of episodic memory.* New York: Oxford University Press.

Tulving, E. (1989). Remembering and knowing the past. *American Scientist, 77,* 361–367.

Tulving, E. (2000). Memory: An overview. In A. Kazdin (Ed.), *Encyclopedia of psychology.* Washington, DC, & New York: American Psychological Association and Oxford U. Press.

Turnbull, C. (1972). *The mountain people.* New York: Simon & Schuster.

Tversky, A., & Fox, C.R. (1995). Weighing risk and uncertainty. *Psychological Review, 102,* 269–283.

Tyler, C. (1983). Sensory processing of binocular disparity. In C.M. Schor & K.J. Ciuffreda (Eds.), *Vergence eye movements.* Boston: Butterworth.

U

Udry, R., Billy, J., Morris, N., Groff, T., & Raj, M. (1985). Serum androgenic hormones motivate sexual behavior in adolescent boys. *Fertility and Sterility, 43,* 90–94.

United Nations. (1992). *1991 demographic yearbook.* New York: United Nations.

Ursano, R.J., & others (1999). Acute and chronic posttraumatic stress disorder in motor vehicle accident victims. *The American Journal of Psychiatry, 156,* 589–595.

V

Vadum, A.E., & Rankin, N.O. (1998). *Psychological research.* New York: McGraw-Hill.

Vaillant, G.E. (1977). *Adaptation to life.* Boston: Little, Brown.

Vaillant, G.E. (1983). *The natural history of alcoholism.* Cambridge, MA: Harvard University Press.

Vaillant, G.E. (1992). Is there a natural history of addiction? In C.P. O'Brien & J.H. Jaffe (Eds.), *Addictive states.* Cambridge, MA: Harvard University Press.

Vallone, R.P., Griffin, D.W., Lin, S., & Ross, L. (1990). Overconfident prediction of future actions and outcomes by self and others. *Journal of Personality and Social Psychology, 58,* 582–592.

Van Deventer, W. (1983, November). Graphoanalysis as a management tool. *United States Banker,* pp. 74–76.

Vedara, K., Schifitto, G., McDermott, M., and the Dana Consortium on Therapy for HIV Dementia and Related Disorders (1999). Disease progression in HIV-positive women with moderate to severe immunosuppression: The role of depression. *Behavioral Medicine, 25,* 53–61.

Vernoy, M.W. (1995). Demonstrating classical conditioning in introductory psychology: Needles do not always make balloons pop! In M.E. Ware & D.E. Johnson (Eds.), *Demonstrations and activities in teaching psychology* (Vol. 2). Mahwah, NJ: Erlbaum.

Vidal, J. (2000). Piaget, Jean. In A. Kazdin (Ed.), *Encyclopedia of psychology.* Washington, DC, & New York: American Psychological Association and Oxford U. Press.

Villani, S., & Sharfstein, S.S. (1999). Evaluating and treating violent adolescents in the managed care era. *The American Journal of Psychiatry, 156,* 458–464.

Vogt, T.M., Mullooly, J.P., Ernst, D., Pople, C.R., & Hollis, J.F. (1992). Social networks as predictors of ischemic heart disease, cancer, stroke, and hypertension. *Journal of Clinical Epidemiology, 45,* 659–666.

Vokey, J.R., & Read, J.D. (1985). Subliminal messages: Between the devil and the media. *American Psychologist, 40,* 1231–1239.

Volpe, E.P., & Rosenbaum, P.A. (2000). *Understanding evolution* (6th ed.). New York: McGraw-Hill.

Von Békésy, G. (1960). Vibratory patterns of the basilar membrane. In E.G. Wever (Ed.), *Experiments in hearing.* New York: McGraw-Hill.

Vygotsky, L.S. (1962). *Thought and language.* Cambridge, MA: MIT Press.

W

Wadden, T.A., Foser, G.D., Stunkard, A.J., & Conill, A.M. (1996). Effects of weight cycling on the resting energy expenditure and body composition of obese women. *Eating Disorders, 19,* 5–12.

Wahlsten, D. (2000). Behavioral genetics. In A. Kazdin (Ed.), *Encyclopedia of psychology.* Washington, DC, & New York: American Psychological Association and Oxford U. Press.

Waits, C., & Shors, D. (1999). *Unabomber.* New York: American World Geographic Publishing.

Walker, L.E. (1999). Psychology and domestic violence around the world. *American Psychologist, 54,* 6–20.

Wallace, R.K., & Benson, H. (1972). The physiology of meditation. *Scientific American, 226,* 83–90.

Wallerstein, R.S. (1989). The psychotherapy research project of the Menninger Foundation: An overview. *Journal of Consulting and Clinical Psychology, 57,* 195–205.

Walsh, W.B. (1995, August). *Person-environment psychology: Contemporary models and perspectives.* Paper presented at the meeting of the American Psychological Association, New York City.

Walsh, W.B., & Betz, N.E. (1995). *Tests and assessment* (3rd ed.). Upper Saddle River, NJ: Prentice-Hall.

Wampold, B.E., Mondin, G.W., Moody, M., Stich, F., Benson, K., & Ahn, H. (1997). A meta-analysis of outcome studies comparing bona fide psychotherapies: Empirically, "All must have prizes." *Psychological Bulletin, 122,* 203–215.

Ward, R.A., & Grashial, A.F. (1995). Using astrology to teach research methods to introductory psychology students. In M.E. Ware & D.E. Johnson (Eds.), *Demonstrations and activities in teaching of psychology* (Vol. 1). Mahwah, NJ: Erlbaum.

Warren, R.M. (1999). *Auditory perception.* New York: Cambridge University Press.

Waters, E., Merrick, S.K., Albersheim, L.J., & Treboux, E. (1995, March.). *Attachment security from infancy to early adulthood.* Paper presented at the meeting of the Society for Research on Adolescence, Boston.

Watkins, C.E., & Guarnaccia, C.A. (1999). Introduction: The future of psychotherapy training: Psychodynamic, experimental, and eclectic perspectives. *Journal of Clinical Psychology, 55* 381–383.

Watson, D.L., & Tharp, R.G. (1989). *Self-directed behavior* (5th ed.). Pacific Grove, CA: Brooks/Cole.

Watson, J.B. (1913). Psychology as the behaviorist views it. *Psychological Review, 20,* 158–177.

Watson, J.B. (1928). *Psychological care of the infant and child.* Philadelphia: Lippincott.

Watson, J.B., & Raynor, R. (1920). Emotional reactions. *Journal of Experimental Psychology, 3,* 1–14.

Webb, W.B. (1993). Functions of sleep. In M.A. Carskadon (Ed.), *Encyclopedia of sleep and dreaming.* New York: Macmillan.

Webb, W.B. (2000). Sleep. In A. Kazdin (Ed.), *Encyclopedia of psychology.* Washington, DC, & New York: American Psychological Association and Oxford U. Press.

Wechsler, D. (1972). "Hold" and "Don't Hold" test. In S.M. Chown (Ed.), *Human aging.* New York: Penguin.

Wechsler, H., Davenport, A., Dowdall, G., Moeykens, B., & Castillo, S. (1994). Health and behavioral consequences of binge drinking in college. *Journal of the American Medical Association, 272,* 1672–1677.

Weidemann, G., Georgilas, A., & Kehoe, E.J. (1999). Temporal specificity in patterning of the rabbit nictitating membrane response. *Animal Learning & Behavior, 27,* 99–109.

Weinberger, D.R., Berman, K.F., & Zec, R.F. (1986). Physiological dysfunction of the dorsalateral prefrontal cortex in schizophrenia. *Archives of General Psychiatry, 43,* 114–124.

Weiner, B. (1986). *An attributional theory of motivation and emotion.* New York: Springer-Verlag.

Weiner, I.B., Exner, J.E., & Sciara, A. (1996). Is the Rorschach welcome in the courtroom? *Journal of Personality Assessment, 67,* 422–424.

Weiss, S.M. (2000). Health psychology. In A. Kazdin (Ed.), *Encyclopedia of psychology.* Washington, DC, & New York: American Psychological Association and Oxford U. Press.

Weissman, M.M., & others (1999). Prevalence of suicide ideation and suicide attempts in nine countries. *Psychological Medicine, 29,* 9–18.

Wellman, B. (1998). Social networks. In H.S. Friedman (Ed.), *Encyclopedia of mental health* (Vol. 3). San Diego: Academic Press.

Wenzlaff, R.M., & Prohaska, M.L. (1989). When misery loves company: Depression, attributions, and responses to others' moods. *Journal of Experimental Social Psychology, 25,* 220–223.

Werner, E.E. (1989). High risk children in young adulthood: A longitudinal study from birth to 32 years. *American Journal of Orthopsychiatry, 59,* 72–81.

Wertheimer, M. (2000). Gestalt therapy. In A. Kazdin (Ed.), *Encyclopedia of psychology.* Washington, DC, & New York: American Psychological Association and Oxford U. Press.

Whipple, B., Ogden, G., & Komisaruk, B. (1992). Analgesia produced in women by genital self-stimulation. *Archives of Sexual Behavior, 9,* 87–99.

Whitbourne, S.K. (2000). Adulthood and aging: Biological processes and physical development. In A. Kazdin (Ed.), *Encyclopedia of psychology.* Washington, DC, & New York: American Psychological Association and Oxford U. Press.

White, N.M., & Milner, P.M. (1992). The psychology of reinforcers. *Annual Review of Psychology, 43,* 443–472.

Whiting, B.B. (1989). *Culture and interpersonal behavior.* Paper presented at the meeting of the Society for Research in Child Development, Kansas City.

Whitley, B.E. (1996). *Principles of research in behavioral science.* Mountain View, CA: Mayfield.

Whorf, B.L. (1956). *Language, thought, and creativity.* New York: Wiley.

Whyte, G. (2000). Groupthink. In A. Kazdin (Ed.), *Encyclopedia of psychology.* Washington, DC, & New York: American Psychological Association and Oxford U. Press.

Wickesberg, R.E. (2000). Hearing: biological organization. In A. Kazdin (Ed.), *Encyclopedia of psychology.* Washington, DC, & New York: American Psychological Association and Oxford U. Press.

Widiger, T.A. (2000). Antisocial personality disorder. In A. Kazdin (Ed.), *Encyclopedia of psychology.* Washington, DC, & New York: American Psychological Association and Oxford U. Press.

Wierzbicki, M. (1999). *Introduction to clinical psychology.* Boston: Allyn & Bacon.

Wiggins, J.S., & Trapnell, P.D. (1997). Personality structure: The return of the big five. In R. Hogan, J. Johnson, & Briggs (Eds.), *Handbook of personality research.* San Diego: Academic Press.

Williams, R.B. (1995). Coronary prone behaviors, hostility, and cardiovascular health. In K. Orth-Gomer & N. Schneiderman (Eds.), *Behavioral medicine approaches to cardiovascular disease prevention.* Mahwah, NJ: Erlbaum.

Willis, S.L., & Schaie, K.W. (1994). Assessing everyday competence in the elderly. In C. Fisher & R. Lerner (Eds.), *Applied developmental psychology.* Mahwah, NJ: Erlbaum.

Wilson, B.J., & Gottman, J.M. (1996). Attention—The shuttle between emotion and cognition: Risk, resiliency, and physiological bases. In E.M. Hetherington & E.A. Blechman (Eds.), *Stress, coping, and resilience in children and families.* Mahwah, NJ: Erlbaum.

Wilson, M.A., & McNaughton, B.L. (1994). Reactivation of hippocampal ensemble memories during sleep. *Science, 265,* 676–678.

Wisch, A.F., & Mahalik, J.R. (1999). Male therapists' clinical bias: Influence of client gender roles and therapist gender role conflict. *Journal of Counseling Psychology, 46,* 51–61.

Wober, M. (1966). Sensotypes. *Journal of Social Psychology, 70,* 181–189.

Wolpe, J. (1963). Behavior therapy in complex neurotic states. *British Journal of Psychiatry, 110,* 28–34.

Wood, J.V. (1989). Theory and research concerning social comparisons of personal attributes. *Psychological Bulletin, 106,* 231–281

Woodruff-Pak, D.S. (1999). New directions for a classical paradigm: Human eyeblink conditioning. *Psychological Science, 10,* 1–3.

Wooley, S.C., & Garner, D.M. (1991). Obesity treatment: The high cost of false hope. *Journal of the American Dietetic Association, 91,* 1248–1251.

Worell, J., & Robinson, D. (1993). Feminist counseling therapy for the 21st century. *Counseling Psychologist, 21,* 92–96.

Wright, B.D. (1999). Fundamental measurement for psychology. In S.E. Embretson & S.L. Hershberger (Eds.), *The new rules of measurement.* Mahwah, NJ: Erlbaum.

Wright, J.C. (1995, March). *Effects of viewing Sesame Street: The longitudinal study of media and time use.* Paper presented at the meeting of the Society for Research in Child Development, Indianapolis.

Wright, R. (1996, March 25). Can machines think? *Time,* pp. 50–56.

Wrightsman, L.S., Nietzel, M.T., & Fortune, W.H. (1998). *Psychology and the legal system* (4th ed.). Pacific Grove, CA: Brooks/Cole.

Yalom, I.D. (1975). *The therapy and practice of group psychotherapy.* New York: Basic Books.

Yalom, I.D. (1995). *The theory and practice of group psychotherapy* (4th ed.). New York: Basic Books.

Yarmey, A.D. (1973). I recognize your face but I can't remember your name: Further evidence for the tip-of-the-tongue phenomenon. *Memory and Cognition, 1,* 287–290.

Yoder, J.D. (1999). *Women and gender: Transforming psychology.* Upper Saddle River, NJ: Prentice-Hall.

Yuille, J.C. (2000). Deception. In A. Kazdin (Ed.), *Encyclopedia of psychology.* Washington, DC, & New York: American Psychological Association and Oxford U. Press.

Zahn, T.P. (2000). Antipsychotic medication. In A. Kazdin (Ed.), *Encyclopedia of psychology.* Washington, DC, & New York: American Psychological Association and Oxford U. Press.

Zajonc, R.B. (1965). Social facilitation. *Science, 149,* 269–274.

Zajonc, R.B. (1984). On the primacy of affect. *American Psychologist, 39,* 117–123.

Zakrajsek, T. (1999). *Instructor's manual for Psychology* (3rd ed.) by J. Halonen and J.S. Santrock. New York: McGraw-Hill.

Zelnik, M., & Kantner, J.F. (1977). Sexual and contraceptive experiences of young unmarried women in the United States, 1976 and 1971. *Family Planning Perspectives, 9,* 55–71.

Zepelin, H., & Rechtschaffen, A. (1974). Mammalian sleep, longevity, and energy metabolism. *Brain, Behavior, and Evolution, 10,* 425–470.

Zeren, A.S., & Makosky, V.P. (1995). Teaching observational methods. In M.E. Ware & D.E. Johnson (Eds.), *Demonstrations and activities in teaching of psychology* (Vol. 1). Mahwah, NJ: Erlbaum.

Ziegert, K.A. (1983). The Wedisih prohibition of corporal punishment: A preliminary report. *Journal of Marriage and the Family, 45,* 917–926.

Zilbergeld, B. (1992). *The new male sexuality.* New York: Bantam Books.

Zillman, D. (1998). Anger. In H.S. Friedman (Ed.), *Encyclopedia of mental health* (Vol. 1). San Diego: Academic Press.

Zimmerman, B.J., Bonner, S., & Lovach, R. (1996). *Developing self-regulated learners.* Washington, DC: American Psychological Association.

Zola, S. (1996, June). *The medial temporal lobe memory system: Findings from human and non-human primates.* Paper presented at the meeting of the American Psychological Society, San Francisco.

Zuckerman, M. (1979). *Sensation seeking.* Hillsdale, NJ: Erlbaum.

Credits

LINE ART AND TEXT

CHAPTER 2

Figure 2.A: © Roy Doty, *Newsweek.*
Figure 2.3: Floyd E. Bloom, et al, *Brain, Mind, and Behavior,* W. H. Freeman and Company, 1985.
Figure 2.5: Leland G. Johnson, *Biology,* 2e, Figure 16.15, p. 396. Copyright © 1987 Times Mirror Higher Education Group, Inc., Dubuque, Iowa. All rights reserved. Reprinted by permission.
Figure 2.19: *Brain, Mind, and Behavior* by Bloom and Lazerson © 1985, 1988 by W. H. Freeman and Company. Used with permission.
Figure 2.20: *The Neurosciences: A Third Study Program,* Schmitt and Wordens (eds.). Copyright © The MIT Press. Reprinted by permission.
Figure 2.23: Leland G. Johnson, *Biology,* 2e, Figure 16.15, p. 396. Copyright © 1987 Times Mirror Higher Education Group, Inc., Dubuque, Iowa. All rights reserved. Reprinted by permission.

CHAPTER 3

Figure 3.3: Sylvia S. Mader, *Biology,* 4th ed. Copyright © 1997 William C. Brown Communications, Inc. Reprinted by permission of The McGraw-Hill Companies.
Figure 3.4: Sylvia S. Mader, *Biology,* 4th ed. Copyright © 1997 William C. Brown Communications, Inc. Reprinted by permission of The McGraw-Hill Companies.
Figure 3.9: Figure from *Introduction to Psychology,* 7th ed. by Richard C. Atkinson, Rita L. Atkinson and Ernest R. Hilgard, copyright © 1979 by Harcourt Inc., reproduced by permission of the publisher.
Figure 3.12: Sylvia S. Mader, *Biology,* 4th ed. Copyright © 1997 William C. Brown Communications, Inc. Reprinted by permission of The McGraw-Hill Companies.
Figure 3.12c: Lester M. Sdorow, *Psychology,* 5/e. Copyright © 1997 William C. Brown Communications, Inc. Reprinted by permission of The McGraw-Hill Companies.
Figure 3.21: Wathern-Dunn, *Models for the Perception of Visual Form.* Copyright © The MIT Press. Reprinted by permission.
Figure 3.23: James J. Gibson, *The Perception of the Visual World.* Copyright © 1951 by Houghton Mifflin Company. Used with permission.

CHAPTER 4

Figure 4.6: Reprinted with permission from Roffwarg, Muzio & Dement, "Ontogenetic development of human dream-sleep cycle," *Science,* 152, 604–609. Copyright © 1966 American Association for the Advancement of Science.
Page 126: *Power Sleep* by James Maas. Copyright © 1988 by James B. Maas, Ph.D. Reprinted by permission of Villard Books, a division of Random House, Inc.

CHAPTER 6

Figure 6.11: Figure from "Retrieval time for semantic memory" by A. M. Collins and M. R. Quillan in *Journal of Verbal Learning and Verbal Behavior,* Volume 3, pp. 240–248. Copyright © 1969 Academic Press, reproduced by permission of the publisher.
Figure 6.12: R. Lachman, et al., *Cognitive Psychology and Information Processing.* Copyright © 1979 Lawrence Erlbaum Associates, Inc. Reprinted with permission.
Figure 6.13: *Brain, Mind, and Behavior* by Bloom and Lazerson © 1985, 1988 by W. H. Freeman and Company. Used with permission.
Figure 6.14: B. Murdock, Jr., *Human Memory: Theory and Data.* Copyright © 1974 Lawrence Erlbaum Associates, Inc. Reprinted by permission of the author.
Figure 6.17: D. C. Rubin and M. Kozin, "Vivid Memories" in *Cognition,* 16:81–95. Copyright © 1984 Associated Scientific Publishers, Amsterdam, Netherlands.

CHAPTER 7

Figure 7.1: W. Labov, "The boundaries of words and their meanings" in *New Ways of Analyzing Variations in English.* Copyright © 1993 Georgetown University Press. Reprinted with permission.
Figure 7.11: Reprinted by permission of Dr. Ulric Neisser.
Figure 7.12: Figure A5 from *Raven's Standard Progressive Matrices.* Reprinted by permission of the copyright owners, J. C. Raven Ltd.

CHAPTER 8

Figure 8.3: W. K. Frankenburg and J. B. Dodds, "The Denver Development Screening Test" in *Journal of Pediatrics,* 71: 181–191. Copyright © 1967 Mosby-Year Book, Inc. Reprinted by permission.

CHAPTER 9

Figure 9.3: Lester M. Sdorow, *Psychology,* 3/e. Copyright © 1997 William C. Brown Communications, Inc. Reprinted by permission of The McGraw-Hill Companies.
Figure 9.5: Reprinted with the permission of Simon & Schuster from *Overweight: Causes, Cost and Control* by Jean Mayer. Copyright © 1968 by Prentice-Hall, Inc.
Figure 9.6: W. H. Masters and V. E. Johnson, *Human Sexual Response,* 1966, Little, Brown and Company. Reprinted by permissions.
Figure 9.12: *Brain, Mind, and Behavior* by Bloom and Lazerson © 1985, 1988 by W. H. Freeman and Company. Used with permission.
Figure 9.17: R. Plutchik, *Emotion: A Psychoevolutionary Synthesis.* Copyright © 1980 by Harper & Row Publishers. Reprinted by permission of Addison-Wesley Educational Publishers Inc.

CHAPTER 10

Figure 10.1: *Psychology: A Scientific Study of Human Behavior,* by L. S. Wrightsman, C. K. Sigelman, and F. H. Sanford. Copyright © 1979, 1975, 1970, 1965, 1961 Brooks/Cole Publishing Company, a division of International Thomson Publishing Inc. By permission of the publisher.
Figure 10.10: Courtesy of Dr. Hans J. Eysenck.

Figure 10.14: N. S. Jacobson, et al., "Toward a behavioral profile of marital distress" in *Journal of Consulting and Clinical Psychology,* 48: 696–703. Copyright © 1980 by the American Psychological Association. All rights reserved.

CHAPTER 11

Table 11.A: *Living with 10- to 15-year-olds: A parent education curriculum.* Copyright © 1982, 1987 by the Center for Early Adolescence, Carrboro, NC. Used with permission.
Figure 11.9: I. I. Gottesman and J. Shields, *Schizophrenia: The Epigenetic Puzzle.* Copyright © 1992 Cambridge University Press. Reprinted with the permission of Cambridge University Press.

CHAPTER 13

Figure 13.1: "Self-Monitoring" from Mark Snyder, *Journal of Personality and Social Psychology,* 30: 562–537. Copyright © 1974 by the American Psychological Association. Reprinted by permission.
Figure 13.5: After Stanley Milgram, "Behavioral Study of Obedience" in *Journal of Abnormal and Social Psychology,* 67: 371–378, 1963.
Figure 13.6: From E. L. Dey, et al., *The American Freshmen: Twenty-Five-Year Trends, 1991;* A. W. Astin, et al., *The American Freshman: National Norms for Fall 1991,* 1991; E. L. Dey, et al., *The American Freshmen: National Norms for Fall 1992,* 1992; A. W. Astin, et al., *The American Freshman: National Norms for Fall 1993,* 1993, and A. W. Astin, et al., *The American Freshman: National Norms for Fall 1994,* 1994. All works © Higher Education Research Institute, UCLA.

PHOTOGRAPHS

CHAPTER 1

Opener: © Michael Tcherevkoff/The Image Bank; **p. 3 (left & right):** AP/Wide World Photos; **p. 6:** © Bettmann/Corbis; **p. 7, 8:** Psychology Archives-University of Akron; **p. 9:** © Bettmann/Corbis; **p. 10:** © Brett Froomer/The Image Bank-Chicago; **p. 11:** © Tom McHugh/Photo Researchers; **p. 12:** Courtesy of Ilavenil Subbiah; **p. 13 (left):** © Jay Dickman; **p. 13 (right):** © Mark Richards/Photo Edit; **p. 14 (top):** AP/Wide World Photos; **p. 14 (bottom):** J.D. Francolon/The Gamma Liaison Network; **1.2:** Wendt, James, Binet, Pavlov: © Bettmann/Corbis; Howard: Courtesy of Ruth Howard; Skinner: Courtesy of Jane Reed/Harvard University; Erikson, Maslow: © Bettmann/Corbis Rogers: Centers for the Study of the Person; Bandura: Courtesy of Albert Bandura; Bem: Courtesy of Sandra Bem; MacCoby: Courtesy of Eleanor MacCoby; Calkins, Hall, Washburn: Courtesy of Archives of the History of American Psychology, University of Akron; Watson: © Bettmann/Corbis; Clark: Courtesy of Keith and Mamie Clark; Horney, Allport, Freud: © Bettmann/Corbis; Sperry: Courtesy of Roger Sperry; Berry: Courtesy of John Berry; photo credit Monica Hurt; Rodin: Courtesy of Judith Rodin; Simon: © Bettman/Corbis; **p. 17:** Courtesy of Mark

R. Rosenzweig; **p. 18:** © Seana O'Sullivan/Sygma; **p. 19:** © Carol Stone/Tony Stone; **p. 21:** Photo by Curt Burgess, University of California, Riverside; **p. 22 Tiger:** © Blos (M. Gunter)/Peter Arnold, Inc.; **p. 22 Chart:** © Bettmann/Corbis; **1.5 (left & right):** Courtesy of Albert Bandura; **p. 30:** © Sharon Beals/Insight; **p. 33:** Reprinted with permission from *Psychology Today Magazine.* Copyright © 1985 Sussex Publishers, Inc. Photograph by John Madere; **p. 34:** © John Amos/Photo Researchers; **1.8:** © Doug Martin/Photo Researchers, Inc.

CHAPTER 2

Opener : © Scott Camazine/Photo Researchers; **p. 43:** © Enrico Ferorelli; **p. 45:** © Ted Thai/Time Magazine; **2.1:** © Will and Deni McIntyre/Photo Researchers; **p. 46:** Courtesy of David M. Buss; **p. 47:** McCandless Photograph, Urbana, IL; **2.4, 2.9:** © Lennart Nilsson/Albert Bonniers Forlag AB; **2.10a:** © Hank Morgan/Photo Researchers; **2.13:** © John Wiley, California Institute of Technology, estate of James Olds; **2.14:** © A. Glauberman/Photo Researchers; **2.16:** From H. Damasio, T. Grabowski, R. Frank, A. M. Galaburda, and A.R. Damasio, "The Return of Phineas Gage: Clues about the brain from a famous patient" in *Science,* 264:1102-1105, 1994. Department of Neurology and Image Analysis Facility, University of Iowa. Copyright © 1994 American Association for the Advancement of Science; **2.17:** © Wilder Penfield Papers/Montreal Neurological Institute; **2.A:** © Roy Doty/Newsweek; **p. 67 (top):** Courtesy of Jerry Levy; **(bottom):** Courtesy of Steven and Cindi Binder; **p. 69:** © Rex USA LTD; **2.21:** © Charles Gupton/Picturesque; **2.22:** © Steven Peterson; **2.24:** Lennart Nilsson/Albert Bonniers Forlag AB

CHAPTER 3

Opener: © Dennis Lisl/The Image Bank-Texas; **p. 80:** © H. Werb/Shooting Star; **p. 81:** Courtesy of Alice O'Toole; **3.5:** © Morris Karol; **3.6:** © Burton McNeely/The Image Bank-Texas; **3.7:** Fritz Goro/Life Magazine © Time, Inc.; **3.8:** Courtesy of Gretac Macbeth; **3.15:** © Chip Simons 1996; **3.15:** © Lennart Nilsson/Albert Bonniers Forlag AB; **3.18:** M. C. Escher's "Relativity" © 1999 Cordon Art B. V.-Baarn-Holland. All rights reserved; **3.22:** © Lawrence Migdale; **p. 104: (bottom):** © The Granger Collection, New York; **p. 106 (left):** Courtesy of Professor Benjamin Harris; **3.27 (left):** © Herman Eisenbeiss/Photo Researchers; **(right):** © Emilio Mercado/Jeroboam; **3.29:** Reprinted with permission from *Psychology Today Magazine.* Copyright © 1976 Sussex Publishers, Inc. Photograph by Don Peterson; **p. 110:** © Dana Fineman/Sygma

CHAPTER 4

Opener: © David Hiser/Photographers Aspen; **4.1 (top to bottom):** © Steve Dunwell Photography/The Image Bank-Texas; © David Young-Wolff/Photo Edit; © David R. Frazier Photolibrary, Inc.; © Randy Duchaine/The Stock Market; © Luis Castaneda/The Image Bank-Chicago; © Cesar Paredes/The Stock Market; © Barry Christensen/Stock Boston; **4.2 (top):** © Stephen Dalton/Photo Researchers; **4.2 (bottom):** © J. Stephens/Superstock; **p. 120 (top):** Courtesy of San Diego Historical Society Union Tribune Collection; **p. 120 (bottom):** Courtesy of

Michel Siffre; **p. 122 (top):** Photo by Charles Herrington; **4.3 (left):** © Will and Dean McIntyre/Photo Researchers; **4.4:** © J. Allan Hobson & Hoffmann-La Rouche, Inc.; **p. 123:** John Foraste/Brown University; **p. 132 (top):** © Jane Steig Parsons/Prints Charming Photography; **p. 132 (bottom):** © James Wilson/Woodfin Camp; **p. 133:** © SPL/Photo Researchers.

CHAPTER 5

Opener: © John W. Thoeming; **p. 145:** © Children's Television Workshop. Sesame Street Muppets. © Jim Henson Company; **p. 147 (top):** © Whitney Lane/The Image Bank-Texas; **p. 147 (bottom):** © The Granger Collection, New York; **p. 151:** Courtesy of Robert Rescorla; **p. 153 (left):** Courtesy of Professor Benjamin Harris; **5.3:** © Marc Romanelli/The Image Bank-Chicago; **p. 158:** © Rita Nannini/Photo Researchers; **5.8:** Nina Leen, Life Magazine © Time, Inc.; **p. 159 (bottom):** © Bob Krist/Leo de Wys; **p. 163:** © Chris Johnson/Stock Boston; **5.15:** Courtesy of Animal Behavior Enterprises, Inc.

CHAPTER 6

Opener: © Grant V. Faint/The Image Bank; **6.6:** © Rokuo Kawakami/The Image Bank-Texas; **p. 184:** Courtesy of Mike Pugh; **p. 188:** Courtesy of Daniel Schacter; **p. 189 (top):** © AP/Wide World Photos; **(bottom):** © James L. Shaffer; **p. 190:** Courtesy of Elizabeth Loftus; **6.15 (left):** © Reuters/H. O./Archive Photos; **6.15 (right):** © Reuters/Rick Wilking/Archive Photos; **p. 196 (left):** © Brad Markel/The Gamma Liaison Network; **p. 196 (right):** © Bassignac-Deville-Merillon-Turpin/The Gamma Liaison Network; **p. 198:** AP/Wide World Photos; **p. 199:** Courtesy of The Wellcome Institute Library, London; **p. 201:** © Joe McNally/Matrix

CHAPTER 7

Opener: © Bob Daemmrich/Stock Boston; **p. 209 (left):** AP/Wide World Photos; **p. 209 (right):** Ted Thai/Time Magazine; **p. 212 (top, middle, bottom):** © John W. Thoeming; **p. 215:** Courtesy of Ellen J. Langer; **7.5 (top):** © Blake Levine/The Gamma Liaison Network; **7.5 (right):** © Cap. Feature/The Image Works; **p. 220:** © 1999 James Balog; **p. 221:** Courtesy of Noam Chomsky; **p. 222:** © Anthony Bannister/Animals Animals/Earth Scenes; **p. 223:** From Curtiss, *Genie: A Psycholinguistic Study of a Modern Day "Wild Child,"* Copyright © 1977 Academic Press, reproduced by permission of the publisher; **7.7:** © Enrico Ferorelli; **p. 226 (insert):** © Superstock; **p. 226 (background):** © Holton/Superstock; **p. 230:** © Stephen Collins/Photo Researchers; **p. 231:** Courtesy of the National Library of Medicine; **p. 233:** © Jay Gardner, 1998; **p. 234:** Courtesy of Robert J. Stemberg; **p. 235:** Reprinted with the permission of The Free Press, a Division of Simon & Schuster, Inc. from *The Bell Curve* by Richard J. Hernstein and Charles Murray. Jacket, Copyright © 1994 by Simon & Schuster, Inc.; **p. 236 (left & right):** © 1998 Ferorelli Enterprises; **p. 241:** Courtesy of Mihaly Csikszentmihalyi; **p. 245 (left, middle, right):** © John W. Thoeming.

CHAPTER 8

Opener: © Nilo Lima/Photo Researchers; **8.2 (a,b,c):** © Lennart Nilsson/Albert Bonniers Forlag AB;

p. 254: Courtesy of Dr. Tiffany Fields; **p. 259:** © Yves DeBraine/Black Star; **8.6 (top & bottom):** © D. Goodman/Monkmeyer Press; **8.7:** © Paul Fusco/Magnum Photo, Inc.; **p. 262:** Courtesy of John Flavell; **8.11 (bottom to top):** © William Hopkins; © Suzanne Szasz/Photo Researchers; © Suzanne Szasz/Photo Researchers; © Melchior Di Giacomo/The Image Bank-Texas; © Sam Zarember/The Image Bank-Texas; © Brett Froomer/The Image Bank-Texas; © Alan Carey/The Image Works; © Art Kane/The Image Bank-Texas; **p. 266 (top):** © Bettmann/Corbis; **8.12:** © Martin Rogers/Stock Boston; **8.13:** Nina Leen/Life Magazine © Time, Inc.; **p. 268:** © Daniel Grogan; **p. 269:** National Association for the Education of Young Children; **p. 273:** © Lampher Production; **p. 276:** © Keith Carter Photography; **p. 277:** © Alan Carey/Image Works; **p. 279:** © William Hubbell/Woodfin Camp; **p. 281:** © Pascal Parrot/Sygma; **p. 282 (left & right):** © Bettman Archives; **p. 356:** © Elizabeth Crews; **8.18:** © Uniphoto; **8.19 (top to bottom):** © John P. Kelly/The Image Bank-Chicago; © Kaz Mori/The Image Bank-Chicago; © David DeLossy/The Image Bank-Chicago; **8.20: (top to bottom)** © Corbis/Jim Richardson; © John Goodman; © Photodisc; © Don Klumpp/The Image Bank-Texas; PhotoDisc; **8.21 (a):** © Jackson Hill/Southern Lights Photography; **(b):** © Spencer Swanger/Tom Stack & Associates.

CHAPTER 9

Opener: © Kaz Mori/The Image Bank; **p. 293:** © AP/Wide World Photos; **9.1 (top to bottom):** © Paul Trummer/The Image Bank-Chicago; © Ted Kawaleski Photograph, Inc./The Image Bank-Texas; © James L. Shaffer; © James L. Shaffer; © Lawrence Migdale; **9.4:** Courtesy of Dr. Philip Teitelbaum, published in *Proceedings of the American Philosophical,* 1964, Vol. 108; **p. 303:** Courtesy of Judith Rodin; **p. 304:** © George Zimbel/Monkmeyer Press; **p. 307 (top left):** © Bob Coyle; **p. 307 (top right):** © Anthony Mercieca/Photo Researchers; **p. 307 (bottom left):** © Seven-Olof Lindblad/Photo Researchers; **p. 307 (bottom right):** © Jan Cannefax/Ekm Nepenthe; **9.7 (top):** © Barry O'Rourke/The Stock Market; **p. 312:** © Randy Taylor/Sygma; **p. 316:** Courtesy of Sandra Graham; **p. 320:** © Bernard Gotfryd/Woodfin Camp; **9.14 (left & right):** © Donald Dutton; **9.15 (left to right):** © Dale Durfee/Tony Stone Images; © SuperStock; © Richard Lord/The Image Works; © SuperStock; © SuperStock; © Index Stock; **9.16 (left to right):** © Photodisc; © Photodisc; © Paul Eckman; © Paul Eckman; **p. 326 (bottom):** © Robert Harding Library; **p. 329:** Courtesy of Ed and Mary Beth Diener; **p. 330:** © Brad Bower/Stock Boston

CHAPTER 10

Opener: © Graham MacFarlane/Tony Stone Images; **p. 335, p. 337:** © Bettmann/Corbis; **10.3 (bottom to top):** © Robert Eckert/Ekm Nepenthe; © Michael Newman/Photo Edit; © Burton McNeely/Image Bank-Texas; © Mark Antman/Image Works; © Richard Hutchings/Photo Researchers; **p. 342:** © Bettmann/Corbis; **p. 343** © Rachel E. Chodorow-Reich; **(bottom):** Corbis-Bettmann; **10.5:** © The Granger Collection, NY; **10.6:** © Lucas Film; **p. 346:** Courtesy of Dr. Walter Mischel; **p. 347:** Courtesy of Albert Bandura; **p. 349:** Center for the Study of the

Person; **p. 350:** © Ann Kaplan/Corbis; **10.8:** © David Frazier Photo Library, Inc.; **10.9:** © Nick Pavloff/ Image Bank; **10.13:** Reprinted by permission of the Publishers from Henry A. Murray, "Thematic Apperception Test," Cambridge, MA: Harvard University Press. Copyright © 1943 by the President and Fellows of Harvard College. © 1971 by Henry A. Murray; **p. 361:** Courtesy of James Butcher; **10.14:** © Michael Newman/PhotoEdit; **10.15 (left to right):** © Bettmann/Corbis; © Joe McNally/Sygma; Center for the Study of the Person; © Bettmann/Corbis

CHAPTER 11

Opener: © Edward Lettau/Photo Researchers; **p. 373:** AP/Wide World Photos; **p. 379:** Scala/Art Resource, NY; **p. 380 (top):** AP/Wide World Photos; **(bottom):** © Rex USA LTD; **11.7:** © 1974, The Washington Post. Photo by Gerald Martineau. Reprinted with permission; **p. 385:** © Erich Lessing/Art Resource, NY; **p. 388:** Courtesy of Martin Seligman; **p. 390:** LANDSCAPE, 1907, by August Neter. Reprinted by permission of Prinzhorn-Sammlung der Psychiatrischen Universitatsklinik Heidelberg; **11.8:** © Mira Schachne/Monkmeyer Press; **p. 392:** © Reuters/NBC-TV/Archive Photos; **p. 394:** AP/Wide World Photos

CHAPTER 12

Opener: © Stacy Pickerell/Tony Stone Images; **12.1:** Courtesy of San Diego Museum of Man; **12.2:** © Historical Pictures/Stock Montage; **p. 401 (bottom):** © The Granger Collection, NY; **12.3:** © Jay Lurie; **p. 406:** © Historical Pictures/Stock Montage; **12.6:** Scala/Art Resource, NY; **p. 409:** Center for the Study of the Person; **p. 411:** Courtesy of Deke Simon; **12.7:** © David Frazier PhotoLibrary, Inc.; **12.8 (top to bottom):** Courtesy of Albert Bandura; Courtesy of Albert Ellis; **p. 416:** © Michael Neman/Photo Edit; **p. 419:** © Bob Daemmrich/Stock Boston; **p. 424 (top):** © Russ Kinne/Comstock, Inc.; **p. 424 (bottom):** © Robert Houser/Comstock, Inc.

CHAPTER 13

Opener: © Ramey/Stock Boston; **p. 423:** AP/Wide World Photos; **13.1:** © Romilly Lockyear/The Image Bank-Chicago; **13.2:** © John P. Kelly/The Image Bank-Chicago; **p. 427:** © Hanson Lightworks Inc./Stock Boston; **p. 431:** Courtesy of New School University, New York, NY; **13.4:** © William Vandivert; **13.5:** Copyright © 1965 by Stanley Milgram. From the film OBEDIENCE distributed by Penn State Media Sales; **p. 437:** Archives of the History of American Psychology-The University of Akron;

p. 438: © AP/Wide World Photos; **p. 439 (inset):** © John P. Kelly/The Image Bank-Texas; **p. 439 (background):** © David Frazier Photolibrary, Inc.; **p. 440 (top to bottom):** © Michael Edrington/The Image Works; © Andrea Pistolesi/The Image Bank-Chicago; © Jean-Marc Loubat/Photo Researchers; **p. 442a:** © AP/Wide World Photos; **p. 442b:** © Alberto Garcia/Gamma Liaison; **p. 443a:** AP/Wide World Photos; **p. 443b:** © Rob Crandall/Stock Boston; **p. 444:** Courtesy of James Jones; **p. 445a:** © Larry Kolvoord/The Image Works; **p. 445b:** © Bob Daemmrich/The Image Works; **p. 445c:** © Bill Gillette/Stock Boston; **p. 445d:** © Spencer Grant/Index Stock Imagery; **p. 447:** © Cleo Freelance Photography; **p. 448:** © Mary Kate Denny/Photo Edit; **p. 451a:** © Bettmann/Corbis; **p. 451b:** © AP/Wide World Photos; **p. 455a:** © Kent Reno/ Jeroboam; **p. 455b:** © David Young-Wolff/Photo Edit; **p. 456** © Randall Hyman/Stock Boston; **13.6:** © David W. Hamilton/The Image Bank-Texas; **p. 459 (top):** Courtesy of the Academy of Motion Picture Arts and Sciences; **p. 459 (bottom):** Courtesy of Ellen Berscheid; **p. 461** © David Young-Wolff/PhotoEdit

Name Index

A

Abnormal behavior
  anxiety disorders, 377–381
  biopsychosocial approach, 374
  and culture, 373
  defined, 370
  Diagnostic and Statistical Manual of Mental Disorders-IV (DSM-IV), 374–377
  dimensions of, 370
  dissociative disorders, 382–383
  gender differences, 373–374
  legal aspects, 371
  medical model, 372, 375–376
  mood disorders, 385–389
  myths/misconceptions about, 371
  personality disorders, 393–396
  prevalence of, 374
  psychological factors, 372–373
  schizophrenia, 389–393
  somatoform disorders, 381–382
Absolute threshold, of sensory system, 78–79
Accommodation
  in Piaget's theory, 258
  visual, 84
Acetylcholine (ACh)
  and Alzheimer's disease, 281
  functions of, 54
Achievement motivation, 313–317
  attribution theory, 315
  and culture, 316–317
  extrinsic and intrinsic motivation, 314–315
  and goal-setting, 315–316
  need for achievement, 314
  and socioeconomic status, 317
Action potential, of neuronal impulse, 53
Activation-synthesis theory, dreams, 130
Activity level, and temperament, 268
Activity theory, aging, 286
Acupuncture, and pain, 96
Addiction, defined, 139
Addiction/drug abuse, 139–140.
  See also Psychoactive drugs
  and brain, 61–62
  disease model, 139
  early intervention, 140
  life-process model, 139
  primary prevention, 139
  secondary prevention, 140
  tertiary prevention, 140
Adler's theory, 343–344. *See also* Individual psychology
Adolescence
  at-risk youth, 277–278

cognitive development, 262, 273–274
  egocentrism in, 274
  Erikson's theory, 265
  events of, 249
  identity development, 276–278
  moral development, 274–276
  physical development, 273
  storm-and-stress view, 271
  violent behavior, 3–4
Adrenal glands, hormones of, 73
Adult development. *See also* Early adulthood; Late adulthood; Middle adulthood
  cohort effects, 286
  Erikson's theory, 285
  life events, 286
  seasons of man's life theory, 285
  social clock theory, 286
  stages and events of, 249–250
Affectionate love, 470
Afferent nerves, function of, 50–51
African-Americans
  intelligence test score issue, 235–236, 238–239
  and prejudice, 454
  stereotyping of, 454
Afterimages, color vision, 89
Aggression, 460–46
  and aversive circumstances, 462–463
  biological theories of, 460–462
  and culture, 462
  frustration-aggression hypothesis, 462
  gender differences, 464
  modeling of, 27–29, 463
  operational definition of, 27–28
  reduction of, 463–464
  and television viewing, 33–34, 463
Aging
  activity theory, 286
  Alzheimer's disease, 281
  cellular clock theory, 280–281
  death and dying, 288–289
  free-radical theory, 281
  life expectancy, 280
  and life review, 287
  life span, 280
  successful aging, elements of, 287
Agonist, defined, 56
Agoraphobia, 379, 380
AIDS
  in infants/children, 253
  and needle-sharing, 137
Albert, classical conditioning of phobia, 152, 153
Alcoholism
  binge drinking, 136
  defined, 136

and fetal alcohol syndrome (FAS), 253
  genetic factors, 136
  recovery, predictors of, 140
Alcohol use, 135–136
  abuse. *See* Alcoholism
  and aggression, 461
  and college students, 136
Algorithms, and problem solving, 213
All-or-none principle, of neuronal impulse, 53
Alpha waves, 122
Altered state of consciousness, 117
Alternative forms reliability, 229
Altruism, 464–468
  biological theories of, 465–466
  bystander effect, 466–467
  and college students, 467
  defined, 464–465
  and egoism, 466
  gender differences, 467–468
Alzheimer's disease
  brain grafts for, 70
  management of, 281
  theories of cause, 281
American Psychiatric Association (APA), classification of mental disorders, 374–377
American Psychological Association (APA), ethical guidelines, 37–38
Amnesia
  anterograde amnesia, 201
  dissociative amnesia, 382
  retrograde amnesia, 201
Amphetamines, 137
Amplitude, sound waves, 91–92
Amygdala
  and emotion, 321–322
  functions of, 59
Analogy, and reasoning, 215–216
Anal stage, 340
Androgens, 306
Anger, 329–330
  and catharsis, 330
  control, steps in, 330
  Freud's theory, 330
  social cognitive theory, 330
Anima/animus, 343
Animal magnetism, 132
Animals
  and dreams, 130
  and language learning, 223–224
  learning, instinctive drift, 169
  research, ethical guidelines, 38
Anorexia nervosa, 304
Antagonist, defined, 56
Anterograde amnesia, 201
Antianxiety drugs, 424–425
Antidepressant drugs, 425
Antipsychotic drugs, 425–426
  side effects, 425–426

Antisocial personality disorder, 393, 394
Anxiety disorders, 377–381
  defined, 377
  drug therapy, 424–425, 427
  generalized anxiety disorders, 377–378
  neurotransmitter related to, 54
  obsessive-compulsive disorder, 380
  panic disorder, 378–379
  phobic disorders, 379–380
  post-traumatic stress disorder, 380–381
Aphasia, 65
Aphrodisiacs, and sexual activity, 307
Apparent movement, types of, 106
Applied behavior analysis, 162–164
  applications of, 163
  defined, 162
  for self-control improvement, 164
Archetypes, Jungian, 343
Arousal. *See also* Emotions
  and nervous system, 318–319
  and performance, 319
  Yerkes-Dodson law, 319
Asch experiment, conformity, 443, 445
Assimilation, in Piaget's theory, 258
Association cortex, functions of, 64–65
Associative learning, classical conditioning as, 148
Astrology, critical thinking about, 22
Asylums, 401
Atkinson-Shiffrin theory, memory, 182
At-risk youth, interventions for, 277–278
Attachment, 266–268
  critical period, 266–267
  defined, 266
  evaluation of theory, 267
  imprinting, 266
  insecure attachment, 267
  and later relationships, 388
  secure attachment, 267
Attention, 100, 102–103
  and memory, 203
  in observational learning, 166
  selective attention, 102
  Stroop effect, 102–103
Attitudes, 440–443
  and behavior, 440–441
  changing, strategies for, 440
  cognitive dissonance, 441–442
  defined, 440
  self-perception theory, 442–443